FINANCIAL ACCOUNTING

A BUSINESS PERSPECTIVE

FINANCIAL ACCOUNTING

SEVENTH EDITION

A BUSINESS PERSPECTIVE

ROGER H. HERMANSON, Ph.D., CPA
Regents Professor of Accounting
Ernst & Young–J.W. Holloway Memorial Professor
School of Accountancy
Georgia State University

JAMES DON EDWARDS, Ph.D., CPA
J.M. Tull Professor of Accounting
J.M. Tull School of Accounting
University of Georgia

Irwin McGraw-Hill

Boston, Massachusetts   Burr Ridge, Illinois   Dubuque, Iowa
Madison, Wisconsin   New York, New York
San Francisco, California   St. Louis, Missouri

Irwin/McGraw-Hill

A Division of The **McGraw·Hill** *Companies*

FINANCIAL ACCOUNTING: A BUSINESS PERSPECTIVE

Copyright © 1998 by The McGraw-Hill Companies, Inc. All rights reserved. Previous edition(s) © 1980, 1983, 1986, 1987, 1989, 1992, and 1995 by Richard D. Irwin, a Times Mirror Higher Education Group, Inc. company. Printed in the United States of America. Except as permitted under the United States Copyright Act of 1976, no part of this publication may be reproduced or distributed in any form or by any means, or stored in a database or retrieval system, without the prior written permission of the publisher.

This book is printed on acid-free paper.

1 2 3 4 5 6 7 8 9 0 VNH/VNH 9 0 9 8 7

ISBN 0-256-24738-2

Vice president and editorial director: *Michael W. Junior*
Publisher: *Jeffrey L. Shelstad*
Associate editor: *Becky Page*
Editorial assistant: *Donna Hayes*
Senior marketing manager: *Rhonda Seelinger*
Project manager: *Kimberly Schau*
Production supervisor: *Lori Koetters*
Senior designer: *Laurie J. Entringer*
Cover designer: *Jenny El-Shanny*
Cover illustration: © *Kevin Short, Stockworks*
Compositor: *Shepard Poorman Communications*
Typeface: *10/12 Times Roman*
Printer: *Von Hoffmann Press, Inc.*

Library of Congress Cataloging-in-Publication Data

Hermanson, Roger H.
    Financial accounting : a business perspective / Roger H. Hermanson,
James Don Edwards. — 7th ed.
       p.   cm.—(The Irwin/McGraw-Hill series in principles of
accounting)
    Includes bibliographical references and index.
    ISBN 0-256-24738-2
    1. Accounting.   I. Edwards, James Don.   II. Title.   III. Series
HF5635.H543   1998
657—dc21   97-33522

http://www.mhhe.com

ABOUT THE AUTHORS

Professor Roger H. Hermanson, Ph.D., CPA

Regents Professor of Accounting and Ernst & Young–
J. W. Holloway Memorial Professor at Georgia State University. He received his doctorate at Michigan State University in 1963 and is a CPA in Georgia. Professor Hermanson taught and later served as chairperson of the Division of Accounting at the University of Maryland. He has authored or coauthored numerous articles for professional and scholarly journals and has coauthored numerous editions of several textbooks, including *Accounting Principles, Financial Accounting, Survey of Financial and Managerial Accounting, Auditing Theory and Practice, Principles of Financial and Managerial Accounting,* and *Computerized Accounting with Peachtree Complete III.* He also has served on the editorial boards of the *Journal of Accounting Education, New Accountant, Accounting Horizons,* and *Management Ac-*

counting. Professor Hermanson has served as coeditor of the Trends in Accounting Education column for *Management Accounting.* He has held the office of vice president of the American Accounting Association and served on its executive committee. He is also a member of the Institute of Management Accountants, the American Institute of Certified Public Accountants, and the Financial Executives Institute.

Professor Hermanson has been awarded two excellence in teaching awards, a doctoral fellow's award, and a Distinguished Alumni Professor award; and he was selected as the Outstanding Faculty Member for 1985 by the Federation of Schools of Accountancy. He has served as a consultant to many companies and organizations. In 1990, Professor Hermanson was named Accounting Educator of the Year by the Georgia Society of CPAs.

Professor James Don Edwards, Ph.D., CPA

J. M. Tull Professor of Accounting in the Terry College of Business at the University of Georgia. He is a graduate of Louisiana State University and has been inducted into the Louisiana State University Alumni Federation's Hall of Distinction. He received his M.B.A. from the University of Denver and his Ph.D. from the University of Texas and is a CPA in Texas and Georgia. He has served as a professor and chairman of the Department of Accounting and Financial Administration at Michigan State University, a professor and dean of the Graduate School of Business Administration at the University of Minnesota, and a Visiting Scholar at Oxford University in Oxford, England.

Professor Edwards is a past president of the American Accounting Association and a past national vice president and executive committee member of the Institute of Management Accountants. He has served on the board of directors of the American Institute of Certified Public Accountants and as chairman of the Georgia State Board of Accountancy. He was an original trustee of the Financial Accounting Foundation, the parent organization of the FASB, and a member of the Public Review Board of Arthur Andersen & Co.

He has published in *The Accounting Review, The Journal of Accountancy, The Journal of Accounting Research, Management Accounting,* and *The Harvard Business History Review.* He is also the author of *History of Public Accounting in the United States.* He has served on various American Institute of Certified Public Accountants committees and

boards, including the Objectives of Financial Statements Committee, Standards of Professional Conduct Committee, and the CPA Board of Examiners. He was the managing editor of the centennial issue of *The Journal of Accountancy.*

In 1974, Beta Alpha Psi, the National Accounting Fraternity, selected Professor Edwards for its first annual Outstanding Accountant of the Year award. This selection is made from industry, government, and educational leaders. In 1975, he was selected by the American Accounting Association as its Outstanding Educator.

He has served the AICPA as president of the Benevolent Fund, chairman of the Awards Committee, member of the Professional Ethics Committee and Program for World Congress of Accountants. He is on the Education Standards Committee of the International Federation of Accountants and the Committee on Planning for the Institute of Management Accountants. He was the director of the Seminar for Management Accountants–Financial Reporting for the American Accounting Association. He is also a member of the Financial Executives Institute.

He received the 1993 AICPA Gold Medal Award, the highest award given by the Institute. A Doctor Honoris Causa (Honorary Doctorate) from the University of Paris was awarded to him in 1994. He is the first accountant to receive this distinction in France. The Academy of Accounting Historians awarded him the 1994 Hourglass Award which is the highest international honor in the field of Accounting History.

PREFACE

PHILOSOPHY AND PURPOSE

Imagine that you have graduated from college without taking an accounting course. You are employed by a company as a sales person, and you eventually become the sales manager of a territory. While attending a sales managers' meeting, financial results are reviewed by the Vice President of Sales and terms such as gross margin percentage, cash flows from operating activities, and LIFO inventory methods are being discussed. The Vice President eventually asks you to discuss these topics as they relate to your territory. You try to do so, but it is obvious to everyone in the meeting that you do not know what you are talking about.

Financial accounting principles courses teach you the "language of business" so you understand terms and concepts used in business decisions. If you understand how accounting information is prepared, you will be in an even stronger position when faced with a management decision based on accounting information.

We wrote this text to give you an understanding of how to use accounting information to analyze business performance and make business decisions. The text takes a business perspective. We use the annual reports of real companies to illustrate many of the accounting concepts. You are familiar with many of the companies we use, such as The Coca-Cola Company, The Home Depot, and Colgate-Palmolive Company.

Gaining an understanding of accounting terminology and concepts, however, is not enough to ensure your success. You also need to be able to find information on the Internet, analyze various business situations, work effectively as a member of a team, and communicate your ideas clearly. This text was developed to help you develop these skills.

CURRICULUM CONCERNS

Significant changes have been recommended for accounting education. Some parties have expressed concern that recent accounting graduates do not possess the necessary set of skills to succeed in an accounting career. The typical accounting graduate seems unable to successfully deal with complex and unstructured "real world" accounting problems and generally lacks communication and interpersonal skills. One recommendation is the greater use of active learning techniques in a reenergized classroom environment. The traditional lecture and structured problem solving method approach would be supplemented or replaced with a more informal classroom setting dealing with cases, simulations, and group projects. Both inside and outside the classroom, there would be two-way communication between (1) profes-

sor and student and (2) student and student. Study groups would be formed so that students could tutor other students. The purposes of these recommendations include enhancing students' critical thinking skills, written and oral communication skills, and interpersonal skills.

One of the most important benefits you can obtain from a college education is that you "learn how to learn." The concept that you gain all of your learning in school and then spend the rest of your life applying that knowledge is not valid. Change is occurring at an increasingly rapid pace. You will probably hold many different jobs during your career, and you will probably work for many different companies. Much of the information you learn in college will be obsolete in just a few years. Therefore, you will be expected to engage in life-long learning. Memorizing is much less important than learning how to think critically.

With this changing environment in mind, we have developed a text that will lend itself to developing the skills that will lead to success in your future career in business. The section at the end of each chapter titled, "Beyond the Numbers—Critical Thinking," provides the opportunity for you to address unstructured case situations, the analysis of real companies' financial situations, ethics cases, team projects, and Internet projects. For many of these items, you will use written and oral communication skills in presenting your results.

OBJECTIVES AND OVERALL APPROACH OF THE SEVENTH EDITION

The Accounting Education Change Commission (AECC) made specific recommendations regarding teaching materials and methods used in the first-year accounting course. As a result, significant changes are taking place in that course at many universities. The AECC states:

The first course in accounting can significantly benefit those who enter business, government, and other organizations, where decision-makers use accounting information. These individuals will be better prepared for their responsibilities if they understand the role of accounting information in decision-making by managers, investors, government regulators, and others. All organizations have accountability responsibilities to their constituents, and accounting, properly used, is a powerful tool in creating information to improve the decisions that affect those constituents.[1]

---

[1]Accounting Education Change Commission, *Position Statement No. Two,* "The First Course in Accounting" (Torrance, CA, June 1992), pp. 1–2.

In making the transition from primarily a preparer's focus to a balanced preparer's and user's focus, in the seventh edition we eliminated chapters on special journals and partnerships and appendixes on (1) payroll and taxes and (2) inflation accounting. We also eliminated the following topics: the net price method for purchases of merchandise, the alternative closing method for a merchandising company, the voucher system, the direct write-off method for receivables, discounting notes receivable, recording capital stock issuances by subscription, and long-term bond investments. The coverage of certain other topics was shortened considerably or relegated to a chapter appendix. For instance, the work sheet for a merchandising company was placed in a chapter appendix.

We retained a solid coverage of accounting that serves business students well regardless of the majors they select. Those who choose not to major in accounting, which is a majority of those taking this course, will become better users of accounting information because they will know something about the preparation of that information.

REVISION APPROACH AND ORGANIZATION

Changes were made in every chapter in this seventh edition, but certain changes deserve special mention.

In Chapter 7, Measuring and Reporting Inventories, we have split the coverage into a section on periodic inventory procedure and a section on perpetual inventory procedure. Some users indicated that they wished to deemphasize the coverage of periodic inventory procedure because of the almost exclusive use of perpetual inventory procedure in accounting software packages. The separation of these topics in Chapter 7 now permits the deemphasis of periodic inventory procedure.

Many users indicate that they desire to have their students engage in *more group (team) projects.* In the sixth edition we had only one group project per chapter. We have added two new group projects per chapter in the seventh edition.

The Internet is expanding daily and contains much information that is useful to accountants. Students need to be knowledgeable about using the Internet, and many of them have used the Internet for purposes other than accounting. We have included *two Internet projects* in each chapter to give students some experience in using the Internet to acquire information pertaining to accounting. We have identified many of the most useful accounting websites (e.g., all of the websites of the Big-Six accounting firms) that students can use, not only for the specific projects assigned, but in later courses and in their working careers. One word of caution is in order. Some entities create websites but either do not revise them to make them current or cancel them. The websites we have selected are ones that we believed would be retained and updated periodically. However, if an Internet project is assigned that involves a website which no longer contains the required information or has been canceled, the student should simply select another Internet project.

The seventh edition contains three types of marginal annotations to help students study the materials. *Notes to the Student* contain examples to illustrate key concepts and alternative presentations of ideas. *Reinforcing problems* indicate which exercises, problems, and cases reinforce coverage of a particular topic. **Real World Examples** give interesting and relevant information about the business world. We hope students and instructors will find these annotations helpful.

A list of check figures is now included at the end of the book. Check figures give key amounts for the problems, business decision cases, other "Beyond the Numbers" items, and comprehensive review problems in the text.

Business Emphasis

Without actual business experience, business students sometimes lack a frame of reference in attempting to apply accounting concepts to business transactions. We seek to involve the business student more in real world business applications as we introduce and explain the subject matter.

- Each part opens with **"A Manager's Perspective,"** which features interviews with managers at The Coca-Cola Company. These opening vignettes provide insight into how managers in various areas in business (marketing, HR, finance, manufacturing, etc.) use accounting information to make decisions.

- **"An Accounting Perspective: Business Insight"** boxes throughout the text provide examples of how companies featured in text examples use accounting information every day, or they provide other useful information.

- **"Accounting Perspective: Uses of Technology"** boxes throughout the text demonstrate how technology has affected the way accounting information is prepared, manipulated, and accessed.

- Some chapters contain **"A Broader Perspective."** These situations, taken from annual reports of real companies and from articles in current business periodicals such as *Accounting Today,* and *Management Accounting,* relate to subject matter discussed in that chapter or present other useful information. These real world examples demonstrate the business relevance of accounting.

- Real world questions and real world business decision cases are included in almost every chapter.

- The Annual Report Booklet included with this text contains significant portions of the 1996 annual reports of The Coca-Cola Company, John H. Harland Company, The Limited, Inc., and the Maytag Corporation. Many of the real world questions and business decision cases are based on these annual reports.

- Numerous illustrations adapted from *Accounting Trends & Techniques* show the frequency of use in business of various accounting techniques. Placed throughout the text, these illustrations give students real world data to consider while learning about different accounting techniques.

- Throughout the text we have included numerous references to the annual reports of over 75 companies. In fact, Chapter 17 and most of Chapter 16 are based on the 1996 annual report of the Colgate-Palmolive Company.

- Most of the chapters contain a section entitled, "Analyzing and Using the Financial Results." This section discusses and illustrates a ratio or other analysis technique that pertains to the content of the chapter. For instance, this section in Chapter 4 discusses the current ratio as it relates to a classified balance sheet.

- Most of the chapters contain end-of-chapter questions, exercises, or business decision cases that require the student to refer to the Annual Report Booklet and answer certain questions. As stated earlier, this booklet is included with the text and contains the significant portions of the 1996 annual reports of four companies: The Coca-Cola Company, Maytag Corporation, The Limited, Inc., and John H. Harland Company.

- Each chapter contains a section entitled, "Beyond the Numbers—Critical Thinking." This section contains business decision cases, annual report analysis problems, writing assignments based on the Ethical Perspective and Broader Perspective boxes, group projects, and Internet projects.

Pedagogy

Students often come into financial accounting courses feeling anxious about learning the subject matter. Recognizing this apprehension, we studied ways to make learning easier and came up with some helpful ideas on how to make this edition work even better for students.

- Improvements in the text's content reflect feedback from adopters, suggestions by reviewers, and a serious study of the learning process itself by the authors and editors. New subject matter is introduced only after the stage has been set by transitional paragraphs between topic headings. These paragraphs provide students with the reasons for proceeding to the new material and explain the progression of topics within the chapter.

- The Introduction contains a section entitled "How to Study the Chapters in This Text," which should be very helpful to students.

  Each chapter has an "Understanding the Learning Objectives" section. These "summaries" enable the student to determine how well the Learning Objectives were accomplished. We were the first authors (1974) to ever include Learning Objectives in an accounting text. These objectives have been included at the beginning of the chapter, as marginal notes within the chapter, at the end of the chapter, and in supplements such as the Test Bank, Instructors' Resource Guide, Computerized Test Bank, and Study Guide. The objectives are also indicated for each exercise and problem.

- Demonstration problems and solutions are included for each chapter, and a different one appears for each chapter in the Study Guide. These demonstration problems help students to assess their own progress by showing them how problems that focus on the topic(s) covered in the chapter are worked before students do assigned homework problems.

- Key terms are printed in another color for emphasis. End-of-chapter glossaries contain the definition and the page number where the new term was first introduced and defined. Students can easily turn back to the original discussion and study the term's significance in context with the chapter material. A "New Terms Index"—an alphabetical list of all key terms in the text with page numbers—is included at the end of the text.

- Each chapter includes a "Self-Test" consisting of true-false and multiple-choice questions. The answers and explanations appear at the end of the chapter. These self-tests are designed to determine whether the student has learned the essential information in each chapter.

- In the margin beside each exercise and problem, we have included a description of the requirements and the related Learning Objective(s). These descriptions let students know what they are expected to do in the problem.

- Throughout the text we use examples taken from everyday life to relate an accounting concept being introduced or discussed to students' experiences.

End-of-Chapter Materials

Describing teaching methods, the AECC stated, "Teachers . . . should place a priority on their interaction with students and on interaction among students. Students' involvement should be promoted by methods such as cases, simulations, and group projects. . . ."[2] A section entitled **"Beyond the Numbers—Critical Thinking"** at the end of every chapter is designed to implement these recommendations. **Business Decision Cases** require critical thinking in complex situations often based on real companies. The **Annual Report Analysis** section requires analyzing annual reports and interpreting the results in writing. The **Ethics Cases** require students to respond in writing to situations they are likely to encounter in their careers. These cases do not necessarily have one right answer. The **Group Projects** for each chapter teach students how to work effectively in teams, a skill that was stressed by the AECC and is becoming increasingly necessary for success in business. The **Internet Projects** teach students how to retrieve useful information from the Internet.

A team approach can also be introduced in the classroom using the regular exercises and problems in the text. Teams can be assigned the task of presenting their solutions to exercises or problems to the rest of the class. Using this team approach in class can help reenergize the classroom by creating an active, informal environment in which students learn from each other. (Two additional group projects are described in the Instructor's Resource Guide. These projects are designed to be used throughout the semester or quarter.)

We have included a vast amount of other resource materials for each chapter *within* the text from which the instructor may draw: (1) one of the largest selections of end-of-chapter questions, exercises, and problems available;

---

[2]Ibid, p. 2.

(2) several comprehensive review problems that allow students to review all major concepts covered to that point; and (3) from one to three business decision cases per chapter. Other key features regarding end-of-chapter material follow.

- A uniform chart of accounts appears on the inside covers of the text. This uniform chart of accounts is used consistently throughout the first 11 chapters. The use of general ledger applications software with this edition necessitated the creation of a uniform chart of accounts. We believe students will benefit from using the same chart of accounts for all homework problems in those chapters.

- A comprehensive review problem at the end of Chapter 4 serves as a mini practice set to test all material covered to that point.

- Many of the end-of-chapter problem materials (questions, exercises, problems, business decision cases, other "Beyond the Numbers" items, and comprehensive review problems) have been revised. Each exercise and problem is identified with the learning objective(s) to which it relates.

- All end-of-chapter exercises and problems have been traced back to the chapters to ensure that nothing is asked of a student that does not appear in the book. This feature was a strength of previous editions, ensuring that instructors could confidently assign problems without having to check for applicability. Also, we took notes while teaching from the text and clarified problem and exercise instructions that seemed confusing to our students.

- Many of the problems, comprehensive review problems, and business decision cases in the text can be solved using software. Those problems that can be solved using *General Ledger Applications Software (GLAS)*, developed by Jack E. Terry of ComSource Associates, are identified in the margin with the symbol below.

This software package can also be used to solve the first two manual practice sets.

Many other exercises, problems, and business decision cases can be solved using *Spreadsheet Applications Template Software (SPATS)* developed by Jack Terry. The exercises and problems solvable with *SPATS* are identified in the margin of the text with the following symbol:

SUPPLEMENTS FOR THE INSTRUCTOR

A complete package of supplemental teaching aids contains all you need to efficiently and effectively teach the course.

Instructor's Resource Guide, Chapters 1–17 This guide contains sample syllabi for both semester- and quarter-based courses. Revised for this edition, each chapter contains: (1) a summary of major concepts; (2) learning objectives from the text; (3) space for the instructor's own notes; (4) an outline of the chapter with an indication of when each exercise can be worked; and (5) detailed lecture notes that also refer to specific end-of-chapter exercise and problem materials illustrating these concepts. Also included are (6) a summary of the estimated time, learning objective(s), level of difficulty, and content of each exercise and problem that is useful in deciding which items to cover in class or to assign as homework; and (7) teaching transparencies masters. The Instructor's Resource Guide for Chapter 17 contains a case study based on Hasbro, Inc. This company is the world's leading manufacturer and marketer of toys, games, puzzles, and infant care products. You may want to assign this case as a special project to individuals or to teams. The results of the analysis, with recommendations, could then be presented to the class.

Solutions Manual, Chapters 1–17 The solutions manual contains suggested discussion points for each ethics case as well as detailed answers to questions, exercises, two series of problems, business decision cases, most "Beyond the Numbers" items, and comprehensive review problems.

Solutions Transparencies Acetate transparencies of solutions to all exercises and *all* problems with excellent clarity are available free to adopters. These transparencies, while useful in many situations, are especially helpful when covering problems in large classroom settings.

Test Bank, Chapters 1–17 The test bank, *revised in this edition,* contains questions and problems to choose from in preparing examinations. This test bank contains true-false questions, multiple-choice questions, and short problems for each chapter. Questions and problems are *classified by the learning objective* to which they relate.

Computest 4 This improved microcomputer version of the Test Bank allows editing of questions; provides up to 99 different versions of each test; and allows question selection based on type of question, level of difficulty, or learning objective. Computest 4 is available on 3.5″ disks.

Teletest Teletest is an in-house testing service that will prepare your exams within 72 working hours after you phone the publisher.

Videos The Irwin/McGraw-Hill Financial Accounting Video Library covers special topics such as the accounting cycle, merchandising, ethics, and international accounting. The subject matter lends itself well to a visual approach in the classroom. A video guide is also provided.

The following items are intended for student use at the option of the instructor.

General Ledger Applications Software (GLAS) Many problems, business decision cases, and comprehensive review problems in the text can be solved using this software.

GLAS is available on 3.5″ disks and can be ordered with the text or as a separate item.

Spreadsheet Applications Template Software (SPATS) Many additional exercises, problems, and business decision cases can be solved using SPATS. It contains innovatively designed templates based on Excel. SPATS is available on 3.5″ disks. SPATS can be ordered with the text or as a separate item.

Peachtree® Complete™ This leading business accounting software is available for site license by contacting your Irwin/McGraw-Hill representative. The version you will receive is the actual "full-featured" commercial software being sold to many U.S. companies.

Windows-based Computerized Tutorials These software packages by Leland Mansuetti of Sierra College include true-false and multiple-choice questions with explanations for both correct and incorrect answers. Upon adoption, these computerized tutorials are available to instructors for classroom or laboratory use. Tutorials are available on 3.5″ disks and can be ordered with the text or as a separate item.

SUPPLEMENTS FOR THE STUDENT

In addition to the text, the package of support items for the student includes the following:

Study Guides, Chapters 1–17 Included for each chapter are learning objectives, a reference outline, a chapter review, and an additional demonstration problem and solution. If students use the study guide throughout the course, their knowledge of accounting will be enhanced significantly. The study guide is a valuable learning tool in that it includes matching, true-false, and multiple-choice questions, completion questions, and exercises. Solutions to all exercises and questions are also included.

Working Papers, Chapters 1–17 A set of working papers is available for completing assigned exercises, problems, business decision cases, other "Beyond the Numbers" items, and comprehensive review problems. In many instances, the working papers are partially filled in to reduce the "pencil pushing" required to solve the problems, yet the working papers are not so complete as to reduce the learning impact.

Manual Practice Sets Four manual practice sets are available.

- *Dominion Lighting Company* illustrates special journals and includes a work sheet for a retailing company. This practice set can be used anytime after Chapter 9.
- *Aspen Mountain Camping Equipment Company* illustrates the use of business papers for a retailing company. It can be used anytime after Chapter 9.
- *Rocky Mountain Clothes Company, Inc.,* illustrates special journals and includes a work sheet for a retailing company. It can be used anytime after Chapter 9. This practice set is also available on our General Ledger Applications Software (GLAS).

Computer Supplements The following computer supplements are available on 3.5″ disks:

- *Granite Bay Jet Ski, Level One,* Second Edition, by Leland Mansuetti and Keith Weidkamp, both of Sierra College, is a computerized simulation that can be used with any Principles of Accounting text using a single proprietorship approach. Level One is intended for use after coverage of the accounting cycle and accounting for cash (Chapter 8).
- *Granite Bay Jet Ski, Inc., Level Two,* Second Edition, by Leland Mansuetti and Keith Weidkamp, both of Sierra College, adds a corporate dimension to the business presented in Level One. It is intended for use after coverage of (1) plant assets and (2) current and long-term liabilities (Chapter 15).

We are indebted to many individuals for reviewing the manuscript of this edition. In addition to those listed on the acknowledgment pages, we are especially indebted to colleagues and students at our respective universities for their helpful suggestions. Our families also provided needed support and showed great patience during the revision process.

Roger H. Hermanson

James Don Edwards

ACKNOWLEDGMENTS

The development of the seventh edition of *Financial Accounting: A Business Perspective* was an evolving and challenging process. Significant changes are taking place in the first course in accounting in schools across the country, and the authors and publisher worked hard throughout the development of this text to stay on top of those changes. The seventh edition is the product of extensive market research including interviews with adopters and nonadopters and comprehensive reviews by faculty. In particular, we are grateful to the following individuals for their valuable contributions and suggestions.

Survey Participants

Diane Adcox
University of North Florida–Jacksonville

Sue Atkinson
Tarleton State University

Ed Bader
Holy Family College

Keith Baker
Oglethorpe University

C. Richard Baker
Fordham University

Audrie Beck
The American University

Joe Bentley
Bunker Hill Community College

Lucille Berry
Webster University

Robert Bricker
Case Western Reserve

William Brosi
Delhi College

Doug Brown
Eastern Montana College

Stuart Brown
Bristol Community College

Janice Buddinseck
Wagner College

Kurt Buerger
Anglo State University

Robert Cantwell
University of Phoenix–Utah

Bruce Cassel
Dutchess Community College

Stan Chu
Borough of Manhattan Community College

Bruce Collier
University of Texas–El Paso

Rosalind Cranor
Virginia Polytech Institute

James Crockett
University of Southern Mississippi

Lee Daugherty
Lorain County Community College

Mary Davis
University of Maryland

Frances Engel
Niagra University

J. Michael Erwin
University of Tennessee

Ali Fekrat
Georgetown University

Bill Felty
Lindenwood College

Clyde J. Galbraith
West Chester University

Susan D. Garr
Wayne State University

John Gercio
Loyola College

Martin Ginsberg
Rockland Community College

Earl Godfrey
Gardner-Webb College

Thomas Grant
Kutztown University

Paul W. Greenough
Assumption College

Roy Gross
Dutchess Community College

Vincent D. R. Guide
Clemson University

Pat Haggerty
Lansing Community College

Paul Hajja
Rivier College

Joh Haney
Lansing Community College

Thomas D. Harris
Indiana State University

Dennis Hart
Manchester Community College

Brenda Hartman
Tomball College

Mary Hatch
Thomas College

Margaret Hicks
Howard University

Patricia H. Holmes
Des Moines Area Community College

Anita Hope
Tarrant County Junior College

Andrew Jackson
Central State University

Donald W. Johnson, Sr.
Siena College

Glenn L. Johnson
Washington State University

Richard W. Jones
Lamar University

Ed Kerr
Bunker Hill Community College

David Kleinerman
Roosevelt University

Jane Konditi
Northwood University

Nathan J. Kranowski
Radford University

Michael Kulper
Santa Barbara Community College

Michael R. Lane
Nassau Community College

Judy Laux
Colorado College

Linda Lessing
SUNY–Farmingdale

Bruce McClane
Hartnell College

Melvin T. McClure
University of Maine

T. J. McCoy
Middlesex Community College

J. Harrison McCraw
West Georgia College

James E. McKinney
Valdosta State

B. J. Michalek
La Roche College

Andrew Miller
Hudson Valley Community College

Cheryl E. Mitchum
Virginia State University

Susan Moncada
Indiana State University

Susan Mulhern
Rivier College

Lee H. Nicholas
University of Southern Iowa

Kristine N. Palmer
Longwood College

Lynn M. Paluska
Nassau Community College

Seong Park
University of Tennessee–Chattanooga

Vikki Passikoff
Dutchess Community College

Barb Pauer
W. Wisconsin Tech Institute

Doug Pfister
Lansing Community College

Sharyll A. Plato
University of Central Oklahoma

Patricia P. Polk
University of Southern Mississippi

Harry Purcell
Ulster Community College

T. J. Regan
Middlesex County College

Ruthie G. Reynolds
Howard University

E. Barry Rice
Loyola College in Maryland

Cheryl Rumler
Monroe County Community College

Francis Sake
Mercer County Community College

Jackie Sanders
Mercer County Community College

Alex J. Sannella
Rutgers University

Thomas Sears
Hartwich College

John Sedensky
Newbury College

Sarah H. Smith
Cedarville College

John Snyder
Mohawk Valley Community College

Leonard E. Stokes
Siena College

Janice Stoudemire
Midlands Technical College–Airport Campus

Marty Stub
DeVry Institute–Chicago

Barbara Sturdevant
Delhi College

William N. Sullivan
Assumption College

Norman A. Sunderman
Angelo State University

Janice M. Swanson
Southern Oregon State College

Norman Swanson
Greenville College

Audrey G. Taylor
Wayne State University

Kayla Tessler
Oklahoma City Community College

Julia Tiernan
Merrimack College

John Vaccaro
Bunker Hill Community College

Al Veragraziano
Santa Barbara Community College

David Wagaman
Kutztown University

Karen Walton
John Carroll University

Linda Wanacott
Portland Community College

Jim Weglin
North Seattle Community College

David P. Weiner
University of San Francisco

L.K. Williams
Morehead State University

Marge Zolldi
Husson College

Reviewers

Lucille Berry
Webster University

Elizabeth L. Boudreau
Newbury College

Wayne G. Bremser
Villanova University

Fred Dial
Stephen F. Austin State University

Larry Falcetto
Emporia State University

Katherine Beal Frazier
North Carolina State University

Al L. Hartgraves
Emory University

Martin G. Jagels
University of South Carolina

Emel Kahya
Rutgers University

Emogene W. King
Tyler Junior College

Jane Konditi
Northwood University

Charles Konkol
University of Wisconsin–Milwaukee

William Lawler
Tomball College

Keith R. Leeseberg
Manatee Junior College–Bradenton

Susan Moncada
Indiana State University

Lee H. Nicholas
University of Northern Iowa

Douglas R. Pfister
Lansing Community College

Patricia P. Polk
University of Southern Mississippi

Richard Rand
Tennessee Technical University

Ruthie G. Reynolds
Howard University

Marilyn Rholl
Lane Community College

E. Berry Rice
Loyola College in Maryland

William Richardson
University of Phoenix

Douglas Sharp
Wichita State University

Janet Stoudemire
Midlands Technical College–Airport Campus

Marilyn Young
Tulsa Junior College–Southeast

Annotations Authors

Diane Adcox
Instructor of Accounting
University of North Florida–Jacksonville

C. Sue Cook
Tulsa Junior College

Alan B. Cryzewski
Indiana State University

Patricia H. Holmes, CPA (Coordinator)
Des Moines Area Community College

Donald W. Johnson, Sr.
Siena College

Linda Lessing
SUNY at Farmingdale

Cheryl E. Mitchem (Coordinator)
Virginia State University

Lee H. Nicholas
University of Northern Iowa

Lynn Mazzola Paluska
Nassau Community College

Benjamin Shlaes, CPA (Coordinator)
Des Moines Area Community College

Margaret Skinner
SUNY at New Paltz

Leonard F. Stokes III, CPA
Siena College

Kathy J. Tam, CPA
Tulsa Junior College

Contents in Brief

CONTENTS

Chapter 3
Adjustments for Financial Reporting 101

Chapter 4
Completing the Accounting Cycle 132

Chapter 5
Accounting Theory Underlying Financial Accounting 173

CHAPTER 6
MERCHANDISING TRANSACTIONS: INTRODUCTION TO INVENTORIES AND CLASSIFIED INCOME STATEMENT 210

CHAPTER 7
MEASURING AND REPORTING INVENTORIES 247

PART III

MANAGEMENT'S PERSPECTIVES IN ACCOUNTING FOR RESOURCES   292

PART IV

SOURCES OF EQUITY CAPITAL FOR MANAGEMENT'S USE IN PRODUCING REVENUE   430

CHAPTER 11
PLANT ASSET DISPOSALS, NATURAL RESOURCES, AND INTANGIBLE ASSETS   399

CHAPTER 12
STOCKHOLDERS' EQUITY: CLASSES OF CAPITAL STOCK   433

CHAPTER 13
CORPORATIONS: PAID-IN CAPITAL, RETAINED EARNINGS, DIVIDENDS, AND TREASURY STOCK   464

CHAPTER 14
STOCK INVESTMENTS: COST, EQUITY, CONSOLIDATIONS; INTERNATIONAL ACCOUNTING   500

PART V
ANALYSIS OF FINANCIAL STATEMENTS: USING THE STATEMENT OF CASH FLOWS   578

CHAPTER 16
ANALYSIS USING THE STATEMENT OF CASH FLOWS   581

CHAPTER 17
ANALYSIS AND INTERPRETATION OF FINANCIAL STATEMENTS   625

FINANCIAL ACCOUNTING
A BUSINESS PERSPECTIVE

INTRODUCTION

THE ACCOUNTING ENVIRONMENT

You have embarked on the challenging and rewarding study of accounting—an old and time-honored discipline. History indicates that all developed societies require certain accounting records. Record-keeping in an accounting sense is thought to have begun about 4000 B.C.

The record-keeping, control, and verification problems of the ancient world had many characteristics similar to those we encounter today. For example, ancient governments also kept records of receipts and disbursements and used procedures to check on the honesty and reliability of employees.

A study of the evolution of accounting suggests that accounting processes have developed primarily in response to business needs. Also, economic progress has affected the development of accounting processes. History shows that the higher the level of civilization, the more elaborate the accounting methods.

The emergence of double-entry bookkeeping was a crucial event in accounting history. In 1494, a Franciscan monk, Luca Pacioli, described the double-entry Method of Venice system in his text called *Summa de Arithmetica, Geometric, Proportion et Proportionalite* (Everything about Arithmetic, Geometry, and Proportion). Many consider Pacioli's *Summa* to be a reworked version of a manuscript that circulated among teachers and pupils of the Venetian school of commerce and arithmetic.

Since Pacioli's days, the roles of accountants and professional accounting organizations have expanded in business and society. As professionals, accountants have a responsibility for placing public service above their commitment to personal economic gain. Complementing their obligation to society, accountants have analytical and evaluative skills needed in the solution of ever-growing world problems. The special abilities of accountants, their independence, and their high ethical standards permit them to make significant and unique contributions to business and areas of public interest.

You probably will find that of all the business knowledge you have acquired or will learn, the study of accounting will be the most useful. Your financial and economic decisions as a student and consumer involve accounting information. When

1

you file income tax returns, accounting information helps determine your taxes payable. Understanding the discipline of accounting also can influence many of your future professional decisions. You cannot escape the effects of accounting information on your personal and professional life.

Every profit-seeking business organization that has economic resources, such as money, machinery, and buildings, uses accounting information. For this reason, accounting is called the *language of business*. Accounting also serves as the language providing financial information about not-for-profit organizations such as governments, churches, charities, fraternities, and hospitals. However, this text concentrates on accounting for business firms.

The accounting system of a profit-seeking business is an information system designed to provide relevant financial information on the resources of a business and the effects of their use. Information is relevant if it has some impact on a decision that must be made. Companies present this relevant information in their financial statements. In preparing these statements, accountants consider the users of the information, such as owners and creditors, and decisions they make that require financial information.

As a background for studying accounting, this Introduction defines accounting and lists the functions accountants perform. In addition to surveying employment opportunities in accounting, it differentiates between financial and managerial accounting. Because accounting information must conform to certain standards, we discuss several prominent organizations contributing to these standards. As you continue your study of accounting in this text, accounting—the language of business—will become your language also. You will realize that you are constantly exposed to accounting information in your everyday life.

ACCOUNTING DEFINED

Objective 1
Define accounting.

The American Accounting Association—one of the accounting organizations discussed later in this Introduction—defines **accounting** as *"the process of identifying, measuring, and communicating economic information to permit informed judgments and decisions by the users of the information."*[1] This information is primarily financial—stated in money terms. Accounting, then, is a measurement and communication process used to report on the activities of profit-seeking business organizations and not-for-profit organizations. As a measurement and communication process for business, accounting supplies information that permits informed judgments and decisions by users of the data.

The accounting process provides financial data for a broad range of individuals whose objectives in studying the data vary widely. Bank officials, for example, may study a company's financial statements to evaluate the company's ability to repay a loan. Prospective investors may compare accounting data from several companies to decide which company represents the best investment. Accounting also supplies management with significant financial data useful for decision making.

Reliable information is necessary before decision makers can make a sound decision involving the allocation of scarce resources. Accounting information is valuable because decision makers can use it to evaluate the financial consequences of various alternatives. Accountants eliminate the need for a crystal ball to estimate the future. They can reduce uncertainty by using professional judgment to quantify the future financial impact of taking action or delaying action.

Although accounting information plays a significant role in reducing uncertainty within the organization, it also provides financial data for persons outside the company. This information tells how management has discharged its responsibility for protecting and managing the company's resources. Stockholders have the right to know how a company is managing its investments. In fulfilling this obligation, accoun-

---

[1]American Accounting Association, *A Statement of Basic Accounting Theory* (Evanston, Ill., 1966), p. 1.

tants prepare financial statements such as an income statement, a statement of retained earnings, a balance sheet, and a statement of cash flows. In addition, they prepare tax returns for federal and state governments, as well as fulfill other governmental filing requirements.

Accounting is often confused with bookkeeping. Bookkeeping is a mechanical process that records the routine economic activities of a business. Accounting includes bookkeeping but goes well beyond it in scope. Accountants analyze and interpret financial information, prepare financial statements, conduct audits, design accounting systems, prepare special business and financial studies, prepare forecasts and budgets, and provide tax services.

Specifically the accounting process consists of the following groups of functions (see Illustration 0.1):

Objective 2
Describe the functions performed by accountants.

1. Accountants *observe* many events (or activities) and *identify* and *measure* in financial terms (dollars) those events considered evidence of economic activity. (Often, these three functions are collectively referred to as *analyze*.) The purchase and sale of goods and services are economic events.

2. Next, the economic events are *recorded, classified* into meaningful groups, and *summarized*.

3. Accountants *report* on economic events (or business activity) by preparing financial statements and special reports. Often accountants *interpret* these statements and reports for various groups such as management, investors, and creditors. Interpretation may involve determining how the business is performing compared to prior years and other similar businesses.

EMPLOYMENT OPPORTUNITIES IN ACCOUNTING

During the last half-century, accounting has gained the same professional status as the medical and legal professions. Today, the accountants in the United States number well over a million. In addition, several million people hold accounting-related positions. Typically, accountants provide services in various branches of accounting. These include public accounting, management (industrial) accounting, governmental or other not-for-profit accounting, and higher education. According to the Bureau of Labor Statistics, the demand for accountants will increase by 40% by the year 2000. This increase is greater than for any other profession. You may want to consider accounting as a career.

Objective 3
Describe employment opportunities in accounting.

Public accounting firms offer professional accounting and related services for a fee to companies, other organizations, and individuals. An accountant may become a **Certified Public Accountant (CPA)** by passing an examination prepared and graded by the American Institute of Certified Public Accountants (AICPA). As of May 1994, the CPA examination became a two-day exam given each May and November. The sections include business law and professional responsibilities, auditing, accounting and reporting, and financial accounting and reporting. The examination contains multiple-choice questions, other objective question formats, and essays or problems. Those who grade the exams consider effective writing skills an important factor when evaluating the essay questions. In addition to passing the exam, CPA candidates must meet other requirements, which include obtaining a state license. These requirements vary by state. A number of states require a CPA candidate to have completed specific accounting courses and earned a certain number of college credits (five years of study in many states); worked a certain number of years in public accounting, industry, or government; and lived in that state a certain length of time before taking the CPA examination. As of the year 2000, five years of course work will be required to become a member of the AICPA.

After a candidate passes the CPA examination, some states (called one-tier states) insist that the candidate meet all requirements before the state grants the CPA certificate and license to practice. Other states (called two-tier states) issue the CPA

Public Accounting

ILLUSTRATION 0.1
Functions Performed
by Accountants

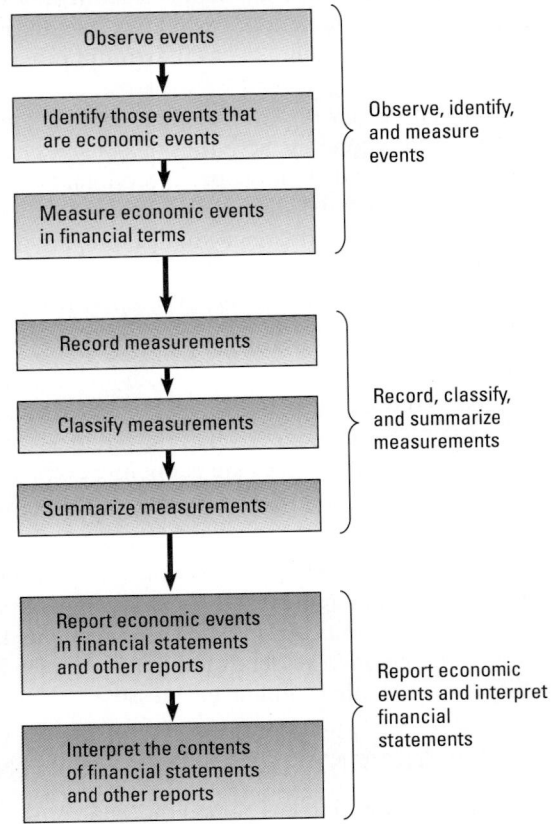

certificate immediately after the candidate passes the exam. However, these states issue the license to practice only after all other requirements have been met. CPAs who want to renew their licenses to practice must stay current through continuing professional education programs and must prove that they have done so. No one can claim to be a CPA and offer the services normally provided by a CPA unless that person holds an active license to practice.

The public accounting profession in the United States consists of the Big-Six international CPA firms, several national firms, many regional firms, and numerous local firms. The Big-Six firms include Arthur Andersen & Co; Coopers & Lybrand; Deloitte & Touche; Ernst & Young; KPMG Peat Marwick; and Price Waterhouse & Co. At all levels, these public accounting firms provide auditing, tax, and management advisory (or consulting) services. In recent years, teams of auditors, tax experts, and consultants have begun specializing in a particular industry (such as health care) and working together to serve the CPA firm's clients in that industry.

AUDITING   A business seeking a loan or attempting to have its securities traded on a stock exchange usually must provide financial statements to support its request. Users of a company's financial statements are more confident that the company is presenting its statements fairly when a CPA has audited the statements. For this reason, companies hire CPA firms to conduct examinations **(independent audits)** of their accounting and related records. **Independent auditors** of the CPA firm check some of the company's records by contacting external sources. For example, the accountant may contact a bank to verify the cash balances of the client. After completing a company audit, independent auditors give an **independent auditor's opinion or report.** (For an example of an auditor's opinion, see The Coca-Cola Company annual report in the separate annual report booklet you received with this text.) This report states whether the company's financial statements fairly (equitably) report the economic performance and financial condition of the business. As you will learn in the next section, auditors within a business also conduct audits, which are not independent audits.

TAX SERVICES   CPAs often provide expert advice on tax planning and preparing federal, state, and local tax returns. The objective in preparing tax returns is to use legal means to minimize the taxes paid. Almost every major business decision has a tax impact. Tax planning helps clients know the tax effects of each financial decision.

MANAGEMENT ADVISORY (OR CONSULTING) SERVICES   Management advisory services constitute the fastest growing service area for most large and many smaller CPA firms. Management frequently identifies projects for which it decides to retain the services of a CPA. For example, management may seek help in selecting new computer hardware and software. Also, the auditing services provided by CPAs often result in suggestions on how clients can improve their operations. For example, CPAs might suggest improvements in the design and installation of an accounting system, the electronic processing of accounting data, inventory control, budgeting, or financial planning. In addition, a relatively fast-growing service area provided by CPAs is financial planning, often for the executives of audit clients.

Management (or Industrial) Accounting

In contrast to public accountants, who provide accounting services for many clients, **management accountants** provide accounting services for a single business. Some companies employ only one management accountant, while others employ a large number. In a company with several management accountants, the person in charge of the accounting activity is often the **controller** or **chief financial officer.**

Management accountants may or may not be CPAs. If management accountants pass an examination prepared and graded by the Institute of Certified Management Accountants (ICMA) and meet certain other requirements, they become **Certified Management Accountants (CMAs).** The ICMA is an affiliate of the Institute of Management Accountants, an organization primarily consisting of management accountants employed in private industry.

Many management accountants specialize in one particular area of accounting. For example, some may specialize in measuring and controlling costs, others in budgeting (the development of plans for future operations), and still others in financial accounting and reporting. Many management accountants become specialists in the design and installation of computerized accounting systems. Other management accountants are **internal auditors** who conduct **internal audits.** They ensure that the company's divisions and departments follow the policies and procedures of management. This last group of management accountants may earn the designation of **Certified Internal Auditor (CIA).** The Institute of Internal Auditors (IIA) grants the CIA certificate to accountants after they have successfully completed the IIA examination and met certain other requirements.

A career in management accounting can be very challenging and rewarding. In recent years, management accountants have realized that to justify their positions they must add value to their organizations through their activities. Management accountants assist managers in implementing **total quality management (TQM).** This technique stresses constantly improving services, products, and the processes that produce them; empowering each member of the organization to make informed decisions; and exceeding customer expectations regarding quality. One tool that management accountants use to help accomplish these goals is **activity based costing (ABC).** Activity based costing identifies the cost of producing a product or performing a service so the inefficiencies can be reduced or eliminated. Later chapters describe this tool in greater detail.

Governmental and Other Not-for-Profit Accounting

Many accountants, including CPAs, work in **governmental and other not-for-profit accounting.** They have essentially the same educational background and training as accountants in public accounting and management accounting.

Governmental agencies at the federal, state, and local levels employ governmental accountants. Often the duties of these accountants relate to tax revenues and expenditures. For example, Internal Revenue Service employees use their accounting backgrounds in reviewing tax returns and investigating tax fraud. Government agencies that regulate business activity, such as a state public service commission that regulates public utilities (e.g., telephone company, electric company), usually employ governmental accountants. These agencies often employ governmental accountants who can review and evaluate the utilities' financial statements and rate increase requests. Also, FBI agents trained as accountants find their accounting backgrounds useful in investigating criminals involved in illegal business activities, such as drugs or gambling.

Not-for-profit organizations, such as churches, charities, fraternities, and universities, need accountants to record and account for funds received and disbursed. Even though these agencies do not have a profit motive, they should operate efficiently and use resources effectively.

Higher Education

Approximately 10,000 accountants are employed in higher education. The activities of these **academic accountants** include teaching accounting courses, conducting scholarly and applied research and publishing the results, and performing service for the institution and the community. Faculty positions exist in two-year colleges, four-year colleges, and universities with graduate programs. A significant shortage of accounting faculty will probably develop due to the anticipated retirement in the late 1990s of many current faculty members. Starting salaries will continue to rise significantly because of the shortage. You may want to talk with some of your professors about the advantages and disadvantages of pursuing an accounting career in higher education.

FINANCIAL ACCOUNTING VERSUS MANAGERIAL ACCOUNTING

Objective 4
Differentiate between financial and managerial accounting.

An accounting information system provides data to help decision makers both outside and inside the business. Decision makers outside the business are affected in some way by the performance of the business. Decision makers inside the business are responsible for the performance of the business. For this reason, accounting is divided into two categories: financial accounting for those outside and managerial accounting for those inside.

Financial Accounting

Financial accounting information appears in financial statements that are intended primarily for external use (although management also uses them for certain internal decisions). Stockholders and creditors are two of the outside parties who need financial accounting information. These outside parties decide on matters pertaining to the entire company, such as whether to increase or decrease their investment in a company or to extend credit to a company. Consequently, financial accounting information relates to the company as a whole, while managerial accounting focuses on the parts or segments of the company.

Management accountants in a company prepare the financial statements. Thus, management accountants must be knowledgeable concerning financial accounting and reporting. The financial statements are the representations of management, not the CPA firm that performs the audit.

The external users of accounting information fall into six groups; each has different interests in the company and wants answers to unique questions. The groups and some of their possible questions are:

1. **Owners and prospective owners.** Has the company earned satisfactory income on its total investment? Should an investment be made in this company? Should

the present investment be increased, decreased, or retained at the same level? Can the company install costly pollution control equipment and still be profitable?

2. **Creditors and lenders.** Should a loan be granted to the company? Will the company be able to pay its debts as they become due?

3. **Employees and their unions.** Does the company have the ability to pay increased wages? Is the company financially able to provide long-term employment for its workforce?

4. **Customers.** Does the company offer useful products at fair prices? Will the company survive long enough to honor its product warranties?

5. **Governmental units.** Is the company, such as a local public utility, charging a fair rate for its services?

6. **General public.** Is the company providing useful products and gainful employment for citizens without causing serious environmental problems?

General-purpose financial statements provide much of the information needed by external users of financial accounting. These **financial statements** are formal reports providing information on a company's financial position, cash inflows and outflows, and the results of operations. Many companies publish these statements in annual reports. (See The Coca-Cola Company annual report in the separate annual report booklet.) The **annual report** also contains the independent auditor's opinion as to the fairness of the financial statements, as well as information about the company's activities, products, and plans.

Financial accounting information is historical in nature, reporting on what has happened in the past. To facilitate comparisons between companies, this information must conform to certain accounting standards or principles called **generally accepted accounting principles (GAAP).** These generally accepted accounting principles for businesses or governmental organizations have developed through accounting practice or been established by an authoritative organization. We describe several of these authoritative organizations in the next major section of the chapter.

Managerial Accounting

Managerial accounting information is for internal use and provides special information for the managers of a company. The information managers use may range from broad, long-range planning data to detailed explanations of why actual costs varied from cost estimates. Managerial accounting information should:

1. Relate to the part of the company for which the manager is responsible. For example, a production manager wants information on costs of production but not of advertising.

2. Involve planning for the future. For instance, a budget would show financial plans for the coming year.

3. Meet two tests: the accounting information must be useful (relevant) and must not cost more to gather and process than it is worth.

Managerial accounting generates information that managers can use to make sound decisions. The four major types of internal management decisions are:

1. **Financial decisions**—deciding what amounts of capital (funds) are needed to run the business and whether to secure these funds from owners (stockholders) or creditors. In this sense, *capital* means money used by the company to purchase resources such as machinery and buildings and to pay expenses of conducting the business.

2. **Resource allocation decisions**—deciding how the total capital of a company is to be invested, such as the amount to be invested in machinery.

3. **Production decisions**—deciding what products are to be produced, by what means, and when.

4. **Marketing decisions**—setting selling prices and advertising budgets; determining the location of a company's markets and how to reach them.

Later chapters discuss managerial accounting in depth.

DEVELOPMENT OF FINANCIAL ACCOUNTING STANDARDS

Objective 5
Identify several organizations that have a role in the development of financial accounting standards.

Several organizations are influential in the establishment of generally accepted accounting principles (GAAP) for businesses or governmental organizations. These are the American Institute of Certified Public Accountants, the Financial Accounting Standards Board, the Governmental Accounting Standards Board, the Securities and Exchange Commission, the American Accounting Association, the Financial Executives Institute, and the Institute of Management Accountants. Each organization has contributed in a different way to the development of GAAP.

American Institute of Certified Public Accountants (AICPA)

The **American Institute of Certified Public Accountants (AICPA)** is a professional organization of CPAs. Many of these CPAs are in public accounting practice. Until recent years, the AICPA was the dominant organization in the development of accounting standards. In a 20-year period ending in 1959, the AICPA Committee on Accounting Procedure issued 51 *Accounting Research Bulletins* recommending certain principles or practices. From 1959 through 1973, the committee's successor, the **Accounting Principles Board (APB),** issued 31 numbered *Opinions* that CPAs generally are required to follow. Through its monthly magazine, the *Journal of Accountancy,* its research division, and its other divisions and committees, the AICPA continues to influence the development of accounting standards and practices. Two of its committees—the Accounting Standards Committee and the Auditing Standards Committee—are particularly influential in providing input to the Financial Accounting Standards Board (the current rule-making body) and to the Securities and Exchange Commission and other regulatory agencies.

Financial Accounting Standards Board (FASB)

In 1973, an independent, seven-member, full-time **Financial Accounting Standards Board (FASB)** replaced the Accounting Principles Board. The FASB has issued numerous *Statements of Financial Accounting Standards.* The old *Accounting Research Bulletins* and *Accounting Principles Board Opinions* are still effective unless specifically superseded by a Financial Accounting Standards Board Statement. The FASB is the *private sector* organization now responsible for the development of new financial accounting standards.

The Emerging Issues Task Force of the FASB interprets official pronouncements for general application by accounting practitioners. The conclusions of this task force must also be followed in filings with the Securities and Exchange Commission.

Governmental Accounting Standards Board (GASB)

In 1984, the **Governmental Accounting Standards Board (GASB)** was established with a full-time chairperson and four part-time members. The GASB issues statements on accounting and financial reporting in the governmental area. This organization is the *private sector* organization now responsible for the development of new governmental accounting concepts and standards. The GASB also has the authority to issue interpretations of these standards.

Securities and Exchange Commission (SEC)

Created under the Securities and Exchange Act of 1934, the **Securities and Exchange Commission (SEC)** is a government agency that administers important acts dealing with the interstate sale of securities (stocks and bonds). The SEC has the authority to prescribe accounting and reporting practices for companies under its jurisdiction. This includes virtually every major U.S. business corporation. Instead of exercising this power, the SEC has adopted a policy of working closely with the accounting profession, especially the FASB, in the development of accounting standards. The SEC indicates to the FASB the accounting topics it believes the FASB should address.

Consisting largely of accounting educators, the **American Accounting Association (AAA)** has sought to encourage research and study at a theoretical level into the concepts, standards, and principles of accounting. One of its quarterly magazines, *The Accounting Review,* carries many articles reporting on scholarly accounting research. Another quarterly journal, *Accounting Horizons,* reports on more practical matters directly related to accounting practice. A third journal, *Issues in Accounting Education,* contains articles relating to accounting education matters. Students may join the AAA as associate members by contacting the American Accounting Association, 5717 Bessie Drive, Sarasota, Florida 34233.

American Accounting Association (AAA)

The **Financial Executives Institute** is an organization established in 1931 whose members are primarily financial policy-making executives. Many of its members are chief financial officers (CFOs) of very large corporations. The role of the CFO has evolved in recent years from number cruncher to strategic planner. These CFOs played a major role in restructuring American businesses in the early 1990s. Slightly more than 14,000 financial officers, representing approximately 7,000 companies in the United States and Canada, are members of the FEI. Through its Committee on Corporate Reporting (CCR) and other means, the FEI is very effective in representing the views of the private financial sector to the FASB and to the Securities and Exchange Commission and other regulatory agencies.

Financial Executives Institute (FEI)

The **Institute of Management Accountants** (formerly the National Association of Accountants) is an organization with approximately 70,000 members, consisting of management accountants in private industry, CPAs, and academics. The primary focus of the organization is on the use of management accounting information for internal decision making. However, management accountants prepare the financial statements for external users. Thus, through its Management Accounting Practices (MAP) Committee and other means, the IMA provides input on financial accounting standards to the Financial Accounting Standards Board and to the Securities and Exchange Commission and other regulatory agencies.

Institute of Management Accountants (IMA)

Many other organizations such as the Financial Analysts Federation (composed of investment advisors and investors), the Securities Industry Associates (composed of investment bankers), and CPA firms have committees or task forces that respond to Exposure Drafts of proposed FASB Statements. Their reactions are in the form of written statements sent to the FASB and testimony given at FASB hearings. Many individuals also make their reactions known to the FASB.

Other Organizations

ETHICAL BEHAVIOR OF ACCOUNTANTS

Several accounting organizations have codes of ethics governing the behavior of their members. For instance, both the American Institute of Certified Public Accountants and the Institute of Management Accountants have formulated such codes. Many business firms have also developed codes of ethics for their employees to follow.

Ethical behavior involves more than merely making sure you are not violating a code of ethics. Most of us sense what is right and wrong. Yet get-rich-quick opportunities can tempt many of us. Almost any day, newspaper headlines reveal public officials and business leaders who did not do the right thing. Greed won out over their sense of right and wrong. These individuals followed slogans such as: "Get yours while the getting is good"; "Do unto others before they do unto you"; and "You have done wrong only if you get caught." More appropriate slogans might be: "If it seems too good to be true, it usually is"; "There are no free lunches"; and the golden rule, "Do unto others as you would have them do unto you."

An accountant's most valuable asset is an honest reputation. Those who take the *high road* of ethical behavior receive praise and honor; they are sought out for their advice and services. They also like themselves and what they represent. Occasionally, accountants do take the *low road* and suffer the consequences. They sometimes find their names mentioned in *The Wall Street Journal* in an unfavorable light, and former friends and colleagues look down on them. Some of these individuals are removed from the profession. Fortunately, the accounting profession has many leaders who have taken the high road, gained the respect of friends and colleagues, and become role models for all of us to follow.

Many chapters in the text include an ethics case entitled, "An Ethical Perspective." We know you will benefit from thinking about the *situational ethics* in these cases. Often you will not have much difficulty in determining "right and wrong." Instead of making the cases "close calls," we have attempted to include situations business students might actually encounter in their careers.

CRITICAL THINKING AND COMMUNICATION SKILLS

Accountants in practice and business executives have generally been dissatisfied with accounting graduates' ability to think critically and to communicate their ideas effectively. The Accounting Education Change Commission has recommended that changes be made in the education of accountants to remove these complaints.

To address these concerns, we have included a section at the end of each chapter entitled, "Beyond the Numbers—Critical Thinking." In that section, you are required to work relatively unstructured business decision cases, analyze real-world annual report data, write about situations involving ethics, and participate in group projects. Most of the other end-of-chapter materials also involve analysis and written communication of ideas.

In some of the cases, analyses, ethics situations, and group projects, you are asked to write a memorandum regarding the situation. In writing such a memorandum, identify your role (auditor, consultant), the audience (management, stockholders, and creditors), and the task (the specific assignment). Present your ideas clearly and concisely.

The purpose of the group projects is to assist you in learning to listen to and work with others. These skills are important in succeeding in the business world. Team players listen to the views of others and work cohesively with them to achieve group goals.

INTERNET SKILLS

The Internet is a fact of life. It is important for accountants and students to be able to use the Internet to find relevant information. Thus, each chapter contains approximately two Internet projects related to accounting. Your instructor might assign some of these, or you could pursue them on your own.

HOW TO STUDY THE CHAPTERS IN THIS TEXT

In studying each chapter:

1. Begin by reading the learning objectives at the beginning of each chapter.
2. Read "Understanding the Learning Objectives" at the end of the chapter for a preview of the chapter content.
3. Read the chapter content. Notice that the learning objectives appear in the margins at the appropriate places in the chapter. Each exercise at the end of the chapters identifies the learning objective(s) to which it pertains. If you learn best by reading about a concept and then working a short exercise that illustrates that concept, work the exercises as you read the chapter. Use the forms in the Working Papers supplement for working these exercises.

4. Reread "Understanding the Learning Objectives" to determine if you have achieved each objective.

5. Study the New Terms to see if you understand each term. If you do not understand a certain term, refer to the page indicated to read about the term in its original context.

6. Take the Self-Test and then check your answers with those at the end of the chapter.

7. Work the Demonstration Problem to further reinforce your understanding of the chapter content. Then, compare your solution to the correct solution that follows immediately.

8. Look over the questions at the end of the chapter and think out an answer to each one. If you cannot answer a particular question, refer back into the chapter for the needed information.

9. Work at least some of the exercises at the end of the chapter.

10. Work the Problems assigned by your instructor, using the forms in the Working Papers supplement.

11. Study the items in the "Beyond the Numbers—Critical Thinking" section and the "Using the Internet—A View of the Real World" section at the end of each chapter to relate what you have learned to real-world situations.

12. Work the Study Guide for the chapter. The Study Guide is a supplement that contains (for each chapter) Learning Objectives; Reference Outline; Chapter Review; Demonstration Problem and Solution (different from the one in the text); Matching, Completion, True-False, and Multiple-Choice Questions; and Solutions to all Questions and Exercises in the Study Guide.

If you perform each of these steps for each chapter, you should do well in the course. A free computerized tutorial is also available that you can use to further test your understanding. Ask your instructor about its availability at your school. Remember that a knowledge of accounting will serve you well regardless of the career you pursue.

I

ACCOUNTING: THE LANGUAGE OF BUSINESS

A MANAGER'S PERSPECTIVE

Ogden Tabb
Deputy Director of Advertising
The Coca-Cola Company

Learning how the numbers fit together in the financial statement and understanding what those numbers mean is crucial. Students can either learn it now in their accounting principles course, or they're going to have to learn it later on the job.

As Deputy Director of Advertising I manage the advertising budget for the production of television, radio, and print advertising for all global brands including Coke, Diet Coke, Sprite, and Fanta. I have little involvement in the creative process; my job

is to produce the ads with an underlying responsibility for the finances. My objective is to get the most for our advertising production dollar.

I began my career at The Coca-Cola Company in the accounting department, and I still rely heavily on that discipline to cover the financial aspects of advertising production.

Estimates for each project are submitted by the ad agencies. These estimates are carefully reviewed on a line-by-line basis by our inhouse staff of executive producers. We know how much we should be paying for each element in the production process.

The lowest estimate is not always necessarily the best one, however, because of the intangibles that exist in advertising. Advertising is only one piece in the marketing mix that drives sales, so it's really hard to quantify what advertising does—we just know we have to do it.

My budget for each brand is based on how much the company plans to spend on media advertising. A general rule is to spend no more than 10% of that amount on production.

The bottom line is that we want great advertising with highest production values at a fair price.

1

ACCOUNTING AND ITS USE IN BUSINESS DECISIONS

The Introduction to this text provided a background for your study of accounting. Now you are ready to learn about the forms of business organizations and the types of business activities they perform. This chapter presents the financial statements used by businesses. These financial statements show the results of decisions made by management. Creditors, investors, and managers use these statements in evaluating management's past decisions and as a basis for making future decisions.

In this chapter, you also study the accounting process (or accounting cycle) that accountants use to prepare those financial statements. This accounting process uses financial data such as the records of sales made to customers and purchases made from suppliers. In a systematic manner, accountants analyze, record, classify, summarize, and finally report these data in the financial statements of businesses. As you study this chapter, you will begin to understand the unique, systematic nature of accounting—the language of business.

FORMS OF BUSINESS ORGANIZATIONS

Accountants frequently refer to a business organization as an *accounting entity* or a *business entity*. A business entity is any business organization, such as a hardware store or grocery store, that exists as an economic unit. For accounting purposes, each business organization or **entity** has an existence separate from its owner(s), creditors, employees, customers, and other businesses.[1] This separate existence of the business organization is known as the **business entity concept.** Thus, in the accounting records

---

---

[1]When first studying any discipline, students encounter new terms. Usually these terms are set in boldface color and defined at their first occurrence. The boldface color terms are also listed and defined at the end of each chapter (see pages 36–37 in this chapter). After the definition of the term in the term list, a page number in parentheses indicates where the term is discussed in the chapter.

15

(concluded)

5. Using the underlying assumptions or concepts, analyze business transactions and determine their effects on items in the financial statements.

6. Prepare an income statement, a statement of retained earnings, and a balance sheet.

7. Analyze and use the financial results—the equity ratio.

of the business entity, the activities of each business should be kept separate from the activities of other businesses and from the personal financial activities of the owner(s).

Assume, for example, that you own two businesses, a physical fitness center and a horse stable. According to the business entity concept, you would consider each business as an independent business unit. Thus, you would normally keep separate accounting records for each business. Now assume your physical fitness center is unprofitable because you are not charging enough for the use of your exercise equipment. You can determine this fact because you are treating your physical fitness center and horse stable as two separate business entities. You must also keep your personal financial activities separate from your two businesses. Therefore, you cannot include the car you drive only for personal use as a business activity of your physical fitness center or your horse stable. However, the use of your truck to pick up feed for your horse stable is a business activity of your horse stable.

As you will see shortly, the business entity concept applies to the three forms of businesses—single proprietorships, partnerships, and corporations. Thus, for accounting purposes, all three business forms are separate from other business entities and from their owner(s). Although corporations are also legally separate from their owners, this is not true for single proprietorships and partnerships. We use the corporate approach in this text and include only a brief discussion of single proprietorships and partnerships.

Single Proprietorship

Objective 1
Identify and describe the three basic forms of business organizations.[2]

A **single proprietorship** is an unincorporated business owned by an individual and often managed by that same person. Single proprietors include physicians, lawyers, electricians, and other people in business for themselves. Many small service businesses and retail establishments are also single proprietorships. No legal formalities are necessary to organize such businesses, and usually business operations can begin with only a limited investment.

In a single proprietorship, the owner is solely responsible for all debts of the business. For accounting purposes, however, the business is a separate entity from the owner. Thus, single proprietors must keep the financial activities of the business, such as the receipt of fees from selling services to the public, separate from their personal financial activities. For example, owners of single proprietorships should not enter the cost of personal houses or car payments in the financial records of their businesses.

Partnership

A **partnership** is an unincorporated business owned by two or more persons associated as partners. Often the same persons who own the business also manage the business. Many small retail establishments and professional practices, such as dentists, physicians, attorneys, and many CPA firms, are partnerships.

A partnership begins with a verbal or written agreement. A written agreement is preferable because it provides a permanent record of the terms of the partnership. These terms include the initial investment of each partner, the duties of each partner, the means of dividing profits or losses between the partners each year, and the settlement after the death or withdrawal of a partner. Each partner may be held liable for all the debts of the partnership and for the actions of each partner within the scope of the business. However, as with the single proprietorship, for accounting purposes, the partnership is a separate business entity.

---

[2]After reading a portion of text material that covers a certain learning objective, some students immediately want to work an exercise that illustrates that material. The exercises at the end of each chapter are labeled with the learning objective to which they pertain. For instance, turn to pages 38–40 to see which learning objective(s) each exercise covers in Chapter 1. Also, "Reinforcing Problems," referring to specific exercises or problems that relate to the concepts being discussed, are mentioned in the margin of the text (e.g., see page 17).

A **corporation** is a business incorporated under the laws of a state and owned by a few stockholders or thousands of stockholders. Almost all large businesses and many small businesses are incorporated.

The corporation is unique in that it is a separate legal business entity. The owners of the corporation are **stockholders, or shareholders.** They buy shares of stock, which are units of ownership, in the corporation. Should the corporation fail, the owners would only lose the amount they paid for their stock. The corporate form of business protects the personal assets of the owners from the creditors of the corporation.[3]

Stockholders do not directly manage the corporation. They elect a board of directors to represent their interests. The board of directors selects the officers of the corporation, such as the president and vice presidents, who manage the corporation for the stockholders.

Accounting is necessary for all three forms of business organizations, and each company must follow generally accepted accounting principles (GAAP). Since corporations have such an important impact on our economy, we use them in this text to illustrate basic accounting principles and concepts.

Corporation

Note to the Student
To illustrate basic forms of business, use the local business section of the telephone directory. Find actual examples representing each form of business and discuss why specific businesses would choose a particular business form.

BUSINESS INSIGHT   Although corporations constitute about 17% of all business organizations, they account for almost 90% of all sales volume. Single proprietorships constitute about 75% of all business organizations but account for less than 10% of sales volume.

AN ACCOUNTING PERSPECTIVE

TYPES OF ACTIVITIES PERFORMED BY BUSINESS ORGANIZATIONS

The forms of business entities discussed in the previous section are classified according to the type of ownership of the business entity. Business entities can also be grouped by the type of business activities they perform—service companies, merchandising companies, and manufacturing companies. Any of these activities can be performed by companies using any of the three forms of business organizations.

Objective 2
Distinguish among the three types of activities performed by business organizations.

1. **Service companies** perform services for a fee. This group includes accounting firms, law firms, and dry cleaning establishments. The early chapters of this text describe accounting for service companies.
2. **Merchandising companies** purchase goods that are ready for sale and then sell them to customers. Merchandising companies include auto dealerships, clothing stores, and supermarkets. We begin the description of accounting for merchandising companies in Chapter 6.
3. **Manufacturing companies** buy materials, convert them into products, and then sell the products to other companies or to the final consumers. Manufacturing companies include steel mills, auto manufacturers, and clothing manufacturers.

Real World Example
Use the local business section of the telephone directory to find local examples of service, merchandising, and manufacturing activities performed by business organizations.

All of these companies produce financial statements as the final end product of their accounting process. These financial statements provide relevant financial information both to those inside the company—management—and to those outside the company—creditors, stockholders, and other interested parties. The next section introduces four common financial statements—the income statement, the statement of retained earnings, the balance sheet, and the statement of cash flows.

Reinforcing Problem
E1–1 Matching exercise

---

[3]When individuals seek a bank loan to finance the formation of a small corporation, the bank often requires those individuals to sign documents making them personally responsible for repaying the loan if the corporation cannot pay. In this instance, the individuals can lose their original investments plus the amount of the loan they are obligated to repay.

FINANCIAL STATEMENTS OF BUSINESS ORGANIZATIONS

Objective 3
Describe the content and purposes of the income statement, statement of retained earnings, balance sheet, and statement of cash flows.

Business entities may have many objectives and goals. For example, one of your objectives in owning a physical fitness center may be to improve *your* physical fitness. However, the two primary objectives of every business are profitability and solvency. **Profitability** is the ability to generate income. **Solvency** is the ability to pay debts as they become due. Unless a business can produce satisfactory income and pay its debts as they become due, the business cannot survive to realize its other objectives.

The financial statement that reflects a company's profitability is the **income statement.** The **statement of retained earnings** shows the change in retained earnings between the beginning and end of a period (e.g., a month or a year). The **balance sheet** reflects a company's solvency. The **statement of cash flows** shows the cash inflows and outflows for a company over a period of time. The headings and elements of each statement are similar from company to company. You have probably noticed this similarity in the financial statements of actual companies in the annual report booklet.

The Income Statement

Real World Example
The Wall Street Journal of December 6, 1996, had an article titled "Net Is a Surprise for National Semiconductor." The article mentioned that National Semiconductor Corporation reported stronger than expected earnings for its fiscal second quarter. Use this as an example for a discussion of the purpose of the income statement.

Reinforcing Problem
E1–2 Compute net income and revenue.

The **income statement,** sometimes called an earnings statement, reports the profitability of a business organization for a *stated period of time.* In accounting, we measure profitability for a period, such as a month or year, by comparing the revenues generated with the expenses incurred to produce these revenues. **Revenues** are the inflows of assets (such as cash) resulting from the sale of products or the rendering of services to customers. We measure revenues by the prices agreed on in the exchanges in which a business delivers goods or renders services. **Expenses** are the costs incurred to produce revenues. Expenses are measured by the assets surrendered or consumed in serving customers. If the revenues of a period exceed the expenses of the same period, **net income** results. Thus,

$$\text{Net income} = \text{Revenues} - \text{Expenses}$$

Net income is often called the *earnings* of the company. When expenses exceed revenues, the business has a **net loss,** and it has operated unprofitably.

In Illustration 1.1, Part A shows the income statement of Metro Courier, Inc., for July 1999. This California corporation performs courier delivery services of documents and packages in San Diego.

Metro's income statement for the month ended July 31, 1999, shows that the revenues (or delivery fees) generated by serving customers for July totaled $5,700. Expenses for the month amounted to $3,600. As a result of these business activities, Metro's net income for July was $2,100. To determine its net income, the company subtracts its expenses of $3,600 from its revenues of $5,700. Even though corporations are taxable entities, we ignore corporate income taxes at this point.

The Statement of Retained Earnings

Real World Example
A *Fortune* magazine article, "This Tough Guy Wants to Give You a Hug," October 14, 1996, stated that EDS could fire its entire marketing department and still count on about $80 billion in revenues over the next 10 years from contracts now on its books. This mention of revenues could be used to consider the placement and effect of revenues on the income statement.

One purpose of the *statement of retained earnings* is to connect the income statement and the balance sheet. The **statement of retained earnings** explains the changes in retained earnings between two balance sheet dates. These changes usually consist of the addition of net income (or deduction of net loss) and the deduction of dividends.

Dividends are the means by which a corporation rewards its stockholders (owners) for providing it with investment funds. A **dividend** is a payment (usually of cash) to the owners of the business; it is a distribution of income to owners rather than an expense of doing business. Because dividends are not an expense, they do not appear on the income statement.

The effect of a dividend is to reduce cash and retained earnings by the amount paid out. Then, the company no longer retains a portion of the income earned but passes it on to the stockholders. Receiving dividends is, of course, one of the primary reasons people invest in corporations.

ILLUSTRATION 1.1

A. Income Statement

METRO COURIER, INC.
Income Statement
For the Month Ended July 31, 1999

Revenues:		
Service revenue		$5,700
Expenses:		
Salaries expense	$2,600	
Rent expense	400	
Gas and oil expense	600	
Total expenses		3,600
Net income		$2,100

B. Statement of Retained Earnings

METRO COURIER, INC.
Statement of Retained Earnings
For the Month Ended July 31, 1999

Retained earnings, July 1	$ –0–
Add: Net income for July	2,100
Retained earnings, July 31	$2,100

C. Balance Sheet

METRO COURIER, INC.
Balance Sheet
July 31, 1999

Assets		Liabilities and Stockholders' Equity*	
Cash	$15,500	Liabilities:	
Accounts receivable	700	Accounts payable	$ 600
Trucks	20,000	Notes payable	6,000
Office equipment	2,500	Total liabilities	$ 6,600
		Stockholders' equity:	
		Capital stock	$30,000
		Retained earnings	2,100
		Total stockholders' equity	$32,100
Total assets	$38,700	Total liabilities and stockholders' equity	$38,700

*The liabilities and stockholders' equity portion of the balance sheet may be shown directly beneath the assets instead of to the right of them, as shown here. When liabilities and stockholders' equity are placed under the assets, the balance sheet is in the *vertical format* or *report form*. The vertical format is as acceptable as the *horizontal format* (or account form) used above.

The statement of retained earnings for Metro Courier, Inc., for July 1999 is relatively simple (see Part B of Illustration 1.1). Organized on June 1, Metro did not earn any revenues or incur any expenses during June. So Metro's beginning retained earnings balance on July 1 is zero. Metro then adds its $2,100 net income for July. Since Metro paid no dividends in July, the $2,100 would be the ending balance.

Next, Metro carries this $2,100 ending balance in retained earnings to the balance sheet (Part C). If there had been a net loss, it would have deducted the loss from the beginning balance on the statement of retained earnings. For instance, if during the next month (August) there is a net loss of $500, the loss would be deducted from the beginning balance in retained earnings of $2,100. The retained earnings balance at the end of August would be $1,600.

Dividends could also have affected the Retained Earnings balance. To give a more realistic illustration, assume that (1) Metro Courier, Inc.'s, net income for August was actually $1,500 (revenues of $5,600 less expenses of $4,100) and (2) the company

Reinforcing Problem

P1–3A Prepare income statement.

declared and paid dividends of $1,000. Then, Metro's statement of retained earnings for August would be:

Reinforcing Problem
E1–3 Compute retained earnings.

METRO COURIER, INC.
Statement of Retained Earnings
For the Month Ended August 31, 1999

Retained earnings, August 1	$2,100
Add: Net income for August	1,500
Total	$3,600
Less: Dividends	1,000
Retained earnings, August 31	$2,600

The Balance Sheet

Note to the Student
Describe a business in a given industry and identify what assets that business would probably have on its balance sheet.

The **balance sheet,** sometimes called the *statement of financial position,* lists the company's assets, liabilities, and stockholders' equity (including dollar amounts) as of a specific moment in time. That specific moment is the close of business on the date of the balance sheet. Notice how the heading of the balance sheet differs from the headings on the income statement and statement of retained earnings. A balance sheet is like a photograph; it captures the financial position of a company at a particular *point* in time. The other two statements are for a *period* of time. As you study about the assets, liabilities, and stockholders' equity contained in a balance sheet, you will understand why this financial statement provides information about the solvency of the business.

Real World Example
A *Fortune* magazine article, "Yahoo! Still Searching for Profits on the Internet," December 9, 1996, discussed the fact that the search companies derive their revenues from advertisers and not from visitors to their sites. For the most recent quarter, the four leading search firms had combined revenues of $16.2 million and combined losses of $16.4 million. How do these losses affect all three financial statements discussed so far?

Assets are things of value owned by the business. They are also called the *resources* of the business. Examples include cash, machines, and buildings. Assets have value because a business can use or exchange them to produce the services or products of the business. In Part C of Illustration 1.1, the assets of Metro Courier, Inc., amount to $38,700. Metro's assets consist of cash, **accounts receivable** (amounts due from customers for services previously rendered), trucks, and office equipment.

Liabilities are the debts owed by a business. Typically, a business must pay its debts by certain dates. A business incurs many of its liabilities by purchasing items on credit. Metro's liabilities consist of **accounts payable** (amounts owed to suppliers for previous purchases) and **notes payable** (written promises to pay a specific sum of money) totaling $6,600.[4]

Metro Courier, Inc., is a corporation. The owners' interest in a corporation is referred to as **stockholders' equity.** Metro's stockholders' equity consists of (1) $30,000 paid for shares of capital stock and (2) retained earnings of $2,100. **Capital stock** shows the amount of the owners' investment in the corporation. **Retained earnings** generally consists of the accumulated net income of the corporation minus dividends distributed to stockholders. We discuss these items later in the text. At this point, simply note that the balance sheet heading includes the name of the organization and the title and date of the statement. Notice also that the dollar amount of the total assets is equal to the claims on (or interest in) those assets. The balance sheet shows these claims under the heading "Liabilities and Stockholders' Equity."

The Statement of Cash Flows

Management is interested in the cash inflows to the company and the cash outflows from the company because these determine the company's cash it has available to pay its bills when due. The **statement of cash flows** shows the cash inflows and cash outflows from operating, investing, and financing activities. *Operating activities* generally include the cash effects of transactions and other events that enter into the determination of net income. *Investing activities* generally include business transactions involving the acquisition or disposal of long-term assets such as land, buildings, and equipment. *Financing activities* generally include the cash effects of transactions and other events involving creditors and owners (stockholders).

---

[4]Most notes bear interest, but in this chapter we assume that all notes bear no interest. Interest is an amount paid by the borrower to the lender (in addition to the amount of the loan) for use of the money over time.

Chapter 16 describes the statement of cash flows in detail. Our purpose here is to merely introduce this important financial statement. Normally, a firm prepares a statement of cash flows for the same time period as the income statement. The following statement, however, shows the cash inflows and outflows for Metro Courier, Inc., since it was formed on June 1, 1999. Thus, this cash flow statement is for two months.

METRO COURIER, INC.
Statement of Cash Flows
For the Two-Month Period Ended July 31, 1999

Cash flows from operating activities:		
Net income		$ 2,100
Adjustments to reconcile net income to net cash provided by operating activities:		
Increase in accounts receivable	(700)	
Increase in accounts payable	600	
Net cash provided by operating activities		$ 2,000
Cash flows from investing activities:		
Purchase of trucks	$(20,000)	
Purchase of office equipment	(2,500)	
Net cash used by investing activities		(22,500)
Cash flows from financing activities:		
Proceeds from notes payable	$ 6,000	
Proceeds from sale of capital stock	30,000	
Net cash provided by financing activities		36,000
Net increase in cash		$ 15,500

At this point in the course, you need to understand what a statement of cash flows is rather than how to prepare it. We do not ask you to prepare such a statement until you have studied Chapter 16.

The income statement, statement of retained earnings, balance sheet, and the statement of cash flows of Metro Courier, Inc., are the result of management's past decisions. They are the end products of the accounting process, which we explain in the next section. These financial statements give a picture of the solvency and profitability of the company. The accounting process details how this picture was made. Management and other interested parties use these statements to make future decisions. Management is the first to know the financial results; then, it publishes the financial statements to inform other users.

USES OF TECHNOLOGY   Accountants and students can find valuable information on the Internet, and it is generally free. To access the Internet you will need minimum hardware of a 486/33 computer, 14.4 modem, 8 megabytes of Random Access Memory, and 2 megabytes of available hard drive. The use of a more powerful computer and faster modem will make more efficient use of your time. You also need software that includes a PPP or SLIP connection and browsing software, such as Netscape Navigator or Microsoft Explorer. Alternatively, you can use the browsers in CompuServe, America Online, or Prodigy to access the Internet. To access a particular web site, under the File menu in many of the browsers select Open URL (stands for Universal Resource Locator) and type in the web address you desire to visit. For instance, you may desire to visit the Web page of the accounting firm, Arthur Andersen. If so, you would type:

http://www.arthurandersen.com

The "http" stands for hypertext transfer protocol. The "www" stands for World Wide Web. The "arthurandersen" is the address of the web server for this company. The "com" means that this entity is a company. Educational entities end their web address with "edu," and organizations, such as the Securities and Exchange Commission, end their web addresses with "org." At any time you are visiting one site and desire to visit a new site, you merely click on the current address and then type in the new address. If you would like to become familiar with using the Internet, you can do so by performing some of the Internet projects at the end of the chapters and/or visiting the websites identified in some of the other Uses of Technology boxes in the text.

AN ACCOUNTING PERSPECTIVE

THE FINANCIAL ACCOUNTING PROCESS

In this section, we explain the accounting equation—the framework for the entire accounting process. Then, we show you how to recognize a business transaction and describe underlying assumptions that accountants use to record business transactions. Next you learn how to analyze and record business transactions.

The Accounting Equation

Objective 4
State the basic accounting equation and describe its relationship to the balance sheet.

In the balance sheet presented in Illustration 1.1 (Part C), the total assets of Metro Courier, Inc., were equal to its total liabilities and stockholders' equity. This equality shows that the assets of a business are equal to its equities; that is,

$$\text{Assets} = \text{Equities}$$

Assets were defined earlier as the things of value owned by the business, or the economic resources of the business. **Equities** are all claims to, or interests in, assets. For example, assume that you purchased a new company automobile for $15,000 by investing $10,000 in your own corporation and borrowing $5,000 in the name of the corporation from a bank. Your equity in the automobile is $10,000, and the bank's equity is $5,000. You can further describe the $5,000 as a liability because the corporation owes the bank $5,000. Also, you can describe your $10,000 equity as stockholders' equity or interest in the asset. Since the owners in a corporation are stockholders, the basic **accounting equation** becomes:

$$\text{Assets (A)} = \text{Liabilities (L)} + \text{Stockholders' equity (SE)}$$

From Metro's balance sheet in Illustration 1.1 (Part C), we can enter in the amount of its assets, liabilities, and stockholders' equity:

$$
\begin{array}{ccccc}
\text{A} & = & \text{L} & + & \text{SE} \\
\$38,700 & = & \$6,600 & + & \$32,100
\end{array}
$$

Remember that someone must provide assets or resources—either a creditor or a stockholder. Therefore, this equation must always be in balance.

You can also look at the right side of this equation in another manner. The liabilities and stockholders' equity show the sources of an existing group of assets. Thus, liabilities are not only claims against assets but also sources of assets.

Reinforcing Problem
E1–4 Compute retained earnings and total assets at beginning of year.

Either creditors or owners provide all the assets in a corporation. The higher the proportion of assets provided by owners, the more solvent the company. However, companies can sometimes improve their profitability by borrowing from creditors and using the funds effectively. As a business engages in economic activity, the dollar amounts and composition of its assets, liabilities, and stockholders' equity change. *However, the equality of the basic accounting equation always holds.*

Analysis of Transactions

Objective 5
Using the underlying assumptions or concepts, analyze business transactions and determine their effects on items in the financial statements.

An accounting **transaction** is a business activity or event that causes a measurable change in the accounting equation, Assets = Liabilities + Stockholders' equity. An exchange of cash for merchandise is a transaction. The exchange takes place at an agreed price that provides an objective measure of economic activity. For example, the objective measure of the exchange may be $5,000. These two factors—evidence and measurement—make possible the recording of a transaction. Merely placing an order for goods is not a recordable transaction because no exchange has taken place.

A *source document* usually supports the evidence of the transaction. A **source document** is any written or printed evidence of a business transaction that describes the essential facts of that transaction. Examples of source documents are receipts for cash paid or received, checks written or received, bills sent to customers for services performed or bills received from suppliers for items purchased, cash register tapes, sales tickets, and notes given or received. We handle source documents constantly in our everyday life. Each source document initiates the process of recording a transaction.

UNDERLYING ASSUMPTIONS OR CONCEPTS In recording business transactions, accountants rely on certain underlying assumptions or concepts. Both preparers and users of financial statements must understand these assumptions:

1. **Business entity concept** (or accounting entity concept). Data gathered in an accounting system relate to a specific business unit or **entity.** The business entity concept assumes that each business has an existence separate from its owners, creditors, employees, customers, other interested parties, and other businesses.

2. **Money measurement concept.** Economic activity is initially recorded and reported in a common monetary unit of measure—the dollar in the United States. This form of measurement is known as *money measurement.*

3. **Exchange-price (or cost) concept (principle).** Most of the amounts in an accounting system are the objective money prices determined in the exchange process. As a result, we record most assets at their acquisition cost. **Cost** is the sacrifice made or the resources given up, measured in money terms, to acquire some desired thing, such as a new truck (asset).

4. **Going-concern (continuity) concept.** Unless strong evidence exists to the contrary, accountants assume that the business entity will continue operations into the indefinite future. Accountants call this assumption the *going-concern or continuity* concept. Assuming that the entity will continue indefinitely allows accountants to value long-term assets, such as land, at cost on the balance sheet since they are to be used rather than sold. Market values of these assets would be relevant only if they were for sale. For instance, accountants would still record land purchased in 1988 at its cost of $100,000 on the December 31, 1999, balance sheet even though its market value has risen to $300,000.

5. **Periodicity (time periods) concept.** According to the *periodicity (time periods)* concept or assumption, an entity's life can be meaningfully subdivided into time periods (such as months or years) to report the results of its economic activities.

Now that you understand business transactions and the five basic accounting assumptions, you are ready to follow some business transactions step by step. To begin, we divide Metro's transactions into two groups: (1) transactions affecting only the balance sheet in June, and (2) transactions affecting the income statement and/or the balance sheet in July. Note that we could also classify these transactions as operating, investing, or financing activities, as shown in the statement of cash flows on page 21.

TRANSACTIONS AFFECTING ONLY THE BALANCE SHEET Since each transaction affecting a business entity must be recorded in the accounting records, analyzing a transaction before actually recording it is an important part of financial accounting. An error in transaction analysis results in incorrect financial statements.

To illustrate the analysis of transactions and their effects on the basic accounting equation, the activities of Metro Courier, Inc., that led to the statements in Illustration 1.1 follow. The first set of transactions (for June), 1a, 2a, and so on, are repeated in the summary of transactions, Illustration 1.2 (Part A) on page 26. The second set of transactions (for July) (1b–6b) are repeated in Illustration 1.3 (Part A) on page 30.

1a. Owners Invested Cash When Metro Courier, Inc., was organized as a corporation on June 1, 1999, the company issued shares of capital stock for $30,000 cash to Ron Chaney, his wife, and their son. This transaction increased assets (cash) of Metro by $30,000 and increased equities (the capital stock element of stockholders' equity) by $30,000. Consequently, the transaction yields the following basic accounting equation:

Reinforcing Problem
E1–5 Analyze transactions.

Note to the Student
Choose a business you would like to start. Develop several transactions for your business and then describe the influence of those transactions on the financial statements.

Trans-action	Explanation	Cash	Accounts Receivable	Trucks	Office Equipment	=	Accounts Payable	Notes Payable	+	Capital Stock
	Beginning balances	$ –0–	$ –0–	$ –0–	$ –0– =		$ –0–	$ –0– +		$ –0–
1a	Stockholders invested cash	+30,000								+30,000
	Balances after transaction	$30,000			=					$30,000

Increased by $30,000 (Cash)   *Increased by $30,000* (Capital Stock)

2a. Borrowed Money   The company borrowed $6,000 from Chaney's father. Chaney signed the note for the company. The note bore no interest and the company promised to repay (recorded as a *note payable*) the amount borrowed within one year. After including the effects of this transaction, the basic equation is:

Trans-action	Explanation	Cash	Accounts Receivable	Trucks	Office Equipment	=	Accounts Payable	Notes Payable	+	Capital Stock
	Balances before transaction	$30,000				=				$30,000
2a	Borrowed money	+6,000						+6,000		
	Balances after transaction	$36,000				=		$6,000 +		$30,000

Increased by $6,000 (Cash)   *Increased by $6,000* (Notes Payable)

3a. Purchased Trucks and Office Equipment for Cash   Metro paid $20,000 cash for two used delivery trucks and $1,500 for office equipment. Trucks and office equipment are assets because the company uses them to earn revenues in the future. Note that this transaction does not change the total amount of assets in the basic equation but only changes the composition of the assets. This transaction decreased cash and increased trucks and office equipment (assets) by the total amount of the cash decrease. Metro received two assets and gave up one asset of equal value. Total assets are still $36,000. The accounting equation now is:

Trans-action	Explanation	Cash	Accounts Receivable	Trucks	Office Equipment	=	Accounts Payable	Notes Payable	+	Capital Stock
	Balances before transaction . . .	$36,000				=		$6,000 +		$30,000
3a	Purchased equipment for cash . .	–21,500		+20,000	+1,500					
	Balances after transaction	$14,500		$20,000	$1,500 =			$6,000 +		$30,000

Decreased by $21,500 (Cash)   *Increased by $20,000* (Trucks)   *Increased by $1,500* (Office Equipment)

4a. Purchased Office Equipment on Account (for Credit)   Metro purchased an additional $1,000 of office equipment on account, agreeing to pay within 10 days after receiving the bill. (To purchase an item *on account* means to buy it on credit.) This transaction increased assets (office equipment) and liabilities (accounts payable) by $1,000. As stated earlier, accounts payable are amounts owed to suppliers for items purchased on credit. Now you can see the $1,000 increase in the assets and liabilities as follows:

Trans-action	Explanation	Cash	Accounts Receiv-able	Trucks	Office Equip-ment	=	Accounts Payable	Notes Payable	+	Capital Stock
	Balances before transaction. . . .	$14,500		$20,000	$1,500 =			$6,000 +		$30,000
4a	Purchased office equipment on account				+1,000		+1,000			
	Balances after transaction	$14,500		$20,000	$2,500 =		$1,000	$6,000 +		$30,000

Increased by $1,000   *Increased by $1,000*

(Assets = Liabilities + Stockholders' Equity)

5a. Paid an Account Payable Eight days after receiving the bill, Metro paid $1,000 for the office equipment purchased on account (transaction 4a). This transaction reduced cash by $1,000 and reduced accounts payable by $1,000. Thus, the assets and liabilities both are reduced by $1,000, and the equation again balances as follows:

Trans-action	Explanation	Cash	Accounts Receiv-able	Trucks	Office Equip-ment	=	Accounts Payable	Notes Payable	+	Capital Stock
	Balances before transaction	$14,500		$20,000	$2,500 =		$1,000	$6,000 +		$30,000
5a	Paid an account payable	−1,000					−1,000			
	End -of-month balances	$13,500	$ –0–	$20,000	$2,500		$ –0–	$6,000 +		$30,000

Decreased by $1,000   *Decreased by $1,000*

(Assets = Liabilities + Stockholders' Equity)

Illustration 1.2, Part A, is a *summary of transactions* prepared in accounting equation form for June. A **summary of transactions** is a teaching tool used to show the effects of transactions on the accounting equation. Note that the stockholders' equity has remained at $30,000. This amount changes as the business begins to earn revenues or incur expenses. You can see how the totals at the bottom of Part A of Illustration 1.2 tie into the balance sheet shown in Part B. The date on the balance sheet is June 30, 1999. These totals become the beginning balances for July 1999.

Thus far, all transactions have consisted of exchanges or acquisitions of assets either by borrowing or by owner investment. We used this procedure to help you focus on the accounting equation as it relates to the balance sheet. However, people do not form a business only to hold present assets. They form businesses so their assets can generate greater amounts of assets. Thus, a business increases its assets by providing goods or services to customers. The results of these activities appear in the income statement. The section that follows shows more of Metro's transactions as it began earning revenues and incurring expenses.

TRANSACTIONS AFFECTING THE INCOME STATEMENT AND/OR BALANCE SHEET
To survive, a business must be profitable. This means that the revenues earned by providing goods and services to customers must exceed the expenses incurred.

In July 1999, Metro Courier, Inc., began selling services and incurring expenses. The explanations of transactions that follow allow you to participate in this process and learn the necessary accounting procedures.

Reinforcing Problems
E1–6 Analyze transactions.
E1–7 Determine effect of transactions on stockholders' equity.

ILLUSTRATION 1.2

A. Summary of Transactions

METRO COURIER, INC.
Summary of Transactions
Month of June 1999

Trans-action	Explanation	Cash	Accounts Receivable	Trucks	Office Equipment	=	Accounts Payable	Notes Payable	+	Capital Stock
				Assets		=	Liabilities		+	Stockholders' Equity
	Beginning balances	$ –0–	$ –0–	$ –0–	$ –0–	=	$ –0–	$ –0–		$ –0–
1a	Stockholders invested cash	+30,000								+30,000
		$30,000				=				$30,000
2a	Borrowed money	+6,000						+6,000		
		$36,000				=		$6,000	+	$30,000
3a	Purchased trucks and office equipment for cash	−21,500		+20,000	+1,500					
		$14,500		$20,000	$1,500	=		$6,000	+	$30,000
4a	Purchased office equipment on account				+1,000		+1,000			
		$14,500		$20,000	$2,500	=	$1,000	$6,000	+	$30,000
5a	Paid an account payable	−1,000					−1,000			
	End-of-month balances	$13,500	$ –0–	$20,000	$2,500	=	$ –0–	$6,000	+	$30,000

B. Balance Sheet

METRO COURIER, INC.
Balance Sheet
June 30, 1999

Assets		Liabilities and Stockholders' Equity	
Cash	$13,500	Liabilities:	
Trucks	20,000	Notes payable	$6,000
Office equipment	2,500	Total liabilities	$ 6,000
		Stockholders' equity:	
		Capital stock	30,000
Total assets	$36,000	Total liabilities and stockholders' equity . . .	$36,000

1b. Earned Service Revenue and Received Cash As its first transaction in July, Metro performed delivery services for customers and received $4,800 cash. This transaction increased an asset (cash) by $4,800. Stockholders' equity (retained earnings) also increased by $4,800, and the accounting equation was in balance.

The $4,800 is a revenue earned by the business and, as such, increases stockholders' equity (in the form of retained earnings) because stockholders prosper when the business earns profits. Likewise, the stockholders would sustain any losses, which would reduce retained earnings.

Revenues increase the amount of retained earnings and expenses and dividends decrease them. (In this first chapter, we show all of these items as immediately affecting retained earnings. In later chapters, the revenues, expenses, and dividends are accounted for separately from retained earnings during the accounting period and are transferred to retained earnings only at the end of the accounting period as part of the closing process described in Chapter 4.) The effects of this $4,800 transaction on the financial status of Metro are:

Trans-action	Explanation	Cash	Accounts Receiv-able	Trucks	Office Equip-ment =	Accounts Payable	Notes Payable	Capital Stock	Re-tained Earn-ings
	Assets				= **Liabilities**		+	**Stockholders' Equity**	
	Beginning balances (Illustration 1.2) . .	$13,500	$ –0–	$20,000	$2,500 =	$ –0–	$6,000 +	$30,000	$ –0–
1b	Earned service revenue and received cash . . .	+4,800							+4,800 (service revenue)
	Balances after transaction	$18,300		$20,000	$2,500 =		$6,000 +	$30,000	$4,800

Increased by $4,800 (Cash)
Increased by $4,800 (Retained Earnings)

Metro would record the increase in stockholders' equity brought about by the revenue transaction as a separate item, retained earnings. This does not increase capital stock because the Capital Stock account increases only when the company issues shares of stock. The expectation is that revenue transactions will exceed expenses and yield net income. If net income is not distributed to stockholders, it is in fact retained. Later chapters show that because of complexities in handling large numbers of transactions, revenues and expenses affect retained earnings only at the end of an accounting period. The preceding procedure is a shortcut used to explain why the accounting equation remains in balance.

2b. Service Revenue Earned on Account (for Credit) Metro performed courier delivery services for a customer who agreed to pay $900 at a later date. The company granted credit rather than requiring the customer to pay cash immediately. This is called earning revenue *on account*. The transaction consists of exchanging services for the customer's promise to pay later. This transaction is similar to the preceding transaction in that stockholders' equity (retained earnings) increases because the company has earned revenues. However, the transaction differs because the company has not received cash. Instead, the company has received another asset, an *account receivable*. As noted earlier, an account receivable is the amount due from a customer for goods or services already provided. The company has a legal right to collect from the customer in the future. Accounting recognizes such claims as assets. The accounting equation, including this $900 item, is as follows:

Trans-action	Explanation	Cash	Accounts Receiv-able	Trucks	Office Equip-ment =	Accounts Payable	Notes Payable	Capital Stock	Re-tained Earn-ings
	Assets				= **Liabilities**		+	**Stockholders' Equity**	
	Balances before transaction	$18,300		$20,000	$2,500 =		$6,000 +	$30,000	$4,800
2b	Earned service revenue on account		+$900						+900 (service revenue)
	Balances after transaction	$18,300	$900	$20,000	$2,500 =		$6,000 +	$30,000	$5,700

Increased by $900 (Accounts Receivable)
Increased by $900 (Retained Earnings)

3b. Collected Cash on Accounts Receivable   Metro collected $200 on account from the customer in transaction 2b. The customer will pay the remaining $700 later. This transaction affects only the balance sheet and consists of giving up a claim on a customer in exchange for cash. The transaction increases cash by $200 and decreases accounts receivable by $200. Note that this transaction consists solely of a change in the composition of the assets. When the company performed the services, it recorded the revenue. Therefore, the company does not record the revenue again when collecting the cash.

Trans-action	Explanation		Assets			=	Liabilities		+	Stockholders' Equity	
		Cash	Accounts Receiv-able	Trucks	Office Equip-ment		Accounts Payable	Notes Payable	Capital Stock	Re-tained Earn-ings	
	Balances before transaction . . .	$18,300	$900	$20,000	$2,500 =				$6,000 + $30,000	$5,700	
3b	Collected cash on account . .	+200	−200								
	Balances after transaction. . . .	$18,500	$700	$20,000	$2,500 =				$6,000 + $30,000	$5,700	

Increased by $200 | Decreased by $200

4b. Paid Salaries   Metro paid employees $2,600 in salaries. This transaction is an exchange of cash for employee services. Typically, companies pay employees for their services after they perform their work. Salaries (or wages) are costs companies incur to produce revenues, and companies consider them an expense. Thus, the accountant treats the transaction as a decrease in an asset (cash) and a decrease in stockholders' equity (retained earnings) because the company has incurred an expense. Expense transactions reduce net income. Since net income becomes a part of the retained earnings balance, expense transactions reduce the retained earnings.

Trans-action	Explanation		Assets			=	Liabilities		+	Stockholders' Equity	
		Cash	Accounts Receiv-able	Trucks	Office Equip-ment		Accounts Payable	Notes Payable	Capital Stock	Re-tained Earn-ings	
	Balances before transaction. . . .	$18,500	$700	$20,000	$2,500 =				$6,000 + $30,000	$5,700	
4b	Paid salaries	−2,600								−2,600 (salaries expense)	
	Balances after transaction. . . .	$15,900	$700	$20,000	$2,500 =				$6,000 + $30,000	$3,100	

Decreased by $2,600   Decreased by $2,600

5b. Paid Rent   In July, Metro paid $400 cash for office space rental. This transaction causes a decrease in cash of $400 and a decrease in retained earnings of $400 because of the incurrence of rent expense.

Transaction 5b has the following effects on the amounts in the accounting equation:

		Assets				=	Liabilities		+	Stockholders' Equity	
Trans-action	Explanation	Cash	Accounts Receiv-able	Trucks	Office Equip-ment		Accounts Payable	Notes Payable		Capital Stock	Re-tained Earn-ings
	Balances before transaction....	$15,900	$700	$20,000	$2,500 =			$6,000	+	$30,000	$3,100
5b	Paid rent......	−400									−400 (rent expense)
	Balances after transaction....	$15,500	$700	$20,000	$2,500 =			$6,000	+	$30,000	$2,700

Decreased by $400

Decreased by $400

6b. Received Bill for Gas and Oil Used At the end of the month, Metro received a $600 bill for gas and oil consumed during the month. This transaction involves an increase in accounts payable (a liability) because Metro has not yet paid the bill and a decrease in retained earnings because Metro has incurred an expense. Metro's accounting equation now reads:

		Assets				=	Liabilities		+	Stockholders' Equity	
Trans-action	Explanation	Cash	Accounts Receiv-able	Trucks	Office Equip-ment		Accounts Payable	Notes Payable		Capital Stock	Re-tained Earn-ings
	Balances before transaction....	$15,500	$700	$20,000	$2,500 =			$6,000	+	$30,000	$2,700
6b	Received bill for gas and oil used ...						+$600				−600 (gas and oil expense)
	End-of-month balances.....	$15,500	$700	$20,000	$2,500 =		$600	$6,000	+	$30,000	$2,100

Increased by $600

Decreased by $600

SUMMARY OF BALANCE SHEET AND INCOME STATEMENT TRANSACTIONS Part A of Illustration 1.3 summarizes the effects of all the preceding transactions on the assets, liabilities, and stockholders' equity of Metro Courier, Inc., in July. The beginning balances are the ending balances in Part A of Illustration 1.2. The summary shows subtotals after each transaction; these subtotals are optional and may be omitted. Note how the accounting equation remains in balance after each transaction and at the end of the month.

The ending balances in each of the columns in Part A of Illustration 1.3 are the dollar amounts in Part B and those reported earlier in the balance sheet in Part C of Illustration 1.1. The itemized data in the Retained Earnings column are the revenue and expense items in Part C of Illustration 1.3 and those reported earlier in the income statement in Part A of Illustration 1.1. The beginning balance in the Retained Earnings column ($–0–) plus net income for the month ($2,100) is equal to the ending balance in retained earnings ($2,100) shown earlier in Part B of Illustration 1.1. Remember that the financial statements are not an end in themselves, but are prepared to assist users of those statements to make informed decisions. Throughout the text we show how people use accounting information in decision making.

DIVIDENDS PAID TO OWNERS (STOCKHOLDERS) Stockholders' equity is (1) increased by capital contributed by stockholders and by revenues earned through operations and (2) decreased by expenses incurred in producing revenues. The payment of

Objective 6
Prepare an income statement, a statement of retained earnings, and a balance sheet.

Reinforcing Problems
E1–8 Analyze transactions.
E1–9 Identify transactions that decrease retained earnings.
E1–10 Prepare income statement.
E1–11 Prepare statement of retained earnings.
E1–12 Prepare balance sheet.

ILLUSTRATION 1.3

A. Summary of Transactions

METRO COURIER, INC.
Summary of Transactions
Month of July 1999

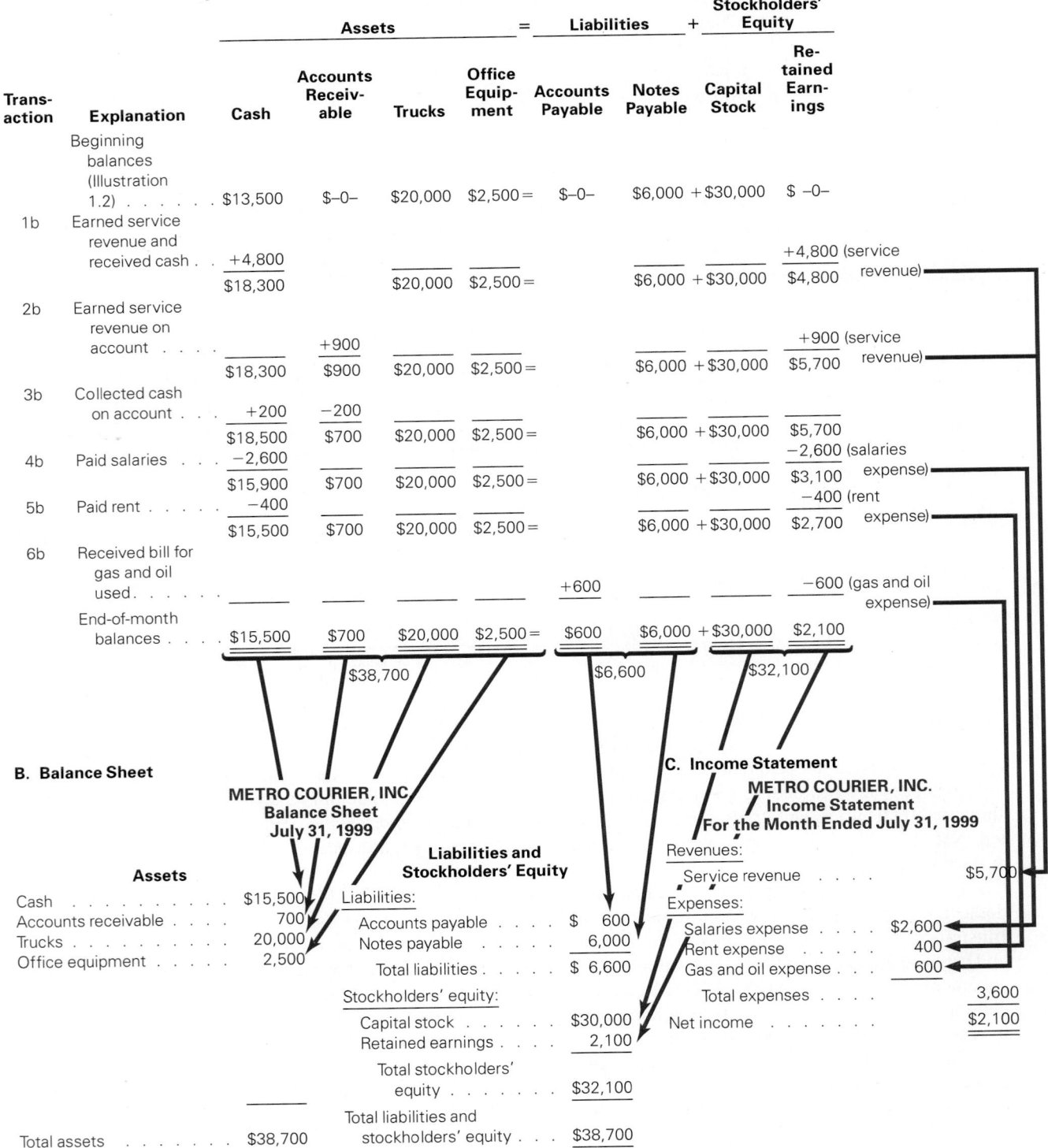

Trans-action	Explanation	Assets				=	Liabilities		+	Stockholders' Equity	
		Cash	Accounts Receivable	Trucks	Office Equipment		Accounts Payable	Notes Payable	Capital Stock	Retained Earnings	
	Beginning balances (Illustration 1.2)	$13,500	$–0–	$20,000	$2,500 =		$–0–	$6,000 +	$30,000	$ –0–	
1b	Earned service revenue and received cash . .	+4,800								+4,800	(service revenue)
		$18,300		$20,000	$2,500 =			$6,000 +	$30,000	$4,800	
2b	Earned service revenue on account		+900							+900	(service revenue)
		$18,300	$900	$20,000	$2,500 =			$6,000 +	$30,000	$5,700	
3b	Collected cash on account . . .	+200	–200								
		$18,500	$700	$20,000	$2,500 =			$6,000 +	$30,000	$5,700	
4b	Paid salaries . . .	–2,600								–2,600	(salaries expense)
		$15,900	$700	$20,000	$2,500 =			$6,000 +	$30,000	$3,100	
5b	Paid rent	–400								–400	(rent expense)
		$15,500	$700	$20,000	$2,500 =			$6,000 +	$30,000	$2,700	
6b	Received bill for gas and oil used.						+600			–600	(gas and oil expense)
	End-of-month balances	$15,500	$700	$20,000	$2,500 =		$600	$6,000 +	$30,000	$2,100	

$38,700 $6,600 $32,100

B. Balance Sheet

METRO COURIER, INC.
Balance Sheet
July 31, 1999

Assets

Cash	$15,500
Accounts receivable	700
Trucks	20,000
Office equipment	2,500
Total assets	$38,700

Liabilities and Stockholders' Equity

Liabilities:

Accounts payable	$ 600
Notes payable	6,000
Total liabilities	$ 6,600

Stockholders' equity:

Capital stock	$30,000
Retained earnings	2,100
Total stockholders' equity	$32,100
Total liabilities and stockholders' equity . . .	$38,700

C. Income Statement

METRO COURIER, INC.
Income Statement
For the Month Ended July 31, 1999

Revenues:

Service revenue	$5,700

Expenses:

Salaries expense	$2,600
Rent expense	400
Gas and oil expense . . .	600
Total expenses	3,600
Net income	$2,100

AN ETHICAL PERSPECTIVE

State University

James Stevens was taking an accounting course at State University. Also, he was helping companies find accounting systems that would fit their information needs. He advised one of his clients to acquire a software computer package that could record the business transactions and prepare the financial statements. The licensing agreement with the software company specified that the basic charge for one site was $4,000 and that $1,000 must be paid for each additional site where the software was used.

James was pleased that his recommendation to acquire the software was followed. However, he was upset that management wanted him to install the software at eight other sites in the company and did not intend to pay the extra $8,000 due the software company. A member of management stated, "The software company will never know the difference and, besides, everyone else seems to be pirating software. If they do find out, we will pay the extra fee at that time. Our expenses are high enough without paying these unnecessary costs." James believed he might lose this client if he did not do as management instructed.

cash or other assets to stockholders in the form of dividends also reduces stockholders' equity. Thus, if the owners receive a cash dividend, the effect would be to reduce the retained earnings part of stockholders' equity; the amount of dividends is not an expense but a distribution of income.

AN ACCOUNTING PERSPECTIVE

USES OF TECHNOLOGY   Accountants and others can access the home pages of companies to find their annual reports and other information, home pages of CPA firms to find employment opportunities and services offered, and home pages of government agencies, universities, and any other agency that has established a home page. By making on-screen choices you can discover all kinds of interesting information about almost anything. You can access libraries, even in foreign countries, newspapers, such as *The Wall Street Journal,* and find addresses and phone numbers of anyone in the nation. We have included some Internet Projects at the end of the chapters to give you some experience at "surfing the net" for accounting applications.

ANALYZING AND USING THE FINANCIAL RESULTS—THE EQUITY RATIO

The two basic sources of equity in a company are stockholders and creditors; their combined interests are called *total equities*. To find the **equity ratio,** divide stockholders' equity by total equities or total assets, since total equities equals total assets. In formula format:

Objective 7
Analyze and use the financial results—the equity ratio.

$$\text{Equity ratio} = \frac{\text{Stockholders' equity}}{\text{Total equities}}$$

Reinforcing Problem
E1–13 Calculate equity ratios for Digital Equipment Corporation.

The higher the proportion of equities (or assets) supplied by the owners, the more solvent the company. However, a high portion of debt may indicate higher profitability because quite often the interest rate on debt is lower than the rate of earnings realized from using the proceeds of the debt.

An example illustrates this concept: Suppose that a company with $100,000 in assets could have raised the funds to acquire those assets in these two ways:

Case 1

Assets . . . . $100,000   Liabilities $20,000
                                          Stockholders' equity 80,000

Case 2

Assets . . . . $100,000   Liabilities $80,000
                                          Stockholders' equity 20,000

When a company suffers operating losses, its assets shrink. In Case 1, the assets would have to shrink by 80% before the liabilities would equal the assets. In Case 2, the assets would have to shrink only 20% before the liabilities would equal the assets. When the liabilities exceed the assets, the company is said to be insolvent. Therefore, creditors are safer in Case 1.

Johnson & Johnson
The world's largest manufacturer of health care products, sells products in more than 150 countries.

GTE
The largest U.S.-based local telephone company and the second largest U.S. cellular service provider.

3M Corporation
One of the world's leading manufacturing companies, produces abrasives, automotive fasteners, specialty films and chemicals, tapes (Scotch tape), electrical/electronic connectors, and imaging and medical products.

General Electric Company
One of the most successful U.S. companies, sells products and services to industries such as aerospace, appliances, industrial and power systems, medical systems, and plastics.

However, if funds borrowed at 10% are used to produce earnings at a 20% rate, Case 2 is preferable in terms of profitability. Therefore, owners are better off in Case 2 if the borrowed funds can earn more than they cost.

Next, we examine the 1995 equity ratios of some actual companies:

Name of Company	Stockholders' Equity ($ millions)	Total Equities ($ millions)	Equity Ratio
Johnson & Johnson	$ 9,045	$ 17,873	50.6%
GTE Corporation	6,871	37,019	18.6
3M Corporation	6,884	14,183	48.5
General Electric Company	29,609	228,035	13.0

As you can see from the preceding data, the equity ratios of actual companies vary widely. Companies such as Johnson & Johnson and 3M Corporation employ a higher proportion of stockholders' equity (a lower proportion of debt) than the others in an effort to have stronger balance sheets (more solvency). The other two companies employ a greater proportion of debt, possibly in an attempt to increase profitability. Every company must strike a balance between solvency and profitability to ensure long-run survival. The correct balance between proportions of stockholder and creditor equities depends on the industry, general business conditions, and management philosophy.

Chapter 1 has introduced two important components of the accounting process—the accounting equation and the business transaction. In Chapter 2, you learn about debits and credits and how accountants use them in recording transactions. Understanding how data are accumulated, classified, and reported in financial statements helps you understand how to use financial statement data in making decisions.

AN ACCOUNTING PERSPECTIVE
——

USES OF TECHNOLOGY   When you apply for your first job after graduation, prospective employers will expect you to know how to use a microcomputer to perform many tasks. Therefore, before you graduate you should be able to use word processing, spreadsheet, and database software. You should be able to use the Internet to find useful information. In many universities, you can learn these skills in courses taken for credit. If your school does not offer credit courses, take noncredit courses or attend a training center.

UNDERSTANDING THE LEARNING OBJECTIVES

Objective 1
Identify and describe the three basic forms of business organizations.

- A single proprietorship is an unincorporated business owned by an individual and often managed by that individual.
- A partnership is an unincorporated business owned by two or more persons associated as partners and is often managed by them.
- A corporation is a business incorporated under the laws of a state and owned by a few stockholders or by thousands of stockholders.

Objective 2
Distinguish among the three types of activities performed by business organizations.

- Service companies perform services for a fee.
- Merchandising companies purchase goods that are ready for sale and then sell them to customers.
- Manufacturing companies buy materials, convert them into products, and then sell the products to other companies or to final customers.

- The income statement reports the revenues and expenses of a company and shows the profitability of that business organization for a stated period of time.
- The statement of retained earnings shows the change in retained earnings between the beginning of the period (e.g., a month) and its end.
- The balance sheet lists the assets, liabilities, and stockholders' equity (including dollar amounts) of a business organization at a specific moment in time.
- The statement of cash flows shows the cash inflows and cash outflows for a company for a stated period of time.

- The accounting equation is Assets = Liabilities + Stockholders' equity.
- The left side of the equation represents the left side of the balance sheet and shows things of value owned by the business.
- The right side of the equation represents the right side of the balance sheet and shows who provided the funds to acquire the things of value (assets).

- Some transactions affect only balance sheet items: assets (such as cash, accounts receivable, and equipment), liabilities (such as accounts payable and notes payable), and stockholders' equity (capital stock). Other transactions affect both balance sheet items and income statement items (revenues, expenses, and eventually retained earnings).
- Illustrations 1.2 (Part A) and 1.3 (Part A) show the effects of business transactions on the accounting equation.

- The income statement appears in Illustrations 1.1 (Part A) and 1.3 (Part C).
- The statement of retained earnings appears in Illustration 1.1 (Part B).
- The balance sheet appears in Illustrations 1.1 (Part C) and 1.3 (Part B).

- The equity ratio is the stockholders' equity divided by total equities (or total assets).
- The equity ratio shows the percentage that assets would have to shrink before a company would become insolvent (liabilities exceed assets).

Objective 3
Describe the content and purposes of the income statement, statement of retained earnings, balance sheet, and statement of cash flows.

Objective 4
State the basic accounting equation and describe its relationship to the balance sheet.

Objective 5
Using the underlying assumptions or concepts, analyze business trans- actions and determine their effects on items in the financial statements.

Objective 6
Prepare an income statement, a statement of retained earnings, and a balance sheet.

Objective 7
Analyze and use the financial results—the equity ratio.

A Comparison of Corporate Accounting with Accounting for a Single Proprietorship and a Partnership

APPENDIX

Some textbook authors use a single proprietorship and a partnership form of business owner- ship to illustrate accounting concepts and practices. In a survey of users and nonusers of our text, we learned that the majority preferred the corporate approach because most students will probably work for or invest in corporations. Also, many small businesses operate as corpora- tions because of the investors' desire for limited liability.

This appendix briefly describes the differences in accounting for these three forms of business ownership. The major difference is in the stockholders' equity or owner's equity section of the balance sheet.

As you learned in this chapter, the stockholders' equity section of the balance sheet for a corporation consists of capital stock and retained earnings. The owner's equity section of the balance sheet for a single proprietorship consists only of the owner's capital account. The owner's equity section of a partnership is similar to that of a single proprietorship except that it shows a capital account and its balance for each partner.

Corporation		Single Proprietorship		Partnership	
Stockholders' equity:		Owner's equity: John Smith,		Partners' capital: John Smith,	
Capital stock. . .	$100,000	Capital	$150,000	Capital	$ 75,000
Retained earnings . . .	50,000			Sam Jones, Capital	75,000
Total	$150,000		$150,000		$150,000

The stockholders' equity section of a corporate balance sheet can become more complex as you will see later in the text. However, the items in the owner's equity section of the balance sheets of a single proprietorship and a partnership always remain as just shown. In a single proprietorship, the owner's capital balance consists of the owner's investments in the business, plus cumulative net income since the beginning of the business, less any amounts withdrawn by the owner. Thus, all of the amounts in the various stockholders' equity accounts for a corporation are in the owner's capital account in a single proprietorship. In a partnership, each partner's capital account balance consists of that partner's investments in the business, plus that partner's cumulative share of net income since that partner became a partner, less any amounts withdrawn by that partner.

The Dividends account in a corporation is similar to an owner's drawing account in a single proprietorship. These accounts both show amounts taken out of the business by the owners. In a partnership, each partner has a drawing account. Accountants treat asset, liability, revenue, and expense accounts similarly in all three forms of organization.

DEMONSTRATION PROBLEM

On June 1, 1999, Green Hills Riding Stable, Incorporated, was organized. The following transactions occurred during June:

June 1 Shares of capital stock were issued for $10,000 cash.
      4 A horse stable and riding equipment were rented (and paid for) for the month at a cost of $1,200.
      8 Horse feed for the month was purchased on credit, $800.
     15 Boarding fees of $3,000 for June were charged to those owning horses boarded at the stable. (This amount is due on July 10.)
     20 Miscellaneous expenses of $600 were paid.
     29 Land was purchased from a savings and loan association by borrowing $40,000 on a note from that association. The loan is due to be repaid in five years. Interest payments are due at the end of each month beginning July 31.
     30 Salaries of $700 for the month were paid.
     30 Riding and lesson fees were billed to customers in the amount of $2,800. (They are due on July 10.)

Required a. Prepare a summary of the preceding transactions. Use columns headed Cash, Accounts Receivable, Land, Accounts Payable, Notes Payable, Capital Stock, and Retained Earnings. Determine balances after each transaction to show that the basic equation is in balance.

b. Prepare an income statement for June 1999.

c. Prepare a statement of retained earnings for June 1999.

d. Prepare a balance sheet as of June 30, 1999.

Solution to Demonstration Problem

a.

GREEN HILLS RIDING STABLE, INCORPORATED
Summary of Transactions
Month of June 1999

Date	Explanation	Cash	Accounts Receivable	Land	Accounts Payable	Notes Payable	Capital Stock	Retained Earnings
June 1	Capital stock issued	$10,000			=		$10,000	
4	Rent expense	−1,200						$−1,200
		$ 8,800			=		$10,000	$−1,200
8	Feed expense				$+800			−800
		$ 8,800			= $ 800		+ $10,000	$−2,000
15	Boarding fees		$+3,000					+3,000
		$ 8,800	$ 3,000		= $ 800		+ $10,000	$ 1,000
20	Miscellaneous expenses	−600						−600
		$ 8,200	$ 3,000		= $ 800		+ $10,000	$ 400
29	Purchased land by borrowing			$+40,000		$+40,000		
		$ 8,200	$ 3,000	$ 40,000 =	$ 800	$ 40,000	+ $10,000	$ 400
30	Salaries paid	−700						−700
		$ 7,500	$ 3,000	$ 40,000 =	$ 800	$ 40,000	+ $10,000	$ −300
30	Riding and lesson fees billed		+2,800					+2,800
		$ 7,500	$ 5,800	$ 40,000	$ 800	$ 40,000	$10,000	$ 2,500

b.

GREEN HILLS RIDING STABLE, INCORPORATED
Income Statement
For the Month Ended June 30, 1999

Revenues:

Horse boarding fees revenue	$3,000	
Riding and lesson fees revenue	2,800	
Total revenues		$5,800

Expenses:

Rent expense	$1,200	
Feed expense	800	
Salaries expense	700	
Miscellaneous expense	600	
Total expenses		3,300
Net income		$2,500

c.

GREEN HILLS RIDING STABLE, INCORPORATED
Statement of Retained Earnings
For the Month Ended June 30, 1999

Retained earnings, June 1	$ –0–
Add: Net income for June	2,500
Total	$2,500
Less: Dividends	–0–
Retained earnings, June 30	$2,500

d.

GREEN HILLS RIDING STABLE, INCORPORATED
Balance Sheet
June 30, 1999
Assets

Cash	$ 7,500
Accounts receivable	5,800
Land	40,000
Total assets	$53,300

Liabilities and Stockholders' Equity

Liabilities:		
Accounts payable		$ 800
Notes payable		40,000
Total liabilities		$40,800
Stockholders' equity:		
Capital stock	$10,000	
Retained earnings	2,500	
Total stockholders' equity		12,500
Total liabilities and stockholders' equity . .		$53,300

NEW TERMS

Accounting equation   Assets = Equities; or Assets = Liabilities + Stockholders' equity. *22*

Accounts payable   Amounts owed to suppliers for goods or services purchased on credit. *20*

Accounts receivable   Amounts due from customers for services already provided. *20*

Assets   Things of value owned by the business. Examples include cash, machines, and buildings. To their owners, assets possess service potential or utility that can be measured and expressed in money terms. *20*

Balance sheet   Financial statement that lists a company's assets, liabilities, and stockholders' equity (including dollar amounts) as of a specific moment in time. Also called a *statement of financial position*. *20*

Business entity concept   The separate existence of the business organization. *15, 23*

Capital stock   The title given to an equity account showing the investment in a business corporation by its stockholders. *20*

Continuity   See *going-concern concept*. *23*

Corporation   Business incorporated under the laws of one of the states and owned by a few stockholders or by thousands of stockholders. *17*

Cost   Sacrifice made or the resources given up, measured in money terms, to acquire some desired thing, such as a new truck (asset). *23*

Dividend   Payment (usually of cash) to the owners of the business; it is a distribution of income to owners rather than an expense of doing business. *18*

Entity   A unit that is deemed to have an existence separate and apart from its owners, creditors, employees, customers, other interested parties, and other businesses, and for which accounting records are maintained. *15, 23*

Equities   Broadly speaking, all claims to, or interests in, assets; includes liabilities and stockholders' equity. *22*

Equity ratio   A ratio found by dividing stockholders' equity by total equities (or total assets). *31*

Exchange-price (or cost) concept (principle)   The objective money prices determined in the exchange process are used to record most assets. *23*

Expenses   Costs incurred to produce revenues, measured by the assets surrendered or consumed in serving customers. *18*

Going-concern (continuity) concept   The assumption by the accountant that unless strong evidence exists to the contrary, a business entity will continue operations into the indefinite future. *23*

Income statement   Financial statement that shows the revenues and expenses and reports the profitability of a business organization for a stated period of time. Sometimes called an *earnings statement*. *18*

Liabilities   Debts owed by a business—or creditors' equity. Examples: notes payable, accounts payable. *20*

Manufacturing companies   Companies that buy materials, convert them into products, and then sell the products to other companies or to final customers. *17*

Merchandising companies   Companies that purchase goods ready for sale and sell them to customers. *17*

Money measurement concept   Recording and reporting economic activity in a common monetary unit of measure such as the dollar. *23*

Net income   Amount by which the revenues of a period exceed the expenses of the same period. *18*

Net loss   Amount by which the expenses of a period exceed the revenues of the same period. *18*

Notes payable   Amounts owed to parties who loan the company money after the owner signs a written agreement (a note) for the company to repay each loan. *20*

Partnership   An unincorporated business owned by two or more persons associated as partners. *16*

Periodicity (time periods) concept   An assumption that an entity's life can be meaningfully subdivided into time periods (such as months or years) for purposes of reporting its economic activities.   *23*

Profitability   Ability to generate income. The income statement reflects a company's profitability.   *18*

Retained earnings   Accumulated net income less dividend distributions to stockholders.   *20*

Revenues   Inflows of assets (such as cash) resulting from the sale of products or the rendering of services to customers.   *18*

Service companies   Companies (such as accounting firms, law firms, or dry cleaning establishments) that perform services for a fee.   *17*

Single proprietorship   An unincorporated business owned by an individual and often managed by that individual.   *16*

Solvency   Ability to pay debts as they become due. The balance sheet reflects a company's solvency.   *18*

Source document   Any written or printed evidence of a business transaction that describes the essential facts of that transaction, such as receipts for cash paid or received.   *22*

Statement of cash flows   Shows cash inflows and outflows for a company over a period of time.   *18, 20*

Statement of retained earnings   Statement used to explain the changes in retained earnings that occurred between two balance sheet dates.   *18*

Stockholders' equity   The owners' interest in a corporation.   *20*

Stockholders or shareholders   Owners of a corporation; they buy shares of stock, which are units of ownership, in the corporation.   *17*

Summary of transactions   Teaching tool used in Chapter 1 to show the effects of transactions on the accounting equation.   *25*

Transaction   A business activity or event that causes a measurable change in the items in the accounting equation, Assets = Liabilities + Stockholders' equity.   *22*

SELF-TEST

TRUE-FALSE

Indicate whether each of the following statements is true or false.

1. The three forms of business organizations are single proprietorship, partnership, and trust.

2. The three types of business activity are service, merchandising, and manufacturing.

3. The income statement shows the profitability of the company and is dated as of a particular date, such as December 31, 1999.

4. The statement of retained earnings shows both the net income for the period and the beginning and ending balances of retained earnings.

5. The balance sheet contains the same major headings as appear in the accounting equation.

MULTIPLE-CHOICE

Select the best answer for each of the following questions.

1. The ending balance in retained earnings is shown in the:
    a. Income statement.
    b. Statement of retained earnings.
    c. Balance sheet.
    d. Both (**b**) and (**c**).

2. Which of the following is *not* a correct form of the accounting equation?
    a. Assets = Equities.
    b. Assets = Liabilities + Stockholders' equity.
    c. Assets − Liabilities = Stockholders' equity.
    d. Assets + Stockholders' equity = Liabilities.

3. Which of the following is *not* one of the five underlying assumptions or concepts mentioned in the chapter?
    a. Exchange-price concept.
    b. Inflation accounting concept.
    c. Business entity concept.
    d. Going-concern concept.

4. When the stockholders invest cash in the business, what is the effect?
    a. Liabilities increase and stockholders' equity increases.
    b. Both assets and liabilities increase.
    c. Both assets and stockholders' equity increase.
    d. None of the above.

5. When services are performed on account, what is the effect?
    a. Both cash and retained earnings decrease.
    b. Both cash and retained earnings increase.
    c. Both accounts receivable and retained earnings increase.
    d. Accounts payable increases and retained earnings decreases.

Now turn to page 48 to check your answers.

QUESTIONS

1. Accounting has often been called the language of business. In what respects would you agree with this description? How might you argue that this description is deficient?
2. Define asset, liability, and stockholders' equity.
3. How do liabilities and stockholders' equity differ? How are they similar?
4. How do accounts payable and notes payable differ? How are they similar?
5. Define revenues. How are revenues measured?
6. Define expenses. How are expenses measured?
7. What is a balance sheet? On what aspect of a business does the balance sheet provide information?
8. What is an income statement? On what aspect of a business does this statement provide information?
9. What information does the statement of retained earnings provide?
10. Identify the three types of activities shown in a statement of cash flows.
11. What is a transaction? What use does the accountant make of transactions? Why?
12. What is the accounting equation? Why must it always balance?
13. Give an example from your personal life that illustrates your use of accounting information in reaching a decision.
14. You have been elected to the governing board of your church. At the first meeting you attend, mention is made of building a new church. What accounting information would the board need in deciding whether or not to go ahead?
15. A company purchased equipment for $2,000 cash. The vendor stated that the equipment was worth $2,400. At what amount should the equipment be recorded?
16. What is meant by money measurement?

17. Of what significance is the exchange-price (or cost) concept? How is the cost to acquire an asset determined?
18. What effect does the going-concern (continuity) concept have on the amounts at which long-term assets are carried on the balance sheet?
19. Of what importance is the periodicity (time periods) concept to the preparation of financial statements?
20. Describe a transaction that would:
    a. Increase both an asset and capital stock.
    b. Increase both an asset and a liability.
    c. Increase one asset and decrease another asset.
    d. Decrease both a liability and an asset.
    e. Increase both an asset and retained earnings.
    f. Decrease both an asset and retained earnings.
    g. Increase a liability and decrease retained earnings.
    h. Decrease both an asset and retained earnings.
21. Identify the causes of increases and decreases in stockholders' equity.

MAYTAG

22. **Real World Question** Refer to the 1996 financial statements of Maytag Corporation in the separate annual report booklet that came with your text. What were the net income or loss amounts in the latest three years? Discuss the meaning of the changes after reading management's discussion and analysis of financial condition and results of operations.

HARLAND

23. **Real World Question** Referring to the financial statements of John H. Harland Company in the separate annual report booklet, has net income improved over the period reported? Has the solvency of the company improved from 1995 to 1996? Discuss.

EXERCISES

Exercise 1–1
Matching (L.O. 1, 2)

Match the descriptions in Column B with the appropriate terms in Column A.

Column A		Column B
1. Corporation.	a.	An unincorporated business owned by an individual.
2. Merchandising company.	b.	The form of organization used by most large businesses.
3. Partnership.	c.	Buys raw materials and converts them into finished products.
4. Manufacturing company.	d.	Buys goods in their finished form and sells them to customers in
5. Service company.		that same form.
6. Single proprietorship.	e.	An unincorporated business with more than one owner.
	f.	Performs services for a fee.

Exercise 1–2
Compute net income and revenue (L.O. 3)

Assume that retained earnings increased by $3,600 from June 30, 1999, to June 30, 2000. A cash dividend of $300 was declared and paid during the year.

a. Compute the net income for the year.
b. Assume expenses for the year were $9,000. Compute the revenue for the year.

Exercise 1–3
Compute retained earnings (L.O. 3, 4)

On December 31, 1999, Perez Company had assets of $150,000, liabilities of $97,500, and capital stock of $30,000. During 2000, Perez earned revenues of $45,000 and incurred expenses of $33,750. Dividends declared and paid amounted to $3,000.

a. Compute the company's retained earnings on December 31, 1999.
b. Compute the company's retained earnings on December 31, 2000.

At the start of the year, a company had liabilities of $50,000 and capital stock of $150,000. At the end of the year, retained earnings amounted to $135,000. Net income for the year was $45,000, and $15,000 of dividends were declared and paid. Compute retained earnings and total assets at the beginning of the year.

Exercise 1–4
Compute retained earnings and total assets at beginning of year (L.O. 3, 4)

For each of the following events, determine if it has an effect on the specific items (such as cash) in the accounting equation. For the events that do have an effect, present an analysis of the transaction showing its two sides or dual nature.

Exercise 1–5
Analyze transactions (L.O. 4, 5)

a. Purchased equipment for cash, $12,000.
b. Purchased a truck for $40,000, signed a note (with no interest) promising payment in 10 days.
c. Paid $1,600 for the current month's utilities.
d. Paid for the truck purchased in (**b**).
e. Employed Mary Childers as a salesperson at $1,200 per month. She is to start work next week.
f. Signed an agreement with a bank in which the bank agreed to lend the company up to $200,000 any time within the next two years.

Bradley Company, engaged in a courier service business, completed the following selected transactions during July 1999:

Exercise 1–6
Indicate effect of transactions on items in the accounting equation (L.O. 4, 5)

a. Purchased office equipment on account.
b. Paid an account payable.
c. Earned service revenue on account.
d. Borrowed money by signing a note at the bank.
e. Paid salaries for month to employees.
f. Received cash on account from a charge customer.
g. Received gas and oil bill for month.
h. Purchased delivery truck for cash.
i. Declared and paid a cash dividend.

Using a tabular form similar to Illustration 1.3 (Part A), indicate the effect of each transaction on the accounting equation using (+) for increase and (−) for decrease. No dollar amounts are needed, and you need not fill in the Explanation column.

Indicate the amount of change (if any) in the stockholders' equity balance based on each of the following transactions:

Exercise 1–7
Determine effect of transactions on stockholders' equity (L.O. 5)

a. The stockholders invested $100,000 cash in the business by purchasing capital stock.
b. Land costing $40,000 was purchased by paying cash.
c. The company performed services for a customer who agreed to pay $18,000 in one month.
d. Paid salaries for the month, $12,000.
e. Paid $14,000 on an account payable.

Give examples of transactions that would have the following effects on the items in a firm's financial statements:

Exercise 1–8
Analyze transactions (L.O. 5)

a. Increase cash; decrease some other asset.
b. Decrease cash; increase some other asset.
c. Increase an asset; increase a liability.
d. Decrease retained earnings; decrease an asset.
e. Increase an asset other than cash; increase retained earnings.
f. Decrease an asset; decrease a liability.

Exercise 1–9
Identify transactions that decrease retained earnings (L.O. 5)

Which of the following transactions results in a decrease in retained earnings? Why?

a. Employees were paid $20,000 for services received during the month.

b. $175,000 was paid to acquire land.

c. Paid an $18,000 note payable. No interest was involved.

d. Paid a $200 account payable.

Exercise 1–10
Prepare income statement (L.O. 6)

Assume that the following items were included in the Retained Earnings column in the summary of transactions for Cinck Company for July 1999:

Salaries expense	$120,000
Service revenue	300,000
Gas and oil expense	27,000
Rent expense	48,000
Dividends paid	40,000

Prepare an income statement for July 1999.

Exercise 1–11
Prepare statement of retained earnings (L.O. 6)

Given the following facts, prepare a statement of retained earnings for Brindle Company, a tanning salon, for August 1999:

Balance in retained earnings at end of July, $188,000.
Dividends paid in August, $63,600.
Net income for August, $72,000.

Exercise 1–12
Prepare balance sheet (L.O. 6)

The column totals of a summary of transactions for Speedy Printer Repair, Inc., as of December 31, 1999, were as follows:

Accounts payable	$ 60,000
Accounts receivable	90,000
Capital stock	100,000
Cash	40,000
Land	80,000
Building	50,000
Equipment	30,000
Notes payable	20,000
Retained earnings	?

Prepare a balance sheet. We have purposely listed the accounts out of order.

Exercise 1–13
Calculate the equity ratios for Digital Equipment Corporation and comment (L.O. 7)

Digital Equipment Corporation is a world leader in implementing and supporting networked platforms and applications in multivendor environments. The company, working with its business partners, provides a complete range of information-processing solutions from personal computers to integrated worldwide networks. The company does business in more than 100 countries. Given the following data for the Digital Equipment Corporation, calculate the equity ratios for 1995 and 1994. Then comment on the results.

	1995	1994
Stockholders' equity	$3,528,280,000	$ 3,279,799,000
Total equities	$9,947,152,000	$10,579,771,000

PROBLEMS

Problem 1–1
Prepare summary of transactions (L.O. 4, 5)

Preston Auto Paint Company had the temporary free use of an old building and completed the following transactions in September 1999:

Sept. 1 The company was organized and received $100,000 cash from the issuance of capital stock.

5 The company bought painting and sanding equipment for cash at a cost of $25,000.

7 The company painted the auto fleet of a customer who agreed to pay $8,000 in one week. The customer furnished the special paint.

14 The company received the $8,000 from the transaction of September 7.

20 Additional sanding equipment that cost $2,800 was acquired today; payment was postponed until September 28.

28 $2,400 was paid on the liability incurred on September 20.

30 Employee salaries for the month, $2,200, were paid.

30 Placed an order for additional painting equipment advertised at $20,000.

Prepare a summary of transactions (see Part A of Illustration 1.3) for the company for these transactions. Use money columns headed Cash, Accounts Receivable, Equipment, Accounts Payable, Capital Stock, and Retained Earnings. Determine balances after each transaction to show that the basic accounting equation balances.

Required

Quick-Start Home Repair Company completed the following transactions in June 1999:

Problem 1–2
Prepare summary of transactions and balance sheet (L.O. 4–6)

June 1 The company was organized and received $200,000 cash from the issuance of capital stock.

4 The company paid $48,000 cash for a truck.

7 The company borrowed $10,000 from its bank on a note.

9 Cash received for repair services performed was $4,500.

12 Expenses of operating the business so far this month were paid in cash, $3,400.

18 Repair services performed for a customer who agreed to pay within a month amounted to $5,400.

25 The company paid $4,065 on its loan from the bank, including $4,050 of principal and $15 of interest. (The principal is the amount of the loan. Interest is an expense, which reduces retained earnings.)

30 Miscellaneous expenses incurred in operating the business from June 13 to date were $3,825 and were paid in cash.

30 An order (contract) was received from a customer for repair services to be performed tomorrow, which will be billed at $3,000.

a. Prepare a summary of transactions (see Part A of Illustration 1.3). Include money columns for Cash, Accounts Receivable, Trucks, Notes Payable, Capital Stock, and Retained Earnings. Determine balances after each transaction to show that the basic accounting equation balances.

b. Prepare a balance sheet as of June 30, 1999.

Required

Following are summarized transaction data for Luxury Apartments, Inc., for the year ending June 30, 1999. The company owns and operates an apartment building.

Problem 1–3
Prepare income statement (L.O. 6)

Rent revenue from building owned	$150,000
Building repairs	2,870
Building cleaning, labor cost	3,185
Property taxes on the building	4,000
Insurance on the building	1,225
Commissions paid to rental agent	5,000
Legal and accounting fees (for preparation of tenant leases)	1,260
Utilities expense	8,225
Cost of new awnings (installed on June 30, will last 10 years)	5,000

Of the $150,000 rent revenue, $5,000 was not collected in cash until July 5, 1999.

Prepare an income statement for the year ended June 30, 1999.

Required

The following data are for Central District Parking Corporation:

Problem 1–4
Prepare summary of transactions, income statement, statement of retained earnings, and balance sheet (L.O. 4–6)

CENTRAL DISTRICT PARKING CORPORATION
Balance Sheet
September 30, 1999

Assets

Cash	$344,000
Accounts receivable	18,000
Total assets	$362,000

Liabilities and Stockholders' Equity

Accounts payable	$ 94,000
Capital stock	232,000
Retained earnings	36,000
Total liabilities and stockholders' equity	$362,000

The summarized transactions for October 1999 are as follows:

Oct. 1   The accounts payable owed as of September 30 ($94,000) were paid.
      1   The company paid rent for the premises for October, $19,200.
      7   The company received cash of $4,200 for parking by daily customers during the week.
      10   The company collected $14,400 of the accounts receivable in the balance sheet at September 30.
      14   Cash receipts for the week from daily customers were $6,600.
      15   Parking revenue earned but not yet collected from fleet customers was $6,000.
      16   The company paid salaries of $2,400 for the period October 1–15.
      19   The company paid advertising expenses of $1,200 for October.
      21   Cash receipts for the week from daily customers were $7,200.
      24   The company incurred miscellaneous expenses of $840. Payment will be due November 10.
      31   Cash receipts for the last 10 days of the month from daily customers were $8,400.
      31   The company paid salaries of $3,000 for the period October 16–31.
      31   Billings to monthly customers totaled $21,600 for October.
      31   Paid cash dividends of $24,000.

Required   a. Prepare a summary of transactions (see Part A of Illustration 1.3) using column headings as given in the preceding balance sheet. Determine balances after each transaction.

b. Prepare an income statement for October 1999.

c. Prepare a statement of retained earnings for October 1999.

d. Prepare a balance sheet as of October 31, 1999.

Problem 1–5
State causes of balance sheet changes (L.O. 3, 6)

The following balance sheets for June 30, 1999, and May 31, 1999, and the income statement for June are for Beach Camping Trailer Storage, Inc. (Common practice is to show the most recent period first.)

BEACH CAMPING TRAILER STORAGE, INC.
Comparative Balance Sheets

	June 30, 1999	May 31, 1999
Assets		
Cash	$ 52,000	$60,000
Accounts receivable	24,000	–0–
Land	36,000	36,000
Total assets	$112,000	$96,000
Liabilities and Stockholders' Equity		
Liabilities	$ 18,000	$24,000
Capital stock	60,000	60,000
Retained earnings	34,000	12,000
Total liabilities and stockholders' equity	$112,000	$96,000

BEACH CAMPING TRAILER STORAGE, INC.
Income Statement
For the Month Ended June 30, 1999

Revenues:		
Service revenue		$100,000
Expenses:		
Salaries expense	$48,000	
Supplies bought and used	24,000	72,000
Net income		$ 28,000

A cash dividend of $6,000 was declared and paid in June.

Required   State the probable causes of the changes in each of the balance sheet accounts from May 31 to June 30, 1999.

ALTERNATE PROBLEMS

Lakewood Personal Finance Company, which provides financial advisory services, engaged in the following transactions during May 1999:

Problem 1–1A
Prepare summary of transactions (L.O. 4, 5)

May 1 Received $300,000 cash for shares of capital stock issued when company was organized.
     2 The company borrowed $40,000 from the bank on a note.
     7 The company bought $182,400 of computer equipment for cash.
    11 Cash received for services performed to date was $15,200.
    14 Services performed for a customer who agreed to pay within a month were $10,000.
    15 Employee wages were paid, $13,200.
    19 The company paid $14,000 on the note to the bank.
    31 Interest paid to the bank for May was $140. (Interest is an expense, which reduces retained earnings.)
    31 The customer of May 14 paid $3,200 of the amount owed to the company.
    31 An order was received from a customer for services to be rendered next week, which will be billed at $12,000.

Prepare a summary of transactions (see Part A of Illustration 1.3). Use money columns headed Cash, Accounts Receivable, Equipment, Notes Payable, Capital Stock, and Retained Earnings. Determine balances after each transaction to show that the accounting equation balances.

Required

Reliable Lawn Care Service, Inc., a company that takes care of lawns and shrubbery of personal residences, engaged in the following transactions in April 1999:

Problem 1–2A
Prepare summary of transactions and balance sheet (L.O. 4–6)

Apr. 1 The company was organized and received $400,000 cash from the owners in exchange for capital stock issued.
      4 The company bought equipment for cash, $101,760.
      9 The company bought additional mowing equipment that cost $9,120 and agreed to pay for it in 30 days.
     15 Cash received for services performed to date was $3,840.
     16 Amount due from a customer for services performed totaled $5,280.
     30 Of the receivable (see April 16), $3,072 was collected in cash.
     30 Miscellaneous operating expenses of $6,240 were paid during the month.
     30 An order was placed for miscellaneous equipment costing $28,800.

a. Prepare a summary of transactions (see Part A of Illustration 1.3). Use money columns headed Cash, Accounts Receivable, Equipment, Accounts Payable, Capital Stock, and Retained Earnings. Determine balances after each transaction to show that the basic accounting equation balances.

b. Prepare a balance sheet as of April 30.

Required

Analysis of the transactions of the Moonlight Drive-In Theater for June 1999 disclosed the following:

Problem 1–3A
Prepare income statement, statement of retained earnings, and balance sheet (L.O. 6)

Ticket revenue	$180,000
Equipment rent expense	50,000
Film rent expense	53,400
Concession revenue	29,600
Advertising expense	18,600
Salaries expense	60,000
Utilities expense	14,100
Cash dividends declared and paid	12,000

Balance sheet figures at June 30 include the following:

Cash	$140,000
Land	148,000
Accounts payable	87,600
Capital stock	114,000
Retained earnings as of June 1, 1999	84,900

a. Prepare an income statement for June 1999.
b. Prepare a statement of retained earnings for June 1999.
c. Prepare a balance sheet as of June 30, 1999.
d. How solvent does this company appear to be?

Required

Problem 1–4A
Prepare income
statement, statement of
retained earnings, and
balance sheet (L.O. 4–6)

Little Folks Baseball, Inc., was formed by a group of parents to meet a need for a place for kids to play baseball. At the beginning of its second year of operations, its balance sheet appeared as follows:

LITTLE FOLKS BASEBALL, INC.
Balance Sheet
April 30, 1999
Assets

Cash	$ 56,000
Accounts receivable	80,000
Land	600,000
Total assets	$736,000

Liabilities and Stockholders' Equity

Liabilities:		
Accounts payable		$ 64,000
Stockholders' equity:		
Capital stock	$400,000	
Retained earnings	272,000	672,000
Total liabilities and stockholders' equity . .		$736,000

The summarized transactions for May 1999 are as follows:

a. Issued additional capital stock for cash, $200,000.

b. Collected $80,000 on accounts receivable.

c. Paid $64,000 on accounts payable.

d. Received membership fees from parents (nonrefundable): in cash, $260,000; and on account, $120,000.

e. Incurred operating expenses: for cash, $60,000; and on account, $160,000.

f. Paid dividends of $16,000.

g. Purchased more land for cash, $96,000.

h. Placed an order for new equipment expected to cost $120,000.

Required   a. Prepare a summary of transactions (see Part A of Illustration 1.3) using column headings as given in the balance sheet. Determine balances after each transaction.

b. Prepare an income statement for May 1999.

c. Prepare a statement of retained earnings for May 1999.

d. Prepare a balance sheet as of May 31, 1999.

Problem 1–5A
State causes of balance
sheet changes (L.O. 3, 6)

The balance sheets for May 31, 1999, and April 30, 1999, and the income statement for May of the Target-Line Golf Driving Range follow. (Common practice is to show the most recent period first.)

TARGET-LINE GOLF DRIVING RANGE
Comparative Balance Sheets

	May 31, 1999	April 30, 1999
Assets		
Cash	$ 56,400	$ 46,800
Land	163,200	144,000
Total assets	$219,600	$190,800
Liabilities and Stockholders' Equity		
Accounts payable	$ 18,000	$ 27,600
Capital stock	144,000	144,000
Retained earnings	57,600	19,200
Total liabilities and stockholders' equity	$219,600	$190,800

TARGET-LINE GOLF DRIVING RANGE
Income Statement
For the Month Ended May 31, 1999

Revenues:			
Service revenue			$ 64,000
Expenses:			
Salaries expense		$ 16,000	
Equipment rental expense		9,600	25,600
Net income			$ 38,400

All revenues earned are on account.

State the probable cause(s) of the change in each of the balance sheet accounts from April 30 to May 31, 1999.

Required

BEYOND THE NUMBERS—CRITICAL THINKING

Upon graduation from high school, Jim Crane went to work for a builder of houses and small apartment buildings. During the next six years, Crane earned a reputation as an excellent employee—hardworking, dedicated, and dependable—in the light construction industry. He could handle almost any job requiring carpentry, electrical, or plumbing skills.

Crane then decided to go into business for himself under the name Jim's Fix-It Shop, Inc. He invested cash, some power tools, and a used truck in his business. He completed many repair and remodeling jobs for homeowners and apartment owners. The demand for his services was so large that he had more work than he could handle. He operated out of his garage, which he had converted into a shop, adding several new pieces of power woodworking equipment.

Now, two years after going into business for himself, Crane must decide whether to continue in his own business or to accept a position as construction supervisor for a home builder. He has been offered an annual salary of $50,000 and a package of fringe benefits (medical and hospitalization insurance, pension contribution, vacation and sick pay, and life insurance) worth approximately $8,000 per year. The offer is attractive to Crane. But he dislikes giving up his business since he has thoroughly enjoyed being his own boss, even though it has led to an average workweek well in excess of the standard 40 hours.

Business Decision Case 1–1
Identify information needed to make decision (L.O. 3)

Suppose Crane comes to you for assistance in gathering the information needed to help him make a decision. He brings along the accounting records that have been maintained for his business by an experienced accountant. Using logic and your own life experiences, indicate the nature of the information Jim needs if he is to make an informed decision. Pay particular attention to the information likely to be found in his business accounting records. Does the accounting information available enter directly into the decision? Write a memorandum to Jim describing the information he will need to make an informed decision. The memo's headings should include Date, To, From, and Subject. (See the format in Group Project 1–5 below.)

Required

Refer to The Coca-Cola Company annual report in the separate annual report booklet that came with your text. Then turn to the section entitled "Selected Financial Data." Recall that in this chapter we showed that the equity ratio is calculated by dividing stockholders' equity by total equities (or total assets). Another format for analyzing solvency is to divide total debt by total equities. This latter calculation tells the proportion of assets financed by debt rather than the proportion of assets financed by stockholders' equity. These two ratios are complements and must add to 100%. Thus, if 25% of assets were financed by debt, 75% were financed by stockholders' equity.

Under "Selected Financial Data" (pages 48–49 of the annual report), The Coca-Cola Company shows "Total-debt-to-total-capital," which is the same as total debt to total equities. These percentages are for 1986 through 1996. Also shown are the "Total debt" amounts for the same period. Study these amounts and comment on the solvency of the company. What does the trend indicate about management's decisions regarding debt?

Annual Report Analysis 1–2
Comment on solvency of The Coca-Cola Company (L.O. 7)

**Annual Report
Analysis 1–3**
Answer questions about
McDonnell Douglas
Corporation's annual report

McDonnell Douglas Corporation is the world's leading producer of military aircraft and the third-largest commercial aircraft manufacturer. The company manufactures helicopters, missiles, sensing systems, and space-launch vehicles and is a major subcontractor on the International Space Station. Included in its 1995 annual report were the following items:

Report of Management Responsibilities

The financial statements of McDonnell Douglas Corporation and consolidated subsidiaries have been prepared under the direction of management in conformity with generally accepted accounting principles and, particularly with respect to long-term contracts and programs, include amounts based on estimates and judgments. The integrity and reliability of data in these financial statements is the responsibility of management. In the opinion of management, the financial statements set forth a fair presentation of the consolidated financial condition of McDonnell Douglas at December 31, 1995 and 1994, and the consolidated results of its operations for the years ended December 31, 1995, 1994, and 1993.

There are inherent limitations in the effectiveness of any system of internal control, including the possibility of human error and the circumvention or overriding of controls. Accordingly, even an effective internal control system can provide only reasonable assurance with respect to financial statement preparation. Furthermore, the effectiveness of an internal control system can change with circumstances.

McDonnell Douglas and its consolidated subsidiaries maintain accounting systems and related internal controls that, in the opinion of management, provide reasonable assurances that transactions are executed in accordance with management's authorization, that financial statements are prepared in accordance with generally accepted accounting principles, and that assets are properly accounted for and safeguarded.

Ethical decision making is a fundamental key in the Company's management philosophy. Management recognizes its responsibility for fostering a strong ethical climate. Written codes of ethics and standards of business conduct are distributed to every employee, and each employee has been trained or is being scheduled to be trained in ethical decision making. The Board of Directors' Corporate Responsibility Committee has oversight responsibilities relative to standards of business conduct.

The Board of Directors has appointed four of its nonemployee members as an Audit Committee. This committee meets periodically with management and the internal and independent auditors. Both internal and independent auditors have unrestricted access to the Audit Committee to discuss the results of their examinations and the adequacy of internal controls. In addition, the Audit Committee makes its recommendation as to the selection of independent auditors to the Board.

Harry C. Stonecipher
President and Chief Executive Officer

J. F. Palmer
Senior Vice President and Chief Financial Officer

January 17, 1996

Report of Ernst & Young LLP, Independent Auditors

Shareholders and Board of Directors
McDonnell Douglas Corporation

We have audited the accompanying balance sheet (including the consolidating data for MDC Aerospace and Financial Services) of McDonnell Douglas Corporation and consolidated subsidiaries (MDC) as of December 31, 1995 and 1994, and the related consolidated statements of operations, shareholders' equity, and cash flows for each of the three years in the period ended December 31, 1995. These financial statements are the responsibility of MDC's management. Our responsibility is to express an opinion on these financial statements based on our audits.

We conducted our audits in accordance with generally accepted auditing standards. Those standards require that we plan and perform the audits to obtain reasonable assurance about whether the financial statements are free of material misstatement. An audit includes examining, on a test basis, evidence supporting the amounts and disclosures in the financial statements. An audit also includes assessing the accounting principles used and significant estimates made by management, as well as evaluating the overall financial statement presentation. We believe that our audits provide a reasonable basis for our opinion.

In our opinion, the financial statements referred to above present fairly, in all material respects, the financial position of McDonnell Douglas Corporation and consolidated subsidiaries at December 31, 1995 and 1994, and the consolidated results of MDC's operations and MDC's cash flows for each of the three years in the period ended December 31, 1995, in conformity with generally accepted accounting principles.

As discussed in Notes 1 and 5 to the consolidated financial statements, in 1995 MDC changed its method of accounting for the MD-11 commercial aircraft program.

Ernst & Young LLP
St. Louis, Missouri
January 17, 1996

Write answers to the following questions:

Required

1. Who is responsible for preparing the financial statements?
2. Of what importance is the internal audit?
3. What is the role of the audit committee?
4. What is the responsibility of the external independent auditor?
5. Does the independent auditor have absolute assurance that the financial statements are free of material misstatement?
6. To what extent does the independent auditor examine evidence?

Refer to "An Ethical Perspective" on page 31. Write a short essay discussing the alternatives James Stevens could pursue and the likely outcomes of those alternatives. Which of the alternatives you have discussed would you recommend?

Ethics Case—Writing Experience 1–4

In teams of two or three students, interview in person or by speaker phone, a businessperson in your community. Ask how that person uses accounting information in making business decisions and obtain specific examples. Each team should write a memorandum to the instructor summarizing the results of the interview. Information contained in the memo should include:

Group Project 1–5
Interview a businessperson

Date:
To:
From:
Subject:

Content of the memo must include the name and title of the person interviewed, name of the company, date of the interview, examples of the use of accounting information for decision making, and any other pertinent information.

With a team composed of one or two other students, conceive of a business that you would like to form after graduation. Then describe approximately 15–20 transactions that the business might undertake in its first month of operations. Prepare a summary of transactions showing how each transaction affects the accounting equation. Identify each asset, liability, and stockholders' equity item in your summary of transactions. For instance, instead of grouping all assets in one number, show cash, accounts receivable, and so on in your accounting equation.

Group Project 1–6
Analyze transactions for a business

With a team of one or two other students and using library sources, write a paper on the American Institute of Certified Public Accountants, their services to members, and their activities. Be careful to cite sources for your information. Direct quotes should be labeled as such and should be single-spaced and indented if relatively long or in quote marks and not indented if relatively short. To quote without giving the source is plagiarism and should be avoided at all costs.

Group Project 1–7
Perform library research

USING THE INTERNET—A VIEW OF THE REAL WORLD

Internet Project 1–8
Investigate company
information

Visit the following website for Peachtree Software:
http://www.peachtree.com
Write a short paper describing company information, products and services, and support available for their products.

Internet Project 1–9
Examine an annual report

Visit the following website for Ford Motor Company:
http://www.ford.com
When the web page appears, click on Stockholder Relations and then click on Ford Motor Company Annual Report. Based on your investigation, write a short paper describing the general content of the annual report.

ANSWERS TO SELF-TEST

TRUE-FALSE

1. **False.** Corporation, not trust, is the third form.
2. **True.** The accounting for all three of these is covered in this text.
3. **False.** The income statement is dated using a period of time, such as "For the Year Ended December 31, 1999."
4. **True.** In addition, the statement of retained earnings shows dividends declared.
5. **True.** Both show assets, liabilities, and stockholders' equity.

MULTIPLE-CHOICE

1. **d.** The ending balance in retained earnings is shown in both the statement of retained earnings and in the balance sheet.
2. **d.** This form of the equation would not balance.
3. **b.** The inflation accounting concept was not one of the ones discussed. The other two were the money measurement concept and the periodicity concept.
4. **c.** When the stockholders invest cash, assets and stockholders' equity increase.
5. **c.** The performance of services on account increases both accounts receivable and retained earnings.

II

PROCESSING INFORMATION FOR DECISIONS AND ESTABLISHING ACCOUNTING POLICY

A MANAGER'S PERSPECTIVE

Eric Thompson
Financial Manager, Marketing
The Coca-Cola Company

As the Financial Manager for the marketing department, I coordinate and monitor the budget for that group. My job is to ensure they have enough money available to accomplish their goals. I do this primarily by comparing requests to amounts requested in previous years. Managers request money based on individual projects and their projected costs, and I evaluate each one to assess whether a request is warranted.

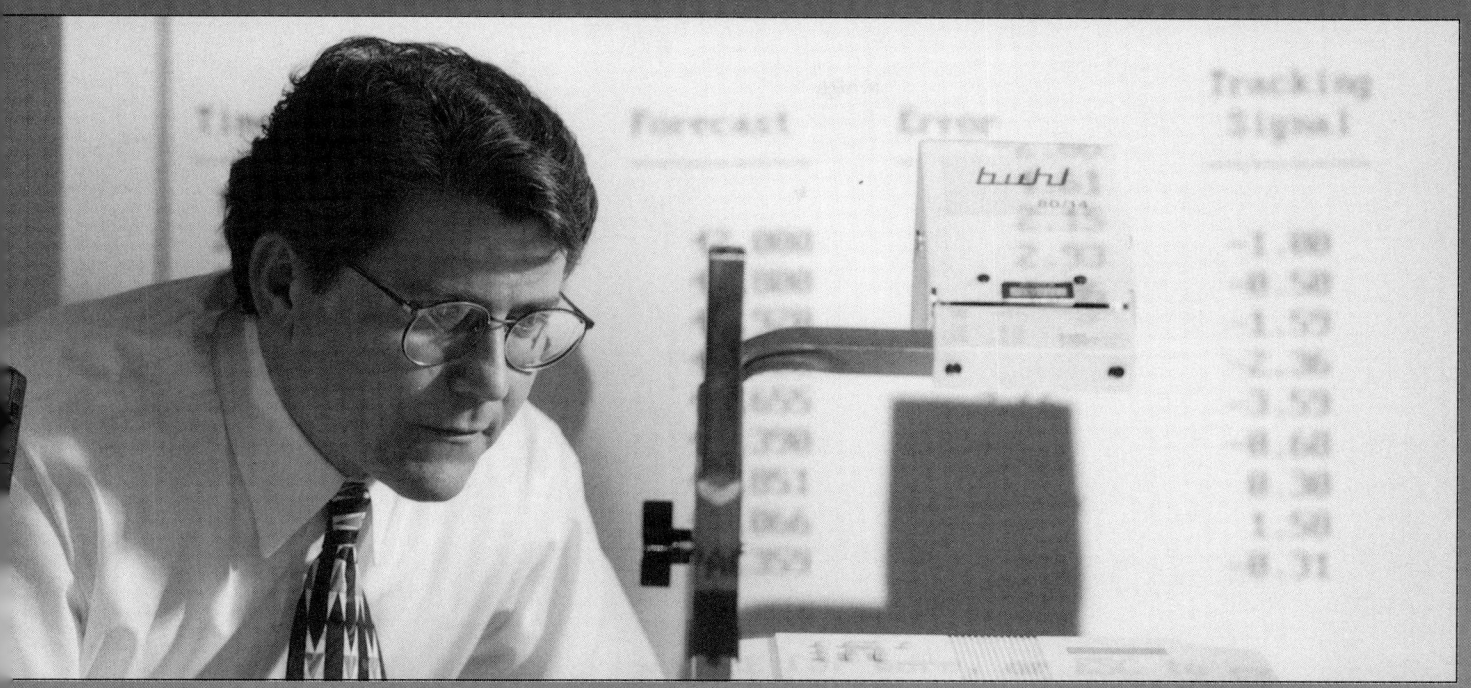

The budget is also used as a benchmark to evaluate the department's overall performance. Each department reports a "rolling estimate" every month, which reviews what they have spent to date and helps managers determine whether they are under or over the budget. Managers prefer to use this figure because the rolling estimate allows time to make corrections and changes. If they were to wait until the actual numbers were available, it would be too late to make adjustments.

I also prepare an annual profit-and-loss statement for each brand. The marketing department uses the profit margin to determine how much to spend on marketing efforts for each product. This also helps the department assess prices for products by analyzing the cost of producing them.

Before deciding to undertake a major new investment such as launching a new product or investing in a new plant, we use discounted cash flow analysis to determine the feasibility of such an expenditure.

Marketing managers must understand the basics of financial information. Too many managers assume the more products you sell, the more value you are creating, and this isn't always true. The more they understand concepts like discounted cash flow analysis, the better they will be as marketeers. Otherwise, they could actually be losing money for the company.

2

RECORDING BUSINESS TRANSACTIONS

In Chapter 1, we illustrated the income statement, statement of retained earnings, balance sheet, and statement of cash flows. These statements are the end products of the financial accounting process, which is based on the accounting equation. The financial accounting process quantifies past management decisions. The results of these decisions are communicated to users—management, creditors, and investors—and serve as a basis for making future decisions.

The raw data of accounting are the business transactions. We recorded the transactions in Chapter 1 as increases or decreases in the assets, liabilities, and stockholders' equity items of the accounting equation. This procedure showed you how various transactions affected the accounting equation. When working through these sample transactions, you probably suspected that listing all transactions as increases or decreases in the transactions summary columns would be too cumbersome in practice. Most businesses, even small ones, enter into many transactions every day. Chapter 2 teaches you how to actually record business transactions in the accounting process.

To explain the dual procedure of recording business transactions with debits and credits, we introduce you to some new tools: the T-account, the journal, and the ledger. You can follow a company through its various business transactions using these tools. Like accountants, you can use a trial balance to check the equality of your recorded debits and credits. This is the double-entry accounting system that the Franciscan monk, Luca Pacioli, described centuries ago. Understanding this system enables you to better understand the content of financial statements so you can use the information provided to make informed business decisions.

THE ACCOUNT AND RULES OF DEBIT AND CREDIT

A business may engage in thousands of transactions during a year. An accountant classifies and summarizes the data in these transactions to create useful information.

(concluded)

6. Prepare a trial balance to test the equality of debits and credits in the journalizing and posting process.

7. Analyze and use the financial results—horizontal and vertical analyses.

The Account

Objective 1
Use the account as the basic classifying and storage unit for accounting information.

Note to the Student
Give an example of a business you would like to start or in which you are presently working. Develop typical transactions of the business and analyze these transactions.

Steps in Recording Business Transactions

Look at Illustration 2.1 to see the steps in recording and posting the effects of a business transaction. Note that source documents provide the evidence that a business transaction occurred. These source documents include such items as bills received from suppliers for goods or services received, bills sent to customers for goods sold or services performed, and cash register tapes. The information in the source document serves as the basis for preparing a journal entry. Then a firm posts (transfers) that information to accounts in the ledger.

You can see from Illustration 2.1 that after you prepare the journal entry, you post it to the accounts in the ledger. However, before you can record the journal entry, you must understand the rules of debit and credit. To teach you these rules, we begin by studying the nature of an account.

Fortunately, most business transactions are repetitive. This makes the task of accountants somewhat easier because they can classify the transactions into groups having common characteristics. For example, a company may have thousands of receipts or payments of cash during a year. As a result, a part of every cash transaction can be recorded and summarized in a single place called an *account*.

An **account** is a part of the accounting system used to classify and summarize the increases, decreases, and balances of each asset, liability, stockholders' equity item, dividend, revenue, and expense. Firms set up accounts for each different business element, such as cash, accounts receivable, and accounts payable. Every business has a Cash account in its accounting system because knowledge of the amount of cash on hand is useful information.

Accountants may differ on the account title (or name) they give the same item. For example, one accountant might name an account Notes Payable and another might call it Loans Payable. Both account titles refer to the amounts borrowed by the company. The account title should be logical to help the accountant group similar transactions into the same account. Once you give an account a title, you must use that same title throughout the accounting records.

The number of accounts in a company's accounting system depends on the information needs of those interested in the business. The main requirement is that each account provides information useful in making decisions. Thus, one account may be set up for all cash rather than having a separate account for each form of cash (coins on hand, currency on hand, and deposits in banks). The amount of cash is useful information; the form of cash often is not.

The T-Account

To illustrate recording the increases and decreases in an account, texts use the **T-account,** which looks like a capital letter T. The name of the account, such as Cash, appears across the top of the T. We record increases on one side of the vertical line of the T and decreases on the other side. A T-account appears as follows:

Title of Account

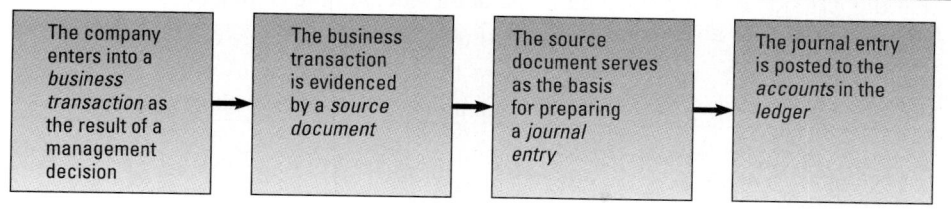

ILLUSTRATION 2.1
The Steps in Recording
and Posting the Effects
of a Business Transaction

In Chapter 1, you saw that each business transaction affects at least two items. For example, if you—an owner—invest cash in your business, the company's assets increase and its stockholders' equity increases. This result was illustrated in the summary of transactions in Illustration 1.3. In the following sections, we use debits and credits and the double-entry procedure to record the increases and decreases caused by business transactions.

Debits and Credits

Objective 2
Express the effects of business transactions in terms of debits and credits to different types of accounts.

Accountants use the term **debit** instead of saying, "Place an entry on the left side of the T-account." They use the term **credit** for "Place an entry on the right side of the T-account." Debit (abbreviated Dr.) simply means left side; credit (abbreviated Cr.) means right side.[1] Thus, for all accounts a debit entry is an entry on the left side, while a credit entry is an entry on the right side.

Any Account	
Left, or debit, side	Right, or credit, side

Double-Entry Procedure

Note to the Student
Debit and *credit* are directional signals. The limited meaning of debit is to record the amount on the left side of the account; the limited meaning of credit is to record the amount on the right side of the account.

After recognizing a business event as a business transaction, we analyze it to determine its increase or decrease effects on the assets, liabilities, stockholders' equity items, dividends, revenues, or expenses of the business. Then we translate these increase or decrease effects into debits and credits.

In each business transaction we record, the total dollar amount of debits must equal the total dollar amount of credits. When we debit one account (or accounts) for $100, we must credit another account (or accounts) for a total of $100. The accounting requirement that each transaction be recorded by an entry that has equal debits and credits is called **double-entry procedure,** or *duality*. This double-entry procedure keeps the accounting equation in balance.

The dual recording process produces two sets of accounts—those with debit balances and those with credit balances. The totals of these two groups of accounts must be equal. Then, some assurance exists that the arithmetic part of the transaction recording process has been properly carried out. Now, let us actually record business transactions in T-accounts using debits and credits.

RECORDING CHANGES IN ASSETS, LIABILITIES, AND STOCKHOLDERS' EQUITY
While recording business transactions, remember that the foundation of the accounting process is the following basic accounting equation:

$$\text{Assets} = \text{Liabilities} + \text{Stockholders' Equity}$$

Recording transactions into the T-accounts is easier when you focus on the equal sign in the accounting equation. Assets, which are on the left of the equal sign, increase on the left side of the T-accounts. Liabilities and stockholders' equity, to the right of the equal sign, increase on the right side of the T-accounts. You already know

---

[1]The abbreviations "Dr." and "Cr." are based on the Latin words "*debere*" and "*credere*." A synonym for *debit* an account is *charge* an account.

that the left side of the T-account is the debit side and the right side is the credit side. So you should be able to fill in the rest of the rules of increases and decreases by deduction, such as:

Assets		=	Liabilities		+	Stockholders' Equity	
Debit for increases	Credit for decreases		Debit for decreases	Credit for increases		Debit for decreases	Credit for increases

To summarize:

1. Assets *increase* by debits (left side) to the T-account and *decrease* by credits (right side) to the T-account.
2. Liabilities and stockholders' equity *decrease* by debits (left side) to the T-account and *increase* by credits (right side) to the T-account.

Applying these two rules keeps the accounting equation in balance. Now we apply the debit and credit rules for assets, liabilities, and stockholders' equity to business transactions.

Assume a corporation issues shares of its capital stock for $10,000 in transaction 1. (Note the figure in parentheses is the number of the transaction and ties the two sides of the transaction together.) The company records the receipt of $10,000 as follows:

(Dr.)	Cash	(Cr.)	(Dr.)	Capital Stock	(Cr.)
(1)	10,000			(1)	10,000

This transaction increases the asset, cash, which is recorded on the left side of the Cash account. Then, the transaction increases stockholders' equity, which is recorded on the right side of the Capital Stock account.

Assume the company borrowed $5,000 from a bank on a note (transaction 2). A **note** is an unconditional written promise to pay to another party (the bank) the amount owed either when demanded or at a specified date, usually with interest at a specified rate. The firm records this transaction as follows:

(Dr.)	Cash	(Cr.)	(Dr.)	Notes Payable	(Cr.)
(1)	10,000			(2)	5,000
(2)	5,000				

Observe that liabilities, Notes Payable, increase with an entry on the right (credit) side of the account.

RECORDING CHANGES IN REVENUES AND EXPENSES   In Chapter 1, we recorded the revenues and expenses directly in the Retained Earnings account. However, this is not done in practice because of the volume of revenue and expense transactions. Instead, businesses treat the expense accounts as if they were subclassifications of the debit side of the Retained Earnings account, and the revenue accounts as if they were subclassifications of the credit side. Since firms need the amounts of revenues and expenses to prepare the income statement, they keep a separate account for each revenue and expense. The recording rules for revenues and expenses are:

• Record increases in revenues on the right (credit) side of the T-account and decreases on the left (debit) side. The reasoning behind this rule is that revenues increase retained earnings, and increases in retained earnings are recorded on the right side.

• Record increases in expenses on the left (debit) side of the T-account and decreases on the right (credit) side. The reasoning behind this rule is that expenses decrease retained earnings, and decreases in retained earnings are recorded on the left side.

To illustrate these rules, assume the same company received $1,000 cash from a customer for services rendered (transaction 3). The Cash account, an asset, increases on the left (debit) side of the T-account; and the Service Revenue account, an increase in retained earnings, increases on the right (credit) side.

(Dr.)	Cash	(Cr.)	(Dr.)	Service Revenue	(Cr.)
(1)	10,000				
(2)	5,000			(3)	1,000
(3)	1,000				

Now assume this company paid $600 in salaries to employees (transaction 4). The Cash account, an asset, decreases on the right (credit) side of the T-account; and the Salaries Expense account, a decrease in retained earnings, increases on the left (debit) side.[2]

(Dr.)	Cash	(Cr.)		(Dr.)	Salaries Expense	(Cr.)
(1)	10,000	(4)	600	(4)	600	
(2)	5,000					
(3)	1,000					

RECORDING CHANGES IN DIVIDENDS   Since dividends decrease retained earnings, increases appear on the left side of the Dividends account and decreases on the right side. Thus, the firm records payment of a $2,000 cash dividend (transaction 5) as follows:

(Dr.)	Cash	(Cr.)		(Dr.)	Dividends[3]	(Cr.)
(1)	10,000	(4)	600	(5)	2,000	
(2)	5,000	(5)	2,000			
(3)	1,000					

At the end of the accounting period, the accountant transfers any balances in the expense, revenue, and Dividends accounts to the Retained Earnings account. This transfer occurs only after the information in the expense and revenue accounts has been used to prepare the income statement. We discuss and illustrate this step in Chapter 4.

To determine the balance of any T-account, total the debits to the account, total the credits to the account, and subtract the smaller sum from the larger. If the sum of the debits exceeds the sum of the credits, the account has a **debit balance.** For example, the following Cash account uses information from the preceding transactions. The account has a debit balance of $13,400, computed as total debits of $16,000 less total credits of $2,600.

Determining the Balance of an Account

(Dr.)	Cash	(Cr.)	
(1)	10,000	(4)	600
(2)	5,000	(5)	2,000
(3)	1,000		
	16,000		2,600
Dr. bal.	13,400		

---

[2]Certain deductions are normally taken out of employees' pay for social security taxes, federal and state withholding, and so on. Those deductions are ignored here.

[3]As we illustrate later in the text, some companies debit dividends directly to the Retained Earnings account rather than to a Dividends account.

If, on the other hand, the sum of the credits exceeds the sum of the debits, the account has a **credit balance.** For instance, assume that a company has an Accounts Payable account with a total of $10,000 in debits and $13,000 in credits. The account has a credit balance of $3,000, as shown in the following T-account:

(Dr.)	Accounts Payable	(Cr.)
10,000		7,000
		6,000
10,000		13,000
	Cr. bal.	3,000

NORMAL BALANCES   Since debits increase asset, expense, and Dividend accounts, they normally have debit (or left-side) balances. Conversely, because credits increase liability, capital stock, retained earnings, and revenue accounts, they normally have credit (or right-side) balances.

The following chart shows the normal balances of the seven accounts we have used:

	Normal Balances	
Types of Accounts	Debit	Credit
Assets	X	
Liabilities		X
Stockholders' equity:		
Capital stock		X
Retained earnings . . .		X
Dividends	X	
Expenses	X	
Revenues		X

Rules of Debit and Credit Summarized

At this point, you should memorize the six rules of debit and credit. Later, as you proceed in your study of accounting, the rules will become automatic. Then, you will no longer ask yourself, "Is this increase a debit or credit?"

Asset accounts increase on the debit side, while liability and stockholders' equity accounts increase on the credit side. When the account balances are totaled, they conform to the following independent equations:

$$\text{Assets} = \text{Liabilities} + \text{Stockholders' Equity}$$

$$\text{Debits} = \text{Credits}$$

The arrangement of these two formulas gives the first three rules of debit and credit:

1. Increases in asset accounts are debits; decreases are credits.
2. Decreases in liability accounts are debits; increases are credits.
3. Decreases in stockholders' equity accounts are debits; increases are credits.

The debit and credit rules for expense and Dividends accounts and for revenue accounts follow logically if you remember that expenses and dividends are decreases in stockholders' equity and revenues are increases in stockholders' equity. Since stockholders' equity accounts decrease on the debit side, expense and Dividend accounts increase on the debit side. Since stockholders' equity accounts increase on the credit side, revenue accounts increase on the credit side. The last three debit and credit rules are:

4. Decreases in revenue accounts are debits; increases are credits.
5. Increases in expense accounts are debits; decreases are credits.
6. Increases in Dividends accounts are debits; decreases are credits.

ILLUSTRATION 2.2 Rules of Debit and Credit

Assets = Liabilities + Stockholders' Equity

Asset Accounts		=	Liability Accounts		+	Stockholders' Equity Account(s) (Capital Stock and Retained Earnings)	
Debit*	Credit		Debit	Credit*		Debit	Credit*
+ Debit for increase	− Credit for decrease		− Debit for decrease	+ Credit for increase		− Debit for decrease	+ Credit for increase

Debits	Credits
1. Increase assets.	1. Decrease assets.
2. Decrease liabilities.	2. Increase liabilities.
3. Decrease stockholders' equity.	3. Increase stockholders' equity.
4. Decrease revenues.	4. Increase revenues.
5. Increase expenses.	5. Decrease expenses.
6. Increase dividends.	6. Decrease dividends.

Expense Accounts and Dividends Account		Revenue Accounts	
Debit*	Credit	Debit	Credit*
+ Debit for increase	− Credit for decrease	− Debit for decrease	+ Credit for increase

*Normal balance.

In Illustration 2.2, we depict these six rules of debit and credit. Note first the treatment of expense and Dividends accounts as if they were subclassifications of the debit side of the Retained Earnings account. Second, note the treatment of the revenue accounts as if they were subclassifications of the credit side of the Retained Earnings account. Next, we discuss the accounting cycle and indicate where steps in the accounting cycle are discussed in Chapters 2 through 4.

THE ACCOUNTING CYCLE

The **accounting cycle** is a series of steps performed during the accounting period (some throughout the period and some at the end) to analyze, record, classify, summarize, and report useful financial information for the purpose of preparing financial statements. Before you can visualize the eight steps in the accounting cycle, you must be able to recognize a business transaction. **Business transactions** are measurable events that affect the financial condition of a business. For example, assume that the owner of a business spilled a pot of coffee in her office or broke her leg while skiing. These two events may briefly interrupt the operation of the business. However, they are not measurable in terms that affect the solvency and profitability of the business.

Business transactions can be the exchange of goods for cash between the business and an external party, such as the sale of a book, or they can involve paying salaries to employees. These events have one fundamental criterion: They must have caused a measurable change in the amounts in the accounting equation, Assets = Liabilities + Stockholders' Equity. The evidence that a business event has occurred is a source document such as a sales ticket, check, and so on. Source documents are important because they are the ultimate proof of business transactions.[4]

After you have determined that an event is a measurable business transaction and have adequate proof of this transaction, mentally analyze the transaction's effects on the accounting equation. You learned how to do this in Chapter 1. This chapter and

Objective 3
List the steps in the accounting cycle.

---

[4]Recently, some companies have been sending and receiving source documents electronically, rather than on paper. In such an electronic computer environment, source documents might exist only in the computer databases of the two parties involved in the transaction.

Chapters 3 and 4 describe other steps in the accounting cycle. The eight steps in the accounting cycle and the chapters that discuss them are:

Performed throughout the accounting period

1. Analyze transactions by examining source documents (Chapters 1 and 2).
2. Journalize transactions in the journal (Chapter 2).
3. Post journal entries to the accounts in the ledger (Chapter 2).

Performed only at end of the accounting period

4. Prepare a trial balance of the accounts (Chapter 2) and complete the work sheet (Chapter 4). (This step includes adjusting entries from Chapter 3.)
5. Prepare financial statements (Chapter 4).
6. Journalize and post adjusting entries (Chapters 3 and 4).
7. Journalize and post closing entries (Chapter 4).
8. Prepare a post-closing trial balance (Chapter 4).

This listing serves as a preview of what you will study in Chapters 2–4. Notice that firms perform the last five steps at the end of the accounting period. Step 5 precedes steps 6 and 7 because management needs the financial statements at the earliest possible date. After the statements have been delivered to management, the adjusting and closing entries can be journalized and posted. In Illustration 2.3, we diagram the eight steps in the accounting cycle.

You can perform many of these steps on a computer with an accounting software package. However, you must understand a manual accounting system and all of the steps in the accounting cycle to understand what the computer is doing. This understanding removes the mystery of what the computer is doing when it takes in raw data and produces financial statements.

THE JOURNAL

Objective 4
Record the effects of business transactions in a journal.

In explaining the rules of debit and credit, we recorded transactions directly in the accounts. Each ledger (general ledger) account shows only the increases and decreases in that account. Thus, all the effects of a single business transaction would not appear in any one account. For example, the Cash account contains only data on changes in cash and does not show how the cash was generated or how it was spent. To have a permanent record of an entire transaction, the accountant uses a book or record known as a *journal*.

A **journal** is a chronological (arranged in order of time) record of business transactions. A *journal entry* is the recording of a business transaction in the journal. A **journal entry** shows all the effects of a business transaction as expressed in debit(s) and credit(s) and may include an explanation of the transaction. *A transaction is entered in a journal before it is entered in ledger accounts.* Because each transaction is initially recorded in a journal rather than directly in the ledger, a journal is called a *book of original entry.*

The General Journal

A business usually has more than one journal. Chapter 4 briefly describes several special journals. In this chapter, we use the basic form of journal, the general journal. As shown in Illustration 2.4, a general journal contains the following columns:

1. **Date column.** The first column on each journal page is for the date. For the first journal entry on a page, this column contains the year, month, and day (number). For all other journal entries on a page, this column contains only the day of the month, until the month changes.

Reinforcing Problems
E2–2 Prepare journal entries
E2–3 Prepare journal entries

2. **Account Titles and Explanation column.** The first line of an entry shows the account debited. The second line shows the account credited. Notice that we indent the credit account title to the right. For instance, in Illustration 2.4 we show the debit to the Cash account and then the credit to the Capital Stock account. Any necessary explanation of a transaction appears on the line(s) below the credit entry and is indented halfway between the accounts debited and

ILLUSTRATION 2.3   Steps in the Accounting Cycle

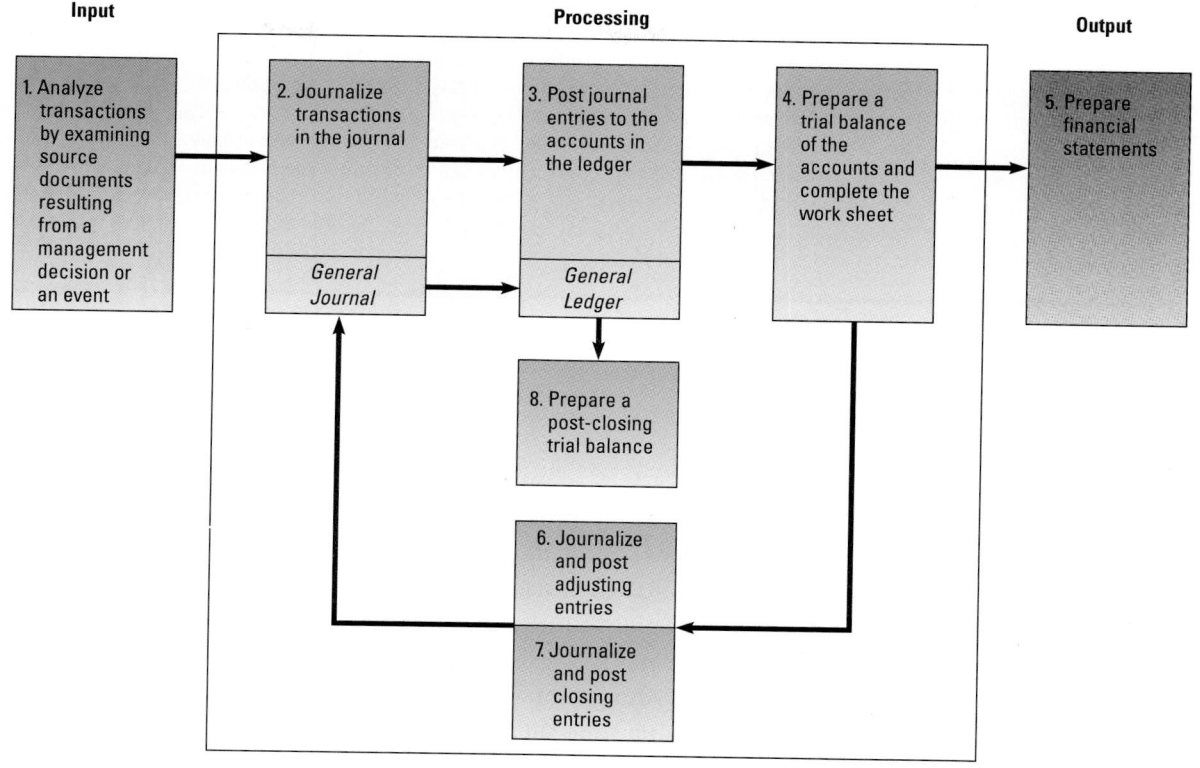

ILLUSTRATION 2.4   General Journal

MICROTRAIN COMPANY
General Journal

Page 1

Date	Account Titles and Explanation	Post. Ref.	Debit	Credit
1999 Nov. 28	Cash	100	5 0 0 0 0	
	Capital Stock	300		5 0 0 0 0
	Stockholders invested $50,000 cash in the business.			

credited. A journal entry explanation should be concise and yet complete enough to describe fully the transaction and prove the entry's accuracy. When a journal entry is self-explanatory, we omit the explanation.

3. **Posting Reference column.** This column shows the account number of the debited or credited account. For instance, in Illustration 2.4, the number 100 in the first entry means that the Cash account number is 100. No number appears in this column until the information has been posted to the appropriate ledger account. We discuss posting later in the chapter.

4. **Debit column.** In the debit column, the amount of the debit is on the same line as the title of the account debited.

5. **Credit column.** In the credit column, the amount of the credit is on the same line as the title of the account credited.

AN ACCOUNTING PERSPECTIVE

USES OF TECHNOLOGY   Preparing journal entries in a computerized system is different than in a manual system. The computer normally asks for the number of the account to be debited. After you type the account number, the computer shows the account title in its proper position. The cursor then moves to the debit column and waits for you to enter the amount of the debit. Then it asks if there are more debits. If not, the computer prompts you for the account number of the credit. After you type the account number, the computer supplies the account name of the credit and enters the same amount debited as the credit. When there is more than one credit, you can override the amount and enter the correct amount. Then you would enter the other credit in the same way. If your debits and credits are not equal, the computer warns you and makes you correct the error. You can supply an explanation for the entry from a standard list or type it in. As you enter the journal entries, the computer automatically posts them to the ledger accounts. At any time, you can have the computer print a trial balance.

Functions and Advantages of a Journal

A summary of the functions and advantages of using a journal follows:

The journal—

1. Records transactions in chronological order.
2. Shows the analysis of each transaction in debits and credits.
3. Supplies an explanation of each transaction when necessary.
4. Serves as a source for future reference to accounting transactions.
5. Eliminates the need for lengthy explanations from the accounts.
6. Makes possible posting to the ledger at convenient times.
7. Assists in maintaining the ledger in balance because the debit(s) must always equal the credit(s) in each journal entry.
8. Aids in tracing errors when the ledger is not in balance.

Reinforcing Problem
P2–1A Prepare journal entries.

THE LEDGER

A **ledger** (general ledger) is the complete collection of all the accounts of a company. The ledger may be in loose-leaf form, in a bound volume, or in computer memory.

Accounts fall into two general groups: (1) *balance sheet accounts* (assets, liabilities, and stockholders' equity) and (2) *income statement accounts* (revenues and expenses). The terms *real accounts* and *permanent accounts* also refer to balance sheet accounts. Balance sheet accounts are **real accounts** because they are not subclassifications or subdivisions of any other account. They are **permanent accounts** because their balances are not transferred (or closed) to any other account at the end of the accounting period. Income statement accounts and the Dividends account are **nominal accounts** because they are merely subclassifications of the stockholders' equity accounts. *Nominal* literally means "in name only." Nominal accounts are also called **temporary accounts** because they temporarily contain revenue, expense, and dividend information that is transferred (or closed) to the Retained Earnings account at the end of the accounting period.

The **chart of accounts** is a complete listing of the titles and numbers of all the accounts in the ledger. The chart of accounts can be compared to a table of contents. The groups of accounts usually appear in this order: assets, liabilities, stockholders' equity, dividends, revenues, and expenses.

Individual accounts are in sequence in the ledger. Each account typically has an identification number and a title to help locate accounts when recording data. For example, a company might number asset accounts, 100–199; liability accounts, 200–299; stockholders' equity accounts and Dividends account, 300–399; revenue accounts, 400–499; and expense accounts, 500–599. We use this numbering system in this text. The uniform chart of accounts used in the first 11 chapters appears on the inside cover of the text. Companies may use other numbering systems. For instance, sometimes a company numbers its accounts in sequence starting with 1, 2, and so on. The important idea is that companies use some numbering system.

Now that you understand how to record debits and credits in an account and how all accounts together form a ledger, you are ready to study the accounting process in operation.

THE ACCOUNTING PROCESS IN OPERATION

MicroTrain Company is a small corporation that provides on-site microcomputer software training using the clients' equipment. The company offers beginning through advanced training with convenient scheduling. A small fleet of trucks transports personnel and teaching supplies to the clients' sites. The company rents a building and is responsible for paying the utilities.

We illustrate the capital stock transaction that occurred to form the company (in November) and the first month of operations (December). The accounting process used by this company is similar to that of any small company. The ledger accounts used by MicroTrain Company are:

	Acct. No.	Account Title	Description
Assets	100	Cash	Bank deposits and cash on hand.
	103	Accounts Receivable	Amounts owed to the company by customers.
	107	Supplies on Hand	Items such as paper, envelopes, writing materials, and other materials used in performing training services for customers or in doing administrative and clerical office work.
	108	Prepaid Insurance	Insurance policy premiums paid in advance of the periods for which the insurance coverage applies.
	112	Prepaid Rent	Rent paid in advance of the periods for which the rent payment applies.
	150	Trucks	Trucks used to transport personnel and training supplies to clients' locations.
Liabilities	200	Accounts Payable	Amounts owed to creditors for items purchased from them.
	216	Unearned Service Fees	Amounts received from customers before the training services have been performed for them.
Stockholders' equity	300	Capital Stock	The stockholders' investment in the business.
	310	Retained Earnings	The earnings retained in the business.
Dividends	320	Dividends	The amount of dividends declared to stockholders.
Revenues	400	Service Revenue	Amounts earned by performing training services for customers.
Expenses	505	Advertising Expense	The cost of advertising incurred in the current period.
	506	Gas and Oil Expense	The cost of gas and oil used in trucks in the current period.
	507	Salaries Expense	The amount of salaries incurred in the current period.
	511	Utilities Expense	The cost of utilities incurred in the current period.

Notice the gaps left between account numbers (100, 103, 107, etc.). These gaps allow the firm to later add new accounts between the existing accounts.

The Recording of Transactions and Their Effects on the Accounts

To begin, a transaction must be *journalized*. **Journalizing** is the process of entering the effects of a transaction in a journal. Then, the information is transferred, or posted, to the proper accounts in the ledger. **Posting** is the process of recording in the ledger accounts the information contained in the journal. We explain posting in more detail later in the chapter.

In the following example, notice that each business transaction affects two or more accounts in the ledger. Also note that the transaction date in both the general journal and the general ledger accounts is the same. In the ledger accounts, the date used is the date that the transaction was recorded in the general journal, even if the entry is not posted until several days later. Our example shows the journal entries posted to T-accounts. In practice, firms post journal entries to three-column ledger accounts, as we show later in the chapter.

Accountants use the *accrual basis of accounting*. Under the **accrual basis of accounting,** they recognize revenues when the company makes a sale or performs a service, regardless of when the company receives the cash. They recognize expenses as incurred, whether or not the company has paid out cash. Chapter 3 discusses the accrual basis of accounting in more detail.

In the following MicroTrain Company example, transaction 1 increases (debits) Cash and increases (credits) Capital Stock by $50,000. First, MicroTrain records the transaction in the general journal; second, it posts the entry to the accounts in the general ledger.

Transaction 1: Nov. 28, 1999 Stockholders invested $50,000 and formed MicroTrain Company.

General Journal

Date	Account Titles and Explanation	Post. Ref.	Debit	Credit
1999 Nov. 28	Cash	100	5 0 0 0 0	
	Capital Stock	300		5 0 0 0 0
	Stockholders invested $50,000 cash in the business.			

General Ledger

(Dr.)	Cash	Acct. No. 100 (Cr.)	(Dr.)	Capital Stock	Acct. No. 300 (Cr.)
1999 Nov. 28	50,000			1999 Nov. 28	50,000

No other transactions occurred in November. The company prepares financial statements at the end of each month. Illustration 2.5 shows the company's balance sheet at November 30, 1999.

The balance sheet reflects ledger account balances as of the close of business on November 30, 1999. These closing balances are the beginning balances on December 1, 1999. The ledger accounts show these closing balances as beginning balances (Beg. bal.).

Now assume that in December 1999, MicroTrain Company engaged in the following transactions. We show the proper recording of each transaction in the journal and then in the ledger accounts (in T-account form), and describe the effects of each transaction.

MICROTRAIN COMPANY
Balance Sheet
November 30, 1999

ILLUSTRATION 2.5
Balance Sheet

Assets		Liabilities and Stockholders' Equity	
Cash	$50,000	Stockholders' equity:	
		Capital stock	$50,000
		Total liabilities and stockholders'	
Total assets	$50,000	equity	$50,000

Transaction 2: Dec. 1 Paid cash for four small trucks, $40,000.

General Journal

Date		Account Titles and Explanation	Post. Ref.	Debit	Credit
1999 Dec.	1	Trucks	150	4 0 0 0 0	
		Cash	100		4 0 0 0 0
		To record the purchase of four trucks.			

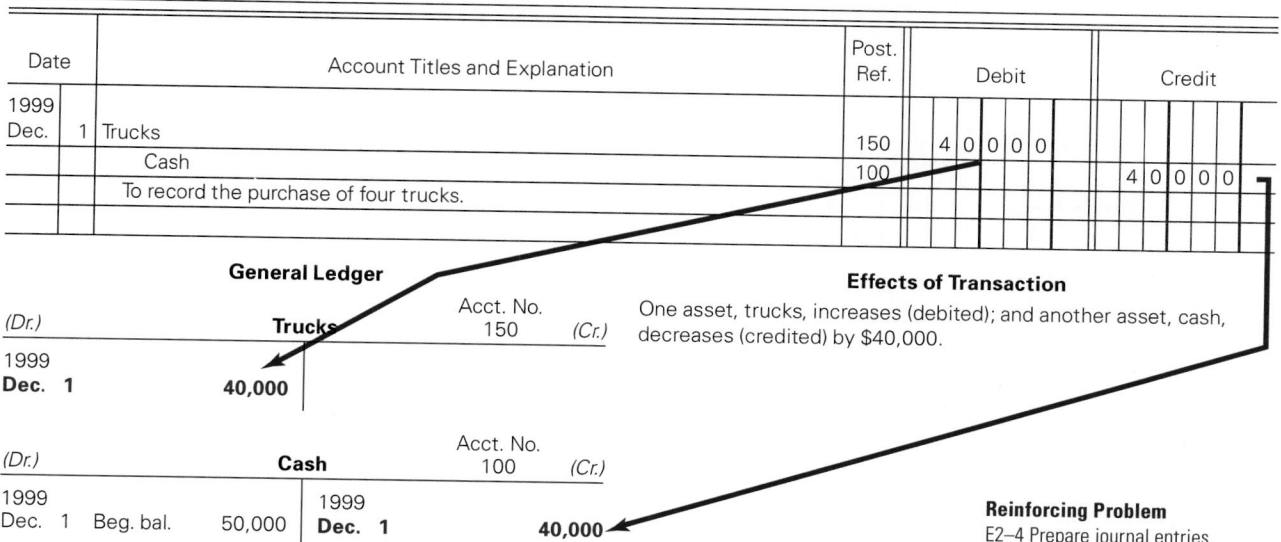

General Ledger

(Dr.) **Trucks** Acct. No. 150 (Cr.)

1999
Dec. 1   40,000

(Dr.) **Cash** Acct. No. 100 (Cr.)

1999
Dec. 1 Beg. bal. 50,000

1999
Dec. 1   40,000

Effects of Transaction

One asset, trucks, increases (debited); and another asset, cash, decreases (credited) by $40,000.

Reinforcing Problem
E2–4 Prepare journal entries.

Transaction 3: Dec. 1 Paid $2,400 cash for insurance on the trucks to cover a one-year period from this date.

General Journal

Date		Account Titles and Explanation	Post. Ref.	Debit	Credit
1999 Dec.	1	Prepaid Insurance	108	2 4 0 0	
		Cash	100		2 4 0 0
		Purchased truck insurance to cover a one-year period.			

General Ledger

(Dr.) **Prepaid Insurance** Acct. No. 108 (Cr.)

1999
Dec. 1   2,400

(Dr.) **Cash** Acct. No. 100 (Cr.)

1999
Dec. 1 Beg. bal. 50,000

1999
Dec. 1   40,000
      1   2,400

Effects of Transaction

An asset, prepaid insurance, increases (debited); and an asset, cash, decreases (credited) by $2,400. The debit is to Prepaid Insurance rather than Insurance Expense because the policy covers more than the current accounting period of December (insurance policies are usually paid one year in advance). As you will see in Chapter 3, prepaid items are expensed as they are used. If this insurance policy was only written for December, the entire $2,400 debit would have been to Insurance Expense.

Transaction 4:   Dec. 1   Rented a building and paid $1,200 to cover a three-month period from this date.

General Journal

Date		Account Titles and Explanation	Post. Ref.	Debit	Credit
1999 Dec.	1	Prepaid Rent	112	1 2 0 0	
		Cash	100		1 2 0 0
		Paid three months' rent on a building.			

General Ledger

(Dr.)   **Prepaid Rent**   Acct. No. 112   *(Cr.)*

| 1999 Dec. 1 | 1,200 | |

(Dr.)   **Cash**   Acct. No. 100   *(Cr.)*

1999 Dec. 1 Beg. bal.	50,000	1999 Dec. 1	40,000
		1	2,400
		1	**1,200**

Effects of Transaction

An asset, prepaid rent, increases (debited); and another asset, cash, decreases (credited) by $1,200. The debit is to Prepaid Rent rather than Rent Expense because the payment covers more than the current month. If the payment had just been for December, the debit would have been to Rent Expense.

Transaction 5:   Dec. 4   Purchased $1,400 of training supplies on account to be used over the next several months.

General Journal

Date		Account Titles and Explanation	Post. Ref.	Debit	Credit
1999 Dec.	4	Supplies on Hand	107	1 4 0 0	
		Accounts Payable	200		1 4 0 0
		To record the purchase of training supplies for future use.			

General Ledger

(Dr.)   **Supplies on Hand**   Acct. No. 107   *(Cr.)*

| 1999 Dec. 4 | 1,400 | |

(Dr.)   **Cash**   Acct. No. 200   *(Cr.)*

| | | 1999 Dec. 4 | 1,400 |

Effects of Transaction

An asset, supplies on hand, increases (debited); and a liability, accounts payable, increases (credited) by $1,400. The debit is to Supplies on Hand rather than Supplies Expense because the supplies are to be used over several accounting periods.

Reinforcing Problem
E2–5 Show entries using journal entries and T-accounts.

In each of the three preceding entries, we debited an asset rather than an expense. The reason is that the expenditure applies to (or benefits) more than just the current accounting period. Whenever a company will not fully use up an item such as insurance, rent, or supplies in the period when purchased, it usually debits an asset. In practice, however, sometimes the expense is initially debited in these situations.

Companies sometimes buy items that they fully use up within the current accounting period. For example, during the first part of the month a company may buy supplies that it intends to consume fully during that month. If the company fully consumes the supplies during the period of purchase, the best practice is to debit Supplies Expense at the time of purchase rather than Supplies on Hand. This same advice applies to insurance and rent. If a company purchases insurance that it fully consumes during the current period, the company should debit Insurance Expense at the time of purchase rather than Prepaid Insurance. Also, if a company pays rent that applies only to the current period, Rent Expense should be debited at the time of purchase rather than Prepaid Rent. As illustrated in Chapter 3, following this advice simplifies the procedures at the end of the accounting period.

Transaction 6:   Dec. 7   Received $4,500 from a customer in payment for future training services.

General Journal

Date	Account Titles and Explanation	Post. Ref.	Debit	Credit
1999 Dec. 7	Cash	100	4 5 0 0	
	Unearned Service Fees	216		4 5 0 0
	To record the receipt of cash from a customer in payment			
	for future training services.			

General Ledger

(Dr.)	**Cash**	Acct. No. 100	(Cr.)
1999 Dec. 1 Beg. bal. 50,000		1999 Dec. 1 40,000	
7 **4,500**		1 2,400	
		1 1,200	

(Dr.)	**Unearned Service Fees**	Acct. No. 216	(Cr.)
		1999 Dec. 7 **4,500**	

Effects of Transaction

An asset, cash, increases (debited); and a liability, unearned service revenue, increases (credited) by $4,500. The credit is to Unearned Service Fees rather than Service Revenue because the $4,500 applies to more than just the current accounting period. Unearned Service Fees is a liability because, if the services are never performed, the $4,500 will have to be refunded. If the payment had been for services to be provided in December, the credit would have been to Service Revenue.

Transaction 7:   Dec. 15   Performed training services for a customer for cash, $5,000.

General Journal

Date	Account Titles and Explanation	Post. Ref.	Debit	Credit
1999 Dec. 15	Cash	100	5 0 0 0	
	Service Revenue	400		5 0 0 0
	To record the receipt of cash for performing training			
	services for a customer.			

General Ledger

(Dr.)	**Cash**	Acct. No. 100	(Cr.)
1999 Dec. 1 Beg. bal. 50,000		1999 Dec. 1 40,000	
7 4,500		1 2,400	
15 **5,000**		1 1,200	

(Dr.)	**Service Revenue**	Acct. No. 400	(Cr.)
		1999 Dec. 15 **5,000**	

Effects of Transaction

An asset, cash, increases (debited); and a revenue, service revenue, increases (credited) by $5,000.

Transaction 8:   Dec. 17   Paid the $1,400 account payable resulting from the transaction of December 4.

General Journal

Date	Account Titles and Explanation	Post. Ref.	Debit	Credit
1999 Dec. 17	Accounts Payable	200	1 4 0 0	
	Cash	100		1 4 0 0
	Paid the account payable arising from the purchase of			
	supplies on December 4.			

General Ledger

Effects of Transaction

A liability, accounts payable, decreases (debited); and an asset, cash, decreases (credited) by $1,400.

		Acct. No.	
(Dr.)	**Accounts Payable**	200	(Cr.)
1999 Dec. 17	**1,400**	1999 Dec. 4	1,400

		Acct. No.	
(Dr.)	**Cash**	100	(Cr.)
1999 Dec. 1 Beg. bal.	50,000	1999 Dec. 1	40,000
7	4,500	1	2,400
15	5,000	1	1,200
		17	**1,400**

Transaction 9:   Dec. 20   Billed a customer for training services performed, $5,700.

General Journal

Date	Account Titles and Explanation	Post. Ref.	Debit	Credit
1999 Dec. 20	Accounts Receivable	103	5 7 0 0	
	Service Revenue	400		5 7 0 0
	To record the performance of training services on account			
	for which a customer was billed.			

General Ledger

Effects of Transaction

An asset, accounts receivable, increases (debited); and a revenue, service revenue, increases (credited) by $5,700.

		Acct. No.	
(Dr.)	**Accounts Receivable**	103	(Cr.)
1999 Dec. 20	**5,700**		

		Acct. No.	
(Dr.)	**Service Revenue**	400	(Cr.)
		1999 Dec. 15	5,000
		20	**5,700**

Transaction 10: Dec. 24 Received a bill for advertising in a local newspaper in December, $50.

General Journal

Date	Account Titles and Explanation	Post. Ref.	Debit	Credit
1999 Dec. 24	Advertising Expense	505	5 0	
	Accounts Payable	200		5 0
	Received a bill for advertising for the month of December.			

General Ledger

(Dr.)   **Advertising Expense**   Acct. No. 505   (Cr.)

1999 Dec. 24	50	

(Dr.)   **Accounts Payable**   Acct. No. 200   (Cr.)

1999 Dec. 17	1,400	1999 Dec. 4	1,400
		24	50

Effects of Transaction

An expense, advertising expense, increases (debited); and a liability, accounts payable, increases (credited) by $50. The reason for debiting an expense rather than an asset is because all the cost pertains to the current accounting period, the month of December. Otherwise, Prepaid Advertising (an asset) would have been debited.

Transaction 11: Dec. 26 Received $500 on accounts receivable from a customer.

General Journal

Date	Account Titles and Explanation	Post. Ref.	Debit	Credit
1999 Dec. 26	Cash	100	5 0 0	
	Accounts Receivable	103		5 0 0
	Received $500 from a customer on accounts receivable.			

General Ledger

(Dr.)   **Cash**   Acct. No. 100   (Cr.)

1999				1999	
Dec. 1	Beg. bal.	50,000		Dec. 1	40,000
7		4,500		1	2,400
15		5,000		1	1,200
26		500		17	1,400

(Dr.)   **Accounts Receivable**   Acct. No. 103   (Cr.)

1999 Dec. 20	5,700	1999 **Dec. 26**	500

Effects of Transaction

One asset, cash, increases (debited); and another asset, accounts receivable, decreases (credited) by $500.

Transaction 12:   Dec. 28   Paid salaries of $3,600 to training personnel for the first four weeks of December. (Payroll and other deductions are to be ignored since they have not yet been discussed.)

General Journal

Date	Account Titles and Explanation	Post. Ref.	Debit	Credit
1999 Dec. 28	Salaries Expense	507	3 6 0 0	
	Cash	100		3 6 0 0
	Paid training personnel salaries for the first four weeks of December.			

General Ledger

(Dr.)	**Salaries Expense**	Acct. No. 507	(Cr.)
1999 **Dec. 28**	**3,600**		

(Dr.)		**Cash**	Acct. No. 100	(Cr.)
1999 Dec. 1	Beg. bal.	50,000	1999 Dec. 1	40,000
7		4,500	1	2,400
15		5,000	1	1,200
26		500	17	1,400
			28	**3,600**

Effects of Transaction

An expense, salaries expense, increases (debited); and an asset, cash, decreases (credited) by $3,600.

Transaction 13:   Dec. 29   Received and paid the utilities bill for December, $150.

General Journal

Date	Account Titles and Explanation	Post. Ref.	Debit	Credit
1999 Dec. 29	Utilities Expense	511	1 5 0	
	Cash	100		1 5 0
	Paid the utilities bill for December.			

General Ledger

(Dr.)	**Utilities Expense**	Acct. No. 511	(Cr.)
1999 **Dec. 29**	**150**		

(Dr.)		**Cash**	Acct. No. 100	(Cr.)
1999 Dec. 1	Beg. bal.	50,000	1999 Dec. 1	40,000
7		4,500	1	2,400
15		5,000	1	1,200
26		500	17	1,400
			28	3,600
			29	**150**

Effects of Transaction

An expense, utilities expense, increases (debited); and an asset, cash, decreases (credited) by $150.

Transaction 14:   Dec. 30   Received a bill for gas and oil used in the trucks for December, $680.

General Journal

Date	Account Titles and Explanation	Post. Ref.	Debit	Credit
1999 Dec.	30	Gas and Oil Expense	506	6 8 0	
		Accounts Payable	200		6 8 0
		Received a bill for gas and oil used in the trucks for December.			

General Ledger

(Dr.)	**Gas and Oil Expense**	Acct. No. 506	(Cr.)
1999 Dec. 30	680		

(Dr.)	**Accounts Payable**	Acct. No. 200	(Cr.)
1999 Dec. 17	1,400	1999 Dec. 4	1,400
		24	50
		30	**680**

Effects of Transaction

An expense, gas and oil expense, increases (debited); and a liability, accounts payable, increases (credited) by $680.

Transaction 15:   Dec. 31   A dividend of $3,000 was paid to stockholders.

General Journal

Date	Account Titles and Explanation	Post. Ref.	Debit	Credit
1999 Dec.	31	Dividends	320	3 0 0 0	
		Cash	100		3 0 0 0
		Dividends were paid to stockholders.			

General Ledger

(Dr.)	**Dividends**	Acct. No. 320	(Cr.)
1999 Dec. 31	3,000		

(Dr.)		**Cash**	Acct. No. 100	(Cr.)
1999 Dec. 1	Beg. bal.	50,000	1999 Dec. 1	40,000
7		4,500	1	2,400
15		5,000	1	1,200
26		500	17	1,400
			28	3,600
			29	150
			31	**3,000**

Effects of Transaction

The Dividends account increases (debited); and an asset, cash, decreases (credited) by $3,000.

Transaction 15 concludes the analysis of the MicroTrain Company transactions. The next section discusses and illustrates posting to three-column ledger accounts and cross-indexing.

THE USE OF THREE-COLUMN LEDGER ACCOUNTS

Posting to Three-Column Ledger Accounts

Objective 5
Post journal entries to the accounts in the ledger.

A journal entry is like a set of instructions. The carrying out of these instructions is known as *posting*. As stated earlier, **posting** is recording in the ledger accounts the information contained in the journal. A journal entry directs the entry of a certain dollar amount as a debit in a specific ledger account and directs the entry of a certain dollar amount as a credit in a specific ledger account. Earlier, we posted the journal entries for MicroTrain Company to T-accounts. In practice, however, companies post these journal entries to three-column ledger accounts.

Using a new example, Jenks Company, we illustrate posting to three-column ledger accounts. Later, we show you how to post the MicroTrain Company journal entries to three-column ledger accounts.

In Illustration 2.6, the first journal entry for the Jenks Company directs that $10,000 be posted in the ledger as a debit to the Cash account and as a credit to the Capital Stock account. We post the debit in the general ledger Cash account by using the following procedure: Enter in the Cash account the date, a short explanation, the journal designation ("G" for general journal) and the journal page number from which the debit is posted, and the $10,000 in the Debit column. Then, enter the number of the account to which the debit is posted in the Posting Reference column of the general journal. Post the credit in a similar manner but as a credit to Account No. 300. The arrows in Illustration 2.6 show how these amounts were posted to the correct accounts.

Illustration 2.6 shows the three-column ledger account. In contrast to the two-sided T-account format shown so far, the three-column format has columns for debit, credit, and balance. The three-column form has the advantage of showing the balance of the account after each item has been posted. In addition, in this chapter, we indicate whether each balance is a debit or a credit. In later chapters and in practice, the nature of the balance is usually not indicated since it is understood. Also, notice that we give an explanation for each item in the ledger accounts. Often accountants omit these explanations because each item can be traced back to the general journal for the explanation.

Posting is always from the journal to the ledger accounts. Postings can be made (1) at the time the transaction is journalized; (2) at the end of the day, week, or month; or (3) as each journal page is filled. The choice is a matter of personal taste. When posting the general journal, the date used in the ledger accounts is the date the transaction was recorded in the journal, not the date the journal entry was posted to the ledger accounts.

Cross-Indexing (Referencing)

Frequently, accountants must check and trace the origin of their transactions, so they provide *cross-indexing*. **Cross-indexing** is the placing of (1) the account number of the ledger account in the general journal and (2) the general journal page number in the ledger account. As shown in Illustration 2.6, the account number of the ledger account to which the posting was made is in the Posting Reference column of the general journal. Note the arrow from Account No. 100 in the ledger to the 100 in the

ILLUSTRATION 2.6   General Journal and General Ledger; Posting and Cross-Indexing

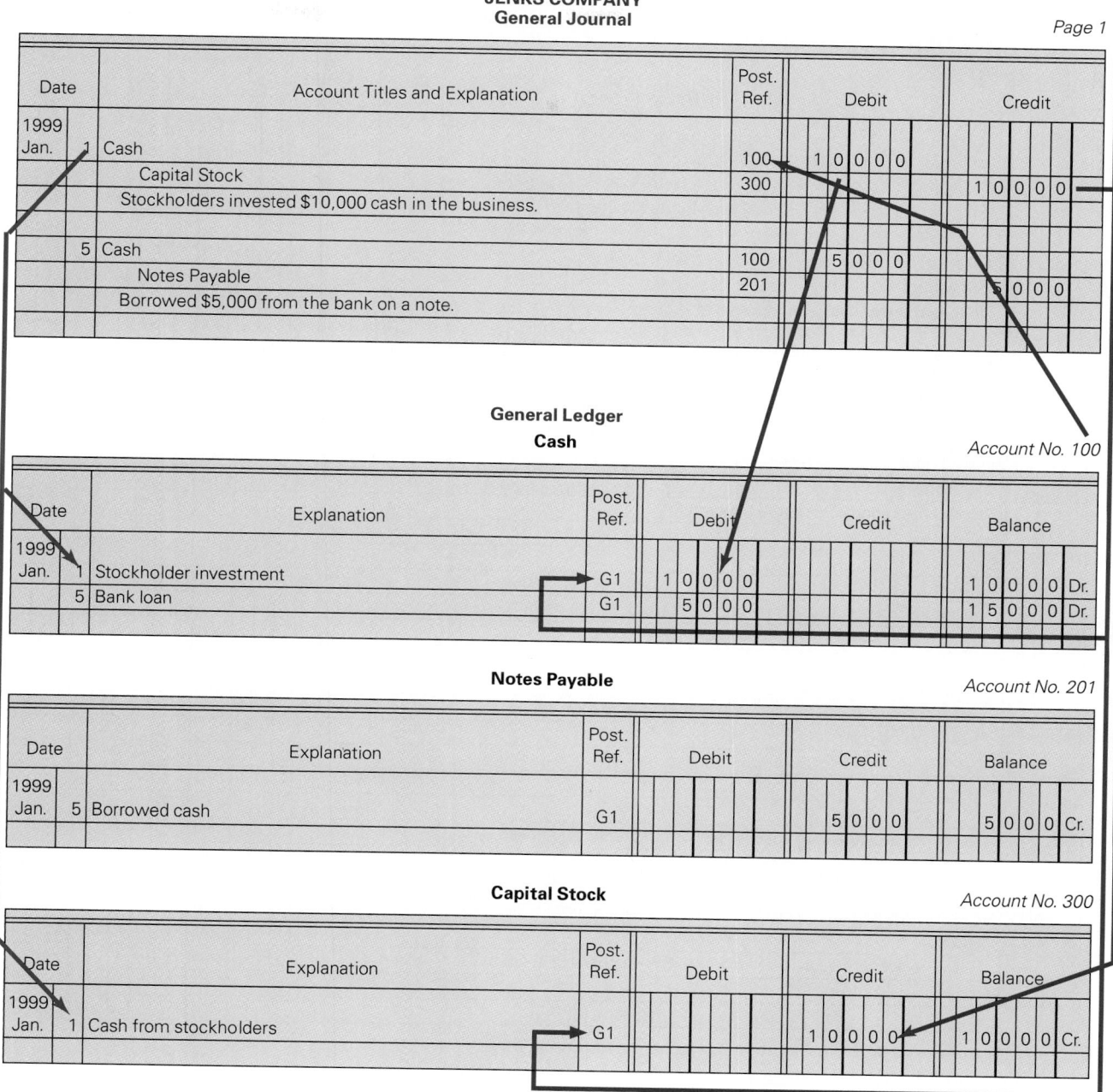

Posting Reference column beside the first debit in the general journal. Accountants place the number of the general journal page from which the entry was posted in the Posting Reference column of the ledger account. Note the arrow from page 1 in the general journal to G1 in the Posting Reference column of the Cash account in the general ledger. The notation "G1" means general journal, page 1. The date of the transaction also appears in the general ledger. Note the arrows from the date in the general journal to the dates in the general ledger.

Cross-indexing aids the tracing of any recorded transaction, either from general journal to general ledger or from general ledger to general journal. Normally, they place cross-reference numbers in the Posting Reference column of the general journal

ILLUSTRATION 2.7   General Journal (after posting)

MICROTRAIN COMPANY
General Journal

Page 1

Date		Account Titles and Explanation	Post. Ref.	Debit	Credit
1999 Nov.	28	Cash	100*	5 0 0 0 0	
		Capital Stock	300		5 0 0 0 0
		Stockholders invested $50,000 cash in the business.			
Dec.	1	Trucks	150	4 0 0 0 0	
		Cash	100		4 0 0 0 0
		To record the purchase of four trucks.			
	1	Prepaid Insurance	108	2 4 0 0	
		Cash	100		2 4 0 0
		Purchased truck insurance to cover a one-year period.			
	1	Prepaid Rent	112	1 2 0 0	
		Cash	100		1 2 0 0
		Paid three months' rent on a building.			
	4	Supplies on Hand	107	1 4 0 0	
		Accounts Payable	200		1 4 0 0
		To record the purchase of training supplies for future use.			
	7	Cash	100	4 5 0 0	
		Unearned Service Fees	216		4 5 0 0
		To record the receipt of cash from a customer in payment for			
		future training services.			
	15	Cash	100	5 0 0 0	
		Service Revenue	400		5 0 0 0
		To record the receipt of cash for performing training services			
		for a customer.			
	17	Accounts Payable	200	1 4 0 0	
		Cash	100		1 4 0 0
		Paid the account payable arising from the purchase of supplies			
		on December 4.			

*These posting references would be entered only after each amount has been posted.

when the entry is posted. If this practice is followed, the cross-reference numbers indicate that the entry has been posted.

     To understand the posting and cross-indexing process, trace the entries from the general journal to the general ledger. The ledger accounts need not contain explanations of all the entries, since any needed explanations can be obtained from the general journal.

Posting and Cross-Indexing—An Illustration

Look at Illustration 2.7 to see how all the November and December transactions of MicroTrain Company presented on pages 64–71 would be journalized. As shown in Illustration 2.7, you skip a line between journal entries to show where one journal

ILLUSTRATION 2.7   (concluded)

General Journal   *Page 2*

Date		Account Titles and Explanation	Post. Ref.	Debit	Credit
1999 Dec.	20	Accounts Receivable	103	5 7 0 0	
		Service Revenue	400		5 7 0 0
		To record the performance of training services on account for			
		which a customer was billed.			
	24	Advertising Expense	505	5 0	
		Accounts Payable	200		5 0
		Received a bill for advertising for the month of December.			
	26	Cash	100	5 0 0	
		Accounts Receivable	103		5 0 0
		Received $500 from a customer on accounts receivable.			
	28	Salaries Expense	507	3 6 0 0	
		Cash	100		3 6 0 0
		Paid training personnel salaries for the first four weeks of December.			
	29	Utilities Expense	511	1 5 0	
		Cash	100		1 5 0
		Paid the utilities bill for December.			
	30	Gas and Oil Expense	506	6 8 0	
		Accounts Payable	200		6 8 0
		Received a bill for gas and oil used in the trucks for December.			
	31	Dividends	320	3 0 0 0	
		Cash	100		3 0 0 0
		Dividends were paid to stockholders.			

entry ends and another begins. This procedure is standard practice among accountants. Note that no dollar signs appear in journals or ledgers. When amounts are in even dollar amounts, accountants leave the cents column blank or use zeros or a dash. When they use lined accounting work papers, commas or decimal points are not needed to record an amount. When they use unlined paper, they add both commas and decimal points.

Next, observe Illustration 2.8, the three-column general ledger accounts of MicroTrain Company after the journal entries have been posted. Each ledger account would appear on a separate page in the ledger. Trace the postings from the general journal to the general ledger to make sure you know how to post journal entries.

Compound Journal Entries

All the journal entries illustrated so far have involved one debit and one credit; these journal entries are called **simple journal entries.** Many business transactions, however, affect more than two accounts. The journal entry for these transactions involves more than one debit and/or credit. Such journal entries are called **compound journal entries.**

As an illustration of a compound journal entry, assume that on January 2, 2000, MicroTrain Company purchased $8,000 of training equipment from Wilson Company.

ILLUSTRATION 2.8   General Ledger—Extended Illustration

MICROTRAIN COMPANY
General Ledger

Cash

Account No. 100

Date	Explanation	Post. Ref.	Debit	Credit	Balance
1999 Dec. 1	Beginning balance*				5 0 0 0 0 Dr.
1	Trucks	G1		4 0 0 0 0	1 0 0 0 0 Dr.
1	Prepaid insurance	G1		2 4 0 0	7 6 0 0 Dr.
1	Prepaid rent	G1		1 2 0 0	6 4 0 0 Dr.
7	Unearned service fees	G1	4 5 0 0		1 0 9 0 0 Dr.
15	Service revenue	G1	5 0 0 0		1 5 9 0 0 Dr.
17	Paid account payable	G1		1 4 0 0	1 4 5 0 0 Dr.
26	Collected account receivable	G2	5 0 0		1 5 0 0 0 Dr.
28	Salaries	G2		3 6 0 0	1 1 4 0 0 Dr.
29	Utilities	G2		1 5 0	1 1 2 5 0 Dr.
31	Dividends	G2		3 0 0 0	8 2 5 0 Dr.

Accounts Receivable

Account No. 103

Date	Explanation	Post. Ref.	Debit	Credit	Balance
1999 Dec. 20	Service revenue	G2	5 7 0 0		5 7 0 0 Dr.
26	Collections	G2		5 0 0	5 2 0 0 Dr.

Supplies on Hand

Account No. 107

Date	Explanation	Post. Ref.	Debit	Credit	Balance
1999 Dec. 4	Purchased on account	G1	1 4 0 0		1 4 0 0 Dr.

Prepaid Insurance

Account No. 108

Date	Explanation	Post. Ref.	Debit	Credit	Balance
1999 Dec. 1	One-year policy on trucks	G1	2 4 0 0		2 4 0 0 Dr.

*Beginning balances result from carrying forward a balance from a preceding page for this account. The Cash account, for example, is likely to use page after page over a period since so many transactions involve cash. This particular beginning balance came from the stockholders' investments in November. Often no explanation is included in the Explanation column since explanations may be found in the general journal or are not relevant.

ILLUSTRATION 2.8   (continued)

General Ledger

Page 2

Prepaid Rent

Account No. 112

Date		Explanation	Post. Ref.	Debit	Credit	Balance
1999 Dec.	1	Three-month payment	G1	1 2 0 0		1 2 0 0 Dr.

Trucks

Account No. 150

Date		Explanation	Post. Ref.	Debit	Credit	Balance
1999 Dec.	1	Paid cash	G1	4 0 0 0 0		4 0 0 0 0 Dr.

Accounts Payable

Account No. 200

Date		Explanation	Post. Ref.	Debit	Credit	Balance
1999 Dec.	4	Supplies	G1		1 4 0 0	1 4 0 0 Cr.
	17	Paid for supplies	G1	1 4 0 0		– 0 –
	24	Advertising	G2		5 0	5 0 Cr.
	30	Gas and oil	G2		6 8 0	7 3 0 Cr.

Unearned Service Fees

Account No. 216

Date		Explanation	Post. Ref.	Debit	Credit	Balance
1999 Dec.	7	Received cash	G1		4 5 0 0	4 5 0 0 Cr.

Capital Stock

Account No. 300

Date		Explanation	Post. Ref.	Debit	Credit	Balance
1999 Dec.	1	Beginning balance				5 0 0 0 0 Cr.

ILLUSTRATION 2.8   (concluded)

General Ledger   *Page 3*

Dividends   *Account No. 320*

Date		Explanation	Post. Ref.	Debit	Credit	Balance
1999 Dec.	31	Cash	G2	3 0 0 0		3 0 0 0 Dr.

Service Revenue   *Account No. 400*

Date		Explanation	Post. Ref.	Debit	Credit	Balance
1999 Dec.	15	Cash	G1		5 0 0 0	5 0 0 0 Cr.
	20	On account	G2		5 7 0 0	1 0 7 0 0 Cr.

Advertising Expense   *Account No. 505*

Date		Explanation	Post. Ref.	Debit	Credit	Balance
1999 Dec.	24	On account	G2	5 0		5 0 Dr.

Gas and Oil Expense   *Account No. 506*

Date		Explanation	Post. Ref.	Debit	Credit	Balance
1999 Dec.	30	On account	G2	6 8 0		6 8 0 Dr.

Salaries Expense   *Account No. 507*

Date		Explanation	Post. Ref.	Debit	Credit	Balance
1999 Dec.	28	Cash paid	G2	3 6 0 0		3 6 0 0 Dr.

Utilities Expense   *Account No. 511*

Date		Explanation	Post. Ref.	Debit	Credit	Balance
1999 Dec.	29	Cash paid	G2	1 5 0		1 5 0 Dr.

MICROTRAIN COMPANY
Trial Balance
December 31, 1999

ILLUSTRATION 2.9
Trial Balance

Acct. No.	Account Title	Debits	Credits
100	Cash	$ 8,250	
103	Accounts Receivable	5,200	
107	Supplies on Hand	1,400	
108	Prepaid Insurance	2,400	
112	Prepaid Rent	1,200	
150	Trucks	40,000	
200	Accounts Payable		$ 730
216	Unearned Service Fees		4,500
300	Capital Stock		50,000
320	Dividends	3,000	
400	Service Revenue		10,700
505	Advertising Expense	50	
506	Gas and Oil Expense	680	
507	Salaries Expense	3,600	
511	Utilities Expense	150	
		$65,930	$65,930

MicroTrain paid $2,000 cash with the balance due on March 3, 2000. The general journal entry for MicroTrain Company is:

			Debit	Credit
2000 Jan.	2	Equipment	8,000	
		Cash		2,000
		Accounts Payable		6,000
		Training equipment purchased from Wilson Company.		

Notes to the Student
Show how this compound journal entry could have been two simple journal entries.

Even in a computerized system, journal entries must be recorded using debits and credits.

Note that the firm credits two accounts, Cash and Accounts Payable, in this one entry. However, the dollar totals of the debits and credits are equal.

Periodically, accountants use a *trial balance* to test the equality of their debits and credits. A **trial balance** is a listing of the ledger accounts and their debit or credit balances to determine that debits equal credits in the recording process. The accounts appear in this order: assets, liabilities, stockholders' equity, dividends, revenues, and expenses. Within the assets category, the most liquid (closest to becoming cash) asset appears first and the least liquid appears last. Within the liabilities, those liabilities with the shortest maturities appear first. Study Illustration 2.9, the trial balance for MicroTrain Company. Note the listing of the account numbers and account titles on the left, the column for debit balances, the column for credit balances, and the equality of the two totals.

When the trial balance does not balance, try retotaling the two columns. If this step does not locate the error, divide the difference in the totals by 2 and then by 9. If the difference is divisible by 2, you may have transferred a debit-balanced account to the trial balance as a credit, or a credit-balanced account as a debit. When the difference is divisible by 2, look for an amount in the trial balance that is equal to one-half of the difference. Thus, if the difference is $800, look for an account with a balance of $400 and see if it is in the wrong column.

If the difference is divisible by 9, you may have made a transposition error in transferring a balance to the trial balance or a slide error. A transposition error occurs when two digits are reversed in an amount (e.g., writing 753 as 573 or 110 as 101). A slide error occurs when you place a decimal point incorrectly (e.g., $1,500 recorded as $15.00). Thus, when a difference is divisible by 9, compare the trial balance amounts with the general ledger account balances to see if you made a transposition or slide error in transferring the amounts.

The Trial Balance

Objective 6
Prepare a trial balance to test the equality of debits and credits in the journalizing and posting process.

AN ETHICAL
PERSPECTIVE

Financial
Deals, Inc.

Larry Fisher was captain of the football team at Prestige University. Later, he earned a master's degree in business administration with a concentration in accounting.

Upon graduation, Larry accepted a position with Financial Deals, Inc., in the accounting and finance division. At first, things were going smoothly. He was tall, good looking, and had an outgoing personality. The president of the company took a liking to him. However, Larry was somewhat bothered when the president started asking him to do some things that were slightly unethical. When he protested mildly, the president said, "Come on, son, this is the way the business world works. You have great potential if you don't let things like this get in your way."

As time went on, Larry was asked to do things that were more unethical, and finally he was performing illegal acts. When he resisted, the president appealed to his loyalty and asked him to be a team player. The president also promised Larry great

wealth sometime in the future. Finally, when he was told to falsify some financial statements by making improper adjusting entries and to sign some documents containing material errors, the president supported his request by stating, "You are in too deep now to refuse to cooperate. If I go down, you are going with me." Through various company schemes, Larry had convinced some friends and relatives to invest about $10 million. Most of this would be lost if the various company schemes were revealed.

Larry could not sleep at night and began each day with a pain in his stomach and by becoming physically ill. He was under great strain and believed that he could lose his mind. He also heard that the president had a shady past and could become violent in retaliating against his enemies. If Larry blows the whistle, he believes he will go to prison for his part in the schemes. (Note: This scenario is based on an actual situation with some facts changed to protect the guilty.)

Reinforcing Problems
E2–7 Prepare a trial balance.
E2–8 Prepare journal entries.
E2–9 Post journal entries in E2–8 to T-accounts.
E2–10 Prepare a trial balance using accounts in E2–9.
E2–11 Determine trial balance errors.

If you still cannot find the error, it may be due to one of the following causes:

1. Failing to post part of a journal entry.
2. Posting a debit as a credit, or vice versa.
3. Incorrectly determining the balance of an account.
4. Recording the balance of an account incorrectly in the trial balance.
5. Omitting an account from the trial balance.
6. Making a transposition or slide error in the accounts or the journal.

Usually, you should work backward through the steps taken to prepare the trial balance. Assuming you have already retotaled the columns and traced the amounts appearing in the trial balance back to the general ledger account balances, use the following steps: Verify the balance of each general ledger account, verify postings to the general ledger, verify general journal entries, and then review the transactions and possibly the source documents.

The equality of the two totals in the trial balance does not necessarily mean that the accounting process has been error-free. Serious errors may have been made, such as failure to record a transaction, or posting a debit or credit to the wrong account. For instance, if a transaction involving payment of a $100 account payable is never recorded, the trial balance totals still balance, but at an amount that is $100 too high. Both cash and accounts payable would be overstated by $100.

Reinforcing Problem
P2–4A Prepare journal entries, post to three-column ledger accounts, and prepare a trial balance.

You can prepare a trial balance at any time—at the end of a day, a week, a month, a quarter, or a year. Typically, you would prepare a trial balance before preparing the financial statements.

AN ACCOUNTING PERSPECTIVE

USES OF TECHNOLOGY Sometimes the computers of persons in a given department or building are connected in a *Local Area Network (LAN)*. These persons can then access simultaneously the programs and databases stored in the LAN and can communicate with all other persons in the LAN through electronic mail. A more advanced type of computer network is called *Client/Server Computing*. Under this structure, any computer in the network can be used to update the information stored elsewhere in the network. For example, accounting information stored in one computer could be updated by authorized persons from a number of other computers in the system. The use of networks is designed to improve efficiency and to reduce software and hardware costs.

ANALYZING AND USING THE FINANCIAL RESULTS—
HORIZONTAL AND VERTICAL ANALYSES

The calculation of dollar and/or percentage changes from one year to the next in an item on financial statements is **horizontal analysis.** For instance, in the following data taken from the 1995 annual report of Hewlett-Packard Company, the amount of cash and cash equivalents increased by $616 million from October 31, 1994, to October 31, 1995. This amount represented a 45% increase. To find the amount of the increase, subtract the 1994 amount from the 1995 amount. To find the percentage change, divide the increase by the 1994 amount.

Objective 7
Analyze and use the financial results—horizontal and vertical analyses.

Knowing the dollar amount and percentage of change in an amount is much more meaningful than merely knowing the amount at one point in time. By analyzing the data, we can see that short-term investments declined in 1995. Their decline at least partially explains the increases in some of the other current assets. We can also see that the company invested in buildings and leasehold improvements, machinery and equipment, and long-term investments and other assets. Any terms in Hewlett-Packard's list of assets that you may not understand are explained in later chapters. At this point, all we want you to understand is the nature of horizontal and vertical analyses.

Vertical analysis shows the percentage that each item in a financial statement is of some significant total such as total assets or sales. For instance, in the Hewlett-Packard data we can see that cash and cash equivalents were 7.0% of total assets as of October 31, 1994, and had risen to 8.1% of total assets by October 31, 1995. Total current assets (cash plus other amounts that will become cash or be used up within one year) remained about 65% of total assets, although the relative composition of current assets changed. Property, plant, and equipment and investments and other assets remained at fairly constant percentages of total assets.

Management performs horizontal and vertical analyses along with other forms of analysis to help evaluate the wisdom of its past decisions and to plan for the future. Other data would have to be examined before decisions could be made regarding the assets shown. For instance, if you discovered the liabilities that would have to be paid within a short time by Hewlett-Packard were more than $10 billion, you might conclude that the company is short of cash even though cash and cash equivalents increased substantially during 1995. We illustrate horizontal and vertical analyses to a much greater extent later in the text.

Reinforcing Problem
E2–12 Perform horizontal and vertical analyses on U.S. Robotics' assets and comment.

Assets (in millions)	1995	1994	Increase or (Decrease) 1995 over 1994 Dollars	Percent	Percent of Total Assets October 31 1995	1994
Current assets:						
Cash and cash equivalents	$ 1,973	$ 1,357	$ 616	45%	8.1%	7.0%
Short-term investments	643	1,121	(478)	(43)	2.6	5.7
Accounts and notes receivable	6,735	5,028	1,707	34	27.6	25.7
Inventories	6,013	4,273	1,740	41	24.6	21.8
Other current assets	875	730	145	20	3.6	3.7
Total current assets	$16,239	$12,509	$3,730	30	66.5%	63.9%
Property, plant, and equipment						
Land	485	508	(23)	(5)	2.0	2.6
Buildings and leasehold improvements	3,810	3,472	338	10	15.6	17.7
Machinery and equipment	4,452	3,958	494	12	18.2	20.2
Accumulated depreciation	(4,036)	(3,610)	(426)	12	(16.5)	(18.4)
Long-term investments and other assets	3,477	2,730	747	27	14.2	14.0
Total assets	$24,427	$19,567	$4,860	25	100.0%	100.0%

Hewlett-Packard Company
Hewlett-Packard Company designs, manufactures, and services products and systems for measurement, computation, and communications.

AN ACCOUNTING PERSPECTIVE	**BUSINESS INSIGHT** Many companies have been restructuring their organizations and reducing the number of employees to cut expenses. General Motors, AT&T, IBM, and numerous other companies have taken this action. One could question whether companies place as much value on their employees as in the past. In previous years it was common to see the following statement in the annual reports of companies: "Our employees are our most valuable asset." Companies are not permitted to show employees as assets on their balance sheets. Do you think they should be allowed to do so?

What you have learned in this chapter is basic to your study of accounting. The entire process of accounting is based on the double-entry concept. Chapter 3 explains that adjustments bring the accounts to their proper balances before accurate financial statements are prepared.

UNDERSTANDING THE LEARNING OBJECTIVES

Objective 1
Use the account as the basic classifying and storage unit for accounting information.

- An account is a storage unit used to classify and summarize money measurements of business activities of a similar nature.
- A firm sets up an account whenever it needs to provide useful information about a particular business item to some party having a valid interest in the business.

Objective 2
Express the effects of business transactions in terms of debits and credits to different types of accounts.

- A T-account resembles the letter T.
- Debits are entries on the left side of a T-account.
- Credits are entries on the right side of a T-account.
- Debits increase asset, expense, and Dividends accounts.
- Credits increase liability, stockholders' equity, and revenue accounts.

Objective 3
List the steps in the accounting cycle.

- Analyze transactions by examining source documents.
- Journalize transactions in the journal.
- Post journal entries to the accounts in the ledger.
- Prepare a trial balance of the accounts and complete the work sheet.
- Prepare financial statements.
- Journalize and post adjusting entries.
- Journalize and post closing entries.
- Prepare a post-closing trial balance.

Objective 4
Record the effects of business transactions in a journal.

- A journal contains a chronological record of the transactions of a business.
- An example of a general journal is shown in Illustration 2.7.
- Journalizing is the process of entering a transaction in a journal.

Objective 5
Post journal entries to the accounts in the ledger.

- Posting is the process of transferring information recorded in the journal to the proper places in the ledger.
- Cross-indexing is the placing of (1) the account number of the ledger account in the general journal and (2) the general journal page number in the ledger account.
- An example of cross-indexing appears in Illustration 2.6.

Objective 6
Prepare a trial balance to test the equality of debits and credits in the journalizing and posting process.

- A trial balance is a listing of the ledger accounts and their debit or credit balances.
- If the trial balance does not balance, an accountant works backward to discover the error.
- A trial balance is shown in Illustration 2.9.

- Horizontal analysis involves calculating the dollar and/or percentage changes in an item from one year to the next.
- Vertical analysis shows the percentage that each item in a financial statement is of some significant total.

Objective 7
Analyze and use the financial results—horizontal and vertical analyses.

DEMONSTRATION PROBLEM

Green Hills Riding Stable, Incorporated, had the following balance sheet on June 30, 1999:

GREEN HILLS RIDING STABLE, INCORPORATED
Balance Sheet
June 30, 1999
Assets

Cash	$ 7,500
Accounts receivable	5,400
Land	40,000
Total assets	$52,900

Liabilities and Stockholders' Equity

Liabilities:

Accounts payable		$ 800
Notes payable		40,000
Total liabilities		$40,800

Stockholders' equity:

Capital stock	$10,000	
Retained earnings	2,100	
Total stockholders' equity		12,100
Total liabilities and stockholders' equity		$52,900

Transactions for July 1999 were as follows:

July 1	Additional shares of capital stock were issued for $25,000 cash.
1	Paid for a prefabricated building constructed on the land at a cost of $24,000.
8	Paid the accounts payable of $800.
10	Collected the accounts receivable of $5,400.
12	Horse feed to be used in July was purchased on credit for $1,100.
15	Boarding fees for July were charged to customers in the amount of $4,500. (This amount is due on August 10.)
24	Miscellaneous expenses of $800 for July were paid.
31	Paid interest expense on the notes payable of $200.
31	Salaries of $1,400 for the month were paid.
31	Riding and lesson fees for July were billed to customers in the amount of $3,600. (They are due on August 10.)
31	Paid a $1,000 dividend to the stockholders.

a. Prepare the journal entries to record the transactions for July 1999.   *Required*

b. Post the journal entries to the ledger accounts after entering the beginning balances in those accounts. Insert cross-indexing references in the journal and ledger. Use the following chart of accounts:

100	Cash	320	Dividends
103	Accounts Receivable	402	Horse Boarding Fees Revenue
130	Land	404	Riding and Lesson Fees Revenue
140	Buildings	507	Salaries Expense
200	Accounts Payable	513	Feed Expense
201	Notes Payable	540	Interest Expense
300	Capital Stock	568	Miscellaneous Expense
310	Retained Earnings		

c. Prepare a trial balance.

SOLUTION TO DEMONSTRATION PROBLEM

a.

GREEN HILLS RIDING STABLE, INCORPORATED
General Journal

Page 1

Date		Account Titles and Explanation	Post. Ref.	Debit	Credit
1999 July	1	Cash	100	2 5 0 0 0	
		Capital Stock	300		2 5 0 0 0
		Additional capital stock issued.			
	1	Buildings	140	2 4 0 0 0	
		Cash	100		2 4 0 0 0
		Paid for building.			
	8	Accounts Payable	200	8 0 0	
		Cash	100		8 0 0
		Paid accounts payable.			
	10	Cash	100	5 4 0 0	
		Accounts Receivable	103		5 4 0 0
		Collected accounts receivable.			
	12	Feed Expense	513	1 1 0 0	
		Accounts Payable	200		1 1 0 0
		Purchased feed on credit.			
	15	Accounts Receivable	103	4 5 0 0	
		Horse Boarding Fees Revenue	402		4 5 0 0
		Billed boarding fees for July.			
	24	Miscellaneous Expense	568	8 0 0	
		Cash	100		8 0 0
		Paid miscellaneous expenses for July.			
	31	Interest Expense	540	2 0 0	
		Cash	100		2 0 0
		Paid interest.			
	31	Salaries Expense	507	1 4 0 0	
		Cash	100		1 4 0 0
		Paid salaries for July.			
	31	Accounts Receivable	103	3 6 0 0	
		Riding and Lesson Fees Revenue	404		3 6 0 0
		Billed riding and lesson fees for July.			
	31	Dividends	320	1 0 0 0	
		Cash	100		1 0 0 0
		Paid a dividend to stockholders.			

b.

GREEN HILLS RIDING STABLE, INCORPORATED
General Ledger

Cash
Account No. 100

Date		Explanation	Post. Ref.	Debit	Credit	Balance
1999 June	30	Balance				7 5 0 0 Dr.
July	1	Stockholders' investment	G1	2 5 0 0 0		3 2 5 0 0 Dr.
	1	Buildings	G1		2 4 0 0 0	8 5 0 0 Dr.
	8	Accounts payable	G1		8 0 0	7 7 0 0 Dr.
	10	Accounts receivable	G1	5 4 0 0		1 3 1 0 0 Dr.
	24	Miscellaneous expense	G1		8 0 0	1 2 3 0 0 Dr.
	31	Interest expense	G1		2 0 0	1 2 1 0 0 Dr.
	31	Salaries expense	G1		1 4 0 0	1 0 7 0 0 Dr.
	31	Dividends	G1		1 0 0 0	9 7 0 0 Dr.

Accounts Receivable
Account No. 103

Date		Explanation	Post. Ref.	Debit	Credit	Balance
1999 June	30	Balance				5 4 0 0 Dr.
July	10	Cash	G1		5 4 0 0	– 0 –
	15	Horse boarding fees	G1	4 5 0 0		4 5 0 0 Dr.
	31	Riding and lesson fees	G1	3 6 0 0		8 1 0 0 Dr.

Land
Account No. 130

Date		Explanation	Post. Ref.	Debit	Credit	Balance
1999 June	30	Balance				4 0 0 0 0 Dr.

Buildings
Account No. 140

Date		Explanation	Post. Ref.	Debit	Credit	Balance
1999 July	1	Cash	G1	2 4 0 0 0		2 4 0 0 0 Dr.

Accounts Payable
Account No. 200

Date		Explanation	Post. Ref.	Debit	Credit	Balance
1999 June	30	Balance				8 0 0 Cr.
July	8	Cash	G1	8 0 0		– 0 –
	12	Feed expense	G1		1 1 0 0	1 1 0 0 Cr.

General Ledger (continued)

Notes Payable

Account No. 201

Date		Explanation	Post. Ref.	Debit	Credit	Balance
1999 June	30	Balance				4 0 0 0 0 Cr.

Capital Stock

Account No. 300

Date		Explanation	Post. Ref.	Debit	Credit	Balance
1999 June	30	Balance				1 0 0 0 0 Cr.
July	1	Cash	G1		2 5 0 0 0	3 5 0 0 0 Cr.

Retained Earnings

Account No. 310

Date		Explanation	Post. Ref.	Debit	Credit	Balance
1999 June	30	Balance				2 1 0 0 Cr.

Dividends

Account No. 320

Date		Explanation	Post. Ref.	Debit	Credit	Balance
1999 July	31	Cash	G1	1 0 0 0		1 0 0 0 Dr.

Horse Boarding Fees Revenue

Account No. 402

Date		Explanation	Post. Ref.	Debit	Credit	Balance
1999 July	15	Accounts receivable	G1		4 5 0 0	4 5 0 0 Cr.

Riding and Lesson Fees Revenue

Account No. 404

Date		Explanation	Post. Ref.	Debit	Credit	Balance
1999 July	31	Accounts receivable	G1		3 6 0 0	3 6 0 0 Cr.

General Ledger (concluded)

Salaries Expense

Account No. 507

Date	Explanation	Post. Ref.	Debit	Credit	Balance
1999 July 31	Cash	G1	1 4 0 0		1 4 0 0 Dr.

Feed Expense

Account No. 513

Date	Explanation	Post. Ref.	Debit	Credit	Balance
1999 July 12	Accounts payable	G1	1 1 0 0		1 1 0 0 Dr.

Interest Expense

Account No. 540

Date	Explanation	Post. Ref.	Debit	Credit	Balance
1999 July 31	Cash	G1	2 0 0		2 0 0 Dr.

Miscellaneous Expense

Account No. 568

Date	Explanation	Post. Ref.	Debit	Credit	Balance
1999 July 24	Cash	G1	8 0 0		8 0 0 Dr.

c.

GREEN HILLS RIDING STABLE, INCORPORATED
Trial Balance
July 31, 1999

Acct. No.	Account Title	Debits	Credits
100	Cash	$ 9,700	
103	Accounts Receivable	8,100	
130	Land	40,000	
140	Buildings	24,000	
200	Accounts Payable		$ 1,100
201	Notes Payable		40,000
300	Capital Stock		35,000
310	Retained Earnings		2,100
320	Dividends	1,000	
402	Horse Boarding Fees Revenue		4,500
404	Riding and Lesson Fees Revenue		3,600
507	Salaries Expense	1,400	
513	Feed Expense	1,100	
540	Interest Expense	200	
568	Miscellaneous Expense	800	
		$86,300	$86,300

NEW TERMS

Account A part of the accounting system used to classify and summarize the increases, decreases, and balances of each asset, liability, stockholders' equity item, dividend, revenue, and expense. The three-column account is normally used. It contains columns for debit, credit, and balance. *54*

Accounting cycle A series of steps performed during the accounting period (some throughout the period and some at the end) to analyze, record, classify, summarize, and report useful financial information for the purpose of preparing financial statements. *59*

Accrual basis of accounting Recognizes revenues when sales are made or services are performed, regardless of when cash is received. Recognizes expenses as incurred, whether or not cash has been paid out. *64*

Business transactions Measurable events that affect the financial condition of a business. *59*

Chart of accounts The complete listing of the account titles and account numbers of all of the accounts in the ledger; somewhat comparable to a table of contents. *62*

Compound journal entry A journal entry with more than one debit and/or credit. *75*

Credit The right side of any account; when used as a verb, to enter a dollar amount on the right side of an account; credits increase liability, stockholders' equity, and revenue accounts and decrease asset, expense, and Dividends accounts. *55*

Credit balance The balance in an account when the sum of the credits to the account exceeds the sum of the debits to that account. *58*

Cross-indexing The placing of (1) the account number of the ledger account in the general journal and (2) the general journal page number in the ledger account. *72*

Debit The left side of any account; when used as a verb, to enter a dollar amount on the left side of an account; debits increase asset, expense, and Dividends accounts and decrease liability, stockholders' equity, and revenue accounts. *55*

Debit balance The balance in an account when the sum of the debits to the account exceeds the sum of the credits to that account. *57*

Double-entry procedure The accounting requirement that each transaction must be recorded by an entry that has equal debits and credits. *55*

Horizontal analysis The calculation of dollar and/or percentage changes in an item on the financial statements from one year to the next. *81*

Journal A chronological (arranged in order of time) record of business transactions; the simplest form of journal is the two-column general journal. *60*

Journal entry Shows all of the effects of a business transaction as expressed in debit(s) and credit(s) and may include an explanation of the transaction. *60*

Journalizing A step in the accounting recording process that consists of entering the effects of a transaction in a journal. *64*

Ledger The complete collection of all of the accounts of a company; often referred to as the *general ledger*. *62*

Nominal accounts See temporary accounts.

Note An unconditional written promise to pay to another party the amount owed either when demanded or at a certain specified date. *56*

Permanent accounts (real accounts) Balance sheet accounts; their balances are not transferred (or closed) to any other account at the end of the accounting period. *62*

Posting Recording in the ledger accounts the information contained in the journal. *64*

Real accounts See *permanent accounts*.

Simple journal entry An entry with one debit and one credit. *75*

T-account An account resembling the letter T, which is used for illustrative purposes only. Debits are entered on the left side of the account, and credits are entered on the right side of the account. *54*

Temporary accounts (nominal accounts) They temporarily contain the revenue, expense, and dividend information that is transferred (or closed) to a stockholders' equity account (Retained Earnings) at the end of the accounting period. *62*

Trial balance A listing of the ledger accounts and their debit or credit balances to determine that debits equal credits in the recording process. *79*

Vertical analysis Shows the percentage that each item in a financial statement is of some significant total such as total assets or sales. *81*

SELF-TEST

TRUE-FALSE

Indicate whether each of the following statements is true or false.

1. All of the steps in the accounting cycle are performed only at the end of the accounting period.

2. A transaction must be journalized in the journal before it can be posted to the ledger accounts.

3. The left side of any account is the credit side.

4. Revenues, liabilities, and Capital Stock accounts are increased by debits.

5. The Dividends account is increased by debits.

6. If the trial balance has equal debit and credit totals, it cannot contain any errors.

MULTIPLE-CHOICE

Select the best answer for each of the following questions.

1. When the stockholders invest cash in the business:
   a. Capital Stock is debited and Cash is credited.
   b. Cash is debited and Dividends is credited.
   c. Cash is debited and Capital Stock is credited.
   d. None of the above.

2. Assume that cash is paid for insurance to cover a three-year period. The recommended debit and credit are:
   a. Debit Insurance Expense, credit Cash.
   b. Debit Prepaid Insurance, credit Cash.
   c. Debit Cash, credit Insurance Expense.
   d. Debit Cash, credit Prepaid Insurance.

3. A company received cash from a customer in payment for future delivery services. The correct debit and credit are:
   a. Debit Cash, credit Unearned Delivery Fees.
   b. Debit Cash, credit Delivery Fee Revenue.
   c. Debit Accounts Receivable, credit Delivery Fee Revenue.
   d. None of the above.

4. A company performed delivery services for a customer for cash. The correct debit and credit are:
   a. Debit Cash, credit Unearned Delivery Fees.
   b. Debit Cash, credit Delivery Fee Revenue.
   c. Debit Accounts Receivable, credit Delivery Fee Revenue.
   d. None of the above.

5. A cash dividend of $500 was declared and paid to stockholders. The correct journal entry is:

   a. Capital Stock. 500
      Cash   500

   b. Cash 500
      Dividends   500

   c. Dividends 500
      Cash   500

   d. Cash 500
      Capital Stock.   500

Now turn to page 100 to check your answers.

QUESTIONS

1. Describe the steps in recording and posting the effects of a business transaction.

2. Give some examples of source documents.

3. Define an account. What are the two basic forms (styles) of accounts illustrated in the chapter?

4. What is meant by the term *double-entry procedure,* or duality?

5. Describe how you would determine the balance of a T-account.

6. Define debit and credit. Name the types of accounts that are:
   a. Increased by a debit.
   b. Decreased by a debit.
   c. Increased by a credit.
   d. Decreased by a credit.
   Do you think this system makes sense? Can you conceive of other possible methods for recording changes in accounts?

7. Which of the steps in the accounting cycle are performed throughout the accounting period?

8. Which of the steps in the accounting cycle are performed only at the end of the accounting period?

9. Why are expense and revenue accounts used when all revenues and expenses could be shown directly in the Retained Earnings account?

10. What is the purpose of the Dividends account and how is it increased?

11. Are the following possibilities conceivable in an entry involving only one debit and one credit? Why?
    a. Increase a liability and increase an expense.
    b. Increase an asset and decrease a liability.
    c. Increase a revenue and decrease an expense.
    d. Decrease an asset and increase another asset.
    e. Decrease an asset and increase a liability.
    f. Decrease a revenue and decrease an asset.
    g. Decrease a liability and increase a revenue.

12. Describe the nature and purposes of the general journal. What does journalizing mean? Give an example of a compound entry in the general journal.

13. Describe a ledger and a chart of accounts. How do these two compare with a book and its table of contents?

14. Describe the act of posting. What difficulties could arise if no cross-indexing existed between the general journal and the ledger accounts?

15. Which of the following cash payments would involve the immediate recording of an expense? Why?
    a. Paid vendors for office supplies previously purchased on account.
    b. Paid an automobile dealer for a new company auto.
    c. Paid the current month's rent.
    d. Paid salaries for the last half of the current month.

16. What types of accounts appear in the unadjusted trial balance? What are the purposes of this trial balance?

17. You have found that the total of the Debits column of the trial balance of Burns Company is $200,000, while the total of the Credits column is $180,000. What are some possible causes of this difference? If the difference between the columns is divisible by 9, what types of errors are possible?

18. Store equipment was purchased for $2,000. Instead of debiting the Store Equipment account, the debit was made to Delivery Equipment. Of what help will the trial balance be in locating this error? Why?

19. A student remembered that the side toward the window in the classroom was the debit side of an account. The student took an examination in a room where the windows were on the other side of the room and became confused and consistently reversed debits and credits. Would the student's trial balance have equal debit and credit totals? If there were no existing balances in any of the accounts to begin with, would the error prevent the student from preparing correct financial statements? Why?

EXERCISES

Exercise 2–1
Indicate rules of debit and credit (L.O. 1, 2)

A diagram of the various types of accounts follows. Show where pluses (+) or minuses (−) should be inserted to indicate the effect debits and credits have on each account.

Asset Accounts		=	Liability Accounts		+	Stockholders' Equity Accounts	
Debit	Credit		Debit	Credit		Debit	Credit

		Expense Accounts and Dividends Accounts		Revenue Accounts	
		Debit	Credit	Debit	Credit

Exercise 2–2
Prepare journal entries
(L.O. 4)

Prepare the journal entry required for each of the following transactions:

a. Cash was received for services performed for customers, $1,200.
b. Services were performed for customers on account, $4,200.

Exercise 2–3
Prepare journal entries
(L.O. 4)

Prepare the journal entry required for each of the following transactions:

a. Capital stock was issued for $100,000.
b. Purchased machinery for cash, $30,000.

Exercise 2–4
Prepare journal entries
(L.O. 4)

Prepare the journal entry required for each of the following transactions:

a. Capital stock was issued for $200,000 cash.
b. A $30,000 loan was arranged with a bank. The bank increased the company's checking account by $30,000 after management of the company signed a written promise to return the $30,000 in 30 days.
c. Cash was received for services performed for customers, $700.
d. Services were performed for customers on account, $1,200.

Exercise 2–5
Show entries using journal entries and T-accounts
(L.O. 4, 5)

For each of the following unrelated transactions, give the journal entry to record the transaction. Then show how the journal entry would be posted to T-accounts. You need not include explanations or account numbers.

a. Capital stock was issued for $100,000 cash.
b. Salaries for a period were paid to employees, $24,000.
c. Services were performed for customers on account, $40,000.

Exercise 2–6
Explain sets of debits and credits (L.O. 1–5)

Explain each of the sets of debits and credits in these accounts for Tuxedos, Inc., a company that rents wedding clothing and accessories. There are 10 transactions to be explained. Each set is designated by the small letters to the left of the amount. For example, the first transaction is the issuance of capital stock for cash and is denoted by the letter (a).

Cash					Dividends	
(a)	200,000	(b)	150,000	(e)	1,000	
(d)	1,800	(e)	1,000			
		(f)	600			
		(g)	2,000			
		(i)	30,000			
Bal.	18,200					

Accounts Receivable			
(c)	1,800	(d)	1,800
(j)	12,000		
Bal.	12,000		

Service Revenue			
		(c)	1,800
		(j)	12,000
		Bal.	13,800

Supplies on Hand		
(b)	150,000	
(i)	30,000	
Bal.	180,000	

Rent Expense		
(f)	600	

Accounts Payable		
	(h)	800

Delivery Expense		
(h)	800	

Capital Stock		
	(a)	200,000

Salaries Expense		
(g)	2,000	

Assume the ledger accounts given in Exercise 2–6 are those of Tuxedos, Inc., as they appear at December 31, 1999. Prepare the trial balance as of that date.

Exercise 2–7
Prepare trial balance
(L.O. 6)

Prepare journal entries to record each of the following transactions for Sanchez Company. Use the letter of the transaction in place of the date. Include an explanation for each entry.

Exercise 2–8
Prepare journal entries
(L.O. 4)

a. Capital stock was issued for cash, $300,000.
b. Purchased trucks by signing a note bearing no interest, $210,000.
c. Earned service revenue on account, $4,800.
d. Collected the account receivable resulting from transaction (c), $4,800.
e. Paid the note payable for the trucks purchased, $210,000.
f. Paid utilities for the month in the amount of $1,800.
g. Paid salaries for the month in the amount of $7,500.
h. Incurred supplies expenses on account in the amount of $1,920.
i. Purchased another truck for cash, $48,000.
j. Performed delivery services on account, $24,000.

Using the data in Exercise 2–8, post the entries to T-accounts. Write the letter of the transaction in the account before the dollar amount. Determine a balance for each account.

Exercise 2–9
Post journal entries to
T-accounts (L.O. 5)

Using your answer for Exercise 2–9, prepare a trial balance. Assume the date of the trial balance is March 31, 1999.

Exercise 2–10
Prepare trial balance
(L.O. 6)

John Adams owns and manages a bowling center called Strike Lanes. He also maintains his own accounting records and was about to prepare financial statements for the year 1999. When he prepared the trial balance from the ledger accounts, the total of the debits column was $435,000, and the total of the credits column was $425,000. What are the possible reasons why the totals of the debits and credits are out of balance? How would you normally proceed to find an error if the two trial balance columns do not agree?

Exercise 2–11
Determine trial balance
errors (L.O. 6)

U.S. Robotics is one of the world's leading suppliers of products and systems that provide access to information. The company designs, manufactures, markets and supports a wide variety of products and systems that connect computers and other equipment over analog, digital, and switched cellular networks, enabling users to gain access to, manage and share data, fax and voice information. The company offers reliable, cost-effective solutions at all points of network access from the data communications center to the mobile user to the

Exercise 2–12
Perform horizontal and
vertical analysis on U.S.
Robotics' assets and
comment (L.O. 7)

desktop. The following data are from U.S. Robotics' 1995 Annual Report. Perform horizontal and vertical analysis, treating total assets as a significant total for vertical analysis. Comment on the results.

(in thousands, except share data)	October 1, 1995	October 2, 1994
ASSETS		
Current Assets		
Cash and cash equivalents	$136,803	$ 58,286
Marketable securities	96,000	8,996
Accounts receivable, less allowances of $7,354 and		
$3,669 for 1995 and 1994, respectively	168,365	93,942
Inventories	103,032	75,604
Deferred income taxes	22,373	7,428
Prepaid expenses and other current assets	7,739	7,029
Total current assets	$534,312	$251,285
Property, Plant, and Equipment—Net	117,156	56,027
Other Assets		
Goodwill	3,016	7,835
Other assets	5,139	8,130
	$659,623	$323,277

PROBLEMS

Problem 2–1
Prepare journal entries
(L.O. 4)

Speedy Laundry Company, Inc., entered into the following transactions in August 1999:

Aug. 1   Received cash for capital stock issued to owners, $400,000.
   3   Paid rent for August on a building and laundry equipment rented, $3,000.
   6   Performed laundry services for $2,000 cash.
   8   Secured an order from a customer for laundry services of $7,000. The services are to be performed next month.
   13   Performed laundry services for $6,300 on account for various customers.
   15   Received and paid a bill for $430 for supplies used in operations.
   23   Cash collected from customers on account, $2,600.
   31   Paid $2,400 salaries to employees for August.
   31   Received the electric and gas bill for August, $385, but did not pay it at this time.
   31   Paid cash dividend, $1,000.

Required   Prepare journal entries for these transactions in the general journal.

Problem 2–2
Record transactions in
journal, post to T-accounts,
and prepare trial balance
(L.O. 4–6)

The transactions listed below are those of Reliable Computer Repair, Inc., for April 1999:

Apr. 1   Cash of $500,000 was received for capital stock issued to the owners.
   3   Rent was paid for April, $3,500.
   6   Trucks were purchased for $56,000 cash.
   7   Office equipment was purchased on account from Wagner Company for $76,800.
   14   Salaries for first two weeks were paid, $12,000.
   15   $28,000 was received for services performed.
   18   An invoice was received from Roger's Gas Station for $400 for gas and oil used during April.
   23   A note was arranged with the bank for $80,000. The cash was received, and a note promising to return the $80,000 on May 30, 1999, was signed.
   29   Purchased trucks for $73,600 by signing a note.
   30   Salaries for the remainder of April were paid, $14,400.

Required   **a.** Prepare journal entries for these transactions.

   b. Post the journal entries to T-accounts. Enter the account number in the Posting Reference column of the journal as you post each amount. Use the following account numbers:

Acct. No.	Account Title
100	Cash
150	Trucks
172	Office Equipment
200	Accounts Payable
201	Notes Payable
300	Capital Stock
400	Service Revenue
506	Gas and Oil Expense
507	Salaries Expense
515	Rent Expense

c. Prepare a trial balance as of April 30, 1999.

Rapid Pick Up & Delivery, Inc., was organized January 1, 1999. Its chart of accounts is as follows:

Problem 2–3
Prepare ledger accounts, journalize transactions, post to three-column ledger accounts, and prepare trial balance (L.O. 4–6)

Acct. No.	Account Title
100	Cash
103	Accounts Receivable
150	Trucks
160	Office Furniture
172	Office Equipment
200	Accounts Payable
201	Notes Payable
300	Capital Stock
310	Retained Earnings
400	Service Revenue
506	Gas and Oil Expense
507	Salaries Expense
511	Utilities Expense
512	Insurance Expense
515	Rent Expense
530	Repairs Expense

Transactions

Jan. 1   The company received $560,000 cash and $240,000 of office furniture in exchange for $800,000 of capital stock.
2   Paid garage rent for January, $6,000.
4   Purchased microcomputers on account, $13,200.
6   Purchased delivery trucks for $280,000; payment was made by giving cash of $150,000 and a 30-day note for the remainder.
12   Purchased insurance for January on the delivery trucks. The cost of the policy, $800, was paid in cash.
15   Received and paid January utilities bills, $960.
15   Paid salaries for first half of January, $3,600.
17   Cash received for delivery services to date amounted to $1,800.
20   Received bill for gasoline purchased and used in January, $180.
23   Purchased delivery trucks for cash, $108,000.
25   Cash sales of delivery services were $2,880.
27   Purchased a copy machine on account, $3,600.
31   Paid salaries for last half of January, $4,800.
31   Sales of delivery services on account amounted to $11,400.
31   Paid for repairs to a delivery truck, $1,120.

Required

a. Prepare general ledger accounts for all these accounts except Retained Earnings. The Retained Earnings account has a beginning balance of zero and maintains this balance throughout the period.

b. Journalize the transactions given for January 1999 in the general journal.

c. Post the journal entries to three-column ledger accounts.

d. Prepare a trial balance as of January 31, 1999.

Problem 2–4
Prepare journal entries, post to three-column ledger accounts, and prepare trial balance (L.O. 4–6)

The trial balance of California Tennis Center, Inc., at the end of the first 11 months of its fiscal year follows:

CALIFORNIA TENNIS CENTER, INC.
Trial Balance
November 30, 1999

Acct. No.	Account Title	Debits	Credits
100	Cash	$ 71,180	
103	Accounts Receivable	81,750	
130	Land	60,000	
200	Accounts Payable		$ 18,750
201	Notes Payable		15,000
300	Capital Stock		50,000
310	Retained Earnings, January 1, 1997		53,700
413	Membership and Lesson Revenue		202,500
505	Advertising Expense	21,000	
507	Salaries Expense	66,000	
511	Utilities Expense	2,100	
515	Rent Expense	33,000	
518	Supplies Expense	2,250	
530	Repairs Expense	1,500	
531	Entertainment Expense	870	
540	Interest Expense	300	
		$339,950	$339,950

Transactions

Dec. 1 Paid building rent for December, $4,000.

2 Paid vendors on account, $18,000.

5 Purchased land for cash, $10,000.

7 Sold memberships on account for December, $27,000.

10 Paid the note payable of $15,000, plus interest of $150.

13 Cash collections from customers on account, $36,000.

19 Received a bill for repairs, $225.

24 Paid the December utilities bill, $180.

28 Received a bill for December advertising, $1,650.

29 Paid the equipment repair bill received on the 19th, $225.

30 Gave tennis lessons for cash, $4,500.

30 Paid salaries, $6,000.

30 Sales of memberships on account since December 7, $18,000 (for the month of December).

30 Costs paid in entertaining customers in December, $350.

30 Paid dividends of $1,500. (The Dividends account is No. 320.)

Required   a. Open three-column general ledger accounts for each of the accounts in the trial balance. Place the word Balance in the explanation space and enter the date December 1, 1999, on this same line. Also open an account for Dividends, No. 320.

b. Prepare entries in the general journal for the transactions during December 1999.

c. Post the journal entries to three-column ledger accounts.

d. Prepare a trial balance as of December 31, 1999.

Problem 2–5
Prepare corrected trial balance (L.O. 6)

Bill Baxter prepared a trial balance for Special Party Rentals, Inc., a company that rents tables, chairs, and other party supplies. The trial balance did not balance. The trial balance he prepared was as follows:

SPECIAL PARTY RENTALS, INC.
Trial Balance
December 31, 1999

Acct. No.	Account Title	Debits	Credits
100	Cash	$ 74,000	
103	Accounts Receivable	50,800	
170	Equipment	160,000	
200	Accounts Payable		$ 34,000
300	Capital Stock		130,000
310	Retained Earnings		44,000
320	Dividends	16,000	
400	Service Revenue		432,000
505	Advertising Expense	1,200	
507	Salaries Expense	176,000	
511	Utilities Expense	44,800	
515	Rent Expense	64,000	
		$586,800	$640,000

In trying to find out why the trial balance did not balance, Baxter discovered the following errors:

1. Equipment was understated (too low) by $12,000 because of an error in addition in determining the balance of that account in the ledger.

2. A credit of $4,800 to Accounts Receivable in the journal was not posted to the ledger account at all.

3. A debit of $16,000 for a semiannual dividend was posted as a credit to the Capital Stock account.

4. The balance of $12,000 in the Advertising Expense account was entered as $1,200 in the trial balance.

5. Miscellaneous Expense (Account No. 568), with a balance of $3,200, was omitted from the trial balance.

Prepare a corrected trial balance as of December 31, 1999. Also, write a description of the effect(s) of each error.   *Required*

ALTERNATE PROBLEMS

The transactions of Lightning Package Delivery Company for March 1999 follow:

Problem 2–1A
Prepare journal entries
(L.O. 4)

Mar. 1 The company was organized and issued capital stock for $300,000 cash.
    2 Paid $6,000 as the rent for March on a completely furnished building.
    5 Paid cash for delivery trucks, $180,000.
    6 Paid $4,000 as the rent for March on two forklift trucks.
    9 Paid $2,200 for supplies received and used in March.
   12 Performed delivery services for customers who promised to pay $27,000 at a later date.
   20 Collected cash of $4,500 from customers on account (see March 12 entry).
   21 Received a bill for $1,200 for advertising in the local newspaper in March.
   27 Paid cash for gas and oil consumed in March, $450.
   31 Paid $2,400 salaries to employees for March.
   31 Received an order for services at $12,000. The services will be performed in April.
   31 Paid cash dividend, $1,000.

Prepare the journal entries required to record these transactions in the general journal of the company.   *Required*

Problem 2–2A
Record transactions in journal, post to T-accounts, and prepare trial balance (L.O. 4–6)

Economy Laundry Company had the following transactions in August 1999:

Aug. 1 Issued capital stock for cash, $150,000.
       3 Borrowed $40,000 from the bank on a note.
       4 Purchased cleaning equipment for $25,000 cash.
       6 Performed services for customers who promised to pay later, $16,000.
       7 Paid this month's rent on a building, $2,800.
      10 Collections were made for the services performed on August 6, $3,200.
      14 Supplies were purchased on account for use this month, $3,000.
      17 A bill for $400 was received for utilities for this month.
      25 Laundry services were performed for customers who paid immediately, $22,000.
      31 Paid employee salaries, $6,000.
      31 Paid cash dividend, $2,000.

Required   **a.** Prepare journal entries for these transactions.

b. Post the journal entries to T-accounts. Enter the account number in the Posting Reference column of the journal as you post each amount. Use the following account numbers:

Acct. No.	Account Title
100	Cash
103	Accounts Receivable
170	Equipment
200	Accounts Payable
201	Notes Payable
300	Capital Stock
320	Dividends
400	Service Revenue
507	Salaries Expense
511	Utilities Expense
515	Rent Expense
518	Supplies Expense

c. Prepare a trial balance as of August 31, 1999.

Problem 2–3A
Prepare ledger accounts, journalize transactions, post to three-column ledger accounts, and prepare trial balance (L.O. 4–6)

Clean-Sweep Janitorial, Inc., a company providing janitorial services, was organized July 1, 1999. The following account numbers and titles constitute the chart of accounts for the company:

Acct. No.	Account Title
100	Cash
103	Accounts Receivable
150	Trucks
160	Office Equipment
170	Equipment
200	Accounts Payable
201	Notes Payable
300	Capital Stock
310	Retained Earnings
320	Dividends
400	Service Revenue
506	Gas and Oil Expense
507	Salaries Expense
511	Utilities Expense
512	Insurance Expense
515	Rent Expense
518	Supplies Expense

Transactions   July 1 The company issued $600,000 of capital stock for cash.
             5 Office space was rented for July, and $5,000 was paid for the rental.
             8 Desks and chairs were purchased for the office on account, $28,800.
            10 Equipment was purchased for $50,000; a note was given, to be paid in 30 days.
            15 Purchased trucks for $150,000, paying $120,000 cash and giving a 60-day note to the dealer for $30,000.

July 18   Paid for supplies received and already used, $2,880.
    23   Received $17,280 cash as service revenue.
    27   Insurance expense for July was paid, $4,500.
    30   Paid for gasoline and oil used by the truck in July, $576.
    31   Billed customers for janitorial services rendered, $40,320.
    31   Paid salaries for July, $51,840.
    31   Paid utilities bills for July, $5,280.
    31   Paid cash dividends, $9,600.

a. Prepare general ledger accounts for all of these accounts except Retained Earnings. The Retained Earnings account has a beginning balance of zero and maintains this balance throughout the period.

b. Journalize the transactions given for July 1999 in the general journal.

c. Post the journal entries to three-column ledger accounts.

d. Prepare a trial balance as of July 31, 1999.

Required

Trim Lawn, Inc., is a lawn care company. Thus, the company earns its revenue from sending its trucks to customers' residences and certain commercial establishments to care for lawns and shrubbery. Trim Lawn's trial balance at the end of the first 11 months of the year follows:

Problem 2–4A
Prepare journal entries, post to three-column ledger accounts, and prepare trial balance (L.O. 4–6)

TRIM LAWN, INC.
Trial Balance
November 30, 1999

Acct. No.	Account Title	Debits	Credits
100	Cash	$ 63,740	
103	Accounts Receivable	88,600	
150	Trucks	102,900	
160	Office Furniture	8,400	
200	Accounts Payable		$ 33,600
300	Capital Stock		30,000
310	Retained Earnings, January 1, 1999		30,540
400	Service Revenue		371,010
505	Advertising Expense	18,300	
506	Gas and Oil Expense	21,900	
507	Salaries Expense	65,850	
511	Utilities Expense	2,310	
515	Rent Expense	15,000	
518	Supplies Expense	75,600	
531	Entertainment Expense	2,550	
		$465,150	$465,150

Dec. 2   Paid rent for December, $3,000.
    5   Paid the accounts payable of $33,600.
    8   Paid advertising for December, $1,500.
   10   Purchased a new office desk on account, $1,050.
   13   Purchased $240 of supplies on account for use in December.
   15   Collected cash from customers on account, $75,000.
   20   Paid for customer entertainment, $450.
   24   Collected an additional $6,000 from customers on account.
   26   Paid for gasoline used in the trucks in December, $270.
   28   Billed customers for services rendered, $79,500.
   30   Paid for more December supplies, $12,000.
   31   Paid December salaries, $15,300.
   31   Paid a $4,000 cash dividend. (The Dividends account is No. 320.)

Transactions

a. Open three-column general ledger accounts for each of the accounts in the trial balance under the date of December 1, 1999. Place the word *Balance* in the explanation space of each account. Also open an account for Dividends, No. 320.

b. Prepare entries in the general journal for the preceding transactions for December 1999.

c. Post the journal entries to three-column general ledger accounts.

d. Prepare a trial balance as of December 31, 1999.

Required

Problem 2–5A
Prepare corrected trial
balance (L.O. 6)

Marc Miller prepared the following trial balance from the ledger of the Quick-Fix TV Repair Company. The trial balance did not balance.

QUICK-FIX TV REPAIR COMPANY
Trial Balance
December 31, 1999

Acct. No.	Account Title	Debits	Credits
100	Cash	$ 69,200	
103	Accounts Receivable	60,800	
160	Office Furniture	120,000	
172	Office Equipment	48,000	
200	Accounts Payable		$ 32,400
300	Capital Stock		180,000
310	Retained Earnings		80,000
320	Dividends	28,800	
400	Service Revenue		360,000
507	Salaries Expense	280,000	
515	Rent Expense	40,000	
568	Miscellaneous Expense	7,200	
		$654,000	$652,400

The difference in totals in the trial balance caused Miller to carefully examine the company's accounting records. In searching back through the accounting records, Miller found that the following errors had been made:

1. One entire entry that included a $10,000 debit to Cash and a $10,000 credit to Accounts Receivable was never posted.

2. In computing the balance of the Accounts Payable account, a credit of $3,200 was omitted from the computation.

3. In preparing the trial balance, the Retained Earnings account balance was shown as $80,000. The ledger account has the balance at its correct amount of $83,200.

4. One debit of $2,400 to the Dividends account was posted as a credit to that account.

5. Office equipment of $12,000 was debited to Office Furniture when purchased.

Required   Prepare a corrected trial balance for the Quick-Fix TV Repair Company as of December 31, 1999. Also, write a description of the effect(s) of each error.

BEYOND THE NUMBERS—CRITICAL THINKING

**Business Decision
Case 2–1**
Prepare journal entries,
post to T-accounts, and
judge profitability
(L.O. 4, 5)

John Jacobs lost his job as a carpenter with a contractor when a recession hit the construction industry. Jacobs had been making $50,000 per year. He decided to form his own company, Jacobs Corporation, and do home repairs.

The following is a summary of the transactions of the business during the first three months of operations in 1999:

Jan. 15   Stockholders invested $40,000 in the business.

Feb. 25   Received payment of $4,400 for remodeling a basement into a recreation room. The homeowner purchased all of the building materials.

Mar. 5   Paid cash for an advertisement that appeared in the local newspaper, $150.

Apr. 10   Received $7,000 for converting a room over a garage into an office for a college professor. The professor purchased all of the materials for the job.

    11   Paid gas and oil expenses for automobile, $900.

    12   Miscellaneous business expenses were paid, $450.

    15   Paid dividends of $2,000.

Required   a. Prepare journal entries for these transactions.

    b. Post the journal entries to T-accounts.

    c. How profitable is this new venture? Should Jacobs stay in this business?

**Annual Report
Analysis 2–2**
Perform horizontal and
vertical analyses and
comment (L.O. 7)

Refer to the balance sheets of John H. Harland Company in the separate annual report booklet. Perform horizontal and vertical analyses of the assets section of the balance sheets for December 31, 1995, and 1996. Horizontal analysis involves showing the dollar amount and percentage increase or decrease of 1996 amounts over 1995 amounts. Vertical analysis involves showing the percentage of total assets that each asset represents as of December 31, 1996, and December 31, 1995. Write comments on any important changes between the two years that are evidence of decisions made by management.

In The Home Depot's recent Annual Report, the following passages appear:

Annual Report Analysis 2–3

The primary key to our success is our 39,000 employees who wear those orange aprons you see in our stores.

Few great achievements—in business or in any aspect of life—are reached and sustained without the support and involvement of large numbers of people committed to shared values and goals they deem worthy. Indeed, one need look no further than the business section of the morning newspaper to read of how yet another "blue chip" American business, entrenched in and isolated by its own bureaucracy, has lost the support of its employees and customers. . .

Frankly, the biggest difference between The Home Depot and our competitors is not the products on our shelves, it's our people and their ability to forge strong bonds of loyalty and trust with our customers. . .

. . . Contrary to conventional management wisdom, those at the top of organization charts are not the source of all wisdom. Many of our best ideas come from the people who work on the sales floor. We encourage our employees to challenge senior management directives if they feel strongly enough about their dissenting opinions. . .

. . . We want our people to be themselves and to be bold enough to apply their talents as individuals. Certainly, people can often perceive great risk acting this way. Thus, we go to great lengths to empower our employees to be mavericks, to express differences of opinion without fear of being fired or demoted. . . We do everything we can to make people feel challenged and inspired at work instead of being threatened and made to feel insecure. An organization can, after all, accomplish more when people work together instead of against each other.

Write answers to the following questions:

Required

a. Do you think The Home Depot management regards its employees more as expenses or assets? Explain.

b. What does The Home Depot regard as its most valuable asset? Explain your answer.

c. Is The Home Depot permitted to list its human resources as assets on its balance sheet? Why or why not?

d. Could its philosophy regarding its employees be the major factor in its outstanding financial performance? Explain.

Refer to "An Ethical Perspective" on page 80. Write out the answers to the following questions:

Ethics Case—Writing Experience 2–4

a. What motivated Larry to go along with unethical and illegal actions? Explain.

b. What are Larry's options now? List each possibility.

c. What would you do if you were Larry? Describe in detail.

d. What do you think the real Larry did? Describe in detail.

In teams of two or three students, interview in person or by speakerphone a new staff member who has worked for a CPA firm for only one or two years. Seek information on the advantages and disadvantages of working for a CPA firm. Also, inquire about the nature of the work and the training programs offered by the firm for new employees. As a team, write a memorandum to the instructor summarizing the results of the interview. The heading of the memorandum should contain the date, to whom it is written, from whom, and the subject matter.

Group Project 2–5
Interview a new staff member at a CPA firm

Using the annual reports booklet that came with the text, your small student group should perform horizontal and vertical analysis on the balance sheet and income statement of one of the four companies. Prepare schedules showing your work and write a report to your instructor commenting on an analysis of the results.

Group Project 2–6
Perform horizontal and vertical analysis

With one or two other students and using library resources, write a report on the life of Luca Pacioli, sometimes referred to as the father of accounting. Pacioli was a Franciscan monk who wrote a book on double-entry accounting in 1494. Be careful to cite sources and treat direct quotes properly. (If you do not know how to do this, ask your instructor.)

Group Project 2–7
Perform library research

USING THE INTERNET—A VIEW OF THE REAL WORLD

Internet Project 2–8
Check on Job Openings

Visit the following website:

http://www.roberthalf.com

Click on Job Listings. Read the information and then click on All Types and All Locations. Then click on Run Search. Read through the job openings and click on any that seem interesting. Write a memo to your instructor about your search and what you learned about certain jobs in accounting.

Internet Project 2–9
Check on accounting salaries

Visit the following website:

http://www.roberthalf.com

Click on Career Corner. Then click on Key Findings from the (latest year) Salary Guide. Print the Salary Guide by clicking on the printer image (or merely prepare notes from the screen) and prepare to make a short report to the class summarizing your findings.

ANSWERS TO SELF-TEST

TRUE-FALSE

1. **False.** Only the last five steps are performed at the end of the period. The first three steps are performed throughout the accounting period.

2. **True.** The journal is the book of original entry. Any amounts appearing in a ledger account must have been posted from the journal.

3. **False.** The left side of any account is the debit side.

4. **False.** These accounts are all increased by credits.

5. **True.** Since dividends reduce stockholders' equity, the Dividends account is increased by debits.

6. **False.** An entire journal entry may not have been posted, or a debit or credit might have been posted to the wrong account.

MULTIPLE-CHOICE

1. **c.** An asset, Cash, is increased by a debit, and the Capital Stock account is increased by a credit.

2. **b.** Since the insurance covers more than the current accounting period, an asset is debited instead of an expense. The credit is to Cash.

3. **a.** The receipt of cash before services are performed creates a liability, Unearned Delivery Fees. To increase a liability, it is credited. Cash is debited to increase its balance.

4. **b.** Cash is increased by the debit, and Delivery Service Revenue is increased by the credit.

5. **c.** Dividends is increased by the debit, and Cash is decreased by the credit.

3

ADJUSTMENTS FOR FINANCIAL REPORTING

Chapters 1 and 2 introduced the accounting process of analyzing, classifying, and summarizing business transactions into accounts. You learned how these transactions are entered into the journal and posted to the ledger accounts. You also know how to use the trial balance to test the equality of debits and credits in the journalizing and posting process. The purpose of the accounting process is to produce accurate financial statements so they may be used for making sound business decisions. At this point in your study of accounting, you are concentrating on three financial statements—the income statement, the statement of retained earnings, and the balance sheet. Detailed coverage of the statement of cash flows appears in Chapter 16.

When you began to analyze business transactions in Chapter 1, you saw that the evidence of the transaction is usually a source document. It is any written or printed evidence that describes the essential facts of a business transaction. Examples are receipts for cash paid or received, checks written or received, bills sent to customers, or bills received from suppliers. The giving, receiving, or creating of source documents triggered the journal entries made in Chapter 2.

The journal entries we discuss in this chapter are *adjusting entries*. The arrival of the end of the accounting period triggers adjusting entries. Accountants use adjusting entries to bring accounts to their proper balances before preparing financial statements. In this chapter, you learn the difference between the cash basis and accrual basis of accounting. Then you learn about the classes and types of adjusting entries and how to prepare them.

CASH VERSUS ACCRUAL BASIS ACCOUNTING

Professionals such as physicians and lawyers and some relatively small businesses may account for their revenues and expenses on a cash basis. The **cash basis of accounting** recognizes revenues when cash is received and recognizes expenses when cash is paid out. For example, under the cash basis, a company would treat services rendered to clients in 1999 for which the company collected cash in 2000 as 2000

ILLUSTRATION 3.1
Cash Basis and Accrual
Basis of Accounting
Compared

	Cash Basis	Accrual Basis
Revenues are recognized	As cash is received	As earned (goods are delivered or services are performed)
Expenses are recognized	As cash is paid	As incurred to produce revenues

Objective 1
Describe the basic
characteristics of the cash
basis and the accrual basis
of accounting.

Reinforcing Problem
E3–1 Answer multiple-choice
questions that emphasize the
differences between cash and
accrual bases of accounting.

revenues. Similarly, under the cash basis, a company would treat expenses incurred in 1999 for which the company disbursed cash in 2000 as 2000 expenses. Under the "pure" cash basis, even the purchase of a building would be debited to an expense. However, under the "modified" cash basis, the purchase of long-lived assets (such as a building) would be debited to an asset and depreciated (gradually charged to expense) over its useful life. Normally the "modified" cash basis is used by those few individuals and small businesses that use the cash basis.

Because the cash basis of accounting does not match expenses incurred and revenues earned, it is generally considered theoretically unacceptable. The cash basis is acceptable in practice only under those circumstances when it approximates the results that a company could obtain under the accrual basis of accounting. Companies using the cash basis do not have to prepare any adjusting entries unless they discover they have made a mistake in preparing an entry during the accounting period. Under certain circumstances, companies may use the cash basis for income tax purposes.

Throughout the text we use the accrual basis of accounting, which matches expenses incurred and revenues earned, because most companies use the accrual basis. The **accrual basis of accounting** recognizes revenues when sales are made or services are performed, regardless of when cash is received. Expenses are recognized as incurred, whether or not cash has been paid out. For instance, assume a company performs services for a customer on account. Although the company has received no cash, the revenue is recorded at the time the company performs the service. Later, when the company receives the cash, no revenue is recorded because the company has already recorded the revenue. Under the accrual basis, adjusting entries are needed to bring the accounts up to date for unrecorded economic activity that has taken place. In Illustration 3.1, we show when revenues and expenses are recognized under the cash basis and under the accrual basis.

THE NEED FOR ADJUSTING ENTRIES

Objective 2
Identify the reasons why
adjusting entries must be
made.

Note to the Student
Every adjusting entry impacts both
a balance sheet and an income
statement account. Therefore, every
adjusting entry impacts net income.
This is not true of all journal entries
made during the accounting period.
    Think of some examples of
journal entries that do affect net
income and some that do not.

The income statement of a business reports all revenues earned and all expenses incurred to generate those revenues during a given period. An income statement that does not report all revenues and expenses is incomplete, inaccurate, and possibly misleading. Similarly, a balance sheet that does not report all of an entity's assets, liabilities, and stockholders' equity at a specific time may be misleading. Each adjusting entry has a dual purpose: (1) to make the income statement report the proper revenue or expense and (2) to make the balance sheet report the proper asset or liability. Thus, every adjusting entry affects at least one income statement account and one balance sheet account.

Since those interested in the activities of a business need timely information, companies must prepare financial statements periodically. To prepare such statements, the accountant divides an entity's life into time periods. These time periods are usually equal in length and are called *accounting periods*. An **accounting period** may be one month, one quarter, or one year. An **accounting year,** or fiscal year, is an accounting period of one year. A **fiscal year** is any 12 consecutive months. The fiscal year may or may not coincide with the **calendar year,** which ends on December 31. As we

	1995	1994	1993	1992
January	23	23	23	21
February	11	12	11	14
March	15	15	16	15
April	8	8	7	7
May	16	16	16	16
June	58	59	62	60
July	14	14	15	15
August	15	15	16	18
September	35	37	35	33
October	23	22	22	22
November	17	17	17	18
Subtotal	**235**	**238**	**240**	**239**
December	365	362	360	361
Total Companies	**600**	**600**	**600**	**600**

Source: American Institute of Certified Public Accountants, *Accounting Trends & Techniques* (New York: AICPA, 1996), p. 27.

ILLUSTRATION 3.2
Summary—Fiscal Year Endings by Month

show in Illustration 3.2, more than half of the companies surveyed have fiscal years that coincide with the calendar year. Companies in certain industries often have a fiscal year that differs from the calendar year. For instance many retail stores end their fiscal year on January 31 to avoid closing their books during their peak sales period. Other companies select a fiscal year ending at a time when inventories and business activity are lowest.

Periodic reporting and the matching principle necessitate the preparation of *adjusting entries*. **Adjusting entries** are journal entries made at the end of an accounting period or at any time financial statements are to be prepared to bring about a proper *matching* of revenues and expenses. The **matching principle** requires that expenses incurred in producing revenues be deducted from the revenues they generated during the accounting period. The matching principle is one of the underlying principles of accounting. This matching of expenses and revenues is necessary for the income statement to present an accurate picture of the profitability of a business. Adjusting entries reflect unrecorded economic activity that has taken place but has not yet been recorded. Why has the company not recorded this activity by the end of the period? One reason is that it is more convenient and economical to wait until the end of the period to record the activity. A second reason is that no source document concerning that activity has yet come to the accountant's attention.

Adjusting entries bring the amounts in the general ledger accounts to their proper balances before the company prepares its financial statements. That is, adjusting entries convert the amounts that are actually in the general ledger accounts to the amounts that should be in the general ledger accounts for proper financial reporting. To make this conversion, the accountants analyze the accounts to determine which need adjustment. For example, assume a company purchased a three-year insurance policy costing $600 at the beginning of the year and debited $600 to Prepaid Insurance. At year-end, the company should remove $200 of the cost from the asset and record it as an expense. Failure to do so misstates assets and net income on the financial statements.

Companies continuously receive benefits from many assets such as prepaid expenses (e.g., prepaid insurance and prepaid rent). Thus, an entry could be made daily to record the expense incurred. Typically, firms do not make the entry until financial statements are to be prepared. Therefore, if monthly financial statements are prepared, monthly adjusting entries are required. By custom, and in some instances by law, businesses report to their owners at least annually. Accordingly, adjusting entries are required at least once a year. Remember, however, that the entry transferring an amount from an asset account to an expense account should transfer only the asset cost that has expired.

Reinforcing Problem
Business Decision Case 3–1 Explain why adjusting entries are made and which accounts need adjustment.

Reinforcing Problem
E3–2 Answer multiple-choice questions concerning the accounting period and why adjusting entries must be made.

ILLUSTRATION 3.3
Two Classes and Four
Types of Adjusting
Entries

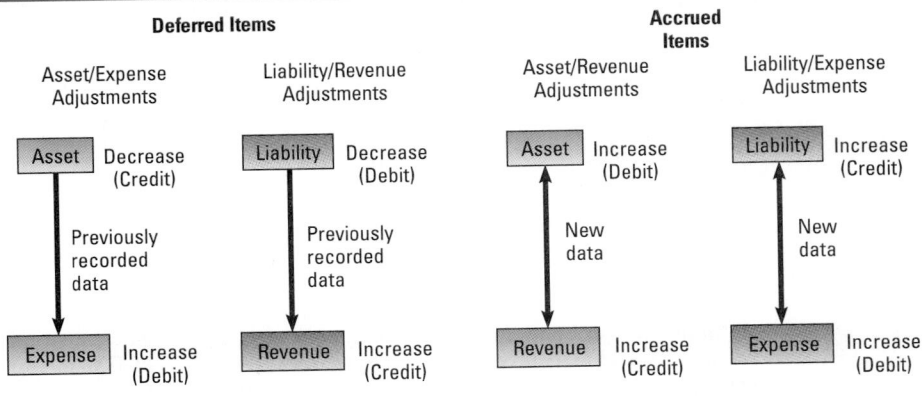

Data previously recorded in an asset account
are transferred to an expense account, or
data previously recorded in a liability account
are transferred to a revenue account.

Data not previously recorded are entered into
an asset account and a revenue account or a
liability account and an expense account.

**AN ACCOUNTING
PERSPECTIVE**

USES OF TECHNOLOGY   Eventually, computers will probably enter adjusting entries continuously on a real-time basis so that up-to-date financial statements can be printed at any time without prior notice. Computers will be fed the facts concerning activities that would normally result in adjusting entries and instructed to seek any necessary information from their own databases or those of other computers to continually adjust the accounts.

CLASSES AND TYPES OF ADJUSTING ENTRIES

Objective 3
Identify the classes and
types of adjusting entries.

Adjusting entries fall into two broad classes: deferred (meaning to postpone or delay) items and accrued (meaning to grow or accumulate) items. **Deferred items** consist of adjusting entries involving data previously recorded in accounts. These entries involve the transfer of data already recorded in asset and liability accounts to expense and revenue accounts, respectively. **Accrued items** consist of adjusting entries relating to activity on which no data have been previously recorded in the accounts. These entries involve the initial, or first, recording of assets and liabilities and the related revenues and expenses (see Illustration 3.3).

Deferred items consist of two types of adjusting entries: asset/expense adjustments and liability/revenue adjustments. For example, prepaid insurance and prepaid rent are assets until they are used up; then they become expenses. Also, unearned revenue is a liability until the company renders the service; then the unearned revenue becomes earned revenue.

Reinforcing Problem
E3–3 Answer multiple-choice
questions that differentiate between deferred and accrued items.

Accrued items consist of two types of adjusting entries: asset/revenue adjustments and liability/expense adjustments. For example, assume a company performs a service for a customer but has not yet billed the customer. The accountant records this transaction as an asset in the form of a receivable and as revenue because the company has earned a revenue. Also, assume a company owes its employees salaries not yet paid. The accountant records this transaction as a liability and an expense because the company has incurred an expense.

In this chapter, we illustrate each of the four types of adjusting entries: asset/ expense, liability/revenue, asset/revenue, and liability/expense. Look at Illustration 3.4, the trial balance of the MicroTrain Company at December 31, 1999. As you can see, MicroTrain must adjust several accounts before it can prepare accurate finan-

MICROTRAIN COMPANY
Trial Balance
December 31, 1999

ILLUSTRATION 3.4
Trial Balance

Acct. No.	Account Title	Debits	Credits
100	Cash	$ 8,250	
103	Accounts Receivable	5,200	
107	Supplies on Hand	1,400	
108	Prepaid Insurance.	2,400	
112	Prepaid Rent	1,200	
150	Trucks.	40,000	
200	Accounts Payable.		$ 730
216	Unearned Service Fees		4,500
300	Capital Stock.		50,000
320	Dividends	3,000	
400	Service Revenue		10,700
505	Advertising Expense	50	
506	Gas and Oil Expense	680	
507	Salaries Expense	3,600	
511	Utilities Expense	150	
		$65,930	$65,930

cial statements. The adjustments for these accounts involve data already recorded in the company's accounts.

In making adjustments for MicroTrain Company, we must add several accounts to the company's chart of accounts shown in Chapter 2 on page 63. These new accounts are:

Type of Account	Acct. No.	Account Title	Description
Asset	121	Interest Receivable	The amount of interest earned but not yet received.
Contra asset*	151	Accumulated Depreciation— Trucks	The total depreciation expense taken on trucks since the acquisition date. The balance of this account is deducted from that of Trucks on the balance sheet.
Liability	206	Salaries Payable	The amount of salaries earned by employees but not yet paid by the company.
Revenue	418	Interest Revenue	The amount of interest earned in the current period.
Expenses	512	Insurance Expense	The cost of insurance incurred in the current period.
	515	Rent Expense	The cost of rent incurred in the current period.
	518	Supplies Expense	The cost of supplies used in the current period.
	521	Depreciation Expense— Trucks	The portion of the cost of the trucks assigned to expense during the current period.

*Accountants deduct the balance of a contra asset from the balance of the related asset account on the balance sheet. We explain the reasons for using a contra asset account later in the chapter.

Now you are ready to follow as MicroTrain Company makes its adjustments for deferred items. If you find the process confusing, review the beginning of this chapter so you clearly understand the purpose of adjusting entries.

ADJUSTMENTS FOR DEFERRED ITEMS

Objective 4
Prepare adjusting entries.

This section discusses the two types of adjustments for deferred items: asset/expense adjustments and liability/revenue adjustments. In the asset/expense group, you learn how to prepare adjusting entries for prepaid expenses and depreciation. In the liability/revenue group, you learn how to prepare adjusting entries for unearned revenues.

Asset/Expense Adjustments— Prepaid Expenses and Depreciation

MicroTrain Company must make several asset/expense adjustments for prepaid expenses. A **prepaid expense** is an asset awaiting assignment to expense, such as prepaid insurance, prepaid rent, and supplies on hand. Note that the nature of these three adjustments is the same.

PREPAID INSURANCE   When a company pays an insurance policy premium in advance, the purchase creates the asset, *prepaid insurance*. This advance payment is an asset because the company will receive insurance coverage in the future. With the passage of time, however, the asset gradually expires. The portion that has expired becomes an expense. To illustrate this point, recall that in Chapter 2, MicroTrain Company purchased for cash an insurance policy on its trucks for the period December 1, 1999, to November 30, 2000. The journal entry made on December 1, 1999, to record the purchase of the policy was:

1999					
Dec.	1	Prepaid Insurance		2,400	
		Cash			2,400
		Purchased truck insurance to cover a one-year period.			

The two accounts relating to insurance are Prepaid Insurance (an asset) and Insurance Expense (an expense). After posting this entry, the Prepaid Insurance account has a $2,400 debit balance on December 1, 1999. The Insurance Expense account has a zero balance on December 1, 1999, because no time has elapsed to use any of the policy's benefits.

(Dr.)	**Prepaid Insurance**	*(Cr.)*	*(Dr.)*	**Insurance Expense**	*(Cr.)*
1999			1999		
Dec. 1			Dec. 1		
Bal.	2,400		Bal.	–0–	

By December 31, 1999, one month of the year covered by the policy has expired. Therefore, part of the **service potential** (or benefit obtained from the asset) has expired. The asset now provides less future services or benefits than when the company acquired it. We recognize this reduction by treating the cost of the services received from the asset as an expense. For the MicroTrain Company example, the service received was one month of insurance coverage. Since the policy provides the same services for every month of its one-year life, we assign an equal amount ($200) of cost to each month. Thus, MicroTrain charges $1/12$ of the annual premium to Insurance Expense on December 31, 1999. The adjusting journal entry is:

1999 Dec.	31	Insurance Expense	200	
		Prepaid Insurance		200
		To record insurance expense for December.		

Adjustment 1—Insurance

After posting these two journal entries, the accounts in T-account format appear as follows:

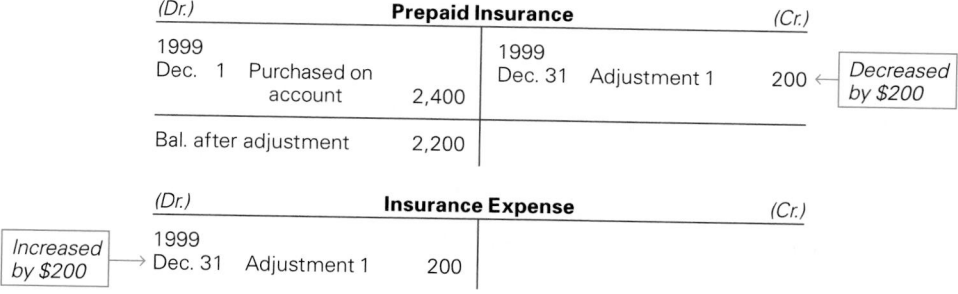

In practice, accountants do not use T-accounts. Instead, they use three-column ledger accounts that have the advantage of showing a balance after each transaction. After posting the preceding two entries, the three-column ledger accounts appear as follows:

Prepaid Insurance   *Account No. 108*

Date		Explanation	Post. Ref.	Debit	Credit	Balance
1999 Dec.	1	Purchased on account	G1	2400		2400 Dr.
	31	Adjustment	G3*		200	2200 Dr.

Insurance Expense   *Account No. 512*

Date		Explanation	Post. Ref.	Debit	Credit	Balance
1999 Dec.	31	Adjustment	G3*	200		200 Dr.

*Assumed journal page number.

Before this adjusting entry was made, the entire $2,400 insurance payment made on December 1, 1999, was a prepaid expense for 12 months of protection. So on December 31, 1999, one month of protection had passed, and an adjusting entry transferred $200 of the $2,400 ($2,400/12 = $200) to Insurance Expense. On the income statement for the year ended December 31, 1999, MicroTrain reports one month of insurance expense, $200, as one of the expenses it incurred in generating that year's revenues. It reports the remaining amount of the prepaid expense, $2,200, as an asset on the balance sheet. The $2,200 prepaid expense represents 11 months of insurance protection that remains as a future benefit.

PREPAID RENT   Prepaid rent is another example of the gradual consumption of a previously recorded asset. Assume a company pays rent in advance to cover more than one accounting period. On the date it pays the rent, the company debits the prepayment to the Prepaid Rent account (an asset account). The company has not yet received benefits resulting from this expenditure. Thus, the expenditure creates an asset.

We measure rent expense similarly to insurance expense. Generally, the rental contract specifies the amount of rent per unit of time. If the prepayment covers a three-month rental, we charge one-third of this rental to each month. Notice that the amount charged is the same each month even though some months have more days than other months.

For example, MicroTrain Company paid $1,200 rent in advance on December 1, 1999, to cover a three-month period beginning on that date. The journal entry would be:

1999				
Dec.	1	Prepaid Rent	1,200	
		Cash		1,200
		Paid three months' rent on a building.		

The two accounts relating to rent are Prepaid Rent (an asset) and Rent Expense. After this entry is posted, the Prepaid Rent account has a $1,200 balance and the Rent Expense account has a zero balance because no part of the rent period has yet elapsed.

(Dr.)	**Prepaid Rent**	*(Cr.)*	*(Dr.)*	**Rent Expense**	*(Cr.)*
1999			1999		
Dec. 1			Dec. 1		
Bal. Cash paid	1,200		Bal.	–0–	

On December 31, 1999, MicroTrain must prepare an adjusting entry. Since one third of the period covered by the prepaid rent has elapsed, it charges one-third of the $1,200 of prepaid rent to expense. The required adjusting entry is:

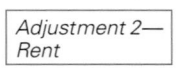
Adjustment 2—Rent

1999				
Dec.	31	Rent Expense.	400	
		Prepaid Rent		400
		To record rent expense for December.		

After posting this adjusting entry, the T-accounts appear as follows:

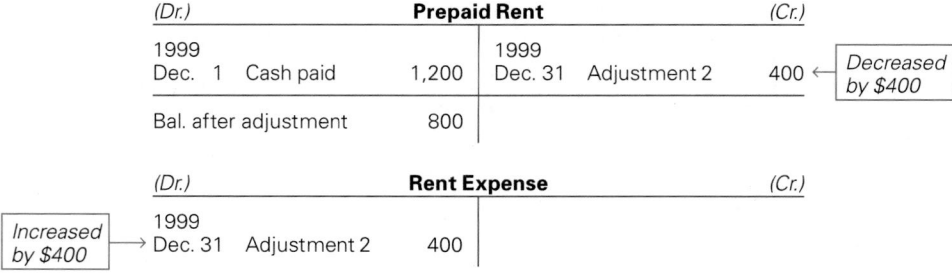

The $400 rent expense appears in the income statement for the year ended December 31, 1999. MicroTrain reports the remaining $800 of prepaid rent as an asset in the balance sheet on December 31, 1999. Thus, the adjusting entries have accomplished their purpose of maintaining the accuracy of the financial statements.

SUPPLIES ON HAND   Almost every business uses supplies in its operations. It may classify supplies simply as supplies (to include all types of supplies), or more specifically as office supplies (paper, stationery, floppy diskettes, pencils), selling supplies (gummed tape, string, paper bags, cartons, wrapping paper), or training supplies (transparencies, training manuals). Frequently, companies buy supplies in bulk. These supplies are an asset until the company uses them. This asset may be called *supplies on hand* or *supplies inventory*. Even though these terms indicate a prepaid expense, the firm does not use *prepaid* in the asset's title.

On December 4, 1999, MicroTrain Company purchased supplies for $1,400 and recorded the transaction as follows:

1999				
Dec.	4	Supplies on Hand	1,400	
		Cash		1,400
		To record the purchase of supplies for future use.		

MicroTrain's two accounts relating to supplies are Supplies on Hand (an asset) and Supplies Expense. After this entry is posted, the Supplies on Hand account shows a debit balance of $1,400 and the Supplies Expense account has a zero balance as shown in the following T-accounts:

(Dr.)	**Supplies on Hand**	(Cr.)	(Dr.)	**Supplies Expense**	(Cr.)
1999			1999		
Dec. 4			Dec. 4		
Bal. Cash paid	1,400		Bal.	–0–	

An actual physical inventory (a count of the supplies on hand) at the end of the month showed only $900 of supplies on hand. Thus, the company must have used $500 of supplies in December. An adjusting journal entry brings the two accounts pertaining to supplies to their proper balances. The adjusting entry recognizes the reduction in the asset (Supplies on Hand) and the recording of an expense (Supplies Expense) by transferring $500 from the asset to the expense. According to the physical inventory, the asset balance should be $900 and the expense balance, $500. So MicroTrain makes the following adjusting entry:

1999				
Dec.	31	Supplies Expense	500	
		Supplies on Hand		500
		To record supplies used during December.		

Adjustment 3— Supplies

After posting this adjusting entry, the T-accounts appear as follows:

(Dr.)	**Supplies on Hand**			(Cr.)	
1999			1999		
Dec. 4	Cash paid	1,400	Dec. 31	Adjustment 3	500 ←
Bal. after adjustment		900			

Decreased by $500

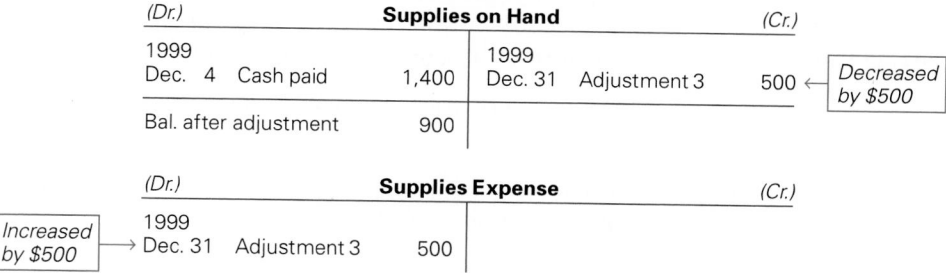

Increased by $500 →

(Dr.)	**Supplies Expense**		(Cr.)
1999			
Dec. 31	Adjustment 3	500	

The entry to record the use of supplies could be made when the supplies are issued from the storeroom. However, such careful accounting for small items each time they are issued is usually too costly a procedure.

Accountants make adjusting entries for supplies on hand, like for any other prepaid expense, before preparing financial statements. Supplies expense appears in the income statement. Supplies on hand is an asset in the balance sheet.

Sometimes companies buy assets relating to insurance, rent, and supplies knowing that they will use them up before the end of the current accounting period (usually one month or one year). If so, an expense account is usually debited at the time of purchase rather than debiting an asset account. This procedure avoids having to make an adjusting entry at the end of the accounting period. Sometimes, too, a company debits an expense even though the asset will benefit more than the current period. Then, at the end of the accounting period, the firm's adjusting entry transfers some of the cost from the expense to the asset. For instance, assume that on January 1, a company paid $1,200 rent to cover a three-year period and debited the $1,200 to Rent Expense. At the end of the year, it transfers $800 from Rent Expense to Prepaid Rent.

Reinforcing Problem
E3–7 Prepare entries for purchase of supplies and adjustment at year-end.

To simplify our approach, we will consistently debit the asset when the asset will benefit more than the current accounting period.

DEPRECIATION   Just as prepaid insurance and prepaid rent indicate a gradual using up of a previously recorded asset, so does depreciation. However, the overall time involved in using up a depreciable asset (such as a building) is much longer and less definite than for prepaid expenses. Also, a prepaid expense generally involves a fairly small amount of money. Depreciable assets, however, usually involve larger sums of money.

A **depreciable asset** is a manufactured asset such as a building, machine, vehicle, or piece of equipment that provides service to a business. In time, these assets lose their utility because of (1) wear and tear from use or (2) obsolescence due to technological change. Since companies gradually use up these assets over time, they record depreciation expense on them. **Depreciation expense** is the amount of asset cost assigned as an expense to a particular period. The process of recording depreciation expense is called **depreciation accounting.** The three factors involved in computing depreciation expense are:

Note to the Student
Depreciation accounting requires the use of estimates in the accounting process. How might these estimates affect the accuracy and credibility of the financial statements?

1. **Asset cost.** The asset cost is the amount that a company paid to purchase the depreciable asset.
2. **Estimated salvage value.** The **estimated salvage value (scrap value)** is the amount that the company can probably sell the asset for at the end of its estimated useful life.
3. **Estimated useful life.** The **estimated useful life** of an asset is the estimated time that a company can use the asset. Useful life is an estimate, not an exact measurement, that a company must make in advance. However, sometimes the useful life is determined by company policy (e.g., keep a fleet of automobiles for three years).

Note to the Student
Why is depreciation an allocation process and not a valuation process even if the end result refers to a *book value* or *carrying value?*

Accountants use different methods for recording depreciation. The method illustrated here is the *straight-line method.* We discuss other depreciation methods in Chapter 10. Straight-line depreciation assigns the same amount of depreciation expense to each accounting period over the life of the asset. The **depreciation formula (straight-line)** to compute straight-line depreciation for a one-year period is:

$$\text{Annual depreciation} = \frac{\text{Asset cost} - \text{Estimated salvage value}}{\text{Estimated years of useful life}}$$

To illustrate the use of this formula, recall that on December 1, MicroTrain Company purchased four small trucks at a cost of $40,000. The journal entry was:

1999				
Dec.	1	Trucks	40,000	
		Cash		40,000
		To record the purchase of four trucks.		

The estimated salvage value for each truck was $1,000, so MicroTrain estimated the total salvage value for all four trucks at $4,000. The company estimated the useful life of each truck to be four years. Using the straight-line depreciation formula, MicroTrain calculated the annual depreciation on the trucks as follows:

$$\text{Annual depreciation} = \frac{\$40,000 - \$4,000}{4 \text{ years}} = \$9,000$$

The amount of depreciation expense for one month would be $\frac{1}{12}$ of the annual amount. Thus, depreciation expense for December is $9,000 \div 12 = \$750$.

The difference between an asset's cost and its estimated salvage value is an asset's **depreciable amount.** To satisfy the matching principle, the firm must allocate the depreciable amount as an expense to the various periods in the asset's useful life. It does this by debiting the amount of depreciation for a period to a depreciation expense account and crediting the amount to an accumulated depreciation account. Micro-Train's depreciation on its delivery trucks for December is $750. The company records the depreciation as follows:

Reinforcing Problem
E3–8 Prepare adjusting entry for depreciation.

1999			
Dec.	31	Depreciation Expense—Trucks	750	
		Accumulated Depreciation—Trucks		750
		To record depreciation expense for December.		

Adjustment 4—
Depreciation

After posting the adjusting entry, the T-accounts appear as follows:

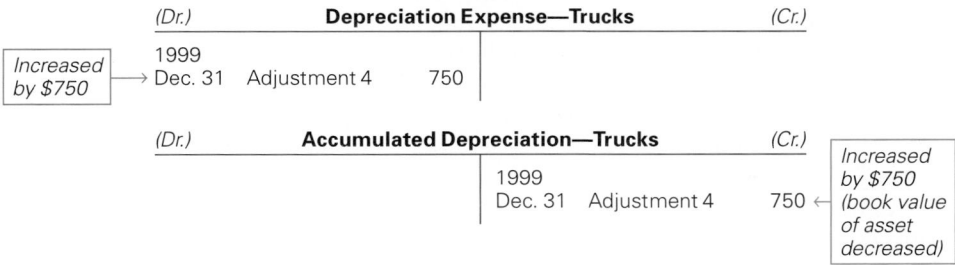

(Dr.)   **Depreciation Expense—Trucks**   *(Cr.)*

Increased by $750 → 1999
Dec. 31   Adjustment 4   750

(Dr.)   **Accumulated Depreciation—Trucks**   *(Cr.)*

1999
Dec. 31   Adjustment 4   750 ←

Increased by $750 (book value of asset decreased)

MicroTrain reports depreciation expense in its income statement. And it reports accumulated depreciation in the balance sheet as a deduction from the related asset.

The **accumulated depreciation account** is a contra asset account that shows the total of all depreciation recorded on the asset *from the date of acquisition up through the balance sheet date*. A **contra asset account** is a deduction from the asset to which it relates in the balance sheet. The purpose of a contra asset account is to reduce the original cost of the asset down to its remaining undepreciated cost or book value. The *accumulated depreciation account* does not represent cash that is being set aside to replace the worn out asset. The *undepreciated cost of the asset* is the debit balance in the asset account (original cost) minus the credit balance in the accumulated depreciation contra account. Accountants also refer to an asset's cost less accumulated depreciation as the **book value** (or net book value) of the asset. Thus, book value is the cost not yet allocated to an expense. In the previous example, the book value of the equipment after the first month is:

Cost	$40,000
Less: Accumulated depreciation	750
Book value (or cost not yet allocated as an expense)	$39,250

MicroTrain credits the depreciation amount to an accumulated depreciation account, which is a contra asset, rather than directly to the asset account. Companies use contra accounts when they want to show statement readers the original amount of the account to which the contra account relates. For instance, for the asset Trucks, it is useful to know both the original cost of the asset and the total accumulated depreciation amount recorded on the asset. Therefore, the asset account shows the original cost. The contra account, Accumulated Depreciation—Trucks, shows the total amount of recorded depreciation from the date of acquisition. By having both original cost and the accumulated depreciation amounts, a user can estimate the approximate percentage of the benefits embodied in the asset that the company has consumed. For instance, assume the accumulated depreciation amount is about three-fourths the cost of the asset. Then, the benefits would be approximately three-fourths consumed, and the company may have to replace the asset soon.

Thus, to provide more complete balance sheet information to users of financial statements, companies show both the original acquisition cost and accumulated depreciation. In the preceding example for adjustment 4, the balance sheet at December 31, 1999, would show the asset and contra asset as follows:

Assets

Trucks	$40,000
Less: Accumulated depreciation	750
	$39,250

As you may expect, the accumulated depreciation account balance increases each period by the amount of depreciation expense recorded until the remaining book value of the asset equals the estimated salvage value.

Liability/Revenue Adjustments— Unearned Revenues

Reinforcing Problems

E3–9 Prepare entries for receipt of subscription fees and adjustment at year-end.

E3–10 Prepare entries for receipt of ticket fees, adjustment for earning revenues, and refund of fees.

A liability/revenue adjustment involving unearned revenues covers situations in which a customer has transferred assets, usually cash, to the selling company before the receipt of merchandise or services. Receiving assets before they are earned creates a liability called **unearned revenue.** The firm debits such receipts to the asset account Cash and credits a liability account. The liability account credited may be Unearned Fees, Revenue Received in Advance, Advances by Customers, or some similar title. The seller must either provide the services or return the customer's money. By performing the services, the company earns revenue and cancels the liability.

Companies receive advance payments for many items, such as training services, delivery services, tickets, and magazine or newspaper subscriptions. Although we illustrate and discuss only advanced receipt of training fees, firms treat the other items similarly.

UNEARNED SERVICE FEES   On December 7, MicroTrain Company received $4,500 from a customer in payment for future training services. The firm recorded the following journal entry:

1999					
Dec.	7	Cash		4,500	
		Unearned Service Fees			4,500
		To record the receipt of cash from a customer in payment for future training services.			

The two T-accounts relating to training fees are Unearned Service Fees (a liability) and Service Revenue. These accounts appear as follows on December 31, 1999 (before adjustment):

(Dr.)	**Unearned Service Fees**	*(Cr.)*
	1999	
	Dec. 7 Cash received	
	in advance 4,500	

(Dr.)	**Service Revenue**	*(Cr.)*
	1999	
	Bal. before adjustment 10,700*	

*The $10,700 balance came from transactions discussed in Chapter 2.

The balance in the Unearned Service Fees liability account established when MicroTrain received the cash will be converted into revenue as the company performs the training services. Before MicroTrain prepares its financial statements, it must make an adjusting entry to transfer the amount of the services performed by the company from a liability account to a revenue account. If we assume that MicroTrain earned one-third of the $4,500 in the Unearned Service Fees account by December 31, then the company transfers $1,500 to the Service Revenue account as follows:

Adjustment 5— Revenue earned

1999					
Dec.	31	Unearned Service Fees		1,500	
		Service Revenue			1,500
		To transfer a portion of training fees from the liability account to the revenue account.			

After posting the adjusting entry, the T-accounts would appear as follows:

(Dr.)	Unearned Service Fees			(Cr.)
Decreased by $1,500 →	1999 Dec. 31 Adjustment 5	1,500	1999 Dec. 7 Cash received in advance	4,500
			Bal. after adjustment	3,000

(Dr.)	Service Revenue		(Cr.)
		1999 Bal. before adjustment	10,700
		Dec. 31 Adjustment 5	1,500 ← *Increased by $1,500*
		Bal. after adjustment	12,200

MicroTrain reports the service revenue in its income statement for 1999. The company reports the $3,000 balance in the Unearned Service Fees account as a liability in the balance sheet. In 2000, the company will likely earn the $3,000 and transfer it to a revenue account.

If MicroTrain does not perform the training services, the company would have to refund the money to the training service customers. For instance, assume that MicroTrain could not perform the remaining $3,000 of training services and would have to refund the money. Then, the company would make the following entry:

Unearned Service Fees	3,000	
Cash		3,000
To record the refund of unearned training fees.		

Thus, the company must either perform the training services or refund the fees. This fact should strengthen your understanding that unearned service fees and similar items are liabilities.

Accountants make the adjusting entries for deferred items for data already recorded in a company's asset and liability accounts. They also make adjusting entries for accrued items, which we discuss in the next section, for business data not yet recorded in the accounting records.

BUSINESS INSIGHT   The U.S. Department of Labor Statistics predicted in 1994 that the need for accountants would rise by 40% by the year 2000. Accounting graduates with a bachelor's degree can expect to earn about $30,000 per year (give or take a few thousand) in their first year of employment. Master's degree holders earn about $4,000 per year more to start. Large firms generally pay more than small firms, and the amounts vary by section of the country. Salaries in both public accounting and in industry rise substantially with advancement. Six-figure incomes are common for partners of CPA firms and for controllers and chief financial officers in corporations. Communication skills, people skills, and critical thinking skills are vital to a successful career in accounting. Why not consider a career in accounting?

AN ACCOUNTING PERSPECTIVE

ADJUSTMENTS FOR ACCRUED ITEMS

Accrued items require two types of adjusting entries: asset/revenue adjustments and liability/expense adjustments. The first group—asset/revenue adjustments—involves accrued assets; the second group—liability/expense adjustments—involves accrued liabilities.

Accrued assets are assets, such as interest receivable or accounts receivable, that have not been recorded by the end of an accounting period. These assets represent rights to receive future payments that are not due at the balance sheet date. To present an accurate picture of the affairs of the business on the balance sheet, firms recognize

Asset/Revenue Adjustments— Accrued Assets

these rights at the end of an accounting period by preparing an adjusting entry to correct the account balances. To indicate the dual nature of these adjustments, they record a related revenue in addition to the asset. We also call these adjustments **accrued revenues** because the revenues must be recorded.

INTEREST REVENUE   Savings accounts literally earn interest moment by moment. Rarely is payment of the interest made on the last day of the accounting period. Thus, the accounting records normally do not show the interest revenue earned (but not yet received), which affects the total assets owned by the investor, unless the company makes an adjusting entry. The adjusting entry at the end of the accounting period debits a receivable account (an asset) and credits a revenue account to record the interest earned and the asset owned.

For example, assume MicroTrain Company has some money in a savings account. On December 31, 1999, the money on deposit has earned one month's interest of $600, although the company has not received the interest. An entry must show the amount of interest earned by December 31, 1999, as well as the amount of the asset, interest receivable (the right to receive this interest). The entry to record the accrual of revenue is:

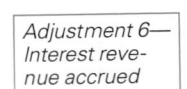

Adjustment 6—Interest revenue accrued	1999 Dec.	31	Interest Receivable	600	
			Interest Revenue		600
			To record one month's interest revenue.		

The T-accounts relating to interest would appear as follows:

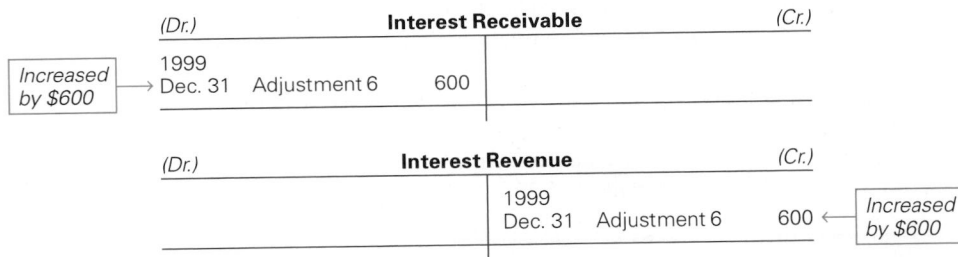

MicroTrain reports the $600 debit balance in Interest Receivable as an asset in the December 31, 1999, balance sheet. This asset accumulates gradually with the passage of time. The $600 credit balance in Interest Revenue is the interest earned during the month. Recall that in recording revenue under accrual basis accounting, it does not matter whether the company collects the actual cash during the year or not. It reports the interest revenue earned during the accounting period in the income statement.

UNBILLED TRAINING FEES   A company may perform services for customers in one accounting period while it bills for the services in a different accounting period.

MicroTrain Company performed $1,000 of training services on account for a client at the end of December. Since it takes time to do the paper work, MicroTrain will bill the client for the services in January. The necessary adjusting journal entry at December 31, 1999, is:

Reinforcing Problems
E3–11 Prepare adjusting entry for accrued legal services revenue.
E3–12 Prepare adjusting entry for accrued interest.

Adjustment 7—Unbilled revenues	1999 Dec.	31	Accounts Receivable (or Service Fees Receivable)	1,000	
			Service Revenue		1,000
			To record unbilled training services performed in December.		

After posting the adjusting entry, the T-accounts appear as follows:

	(Dr.)	**Accounts Receivable**		(Cr.)
	1999			
Increased by $1,000	Previous bal.	5,200*		
	Dec. 31 Adjustment 7	1,000		
	Bal. after adjustment	6,200		

*This previous balance came from transactions discussed in Chapter 2.

	(Dr.)	**Service Revenue**		(Cr.)	
		1999			
		Bal. before adjustment	10,700		
		Dec. 31 Adjustment 5—			
		previously			
		unearned			
		revenue	1,500		Increased by $1,000
		31 Adjustment 7	1,000		
		Bal. after both			
		adjustments	13,200		

The service revenue appears in the income statement; the asset, accounts receivable, appears in the balance sheet.

Accrued liabilities are liabilities not yet recorded at the end of an accounting period. They represent obligations to make payments not legally due at the balance sheet date, such as employee salaries. At the end of the accounting period, the company recognizes these obligations by preparing an adjusting entry including both a liability and an expense. For this reason, we also call these obligations **accrued expenses.**

SALARIES   The recording of the payment of employee salaries usually involves a debit to an expense account and a credit to Cash. Unless a company pays salaries on

Note to the Student
Which accounting period should be associated with the training services performed? Should it be the period in which the actual service was performed, or the period in which the bill was sent out and presumably collected?

Liability/Expense Adjustments— Accrued Liabilities

the last day of the accounting period for a pay period ending on that date, it must make an adjusting entry to record any salaries incurred but not yet paid.

MicroTrain Company paid $3,600 of salaries on Friday, December 28, 1999, to cover the first four weeks of December. The entry made at that time was:

1999					
Dec.	28	Salaries Expense	3,600	
		Cash		3,600
		Paid training employee salaries for the first four weeks of December.		

Assuming that the last day of December 1999 falls on a Monday, this expense account does not show salaries earned by employees for the last day of the month. Nor does any account show the employer's obligation to pay these salaries. The T-accounts pertaining to salaries appear as follows before adjustment:

(Dr.)	**Salaries Expense**	*(Cr.)*	*(Dr.)*	**Salaries Payable**	*(Cr.)*
1999 Dec. 28	3,600			1999 Dec. 28 Bal.	–0–

If salaries are $3,600 for four weeks, they are $900 per week. For a five-day work-week, daily salaries are $180. MicroTrain makes the following adjusting entry on December 31 to accrue salaries for one day:

1999					
Dec.	31	Salaries Expense	180	
		Salaries Payable.		180
		To accrue one day's salaries that were earned but are unpaid.		

After adjustment, the two T-accounts involved appear as follows:

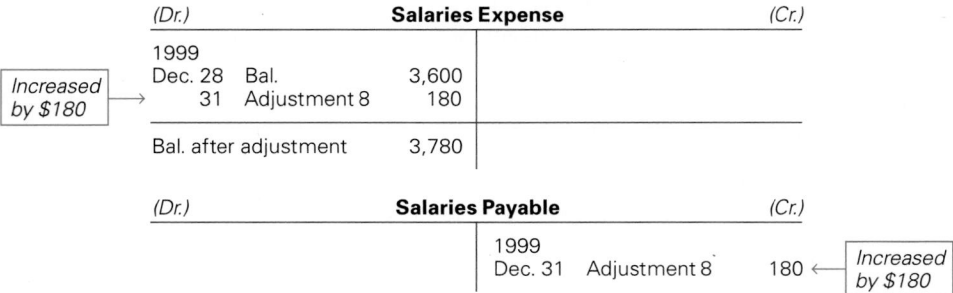

The debit in the adjusting journal entry brings the month's salaries expense up to its correct $3,780 amount for income statement purposes. The credit to Salaries Payable records the $180 salary liability to employees. The balance sheet shows salaries payable as a liability.

Another example of a liability/expense adjustment is when a company incurs interest on a note payable. The debit would be to Interest Expense, and the credit would be to Interest Payable. We discuss this adjustment in Chapter 9.

EFFECTS OF FAILING TO PREPARE ADJUSTING ENTRIES

Failure to prepare proper adjusting entries causes net income and the balance sheet to be in error. You can see the effect of failing to record each of the major types of adjusting entries on net income and balance sheet items in Illustration 3.5.

Failure to Recognize	Effect on Net Income	Effect on Balance Sheet Items
1. Consumption of the benefits of an asset (prepaid expense)	Overstates net income	Overstates assets Overstates retained earnings
2. Earning of previously unearned revenues	Understates net income	Overstates liabilities Understates retained earnings
3. Accrual of assets	Understates net income	Understates assets Understates retained earnings
4. Accrual of liabilities	Overstates net income	Understates liabilities Overstates retained earnings

ILLUSTRATION 3.5
Effects of Failure to Recognize Adjustments

Reinforcing Problems
E3–14 Determine effect on net income from failing to record adjusting entries.
E3–15 Show the effects of failing to recognize indicated adjustments.

Using MicroTrain Company as an example, this chapter has discussed and illustrated many of the typical entries that companies must make at the end of an accounting period. Later chapters explain other examples of adjusting entries.

Objective 5
Determine the effects of failing to prepare adjusting entries.

ANALYZING AND USING THE FINANCIAL RESULTS—TREND PERCENTAGES

It is sometimes more informative to express all the dollar amounts as a percentage of one of the amounts in the base year rather than to look only at the dollar amount of the item in the financial statements. You can calculate **trend percentages** by dividing the amount for each year for an item, such as net income or net sales, by the amount of that item for the base year:

$$\text{Trend percentage} = \frac{\text{Current year amount}}{\text{Base year amount}}$$

To illustrate, Wal-Mart Stores, Inc., and its subsidiaries reported the following net income for the years ended January 31, 1985, through 1995. The last column expresses these dollar amounts as a percentage of the 1985 amount. For instance, we would calculate the 121% for 1986 as:

$$\left[\left(\frac{\$327,000,000}{\$271,000,000} \right) \times 100 \right]$$

Objective 6
Analyze and use the financial results—trend percentages.

Wal-Mart
Wal-Mart Stores, Inc., is a mass consumer goods merchandiser with about 2,000 Wal-Mart stores and 430 Sam's Club stores throughout the nation.

	Dollar Amount of Net Income (millions)	Percentage of 1985 Net Income
1985	$ 271	100%
1986	327	121
1987	451	166
1988	628	232
1989	838	309
1990	1,076	397
1991	1,291	476
1992	1,609	594
1993	1,995	736
1994	2,333	861
1995	2,681	989

Reinforcing Problem
E3–16 Calculate the trend percentages for net income (loss) for Chrysler Corporation and comment.

Examining the trend percentages, we can see that Wal-Mart's net income has increased steadily over the 10-year period. The 1995 net income is almost 10 times as much as the 1985 amount. This is the kind of performance that management and stockholders seek. Sam Walton started and built this company; when he died in 1993, he was one of the world's richest individuals. Walton spent considerable time at his stores talking with employees and customers. Wal-Mart currently is considered to be one of the greatest success stories in American business.

In the first three chapters of this text, you have learned most of the steps of the accounting process. Chapter 4 shows the final steps in the accounting cycle.

<table>
<tr><td rowspan="2">AN ACCOUNTING
PERSPECTIVE</td><td colspan="2">USES OF TECHNOLOGY   The Internet sites of the Big-6 accounting firms are as follows:</td></tr>
<tr><td>Arthur Andersen & Co. LLP
Coopers & Lybrand LLP
Deloitte & Touche LLP
Ernst & Young LLP
KPMG Peat Marwick LLP
Price Waterhouse LLP</td><td>http://www.arthurandersen.com
http://www.colybrand.com
http://www.dttus.com
http://www.ey.com
http://www.kpmg.com
http://www.pw.com</td></tr>
</table>

You might want to visit these sites to learn more about a possible career in accounting.

UNDERSTANDING THE LEARNING OBJECTIVES

Objective 1
Describe the basic characteristics of the cash basis and the accrual basis of accounting.

- The cash basis of accounting recognizes revenues when cash is received and recognizes expenses when cash is paid out.
- The accrual basis of accounting recognizes revenues when sales are made or services are performed, regardless of when cash is received; expenses are recognized as incurred, whether or not cash has been paid out.
- The accrual basis is more generally accepted than the cash basis because it provides a better matching of revenues and expenses.

Objective 2
Identify the reasons why adjusting entries must be made.

- Adjusting entries convert the amounts that are actually in the accounts to the amounts that should be in the accounts for proper periodic financial reporting.
- Adjusting entries reflect unrecorded economic activity that has taken place but has not yet been recorded.

Objective 3
Identify the classes and types of adjusting entries.

- Deferred items consist of adjusting entries involving data previously recorded in accounts. Adjusting entries in this class normally involve moving data from asset and liability accounts to expense and revenue accounts. The two types of adjustments within this deferred items class are asset/expense adjustments and liability/revenue adjustments.
- Accrued items consist of adjusting entries relating to activity on which no data have been previously recorded in the accounts. These entries involve the initial recording of assets and liabilities and the related revenues and expenses. The two types of adjustments within this accrued items class are asset/revenue adjustments and liability/expense adjustments.

Objective 4
Prepare adjusting entries.

- This chapter illustrates entries for deferred items and accrued items.

Objective 5
Determine the effects of failing to prepare adjusting entries.

- Failure to prepare adjusting entries causes net income and the balance sheet to be in error.

Objective 6
Analyze and use the financial results—trend percentages.

- For a particular item such as sales or net income select a base year and express all dollar amounts in other years as a percentage of the base year dollar amount.

DEMONSTRATION PROBLEM

Among other items, the trial balance of Korman Company for December 31, 1999, includes the following account balances:

	Debits	**Credits**
Supplies on Hand	$ 6,000	
Prepaid Rent	25,200	
Buildings	200,000	
Accumulated Depreciation—Buildings		$33,250
Salaries Expense	124,000	
Unearned Delivery Fees		4,000

1. Some of the supplies represented by the $6,000 balance of the Supplies on Hand account *Additional data* have been consumed. An inventory count of the supplies actually on hand at December 31 totaled $2,400.

2. On May 1 of the current year, a rental payment of $25,200 was made for 12 months' rent; it was debited to Prepaid Rent.

3. The annual depreciation for the buildings is based on the cost shown in the Buildings account less an estimated salvage value of $10,000. The estimated useful lives of the buildings are 40 years each.

4. The salaries expense of $124,000 does not include $6,000 of unpaid salaries earned since the last payday.

5. The company has earned one-fourth of the unearned delivery fees by December 31.

6. Delivery services of $600 were performed for a customer, but a bill has not yet been sent.

a. Prepare the adjusting journal entries for December 31, assuming adjusting entries are *Required* prepared only at year-end.

b. Based on the adjusted balance shown in the Accumulated Depreciation—Buildings account, how many years has Korman Company owned the building?

SOLUTION TO DEMONSTRATION PROBLEM

a.

KORMAN COMPANY
General Journal

Date		Account Titles and Explanation	Post. Ref.	Debit	Credit
1999					
Dec.	31	Supplies Expense		3 6 0 0	
		Supplies on Hand			3 6 0 0
		To record supplies expense ($6,000 − $2,400).			
	31	Rent Expense		1 6 8 0 0	
		Prepaid Rent			1 6 8 0 0
		To record rent expense ($25,200 × 8/12).			
	31	Depreciation Expense—Buildings		4 7 5 0	
		Accumulated Depreciation—Buildings			4 7 5 0
		To record depreciation [($200,000 − $10,000) ÷ 40 years].			
	31	Salaries Expense		6 0 0 0	
		Salaries Payable			6 0 0 0
		To record accrued salaries.			
	31	Unearned Delivery Fees		1 0 0 0	
		Service Revenue			1 0 0 0
		To record delivery fees earned.			
	31	Accounts Receivable		6 0 0	
		Service Revenue			6 0 0
		To record delivery fees earned.			

b.   Eight years; computed as:

$$\frac{\text{Total accumulated depreciation}}{\text{Annual depreciation expense}} = \frac{\$33,250 + \$4,750}{\$4,750} = 8$$

New Terms

Accounting period   A time period normally of one month, one quarter, or one year into which an entity's life is arbitrarily divided for financial reporting purposes.   *102*

Accounting year   An accounting period of one year. The accounting year may or may not coincide with the calendar year.   *102*

Accrual basis of accounting   Recognizes revenues when sales are made or services are performed, regardless of when cash is received. Recognizes expenses as incurred, whether or not cash has been paid out.   *102*

Accrued assets and liabilities   Assets and liabilities that exist at the end of an accounting period but have not yet been recorded; they represent rights to receive, or obligations to make, payments that are not legally due at the balance sheet date. Examples are accrued fees receivable and salaries payable.   *113, 115*

Accrued items   Adjusting entries relating to activity on which no data have been previously recorded in the accounts. Also, see *accrued assets and liabilities.*

Accrued revenues and expenses   Other names for accrued assets and liabilities.   *114, 115*

Accumulated depreciation account   A contra asset account that shows the total of all depreciation recorded on the asset up through the balance sheet date.   *111*

Adjusting entries   Journal entries made at the end of an accounting period to bring about a proper matching of revenues and expenses; they reflect economic activity that has taken place but has not yet been recorded. Adjusting entries are made to bring the accounts to their proper balances before financial statements are prepared.   *103*

Book value   For depreciable assets, book value equals cost less accumulated depreciation.   *111*

Calendar year   The normal year, which ends on December 31.   *102*

Cash basis of accounting   Recognizes revenues when cash is received and recognizes expenses when cash is paid out.   *101*

Contra asset account   An account shown as a deduction from the asset to which it relates in the balance sheet; used to reduce the original cost of the asset down to its remaining undepreciated cost or book value.   *111*

Deferred items   Adjusting entries involving data previously recorded in the accounts. Data are transferred from asset and liability accounts to expense and revenue accounts. Examples are prepaid expenses, depreciation, and unearned revenues.   *104*

Depreciable amount   The difference between an asset's cost and its estimated salvage value.   *110*

Depreciable asset   A manufactured asset such as a building, machine, vehicle, or equipment on which depreciation expense is recorded.   *110*

Depreciation accounting   The process of recording depreciation expense.   *110*

Depreciation expense   The amount of asset cost assigned as an expense to a particular time period.   *110*

Depreciation formula (straight-line):

$$\text{Annual depreciation} = \frac{\text{Asset cost} - \text{Estimated salvage value}}{\text{Estimated years of useful life}} \qquad 110$$

Estimated salvage value (scrap value)   The amount that the company can probably sell the asset for at the end of its estimated useful life.   *110*

Estimated useful life   The estimated time periods that a company can make use of the asset.   *110*

Fiscal year   An accounting year of any 12 consecutive months that may or may not coincide with the calendar year. For example, a company may have an accounting, or fiscal, year that runs from April 1 of one year to March 31 of the next.   *102*

Matching principle   An accounting principle requiring that expenses incurred in producing revenues be deducted from the revenues they generated during the accounting period.   *103*

Prepaid expense   An asset awaiting assignment to expense. An example is prepaid insurance. Assets such as cash and accounts receivable are not prepaid expenses.   *106*

Service potential   The benefits that can be obtained from assets. The future services that assets can render make assets "things of value" to a business.   *106*

Trend percentages   Calculated by dividing the amount of an item for each year by the amount of that item for the base year.   *117*

Unearned revenue   Assets received from customers before services are performed for them. Since the revenue has not been earned, it is a liability, often called *revenue received in advance* or *advances by customers.*   *112*

SELF-TEST

TRUE-FALSE

1. Every adjusting entry affects at least one income statement account and one balance sheet account.

2. All calendar years are also fiscal years, but not all fiscal years are calendar years.

3. The accumulated depreciation account is an asset account that shows the amount of depreciation for the current year only.

4. The Unearned Delivery Fees account is a revenue account.

5. If all of the adjusting entries are not made, the financial statements are incorrect.

MULTIPLE-CHOICE

Select the best answer for each of the following questions.

1. An insurance policy premium of $1,200 was paid on September 1, 1999, to cover a one-year period from that date. An asset was debited on that date. Adjusting entries are prepared once a year, at year-end. The necessary adjusting entry at the company's year-end, December 31, 1999, is:

   a. Prepaid Insurance 400
   　　Insurance Expense . . . 　　　400
   b. Insurance Expense 800
   　　Prepaid Insurance . . . . 　　　800
   c. Prepaid Insurance 800
   　　Insurance Expense . . . 　　　800
   d. Insurance Expense 400
   　　Prepaid Insurance . . . . 　　　400

2. The Supplies on Hand account has a balance of $1,500 at year-end. The actual amount of supplies on hand at the end of the period was $400. The necessary adjusting entry is:

   a. Supplies Expense 1,100
   　　Supplies on Hand . . . . 　　　1,100
   b. Supplies Expense 400
   　　Supplies on Hand . . . . 　　　400
   c. Supplies on Hand 1,100
   　　Supplies Expense . . . . 　　　1,100
   d. Supplies on Hand 400
   　　Supplies Expense . . . . 　　　400

3. A company purchased a truck for $20,000 on January 1, 1999. The truck has an estimated salvage value of $5,000 and is expected to last five years. Adjusting entries are prepared only at year-end. The necessary adjusting entry at December 31, 1999, the company's year-end, is:

   a. Depreciation Expense—Trucks 4,000
   　　Accumulated Deprecia-
   　　tion—Trucks . . . . . 　　　4,000
   b. Depreciation Expense—Trucks 3,000
   　　Trucks . . . . 　　　3,000
   c. Depreciation Expense—Trucks 3,000
   　　Accumulated Deprecia-
   　　tion—Trucks . . . . . 　　　3,000

   d. Accumulated Depreciation
   　　Trucks 3,000
   　　Depreciation Expense—
   　　Trucks . . . . 　　　3,000

4. A company received cash of $24,000 on October 1, 1999, as subscriptions for a one-year period from that date. A liability account was credited when the cash was received. The magazine is to be published by the company and delivered to subscribers each month. The company prepares adjusting entries at the end of each month because it prepares financial statements each month. The adjusting entry the company would make at the end of each of the next 12 months would be:

   a. Unearned Subscription Fees. . 6,000
   　　Subscription Fee Revenue 　　　6,000
   b. Unearned Subscription Fees. . 2,000
   　　Subscription Fee Revenue 　　　2,000
   c. Unearned Subscription Fees. . 18,000
   　　Subscription Fee Revenue 　　　18,000
   d. Subscription Fee Revenue. . . 2,000
   　　Unearned Subscription
   　　Fees . . . . 　　　2,000

5. When a company earns interest on a note receivable or on a bank account, the debit and credit are as follows:

	Debit	**Credit**
a.	Accounts Receivable	Interest Revenue
b.	Interest Receivable	Interest Revenue
c.	Interest Revenue	Accounts Receivable
d.	Interest Revenue	Interest Receivable

6. If $3,000 has been earned by a company's workers since the last payday in an accounting period, the necessary adjusting entry would be:

   a. Debit an expense and credit a liability.
   b. Debit an expense and credit an asset.
   c. Debit a liability and credit an asset.
   d. Debit a liability and credit an expense.

Now turn to page 131 to check your answers.

QUESTIONS

1. Which events during an accounting period trigger the recording of normal journal entries? Which event triggers the making of adjusting entries?

2. Describe the difference between the cash basis and accrual basis of accounting.

3. Why are adjusting entries necessary? Why not treat every cash disbursement as an expense and every cash receipt as a revenue when the cash changes hands?

4. "Adjusting entries would not be necessary if the 'pure' cash basis of accounting were followed (assuming no mistakes were made in recording cash transactions as they occurred). Under the cash basis, receipts that are of a revenue nature are considered revenue when received, and expenditures that are of an expense nature are considered expenses when paid. It is the use of the accrual basis of accounting, where an effort is made to match expenses incurred against the revenues they create, that makes adjusting entries necessary." Do you agree with this statement? Why?

5. Why don't accountants keep all the accounts at their proper balances continuously throughout the period so that adjusting entries would not have to be made before financial statements are prepared?

6. What is the fundamental difference between deferred items and accrued items?

7. Identify the types of adjusting entries included in each of the two major classes of adjusting entries.

8. Give an example of a journal entry for each of the following:
   a. Equal growth of an expense and a liability.
   b. Earning of revenue that was previously recorded as unearned revenue.
   c. Equal growth of an asset and a revenue.
   d. Increase in an expense and decrease in an asset.

9. A fellow student makes the following statement: "You can easily tell whether a company is using the cash or accrual basis of accounting. When an amount is paid for future rent or insurance services, a firm that is using the cash basis debits an expense account while a firm that is using the accrual basis debits an asset account." Is the student correct?

10. You notice that the Supplies on Hand account has a debit balance of $2,700 at the end of the accounting period. How would you determine the extent to which this account needs adjustment?

11. Some assets are converted into expenses as they expire and some liabilities become revenues as they are earned. Give examples of asset and liability accounts for which this statement is true. Give examples of asset and liability accounts to which the statement does not apply.

12. Give the depreciation formula to compute straight-line depreciation for a one-year period.

13. What does the term *accrued liability* mean?

14. What is meant by the term *service potential?*

15. When assets are received before they are earned, what type of an account is credited? As the amounts are earned, what type of account is credited?

16. What does the word *accrued* mean? Is there a conceptual difference between interest payable and accrued interest payable?

17. Matching expenses incurred with revenues earned is more difficult than matching expenses paid with revenues received. Do you think the effort is worthwhile?

18. Refer to "A Broader Perspective" on page 115. What type of adjusting entry is involved? How do you think the managements of some companies might react to having to record postretirement benefits in this way?

The Coca-Cola Company

19. **Real World Question** Refer to the financial statements of The Coca-Cola Company in its annual report in the annual report booklet. Approximately what percentage of the depreciable assets under property, plant, and equipment has been depreciated as of December 31, 1996?

MAYTAG

20. **Real World Question** Refer to the financial statements of Maytag Corporation in the annual report booklet. What percentage of depreciable property, plant, and equipment has been depreciated as of December 31, 1996? (Construction in progress is not a depreciable asset.)

EXERCISES

Exercise 3–1
Answer multiple-choice questions (L.O. 1)

Select the correct response for each of the following multiple-choice questions:

1. The cash basis of accounting:
   a. Recognizes revenues when sales are made or services are rendered.
   b. Recognizes expenses as incurred.
   c. Is typically used by some relatively small businesses and professional persons.
   d. Recognizes revenues when cash is received and recognizes expenses when incurred.

2. The accrual basis of accounting:
   a. Recognizes revenues only when cash is received.
   b. Is used by almost all companies.
   c. Recognizes expenses only when cash is paid out.

d. Recognizes revenues when sales are made or services are performed and recognizes expenses only when cash is paid out.

Select the correct response for each of the following multiple-choice questions:

1. The least common accounting period among the following is:
   a. One month.
   b. Two months.
   c. Three months.
   d. Twelve months.

2. The need for adjusting entries is based on:
   a. The matching principle.
   b. Source documents.
   c. The cash basis of accounting.
   d. Activity that has already been recorded in the proper accounts.

Exercise 3–2
Answer multiple-choice questions (L.O. 2)

Select the correct response for each of the following multiple-choice questions:

1. Which of the following types of adjustments belongs to the deferred items class?
   a. Asset/revenue adjustments.
   b. Liability/expense adjustments.
   c. Asset/expense adjustments.
   d. Asset/liability adjustments.

2. Which of the following types of adjustments belongs to the accrued items class?
   a. Asset/expense adjustments.
   b. Liability/revenue adjustments.
   c. Asset/liability adjustments.
   d. Liability/expense adjustments.

Exercise 3–3
Answer multiple-choice questions (L.O. 3)

a. A one-year insurance policy was purchased on August 1 for $2,400, and the following entry was made at that time:

Prepaid Insurance	2,400	
Cash		2,400

What adjusting entry is necessary at December 31, the end of the accounting year?

b. Show how the T-accounts for Prepaid Insurance and Insurance Expense would appear after the entries are posted.

Exercise 3–4
Prepare and post adjusting entry for insurance (L.O. 4)

Assume that rent of $12,000 was paid on September 1, 1999, to cover a one-year period from that date. Prepaid Rent was debited. If financial statements are prepared only on December 31 of each year, what adjusting entry is necessary on December 31, 1999, to bring the accounts involved to their proper balances?

Exercise 3–5
Prepare adjusting entry for rent (L.O. 4)

At December 31, 1999, an adjusting entry was made as follows:

Rent Expense	1,500	
Prepaid Rent		1,500

Exercise 3–6
Determine date and entry for rent paid (L.O. 4)

You know that the gross amount of rent paid was $4,500, which was to cover a one-year period. Determine:

a. The opening date of the year to which the $4,500 of rent applies.
b. The entry that was made on the date the rent was paid.

Supplies were purchased for cash on May 2, 1999, for $8,000. Show how this purchase would be recorded. Then show the adjusting entry that would be necessary, assuming that $2,500 of the supplies remained at the end of the year.

Exercise 3–7
Prepare entries for purchase of supplies and adjustment at year-end (L.O. 4)

Assume that a company acquired a building on January 1, 1999, at a cost of $1,000,000. The building has an estimated useful life of 40 years and an estimated salvage value of $200,000. What adjusting entry is needed on December 31, 1999, to record the depreciation for the entire year 1999?

Exercise 3–8
Prepare adjusting entry for depreciation (L.O. 4)

Exercise 3–9
Prepare entries for receipt of subscription fees and adjustment at year-end (L.O. 4)

On September 1, 1999, Professional Golfer Journal, Inc., received a total of $120,000 as payment in advance for one-year subscriptions to a monthly magazine. A liability account was credited to record this cash receipt. By the end of the year, one-third of the magazines paid for in advance had been delivered. Give the entries to record the receipt of the subscription fees and to adjust the accounts at December 31, assuming annual financial statements are prepared at year-end.

Exercise 3–10
Prepare entries for receipt of ticket fees, adjustment for earning revenue, and refund of fees (L.O. 4)

On April 15, 1999, Rialto Theater sold $90,000 in tickets for the summer musicals to be performed (one per month) during June, July, and August. On July 15, 1999, Rialto Theater discovered that the group that was to perform the July and August musicals could not do so. It was too late to find another group qualified to perform the musicals. A decision was made to refund the remaining unearned ticket revenue to its ticket holders, and this was done on July 20. Show the appropriate journal entries to be made on April 15, June 30, and July 20. Rialto has a June 30th year-end.

Exercise 3–11
Prepare adjusting entry for accrued legal services (L.O. 4)

Guilty & Innocent, a law firm, performed legal services in late December 1999 for clients. The $30,000 of services would be billed to the clients in January 2000. Give the adjusting entry that is necessary on December 31, 1999, if financial statements are prepared at the end of each month.

Exercise 3–12
Prepare adjusting entry for accrued interest (L.O. 4)

A firm borrowed $30,000 on November 1. By December 31, $300 of interest had been incurred. Prepare the adjusting entry required on December 31.

Exercise 3–13
Prepare adjusting entry for accrued salaries (L.O. 4)

Convenient Mailing Services, Inc., incurs salaries at the rate of $3,000 per day. The last payday in January is Friday, January 27. Salaries for Monday and Tuesday of the next week have not been recorded or paid as of January 31. Financial statements are prepared monthly. Give the necessary adjusting entry on January 31.

Exercise 3–14
Determine effect on net income from failing to record adjusting entries (L.O. 5)

State the effect that each of the following independent situations would have on the amount of annual net income reported for 1999 and 2000.

a. No adjustment was made for accrued salaries of $8,000 as of December 31, 1999.

b. The collection of $5,000 for services yet unperformed as of December 31, 1999, was credited to a revenue account and not adjusted. The services are performed in 2000.

Exercise 3–15
Show the effects of failing to recognize indicated adjustments (L.O. 5)

In the following table, indicate the effects of failing to recognize each of the indicated adjustments by writing "O" for overstated and "U" for understated.

| | | | Effect on Balance Sheet Items | |
| | Effect on Net Income | Assets | Liabilities | Stockholders' Equity |
Failure to Recognize				
1. Depreciation on a building				
2. Consumption of supplies on hand				
3. The earning of ticket revenue received in advance				
4. The earning of interest on a bank account				
5. Salaries incurred but unpaid				

Exercise 3–16
Calculate the trend percentages for net income (loss) for Chrysler Corporation and comment (L.O. 6)

The following data regarding net income (earnings) are for the Chrysler Corporation for the period 1986–95. Chrysler Corporation is one of the world's largest auto manufacturers.

	Net Income (Earnings) ($ millions)		Net Income (Earnings) ($ millions)
1986	1,389	1991	(795)
1987	1,290	1992	723
1988	1,050	1993	(2,551)
1989	359	1994	3,713
1990	68	1995	2,025

Using 1986 as the base year, calculate the trend percentages, and comment on the results.

PROBLEMS

The trial balance of Caribbean Vacation Tours, Inc., at December 31 of the current year includes, among other items, the following account balances:

	Debits	Credits
Prepaid Insurance	$ 24,000	
Prepaid Rent	24,000	
Buildings	188,000	
Accumulated Depreciation—Buildings		$31,600
Salaries Expense	200,000	

1. The balance in the Prepaid Insurance account is the advance premium for one year from September 1 of the current year.
2. The buildings are expected to last 25 years, with an expected salvage value of $30,000.
3. Salaries incurred but not paid as of December 31 amount to $8,400.
4. The balance in Prepaid Rent is for a one-year period that started March 1 of the current year.

Prepare the annual year-end adjusting journal entries at December 31.

Problem 3–1
Prepare adjusting entries
(L.O. 4)

Additional data

Required

Among the account balances shown in the trial balance of Dunwoody Mail Station, Inc., at December 31 of the current year are the following:

	Debits	Credits
Supplies on Hand	$ 10,000	
Prepaid Insurance	6,000	
Buildings	168,000	
Accumulated Depreciation—Buildings		$39,000

1. The inventory of supplies on hand at December 31 amounts to $3,000.
2. The balance in the Prepaid Insurance account is for a two-year policy taken out June 1 of the current year.
3. Depreciation for the buildings is based on the cost shown in the Buildings account, less salvage value estimated at $18,000. When acquired, the lives of the buildings were estimated at 50 years each.

a. Prepare the year-end adjusting journal entries at December 31. Assume you used page 27 of the general journal to record the journal entries.
b. Open ledger accounts for each of the accounts involved, enter the balances as shown in the trial balance, post the adjusting journal entries, and calculate year-end balances.

Problem 3–2
Prepare adjusting entries
and post to ledger accounts
(L.O. 4)

Additional data

Required

Nevada Camping Equipment Rental Company occupies rented quarters on the main street of Las Vegas. To get this location, the company rented a store larger than needed and subleased (rented) a portion of the area to Max's Restaurant. The partial trial balance of Nevada Camping Equipment Rental Company as of December 31, 1999, is as follows:

Problem 3–3
Prepare adjusting entries
(L.O. 4)

NEVADA CAMPING EQUIPMENT RENTAL COMPANY
Partial Trial Balance
December 31, 1999

	Debits	Credits
Cash	$100,000	
Prepaid Insurance	11,400	
Supplies on Hand	20,000	
Camping Equipment	176,000	
Accumulated Depreciation—Camping Equipment		$ 19,200
Notes Payable		40,000
Equipment Rental Revenue		1,500,000
Sublease Rental Revenue		8,800
Building Rent Expense	14,400	
Salaries Expense	196,000	

a. Salaries of employees amount to $300 per day and were last paid through Wednesday, December 27. December 31 is a Sunday. The store is closed Sundays.

Additional data

b. An analysis of the Camping Equipment account disclosed:

Balance, January 1, 1999	$128,000
Addition, July 1, 1999	48,000
Balance, December 31, 1997, per trial balance . . .	$176,000

The company estimates that all equipment will last 20 years from the date they were acquired and that the salvage value will be zero.

c. The store carries one combined insurance policy, which is taken out once a year effective August 1. The premium on the policy now in force amounts to $7,200 per year.

d. Unused supplies on hand at December 31, 1999, have a cost of $9,200.

e. December's rent from Max's Restaurant has not yet been received, $800.

f. Interest accrued on the note payable is $700.

Required   Prepare the annual year-end entries required by the preceding statement of facts.

Problem 3–4
Calculate correct net income (L.O. 5)

The reported net income amounts for Safety Waste Control Company were 1999, $200,000; and 2000, $230,000. *No* annual adjusting entries were made at either year-end for any of these transactions:

a. A building was rented on April 1, 1999. Cash of $14,400 was paid on that date to cover a two-year period. Prepaid Rent was debited.

b. The balance in the Office Supplies on Hand account on December 31, 1999, was $6,000. An inventory of the supplies on December 31, 1999, revealed that only $3,500 were actually on hand at that date. No new supplies were purchased during 1998. At December 31, 2000, an inventory of the supplies revealed that $800 were on hand.

c. A building costing $1,200,000 and having an estimated useful life of 40 years and a salvage value of $240,000 was put into service on January 1, 1999.

d. Services were performed for customers in December 1999. The $24,000 bill for these services was not sent until January 2000. The only transaction that was recorded was a debit to Cash and a credit to Service Revenue when payment was received in January.

Required   Calculate the correct net income for 1999 and 2000. In your answer, start with the reported net income amounts. Then show the effects of each correction (adjustment) using a plus or a minus to indicate whether reported income should be increased or decreased as a result of the correction. When the corrections are added to or deducted from the reported net income amounts, the result should be the correct net income amounts. The answer format should be as follows:

Explanation of Corrections	**1999**	**2000**
Reported net income	$200,000	$230,000
To correct error in accounting for:		
a. Prepaid rent:		
Correct expense in 1999	−5,400	
Correct expense in 2000		−7,200

Problem 3–5
Prepare journal entries under cash basis and accrual basis (L.O. 1, 4)

On June 1, 1999, Richard Cross opened a swimming pool cleaning and maintenance service, Cross Pool Company. He vaguely recalled the process of making journal entries and establishing ledger accounts from a high school bookkeeping course he had taken some years ago. At the end of June, he prepared an income statement for the month of June, but he had the feeling that he had not proceeded correctly. He contacted his brother, John, a recent college graduate with a major in accounting, for assistance. John immediately noted that his brother had kept his records on a cash basis.

Transactions   June 1   Received cash of $28,000 from various customers in exchange for service agreements to clean and maintain their pools for June, July, August, and September.

5   Paid rent for automotive and cleaning equipment to be used during the period June through September, $8,000. The payment covered the entire period.

8   Purchased a two-year liability insurance policy effective June 1 for $12,000 cash.

10   Received an advance of $9,000 from a Florida building contractor in exchange for an agreement to help service pools in his housing development during October through May.

June 16   Paid salaries for the first half of June, $8,400.

17   Paid $900 for advertising to be run in a local newspaper for two weeks in June and four weeks in July.

19   Paid the rent of $24,000 under a four-month lease on a building rented and occupied on June 1.

26   Purchased $5,400 of supplies for cash. (Only $900 of these supplies were used in June.)

29   Billed various customers for services rendered, $16,000.

30   Unpaid employee services received in the last half of June amounted to $12,600.

30   Received a bill for $600 for gas and oil used in June.

a.   Prepare the entries for the transactions as Richard must have recorded them under the cash basis of accounting.

Required

b.   Prepare journal entries as they would have been prepared under the accrual basis. Where the entry is the same as under the cash basis, merely indicate "same." Where possible, record the original transaction so that no adjusting entry would be necessary at the end of the month. Ignore explanations.

Alternate Problems

Among other items, the trial balance of Filmblaster, Inc., a movie rental company, at December 31 of the current year includes the following account balances:

Problem 3–1A
Prepare adjusting entries
(L.O. 4)

	Debits
Prepaid Insurance	$10,000
Prepaid Rent	14,400
Supplies on Hand	2,800

Examination of the records shows that adjustments should be made for the following items:

a.   Of the prepaid insurance in the trial balance, $4,000 is for coverage during the months after December 31 of the current year.

b.   The balance in the Prepaid Rent account is for a 12-month period that started October 1 of the current year.

c. $300 of interest has been earned but not received.

d.   Supplies used during the year amount to $1,800.

Prepare the annual year-end adjusting journal entries at December 31.

Required

Marathon Magazine, Inc., has the following account balances, among others, in its trial balance at December 31 of the current year:

Problem 3–2A
Prepare adjusting entries
and post to ledger accounts
(L.O. 4)

	Debits	**Credits**
Supplies on Hand	$ 3,720	
Prepaid Rent	7,200	
Unearned Subscription Fees		$ 15,000
Subscriptions Revenue		261,000
Salaries Expense	123,000	

1.   The inventory of supplies on hand at December 31 amounts to $720.

Additional data

2.   The balance in the Prepaid Rent account is for a one-year period starting October 1 of the current year.

3.   One-third of the $15,000 balance in Unearned Subscription Fees has been earned.

4.   Since the last payday, the employees of the company have earned additional salaries in the amount of $5,430.

a.   Prepare the year-end adjusting journal entries at December 31. Assume you used page 22 of the general journal to record the journal entries.

Required

b.   Open ledger accounts for each of the accounts involved, enter the balances as shown in the trial balance, post the adjusting journal entries, and calculate year-end balances.

Hillside Apartments, Inc., adjusts and closes its books each December 31. Assume the accounts for all prior years have been properly adjusted and closed. Following are some of the company's account balances prior to adjustment on December 31, 1999:

Problem 3–3A
Prepare adjusting entries
(L.O. 4)

HILLSIDE APARTMENTS, INC.
Partial Trial Balance
December 31, 1999

	Debits	Credits
Prepaid Insurance	$ 7,500	
Supplies on Hand	7,000	
Buildings	255,000	
Accumulated Depreciation—Buildings		$ 96,000
Unearned Rent		2,700
Salaries Expense	69,000	
Rental Revenue		277,500

Additional data

1. The Prepaid Insurance account balance represents the remaining cost of a four-year insurance policy dated June 30, 1997, having a total premium of $12,000.

2. The physical inventory of the office supply stockroom indicates that the supplies on hand cost $3,000.

3. The building was originally acquired on January 1, 1983, at which time management estimated that the building would last 40 years and have a salvage value of $15,000.

4. Salaries earned since the last payday but unpaid at December 31 amount to $5,000.

5. Interest earned but not collected on a savings account during the year amounts to $400.

6. The Unearned Rent account arose through the prepayment of rent by a tenant in the building for 12 months beginning October 1, 1999.

Required   Prepare the annual year-end adjusting entries indicated by the additional data.

Problem 3–4A
Calculate correct net income (L.O. 5)

The reported net income amounts for Gulf Coast Magazine, Inc., for calendar years 1999 and 2000 were $200,000 and $222,000, respectively. No annual adjusting entries were made at either year-end for any of the following transactions:

1. A fire insurance policy to cover a three-year period from the date of payment was purchased on March 1, 1999, for $3,600. The Prepaid Insurance account was debited at the date of purchase.

2. Subscriptions for magazines in the amount of $72,000 to cover an 18-month period from May 1, 1999, were received on April 15, 1999. The Unearned Subscription Fees account was credited when the payments were received.

3. A building costing $180,000 and having an estimated useful life of 50 years and a salvage value of $30,000 was purchased and put into service on January 1, 1999.

4. On January 12, 2000, salaries of $9,600 were paid to employees. The account debited was Salaries Expense. One-third of the amount paid was earned by employees in December of 1999.

Required   Calculate the correct net income for 1999 and 2000. In your answer, start with the reported net income. Then show the effects of each correction (adjustment), using a plus or a minus to indicate whether reported income should be increased or decreased as a result of the correction. When the corrections are added to or deducted from the reported net income amounts, the result should be the correct net income amounts. The answer format should appear as follows:

Explanation of Corrections	1999	2000
Reported net income	$200,000	$222,000
To correct error in accounting for:		
a. Fire insurance policy premium:		
Correct expense in 1999	−1,000	
Correct expense in 2000		−1,200

Problem 3–5A
Prepare journal entries under cash basis and accrual basis (L.O. 1, 4)

Jupiter Publishing Company began operations on December 1, 1999. The company's bookkeeper intended to use the cash basis of accounting. Consequently, the bookkeeper recorded all cash receipts and disbursements for items relating to operations in revenue and expense accounts. No adjusting entries were made prior to preparing the financial statements for December.

Transactions   Dec. 1   Issued capital stock for $300,000 cash.

3   Received $144,000 for magazine subscriptions to run for two years from this date. The magazine is published monthly on the 23rd.

Dec. 4 Paid for advertising to be run in a national periodical for six months (starting this month). The cost was $36,000.

7 Purchased for cash an insurance policy to cover a two-year period beginning December 15, $24,000.

12 Paid the annual rent on the building, $36,000, effective through November 30, 2000.

15 Received $216,000 cash for two-year subscriptions starting with the December issue.

15 Salaries for the period December 1–15 amounted to $48,000. Beginning as of this date, salaries will be paid on the 5th and 20th of each month for the preceding two-week period.

20 Salaries for the period December 1–15 were paid.

23 Supplies purchased for cash, $21,600. (Only $1,800 of these were subsequently used in 1999.)

27 Printing costs applicable equally to the next six issues beginning with the December issue were paid in cash, $144,000.

31 Cash sales of the December issue, $84,000.

31 Unpaid salaries for the period December 16–31 amounted to $22,000.

31 Sales on account of December issue, $14,000.

a. Prepare journal entries for the transactions as the bookkeeper prepared them.

b. Prepare journal entries as they would have been prepared under the accrual basis. Where the entry is the same as under the cash basis, merely indicate "same." Where possible, record the original transaction so that no adjusting entry would be necessary at the end of the month. Ignore explanations.

Required

Beyond the Numbers—Critical Thinking

You have just been hired by Top Executive Employment Agency, Inc., to help prepare adjusting entries at the end of an accounting period. It becomes obvious to you that management does not seem to have much of an understanding about the necessity for adjusting entries or which accounts might possibly need adjustment. The first step you take is to prepare the following unadjusted trial balance from the general ledger. Only those ledger accounts that had end-of-year balances are included in the trial balance.

Business Decision Case 3–1
Explain why adjusting entries are made and which accounts need adjustment (L.O. 2, 4)

	Debits	Credits
Cash	$ 80,000	
Accounts Receivable	28,000	
Supplies on Hand	3,000	
Prepaid Insurance	2,700	
Office Equipment	120,000	
Accumulated Depreciation—Office Equipment		$ 45,000
Buildings	360,000	
Accumulated Depreciation—Buildings		105,000
Accounts Payable		9,000
Loan Payable (Bank)		15,000
Unearned Commission Fees		30,000
Capital Stock		160,000
Retained Earnings		89,300
Commissions Revenue		270,000
Advertising Expense	6,000	
Salaries Expense	112,500	
Utilities Expense	7,500	
Miscellaneous Expense	3,600	
	$723,300	$723,300

a. Explain to management why adjusting entries in general are made.

b. Explain to management why some of the specific accounts appearing in the trial balance may need adjustment and what the nature of each adjustment might be (do not worry about specific dollar amounts).

Required

Business Decision Case 3–2

Prepare an appraisal and an approximate income statement (L.O. 1, 4)

A friend of yours, Jack Andrews, is quite excited over the opportunity he has to purchase the land and several miscellaneous assets of Drake Bowling Lanes Company for $400,000. Andrews tells you that Mr. and Mrs. Drake (the sole stockholders in the company) are moving due to Mr. Drake's ill health. The annual rent on the building and equipment is $54,000.

Drake reports that the business earned a profit of $100,000 in 1999 (last year). Andrews believes an annual profit of $100,000 on an investment of $400,000 is a really good deal. But, before completing the deal, he asks you to look it over. You agree and discover the following:

1. Drake has computed his annual profit for 1999 as the sum of his cash dividends plus the increase in the Cash account: Dividends of $60,000 + Increase in Cash account of $40,000 = $100,000 profit.

2. As buyer of the business, Andrews will take over responsibility for repayment of a $300,000 loan (plus interest) on the land. The land was acquired at a cost of $624,000 seven years ago.

3. An analysis of the Cash account shows the following for 1999:

Rental revenues received		$465,000
Cash paid out in 1999 for—		
Salaries paid to employees	$260,000	
Utilities paid	18,000	
Advertising expenses paid	15,000	
Supplies purchased and used	24,000	
Interest paid on loan	18,000	
Loan principal paid	30,000	
Cash dividends	60,000	425,000
Increase in cash balance for the year		$ 40,000

4. You also find that the annual rent of $54,000, a December utility bill of $4,000, and an advertising bill of $6,000 have not been paid.

Required

a. Prepare a written report for Andrews giving your appraisal of Drake Bowling Lanes Company as an investment. Comment on Drake's method of computing the annual profit of the business.

b. Include in your report an approximate income statement for 1999.

Annual Report Analysis 3–3

Develop trend percentages for The Coca-Cola Company's net income and comment (L.O. 6)

Turn to the "Selected Financial Data" section of The Coca-Cola Company's annual report in the annual report booklet. Prepare trend percentages for the net income amounts using 1986 as the base year. Comment on the trend of performance.

Group Project 3–4

Undertake library project concerning annual reports (L.O. 6)

In teams of two or three students, go to the library to locate one company's annual report for the most recent year. (The university may have received the annual reports of companies either in published form, in microfiche form, or in computer readable format.) Identify the name of the company and the major products or services offered, as well as gross revenues, major expenses, and the trend of profits over the last three years. Calculate trend percentages for revenues, expenses, and profits using the oldest year as the base year. Each team should write a memorandum to management summarizing the data and commenting on the trend percentages. The heading of the memorandum should contain the date, to whom it is written, from whom, and the subject matter.

Group Project 3–5

Perform library research

With one or two other students and using library sources, write a paper on *Statement of Accounting Standards No. 106,* "Accounting for Postretirement Benefits Other Than Pensions." This standard resulted in some of the largest adjusting entries ever made. Companies had to record an expense and a liability to account for these costs on an accrual basis. In the past they typically had recorded this expense on a cash basis, recognizing the expense only when cash was paid to retirees. Be sure to cite your sources and treat direct quotes properly.

Group Project 3–6

Perform library research

With one or two other students and using library sources, write a paper on human resource accounting. Generally accepted accounting principles do not allow "human assets" to be included among assets on the balance sheet. Why is this? Be sure to cite your sources and to treat direct quotes properly.

USING THE INTERNET—A VIEW OF THE REAL WORLD

Visit the website:

http://www.arthurandersen.com

Click on Career Opportunities. Then click on Explore the Work We Do. Summarize the services they provide and click on one of those services for more detailed information and then click on any other information that looks interesting. Write a report to your instructor summarizing your findings.

Visit the website:

http://www.dttus.com

Then click on Supporting Work/Life Balance. Read the information and then return to the home page and click on D&T Initiatives for Women. Read the information and click on any subtopics that look interesting. Give an oral report to your class on your findings.

Internet Project 3–7
Check out Arthur
Andersen

Internet Project 3–8
Check out Deloitte
& Touche

ANSWERS TO SELF-TEST

TRUE-FALSE

1. **True.** Every adjusting entry involves either moving previously recorded data from an asset account to an expense account or from a liability account to a revenue account (or in the opposite direction) or simultaneously entering new data in an asset account and a revenue account or in a liability account and an expense account.

2. **True.** A fiscal year is any 12 consecutive months, so all calendar years are also fiscal years. A calendar year, however, must end on December 31, so it does not include fiscal years that end on any date other than December 31 (such as June 30).

3. **False.** The accumulated depreciation account is a *contra asset* that shows the total of all depreciation recorded on an asset from its acquisition date up through the balance sheet date.

4. **False.** The Unearned Delivery Fees account is a liability. As the fees are earned, the amount in that account is transferred to a revenue account.

5. **True.** If an adjusting entry is overlooked and not made, at least one income statement account and one balance sheet account will be incorrect.

MULTIPLE-CHOICE

1. **d.** One-third of the benefits have expired. Therefore, $400 must be moved from the asset (credit) to an expense (debit).

2. **a.** $1,100 of the supplies have been used, so that amount must be moved from the asset (credit) to an expense (debit).

3. **c.** The amount of annual depreciation is determined as ($20,000 − $5,000) divided by 5 = $3,000. The debit is to Depreciation Expense—Trucks, and the credit is to Accumulated Depreciation—Trucks, a contra asset account.

4. **b.** Each month $2,000 would be transferred from the liability account (debit), Unearned Subscription Fees, to a revenue account (credit).

5. **b.** An asset, Interest Receivable, is debited, and Interest Revenue is credited.

6. **a.** The debit would be to Salaries Expense, and the credit would be to Salaries Payable.

4

COMPLETING THE ACCOUNTING CYCLE

This chapter explains two new steps in the **accounting cycle**—the preparation of the work sheet and closing entries. In addition, we briefly discuss the evolution of accounting systems and present a classified balance sheet. This balance sheet format more closely resembles actual company balance sheets, such as those in the annual report booklet. After completing this chapter, you will understand how accounting begins with source documents that are evidence of a business entity's transactions and ends with financial statements that show the solvency and profitability of the entity.

THE ACCOUNTING CYCLE SUMMARIZED

In Chapter 1, you learned that when an event is a measureable business transaction, you need adequate proof of this transaction. Then, you analyze the transaction's effects on the accounting equation, Assets = Liabilities + Stockholders' equity. In Chapters 2 and 3, you performed other steps in the accounting cycle. Chapter 2 presented the eight steps in the accounting cycle as a preview of the content of Chapters 2 through 4. As a review, study the diagram of the eight steps in the accounting cycle in Illustration 4.1 (page 134). Remember that the first three steps occur during the accounting period and the last five occur at the end. The next section explains how to use the work sheet to facilitate the completion of the accounting cycle.

THE WORK SHEET

The **work sheet** is a columnar sheet of paper or a computer spreadsheet on which accountants summarize information needed to make the adjusting and closing entries and to prepare the financial statements. Usually, they save these work sheets to document the end-of-period entries. A work sheet is only an accounting tool and not part of the formal accounting records. Therefore, work sheets may vary in format; some are prepared in pencil so that errors can be corrected easily. Other work sheets are prepared on personal computers with spreadsheet software. Accountants prepare work sheets each time financial statements are needed—monthly, quarterly, or at the end of the accounting year.

This chapter illustrates a 12-column work sheet that includes sets of columns for an unadjusted trial balance, adjustments, adjusted trial balance, income statement, statement of retained earnings, and balance sheet. Each set has a debit and a credit column. (See Illustration 4.2 on page 135.)

Accountants use these initial steps in preparing the work sheet. The following sections describe the detailed steps for completing the work sheet.

1. Enter the titles and balances of ledger accounts in the Trial Balance columns.
2. Enter adjustments in the Adjustments columns.
3. Enter adjusted account balances in the Adjusted Trial Balance columns.
4. Extend adjusted balances of revenue and expense accounts from the Adjusted Trial Balance columns to the Income Statement columns.
5. Extend any balances in the Retained Earnings and Dividends accounts to the Statement of Retained Earnings columns.
6. Extend adjusted balances of asset, liability, and capital stock accounts from the Adjusted Trial Balance columns to the Balance Sheet columns.

Instead of preparing a separate trial balance as we did in Chapter 2, accountants use the Trial Balance columns on a work sheet. Look at Illustration 4.2 and note that the numbers and titles of the ledger accounts of MicroTrain Company are on the left portion of the work sheet. Usually, only those accounts with balances as of the end of the accounting period are listed. (Some accountants do list the entire chart of accounts, even those with zero balances.) Assume you are MicroTrain's accountant. You list the Retained Earnings account in the trial balance even though it has a zero balance to (1) show its relative position among the accounts and (2) indicate that December 1999 is the first month of operations for this company. Next, you enter the balances of the ledger accounts in the Trial Balance columns. The accounts are in the order in which they appear in the general ledger: assets, liabilities, stockholders' equity, dividends, revenues, and expenses. Then, total the columns. If the debit and credit column totals are not equal, an error exists that must be corrected before you proceed with the work sheet.

As you learned in Chapter 3, adjustments bring the accounts to their proper balances before accountants prepare the income statement, statement of retained earnings, and balance sheet. You enter these adjustments in the Adjustments columns of the work sheet. Also, you cross-reference the debits and credits of the entries by placing a key number or letter to the left of the amounts. This key number facilitates the actual journalizing of the adjusting entries later because you do not have to rethink the adjustments to record them. For example, the number *(1)* identifies the adjustment debiting Insurance Expense and crediting Prepaid Insurance. Note in the Account Titles column that the Insurance Expense account title is below the trial balance totals because the Insurance Expense account did not have a balance before the adjustment and, therefore, did not appear in the trial balance.

Work sheet preparers often provide brief explanations at the bottom for the keyed entries as in Illustration 4.2. Although these explanations are optional, they provide valuable information for those who review the work sheet later.

The adjustments (which were discussed and illustrated in Chapter 3) for MicroTrain Company are:

- Entry *(1)* records the expiration of $200 of prepaid insurance in December.
- Entry *(2)* records the expiration of $400 of prepaid rent in December.
- Entry *(3)* records the using up of $500 of supplies during the month.

(concluded)

6. Describe the evolution of accounting systems.

7. Prepare a classified balance sheet.

8. Analyze and use the financial results—the current ratio.

Objective 1
Summarize the steps in the accounting cycle.

Objective 2
Prepare a work sheet for a service company.

The Trial Balance Columns

Note to the Student
1. The work sheet is not a formal financial statement; usually only the accountant sees it.
2. Its major purpose is to organize data into a convenient form prior to preparing the financial statements.
3. Some accountants do not prepare a work sheet; however, many believe it makes the end-of-period work easier.

The Adjustments Columns

Reinforcing Problem
E4–1 Identify the steps in the accounting cycle.

ILLUSTRATION 4.1   Steps in the Accounting Cycle

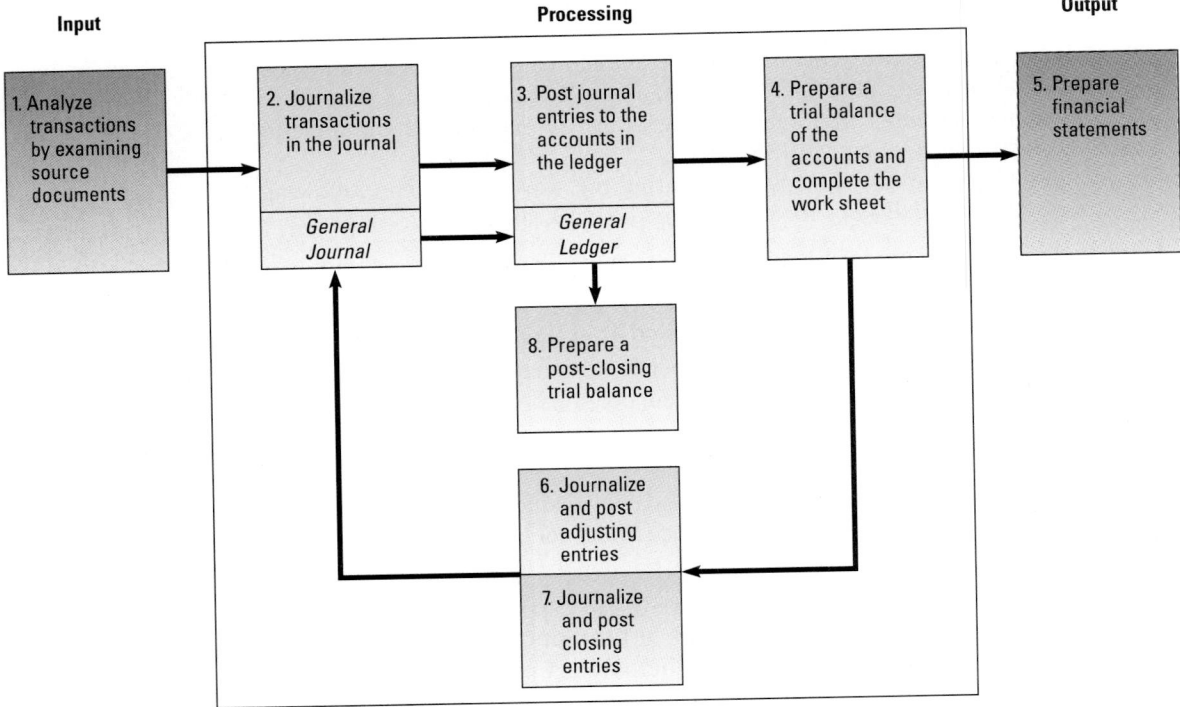

- Entry *(4)* records $750 depreciation expense on the trucks for the month. MicroTrain acquired the trucks at the beginning of December.
- Entry *(5)* records the earning of $1,500 of the $4,500 in the Unearned Service Fees account.
- Entry *(6)* records $600 of interest earned in December.
- Entry *(7)* records $1,000 of unbilled training services performed in December.
- Entry *(8)* records the $180 accrual of salaries expense at the end of the month.

Often it is difficult to discover all the adjusting entries that should be made. The following steps are helpful:

1. Examine adjusting entries made at the end of the preceding accounting period. The same types of entries often are necessary period after period.
2. Examine the account titles in the trial balance. For example, if the company has an account titled Trucks, an entry must be made for depreciation.
3. Examine various business documents (such as bills for services received or rendered) to discover other assets, liabilities, revenues, and expenses that have not yet been recorded.
4. Ask the manager or other personnel specific questions regarding adjustments that may be necessary. For example, "Were any services performed during the month that have not yet been billed?"

After all the adjusting entries are entered in the Adjustments columns, total the two columns. The totals of these two columns should be equal when all debits and credits are entered properly.

The Adjusted Trial Balance Columns

After MicroTrain's adjustments, compute the adjusted balance of each account and enter these in the Adjusted Trial Balance columns. For example, Supplies on Hand (Account No. 107) had an unadjusted balance of $1,400. Adjusting entry *(3)* credited

ILLUSTRATION 4.2 Completed Work Sheet

MICROTRAIN COMPANY
Work Sheet
For the Month Ended December 31, 1999

Acct. No.	Account Titles	Trial Balance Debit	Trial Balance Credit	Adjustments Debit	Adjustments Credit	Adjusted Trial Balance Debit	Adjusted Trial Balance Credit	Income Statement Debit	Income Statement Credit	Statement of Retained Earnings Debit	Statement of Retained Earnings Credit	Balance Sheet Debit	Balance Sheet Credit
100	Cash	8,250				8,250						8,250	
103	Accounts Receivable	5,200		(7) 1,000		6,200						6,200	
107	Supplies on Hand	1,400			(3) 500	900						900	
108	Prepaid Insurance	2,400			(1) 200	2,200						2,200	
112	Prepaid Rent	1,200			(2) 400	800						800	
150	Trucks	40,000				40,000						40,000	
200	Accounts Payable		730				730						730
216	Unearned Service Fees		4,500	(5) 1,500			3,000						3,000
300	Capital Stock		50,000				50,000						50,000
310	Retained Earnings, 12/1/99		–0–				–0–				–0–		
320	Dividends	3,000				3,000				3,000			
400	Service Revenue		10,700		(5) 1,500 (7) 1,000		13,200		13,200				
505	Advertising Expense	50				50		50					
506	Gas and Oil Expense	680				680		680					
507	Salaries Expense	3,600		(8) 180		3,780		3,780					
511	Utilities Expense	150				150		150					
		65,930	65,930										
512	Insurance Expense			(1) 200		200		200					
515	Rent Expense			(2) 400		400		400					
518	Supplies Expense			(3) 500		500		500					
521	Depreciation Expense—Trucks			(4) 750		750		750					
151	Accumulated Depreciation—Trucks				(4) 750		750						750
121	Interest Receivable			(6) 600		600						600	
418	Interest Revenue				(6) 600		600		600				
206	Salaries Payable				(8) 180		180						180
				5,130	5,130	68,460	68,460	6,510	13,800				
	Net Income							7,290			7,290		
								13,800	13,800	3,000	7,290		
	Retained Earnings, 12/31/99									4,290			4,290
										7,290	7,290	58,950	58,950

Adjustments explanations:

(1) To record insurance expense for December.
(2) To record rent expense for December.
(3) To record supplies expense for December.
(4) To record depreciation expense for December.
(5) To transfer fees for services provided in December from the liability account to the revenue account.
(6) To record one month's interest revenue.
(7) To record unbilled training services performed in December.
(8) To accrue one day's salaries that were earned but are unpaid.

the account for $500, leaving a debit balance of $900. This amount is a debit in the Adjusted Trial Balance columns.

Next, extend all accounts having balances to the Adjusted Trial Balance columns. Note carefully how the rules of debit and credit apply in determining whether an adjustment increases or decreases the account balance. For example, Salaries Expense (Account No. 507) has a $3,600 debit balance in the Trial Balance columns. A $180 debit adjustment increases this account, which has a $3,780 debit balance in the Adjusted Trial Balance columns.

Note to the Student

In computing the Adjusted Trial Balance column amounts, the process is to *add* debits plus debits and credits plus credits in the Trial Balance and Adjustments columns, and to *subtract* debits and credits.

Some account balances remain the same because no adjustments have affected them. For example, the balance in Accounts Payable (Account No. 200) does not change and is simply extended to the Adjusted Trial Balance columns.

Now, total the Adjusted Trial Balance debit and credit columns. The totals must be equal before taking the next step in completing the work sheet. When the Trial Balance and Adjustments columns both balance but the Adjusted Trial Balance columns do not, the most probable cause is a math error or an error in extension. The Adjusted Trial Balance columns make the next step of sorting the amounts to the Income Statement, the Statement of Retained Earnings, and the Balance Sheet columns much easier.

The Income Statement Columns

Begin by extending all of MicroTrain's revenue and expense account balances in the Adjusted Trial Balance columns to the Income Statement columns. Since revenues carry credit balances, extend them to the credit column. After extending expenses to the debit column, subtotal each column. MicroTrain's total expenses are $6,510 and total revenues are $13,800. Thus, net income for the period is $7,290 ($13,800 − $6,510). Enter this $7,290 income in the debit column to make the two column totals balance. You would record a net loss in the opposite manner; expenses (debits) would have been larger than revenues (credits) so a net loss would be entered in the credit column to make the columns balance.

The Statement of Retained Earnings Columns

Note to the Student
Conceptually, retained earnings increases because revenues exceeded expenses resulting in net income. Procedurally, the result is a net credit, and stockholders' equity (retained earnings) increases with a credit.

Next, complete the Statement of Retained Earnings columns. Enter the $7,290 net income amount for December in the credit Statement of Retained Earnings column. Thus, this net income amount is the balancing figure for the Income Statement columns and is also in the credit Statement of Retained Earnings column. Net income appears in the Statement of Retained Earnings credit column because it causes an increase in retained earnings. Add the $7,290 net income to the beginning retained earnings balance of $–0–, and deduct the dividends of $3,000. As a result, the ending balance of the Retained Earnings account is $4,290.

The Balance Sheet Columns

Reinforcing Problems
E4–6 Prepare a work sheet.
P4–4 Prepare a work sheet and closing entries.

Now extend the assets, liabilities, and capital stock accounts in the Adjusted Trial Balance columns to the Balance Sheet columns. Extend asset amounts as debits and liability and capital stock amounts as credits.

Note that the ending retained earnings amount determined in the Statement of Retained Earnings columns appears again as a credit in the Balance Sheet columns. The ending retained earnings amount is a debit in the Statement of Retained Earnings columns to balance the Statement of Retained Earnings columns. The ending retained earnings is a credit in the Balance Sheet columns because it increases stockholders' equity, and increases in stockholders' equity are credits. (Retained earnings would have a debit ending balance only if cumulative losses and dividends exceed cumulative earnings.) With the inclusion of the ending retained earnings amount, the Balance Sheet columns balance.

Locating Errors

Reinforcing Problem
E4–5 Find the causes of Balance Sheet columns not in balance.

When the Balance Sheet column totals do not agree on the first attempt, work backward through the process used in preparing the work sheet. Specifically, take the following steps until you discover the error:

1. Retotal the two Balance Sheet columns to see if you made an error in addition. If the column totals do not agree, check to see if you did not extend a balance sheet item or if you made an incorrect extension from the Adjusted Trial Balance columns.

MICROTRAIN COMPANY
Income Statement
For the Month Ended December 31, 1999

Revenues:		
Service revenue		$13,200
Interest revenue		600
Total revenue		$13,800
Expenses:		
Advertising expense	$ 50	
Gas and oil expense	680	
Salaries expense	3,780	
Utilities expense	150	
Insurance expense	200	
Rent expense	400	
Supplies expense	500	
Depreciation expense—trucks	750	
Total expenses		6,510
Net income		$ 7,290

ILLUSTRATION 4.3
Income Statement

2. Retotal the Statement of Retained Earnings columns and determine whether you entered the correct amount of retained earnings in the appropriate Statement of Retained Earnings and Balance Sheet columns.

3. Retotal the Income Statement columns and determine whether you entered the correct amount of net income or net loss for the period in the appropriate Income Statement and Statement of Retained Earnings columns.

USES OF TECHNOLOGY   Electronic spreadsheets have numerous applications in accounting. An electronic spreadsheet is simply a large blank page that contains rows and columns on the computer screen. The blocks created by the intersection of the rows and columns are cells; each cell can hold one or more words, a number, or the product of a mathematical formula. Spreadsheets are ideal for creating large work sheets, trial balances, and other schedules, and for performing large volumes of calculations such as depreciation calculations. Some of the most popular spreadsheet programs are Lotus 1–2–3®, Microsoft Excel®, QuattroPro®, and AppleWorks®.

AN ACCOUNTING PERSPECTIVE

PREPARING FINANCIAL STATEMENTS FROM THE WORK SHEET

When the work sheet is completed, all the necessary information to prepare the income statement, statement of retained earnings, and balance sheet is readily available. Now, you need only recast the information into the appropriate financial statement format.

Income Statement

The information you need to prepare the income statement in Illustration 4.3 is in the work sheet's Income Statement columns in Illustration 4.2.

The information you need to prepare the statement of retained earnings is taken from the Statement of Retained Earnings columns in the work sheet. Look at Illustration 4.4, MicroTrain Company's statement of retained earnings for the month ended December 31, 1999. To prepare this statement, use the beginning Retained Earnings account balance (Account No. 310), add the net income (or deduct the net loss), and then subtract the Dividends (Account No. 320). Carry the ending Retained Earnings

Objective 3
Prepare an income statement, statement of retained earnings, and balance sheet using information contained in the work sheet.

Statement of Retained Earnings

Reinforcing Problem
E4–7 Prepare statement of retained earnings.

ILLUSTRATION 4.4
Statement of Retained
Earnings

MICROTRAIN COMPANY
Statement of Retained Earnings
For the Month Ended December 31, 1999

Retained earnings, December 1, 1999	$ –0–
Net income for December	7,290
Total	$7,290
Less: Dividends	3,000
Retained earnings, December 31, 1999	$4,290

ILLUSTRATION 4.5
Balance Sheet

MICROTRAIN COMPANY
Balance Sheet
December 31, 1999

Assets

Cash		$ 8,250
Accounts receivable		6,200
Supplies on hand		900
Prepaid insurance		2,200
Prepaid rent		800
Interest receivable		600
Trucks	$40,000	
Less: Accumulated depreciation	750	39,250
Total assets		$58,200

Liabilities and Stockholders' Equity

Liabilities:		
Accounts payable		$ 730
Unearned service fees		3,000
Salaries payable		180
Total liabilities		$ 3,910
Stockholders' equity:		
Capital stock	$50,000	
Retained earnings	4,290	
Total stockholders' equity		54,290
Total liabilities and stockholders' equity . . .		$58,200

Real World Example
A December 23, 1996, *Business Week* article, "The First Name in Modems Gets a Second Chance," revealed that the new CEO of Hayes Microcomputers has streamlined management, nearly halved expenses, slashed inventories, and reduced the number of products to those having high margins. Consider how these events affect the financial statements.

balance forward to the balance sheet. Remember that the statement of retained earnings helps to relate income statement information to balance sheet information. It does this by indicating how net income on the income statement relates to retained earnings on the balance sheet.

Balance Sheet

The information needed to prepare a balance sheet comes from the Balance Sheet columns of MicroTrain's work sheet (Illustration 4.2). As stated earlier, the correct amount for the ending retained earnings appears on the statement of retained earnings. See the completed balance sheet for MicroTrain in Illustration 4.5.

JOURNALIZING ADJUSTING ENTRIES

Objective 4
Prepare adjusting and closing entries using information contained in the work sheet.

After completing MicroTrain's financial statements from the work sheet, you should enter the adjusting entries in the general journal and post them to the appropriate ledger accounts. You would prepare these adjusting entries as you learned in Chapter 3, except that the work sheet is now your source for making the entries. The preparation of a work sheet does not eliminate the need to prepare and post adjusting entries because the work sheet is only an informal accounting tool and is not part of the formal accounting records.

The numerical notations in the Adjustments columns and the adjustments explanations at the bottom of the work sheet identify each adjusting entry. The Adjustments columns show each entry with its appropriate debit and credit. MicroTrain's adjusting entries as they would appear in the general journal after posting are:

Reinforcing Problem
E4–8 Prepare adjusting entries and determine the correct net income.

MICROTRAIN COMPANY
General Journal

Page 3

Date		Account Titles and Explanation	Post. Ref.	Debit	Credit
1999		**Adjusting Entries**			
Dec.	31	Insurance Expense	512	2 0 0	
		Prepaid Insurance	108		2 0 0
		To record insurance expense for December.			
	31	Rent Expense	515	4 0 0	
		Prepaid Rent	112		4 0 0
		To record rent expense for December.			
	31	Supplies Expense	518	5 0 0	
		Supplies on Hand	107		5 0 0
		To record supplies used during December.			
	31	Depreciation Expense—Trucks	521	7 5 0	
		Accumulated Depreciation—Trucks	151		7 5 0
		To record depreciation expense for December.			
	31	Unearned Service Fees	216	1 5 0 0	
		Service Revenue	400		1 5 0 0
		To transfer a portion of training fees from the liability account to the revenue account.			
	31	Interest Receivable	121	6 0 0	
		Interest Revenue	418		6 0 0
		To record one month's interest revenue.			
	31	Accounts Receivable	103	1 0 0 0	
		Service Revenue	400		1 0 0 0
		To record unbilled training services performed in December.			
	31	Salaries Expense	507	1 8 0	
		Salaries Payable	206		1 8 0
		To accrue one day's salaries that were earned but are unpaid.			

THE CLOSING PROCESS

In Chapter 2, you learned that revenue, expense, and Dividends accounts are nominal (temporary) accounts that are merely subclassifications of a real (permanent) account, Retained Earnings. And you learned that we prepare financial statements for certain accounting periods. The **closing process** transfers (1) the balances in the revenue and expense accounts to a clearing account called *Income Summary* and then to Retained Earnings and (2) the balance in the Dividends account to the Retained Earnings account. The closing process reduces revenue, expense, and Dividends account balances to zero so they are ready to receive data for the next accounting period. Accountants may perform the closing process monthly or annually.

The **Income Summary account** is a clearing account used only at the end of an accounting period to summarize revenues and expenses for the period. After transferring all revenue and expense account balances to Income Summary, the balance in the Income Summary account represents the net income or net loss for the period. Closing or transferring the balance in the Income Summary account to the Retained Earnings account results in a zero balance in Income Summary.

Also closed at the end of the accounting period is the Dividends account containing the dividends declared by the board of directors to the stockholders. We close the Dividends account directly to the Retained Earnings account and not to Income Summary because dividends have no effect on income or loss for the period.

In accounting, we often refer to the process of closing as closing the books. Remember that only revenue, expense, and Dividend accounts are closed—not asset, liability, Capital Stock, or Retained Earnings accounts. The four basic steps in the closing process are:

Notes to the Student
Review the previous steps in the accounting cycle. Describe the purpose of each step as the cycle is completed.

Identify which accounts on a trial balance are permanent (real) or temporary (nominal).

1. **Closing the revenue accounts**—transferring the balances in the revenue accounts to a clearing account called Income Summary.
2. **Closing the expense accounts**—transferring the balances in the expense accounts to a clearing account called Income Summary.
3. **Closing the Income Summary account**—transferring the balance of the Income Summary account to the Retained Earnings account.
4. **Closing the Dividends account**—transferring the balance of the Dividends account to the Retained Earnings account.

Step 1: Closing the Revenue Accounts

Revenues appear in the Income Statement credit column of the work sheet. The two revenue accounts in the Income Statement credit column for MicroTrain Company are service revenue of $13,200 and interest revenue of $600 (Illustration 4.2). Because revenue accounts have credit balances, you must debit them for an amount equal to their balance to bring them to a zero balance. When you debit Service Revenue and Interest Revenue, credit Income Summary (Account No. 600). Enter the account numbers in the Posting Reference column when the journal entry has been posted to the ledger. Do this for all other closing journal entries.

MICROTRAIN COMPANY
General Journal   *Page 4*

Date		Account Titles and Explanation	Post. Ref.	Debit	Credit
1999		**Closing Entries**			
Dec.	31	Service Revenue	400	1 3 2 0 0	
		Interest Revenue	418	6 0 0	
		Income Summary	600		1 3 8 0 0
		To close the revenue accounts in the Income Statement credit			
		column to Income Summary.			

After the closing entries have been posted, the Service Revenue and Interest Revenue accounts (in T-account format) of MicroTrain appear as follows. Note that the accounts now have zero balances.

	Service Revenue	*Account No. 400*
1999		Bal. before closing	13,200
Dec. 31 To close to Income Summary 13,200		

Decreased by $13,200 →

| | Bal. after closing | –0– |

	Interest Revenue	*Account No. 418*

	1999				Bal. before closing	600

Decreased by $600 → | Dec. 31 | To close to Income Summary | | 600 |

| | | | | | Bal. after closing | –0– |

As a result of the previous entry, you would credit the Income Summary account for $13,800. We show the Income Summary account in Step 3.

Expenses appear in the Income Statement debit column of the work sheet. MicroTrain Company has eight expenses in the Income Statement debit column. As shown by the column subtotal, these expenses add up to $6,510. Since expense accounts have debit balances, credit each account to bring it to a zero balance. Then, make the debit in the closing entry to the Income Summary account for $6,510. Thus, to close the expense accounts, MicroTrain makes the following entry:

Step 2: Closing the Expense Accounts

MICROTRAIN COMPANY
General Journal

Page 4

Date	Account Titles and Explanation	Post. Ref.	Debit	Credit
1999				
Dec. 31	Income Summary	600	6 5 1 0	
	Advertising Expense	505		5 0
	Gas and Oil Expense	506		6 8 0
	Salaries Expense	507		3 7 8 0
	Utilities Expense	511		1 5 0
	Insurance Expense	512		2 0 0
	Rent Expense	515		4 0 0
	Supplies Expense	518		5 0 0
	Depreciation Expense—Trucks	521		7 5 0
	To close the expense accounts appearing in the Income Statement			
	debit column to Income Summary.			

The debit of $6,510 to the Income Summary account agrees with the Income Statement debit column subtotal in the work sheet. This comparison with the work sheet serves as a check that all revenue and expense items have been listed and closed. If the debit in the preceding entry was made for a different amount than the column subtotal, the company would have an error in the closing entry for expenses.

After they have been closed, MicroTrain's expense accounts appear as follows. Note that each account has a zero balance after closing.

	Advertising Expense	*Account No. 505*

Bal. before closing	50	1999		
		Dec. 31	To close to Income Summary	50	← *Decreased by $50*
Bal. after closing	–0–			

	Gas and Oil Expense	*Account No. 506*

Bal. before closing	680	1999		
		Dec. 31	To close to Income Summary	680	← *Decreased by $680*
Bal. after closing	–0–			

Reinforcing Problems

E4–9 Prepare adjusting and closing entries.

E4–11 Show how closing entries would be posted to T-accounts.

E4–12 Prepare closing entries.

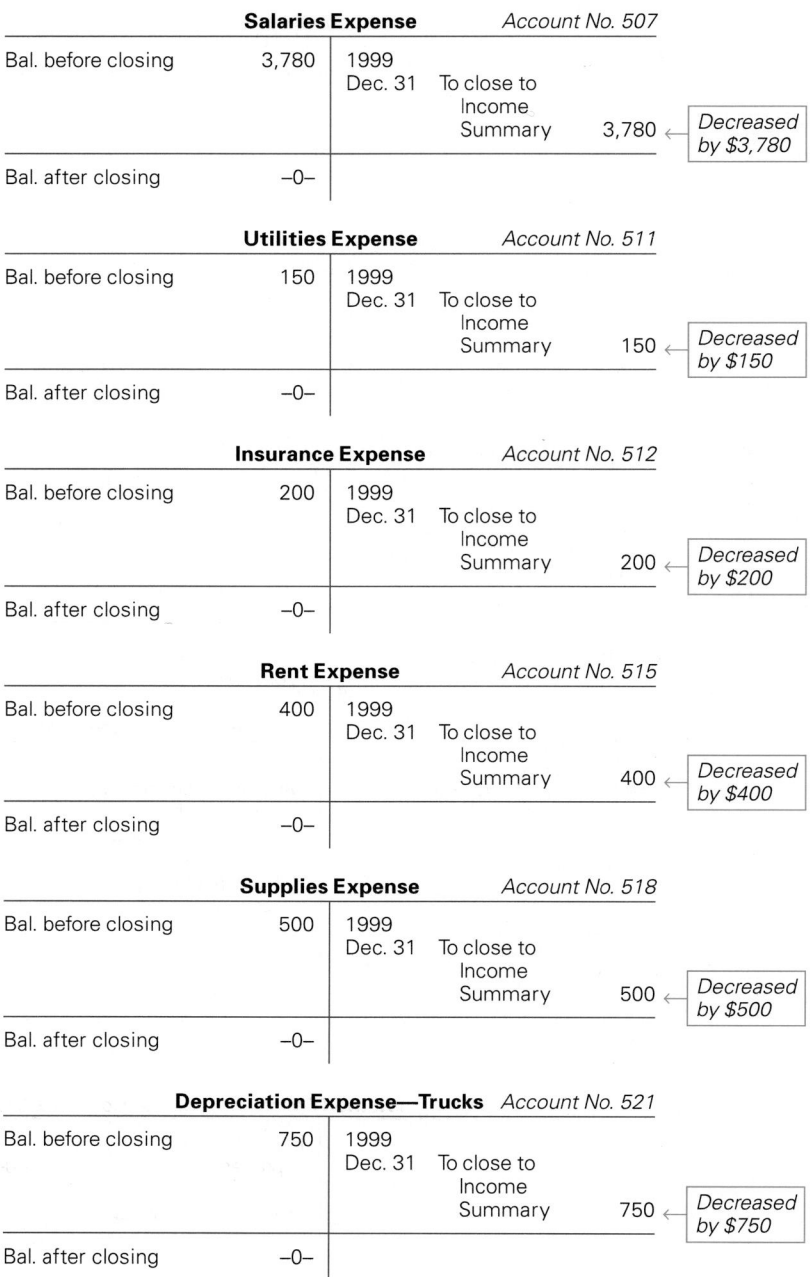

The expense accounts could be closed before the revenue accounts; the end result is the same.

Step 3: Closing the Income Summary Account

As the result of closing the revenues and expenses of MicroTrain, the total revenues and expenses have been transferred to the Income Summary account.

	Income Summary	
If total expenses exceed total revenues, the account has a debit balance, which is the net loss for the period.	Total expenses	Total revenues	If total revenues exceed total expenses, the account has a credit balance, which is the net income for the period.

MicroTrain's Income Summary account now has a credit balance of $7,290, the company's net income for December.

Income Summary

1999			1999		
Dec. 31	From closing the expense accounts	6,510	Dec. 31	From closing the revenue accounts	13,800
				Bal. before closing this account (net income)	7,290

Reinforcing Problem
E4–10 Post to Income Summary account from Income Statement column totals.

Next, close MicroTrain's Income Summary account to its Retained Earnings account. The journal entry to do this is:

MICROTRAIN COMPANY
General Journal   *Page 4*

Date		Account Titles and Explanation	Post. Ref.	Debit	Credit
1999 Dec.	31	Income Summary	600	7 2 9 0	
		Retained Earnings	310		7 2 9 0
		To close the Income Summary account to the Retained Earnings account.			

After its Income Summary account is closed, the company's Income Summary and Retained Earnings accounts appear as follows:

Income Summary   *Account No. 600*

1999			1999		
Dec. 31	From closing the expense accounts	6,510	Dec. 31	From closing the revenue accounts	13,800
				Bal. before closing account (net Income)	7,290
Dec. 31	To close this account to Retained Earnings	7,290			
				Bal. after closing	–0–

Decreased by $7,290 →

Retained Earnings   *Account No. 310*

			Bal. before closing process	–0–
		1999 Dec. 31	From Income Summary	7,290 ←

Increased by $7,290

Note to the Student
Points to remember:
1. The Income Summary account is a temporary account. It is opened and closed during the closing process.
2. The Income Summary account does not have a normal balance. It is used to close and clear the balances of the revenue and expense accounts.
3. An important function of the Income Summary account is to avoid unnecessary detail in the Retained Earnings account when closing the revenue and expense accounts.

The last closing entry closes MicroTrain's Dividends account. This account has a debit balance before closing. To close the account, credit the Dividends account and debit the Retained Earnings account. The Dividends account is not closed to the Income Summary because it is not an expense and does not enter into income determination. The journal entry to close MicroTrain's Dividends account is:

Step 4: Closing the Dividends Account

MICROTRAIN COMPANY
General Journal   *Page 4*

Date		Account Titles and Explanation	Post. Ref.	Debit	Credit
1999 Dec.	31	Retained Earnings	310	3 0 0 0	
		Dividends	320		3 0 0 0
		To close the Dividends account to the Retained Earnings account.			

After this closing entry is posted, the company's Dividends and Retained Earnings accounts appear as follows:

Note to the Student
Retained Earnings contains single closing entries for each year presenting a historical summary of annual dividends paid and annual income or loss. For many years, the only increases or decreases in stockholders' equity take place through changes in retained earnings. Consider why this is usually the case.

Dividends			Account No. 320
Bal. before closing	3,000	1999 Dec. 31 To close to Retained Earnings	3,000 ← *Decreased by $3,000*
Bal. after closing	–0–		

Retained Earnings			Account No. 310
1999		Bal. before closing process	–0–
Decreased by $3,000 → Dec. 31 From Dividends	3,000	1999 Dec. 31 From Income Summary	7,290
		Bal. after closing process is complete	4,290

Post-Closing Trial Balance

Objective 5
Prepare a post-closing trial balance.

Reinforcing Problem
E4–13 Identify accounts in the post-closing trial balance.

After you have completed the closing process, the only accounts in the general ledger that have not been closed are the permanent balance sheet accounts. Because these accounts contain the opening balances for the coming accounting period, debit balance totals must equal credit balance totals. The preparation of a post-closing trial balance serves as a check on the accuracy of the closing process and ensures that the books are in balance at the start of the new accounting period. The post-closing trial balance differs from the adjusted trial balance in only two important respects: (1) it excludes all temporary accounts since they have been closed; and (2) it updates the Retained Earnings account to its proper ending balance.

A **post-closing trial balance** is a trial balance taken after the closing entries have been posted. The only accounts that should be open are assets, liabilities, capital stock, and Retained Earnings accounts. List all the account balances in the debit and credit columns and total them to make sure debits and credits are equal.

Look at Illustration 4.6, a post-closing trial balance for MicroTrain Company as of December 31, 1999. The amounts in the post-closing trial balance are from the ledger after the closing entries have been posted.

The next section briefly describes the evolution of accounting systems from the one-journal, one-ledger manual system you have been studying to computerized systems. Then, we discuss the role of an accounting system.

AN ACCOUNTING PERSPECTIVE —

USES OF TECHNOLOGY   You may want to visit the American Institute of Public Accountants website at:

http://www.aicpa.org

You will find information about the CPA exam, about becoming a CPA, hot accounting topics, and various other topics, such as the states that have passed a 150-hour requirement to sit for the CPA exam. You can also learn such things as the states that have approved limited liability companies (LLCs) and limited liability partnerships (LLPs). These forms of organization serve to place limits on accountants' liability. You can also find the phone numbers and mailing addresses of state boards of accountancy and state societies of CPAs. Browse around this site to investigate anything else that is of interest.

ACCOUNTING SYSTEMS: FROM MANUAL TO COMPUTERIZED

Objective 6
Describe the evolution of accounting systems.

The manual accounting system with only one general journal and one general ledger has been in use for hundreds of years and is still used by some very small companies. Gradually, some manual systems evolved to include multiple journals and ledgers for increased efficiency. For instance, a manual system with multiple journals and ledgers

MICROTRAIN COMPANY
Post-Closing Trial Balance
December 31, 1999

Acct. No.	Account Title	Debits	Credits
100	Cash.	$ 8,250	
103	Accounts Receivable.	6,200	
107	Supplies on Hand	900	
108	Prepaid Insurance	2,200	
112	Prepaid Rent	800	
121	Interest Receivable	600	
150	Trucks	40,000	
151	Accumulated Depreciation—Trucks		$ 750
200	Accounts Payable.		730
206	Salaries Payable.		180
216	Unearned Service Fees.		3,000
300	Capital Stock		50,000
310	Retained Earnings.		4,290
		$58,950	$58,950

ILLUSTRATION 4.6
Post-Closing Trial Balance

often includes (1) a sales journal to record all credit sales, (2) a purchases journal to record all credit purchases, (3) a cash receipts journal to record all cash receipts, and (4) a cash disbursements journal to record all cash payments. Still recorded in the general journal are adjusting and closing entries and any other entries that do not fit in one of the special journals. Besides the general ledger, such a system normally has subsidiary ledgers for accounts receivable and accounts payable showing how much each customer owes and how much is owed to each supplier. The general ledger shows the total amount of accounts receivable and accounts payable, but the details in the subsidiary ledgers allow companies to send bills to customers and pay bills to suppliers.

BUSINESS INSIGHT   Imagine a company with an Accounts Receivable account and an Accounts Payable account in its general ledger and no Accounts Receivable Subsidiary Ledger or Accounts Payable Subsidiary Ledger. How would this company know to whom to send bills and in what amounts? Also, how would employees know for which suppliers to write checks and in what amounts? Such subsidiary records are necessary either on paper or in a computer file.

AN ACCOUNTING PERSPECTIVE

Here is how the general ledger and subsidiary ledgers might look:

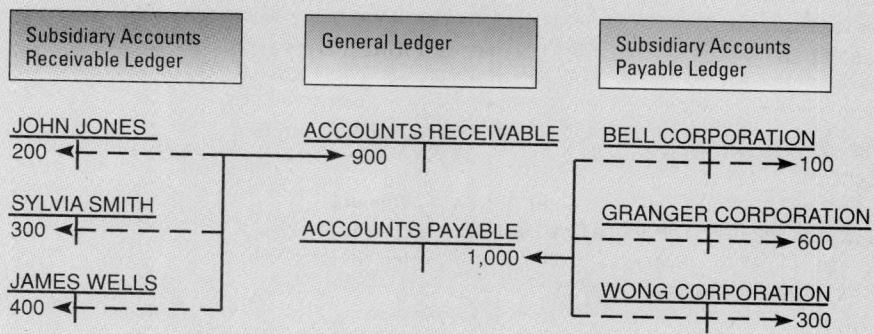

When a sale on account is made to John Jones, the debit is posted to both the control account, Accounts Receivable, in the General Ledger and the subsidiary account, John Jones, in the Subsidiary Accounts Receivable Ledger. Likewise, when a purchase on account is made from Bell Corporation, the credit is posted to both the control account, Accounts Payable, in the General Ledger and to the subsidiary account, Bell Corporation, in the Subsidiary Accounts Payable Ledger. At the end of the accounting period, the balances in each of the control accounts in the General Ledger must agree with the totals of the accounts in their respective subsidiary ledgers as shown above. A given company could have hundreds or even thousands of accounts in their subsidiary ledgers that show the detail not supplied by the totals in the control accounts.

The decision has been made: You [Tracy] have opted to start your career by joining an international accounting firm. But you can't help wondering if you have the right skills both for short- and long-term success in public accounting. . . .

Most students understand that accounting knowledge, organizational ability and interpersonal skills are critical to success in public accounting. But it is important for the beginner to realize that different skills are emphasized at different points in a public accountant's career. . . .

Let's examine the duties and skills needed at each level—Staff Accountant (years 1–2), Senior Accountant (years 3–4), Manager/Senior Manager (years 5–11) and Partner (years 11 +).

Staff accountant—Enthusiastic learner

Let's travel with Tracy as she begins her career at the staff level. At the outset, she works directly under a senior accountant on each of her audits and is responsible for completing audits and administrative tasks assigned to her. Her duties include documenting workpapers, interacting with client accounting staff, clerical tasks and discussing questions that arise with her senior. Tracy will work on different audit engagements during her first year and learn the firm's audit approach. She will be introduced to various industries and accounting systems.

The two most important traits to be demonstrated at the staff level are (1) a positive attitude and (2) the ability to learn quickly while adapting to unfamiliar situations. . . .

Senior accountant—Organizer and teacher

As a senior accountant, Tracy will be responsible for the day-to-day management of several audit engagements during the year. She will plan the audits, oversee the performance of interim audit testing and direct year-end field work. She will also perform much of the final wrap-up work, such as preparing checklists, writing the management letter and reviewing or drafting the financial statements. Throughout this process, Tracy will spend a substantial amount of time instructing and supervising staff accountants.

The two most critical skills needed at the senior level are (1) the ability to organize and control an audit and (2) the ability to teach staff accountants how to audit. . . .

Manager/senior manager—General manager and salesperson

Upon promotion to manager, Tracy will begin the transformation from auditor to executive. She will manage several audits at one time and become active in billing clients as well as negotiating audit fees. She will handle many important client meetings and closing conferences. Tracy will also become more involved in the firm's administrative tasks. . . . Finally, outside of her client service and administrative duties, Tracy will be evaluated to a large extent on her community involvement and ability to assist the partners in generating new business for the firm.

The two skills most emphasized at the manager level are (1) general management ability and (2) sales and communication skills. . . .

Partner—Leader and expert

As a partner in the firm, Tracy will have many broad responsibilities. She will engage in high-level client service activities, business development, recruiting, strategic planning, office administration and counseling. Besides serving as the engagement partner on several audits, she will have ultimate responsibility for the quality of service provided to each of her clients. Although a certain industry or administrative function will become her specialty, she will often be called upon to perform a wide variety of audit and administrative duties when other partners have scheduling conflicts. She will be expected to serve as a positive example to those who work for her and will train others in her areas of expertise.

At the partnership level, what's looked for is leadership ability plus the ability to become an expert in a specific industry or administrative function. . . .

In the meantime

Those planning on a public accounting career should do more than just learn accounting. To develop the needed skills, a broad education background in business and nonbusiness courses is required plus participation in extracurricular activities that promote leadership and communication skills. It is never too early to start building the skills for long-term success.

Source: Dana R. Hermanson and Heather M. Hermanson, *New Accountant*, January 1990, pp. 24–26, © 1990, New DuBois Corporation.

A BROADER PERSPECTIVE

Skills for the Long Haul

Another innovation in manual systems was the "one write" or pegboard system. By creating one document and aligning other records under it on a pegboard, companies could record transactions more efficiently. These systems permit the writing of a check and the simultaneous recording of the check in the cash disbursements journal. Even though some of these systems are still in use today, computers make them obsolete.

During the 1950s, companies also used bookkeeping machines to supplement manual systems. These machines recorded recurring transactions such as sales on account. They posted transactions to the general ledger and subsidiary ledger accounts and computed new balances. With the development of computers, bookkeeping machines became obsolete. They were quite expensive, and computers easily outperformed them. In the mid-1950s, large companies began using mainframe computers. Early accounting applications were in payroll, accounts receivable, accounts payable, and inventory. Within a few years, programs existed for all phases of accounting, including manufacturing operations and the total integration of other accounting programs with the general ledger. Until the 1980s, small and medium-sized companies either continued with a manual system, rented time on another company's computer, or hired a service bureau to perform at least some accounting functions.

The development of the microcomputer in 1975 and its widespread use a decade later drastically changed the accounting systems of small and medium-sized businesses. The number and quality of accounting software packages for these computers and the power of the microcomputers quickly increased. Soon small and medium-sized businesses could maintain all accounting functions on a microcomputer. By the 1990s, the cost of microcomputers and accounting software packages had decreased significantly, accounting software packages had become more user-friendly, and computer literacy had increased so much that many very small businesses converted from manual to computerized systems. However, some small business owners still use manual systems because they are familiar and meet their needs, and the persons keeping the records may not be computer literate.

Your knowledge of the basic manual accounting system described in these first four chapters enables you to better understand a computerized accounting system. The computer automatically performs some of the steps in the accounting cycle, such as posting journal entries to the ledger accounts, closing the books, and preparing the financial statements. However, if you understand all of the steps in the accounting cycle, you will better understand how to use the resulting data in decision making.

USES OF TECHNOLOGY Numerous microcomputer accounting systems are currently available; prices range from about $100 to $2,500. Some of the most popular are Peachtree Complete Accounting®, MAS Master Accounting®, Acc Pac Plus®, and Dac Easy Accounting®. Using these programs, small to medium-sized businesses can greatly reduce the clerical work performed by their accounting staffs. Although employees must journalize transactions during the accounting period and make adjusting entries, computerized systems automatically prepare postings, closing entries, and financial statements.

AN ACCOUNTING PERSPECTIVE

The Role of an Accounting System

As we show in Illustration 4.7, an **accounting system** is a set of records and the procedures and equipment used to perform the accounting functions. Manual systems consist of journals and ledgers on paper. Computerized accounting systems consist of accounting software, computer files, computers, and related peripheral equipment such as printers.

Regardless of the system, the functions of accountants include: (1) observing, identifying, and measuring economic events; (2) recording, classifying, and summarizing measurements; and (3) reporting economic events and interpreting financial statements. Both internal and external users tell accountants their information needs. The accounting system enables a company's accounting staff to supply relevant accounting information to meet those needs. As internal and external users make decisions that become economic events, the cycle of information, decisions, and economic events begins again.

The primary focus of the first four chapters has been on how you can use an accounting system to prepare financial statements. However, we also discussed how to use that information in making decisions. Later chapters also show how to prepare

ILLUSTRATION 4.7   The Role of an Accounting System

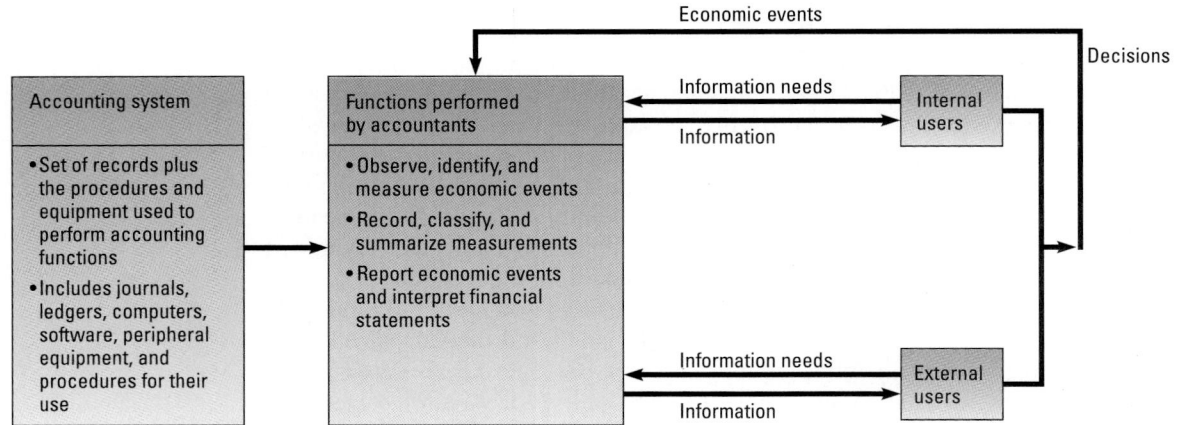

information and how that information helps users to make informed decisions. *We have not eliminated the preparation aspects because we believe that the most informed users are ones who also understand how the information was prepared.* These users understand not only the limitations of the information but also its relevance for decision making.

The next section discusses and illustrates the classified balance sheet, which aids in the analysis of the financial position of companies. One example of this analysis is the current ratio and its use in analyzing the short-term debt-paying ability of a company.

AN ACCOUNTING PERSPECTIVE
——

USES OF TECHNOLOGY   Accounting software packages are typically menu driven and organized into modules such as general ledger, accounts payable, accounts receivable, invoicing, inventory, payroll, fixed assets, job cost, and purchase order. For instance, general journal entries are made in the general ledger module, and this module contains all of the company's accounts. The accounts payable module records all transactions involving credit purchases from suppliers and payments made to those suppliers. The accounts receivable module records all sales on credit to various customers and amounts received from customers.

A CLASSIFIED BALANCE SHEET

Objective 7
Prepare a classified balance sheet.

The balance sheets we presented so far have been unclassified balance sheets. As shown in Illustration 4.5, an **unclassified balance sheet** has three major categories: assets, liabilities, and stockholders' equity. A **classified balance sheet** contains the same three major categories and subdivides them to provide useful information for interpretation and analysis by users of financial statements.

Illustration 4.8 on page 149, shows a slightly revised classified balance sheet for The Home Depot, Inc., and subsidiaries.[1] Note that The Home Depot classified balance sheet is in a vertical format (assets appearing above liabilities and stockholders' equity) rather than the horizontal format (assets on the left and liabilities and stockholders' equity on the right). The two formats are equally acceptable.

The Home Depot classified balance sheet subdivides two of its three major categories. The Home Depot subdivides its assets into current assets, property and

---

[1]Founded in 1978, The Home Depot is America's largest home improvement retailer and ranks among the nation's 30 largest retailers. The company has more than 420 full-service warehouse stores. Their primary customers are do-it-yourselfers.

THE HOME DEPOT, INC. AND SUBSIDIARIES
Consolidated Balance Sheet
January 28, 1996
(amounts in thousands, except share data)

ILLUSTRATION 4.8
A Classified Balance
Sheet

Reinforcing Problem
E4–14 Categorize items for
classified balance sheet.

	January 28, 1996	
Assets		
Current Assets:		
Cash and Cash Equivalents	$ 53,269	
Short-Term Investments, including current maturities of long-term investments (note 7)	54,756	
Receivables, Net	325,384	
Merchandise Inventories	2,180,318	
Other Current Assets	58,242	
Total Current Assets		$2,671,969
Property and Equipment, at cost:		
Land	$1,510,619	
Buildings	1,885,742	
Furniture, Fixtures, and Equipment	857,082	
Leasehold Improvements	314,933	
Construction in Progress	308,365	
Capital Leases	92,154	
Gross Property and Equipment	$4,968,895	
Less: Accumulated Depreciation and Amortization	507,871	
Net Property and Equipment	$4,461,024	
Long-Term Investments	25,436	
Notes Receivable	54,715	
Cost in Excess of the Fair Value of Net Assets Acquired, net of accumulated amortization of $10,536 at January 28, 1996	87,238	
Other	53,651	
Total Long-Term Assets		4,682,064
Total Assets		$7,354,033
Liabilities and Stockholders' Equity		
Current Liabilities:		
Accounts Payable	$ 824,808	
Accrued Salaries and Related Expenses	198,208	
Sales Taxes Payable	113,066	
Other Accrued Expenses	242,859	
Income Taxes Payable	35,214	
Current Installments of Long-Term Debt	2,327	
Total Current Liabilities		$1,416,482
Long-Term Debt, excluding current installments	$ 720,080	
Other Long-Term Liabilities	115,917	
Deferred Income Taxes	37,225	
Total Long-Term Liabilities		873,222
Minority Interest		76,563
Stockholders' Equity:		
Common Stock, par value $0.05. Authorized: 1,000,000,000 shares; issued and outstanding—477,106,000 shares at January 28, 1996	$ 23,855	
Paid-in Capital	2,407,815	
Retained Earnings	2,579,059	
Cumulative Translation Adjustments	(6,131)	
Unrealized Loss on Investments, Net	(47)	
	$5,004,551	
Less: Notes Receivable from ESOP	16,539	
Shares Held in Employee Benefit Trust	246	
Total Stockholders' Equity		4,987,766
Total Liabilities and Stockholders' Equity		$7,354,033

equipment, long-term investments, long-term notes receivable, intangible assets (cost in excess of the fair value of net assets acquired), and other assets. The company subdivides its liabilities into current liabilities and long-term liabilities (including deferred income taxes). A later chapter describes minority interest. Stockholders' equity is the same in a classified balance sheet as in an unclassified balance sheet. Later chapters describe further subdivisions of the stockholders' equity section.

We discuss the individual items in the classified balance sheet later in the text. Our only purpose here is to briefly describe the items that can be listed under each category. Some of these items are not in The Home Depot's balance sheet.

Current Assets

Notes to the Student

During the operating cycle, management needs to monitor the company's liquidity and solvency. Much of the monitoring is performed by various levels of management using a variety of information besides the general ledger account balances including ratios, unfilled orders, sales backlog, and customer counts.

It's important to remember that current assets are listed on the balance sheet according to liquidity—how quickly they can be turned back to cash or how quickly they can be consumed or expire.

Current assets are cash and other assets that a business can convert to cash or uses up in a relatively short period—one year or one operating cycle, whichever is longer. An **operating cycle** is the time it takes to start with cash, buy necessary items to produce revenues (such as materials, supplies, labor, and/or finished goods), sell services or goods, and receive cash by collecting the resulting receivables. Companies in service industries and merchandising industries generally have operating cycles shorter than one year. Companies in some manufacturing industries, such as distilling and lumber, have operating cycles longer than one year. However, since most operating cycles are shorter than one year, the one-year period is usually used in identifying current assets and current liabilities. Common current assets in a service business include cash, marketable securities, accounts receivable, notes receivable, interest receivable, and prepaid expenses. Note that on a balance sheet, current assets are in order of how easily they are convertible to cash, from most liquid to least liquid.

Cash includes deposits in banks available for current operations at the balance sheet date plus cash on hand consisting of currency, undeposited checks, drafts, and money orders. Cash is the first current asset to appear on a balance sheet. The term *cash* normally includes cash equivalents.

Cash equivalents are highly liquid, short-term investments acquired with temporarily idle cash and easily convertible into a known cash amount. Examples are Treasury bills, short-term notes maturing within 90 days, certificates of deposit, and money market funds.

Marketable securities are temporary investments such as short-term ownership of stocks and bonds of other companies. Such investments do not qualify as cash equivalents. These investments earn additional money on cash that the business does not need at present but will probably need within one year.

Accounts receivable (also called *trade accounts receivable*) are amounts owed to a business by customers. An account receivable arises when a company performs a service or sells merchandise on credit. Customers normally provide no written evidence of indebtedness on sales invoices or delivery tickets except their signatures. Notice the term *net* in the balance sheet of The Home Depot (Illustration 4.8). This term indicates the possibility that the company may not collect some of its accounts receivable. In the balance sheet, the accounts receivable amount is the sum of the individual accounts receivable from customers shown in a subsidiary ledger or file.

Merchandise inventories are goods held for sale. Chapter 6 begins our discussion of merchandise inventories.

A **note** is an unconditional written promise to pay another party the amount owed either when demanded or at a certain specified date, usually with interest (a charge made for use of the money) at a specified rate. A *note receivable* appears on the balance sheet of the company to which the note is given. A note receivable arises (1) when a company makes a sale and receives a note from the customer, (2) when a customer gives a note for an amount due on an account receivable, or (3) when a company loans money and receives a note in return. Chapter 9 discusses notes at length.

Other current assets might include interest receivable and prepaid expenses. **Interest receivable** arises when a company has earned but not collected interest by the balance sheet date. Usually, the amount is not due until later. **Prepaid expenses** include rent, insurance, and supplies that have been paid for but from which all the benefits have not yet been realized (or consumed). If prepaid expenses had not been paid for in advance, they would require the future disbursement of cash. Furthermore, prepaid expenses are considered assets because they have service potential.

Long-term assets are assets that a business has on hand or uses for a relatively long time. Examples include property, plant, and equipment; long-term investments; and intangible assets.

Long-Term Assets

PROPERTY, PLANT, AND EQUIPMENT **Property, plant, and equipment** are assets with useful lives of more than one year; a company acquires them for use in the business rather than for resale. (These assets are called property and equipment in The Home Depot's balance sheet.) The terms *plant assets* or *fixed assets* are also used for property, plant, and equipment. To agree with the order in the heading, balance sheets generally list property first, plant next, and equipment last. These items are *fixed assets* because the company uses them for long-term purposes. We describe several types of property, plant, and equipment next.

Land is ground the company uses for business operations; this includes ground on which the company locates its business buildings and that is used for outside storage space or parking. Land owned for investment is not a plant asset because it is a long-term investment.

Buildings are structures the company uses to carry on its business. Again, the buildings that a company owns as investments are not plant assets.

Office furniture includes file cabinets, desks, chairs, and shelves.

Office equipment includes computers, copiers, FAX machines, and phone answering machines.

Leasehold improvements are any physical alterations made by the lessee to the leased property when these benefits are expected to last beyond the current accounting period. An example is when the lessee builds room partitions in a leased building. (The lessee is the one obtaining the rights to possess and use the property.)

Construction in progress represents the partially completed stores or other buildings that a company such as The Home Depot plans to occupy when completed.

Accumulated depreciation is a contra asset account to depreciable assets such as buildings, machinery, and equipment. This account shows the total depreciation taken for the depreciable assets. On the balance sheet, companies deduct the accumulated depreciation (as a contra asset) from its related asset.

LONG-TERM INVESTMENTS A **long-term investment** usually consists of securities of another company held with the intention of (1) obtaining control of another company, (2) securing a permanent source of income for the investor, or (3) establishing friendly business relations. The long-term investment classification in the balance sheet does not include those securities purchased for short-term purposes. For most businesses, long-term investments may be stocks or bonds of other corporations. Occasionally, long-term investments include funds accumulated for specific purposes, rental properties, and plant sites for future use.

INTANGIBLE ASSETS **Intangible assets** consist of the noncurrent, nonmonetary, nonphysical assets of a business. Companies must charge the costs of intangible assets to expense over the period benefited up to a maximum of 40 years. Among the intangible assets are rights granted by governmental bodies, such as patents and copyrights. Other intangible assets include leaseholds and goodwill.

A **patent** is a right granted by the federal government; it gives the owner of an invention the authority to manufacture a product or to use a process for a specified time.

A **copyright** granted by the federal government gives the owner the exclusive privilege of publishing written material for a specified time.

Leaseholds are rights to use rented properties, usually for several years.

Goodwill is an intangible value attached to a business, evidenced by the ability to earn larger net income per dollar of investment than that earned by competitors in the same industry. The ability to produce superior profits is a valuable resource of a business. Normally, companies record goodwill only at the time of purchase and then only at the price paid for it. The Home Depot has labeled its goodwill "cost in excess of the fair value of net assets acquired."

Accumulated amortization is a contra asset account to intangible assets. This account shows the total amortization taken on the intangible assets.

Current Liabilities

Current liabilities are debts due within one year or one operating cycle, whichever is longer. The payment of current liabilities normally requires the use of current assets. Balance sheets list current liabilities in the order they must be paid; the sooner a liability must be paid, the earlier it is listed. Examples of current liabilities follow.

Accounts payable are amounts owed to suppliers for goods or services purchased on credit. Accounts payable are generally due in 30 or 60 days and do not bear interest. In the balance sheet, the accounts payable amount is the sum of the individual accounts payable to suppliers shown in a subsidiary ledger or file.

Notes payable are unconditional written promises by the company to pay a specific sum of money at a certain future date. The notes may arise from borrowing money from a bank, from the purchase of assets, or from the giving of a note in settlement of an account payable. Generally, only notes payable due in one year or less are included as current liabilities.

Salaries payable are amounts owed to employees for services rendered. The company has not paid these salaries by the balance sheet date because they are not due until later.

Sales taxes payable are the taxes a company has collected from customers but not yet remitted to the taxing authority, usually the state.

Other accrued expenses might include taxes withheld from employees, income taxes payable, and interest payable. **Taxes withheld from employees** include federal income taxes, state income taxes, and social security taxes withheld from employees' paychecks. The company plans to pay these amounts to the proper governmental agencies within a short period. **Income taxes payable** are the taxes paid to the state and federal governments by a corporation on its income. **Interest payable** is interest that the company has accumulated on notes or bonds but has not paid by the balance sheet date because it is not due until later.

Dividends payable, or amounts the company has declared payable to stockholders, represent a distribution of income. Since the corporation has not paid these declared dividends by the balance sheet date, they are a liability.

Unearned revenues (revenues received in advance) result when a company receives payment for goods or services before earning the revenue, such as payments for subscriptions to a magazine. These unearned revenues represent a liability to perform the agreed services or other contractual requirements or to return the assets received.

Companies report any current installment on long-term debt due within one year under current liabilities. The remaining portion continues to be reported as a long-term liability.

Long-Term Liabilities

Long-term liabilities are debts such as a mortgage payable and bonds payable that are not due for more than one year. Companies should show maturity dates in the balance sheet for all long-term liabilities. Normally, the liabilities with the earliest due dates are listed first.

Notes payable with maturity dates at least one year beyond the balance sheet date are long-term liabilities.

Bonds payable are long-term liabilities and are evidenced by formal printed certificates sometimes secured by liens (claims) on property, such as mortgages. Maturity dates should appear on the balance sheet for all major long-term liabilities.

The deferred income taxes on The Home Depot's balance sheet result from a difference between income tax expense in the accounting records and the income tax payable on the company's tax return.

Stockholders' equity shows the owners' interest in the business. This interest is equal to the amount contributed plus the income left in the business.

Stockholders' Equity

The items under stockholders' equity in The Home Depot's balance sheet are paid-in capital (including common stock) and retained earnings. **Paid-in capital** shows the capital paid into the company as the owners' investment. **Retained earnings** shows the cumulative income of the company less the amounts distributed to the owners in the form of dividends. Cumulative translation adjustments result from translating foreign currencies into U.S. dollars (a topic discussed in advanced accounting courses). The unrealized loss on investments is discussed in Chapter 14.

The next section shows how two categories on the classified balance sheet relate to each other. Together they help reveal a company's short-term debt-paying ability.

ANALYZING AND USING THE FINANCIAL RESULTS—THE CURRENT RATIO

The current ratio indicates the short-term debt-paying ability of a company. To find the **current ratio,** we divide current assets by current liabilities. For instance, Illustration 4.8 shows that The Home Depot's current assets as of January 28, 1996, were $2,671,969,000 and its current liabilities were $1,416,482,000. Thus, its current ratio was:

Objective 8
Analyze and use the financial results—the current ratio.

Current asset

C   Current ratio = = = 1.89 : 1

The current ratio of 1.89 : 1 for The Home Depot means that it has almost twice as many current assets as current liabilities. Because current liabilities are normally paid with current assets, the company appears to be able to pay its short-term obligations easily.

In evaluating a company's short-term debt-paying ability, you should also examine the quality of the current assets. If they include large amounts of uncollectable accounts receivable and/or obsolete and unsalable inventory, even a 2 : 1 current ratio may be inadequate to allow the company to pay its current liabilities. The Home Depot undoubtedly does not have such a problem.

Reinforcing Problem
E4–15 Calculate current ratios for The Procter & Gamble Company and subsidiaries and comment.

The current assets, current liabilities, and current ratios of some other companies as of the end of 1995 were:

Company	Current Assets	Current Liabilities	Current Ratio
Chevron Corporation	$ 7,667,000,000	$9,445,000,000	.81 : 1
Wal-Mart Stores, Inc.*	15,338,000,000	9,973,000,000	1.54 : 1
3M Corporation*	6,395,000,000	3,724,000,000	1.72 : 1
GTE Corporation*	5,892,000,000	8,312,000,000	.71 : 1
Sprint Corporation	3,619,400,000	5,142,100,000	.70 : 1

*We described these companies earlier in the text.

Chevron Corporation
Chevron Corporation is one of the world's largest oil companies.

Sprint
Sprint Corporation is a diversified telecommunications company providing global voice, data, and videoconferencing services and related products.

As you can see from these comparisons, the current ratios vary a great deal. An old rule of thumb is that the current ratio should be at least 2 : 1. However, what constitutes an adequate current ratio depends on available lines of credit, the cash-generating ability of the company, and the nature of the industry in which the company operates. For instance, companies in the airline industry are able to generate huge amounts of cash on a daily basis and may be able to pay their current liabilities even if their current ratio is less than 1 : 1. Comparing a company's current ratio with other companies in the same industry makes sense because all of these companies face about the same economic conditions. A company with the lowest current ratio in its industry may be unable to pay its short-term obligations on a timely basis, unless it can borrow funds from a bank on a line of credit. A company with the highest current ratio in its industry may have on hand too many current assets, such as cash and marketable securities, which could be invested in more productive assets.

The next chapter describes the assumptions, concepts, and principles that constitute the accounting theory underlying financial accounting. Thus, accounting theory dictates the standards and procedures applied to the reporting of financial information in the financial statements.

UNDERSTANDING THE LEARNING OBJECTIVES

Objective 1
Summarize the steps in the accounting cycle.

- Analyze transactions by examining source documents.
- Journalize transactions in the journal.
- Post journal entries to the accounts in the ledger.
- Prepare a trial balance of the accounts and complete the work sheet.
- Prepare financial statements.
- Journalize and post adjusting entries.
- Journalize and post closing entries.
- Prepare a post-closing trial balance.

Objective 2
Prepare a work sheet for a service company.

- The work sheet is a columnar sheet of paper on which accountants summarize information needed to make the adjusting and closing entries and to prepare the financial statements.
- Work sheets may vary in format. The work sheet illustrated in the chapter has 12 columns—two each for trial balance, adjustments, adjusted trial balance, income statement, statement of retained earnings, and balance sheet.

Objective 3
Prepare an income statement, statement of retained earnings, and balance sheet using information contained in the work sheet.

- The information needed to prepare the income statement is in the Income Statement columns of the work sheet. Net income for the period is the amount needed to balance the two Income Statement columns in the work sheet.
- The information needed to prepare the statement of retained earnings is in the Statement of Retained Earnings columns of the work sheet. The ending Retained Earnings balance is carried forward to the balance sheet.
- The information needed to prepare the balance sheet is in the Balance Sheet columns of the work sheet.

Objective 4
Prepare adjusting and closing entries using information contained in the work sheet.

- As explained in Chapter 3, adjusting entries are necessary to bring the accounts to their proper balances before preparing the financial statements.
- Closing entries are necessary to reduce the balances of revenue, expense, and Dividends accounts to zero so they are ready to receive data for the next accounting period.
- Revenue accounts are closed by debiting them and crediting the Income Summary account.
- Expense accounts are closed by crediting them and debiting the Income Summary account.
- The balance in the Income Summary account represents the net income or net loss for the period.
- To close the Income Summary account, the balance is transferred to the Retained Earnings account.
- To close the Dividends account, the balance is transferred to the Retained Earnings account.

- Only the balance sheet accounts have balances and appear on the post-closing trial balance.

- All revenue, expense, and Dividends accounts have zero balances and are not included in the post-closing trial balance.

- Manual systems and computerized systems perform the same accounting functions.
- The ease of accounting with a microcomputer has encouraged even small companies to convert to computerized systems.

- A classified balance sheet subdivides the major categories on the balance sheet. For instance, a classified balance sheet subdivides assets into current assets; long-term investments; property, plant, and equipment; and intangible assets. It subdivides liabilities into current liabilities and long-term liabilities. Later chapters show more accounts in the stockholders' equity section, but the subdivisions remain basically the same.

- The current ratio gives some indication of the short-term debt-paying ability of a company.
- To find the current ratio, divide current assets by current liabilities.

Objective 5
Prepare a post-closing trial balance.

Objective 6
Describe the evolution of accounting systems.

Objective 7
Prepare a classified balance sheet.

Objective 8
Analyze and use the financial results—the current ratio.

DEMONSTRATION PROBLEM

This problem involves using a work sheet for Green Hills Riding Stable, Incorporated, for the month ended July 31, 1999, and performing the closing process. The trial balance for Green Hills Riding Stable, Incorporated, as of July 31, 1999, was as follows:

GREEN HILLS RIDING STABLE, INCORPORATED
Trial Balance
July 31, 1999

Acct. No.	Account Title	Debits	Credits
100	Cash.	$10,700	
103	Accounts Receivable.	8,100	
130	Land.	40,000	
140	Buildings	24,000	
200	Accounts Payable		$ 1,100
201	Notes Payable.		40,000
300	Capital Stock		35,000
310	Retained Earnings, July 1, 1997		3,100
320	Dividends.	1,000	
402	Horse Boarding Fees Revenue.		4,500
404	Riding and Lesson Fees Revenue		3,600
507	Salaries Expense	1,400	
513	Feed Expense.	1,100	
540	Interest Expense	200	
568	Miscellaneous Expense	800	
		$87,300	$87,300

Depreciation expense for the month is $200. Accrued salaries on July 31 are $300.

a. Prepare a 12-column work sheet for the month ended July 31, 1999.
b. Journalize the adjusting entries.
c. Journalize the closing entries.

Additional data

Required

SOLUTION TO DEMONSTRATION PROBLEM

a. See the work sheet below.

GREEN HILLS RIDING STABLE, INCORPORATED
Work Sheet
For the Month Ended July 31, 1999

Acct. No.	Account Titles	Trial Balance Debit	Trial Balance Credit	Adjustments Debit	Adjustments Credit	Adjusted Trial Balance Debit	Adjusted Trial Balance Credit	Income Statement Debit	Income Statement Credit	Statement of Retained Earnings Debit	Statement of Retained Earnings Credit	Balance Sheet Debit	Balance Sheet Credit
100	Cash	10,700				10,700						10,700	
103	Accounts Receivable	8,100				8,100						8,100	
130	Land	40,000				40,000						40,000	
140	Buildings	24,000				24,000						24,000	
200	Accounts Payable		1,100				1,100						1,100
201	Notes Payable		40,000				40,000						40,000
300	Capital Stock		35,000				35,000						35,000
310	Retained Earnings, July 1, 1999		3,100				3,100				3,100		
320	Dividends	1,000				1,000				1,000			
402	Horse Boarding Fees Revenue		4,500				4,500		4,500				
404	Riding and Lesson Fees Revenue		3,600				3,600		3,600				
507	Salaries Expense	1,400		(2) 300		1,700		1,700					
513	Feed Expense	1,100				1,100		1,100					
540	Interest Expense	200				200		200					
568	Miscellaneous Expense	800				800		800					
		87,300	87,300										
520	Depreciation Expense—Buildings			(1) 200		200		200					
141	Accumulated Depreciation—Buildings				(1) 200		200						200
206	Salaries Payable				(2) 300		300						300
				500	500	87,800	87,800						
								4,000	8,100				
	Net Income							4,100			4,100		
								8,100	8,100	1,000	7,200	82,800	76,600
										6,200			6,200
	Retained Earnings, July 31, 1999									7,200	7,200	82,800	82,800

Adjustments:
(1) To record depreciation of building for July.
(2) To record accrued salaries of $300.

b.

GREEN HILLS RIDING STABLE, INCORPORATED
General Journal

Page 4

Date		Account Titles and Explanation	Post. Ref.	Debit	Credit
1999		**Adjusting Entries**			
July	31	Depreciation Expense—Buildings	520	200	
		Accumulated Depreciation—Buildings	141		200
		To record depreciation expense.			
	31	Salaries Expense	507	300	
		Salaries Payable	206		300
		To record accrued salaries.			

c.

GREEN HILLS RIDING STABLE, INCORPORATED
General Journal

Page 4

Date		Account Titles and Explanation	Post. Ref.	Debit	Credit
1999		**Closing Entries**			
July	31	Horse Boarding Fees Revenue	402	4 5 0 0	
		Riding and Lesson Fees Revenue	404	3 6 0 0	
		Income Summary	600		8 1 0 0
		To close revenue accounts.			
	31	Income Summary	600	4 0 0 0	
		Salaries Expense	507		1 7 0 0
		Feed Expense	513		1 1 0 0
		Interest Expense	540		2 0 0
		Miscellaneous Expense	568		8 0 0
		Depreciation Expense—Buildings	520		2 0 0
		To close expense accounts.			
	31	Income Summary	600	4 1 0 0	
		Retained Earnings	310		4 1 0 0
		To close Income Summary account.			
	31	Retained Earnings	310	1 0 0 0	
		Dividends	320		1 0 0 0
		To close Dividends account.			

New Terms*

Accounting cycle Series of steps performed during the accounting period to analyze, record, classify, summarize, and report useful financial information for the purpose of preparing financial statements. The steps include analyzing transactions, journalizing transactions, posting journal entries, taking a trial balance and completing the work sheet, preparing financial statements, journalizing and posting adjusting entries, journalizing and posting closing entries, and taking a post-closing trial balance. *132*

Accounting system A set of records and the procedures and equipment used to perform accounting functions. *147*

Accounts payable Amounts owed to suppliers for goods or services purchased on credit. *152*

Accounts receivable Amounts due from customers for services performed or merchandise sold on credit. *150*

Accumulated amortization A contra account to intangible assets. *152*

Accumulated depreciation A contra account to depreciable assets such as buildings, machinery, and equipment. *151*

Bonds payable Written promises to pay a definite sum at a certain date as evidenced by formal printed certificates that are sometimes secured by liens on property, such as mortgages. *153*

Buildings Structures used to carry on the business. *151*

Cash Includes deposits in banks available for current operations at the balance sheet date plus cash on hand consisting of currency, undeposited checks, drafts, and money orders. *150*

Cash equivalents Highly liquid, short-term investments acquired with temporarily idle cash. *150*

Classified balance sheet Subdivides the three major balance sheet categories (assets, liabilities, and stockholders' equity) to provide more information for users of financial statements. Assets may be divided into current assets; long-term investments; property, plant, and equipment; and intangible assets. Liabilities may be divided into current liabilities and long-term liabilities. *148*

Closing process The act of transferring the balances in the revenue and expense accounts to a clearing account called *Income Summary* and then to the Retained Earnings account. The balance in the Dividends account is also transferred to the Retained Earnings account. *139*

Construction in progress Represents the partially completed stores or other buildings that a company plans to occupy when completed. *151*

Copyright Grants the owner the exclusive privilege of publication of written material for a specific time. *151*

Current assets Cash and other assets that a business can convert into cash or use up in one year or one operating cycle, whichever is longer. *150*

Current liabilities Debts due within one year or one operating cycle, whichever is longer. The payment of current liabilities normally requires the use of current assets. *152*

*Some of these terms have been defined in earlier chapters but are included here for your convenience.

Current ratio   Calculated by dividing current assets by current liabilities.   *153*

Dividends payable   Amounts declared payable to stockholders and that represent a distribution of income.   *152*

Goodwill   An intangible value attached to a business, evidenced by the ability to earn larger net income per dollar of investment than that earned by competitors in the same industry.   *152*

Income Summary account   A clearing account used only at the end of an accounting period to summarize revenues and expenses for the period.   *140*

Income taxes payable   Are the taxes payable to the state and federal governments by a corporation based on its income.   *152*

Intangible assets   Noncurrent, nonmonetary, nonphysical assets of a business.   *151*

Interest payable   Interest that has accumulated on debts, such as notes or bonds. This accrued interest has not been paid at the balance sheet date because it is not due until later.   *152*

Interest receivable   Arises when interest has been earned but not collected at the balance sheet date.   *150*

Land   Ground the company uses for business operations. Land could include ground on which the company locates its business buildings and that used for outside storage space or a parking lot.   *151*

Leasehold improvements   Are any physical alterations made by the lessee to the leased property when these benefits are expected to last beyond the current accounting period.   *151*

Leaseholds   Rights to use rented properties.   *152*

Long-term assets   Assets that are on hand or used by a business for a relatively long time. Examples include long-term investments; property, plant, and equipment; and intangible assets.   *151*

Long-term investment   Usually securities of another company held with the intention of *(1)* obtaining control of another company, *(2)* securing a permanent source of income for the investor, or *(3)* establishing friendly business relations.   *151*

Long-term liabilities   Debts such as a mortgage payable and bonds payable that are not due for more than one year.   *152*

Marketable securities   Temporary investments that a company makes to earn a return on idle cash.   *150*

Merchandise inventory   Goods held for sale.   *150*

Note   An unconditional written promise to pay to another party the amount owed either when demanded or at a certain date.   *150*

Notes payable   Unconditional written promises by a company to pay a specific sum of money at a certain future date.   *152*

Office equipment   Includes computers, copiers, FAX machines, and phone answering machines.   *151*

Office furniture   Includes file cabinets, desks, chairs, and shelves.   *151*

Operating cycle   The time it takes to start with cash, buy necessary items to produce revenues (such as materials, supplies, labor, and/or inventories), sell services or goods, and receive cash by collecting the resulting receivables.   *150*

Paid-in capital   Shows the capital paid into the company as the owners' investment.   *153*

Patent   A right granted by the federal government authorizing the owner of an invention to manufacture a product or to use a process for a specific time.   *151*

Post-closing trial balance   A trial balance taken after the closing entries have been posted.   *144*

Prepaid expenses   Assets awaiting assignment to expense. Items such as rent, insurance, and supplies that have been paid for but from which all of the benefits have not yet been realized (or consumed). Prepaid expenses are classified as current assets.   *150*

Property, plant, and equipment   Assets with useful lives of more than one year that a company acquired for use in a business rather than for resale; also called *plant assets* or *fixed assets.*   *151*

Retained earnings   Shows the cumulative income of the company less the amounts distributed to the owners in the form of dividends.   *153*

Salaries payable   Amounts owed to employees for services rendered.   *152*

Sales taxes payable   Are taxes a company has collected from customers but has not remitted to the taxing authority, usually the state.   *152*

Stockholders' equity   Shows the owners' interest (equity) in the business.   *153*

Taxes withheld from employees   Items such as federal income taxes, state income taxes, and social security taxes withheld from employees' paychecks.   *152*

Unclassified balance sheet   A balance sheet showing only three major categories: assets, liabilities, and stockholders' equity.   *148*

Unearned revenues (revenues received in advance)   Result when payment is received for goods or services before revenue has been earned.   *152*

Work sheet   A columnar sheet of paper on which accountants have summarized information needed to make the adjusting and closing entries and to prepare the financial statements.   *132*

SELF-TEST

TRUE-FALSE

Indicate whether each of the following statements is true or false.

1.   At the end of the accounting period, three trial balances are prepared.

2.   The amounts in the Adjustments columns are always added to the amounts in the Trial Balance columns to determine the amounts in the Adjusted Trial Balance columns.

3. If a net loss occurs, it appears in the Income Statement credit column and Statement of Retained Earnings debit column.

4. After the closing process is complete, no balance can exist in any revenue, expense, Dividends, or Income Summary account.

5. The post-closing trial balance may contain revenue and expense accounts.

6. All accounting systems currently in use are computerized.

MULTIPLE-CHOICE

Select the best answer for each of the following questions.

1. Which of the following accounts is *least* likely to be adjusted on the work sheet?
   a. Supplies on Hand.
   b. Land.
   c. Prepaid Rent.
   d. Unearned Delivery Fees.

2. If the Balance Sheet columns do not balance, the error is most likely to exist in the:
   a. General journal.
   b. General ledger.
   c. Last six columns of the work sheet.
   d. First six columns of the work sheet.

3. Net income for a period appears in all but which one of the following?
   a. Income Statement debit column of the work sheet.
   b. Statement of Retained Earnings credit column of the work sheet.
   c. Statement of retained earnings.
   d. Balance sheet.

4. Which of the following statements is *false* regarding the closing process?
   a. The Dividends account is closed to Income Summary.
   b. The closing of expense accounts results in a debit to Income Summary.
   c. The closing of revenues results in a credit to Income Summary.
   d. The Income Summary account is closed to the Retained Earnings account.

5. Which of the following statements is *true* regarding the classified balance sheet?
   a. Current assets include cash, accounts receivable, and equipment.
   b. Plant, property, and equipment is one category of long-term assets.
   c. Current liabilities include accounts payable, salaries payable, and notes receivable.
   d. Stockholders' equity is subdivided into current and long-term categories.

Now turn to page 170 to check your answers.

QUESTIONS

1. At which stage of the accounting cycle is a work sheet usually prepared?

2. Why are the financial statements prepared before the adjusting and closing entries are journalized and posted?

3. Describe the purposes for which the work sheet is prepared.

4. You have taken over a set of accounting books for a small business as a part-time job. At the end of the first accounting period, you have partially completed the work sheet by entering the proper ledger accounts and balances in the Trial Balance columns. You turn to the manager and ask, "Where is the list of additional information I can use in entering the adjusting entries?" The manager indicates there is no such list. (In all the text problems you have done, you have always been given this information.) How would you obtain the information for this real-life situation? What are the consequences of not making all of the required adjustments at the end of the accounting period?

5. How are the amounts in the Adjusted Trial Balance columns of a work sheet determined?

6. The work sheet for Bridges Company shows net income of $40,000. The following four adjustments were ignored:
   1. Subscriptions Fees earned, $1,200.
   2. Depreciation of equipment, $4,000.

3. Depreciation of building, $10,000.
4. Salaries accrued, $3,000.
What is the correct net income?

7. After the Adjusted Trial Balance columns of a work sheet have been totaled, which account balances are extended to the Income Statement columns, which account balances are extended to the Statement of Retained Earnings columns, and which account balances are extended to the Balance Sheet columns?

8. How is the statement of retained earnings prepared?

9. What is the purpose of closing entries? What accounts are not affected by closing entries?

10. A company has net income of $50,000 for the year. In which columns of the work sheet would net income appear?

11. Is it possible to prepare monthly financial statements without journalizing and posting adjusting and closing entries? How?

12. What is the purpose of a post-closing trial balance?

13. Describe some of the ways in which the manual accounting system has evolved.

14. When did computerized accounting systems come into use?

15. Define an accounting system.

16. How is a classified balance sheet different than an unclassified balance sheet?

17. **Real World Question** Refer to "A Broader Perspective" on page 146 to answer the following true-false questions:
    a. The same skills are needed at each level in a CPA firm.
    b. The two most important traits at the staff accountant level are a positive attitude and the ability to learn quickly while adapting to unfamiliar situations.
    c. The senior accountant needs management skills in addition to technical skills.
    d. Partners become increasingly involved in technical matters and have less and less interaction with people.

18. **Real World Question** Referring to the annual report booklet, identify the classifications (or categories) of assets used by The Coca-Cola Company, Maytag Corporation, The Limited, Inc., and John H. Harland Company in their respective balance sheets.

19. **Real World Question** Referring to the annual report booklet, identify the classifications (or categories) of liabilities used by The Coca-Cola Company, Maytag Corporation, The Limited, Inc., and John H. Harland Company in their respective balance sheets.

EXERCISES

Exercise 4–1
Identify the steps in the accounting cycle (L.O. 1)

List the steps in the accounting cycle. Would the system still work if any of the steps were performed out of order?

Exercise 4–2
Determine where items would appear in the work sheet (L.O. 2)

Three of the major column headings on a work sheet are Trial Balance, Income Statement, and Balance Sheet. Determine under which major column headings each of the following items would appear and whether it would be a debit or credit. (For example, Cash would appear on the debit side of the Trial Balance and Balance Sheet columns.)

	Account Titles	Trial Balance		Income Statement		Statement of Retained Earnings		Balance Sheet	
		Debit	Credit	Debit	Credit	Debit	Credit	Debit	Credit
a.	Accounts Receivable								
b.	Accounts Payable								
c.	Interest Revenue								
d.	Advertising Expense								
e.	Capital Stock								
f.	Retained Earnings (Beg.)								
g.	Net income for the month								
h.	Retained Earnings (Endg.)								

Exercise 4–3
Determine where items would appear in the work sheet (L.O. 2)

Assume a beginning balance in Retained Earnings of $84,000 and net income for the year of $36,000. Illustrate how these would appear in the Statement of Retained Earnings columns and Balance Sheet columns in the work sheet.

Exercise 4–4
Determine where items would appear in the work sheet (L.O. 2)

In Exercise 4–3, if there was a debit balance of $216,000 in the Retained Earnings account as of the beginning of the year and a net loss of $192,000 for the year, show how these would be treated in the work sheet.

Exercise 4–5
Find cause of Balance Sheet columns not in balance (L.O. 2)

Damon Davis was preparing the work sheet for Drano Plumbing Company. He calculated the net income to be $50,000. When he totaled the Balance Sheet columns, the column totals were debit, $400,000; and credit, $300,000. What was the probable cause of this difference? If this was not the cause, what should he do to find the error?

Exercise 4–6
Prepare a work sheet (L.O. 2)

The Trial Balance of the Printer Repair Company at December 31, 1999, contains the following account balances listed in alphabetical order to increase your skill in sorting amounts to the proper work sheet columns.

PRINTER REPAIR COMPANY
Trial Balance Account Balances
December 31, 1999

Accounts Payable	$ 41,000
Accounts Receivable	92,000
Accumulated Depreciation—Buildings	25,000
Accumulated Depreciation—Equipment	9,000
Buildings	140,000
Capital Stock	65,000
Cash	60,000
Equipment	36,000
Prepaid Insurance	3,600
Retained Earnings, January 1, 1999	4,800
Salaries Expense	96,000
Service Revenue	290,000
Supplies on Hand	4,000
Utilities Expense	3,200

Using these account balances and the following additional information, prepare a work sheet for Printer Repair Company. Arrange the accounts in their approximate usual order.

1. Supplies on hand at December 31, 1999, have a cost of $2,400.

2. The balance in the Prepaid Insurance account represents the cost of a two-year insurance policy covering the period from January 1, 1999, through December 31, 2000.

3. The estimated lives of depreciable assets are buildings, 40 years, and equipment, 20 years. No salvage values are anticipated.

Additional data

Texban Corporation had a January 1, 1999, balance in its Retained Earnings account of $90,000. For the year 1999, net income was $50,000 and dividends declared and paid were $24,000. Prepare a statement of retained earnings for the year ended December 31, 1999.

Exercise 4–7
Prepare statement of retained earnings (L.O. 3)

Rubino Company reported net income of $100,000 for the current year. Examination of the work sheet and supporting data indicates that the following items were ignored:

1. Accrued salaries were $6,000 at December 31.

2. Depreciation on equipment acquired on July 1 amounted to $4,000.

Based on this information, *(a)* what adjusting journal entries should have been made at December 31, and *(b)* what is the correct net income?

Exercise 4–8
Prepare adjusting entries and determine correct net income (L.O. 4)

Refer to the work sheet prepared in Exercise 4–6. Prepare the adjusting and closing journal entries.

Exercise 4–9
Prepare adjusting and closing entries (L.O. 4)

The Income Statement column totals on a work sheet prepared at December 31, 1999, are debit, $500,000; and credit, $900,000. In T-account format, show how the postings to the Income Summary account would appear as a result of the closing process. Identify what each posting represents.

Exercise 4–10
Post to Income Summary account from Income Statement column totals (L.O. 4)

After adjustment, these selected account balances of Cold Stream Campground are:

Exercise 4–11
Show how closing entries would be posted to T-accounts (L.O. 4)

	Debits	Credits
Retained Earnings		$540,000
Rental Revenue		960,000
Salaries Expense	$336,000	
Depreciation Expense—Buildings	64,000	
Utilities Expense	208,000	
Dividends	32,000	

In T-account format, show how journal entries to close the books for the period would be posted. (You do not need to show the closing journal entries.) Enter these balances in the accounts before doing so. Key the postings from the first closing entry with the number (1), the second with the number (2), and so on.

The following account balances appeared in the Income Statement columns of the work sheet prepared for Liu Company for the year ended December 31, 1999:

Exercise 4–12
Prepare closing entries (L.O. 4)

	Income Statement	
Account Titles	**Debit**	**Credit**
Service Revenue		330,000
Advertising Expense	1,350	
Salaries Expense	130,000	
Utilities Expense	2,250	
Insurance Expense	900	
Rent Expense	6,750	
Supplies Expense	2,250	
Depreciation Expense—Equipment	4,500	
Interest Expense	562	
Interest Revenue		1,125
	148,562	331,125
Net Income	182,563	
	331,125	331,125

Prepare the closing journal entries.

Exercise 4–13
Identify accounts in the post-closing trial balance (L.O. 5)

Which of the following accounts are likely to appear in the post-closing trial balance for the Blake Company?

1. Accounts Receivable
2. Cash
3. Service Revenue
4. Buildings
5. Salaries Expense
6. Capital Stock
7. Dividends
8. Accounts Payable
9. Income Summary
10. Unearned Subscription Fees

Exercise 4–14
Categorize items for classified balance sheet (L.O. 7)

Using the legend at the right, determine the category (number) into which you would place each of these items.

Item	Legend
_____ **a.** Land.	**1.** Current assets.
_____ **b.** Marketable securities.	**2.** Long-term investments.
_____ **c.** Notes payable, due in three years.	**3.** Property, plant, and equipment.
_____ **d.** Taxes withheld from employees.	**4.** Intangible assets.
_____ **e.** Patents.	**5.** Current liabilities.
_____ **f.** Retained earnings.	**6.** Long-term liabilities.
_____ **g.** Unearned subscription fees.	**7.** Stockholders' equity.
_____ **h.** Bonds of another corporation (a 20-year investment).	
_____ **i.** Notes payable, due in six months.	
_____ **j.** Accumulated depreciation.	

Exercise 4–15
Calculate current ratios for The Procter & Gamble Company and subsidiaries and comment (L.O. 8)

The following data are from the 1995 annual report of The Procter & Gamble Company and its subsidiaries. This company markets a broad range of laundry, cleaning, paper, beauty care, health care, food, and beverage products in more than 140 countries around the world. Leading brands include Ariel, Crest, Pampers, Pantene, Crisco, Vicks, and Max Factor. The dollar amounts are in millions.

	June 30	
	1995	**1994**
Current assets	$10,842	$9,988
Current liabilities	8,648	8,040

Calculate the current ratios for the two years. Comment on whether the trend is favorable or unfavorable.

PROBLEMS

The following adjusted trial balance is for Dream Home Realty Company:

DREAM HOME REALTY COMPANY
Adjusted Trial Balance
June 30, 1999

	Debits	Credits
Cash	$ 98,000	
Accounts Receivable	40,000	
Office Equipment	35,000	
Accumulated Depreciation—Office Equipment		$ 14,000
Automobiles	40,000	
Accumulated Depreciation—Automobiles		20,000
Accounts Payable		63,000
Capital Stock		75,000
Retained Earnings, July 1, 1998		54,700
Dividends	5,000	
Commissions Revenue		170,000
Salaries Expense	25,000	
Commissions Expense	120,000	
Gas and Oil Expense	4,000	
Rent Expense	14,800	
Supplies Expense	1,400	
Utilities Expense	2,000	
Depreciation Expense—Office Equipment	3,500	
Depreciation Expense—Automobiles	8,000	
	$396,700	$396,700

Prepare the closing journal entries at the end of the fiscal year, June 30, 1999.

The adjusted trial balance for Penrod Insurance Consultants, Inc., follows:

PENROD INSURANCE CONSULTANTS, INC.
Adjusted Trial Balance
December 31, 1999

	Debits	Credits
Cash	$107,200	
Accounts Receivable	68,000	
Interest Receivable	400	
Notes Receivable	20,000	
Prepaid Insurance	2,400	
Supplies on Hand	1,800	
Land	32,000	
Buildings	190,000	
Accumulated Depreciation—Buildings		$ 40,000
Office Equipment	28,000	
Accumulated Depreciation—Office Equipment		8,000
Accounts Payable		48,000
Salaries Payable		8,500
Interest Payable		900
Notes Payable (due 1998)		64,000
Capital Stock		120,000
Retained Earnings, January 1, 2000		42,800
Dividends	40,000	
Commissions Revenue		392,520
Advertising Expense	24,000	
Commissions Expense	75,440	
Travel Expense	12,880	
Depreciation Expense—Buildings	8,500	
Salaries Expense	98,400	
Depreciation Expense—Office Equipment	2,800	
Supplies Expense	3,800	
Insurance Expense	3,600	
Repairs Expense	1,900	
Utilities Expense	3,400	
Interest Expense	1,800	
Interest Revenue		1,600
	$726,320	$726,320

Problem 4–1
Prepare closing entries
(L.O. 4)

Required

Problem 4–2
Prepare income statement,
statement of retained
earnings, classified balance
sheet, closing entries, and
post-closing trial balance
(L.O. 3–5, 7)

Required
  a. Prepare an income statement for the year ended December 31, 1999.

  b. Prepare a statement of retained earnings.

  c. Prepare a classified balance sheet.

  d. Prepare the closing journal entries.

  e. Show the post-closing trial balance assuming you had posted the closing entries to the general ledger.

Problem 4–3
Prepare work sheet, adjusting entries, and closing entries (L.O. 2, 4)

The following trial balance and additional data are for Ramon Data Processing Company:

RAMON DATA PROCESSING COMPANY
Trial Balance
December 31, 1999

	Debits	Credits
Cash	$ 76,000	
Accounts Receivable	98,000	
Prepaid Rent	7,200	
Prepaid Insurance	2,400	
Equipment	80,000	
Accumulated Depreciation—Equipment		$ 40,000
Accounts Payable		30,000
Capital Stock		100,000
Retained Earnings, January 1, 1999		65,600
Dividends	24,000	
Service Revenue		370,000
Commissions Expense	270,000	
Travel Expense	36,000	
Miscellaneous Expense	12,000	
	$605,600	$605,600

Additional data
  1. The prepaid rent is for the period January 1, 1999, to December 31, 2000.

  2. The equipment is expected to last 10 years with no salvage value.

  3. The prepaid insurance was for the period April 1, 1999, to March 31, 2000.

  4. Accrued commissions payable total $3,000 at December 31.

Required
  a. Prepare a 12-column work sheet for the year ended December 31, 1999. You need not include account numbers or explanations of adjustments.

  b. Prepare the adjusting journal entries.

  c. Prepare the closing journal entries.

Problem 4–4
Prepare work sheet and closing entries (L.O. 2, 4)

The following trial balance and additional data are for Best-Friend Pet Hospital, Inc.:

BEST-FRIEND PET HOSPITAL, INC.
Trial Balance
December 31, 1999

	Debits	Credits
Cash	$ 16,490	
Accounts Receivable	54,390	
Supplies on Hand	900	
Prepaid Fire Insurance	1,800	
Prepaid Rent	21,600	
Equipment	125,000	
Accumulated Depreciation—Equipment		$ 25,000
Accounts Payable		29,550
Notes Payable		9,000
Capital Stock		150,000
Retained Earnings, January 1, 1999		20,685
Service Revenue		179,010
Interest Expense	225	
Salaries Expense	142,200	
Advertising Expense	29,250	
Supplies Expense	2,135	
Miscellaneous Expense	3,705	
Legal and Accounting Expense	13,750	
Utilities Expense	1,800	
	$413,245	$413,245

The company consistently followed the policy of initially debiting all prepaid items to asset accounts.

Additional data

1. Prepaid fire insurance is $600 as of the end of the year.
2. Supplies on hand are $638 as of the end of the year.
3. Prepaid rent is $2,625 as of the end of the year.
4. The equipment is expected to last 10 years with no salvage value.
5. Accrued salaries are $2,625.

Required

a. Prepare a 12-column work sheet for the year ended December 31, 1999. You need not include account numbers. Briefly explain the entries in the Adjustments columns at the bottom of the work sheet, as was done in Illustration 4.2.
b. Prepare the December 31, 1999, closing entries.

The following trial balance and additional data are for Roswell Interior Decorators, Inc.:

Problem 4–5
Prepare work sheet, income statement, statement of retained earnings, classified balance sheet, and adjusting and closing entries (L.O. 2–5, 7)

ROSWELL INTERIOR DECORATORS, INC.
Trial Balance
December 31, 1999

	Debits	Credits
Cash	$ 85,400	
Accounts Receivable	81,600	
Supplies on Hand	4,000	
Prepaid Rent	12,240	
Prepaid Advertising	2,880	
Prepaid Insurance	4,400	
Office Equipment	7,600	
Accumulated Depreciation—Office Equipment		$ 2,760
Office Furniture	29,200	
Accumulated Depreciation—Office Furniture		8,280
Accounts Payable		25,200
Notes Payable (due 2000)		4,000
Capital Stock		100,000
Retained Earnings, January 1, 1999		22,400
Dividends	42,520	
Service Revenue		250,000
Salaries Expense	98,800	
Utilities Expense	20,000	
Miscellaneous Expense	24,000	
	$412,640	$412,640

Additional data

1. Supplies on hand at December 31, 1999, are $1,000.
2. Rent expense for 1999 is $10,000.
3. Advertising expense for 1999 is $2,304.
4. Insurance expense for 1999 is $2,400.
5. Depreciation expense is office equipment, $912, and office furniture, $3,000.
6. Accrued interest on notes payable is $150.
7. Accrued salaries are $4,200.

Required

a. Prepare a 12-column work sheet for the year ended December 31, 1999. You need not include account numbers or explanations of adjustments.
b. Prepare an income statement.
c. Prepare a statement of retained earnings.
d. Prepare a classified balance sheet.
e. Prepare adjusting and closing entries.

ALTERNATE PROBLEMS

Problem 4–1A
Prepare closing entries
(L.O. 4)

The following adjusted trial balance is for Jasper Appliance Repair Company:

JASPER APPLIANCE REPAIR COMPANY
Adjusted Trial Balance
June 30, 1999

	Debits	Credits
Cash	$ 63,000	
Accounts Receivable	42,000	
Trucks	110,000	
Accumulated Depreciation—Trucks		$ 30,000
Accounts Payable		10,800
Notes Payable		20,000
Capital Stock		50,000
Retained Earnings, July 1, 1998		5,500
Dividends	10,000	
Service Revenue		230,000
Rent Expense	12,000	
Advertising Expense	5,000	
Salaries Expense	90,000	
Supplies Expense	1,500	
Insurance Expense	1,200	
Depreciation Expense—Trucks	10,000	
Interest Expense	1,000	
Miscellaneous Expense	600	
	$346,300	$346,300

Required   Prepare the closing journal entries at the end of the fiscal year, June 30, 1999.

Problem 4–2A
Prepare income
statement, statement of
retained earnings, classified
balance sheet, closing
entries, and post-closing
trial balance (L.O. 3–5, 7)

The adjusted trial balance for Denver Architects, Inc., follows.

DENVER ARCHITECTS, INC.
Adjusted Trial Balance
December 31, 1999

	Debits	Credits
Cash	$ 90,000	
Accounts Receivable	20,000	
Interest Receivable	200	
Notes Receivable	4,000	
Prepaid Insurance	960	
Prepaid Rent	2,400	
Supplies on Hand	600	
Equipment	60,000	
Accumulated Depreciation—Equipment		$ 12,500
Buildings	140,000	
Accumulated Depreciation—Buildings		15,000
Land	56,240	
Accounts Payable		60,000
Notes Payable		10,000
Interest Payable		750
Salaries Payable		7,000
Capital Stock		100,000
Retained Earnings, January 1, 1999		20,200
Dividends	40,000	
Service Revenue		360,000
Insurance Expense	1,920	
Rent Expense	9,600	
Advertising Expense	1,200	
Depreciation Expense—Equipment	2,500	
Depreciation Expense—Buildings	3,000	
Supplies Expense	2,280	
Salaries Expense	150,000	
Interest Expense	750	
Interest Revenue		200
	$585,650	$585,650

a. Prepare an income statement.

b. Prepare a statement of retained earnings.

c. Prepare a classified balance sheet.

d. Prepare the closing journal entries.

e. Show the post-closing trial balance assuming you had posted the closing entries to the general ledger.

Required

The following trial balance and additional data are for Sure Sale Realty Company:

Problem 4–3A
Prepare work sheet, adjusting entries, and closing entries (L.O. 2, 4)

SURE SALE REALTY COMPANY
Trial Balance
December 31, 1999

	Debits	Credits
Cash	$ 62,800	
Accounts Receivable	117,120	
Prepaid Rent	46,080	
Equipment	173,760	
Accumulated Depreciation—Equipment		$ 21,120
Accounts Payable		62,400
Capital Stock		96,000
Retained Earnings, January 1, 1999		49,920
Dividends	46,080	
Commissions Revenue		653,200
Salaries Expense	321,600	
Travel Expense	96,480	
Miscellaneous Expense	18,720	
	$882,640	$882,640

1. The prepaid rent is for the period July 1, 1999, to June 30, 2000.

2. The equipment has an expected life of 10 years with no salvage value.

3. Accrued salaries are $11,520.

4. Travel expenses accrued but unreimbursed to sales staff at December 31 were $17,280.

Additional data

a. Prepare a 12-column work sheet for the year ended December 31, 1999. You need not include account numbers or explanations of adjustments.

b. Prepare adjusting journal entries.

c. Prepare closing journal entries.

Required

The following trial balance and additional data are for South Sea Tours, Inc.:

Problem 4–4A
Prepare work sheet and closing entries (L.O. 2, 4)

SOUTH SEA TOURS, INC.
Trial Balance
December 31, 1999

	Debits	Credits
Cash	$109,050	
Accounts Receivable	133,750	
Prepaid Insurance	4,350	
Prepaid Advertising	18,000	
Notes Receivable	11,250	
Land	90,000	
Buildings	165,000	
Accumulated Depreciation—Buildings		$ 49,500
Office Equipment	83,400	
Accumulated Depreciation—Office Equipment		16,680
Accounts Payable		56,850
Notes Payable		75,000
Capital Stock		240,000
Retained Earnings, January 1, 1999		47,820
Dividends	30,000	
Service Revenue		368,350
Salaries Expense	96,000	
Travel Expense	111,000	
Interest Revenue		600
Interest Expense	3,000	
	$854,800	$854,800

The company consistently followed the policy of initially debiting all prepaid items to asset accounts.

Additional data

1. The buildings have an expected life of 50 years with no salvage value.
2. The office equipment has an expected life of 10 years with no salvage value.
3. Accrued interest on notes receivable is $450.
4. Accrued interest on the notes payable is $1,000.
5. Accrued salaries are $2,100.
6. Expired prepaid insurance is $3,750.
7. Expired prepaid advertising is $16,500.

Required

a. Prepare a 12-column work sheet for the year ended December 31, 1999. You need not include account numbers. Briefly explain the entries in the Adjustments columns at the bottom of the work sheet, as was done in Illustration 4.2.

b. Prepare the required closing entries.

Problem 4–5A
Prepare work sheet, income statement, statement of retained earnings, classified balance sheet, and adjusting and closing entries (L.O. 2–5, 7)

The following trial balance and additional data are for Florida Time-Share Property Management Company:

FLORIDA TIME-SHARE PROPERTY MANAGEMENT COMPANY
Trial Balance
December 31, 1999

	Debits	Credits
Cash	$424,000	
Prepaid Rent	28,800	
Prepaid Insurance	7,680	
Supplies on Hand	2,400	
Office Equipment	24,000	
Accumulated Depreciation—Office Equipment		$ 5,760
Automobiles	64,000	
Accumulated Depreciation—Automobiles		16,000
Accounts Payable		2,880
Unearned Management Fees		12,480
Capital Stock		360,000
Retained Earnings, January 1, 1999		120,640
Dividends	28,000	
Commissions Revenue		260,000
Management Fee Revenue		19,200
Salaries Expense	199,840	
Advertising Expense	2,400	
Gas and Oil Expense	14,240	
Miscellaneous Expense	1,600	
	$796,960	$796,960

Additional data

1. Insurance expense for the year, $3,840.
2. Rent expense for the year, $19,200.
3. Depreciation expense: office equipment, $2,880; and automobiles, $12,800.
4. Salaries earned but unpaid at December 31, $26,640.
5. Supplies on hand at December 31, $1,000.
6. The unearned management fees were received and recorded on November 1, 1999. The advance payment covered six months' management of an apartment building.

Required

a. Prepare a 12-column work sheet for the year ended December 31, 1999. You need not include account numbers or explanations of adjustments.

b. Prepare an income statement.

c. Prepare a statement of retained earnings.

d. Prepare a classified balance sheet.

e. Prepare adjusting and closing entries.

BEYOND THE NUMBERS—CRITICAL THINKING

Heather and Dan Holt met while both were employed in the interior trim and upholstery department of an auto manufacturer. After their marriage, they decided to earn some extra income by doing small jobs involving canvas, vinyl, and upholstered products. Their work was considered excellent, and at the urging of their customers, they decided to go into business for themselves, operating out of the basement of the house they owned. To do this, they invested $120,000 cash in their business. They spent $10,500 for a sewing machine (expected life, 10 years) and $12,000 for other miscellaneous tools and equipment (expected life, 5 years). They undertook only custom work, with the customers purchasing the required materials, to avoid stocking any inventory other than supplies. Generally, they required an advance deposit on all jobs.

The business seemed successful from the start, as the Holts received orders from many customers. But they felt something was wrong. They worked hard and charged competitive prices. Yet there seemed to be barely enough cash available from the business to cover immediate personal needs. Summarized, the checkbook of the business for 1999, their second year of operations, showed:

**Business Decision
Case 4–1**
Prepare report on profit-
ability of business (L.O. 3)

Balance, January 1, 1999		$ 99,200
Cash received from customers:		
For work done in 1998	$ 36,000	
For work done in 1999	200,000	
For work to be done in 2000	48,000	284,000
		$383,200
Cash paid out:		
Two-year insurance policy dated January 1, 1999	$ 19,200	
Utilities	48,000	
Supplies	104,000	
Other expenses	72,000	
Taxes, including sales taxes	26,400	
Dividends	40,000	309,600
Balance, December 31, 1999		$ 73,600

Considering how much they worked, the Holts were concerned that the cash balance decreased by $25,600 even though they only received dividends of $40,000. Their combined income from the auto manufacturer had been $45,000. They were seriously considering giving up their business and going back to work for the auto manufacturer. They turned to you for advice. You discovered the following:

1. Of the supplies purchased in 1999, $24,000 were used on jobs billed to customers in 1999; no supplies were used for any other work.

2. Work completed in 1999 and billed to customers for which cash had not yet been received by year-end amounted to $40,000.

Prepare a written report for the Holts, responding to their belief that their business is not sufficiently profitable. (Hint: Prepare an income statement for 1999 and include it in your report.)

Required

Using the annual report booklet, calculate the current ratios for the two years shown for The Coca-Cola Company, The Limited, Inc., Maytag Corporation, and John H. Harland Company. Write a summary of the results of your calculations. Also, look at some of the other data provided by the companies in preparing your comments. For instance, look at the net income for the last three years.

**Annual Report
Analysis 4–2**
Calculate current ratios
for four real companies
(L.O. 8)

Read the "A Broader Perspective" on page 146. Write a description of a career in public accounting at each level within the firm. Discuss the skills needed and how you could develop these skills.

**Broader Perspective—
Writing Experience 4–3**

In teams of two or three students, interview a management accountant in person or by speaker phone. Management accountants may have the title of chief financial officer (CFO), controller, or some other accounting title within a company. Seek information on the advantages and disadvantages of working as a management accountant. Also inquire about the nature of the work and any training programs offered by the company. As a team, write a memorandum to

Group Project 4–4
Interview a management
accountant

the instructor summarizing the results of the interview. The heading of the memorandum should contain the date, to whom it is written, from whom, and the subject matter.

Group Project 4–5
Perform annual report analysis

With a small group of students, obtain an annual report of a company in which you have some interest. You may obtain the annual report from your instructor, the library, the Internet, or the company. Describe the nature of each item on the classified balance sheet. You may have to do library research on some of the items. Also, calculate the current ratio for the most recent two years and comment. Write a report to your instructor summarizing the results of the project.

Group Project 4–6
Evaluate accounting software packages

With a small group of students and using library sources, write a paper comparing the features of three different accounting software packages (such as Peachtree Complete, DacEasy Accounting, Great Plains Accounting Dynamics, Open Systems Accounting Software, and Solomon for Windows). Give the strengths and weaknesses of each. Cite sources for the information and treat direct quotes properly.

USING THE INTERNET—A VIEW OF THE REAL WORLD

Internet Project 4–7
Investigate a consolidated balance sheet

Visit the following Internet site:

http://www.merck.com

Pursue choices you are offered on the screen until you locate the consolidated balance sheet. In a short report to your instructor, describe how you got to the balance sheet and identify the major headings used by Merck & Co., Inc., in the balance sheet. For instance, the first such heading is Current Assets. Also, calculate the current ratio and show how you found it.

Internet Project 4–8
Investigate a consolidated balance sheet

Visit the following Internet site:

http://www.mobil.com

Using the choices provided on the screen, locate the annual report and the consolidated balance sheet. Identify the major headings within the balance sheet for Mobil Corporation and calculate the current ratio for the two years shown. Show your calculations and comment on the results. Write a memo to your instructor summarizing your findings.

ANSWERS TO SELF-TEST

TRUE-FALSE

1. **True.** The three trial balances are the unadjusted trial balance, the adjusted trial balance, and the post-closing trial balance. The first two trial balances appear on the work sheet.

2. **False.** If a debit-balance account (such as Prepaid Rent) is credited in the adjustment, the amount in the Adjustments columns is deducted from the amount in the Trial Balance columns to determine the amount for that item in the Adjusted Trial Balance columns.

3. **True.** The net loss appears in the Income Statement credit column to balance the Income Statement columns. Then the loss appears in the Statement of Retained Earnings debit column because it reduces Retained Earnings.

4. **True.** All of these accounts are closed, or reduced to zero balances, as a result of the closing process.

5. **False.** All revenue and expense accounts have zero balances after closing.

6. **False.** Some manual accounting systems are still in use.

MULTIPLE-CHOICE

1. **b.** The other accounts are very likely to be adjusted. The Land account would be adjusted only if an error has been made involving that account.

2. **c.** The Adjusted Trial Balance columns should balance before items are spread to the Income Statement, Statement of Retained Earnings, and Balance Sheet columns. Therefore, if the Balance Sheet columns do not balance, the error is likely to exist in the last six columns of the work sheet.

3. **d.** The net income for the period does not appear in the balance sheet. It does appear in all of the other places listed.

4. **a.** The Dividends account is closed to the Retained Earnings account rather than to the Income Summary account.

5. **b.** Plant, property, and equipment is one of the long-term asset categories. Response **a** should not include equipment. Response **c** should not include notes receivable. Stockholders' equity is not subdivided into current and long-term categories.

COMPREHENSIVE REVIEW PROBLEM

Lopez Delivery Service Company has the following chart of accounts:

Acct. No.	Account Title	Acct. No.	Account Title
100	Cash	310	Retained Earnings
103	Accounts Receivable	320	Dividends
107	Supplies on Hand	400	Service Revenue
108	Prepaid Insurance	507	Salaries Expense
112	Prepaid Rent	511	Utilities Expense
140	Buildings	512	Insurance Expense
141	Accumulated Depreciation—Buildings	515	Rent Expense
150	Trucks	518	Supplies Expense
151	Accumulated Depreciation—Trucks	520	Depreciation Expense—Buildings
200	Accounts Payable	521	Depreciation Expense—Trucks
206	Salaries Payable	568	Miscellaneous Expense
300	Capital Stock	600	Income Summary

Problem covers all steps in the accounting cycle covered in Chapters 1–4. Open ledger accounts and enter beginning balances. Journalize transactions and post to ledger accounts. Prepare work sheet, income statement, statement of retained earnings, classified balance sheet, adjusting and closing entries, and post-closing trial balance.

The post-closing trial balance as of May 31, 1999, was as follows:

LOPEZ DELIVERY SERVICE COMPANY
Post-Closing Trial Balance
May 31, 1999

Acct. No.	Account Title	Debits	Credits
100	Cash	$ 80,000	
103	Accounts Receivable	30,000	
107	Supplies on Hand	14,000	
108	Prepaid Insurance	4,800	
112	Prepaid Rent	12,000	
140	Buildings	320,000	
141	Accumulated Depreciation—Buildings		$ 36,000
150	Trucks	80,000	
151	Accumulated Depreciation—Trucks		30,000
200	Accounts Payable		24,000
300	Capital Stock		300,000
310	Retained Earnings		150,800
		$540,800	$540,800

The transactions for June 1999 were as follows:

June 1 Performed delivery services for customers on account, $60,000.
      3 Paid dividends, $10,000.
      4 Purchased a $20,000 truck on account.
      7 Collected $22,000 of the accounts receivable.
      8 Paid $16,000 of the accounts payable.
   11 Purchased $4,000 of supplies on account. The asset account for supplies was debited.
   17 Performed delivery services for cash, $32,000.
   20 Paid the utilities bills for June, $1,200.
   23 Paid miscellaneous expenses for June, $600.
   28 Paid salaries of $28,000 for June.

Additional data

1. Depreciation expense on the buildings for June is $800.
2. Depreciation expense on the trucks for June is $400.
3. Accrued salaries at June 30 are $4,000.
4. A physical count showed $12,000 of supplies on hand on June 30.
5. The prepaid insurance balance of $4,800 applies to a two-year period beginning June 1, 1999.
6. The prepaid rent of $12,000 applies to a one-year period beginning June 1, 1999.
7. Performed $12,000 of delivery services for customers as of June 30 that will not be billed to those customers until July.

Required

a. Open three-column ledger accounts for the accounts listed in the chart of accounts.

b. Enter the May 31, 1999, account balances in the accounts.

c. Journalize the transactions for June 1999.

d. Post the June journal entries and include cross-references (assume all journal entries appear on page 10 of the journal).

e. Prepare a 12-column work sheet as of June 30, 1999.

f. Prepare an income statement, a statement of retained earnings, and a classified balance sheet.

g. Prepare and post the adjusting entries (assume they appear on page 11 of the general journal).

h. Prepare and post the closing entries (assume they appear on page 12 of the general journal).

i. Prepare a post-closing trial balance.

5

ACCOUNTING THEORY UNDERLYING FINANCIAL ACCOUNTING

Chapter 1 briefly introduced the body of theory underlying accounting procedures. In this chapter, we discuss accounting theory in greater depth. Now that you have learned some accounting procedures, you are better able to relate these theoretical concepts to accounting practice. **Accounting theory** is "a set of basic concepts and assumptions and related principles that explain and guide the accountant's actions in identifying, measuring, and communicating economic information."[1]

To some people, the word *theory* implies something abstract and out of reach. Understanding the theory behind the accounting process, however, helps one make decisions in diverse accounting situations. Accounting theory provides a logical framework for accounting practice.

The first part of the chapter describes underlying accounting assumptions or concepts, the measurement process, major principles, and modifying conventions or constraints. Accounting theory has developed over the years and is contained in authoritative accounting literature and textbooks. The next part of the chapter describes the development of the Financial Accounting Standards Board's conceptual framework for accounting. This framework builds on accounting theory developed over time and serves as a basis for formulating accounting standards in the future. Presenting the traditional body of theory first and the conceptual framework second gives you a sense of the historical development of accounting theory. Despite some overlap between the two parts of the chapter, remember that FASB's conceptual framework builds on traditional theory rather than replaces it. The final part of the chapter discusses (1) the information needs of investors and creditors as identified by a committee of the American Institute of Certified Public Accountants and (2) significant accounting policies contained in annual reports issued by companies.

[1]American Accounting Association, *A Statement of Basic Accounting Theory* (Sarasota, Fla., 1966), pp. 1–2.

LEARNING OBJECTIVES

After studying this chapter, you should be able to:

1. Identify and discuss the underlying assumptions or concepts of accounting.

2. Identify and discuss the major principles of accounting.

3. Identify and discuss the modifying conventions (or constraints) of accounting.

4. Describe the conceptual framework project of the Financial Accounting Standards Board.

(continued)

TRADITIONAL ACCOUNTING THEORY

Traditional accounting theory consists of underlying assumptions, rules of measurement, major principles, and modifying conventions (or constraints). The following sections describe these aspects of accounting theory that greatly influence accounting practice.

UNDERLYING ASSUMPTIONS OR CONCEPTS

The major underlying assumptions or concepts of accounting are (1) business entity, (2) going concern (continuity), (3) money measurement, (4) stable dollar, and (5) periodicity. This section discusses the effects of these assumptions on the accounting process.

Business Entity

Objective 1
Identify and discuss the underlying assumptions or concepts of accounting.

Real World Example
PepsiCo, Inc., is a business entity made up of different legal entities including, among others, Pizza Hut, Taco Bell, KFC, and Frito-Lay, Inc.

Data gathered in an accounting system must relate to a specific business unit or entity. The **business entity concept** assumes that each business has an existence separate from its owners, creditors, employees, customers, interested parties, and other businesses. For each business (such as a horse stable or a fitness center), the business, not the business owner, is the accounting entity. Therefore, financial statements are identified as belonging to a particular business entity. The content of these financial statements reports only on the activities, resources, and obligations of that entity.

A business entity may be made up of several different legal entities. For instance, a large business (such as General Motors Corporation) may consist of several separate corporations, each of which is a separate legal entity. For reporting purposes, however, the corporations may be considered as one business entity because they have a common ownership. Chapter 14 illustrates this concept.

Going Concern (Continuity)

Note to the Student
The going-concern concept is linked to depreciation by the assumption that a business will continue at least as long as its longest lived plant asset.

When accountants record business transactions for an entity, they assume it is a going concern. The **going-concern (continuity) assumption** states that an entity will continue to operate indefinitely unless strong evidence exists that the entity will terminate. The termination of an entity occurs when a company ceases business operations and sells its assets. The process of termination is called **liquidation.** If liquidation appears likely, the going-concern assumption is no longer valid.

Accountants often cite the going-concern assumption to justify using historical costs rather than market values in measuring assets. Market values are of little or no significance to an entity using its assets rather than selling them. On the other hand, if an entity is liquidating, it should use liquidation values to report assets.

The going-concern assumption permits the accountant to record certain items as assets. For example, printed advertising matter may promote a special sale next month. This advertising material may have little, if any, value to anyone but its owner. However, since management expects to continue operating long enough to benefit from the advertising, the accountant classifies the expenditure as an asset, prepaid advertising, and not an expense.

Money Measurement

The economic activity of a business is normally recorded and reported in money terms. **Money measurement** is the use of a monetary unit such as the dollar instead of physical or other units of measurement. Using a particular monetary unit provides accountants with a common unit of measurement to report economic activity. Without a monetary unit, it would be impossible to add such items as buildings, equipment, and inventory on a balance sheet.

Financial statements identify their unit of measure (the dollar in the United States) so the statement user can make valid comparisons of amounts. For example, it would be difficult to compare relative asset amounts or profitability of a company reporting in U.S. dollars with a company reporting in Japanese yen.

In the United States, accountants make another assumption regarding money measurement—the stable dollar assumption. Under the **stable dollar assumption,** the dollar is accepted as a reasonably stable unit of measurement. Thus, accountants make no adjustments for the changing value of the dollar in the primary financial statements.

Using the stable dollar assumption creates a difficulty in depreciation accounting. Assume, for example, that a company acquired a building in 1969 and computed the 30-year straight-line depreciation on the building without adjusting for any changes in the value of the dollar. Thus, the depreciation deducted in 1999 is the same as the depreciation deducted in 1969. The company makes no adjustments for the difference between the values of the 1969 dollar and the 1999 dollar. Both dollars are treated as equal monetary units of measurement despite substantial price inflation over the 30-year period. Accountants and business executives have expressed concern over this inflation problem, especially during periods of high inflation.

Stable Dollar

According to the **periodicity (time periods) assumption,** accountants divide an entity's life into months or years to report its economic activities. Then, accountants attempt to prepare accurate reports on the entity's activities for these periods. Although these time-period reports provide useful and timely financial information for investors and creditors, they may be inaccurate for some of these time periods because accountants must estimate depreciation expense and certain other adjusting entries.

Accounting reports cover relatively short periods. These time periods are usually of equal length so that statement users can make valid comparisons of a company's performance from period to period. The length of the accounting period must be stated in the financial statements. For instance, so far, the income statements in this text were for either one month or one year. Companies that publish their financial statements, such as publicly held corporations, generally prepare monthly statements for internal management and publish financial statements quarterly and annually for external statement users.

Periodicity (Time Periods)

ACCRUAL BASIS AND PERIODICITY Chapter 3 demonstrated that financial statements more accurately reflect the financial status and operations of a company when prepared under the accrual basis rather than the cash basis of accounting. Under the cash basis, we record revenues when cash is received and expenses when cash is paid. Under the accrual basis, however, we record revenues when services are rendered or products are sold and expenses when incurred.

The periodicity assumption requires preparing adjusting entries under the accrual basis. Without the periodicity assumption, a business would have only one time period running from its inception to its termination. Then, the concepts of cash basis and accrual basis accounting would be irrelevant because all revenues and all expenses would be recorded in that one time period and would not have to be assigned to artificially short periods of one year or less.

APPROXIMATION AND JUDGMENT BECAUSE OF PERIODICITY To provide periodic financial information, accountants must often estimate expected uncollectible accounts (see Chapter 9) and the useful lives of depreciable assets. Uncertainty about future events prevents precise measurement and makes estimates necessary in accounting. Fortunately, these estimates are often reasonably accurate.

OTHER BASIC CONCEPTS

Other basic accounting concepts that affect accounting for entities are (1) general-purpose financial statements, (2) substance over form, (3) consistency, (4) double entry, and (5) articulation. We discuss these basic accounting concepts next.

General-Purpose Financial Statements	Accountants prepare general-purpose financial statements at regular intervals to meet many of the information needs of external parties and top-level internal managers. In contrast, accountants can gather special-purpose financial information for a specific decision, usually on a one-time basis. For example, management may need specific information to decide whether to purchase a new computer. Since special-purpose financial information must be specific, this information is best obtained from the detailed accounting records rather than from the financial statements.
Substance over Form	In some business transactions, the economic substance of the transaction conflicts with its legal form. For example, a contract that is legally a lease may, in fact, be equivalent to a purchase. A company may have a three-year contract to lease (rent) an automobile at a stated monthly rental fee. At the end of the lease period, the company receives title to the auto after paying a nominal sum (say, $1). The economic substance of this transaction is a purchase rather than a lease of the auto. Thus, under the substance-over-form concept, the auto is an asset on the balance sheet and is depreciated instead of showing rent expense on the income statement. Accountants record a transaction's *economic substance* rather than its *legal form*.
Consistency	**Consistency** generally requires that a company use the same accounting principles and reporting practices through time. This concept prohibits indiscriminate switching of accounting principles or methods, such as changing inventory methods every year. However, consistency does not prohibit a change in accounting principles if the information needs of financial statement users are better served by the change. When a company makes a change in accounting principles, it must make the following disclosures in the financial statements: (1) nature of the change; (2) reasons for the change; (3) effect of the change on current net income, if significant; and (4) cumulative effect of the change on past income.
Double Entry	Chapter 2 introduced the basic accounting concept of the double-entry method of recording transactions. Under the double-entry approach, every transaction has a two-sided effect on each party engaging in the transaction. Thus, to record a transaction, each party debits at least one account and credits at least one account. The total debits equal the total credits in each journal entry.
Articulation	When learning how to prepare work sheets in Chapter 4, you learned that financial statements are fundamentally related and *articulate* (interact) with each other. For example, we carry the amount of net income from the income statement to the statement of retained earnings. Then we carry the ending balance on the statement of retained earnings to the balance sheet to bring total assets and total equities into balance. In Illustration 5.1 we summarize the underlying assumptions or concepts. The next section discusses the measurement process used in accounting.

MEASUREMENT IN ACCOUNTING

Earlier, we defined accounting as "the process of identifying, measuring, and communicating economic information to permit informed judgments and decisions by the users of the information."[2] In this section, we focus on the *measurement* process of accounting.

---

[2]Ibid., p. 1.

ILLUSTRATION 5.1 The Underlying Assumptions or Concepts

Assumption or Concept	Description	Importance
Business entity	Each business has an existence separate from its owners, creditors, employees, customers, other interested parties, and other businesses.	Defines the scope of the business such as a horse stable or physical fitness center. Identifies which transactions should be recorded on the company's books.
Going concern (continuity)	An entity will continue to operate indefinitely unless strong evidence exists that the entity will terminate.	Allows a company to continue carrying plant assets at their historical costs in spite of a change in their market values.
Money measurement	Each business uses a monetary unit of measurement, such as the dollar, instead of physical or other units of measurement.	Provides accountants with a common unit of measure to report economic activity. This concept permits us to add and subtract items on the financial statements.
Stable dollar	The dollar is accepted as a reasonably stable unit of measure.	Permits us to make no adjustments in the financial statements for the changing value of the dollar. This assumption works fairly well in the United States because of our relatively low rate of inflation.
Periodicity (time periods)	An entity's life can be subdivided into months or years to report its economic activities.	Permits us to prepare financial statements that cover periods shorter than the entire life of a business. Thus, we know how well a business is performing before it terminates its operations. The need for adjusting entries arises because of this concept and the use of accrual accounting.
General-purpose financial statements	One set of financial statements serves the needs of all users.	Allows companies to prepare only one set of financial statements instead of a separate set for each potential type of user of those statements. The financial statements should be free of bias so they do not favor the interests of any one type of user.
Substance over form	Accountants should record the economic substance of a transaction rather than its legal form.	Encourages the accountant to record the true nature of a transaction rather than its apparent nature. This approach is the accounting equivalent of "tell it like it is." An apparent lease transaction that has all the characteristics of a purchase should be recorded as a purchase.
Consistency	Generally requires that a company use the same accounting principles and reporting practices every accounting period.	Prevents a company from changing accounting methods whenever it likes to present a better picture or to manipulate income. The inventory and depreciation chapters (Chapters 7 and 10) both mention the importance of this concept.
Double entry	Every transaction has a two-sided effect on each company or party engaging in the transaction.	Uses a system of checks and balances to help identify whether or not errors have been made in recording transactions. When the debits do not equal the credits, this inequality immediately signals us to stop and find the error.
Articulation	Financial statements are fundamentally related and articulate (interact) with each other.	Changes in account balances during an accounting period are reflected in financial statements that are related to one another. For instance, earning revenue increases net income on the income statement, retained earnings on the statement of retained earnings, and assets and retained earnings on the balance sheet. The statement of retained earnings ties the income statement and balance sheet together.

Accountants measure a business entity's assets, liabilities, and stockholders' equity and any changes that occur in them. By assigning the effects of these changes to particular time periods (periodicity), they can find the net income or net loss of the accounting entity for those periods.

Measuring Assets and Liabilities

Accountants measure the various assets of a business in different ways. They measure cash at its specified amount. Chapter 9 explains how they measure claims to cash, such as accounts receivable, at their expected cash inflows, taking into consideration possible uncollectibles. They measure inventories, prepaid expenses, plant assets, and intangibles at their historical costs (actual amounts paid). After the acquisition date, they carry some items, such as inventory, at the lower-of-cost-or-market value. After the acquisition date, they carry plant assets and intangibles at original cost less accumulated depreciation or amortization. They measure liabilities at the amount of cash that will be paid or the value of services that will be performed to satisfy the liabilities.

Measuring Changes in Assets and Liabilities

Accountants can easily measure some changes in assets and liabilities, such as the acquisition of an asset on credit and the payment of a liability. Other changes in assets and liabilities, such as those recorded in adjusting entries, are more difficult to measure because they often involve estimates and/or calculations. The accountant must determine when a change has taken place and the amount of the change. These decisions involve matching revenues and expenses and are guided by the principles discussed next.

THE MAJOR PRINCIPLES

Objective 2
Identify and discuss the major principles of accounting.

Generally accepted accounting principles (GAAP) set forth standards or methods for presenting financial accounting information. A standardized presentation format enables users to compare the financial information of different companies more easily. Generally accepted accounting principles have been either developed through accounting practice or established by authoritative organizations. Organizations that have contributed to the development of the principles are the American Institute of Certified Public Accountants (AICPA), the Financial Accounting Standards Board (FASB), the Securities and Exchange Commission (SEC), the American Accounting Association (AAA), the Financial Executives Institute (FEI), and the Institute of Management Accounting (IMA). This section explains the following major principles:

Reinforcing Problem
E5–1 Match theory terms with definitions.

1. Exchange-price (or cost) principle.
2. Matching principle.
3. Revenue recognition principle.
4. Expense recognition principle.
5. Gain and loss recognition principle.
6. Full disclosure principle.

Exchange-Price (or Cost) Principle

Whenever resources are transferred between two parties, such as buying merchandise on account, the accountant must follow the *exchange-price (or cost) principle* in presenting that information. The **exchange-price (or cost) principle** requires an accountant to record transfers of resources at prices agreed on by the parties to the exchange at the time of exchange. This principle sets forth (1) what goes into the accounting system—transaction data; (2) when it is recorded—at the time of exchange; and (3) the amounts—exchange prices—at which assets, liabilities, stockholders' equity, revenues, and expenses are recorded.

As applied to most assets, this principle is often called the **cost principle.** It dictates that purchased or self-constructed assets are initially recorded at historical cost. **Historical cost** is the amount paid, or the fair market value of the liability incurred or other resources surrendered, to acquire an asset and place it in a condition and position for its intended use. For instance, when the cost of a plant asset (such as a machine) is recorded, its cost includes the net purchase price plus any costs of reconditioning, testing, transporting, and placing the asset in the location for its intended use. Accountants prefer the term *exchange-price principle* to cost principle because it seems inappropriate to refer to liabilities, stockholders' equity, and such assets as cash and accounts receivable as being measured in terms of cost.

Using the **matching principle,** we determine the net income of a period by associating or relating revenues earned with expenses incurred to generate those revenues. The logic underlying this principle is that whenever economic resources are used, someone wants to know what was accomplished and at what cost. Every evaluation of economic activity involves matching benefit with sacrifice. We discuss and illustrate the application of the matching principle later in this chapter.

Matching Principle

Reinforcing Problem
E5–4 Compute the effect on financial statements of incorrectly expensing an asset.

BUSINESS INSIGHT   In some European countries, the financial statements contain *secret reserves.* These secret reserves arise from a company not reporting all of its profits when it has a very good year. The justification is that the stockholders vote on the amount of dividends they receive each year; if all profits were reported, the stockholders might vote to pay the entire amount out as dividends. By holding back some profits, not only are the creditors more protected but the company is also more solvent and has more resources to invest in productive assets.

AN ACCOUNTING PERSPECTIVE

Revenue is not difficult to define or measure; it is the inflow of assets from the sale of goods and services to customers, measured by the cash expected to be received from customers. However, the crucial question for the accountant is when to record a revenue. Under the **revenue recognition principle,** revenues should be earned and realized before they are recognized (recorded).

Revenue Recognition Principle

EARNING OF REVENUE   All economic activities undertaken by a company to create revenues are part of the earning process. Many activities may have preceded the actual receipt of cash from a customer, including (1) placing advertisements, (2) calling on the customer several times, (3) submitting samples, (4) acquiring or manufacturing goods, and (5) selling and delivering goods. For these activities, the company incurs costs. Although revenue was actually being earned by these activities, accountants do not recognize revenue until the time of sale because of the requirement that revenue be *substantially* earned before it is recognized (recorded). This requirement is the **earning principle**

REALIZATION OF REVENUE   Under the **realization principle,** the accountant does not recognize (record) revenue until the seller acquires the right to receive payment from the buyer. The seller acquires this right from the buyer at the time of sale for merchandise transactions or when services have been performed in service transactions. Legally, a sale of merchandise occurs when title to the goods passes to the buyer. The time at which title passes normally depends on the shipping terms—FOB shipping point or FOB destination (as we discuss in Chapter 6). As a practical matter, accountants generally record revenue when goods are delivered.

The advantages of recognizing revenue at the time of sale are (1) the actual transaction—delivery of goods—is an observable event; (2) revenue is easily measured; (3) risk of loss due to price decline or destruction of the goods has passed to the buyer; (4) revenue has been earned, or substantially so; and (5) because the revenue has been earned, expenses and net income can be determined. As discussed later, the disadvantage of recognizing revenue at the time of sale is that the revenue might not be recorded in the period during which most of the activity creating it occurred.

EXCEPTIONS TO THE REALIZATION PRINCIPLE   The following examples are instances when practical considerations may cause accountants to vary the point of revenue recognition from the time of sale. These examples illustrate the effect that the business environment has on the development of accounting principles and standards.

Cash Collection as Point of Revenue Recognition   Some small companies record revenues and expenses at the time of cash collection and payment, which may not occur at the time of sale. This procedure is the cash basis of accounting. The cash basis is acceptable primarily in service enterprises that do not have substantial credit transactions or inventories, such as business entities of doctors or dentists.

Installment Basis of Revenue Recognition   When collecting the selling price of goods sold in monthly or annual installments and considerable doubt exists as to collectibility, the company may use the installment basis of accounting. Companies make these sales in spite of the doubtful collectibility of the account because their margin of profit is high and the goods can be repossessed if the payments are not received. Under the **installment basis,** the percentage of total gross margin (selling price of a good minus its cost) recognized in a period is equal to the percentage of total cash from a sale that is received in that period. Thus, the gross margin recognized in a period is equal to the cash received times the gross margin percentage (gross margin divided by selling price). The formula to recognize gross profit on cash collections made on installment sales of a certain year is:

$$\frac{\text{Cash}}{\text{collections}} \times \frac{\text{Gross margin}}{\text{percentage}} = \frac{\text{Gross margin}}{\text{recognized}}$$

To be more precise, we expand the descriptions in the formula as follows:

$$\begin{matrix}\text{Cash collections} \\ \text{this year resulting} \\ \text{from installment} \\ \text{sales made in a} \\ \text{certain year}\end{matrix} \times \begin{matrix}\text{Gross margin} \\ \text{percentage} \\ \text{for the year} \\ \text{of sale}\end{matrix} = \begin{matrix}\text{Gross margin} \\ \text{recognized this year} \\ \text{on cash collections} \\ \text{this year from} \\ \text{installment sales made} \\ \text{in a certain year}\end{matrix}$$

Reinforcing Problems
E5–2 Compute net income under accrual basis and under installment basis.
P5–2 Compute net income assuming revenues are recognized at time of sale and then assuming installment basis is used.

To illustrate, assume a company sold a stereo set. The facts of the sale are:

Date of Sale	Selling Price	Cost	Gross Margin (Selling price − Cost)	Gross Margin Percentage (Gross margin ÷ Selling price)
October 1, 1999	$500	$300	($500 − $300) = $200	($200 ÷ $500) = 40%

The buyer makes 10 equal monthly installment payments of $50 to pay for the set (10 × $50 = $500). If the company receives three monthly payments in 1999, the total amount of cash received in 1999 is $150 (3 × $50). The gross margin to recognize in 1999 is:

$$\begin{matrix}\text{1999 cash} \\ \text{collections from} \\ \text{1999 installment} \\ \text{sales}\end{matrix} \times \begin{matrix}\text{Gross margin} \\ \text{percentage} \\ \text{on 1999} \\ \text{installment} \\ \text{sales}\end{matrix} = \begin{matrix}\text{1999 gross margin} \\ \text{recognized on 1999} \\ \text{cash collections} \\ \text{from 1999 installment} \\ \text{sales}\end{matrix}$$

$$\mathbf{\$150} \quad \times \quad \mathbf{40\%} \quad = \quad \mathbf{\$60}$$

The company collects the other installments when due so it receives a total of $350 in 2000 from 1999 installment sales. The gross margin to recognize in 2000 on these cash collections is as follows:

Eighteen ay lustum dudit policy.

$1000 \times 60\% = 600$

$\frac{6}{10} = \frac{3}{5}$

Photo ID Cards

1 accountant
Function — approving bills for payment
preparing and signing checks,
almost all other financial duties
receiving, approving & paying invoices

Steps required to prevent one person to control
almost all functions of the accounting program would be

Later Steps they may prevent theft of this nature

* Segregation of Duties — even though this
is a small business should not be difficult
to establish.

* Assign specific duties of each employee.

* Rotate employee job assignments

* maintain complete and accurate accounting records

* Establish written procedure for approval of purchases
this would include:
Purchase requisition
purchase order
invoice
receiving report

$$
\begin{array}{ccc}
\begin{array}{c}\text{2000 cash}\\\text{collections from}\\\text{1999 installment}\\\text{sales}\end{array} & \times & \begin{array}{c}\text{Gross margin}\\\text{percentage}\\\text{on 1999}\\\text{installment}\\\text{sales}\end{array} & = & \begin{array}{c}\text{2000 gross margin}\\\text{recognized on 2000}\\\text{cash collections}\\\text{from 1999 installment}\\\text{sales}\end{array}\\
\\
\mathbf{\$350} & \times & \mathbf{40\%} & = & \mathbf{\$140}
\end{array}
$$

In summary, the total receipts and gross margin recognized in the two years are as follows:

Note to the Student
The installment basis of revenue recognition is acceptable only when considerable doubt exists about the collectibility of the installment. The installment basis delays revenue recognition beyond the time of sale.

Year	Total Amount of Cash Received	Gross Margin Recognized
1999	$150 (30%)	$ 60 (30%)
2000	350 (70%)	140 (70%)
Total	$500 100%	$200 100%

An accountant may use the installment basis of revenue recognition for tax purposes only in very limited circumstances. Because the installment basis delays revenue recognition beyond the time of sale, it is acceptable for accounting purposes only when considerable doubt exists as to collectibility of the installments.

Revenue Recognition on Long-Term Construction Projects   Companies recognize revenue from a long-term construction project under two different methods: (1) the completed-contract method or (2) the percentage-of-completion method. The **completed-contract method** does not recognize any revenue until the project is completed. In that period, they recognize all revenue even though the contract may have required three years to complete. Thus, the completed-contract method recognizes revenues at the time of sale, as is true for most sales transactions. Companies carry costs incurred on the project forward in an inventory account (Construction in Process) and charge them to expense in the period in which the revenue is recognized.

Some accountants argue that waiting so long to recognize any revenue is unreasonable. They believe that because revenue-producing activities have been performed during each year of construction, revenue should be recognized in each year of construction even if estimates are needed. The **percentage-of-completion method** recognizes revenue based on the estimated stage of completion of a long-term project. To measure the stage of completion, firms compare actual costs incurred in a period with the total estimated costs to be incurred on the project.

Reinforcing Problems
E5–3 Recognize revenue under percentage-of-completion method.
P5–3 Compute income under completed-contract and percentage-of-completion methods.

To illustrate, assume that a company has a contract to build a dam for $44 million. The estimated construction cost is $40 million. You calculate the estimated gross margin as follows:

Sales Price of Dam	Estimated Costs to Construct Dam	Estimated Gross Margin (Sales price − Estimated costs)
$44 million	$40 million	($44 million − $40 million) = $4 million

Real World Example
The Tax Reform Act of 1986 allows only small contractors to use the completed-contract method for tax purposes. Large contractors must use one of two variations of the percentage-of-completion method.

The firm recognizes the $4 million gross margin in the financial statements by recording the assigned revenue for the year and then deducting actual costs incurred that year. The formula to recognize revenue is:

$$
\left(\begin{array}{c}\text{Actual construction}\\\text{costs incurred during}\\\text{the period}\end{array} \div \begin{array}{c}\text{Total estimated}\\\text{construction costs}\\\text{for the entire project}\end{array}\right) \times \begin{array}{c}\text{Total}\\\text{sales}\\\text{price}\end{array} = \begin{array}{c}\text{Revenue}\\\text{recognized}\\\text{for period}\end{array}
$$

Suppose that by the end of the first year (1999), the company had incurred actual construction costs of $30 million. These costs are 75% of the total estimated construction costs ($30 million ÷ $40 million = 75%). Under the percentage-of-completion method, the firm would use the 75% figure to assign revenue to the first year. In 2000, it incurs another $6 million of construction costs. In 2001, it incurs the final $4 million of construction costs. The amount of revenue to assign to each year is as follows:

Year	Ratio of Actual Construction Costs to Total Estimated Construction Costs	×	Agreed Price of Dam	=	Amount of Revenue to Recognize (Assign)
1999. . .	($30 million ÷ $40 million) = 75%				
	75%	×	$44 million	=	$33 million
2000. . .	($6 million ÷ $40 million) = 15%				
	15%	×	$44 million	=	$6.6 million
2001. . .	($4 million ÷ $40 million) = 10%				
	10%	×	$44 million	=	$4.4 million

The amount of gross margin to recognize in each year is as follows:

Year	Assigned Revenues	−	Actual Construction Costs	=	Recognized Gross Margin
1999	$33.0 million	−	$30.0 million	=	$3.0 million
2000	6.6	−	6.0	=	0.6
2001	4.4	−	4.0	=	0.4
Total	$44.0 million	−	$40.0 million	=	$4.0 million

This company would deduct other costs incurred in the accounting period, such as general and administrative expenses, from gross margin to determine net income. For instance, assuming general and administrative expenses were $100,000 in 1999, net income would be ($3,000,000 − $100,000) = $2,900,000.

In Illustration 5.2, you can see which methods of accounting for long-term contracts are used most often in the financial statements of a group of companies involved in these types of projects. The percentage-of-completion method is the most widely used. (Units of delivery is a form of the percentage-of-completion method.)

REVENUE RECOGNITION AT COMPLETION OF PRODUCTION   Businesses that recognize revenue at the time of completion of production or extraction use the **production basis.** The production basis is an acceptable procedure when accounting for many farm products (wheat, corn, and soybeans) and for certain precious metals (gold). Accountants justify recognizing revenue before the sale of these products because (1) the products are homogeneous in nature, (2) they can usually be sold at their market prices, and (3) unit production costs for these products are often difficult to determine.

To recognize revenue on completion of production or extraction, they debit inventory (an asset) and credit a revenue account for the expected selling price of the goods. Then they treat all costs incurred in the period as expenses. For example, assume that a firm mined 1,000 ounces of gold at a time when gold sold for $400 per ounce. The entry to record the extraction of 1,000 ounces of gold would be:

Reinforcing Problem
E5–5 Compute gross margin under GAAP and then as production is completed.

Inventory of Gold	400,000	
Revenue from Extraction of Gold		400,000
To record extraction of 1,000 ounces of gold. Selling price is $400 per ounce.		

Later, if the company sells the gold at $400 per ounce, it debits Cash and credits Inventory of Gold for $400,000 as follows:

Cash	400,000	
Inventory of Gold		400,000
To record sale of 1,000 ounces of gold at $400 per ounce.		

If expenses in producing the gold amounted to $300,000, net income on the gold mined would be $100,000.

	Number of Companies			
	1995	**1994**	**1993**	**1992**
Percentage of completion	80	90	91	94
Units of delivery	28	33	27	35
Completed contract	4	2	4	5
Not determinable	3	1	1	1

Source: American Institute of Certified Public Accountants, *Accounting Trends & Techniques* (New York: AICPA, 1996), p. 382.

ILLUSTRATION 5.2
Methods of Accounting
for Long-Term Contracts

Expense Recognition Principle

Expense recognition is closely related to, and sometimes discussed as part of, the revenue recognition principle. The **expense recognition principle** states that expenses should be recognized (recorded) as they are incurred to produce revenues. An expense is the outflow or using up of assets in the generation of revenue. Firms voluntarily incur expense to produce revenue. For instance, a television set delivered by a dealer to a customer in exchange for cash is an asset consumed to produce revenue; its cost becomes an expense. Similarly, the cost of services such as labor are voluntarily incurred to produce revenue.

THE MEASUREMENT OF EXPENSE   Accountants measure most assets used in operating a business by their historical costs. Therefore, they measure a depreciation expense resulting from the consumption of those assets by the historical costs of those assets. They measure other expenses, such as wages that are paid for currently, at their current costs.

THE TIMING OF EXPENSE RECOGNITION   The matching principle implies that a relationship exists between expenses and revenues. For certain expenses, such as costs of acquiring or producing the products sold, you can easily see this relationship. However, when a direct relationship cannot be seen, we charge the costs of assets with limited lives to expense in the periods benefited on a systematic and rational allocation basis. Depreciation of plant assets is an example.

Product costs are costs incurred in the acquisition or manufacture of goods. As you will see in the next chapter, included as product costs for purchased goods are invoice, freight, and insurance-in-transit costs. For manufacturing companies, product costs include all costs of materials, labor, and factory operations necessary to produce the goods. Product costs attach to the goods purchased or produced and remain in inventory accounts as long as the goods are on hand. We charge product costs to expense when the goods are sold. The result is a precise matching of cost of goods sold expense to its related revenue.

Period costs are costs not traceable to specific products and expensed in the period incurred. Selling and administrative costs are period costs.

AN ACCOUNTING PERSPECTIVE

USES OF TECHNOLOGY   An interesting website on the Internet is:
http://www.aicpa.org/members/div/career/index.htm
By visiting this site you will learn about the work of the AICPA's Academic and Career Development Team. The objectives of this team are to encourage highly qualified people to enter the profession, to improve the quality and value of the education of accountants, to recruit minorities into the profession and enhance their upward mobility, and to enhance the upward mobility of women in the profession, and help males and females balance their work, family, and personal lives. You might want to browse around this site to learn about these important initiatives.

Gain and Loss Recognition Principle

The **gain and loss recognition principle** states that we record gains only when realized, but losses when they first become evident. Thus, we recognize losses at an earlier point than gains. This principle is related to the conservatism concept.

Gains typically result from the sale of long-term assets for more than their book value. Firms should not recognize gains until they are realized through sale or exchange. Recognizing potential gains before they are actually realized is generally forbidden in accounting.

Losses consume assets, as do expenses. However, unlike expenses, they do not produce revenues. Losses are usually *involuntary,* such as the loss suffered from destruction by fire on an uninsured building. A loss on the sale of a building may be voluntary when management decides to sell the building even though incurring a loss.

Full Disclosure Principle

The **full disclosure principle** states that information important enough to influence the decisions of an informed user of the financial statements should be disclosed. Depending on its nature, companies should disclose this information either in the financial statements, in notes to the financial statements, or in supplemental statements. For instance, the annual report booklet illustrates how The Coca-Cola Company discloses information in notes to its financial statements. In judging whether or not to disclose information, it is better to err on the side of too much disclosure rather than too little. Many lawsuits against CPAs and their clients have resulted from inadequate or misleading disclosure of the underlying facts.

We summarize the major principles and describe the importance of each in Illustration 5.3.

AN ACCOUNTING PERSPECTIVE
—

BUSINESS INSIGHT   The accounting model involves reporting revenues earned and expenses incurred by the company. Some have argued that social benefits and social costs created by the company should also be reported. Suppose, for instance, that a company is dumping toxic waste into a river and this action causes cancer among the citizens downstream. Should this cost be reported when preparing financial statements showing the performance of the company? What do you think?

MODIFYING CONVENTIONS (OR CONSTRAINTS)

Objective 3
Identify and discuss the
modifying conventions (or
constraints) of accounting.

In certain instances, companies do not strictly apply accounting principles because of modifying conventions (or constraints). **Modifying conventions** are customs emerging from accounting practice that alter the results obtained from a strict application of accounting principles. Three modifying conventions are cost-benefit, materiality, and conservatism.

COST-BENEFIT   The **cost-benefit consideration** involves deciding whether the benefits of including optional information in financial statements exceed the costs of providing the information. Users tend to think information is cost free since they incur none of the costs of providing the information. Preparers realize that providing information is costly. The benefits of using information should exceed the costs of providing it. The measurement of benefits is nebulous and inexact, which makes application of this modifying convention difficult in practice.

MATERIALITY   **Materiality** is a modifying convention that allows accountants to deal with immaterial (unimportant) items in an expedient but theoretically incorrect manner. The fundamental question accountants must ask in judging the materiality of an item is whether a knowledgeable user's decisions would be different if the information were presented in the theoretically correct manner. If not, the item is immaterial and may be reported in a theoretically incorrect but expedient manner. For instance, because inexpensive items such as calculators often do not make a difference in a statement user's decision to invest in the company, they are *immaterial* (unimportant) and may be expensed when purchased. However, because expensive items such as mainframe computers usually do make a difference in such a decision, they are

ILLUSTRATION 5.3   The Major Principles

Principle	Description	Importance
Exchange-price (or cost)	Requires transfers of resources to be recorded at prices agreed on by the parties to the exchange at the time of the exchange.	Tells the accountant to record a transfer of resources at an objectively determinable amount at the time of the exchange. Also, self-constructed assets are recorded at their actual cost rather than at some estimate of what they would have cost if they had been purchased.
Matching	Net income of a period is determined by associating or relating revenues earned in a period with expenses incurred to generate those revenues.	Identifies how to calculate net income under the accrual concept of income. In Chapter 3 we illustrated the matching principle; all chapters reinforce the importance of this fundamental principle.
Revenue recognition	Revenues should be earned and realized before they are recognized (recorded).	Informs accountant that revenues generally should be recognized when services are performed or goods are sold. Exceptions are made for installment sales, long-term construction projects, certain farm products, and precious metals.
Expense recognition	Expenses should be recognized (recorded) as they are incurred to produce revenues.	Indicates that expenses are to be recorded as soon as they are incurred rather than waiting until some future time.
Gain and loss recognition	Gains may be recorded only when realized, but losses should be recorded when they first become evident.	Tells the accountant to be conservative when recognizing gains and losses. Gains can only be recognized when they have been realized through sale or exchange. Losses should be recognized as soon as they become evident. Thus, potential losses can be recorded, but only gains that have actually been realized can be recorded.
Full disclosure	Information important enough to influence the decisions of an informed user of the financial statements should be disclosed.	Requires the accountant to disclose everything that is important. A good rule to follow is—if in doubt, disclose. Another good rule is—if you are not consistent, disclose all the facts and the effect on income.

material (important) and should be recorded as assets and depreciated. Accountants should record all material items in a theoretically correct manner. They may record immaterial items in a theoretically incorrect manner simply because it is more convenient and less expensive to do so. For example, they may debit the cost of a wastebasket to an expense account rather than an asset account even though the wastebasket has an expected useful life of 30 years. It simply is not worth the cost of recording depreciation expense on such a small item over its life.

The FASB defines materiality as "the magnitude of an omission or misstatement of accounting information that, in the light of surrounding circumstances, makes it probable that the judgment of a reasonable person relying on the information would have been changed or influenced by the omission or misstatement."[3] The term *magnitude* in this definition suggests that the materiality of an item may be assessed by looking at its relative size. A $10,000 error in an expense in a company with earnings of $30,000 is material. The same error in a company earning $30,000,000 may not be material.

Materiality involves more than the relative dollar amounts. Often the nature of the item makes it material. For example, it may be quite significant to know that a company is paying bribes or making illegal political contributions, even if the dollar amounts of such items are relatively small.

---

[3]FASB, *Statement of Financial Accounting Concepts No. 2*, "Qualitative Characteristics of Accounting Information" (Stamford, Conn., 1980), p. xv. Copyright © by the Financial Accounting Standards Board, High Ridge Park, Stamford, Connecticut 06905, U.S.A. Quoted (or excerpted) with permission. Copies of the complete documents are available from the FASB.

ILLUSTRATION 5.4 Modifying Conventions

Modifying Convention	Description	Importance
Cost-benefit	Optional information should be included in financial statements only if the benefits of providing it exceed its costs.	Lets the accountant know that information that is not required should be made available only if its benefits exceed its costs. An example may be companies going to the expense of providing information on the effects of inflation when the inflation rate is low and/or users do not seem to benefit significantly from the information.
Materiality	Only items that would affect a knowledgeable user's decision are material (important) and must be reported in a theoretically correct way.	Allows accountants to treat immaterial (relatively small dollar amount) information in a theoretically incorrect but expedient manner. For instance, a wastebasket can be expensed rather than capitalized and depreciated even though it may last for 30 years.
Conservatism	Transactions should be recorded so that net assets and net income are not overstated.	Warns accountants that net assets and net income are not to be overstated. "Anticipate (and record) all possible losses and do not anticipate (or record) any possible gains" is common advice under this constraint. Also, conservative application of the matching principle involves making sure that adjustments for expenses for such items as uncollectible accounts, warranties, and depreciation are adequate.

CONSERVATISM   **Conservatism** means being cautious or prudent and making sure that net assets and net income are not overstated. Such overstatements can mislead potential investors in the company and creditors making loans to the company. We apply conservatism when the lower-of-cost-or-market rule is used for inventory (see Chapter 7). Accountants must realize a fine line exists between conservative and incorrect accounting.

See Illustration 5.4 for a summary of the modifying conventions and their importance.

The next section of this chapter discusses the conceptual framework project of the Financial Accounting Standards Board. The FASB designed the conceptual framework project to resolve some disagreements about the proper theoretical foundation for accounting. We present only the portions of the project relevant to this text.

THE FINANCIAL ACCOUNTING STANDARDS BOARD'S CONCEPTUAL FRAMEWORK PROJECT

Objective 4
Describe the conceptual framework project of the Financial Accounting Standards Board.

Experts have debated the exact nature of the basic concepts and related principles composing accounting theory for years. The debate continues today despite numerous references to generally accepted accounting principles (GAAP). To date, all attempts to present a concise statement of GAAP have received only limited acceptance.

Due to this limited success, many accountants suggest that the starting point in reaching a concise statement of GAAP is to seek agreement on the objectives of financial accounting and reporting. The belief is that if a person (1) carefully studies the environment, (2) knows what objectives are sought, (3) can identify certain qualitative traits of accounting information, and (4) can define the basic elements of financial statements, that person can discover the principles and standards leading to the stated objectives. The FASB completed the first three goals by publishing "Objectives of Financial Reporting by Business Enterprises" and "Qualitative Characteristics of Accounting Information."[4] Addressing the fourth goal are concepts statements

---

[4]FASB, *Statement of Financial Accounting Concepts No. 1*, "Objectives of Financial Reporting by Business Enterprises" (Stamford, Conn., 1978); and *Statement of Financial Accounting Concepts No. 2*, "Qualitative Characteristics of Accounting Information" (Stamford, Conn., 1980). Copyright © by the Financial Accounting Standards Board, High Ridge Park, Stamford, Connecticut 06905, U.S.A. Quoted (or excerpted) with permission. Copies of the complete documents are available from the FASB.

entitled "Elements of Financial Statements of Business Enterprises" and "Elements of Financial Statements."[5]

Objectives of Financial Reporting

Financial reporting objectives are the broad overriding goals sought by accountants engaging in financial reporting. According to the FASB, the first objective of financial reporting is to:

provide information that is useful to present and potential investors and creditors and other users in making rational investment, credit, and similar decisions. The information should be comprehensible to those who have a reasonable understanding of business and economic activities and are willing to study the information with reasonable diligence.[6]

Interpreted broadly, the term *other users* includes employees, security analysts, brokers, and lawyers. Financial reporting should provide information to all who are willing to learn to use it properly.

The second objective of financial reporting is to:

provide information to help present and potential investors and creditors and other users in assessing the amounts, timing, and uncertainty of prospective cash receipts from dividends [owner withdrawals] or interest and the proceeds from the sale, redemption, or maturity of securities or loans. Since investors' and creditors' cash flows are related to enterprise cash flows, financial reporting should provide information to help investors, creditors, and others assess the amounts, timing, and uncertainty of prospective net cash inflows to the related enterprise.[7]

This objective ties the cash flows of investors (owners) and creditors to the cash flows of the enterprise, a tie-in that appears entirely logical. Enterprise cash inflows are the source of cash for dividends, interest, and the redemption of maturing debt.

Third, financial reporting should:

provide information about the economic resources of an enterprise, the claims to those resources (obligations of the enterprise to transfer resources to other entities and owners' equity), and the effects of transactions, events, and circumstances that change its resources and claims to those resources.[8]

We can draw some conclusions from these three objectives and from a study of the environment in which financial reporting is carried out. For example, financial reporting should:

1. Provide information about an enterprise's past performance because such information is a basis for predicting future enterprise performance.
2. Focus on earnings and its components, despite the emphasis in the objectives on cash flows. (Earnings computed under the accrual basis generally provide a better indicator of ability to generate favorable cash flows than do statements prepared under the cash basis.)

On the other hand, financial reporting does not seek to:

1. Measure the value of an enterprise but to provide information useful in determining its value.
2. Evaluate management's performance, predict earnings, assess risk, or estimate

---

[5]FASB, *Statement of Financial Accounting Concepts No. 3*, "Elements of Financial Statements of Business Enterprises" (Stamford, Conn., 1980); and *Statement of Financial Accounting Concepts No. 6*, "Elements of Financial Statements" (Stamford, Conn., 1985). Copyright © by the Financial Accounting Standards Board, High Ridge Park, Stamford, Connecticut 06905, U.S.A. Quoted (or excerpted) with permission. Copies of the complete documents are available from the FASB.

[6]FASB, *Statement of Financial Accounting Concepts No. 1*, p. viii.

[7]Ibid.

[8]Ibid.

earning power but to provide information to persons who wish to make these evaluations.

These conclusions are some of those reached in *Statement of Financial Accounting Concepts No. 1.* As the Board stated, these statements "are intended to establish the objectives and concepts that the Financial Accounting Standards Board will use in developing standards of financial accounting and reporting."[9] How successful the Board will be in the approach adopted remains to be seen.

QUALITATIVE CHARACTERISTICS

Accounting information should possess **qualitative characteristics** to be useful in decision making. This criterion is difficult to apply. The usefulness of accounting information in a given instance depends not only on information characteristics but also on the capabilities of the decision makers and their professional advisers. Accountants cannot specify who the decision makers are, their characteristics, the decisions to be made, or the methods chosen to make the decisions. Therefore, they direct their attention to the characteristics of accounting information. Note the FASB's graphic summarization of the qualities accountants consider in Illustration 5.5.[10]

Relevance

To have **relevance,** information must be pertinent to or affect a decision. The information must make a difference to someone who does not already have it. Relevant information makes a difference in a decision either by affecting users' predictions of outcomes of past, present, or future events or by confirming or correcting expectations. Note that information need not be a prediction to be useful in developing, confirming, or altering expectations. Expectations are commonly based on the present or past. For example, any attempt to predict future earnings of a company would quite likely start with a review of present and past earnings. Although information that merely confirms prior expectations may be less useful, it is still relevant because it reduces uncertainty.

Critics have alleged that certain types of accounting information lack relevance. For example, some argue that a cost of $1 million paid for a tract of land 40 years ago and reported in the current balance sheet at that amount is irrelevant (except for possible tax implications) to users for decision making today. Such criticism has encouraged research into the types of information relevant to users. Some suggest using a different valuation basis, such as current cost, in reporting such assets.

PREDICTIVE VALUE AND FEEDBACK VALUE   Since actions taken now can affect only future events, information is obviously relevant when it possesses **predictive value,** or improves users' abilities to predict outcomes of events. Information that reveals the relative success of users in predicting outcomes possesses **feedback value.** Feedback reports on past activities and can make a difference in decision making by (1) reducing uncertainty in a situation, (2) refuting or confirming prior expectations, and (3) providing a basis for further predictions. For example, a report on the first quarter's earnings of a company reduces the uncertainty surrounding the amount of such earnings, confirms or refutes the predicted amount of such earnings, and provides a possible basis on which to predict earnings for the full year. Remember that although accounting information may possess predictive value, it does not consist of predictions. Making predictions is a function performed by the decision maker, not the accountant.

TIMELINESS   **Timeliness** requires accountants to provide accounting information at a time when it may be considered in reaching a decision. Utility of information

---

[9]Ibid., p. i.

[10]FASB, *Statement of Financial Accounting Concepts No. 2,* p. 15.

ILLUSTRATION 5.5   A Hierarchy of Accounting Qualities

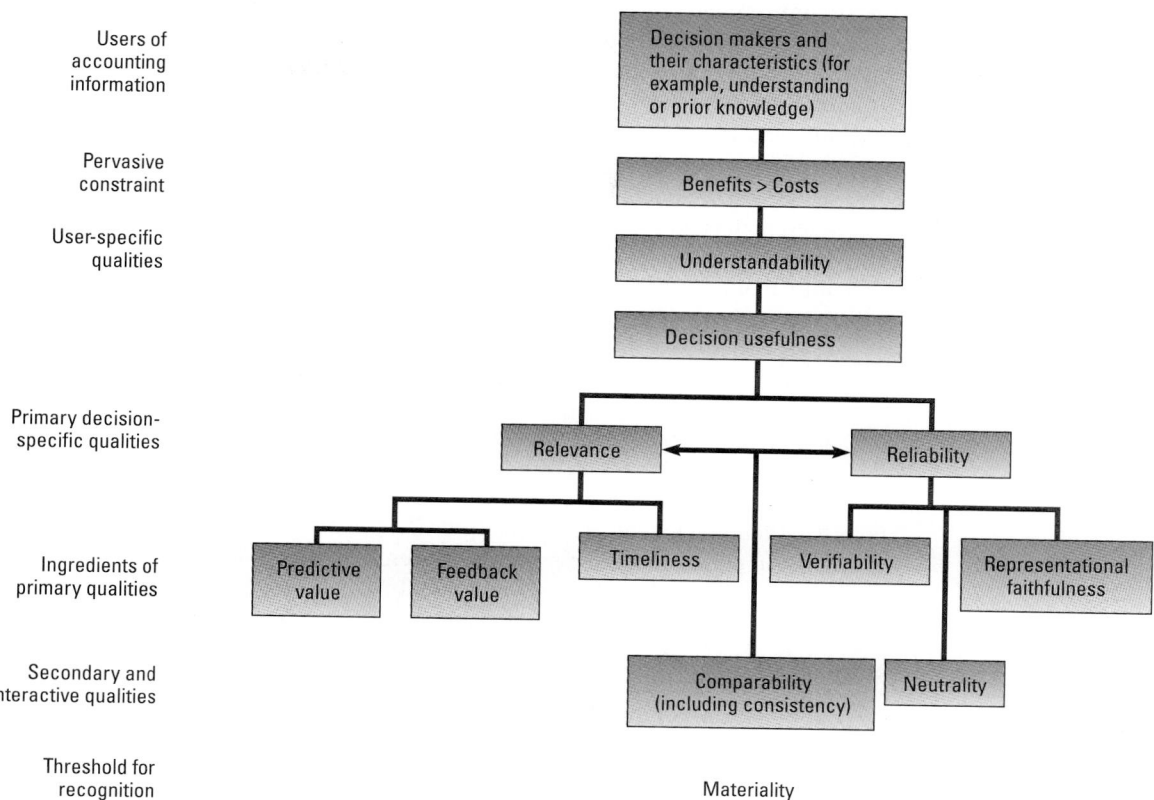

decreases with age—to know what the net income for 1999 was in early 2000 is much more useful than receiving this information a year later. If information is to be of any value in decision making, it must be available before the decision is made. If not, the information is of little value. In determining what constitutes timely information, accountants consider the other qualitative characteristics and the cost of gathering information. For example, a timely estimate for uncollectible accounts may be more valuable than a later, verified actual amount. Timeliness alone cannot make information relevant, but potentially relevant information can be rendered irrelevant by a lack of timeliness.

Reliability

In addition to being relevant, information must be reliable to be useful. Information has **reliability** when it faithfully depicts for users what it purports to represent. Thus, accounting information is reliable if users can depend on it to reflect the underlying economic activities of the organization. The reliability of information depends on its representational faithfulness, verifiability, and neutrality. The information must also be complete and free of bias.

REPRESENTATIONAL FAITHFULNESS   To gain insight into this quality, consider a map. When it shows roads and bridges where roads and bridges actually exist, a map possesses representational faithfulness. A correspondence exists between what is on the map and what is present physically. Similarly, **representational faithfulness** exists when accounting statements on economic activity correspond to the actual underlying activity. Where there is no correspondence, the cause may be (1) bias or (2) lack of completeness.

1.   **Effects of bias.** Accounting measurements contain **bias** if they are consistently too high or too low. Accountants create bias in accounting measurements by

choosing the wrong measurement method or introducing bias either deliberately or through lack of skill.

2. **Completeness.** To be free from bias, information must be sufficiently complete to ensure that it validly represents underlying events and conditions. **Completeness** means disclosing all significant information in a way that aids understanding and does not mislead. Firms can reduce the relevance of information by omitting information that would make a difference to users. Currently, full disclosure requires presentation of a balance sheet, an income statement, a statement of cash flows, and necessary notes to the financial statements and supporting schedules. Also required in annual reports of corporations are statements of changes in stockholders' equity which contain information included in a statement of retained earnings. Such statements must be complete, with items properly classified and segregated (such as reporting sales revenue separately from other revenues). Required disclosures may be made in (1) the body of the financial statements, (2) the notes to such statements, (3) special communications, and/or (4) the president's letter or other management reports in the annual report.

Another aspect of completeness is fully disclosing all changes in accounting principles and their effects.[11] Disclosure should include unusual activities (loans to officers), changes in expectations (losses on inventory), depreciation expense for the period, long-term obligations entered into that are not recorded by the accountant (a 20-year lease on a building), new arrangements with certain groups (pension and profit-sharing plans for employees), and significant events that occur after the date of the statements (loss of a major customer). Firms must also disclose accounting policies (major principles and their manner of application) followed in preparing the financial statements.[12] Because of its emphasis on disclosure, we often call this aspect of reliability the *full disclosure principle*.

VERIFIABILITY   Financial information has **verifiability** when independent measurers can substantially duplicate it by using the same measurement methods. Verifiability eliminates measurer bias, rather than measurement method bias. The requirement that financial information be based on objective evidence arises from the demonstrated needs of users for reliable, unbiased financial information. Unbiased information is especially necessary when parties with opposing interests (credit seekers and credit grantors) rely on the same information. If the information is verifiable, this enhances the reliability of information.

Financial information is never free of subjective opinion and judgment; it always possesses varying degrees of verifiability. Canceled checks and invoices support some measurements. Accountants can never verify other measurements, such as periodic depreciation charges, because of their very nature. Thus, financial information in many instances is verifiable only in that it represents a consensus of what other accountants would report if they followed the same procedures.

Reinforcing Problems
E5–6 Match accounting qualities with proper descriptions.
P5–5 Answer multiple choice questions regarding the conceptual framework project.

NEUTRALITY   **Neutrality** means that the accounting information should be free of measurement method bias. The primary concern should be relevance and reliability of the information that results from application of the principle, not the effect that the principle may have on a particular interest. Nonneutral accounting information favors one set of interested parties over others. For example, a particular form of measurement might favor stockholders over creditors, or vice versa. "To be neutral, accounting information must report economic activity as faithfully as possible, without coloring the image it communicates for the purpose of influencing behavior in *some*

---

[11]APB, *APB Opinion No. 20*, "Accounting Changes" (New York: AICPA, July 1971).

[12]APB, *APB Opinion No. 22*, "Disclosure of Accounting Policies" (New York: AICPA, April 1972).

particular direction."[13] Accounting standards are not like tax regulations that deliberately foster or restrain certain types of activity. Verifiability seeks to eliminate measurer bias; neutrality seeks to eliminate measurement method bias.

When **comparability** exists, reported differences and similarities in financial information are real and not the result of differing accounting treatments. Comparable information reveals relative strengths and weaknesses in a single company through time and between two or more companies at the same time.

Comparability (and Consistency)

   Consistency requires that a company use the same accounting principles and reporting practices through time. Consistency leads to comparability of financial information for a single company through time. Comparability between companies is more difficult because they may account for the same activities in different ways. For example, Company B may use one method of depreciation, while Company C accounts for an identical asset in similar circumstances using another method. A high degree of intercompany comparability in accounting information does not exist unless accountants are required to account for the same activities in the same manner across companies and through time.

As we show in Illustration 5.5, accountants must consider one pervasive constraint and one threshold for recognition in providing useful information. First, the benefits secured from the information must be greater than the costs of providing that information. Second, only material items need be disclosed and accounted for strictly in accordance with generally accepted accounting principles (GAAP). We discussed cost-benefit and materiality earlier in the chapter.

Pervasive Constraint and Threshold for Recognition

USE OF TECHNOLOGY   You may want to visit the home page of the Financial Accounting Standards Board at:

AN ACCOUNTING PERSPECTIVE

http://www.fasb.org

You can check out the latest developments at the FASB to see how the rules of accounting might be changing. You can investigate facts about the FASB, press releases, exposure drafts, publications, emerging issues, board actions, forthcoming meetings, and many other topics.

THE BASIC ELEMENTS OF FINANCIAL STATEMENTS

Thus far we have discussed objectives of financial reporting and qualitative characteristics of accounting information. A third important task in developing a conceptual framework for any discipline is identifying and defining its basic elements. The FASB identified and defined the basic elements of financial statements in *Concepts Statement No. 3*. Later, *Concepts Statement No. 6* revised some of the definitions. We defined most of the terms earlier in this text in a less technical way; the more technical definitions follow. (These items are not repeated in this chapter's New Terms.)

   Assets are probable future economic benefits obtained or controlled by a particular entity as a result of past transactions or events.

   Liabilities are probable future sacrifices of economic benefits arising from present obligations of a particular entity to transfer assets or provide services to other entities in the future as a result of past transactions or events.

   Equity or net assets is the residual interest in the assets of an entity that remains after deducting its liabilities. In a business enterprise, the equity is the ownership interest. In a not-for-profit organization, which has no ownership interest in the same sense as a business enterprise, net assets is divided into three classes based

Note to the Student
Review the definitions of all the terms listed.

---

[13]FASB, *Statement of Financial Accounting Concepts No. 2*, par. 100.

on the presence or absence of donor-imposed restrictions—permanently restricted, temporarily restricted, and unrestricted net assets.

Comprehensive income is the change in equity of a business enterprise during a period from transactions and other events and circumstances from nonowner sources. It includes all changes in equity during a period except those resulting from investments by owners and distributions to owners.

Revenues are inflows or other enhancements of assets of any entity or settlements of its liabilities (or a combination of both) from delivering or producing goods, rendering services, or other activities that constitute the entity's ongoing major or central operations.

Expenses are outflows or other using up of assets or incurrences of liabilities (or a combination of both) from delivering or producing goods, rendering services, or carrying out other activities that constitute the entity's ongoing major or central operations.

Gains are increases in equity (net assets) from peripheral or incidental transactions of an entity and from all other transactions and other events and circumstances affecting the entity except those that result from revenues or investments by owners.

Losses are decreases in equity (net assets) from peripheral or incidental transactions of an entity and from all other transactions and other events and circumstances affecting the entity except those that result from expenses or distributions to owners.

Investments by owners are increases in equity of a particular business enterprise resulting from transfers to it from other entities of something valuable to obtain or increase ownership interests (or equity) in it. Assets are most commonly received as investments by owners, but that which is received may also include services or satisfaction or conversion of liabilities of the enterprise.

Distributions to owners are decreases in equity of a particular business enterprise resulting from transferring assets, rendering services, or incurring liabilities by the enterprise to owners. Distributions to owners decrease ownership interest (or equity) in an enterprise.[14]

AN ACCOUNTING PERSPECTIVE	**BUSINESS INSIGHT** Accountants record expenditures on physical resources such as land, buildings, and equipment that benefit future periods as assets. However, they expense expenditures on human resources for hiring and training that benefit future periods. Also, when a computer is dropped and destroyed, accountants record a loss. However, when the president of the company dies, they record no loss. Should the accounting model be changed regarding the accounting for human resources?

Note the requirement that assets and liabilities be based on past transactions normally rules out the recording of contracts that are mutual promises to do something, such as entering into an employment contract with an officer. For a similar reason, the accountant refuses to record an asset and a liability when a contract is signed whereby the entity agrees to purchase a certain amount of a product over a future period.

RECOGNITION AND MEASUREMENT IN FINANCIAL STATEMENTS

In December 1984, the FASB issued *Statement of Financial Accounting Concepts No. 5,* "Recognition and Measurement in Financial Statements of Business Enterprises," describing recognition criteria and providing guidance for the timing and

---

[14]FASB, *Statement of Financial Accounting Concepts No. 6.*

Maplehurst Company manufactures large spinning machines for the textile industry. The company had purchased $100,000 of small hand tools to use in its business. The company's accountant recorded the tools in an asset account and was going to write them off over 20 years. Management wanted to write these tools off as an expense of this year because revenues this year had been abnormally high and were expected to be lower in the future. Management's goal was to smooth out income rather than showing sharp increases and decreases. When told by the accountant that $100,000 was a material item that must be accounted for in a theoretically correct manner, management decided to consider the tools as consisting of 10 groups, each having a cost of $10,000. Since amounts under $20,000 are considered immaterial for this company, all of the tools could then be charged to expense this year.

The accountant is concerned about this treatment. She doubts that she could successfully defend management's position if the auditors challenge the expensing of these items.

AN ETHICAL PERSPECTIVE

Maplehurst Company

nature of information included in financial statements.[15] The recognition criteria established in the *Statement* are fairly consistent with those used in current practice. The *Statement* indicates, however, that when information more useful than currently reported information is available at a reasonable cost, it should be included in financial statements.

MEETING THE INFORMATION NEEDS OF INVESTORS AND CREDITORS

In 1991 the Board of Directors of the American Institute of Certified Public Accountants (AICPA) appointed The AICPA Special Committee on Financial Reporting to address increasing concerns about the relevance and usefulness of financial reporting. The committee's specific charge was "to recommend (1) the nature and extent of information that should be made available to others by management and (2) the extent to which auditors should report on the various elements of that information." Before making recommendations, the committee decided to research and identify the information needs of investors and creditors. The committee's final recommendations were published in 1994.[16]

The committee is not a standard-setting body. However, its recommendations are likely to affect financial accounting theory and practice in the future by influencing the output of the Financial Accounting Standards Board.

The committee examined the published research of others and the types of information included in financial analysts' reports. It also held meetings with portfolio managers, analysts, bankers, certain knowledgeable committees of financial accounting policy organizations, and investors and creditors.

The committee's recommendations regarding user needs (quoted from the report) were as follows:

Improving the Types of Information in Business Reporting

Recommendation 1: Standard setters should develop a comprehensive model of business reporting indicating the types and timing of information that users need to value and assess the risk of their investments.

Objective 5
Describe the recommendations for meeting the information needs of investors and creditors.

---

[15]FASB, *Statement of Financial Accounting Concepts No. 5*, "Recognition and Measurement in Financial Statements of Business Enterprises" (Stamford, Conn., 1984). Copyright © by the Financial Accounting Standards Board, High Ridge Park, Stamford, Connecticut 06905, U.S.A. Copies of the complete document are available from the FASB. (In case you are wondering why we do not mention *Statement of Financial Accounting Concepts No. 4*, it pertains to accounting for not-for-profit organizations and is, therefore, not relevant to this text.)

[16]The AICPA Special Committee on Financial Reporting, *Improving Business Reporting—A Customer Focus: Meeting the Information Needs of Investors and Creditors*, "A Report on the AICPA Special Committee's Study of the Information Needs of Today's Users of Financial Reporting," 1994, Copyright © 1994 by American Institute of Certified Public Accountants, Inc., New York, NY (197 pp.).

Recommendation 2: Improve understanding of costs and benefits of business reporting, recognizing that definitive quantification of costs and benefits is not possible.

Financial Statements and Related Disclosures

Recommendation 1: Improve disclosure of business segment information.

Recommendation 2: Address the disclosures and accounting for innovative financial instruments.

Recommendation 3: Improve disclosures about the identity, opportunities, and risks of off-balance-sheet financing arrangements and reconsider the accounting for those arrangements.

Recommendation 4: Report separately the effects of core and noncore activities and events, and measure at fair value noncore assets and liabilities.

Recommendation 5: Improve disclosures about the uncertainty of measurements of certain assets and liabilities.

Recommendation 6: Improve quarterly reporting by reporting on the fourth quarter separately and including business segment data.

Recommendation 7: Standard setters should search for and eliminate less relevant disclosures.

Other recommendations

- *Display of information in financial statements*
  — In general, companies should increase the amount of detail in financial statements, particularly in the income statement

- *Interim reporting*
  — Interim reporting should include quarterly cash flow statements.
  — Interim information should include uncondensed financial statements; however, condensed note disclosures remain appropriate at interim periods.
  — Companies should disclose the methods of computing reported amounts used in interim periods that differ from the methods used at year-end.

- *Comparability and consistency of information*
  — Companies should restate or reclassify information in more circumstances than allowed in current practice for dispositions, accounting changes, changes on the definitions of business segments, and possibly other items as well if the restated or reclassified information can be assembled reasonably and is necessary for a better and more complete understanding of the business.
  — Standard setters should consider simplifying the procedure for adopting new pronouncements by making them effective for all companies in a single year and prescribing only one method of adoption.

- *Key statistics and ratios*
  — Companies should provide a summary of key financial and non-financial data on a consolidated basis as well as for each business segment.
  — A company and the users of its business reporting should agree on the periods to be reported for the summary information, which generally need not exceed five years.

- *Lower priority issues*
  — Standard setters should defer considering issues that have low priority according to the current evidence of users' needs. The Committee's study identified the following five areas that standard setters should not devote attention to at this time:
    1. Value-based accounting model.
    2. Accounting for intangible assets, including goodwill.
    3. Forecasted financial statements.
    4. Accounting for business combinations.
    5. Alternative accounting principles.

Auditor Association with Business Reporting

Recommendation 1: Allow for flexible auditor association with business reporting, whereby the elements of information on which auditors report and the level of auditor involvement with those elements are decided by agreement between a company and the users of its business reporting.

Recommendation 2: The auditing profession should prepare to be involved with all the information in the comprehensive model, so companies and users can call on it to provide assurance on any of the model's elements.

Recommendation 3: The newly formed AICPA Special Committee on Assurance Services should research and formulate conclusions on analytical commentary in auditors' reports within the context of the Committee's model, focusing on users' needs for information.

Recommendation 4: The profession should continue its projects on other matters related to auditor association with business reporting.

Facilitating Change in Business Reporting

Recommendation 1: National and international standard setters and regulators should increase their focus on the information needs of users, and users should be encouraged to work with standard setters to increase the level of their involvement in the standard-setting process.

Recommendation 2: U.S. standard setters and regulators should continue to work with their non-U.S. counterparts and international standard setters to develop international accounting standards, provided the resulting standards meet users' needs for information.

Recommendation 3: Lawmakers, regulators, and standard setters should develop more effective deterrents to unwarranted litigation that discourages companies from disclosing forward-looking information.

Recommendation 4: Companies should be encouraged to experiment voluntarily with ways to improve the usefulness of reporting consistent with the Committee's model. Standard setters and regulators should consider allowing companies that experiment to substitute information specified by the model for information currently required.

Recommendation 5: Standard setters should adopt a longer term focus by developing a vision of the future business environment and users' needs for information in that environment. Standards should be consistent directionally with that long-term vision.

Recommendation 6: Regulators should consider whether there are any alternatives to the current requirement that public companies make all disclosures publicly available.

Recommendation 7: The AICPA should establish a Coordinating Committee charged to ensure that the recommendations in this report are given adequate consideration by those who can act on them.

The committee's recommendations are responsive to the users' needs as identified by the committee's research. The Financial Accounting Standards Board is aware of the recommendations and will probably be influenced by them in future deliberations. For a discussion of any of the recommendations, you should refer to the full report.

SUMMARY OF SIGNIFICANT ACCOUNTING POLICIES

As part of their annual reports, companies include summaries of significant account-ing policies. These policies assist users in interpreting the financial statements. To a large extent, accounting theory determines the nature of these policies. Companies must follow generally accepted accounting principles in preparing their financial statements.

Objective 6
Discuss the nature of a company's summary of significant accounting policies in its annual report.

The accounting policies of The Walt Disney Company, one of the world's leading entertainment companies, as contained in its 1995 annual report follow. After each, the chapter of this text where we discuss that particular policy is in parentheses. While a few of the items have already been covered, the remainder offer a preview of the concepts explained in later chapters.

Significant Accounting Policies
Principles of Consolidation
The consolidated financial statements of the Company include the accounts of The Walt Disney Company and its subsidiaries after elimination of intercompany accounts and

transactions. Investments in affiliated companies are accounted for using the equity method. (Chapter 14)

Accounting Changes

Effective October 1, 1994, the Company adopted *Statement of Financial Accounting Standards ("SFAS") 115* "Accounting for Certain Investments in Debt and Equity Securities" (see Note 14), the impact of which was not material. Effective October 1, 1992, the Company adopted *SFAS 106,* "Employers' Accounting for Postretirement Benefits Other Than Pensions" (see Note 8) and SFAS 109, "Accounting for Income Taxes" (see Note 7) and changed its method of accounting for pre-opening costs (see Note 12). These changes had no cash impact.

The pro forma amounts presented in the consolidated statement of income reflect the effect of retroactive application of expensing pre-opening costs. (Chapters 13 and 14)

Revenue Recognition

Revenues from the theatrical distribution of motion pictures are recognized when motion pictures are exhibited. Television licensing revenues are recorded when the program material is available for telecasting by the licensee and when certain other conditions are met. Revenues from video sales are recognized on the date that video units are made widely available for sale by retailers.

Revenues from participants and sponsors at the theme parks are generally recorded over the period of the applicable agreements commencing with the opening of the related attraction. (Chapter 5)

Cash, Cash Equivalents and Investments

Cash and cash equivalents consist of cash on hand and marketable securities with original maturities of three months or less. (Chapter 8)

SFAS 115, adopted in 1995, requires that certain investments in debt and equity securities be classified into one of three categories. Debt securities that the Company has the positive intent and ability to hold to maturity are classified as "held-to-maturity" and reported at amortized cost. Debt securities not classified as held-to-maturity and marketable equity securities are classified as either "trading" or "available-for-sale," and are recorded at fair value with unrealized gains and losses included in earnings or stockholders' equity, respectively. Prior to 1995, debt securities were carried at cost, adjusted for unamortized premium or discount. Marketable equity securities were carried at the lower of aggregate cost or market. Realized gains and losses were determined on an average cost basis. (Chapter 14)

Merchandise Inventories

Carrying amounts of merchandise, materials and supplies inventories are generally determined on a moving average cost basis and are stated at the lower of cost or market. (Chapter 7)

Film and Television Costs

Film and television production and participation costs are expensed based on the ratio of the current period's gross revenues to estimated total gross revenues from all sources on an individual production basis. Estimates of total gross revenues are reviewed periodically and amortization is adjusted accordingly.

Television broadcast rights are amortized principally on an accelerated basis over the estimated useful lives of the programs. (Chapter 11)

Theme Parks, Resorts and Other Property

Theme parks, resorts and other property are carried at cost. Depreciation is computed on the straight-line method based upon estimated useful lives ranging from three to fifty years. (Chapter 3)

Other Assets

Rights to the name, likeness and portrait of Walt Disney, goodwill and other intangible assets are amortized over periods ranging from two to forty years. (Chapter 11)

Risk Management Contracts

In the normal course of business, the Company employs a variety of off-balance-sheet financial instruments to manage its exposure to fluctuations in interest and foreign currency exchange rates, including interest rate and cross-currency swap agreements, forward and option contracts, and interest rate exchange-traded futures. The company designates interest rate and cross-currency swaps as hedges of investments and debt, and accrues the differential to be paid or received under the agreements as interest rates change over the lives of the contracts. Differences paid or received on swap agreements are recognized as adjustments to interest income or expense over the life of the swaps, thereby adjusting the effective interest rate on the underlying investment or obligation. Gains and losses on the termination of swap agreements, prior to the original maturity, are deferred and amortized to interest income or expense over the original term of the swaps. Gains and losses arising from interest rate futures, forwards and option contracts, and foreign currency forward and option contracts are recognized in income or expense as offsets of gains and losses resulting from the underlying hedged transactions. (Not covered in this text)

Cash flows from interest rate and foreign exchange risk management activities are classified in the same category as the cash flows from the related investment, borrowing or foreign exchange activity. (Chapter 16)

The Company classifies its derivative financial instruments as held or issued for purposes other than trading. (Chapter 14)

Earnings Per Share

Earnings per share amounts are based upon the weighted average number of common and common equivalent shares outstanding during the year. Common equivalent shares are excluded from the computation in periods in which they have an antidilutive effect. (Chapter 13)

Reclassifications

Certain reclassifications have been made in the 1994 and 1993 financial statements to conform to the 1995 presentations.

As you proceed through the remaining chapters, you can see the accounting theories introduced in this chapter being applied. In Chapter 6, for instance, we discuss why sales revenue is recognized and recorded only after goods have been delivered to the customer. So far, we have used service companies to illustrate accounting techniques. Chapter 6 introduces merchandising operations. Merchandising companies, such as clothing stores, buy goods in their finished form and sell them to customers.

UNDERSTANDING THE LEARNING OBJECTIVES

- The major underlying assumptions or concepts of accounting are (1) business entity, (2) going concern (continuity), (3) money measurement, (4) stable dollar, and (5) periodicity.

Objective 1
Identify and discuss the underlying assumptions or concepts of accounting.

- Other basic accounting concepts that affect the accounting for entities are (1) general-purpose financial statements, (2) substance over form, (3) consistency, (4) double entry, and (5) articulation.

- The major principles include exchange-price (or cost), matching, revenue recognition, expense recognition, gain and loss recognition, and full disclosure. Major exceptions to the realization principle include cash collection as point of revenue recognition, installment basis of revenue recognition, the percentage-of-completion method of recognizing revenue on long-term construction projects, and revenue recognition at completion of production.

Objective 2
Identify and discuss the major principles of accounting.

- Modifying conventions include cost-benefit, materiality, and conservatism.

Objective 3
Identify and discuss the modifying conventions (or constraints) of accounting.

- The FASB has defined the objectives of financial reporting, qualitative characteristics of accounting information, and elements of financial statements.
- Financial reporting objectives are the broad overriding goals sought by accountants engaging in financial reporting.
- Qualitative characteristics are those that accounting information should possess to be useful in decision making. The two primary qualitative characteristics are relevance and reliability. Another qualitative characteristic is comparability.

Objective 4
Describe the conceptual framework project of the Financial Accounting Standards Board.

- Pervasive constraints include cost-benefit analysis and materiality.
- The FASB has identified and defined the basic elements of financial statements.
- The FASB has also described revenue recognition criteria and provided guidance as to the timing and nature of information to be included in financial statements.

Objective 5
Describe the recommendations for meeting the information needs of investors and creditors.

- A committee of the American Institute of Certified Public Accountants was assigned to address increasing concerns about the relevance and usefulness of financial reporting.
- The committee's final recommendations were published in 1994.

Objective 6
Discuss the nature and content of a company's summary of significant accounting policies in its annual report.

- These policies aid users in interpreting the financial statements.
- To a large extent, accounting theory determines the nature of those policies.

DEMONSTRATION PROBLEM

For each of the following transactions or circumstances and the entries made, state which, if any, of the assumptions, concepts, principles, or modifying conventions of accounting have been violated. For each violation, give the entry to correct the improper accounting assuming the books have not been closed.

During the year, Dorsey Company did the following:

1. Had its buildings appraised. They were found to have a market value of $410,000, although their book value was only $380,000. The accountant debited the Buildings and Accumulated Depreciation—Buildings accounts for $15,000 each and credited Paid-in Capital—From Appreciation. No separate mention was made of this action in the financial statements.
2. Purchased new electric pencil sharpeners for its offices at a total cost of $60. These pencil sharpeners were recorded as assets and are being depreciated over five years.
3. Produced agricultural products at a cost of $26,000. These costs were charged to expense when the products were harvested. The products were set up in inventory at their net market value of $35,000, and the Farm Revenues Earned account was credited for $35,000.

SOLUTION TO DEMONSTRATION PROBLEM

1. The realization principle and the modifying convention of conservatism may have been violated. Such write-ups simply are not looked on with favor in accounting. To correct the situation, the entry made needs to be reversed:

Paid-in Capital—From Appreciation	30,000	
Buildings		15,000
Accumulated Depreciation—Buildings		15,000

2. Theoretically, no violations occurred, but the cost of compiling insignificant information could be considered a violation of acceptable accounting practice. As a practical matter, the $60 could have been expensed on materiality grounds.
3. No violations occurred. The procedures followed are considered acceptable for farm products that are interchangeable and readily marketable. No correcting entry is needed, provided due allowance has been made for the costs to be incurred in delivering the products to the market.

NEW TERMS

Accounting theory "A set of basic concepts and assumptions and related principles that explain and guide the accountant's actions in identifying, measuring, and communicating economic information." *173*

Bias Exists when accounting measurements are consistently too high or too low. *189*

Business entity concept The specific unit for which accounting information is gathered. Business entities have a separate existence from owners, creditors, employees, customers, other interested parties, and other businesses. *174*

Comparability A qualitative characteristic of accounting information; when information is comparable, it reveals differences and similarities that are real and are not the result of differing accounting treatments. *191*

Completed-contract method A method of recognizing revenue on long-term projects under which no revenue is recognized until the period in which the project is completed; similar to recognizing revenue upon the completion of a sale. *181*

Completeness A qualitative characteristic of accounting information; requires disclosure of all significant information in a way that aids understanding and does not mislead; sometimes called the *full disclosure principle*. *190*

Conservatism Being cautious or prudent and making sure that net assets and net income are not overstated. *186*

Consistency Requires a company to use the same accounting principles and reporting practices through time. *176, 191*

Cost-benefit consideration Determining whether benefits of including information in financial statements exceed costs. *184*

Cost principle See Exchange-price principle.

Earning principle The requirement that revenue be substantially earned before it is recognized (recorded). *179*

Exchange-price (or cost) principle Transfers of resources are recorded at prices agreed on by the parties at the time of the exchange. *178*

Expense recognition principle Expenses should be recognized as they are incurred to produce revenues. *183*

Feedback value A qualitative characteristic that information has when it reveals the relative success of users in predicting outcomes. *188*

Financial reporting objectives The broad overriding goals sought by accountants engaging in financial reporting. *187*

Full disclosure principle Information important enough to influence the decisions of an informed user of the financial statements should be disclosed. *184*

Gain and loss recognition principle Gains may be recorded only when realized, but losses should be recorded when they first become evident. *183*

Gains Typically result from the sale of long-term assets for more than their book value. *184*

Going-concern (continuity) assumption The assumption that an entity will continue to operate indefinitely unless strong evidence exists that the entity will terminate. *174*

Historical cost The amount paid, or the fair market value of a liability incurred or other resources surrendered, to acquire an asset and place it in a condition and position for its intended use. *179*

Installment basis A revenue recognition procedure in which the percentage of total gross margin recognized in a period on an installment sale is equal to the percentage of total cash from the sale that is received in that period. *180*

Liquidation Terminating a business by ceasing business operations and selling off its assets. *174*

Losses Asset expirations that are usually involuntary and do not create revenues. *184*

Matching principle The principle that net income of a period is determined by associating or relating revenues earned in a period with expenses incurred to generate those revenues. *179*

Materiality A modifying convention that allows the accountant to deal with immaterial (unimportant) items in an expedient but theoretically incorrect manner; also a qualitative characteristic specifying that financial accounting report only information significant enough to influence decisions or evaluations. *184*

Modifying conventions Customs emerging from accounting practice that alter the results obtained from a strict application of accounting principles; conservatism is an example. *184*

Money measurement Use of a monetary unit of measurement, such as the dollar, instead of physical or other units of measurement—feet, inches, grams, and so on. *174*

Neutrality A qualitative characteristic that requires accounting information to be free of measurement method bias. *190*

Percentage-of-completion method A method of recognizing revenue based on the estimated stage of completion of a long-term project. The stage of completion is measured by comparing actual costs incurred in a period with total estimated costs to be incurred in all periods. *181*

Period costs Costs that cannot be traced to specific products and are expensed in the period incurred. *183*

Periodicity (time periods) assumption An assumption of the accountant that an entity's life can be divided into time periods for reporting its economic activities. *175*

Predictive value A qualitative characteristic that information has when it improves users' abilities to predict outcomes of events. *188*

Product costs Costs incurred in the acquisition or manufacture of goods. Product costs are accounted for as if they were attached to the goods, with the result that they are charged to expense when the goods are sold. *183*

Production basis A method of revenue recognition used in limited circumstances that recognizes revenue at the time of completion of production or extraction. *182*

Qualitative characteristics   Characteristics that accounting information should possess to be useful in decision making.   *188*

Realization principle   A principle that directs that revenue is recognized only after the seller acquires the right to receive payment from the buyer.   *179*

Relevance   A qualitative characteristic requiring that information be pertinent to or affect a decision.   *188*

Reliability   A qualitative characteristic requiring that information faithfully depict for users what it purports to represent.   *189*

Representational faithfulness   A qualitative characteristic requiring that accounting statements on economic activity correspond to the actual underlying activity.   *189*

Revenue recognition principle   The principle that revenues should be earned and realized before they are recognized (recorded).   *179*

Stable dollar assumption   An assumption that the dollar is a reasonably stable unit of measurement.   *175*

Timeliness   A qualitative characteristic requiring that accounting information be provided at a time when it may be considered before making a decision.   *188*

Verifiability   A qualitative characteristic of accounting information; information is verifiable when it can be substantially duplicated by independent measurers using the same measurement methods.   *190*

SELF-TEST

TRUE-FALSE

Indicate whether each of the following statements is true or false.

1. The business entity concept assumes that each business has an existence separate from all parties except its owners.

2. When the substance of a transaction differs from its legal form, the accountant should record the economic substance.

3. The matching principle is fundamental to the accrual basis of accounting.

4. Exceptions to the realization principle include the installment basis of revenue recognition for sales revenue and the completed-contract method for long-term construction projects.

5. Immaterial items do not have to be recorded at all.

6. The conceptual framework project resulted in identifying two primary qualitative characteristics that accounting information should possess—relevance and reliability.

MULTIPLE-CHOICE

1. The underlying assumptions of accounting include all the following except:
    a. Business entity.
    b. Going concern.
    c. Matching.
    d. Money measurement and periodicity.

2. The concept that requires all companies to use the same accounting practices and reporting practices through time is:
    a. Substance over form.
    b. Consistency.
    c. Articulation.
    d. None of the above.

3. Which of the following statements is false regarding the revenue recognition principle?
    a. Revenue must be substantially earned before it is recognized.
    b. The accountant usually recognizes revenue before the seller acquires the right to receive payment from the buyer.
    c. Some small companies use the cash basis of accounting.
    d. Under the installment basis, the gross margin recognized in a period is equal to the amount of cash received from installment sales times the gross margin percentage for the year of sale.

4. Assume the following facts regarding the construction of a bridge:

Construction costs this period	$ 3,000,000
Total estimated construction costs . . .	10,000,000
Total sales price	15,000,000

    The revenue that should be recognized this period is:
    a. $3,000,000.
    b. $4,500,000.
    c. $5,000,000.
    d. $6,500,000.

5. Modifying conventions include all of the following except:
    a. Periodicity.
    b. Cost-benefit.
    c. Materiality.
    d. Conservatism.

6. Which of the following is not part of the conceptual framework project?
    a. Objectives of financial reporting.
    b. Quantitative characteristics.
    c. Qualitative characteristics.
    d. Basic elements of financial statements.

Now turn to page 209 to check your answers.

Questions

1. Name the assumptions underlying generally accepted accounting principles. Comment on the validity of the stable unit of measurement assumption during periods of high inflation.

2. Why does the accountant use the business entity concept?

3. When is the going-concern assumption not to be used?

4. What is meant by the term *accrual basis of accounting?* What is its alternative?

5. What does it mean to say that accountants record substance rather than form?

6. If a company changes an accounting principle because the change better meets the information needs of users, what disclosures must be made?

7. What is the exchange-price (or cost) principle? What is the significance of adhering to this principle?

8. What two requirements generally must be met before recognizing revenue in a period?

9. Under what circumstances, if any, is the receipt of cash an acceptable time to recognize revenue?

10. What two methods may be used in recognizing revenues on long-term construction contracts?

11. Define expense. What principles guide the recognition of expense?

12. How does an expense differ from a loss?

13. What is the full disclosure principle?

14. What role does cost-benefit play in financial reporting?

15. What is meant by the accounting term *conservatism?* How does it affect the amounts reported in the financial statements?

16. Does materiality relate only to the relative size of dollar amounts?

17. Identify the three major parts of the conceptual framework project.

18. What are the two primary qualitative characteristics?

19. **Real World Question** A recent annual report of the American Ship Building Company stated:

   Revenues, costs, and profits applicable to construction and conversion contracts are included in the consolidated statements of operations using the . . . percentage-of-completion accounting method. . . . The completed contract method was used for income tax reporting in the years this method was allowed.

   Why might the management of a company want to use two different methods for accounting and tax purposes?

20. **Real World Question** A recent annual report of Chevron Corporation stated:

   Environmental expenditures that relate to current or future revenues are expensed or capitalized as appropriate. Expenditures that relate to an existing condition caused by past operations, and do not contribute to current or future revenue generation, are expensed.

   Which principle of accounting is being followed by this policy?

21. The AICPA Special Committee on Financial Reporting issued a report on the information needs of investors and creditors. What was the overriding consideration in making the recommendations? Identify four of the committee's recommendations regarding financial statements and related disclosures.

22. Identify some of the "lower priority issues" to which the AICPA Special Committee on Financial Reporting recommended standard setters not devote attention at that time.

23. What is the purpose of including a "Summary of Significant Accounting Policies" in the company's annual report?

Exercises

Match the items in Column A with the proper descriptions in Column B.

Exercise 5–1
Match theory terms with definitions (L.O. 1–3)

Column A

1. Going concern (continuity).
2. Consistency.
3. Disclosure.
4. Periodicity.
5. Conservatism.
6. Stable dollar.
7. Matching.
8. Materiality.
9. Exchange-price.
10. Business entity.

Column B

a. An assumption relied on in the preparation of the primary financial statements that would be unreasonable when the inflation rate is high.
b. Concerned with relative dollar amounts.
c. The usual basis for the recording of assets.
d. Required if the accounting treatment differs from that previously used for a particular item.
e. An assumption that would be unreasonable to use in reporting on a firm that had become insolvent.
f. None of these.
g. Requires a company to use the same accounting procedures and practices through time.
h. An assumption that the life of an entity can be subdivided into time periods for reporting purposes.
i. Discourages undue optimism in measuring and reporting net assets and net income.
j. Requires separation of personal from business activities in the recording and reporting processes.

Exercise 5–2
Compute net income under accrual basis and under installment basis (L.O. 2)

Parker Clothing Company sells its products on an installment sales basis. Data for 1999 and 2000 follow:

	1999	2000
Installment sales	$800,000	$960,000
Cost of goods sold on installment sales	560,000	720,000
Other expenses	120,000	160,000
Cash collected from 1999 sales	480,000	240,000
Cash collected from 2000 sales		640,000

a. Compute the net income for 2000, assuming use of the accrual (sales) basis of revenue recognition.

b. Compute the net income for 2000, assuming use of the installment basis of recognizing gross margin.

Exercise 5–3
Recognize revenue under percentage-of-completion method (L.O. 2)

A company has a contract to build a ship at a price of $500 million and an estimated cost of $400 million. In 1999, costs of $100 million were incurred. Under the percentage-of-completion method, how much revenue would be recognized in 1999?

Exercise 5–4
Compute the effect on financial statements of incorrectly expensing an asset (L.O. 2)

A company follows a practice of expensing the premium on its fire insurance policy when the policy is paid. In 1999, the company charged to expense the $6,000 premium paid on a three-year policy covering the period July 1, 1999, to June 30, 2002. In 1996, a premium of $5,400 was charged to expense on the same policy for the period July 1, 1996, to June 30, 1999.

a. State the principle of accounting that was violated by this practice.

b. Compute the effects of this violation on the financial statements for the calendar year 1999.

c. State the basis on which the company's practice might be justified.

Exercise 5–5
Compute gross margin under GAAP and then as production is completed (L.O. 2)

Maryland Patio Umbrella Company produces umbrellas at a cost of $60 per unit that it sells for $100. The company has been very successful and sells all of the units it can produce. During 1999, the company manufactured 50,000 units, but (because of a transportation strike) sold and delivered only 40,000 units.

a. Compute the gross margin for 1999 following the realization principle. The cost of the units sold should be entitled "cost of goods sold" and treated as an expense.

b. Compute the gross margin for 1999, assuming the realization principle is ignored and revenue is recognized as production is completed.

Exercise 5–6
Match accounting qualities with proper descriptions (L.O. 4)

Match the descriptions in Column B with the accounting qualities in Column A. Use some descriptions more than once.

Column A: Accounting Qualities	Column B: Descriptions
1. Relevance.	a. Users of accounting information.
2. Feedback value.	b. Pervasive constraint.
3. Decision makers.	c. User-specific qualities.
4. Representational faithfulness.	d. Primary decision-specific qualities.
5. Reliability.	e. Ingredients of primary qualities.
6. Comparability.	f. Secondary and interactive qualities.
7. Benefits exceed costs.	g. Threshold for recognition.
8. Predictive value.	
9. Timeliness.	
10. Decision usefulness.	
11. Verifiability.	
12. Understandability.	
13. Neutrality.	
14. Materiality.	

PROBLEMS

Problem 5–1
Answer multiple-choice questions regarding accounting theory (L.O. 1–3)

Select the best answer to each of the following questions:

1. A set of basic concepts and assumptions and related principles that explain and guide the accountant's actions in identifying, measuring, and communicating economic information is called:

  a. Accounting theory.

   b. Accounting rules.

   c. Accrual basis.

   d. Matching concept.

2. Which of the following statements is false?

   a. Several separate legal entities properly may be considered to be one accounting entity.

   b. The stable dollar assumption is used only when the dollar is absolutely stable.

   c. Publicly held corporations generally prepare monthly financial statements for internal management and publish quarterly and annual financial statements for users outside the company.

   d. Without the periodicity assumption, a business would have only one time period running from the inception of the business to its termination.

3. Which of the following statements is true?

   a. When the substance of a transaction conflicts with the legal form of the transaction, the accountant should be guided by the legal form in recording the transaction.

   b. The consistency concept prohibits a change in accounting principle even when such a change would better meet the information needs of financial statement users.

   c. Under the double-entry approach, each transaction must be recorded with one debit and one credit of equal dollar amounts.

   d. Special-purpose financial information for a specific decision, such as whether or not to purchase a new machine, is best obtained from the detailed accounting records rather than from the financial statements.

4. Which of the following statements is true?

   a. All assets are carried indefinitely at their original costs in the financial statements.

   b. Liabilities are measured in the cash to be paid or the value of services to be performed to satisfy the liabilities.

   c. Accounting principles are derived by merely summarizing accounting practices used to date.

   d. Accountants can easily measure all changes in assets and liabilities since they never involve estimates or calculations.

5. Which of the following statements is false?

   a. The exchange-price principle is also called the cost principle.

   b. The matching principle is closely related to the revenue recognition principle and the expense recognition principle.

   c. The installment sales method recognizes revenue sooner than it would normally be recognized.

   d. The percentage-of-completion method recognizes revenue sooner than the completed-contract method.

Problem 5–2
Compute net income assuming revenues are recognized at time of sale and then assuming the installment basis is used (L.O. 2)

Nevada Real Estate Sales Company sells lots in its development in Dry Creek Canyon under terms calling for small cash down payments with monthly installment payments spread over a few years. Following are data on the company's operations for its first three years:

	1997	1998	1999
Gross margin rate	45%	48%	50%
Cash collected in 1999 from			
sales of lots made in	$640,000	$800,000	$900,000

The total selling price of the lots sold in 1999 was $3,000,000, while general and administrative expenses (which are not included in the costs used to determine gross margin) were $800,000.

Required

a. Compute net income for 1999 assuming revenue is recognized on the sale of a lot.

b. Compute net income for 1999 assuming use of the installment basis of accounting for sales and gross margin.

Problem 5–3
Compute net income under completed-contract and percentage-of-completion methods (L.O. 2)

The following contract prices and costs relate to all of Orlando Construction Company's long-term construction projects (in millions of dollars):

	Contract Price	Costs Incurred		Cost to Be Incurred in Future Years
		Prior to 1999	In 1999	
On projects completed in 1999 . . .	$ 46	$ 4	$36	$–0–
On incomplete projects	144	24	48	48

General and administrative expenses for 1999 amounted to $1,200,000. Assume that the general and administrative expenses are not to be treated as a part of the construction cost.

Required

a. Compute net income for 1999 using the completed-contract method.
b. Compute net income for 1999 using the percentage-of-completion method.

Problem 5–4
Indicate agreement or disagreement with accounting practices followed and comment (L.O. 1–3)

In each of these circumstances, the accounting practices may be questioned. Indicate whether you agree or disagree with the accounting practice employed and state the assumptions, concepts, or principles that justify your position.

1. The salaries paid to the top officers of the company were charged to expense in the period in which they were incurred even though the officers spent over half of their time planning next year's activities.
2. No entry was made to record the belief that the market value of the land owned (carried in the accounts at $800,000) had increased.
3. The acquisition of a tract of land was recorded at the price paid for it of $400,000, even though the company would have been willing to pay $600,000.
4. A truck acquired at the beginning of the year was reported at year-end at 80% of its acquisition price even though its market value then was only 65% of its original acquisition price.

Problem 5–5
Answer multiple-choice questions regarding the conceptual framework project (L.O. 4)

Select the best answer to each of the following questions:

1. In the conceptual framework project, how many financial reporting objectives were identified by the FASB?
   a. One.
   b. Two.
   c. Three.
   d. Four.
2. The two primary qualitative characteristics are:
   a. Predictive value and feedback value.
   b. Timeliness and verifiability.
   c. Comparability and neutrality.
   d. Relevance and reliability.
3. A pervasive constraint of accounting information is that:
   a. Benefits must exceed costs.
   b. The information must be timely.
   c. The information must be neutral.
   d. The information must be verifiable.
4. To be reliable, information must (identify the *incorrect* quality):
   a. Be verifiable.
   b. Be timely.
   c. Have representational faithfulness.
   d. Be neutral.
5. The *basic elements* of financial statements consist of:
   a. Terms and their definitions.
   b. The objectives of financial reporting.
   c. The qualitative characteristics.
   d. The new income statement format.

ALTERNATE PROBLEMS

Problem 5–1A
Answer multiple-choice questions regarding accounting theory (L.O. 1–3)

Select the best answer to each of the following questions:

1. The assumption that each business has an existence separate from its owners, creditors, employees, customers, other interested parties, and other businesses is the:
   a. Going-concern assumption.
   b. Business entity concept.
   c. Separate entity concept.
   d. Corporation concept.

2. Companies should use liquidation values to report assets if which of the following conditions exists?
   a. There are changes in the value of the dollar.
   b. The periodicity assumption is applied.
   c. The company is not a going concern and will be dissolved.
   d. The accrual basis of accounting is not used.

3. Assume that a company has paid for advertising and that the ad has already appeared. The company chose to report the item as prepaid advertising and includes it among the assets on the balance sheet. Previously, the company had always expensed expenditures such as this. This practice is a violation of:
   a. Generally accepted accounting principles.
   b. The matching concept.
   c. The consistency concept.
   d. All of the above.

4. Recording revenue only after the seller has obtained the right to receive payment from the buyer for merchandise sold or services performed is called the:
   a. Earning principle.
   b. Installment basis.
   c. Realization principle.
   d. Completed-contract method.

5. Assume that 2,000 ounces of gold were mined at a time when gold sold for $500 an ounce. The cost to extract the gold was $300 per ounce. Revenue was recognized under the production basis. The gold has not yet been sold. The entry to record the extraction of the gold would include:
   a. A debit to Inventory of Gold for $600,000.
   b. A credit to Revenue from Extraction of Gold of $1,000,000.
   c. A debit to Cash of $1,000,000.
   d. A credit to Inventory of Gold of $1,000,000.

Problem 5–2A

Compute income assuming revenues are recognized at time of sale and then assuming installment method is used (L.O. 2)

Ramirez Video, Inc., sells video recorders under terms calling for a small down payment and monthly payments spread over three years. Following are data for the first three years of the company's operations:

	1997	1998	1999
Gross margin rate	30%	40%	50%
Cash collected in 1999:			
From sales in	$216,000		
From sales in		$288,000	
From sales in			$480,000

Total sales for 1999 were $1,600,000, while general and selling expenses amounted to $400,000.

Required

a. Compute net income for 1999, assuming revenues are recognized at the time of sale.
b. Compute net income for 1999, using the installment method of accounting for sales and gross margin.

Problem 5–3A

Compute income under completed-contract and percentage-of-completion methods (L.O. 2)

The following data relate to Merit Construction Company's long-term construction projects for the year 1999:

	Completed Projects	Incomplete Projects
Contract price	$20,000,000	$100,000,000
Costs incurred prior to 1999	3,700,000	16,000,000
Costs incurred in 1999	11,100,000	32,000,000
Estimated costs to be incurred		
in future years	–0–	32,000,000

General and administrative expenses incurred in 1999 amounted to $2 million, none of which is to be considered a construction cost.

Required

a. Compute net income for 1999 under the completed-contract method.
b. Compute net income for 1999 under the percentage-of-completion method.

Problem 5–4A
Match principles,
assumptions, or concepts
with certain accounting
procedures followed
(L.O. 1–3)

For each of the following numbered items, state the letter or letters of the principle(s), assumption(s), or concept(s) used to justify the accounting procedure followed. The accounting procedures are all correct.

a. Business entity.
b. Conservatism.
c. Earning principle of revenue recognition.
d. Going concern (continuity).
e. Exchange-price principle.
f. Matching principle.
g. Period cost (or principle of immediate recognition of expense).
h. Realization principle.
i. Stable dollar assumption.

1. The estimated liability for federal income taxes was increased by $10,000 over the amount reported on the tax return to cover possible differences found by the Internal Revenue Service in determining the income taxes payable.
2. A truck purchased in January was reported at 80% of its cost even though its market value at year-end was only 70% of its cost.
3. The collection of $40,000 of cash for services to be performed next year was reported as a current liability.
4. The president's salary was treated as an expense of the year even though he spent most of his time planning the next two years' activities.
5. No entry was made to record the company's receipt of an offer of $800,000 for land carried in its accounts at $435,000.
6. A supply of printed stationery, checks, and invoices with a cost of $8,500 was treated as a current asset at year-end even though it had no value to others.
7. A tract of land acquired for $180,000 was recorded at that price even though it was appraised at $230,000, and the company would have been willing to pay that amount.
8. The company paid and charged to expense the $4,200 paid to Craig Nelson for rent of a truck owned by him. Craig Nelson is the sole stockholder of the company.

Problem 5–5A
Answer matching question
regarding the conceptual
framework project (L.O. 4)

Match the descriptions in Column B with the proper terms in Column A.

Column A

1. Financial reporting objectives.
2. Qualitative characteristics.
3. Relevance.
4. Predictive value.
5. Feedback value.
6. Timeliness.
7. Reliability.
8. Representational faithfulness.
9. Verifiability.
10. Neutrality.
11. Comparability.
12. Consistency.
13. Cost-benefit.
14. Materiality.

Column B

a. Information is free of measurement method bias.
b. The benefits exceed the costs.
c. Relatively large items must be accounted for in a theoretically correct way.
d. The information can be substantially duplicated by independent measurers using the same measurement methods.
e. When information improves users' ability to predict outcomes of events.
f. Broad overriding goals sought by accountants engaging in financial reporting.
g. When information is pertinent or bears on a decision.
h. The characteristics that accounting information should possess to be useful in decision making.
i. Information that reveals the relative success of users in predicting outcomes.
j. When accounting statements on economic activity correspond to the actual underlying activity.
k. When information is provided soon enough that it may be considered in decision making.
l. When information faithfully depicts for users what it purports to represent.
m. Requires a company to use the same accounting principles and reporting practices through time.
n. When reported differences and similarities in information are real and not the result of differing accounting treatments.

BEYOND THE NUMBERS—CRITICAL THINKING

Jim Casey recently received his accounting degree from State University and went to work for a Big-Six CPA firm. After he had been with the firm for about six months, he was sent to the Ling Clothing Company to work on the audit. He was not very confident of his knowledge at this early point in his career. He noticed, however, that some of the company's transactions and events were recorded in a way that might be in violation of accounting theory and generally accepted accounting principles.

Business Decision Case 5–1
Evaluate correctness of accounting practices and give reasons for conclusions (L.O. 1–3)

Required

Study each of the following facts to see if the auditors should challenge the financial accounting practices used or the intentions of management. Write your decisions and the reasoning behind your conclusions.

This problem can serve as an opportunity to apply accounting theory to situations with which you are not yet familiar and as a preview of future chapters. Some of the following situations relate to material you have already covered, and some situations relate to material to be covered in future chapters. After each item, we have given an indication of the chapter in which that item is discussed. You may research future chapters to find the correct answer. Alternatively, you could use your present knowledge of accounting theory to determine whether or not Casey should challenge each of the financial accounting practices used. Realize, however, that some generally accepted accounting practices were based on compromise and seem to differ with accounting theory as described in this chapter.

1. One of the senior members of management stated the company planned to replace all of the furniture next year. He said that the cash in the Accumulated Depreciation account would be used to pay for the furniture. (Ch. 3)

2. The company held the books open at the end of 1999 so they could record some early 2000 sales as 1999 revenue. The justification for this practice was that 1999 was not a good year for profits. (Ch. 3, 5, 6)

3. The company's buildings were appraised for insurance purposes. The appraised values were $10,000,000 higher than the book value. The accountant debited Buildings and credited Paid-in Capital from Appreciation for the difference. (Ch. 5)

4. The company recorded purchases of merchandise at the list price rather than the gross selling (invoice) price. (Ch. 6)

5. Goods shipped to the company from a supplier, FOB destination, were debited to Purchases. The goods were not included in ending inventory because the goods had not yet arrived. (Ch. 5, 6)

6. The company counted some items twice in taking the physical inventory at the end of the year. The person taking the inventory said he had forgotten to include some items in last year's physical inventory, and counting some items twice would make up for the items missed last year so that net income this year would be about correct. (Ch. 7)

7. The company switched from FIFO to LIFO in accounting for inventories. The preceding year it had switched from the weighted-average method to FIFO. The reason given for the most recent change was that federal income taxes would be lower. No indication of this switch was to appear in the financial statements. (Ch. 5, 7)

8. Since things were pretty hectic at year-end, the accountant made no effort to reconcile the bank account. His reason was that the bank probably had not made any errors. The bank balance was lower than the book balance, so the accountant debited Miscellaneous Expense and credited Cash for the difference. (Ch. 8)

9. When a customer failed to pay the amount due, the accountant debited Allowance for Uncollectible Accounts and credited Accounts Receivable. The amount of accounts written off in this manner was huge. (Ch. 9)

10. A completely depreciated machine was still being used. The accountant left the asset and its related accumulated depreciation on the books, stopped recording depreciation on the machine, and did not go back and correct earlier years' net income and reduce accumulated depreciation. (Ch. 10)

11. The accountant stated that even though research and development costs incurred to develop a new product would benefit future periods, these costs must be expensed as incurred. This year $200,000 of these costs were charged to expense. (Ch. 11)

12. An old truck was traded for a new truck. Since the trade-in value of the old truck was higher than its book value, a gain was recorded on the transaction. (Ch. 11)

13. The company paid for a franchise giving it the exclusive right to operate in a given geographical area for 60 years. The accountant is amortizing the asset over 60 years. (Ch. 11)

14. The company leases a building and has a nonrenewable lease that expires in 15 years. The company made some improvements to the building. Since the improvements will last 30 years, they are being written off over 30 years. (Ch. 11)

Annual Report Analysis 5–2
List "Summary of Significant Accounting Policies" for four real companies (L.O. 6)

Refer to the "Summary of Significant Accounting Policies" in the annual reports of The Coca-Cola Company, Maytag Corporation, The Limited, Inc., and John H. Harland Company in the annual report booklet. For each company, list the policies discussed. Then place a check (✔) by the topics common to at least two of the companies. For each of the common policies, explain in writing what the company is trying to communicate.

Ethics—A Writing Experience 5–3
Answer questions regarding ethics case

Refer to the item "An Ethical Perspective" on page 193. Write out the answers to the following questions:

Is management being ethical in this situation? Explain.

Is the accountant correct in believing that management's position could not be successfully defended? Explain.

What would you do if you were the accountant? Describe in detail.

Group Project 5–4
Undertake library project concerning annual reports

In teams of two or three students, go to the library to locate one company's annual report for the most recent year. (The university may have received the annual reports of companies in either published form, microfiche form, or a computer readable format.) Examine the "Summary of Accounting Policies," which is part of the "Notes to Financial Statements" section immediately following the financial statements. As a team, write a memorandum to the instructor detailing the significant accounting policies of the company. The heading of the memorandum should contain the date, to whom it is written, from whom, and the subject matter.

Group Project 5–5
Perform library research

With one or two other students and using library sources, write a paper on the history and achievements of the Financial Accounting Standards Board. This board is responsible for establishing the accounting standards and principles for financial accounting in the private sector. It was formed in 1973 and took over the rule setting function from the Accounting Principles Board of the American Institute of Certified Public Accountants at that time. Be sure to cite sources used and to treat direct quotes properly.

Group Project 5–6
Perform library research

Your team of students should obtain a copy of the report, "Improving Business Reporting—A Customer Focus" by the AICPA Special Committee on Financial Reporting (1994). Your library might have a copy. If not, it can be obtained from the AICPA [Product No. 019303, Order Department, AICPA, Harborside Financial Center, 201 Plaza Three, Jersey City, NJ 07311-3881] [Toll free number 1-800-862-4272; FAX 1-800-362-5066]. Write a report giving a more complete description of the recommendations of the committee as contained in this chapter of the text. Be sure to cite sources used and treat direct quotes properly.

USING THE INTERNET—A VIEW OF THE REAL WORLD

Internet Project 5–7
Check out significant accounting policies

Visit the following Internet site for Motorola, Inc.:
http://www.mot.com
Using the choices provided on the screen, find the annual report, and then the Significant Accounting Policies within that report. Print a copy of the Significant Accounting Policies. Write a short report to your instructor summarizing your findings.

Visit the following Internet site for Sun Microsystems, Inc.:

http://www.sun.com

Click on Company Information, then on Environmental Policies. Write a short report for your instructor on what this company is doing to protect the environment.

Internet Project 5–8
Check on company environmental policies

ANSWERS TO SELF-TEST

TRUE-FALSE

1. **False.** The business entity concept assumes that each business has an existence separate from its owners, creditors, employees, customers, other interested parties, and other businesses.

2. **True.** Accountants should be guided by the economic substance of a transaction rather than its legal form.

3. **True.** The accrual basis of accounting seeks to match effort and accomplishment by matching expenses against the revenues they created.

4. **False.** Exceptions include the installment basis of revenue recognition for sales and the percentage-of-completion method for long-term construction projects.

5. **False.** Immaterial items do have to be recorded, but they can be recorded in a theoretically incorrect way (e.g., expensing a wastebasket that will last many years).

6. **True.** Relevance and reliability are the two primary characteristics.

MULTIPLE-CHOICE

1. **c.** The matching concept is one of the major principles of accounting rather than an assumption.

2. **d.** If you answered **(b)**, note that the consistency concept requires that a given company (not all companies) use the same accounting principles and reporting practices through time.

3. **b.** Usually, the accountant does not recognize revenue until the seller acquires the right to receive payment from the buyer.

4. **b.** $3,000,000/$10,000,000 \times $15,000,000 = $4,500,000.

5. **a.** Periodicity is an underlying assumption rather than a modifying convention.

6. **b.** The category, quantitative characteristics, is not part of the conceptual framework project.

6

MERCHANDISING TRANSACTIONS
INTRODUCTION TO INVENTORIES AND CLASSIFIED INCOME STATEMENT

Your study of accounting began with service companies as examples because they are the least complicated type of business. You are now ready to apply the accounting process to a more complex business—a merchandising company. Although the fundamental accounting concepts for service businesses apply to merchandising businesses, they require some additional accounts and techniques to record sales and purchases.

The normal flow of goods from manufacturer to final customer is as follows:

Merchandising Companies

Manufacturer → Wholesaler → Retailer → Final customer

Manufacturers produce goods from raw materials and normally sell them to wholesalers. After performing certain functions, such as packaging or labeling, **wholesalers** sell the goods to retailers. **Retailers** sell the goods to final customers. The two middle boxes in the diagram represent merchandising companies. These companies buy goods in finished form for resale.

This chapter compares the income statement of a service company with that of a merchandising company. Then, we describe (1) how to record merchandise-related transactions (2) a classified income statement and (3) the gross margin percentage. Finally, in the appendix we explain the work sheet and the closing process for a merchandising company.

TWO INCOME STATEMENTS COMPARED—SERVICE COMPANY AND MERCHANDISING COMPANY

In Illustration 6.1 we compare the main divisions of an income statement for a service company with those for a merchandising company. To determine profitability or net

ILLUSTRATION 6.1   Condensed Income Statements of a Service Company and a Merchandising Company Compared

SERVICE COMPANY Income Statement For the Year Ended December 31, 1999		MERCHANDISING COMPANY Income Statement For the Year Ended December 31, 1999	
Service revenues	$13,200	Sales revenues	$262,000
		Cost of goods sold	159,000
		Gross margin	$103,000
Expenses	6,510	Expenses	74,900
Net income	$ 6,690	Net income	$ 28,100

income, a service company deducts total expenses incurred from revenues earned. A merchandising company is a more complex business and, therefore, has a more complex income statement.

As shown in Illustration 6.1, merchandising companies must deduct from revenues the cost of the goods they sell to customers. Then, they deduct other expenses. The income statement of a merchandising company has three main divisions: (1) sales revenues, which result from the sale of goods by the company; (2) cost of goods sold, which is an expense that indicates how much the company paid for the goods sold; and (3) expenses, which are the company's other expenses in running the business.

In the next two sections we discuss the first two main divisions of the income statement of a merchandising company. The third division (expenses) is similar to expenses for a service company, which we illustrated in preceding chapters. As you study these sections, keep in mind how the divisions of the merchandising income statement are related to each other and produce the final figure—net income or net loss—which indicates the profitability of the company.

(concluded)

6. Prepare a classified income statement.

7. Analyze and use the financial results—gross margin percentage.

8. Prepare a work sheet and closing entries for a merchandising company (Appendix).

SALES REVENUES

The sale of goods occurs between two parties. The seller of the goods transfers them to the buyer in exchange for cash or a promise to pay at a later date. This exchange is a relatively simple business transaction. Sellers make sales to create revenues; this inflow of assets results from selling goods to customers.

In Illustration 6.1, we show a condensed income statement to emphasize its major divisions. Next, we describe the more complete income statement actually prepared by accountants. The merchandising company that we use to illustrate the income statement is Hanlon Retail Food Store. This section explains how to record sales revenues, including the effect of trade discounts. Then, we explain how to record two deductions from sales revenues—sales discounts and sales returns and allowances (Illustration 6.2). The amount that remains is **net sales.** The formula, then, for determining net sales is:

Net sales = Gross sales − (Sales discounts + Sales returns and allowances)

In a sales transaction, the seller transfers the legal ownership (title) of the goods to the buyer. Usually, the physical delivery of the goods occurs at the same time as the sale of the goods. A business document called an *invoice* (a *sales invoice* for the seller and a *purchase invoice* for the buyer) becomes the basis for recording the sale.

An **invoice** is a document prepared by the seller of merchandise and sent to the buyer. The invoice contains the details of a sale, such as the number of units sold, unit price, total price billed, terms of sale, and manner of shipment. A retail company prepares the invoice at the point of sale. A wholesale company, which supplies goods to retailers, prepares the invoice after the shipping department notifies the accounting

Objective 1
Record journal entries for sales transactions involving merchandise.

Recording Gross Sales

Note to the Student
A common example of an invoice is a sales ticket. It serves as the merchant's sales invoice and the customer's purchase invoice.

ILLUSTRATION 6.2
Partial Income Statement
of Merchandising
Company

HANLON RETAIL FOOD STORE
Partial Income Statement
For the Year Ended December 31, 1999

Operating revenues:			
Gross sales			$282,000
Less: Sales discounts	$ 5,000		
Sales returns and allowances . . .	15,000	20,000	
Net sales			$262,000

ILLUSTRATION 6.3
Invoice

BRYAN WHOLESALE CO.
476 Mason Street
Detroit, Michigan 48823

Invoice No.: 1258
Date: Dec. 19, 1999

Customer's Order No.: 218
Sold to: Baier Company
Address: 2255 Hannon Street
Big Rapids, Michigan 48106
Terms: Net 30, FOB Destination

Date Shipped: Dec. 19, 1999
Shipped by: Nagel Trucking Co.

Description	Item Number	Quantity	Price per Unit	Total Amount
True-tone stereo radios	Model No. 5868-24393	200	$100	$20,000
		Total		$20,000

department that it has shipped the goods to the retailer. See Illustration 6.3, an invoice prepared by a wholesale company for goods sold to a retail company.

Using the invoice as the source document, a wholesale company records the revenue from the sale at the time of the sale for the following reasons:

1. The seller has passed *legal title* of the goods to the buyer, and the goods are now the responsibility and property of the buyer.
2. The seller has established the selling price of the goods.
3. The seller has completed its obligation.
4. The seller has exchanged the goods for another asset, such as cash or accounts receivable.
5. The seller can determine the costs incurred in selling the goods.

Each time a company makes a sale, the company earns revenue. This revenue increases a revenue account called *Sales*. Recall from Chapter 2 that credits increase revenues. Therefore, the firm credits the Sales account for the amount of the sale.

Usually sales are for cash or on account. When a sale is for cash, the company credits the Sales account and debits Cash. When a sale is on account, it credits the Sales account and debits Accounts Receivable. For example, it records a $20,000 sale for cash as follows:

Cash	20,000	
Sales		20,000
To record the sale of merchandise for cash.		

This entry records a $20,000 sale on account:

Accounts Receivable	20,000	
Sales		20,000
To record the sale of merchandise on account.		

Usually, a seller quotes the gross selling price, also called the invoice price, of goods to the buyer; sometimes a seller quotes a list price of goods along with available trade discounts. In this latter situation, the buyer must calculate the gross selling price. The list price less all trade discounts is the **gross selling price.** Merchandising companies that sell goods use the gross selling price as the credit to sales.

AN ACCOUNTING PERSPECTIVE

A **trade discount** is a percentage deduction, or discount, from the specified list price or catalog price of merchandise. Companies use trade discounts to:

1. Reduce the cost of catalog publication. A seller can use a catalog for a longer time by printing list prices in the catalog and giving separate discount sheets to salespersons whenever prices change.
2. Grant quantity discounts.
3. Allow quotation of different prices to various customers, such as retailers and wholesalers.

The seller's invoice may show trade discounts. However, sellers do not record trade discounts in their accounting records because the discounts are used only to calculate the gross selling price. Nor do trade discounts appear on the books of the purchaser. To illustrate, assume an invoice contains the following data:

List price, 200 swimsuits at $24	$4,800
Less: Trade discount, 30%	1,440
Gross selling price (invoice price)	$3,360

The seller records a sale of $3,360. The purchaser records a purchase of $3,360. Thus, neither the seller nor the purchaser enters list prices and trade discounts on their books.

Sometimes the list price of a product is subject to several trade discounts; this series of discounts is a **chain discount.** Chain discounts exist, for example, when a wholesaler receives two trade discounts for services performed, such as packaging and distributing. When more than one discount is given, the buyer applies each discount to the declining balance successively. If a product has a list price of $100 and is subject to trade discounts of 20% and 10%, the gross selling price (invoice price) would be $100 - 0.2($100) = $80; $80 - 0.1($80) = $72, computed as follows:

List price	$100
Less 20%	- 20
	$ 80
Less 10%	- 8
Gross selling price (invoice price)	$ 72

You could obtain the same results by multiplying the list price by the complements of the trade discounts allowed. The complement of 20% is 80% because 20% + 80% = 100%. The complement of 10% is 90% because 10% + 90% = 100%. Thus, the gross selling price is $100 \times 0.8 \times 0.9 = $72.

Determining Gross Selling Price when Companies Offer Trade Discounts

Note to the Student
Have you ever noticed at a paint store or a plumbing supplies shop that professional painters and plumbers generally pay less for the paint and plumbing supplies they use in their businesses than you have to pay? Painters and plumbers have to make a profit on items they must use in their businesses. A portion of this profit arises from trade discounts received on their purchases.

Note to the Student
The order in which the discounts are applied does not matter because the result is the same. Here is proof:

Example: A $100 sale with a chain trade discount of 5%, 3%, and 1%.
Solution:
$100 \times 95\% \times 97\% \times 99\%$
$= 91.22
$100 \times 99\% \times 95\% \times 97\%$
$= 91.22

Recording Deductions from Gross Sales

Two common deductions from gross sales are (1) sales discounts and (2) sales returns and allowances. Sellers record these deductions in contra revenue accounts to the Sales account. Contra accounts have normal balances that are opposite the balance of the account they reduce. For example, since the Sales account normally has a credit balance, the Sales Discounts account and Sales Returns and Allowances account have debit balances. We explain the methods of recording these contra revenue accounts next.

SALES DISCOUNTS   Whenever a company sells goods on account, it clearly specifies terms of payment on the invoice. For example, the invoice in Illustration 6.3 states the terms of payment as "net 30."

Net 30 is sometimes written as "n/30." Either way, this term means that the buyer may not take a discount and must pay the entire amount of the invoice ($20,000) on or before 30 days after December 19, 1999 (invoice date)—or January 18, 2000. In Illustration 6.3, if the terms had read "n/10/EOM" (EOM means end of month), the buyer could not take a discount, and the invoice would be due on the 10th day of the month following the month of sale—or January 10, 2000. Credit terms vary from industry to industry.

In some industries, credit terms include a *cash discount* of 1% to 3% to induce early payment of an amount due. A **cash discount** is a deduction from the invoice price that can be taken only if the invoice is paid within a specified time. A cash discount differs from a trade discount in that a cash discount is a deduction from the gross selling price for the prompt payment of an invoice. Whereas a trade discount is a deduction from the list price to determine the gross selling price (or invoice price). Sellers call a cash discount a **sales discount** and buyers call it a **purchase discount.**

Companies often state cash discount terms as follows:

- **2/10, n/30**—means a buyer who pays within 10 days following the invoice date may deduct a discount of 2% of the invoice price. If payment is not made within the discount period, the entire invoice price is due 30 days from the invoice date.
- **2/EOM, n/60**—means a buyer who pays by the end of the month of purchase may deduct a 2% discount from the invoice price. If payment is not made within the discount period, the entire invoice price is due 60 days from the invoice date.
- **2/10/EOM, n/60**—means a buyer who pays by the 10th of the month following the month of purchase may deduct a 2% discount from the invoice price. If payment is not made within the discount period, the entire invoice price is due 60 days from the invoice date.

Sellers cannot record the sales discount before they receive payment since they do not know when the buyer will pay the invoice. A cash discount taken by the buyer reduces the cash that the seller actually collects from the sale of the goods, so the seller must indicate this fact in its accounting records. The following entries show how to record a sale and a subsequent sales discount.

Assume that on July 12, a business sold merchandise for $2,000 on account; terms are 2/10, n/30. On July 21 (nine days after invoice date), the business received a $1,960 check in payment of the account. The required journal entries for the seller are:

July	12	Accounts Receivable.	2,000	
		Sales		2,000
		To record sale on account; terms 2/10, n/30.		
	21	Cash	1,960	
		Sales Discounts.	40	
		Accounts Receivable.		2,000
		To record collection on account, less discount.		

The **Sales Discounts account** is a contra revenue account to the Sales account. In the income statement, the seller deducts this contra revenue account from gross sales. Sellers use the Sales Discounts account (rather than directly reducing the Sales account) so management can examine the sales discounts figure to evaluate the company's sales discount policy. Note that the Sales Discounts account is not an expense incurred in generating revenue. Rather, the purpose of the account is to reduce recorded revenue to the amount actually realized from the sale.

SALES RETURNS AND ALLOWANCES   Merchandising companies usually allow customers to return goods that are defective or unsatisfactory for a variety of reasons, such as wrong color, wrong size, wrong style, wrong amounts, or inferior quality. In fact, when their policy is satisfaction guaranteed, some companies allow customers to return goods simply because they do not like the merchandise. A **sales return** is merchandise returned by a buyer. Sellers and buyers regard a sales return as a cancellation of a sale. Alternatively, some customers keep unsatisfactory goods, and the seller gives them an allowance off the original price. A **sales allowance** is a deduction from the original invoiced sales price granted when the customer keeps the merchandise but is dissatisfied for any of a number of reasons, including inferior quality, damage, or deterioration in transit. When a seller agrees to the sales return or sales allowance, the seller sends the buyer a credit memorandum indicating a reduction (crediting) of the buyer's account receivable. A credit memorandum is a document that provides space for the name and address of the concerned parties and contains the preprinted words, "WE CREDIT YOUR ACCOUNT," followed by a space for the reason for the credit and the amount to be credited. A credit memorandum becomes the basis for recording a sales return or a sales allowance.

In theory, sellers could record both sales returns and sales allowances as debits to the Sales account because they cancel part of the recorded selling price. However, because the amount of sales returns and sales allowances is useful information to management, it should be shown separately. The amount of returns and allowances in relation to goods sold can indicate the quality of the goods (high-return percentage, low quality) or of pressure applied by salespersons (high-return percentage, high-pressure sales). Thus, sellers record sales returns and sales allowances in a separate *Sales Returns and Allowances account*. The **Sales Returns and Allowances account** is a contra revenue account (to Sales) that records the selling price of merchandise returned by buyers or reductions in selling prices granted. (Some companies use separate accounts for sales returns and for sales allowances, but this text does not.)

Following are two examples illustrating the recording of sales returns in the Sales Returns and Allowances account:

1. Assume that a customer returns $300 of goods sold on account. If payment has not yet been received, the required entry is:

Sales Returns and Allowances	300	
Accounts Receivable		300
To record a sales return from a customer.		

2. Assume that the customer has already paid the account and the seller gives the customer a cash refund. Now, the credit is to Cash rather than to Accounts Receivable. If the customer has taken a 2% discount when paying the account, the company would return to the customer the sales price less the sales discount amount. For example, if a customer returns goods that sold for $300, on which a 2% discount was taken, the following entry would be made:

Sales Returns and Allowances	300	
Cash		294
Sales Discounts		6
To record a sales return from a customer who had taken a discount and was sent a cash refund.		

The debit to the Sales Returns and Allowances account is for the full selling price of the purchase. The credit of $6 reduces the balance of the Sales Discounts account.

ILLUSTRATION 6.4
Partial Income
Statement*

HANLON RETAIL FOOD STORE
Partial Income Statement
For the Year Ended December 31, 1999

Operating revenues:

Gross sales		$282,000
Less: Sales discounts	$ 5,000	
Sales returns and allowances	15,000	20,000
Net sales		$262,000

*This illustration is the same as Illustration 6.2, repeated here for your convenience.

Next, we illustrate the recording of a sales allowance in the Sales Returns and Allowances account. Assume that a company grants a $400 allowance to a customer for damage resulting from improperly packed merchandise. If the customer has not yet paid the account, the required entry would be:

Sales Returns and Allowances	400	
Accounts Receivable		400
To record sales allowance granted for damaged merchandise.		

If the customer has already paid the account, the credit is to Cash instead of Accounts Receivable. If the customer took a 2% discount when paying the account, the company would refund only the net amount ($392). Sales Discounts would be credited for $8. The entry would be:

Sales Returns and Allowances	400	
Cash		392
Sales Discounts		8
To record sales allowance when a customer has paid and taken a 2% discount.		

Reporting Net Sales in the Income Statement

Illustration 6.4 shows how a company could report sales, sales discounts, and sales returns and allowances in the income statement. More often, the income statement in a company's annual report begins with "Net sales" because sales details are not important to external financial statement users.

AN ACCOUNTING PERSPECTIVE

BUSINESS INSIGHT   When examining a company's sales cycle, management and users of financial data should be aware of any seasonal changes that may affect its reported sales. CompUSA, Inc., is a national retailer of personal computers and related products and services. CompUSA includes the following paragraph in its 1996 Annual Report describing seasonality.

Seasonality

Based upon its operating history, the company believes that its business is seasonal. Excluding the effects of new store openings, net sales and earnings are generally lower during the first and fourth fiscal quarters than in the second and third fiscal quarters.

AN ACCOUNTING PERSPECTIVE

BUSINESS INSIGHT   For many retailers a large percentage of their annual sales occurs during the period from Thanksgiving to Christmas. They attempt to stock just the right amount of goods to meet demand. Since this is a difficult estimate to make accurately, many retailers end up with a large amount of unsold goods at the end of this season. The only way they can unload these goods is to offer huge discounts during the following period. In both 1995 and 1996 many retailers overestimated their holiday season sales and had to offer huge discounts in January to clear the merchandise.

Cost of goods sold:

Merchandise inventory, January 1, 1999			$ 24,000
Purchases		$167,000	
Less: Purchase discounts	$3,000		
Purchase returns and allowances	8,000	11,000	
Net purchases		$156,000	
Add: Transportation-in		10,000	
Net cost of purchases			166,000
Cost of goods available for sale			$190,000
Less: Merchandise inventory, December 31, 1999			31,000
Cost of goods sold			$159,000

ILLUSTRATION 6.5
Determination of Cost of Goods Sold for Hanlon Retail Food Store

COST OF GOODS SOLD

The second main division of an income statement for a merchandising business is cost of goods sold. **Cost of goods sold** is the cost to the seller of the goods sold to customers. For a merchandising company, the cost of goods sold can be relatively large. All merchandising companies have a quantity of goods on hand called *merchandise inventory* to sell to customers. **Merchandise inventory** (or *inventory*) is the quantity of goods available for sale at any given time. Cost of goods sold is determined by computing the cost of (1) the beginning inventory, (2) the net cost of goods purchased, and (3) the ending inventory.

Look at the cost of goods sold section of Hanlon Retail Food Store's income statement in Illustration 6.5. The merchandise inventory on January 1, 1999, was $24,000. The net cost of purchases for the year was $166,000. Thus, Hanlon had $190,000 of merchandise available for sale during 1999. On December 31, 1999, the merchandise inventory was $31,000, meaning that this amount was left unsold. Subtracting the unsold inventory (the ending inventory), $31,000, from the amount Hanlon had available for sale during the year, $190,000, gives the cost of goods sold for the year of $159,000. Understanding this relationship shown on Hanlon Retail Food Store's partial income statement gives you the necessary background to determine the cost of goods sold as presented in this section.

Objective 2
Describe briefly cost of goods sold and the distinction between perpetual and periodic inventory procedures.

Real World Example
In its 1995 annual report, Safeway Inc., one of the world's largest food retailers, reports the first two lines of its income statement as *Sales* and *Cost of goods sold*. The cost of goods sold is about 73% of sales.

Two Procedures for Accounting for Inventories

To determine the cost of goods sold, accountants must have accurate merchandise inventory figures. Accountants use two basic methods for determining the amount of merchandise inventory—perpetual inventory procedure and periodic inventory procedure. We mention perpetual inventory procedure only briefly here as periodic inventory procedure is used extensively in this chapter. In the next chapter, we emphasize perpetual inventory procedure and further compare it with periodic inventory procedure.

When discussing inventory, we need to clarify whether we are referring to the physical goods on hand or the Merchandise Inventory account, which is the financial representation of the physical goods on hand. The difference between perpetual and periodic inventory procedures is the frequency with which the Merchandise Inventory account is updated to reflect what is physically on hand. Under **perpetual inventory procedure,** the Merchandise Inventory account is continuously updated to reflect items on hand. For example, your supermarket uses a scanner to ring up your purchases. When your box of Rice Krispies crosses the scanner, the Merchandise Inventory account shows that one less box of Rice Krispies is on hand.

Under **periodic inventory procedure,** the Merchandise Inventory account is updated periodically after a physical count has been made. Usually, the physical count takes place immediately before the preparation of financial statements.

PERPETUAL INVENTORY PROCEDURE   Companies use perpetual inventory procedure in a variety of business settings. Historically, companies that sold merchandise with a high individual unit value, such as automobiles, furniture, and appliances, used perpetual inventory procedure. Today, computerized cash registers, scanners, and accounting software programs automatically keep track of inflows and outflows of each inventory item. Computerization makes it economical for many retail stores to use perpetual inventory procedure for goods of low unit value, such as groceries.

Under perpetual inventory procedure, the Merchandise Inventory account provides close control by showing the cost of the goods that are supposed to be on hand at any particular time. Companies debit the Merchandise Inventory account for each purchase and credit it for each sale so that the current balance is shown in the account at all times. Usually, firms also maintain detailed unit records showing the quantities of each type of goods that should be on hand. At the end of the accounting period, company personnel take a physical inventory by actually counting the units of inventory on hand. Then they compare this physical count with the records showing the units that should be on hand. Chapter 7 describes perpetual inventory procedure in more detail.

PERIODIC INVENTORY PROCEDURE   Merchandising companies selling low unit value merchandise (such as nuts and bolts, nails, Christmas cards, or pencils) that have not computerized their inventory systems often find that the extra costs of record-keeping under perpetual inventory procedure more than outweigh the benefits. These merchandising companies often use periodic inventory procedure.

Under periodic inventory procedure, companies do not use the Merchandise Inventory account to record each purchase and sale of merchandise. Instead, a company corrects the balance in the Merchandise Inventory account as the result of a physical inventory count at the end of the accounting period. Also, the company usually does not maintain other records showing the exact number of units that should be on hand. Although periodic inventory procedure reduces record-keeping considerably, it also reduces control over inventory items.

Companies using periodic inventory procedure make no entries to the Merchandise Inventory account nor do they maintain unit records during the accounting period. Thus, these companies have no up-to-date balance against which to compare the physical inventory count at the end of the period. Also, these companies make no attempt to determine the cost of goods sold at the time of each sale. Instead, they calculate the cost of all the goods sold during the accounting period at the *end* of the period. To determine the cost of goods sold, a company must know:

1. Beginning inventory (cost of goods on hand at the beginning of the period).
2. Net cost of purchases during the period.
3. Ending inventory (cost of unsold goods at the end of the period).

The company would show this information as follows:

Beginning inventory	$ 34,000
Add: Net cost of purchases during the period	140,000
Cost of goods available for sale during the period	$174,000
Deduct: Ending inventory	20,000
Cost of goods sold during the period	$154,000

In this schedule, notice that the company began the accounting period with $34,000 of merchandise and purchased an additional $140,000, making a total of $174,000 of goods that could have been sold during the period. Then, a physical inventory showed that $20,000 remained unsold, which implies that $154,000 was the cost of goods sold during the period. Of course, the $154,000 is not necessarily the precise amount of goods sold because no actual record was made of the dollar cost of the goods sold. Periodic inventory procedure basically assumes that everything not on hand at the end of the period has been sold. This method disregards problems such as theft or breakage because the Merchandise Inventory account contains no up-to-date balance at the end of the accounting period against which to compare the physical count.

Because this chapter emphasizes periodic inventory, an in-depth discussion of the accounts and journal entries used under periodic inventory procedure follows.

Under periodic inventory procedure, a merchandising company uses the **Purchases account** to record the cost of merchandise bought for resale during the current accounting period. The Purchases account, which is increased by debits, appears with the income statement accounts in the chart of accounts.

To illustrate entries affecting the Purchases account, assume that Hanlon Retail Food Store made two purchases of merchandise from Smith Wholesale Company. Hanlon purchased $30,000 of merchandise on credit (on account) on May 4, and on May 21 purchased $20,000 of merchandise for cash. The required journal entries for Hanlon are:

May	4	Purchases	30,000	
		Accounts Payable		30,000
		To record purchase of merchandise on account.		
	21	Purchases	20,000	
		Cash		20,000
		To record purchase of merchandise for cash.		

The buyer deducts purchase discounts and purchase returns and allowances from purchases to arrive at net purchases. The accountant records these items in contra accounts to the Purchases account.

PURCHASE DISCOUNTS Often companies purchase merchandise under credit terms that permit them to deduct a stated cash discount if they pay invoices within a specifed time. Assume that credit terms for Hanlon's May 4 purchase are 2/10, n/30. If Hanlon pays for the merchandise by May 14, the store may take a 2% discount. Thus, Hanlon must pay only $29,400 to settle the $30,000 account payable. The entry to record the payment of the invoice on May 14 is:

May	14	Accounts Payable	30,000	
		Cash		29,400
		Purchase Discounts		600
		To record payment on account within discount period.		

The buyer records the purchase discount only when the invoice is paid within the discount period and the discount is taken. The **Purchase Discounts account** is a contra account to Purchases that reduces the recorded invoice price of the goods purchased to the price actually paid. Hanlon reports purchase discounts in the income statement as a deduction from purchases.

Companies base purchase discounts on the invoice price of goods. If an invoice shows purchase returns or allowances, they must be deducted from the invoice price before calculating purchase discounts. For example, in the previous transaction, the invoice price of goods purchased was $30,000. If Hanlon returned $2,000 of the goods, the seller calculates the purchase discount on $28,000.

INTEREST RATE IMPLIED IN CASH DISCOUNTS To decide whether you should take advantage of discounts by using your cash or borrowing, make this simple analysis. Assume that you must pay $10,000 within 30 days or $9,800 within 10 days to settle a $10,000 invoice with terms of 2/10, n/30. By advancing payment 20 days from the

Purchases of Merchandise

Objective 3
Record journal entries for purchase transactions involving merchandise.

Reinforcing Problem
E6–1 Apply rules of debit and credit for merchandise-related accounts.

Deductions from Purchases

Reinforcing Problems
E6–2 Prepare entries for merchandise purchase/sale, return, and allowance on both buyer's and seller's books.
E6–3 Determine end of the discount period and prepare an entry to record payment.
E6–4 Calculate the effect of trade and cash discounts on payment.

final due date, you can secure a discount of $200. The interest expense incurred to borrow $9,800 at 12% per year for 20 days is $65.33. You would save $134.67 ($200 − $65.33) by borrowing the money and paying the invoice within the discount period.

In terms of an annual rate of interest, the 2% rate of discount for 20 days is equivalent to a 36% annual rate: (360 ÷ 20) × 2%. The formula is:

$$\text{Equivalent annual rate of interest} = \frac{\text{The number of days in a year (assumed to be 360)}}{\text{The number of days from the end of the discount period until the final due date}} \times \text{The percentage rate of discount}$$

You can convert all cash discount terms to their approximate annual interest rate equivalents by use of this formula. Thus, a company could afford to pay up to 36% [(360 ÷ 20) × 2%] on borrowed funds to take advantage of discount terms of 2/10, n/30. The company could pay 18% on terms of 1/10, n/30.

PURCHASE RETURNS AND ALLOWANCES   A purchase return occurs when a buyer returns merchandise to a seller. When a buyer receives a reduction in the price of goods shipped, a purchase allowance results. Then, the buyer commonly uses a debit memorandum to notify the seller that the account payable with the seller is being reduced (Accounts Payable is debited). A debit memorandum is similar to a credit memorandum except for the preprinted words, "WE DEBIT YOUR ACCOUNT." The buyer may use a copy of a debit memorandum to record the returns or allowances or may wait for confirmation, usually a credit memorandum, from the seller.

Both returns and allowances reduce the buyer's debt to the seller and decrease the cost of the goods purchased. The buyer may want to know the amount of returns and allowances as the first step in controlling the costs incurred in returning unsatisfactory merchandise or negotiating purchase allowances. For this reason, buyers record purchase returns and allowances in a separate **Purchase Returns and Allowances account.** If Hanlon returned $350 of merchandise to Smith Wholesale before paying for the goods, it would make this journal entry:

Accounts Payable	350	
Purchase Returns and Allowances		350
To record return of damaged merchandise to supplier.		

The entry would have been the same to record a $350 allowance. Only the explanation would change.

If Hanlon had already paid the account, the debit would be to Cash instead of Accounts Payable, since Hanlon would receive a refund of cash. If the company took a discount at the time it paid the account, only the net amount would be refunded. For instance, if a 2% discount had been taken, Hanlon's journal entry for the return would be:

Cash	343	
Purchase Discounts	7	
Purchase Returns and Allowances		350
To record return of damaged merchandise to supplier and record receipt of cash.		

Purchase Returns and Allowances is a contra account to the Purchases account, and the income statement shows it as a deduction from purchases. When both purchase discounts and purchase returns and allowances are deducted from purchases, the result is **net purchases.**

Transportation costs are an important part of cost of goods sold. To understand how to account for transportation costs, you must know the meaning of the following terms:

- **FOB shipping point** means "free on board at shipping point." The buyer incurs all transportation costs after the merchandise has been loaded on a railroad car or truck at the point of shipment. Thus, the buyer is responsible for *ultimately* paying the freight charges.
- **FOB destination** means "free on board at destination." The seller ships the goods to their destination without charge to the buyer. Thus, the seller is *ultimately* responsible for paying the freight charges.
- **Passage of title** is a term that indicates the transfer of the legal ownership of goods. Title to the goods normally passes from seller to buyer at the FOB point. Thus, when goods are shipped FOB shipping point, title usually passes to the buyer at the shipping point. When goods are shipped FOB destination, title usually passes at the destination.
- **Freight prepaid** means the *seller* must *initially* pay the freight at the time of shipment.
- **Freight collect** indicates the *buyer* must *initially* pay the freight bill on the arrival of the goods.

To illustrate the use of these terms, assume that a company ships goods FOB shipping point, freight collect. Title passes at the shipping point. The buyer is responsible for paying the $100 freight costs and does so. The seller makes no entry for freight charges; the entry on the *buyer's books* is:

Transportation-In (or Freight-In)	100	
Cash		100
To record payment of freight bill on goods purchased.		

The **Transportation-In account** records the inward freight costs of acquiring merchandise. Transportation-In is an adjunct account in that it is added to net purchases to arrive at **net cost of purchases**. An **adjunct account** is closely related to another account (Purchases, in this instance), and its balance is added to the balance of the related account in the financial statements. Recall that a contra account is just the opposite of an adjunct account. Buyers deduct a contra account, such as accumulated depreciation, from the related account in the financial statements.

When shipping goods FOB destination, freight prepaid, the seller is responsible for and pays the freight bill. Because the seller cannot bill a separate freight cost to the buyer, the buyer shows no entry for freight on its books. The seller, however, has undoubtedly considered the freight cost in setting selling prices. The following entry is required on the *seller's books*:

Delivery Expense (or Transportation-Out Expense)	100	
Cash		100
To record freight cost on goods sold.		

When the terms are FOB destination, the seller records the freight costs as **delivery expense;** this selling expense appears on the income statement with other selling expenses.

FOB terms are especially important at the end of an accounting period. Goods in transit then belong to either the seller or the buyer, and one of these parties must include these goods in its ending inventory. Goods shipped FOB destination belong to the seller while in transit, and the seller includes these goods in its ending inventory. Goods shipped FOB shipping point belong to the buyer while in transit, and the buyer records these goods as a purchase and includes them in its ending inventory. For

Transportation Costs

Objective 4
Describe the freight terms and record transportation costs.

Reinforcing Problem
E6–6 Determine cash discount available and amount of cash paid.

Note to the Students
An easy way to interpret FOB terms is to identify either the destination or shipping point as the location where the goods change ownership.

example, assume that a seller ships goods on December 30, 1998, and they arrive at their destination on January 5, 1999. If terms are FOB destination, the seller includes the goods in its December 31, 1998, inventory, and neither seller nor buyer records the exchange transaction until January 5, 1999. If terms are FOB shipping point, the buyer includes the goods in its December 31, 1998, inventory, and both parties record the exchange transaction as of December 30, 1998.

Sometimes the seller prepays the freight as a convenience to the buyer, even though the buyer is ultimately responsible for it. The buyer merely reimburses the seller for the freight paid. For example, assume that Wood Company sold merchandise to Loud Company with terms of FOB shipping point, freight prepaid. The freight charges were $100. The following entries are necessary on the books of the buyer and the seller:

Buyer—Loud Company			**Seller—Wood Company**		
Transportation-In	100		Accounts Receivable . . .	100	
Accounts Payable . . .		100	Cash		100

Reinforcing Problems
E6–7 Prepare entries for purchase, transportation-in, purchase discounts, and payment.
P6–1 Journalize merchandise transactions for two different companies.
P6–2 Journalize merchandise transactions on both the buyer's and seller's books.

Such entries are necessary because Wood initially paid the freight charges when not required to do so. Therefore, Loud Company must reimburse Wood for the charges. If the buyer pays freight for the seller (e.g., FOB destination, freight collect), the buyer merely deducts the freight paid from the amount owed to the seller. The following entries are necessary on the books of the buyer and the seller:

Buyer—Loud Company			**Seller—Wood Company**		
Accounts Payable	100		Delivery Expense	100	
Cash		100	Accounts Receivable		100

Purchase discounts may be taken only on the purchase price of goods. Therefore, a buyer who owes the seller for freight charges cannot take a discount on the freight charges owed, even if the buyer makes payment within the discount period. We summarize our discussion of freight terms and the resulting journal entries to record the freight charges in Illustration 6.6.

Merchandise Inventories

Merchandise inventory is the cost of goods on hand and available for sale at any given time. To determine the cost of goods sold in any accounting period, management needs inventory information. Management must know its cost of goods on hand at the start of the period (beginning inventory), the net cost of purchases during the period, and the cost of goods on hand at the close of the period (ending inventory). Since the ending inventory of the preceding period is the beginning inventory for the current period, management already knows the cost of the beginning inventory. Companies record purchases, purchase discounts, purchase returns and allowances, and transportation-in throughout the period. Therefore, management needs to determine only the cost of the ending inventory at the end of the period in order to calculate cost of goods sold.

Note to the Student
A physical inventory is required whether the inventory system is periodic or perpetual. A complicating factor is placing a value on the unsold inventory that has been counted. We discuss several approaches to pricing the unsold items in a later chapter.

Taking a Physical Inventory   Under periodic inventory procedure, company personnel determine ending inventory cost by taking a *physical inventory*. Taking a **physical inventory** consists of counting physical units of each type of merchandise on hand. To calculate inventory cost, they multiply the number of each kind of merchandise by its unit cost. Then, they combine the total costs of the various kinds of merchandise to provide the total ending inventory cost.

In taking a physical inventory, company personnel must be careful to count all goods owned, regardless of where they are located, and include them in the inventory. Thus, companies should include goods shipped to potential customers on approval in their inventories. Similarly, companies should not record **consigned goods** (goods delivered to another party who attempts to sell them for a commission) as sold goods.

Shipping point: Detroit

Destination: San Diego

ILLUSTRATION 6.6
Summary of Shipping Terms

Goods travel from shipping point to destination

If shipping terms are:

FOB shipping point—Buyer incurs the freight charges

Freight prepaid—Seller initially pays the freight charges

FOB destination—Seller incurs the freight charge

Freight collect—Buyer initially pays the freight charges

If the freight terms are combined as follows:

Terms	Party that Initially Pays	Party that Ultimately Bears Expense
(1) FOB shipping point, freight collect	Buyer	Buyer
(2) FOB destination, freight prepaid	Seller	Seller
(3) FOB shipping point, freight prepaid	Seller	Buyer
(4) FOB destination, freight collect	Buyer	Seller

Explanations:

FOB shipping point, freight collect—Buyer both incurs and initially pays the freight charges. The proper party paid the freight. The buyer debits Transportation-In and credits Cash.

FOB destination, freight prepaid—Seller both incurs and initially pays the freight charges. The proper party paid the freight. The seller debits Delivery Expense and credits Cash.

FOB shipping point, freight prepaid—Buyer incurs the freight charges, and seller initially pays the freight charges. Buyer must reimburse seller for freight charges. The seller debits Accounts Receivable and credits Cash upon paying the freight. The buyer debits Transportation-In and credits Accounts Payable when informed of the freight charges.

FOB destination, freight collect—Seller incurs freight charges, and buyer initially pays freight charges. Buyer deducts freight charges from amount owed to seller. The buyer debits Accounts Payable and credits Cash when paying the freight. The seller debits Delivery Expense and credits Accounts Receivable when informed of the freight charges.

These goods remain the property of the owner (consignor) until sold by the consignee and must be included in the owner's inventory.

Merchandise in transit is merchandise in the hands of a freight company on the date of a physical inventory. As stated above, buyers must record merchandise in transit at the end of the accounting period as a purchase if the goods were shipped FOB shipping point and they have received title to the merchandise. In general, the goods belong to the party who ultimately bears the transportation charges.

When accounting personnel know the beginning and ending inventories and the various items making up the net cost of purchases, they can determine the cost of goods sold. To illustrate, assume the following account balances for Hanlon Retail Food Store as of December 31, 1999:

Determining Cost of Goods Sold

Objective 5
Determine cost of goods sold.

Reinforcing Problem
E6–8 Determine cost of goods sold.

Merchandise Inventory, January 1, 1999	$ 24,000 Dr.
Purchases	167,000 Dr.
Purchase Discounts	3,000 Cr.
Purchase Returns and Allowances	8,000 Cr.
Transportation-In	10,000 Dr.

By taking a physical inventory, Hanlon determined the December 31, 1999, merchandise inventory to be $31,000. Hanlon then calculated its cost of goods sold as shown in Illustration 6.7. This computation appears in a section of the income statement directly below the calculation of net sales.

In Illustration 6.7, Hanlon's beginning inventory ($24,000) plus net cost of purchases ($166,000) is equal to **cost of goods available for sale** ($190,000). The firm

ILLUSTRATION 6.7
Determination of Cost of
Goods Sold for Hanlon
Retail Food Store*

Cost of goods sold:

Merchandise inventory, January 1, 1999			$ 24,000
Purchases		$167,000	
Less: Purchase discounts	$3,000		
Purchase returns and allowances	8,000	11,000	
Net purchases		$156,000	
Add: Transportation-in		10,000	
Net cost of purchases			166,000
Cost of goods available for sale			$190,000
Less: Merchandise inventory, December 31, 1999			31,000
Cost of goods sold			$159,000

*This illustration is the same as Illustration 6.5, repeated here for your convenience.

deducts the ending inventory cost ($31,000) from cost of goods available for sale to arrive at cost of goods sold ($159,000).

Another way of looking at this relationship is the following diagram:

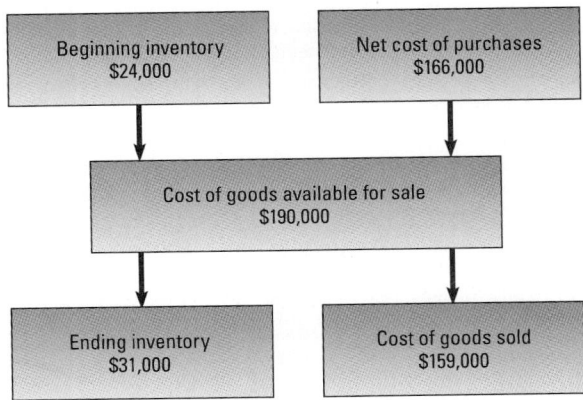

Beginning inventory and net cost of purchases combine to form cost of goods available for sale. Hanlon divides the cost of goods available for sale into ending inventory (which is the cost of goods not sold) and cost of goods sold.

To continue the calculation appearing in Illustration 6.7, net cost of purchases ($166,000) is equal to purchases ($167,000), *less* purchase discounts ($3,000) and purchase returns and allowances ($8,000), *plus* transportation-in ($10,000).

As shown in Illustration 6.7, ending inventory cost (merchandise inventory) appears in the income statement as a deduction from cost of goods available for sale to compute cost of goods sold. Ending inventory cost (merchandise inventory) is also a current asset in the end-of-period balance sheet.

Lack of Control under Periodic Inventory Procedure

Note to the Student
The word *stolen* often implies a burglar entering and taking a company's assets. However stolen also includes goods taken by employees or by shoplifting customers. An executive of a Midwest department store chain remarked that stealing by employees was much more frequent than shoplifting by customers.

Companies use periodic inventory procedure because of its simplicity and relatively low cost. However, periodic inventory procedure provides little control over inventory. Firms assume any items not included in the physical count of inventory at the end of the period have been sold. Thus, they mistakenly assume items that have been stolen have been sold and include their cost in cost of goods sold.

To illustrate, suppose that the cost of goods available for sale was $200,000 and ending inventory was $60,000. These figures suggest that the cost of goods sold was $140,000. Now suppose that $2,000 of goods were actually shoplifted during the year. If such goods had not been stolen, the ending inventory would have been $62,000 and the cost of goods sold only $138,000. Thus, the $140,000 cost of goods sold calculated under periodic inventory procedure includes both the cost of the merchandise delivered to customers and the cost of merchandise stolen.

CLASSIFIED INCOME STATEMENT

In preceding chapters, we illustrated the unclassified (or single-step) income statement. An **unclassified income statement** has only two categories—revenues and expenses. In contrast, a **classified income statement** divides both revenues and expenses into operating and nonoperating items. The statement also separates operating expenses into selling and administrative expenses. A classified income statement is also called a multiple-step income statement.

Objective 6
Prepare a classified income statement.

In Illustration 6.8, we present a classified income statement for Hanlon Retail Food Store. This statement uses the previously presented data on sales (Illustration 6.4) and cost of goods sold (Illustration 6.7), together with additional assumed data on operating expenses and other expenses and revenues. Note in Illustration 6.8 that a classified income statement has the following four major sections:

1.   Operating revenues.
2.   Cost of goods sold.
3.   Operating expenses.
4.   Nonoperating revenues and expenses (other revenues and other expenses).

The classified income statement shows important relationships that help in analyzing how well the company is performing. For example, by deducting cost of goods sold from operating revenues, you can determine by what amount sales revenues exceed the cost of items being sold. If this margin, called gross margin, is lower than desired, a company may need to increase its selling prices and/or decrease its cost of goods sold. The classified income statement subdivides operating expenses into selling and administrative expenses. Thus, statement users can see how much expense is incurred in selling the product and how much in administering the business. Statement users can also make comparisons with other years' data for the same business and with other businesses. Nonoperating revenues and expenses appear at the bottom of the income statement because they are less significant in assessing the profitability of the business.

Reinforcing Problems
P6–3 Prepare and post journal entries, and prepare a trial balance and classified income statement. Annual Report Analysis 6–3 Classify income statement items and calculate gross margin percentages.

Next, we explain the major headings of the classified income statement in Illustration 6.8. The terms in some of these headings are already familiar to you. Although future illustrations of classified income statements may vary somewhat in form, we retain the basic organization.

   1.   Operating revenues are the revenues generated by the major activities of the business—usually the sale of products or services or both.

   2.   Cost of goods sold is the major expense in merchandising companies. Note the cost of goods sold section of the classified income statement in Illustration 6.8. This chapter has already discussed the items used in calculating cost of goods sold. Merchandisers usually highlight the amount by which sales revenues exceed the cost of goods sold in the top part of the income statement. The excess of net sales over cost of goods sold is the **gross margin or gross profit.** To express gross margin as a

Note to the Student
What do you think the gross margin rates for different types of retail stores in your area, such as jewelry versus groceries, would be? Would you rather purchase goods from a store with a high or low gross margin rate?

ILLUSTRATION 6.8   Classified Income Statement for a Merchandising Company

HANLON RETAIL FOOD STORE
Income Statement
For the Year Ended December 31, 1999

Operating revenues:			
Gross sales			$282,000
Less: Sales discounts		$ 5,000	
Sales returns and allowances		15,000	20,000
Net sales			$262,000
Cost of goods sold:			
Merchandise inventory, January 1, 1999		$ 24,000	
Purchases	$167,000		
Less: Purchase discounts	$3,000		
Purchase returns and allowances	8,000	11,000	
Net purchases	$156,000		
Add: Transportation-in	10,000		
Net cost of purchases		166,000	
Cost of goods available for sale		$190,000	
Less: Merchandise inventory, December 31, 1999		31,000	
Cost of goods sold			159,000
Gross margin			$103,000
Operating expenses:			
Selling expenses:			
Sales salaries and commissions expense	$ 26,000		
Salespersons' travel expense	3,000		
Delivery expense	2,000		
Advertising expense	4,000		
Rent expense—store building	2,500		
Supplies expense	1,000		
Utilities expense	1,800		
Depreciation expense—store equipment	700		
Other selling expense	400	$ 41,400	
Administrative expenses:			
Salaries expense, executive	$ 29,000		
Rent expense—administrative building	1,600		
Insurance expense	1,500		
Supplies expense	800		
Depreciation expense—office equipment	1,100		
Other administrative expenses	300	34,300	
Total operating expenses			75,700
Income from operations			$ 27,300
Nonoperating revenues and expenses:			
Nonoperating revenues:			
Interest revenue			1,400
			$ 28,700
Nonoperating expenses:			
Interest expense			600
Net income			$ 28,100

percentage rate, we divide gross margin by net sales. In Illustration 6.8, the gross margin rate is approximately 39.3% ($103,000/$262,000). The gross margin rate indicates that out of each sales dollar, approximately 39 cents is available to cover other expenses and produce income. Business owners watch the gross margin rate closely since a small percentage fluctuation can cause a large dollar change in net income. Also, a downward trend in the gross margin rate may indicate a problem, such as theft of merchandise. For instance, one Southeastern sporting goods company, SportsTown, Inc., suffered significant gross margin deterioration in fiscal year 1994 from increased shoplifting and employee theft.

3. **Operating expenses** for a merchandising company are those expenses, other than cost of goods sold, incurred in the normal business functions of a company. Usually, operating expenses are either selling expenses or administrative expenses. **Selling expenses** are expenses a company incurs in selling and marketing efforts. Examples include salaries and commissions of salespersons, expenses for salespersons' travel, delivery, advertising, rent (or depreciation, if owned) and utilities on a sales building, sales supplies used, and depreciation on delivery trucks used in sales. **Administrative expenses** are expenses a company incurs in the overall management of a business. Examples include administrative salaries, rent (or depreciation, if owned) and utilities on an administrative building, insurance expense, administrative supplies used, and depreciation on office equipment.

Certain operating expenses may be shared by the selling and administrative functions. For example, a company might incur rent, taxes, and insurance on a building for both sales and administrative purposes. Expenses covering both the selling and administrative functions must be analyzed and prorated between the two functions on the income statement. For instance, if $1,000 of depreciation expense relates 60% to selling and 40% to administrative based on the square footage or number of employees, the income statement would show $600 as a selling expense and $400 as an administrative expense.

4. **Nonoperating revenues (other revenues)** and **nonoperating expenses (other expenses)** are revenues and expenses not related to the sale of products or services regularly offered for sale by a business. An example of a nonoperating revenue is interest that a business earns on notes receivable. An example of a nonoperating expense is interest incurred on money borrowed by the company.

Real World Example
In its 1995 annual report, J. C. Penney Company stated that, "In 1994, gross margin increased as a result of favorable sales performance and improved inventory management. As a percentage of sales, gross margin decreased to 30.3 percent in 1995 from 31.5 percent in 1994 and 1993."

To summarize the more important relationships in the income statement of a merchandising firm in equation form:

1. **Net sales** = Gross sales − (Sales discounts + Sales returns and allowances).
2. **Net purchases** = Purchases − (Purchase discounts + Purchase returns and allowances).
3. **Net cost of purchases** = Net purchases + Transportation-in.
4. **Cost of goods sold** = Beginning inventory + Net cost of purchases − Ending inventory.
5. **Gross margin** = Net sales − Cost of goods sold.
6. **Income from operations** = Gross margin − Operating (selling and administrative) expenses.
7. **Net income** = Income from operations + Nonoperating revenues − Nonoperating expenses.

Each of these relationships is important because of the way it relates to an overall measure of business profitability. For example, a company may produce a high gross margin on sales. However, because of large sales commissions and delivery expenses, the owner may realize only a very small percentage of the gross margin as profit. The classifications in the income statement allow a user to focus on the whole picture as well as on how net income was derived (statement relationships).

Important Relationships in the Income Statement

Reinforcing Problems
E6–9 Supply missing amounts in the income statement.
E6–10 Supply missing terms in formulas showing income statement relationships.

ANALYZING AND USING THE FINANCIAL RESULTS— GROSS MARGIN PERCENTAGE

As discussed on pages 225–226, you can calculate the **gross margin percentage** by using the following formula:

$$\text{Gross margin percentage} = \frac{\text{Gross margin}}{\text{Net sales}}$$

Objective 7
Analyze and use the financial results—gross margin percentage.

AN ETHICAL PERSPECTIVE

World Auto Parts Corporation

John Bentley is the chief financial officer for World Auto Parts Corporation. The company buys approximately $500 million of auto parts each year from small suppliers all over the world and resells them to auto repair shops in the United States.

Most of the suppliers have cash discount terms of 2/10, n/30. John has instructed his personnel to pay invoices on the 30th day after the invoice date but to take the 2% discount even though they are not entitled to do so. Whenever a supplier complains, John instructs his purchasing agent to find another supplier who will go along with this practice. When some of his own employees questioned the practice, John responded as follows:

This practice really does no harm. These small suppliers are much better off to go along and have our business than to not go along and lose it. For most of them, we are their largest customer. Besides, if they are willing to sell to others at a 2% discount, why should they not be willing to sell to us at that same discount even though we pay a little later? The benefit to our company is very significant. Last year our profits were $100 million. A total of $10 million of the profits was attributable to this practice. Do you really want me to change this practice and give up 10% of our profits?

To demonstrate the use of this ratio, consider the following information from the 1996 Annual Report of Western Digital Corporation.

Western Digital Corporation
Western Digital Corporation produces information storage products, such as hard drives.

($ millions)	**1996**	**1995**	**1994**
Revenues	$2,865.2	$2,130.9	$1,539.7
Gross profit	$ 382.1	$ 394.1	$ 317.9
Gross profit (margin) percentage	$\frac{\$382.1}{\$2,865.2} = 13.33\%$	$\frac{\$394.1}{\$2,130.9} = 18.49\%$	$\frac{\$317.9}{\$1,539.7} = 20.65\%$

Western Digital Corporation's downward trend in gross margin percentages could indicate a problem such as theft of merchandise. Alternatively, maybe severe competition has reduced selling prices.

AN ACCOUNTING PERSPECTIVE

BUSINESS INSIGHT   Perkin-Elmer develops, manufactures, and markets life science systems and analytical instruments used in such markets as environmental testing and food. Management often watches gross margin percentage to see if trends can be explained. Take, for example, Perkin-Elmer's 1996 Annual Report. Under Management's Discussion and Analysis, Perkin-Elmer's management discusses the gross margin as follows:

Gross margin as a percentage of net revenues was 48.8% in fiscal 1996 compared with 47.3% in fiscal 1995. The improvement was the result of increased unit sales of higher margin life science products. This was partially offset by lower margins in the United States analytical instruments market.

You should now understand the distinction between accounting for a service company and a merchandising company. The next chapter continues the discussion of merchandise inventory carried by merchandising companies.

UNDERSTANDING THE LEARNING OBJECTIVES

Objective 1
Record journal entries for sales transactions involving merchandise.

- In a sales transaction, the seller transfers the legal ownership (title) of the goods to the buyer.
- An invoice is a document, prepared by the seller of merchandise and sent to the buyer, that contains the details of a sale, such as the number of units sold, unit price, total price, terms of sale, and manner of shipment.
- Usually sales are for cash or on account. When a sale is for cash, the debit is to Cash and the credit is to Sales. When a sale is on account, the debit is to Accounts Receivable and the credit is to Sales.
- When companies offer trade discounts, the gross selling price (gross invoice price) at which the sale is recorded is equal to the list price minus any trade discounts.
- Two common deductions from gross sales are (1) sales discounts and (2) sales returns and allowances. These deductions are recorded in contra revenue accounts to the Sales account. Both the Sales Discounts account and the Sales Returns and Allowances

account normally have debit balances. Net sales = Sales − (Sales discounts + Sales returns and allowances).

- Sales discounts arise when the seller offers the buyer a cash discount of 1% to 3% to induce early payment of an amount due.

- Sales returns result from merchandise being returned by a buyer because the goods are considered unsatisfactory or have been damaged. A sales allowance is a deduction from the original invoiced sales price granted to a customer when the customer keeps the merchandise but is dissatisfied.

- Cost of goods sold = Beginning inventory + Net cost of purchases − Ending inventory. Net cost of purchases = Purchases − (Purchase discounts + Purchase returns and allowances) + Transportation-in.

- Two methods of accounting for inventory are perpetual inventory procedure and periodic inventory procedure. Under perpetual inventory procedure, the inventory account is continuously updated during the accounting period. Under periodic inventory procedure, the inventory account is updated only periodically—after a physical count has been made.

- Purchases of merchandise are recorded by debiting Purchases and crediting Cash (for cash purchases) or crediting Accounts Payable (for purchases on account).

- Two common deductions from purchases are (1) purchase discounts and (2) purchase returns and allowances. In the general ledger, both of these items normally carry credit balances. From the buyer's side of the transactions, cash discounts are purchase discounts, and merchandise returns and allowances are purchase returns and allowances.

- FOB shipping point means free on board at shipping point—the buyer incurs the freight.

- FOB destination means free on board at destination—the seller incurs the freight.

- Passage of title is a term indicating the transfer of the legal ownership of goods.

- Freight prepaid is when the seller must initially pay the freight at the time of shipment.

- Freight collect is when the buyer must initially pay the freight on the arrival of the goods.

- Expansion and application of the relationship introduced in Learning Objective 2. Beginning inventory + Net cost of purchases = Cost of goods available for sale. Cost of goods available for sale − Ending inventory = Cost of goods sold.

- A classified income statement has four major sections—operating revenues, cost of goods sold, operating expenses, and nonoperating revenues and expenses.

- Operating revenues are the revenues generated by the major activities of the business—usually the sale of products or services or both.

- Cost of goods sold is the major expense in merchandising companies.

- Operating expenses for a merchandising company are those expenses other than cost of goods sold incurred in the normal business functions of a company. Usually, operating expenses are classified as either selling expenses or administrative expenses.

- Nonoperating revenues and expenses are revenues and expenses not related to the sale of products or services regularly offered for sale by a business.

- Gross margin percentage = Gross margin/Net sales.

- The gross margin rate indicates the amount of sales dollars available to cover expenses and produce income.

- Except for the merchandise-related accounts, the work sheet for a merchandising company is the same as for a service company.

- Any revenue accounts and contra purchases accounts in the Adjusted Trial Balance credit column of the work sheet are carried to the Income Statement credit column.

- Beginning inventory, contra revenue accounts, Purchases, Transportation-In, and expense accounts in the Adjusted Trial Balance debit column are carried to the Income Statement debit column.

Objective 2
Describe briefly cost of goods sold and the distinction between perpetual and periodic inventory procedures.

Objective 3
Record journal entries for purchase transactions involving merchandise.

Objective 4
Describe the freight terms and record transportation costs.

Objective 5
Determine cost of goods sold.

Objective 6
Prepare a classified income statement.

Objective 7
Analyze and use the financial results—gross margin percentage.

Objective 8
Prepare a work sheet and closing entries for a merchandising company (Appendix).

- Ending merchandise inventory is entered in the Income Statement credit column and in the Balance Sheet debit column.
- Closing entries may be prepared directly from the work sheet. The first journal entry debits all items appearing in the Income Statement credit column and credits Income Summary. The second entry credits all items appearing in the Income Statement debit column and debits Income Summary. The third entry debits Income Summary and credits the Retained Earnings account (assuming positive net income). The fourth entry debits the Retained Earnings account and credits the Dividends account.

APPENDIX

THE WORK SHEET FOR A MERCHANDISING COMPANY

Objective 8
Prepare a work sheet and closing entries for a merchandising company.

Reinforcing Problem
E6–11 Prepare a partial work sheet using merchandise-related accounts.

Illustration 6.9 shows a work sheet for a merchandising company. Lyons Company is a small sporting goods firm. The illustration for Lyons Company focuses on merchandise-related accounts. Thus, we do not show the fixed assets (land, building, and equipment). Except for the merchandise-related accounts, the work sheet for a merchandising company is the same as for a service company. Recall that use of a work sheet assists in the preparation of the adjusting and closing entries. The work sheet also contains all the information needed for the preparation of the financial statements.

To further simplify this illustration, assume Lyons needs no adjusting entries at month-end. The trial balance is from the ledger accounts at December 31, 1999. The $7,000 merchandise inventory in the trial balance is the beginning inventory. The sales and sales-related accounts and the purchases and purchases-related accounts summarize the merchandising activity for December 1999.

Completing the Work Sheet

Note to the Student
Illustrate the placement of the beginning and ending inventory amounts in the work sheet using the BEE approach, where B stands for beginning and E stands for ending. Place the beginning inventory in the Income Statement debit column. Place the ending inventory in the Income Statement credit column. Place the ending inventory in the Balance Sheet debit column. The word *BEE* is spelled out on the work sheet.

Lyons carries any revenue accounts (Sales) and contra purchases accounts (Purchase Discounts, Purchase Returns and Allowances) in the Adjusted Trial Balance credit columns of the work sheet to the Income Statement credit column. It carries beginning inventory, contra revenue accounts (Sales Discounts, Sales Returns and Allowances), Purchases, Transportation-In, and expense accounts (Selling Expenses, Administrative Expenses) in the Adjusted Trial Balance debit column to the Income Statement debit column.

Assume that ending inventory is $8,000. Lyons enters this amount in the Income Statement credit column because it is deducted from cost of goods available for sale (beginning inventory plus net cost of purchases) in determining cost of goods sold. It also enters the ending inventory in the Balance Sheet debit column to establish the proper balance in the Merchandise Inventory account. The beginning and ending inventories are on the Income Statement because Lyons uses both to calculate cost of goods sold in the income statement. Net income of $5,843 for the period balances the Income Statement columns. The firm carries the net income to the Statement of Retained Earnings credit column. Retained earnings of $18,843 balances the Statement of Retained Earnings columns. Lyons Company carries the retained earnings to the Balance Sheet credit column.

Lyons carries all other asset account balances (Cash, Accounts Receivable, and ending Merchandise Inventory) to the Balance Sheet debit column. It also carries the liability (Accounts Payable) and Capital Stock account balances to the Balance Sheet credit column. The balance sheet columns total to $29,543.

Financial Statements for a Merchandising Company

Reinforcing Problems
P6–5 and P6–5A Prepare a work sheet, classified income statement, statement of retained earnings, classified balance sheet, and closing entries.

Once the work sheet has been completed, Lyons prepares the financial statements. After entering any adjusting and closing entries in the journal, the firm posts them to the ledger. This process clears the records for the next accounting period. Finally, it prepares a post-closing trial balance.

INCOME STATEMENT   Illustration 6.10 shows the income statement Lyons prepared from its work sheet in Illustration 6.9. The focus in this income statement is on determining the cost of goods sold.

STATEMENT OF RETAINED EARNINGS   The statement of retained earnings, as you recall, is a financial statement that summarizes the transactions affecting the Retained Earnings account balance. In Illustration 6.11, the statement of retained earnings shows an increase in equity resulting from net income and a decrease in equity resulting from dividends.

ILLUSTRATION 6.9 Work Sheet for a Merchandising Company

LYONS COMPANY
Work Sheet
For the Month Ended December 31, 1999

Acct. No.	Account Titles	Trial Balance Debit	Trial Balance Credit	Adjustments Debit	Adjustments Credit	Adjusted Trial Balance Debit	Adjusted Trial Balance Credit	Income Statement Debit	Income Statement Credit	Statement of Retained Earnings Debit	Statement of Retained Earnings Credit	Balance Sheet Debit	Balance Sheet Credit
100	Cash	19,663				19,663						19,663	
103	Accounts Receivable	1,880				1,880						1,880	
105	Merchandise Inventory, December 1	7,000				7,000		7,000	8,000			8,000	
200	Accounts Payable		700				700						700
300	Capital Stock		10,000				10,000						10,000
310	Retained Earnings, December 1		15,000				15,000				15,000		
320	Dividends	2,000				2,000				2,000			
410	Sales		14,600				14,600		14,600				
411	Sales Discounts	44				44		44					
412	Sales Returns and Allowances	20				20		20					
500	Purchases	6,000				6,000		6,000					
501	Purchases Discounts		82				82		82				
502	Purchase Returns and Allowances		100				100		100				
503	Transportation-In	75				75		75					
557	Miscellaneous Selling Expenses	2,650				2,650		2,650					
567	Miscellaneous Administrative Expenses	1,150				1,150		1,150					
		40,482	40,482			40,482	40,482	16,939	22,782				
	Net Income							5,843			5,843		
								22,782	22,782	2,000	20,843	29,543	10,700
	Retained Earnings, December 31									18,843			18,843
										20,843	20,843	29,543	29,543

LYONS COMPANY
Income Statement
For the Month Ended December 31, 1999

Operating revenues:

Gross sales $14,600

Less: Sales discounts . . . . $ 44

Sales returns and allowances 20   64

Net sales $14,536

Cost of goods sold:

Merchandise inventory, December 1, 1999 . . . . $ 7,000

Purchases $6,000

Less: Purchase discounts . . . . $ 82

Purchase returns and allowances 100   182

Net purchases $5,818

Add: Transportation-in 75

Net cost of purchases 5,893

Cost of goods available for sale $12,893

Less: Merchandise inventory, December 31, 1999 8,000

Cost of goods sold 4,893

Gross margin . . . . $ 9,643

Operating expenses:

Miscellaneous selling expenses . . . . $ 2,650

Miscellaneous administrative expenses 1,150

Total operating expenses 3,800

Net income . . . . $ 5,843

ILLUSTRATION 6.10
Income Statement for a Merchandising Company

ILLUSTRATION 6.11
Statement of Retained
Earnings

LYONS COMPANY
Statement of Retained Earnings
For the Month Ended December 31, 1999

Retained earnings, December 1, 1999	$15,000
Add: Net income for the month	5,843
Total	$20,843
Deduct: Dividends	2,000
Retained earnings, December 31, 1999	$18,843

ILLUSTRATION 6.12
Balance Sheet for a
Merchandising Company

LYONS COMPANY
Balance Sheet
December 31, 1999
Assets

Current assets:		
Cash		$19,663
Accounts receivable		1,880
Merchandise inventory		8,000
Total assets		$29,543

Liabilities and Stockholders' Equity

Current liabilities:		
Accounts payable		$ 700
Stockholders' equity:		
Capital stock	$10,000	
Retained earnings	18,843	
Total stockholders' equity		28,843
Total liabilities and stockholders' equity		$29,543

BALANCE SHEET   The balance sheet, Illustration 6.12, contains the assets, liabilities, and stockholders' equity items taken from the work sheet. Note the $8,000 ending inventory is a current asset. The Retained Earnings account balance comes from the statement of retained earnings.

Closing Entries

Reinforcing Problem
E6–12 Prepare and post closing entries using T-accounts.

Recall from Chapter 4 that the closing process normally takes place after the accountant has prepared the financial statements for the period. The closing process closes revenue and expense accounts by transferring their balances to a clearing account called Income Summary and then to Retained Earnings. The closing process reduces the revenue and expense account balances to zero so that information for each accounting period may be accumulated separately.

Lyons's accountant would prepare closing entries directly from the work sheet in Illustration 6.9 using the same procedure presented in Chapter 4. The closing entries for Lyons Company follow.

The first journal entry *debits* all items appearing in the Income Statement credit column of the work sheet and *credits* Income Summary for the total of the column, $22,782.

1st entry	1999 Dec.	31	Merchandise Inventory (ending)	8,000	
			Sales	14,600	
			Purchase Discounts	82	
			Purchase Returns and Allowances	100	
			Income Summary		22,782
			To close accounts with a credit balance in the Income Statement columns and to establish ending merchandise inventory.		

The second entry *credits* all items appearing in the Income Statement debit column and *debits* Income Summary for the total of that column, $16,939.[1]

Dec.	31	Income Summary	16,939		2nd entry
		Merchandise Inventory (beginning).		7,000	
		Sales Discounts.		44	
		Sales Returns and Allowances		20	
		Purchases		6,000	
		Transportation-In		75	
		Miscellaneous Selling Expenses.		2,650	
		Miscellaneous Administrative Expenses		1,150	
		To close accounts with a debit balance in the Income Statement columns.			

Note to the Student
How would this closing entry be different if the company had a net loss?

The third entry closes the credit balance in the Income Summary account of $5,843 to the Retained Earnings account.

Dec.	31	Income Summary	5,843		3rd entry
		Retained Earnings.		5,843	
		To close the Income Summary account to the Retained Earnings account.			

The fourth entry closes the Dividends account balance of $2,000 to the Retained Earnings account by debiting Retained Earnings and crediting Dividends.

Dec.	31	Retained Earnings.	2,000		4th entry
		Dividends		2,000	
		To close the Dividends account to the Retained Earnings account.			

Note how the first three closing entries tie into the totals in the Income Statement columns of the work sheet in Illustration 6.9. In the first closing journal entry, the credit to the Income Summary account is equal to the total of the Income Statement credit column. In the second entry, the debit to the Income Summary account is equal to the subtotal of the Income Statement debit column. The difference between the totals of the two Income Statement columns ($5,843) represents net income and is the amount of the third closing entry.

DEMONSTRATION PROBLEM

The following transactions occurred between Companies C and D in June of 1999:

June 10   Company C purchased merchandise from Company D for $80,000; terms 2/10/EOM, n/60, FOB destination, freight prepaid.
11   Company D paid freight of $1,200.
14   Company C received an allowance of $4,000 from the gross selling price because of damaged goods.
23   Company C returned $8,000 of goods purchased because they were not the quality ordered.
30   Company D received payment in full from Company C.

a.   Journalize the transactions for Company C.
b.   Journalize the transactions for Company D.

Required

---

[1]You may close debit balanced accounts (in the income statement) before credit balanced accounts. This practice does not affect the balance of the Income Summary account or the amount of net income.

SOLUTION TO DEMONSTRATION PROBLEM

a.

General Journal

Date		Account Titles and Explanation	Post. Ref.	Debit	Credit
		Company C			
1999 June	10	Purchases		8 0 0 0 0	
		Accounts Payable			8 0 0 0 0
		Purchased merchandise from Company D; terms 2/10/EOM, n/60.			
	14	Accounts Payable		4 0 0 0	
		Purchase Returns and Allowances			4 0 0 0
		Received an allowance from Company D for damaged goods.			
	23	Accounts Payable		8 0 0 0	
		Purchase Returns and Allowances			8 0 0 0
		Returned merchandise to Company D because of improper quality.			
	30	Accounts Payable ($80,000 − $4,000 − $8,000)		6 8 0 0 0	
		Purchase Discounts ($68,000 × 0.02)			1 3 6 0
		Cash ($68,000 − $1,360)			6 6 6 4 0
		Paid the amount due to Company D.			

b.

General Journal

Date		Account Titles and Explanation	Post. Ref.	Debit	Credit
		Company D			
1999 June	10	Accounts Receivable		8 0 0 0 0	
		Sales			8 0 0 0 0
		Sold merchandise to Company C; terms 2/10/EOM, n/60.			
	11	Delivery Expense		1 2 0 0	
		Cash			1 2 0 0
		Paid freight on sale of merchandise shipped FOB destination, freight prepaid.			
	14	Sales Returns and Allowances		4 0 0 0	
		Accounts Receivable			4 0 0 0
		Granted an allowance to Company C for damaged goods.			
	23	Sales Returns and Allowances		8 0 0 0	
		Accounts Receivable			8 0 0 0
		Merchandise returned from Company C due to improper quality.			
	30	Cash ($68,000 − $1,360)		6 6 6 4 0	
		Sales Discounts ($68,000 × 0.02)		1 3 6 0	
		Accounts Receivable ($80,000 − $4,000 − $8,000)			6 8 0 0 0
		Received the amount due from Company C.			

NEW TERMS

Adjunct account   Closely related to another account; its balance is added to the balance of the related account in the financial statements.   *221*

Administrative expenses   Expenses a company incurs in the overall management of a business.   *227*

Cash discount   A deduction from the invoice price that can be taken only if the invoice is paid within a specified time. To the seller, it is a sales discount; to the buyer, it is a purchase discount.   *214*

Chain discount   Occurs when the list price of a product is subject to a series of trade discounts.   *213*

Classified income statement   Divides both revenues and expenses into operating and nonoperating items. The statement also separates operating expenses into selling and administrative expenses. Also called the multiple-step income statement.   *225*

Consigned goods   Goods delivered to another party who attempts to sell the goods for the owner at a commission.   *222*

Cost of goods available for sale   Equal to beginning inventory plus net cost of purchases.   *223*

Cost of goods sold   Shows the cost to the seller of the goods sold to customers; under periodic inventory procedure, cost of goods sold is computed as Beginning inventory + Net cost of purchases − Ending inventory.   *217, 227*

Delivery expense   A selling expense recorded by the seller for freight costs incurred when terms are FOB destination.   *221*

FOB destination   Means free on board at destination; goods are shipped to their destination without charge to the buyer; the seller is responsible for paying the freight charges.   *221*

FOB shipping point   Means free on board at shipping point; buyer incurs all transportation costs after the merchandise is loaded on a railroad car or truck at the point of shipment.   *221*

Freight collect   Terms that require the buyer to pay the freight bill on arrival of the goods.   *221*

Freight prepaid   Terms that indicate the seller has paid the freight bill at the time of shipment.   *221*

Gross margin or gross profit   Net sales − Cost of goods sold; identifies the number of dollars available to cover expenses other than cost of goods sold.   *225, 227*

Gross margin percentage   Gross margin divided by net sales.   *227*

Gross selling price   (also called the invoice price) The list price less all trade discounts.   *213*

Income from operations   Gross margin − Operating (selling and administrative) expenses.   *227*

Invoice   A document prepared by the seller of merchandise and sent to the buyer. It contains the details of a sale, such as the number of units sold, unit price, total price billed, terms of sale, and manner of shipment. It is a purchase invoice from the buyer's point of view and a sales invoice from the seller's point of view.   *211*

Manufacturers   Companies that produce goods from raw materials and normally sell them to wholesalers.   *210*

Merchandise in transit   Merchandise in the hands of a freight company on the date of a physical inventory.   *223*

Merchandise inventory   The quantity of goods available for sale at any given time.   *217, 222*

Net cost of purchases   Net purchases + Transportation-in.   *221, 227*

Net income   Income from operations + Nonoperating revenues − Nonoperating expenses.   *227*

Net purchases   Purchases − (Purchase discounts + Purchase returns and allowances).   *227*

Net sales   Gross sales − (Sales discounts + Sales returns and allowances).   *211, 227*

Nonoperating expenses (other expenses)   Expenses incurred by a business that are not related to the acquisition and sale of the products or services regularly offered for sale.   *227*

Nonoperating revenues (other revenues)   Revenues not related to the sale of products or services regularly offered for sale by a business.   *227*

Operating expenses   Those expenses other than cost of goods sold incurred in the normal business functions of a company.   *227*

Operating revenues   Those revenues generated by the major activities of a business.   *225*

Passage of title   A legal term used to indicate transfer of legal ownership of goods.   *221*

Periodic inventory procedure   A method of accounting for merchandise acquired for sale to customers wherein the cost of merchandise sold and the cost of merchandise on hand are determined only at the end of the accounting period by taking a physical inventory.   *217*

Perpetual inventory procedure   A method of accounting for merchandise acquired for sale to customers wherein the Merchandise Inventory account is continuously updated to reflect items on hand; this account is debited for each purchase and credited for each sale so that the current balance is shown in the account at all times.   *217*

Physical inventory   Consists of counting physical units of each type of merchandise on hand.   *222*

Purchase discount   See Cash discount.

Purchase Discounts account   A contra account to Purchases that reduces the recorded gross invoice cost of the purchase to the price actually paid.   *219*

Purchase Returns and Allowances account   An account used under periodic inventory procedure to record the cost of merchandise returned to a seller and to record reductions in selling prices granted by a seller because merchandise was not satisfactory to a buyer; viewed as a reduction in the recorded cost of purchases.   *220*

Purchases account   An account used under periodic inventory procedure to record the cost of goods or merchandise bought for resale during the current accounting period.   *219*

Retailers Companies that sell goods to final consumers. *210*

Sales allowance A deduction from original invoiced sales price granted to a customer when the customer keeps the merchandise but is dissatisfied for any of a number of reasons, including inferior quality, damage, or deterioration in transit. *215*

Sales discount See Cash discount.

Sales Discounts account A contra revenue account to Sales; it is shown as a deduction from gross sales in the income statement. *214*

Sales return From the seller's point of view, merchandise returned by a buyer for any of a variety of reasons; to the buyer, a purchase return. *215*

Sales Returns and Allowances account A contra revenue account to Sales used to record the selling price of merchandise returned by buyers or reductions in selling prices granted. *215*

Selling expenses Expenses a company incurs in selling and marketing efforts. *227*

Trade discount A percentage deduction, or discount, from the specified list price or catalog price of merchandise to arrive at the gross invoice price; granted to particular categories of customers (e.g., retailers and wholesalers). Also see Chain discount. *213*

Transportation-In account An account used under periodic inventory procedure to record inward freight costs incurred in the acquisition of merchandise; a part of cost of goods sold. *221*

Unclassified income statement Shows only major categories for revenues and expenses. Also called the single-step income statement. *225*

Wholesalers Companies that normally sell goods to other companies (retailers) for resale. *210*

SELF-TEST

TRUE-FALSE

Indicate whether each of the following statements is true or false.

1. To compute net sales, sales discounts are added to, and sales returns and allowances are deducted from, gross sales.

2. Under perpetual inventory procedure, the Merchandise Inventory account is debited for each purchase and credited for each sale.

3. Purchase discounts and purchase returns and allow-ances are recorded in contra accounts to the Purchases account.

4. In taking a physical inventory, consigned goods are delivered to another party who attempts to sell the goods not included in the ending inventory of the company that sent the goods.

5. A classified income statement consists of only two categories of items, revenues and expenses.

MULTIPLE-CHOICE

Select the best answer for each of the following questions.

1. A seller sold merchandise which has a list price of $4,000 on account, giving a trade discount of 20%. The entry on the books of the seller is:

a.	Accounts Receivable	3,200	
	Trade Discounts	800	
	Sales		4,000
b.	Accounts Receivable	4,000	
	Sales		4,000
c.	Accounts Receivable	3,200	
	Sales Discounts	800	
	Sales		4,000
d.	Accounts Receivable	3,200	
	Sales		3,200

e. None of the above.

2. X Company began the accounting period with $60,000 of merchandise, and net cost of purchases was $240,000. A physical inventory showed $72,000 of merchandise unsold at the end of the period. The cost of goods sold of Y Company for the period is:
   a. $300,000.
   b. $228,000.
   c. $252,000.
   d. $168,000.
   e. None of the above.

3. A business purchased merchandise for $12,000 on account; terms are 2/10, n/30. If $2,000 of the merchandise was returned and the remaining amount due was paid within the discount period, the purchase discount would be:
   a. $240.
   b. $200.
   c. $1,200.
   d. $1,000.
   e. $3,600.

4. A classified income statement consists of all of the following major sections except for:
   a. Operating revenues.
   b. Cost of goods sold.
   c. Operating expenses.
   d. Nonoperating revenues and expenses.
   e. Current assets.

5. (Appendix) Closing entries for merchandise-related accounts include all of the following except for:
   a. A credit to Sales Discounts.
   b. A credit to Merchandise Inventory for the cost of ending inventory.
   c. A debit to Purchase Discounts.
   d. A credit to Transportation-In.
   e. A debit to Sales.

Now turn to page 246 to check your answers.

QUESTIONS

1. Which account titles are likely to appear in a merchandising company's ledger that do not appear in the ledger of a service enterprise?

2. What entry is made to record a sale of merchandise on account under periodic inventory procedure?

3. Describe trade discounts and chain discounts.

4. Sales discounts and sales returns and allowances are deducted from sales on the income statement to arrive at net sales. Why not deduct these directly from the Sales account by debiting Sales each time a sales discount, return, or allowance occurs?

5. What are the two basic procedures for accounting for inventory? How do these two procedures differ?

6. What useful purpose does the Purchases account serve?

7. What do the letters FOB stand for? When terms are *FOB destination*, who incurs the cost of freight?

8. What type of an expense is delivery expense? Where is this expense reported in the income statement?

9. Periodic inventory procedure is said to afford little control over inventory. Explain why.

10. How does the accountant arrive at the total dollar amount of the inventory after taking a physical inventory?

11. How is cost of goods sold determined under periodic inventory procedure?

12. If the cost of goods available for sale and the cost of the ending inventory are known, what other amount appearing on the income statement can be calculated?

13. What are the major sections in a classified income statement for a merchandising company, and in what order do these sections appear?

14. What is gross margin? Why might management be interested in the percentage of gross margin to net sales?

15. (Appendix) After closing entries are posted to the ledger, which types of accounts have balances? Why?

MAYTAG

16. **Real World Question** Based on the financial statements of Maytag Corporation contained in the annual report booklet, what were the 1996 selling, general, and administrative expenses? For each of the three years shown, what percentage of net sales were these expenses? Is the trend favorable or unfavorable?

THE LIMITED, INC.

17. **Real World Question** Based on the financial statements of The Limited, Inc., contained in the annual report booklet, what were the 1996 cost of goods sold, occupancy, and buying costs? For each of the three years shown, what percentage of net sales were these expenses? Is the trend favorable or unfavorable?

HARLAND

18. **Real World Question** Based on the financial statements of John H. Harland Company contained in the annual report booklet, what was the 1996 income from operations? For each of the three years shown, what percentage of net sales was income from operations? Is the trend favorable or unfavorable?

EXERCISES

In the following table, indicate how to increase or decrease (debit or credit) each account, and indicate its normal balance (debit or credit).

Exercise 6–1
Apply rules of debit and credit for merchandise-related accounts (L.O. 1, 3)

Title of Account	Increased by (debit or credit)	Decreased by (debit or credit)	Normal Balance (debit or credit)
Merchandise Inventory			
Sales			
Sales Returns and Allowances			
Sales Discounts			
Accounts Receivable			
Purchases			
Purchase Returns and Allowances			
Purchase Discounts			
Accounts Payable			
Transportation-In			

a. Silver Company purchased $56,000 of merchandise from Milton Company on account. Before paying its account, Silver Company returned damaged merchandise with an invoice price of $11,680. Assuming use of periodic inventory procedure, prepare entries on both companies' books to record both the purchase/sale and the return.

b. Show how any of the required entries would change assuming that Milton Company granted an allowance of $3,360 on the damaged goods instead of giving permission to return the merchandise.

Exercise 6–2
Prepare entries for merchandise purchase/sale, return, and allowance on both buyer's and seller's books (L.O. 1, 3)

Exercise 6–3
Determine end of discount period and prepare an entry to record payment (L.O. 1, 3)

What is the last payment date on which the cash discount can be taken on goods sold on March 5 for $51,200; terms 3/10/EOM, n/60? Assume that the bill is paid on this date and prepare the correct entries on both the buyer's and seller's books to record the payment.

Exercise 6–4
Calculate effect of trade and cash discounts on payment (L.O. 1, 3)

You have purchased merchandise with a list price of $36,000. Because you are a wholesaler, you are granted trade discounts of 30%, 20%, and 10%. The cash discount terms are 2/EOM, n/60. How much will you remit if you pay the invoice by the end of the month of purchase? How much will you remit if you do not pay the invoice until the following month?

Exercise 6–5
Calculate gross selling price and final payment (L.O. 1, 3)

Lasky Company sold merchandise with a list price of $60,000 on July 1, 1999. For each of the following independent assumptions, calculate (1) the gross selling price used to record the sale and (2) the amount that the buyer would have to remit when paying the invoice.

	Trade Discount Granted	Credit Terms	Date Paid
a.	30%, 20%	2/10, n/30	July 10
b.	40%, 10%	2/EOM, n/60	August 10
c.	30%, 10%, 5%	3/10/EOM, n/60	August 10
d.	40%	1/10, n/30	July 12

Exercise 6–6
Determine cash discount available and amount of cash paid (L.O. 1, 3, 4)

Raiser Company purchased goods at a gross selling price of $2,400 on August 1, 1999. Discount terms of 2/10, n/30 were available. For each of the following independent situations, determine (1) the cash discount available on the final payment and (2) the amount paid if payment is made within the discount period.

	Transportation Terms	Freight Paid (by)	Purchase Allowance Granted
a.	FOB shipping point	$240 (buyer)	$480
b.	FOB destination	120 (seller)	240
c.	FOB shipping point	180 (seller)	720
d.	FOB destination	192 (buyer)	120

Exercise 6–7
Prepare entries for purchase, transportation-in, purchase discounts, and payment (LO. 3, 4)

Stuart Company purchased goods for $84,000 on June 14, 1999, under the following terms: 3/10, n/30; FOB shipping point, freight collect. The bill for the freight was paid on June 15, $1,200.

a. Assume that the invoice was paid on June 24, and prepare all entries required on Stuart Company's books.

b. Assume that the invoice was paid on July 11. Prepare the entry to record the payment made on that date.

Exercise 6–8
Determine cost of goods sold (LO. 2, 3, 5)

Cramer Company uses periodic inventory procedure. Determine the cost of goods sold for the company assuming purchases during the period were $40,000, transportation-in was $300, purchase returns and allowances were $1,000, beginning inventory was $25,000, purchase discounts were $2,000, and ending inventory was $13,000.

Exercise 6–9
Supply missing amounts in the income statement (LO. 1–4, 6)

In each case, use the following information to calculate the missing information:

	Case 1	Case 2	Case 3
Gross sales	$640,000	$?	$?
Sales discounts	?	25,600	19,200
Sales returns and allowances	19,200	44,800	32,000
Net sales	608,000	1,209,600	?
Merchandise inventory, January 1	256,000	?	384,000
Purchases	384,000	768,000	?
Purchase discounts	7,680	13,440	12,800
Purchase returns and allowances	24,320	31,360	32,000
Net purchases	352,000	?	672,000
Transportation-in	25,600	38,400	32,000
Net cost of purchases	377,600	761,600	?
Cost of goods available for sale	?	1,081,600	1,088,000
Merchandise inventory, December 31	?	384,000	448,000
Cost of goods sold	320,000	?	640,000
Gross margin	?	512,000	320,000

In each of the following equations supply the missing term(s):

a. Net sales = Gross sales − (_____ _____ + Sales returns and allowances).

b. Cost of goods sold = Beginning inventory + Net cost of purchases − _____ _____.

c. Gross margin = _____ _____ − Cost of goods sold.

d. Income from operations = _____ _____ − Operating expenses.

e. Net income = Income from operations + _____ _____ − _____ _____.

Exercise 6–10
Supply missing terms in formulas showing income statement relationships (L.O. 6)

Given the balances in this partial trial balance, indicate how the balances would be treated in the work sheet. The ending inventory is $96. (The amounts are unusually small for ease in rewriting the numbers. We purposely left out the Statement of Retained Earnings columns since they are not used.)

Exercise 6–11
Prepare a partial work sheet using merchandise-related accounts (based on Appendix) (L.O. 8)

Account Titles	Trial Balance Debit	Trial Balance Credit	Adjustments Debit	Adjustments Credit	Adjusted Trial Balance Debit	Adjusted Trial Balance Credit	Income Statement Debit	Income Statement Credit	Balance Sheet Debit	Balance Sheet Credit
Merchandise Inventory	120									
Sales		840								
Sales Discounts	18									
Sales Returns and Allowances	48									
Purchases	600									
Purchase Discounts		12								
Purchase Returns and Allowances		24								
Transportation-In	36									

Using the data in Exercise 6–11 prepare closing entries for the preceding accounts. Do not close the Income Summary account.

Exercise 6–12
Prepare and post closing entries using T-accounts (based on Appendix) (L.O. 8)

PROBLEMS

a. Candle Carpet Company engaged in the following transactions in August 1999:

Problem 6–1
Journalize merchandise transactions for two different companies (L.O. 1, 3, 4)

Aug. 2 Sold merchandise on account for $300,000; terms 2/10, n/30, FOB shipping point, freight collect.
   18 Received payment for the sale of August 2.
   20 A total of $10,000 of the merchandise sold on August 2 was returned, and a full refund was made because it was the wrong merchandise.
   28 An allowance of $16,000 was granted on the sale of August 2 because some merchandise was found to be damaged; $16,000 cash was returned to the customer.

b. Lee Furniture Company engaged in the following transactions in August 1999:

Aug. 4 Purchased merchandise on account at a cost of $140,000; terms 2/10, n/30, FOB shipping point, freight collect.
    6 Paid freight of $2,000 on the purchase of August 4.
   10 Sold goods for $100,000; terms 2/10, n/30.
   12 Returned $24,000 of the merchandise purchased on August 4.
   14 Paid the amount due on the purchase of August 4.

Prepare journal entries for the transactions.

Required

Problem 6–2
Journalize merchandise
transactions on both
buyer's and seller's books
(L.O. 1, 3, 4)

Edwardo Auto Parts Company and Spoon Company engaged in the following transactions
with each other during August 1999:

Aug. 15   Edwardo Auto Parts Company purchased merchandise on account with a list
price of $192,000 from Spoon Company. Trade discounts of 20% and 10%
were allowed. Terms were 2/10, n/30, FOB destination, freight prepaid.

16   The seller paid the freight charges, $2,400.

17   The buyer requested an allowance of $4,512 against the amount due because
the goods were damaged in transit.

20   The seller granted the allowance requested on August 17.

The buyer paid the amount due on the last day of the discount period.

Required   Record all of the entries required on the books of both the buyer and the seller.

Problem 6–3
Prepare and post journal
entries, and prepare trial
balance and classified
income statement
(L.O. 1–6)

Gardner Company engaged in the following transactions in June 1999, the company's first
month of operations:

June 1   Stockholders invested $384,000 cash and $144,000 of merchandise inventory
in the business in exchange for capital stock.

3   Merchandise was purchased on account, $192,000; terms 2/10, n/30,
FOB shipping point, freight collect.

4   Paid freight on the June 3 purchase, $5,280.

7   Merchandise was purchased on account, $96,000; terms 2/10, n/30,
FOB destination, freight prepaid.

10   Sold merchandise on account, $230,400; terms 2/10, n/30, FOB shipping
point, freight collect.

11   Returned $28,800 of the merchandise purchased on June 3.

12   Paid the amount due on the purchase of June 3.

13   Sold merchandise on account, $240,000; terms 2/10, n/30, FOB destination,
freight prepaid.

14   Paid freight on sale of June 13, $14,400.

20   Paid the amount due on the purchase of June 7.

21   $48,000 of the goods sold on June 13 were returned for credit.

22   Received the amount due on sale of June 13.

25   Received the amount due on sale of June 10.

29   Paid rent for the administration building for June, $19,200.

30   Paid sales salaries of $57,600 for June.

30   Purchased merchandise on account, $48,000; terms 2/10, n/30,
FOB destination, freight prepaid.

Additional data   The inventory on hand on June 30 was $288,000.

Required   **a.**   Prepare journal entries for the transactions.

b.   Post the journal entries to the proper ledger accounts. Use the account numbers in the
chart of accounts on the inside covers of the text. Assume that all postings are from
page 10 of the general journal.

c.   Prepare a trial balance as of June 30, 1999.

d.   Prepare a classified income statement for the month ended June 30, 1999. No adjusting
entries are needed.

Problem 6–4
Prepare and post journal
entries; prepare trial
balance and classified
income statement
(L.O. 1–6)

Organized on May 1, 1999, Noah Cabinet Company engaged in the following transactions:

May 1   The stockholders invested $900,000 in this new business by purchasing capital
stock.

1   Purchased merchandise on account from String Company, $46,800; terms
n/60, FOB shipping point, freight collect.

3   Sold merchandise for cash, $28,800.

6   Paid transportation charges on May 1 purchase, $1,440 cash.

7   Returned $3,600 of merchandise to String Company due to improper size.

10   Requested and received an allowance of $1,800 from String Company for
improper quality of certain items.

14   Sold merchandise on account to Texas Company, $18,000; terms 2/20, n/30,
FOB shipping point, freight collect.

May 16   Issued cash refund for return of merchandise relating to sale made on May 3, $180.

18   Purchased merchandise on account from Tan Company invoiced at $28,800; terms 2/15, n/30, FOB shipping point, freight collect.

18   Received a bill for freight charges of $900 from Ball Trucking Company on the purchase from Tan Company.

19   Texas Company returned $360 of merchandise purchased on May 14.

24   Returned $2,880 of defective merchandise to Tan Company. Received full credit.

28   Texas Company remitted balance due on sale of May 14.

31   Paid Tan Company for the purchase of May 18 after adjusting for transaction of May 24.

31   Paid miscellaneous selling expenses of $7,200.

31   Paid miscellaneous administrative expenses of $10,800.

The May 31st inventory is $57,600.

From the data for Noah Cabinet Company:

a.   Journalize the transactions. Round all amounts to the nearest dollar.

b.   Post the entries to the proper ledger accounts. Use the account numbers appearing in the chart of accounts on the inside covers of the text. Assume all postings are from page 5 of the general journal. (There were no adjusting journal entries.)

c.   Prepare a trial balance.

d.   Prepare a classified income statement for the month ended May 31, 1999.

Additional data

Required

The following data are for Bayer Lamp Company:

Problem 6–5
Prepare a work sheet, classified income statement, statement of retained earnings, classified balance sheet, and closing entries (based on Appendix)
(L.O. 5–8)

BAYER LAMP COMPANY
Trial Balance
December 31, 1999

Acct. No.	Account Title	Debits	Credits
100	Cash	$ 228,800	
103	Accounts Receivable	193,200	
105	Merchandise Inventory, January 1, 1999	166,400	
108	Prepaid Insurance	11,600	
130	Land	240,000	
140	Buildings	440,000	
141	Accumulated Depreciation—Buildings		$ 132,000
174	Store Fixtures	222,400	
175	Accumulated Depreciation—Store Fixtures		44,480
200	Accounts Payable		151,600
300	Capital Stock		400,000
310	Retained Earnings, 1/1/99		480,720
410	Sales		2,206,000
411	Sales Discounts	14,800	
412	Sales Returns and Allowances	8,000	
418	Interest Revenue		1,600
500	Purchases	1,251,600	
501	Purchase Discounts		10,400
502	Purchase Returns and Allowances		5,600
503	Transportation-In	29,200	
505	Advertising Expense	48,000	
508	Sales Salaries Expense	256,000	
509	Office Salaries Expense	296,000	
519	Delivery Expense	18,400	
540	Interest Expense	8,000	
		$3,432,400	$3,432,400

1.   Depreciation expense on the store building is $8,800.

2.   Depreciation expense on the store fixtures is $22,240.

3.   Accrued sales salaries are $5,600.

4.   Insurance expired in 1999 is $10,000.

5.   Cost of merchandise inventory on hand December 31, 1999, is $222,000.

Additional data

Required   Prepare the following:

a.   A work sheet for the year ended December 31, 1999. Refer to the chart of accounts on the inside covers of the text for any other account numbers you need.

b.   A classified income statement. The only administrative expenses are office salaries and insurance. The building depreciation is on the store building.

c.   A statement of retained earnings.

d.   A classified balance sheet.

e.   The required closing entries.

ALTERNATE PROBLEMS

Problem 6–1A
Journalize merchandise transactions for two different companies (L.O. 1, 3, 4)

a.   Spencer Sporting Goods Company engaged in the following transactions in April 1999:

Apr. 1   Sold merchandise on account for $288,000; terms 2/10, n/30, FOB shipping point, freight collect.
     5   $43,200 of the goods sold on account on April 1 were returned for a full credit. Payment for these goods had not yet been received.
     8   A sales allowance of $5,760 was granted on the merchandise sold on April 1 because the merchandise was damaged in shipment.
    10   Payment was received for the net amount due from the sale of April 1.

b.   High Stereo Company engaged in the following transactions in July 1999:

July 2   Purchased stereo merchandise on account at a cost of $43,200; terms 2/10, n/30, FOB destination, freight prepaid.
     15   Sold merchandise for $64,800, terms 2/10, n/30, FOB destination, freight prepaid.
     16   Paid freight costs on the merchandise sold, $2,160.
     20   High Stereo Company was granted an allowance of $2,880 on the purchase of July 2 because of damaged merchandise.
     31   Paid the amount due on the purchase of July 2.

Required   Prepare journal entries to record the transactions.

Problem 6–2A
Journalize merchandise transactions on both buyer's and seller's books (L.O. 1, 3, 4)

Mars Musical Instrument Company and Tiger Company engaged in the following transactions with each other during July 1999:

July 2   Mars Musical Instrument Company purchased merchandise on account with a list price of $48,000 from Tiger Company. The terms were 3/EOM, n/60, FOB shipping point, freight collect. Trade discounts of 15%, 10%, and 5% were granted by Tiger Company.
     5   The buyer paid the freight bill on the purchase of July 2, $1,104.
     6   The buyer returned damaged merchandise with an invoice price of $2,790 to the seller and received full credit.

On the last day of the discount period, the buyer paid the seller for the merchandise.

Required   Prepare all the necessary journal entries for the buyer and the seller.

Problem 6–3A
Prepare and post journal entries, and prepare a trial balance and classified income statement (L.O. 1–6)

The following data for June 1999 are for Rusk Company's first month of operations:

June 1   Rusk Company was organized, and the stockholders invested $1,008,000 cash, $336,000 of merchandise inventory, and a $288,000 plot of land in exchange for capital stock.
     4   Merchandise was purchased for cash, $432,000; FOB shipping point, freight collect.
     9   Cash of $10,080 was paid to a trucking company for delivery of the merchandise purchased June 4.
    13   The company sold merchandise on account, $288,000; terms 2/10, n/30.
    15   The company sold merchandise on account, $230,400; terms 2/10, n/30.
    16   Of the merchandise sold June 13, $31,680 was returned for credit.
    20   Salaries for services received were paid as follows: to office employees, $31,680; to salespersons, $83,520.
    22   The company collected the amount due on the remaining $256,320 of accounts receivable arising from the sale of June 13.

June 24 The company purchased merchandise on account at a cost of $345,600; terms 2/10, n/30, FOB shipping point, freight collect.

26 The company returned $57,600 of the merchandise purchased June 24 to the vendor for credit.

27 A trucking company was paid $7,200 for delivery to Rusk Company of the goods purchased June 24.

29 The company sold merchandise on account, $384,000; terms 2/10, n/30.

30 Sold merchandise for cash, $172,800.

30 Payment was received for the sale of June 15.

30 Paid store rent for June, $43,200.

30 Paid the amount due on the purchase of June 24.

The inventory on hand at the close of business June 30 was $672,000 at cost.

Additional data

Required

a. Prepare journal entries for the transactions.

b. Post the journal entries to the proper ledger accounts. Use the account numbers in the chart of accounts on the inside covers of the text. Assume that all postings are from page 20 of the general journal.

c. Prepare a trial balance as of June 30, 1999.

d. Prepare a classified income statement for the month ended June 30, 1999. No adjusting entries are needed.

The Western Wear Company, a wholesaler of western wear clothing, sells to retailers. The company entered into the following transactions in May 1999:

Problem 6–4A
Prepare and post journal entries, prepare trial balance, classified income statement, and classified balance sheet (L.O. 1–6)

May 1 The Western Wear Company was organized as a corporation. The stockholders purchased stock at par for the following assets in the business: $462,000 cash, $168,000 merchandise, and $105,000 land.

1 Paid rent on administrative offices for May, $25,200.

5 The company purchased merchandise from Carl Company on account, $189,000; terms 2/10, n/30. Freight terms were FOB shipping point, freight collect.

8 Cash of $8,400 was paid to a trucking company for delivery of the merchandise purchased May 5.

14 The company sold merchandise on account, $315,000; terms 2/10, n/30.

15 Paid Carl Company the amount due on the purchase of May 5.

16 Of the merchandise sold May 14, $13,860 was returned for credit.

19 Salaries for services received were paid for May as follows: office employees, $16,800; salespersons, $33,600.

24 The company collected the amount due on $126,000 of the accounts receivable arising from the sale of May 14.

25 The company purchased merchandise on account from Bond Company, $151,200; terms 2/10, n/30. Freight terms were FOB shipping point, freight collect.

27 Of the merchandise purchased May 25, $25,200 was returned to the vendor.

28 A trucking company was paid $2,100 for delivery to The Western Wear Company of the goods purchased May 25.

29 The company sold merchandise on open account, $15,120; terms 2/10, n/30.

30 Cash sales were $74,088.

30 Cash of $100,800 was received from the sale of May 14.

31 Paid Bond Company for the merchandise purchased on May 25, taking into consideration the merchandise returned on May 27.

The inventory on hand at the close of business on May 31 is $299,040.

From the data given for The Western Wear Company:

Additional data

Required

a. Prepare journal entries for the transactions.

b. Post the journal entries to the proper ledger accounts. Use the account numbers in the chart of accounts on the inside covers of the text. Assume that all postings are from page 15 of the general journal. (There were no adjusting journal entries.)

c. Prepare a trial balance.

d. Prepare a classified income statement for the month ended May 31, 1999.

e. Prepare a classified balance sheet as of May 31, 1999.

Problem 6–5A
Prepare work sheet,
classified income state-
ment, statement of retained
earnings, classified balance
sheet, and closing entries
(based on Appendix)
(L.O. 5–8)

The following data are for Leone Lumber Company:

LEONE LUMBER COMPANY
Trial Balance
December 31, 1999

Acct. No.	Account Title	Debits	Credits
100	Cash	$ 70,640	
103	Accounts Receivable	159,520	
105	Merchandise Inventory	285,200	
107	Supplies on Hand	5,360	
108	Prepaid Insurance	4,800	
112	Prepaid Rent	57,600	
170	Equipment	88,000	
171	Accumulated Depreciation—Equipment		$ 17,600
200	Accounts Payable		102,800
300	Capital Stock		200,000
310	Retained Earnings, 1/1/99		219,640
410	Sales		1,122,360
412	Sales Returns and Allowances	5,160	
418	Interest Revenue		1,000
500	Purchases	500,840	
502	Purchase Returns and Allowances		4,040
503	Transportation-In	7,840	
505	Advertising Expense	78,000	
508	Sales Salaries Expense	138,400	
509	Office Salaries Expense	80,800	
510	Officers' Salaries Expense	160,000	
511	Utilities Expense	4,800	
536	Legal and Accounting Expense	10,000	
540	Interest Expense	600	
567	Miscellaneous Administrative Expense	9,880	
		$1,667,440	$1,667,440

Additional data

1. A total of $3,400 of the prepaid insurance has expired.
2. An inventory of supplies showed that $1,700 are still on hand.
3. Prepaid rent expired during the year is $50,600.
4. Depreciation expense on store equipment is $8,800.
5. Accrued sales salaries are $4,000.
6. Accrued office salaries are $3,000.
7. Merchandise inventory on hand is $350,000.

Required   Prepare the following:

a. A work sheet for the year ended December 31, 1999. Refer to the chart of accounts on the inside covers of the text for any other account numbers you need.
b. A classified income statement. The only selling expenses are sales salaries, advertising, supplies, and depreciation expense—equipment.
c. A statement of retained earnings.
d. A classified balance sheet.
e. The December 31, 1999, closing entries.

BEYOND THE NUMBERS—CRITICAL THINKING

**Business Decision
Case 6–1**
Prepare income statements
and evaluate feasibility
(L.O. 5, 6)

Candy's Shirts, Inc., has an opportunity to purchase 40,000 shirts with the logo of the 2000 Olympics in January 1998. Candy, who is not currently in business, is considering buying these shirts and then renting a display cart from which to sell these shirts (called a kiosk) in an Australian shopping mall. Based on the following information and estimates, Candy needs to decide if the business would be profitable:

1. Cost of the 40,000 shirts, all of which must be purchased in January 1998, is $440,000.
2. Candy thinks it would take two years to sell all of the shirts. She estimates her sales at 25,000 shirts in 1998 and 15,000 shirts in 1999.

3. Rent of the kiosk would be $1,500 per month in 1998 and $1,600 per month in 1999.

4. Candy can buy some counters on which to display the merchandise for $4,000. She could sell the counters for $500 at the end of the second year.

5. Candy estimates the cost to decorate her kiosk would be $2,500.

6. Candy would hire employees and pay them $1 per shirt sold.

7. Candy plans to sell the shirts for $17 each.

8. Candy and her husband purchased $100,000 of capital stock in the business. Therefore, she plans to borrow $400,000 from their family banker. Interest expense on this loan will be $52,000 in 1998 and $6,500 in 1999. Candy plans to repay $300,000 on January 2, 1999, and the remaining $100,000 on July 1, 1999.

9. Candy needs to rent some storage space because all 40,000 shirts cannot be stored at the kiosk. Storage space costs $2,500 per year.

a. Prepare estimated income statements for 1998 and 1999 for Candy's business. Does it appear that the business will be profitable?

b. Will Candy have the cash available to pay the bank loan as she planned?

Required

Perkin-Elmer is one of the leaders in the life science systems and analytical instrument markets. Using the following information from Perkin-Elmer's 1996 annual report, calculate the gross margin percentage and write an explanation of what the results mean.

Business Decision Case 6–2
Analyze the importance of the gross margin percentage (L.O. 7)

($ thousands)	1996	1995	1994
Net revenues	$1,162,949	$1,063,506	$1,024,467
Cost of sales	595,857	560,402	535,178
Gross margin	$ 567,092	$ 503,104	$ 489,289

Refer to the consolidated statements of income of The Coca-Cola Company in the annual reports booklet. Identify the 1996 net operating revenues; cost of goods sold; gross profit; selling, administrative, and general expenses; and operating income. Do the results of 1996 compare favorably with those of 1995? Also calculate the gross profit (margin) percentages and comment.

Annual Report Analysis 6–3
Classify income statement items and calculate gross margin percentages (L.O. 6, 7)

Based on the ethics case related to World Auto Parts Corporation on page 228, respond in writing to the following questions:

a. Do you agree that the total impact of this practice could be as much as $10 million?

b. Are the small suppliers probably better off going along with the practice?

c. Is this practice ethical?

Ethics Case—Writing Experience 6–4
Respond to questions regarding ethics case

In teams of two or three students, go to the library to locate one merchandising company's annual report for the most recent year. Calculate the company's gross margin percentage for each of the most recent three years. As a team, write a memorandum to the instructor showing your calculations and commenting on the results. The heading of the memorandum should contain the date, to whom it is written, from whom, and the subject matter.

Group Project 6–5
Undertake library project concerning annual reports—gross margin percentages (L.O. 7)

In a team of two or three students, contact a variety of businesses in your area and inquire as to the types of sales discount terms they offer to credit customers and the types of purchase discount terms they are offered by their suppliers. Calculate the approximate annual rate of interest implied in several of the more common discount terms. For instance, the book states that the implied annual rate of interest on terms of 2/10, n/60 is 36%, assuming we use a 360-day year. Present your findings in a written report to your instructor.

Group Project 6–6
Investigate sales and purchase discounts offered

Group Project 6–7
Study income statements in annual reports

In a team of two or three students, obtain access to several annual reports of companies in different industries. Examine their income statements and identify differences in their formats. Discuss these differences within your group and then present your findings in a report to your instructor.

USING THE INTERNET—A VIEW OF THE REAL WORLD

Internet Project 6–8
Investigate the Coca-Cola website

Visit the Coca-Cola Company website at:
http://www.cocacola.com
Browse around the site for interesting information. How does the information at this website differ from the information you can find in the annual reports booklet that came with this text? What did you like about the site and what improvements could be made? Was any information found both in the annual report and at the website? Write a report to your instructor summarizing your experience at this site.

Internet Project 6–9
Catch up on some late developing accounting news

Visit the Accounting Professionals Resource Center site at:
http://www.kentis.com
Check out some of the news items at this site. Also look at anything else that looks interesting. Write a brief summary of some of the news items and summarize what else is available at this site. Turn in your report to your instructor and be prepared to make a brief report to the class.

ANSWERS TO SELF-TEST

TRUE-FALSE

1. **False.** Sales discounts, as well as sales returns and allowances, are deducted from gross sales.

2. **True.** Under perpetual inventory procedure, the Merchandise Inventory account is debited for each purchase and credited for each sale.

3. **True.** Purchase Discounts and Purchase Returns and Allowances are contra accounts to the Purchases account. The balances of those accounts are deducted from purchases to arrive at net purchases.

4. **False.** Consigned goods delivered to another party for attempted sale are included in the ending inventory of the company that sent the goods.

5. **False.** An unclassified income statement, not a classified income statement, has only two categories of items.

MULTIPLE-CHOICE

1. **d.** Trade discounts are not recorded on the books of either a buyer or a seller. In other words, the invoice price of sales (purchases) is recorded:

$$\$4,000 \times 0.8 = \$3,200$$

2. **b.** The cost of goods sold is computed as follows:

Beginning inventory	$ 60,000
Net cost of purchases	240,000
Cost of goods available for sale	$300,000
Ending inventory	72,000
Cost of goods sold	$228,000

3. **b.** Purchase discounts are based on invoice prices less purchase returns and allowances, if any.

$$\frac{\text{Purchase}}{\text{discount}} = (\$12,000 - \$2,000) \times 0.02 = \$200$$

4. **e.** All of the sections mentioned in **(a–d)** appear in a classified income statement. Current assets appear on a classified balance sheet.

5. **b.** Merchandise Inventory is debited for the cost of ending inventory.

7

MEASURING AND REPORTING INVENTORIES

Have you ever taken advantage of a pre-inventory sale at your favorite retail store? Many stores offer bargain prices to reduce the merchandise on hand and to minimize the time and expense of taking the inventory. A smaller inventory also enhances the probability of taking an accurate inventory since the store has less merchandise to count. From Chapter 6 you know that companies use inventory amounts to determine the cost of goods sold; this major expense affects a merchandising company's net income. In this chapter, you learn how important inventories are in preparing an accurate income statement, statement of retained earnings, and balance sheet.

This chapter discusses merchandise inventory carried by merchandising retailers and wholesalers. A later chapter discusses other types of inventory carried by manufacturers. **Merchandise inventory** is the quantity of goods held by a merchandising company for resale to customers. Merchandising companies determine the quantity of inventory items by a physical count.

The merchandise inventory figure used by accountants depends on the quantity of inventory items and the cost of the items. This chapter discusses four accepted methods of costing the items: (1) specific identification; (2) first-in, first-out (FIFO); (3) last-in, first-out (LIFO); and (4) weighted-average. Each method has advantages and disadvantages.

This chapter stresses the importance of having accurate inventory figures and the serious consequences of using inaccurate inventory figures. This explains why your favorite retail store closes early to take inventory or why its employees work late to take inventory. When you finish this chapter, you should understand how taking inventory connects with the cost of goods sold figure on the store's income statement, the retained earnings amount on the statement of retained earnings, and both the inventory figure and the retained earnings amount on the store's balance sheet.

LEARNING OBJECTIVES

After studying this chapter, you should be able to:

1. Explain and calculate the effects of inventory errors on certain financial statement items.

2. Indicate which costs are properly included in inventory.

3. Calculate cost of ending inventory and cost of goods sold under the four major inventory costing methods using periodic and perpetual inventory procedures.

4. Explain the advantages and disadvantages of the four major inventory costing methods.

(*continued*)

Objective 1
Explain and calculate the effects of inventory errors on certain financial statement items.

Real World Example
Winn-Dixie Stores, Inc., a large grocery store chain, sells the equivalent of its entire inventory every three days.

Reinforcing Problems
E7–1 Determine effects of inventory errors.
P7–1A Compute corrected net income given inventory errors.
P7–2A Compute corrected net income given inventory errors; indicate balance sheet errors and comment.

INVENTORIES AND COST OF GOODS SOLD

Inventory is often the largest and most important asset owned by a merchandising business. The inventory of some companies, like car dealerships or jewelry stores, may cost several times more than any other asset the company owns. As an asset, the inventory figure has a direct impact on reporting the solvency of the company in the balance sheet. As a factor in determining cost of goods sold, the inventory figure has a direct impact on the profitability of the company's operations as reported in the income statement. Thus, the importance of the inventory figure should not be underestimated.

Importance of Proper Inventory Valuation

A merchandising company can prepare accurate income statements, statements of retained earnings, and balance sheets only if its inventory is correctly valued. On the income statement, a company using periodic inventory procedure takes a physical inventory to determine the cost of goods sold. Since the cost of goods sold figure affects the company's net income, it also affects the balance of retained earnings on the statement of retained earnings. On the balance sheet, incorrect inventory amounts affect both the reported ending inventory and retained earnings. Inventories appear on the balance sheet under the heading "Current Assets," which reports current assets in a descending order of liquidity. Because inventories are consumed or converted into cash within a year or one operating cycle, whichever is longer, inventories usually follow cash and receivables on the balance sheet.

Recall that under periodic inventory procedure we determine the cost of goods sold figure by adding the beginning inventory to the net cost of purchases and deducting the ending inventory. In each accounting period, the appropriate expenses must be matched with the revenues of that period to determine the net income. Applied to inventory, matching involves determining (1) how much of the cost of goods available for sale during the period should be deducted from current revenues and (2) how much should be allocated to goods on hand and thus carried forward as an asset (merchandise inventory) in the balance sheet to be matched against future revenues. Because we determine the cost of goods sold by deducting the ending inventory from the cost of goods available for sale, a highly significant relationship exists: *Net income for an accounting period depends directly on the valuation of ending inventory.* This relationship involves three items:

First, a merchandising company must be sure that it has properly valued its ending inventory. If the ending inventory is overstated, cost of goods sold is understated, resulting in an overstatement of gross margin and net income. Also, overstatement of ending inventory causes current assets, total assets, and retained earnings to be overstated. Thus, any change in the calculation of ending inventory is reflected, dollar for dollar (ignoring any income tax effects), in net income, current assets, total assets, and retained earnings.

Second, when a company misstates its ending inventory in the current year, the company carries forward that misstatement into the next year. This misstatement occurs because the ending inventory amount of the current year is the beginning inventory amount for the next year.

Third, an error in one period's ending inventory automatically causes an error in net income in the opposite direction in the next period. After two years, however, the error washes out, and assets and retained earnings are properly stated.

Illustrations 7.1 and 7.2 prove that net income for an accounting period depends directly on the valuation of the inventory. Allen Company's income statements and the statements of retained earnings for years 1998 and 1999 show this relationship.

In Illustration 7.1, the correctly stated ending inventory for the year 1998 is $35,000. As a result, Allen has a gross margin of $135,000 and net income of $50,000. The statement of retained earnings shows a beginning retained earnings of $120,000

ALLEN COMPANY

For Year Ended December 31, 1998

Income Statement	Ending Inventory Correctly Stated		Ending Inventory Overstated by $5,000	
Sales		$400,000		$400,000
Cost of goods available for sale	$300,000		$300,000	
Ending inventory	35,000		40,000	
Cost of goods sold		265,000		260,000
Gross margin		$135,000		$140,000
Other expenses		85,000		85,000
Net income		$ 50,000		$ 55,000
Statement of Retained Earnings				
Beginning retained earnings		$120,000		$120,000
Net income		50,000		55,000
Ending retained earnings		$170,000		$175,000

ILLUSTRATION 7.1
Effects of an Overstated
Ending Inventory

Note to the Student
The concept of cost of goods sold versus ending inventory is sometimes difficult to understand. Refer to the text illustration showing that Goods Available for Sale is divided between cost of goods sold and ending inventory. This means that everything available for sale is either sold or not sold. If it is sold, it is a part of cost of goods sold. If it is not sold, it is part of ending inventory.

ALLEN COMPANY

For Year Ended December 31, 1999

Income Statement	Beginning Inventory Correctly Stated		Beginning Inventory Overstated by $5,000	
Sales		$425,000		$425,000
Beginning inventory	$ 35,000		$ 40,000	
Purchases	290,000		290,000	
Cost of goods available for sale	$325,000		$330,000	
Ending inventory	45,000		45,000	
Cost of goods sold		280,000		285,000
Gross margin		$145,000		$140,000
Other expenses		53,500		53,500
Net income		$ 91,500		$ 86,500
Statement of Retained Earnings				
Beginning retained earnings		$170,000		$175,000
Net income		91,500		86,500
Ending retained earnings		$261,500		$261,500

ILLUSTRATION 7.2
Effects of an
Overstated Beginning
Inventory

and an ending retained earnings of $170,000. When the ending inventory is overstated by $5,000, as shown on the right in Illustration 7.1, the gross margin is $140,000, and net income is $55,000. The statement of retained earnings then has an ending retained earnings of $175,000. The ending inventory overstatement of $5,000 causes a $5,000 overstatement of net income and a $5,000 overstatement of retained earnings. The balance sheet would show both an overstated inventory and an overstated retained earnings. Due to the error in ending inventory, both the stockholders and creditors may overestimate the profitability of the business.

Illustration 7.2 is a continuation of Illustration 7.1 and contains Allen's operating results for the year ended December 31, 1999. Note that the ending inventory in Illustration 7.1 now becomes the beginning inventory of Illustration 7.2. However, Allen's inventory at December 31, 1999, is now an accurate inventory of $45,000. As a result, the gross margin in the income statement with the beginning inventory correctly stated is $145,000, and Allen Company has net income of $91,500 and an ending retained earnings of $261,500. In the income statement columns at the right, in which the beginning inventory is overstated by $5,000, the gross margin is $140,000 and net income is $86,500, with the ending retained earnings also at $261,500.

Thus, in contrast to an overstated ending inventory, resulting in an overstatement of net income, an overstated beginning inventory results in an understatement of net income. If the beginning inventory is overstated, then cost of goods available for sale and cost of goods sold also are overstated. Consequently, gross margin and net income are understated. Note, however, that when net income in the second year is closed to retained earnings, the retained earnings account is stated at its proper amount. The overstatement of net income in the first year is offset by the understatement of net income in the second year. For the two years combined the net income is correct. At the end of the second year, the balance sheet contains the correct amounts for both inventory and retained earnings. To summarize the effects of errors of inventory valuation:

	Ending Inventory		Beginning Inventory	
	Understated	Overstated	Understated	Overstated
Cost of goods sold	Overstated	Understated	Understated	Overstated
Net income	Understated	Overstated	Overstated	Understated

DETERMINING INVENTORY COST

To place the proper valuation on inventory, a business must answer the question: Which costs should be included in inventory cost? Then, when the business purchases identical goods at different costs, it must answer the question: Which cost should be assigned to the items sold? In this section, you learn how accountants answer these questions.

Objective 2
Indicate which costs are properly included in inventory.

The costs included in inventory depend on two variables: quantity and price. To arrive at a current inventory figure, companies must begin with an accurate physical count of inventory items. They multiply the quantity of inventory by the unit cost to compute the cost of ending inventory. This section discusses the taking of a physical inventory and the methods of costing the physical inventory under both perpetual and periodic inventory procedures. The remainder of the chapter discusses departures from the cost basis of inventory measurement.

Taking a Physical Inventory

As briefly described in Chapter 6, to take a physical inventory, a company must count, weigh, measure, or estimate the physical quantities of the goods on hand. For example, a clothing store may count its suits; a hardware store may weigh bolts, washers, and nails; a gasoline company may measure gasoline in storage tanks; and a lumberyard may estimate quantities of lumber, coal, or other bulky materials. Throughout the taking of a physical inventory, the goal should be accuracy.

Taking a physical inventory may disrupt the normal operations of a business. Thus, the count should be administered as quickly and as efficiently as possible. The actual taking of the inventory is not an accounting function; however, accountants often plan and coordinate the count. Proper forms are required to record accurate counts and determine totals. Identification names or symbols must be chosen, and those persons who count, weigh, or measure the inventory items must know these symbols.

Taking a physical inventory often involves using inventory tags, such as that in Illustration 7.3. These tags are consecutively numbered for control purposes. A tag usually consists of a stub and a detachable duplicate section. The duplicate section facilitates checking discrepancies. The format of the tags can vary. However, the tag usually provides space for (1) a detailed description and identification of inventory items by product, class, and model; (2) location of items; (3) quantity of items on hand; and (4) initials of the counters and checkers.

The descriptive information and count may be entered on one copy of the tag by one team of counters. Another team of counters may record its count on the duplicate

```
┌─────────────────────────────────────────────┐
│             Inventory Tag                    │
│             JMA Corp.                        │
│                                              │
│  Inventory Tag No.  _281_    Date _____    │
│  Description _____  │
│              _____  │
│  Location _____ │
│  Quantity Counted _____                 │
│  Counted by _____                       │
│  Checked by _____                       │
│ ─ ─ ─ ─ ─ ─ ─ ─ ─ ─ ─ ─ ─ ─ ─ ─ ─ ─ ─ ─ ─  │
│          Duplicate Inventory Tag             │
│  Inventory Tag No.  _281_    Date _____    │
│  Description _____  │
│              _____  │
│  Location _____ │
│  Quantity Counted _____                 │
│  Counted by _____                       │
│  Checked by _____                       │
└─────────────────────────────────────────────┘
```

ILLUSTRATION 7.3
Inventory Tag

copy of the tag. Discrepancies between counts of the same items by different teams are reconciled by supervisors, and the correct counts are assembled on intermediate inventory sheets. Only when the inventory counts are completed and checked does management send the final sheets to the accounting department for pricing and extensions (quantity × price). The tabulated result is the dollar amount of the physical inventory. Later in the chapter we explain the different methods accountants use to cost inventory.

Usually, inventory cost includes all the necessary outlays to obtain the goods, get the goods ready to sell, and have the goods in the desired location for sale to customers. Thus, inventory cost includes:

Costs Included in Inventory Cost

1. Seller's invoice price less any purchase discount.
2. Cost of the buyer's insurance to cover the goods while in transit.
3. Transportation charges when borne by the buyer.
4. Handling costs, such as the cost of pressing clothes wrinkled during shipment.

In theory, the cost of each unit of inventory should include its net invoice price plus its share of other costs incurred in shipment. The 1986 Tax Reform Act requires companies to assign these costs to inventory for tax purposes. For accounting purposes, these cost assignments are recommended but not required.

Practical difficulties arise in allocating some of these costs to inventory items. Assume, for example, that the freight bill on a shipment of clothes does not separate out the cost of shipping one shirt. Also, assume that the company wants to include the freight cost as part of the inventory cost of the shirt. Then, the freight cost would have to be *allocated* to each unit because it cannot be measured directly. In practice, allocations of freight, insurance, and handling costs to the individual units of inventory purchased are often not worth the additional cost. Consequently, in the past many companies have not assigned the costs of freight, insurance, and handling to inventory. Instead, they have expensed these costs as incurred. When companies omit these costs from both beginning and ending inventories, they minimize the effect of expensing these costs on net income. The required allocation for tax purposes has probably resulted in many companies using the same inventory amounts in their financial statements.

Even if a company derives a cost for each unit in inventory, the inventory valuation problem is not solved. Management must consider two other aspects of the problem:

1.   If goods were purchased at varying unit costs, how should the cost of goods available for sale be allocated between the units sold and those that remain in inventory? For example, assume Hi-Fi Buys, Inc., purchased two identical VCRs for resale. One cost $250 and the other, $200. If one recorder was sold during the period, should Hi-Fi Buys assign it a cost of $250, $200, or an average cost of $225?

2.   Does the fact that current replacement costs are less than the costs of some units in inventory have any bearing on the amount at which inventory should be carried? Using the same example, if Hi-Fi Buys can currently buy all VCRs for $200, is it reasonable to carry some units in inventory at $250 rather than $200?

We answer these questions in the next section.

Inventory Valuation under Changing Prices

Generally companies should account for inventories at historical cost; that is, the cost at which the items were purchased. However, this rule does not indicate how to assign costs to ending inventory and to cost of goods sold when the goods have been purchased at different unit costs. For example, suppose a retailer has three shirts on hand. One unit cost $20; another, $22; and a third, $24. If the retailer sells two shirts for $30 each, what is the cost of the two shirts sold?

Methods of Determining Inventory Cost

Accountants developed these four inventory costing methods to solve costing problems: (1) specific identification; (2) first-in, first-out (FIFO); (3) last-in, first-out (LIFO); and (4) weighted-average. Look at Illustration 7.4 to see how often a group of representative companies used these methods for the years 1992–1995. Obviously, some companies use one method for certain inventory items and another method for other inventory items.

Before explaining the inventory costing methods, we briefly introduce perpetual inventory procedure and compare periodic and perpetual inventory procedures.

Perpetual Inventory Procedure

In Chapter 6, the emphasis was on periodic inventory procedure. Under periodic inventory procedure, firms debit the Purchases account when goods are acquired; they use other accounts, such as Purchase Discounts, Purchase Returns and Allowances, and Transportation-In, for purchase-related transactions. Companies determine cost of goods sold only at the end of the period as the difference between cost of goods available for sale and ending inventory. They keep no records of the cost of items as they are sold, and have no information on possible inventory shortages. They assume any goods not in ending inventory have been sold.

The availability of inventory management software packages is causing more and more businesses to change from periodic to perpetual inventory procedure. Under perpetual inventory procedure, companies have no Purchases and purchase-related accounts. Instead, they make all entries involving merchandise purchased for sale to customers directly in the Merchandise Inventory account. Thus, they debit or credit Merchandise Inventory in place of debiting or crediting Purchases, Purchase Discounts, Purchase Returns and Allowances, and Transportation-In. At the time of each sale, firms make two entries: the first debits Accounts Receivable or Cash and credits Sales at the retail selling price. The second debits Cost of Goods Sold and credits Merchandise Inventory at cost. Therefore, at the end of the period the Merchandise Inventory account shows the cost of the inventory that should be on hand. Comparison of this amount with the cost obtained by taking and pricing a physical inventory may reveal inventory shortages. Thus, perpetual inventory procedure is an important element in providing internal control over goods in inventory.

Methods	**Number of Companies**			
	1995	**1994**	**1993**	**1992**
First-in, first-out (FIFO)	411	417	417	415
Last-in, first-out (LIFO)	347	351	350	358
Average cost	185	192	189	193
Other	40	42	42	45
Use of LIFO				
All inventories	14	17	17	23
50% or more of inventories	191	186	191	189
Less than 50% of inventories	88	98	92	91
Not determinable	54	50	50	55
Companies using LIFO	**347**	**351**	**350**	**358**

Source: Based on American Institute of Certified Public Accountants, *Accounting Trends & Techniques* (New York: AICPA, 1996), p. 166.

ILLUSTRATION 7.4
Frequency of Use of Inventory Methods

Item	TV-96874		Maximum	26	
Location			Minimum	6	

1996 Date	**Purchased**			**Sold**			**Balance**		
	Units	Unit Cost	Total Cost	Units	Unit Cost	Total Cost	Units	Unit Cost	Total
Beg. inv.							8	$300	$2,400
July 5	10	$300	$3,000				18	300	5,400
7				12	$300	$3,600	6	300	1,800
12	10	315	3,150				{ 6	300	1,800
							{ 10	315	3,150
22				{ 6	300	1,800			
				{ 2	315	630	8	315	2,520
24	8	320	2,560				{ 8	315	2,520
							{ 8	320	2,560

ILLUSTRATION 7.5
Perpetual Inventory Record (FIFO method)

PERPETUAL INVENTORY RECORDS Even though companies could apply perpetual inventory procedure manually, tracking units and dollars in and out of inventory is much easier using a computer. Both manual and computer processing maintain a record for each item in inventory. Look at Illustration 7.5, an inventory record for Entertainment World, a firm that sells many different brands of television sets. This inventory record shows the information on one particular brand and model of television set carried in inventory. Other information on the record includes (1) the maximum and minimum number of units the company wishes to stock at any time, (2) when and how many units were acquired and at what cost, and (3) when and how many units were sold and what cost was assigned to cost of goods sold. The number of units on hand and their cost are readily available also. Entertainment World assumes that the first units acquired are the first units sold. This assumption is the first-in, first-out (FIFO) method of inventory costing; we will discuss it later.

USES OF TECHNOLOGY Keeping track of inventories under a perpetual inventory system is much more cost-effective with computers. Under a manual system, the cost of an up-to-date inventory for stores with high turnover would outweigh the benefit. Most retail stores use scanning devices to read the inventory numbers of products purchased at the cash register. These scanning tags not only provide accurate sales prices but also record the merchandise sold so that the total cost of the store's inventory is always up to date.

AN ACCOUNTING PERSPECTIVE

Comparing Journal Entries under Periodic and Perpetual Inventory Procedures

The following comparison reveals several differences between accounting for inventories under periodic and perpetual procedures. We explain these differences by using data from Illustration 7.5 and making additional assumptions. Later, we discuss other journal entries under perpetual inventory procedure.

These entries record the purchase on July 5 under each of the methods:

Periodic Procedure			Perpetual Procedure		
Purchases	3,000		Merchandise Inventory . . .	3,000	
Accounts Payable . . .		3,000	Accounts Payable . . .		3,000

Assuming the merchandise sold on July 7 was priced at $4,800, these entries record the sale:

Periodic Procedure			Perpetual Procedure		
Accounts Receivable	4,800		Accounts Receivable	4,800	
Sales		4,800	Sales		4,800
			Cost of Goods Sold	3,600	
			Merchandise Inventory		3,600

Several other transactions not included in Illustration 7.5 could occur:

1. Assume that two of the units purchased on July 5 were returned to the supplier because they were defective. The entries would be:

Periodic Procedure			Perpetual Procedure		
Accounts Payable	600		Accounts Payable	600	
Purchase			Merchandise		
Returns and			Inventory		600
Allowances		600			

2. Assume that the supplier instead granted an allowance of $600 to the company because of the defective merchandise. The entries would be:

Periodic Procedure			Perpetual Procedure		
Accounts Payable	600		Accounts Payable	600	
Purchase			Merchandise		
Returns and			Inventory		600
Allowances		600			

Note to the Student
If Purchase Discounts and Purchase Returns and Allowances accounts are used, they appear as deductions from Purchases on the income statement. Since we have no Purchases account, we cannot deduct any amounts from it, so these accounts cannot exist.

3. Assume that the company incurred and paid freight charges of $100 on the purchase of July 5. The entries would be:

Periodic Procedure			Perpetual Procedure		
Transportation-In	100		Merchandise Inventory . .	100	
Cash		100	Cash		100

In these entries, notice that under perpetual inventory procedure the Merchandise Inventory account records purchases, purchase returns and allowances, purchase discounts, and transportation-in. Also, when goods are sold, the seller debits (increases) Cost of Goods Sold and credits or reduces Merchandise Inventory.

At the end of the accounting period, under perpetual inventory procedure, the only merchandise-related expense account to be closed is Cost of Goods Sold. The Purchases, Purchase Returns and Allowances, Purchase Discounts, and Transportation-In accounts do not even exist.

ILLUSTRATION 7.6 Beginning Inventory, Purchases, and Sales

Beginning Inventory and Purchases					Sales			
Date	**Units**	**Unit Cost**	**Total Cost**		**Date**	**Units**	**Price**	**Total**
Beginning inventory	10	$8.00	$ 80		March 10	10	$12.00	$120
March 2	10	8.50	85		July 14	20	12.00	240
May 28	20	8.40	168		September 7	10	14.00	140
August 12	10	9.00	90		November 22	20	14.00	280
October 12	20	8.80	176					
December 21	10	9.10	91					
	80		$690			60		$780

Ending inventory = 20 units, determined by taking a physical inventory.

BUSINESS INSIGHT   When you buy a box of breakfast cereal at the supermarket, the cashier scans the bar code on the box. The name of the item and the price appear on a video display that you can see. The information is also printed on the sales slip so that you can later compare the items paid for with the items received. But this is not the end of the story. The information is also fed to the store's computer to update the inventory records. The information is included with other information and is used to order more merchandise from the warehouse so the items can be replenished in the store. At a certain point, the company also uses the reduced inventory levels to order more merchandise from suppliers, such as wholesalers that supply the region with breakfast cereals and other goods. The paperwork for the purchase and payment are often handled electronically through a process called *electronic data inter-change (EDI)* and *electronic funds transfer (EFT)*.

AN ACCOUNTING PERSPECTIVE

Using the data for purchases, sales, and beginning inventory in Illustration 7.6, next we explain the four inventory costing methods. Except for the specific identification method, we first present all of the methods using periodic inventory procedure and then present all of the methods using perpetual inventory procedure. Total goods available for sale consist of 80 units with a total cost of $690. A physical inventory determined that 20 units are on hand at the end of the period. Sales revenue for the 60 units sold was $780. The questions to be answered are: What is the cost of the 20 units in inventory? What is the cost of the 60 units sold?

SPECIFIC IDENTIFICATION   The **specific identification method** of inventory costing attaches the actual cost to an identifiable unit of product. Firms find this method easy to apply when purchasing and selling large inventory items such as autos. Under the specific identification method, the firm must identify each unit in inventory, unless it is unique, with a serial number plate or identification tag.

To illustrate, assume that the company in Illustration 7.6 can identify the 20 units on hand at year-end as 10 units from the August 12 purchase and 10 units from the December 21 purchase. The company computes the ending inventory as shown in Illustration 7.7; it subtracts the $181 ending inventory cost from the $690 cost of goods available for sale to obtain the $509 cost of goods sold. Note that you can also determine the cost of goods sold for the year by recording the cost of each unit sold. The $509 cost of goods sold is an expense on the income statement, and the $181 ending inventory is a current asset on the balance sheet.

The specific identification costing method attaches cost to an identifiable unit of inventory. The method does not involve any assumptions about the flow of the costs

An Extended Illustration of Four Inventory Methods under Periodic and Perpetual Inventory Procedures

Objective 3
Calculate cost of ending inventory and cost of goods sold under the four major inventory costing methods using periodic and perpetual inventory procedures (applies to each method separately).

Reinforcing Problems
E7–2 Compute the impact on net income under specific identification.
P7–3 Maximize and minimize gross margin using specific identification.

ILLUSTRATION 7.7
Determining Ending
Inventory under
Specific Identification

	Units	Unit Cost	Total Cost
Ending inventory composed of purchases made on:			
August 12	10	$9.00	$ 90
December 21	10	9.10	91
Ending inventory	20		$181
Cost of goods sold composed of:			
Beginning inventory	10	8.00	$ 80
Purchases made on:			
March 2	10	8.50	85
May 28	20	8.40	168
October 12	20	8.80	176
			$509
Cost of goods available for sale			$690
Ending inventory			181
Cost of goods sold			$509

as in the other inventory costing methods. Conceptually, the method matches the cost to the physical flow of the inventory and eliminates the emphasis on the timing of the cost determination. Therefore, periodic and perpetual inventory procedures produce the same results for the specific identification method.

Periodic Inventory Procedure

Real World Example
The Raymond Corporation's financial statements included the following note relating to inventories: Inventories are stated principally at the lower of cost (FIFO—first-in, first-out method) or market.

Note to the Student
When determining the ending inventory using FIFO, you can also use the acronym, LISH, which stands for last in, still here.

FIFO (FIRST-IN, FIRST-OUT) UNDER PERIODIC INVENTORY PROCEDURE   Some companies use a method based on a cost flow assumption rather than specific identification. The **FIFO (first-in, first-out)** method of inventory costing assumes that the costs of the first goods purchased are those charged to cost of goods sold when the company actually sells goods. This method assumes the first goods purchased are the first goods sold. In some companies, the first units in (bought) must be the first units out (sold) to avoid large losses from spoilage. Such items as fresh dairy products, fruits, and vegetables should be sold on a FIFO basis. In these cases, an assumed first-in, first-out flow corresponds with the actual physical flow of goods.

Because a company using FIFO assumes the older units are sold first and the newer units are still on hand, the ending inventory consists of the most recent purchases. When using periodic inventory procedure, to determine the cost of the ending inventory at the end of the period under FIFO, you would begin by listing the cost of the most recent purchase. If the ending inventory contains more units than acquired in the most recent purchase, it also includes units from the next-to-the-latest purchase at the unit cost incurred, and so on. You would list these units from the latest purchases until that number agrees with the units in the ending inventory.

In Illustration 7.8, you can see how to determine the cost of ending inventory under FIFO using periodic inventory procedure. The company assumes that the 20 units in inventory consist of 10 units purchased December 21 and 10 units purchased October 12. The total cost of ending inventory is $179, and the cost of goods sold is $511.

We show the relationship between the cost of goods sold and the cost of ending inventory under FIFO using periodic inventory procedure in Illustration 7.9. The 80 units in cost of goods available for sale consists of the beginning inventory and all of the purchases during the period. Under FIFO, the ending inventory of 20 units consists of the most recent purchases—10 units of December 21 purchase and 10 units of October 12 purchase—costing $179. We assume the beginning inventory and other earlier purchases have been sold during the period, representing the cost of goods sold of $511.

ILLUSTRATION 7.8   Determining FIFO Cost of Ending Inventory under Periodic Inventory Procedure

	Units	Unit Cost	Total Cost
Ending inventory composed of purchases made on:			
December 21	10	$9.10	$ 91
October 12	10	8.80	88
Ending inventory	20		$179
Cost of goods sold composed of:			
Beginning inventory	10	8.00	$ 80
Purchases made on:			
March 2	10	8.50	85
May 28	20	8.40	168
August 12	10	9.00	90
October 12	10	8.80	88
			$511

Cost of goods available for sale	$690	
Ending inventory	179	← Used to establish the ending balance in the Merchandise Inventory account
Cost of goods sold	$511	

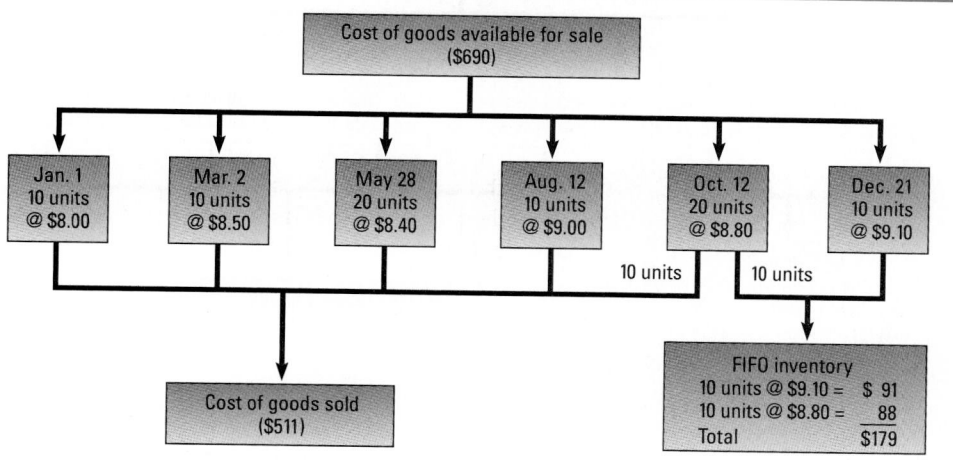

ILLUSTRATION 7.9
FIFO Flow of Costs

LIFO (LAST-IN, FIRST-OUT) UNDER PERIODIC INVENTORY PROCEDURE   The LIFO (last-in, first-out) method of inventory costing assumes that the costs of the most recent purchases are the first costs charged to cost of goods sold when the company actually sells the goods.

In Illustration 7.10, we show the use of LIFO under periodic inventory procedure. Since the company charges the latest costs to cost of goods sold under periodic inventory procedure, the ending inventory always consists of the oldest costs. Therefore, when determining the cost of inventory under periodic inventory procedure, the company lists the oldest units and their costs. The first units listed are those in beginning inventory, then the first purchase, and so on, until the number listed agrees with the units in ending inventory. Thus, ending inventory in Illustration 7.10 consists of the 10 units from beginning inventory and the 10 units purchased on March 2. The total cost of these 20 units, $165, is the ending inventory cost; the cost of goods sold is $525. Illustration 7.11 is a graphic representation of the LIFO flow of costs under periodic inventory procedure.

Note to the Student
When determining the ending inventory using LIFO, you can also use the acronym, FISH, which stands for first in, still here.

ILLUSTRATION 7.10
Determining LIFO Cost
of Ending Inventory
under Periodic
Inventory Procedure

	Units	Unit Cost	Total Cost
Ending inventory composed of:			
Beginning inventory	10	$8.00	$ 80
March 2 purchase	10	8.50	85
Ending inventory	20		$165
Cost of goods sold composed of purchases made on:			
December 21	10	9.10	$ 91
October 12	20	8.80	176
August 12	10	9.00	90
May 28	20	8.40	168
			$525
Cost of goods available for sale			$690
Ending inventory			165
Cost of goods sold			$525

ILLUSTRATION 7.11
LIFO Flow of Costs
under Periodic
Inventory Procedure

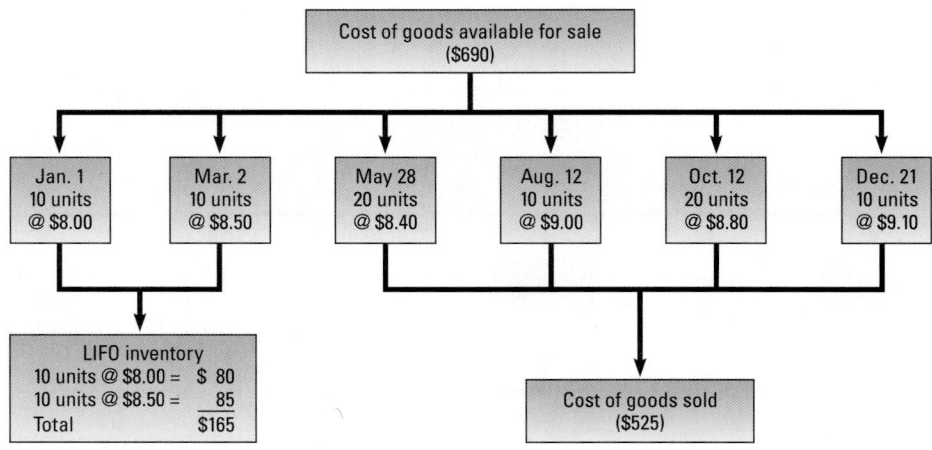

Reinforcing Problem
E7–10 Prepare journal entries
affecting inventory using weighted-
average periodic inventory
procedure.

WEIGHTED-AVERAGE UNDER PERIODIC INVENTORY PROCEDURE   The **weighted-average method** of inventory costing is a means of costing ending inventory using a weighted-average unit cost. Companies most often use the weighted-average method to determine a cost for units that are basically the same, such as identical games in a toy store or identical electrical tools in a hardware store. Since the units are alike, firms can assign the same unit cost to them.

Under periodic inventory procedure, a company determines the average cost at the end of the accounting period by dividing the total units purchased plus those in beginning inventory into total cost of goods available for sale. The ending inventory is carried at this per unit cost. To see how a company uses the weighted-average method to determine inventory costs using periodic inventory procedure, look at Illustration 7.12. Note that we compute weighted-average cost per unit by dividing the cost of units available for sale, $690, by the total number of units available for sale, 80. Thus, the weighted-average cost per unit is $8.625, meaning that each unit sold or remaining in inventory is valued at $8.625.

Perpetual Inventory Procedure

FIFO UNDER PERPETUAL INVENTORY PROCEDURE   Under perpetual inventory procedure, the ending balance in the Merchandise Inventory account reflects these most recent purchases as a result of making the required entries during the period.

	Units	Unit Cost	Total Cost
Beginning inventory	10	$8.00	$ 80.00
Purchases			
March 2	10	8.50	85.00
May 28	20	8.40	168.00
August 12	10	9.00	90.00
October 12	20	8.80	176.00
December 21	10	9.10	91.00
Total	80		$690.00

Weighted-average unit cost is
$690 ÷ 80, or $8.625.
Ending inventory then is $8.625 × 20 . . . . 172.50

Cost of goods sold:
$8.625 × 60 . . . . $517.50

ILLUSTRATION 7.12
Determining Ending Inventory under Weighted-Average Method Using Periodic Inventory Procedure

ILLUSTRATION 7.13 Determining FIFO Cost of Ending Inventory under Perpetual Inventory Procedure

Date	Purchased Units	Purchased Unit Cost	Purchased Total Cost	Sold Units	Sold Unit Cost	Sold Total Cost	Balance Units	Balance Unit Cost	Balance Total
Beg. inv.							10	$8.00	$ 80
Mar. 2	10	$8.50	$ 85				10 / 10	8.00 / 8.50	80 / 85
Mar. 10				10	$8.00	$80 ←	10	8.50	85
May 28	20	8.40	168				10 / 20	8.50 / 8.40	85 / 168
July 14				10 / 10	8.50 / 8.40	85 ← / 84 ←	10	8.40	84
Aug. 12	10	9.00	90				10 / 10	8.40 / 9.00	84 / 90
Sept. 7				10	8.40	84 ←	10	9.00	90
Oct. 12	20	8.80	176				10 / 20	9.00 / 8.80	90 / 176
Nov. 22				10 / 10	9.00 / 8.80	90 ← / 88 ←	10	8.80	88
Dec. 21	10	9.10	91				10 / 10	8.80 / 9.10	88 / 91

Sales are assumed to be from the oldest units on hand.

Total of $179 would agree with balance already existing in Merchandise Inventory account.

Total cost of ending inventory = $179

Also, the firm has already recorded the cost of goods sold in the Cost of Goods Sold account. Illustration 7.13 shows how to determine the cost of ending inventory under FIFO using perpetual inventory procedure. This illustration uses the same format as the earlier perpetual inventory record. The company keeps a record of the balance in the inventory account as it makes purchases and sells items from inventory. Notice in Illustration 7.13 that each time a sale occurs, the company assumes the items sold are the oldest on hand. Thus, after each transaction, it can readily determine the balance in the Merchandise Inventory account from the perpetual inventory record. The balance after the December 21 purchase represents the 20 units from the most recent

Reinforcing Problems
E7–3 Compute ending inventory using FIFO perpetual inventory procedure.
P7–4 Compute cost of goods sold using FIFO for both perpetual and periodic inventory procedures.

ILLUSTRATION 7.14   Determining LIFO Cost of Ending Inventory under Perpetual Inventory Procedure

Date	Purchased Units	Unit Cost	Total Cost	Sold Units	Unit Cost	Total Cost	Balance Units	Unit Cost	Total
Beg. inv.							10	$8.00	$ 80
Mar. 2	10	$8.50	$ 85				10 10	8.00 8.50	80 85
Mar. 10				10	$8.50	$ 85 ←	10	8.00	80
May 28	20	8.40	168				10 20	8.00 8.40	80 168
July 14				20	8.40	168 ←	10	8.00	80
Aug. 12	10	9.00	90				10 10	8.00 9.00	80 90
Sept. 7				10	9.00	90 ←	10	8.00	80
Oct. 12	20	8.80	176				10 20	8.00 8.80	80 176
Nov. 22				20	8.80	176 ←	10	8.00	80
Dec. 21	10	9.10	91				10 10	8.00 9.10	80 91

Sales are assumed to be from the most recent purchases.

Balance of $171 would agree with balance already existing in the Merchandise Inventory account.

Total cost of ending inventory = $171

purchases. The total cost of ending inventory is $179, which the company reports as a current asset on the balance sheet. During the accounting period, as sales occurred the firm would have debited a total of $511 to Cost of Goods Sold. Adding this $511 to the ending inventory of $179 accounts for the $690 cost of goods available for sale. *Under FIFO, using either perpetual or periodic inventory procedures results in the same total amounts for ending inventory and for cost of goods sold.*

Reinforcing Problem
E7–4 Compute ending inventory under LIFO perpetual inventory procedure.

LIFO UNDER PERPETUAL INVENTORY PROCEDURE   Look at Illustration 7.14 to see the LIFO method using perpetual inventory procedure. Under this procedure, the inventory composition and balance are updated with each purchase and sale. Notice in Illustration 7.14 that each time a sale occurs, the items sold are assumed to be the most recent ones acquired. Despite numerous purchases and sales during the year, the ending inventory still includes the 10 units from beginning inventory in our example. The remainder of the ending inventory consists of the last purchase because no sale occurred after the December 21 purchase. The total cost of the 20 units in ending inventory is $171; the cost of goods sold is $519. Illustration 7.15 shows graphically the LIFO flow of costs under perpetual inventory procedure.

Applying LIFO on a perpetual basis during the accounting period, as shown in Illustration 7.14, results in different ending inventory and cost of goods sold figures than applying LIFO only at year-end using periodic inventory procedure. (Compare Illustrations 7.14 and 7.10 to verify that ending inventory and cost of goods sold are different under the two procedures.) For this reason, if LIFO is applied on a perpetual basis during the period, special adjustments are sometimes necessary at year-end to take full advantage of using LIFO for tax purposes. Complicated applications of LIFO perpetual inventory procedures that require such adjustments are beyond the scope of this text.

Look at Illustrations 7.15 and 7.11, the flow of inventory costs under LIFO using both the perpetual and periodic inventory procedures. Note that ending inventory and cost of goods sold are different under the two procedures.

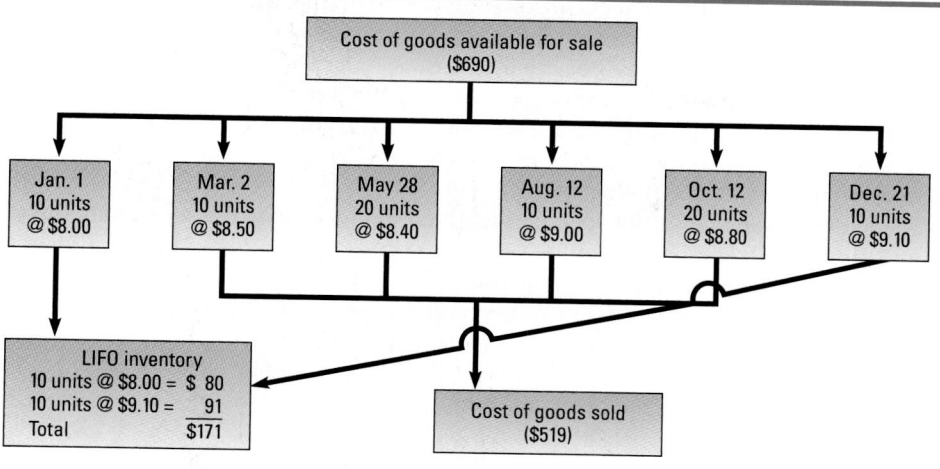

ILLUSTRATION 7.15
LIFO Flow of Costs under Perpetual Inventory Procedure

ILLUSTRATION 7.16 Determining Ending Inventory under Weighted-Average Method Using Perpetual Inventory Procedure

Date	Purchased Units	Purchased Unit Cost	Purchased Total Cost	Sold Units	Sold Unit Cost	Sold Total Cost	Balance Units	Balance Unit Cost	Balance Total	
Beg. inv.							10	$8.00	$ 80.00	*A new unit cost is calculated after each purchase.*
Mar. 2	10	$8.50	$ 85				20	8.25[a]	165.00	
Mar. 10				10	$8.25	$ 82.50	10	8.25	82.50	*The unit cost of sales is the most recently calculated unit cost.*
May 28	20	8.40	168				30	8.35[b]	250.50	
July 14				20	8.35	167.00	10	8.35	83.50	
Aug. 12	10	9.00	90				20	8.675[c]	173.50	*Balance of $178.58 would agree with balance already existing in the Merchandise Inventory account.*
Sept. 7				10	8.675	86.75	10	8.675	86.75	
Oct. 12	20	8.80	176				30	8.758[d]	262.75	
Nov. 22				20	8.758	175.17*	10	8.758	87.58	
Dec. 21	10	9.10	91				20	$8.929[e]	$178.58	

[a]$165.00/20 = $8.25. [b]$250.50/30 = $8.35. [c]$173.50/20 = $8.675. [d]$262.75/30 = $8.758. [e]$178.58/20 = $8.929. *Rounding difference.

WEIGHTED-AVERAGE UNDER PERPETUAL INVENTORY PROCEDURE Under perpetual inventory procedure, firms compute a new weighted-average unit cost after each purchase by dividing total cost of goods available for sale by total units available for sale. The unit cost is a moving weighted-average because it changes after each purchase. In Illustration 7.16, you can see how to compute the moving weighted-average using perpetual inventory procedure. The new weighted-average unit cost computed after each purchase is the unit cost for inventory items sold until a new purchase is made. The unit cost of the 20 units in ending inventory is $8.929 for a total inventory cost of $178.58. Cost of goods sold under this procedure is $690 minus the $178.58, or $511.42.

Reinforcing Problem
E7–5 Compute ending inventory under weighted-average perpetual inventory procedure.

Advantages and Disadvantages of Inventory Methods

Objective 4
Explain the advantages and disadvantages of the four major inventory costing methods (applies to each method separately).

ADVANTAGES AND DISADVANTAGES OF SPECIFIC IDENTIFICATION   Companies that use the specific identification method of inventory costing state their cost of goods sold and ending inventory at the actual cost of specific units sold and on hand. Some accountants argue that this method provides the most precise matching of costs and revenues and is, therefore, the most theoretically sound method. This statement is true for some one-of-a-kind items, such as autos or real estate. For these items, use of any other method would seem illogical.

One disadvantage of the specific identification method is that it permits the manipulation of income. For example, assume that a company bought three identical units of a given product at different prices. One unit cost $2,000, the second cost $2,100, and the third cost $2,200. The company sold one unit for $2,800. The units are alike, so the customer does not care which of the identical units the company ships. However, the gross margin on the sale could be either $800, $700, or $600, depending on which unit the company ships.

ADVANTAGES AND DISADVANTAGES OF FIFO   The FIFO method has four major advantages: (1) it is easy to apply, (2) the assumed flow of costs corresponds with the normal physical flow of goods, (3) no manipulation of income is possible, and (4) the balance sheet amount for inventory is likely to approximate the current market value. All the advantages of FIFO occur because when a company sells goods, the first costs it removes from inventory are the oldest unit costs. A company cannot manipulate income by choosing which unit to ship because the cost of a unit sold is not determined by a serial number. Instead, the cost attached to the unit sold is always the oldest cost. Under FIFO, purchases at the end of the period have no effect on cost of goods sold or net income.

The disadvantages of FIFO include (1) the recognition of paper profits and (2) a heavier tax burden if used for tax purposes in periods of inflation. We discuss these disadvantages later as advantages of LIFO.

ADVANTAGES AND DISADVANTAGES OF LIFO   The advantages of the LIFO method are based on the fact that prices have risen almost constantly for decades. LIFO supporters claim this upward trend in prices leads to *inventory, or paper, profits* if the FIFO method is used. **Inventory, or paper, profits** are equal to the current replacement cost of a unit of inventory at the time of sale minus the unit's historical cost.

For example, assume a company has three units of a product on hand, each purchased at a different cost: $12, $15, and $20 (the most recent cost). The sales price of the unit normally rises because the unit's replacement cost is rising. Assume that the company sells one unit for $30. FIFO gross margin would be $18 ($30 − $12), while LIFO would show a gross margin of $10 ($30 − $20). LIFO supporters would say that the extra $8 gross margin shown under FIFO represents inventory (paper) profit; it is merely the additional amount that the company must spend over cost of goods sold to purchase another unit of inventory ($8 + $12 = $20). Thus, the profit is not real; it exists only on paper. The company cannot distribute the $8 to owners, but must retain it to continue handling that particular product. LIFO shows the actual profits that the company can distribute to the owners while still replenishing inventory.

During periods of inflation, LIFO shows the largest cost of goods sold of any of the costing methods because the newest costs charged to cost of goods sold are also the highest costs. The larger the cost of goods sold, the smaller the net income.

Those who favor LIFO argue that its use leads to a better matching of costs and revenues than the other methods. When a company uses LIFO, the income statement reports both sales revenue and cost of goods sold in current dollars. The resulting gross margin is a better indicator of management's ability to generate income than gross margin computed using FIFO, which may include substantial inventory (paper) profits.

Supporters of FIFO argue that LIFO (1) matches the cost of goods not sold against revenues, (2) grossly understates inventory, and (3) permits income manipulation.

The first criticism—that LIFO matches the cost of goods not sold against revenues—is an extension of the debate over whether the assumed flow of costs should agree with the physical flow of goods. LIFO supporters contend that it makes more sense to match current costs against current revenues than to worry about matching costs for the physical flow of goods.

The second criticism—that LIFO grossly understates inventory—is valid. A company may report LIFO inventory at a fraction of its current replacement cost, especially if the historical costs are from several decades ago. LIFO supporters contend that the increased usefulness of the income statement more than offsets the negative effect of this undervaluation of inventory on the balance sheet.

The third criticism—that LIFO permits income manipulation—is also valid. Income manipulation is possible under LIFO. For example, assume that management wishes to reduce income. The company could purchase an abnormal amount of goods at current high prices near the end of the current period, with the purpose of selling the goods in the next period. Under LIFO, these higher costs are charged to cost of goods sold in the current period, resulting in a substantial decline in reported net income. To obtain higher income, management could delay making the normal amount of purchases until the next period and thus include some of the older, lower costs in cost of goods sold.

Tax Benefit of LIFO   The LIFO method results in the lowest taxable income, and thus the lowest income taxes, when prices are rising. The Internal Revenue Service allows companies to use LIFO for tax purposes only if they use LIFO for financial reporting purposes. Companies may also report an alternative inventory amount in the notes to their financial statements for comparison purposes. Because of high inflation during the 1970s, many companies switched from FIFO to LIFO for tax advantages.

ADVANTAGES AND DISADVANTAGES OF WEIGHTED-AVERAGE   When a company uses the weighted-average method and prices are rising, its cost of goods sold is less than that obtained under LIFO, but more than that obtained under FIFO. Inventory is not as badly understated as under LIFO, but it is not as up to date as under FIFO. Weighted-average costing takes a middle-of-the-road approach. A company can manipulate income under the weighted-average costing method by buying or failing to buy goods near year-end. However, the averaging process reduces the effects of buying or not buying.

Differences in Costing Methods Summarized

The four inventory costing methods—specific identification, FIFO, LIFO, and weighted-average—involve assumptions about how costs flow through a business. In some instances, assumed cost flows may correspond with the actual physical flow of goods. For example, fresh meats and dairy products must flow in a FIFO manner to avoid spoilage losses. In contrast, firms use lumber or coal stacked in a pile in a LIFO manner because the newest units purchased are unloaded on top of the pile and sold first. Gasoline held in a tank is a good example of an inventory that has an average physical flow. As the tank is refilled, the new gasoline mixes with the old. Thus, any amount used is a blend of the old gas with the new.

Although physical flows are sometimes cited as support for an inventory method, accountants now recognize that an inventory method's assumed cost flows need not necessarily correspond with the actual physical flow of the goods. In fact, good reasons exist for simply ignoring physical flows and choosing an inventory method based on more significant criteria.

In Illustrations 7.17 and 7.18, we use data from Illustration 7.6 to show the cost of goods sold, inventory cost, and gross margin for each of the four basic costing methods using perpetual and periodic inventory procedures. The differences for the four methods occur because the company paid different prices for goods purchased. No differences would occur if purchase prices were constant. Since a company's

Reinforcing Problems
P7–5A Compute ending inventory under FIFO, LIFO, and weighted-average using perpetual and periodic inventory procedures.
P7–7A Compute ending inventory and cost of goods sold under FIFO, LIFO, and weighted-average using perpetual and periodic inventory procedures.
P7–8A Compute gross margin using FIFO and LIFO illustrating effects of end-of-year purchases.

ILLUSTRATION 7.17
Effects of Different
Inventory Costing
Methods Using Perpetual
Inventory Procedure

	Specific Identification	FIFO	LIFO	Weighted-Average
Sales	$780.00	$780.00	$780.00	$780.00
Cost of goods sold:				
Beginning inventory	$ 80.00	$ 80.00	$ 80.00	$ 80.00
Purchases	610.00	610.00	610.00	610.00
Cost of goods available for sale	$690.00	$690.00	$690.00	$690.00
Ending inventory	181.00	179.00	171.00	178.58
Cost of goods sold	$509.00	$511.00	$519.00	$511.42
Gross margin	$271.00	$269.00	$261.00	$268.58

ILLUSTRATION 7.18
Effects of Different
Inventory Costing
Methods Using Periodic
Inventory Procedure

	Specific Identification	FIFO	LIFO	Weighted-Average
Sales	$780.00	$780.00	$780.00	$780.00
Cost of goods sold:				
Beginning inventory	$ 80.00	$ 80.00	$ 80.00	$ 80.00
Purchases	610.00	610.00	610.00	610.00
Cost of goods available for sale	$690.00	$690.00	$690.00	$690.00
Ending inventory	181.00	179.00	165.00	172.50
Cost of goods sold	$509.00	$511.00	$525.00	$517.50
Gross margin	$271.00	$269.00	$255.00	$262.50

Reinforcing Problem
E7–6 Compute cost of ending inventory using FIFO, LIFO, and weighted-average under periodic inventory procedure.

purchase prices are seldom constant, inventory costing method affects cost of goods sold, inventory cost, gross margin, and net income. Therefore, companies must disclose on their financial statements which inventory costing methods were used.

WHICH IS THE CORRECT METHOD?   All four methods of inventory costing are acceptable; no single method is the only correct method. Different methods are attractive under different conditions.

If a company wants to match sales revenue with current cost of goods sold, it would use LIFO. If a company seeks to reduce its income taxes in a period of rising prices, it would also use LIFO. On the other hand, LIFO often charges against revenues the cost of goods not actually sold. Also, LIFO may allow the company to manipulate net income by changing the timing of additional purchases.

The FIFO and specific identification methods result in a more precise matching of historical cost with revenue. However, FIFO can give rise to paper profits, while specific identification can give rise to income manipulation. The weighted-average method also allows manipulation of income. Only under FIFO is the manipulation of net income not possible.

AN ACCOUNTING PERSPECTIVE
—

BUSINESS INSIGHT   Management decides which inventory costing method or methods (LIFO, FIFO, etc.) to use. Also, management must determine which method is the most meaningful and useful in representing economic results. Then, it must use the selected method consistently.

The principal business of Kellwood Company is the marketing, merchandising, and manufacturing of apparel, primarily for women. Note in the following footnote from Kellwood's 1996 financial statements that it, like other companies, uses several costing methods within the same enterprise:

Summary of Significant Accounting Policies
3. Inventories and Revenue Recognition
Inventories are stated at the lower of cost or market. The first-in, first-out (FIFO) method is used to determine the value of 46% of the domestic inventories, and the last-in, first-out (LIFO) method is used to value the remaining domestic inventories. Inventories of foreign subsidiaries are valued using the specific identification method. Sales are recognized when goods are shipped.

Generally, companies use the inventory method that best fits their individual circum- stances. However, this freedom of choice does not include changing inventory methods every year or so, especially if the goal is to report higher income. Continuous switch- ing of methods violates the accounting principle of *consistency,* which requires using the same accounting methods from period to period in preparing financial statements. Consistency of methods in preparing financial statements enables financial statement users to compare statements of a company from period to period and determine trends.

Changing Inventory Methods

BUSINESS INSIGHT   Sometimes, companies change inventory methods in spite of the principle of consistency. Improved financial reporting is the only justification for a change in inventory method. A company that changes its inventory method must make a full disclosure of the change. Usually, the company makes a full disclosure in a footnote to the financial statements. The footnote consists of a complete description of the change, the reasons why the change was made, and, if possible, the effect of the change on net income.

J. M. Tull Industries, Inc., sells a diverse range of metals (aluminum, brass, copper, steel, stainless steel, and nickel alloys) for severe corrosion conditions and high-temperature applications. For example, when J. M. Tull changed from lower of average cost or market to LIFO, the following footnote appeared in its annual report:

Note B. Change in accounting method for inventory
Effective with the year ending December 31, 1975, the company changed its method of determining inventory cost from the lower of average cost or market method to the last-in, first-out (LIFO) method for substantially all inventory. This change was made because management believes LIFO more clearly reflects income by providing a closer matching of current cost against current revenue.

AN ACCOUNTING PERSPECTIVE

Now we illustrate in more detail the journal entries made when using perpetual inven- tory procedure. Data from Illustration 7.13 serve as the basis for some of the entries.

You would debit the Merchandise Inventory account to record the increases in the asset due to purchase costs and transportation-in costs. And you would credit Mer- chandise Inventory to record the decreases in the asset brought about by purchase returns and allowances, purchase discounts, and cost of goods sold to customers. The balance in the account is the cost of the inventory that should be on hand at any date. This entry records the purchase of 10 units on March 2 in Illustration 7.13:

Journal Entries under Perpetual Inventory Procedure

Objective 5
Record merchandise trans- actions under perpetual inventory procedure.

Mar.	2	Merchandise Inventory	85	
		Accounts Payable		85
		To record purchase of 10 units at $8.50 on account.		

You would also record the 10 units sold on the perpetual inventory record in Illustration 7.13 on page 259. Perpetual inventory procedure requires two journal entries for each sale. One entry is at selling price—a debit to Accounts Receivable (or Cash) and a credit to Sales. The other entry is at cost—a debit to Cost of Goods Sold and a credit to Merchandise Inventory. Assuming that the 10 units sold on March 10 in Illustration 7.13 had a retail price of $13 each, you would record the following entries:

Mar.	10	Accounts Receivable	130	
		Sales		130
		To record 10 units sold at $13 each on account.		
	10	Cost of Goods Sold	80	
		Merchandise Inventory		80
		To record cost of $8 on each of the 10 units sold.		

Reinforcing Problems
E7–7 Prepare journal entries for inventory under FIFO perpetual inventory procedure.
E7–8 Prepare journal entries under FIFO perpetual inventory procedure.
E7–9 Prepare journal entries affect- ing inventory using LIFO perpetual inventory procedure.
P7–6 Record journal entries for purchases and sales under FIFO perpetual and periodic procedures.

When a company sells merchandise to customers, it transfers the cost of the merchandise from an asset account (Merchandise Inventory) to an expense account (Cost of Goods Sold). The company makes this transfer because the sale reduces the asset, and the cost of the goods sold is one of the expenses of making the sale. Thus, the Cost of Goods Sold account accumulates the cost of all the merchandise that the company sells during a period.

A sales return also requires two entries, one at selling price and one at cost. Assume that a customer returned merchandise that cost $20 and originally sold for $32. The entry to reduce the accounts receivable and to record the sales return of $32 is:

Mar.	17	Sales Returns and Allowances	32	
		Accounts Receivable.		32
		To record the reduction in amount owed by a customer upon return of goods.		

The entry that increases the Merchandise Inventory account and decreases the Cost of Goods Sold account by $20 is as follows:

Mar.	17	Merchandise Inventory.	20	
		Cost of Goods Sold		20
		To record replacement of goods returned to inventory.		

Sales returns affect both revenues and cost of goods sold because the goods charged to cost of goods sold are actually returned to the seller. In contrast, sales allowances granted to customers affect only revenues because the customers do not have to return goods. Thus, if the company had granted a sales allowance of $32 on March 17, only the first entry would be required.

The balance of the Merchandise Inventory account is the cost of the inventory that should be on hand. This fact is a major reason some companies choose to use perpetual inventory procedure. The cost of inventory that should be on hand is readily available. Periodically, usually at year-end, a physical inventory determines the accuracy of the account balance. Management may investigate any major discrepancies between the balance in the account and the cost based on the physical count. It thereby achieves greater control over inventory. When a shortage is discovered, an adjusting entry is required. Assuming a $15 shortage (at cost) is discovered, the entry is:

Dec.	31	Loss from Inventory Shortage.	15	
		Merchandise Inventory.		15
		To record inventory shortage.		

Assume that the Cost of Goods Sold account had a balance of $200,000 by year-end when it is closed to Income Summary. There are no other purchase-related accounts to be closed. The entry to close the Cost of Goods Sold account is:

Dec.	31	Income Summary	200,000	
		Cost of Goods Sold		200,000
		To close Cost of Goods Sold account to Income Summary at the end of the year.		

AN ACCOUNTING PERSPECTIVE

USE OF TECHNOLOGY   A particularly useful website is:
http://www.news.com
This site contains the latest news about the Internet, computing, business, rumor mill, and other business and computer-related topics. It also offers hardware and software reviews, programs available for downloading, and other items. This site is updated every few hours, so the news is very current. You might want to visit this site to see for yourself how interesting and current it is in providing useful information about business and computing.

DEPARTURES FROM COST BASIS OF INVENTORY MEASUREMENT

Generally, companies should use historical cost to value inventories and cost of goods sold. However, some circumstances justify departures from historical cost. One of these circumstances is when the utility or value of inventory items is less than their cost. A decline in the selling price of the goods or their replacement cost may indicate such a loss of utility. This section explains how accountants handle some of these departures from the cost basis of inventory measurement.

Companies should not carry goods in inventory at more than their net realizable value. **Net realizable value** is the estimated selling price of an item less the estimated costs that the company incurs in preparing the item for sale and selling it. Damaged, obsolete, or shopworn goods often have a net realizable value lower than their historical cost and must be written down to their net realizable value. However, goods do not have to be damaged, obsolete, or shopworn for this situation to occur. Technological changes and increased competition have caused significant reductions in selling prices for such products as computers, VCRs, calculators, and microwave ovens.

To illustrate a necessary write-down in the cost of inventory, assume that an automobile dealer has a demonstrator on hand. The dealer acquired the auto at a cost of $18,000. The auto had an original selling price of $19,600. Since the dealer used the auto as a demonstrator and the new models are coming in, the auto now has an estimated selling price of only $18,100. However, the dealer can get the $18,100 only if the demonstrator receives some scheduled maintenance, including a tune-up and some paint damage repairs. This work and the sales commission cost $300. The net realizable value of the demonstrator, then, is $17,800 (selling price of $18,100 less costs of $300). For inventory purposes, the required journal entry is:

Loss Due to Decline in Market Value of Inventory	200	
Merchandise Inventory		200
To write down inventory to net realizable value ($18,000 − $17,800).		

This entry treats the $200 inventory decline as a loss in the period in which the decline in utility occurred. Such an entry is necessary only when the net realizable value is less than cost. If net realizable value declines but still exceeds cost, the dealer would continue to carry the item at cost.

The **lower-of-cost-or-market (LCM) method** is an inventory costing method that values inventory at the lower of its historical cost or its current market (replacement) cost. The term *cost* refers to historical cost of inventory as determined under the specific identification, FIFO, LIFO, or weighted-average inventory method. *Market* generally refers to a merchandise item's replacement cost in the quantity usually purchased. The basic assumption of the LCM method is that if the purchase price of an item has fallen, its selling price also has fallen or will fall. The LCM method has long been accepted in accounting.

Under LCM, inventory items are written down to market value when the market value is less than the cost of the items. For example, assume that the market value of the inventory is $39,600 and its cost is $40,000. Then, the company would record a $400 loss because the inventory has lost some of its revenue-generating ability. The company must recognize the loss in the period the loss occurred. On the other hand, if ending inventory has a market value of $45,000 and a cost of $40,000, the company would not recognize this increase in value. To do so would recognize revenue before the time of sale.

LCM APPLIED   A company may apply LCM to each inventory item (such as Trivial Pursuit), each inventory class (such as games), or total inventory. To see how the company would apply the method to individual items and total inventory, look at Illustration 7.19.

Net Realizable Value

Objective 6
Apply net realizable value and the lower-of-cost-or-market method to inventory.

Reinforcing Problems
E7–13 Using net realizable value, compute carrying cost of inventory item.
E7–14 Determine the proper carrying value of damaged goods.

Lower-of-Cost-or Market Method

Real World Example
Merck & Co. reported the following concerning its inventories in the notes to its 1995 financial statements: "The majority of domestic inventories are valued at the lower of last-in, first-out (LIFO) cost or market. Remaining inventories are valued at the lower of first-in (FIFO) cost or market."

ILLUSTRATION 7.19
Application of
Lower-of-Cost-or-Market
Method

Item	Quantity	Unit Cost	Unit Market	Total Cost	Total Market	LCM on Item-by-Item Basis
1	100 units	$10	$9.00	$1,000	$ 900	$ 900
2	200 units	8	8.75	1,600	1,750	1,600
3	500 units	5	5.00	2,500	2,500	2,500
				$5,100	$5,150	$5,000

Reinforcing Problems
E7–15 Compute value of ending inventory using LCM applied on item-by-item basis.
E7–16 Compute value of total inventory using LCM.
P7–9A Compute ending inventory using LCM.

If LCM is applied on an item-by-item basis, ending inventory would be $5,000. The company would deduct the $5,000 ending inventory from cost of goods available for sale on the income statement and report this inventory in the current assets section of the balance sheet. Under the class method, a company applies LCM to the total cost and total market for each class of items compared. One class might be games; another might be toys. Then, the company values each class at the lower of its cost or market amount. If LCM is applied on a total inventory basis, ending inventory would be $5,100, since total cost of $5,100 is lower than total market of $5,150.

An annual report of Du Pont contains an actual example of applying LCM. The report states that "substantially all inventories are valued at cost as determined by the last-in, first-out (LIFO) method; in the aggregate, such valuations are not in excess of market." The term *in the aggregate* means that Du Pont applied LCM to total inventory.

AN ACCOUNTING PERSPECTIVE

BUSINESS INSIGHT   Procter & Gamble markets a broad range of laundry, cleaning, paper, beauty care, health care, food, and beverage products around the world. Procter & Gamble's footnote in its Notes to Consolidated Financial Statements in its 1995 annual report illustrates that companies often disclose LCM in their notes to financial statements.

Inventories are valued at cost, which is not in excess of current market price. Cost is primarily determined by either the average cost or the first-in, first-out method. The replacement cost of last-in, first-out inventories exceeds carrying value by approximately $169 [million].

Estimating Inventory

Objective 7
Estimate cost of ending inventory using the gross margin and retail inventory methods.

Note to the Student
Auditors sometimes use the gross margin method of estimating inventory to check that the amount reported by the company as ending inventory is reasonable.

Reinforcing Problems
E7–17 Estimate ending inventory using gross margin method.
E7–18 Estimate ending inventory using gross margin method.
P7–10 Estimate inventory using gross margin method.

A company using periodic inventory procedure may estimate its inventory for any of the following reasons:

1. To obtain an inventory cost for use in monthly or quarterly financial statements without taking a physical inventory. The effort of taking a physical inventory can be very expensive and disrupts normal business operations; once a year is often enough.

2. To compare with physical inventories to determine whether shortages exist.

3. To determine the amount recoverable from an insurance company when fire has destroyed inventory or the inventory has been stolen.

Next, we introduce two recognized methods of estimating the cost of ending inventory when a company has not taken a physical inventory—the gross margin method and the retail inventory method.

GROSS MARGIN METHOD   The steps in calculating ending inventory under the gross margin method are:

1. Estimate gross margin (based on net sales) using the same gross margin rate experienced in prior accounting periods.

2. Determine estimated cost of goods sold by deducting estimated gross margin from net sales.

3. Determine estimated ending inventory by deducting estimated cost of goods sold from cost of goods available for sale.

Merchandise inventory, January 1, 1999		$ 40,000
Net cost of purchases		480,000
Cost of goods available for sale		$520,000
Less estimated cost of goods sold:		
Net sales	$700,000	
Gross margin (30% of $700,000)	210,000	
Estimated cost of goods sold		490,000
Estimated inventory, December 31, 1999		$ 30,000

ILLUSTRATION 7.20
Inventory Estimation
Using Gross Margin
Method

Thus, the **gross margin method** estimates ending inventory by deducting estimated cost of goods sold from cost of goods available for sale.

The gross margin method assumes that a fairly stable relationship exists between gross margin and net sales. In other words, gross margin has been a fairly constant percentage of net sales, and this relationship has continued into the current period. If this percentage relationship has changed, the gross margin method does not yield satisfactory results.

To illustrate the gross margin method of computing inventory, assume that for several years Field Company has maintained a 30% gross margin on net sales. The following data for 1999 are available: The January 1 inventory was $40,000; net cost of purchases of merchandise was $480,000; and net sales of merchandise were $700,000. As shown in Illustration 7.20, Field can estimate the inventory for December 31, 1999, by deducting the estimated cost of goods sold from the actual cost of goods available for sale.

An alternative format for calculating estimated ending inventory uses the standard income statement format and solves for the one unknown (ending inventory):

Net sales		$700,000
Less cost of goods sold:		
Merchandise inventory, January 1, 1999	$ 40,000	
Net cost of purchases	480,000	
Cost of goods available for sale	$520,000	
Less estimated inventory, December 31, 1999	?	
Estimated cost of goods sold		490,000 (70% of net sales)
Estimated gross margin		$210,000 (30% of net sales)

We know that:

$$\frac{\text{Cost of goods}}{\text{available for sale}} - \frac{\text{Ending}}{\text{inventory}} = \frac{\text{Cost of}}{\text{goods sold}}$$

Therefore (let X = Ending inventory):

$$\$520,000 - X = \$490,000$$
$$X = \$30,000$$

The gross margin method is not precise enough to be used for year-end financial statements. At year-end, a physical inventory must be taken and valued by either the specific identification, FIFO, LIFO, or weighted-average methods.

RETAIL INVENTORY METHOD   Retail stores frequently use the retail inventory method to estimate ending inventory at times other than year-end. Taking a physical inventory during an accounting period (such as monthly or quarterly) is too time consuming and significantly interferes with business operations. The **retail inventory method** estimates the cost of the ending inventory by applying a cost/retail price ratio to ending inventory stated at retail prices. The advantage of this method is that companies can estimate ending inventory (at cost) without taking a physical inventory. Thus, the use of this estimate permits the preparation of interim financial statements

Note to the Student
It seems that it would be just as easy to physically count and determine the actual inventory instead of keeping retail records and calculating an estimate. However, a physical inventory involves applying a cost flow method and takes longer than keeping retail records as goods are purchased.

ILLUSTRATION 7.21
Inventory Estimation

	Cost	Retail
Merchandise inventory, January 1, 1999	$ 22,000	$ 40,000
Purchases	182,000	303,000
Purchase returns	(2,000)	(3,000)
Purchase allowances	(3,000)	
Transportation-in	5,000	
Goods available for sale	$204,000	$340,000
Cost/retail price ratio: $204,000/$340,000 = 60%		
Sales		280,000
Ending inventory at retail prices		$ 60,000
Times cost/retail price ratio		×60%
Ending inventory at cost, March 31, 1999.	$ 36,000	

Reinforcing Problem
E7–19 Estimate ending inventory using retail inventory method.

(monthly or quarterly) without taking a physical inventory. The steps for finding the ending inventory by the retail inventory method are:

1. Total the beginning inventory and the net amount of goods purchased during the period at both cost and retail prices.
2. Divide the cost of goods available for sale by the retail price of the goods available for sale to find the cost/retail price ratio.
3. Deduct the retail sales from the retail price of the goods available for sale to determine ending inventory at retail.
4. Multiply the cost/retail price ratio or percentage by the ending inventory at retail prices to reduce it to the ending inventory at cost.

In Illustration 7.21, we show the retail inventory method. In the illustration, the cost ($22,000) and retail ($40,000) amounts for beginning inventory are available from the preceding period's computation. The amounts for the first quarter purchases, purchase returns, purchase allowances, and transportation-in came from the accounting records. The amounts for purchase allowances and transportation-in appear only in the cost column. The first quarter sales amount ($280,000) is from the Sales account and stated at retail (sales) prices. The difference between what was available for sale at retail prices and what was sold at retail prices (which is sales) equals what should be on hand (March 31 inventory of $60,000) expressed in retail prices. The retail price of the March 31 inventory needs to be converted into cost for use in the financial statements. We do this by multiplying it times the cost/retail price ratio. In the example, the cost/retail price ratio is 60%, which means that on the average, 60 cents of each sales dollar is cost of goods sold. To find the March 31, 1999, inventory at cost ($36,000), we multiplied the ending inventory at retail ($60,000) by 60%.

Once the March 31 inventory has been estimated at cost ($36,000), we deduct the cost of the inventory from cost of goods available for sale ($204,000) to determine cost of goods sold ($168,000). We can also find the cost of goods sold by multiplying the cost/retail price ratio of 60% by sales of $280,000.

For the next quarterly period, the $36,000 and $60,000 amounts would appear on the schedule as beginning inventory at cost and retail, respectively. We would include other quarterly data regarding purchases, purchase returns, purchase allowances, and transportation-in to determine goods available for sale at cost and at retail. From these amounts, we could compute a new cost/retail price ratio for the second quarter.

At the end of each year, merchandisers usually take a physical inventory at retail prices. Since the retail prices are on the individual items (while the cost is not), taking an inventory at retail prices is more convenient than taking an inventory at cost. Accountants can then compare the results of the physical inventory to the calculation of inventory at retail under the retail inventory method for the fourth quarter to determine whether a shortage exists.

Terry Dorsey started Dorsey Hardware, a small hardware store, two years ago and has struggled to make it successful. The first year of operations resulted in a substantial loss; in the second year, there was a small net income. His initial cash investment was almost depleted because he had to withdraw money for living expenses. The current year of operations looked much better. His customer base was growing and seemed to be loyal. To increase sales, however, Terry had to invest his remaining funds and the proceeds of a $40,000 bank loan into doubling the size of his inventory and purchasing some new display shelves and a new truck.

At the end of the third year, Terry's accountant asked him for his ending inventory figure and later told him that initial estimates indicated that net income (and taxable income) for the year would be approximately $80,000. Terry was delighted until he learned that the federal income taxes on that income would be about $17,250. He told the accountant that he did not have enough cash to pay the taxes and could not even borrow it, since he already had an outstanding loan at the bank.

Terry asked the accountant for a copy of the income statement figures so he could see if any items had been overlooked that might reduce his net income. He noticed that ending inventory of $160,000 had been deducted from cost of goods available for sale of $640,000 to arrive at cost of goods sold of $480,000. Net sales of $720,000 and expenses of $160,000 could not be changed. But Terry hit on a scheme to reduce his net income. The next day he told his accountant that he had made an error in determining ending inventory and that its correct amount was $120,000. This lower inventory amount would increase cost of goods sold by $40,000 and reduce net income by that same amount. The resulting income taxes would be about $6,000, which was just about what Terry had paid in estimated taxes.

To justify his action in his own mind, Terry used the following arguments: (1) federal taxes are too high, and the federal government seems to be taxing the little guy out of existence; (2) no harm is really done because, when the business becomes more profitable, I will use correct inventory amounts, and this loan from the government will be paid back; (3) since I am the only one who knows the correct ending inventory I will not get caught; and (4) I'll bet a lot of other people do this same thing.

Both the gross margin and the retail inventory methods can help you detect inventory shortages. To illustrate how you can determine inventory shortages using the retail method, assume that a physical inventory taken on December 31, 1999, showed only $62,000 of retail-priced goods in the store. Assume that use of the retail method for the fourth quarter showed that $66,000 of goods should be on hand, thus indicating a $4,000 inventory shortage at retail. After converting the $4,000 to $2,400 of cost ($4,000 × 0.60) you would report this as a "Loss from inventory shortage" in the income statement. Knowledge of such shortages may lead management to reduce or prevent them, by increasing security or improving the training of employees.

Reinforcing Problem
P7–11A Estimate ending inventory using retail inventory method.

ANALYZING AND USING FINANCIAL RESULTS—INVENTORY TURNOVER RATIO

An important ratio for managers, investors, and creditors to consider when analyzing a company's inventory is the inventory turnover ratio. This ratio tests whether a company is generating a sufficient volume of business based on its inventory. To calculate the **inventory turnover ratio:**

Objective 8
Analyze and use the financial results—inventory turnover ratio.

$$\text{Inventory turnover ratio} = \frac{\text{Cost of goods sold}}{\text{Average inventory}}$$

Inventory turnover measures the efficiency of the firm in managing and selling inventory: thus, it gauges the liquidity of the firm's inventory. A high inventory turnover is generally a sign of efficient inventory management and profit for the firm; the faster inventory sells, the less time funds are tied up in inventory. A relatively low turnover could be the result of a company carrying too much inventory or stocking inventory that is obsolete, slow-moving, or inferior.

In assessing inventory turnover, analysts also consider the type of industry. When making comparisons among firms, they check the cost-flow assumption used to value inventory and cost of products sold.

Procter & Gamble
Procter & Gamble markets a broad range of laundry, cleaning, paper, beauty care, health care, food, and beverage products around the world.

The Procter & Gamble Company (P&G) and its subsidiaries reported the following financial data for 1995 (in millions):

Cost of goods sold	$19,623
Beginning inventory	2,877
Ending inventory	3,453

P&G's inventory turnover is:

$$\$19,623/[(\$2,877 + \$3,453)/2] = 6.2 \text{ times}$$

You should now understand the importance of taking an accurate physical inventory and knowing how to value this inventory. In the next chapter, you will learn the general principles of internal control and how to control cash. Cash is one of a company's most important and mobile assets.

UNDERSTANDING THE LEARNING OBJECTIVES

Objective 1
Explain and calculate the effects of inventory errors on certain financial statement items.

- Net income for an accounting period depends directly on the valuation of ending inventory.
- If ending inventory is overstated, cost of goods sold is understated, resulting in an overstatement of gross margin, net income, and retained earnings.
- When ending inventory is misstated in the current year, companies carry that misstatement forward into the next year.
- An error in the net income of one year caused by misstated ending inventory automatically causes an error in net income in the opposite direction in the next period because of the misstated beginning inventory.

Objective 2
Indicate which costs are properly included in inventory.

- Inventory cost includes all necessary outlays to obtain the goods, get the goods ready to sell, and have the goods in the desired location for sale to customers.
- Inventory cost includes:
  a. Seller's gross selling price less purchase discount.
  b. Cost of insurance on the goods while in transit.
  c. Transportation charges when borne by the buyer.
  d. Handling costs, such as the cost of pressing clothes wrinkled during shipment.

Objective 3
Calculate cost of ending inventory and cost of goods sold under the four major inventory costing methods using periodic and perpetual inventory procedures.

- **Specific identification:** Attaches actual cost of each unit of product to units in ending inventory and cost of goods sold. Specific identification creates precise matching in determining net income.
- **FIFO (first-in, first-out):** Ending inventory consists of the most recent purchases. FIFO assumes that the costs of the first goods purchased are those charged to cost of goods sold when goods are sold. During periods of rising prices, FIFO creates higher net income since the costs charged to cost of goods sold are lower.
- **LIFO (last-in, first-out):** Ending inventory consists of the oldest costs. LIFO assumes that the costs of the most recent purchases are the first costs charged to cost of goods sold. Net income is usually lower under LIFO since the costs charged to cost of goods sold are higher due to inflation. The ending inventory may differ between perpetual and periodic inventory procedures.
- **Weighted-average:** Ending inventory is priced using a weighted-average unit cost. Under perpetual inventory procedure, a new weighted-average is determined after each purchase. Under periodic procedure, the average is determined at the end of the accounting period by dividing the total number of units purchased plus those in beginning inventory into total cost of goods available for sale. In determining cost of goods sold, this average unit cost is applied to each item. Under the weighted-average method, in a period of rising prices net income is usually higher than income under LIFO and lower than income under FIFO.

Objective 4
Explain the advantages and disadvantages of the four major inventory costing methods.

- **Specific identification:** *Advantages:* (1) States cost of goods sold and ending inventory at the actual cost of specific units sold and on hand, and (2) provides the most precise matching of costs and revenues. *Disadvantage:* Income manipulation is possible.
- **FIFO:** *Advantages:* (1) FIFO is easy to apply, (2) the assumed flow of costs often corresponds with the normal physical flow of goods, (3) no manipulation of income is

possible, and (4) the balance sheet amount for inventory is likely to approximate the current market value.   *Disadvantages:* (1) Recognizes paper profits, and (2) tax burden is heavier if used for tax purposes when prices are rising.

- **LIFO:**   *Advantages:* (1) LIFO reports both sales revenue and cost of goods sold in current dollars, and (2) lower income taxes result if used for tax purposes when prices are rising.   *Disadvantages:* (1) Often matches the cost of goods *not* sold against revenues, (2) grossly understates inventory, and (3) permits income manipulation.

- **Weighted-average:**   *Advantages:* Due to the averaging process, the effects of year-end buying or not buying are lessened.   *Disadvantage:* Manipulation of income is possible.

- Perpetual inventory procedure requires an entry to Merchandise Inventory whenever goods are purchased, returned, sold, or otherwise adjusted, so that inventory records reflect actual units on hand at all times. Thus, an entry is required to record cost of goods sold for each sale.

Objective 5
Record merchandise transactions under perpetual inventory procedure.

- Companies should not carry goods in inventory at more than their net realizable value. Net realizable value is the estimated selling price of an item less the estimated costs incurred in preparing the item for sale and selling it.

- Inventory items are written down to market value when the market value is less than the cost of the items. If market value is greater than cost, the increase in value is not recognized. LCM may be applied to each inventory item, each inventory class, or total inventory.

Objective 6
Apply net realizable value and the lower-of-cost-or-market method to inventory.

- The steps in calculating ending inventory under the gross margin method are:
    a. Estimate gross margin (based on net sales) using the same gross margin rate experienced in prior accounting periods.
    b. Determine estimated cost of goods sold by deducting estimated gross margin from net sales.
    c. Determine estimated ending inventory by deducting estimated cost of goods sold from cost of goods available for sale.

Objective 7
Estimate cost of ending inventory using the gross margin and retail inventory methods.

- The retail inventory method estimates the cost of the ending inventory by applying a cost/retail price ratio to ending inventory stated at retail prices. To find the cost/retail price ratio, divide the cost of goods available for sale by the retail price of the goods available for sale.

- Inventory turnover ratio $= \dfrac{\text{Cost of goods sold}}{\text{Average inventory}}$

- Inventory turnover measures the efficiency of the firm in managing and selling inventory. It gauges the liquidity of the firm's inventory.

Objective 8
Analyze and use the financial results—inventory turnover ratio.

DEMONSTRATION PROBLEM 7–A

Following are data related to Adler Company's beginning inventory, purchases, and sales for the year 1999:

Beginning Inventory and Purchases	Units		Unit Cost	Sales	Units
Beginning inventory	6,250	@	$3.00	February 3	5,250
March 15	5,000	@	3.12	May 4	4,500
May 10	8,750	@	3.30	September 16	8,000
August 12	6,250	@	3.48	October 9	7,250
November 20	3,750	@	3.72		
	30,000				25,000

a. Compute the ending inventory under each of the following methods:
  1. Specific identification (assume ending inventory is taken equally from the August 12 and November 20 purchases).
  2. FIFO: *(a)* Assume use of perpetual inventory procedure.
         (b) Assume use of periodic inventory procedure.

Required

  3. LIFO: *(a)* Assume use of perpetual inventory procedure.
     (b) Assume use of periodic inventory procedure.
  4. Weighted-average: *(a)* Assume use of perpetual inventory procedure.
     (b) Assume use of periodic inventory procedure.
     (Carry unit cost to four decimal places and round total cost to nearest dollar.)
b. Give the journal entries to record the individual purchases and sales (Cost of Goods Sold entry only) under the LIFO method and perpetual procedure.

SOLUTION TO DEMONSTRATION PROBLEM 7-A

a. The ending inventory is 5,000 units, calculated as follows:

	Units
Beginning inventory	6,250
Purchases	23,750
Goods available	30,000
Sales	25,000
Ending inventory	5,000

1. Ending inventory under specific identification:

Purchased	Units	Unit Cost	Total Cost
November 20	2,500	$3.72	$ 9,300
August 12	2,500	3.48	8,700
			$18,000

2. Ending inventory under FIFO:
   (a) Perpetual:

	Purchased			Sold			Balance		
Date	Units	Unit Cost	Total Cost	Units	Unit cost	Total Cost	Units	Unit Cost	Total Cost
Beg. inv.							6,250	$3.00	$18,750
Feb. 3				5,250	$3.00	$15,750	1,000	3.00	3,000
Mar. 15	5,000	$3.12	$15,600				1,000	3.00	3,000
							5,000	3.12	15,600
May 4				1,000	3.00	3,000			
				3,500	3.12	10,920	1,500	3.12	4,680
May 10	8,750	3.30	28,875				1,500	3.12	4,680
							8,750	3.30	28,875
Aug. 12	6,250	3.48	21,750				1,500	3.12	4,680
							8,750	3.30	28,875
							6,250	3.48	21,750
Sept. 16				1,500	3.12	4,680			
				6,500	3.30	21,450	2,250	3.30	7,425
							6,250	3.48	21,750
Oct. 9				2,250	3.30	7,425			
				5,000	3.48	17,400	1,250	3.48	4,350
Nov. 20	3,750	3.72	13,950				1,250	3.48	4,350
							3,750	3.72	13,950

Ending inventory = (1,250 × $3.48) + (3,750 × $3.72) = $18,300

   (b) Periodic:

Purchased	Units	Unit Cost	Total Cost
November 20	3,750	$3.72	$13,950
August 12	1,250	3.48	4,350
	5,000		$18,300*

*Note that the cost of ending inventory is the same as under perpetual.

3. Ending inventory under LIFO:
   (a) Perpetual:

Date	Purchased			Sold			Balance		
	Units	Unit Cost	Total Cost	Units	Unit Cost	Total Cost	Units	Unit Cost	Total Cost
Beg. inv.							6,250	$3.00	$18,750
Feb. 3				5,250	$3.00	$15,750	1,000	3.00	3,000
Mar. 15	5,000	$3.12	$15,600				1,000	3.00	3,000
							5,000	3.12	15,600
May 4				4,500	3.12	14,040	1,000	3.00	3,000
							500	3.12	1,560
May 10	8,750	3.30	28,875				1,000	3.00	3,000
							500	3.12	1,560
							8,750	3.30	28,875
Aug. 12	6,250	3.48	21,750				1,000	3.00	3,000
							500	3.12	1,560
							8,750	3.30	28,875
							6,250	3.48	21,750
Sept. 16				6,250	3.48	21,750			
				1,750	3.30	5,775	1,000	3.00	3,000
							500	3.12	1,560
							7,000	3.30	23,100
Oct. 9				7,000	3.30	23,100			
				250	3.12	780	1,000	3.00	3,000
							250	3.12	780
Nov. 20	3,750	3.72	13,950				1,000	3.00	3,000
							250	3.12	780
							3,750	3.72	13,950

Ending inventory = (1,000 × $3.00) + (250 × $3.12) + (3,750 × $3.72) = $17,730

   (b) Periodic:

	Units	Unit Cost	Total Cost
Merchandise inventory, January 1	5,000	$3.00	$15,000

4. Ending inventory under weighted-average:
   (a) Perpetual:

Date	Purchased			Sold			Balance		
	Units	Unit Cost	Total Cost	Units	Unit Cost	Total Cost	Units	Unit Cost	Total Cost
Beg. inv.							6,250	$3.0000	$18,750
Feb. 3				5,250	$3.00	$15,750	1,000	3.0000	3,000
Mar. 15	5,000	$3.12	$15,600				6,000	3.1000[a]	18,600
May 4				4,500	3.10	13,950	1,500	3.1000	4,650
May 10	8,750	3.30	28,875				10,250	3.2707[b]	33,525
Aug. 12	6,250	3.48	21,750				16,500	3.3500[c]	55,275
Sept. 16				8,000	3.3500	26,800	8,500	3.3500	28,475*
Oct. 9				7,250	3.3500	24,288	1,250	3.3500	4,187*
Nov. 20	3,750	3.72	13,950				5,000	3.6274[d]	18,137

Ending inventory = (5,000 × $3.6274) = $18,137

[a]$\dfrac{\$18,600}{6,000} = \$3.1000.$ [b]$\dfrac{\$33,525}{10,250} = \$3.2707.$ [c]$\dfrac{\$55,275}{16,500} = \$3.3500.$ [d]$\dfrac{\$18,137}{5,000} = \$3.6274.$

*Rounding difference.

(b) Periodic:

Purchased	Units	Unit Cost	Total Cost
Merchandise inventory, January 1	6,250	$3.00	$18,750
March 15	5,000	3.12	15,600
May 10	8,750	3.30	28,875
August 12	6,250	3.48	21,750
November 20	3,750	3.72	13,950
	30,000		$98,925

Weighted-average unit cost = $98,925 ÷ 30,000 = $3.2975
Ending inventory cost = $3.2975 × 5,000 = $16,488*

*Rounding difference.

b. Journal entries under LIFO perpetual:

Feb.	3	Cost of Goods Sold	15,750	
		Merchandise Inventory		15,750
		To record cost of $3 on 5,250 units sold.		
Mar.	15	Merchandise Inventory	15,600	
		Accounts Payable.		15,600
		To record purchase of 5,000 units at $3.12 on account.		
May	4	Cost of Goods Sold	14,040	
		Merchandise Inventory		14,040
		To record cost of $3.12 on 4,500 units sold.		
	10	Merchandise Inventory	28,875	
		Accounts Payable.		28,875
		To record purchase of 8,750 units at $3.30 on account.		
Aug.	12	Merchandise Inventory	21,750	
		Accounts Payable.		21,750
		To record purchase of 6,250 units at $3.48 on account.		
Sept.	16	Cost of Goods Sold	27,525	
		Merchandise Inventory		27,525
		To record costs of $3.48 and $3.30 on 6,250 units and 1,750 units sold, respectively.		
Oct.	9	Cost of Goods Sold	23,880	
		Merchandise Inventory		23,880
		To record costs of $3.30 and $3.12 on 7,000 units and 250 units sold, respectively.		
Nov.	20	Merchandise Inventory	13,950	
		Accounts Payable.		13,950
		To record purchase of 3,750 units at $3.72 on account.		

DEMONSTRATION PROBLEM 7–B

a. Joel Company reported annual net income as follows:

1996	$27,200
1997	28,400
1998	24,000

Analysis of the inventories shows that certain clerical errors were made with the following results:

	Incorrect Inventory Amount	Correct Inventory Amount
December 31, 1996	$4,800	$5,680
December 31, 1997	5,600	4,680

Required What is the corrected net income for 1996, 1997, and 1998?

b. The records of Little Corporation show the following account balances on the day a fire destroyed the company's inventory:

Merchandise inventory, January 1	$ 40,000
Net cost of purchases (to date)	200,000
Sales (to date)	300,000
Average rate of gross margin for the past five years	30% of net sales

Compute an estimated value of the ending inventory using the gross margin method.   *Required*

c. The records of Draper Company show the following account balances at year-end:

	Cost	Retail
Merchandise inventory, January 1	$17,600	$ 25,000
Purchases	68,000	100,000
Transportation-in	1,900	
Sales		101,000

Compute the estimated ending inventory at cost using the retail inventory method.   *Required*

SOLUTION TO DEMONSTRATION PROBLEM 7–B

a. Corrected net income:

	1996	1997	1998	Total
Net income as reported	$27,200	$28,400	$24,000	$79,600
Adjustments:				
(1)	880			
(2)		(880)		
		(920)		
(3)			920	
Corrected net income	$28,080	$26,600	$24,920	$79,600

(1) Ending inventory understated ($5,680 − $4,800 = $880).
(2) Beginning inventory understated ($5,680 − $4,800 = $880).
     Ending inventory overstated ($5,600 − $4,680 = $920).
(3) Beginning inventory overstated ($5,600 − $4,680 = $920).

b. Computation of inventory:

Merchandise inventory, January 1		$ 40,000
Net cost of purchases		200,000
Cost of goods available for sale		$240,000
Less estimated cost of goods sold:		
Net sales	$300,000	
Gross margin ($300,000 × 0.30)	90,000	
Estimated cost of goods sold		210,000
Inventory at cost, estimated by gross margin method		$ 30,000

c. Computation of inventory:

	Cost	Retail
Merchandise inventory, January 1	$17,600	$ 25,000
Purchases	68,000	100,000
Transportation-in	1,900	—
Goods available for sale	$87,500	$125,000
Cost/retail price ratio:		
$87,500/$125,000 = 70%		
Sales		101,000
Ending inventory at retail price		$ 24,000
Times cost/retail price ratio		× 70%
Ending inventory at cost, December 31	$16,800	

NEW TERMS

FIFO (first-in, first-out)   A method of costing inventory that assumes the costs of the first goods purchased are those charged to cost of goods sold when the company actually sells goods.   *256*

Gross margin method   A procedure for estimating inventory cost in which estimated cost of goods sold (determined using an estimated gross margin) is deducted from the cost of goods available for sale to determine estimated ending inventory. The estimated gross margin is calculated using gross margin rates (in relation to net sales) of prior periods.   *269*

Inventory, or paper, profits   Equal to the current replacement cost to purchase a unit of inventory at time of sale minus the unit's historical cost.   *262*

Inventory turnover ratio   Cost of goods sold ÷ Average inventory.   *271*

LIFO (last-in, first-out)   A method of costing inventory that assumes the costs of the most recent purchases are the first costs charged to cost of goods sold when the company actually sells the goods.   *257*

Lower-of-cost-or-market (LCM) method   An inventory costing method that values inventory at the lower of its

historical cost or its current market (replacement) cost.   *267*

Merchandise inventory   The quantity of goods held by a merchandising company for resale to customers.   *247*

Net realizable value   Estimated selling price of an item less the estimated costs incurred in preparing the item for sale and selling it.   *267*

Retail inventory method   A procedure for estimating the cost of the ending inventory by applying a cost/retail price ratio to ending inventory stated at retail prices.   *269*

Specific identification method   An inventory costing method that attaches the actual cost to an identifiable unit of product.   *255*

Weighted-average method   A method of costing ending inventory using a weighted-average unit cost. Under perpetual inventory procedure, a new weighted-average is calculated after each purchase. Under periodic procedure, the weighted-average is determined by dividing the total number of units purchased plus those in beginning inventory into total cost of goods available for sale. Units in the ending inventory are carried at this per unit cost.   *258*

SELF-TEST

TRUE-FALSE

Indicate whether each of the following statements is true or false.

1. Overstated ending inventory results in an overstatement of cost of goods sold and an understatement of gross margin and net income.

2. In a period of rising prices, FIFO results in the lowest cost of goods sold.

3. Under LCM, inventory is written down to market value when the market value is less than the cost, and inventory is written up to market value when the market value is greater than the cost.

4. Under the gross margin method, an estimate must be made of gross margin to determine estimated cost of goods sold and estimated ending inventory.

5. To use the retail inventory method, both cost and retail prices must be known for the goods available for sale.

6. Under perpetual procedure, cost of goods sold is determined as a result of the closing entries made at the end of the period.

MULTIPLE-CHOICE

Select the best answer for each of the following questions.

On July 1, 1999, Jack Company began the accounting period with inventory of 3,000 units at $30 each. During the period, the company purchased an additional 5,000 units at $36 each and sold 4,600 units. Assume the use of periodic inventory procedure for Questions 1–6.

1. Cost of ending inventory using FIFO is:
    a. $104,400.
    b. $122,400.
    c. $120,000.
    d. $147,600.
    e. None of the above.

2. Cost of goods sold using FIFO is:
    a. $165,600.
    b. $150,000.

    c. $147,600.
    d. $122,400.
    e. None of the above.

3. Cost of ending inventory using LIFO is:
    a. $104,400.
    b. $114,750.
    c. $156,000.
    d. $122,400.
    e. None of the above.

4. Cost of goods sold using LIFO is:
    a. $155,250.
    b. $114,000.
    c. $147,600.
    d. $165,600.
    e. None of the above.

5. Cost of ending inventory using weighted-average is:
   a. $114,750.
   b. $157,600.
   c. $122,400.
   d. $109,650.
   e. None of the above.

6. Cost of goods sold using weighted-average is:
   a. $147,200.
   b. $160,350.
   c. $155,250.
   d. $114,000.
   e. None of the above.

7. During a period of rising prices, which inventory method might be expected to give the highest net income?
   a. Weighted-average.
   b. FIFO.
   c. LIFO.
   d. Specific identification.
   e. Cannot determine.

Now turn to page 290 to check your answers.

QUESTIONS

1. Why is proper inventory valuation so important?
2. Why does an understated ending inventory understate net income for the period by the same amount?
3. Why does an error in ending inventory affect two accounting periods?
4. What is the meaning of taking a physical inventory?
5. What is the accountant's responsibility regarding taking a physical inventory?
6. Which cost elements are included in inventory? What practical problems arise by including the costs of such elements?
7. Which accounts that are used under periodic inventory procedure are not used under perpetual inventory procedure?
8. What entries are necessary under perpetual inventory procedure when goods are sold?
9. Why is there closer control over inventory under perpetual inventory procedure than under periodic inventory procedure?
10. Why is perpetual inventory procedure being used increasingly in business?
11. What is the cost flow assumption? What is meant by the physical flow of goods? Does a relationship between cost flows and the physical flow of goods exist, or should such a relationship exist?
12. Indicate how a company can manipulate its net income if it uses LIFO. Is the same opportunity available under FIFO? Why or why not?
13. What are the main advantages of using FIFO and LIFO?
14. Which inventory method is the correct one? Can a company change inventory methods?
15. Why are ending inventory and cost of goods sold the same under FIFO perpetual and FIFO periodic?
16. Would you agree with the following statement? Reducing the amount of taxes payable currently is a valid objective of business management and, since LIFO results in such a reduction, all businesses should use LIFO.
17. What is net realizable value, and how is it used?
18. Why is it acceptable accounting practice to recognize a loss by writing down an item in inventory to market, but unacceptable to recognize a gain by writing up an inventory item?
19. Under what conditions would the gross margin method of computing an estimated inventory yield approximately correct amounts?
20. What are the main reasons for estimating ending inventory?
21. Should a company rely exclusively on the gross margin method to determine the ending inventory and cost of goods sold for the end-of-year financial statements?
22. How can the retail method be used to estimate inventory?

MAYTAG

23. **Real World Question** Based on the notes to the financial statements of Maytag Corporation contained in the annual report booklet, what inventory methods were used?

THE LIMITED, INC.

24. **Real World Question** Based on the notes to the financial statements of The Limited, Inc., contained in the annual report booklet, what inventory methods were used?

HARLAND

25. **Real World Question** Based on the notes to the financial statements of John H. Harland Company contained in the annual report booklet, what inventory methods were used?

EXERCISES

Crocker Company reported annual net income as follows:

1997	$484,480
1998	487,680
1999	409,984

Exercise 7–1
Determine effects of inventory errors (L.O. 1)

Analysis of its inventories revealed the following incorrect inventory amounts and these correct amounts:

	Incorrect Inventory Amount	Correct Inventory Amount
December 31, 1997	$76,800	$89,600
December 31, 1998	86,400	77,600

Compute the annual net income for each of the three years assuming the correct inventories had been used.

Exercise 7–2
Compute the impact on net income under specific identification (L.O. 3, 4)

Slate Truck Company manufactures trucks and identifies each truck with a unique serial plate. On December 31, a customer ordered 5 trucks from the company, which currently has 20 trucks in its inventory. Ten of these trucks cost $20,000 each, and the other 10 cost $25,000 each. If Slate wished to minimize its net income, which trucks would it ship? By how much could Slate reduce net income by selecting units from one group versus the other group?

Exercise 7–3
Compute ending inventory using FIFO perpetual inventory procedure (L.O. 3)

Miami Discount Company inventory records show:

	Units	Unit Cost	Total Cost
Beginning inventory . . .	3,000	$38.00	$114,000
Purchases:			
February 14	900	39.00	35,100
March 18	2,400	40.00	96,000
July 21	1,800	40.30	72,540
September 27	1,800	40.60	73,080
November 27	600	41.00	24,600
Sales:			
April 15	2,800		
August 20	2,000		
October 3	1,500		

The December 31 inventory was 4,200 units. Miami Discount Company uses perpetual inventory procedure. Present a schedule showing the measurement of the ending inventory using FIFO perpetual inventory procedure.

Exercise 7–4
Compute ending inventory under LIFO perpetual inventory procedure (L.O. 3)

Using the data in Exercise 7–3 for Miami Discount Company, present a schedule showing the measurement of the ending inventory using LIFO perpetual inventory procedure.

Exercise 7–5
Compute ending inventory under weighted-average perpetual inventory procedure (L.O. 3)

London Company had a beginning inventory of 160 units at $24 (total = $3,840) and the following inventory transactions during 1998:

1. January 8, sold 40 units.
2. January 11, purchased 80 units at $30.00.
3. January 15, purchased 80 units at $32.00.
4. January 22, sold 80 units.

Using the preceding information, price the ending inventory at its weighted-average cost, assuming perpetual inventory procedure.

Exercise 7–6
Compute cost of ending inventory using FIFO, LIFO, and weighted-average under periodic inventory procedure (L.O. 3)

Kettle Company made the following purchases of Product A in its first year of operations:

	Units	Unit Cost
January 2	1,400 @	$7.40
March 31	1,200 @	7.00
July 5	2,400 @	7.60
November 1	1,800 @	8.00

The ending inventory that year consisted of 2,400 units. Kettle uses periodic inventory procedure.

a. Compute the cost of the ending inventory using each of the following methods:
   (1) FIFO, (2) LIFO, and (3) weighted-average.

b. Which method would yield the highest amount of gross margin? Explain why it does.

The following are selected transactions and other data of the Custer Company:

1. Purchased 20 units @ $360 per unit on account on September 18, 1999.
2. Sold 6 units on account for $576 per unit on September 20, 1999.
3. Discovered a shortage of $2,640 at year-end after a physical inventory.

Prepare journal entries for these transactions using FIFO perpetual inventory procedure. Assume the beginning inventory consists of 20 units @ $336 per unit.

Exercise 7–7
Prepare journal entries for inventory under FIFO perpetual inventory procedure (L.O. 3, 5)

Following are selected transactions of Gamble Company:

1. Purchased 100 units of merchandise at $240 each; terms 2/10, n/30.
2. Paid the invoice in transaction 1 within the discount period.
3. Sold 80 units at $384 each for cash.
4. Purchased 100 units at $360; terms 2/10, n/30.
5. Paid the invoice in transaction 4 within the discount period.
6. Sold 60 units at $552 each for cash.

Prepare journal entries for the six preceding items. Assume Gamble uses FIFO perpetual inventory procedure.

Exercise 7–8
Prepare journal entries under FIFO perpetual inventory procedure (L.O. 3, 5)

Wells Company had the following transactions during February:

1. Purchased 135 units at $65 on account.
2. Sold 108 units at $90 on account.
3. Purchased 170 units at $75 on account.
4. Sold 122 units at $95 on account.
5. Sold 67 units at $100 on account.

The beginning inventory consisted of 67 units purchased at a cost of $55.

Prepare the journal entries relating to inventory for these five transactions, assuming Wells accounts for inventory using perpetual inventory procedure and the LIFO inventory method. Do not record the entries for sales.

Exercise 7–9
Prepare journal entries affecting inventory using LIFO perpetual inventory procedure (L.O. 3, 5)

Following are inventory data for 1999 for Kintech Company:

1. January 1 inventory on hand, 400 units @ $28.80.
2. January sales were 80 units.
3. February sales totaled 120 units.
4. March 1, purchased 200 units @ $30.24.
5. Sales for March through August were 160 units.
6. September 1, purchased 40 units @ $33.12.
7. September through December sales were 180 units.

A physical inventory on December 31, 1999, showed 100 units on hand. Determine the cost of the ending inventory using the weighted-average method under periodic inventory procedure.

Exercise 7–10
Prepare journal entries affecting inventory using weighted-average periodic inventory procedure (L.O. 3)

A company purchased 1,000 units of a product at $12.00 and 2,000 units at $13.20. It sold all of these units at $18.00 each at a time when the current cost to replace the units sold was $13.80. Compute the amount of gross margin under FIFO that LIFO supporters would call inventory, or paper, profits.

Exercise 7–11
Compute inventory (paper) profit under FIFO (L.O. 3, 4)

Clayton Company's inventory was 12,000 units with a cost of $160 each on January 1, 1999. During 1999, numerous units were purchased and sold. Also during 1999, the purchase price of this product fell steadily until at year-end it was $120. The inventory at year-end was 18,000 units. State which method of inventory measurement, LIFO or FIFO, would have resulted in higher reported net income, and explain briefly.

Exercise 7–12
Indicate whether FIFO or LIFO would yield the higher net income (L.O. 3, 4)

Levi Motor Company owns a luxury automobile that it has used as a demonstrator for eight months. The auto has a list or sticker price of $85,000 and cost Levi $75,000. At the end of the fiscal year, the auto is on hand and has an expected selling price of $80,000. Costs expected to be incurred to sell the auto include tune-up and maintenance costs of $3,000, advertising of

Exercise 7–13
Using net realizable value, compute carrying cost of inventory item (L.O. 6)

$1,000, and a commission of 5% of selling price to the employee selling the auto. Compute the amount at which the auto should be carried in inventory.

Exercise 7–14
Determine the proper carrying value of damaged goods (L.O. 6)

Pure Sound Systems used one sound system as a floor model. It cost $3,600 and had an original selling price of $4,800. After six months, the sound system was damaged and replaced by a newer model. The sound system had an estimated selling price of $2,880, but when the company performed $480 in repairs, it could be sold for $3,840. Prepare the journal entry, if any, that must be made on Pure Sound's books to record the decline in market value.

Exercise 7–15
Compute value of ending inventory using LCM applied on an item-by-item basis (L.O. 6)

Your assistant has compiled the following data:

Item	Quantity (units)	Unit Cost	Unit Market	Total Cost	Total Market
A	300	$57.60	$55.20	$17,280	$16,560
B	300	28.80	33.60	8,640	10,080
C	900	21.60	21.60	19,440	19,440
D	500	12.00	13.20	6,000	6,600

Calculate the dollar amount of the ending inventory using the LCM method, applied on an item-by-item basis, and the amount of the decline from cost to lower-of-cost-or-market.

Exercise 7–16
Compute value of total inventory using LCM (L.O. 6)

Use the data in Exercise 7–15 to compute the cost of the ending inventory using the LCM method applied to the total inventory.

Exercise 7–17
Estimate ending inventory using gross margin method (L.O. 7)

Tilley-Mill Company takes a physical inventory at the end of each calendar-year accounting period to establish the ending inventory amount for financial statement purposes. Its financial statements for the past few years indicate an average gross margin on net sales of 25%. On July 18, a fire destroyed the entire store building and its contents. The records in a fireproof vault were intact. Through July 17, these records show:

Merchandise inventory, January 1	$ 672,000
Merchandise purchases	9,408,000
Purchase returns	134,400
Transportation-in	504,000
Sales	14,336,000
Sales returns	672,000

The company was fully covered by insurance and asks you to determine the amount of its claim for loss of merchandise.

Exercise 7–18
Estimate ending inventory using gross margin method (L.O. 7)

Ryan Company takes a physical inventory at the end of each calendar-year accounting period. Its financial statements for the past few years indicate an average gross margin on net sales of 30%.

On June 12, a fire destroyed the entire store building and the inventory. The records in a fireproof vault were intact. Through June 11, these records show:

Merchandise inventory, January 1	$ 120,000
Merchandise purchases	3,000,000
Purchase returns	36,000
Transportation-in	204,000
Sales	3,720,000

The company was fully covered by insurance and asks you to determine the amount of its claim for loss of merchandise.

Exercise 7–19
Estimate ending inventory using retail inventory method (L.O. 7)

Victoria Falls Company, Inc., records show the following account balances for the year ending December 31, 1999:

	Cost	Retail
Beginning inventory	$42,000	$57,500
Purchases	25,000	37,500
Transportation-in	500	
Sales		52,500

Using these data, compute the estimated cost of ending inventory using the retail method of inventory valuation.

PROBLEMS

Harris Company reported net income of $312,000 for 1998, $324,000 for 1999, and $348,000 for 2000, using the incorrect inventory amounts shown for December 31, 1998, and 1999. Recently Harris corrected these inventory amounts. Harris used the correct December 31, 2000, inventory amount in calculating 2000 net income.

Problem 7–1
Compute corrected net income given inventory errors (L.O. 1)

	Incorrect	Correct
December 31, 1998	$96,000	$108,000
December 31, 1999	91,200	84,000

Prepare a schedule that shows: *(a)* the reported net income for each year, *(b)* the amount of correction needed for each year, and *(c)* the correct net income for each year.

Required

An examination of the financial records of Jersey Company on December 31, 1998, disclosed the following with regard to merchandise inventory for 1998 and prior years:

Problem 7–2
Compute corrected net income given inventory errors; indicate balance sheet errors and comment (L.O. 1)

1. December 31, 1994, inventory was correct.
2. December 31, 1995, inventory was understated $50,000.
3. December 31, 1996, inventory was overstated $35,000.
4. December 31, 1997, inventory was understated $30,000.
5. December 31, 1998, inventory was correct.

The reported net income for each year was:

1995	$292,500
1996	355,000
1997	382,500
1998	350,000

a. Prepare a schedule of corrected net income for each of the four years—1995–1998.
b. What errors would have been included in each December 31 balance sheet? Assume each year's error is independent of the other years' errors.
c. Comment on the implications of the corrected net income as contrasted with reported net income.

Required

High Surf Company sells the Ultra-Light model wind surfer and uses the specific identification method to account for its inventory. The Ultra-Lights are identical except for identifying serial numbers. On August 1, 1998, the company had three Ultra-Lights that cost $14,000 each in its inventory. During the month, the company purchased the following:

Problem 7–3
Maximize and minimize gross margin using specific identification (L.O. 3, 4)

	Units	Unit Cost
August 3	5	@ $13,000
August 17	6	@ 14,500
August 28	6	@ 15,000

High Surf Company sold 13 Ultra-Lights in August at $20,000 each.

a. Compute the gross margin earned by the company in August if it shipped the units that would maximize gross margin.
b. Repeat part **a** assuming the company shipped the units that would minimize gross margin.
c. Do you think High Surf Company should be permitted to use the specific identification method of accounting for Ultra-Lights in view of the manipulation possible as shown by your calculations in **a** and **b**?

Required

The inventory records of Coral Company show the following:

Problem 7–4
Compute cost of goods sold using FIFO for both perpetual and periodic inventory procedures (L.O. 3, 5)

Jan.	1	Beginning inventory consists of 12 units costing $48 per unit.
	5	Purchased 15 units @ $49.92 per unit.
	10	Sold 9 units @ $108 per unit.
	12	Sold 7 units @ $108 per unit.
	20	Purchased 20 units @ $50.16 per unit.
	22	Purchased 5 units @ $48 per unit.
	30	Sold 20 units @ $110.40 per unit.

Assume all purchases and sales are made on account.

Required

a. Using FIFO perpetual inventory procedure, compute cost of goods sold for January.

b. Using FIFO perpetual inventory procedure, prepare the journal entries for January.

c. Compute the cost of goods sold under FIFO periodic inventory procedure. Is there a difference between the amount computed using the two different procedures?

Problem 7–5
Compute ending inventory under FIFO, LIFO, and weighted-average using perpetual and periodic inventory procedures (L.O. 3)

Following are data for Dandy Company for the year 1999:

	Units	Unit Cost
Merchandise inventory, January 1	700 @	$20.40
Purchases:		
February 2	500 @	21.00
April 5	1,000 @	24.00
June 15	600 @	27.00
September 30	700 @	30.00
November 28	900 @	31.20
	4,400	
Sales:		
March 5	400	
July 18	1,200	
August 12	800	
October 15	900	
	3,300	

Required

a. Compute the ending inventory as of December 31, 1999, assuming use of perpetual inventory procedure, under each of the following methods: (1) FIFO, (2) LIFO, and (3) weighted-average (carry unit cost to four decimal places and round total cost to nearest dollar).

b. Compute the ending inventory as of December 31, 1999, assuming use of periodic inventory procedure, under each of the following methods: (1) FIFO, (2) LIFO, and (3) weighted-average.

Problem 7–6
Record journal entries for purchases and sales under FIFO perpetual and periodic inventory procedures (L.O. 5)

Refer to the data in Problem 7–5.

Required

a. Give the journal entries to record the purchases and sales (Cost of Goods Sold entry only) for the year under FIFO perpetual.

b. Give the journal entries to record the purchases for the year and necessary year-end entries to charge Income Summary with the cost of goods sold for the year under FIFO periodic. (Note: You may want to refer to the Appendix in Chapter 6 for this part.)

Problem 7–7
Compute ending inventory and cost of goods sold under FIFO, LIFO, and weighted-average using perpetual and periodic inventory procedures (L.O. 3)

Following are data related to a product of Coen Company for the year 1999:

	Units	Unit Cost
Merchandise inventory, January 1	2,100 @	$12.60
Purchases:		
March 10	1,500 @	12.00
May 24	3,000 @	11.20
July 15	1,800 @	10.50
September 20	2,100 @	9.00
December 1	2,700 @	10.00
Sales:		
April 5	1,400	
June 13	2,900	
October 9	2,300	
November 21	1,700	

a. Assuming use of perpetual inventory procedure, compute the ending inventory and cost of goods sold under each of the following methods: (1) FIFO, (2) LIFO, and (3) weighted-average (carry unit cost to four decimal places and round total cost to nearest dollar).

b. Assuming use of periodic inventory procedure, compute the ending inventory and cost of goods sold under each of the following methods: (1) FIFO, (2), LIFO, and (3) weighted-average (carry unit cost to four decimal places and round total cost to nearest dollar).

Required

Star Company accounts for its inventory using the LIFO method under periodic inventory procedure. Data on purchases, sales, and inventory for the year ended December 31, 1998, are:

Problem 7–8
Compute gross margin using FIFO and LIFO illustrating effects of end-of-year purchases (L.O. 3, 4)

	Units	Unit Cost
Merchandise inventory, January 1	2,000 @	$20
Purchases:		
January 7	5,000 @	24
July 7	10,000 @	28
December 21	6,000 @	32

During 1998, 16,000 units were sold for $1,280,000, leaving an inventory on December 31, 1998, of 7,000 units.

a. Compute the gross margin earned on sales during 1998.

b. Compute the change in gross margin that would have resulted if the purchase of December 21 had been delayed until January 6, 1999.

c. Recompute the gross margin assuming that 9,000 units rather than 6,000 units were purchased on December 21 at the same cost per unit.

d. Solve parts **a, b,** and **c** using the FIFO method.

Required

Data on the ending inventory of Jannis Company on December 31, 1998, are:

Problem 7–9
Compute ending inventory using LCM (L.O. 6)

Item	Quantity	Unit Cost	Unit Market
1	8,400	$3.20	$3.12
2	16,800	2.88	3.04
3	5,600	2.80	2.88
4	14,000	3.84	3.60
5	11,200	3.60	3.68
6	2,800	3.04	2.88

a. Compute the ending inventory applying the LCM method to the total inventory.

b. Determine the ending inventory by applying the LCM method on an item-by-item basis.

Required

The sales and cost of goods sold for Lively Company for the past five years were as follows:

Problem 7–10
Estimate inventory using gross margin method (L.O. 7)

Year	Sales (net)	Cost of Goods Sold
1993	$ 9,984,960	$6,240,600
1994	10,794,240	6,746,400
1995	12,346,560	7,716,600
1996	11,926,080	7,272,000
1997	12,747,840	7,920,000

The following information is for the seven months ended July 31, 1998:

Sales	$7,748,000
Purchases	4,588,800
Purchase returns	28,800
Sales returns	173,760
Merchandise inventory, January 1, 1999	948,000

To secure a loan, Lively Company has been asked to present current financial statements. However, the company does not wish to take a complete physical inventory as of July 31, 1998.

Required   a.   Indicate how financial statements can be prepared without taking a complete physical inventory.

b.   From the data given, compute the estimated inventory as of July 31, 1999.

Problem 7–11
Estimate ending inventory using retail inventory method (L.O. 7)

Apple Company's records contained the following inventory information for 1997:

	Cost	Retail
Sales	—	$420,000
Purchases	$396,000	582,000
Purchase returns	8,400	12,000
Transportation-in	10,800	—
Merchandise inventory,		
January 1	21,600	30,000

Required   Compute the estimated year-end inventory balance at cost using the retail method of inventory valuation.

ALTERNATE PROBLEMS

Problem 7–1A
Compute corrected net income given inventory errors (L.O. 1)

Kelley Company reported net income of $358,050 for 1998, $371,400 for 1999, and $325,800 for 2000, using the incorrect inventory amounts shown for December 31, 1998, and 1999. Recently, Kelley corrected the inventory amounts for those dates. Kelley used the correct December 31, 2000, inventory amount in calculating 2000 net income.

	Incorrect	Correct
December 31, 1998	$72,600	$85,200
December 31, 1999	84,000	70,200

Required   Prepare a schedule that shows: *(a)* the reported net income for each year, *(b)* the amount of correction needed for each year, and *(c)* the correct net income for each year.

Problem 7–2A
Compute corrected net income given inventory errors; indicate balance sheet errors and comment (L.O. 1)

An examination of the financial records of Lanal Company on December 31, 1998, disclosed the following with regard to merchandise inventory for 1998 and prior years:

1.   December 31, 1994, inventory was correct.
2.   December 31, 1995, inventory was overstated $200,000.
3.   December 31, 1996, inventory was overstated $100,000.
4.   December 31, 1997, inventory was understated $220,000.
5.   December 31, 1998, inventory was correct.

The reported net income for each year was:

1995	$384,000
1996	544,000
1997	670,000
1998	846,000

Required   a.   Prepare a schedule of corrected net income for each of the four years—1995–1998.

b.   What error(s) would have been included in each December 31 balance sheet? Assume each year's error is independent of the other years' errors.

c.   Comment on the implications of your corrected net income as contrasted with reported net income.

Problem 7–3A
Maximize and minimize gross margin using specific identification (L.O. 3, 4)

Brett Company sells minicomputers and uses the specific identification method to account for its inventory. On November 30, 1999, the company had 46 Orange III minicomputers on hand that were acquired on the following dates and at these stated costs:

	Units	Unit Cost
July 3	10	@ $10,080
September 10	20	@ 9,600
November 29	16	@ 10,700

Brett sold 36 Orange III computers at $12,720 each in December. There were no purchases of this model in December.

Required   a.   Compute the gross margin on December sales of Orange III computers assuming the company shipped those units that would maximize reported gross margin.

b. Repeat part **a** assuming the company shipped those units that would minimize reported gross margin for December.

c. In view of your answers to parts **a** and **b,** what would be your reaction to an assertion that the specific identification method should not be considered an acceptable method for costing inventory?

The inventory records of Thimble Company show the following:

Mar. 1 Beginning inventory consists of 10 units costing $40 per unit.
3 Sold 5 units at $94 per unit.
10 Purchased 16 units at $48 per unit.
12 Sold 8 units at $96 per unit.
20 Sold 7 units at $96 per unit.
25 Purchased 16 units at $50 per unit.
31 Sold 8 units at $96 per unit.

Assume all purchases and sales are made on credit.

Using FIFO perpetual inventory procedure, prepare the appropriate journal entries for March.

Problem 7–4A
Prepare journal entries for purchases and sales using FIFO perpetual inventory procedure (L.O. 3, 5)

Required

The following purchases and sales for Ripple Company are for April 1999. There was no inventory on April 1.

Problem 7–5A
Compute ending inventory under FIFO, LIFO, and weighted-average using perpetual and periodic inventory procedures (L.O. 3)

Purchases			Sales	
	Units	**Unit Cost**		**Units**
April 3	3,200 @	$33.00	April 6	1,500
April 10	1,600 @	34.00	April 12	1,400
April 22	2,000 @	35.00	April 25	2,300
April 28	1,800 @	36.00		

a. Compute the ending inventory as of April 30, 1998, using perpetual inventory procedure, under each of the following methods: (1) FIFO, (2) LIFO, and (3) weighted-average (carry unit cost to four decimal places and round total cost to nearest dollar).

b. Repeat **a** using periodic inventory procedure.

Required

Refer to the data in Problem 7–5A.

Problem 7–6A
Prepare journal entries for purchases and sales using LIFO perpetual and periodic inventory procedures (L.O. 5)

Required

a. Using LIFO perpetual inventory procedure, prepare the journal entries for the purchases and sales (Cost of Goods Sold entry only).

b. Repeat **a** using LIFO periodic inventory procedure, including closing entries. (Note: You may want to refer to the Appendix in Chapter 6 for this part.)

The following data relate to the beginning inventory, purchases, and sales of Braxton Company for the year 1999:

Problem 7–7A
Compute ending inventory and cost of goods sold under FIFO, LIFO, and weighted-average using perpetual and periodic inventory procedures (L.O. 3)

	Units	**Unit Cost**
Merchandise inventory,		
January 1	1,400 @	$5.04
Purchases:		
February 2	1,000 @	4.80
April 5	2,000 @	3.60
June 15	1,200 @	3.00
September 30	1,400 @	2.88
November 28	1,800 @	4.20
Sales:		
March 10	900	
May 15	1,800	
July 6	800	
August 23	600	
December 22	2,500	

Required   a. Assuming use of perpetual inventory procedure, compute the ending inventory and cost of goods sold under each of the following methods: (1) FIFO, (2) LIFO, and (3) weighted-average (carry unit cost to four decimal places and round total cost to nearest dollar).

b. Repeat **a** assuming use of periodic inventory procedure.

Problem 7–8A
Compute gross margin using LIFO and FIFO illustrating effects of end-of-year purchases (L.O. 3, 4)

Welch Company accounts for a product it sells using LIFO periodic inventory procedure. Product data for the year ended December 31, 1998, follow. Merchandise inventory on January 1 was 3,000 units at $14.40 each.

Purchases			**Sales**		
	Units	**Unit Cost**		**Units**	**Unit Cost**
January 5	6,000 @	$18.00	January 10	4,000 @	$28.80
March 31	18,000 @	21.60	April 2	15,000 @	32.40
August 12	12,000 @	27.00	August 22	16,000 @	36.00
December 26	6,000 @	28.80	December 24	3,000 @	39.60

Required   a. Compute the gross margin earned on sales of this product for 1998.

b. Repeat part **a** assuming that the December 26 purchase was made in January of 1999.

c. Recompute the gross margin assuming that 10,000 rather than 6,000 units were purchased on December 26 at the same cost per unit.

d. Solve parts **a, b,** and **c** using the FIFO method.

Problem 7–9A
Compute ending inventory using LCM (L.O. 6)

The accountant for Gentry Company prepared the following schedule of the company's inventory at December 31, 1998, and used the LCM method applied to total inventory in determining cost of goods sold:

Item	Quantity	Unit Cost	Unit Market
Q . . .	4,200	$7.20	$7.20
R	2,400	6.00	5.76
S	5,400	4.80	4.56
T	4,800	4.20	4.32

Required   a. State whether this approach is an acceptable method of inventory measurement and show the calculations used to determine the amounts.

b. Compute the amount of the ending inventory using the LCM method on an item-by-item basis.

c. State the effect on net income in 1998 if the method in **b** was used rather than the method referred to in **a**.

Problem 7–10A
Prepare quarterly and six-month income statements using the gross margin method (L.O. 6)

As part of a loan agreement with a local bank, Brazos Company must present quarterly and cumulative income statements for the year 1998. The company uses periodic inventory procedure and marks its merchandise to sell at a price yielding a gross margin of 30%. Selected data for the first six months of 1998 are as follows:

	First Quarter	Second Quarter
Sales	$248,000	$256,000
Purchases	160,000	184,000
Purchase returns and allowances	9,600	11,200
Purchase discounts	3,200	3,520
Sales returns and allowances	8,000	4,800
Transportation-in	8,000	8,320
Miscellaneous selling expenses	25,600	24,000
Miscellaneous administrative expenses	9,600	8,000

The cost of the physical inventory taken December 31, 1997, was $30,400.

Required   a. Indicate how income statements can be prepared without taking a physical inventory at the end of each of the first two quarters of 1998.

b. Prepare income statements for the first quarter, the second quarter, and the first six months of 1998.

Cobb Company records show the following information for 1999:

	Cost	Retail
Sales	—	$350,400
Purchases	$270,000	420,000
Transportation-in	26,280	—
Merchandise inventory,		
January 1	12,000	17,400
Purchase returns	15,120	18,600

Compute the estimated year-end inventory balance at cost using the retail method of estimating inventory.

Problem 7–11A
Estimate ending inventory using retail inventory method (L.O. 7)

Required

BEYOND THE NUMBERS—CRITICAL THINKING

Two sisters, Susan Green and Carol Lewis, were interested in starting part-time business activities to supplement their family incomes. Both heard a presentation by the manufacturer of an exercise device and decided to become a distributor of this exerciser. Green's sales territory is Cobb County, and Lewis's sales territory is Gwinett County. Each owns her own business.

To induce Green and Lewis to become distributors, the manufacturer made price concessions on the first 1,000 units that each sister purchased. The manufacturer sold the first 200 units at $15 each, the next 300 at $18 per unit, and the next 500 at $19 per unit. After that, Green and Lewis had to pay $20 per unit.

During the first year, each sister bought 1,200 units; coincidentally, both sold exactly 950 units for $27 each. Green had $2,600 of selling expenses; Lewis incurred $1,700 of selling expenses. (Green's expenses were considerably higher because on December 28 she distributed 4,000 sales brochures to households in her territory at a cost of $800. The brochures stressed that people would want to take off the extra pounds gained during the holiday season; also, these exercisers were inexpensive and could be used at home.)

At the end of the year, both sisters had to determine their net incomes. Green received a B in the accounting course she took at State University. She remembered the FIFO inventory method and plans to use it. Lewis knows nothing about inventory costing methods. However, her husband is acquainted with the LIFO inventory method used at the company where he works. He will help her compute the cost of the ending inventory and the cost of goods using LIFO.

a. Prepare income statements for Green and Lewis.

b. Which sister's business has performed better? Explain why.

c. Determine the inventory turnovers for both sisters.

Business Decision Case 7–1
Prepare income statement using LIFO and FIFO. Determine inventory turnover (L.O. 3, 4, 8)

Required

Connie Dalton owns and operates a sporting goods store. On February 2, 1998, the store suffered extensive fire damage, and all of the inventory was destroyed. Dalton uses periodic inventory procedure and has the following information in her accounting records, which were undamaged:

Merchandise inventory,	
January 1	$ 80,000
Purchases:	
January 8	32,000
January 20	48,000
January 30	64,000
Net sales:	
During January	240,000
February 1 and 2	16,000

Business Decision Case 7–2
Determine insurance settlement using gross margin method (L.O. 7)

Dalton's gross margin rate on net sales has been 40% for the past three years. Her insurance company offered to pay $56,000 to settle this inventory loss unless Dalton can show that she suffered a greater loss. She has asked you, her CPA, to help her in determining her loss.

Answer these questions: Based on your analysis, should Dalton settle for $56,000? If not, how can she show that she suffered a greater loss? What is your estimate of her loss?

Required

Annual Report Analysis 7–3
Determine inventory method and inventory turnover rate (L.O. 6)

Refer to the financial statements of The Coca-Cola Company in the annual report booklet. Describe how inventory values are determined (see Footnote 1). Also, determine the inventory turnover rate for 1996.

Ethics Case—Writing Experience 7–4

Respond in writing to the following questions based on the ethics case concerning Terry Dorsey on page 271:

a. Do you believe that Terry's scheme will work?

b. What would you do if you were Terry's accountant?

c. Comment on each of Terry's points of justification.

Group Project 7–5
Inventory control and measurement—interview with manager of merchandising company

In teams of two or three students, interview the manager of a merchandising company (in person or by speakerphone). Inquire about inventory control methods, inventory costing methods, and any other information about the company's inventory procedures. As a team, write a memorandum to your instructor summarizing the results of the interview. The heading of the memorandum should include the date, to whom it is written, from whom, and the subject matter.

Group Project 7–6
Examine use of computer in inventory management

In a team of two or three students, locate and visit a nearby retail store that uses perpetual inventory procedure and a computerized inventory management system. Investigate how the system works by interviewing a knowledgeable person in the company. Write a report to your instructor and make a short presentation to the class on your findings.

Group Project 7–7
Examine use of the retail inventory method

With a small group of students, identify and visit a retail store that uses periodic inventory procedure and uses the retail inventory method for preparing interim (monthly or quarterly) financial reports. Discover how the retail inventory method is applied and how the end-of-year inventory amount is calculated. Write a report to your instructor summarizing your findings.

USING THE INTERNET—A VIEW OF THE REAL WORLD

Internet Project 7–8
Locate state boards of accountancy

Visit the National Association of State Boards of Accountancy website at:
http://www.nasba.org/stateB.htm
Find the address of the state board of accountancy in your state. Also check out some of the information provided at websites of other state boards by clicking on any sites that appear at the end of a listing for a particular state. In a report to your instructor, summarize what you learned about state boards at some of these sites.

Internet Project 7–9
Investigate the Lexis-Nexis website

Visit the Lexis-Nexis website at:
http://www.lexis-nexis.com
Determine the kinds of information that can be obtained at this site. Specifically, what kinds of products and services are available? What is the background of Lexis-Nexis? What pricing information is available for using its services? Write a report to your instructor summarizing your findings.

ANSWERS TO SELF-TEST

TRUE-FALSE

1. **False.** Overstated ending inventory results in an understatement of cost of goods sold and an overstatement of gross margin and net income.

2. **True.** The cost of goods sold consists of the earliest purchases at the lowest costs in a period of rising prices.

3.   **False.** Under LCM, inventory is adjusted to market value only when the market (replacement) value is less than the cost.

4.   **True.** The first step in the gross margin method is to estimate gross margin using the gross margin rate experienced in the past.

5.   **True.** The cost/retail ratio is computed by dividing the cost of goods available for sale by the retail price of the goods available for sale.

6.   **False.** Under perpetual procedure, the Cost of Goods Sold account is updated as sales occur.

MULTIPLE-CHOICE

1.   **b.** The cost of ending inventory using FIFO consists of the most recent purchase:

$$\text{Cost of ending inventory} = 3{,}400 \times \$36$$
$$= \$122{,}400$$

2.   **c.** The cost of goods sold using FIFO is:

$$\text{Cost of goods available for sale} = (3{,}000 \times \$30) + (5{,}000 \times \$36)$$
$$= \$270{,}000$$

$$\text{Cost of goods sold} = \$270{,}000 - \$122{,}400$$
$$= \$147{,}600$$

3.   **a.** The cost of ending inventory using LIFO is:

$$(3{,}000 \times \$30) + (400 \times \$36) = \$104{,}400$$

4.   **d.** The cost of goods sold using LIFO is:

$$\$270{,}000 - \$104{,}400 = \$165{,}600$$

5.   **a.** The cost of ending inventory using weighted-average cost is computed:

$$\text{Unit cost} = \$270{,}000 \div 8{,}000 = \$33.75$$

$$\text{Cost of ending inventory} = 3{,}400 \times \$33.75$$
$$= \$114{,}750$$

6.   **c.** The cost of goods sold using weighted-average cost is:

$$\$270{,}000 - \$114{,}750 = \$155{,}250$$

7.   **b.** During a period of rising prices, FIFO results in the lowest cost of goods sold, thus the highest net income.

III

Management's Perspectives in Accounting for Resources

A Manager's Perspective

Ann Stapinski
Staffing, Processing Project Leader
Human Resources
The Coca-Cola Company

I am responsible for staffing at The Coca-Cola Company, and I also handle special projects pertaining to general human resources activities. I have to understand basic financial information because I am often a job candidate's first impression of the company. Good candidates ask about the

company's financials and information in the annual report during the hiring process, and I need to be able to respond well to those queries in order to attract bright people to the company.

Human resources managers (or generalists) often work with managers from various other departments within the corporation to help resolve individual management issues, so they must understand the nature of each manager's business in order to be a helpful resource.

At the department level, we rely on a budget in human resources to make decisions about head count, capital expenditures, and merit increases.

Another important function in human resources is compensation planning. We evaluate current salary structures and expected economic changes to forecast salary increases and incentive pay expenses.

In every profession, accounting—budget structures and so forth—serves as a framework for evaluating business results. If you don't understand how the numbers fit together, you won't be able to understand general business principles or make sound decisions.

8

CONTROL OF CASH

In a small corporation the president might make all the important decisions and will usually maintain a close watch over the affairs of the business. However, as the business grows and the need arises for additional employees, officers, and managers, the president begins to lose absolute control. Realizing that precautions are necessary to protect the company's interests, the company establishes an internal control structure at this point.

The **internal control structure** of a company consists of "the policies and procedures established to provide reasonable assurance that specific entity objectives will be achieved."[1] The three elements of an internal control structure are the control environment, the accounting system, and the control procedures.

The **control environment** reflects the overall attitude, awareness, and actions of the board of directors, management, and stockholders. The **accounting system** consists of the methods and records that identify, assemble, analyze, classify, record, and report an entity's transactions to provide complete, accurate, and timely financial information. The **control procedures** of a company are additional policies and procedures that management establishes to provide reasonable assurance that the company achieves its specific objectives. These control procedures may pertain to proper authorization, segregation of duties, design and use of adequate documents and records, adequate safeguards over access to assets, and independent checks on performance.

Internal control not only prevents theft and fraud but also serves many purposes: (1) Companies must implement policies requiring compliance with federal law; (2) personnel must perform their assigned duties to promote efficiency of operations; and (3) correct accounting records must supply accurate and reliable information in the accounting reports.

LEARNING OBJECTIVES

After studying this chapter, you should be able to:

1. Describe the necessity for and features of internal control.

2. Define cash and list the objectives sought by management in handling a company's cash.

3. Identify procedures for controlling cash receipts and disbursements.

4. Prepare a bank reconciliation and make necessary journal entries based on that schedule.

(continued)

[1]AICPA, *Statement on Auditing Standards No. 55,* "Consideration of the Internal Control Structure in a Financial Statement Audit" (New York, 1988), p. 4. The sixth and seventh editions of this text use the terminology (internal control structure) of the AICPA. Previous editions referred to the "internal control system."

(concluded)

5. Explain why a company uses a petty cash fund, describe its operations, and make the necessary journal entries.

6. Analyze and use the financial results—quick ratio.

Objective 1
Describe the necessity for and features of internal control.

Real World Example
In a recent GAO report, 70% of the audit committees surveyed considered monitoring adherence to established codes of conduct as their primary responsibility.

This chapter discusses the internal control structure that a company establishes to protect its assets and promote the accuracy of its accounting records. You will learn how to establish internal control through control of cash receipts and cash disbursements, proper use of the bank checking account, preparation of the bank reconciliation, and protection of petty cash funds. The internal control structure is enhanced by hiring competent and trustworthy employees, a fact you will appreciate if you become a business owner.

INTERNAL CONTROL

An effective **internal control structure** includes a company's plan of organization and all the procedures and actions it takes to:

1. Protect its assets against theft and waste.
2. Ensure compliance with company policies and federal law.
3. Evaluate the performance of all personnel to promote efficient operations.
4. Ensure accurate and reliable operating data and accounting reports.

As you study the basic procedures and actions of an effective internal control structure, remember that even small companies can benefit from using some internal control measures. Preventing theft and waste is only a part of internal control.

In general terms, the purpose of internal control is to ensure the efficient operations of a business, thus enabling the business to effectively reach its goals. Since additional control procedures are necessary in a computer environment, a discussion of these controls concludes this section on internal control.

AN ACCOUNTING PERSPECTIVE

BUSINESS INSIGHT   When performing an audit, one of an outside auditor's first duties is to examine the internal control structure of the corporation. To understand the internal control structure, an auditor focuses mainly on management's attitude and awareness concerning controls and the accounting system's processing of transactions. To increase understanding, the auditor inspects documents in the accounting system, discusses external influences on the company with management, reads accounting manuals, and observes the happenings in the company. This understanding of the company's control environment helps the auditor to plan the audit and to determine the nature, timing, and extent of tests of account balances.

Protection of Assets

Companies protect their assets by (1) segregating employee duties, (2) assigning specific duties to each employee, (3) rotating employee job assignments, and (4) using mechanical devices.

Real World Example
Even a small business should have internal controls and separation of duties. If the accountant writes the checks and keeps the ledger, the owner should sign the checks and reconcile the bank statements.

SEGREGATION OF EMPLOYEE DUTIES   **Segregation of duties** requires that someone other than the employee responsible for safeguarding an asset must maintain the accounting records for that asset. Also, employees share responsibility for related transactions so that one employee's work serves as a check on the work of other employees.

When a company segregates the duties of employees, it minimizes the probability of an employee being able to steal assets and cover up the theft. For example, an employee could not steal cash from a company and have the theft go undetected unless someone changes the cash records to cover the shortage. To change the records, the employee stealing the cash must also maintain the cash records or be in collusion with the employee who maintains the cash records.

ASSIGNMENT OF SPECIFIC DUTIES TO EACH EMPLOYEE   When the responsibility for a particular work function is assigned to one employee, that employee is accountable for specific tasks. Should a problem occur, the company can quickly identify the responsible employee.

When a company gives each employee specific duties, it can trace lost documents or determine how a particular transaction was recorded. Also, the employee responsible for a given task can provide information about that task. Being responsible for specific duties gives people a sense of pride and importance that usually makes them want to perform to the best of their ability.

ROTATION OF EMPLOYEE JOB ASSIGNMENTS   Some companies rotate job assignments to discourage employees from engaging in long-term schemes to steal from them. Employees realize that if they steal from the company, the next employees assigned to their positions may discover the theft.

Frequently, companies have the policy that all employees must take an annual vacation. This policy also discourages theft because many dishonest schemes collapse when the employee does not attend to the scheme on a daily basis.

USE OF MECHANICAL DEVICES   Companies use several mechanical devices to help protect their assets. Check protectors (machines that perforate the check amount into the check), cash registers, and time clocks make it extremely difficult for employees to alter certain company documents and records.

Real World Example
Many companies have a mandatory vacation policy for employees. Most require a minimum of one week, many require two weeks.

Compliance with Company Policies and Federal Law

Internal control policies are effective only when employees follow them. To ensure that they carry out its internal control policies, a company must hire competent and trustworthy employees. Thus, the execution of effective internal control begins with the time and effort a company expends in hiring employees. Once the company hires the employees, it must train those employees and clearly communicate to them company policies, such as obtaining proper authorization before making a cash disbursement. Frequently, written job descriptions establish the responsibilities and duties of employees. The initial training of employees should include a clear explanation of their duties and how to perform them.

In publicly held corporations, the company's internal control structure must satisfy the requirements of federal law. In December 1977, Congress enacted the Foreign Corrupt Practices Act (FCPA). This law requires a publicly held corporation to devise and maintain an effective internal control structure and to keep accurate accounting records. This law came about partly because company accounting records covered up bribes and kickbacks made to foreign governments or government officials. The FCPA made this specific type of bribery illegal.

Evaluation of Personnel Performance

To evaluate how well employees are doing their jobs, many companies use an internal auditing staff. **Internal auditing** consists of investigating and evaluating employees' compliance with the company's policies and procedures. Companies employ **internal auditors** to perform these audits. Once trained in company policies and internal auditing duties, internal auditors periodically test the effectiveness of controls and procedures throughout the company.

Internal auditors encourage operating efficiency throughout the company and are constantly alert for breakdowns in the company's internal control structure. In addition, internal auditors make recommendations for the improvement of the company's internal control structure. All companies and nonprofit organizations can benefit from internal auditing. However, internal auditing is especially necessary in large organizations because the owners (stockholders) cannot be involved personally with all aspects of the business.

Accuracy of Accounting Records

Companies should maintain complete and accurate accounting records. The best method to ensure such accounting records is to hire and train competent and honest individuals. Periodically, supervisors evaluate an employee's performance to make sure the employee is following company policies. Inaccurate or inadequate accounting

ILLUSTRATION 8.1
Purchase Requisition

PURCHASE REQUISITION		No. _2416_	
BRYAN WHOLESALE COMPANY			

From: _Automotive Supplies Department_   **Date:** _November 20, 1999_

To: _Purchasing Department_

Suggested supplier: _Wilkes Radio Company_

Please purchase the following items:

Description	Item Number	Quantity	Esitmated Price
True-tone stereo radios	Model No. 5868-24393	200	$50 per unit

Reason for request:
Customer order
Baier Company

To be filled in by purchasing department:
Date ordered _11/21/99_
Purchase order number _N-145_
Approved _R.S.T._

records serve as an invitation to theft by dishonest employees because theft can be concealed more easily.

One or more business documents support most accounting transactions. These source documents are an integral part of the internal control structure. For optimal control, source documents should be serially numbered. (Transaction documentation and related aspects of internal control are presented throughout the text.)

Since source documents serve as documentation of business transactions, from time to time firms check the validity of these documents. For example, to review a merchandise transaction, they check the documents used to record the transaction against the proper accounting records. When the accounting department records a merchandise transaction, it should receive copies of the following four documents:

1. A **purchase requisition** (Illustration 8.1) is a written request from an employee inside the company to the purchasing department to purchase certain items.

2. A **purchase order** (Illustration 8.2) is a document sent from the purchasing department to a supplier requesting that merchandise or other items be shipped to the purchaser.

3. An **invoice** (Illustration 8.3) is the statement sent by the supplier to the purchaser requesting payment for the merchandise shipped.

4. A **receiving report** is a document prepared by the receiving department showing the descriptions and quantities of all items received from a supplier in a particular shipment. A copy of the purchase order can serve as a receiving report if the quantity ordered is omitted. Then, because receiving department personnel do not know what quantity to expect, they will count the quantity received more accurately.

These four documents together serve as authorization to pay for merchandise and should be checked against the accounting records. Without these documents, a company might fail to pay a legitimate invoice, pay fictitious invoices, or pay an invoice more than once. Companies can accomplish proper internal control only by periodically checking the source documents of business transactions with the accounting records of those transactions. In Illustration 8.4 on page 301, we show the flow of documents and goods in a merchandise transaction.

Unfortunately, even though a company implements all of these features in its internal control structure, theft may still occur. If employees are dishonest, they can usually figure out a way to steal from a company, thus circumventing even the most effective internal control structure. Therefore, companies should carry adequate

Real World Example
Prenumbering of documents is not an effective control unless unused documents are safeguarded and all numbered documents are accounted for—never destroyed. Examples: void checks, void purchase orders, or canceled sales invoices.

```
                    PURCHASE ORDER                     No.  N-145

                 BRYAN WHOLESALE COMPANY
                       476 Mason Street
                    Detroit, Michigan 48823

To:  Wilkes Radio Company
     2515 West Peachtree Street      Date:  November 21, 1999
     Atlanta, Georgia 30303          Ship by:  December 20, 1999
Ship to:  Above address              FOB terms requested:  Destination
                                     Discount terms requested:  2/10, n/30
Please send the following items:
```

Description	Item Number	Quantity	Price per Unit	Total Amount
True-tone stereo radios	5868-24393	200	$50	$10,000

```
Ordered by:  Jane Knight              Please include order number on all
                                      invoices and shipments.
```

ILLUSTRATION 8.2
Purchase Order

casualty insurance on assets. This insurance reimburses the company for loss of a nonmonetary asset such as specialized equipment. Companies should also have **fidelity bonds** on employees handling cash and other negotiable instruments. These bonds ensure that a company is reimbursed for losses due to theft of cash and other monetary assets. With both casualty insurance on assets and fidelity bonds on employees, a company can recover at least a portion of any loss that occurs.

Components of Internal Control

According to the Committee of Sponsoring Organizations of the Treadway Commission, there are five components of an internal control structure. When these components are linked to the organization's operations, they can quickly respond to shifting conditions. The components are:

1. **Control environment.** The control environment is the basis for all other elements of the internal control structure. The control environment includes many factors such as ethical values, management's philosophy, the integrity of the employees of the corporation, and the guidance provided by management or the board of directors.

2. **Risk assessment.** After the entity sets objectives, the risks (such as theft and waste of assets) from external and internal sources must be assessed. Examining the risks associated with each objective allows management to develop the means to control these risks.

3. **Control activities.** To address the risks associated with each objective, management establishes control activities. These activities include procedures that employees must follow. Examples include procedures to protect the assets through segregation of employee duties and the other means we discussed earlier.

4. **Information and communication.** Information relevant to decision making must be collected and reported in a timely manner. The events that yield these data may come from internal or external sources. Communication throughout the entity is important to achieve management's goals. Employees must understand what is expected of them and how their responsibilities relate to the work of others. Communication with external parties such as suppliers and shareholders is also important.

ILLUSTRATION 8.3
Invoice

INVOICE			Invoice No.: _1574_	
			Date: _Dec. 15, 1999_	

WILKES RADIO COMPANY
2515 West Peachtree Street
Atlanta, Georgia 30303

Customer's Order No.: _N-145_
Sold to: _Bryan Wholesale Co._
Address: _476 Mason Street_
        Detroit, Michigan 48823
Terms: _2/10, n/30, FOB destination_   **Date shipped:** _Dec. 15, 1999_
        Shipped by: _Nagel Trucking Co._

Description	Item Number	Quantity	Price per Unit	Total Amount
True-tone stereo radios	_Model No. 5868-24393_	_200_	_$50_	_$10,000_
		Total		_$10,000_

5. **Monitoring.** After the internal control structure is in place, the firm should monitor its effectiveness so that it can make changes before serious problems arise. In testing components of the internal control structure, companies base their thoroughness on the risk assigned to those components.

Responsibility for Internal Control

Internal control is the general responsibility of all members in an organization. However, the following three groups have specific responsibilities regarding the internal control structure.

Management holds ultimate responsibility for establishing and maintaining an effective internal control structure. Through leadership and example, management demonstrates ethical behavior and integrity within the company.

The *board of directors* provides guidance to management. Because board members have a working knowledge of the functions of the company, they help shield the company from managers who try to override some control procedures for dishonest purposes. Often, an efficient board that has access to the company's internal auditors can discover such fraud.

Auditors within the organization evaluate the effectiveness of the internal control structure and determine whether company policies and procedures are being followed. All employees are part of a communications network that enables an internal control structure to work effectively.

Internal Control in a Computer Environment

Computerized financial records require the same internal control principles of separation of duties and control over access as a manual accounting system. The exact control steps depend on whether a company is using mainframe computers and minicomputers or microcomputers.

Large corporations might use all three types of computers in their accounting environments. The size and complexity of mainframe computers and minicomputers require specially trained persons to keep these systems operating. While systems specialists operate the computer system itself, programmers develop the programs that direct the computer to perform specific tasks. In a mainframe or minicomputer environment, internal control should include the following:

- Control computer access by placing the computer in an easily secured room, and allow only persons authorized to operate the computer to enter the room.

Purchasing Company

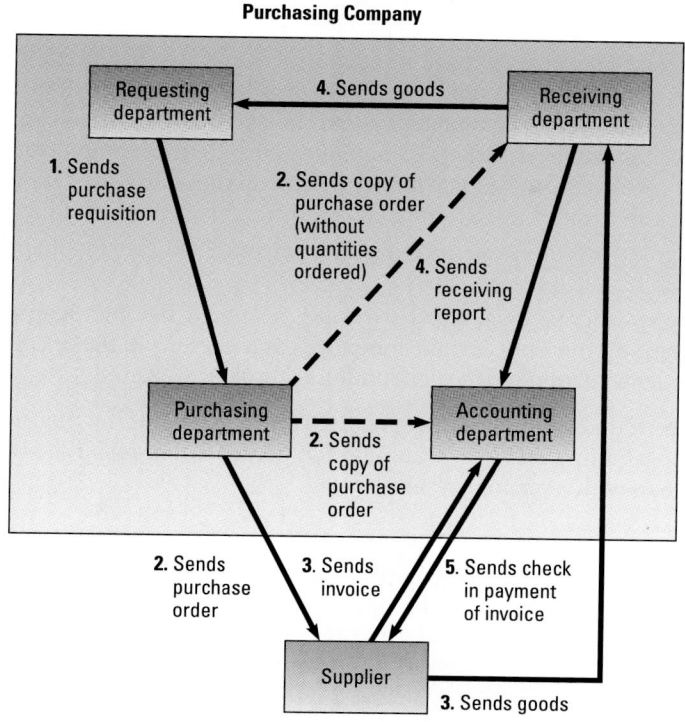

ILLUSTRATION 8.4
Flow of Documents and Goods in a Merchandising Transaction

Steps

1. Requesting department sends purchase requisition to purchasing department.
2. Purchasing department sends purchase order to supplier, with copies going to the receiving department (without quantities ordered) and the accounting department.
3. Supplier sends goods to receiving department, where goods received are checked against purchase order, and sends invoice to accounting department.
4. Receiving department sends goods to requesting department and sends receiving report to accounting department.
5. Accounting department checks receiving report against purchase order and invoice and sends check in payment of invoice to the supplier.

- Restrict the access of systems specialists (who operate the computer) to software programs and the access of programmers to the computer. This policy prevents the running of unauthorized, altered programs.

- Run some programs, such as ones used to print monthly accounts receivable statements to send to credit customers, only during an authorized time period. If programs and data are stored on magnetic tape, store the tapes under lock and key and under the control of a tape librarian. The librarian should be independent of the computer systems and programming functions.

Many smaller companies use microcomputers instead of a mainframe or a minicomputer. Also, large companies might supply certain employees with microcomputers. The use of microcomputers changes the control environment somewhat. Small companies generally do not employ systems specialists and programmers. Instead, these companies use off-the-shelf programs such as accounting, spreadsheet, database management, and word processing packages. The data created by use of these programs are valuable (e.g., the company's accounting records) and often sensitive. Thus, controls are also important. In a microcomputer environment, the following controls can be useful:

Reinforcing Problems
E8–1 Answer true-false questions about internal control.
E8–2 Answer multiple-choice question about internal control.

- Keep each microcomputer locked when not in use and give keys only to persons authorized to use that computer.
- Require computer users to have tight control over their diskettes on which programs and data are stored. Just as one person maintains custody over a certain set of records in a manual system, in a computer system one person maintains custody over diskettes containing certain information (such as the accounts receivable subsidiary ledger). Lock up these diskettes at night, and make backup copies that are retained in a different secured location.
- Require passwords (kept secret) to gain entry into data files maintained on the hard disk.
- In situations where a local area network (LAN) links the microcomputers into one system, permit only certain computers and persons in the network to have access to some data files (the accounting records, for example).

Computerized accounting systems do not lessen the need for internal control. In fact, access to a computer by an unauthorized person could result in significant theft in less time than with a manual system.

AN ACCOUNTING PERSPECTIVE   **BUSINESS INSIGHT**   A serious millennium "bug" awaits on the horizon. When the year 2000 arrives, many computers will advance the year to "00" and interpret this as 1900 instead of 2000. This problem is caused by the fact that a substantial portion of computer code was written using only two digits to indicate the year. Business documents might look 99 years old, maturity dates for notes may be miscalculated, and many other problems could occur. Much of the computer code, especially in mainframe computers, will have to be rewritten, at an estimated cost of over $100 billion, to avoid serious consequences.

CONTROLLING CASH

Objective 2
Define cash and list the objectives sought by management in handling a company's cash.

Since cash is the most liquid of all assets, a business cannot survive and prosper if it does not have adequate control over its cash. In accounting, **cash** includes coins; currency; undeposited negotiable instruments such as checks, bank drafts, and money orders; amounts in checking and savings accounts; and demand certificates of deposit. A **certificate of deposit (CD)** is an interest-bearing deposit that can be withdrawn from a bank at will (demand CD) or at a fixed maturity date (time CD). Cash only includes demand CDs that may be withdrawn at any time without prior notice or penalty. Cash does not include postage stamps, IOUs, time CDs, or notes receivable.

In its general ledger, a company usually maintains two cash accounts—Cash and Petty Cash. On the company's balance sheet, it combines the balances of these two accounts into one amount reported as Cash.

AN ACCOUNTING PERSPECTIVE   **BUSINESS INSIGHT**   Users of financial data must look to see the real meaning behind the numbers. Reader's Digest publishes the world's most widely read magazine as well as various other books, home entertainment products, and special interest magazines. In Reader's Digest's 1996 annual report, for example, the company defines cash and cash equivalents in this footnote:

The company considers all highly liquid debt instruments with original maturities of three months or less to be cash equivalents.

The footnote provides more insight to the number on the financial statement.

Since many business transactions involve cash, it is a vital factor in the operation of a business. Of all the company's assets, cash is the most easily mishandled either through theft or carelessness. To control and manage its cash, a company should:

1. Account for all cash transactions accurately so that correct information is available regarding cash flows and balances.

2. Make certain that enough cash is available to pay bills as they come due.
3. Avoid holding too much idle cash because excess cash could be invested to generate income, such as interest.
4. Prevent loss of cash due to theft or fraud.

The need to control cash is clearly evident and has many aspects. Without the proper timing of cash flows and the protection of idle cash, a business cannot survive. This section discusses cash receipts and cash disbursements. Later in the chapter, we explain the importance of preparing a bank reconciliation for each bank checking account and controlling the petty cash fund.

Controlling Cash Receipts

Objective 3
Identify procedures for controlling cash receipts and disbursements.

When a merchandising company sells its merchandise, it may receive cash immediately or several days or weeks later. A clerk receives the cash immediately *over the counter*, records it, and places it in a cash register. The presence of the customer as the sale is *rung up* usually ensures that the cashier enters the correct amount of the sale in the cash register. At the end of each day, stores reconcile the cash in each cash register with the cash register tape or computer printout for that register. Payments received later are almost always in the form of checks. Stores prepare a record of the checks received as soon as they are received. Some merchandising companies receive all their cash receipts on a delayed basis as payments on accounts receivable. (See the cash receipts cycle for merchandise transactions in Illustration 8.5.)

Although businesses vary their specific procedures for controlling cash receipts, they usually observe the following principles:

1. Prepare a record of all cash receipts as soon as cash is received. Most thefts of cash occur before a record is made of the receipt. Once a record is made, it is easier to trace a theft.
2. Deposit all cash receipts intact as soon as feasible, preferably on the day they are received or on the next business day. Undeposited cash is more susceptible to misappropriation.
3. Arrange duties so that the employee who handles cash receipts does not record the receipts in the accounting records. This control feature follows the general principle of *segregation of duties* given earlier in the chapter, as does item 4.
4. Arrange duties so that the employee who receives the cash does not disburse the cash. This control measure is possible in all but the smallest companies.

Real World Example
What internal control procedures over cash might be implemented in a retail business? *Answer:* Internal and external cash register tapes. In addition, customers might receive a bonus if they are not provided receipts.

Note to the Student
A bank account is like friendship. You cannot continue to draw from it without making deposits.

Controlling Cash Disbursements

Companies also need controls over cash disbursements. Since a company spends most of its cash by check, many of the internal controls for cash disbursements deal with checks and authorizations for cash payments. The basic principle of segregation of duties also applies in controlling cash disbursements. Following are some basic control procedures for cash disbursements:

- Make all disbursements by check or from petty cash. Obtain proper approval for all disbursements and create a permanent record of each disbursement. Many retail stores make refunds for returned merchandise from the cash register. When this practice is followed, clerks should have refund tickets approved by a supervisor before refunding cash.
- Require all checks to be serially numbered and limit access to checks to employees authorized to write checks.
- Require two signatures on each check so that one person cannot withdraw funds from the bank account.
- Arrange duties so that the employee who authorizes payment of a bill does not sign checks. Otherwise, the checks could be written to friends in payment of fictitious invoices.
- Require approved documents to support all checks issued.

ILLUSTRATION 8.5
Cash Receipts Cycle
for Merchandise
Transactions

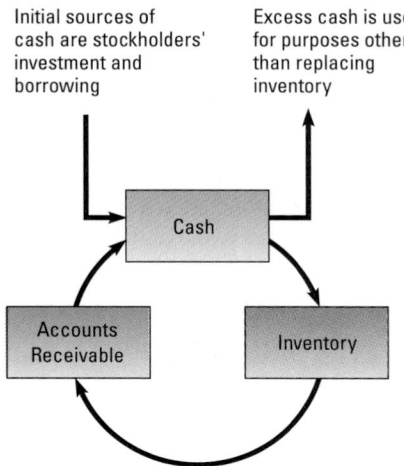

Initial sources of
cash are stockholders'
investment and
borrowing

Excess cash is used
for purposes other
than replacing
inventory

Cash initially comes into the business from
stockholders' investment and borrowing. Cash
is then invested in inventory and other assets.
When inventory is sold, cash may be received
immediately, or receipt may be delayed and
involve accounts receivable. The inventory
generally is sold at more than cost so the
company can make a profit. Each time the
cycle is completed, the amount of cash
grows and may be used for purposes other
than replacing inventory.

- Instruct the employee authorizing cash disbursements to make certain that payment is for a legitimate purpose and is made out for the exact amount and to the proper party.
- Stamp the supporting documents *paid* when liabilities are paid and indicate the date and number of the check issued. These procedures lessen the chance of paying the same debt more than once.
- Arrange duties so that those employees who sign checks neither have access to canceled checks nor prepare the bank reconciliation. This policy makes it more difficult for an employee to conceal a theft.
- Have an employee who has no other cash duties prepare the bank reconciliation each month, so that errors and shortages can be discovered quickly.
- Void all checks incorrectly prepared. Mark these checks void and retain them to prevent unauthorized use.

Real World Example
Texas Instruments requires all of its vendors to be Electronic Data Interchange (EDI) capable. EDI systems enable trading partners to conduct business such as ordering, shipping, billing, and payment transactions over computer networks rather than sending paper copies of documents. "A Guide to Electronic Commerce," *Management Accounting*, September 1996, p. 43.

Illustration 8.6 shows an overview of some of the internal control considerations relating to cash.

Most companies use checking accounts to handle their cash transactions. The company deposits its cash receipts in a bank checking account and writes checks to pay its bills. The bank sends the company a statement each month. The company checks this statement against its records to determine if it must make any corrections or adjustments in either the company's balance or the bank's balance. You learn how to do this bank reconciliation later. In the next section, we discuss the bank checking account. If you have a personal checking account, some of this information will be familiar to you.

**AN ACCOUNTING
PERSPECTIVE**

USES OF TECHNOLOGY   Many companies are using Electronic Data Interchange (EDI) to transmit business documents such as purchase orders, invoices, and even payments for goods and services. Instead of mailing paper copies of these documents, the entire transaction is done electronically. This procedure speeds up the transaction and eliminates the expense of sending paper copies. One concern of such procedures is the security of the transaction. Since this issue is being successfully addressed by various methods, including encrypting the data, we can expect the use of EDI to increase dramatically in the future.

THE BANK CHECKING ACCOUNT

Banks earn income by providing a variety of services to individuals, businesses, and other entities such as churches or libraries. One of these services is the checking

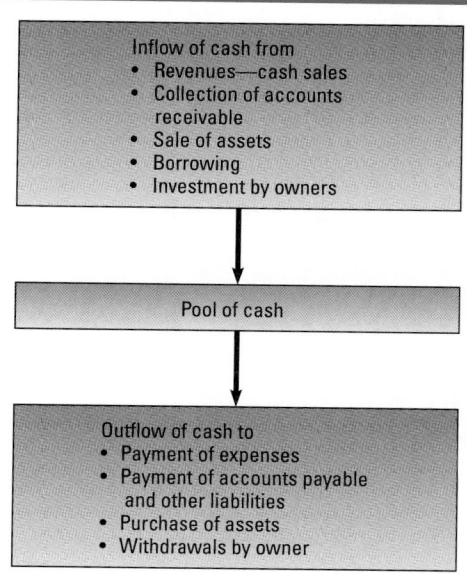

Internal control considerations

1. Are all cash receipts being properly recorded and actually going into the company's pool of cash, or are individuals siphoning off some of these receipts for their own use?
2. Is the pool of cash protected from theft? Is the cash on hand managed so as to produce income for the company and yet be available when needed to make legitimate disbursements?
3. Is there close control over cash disbursements to ensure that only legitimate disbursements are made in the proper amounts and on a timely basis?

ILLUSTRATION 8.6
Internal Control Considerations Regarding Cash

account. A **checking account** is a money balance maintained in the bank; it is subject to withdrawal by the depositor, or owner of the money, on demand. To provide depositors with an accurate record of depositor funds received and disbursed, a bank uses the business documents discussed in this section.[2]

A bank requires a new depositor to complete a **signature card,** which provides the signatures of persons authorized to sign checks drawn on an account. The bank retains the card and uses it to identify signatures on checks it pays. The bank does not compare every check with this signature card. Usually, it makes a comparison only when the depositor disputes the validity of a check paid by the bank or when someone presents a check for an unusually large sum for payment.

Signature Card

Note to the Student
The bank has the responsibility of verifying the signature on checks. Since this is not always feasible with the high volume of checks, the bank sometimes incurs a loss.

When depositors make a bank deposit, they prepare a deposit ticket or slip. A **deposit ticket** is a form that shows the date and the items that make up the deposit (Illustration 8.7). Often, the ticket is preprinted to show the depositor's name, address, and account number. A depositor enters the items constituting the deposit—cash and a list of checks—on the ticket when making the deposit. The depositor receives a receipt showing the date of deposit and the amount deposited.

Deposit Ticket

A **check** is a written order to a bank to pay a specific sum of money to the party designated as the payee by the party issuing the check. Thus, every check transaction involves three parties: the *bank,* the **payee** (party to whom the check is made payable), and the **drawer** (depositor). Most depositors use serially numbered checks preprinted with information about the depositor, such as name, address, and telephone number. Often a business check has an attached remittance advice. A **remittance advice** informs the payee why the **drawer** (or maker) of the check is making this payment. Before cashing or depositing it, the payee detaches the remittance advice from the check (Illustration 8.8).

Check

---

[2]Due to relaxed federal regulations, institutions other than banks—such as savings and loan associations and credit unions—now offer checking account services. All of these institutions function somewhat similarly; but, for simplicity's sake, we discuss only banks here.

ILLUSTRATION 8.7
Deposit Ticket

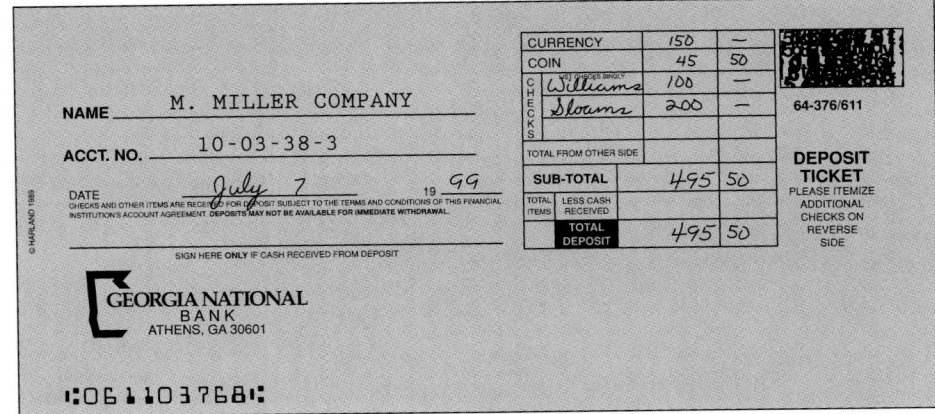

ILLUSTRATION 8.8
Check with Attached
Remittance Advice

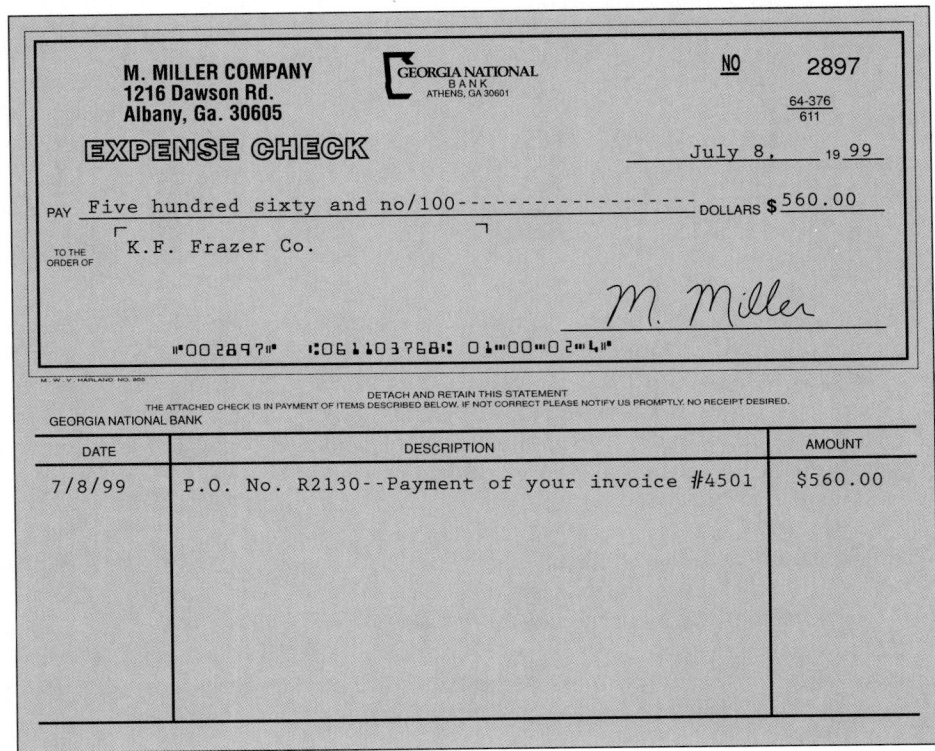

Bank Statement

Note to the Student

A bank statement balance does not usually represent the amount that appears in the ledger account; deposits in transit and outstanding checks have not been recorded by the bank as of the statement date.

A **bank statement** is a statement issued (usually monthly) by a bank describing the activities in a depositor's checking account during the period. Illustration 8.9 shows a bank statement that includes the following data:

1. Deposits made to the checking account during the period.
2. Checks paid out of the depositor's checking account by the bank during the period. These checks have *cleared* the bank and are *canceled*.
3. Other deductions from the checking account for service charges, NSF (not sufficient funds) checks, safe-deposit box rent, and check printing fees. Banks assess **service charges** on the depositor to cover the cost of handling the checking account, such as check clearing charges. An **NSF (not sufficient**

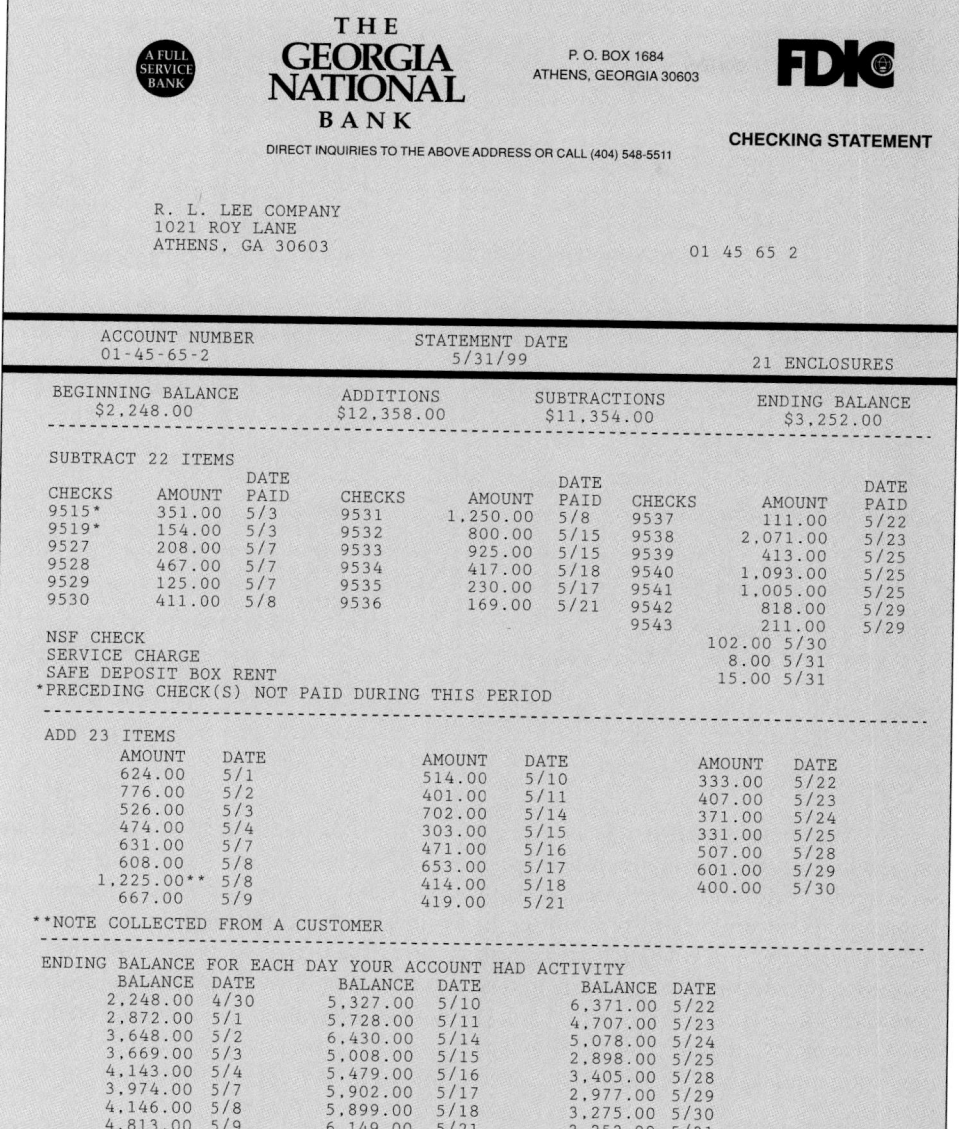

ILLUSTRATION 8.9
Bank Statement

funds) check is a customer's check returned from the customer's bank to the depositor's bank because the funds in the customer's checking account balance were insufficient to cover the check. The depositor's bank deducts the amount of the returned check from the depositor's checking account. Since the customer still owes the depositor money, the depositor restores the amount of the NSF check to the account receivable for that customer in the company's books.

4. Other additions to the checking account from proceeds of a note collected by the bank for the depositor and interest earned on the account.

In addition to the data in the bank statement in Illustration 8.9, bank statements also can show nonroutine deposits made to the depositor's checking account. Such deposits are made by a third party. For example, the bank may have received a wire transfer of funds for the depositor.

Reinforcing Problem

E8–3 Determine available cash balance from bank statement and Cash account data.

ILLUSTRATION 8.10
Debit Memorandum (top) and Credit Memorandum (bottom)

GENERAL LEDGER **DEBIT** ACCT. TITLE	R. L. Lee Company 1021 Roy Lane Athens, GA 30603	Acct. No. 01 45 65 2 DATE May 31, 1999

DESCRIPTION	AMOUNT
Safe Deposit Box Rental	
CONTRA ENTRY	
DRAWN BY CWT CENTER APPROVED BY MRC TOTAL	15 00

BANKERS SYSTEMS, INC., ST. CLOUD, MN 56301

⑈037600800⑈

GENERAL LEDGER **CREDIT** ACCT. TITLE	R. L. Lee Company 1021 Roy Lane Athens, GA 30603	Acct. No. 01 45 65 2 DATE 5/8/99

DESCRIPTION	AMOUNT
Collection of note for the Lee Company from X Company	
CONTRA ENTRY	
DRAWN BY CWT CENTER APPROVED BY MRC TOTAL	1,225 00

BANKERS SYSTEMS, INC., ST. CLOUD, MN 56301

⑈037600208⑈

Real World Example
A business must keep a separate cash account in the general ledger for each bank account or a subsidiary ledger of accounts. Otherwise, reconciliation of individual bank accounts would not be possible.

A **wire transfer of funds** is an interbank transfer of funds by telephone. Companies that operate in many widely scattered locations and have checking accounts with several different local banks often use interbank transfers of funds. These companies may set up special procedures to avoid accumulating too much idle cash in local bank accounts. One such procedure involves the use of special-instruction bank accounts. For example, a company may set up **transfer bank accounts** so local banks automatically transfer to a central bank (by wire or bank draft) all amounts on deposit in excess of a stated amount. In this way, transfers move funds not needed for local operations quickly to headquarters, where the company can use the funds or invest them.

Frequently, the bank returns canceled checks and original deposit tickets with the bank statement. Since it is expensive to sort, handle, and mail these items, some banks no longer return them to depositors. These banks usually store the documents on microfilm, with photocopies available if needed. Most depositors need only a detailed bank statement, as shown in Illustration 8.9, and not the original documents to show what transactions occurred during a given period.

When banks debit or credit a depositor's checking account, they prepare debit and credit memoranda (memos). Banks may also return these memos with the bank statement. A **debit memo** is a form used by a bank to explain a deduction from the depositor's account; a **credit memo** explains an addition to the depositor's account. The terms *debit memo* and *credit memo* may seem reversed, but remember that the depositor's checking account is a liability—an account payable—of the bank. So, when the bank seeks to reduce a depositor's balance, it prepares a debit memo. To increase the balance, it prepares a credit memo. Illustration 8.10 contains examples of debit and credit memos. Some banks no longer mail these documents to the depositor and rely instead on explanations in the bank statements.

Information that the depositor did not know before receiving the bank statement (items 3 and 4 on pages 306–7) requires new journal entries on the company's books.

After the entries have been made to record the new information, the balance in the Cash account is the actual cash available to the company. When the depositor has already received notice of NSF checks and other bank charges or credits, the needed journal entries may have been made earlier. In this chapter, we assume no entries have been made for these items unless stated otherwise.

When a company receives its bank statement, it must reconcile the balance shown by the bank with the cash balance in the company's books. If you have a personal checking account, you also should reconcile your bank statement with your checkbook. You can use the reconciliation form on the back of the bank statement to list your checks that have not yet been paid by the bank and your deposits not yet shown on the bank statement. Some small businesses use this form. Others prepare a separate bank reconciliation, which we discuss in the next section.

BANK RECONCILIATION

A **bank reconciliation,** often called a *bank reconciliation statement* or *schedule,* is a schedule the company (depositor) prepares to reconcile, or explain, the difference between the cash balance on the bank statement and the cash balance on the company's books. The company prepares a bank reconciliation to determine its actual cash balance and prepare the entry(ies) to correct the cash balance in the ledger.

Objective 4
Prepare a bank reconciliation and make necessary journal entries based on that schedule.

BUSINESS INSIGHT   Within the internal control structure, segregation of duties is an important way to prevent fraud. One place to segregate duties is between the cash disbursement cycle and bank reconciliations. To prevent collusion among employees, the person who reconciles the bank account should not be involved in the cash disbursement cycle. Also, the bank should mail the statement directly to the person who reconciles the bank account each month. Sending the statement directly limits the number of employees who would have an opportunity to tamper with the statement.

AN ACCOUNTING PERSPECTIVE

Look at Illustration 8.11; the bank reconciliation has two main sections. The top section begins with the balance on the bank statement. The bottom section begins with the balance on the company's books. After the company makes adjustments to both the *bank* and *book* balances, both adjusted balances should be the same. The steps in preparing a bank reconciliation are as follows:

Deposits. Compare the deposits listed on the bank statement with the deposits on the company's books. To make this comparison, place check marks in the bank statement and in the company's books by the deposits that agree. Then determine the deposits in transit. A **deposit in transit** is typically a day's cash receipts recorded in the depositor's books in one period but recorded as a deposit by the bank in the succeeding period. The most common deposit in transit is the cash receipts deposited on the last business day of the month. Normally, deposits in transit occur only near the end of the period covered by the bank statement. For example, a deposit made in a bank's night depository on May 31 would be recorded by the company on May 31 and by the bank on June 1. Thus, the deposit does not appear on a bank statement for the month ended May 31. Also check the deposits in transit listed in last month's bank reconciliation against the bank statement. Immediately investigate any deposit made during the month but missing from the bank statement (unless it involves a deposit made at the end of the period).

Paid checks. If canceled checks are returned with the bank statement, compare them to the statement to be sure both amounts agree. Then, sort the checks in numerical order. Next, determine which checks are outstanding. **Outstanding checks** are those issued by a depositor but not paid by the bank on which they

ILLUSTRATION 8.11
Bank Reconciliation

R. L. LEE COMPANY
Bank Reconciliation
May 31, 1999

①	Balance per bank statement, May 31, 1999		$3,252
②	Add: Deposit in transit		452
			$3,704
③	Less: Outstanding checks:		
	No. 9544	$322	
	No. 9545	168	
	No. 9546	223	713
	Adjusted balance, May 31, 1999		$2,991
①	Balance per ledger, May 31, 1999.		$1,891
④	Add: Note collected (including interest of $25)		1,225
			$3,116
⑤	Less: NSF check (R. Johnson)	$102	
⑥	Safe-deposit box rent	15	
⑥	Service charges.	8	125
	Adjusted balance, May 31, 1999		$2,991

are drawn. The party receiving the check may not have deposited it immediately. Once deposited, checks may take several days to clear the banking system, although this process has been expedited in recent years. Determine the outstanding checks by comparing the check numbers that have cleared the bank with the check numbers issued by the company. Use check marks in the company's record of checks issued to identify those checks returned by the bank. Checks issued that have not yet been returned by the bank are the outstanding checks. If the bank does not return checks but only lists the cleared checks on the bank statement, determine the outstanding checks by comparing this list with the company's record of checks issued.

Sometimes checks written long ago are still outstanding. Checks outstanding as of the beginning of the month appear on the prior month's bank reconciliation. Most of these have cleared during the current month; list those that have not cleared as still outstanding on the current month's reconciliation.

Bank debit and credit memos. Verify all debit and credit memos on the bank statement. Debit memos reflect deductions for such items as service charges, NSF checks, safe-deposit box rent, and notes paid by the bank for the depositor. Credit memos reflect additions for such items as notes collected for the depositor by the bank and wire transfers of funds from another bank in which the company sends funds to the home office bank. Check the bank debit and credit memos with the depositor's books to see if they have already been recorded. Make journal entries for any items not already recorded in the company's books.

Errors. List any errors. A common error by depositors is recording a check in the accounting records at an amount that differs from the actual amount. For example, a $47 check may be recorded as $74. Although the check clears the bank at the amount written on the check ($47), the depositor frequently does not catch the error until reviewing the bank statement or canceled checks.

Deposits in transit, outstanding checks, and bank service charges usually account for the difference between the company's Cash account balance and the bank balance. (These same items can cause a difference between your personal checkbook balance and the balance on your bank statement.) Remember that all items shown on the bank reconciliation as adjustments of the book (ledger) balance require journal entries to adjust the Cash account (items 4, 5, and 6 in Illustration 8.11 and in the following example). Items appearing as adjustments to the balance per bank statement do not require entries by the depositor (items 2 and 3). Of course, you should call any bank errors to the bank's attention.

To illustrate the preparation of the bank reconciliation in Illustration 8.11, assume the following (these items are keyed to numbers in that illustration):

Reinforcing Problem
E8–7 Determine deposits in transit.

1. On May 31, 1999, R. L. Lee Company showed a balance in its Cash account of $1,891. On June 2, Lee received its bank statement for the month ended May 31, which showed an ending balance of $3,252.

2. A matching of debits to the Cash account on the books with deposits on the bank statement showed that the $452 receipts of May 31 were included in Cash but not included as a deposit on the bank statement. This deposit was in the bank's night deposit chute on May 31.

3. A comparison of checks issued with checks that had cleared the bank showed three checks outstanding:

Reinforcing Problem
E8–6 Determine checks outstanding.

No. 9544	$322
No. 9545	168
No. 9546	223
Total	$713

4. Included with the bank statement was a credit memo for $1,225 (principal of $1,200 + interest of $25) for collection of a note owed to Lee by Shipley Company.

5. Included with the bank statement was a $102 debit memo for an NSF check written by R. Johnson and deposited by Lee.

6. Charges made to Lee's account include $15 for safe-deposit box rent and $8 for service charges.

After reconciling the book and bank balances as shown in Illustration 8.11, Lee Company finds that its actual cash balance is $2,991. The following entries record information from the bank reconciliation:

④	Cash	1,225	
	Notes Receivable—Shipley Company		1,200
	Interest Revenue		25
	To record note collected from Shipley Company.		
⑤	Accounts Receivable—R. Johnson*	102	
	Cash		102
	To charge NSF check back to customer, R. Johnson.		
⑥	Bank Service Charge Expense (or Miscellaneous Expense)	23	
	Cash		23
	To record bank service charges.		

*This debit would be posted to the Accounts Receivable control account in the general ledger and to R. Johnson's account in the accounts receivable subsidiary ledger.

The income statement for the period ending May 31, 1999, would include the $23 bank service charge as an expense and the $25 interest as revenue. The May 31 balance sheet would show $2,991 cash, the actual cash balance. You could combine the preceding three entries into one compound entry as follows:

	Cash	1,100	
	Bank Service Charge Expense	23	
	Accounts Receivable—R. Johnson	102	
	Notes Receivable		1,200
	Interest Revenue		25
	To correct the accounts for needed changes identified in the bank reconciliation.		

Reinforcing Problems
E8–4 Prepare a bank reconciliation and specify cash available.
E8–5 Record necessary journal entry or entries to correct cash balance.
E8–8 Prepare a bank reconciliation and necessary journal entry or entries.

The bank routinely handles the deposit in transit and any outstanding checks already recorded in the depositor's books. Since these items appear on the bank balance side of the reconciliation, they require no entry in the company's books. The bank processes these items in the subsequent period.

When a company maintains more than one checking account, it must reconcile each account separately with the balance on the bank statement for that account. The depositor should also check carefully to see that the bank did not combine the transactions of the two accounts.

Certified and Cashier's Checks

To make sure a check cannot *bounce* and become an NSF check, a payee may demand a certified or cashier's check from the maker. Both certified checks and cashier's checks are liabilities of the issuing bank rather than the depositor. As a result, payees usually accept these checks without question.

- A **certified check** is a check written, or drawn, by a depositor and taken to the depositor's bank for certification. The bank stamps certified across the face of the check and inserts the name of the bank and the date; a bank official signs the certification. The bank certifies a check only when the depositor's balance is large enough to cover the check. The bank deducts the amount of the check from the depositor's account at the time it certifies the check.
- A **cashier's check** is a check made out to either the depositor or a third party and written, or drawn, by a bank after deducting that amount from the depositor's account or receiving cash from the depositor.

In this section, you learned that all cash receipts should be deposited in the bank and all cash disbursements should be made by check. However, the next section explains the convenience of having small amounts of cash (petty cash) available for minor expenditures.

AN ACCOUNTING PERSPECTIVE	**USES OF TECHNOLOGY** Some companies now offer to deposit employees' paychecks directly into their bank accounts. This process of transferring money by telephone, computer, or wire is called *electronic fund transferring*. Often companies prefer this method because it limits the number of employees involved in the payroll process. Manipulation and fraud can still occur whenever firms do not separate duties; however, limiting access to the payroll function may eliminate some of the risk associated with internal control weaknesses.

PETTY CASH FUNDS

Objective 5
Explain why a company uses a petty cash fund, describe its operations, and make the necessary journal entries.

At times, every business finds it convenient to have small amounts of cash available for immediate payment of items such as delivery charges, postage stamps, taxi fares, supper money for employees working overtime, and other small items. To permit these cash disbursements and still maintain adequate control over cash, companies frequently establish a **petty cash fund** of a round figure such as $100 or $500.

Usually one individual, called the *petty cash custodian* or *cashier,* is responsible for the control of the petty cash fund and documenting the disbursements made from the fund. By assigning the responsibility for the fund to one individual, the company has internal control over the cash in the fund.

Establishing the Fund

A business establishes a petty cash fund by writing a check for, say, $100. It is payable to the petty cash custodian. The petty cash fund should be large enough to make disbursements for a reasonable period, such as a month. The following entry records this transaction as follows:

Petty Cash	100	
Cash		100
To establish a petty cash fund.		

```
                PETTY CASH VOUCHER NO.  359
    To   Local Cartage, Inc.                    Date  June 29,  1999

         EXPLANATION          ACCT. NO.        AMOUNT

      Freight on parts            27          12 | 57



        APPROVED                    RECEIVED  Ken Black
    BY   A.E.S.                     PAYMENT
```

ILLUSTRATION 8.12
Petty Cash Voucher

After the check is cashed, the petty cash custodian normally places the money in a small box that can be locked. The fund is now ready to be disbursed as needed.

Operating the Fund

One of the conveniences of the petty cash fund is that payments from the fund require no journal entries at the time of payment. Thus, using a petty cash fund avoids the need for making many entries for small amounts. Only when the fund is reimbursed, or when the end of the accounting period arrives, does the firm make an entry in the journal.

When disbursing cash from the fund, the petty cash custodian prepares a petty cash voucher, which should be signed by the person receiving the funds. A **petty cash voucher** (Illustration 8.12) is a document or form that shows the amount of and reason for a petty cash disbursement. The custodian should prepare a voucher for each disbursement and staple any invoices for expenditures to the petty cash voucher. At all times, the employee responsible for petty cash is accountable for having cash and petty cash vouchers equal to the total amount of the fund.

Replenishing the Fund

Companies replenish the petty cash fund at the end of the accounting period, or sooner if it becomes low. The reason for replenishing the fund at the end of the accounting period is that no record of the fund expenditures is in the accounts until the check is written and a journal entry is made. (Sometimes we refer to this fund as an *imprest* fund since it is replenished when it becomes low.) The petty cash custodian presents the vouchers to the employee having authority to order that the fund be reimbursed. After the vouchers are examined, if all is in order, that employee draws a check to restore the fund to its original amount.

To determine which accounts to debit, an employee summarizes the petty cash vouchers according to the reasons for expenditure. Next, that person stamps or defaces the petty cash vouchers to prevent reuse. The journal entry to record replenishing the fund would debit the various accounts indicated by the summary and credit Cash.

For example, assume the $100 petty cash fund currently has a money balance of $7.40. A summary of the vouchers shows payments of $22.75 for transportation-in, $50.80 for stamps, and $19.05 for an advance to an employee; these payments total $92.60. After the vouchers have been examined and approved, an employee draws a check for $92.60 which, when cashed, restores the cash in the fund to its $100 balance. The journal entry to record replenishment is:

Note to the Student
When the petty cash fund is replenished, the Petty Cash account is neither debited nor credited.

Transportation-In	22.75	
Postage Expense	50.80	
Receivable from Employees (or Advances to Employees)	19.05	
Cash		92.60
To replenish a petty cash fund.		

Note that the entry to record replenishing the fund does not credit the Petty Cash account. We make entries to the Petty Cash account only when the fund is established, when the end of the accounting period arrives and the fund is not replenished, or when the size of the fund is changed.

At the end of an accounting period, the firm records any petty cash disbursements for which the fund has not yet been replenished. Since the fund has not been replenished, the credit would be to Petty Cash rather than Cash. Failure to make an entry at the end of an accounting period would cause errors in both the income statement and balance sheet. The easiest way to record these disbursements is to replenish the fund.

After a time, if the petty cash custodian finds that the petty cash fund is larger than needed, the excess petty cash should be deposited in the company's checking account. The required entry to record a decrease in the fund debits Cash and credits Petty Cash for the amount returned and deposited. On the other hand, a petty cash fund may be too small, requiring replenishment every few days. The entry to record an increase in the fund debits Petty Cash and credits Cash for the amount of the increase.

To illustrate, the entry to *decrease* the petty cash fund by $50 would be:

Cash	50	
Petty Cash		50
To decrease the size of the petty cash fund by $50.		

The entry to *increase* the petty cash fund by $600 would be:

Petty Cash	600	
Cash		600
To increase the size of the petty cash fund by $600.		

The following rules summarize how the Petty Cash account is debited and credited:

Debited to establish

Debited to increase

Credited to decrease

Credited to terminate

Cash Short and Over

Sometimes, the petty cash custodian makes errors in making change from the fund. These errors cause the cash in the fund to be more or less than the amount of the fund less the total vouchers. When the fund is restored to its original amount, the credit to Cash is for the difference between the established amount and the actual cash in the fund. We would debit all vouchered items. Any discrepancy should be debited or credited to an account called *Cash Short and Over*. The Cash Short and Over account is an expense or a revenue, depending on whether it has a debit or credit balance.

To illustrate, assume in the preceding example that the balance in the fund was only $6.10 instead of $7.40. Restoring the fund to $100 requires a check for $93.90. Since the petty cash vouchers total only $92.60, the fund is short $1.30. The entry for replenishment is:

Reinforcing Problems
E8–9 and E8–10 Record the reimbursement of petty cash fund.
E8–11 Prepare journal entries regarding petty cash.

Transportation-In	22.75	
Postage Expense	50.80	
Receivable from Employees	19.05	
Cash Short and Over	1.30	
Cash		93.90
To replenish petty cash fund.		

Entries in the Cash Short and Over account also result from other change-making activities. For example, assume that a clerk accidentally shortchanges a customer $1 and that total cash sales for the day are $740.50. At the end of the day, actual cash is

$1 over the sum of the sales tickets or the total of the cash register tape. The journal entry to record the day's cash sales is:

Cash	741.50	
Sales		740.50
Cash Short and Over		1.00
To record cash sales for the day.		

ANALYZING AND USING THE FINANCIAL RESULTS—THE QUICK RATIO

The **quick ratio** measures a company's short-term debt-paying ability. It is the ratio of quick assets (cash, marketable securities, and net receivables) to current liabilities. When computing quick assets, we do not include inventories and prepaid expenses because they might not be readily convertible into cash. A rule of thumb is that the ratio of quick assets to current liabilities should be 1:1 or higher. However, a lower quick ratio is satisfactory in companies that generate a steady flow of cash in their operations. Short-term creditors are interested in this ratio since it relates the pool of cash and immediate cash inflows to immediate cash outflows. The formula for the quick ratio is:

Objective 6
Analyze and use the financial results—quick ratio.

$$\text{Quick ratio} = \frac{\text{Quick assets}}{\text{Current liabilities}}$$

Based on the following information, we can determine that Bay Network's 1996 and 1995 quick ratios are 6.85 and 6.84, respectively:

Bay Networks
Bay Networks is a relatively new networking and telecommunications company. The company works to connect network users through the use of switches that transport data and has one of the most complete switching lines in the industry.

	1996	1995
Cash	$315,064	$283,913
Short-term investments	119,093	314,872
Net receivables	320,892	177,300
Total quick assets	$755,049	$776,085
Current liabilities	$110,147	$113,430
	$\frac{\$755,049}{\$110,147} = 6.85$	$\frac{\$776,085}{\$113,430} = 6.84$

Now that you have learned how to control a company's most liquid asset, cash, in the next chapter you are ready to study receivables and payables. As you realize, the backbone of our economy is credit. In all probability, the next automobile you plan to buy will be financed. Companies are anxious to offer credit to worthy customers and prospective customers. The many offers of credit we receive from various businesses are evidence of the importance companies place on credit as a method of stimulating sales and expanding their business.

UNDERSTANDING THE LEARNING OBJECTIVES

Objective 1
Describe the necessity for and features of internal control.

- The internal control structure of a company includes its plan of organization and all the procedures and actions taken by the company to protect its assets against theft and waste, ensure compliance with company policies and federal law, evaluate the performance of all personnel in the company to promote efficiency of operations, and ensure accurate and reliable operating data and accounting records.
- The purpose of internal control is to ensure the efficient operation of a business.

Objective 2
Define cash and list the objectives sought by management in handling a company's cash.

- Cash includes coins; currency; undeposited negotiable instruments such as checks, bank drafts, and money orders; amounts in checking and saving accounts; and demand certificates of deposit.
- To protect their cash, companies should account for all cash transactions accurately, make certain enough cash is available to pay bills as they come due, avoid holding too much idle cash, and prevent loss of cash due to theft or fraud.

Objective 3
Identify procedures for controlling cash receipts and disbursements.

- Procedures for controlling cash receipts include such basic principles as recording all cash receipts as soon as cash is received; depositing all cash receipts on the day they are received or on the next business day; and preventing the employee who handles cash receipts from also recording the receipts in the accounting records or from disbursing cash.
- Procedures for controlling cash disbursements include, among others, making all disbursements by check or from petty cash, using checks that are serially numbered, requiring two signatures on each check, and having a different person authorize payment of a bill than the persons allowed to sign checks.

Objective 4
Prepare a bank reconciliation and make necessary journal entries based on that schedule.

- A bank reconciliation is prepared to *reconcile,* or explain, the difference between the cash balance on the bank statement and the cash balance on the company's books and to make the required entry(ies) to correct the cash balance in the ledger.
- A bank reconciliation is shown in Illustration 8.11.
- Journal entries are needed for all items that appear in the bank reconciliation as adjustments to the balance per ledger to arrive at the adjusted cash balance.

Objective 5
Explain why a company uses a petty cash fund, describe its operations, and make the necessary journal entries.

- Companies establish a petty cash fund to permit minor cash disbursements and still maintain adequate control over cash.
- When the cash in the petty cash fund becomes low, the fund should be replenished. A journal entry is necessary to record the replenishment.

Objective 6
Analyze and use the financial results—quick ratio.

- Quick ratio equals cash, marketable securities, and net receivables divided by current liabilities.
- The quick ratio measures a company's short-term debt-paying ability.

DEMONSTRATION PROBLEM 8–A

You are the manager of a restaurant that has an ice cream parlor as a separate unit. Your accountant comes in once a year to prepare financial statements and the tax return. In the current year, you have a feeling that even though business seems good, net income is going to be lower. You ask the accountant to prepare condensed statements on a monthly basis. All sales are priced to yield an estimated gross margin of 40%. You, your accountant, and several of the accountant's assistants take physical inventories at the end of each of the following four months. The resulting sales, cost of goods sold, and gross margins are:

	March		April		May		June	
	Restaurant	Ice Cream Parlor	Restaurant	Ice Cream Parlor	Restaurant	Ice Cream Parlor	Restaurant	Ice Cream Parlor
Sales	$36,300	$53,000	$39,050	$42,750	$38,100	$39,000	$41,250	$35,500
Cost of goods sold	23,275	31,500	23,800	31,000	22,975	30,750	25,500	31,125
Gross margin	$13,025	$21,500	$15,250	$11,750	$15,125	$ 8,250	$15,750	$ 4,375

What would you suspect after analyzing these reports? What sales control procedures would *Required* you recommend to correct the situation? All of the points in this problem were not specifically covered in the chapter, although the principles were. Use logic, common sense, and knowledge gained elsewhere in coming up with some of the control procedures.

SOLUTION TO DEMONSTRATION PROBLEM 8–A

The gross margin percentages are as follows:

	March	April	May	June
Restaurant	35.88%	39.05%	39.70%	38.18%
Ice cream parlor	40.57	27.49	21.15	12.32

Either cash or inventory is being stolen or given away in the ice cream parlor. Employees or outsiders may be pocketing cash. Or the employees may be giving extra-large ice cream cones to friends, or eating the ice cream themselves. Several things could be done to improve the sales control procedures:

1. The manager could hire an investigator to come in and watch the employees in action. If cash is being pocketed, the employees could be fired.
2. The prices of ice cream cones could be changed to odd amounts so that employees would not be as able to make change without going to the cash register. Also, the No Sale lever could be removed from the cash register.
3. The customers could be encouraged to ask for their cash register receipts by having a monthly drawing (for some prize) by cash register receipt number.
4. The cash register should be placed in a prominent position so that each customer could see the amount recorded for each sale. No customer is going to be willing to pay 65 cents when the employee rings up 50 cents.
5. The cash register tapes should be inaccessible to the employees. The manager (and possibly assistant manager) should have the only keys to the cash registers.
6. Mention to the employees that you have an effective internal control structure. The employees do not have to know what the structure is.
7. Pay the employees a competitive wage.
8. Require that all sales be rung up immediately after the sale.
9. The manager or assistant manager should reconcile the cash register tapes at the end of each day.

DEMONSTRATION PROBLEM 8–B

The following data pertain to Carr Company:

1. Balance per bank statement, dated March 31, 1999, is $4,450.
2. Balance of the Cash account on the company's books as of March 31, 1999, is $4,459.
3. The $1,300 deposit of March 31 was not on the bank statement.
4. Of the checks recorded as cash disbursements in March, some checks, totaling $1,050, have not yet cleared the bank.
5. Service and collection charges for the month were $10.
6. The bank erroneously charged the Carr Company account for the $200 check of another company. The check was included with the canceled checks returned with the bank statement.
7. The bank credited the company's account with the $1,000 proceeds of a noninterest-bearing note that it collected for the company.
8. A customer's $75 check marked NSF was returned with the bank statement.
9. As directed, the bank paid and charged to the company's account a $507.50 noninterest-bearing note of Carr Company. This payment has not been recorded by the company.
10. An examination of the cash receipts and the deposit tickets revealed that the bookkeeper erroneously recorded a customer's check of $148.50 as $135.00.
11. The bank credited the company's checking account for $20 interest earned.

a. Prepare a bank reconciliation as of March 31, 1999. *Required*
b. Prepare the necessary journal entry or entries to adjust the Cash account.

Solution to Demonstration Problem 8–B

a.

CARR COMPANY
Bank Reconciliation
March 31, 1999

Balance per bank statement, March 31, 1999		$4,450.00
Add: Deposit in transit	$1,300.00	
Check charged in error	200.00	1,500.00
		$5,950.00
Less: Outstanding checks		1,050.00
Adjusted balance, March 31, 1999		$4,900.00
Balance per ledger, March 31, 1999		$4,459.00
Add: Note collected	$1,000.00	
Interest earned on checking account	20.00	
Error in recording customer's check	13.50	1,033.50
		$5,492.50
Less: Service and collection charges	$ 10.00	
NSF check	75.00	
Carr Company note charged against account	507.50	592.50
Adjusted balance, March 31, 1999		$4,900.00

b.

1999					
Mar.	31	Cash		441.00	
		Bank Service Charge Expense		10.00	
		Accounts Receivable		75.00	
		Notes Payable		507.50	
		Notes Receivable			1,000.00
		Interest Revenue			20.00
		Accounts Receivable			13.50
		To record adjustments to Cash account.			

Alternatively:

1999					
Mar.	31	Cash		1,033.50	
		Notes Receivable			1,000.00
		Interest Revenue			20.00
		Accounts Receivable			13.50
		To record additions to Cash account.			
		Bank Service Charge Expense		10.00	
		Accounts Receivable		75.00	
		Notes Payable		507.50	
		Cash			592.50
		To record deductions from Cash account.			

New Terms

Accounting system   Methods and records established to identify, assemble, analyze, classify, record, and report an entity's transactions to provide complete, accurate, and timely financial information. *295*

Bank reconciliation   A schedule the company (depositor) prepares to *reconcile*, or explain, the difference between the cash balance on the bank statement and the cash balance on the company's books; often called a *bank reconciliation statement* or *schedule*. *309*

Bank statement   A statement issued (usually monthly) by a bank describing the activities in a depositor's checking account during the period. *306*

Cash   Includes coins; currency; certain undeposited negotiable instruments such as checks, bank drafts, and money orders; amounts in checking and savings accounts; and demand certificates of deposit. *302*

Cashier's check   A check made out to either the depositor or a third party and written, or drawn, by a bank after deducting the amount of the check from the depositor's account or receiving cash from the depositor. *312*

Certificate of deposit (CD)   An interest-bearing deposit that can be withdrawn from a bank at will (demand CD) or at a fixed maturity date (time CD). *302*

Certified check   A check written, or drawn, by a depositor and taken to the depositor's bank for certification. The check is deducted from the depositor's balance immediately and becomes a liability of the bank. Thus, it usually is accepted without question.   *312*

Check   A written order to a bank to pay a specific sum of money to the party designated as the payee by the party issuing the check.   *305*

Checking account   A money balance maintained in a bank that is subject to withdrawal by the depositor, or owner of the money, on demand.   *305*

Control environment   Reflects the overall attitude, awareness, and actions of the board of directors, management, and stockholders.   *295*

Control procedures   Policies and procedures in addition to the control environment and the accounting system that management has established to provide reasonable assurance that the company will achieve its specific objectives.   *295*

Credit memo   A form used by a bank to explain an addition to the depositor's account.   *308*

Debit memo   A form used by a bank to explain a deduction from the depositor's account.   *308*

Deposit in transit   Typically, a day's cash receipts recorded in the depositor's books in one period but recorded as a deposit by the bank in the succeeding period.   *309*

Deposit ticket   A form that shows the date and the items that make up the deposit.   *305*

Drawer   The party (depositor) writing a check.   *305*

Fidelity bonds   Ensure that a company is reimbursed for losses due to theft of cash and other monetary assets.   *299*

Internal auditing   Consists of investigating and evaluating employees' compliance with the company's policies and procedures. Internal auditing is performed by company personnel.   *297*

Internal auditors   Auditors employed by the company to perform internal audits. These auditors are trained in company policies and in internal auditing duties such as testing effectiveness of controls and procedures involving cash receipts and cash disbursements.   *297*

Internal control structure   Policies and procedures established to provide reasonable assurance that specific entity objectives will be achieved.   *295, 296*

Invoice   Statement sent by the supplier to the purchaser requesting payment for the merchandise shipped.   *298*

NSF (not sufficient funds) check   A customer's check returned from the customer's bank to the depositor's bank because the funds in the customer's checking account balance were insufficient to cover the check.   *306*

Outstanding checks   Checks issued by a depositor that have not yet been paid by the bank on which they are drawn.   *309*

Payee   The party to whom a check is made payable.   *305*

Petty cash fund   A nominal sum of money established as a separate fund from which minor cash disbursements for valid business purposes are made. The cash in the fund plus the vouchers covering disbursements should always equal the balance at which the fund was established and at which it is carried in the Petty Cash account.   *312*

Petty cash voucher   A document or form that shows the amount of, and reason for, a petty cash disbursement.   *313*

Purchase order   A document sent from the purchasing department to a supplier requesting that merchandise or other items be shipped to the purchaser.   *298*

Purchase requisition   A written request from an employee inside the company to the purchasing department to purchase certain items.   *298*

Quick ratio   The ratio of quick assets (cash, marketable securities, and net receivables) to current liabilities. The quick ratio measures a company's short-term debt-paying ability.   *315*

Receiving report   A document prepared by the receiving department showing the descriptions and quantities of all items received from a supplier in a particular shipment.   *298*

Remittance advice   Informs the payee why the drawer (or maker) of the check is making this payment.   *305*

Segregation of duties   Having one employee responsible for safeguarding an asset and a second employee responsible for maintaining the accounting records for that asset.   *296*

Service charges   Charges assessed by the bank on the depositor to cover the cost of handling the checking account.   *306*

Signature card   Provides the signatures of persons authorized to sign checks drawn on an account.   *305*

Transfer bank accounts   Bank accounts set up so that local banks automatically transfer to a central bank (by wire or written bank draft) all amounts on deposit in excess of a stated amount.   *308*

Wire transfer of funds   Interbank transfer of funds by telephone.   *308*

Self-Test

True-False

Indicate whether each of the following statements is true or false.

1. Cash includes coin, currency, postdated checks, money orders, and money on deposit with banks.

2. To effectively manage its cash, a company should make certain that enough cash is available to pay bills as they come due.

3. The cash balance on the bank statement is usually equal to the cash balance in the depositor's books.

4. A deposit in transit requires an entry in the depositor's books after the bank reconciliation is prepared.

5. For control purposes, a company should issue checks for every payment, regardless of its amount.

MULTIPLE-CHOICE

Select the best answer for each of the following questions.

1. The objectives of the internal control structure of a company include all of the following except:
   a. Compliance with company policies and federal law.
   b. Protection of its assets.
   c. Increase in accuracy and reliability of accounting data.
   d. Guarantee of a certain level of profit.
   e. Evaluation of personnel performance to promote efficiency of operations.

Use the following information to answer Questions 2–4:

Balance per bank statement	$1,951.20
Balance per ledger	1,869.60
Deposits in transit	271.20
Outstanding checks	427.80
NSF check	61.20
Service charges	13.80

2. The adjusted cash balance is:
   a. $1,794.60.
   b. $1,719.60.
   c. $1,638.00.

   d. $1,713.00.
   e. $1,876.20.

3. In a bank reconciliation, deposits in transit should be:
   a. Deducted from the balance per books.
   b. Deducted from the balance per bank statement.
   c. Added to the balance per ledger.
   d. Added to the balance per bank statement.
   e. Disregarded in the bank reconciliation.

4. After the bank reconciliation is prepared, the entry to record bank service charges would have a credit to:
   a. Bank Service Charge Expense.
   b. Cash.
   c. Petty Cash.
   d. Cash Short and Over.
   e. None of the above.

5. The entry to replenish the petty cash fund for disbursements made for stamps includes:
   a. A credit to Petty Cash.
   b. A credit to Postage Expense.
   c. A debit to Accounts Payable.
   d. A credit to Cash.
   e. None of the above.

Now turn to page 329 to check your answers.

QUESTIONS

1. Why should a company establish an internal control structure?
2. Why are mechanical devices used in an internal control structure?
3. Identify some features that could strengthen an internal control structure.
4. Name several control documents used in merchandise transactions.
5. What are the four objectives sought in effective cash management?
6. List four essential features of internal control over cash receipts.
7. The bookkeeper of a given company was stealing cash received from customers in payment of their accounts. To conceal the theft, the bookkeeper made out false credit memos indicating returns and allowances made by or granted to customers. What feature of internal control would have prevented the thefts?
8. List six essential features of internal control over cash disbursements.
9. What types of items cause the balance per ledger and the balance per bank statement to disagree?
10. "The difference between a company's Cash account balance and the balance on its bank statement is usually a matter of timing." Do you agree or disagree? Why?
11. Explain how transfer bank accounts can help bring about effective cash management.

12. Describe the operation of a petty cash fund and its advantages. Indicate how control is maintained over petty cash transactions.
13. When are entries made to the Petty Cash account?

The Coca-Cola Company

14. **Real World Question** From the consolidated balance sheet of The Coca-Cola Company in the annual report booklet, identify the total 1996 cash and marketable securities. Explain the definition of cash equivalents and marketable securities in accordance with footnote 1—Accounting Policies.

MAYTAG

15. **Real World Question** Based on the financial statements of Maytag Corporation contained in the annual report booklet, what was the 1996 ending cash and cash equivalents balance? What percentage of current assets does the amount of cash and cash equivalents represent for each of the two years shown?

THE LIMITED, INC.

16. **Real World Question** Based on the financial statements of The Limited, Inc., in the annual report booklet, what was the 1996 ending cash and cash equivalents

balance? What percentage of current assets does the amount of cash and cash equivalents represent for each of the two years shown?

HARLAND

17. **Real World Question** Based on the financial statements of John H. Harland Company contained in the annual report booklet, what was the 1996 ending short-term investments balance? How does this compare with the preceding year?

EXERCISES

State whether each of the following statements about internal control is *true* or *false*:

a. Those employees responsible for safeguarding an asset should maintain the accounting records for that asset.

b. Complete, accurate, and up-to-date accounting records should be maintained.

c. Whenever possible, responsibilities should be assigned and duties subdivided in such a way that only one employee is responsible for a given function.

d. Employees should be assigned to one job and should remain in that job so that skill levels will be as high as possible.

e. The use of check protectors, cash registers, and time clocks is recommended.

f. An internal auditing function should not be implemented because it leads the employees to believe that management does not trust them.

g. One of the best protections against theft is to hire honest, competent employees.

h. A foolproof internal control structure can be devised if management puts forth the effort.

Exercise 8–1
Answer true-false questions about internal control (L.O. 1)

Concerning internal control, which one of the following statements is correct? Explain.

a. Broadly speaking, an internal control structure is only necessary in large organizations.

b. The purposes of internal control are to check the accuracy of accounting data, safeguard assets against theft, promote efficiency of operations, and ensure that management's policies are being followed.

c. Once an internal control structure has been established, it should be effective as long as the formal organization remains unchanged.

d. An example of internal control is having one employee count the day's cash receipts and compare the total with the total of the cash register tapes.

Exercise 8–2
Answer multiple-choice question about internal control (L.O. 1)

The bank statement for Yarley Company at the end of August showed a balance of $12,862. Checks outstanding totaled $3,937, and deposits in transit were $5,990. If these amounts are the only pertinent data available to you, what was the adjusted balance of cash at the end of August?

Exercise 8–3
Determine available cash balance from bank statement and Cash account data (L.O. 4)

From the following data, prepare a bank reconciliation and determine the correct available cash balance for Reed Company as of October 31, 1999.

Exercise 8–4
Prepare a bank reconciliation and specify cash available (L.O. 4)

Balance per bank statement, October 31, 1999	$13,974
Ledger account balance, October 31, 1999	8,088
Proceeds of a note collected by bank not yet entered in ledger (includes $500 of interest)	6,000
Bank service charges not yet entered by Reed Company	18
Deposit in transit	1,680
Outstanding checks:	
No. 327	654
No. 328	288
No. 329	390
No. 331	252

Exercise 8–5
Record necessary journal entry or entries to correct cash balance (L.O. 4)

The following is a bank reconciliation for Brian Company as of August 31, 1999.

Balance per bank statement, August 31, 1999		$ 7,470
Add: Deposit in transit		5,676
		$13,146
Less: Outstanding checks		6,024
Adjusted balance, August 31, 1999		$ 7,122
Balance per ledger, August 31, 1999		$ 7,248
Add: Error correction.		54*
		$ 7,302
Less: NSF check	$150	
Service charges	30	180
Adjusted balance, August 31, 1999		$ 7,122

*The error occurred when the bookkeeper debited Accounts Payable and credited Cash for $93.00, instead of the correct amount, $39.00.

Prepare the journal entry or entries needed to adjust or correct the Cash account.

Exercise 8–6
Determine checks outstanding (L.O. 4)

On March 1 of the current year, Shelbey Company had outstanding checks of $15,000. During March, the company issued an additional $57,000 of checks. As of March 31, the bank statement showed $48,000 of checks had cleared the bank during the month. What is the amount of outstanding checks on March 31?

Exercise 8–7
Determine deposits in transit (L.O. 4)

Matson Company's bank statement as of August 31, 1999, shows total deposits into the company's account of $15,000 and a total of 14 separate deposits. On July 31, deposits of $410 and $330 were in transit. The total cash receipts for August were $19,000, and the company's records show 13 deposits made in August. What is the amount of deposits in transit at August 31?

Exercise 8–8
Prepare a bank reconciliation and necessary journal entry or entries (L.O. 4)

Holder Company deposits all cash receipts intact each day and makes all payments by check. On October 31, after all posting was completed, its Cash account had a debit balance of $4,325. The bank statement for the month ended on October 31 showed a balance of $3,988. Other data are:

1. Outstanding checks total $425.
2. October 31 cash receipts of $838 were placed in the bank's night depository and do not appear on the bank statement.
3. Bank service charges for October are $14.
4. Check No. 772 for store supplies on hand was entered at $405, but paid by the bank at its actual amount of $315.

Prepare a bank reconciliation for Holder Company as of October 31. Also prepare any necessary journal entry or entries.

Exercise 8–9
Record the reimbursement of petty cash fund (L.O. 5)

On August 31, 1999, Brighton Company's petty cash fund contained coins and currency of $260, an IOU from an employee of $30, and vouchers showing expenditures of $120 for postage, $52 for taxi fare, and $138 to entertain a customer. The Petty Cash account shows a balance of $600. The fund is replenished on August 31 because financial statements are to be prepared. What journal entry is required on August 31?

Exercise 8–10
Record the reimbursement of petty cash fund (L.O. 5)

Use the data in Exercise 8–9. What entry would have been required if the amount of coin and currency had been $247.20? Which of the accounts debited would not appear in the income statement?

Exercise 8–11
Prepare journal entries regarding petty cash (L.O. 5)

Rock Company has a $450 petty cash fund. The following transactions occurred in December:

Dec. 2 The petty cash fund was increased to $1,350.
     8 Petty Cash Voucher No. 318 for $14.20 delivery expense was prepared and paid. The fund was not replenished at this time.
   20 The company decided that the fund was too large and reduced it to $1,120.

Prepare any necessary journal entries for these transactions.

PROBLEMS

The following data pertain to England Company:

1. Balance per the bank statement dated June 30, 1999, is $30,000.
2. Balance of the Cash in Bank account on the company books as of June 30, 1999, is $8,795.
3. Outstanding checks as of June 30, 1999, total $14,300.
4. Bank deposit of June 30 for $2,735 was not included in the deposits per the bank statement.
5. The bank had collected proceeds of a note, $22,612 (of which $112 was interest), that it credited to the England Company account. The bank charged the company a collection fee of $15 on the note.
6. The bank erroneously charged the England Company account for a $10,500 debit memo of another company that has a similar name.
7. Bank service charges for June, exclusive of the collection fee, amounted to $95.
8. Among the canceled checks was one for $700 given in payment of an account. The bookkeeper had recorded the check at $920 in the company records.
9. A check of Crosby, a customer, for $2,447, deposited on June 20, was returned by the bank marked NSF. No entry has been made to reflect the returned check on the company records.
10. A check for $1,435 of Malcolm, a customer, which had been deposited in the bank, was erroneously recorded by the bookkeeper as $1,570. The check had been received as a payment on the customer's account receivable.

Prepare a bank reconciliation as of June 30, 1999, and any necessary journal entry or entries to correct the accounts.

Problem 8–1
Prepare bank reconciliation with necessary journal entry or entries (L.O. 4)

Required

The bank statement of Irish Company's checking account with the 2nd National Bank shows:

Balance, June 30, 1999		$166,118
Deposits		245,700
		$411,818
Less: Checks deducted	$243,001	
Service charges	67	243,068
Balance, July 31, 1999		$168,750

The following additional data are available:

1. Balance per ledger account as of July 31 was $128,209.
2. A credit memo included with the bank statement indicated the collection of a note by the bank for Irish Company. Proceeds were $13,500, of which $375 was interest.
3. An NSF check in the amount of $6,210 was returned by the bank and included in the total of checks deducted on the bank statement.
4. Deposits in transit as of July 31 totaled $33,750.
5. Checks outstanding as of July 31 were $55,350.
6. The bank added the $29,025 deposit of another company to Irish's account in error.
7. The bank deducted one of Irish's checks as $20,250 instead of the correct amount of $2,025.
8. Deposit of July 21 was recorded by the company as $4,299.75 and by the bank at the actual amount of $4,542.75. The receipts for the day were from collections on account.
9. The deposits amount shown on the bank statement includes $675 of interest earned by Irish on its checking account with the bank.

a. Prepare a bank reconciliation as of July 31, 1999, for Irish Company.
b. Prepare any journal entry or entries needed at July 31, 1999.

Problem 8–2
Prepare bank reconciliation with necessary journal entry or entries (L.O. 4)

Required

Problem 8–3
Prepare journal entries to
record establishment and
reimbursement of petty
cash fund (L.O. 5)

Transactions involving the petty cash fund of Sonar Company during 1999 are as follows:

Mar. 1   Established a petty cash fund of $750, which will be under the control of the
assistant office manager.

31   Fund was replenished on this date. Prior to replenishment, the fund consisted
of the following:

Coins and currency	$491.50
Petty cash vouchers indicating disbursements for:	
Postage stamps	82.00
Supper money for office employees working overtime	36.00
Office supplies	32.70
Window washing service	60.00
Flowers for wedding of employee	15.00
Flowers for hospitalized employee	15.00
Employee's IOU	15.00

Required   Present journal entries for these transactions. Use the Cash Short and Over account for any
shortage or overage in the fund.

Problem 8–4
Prepare journal entries to
record establishment,
reimbursement, and
increase of petty cash fund
(L.O. 5)

Sun Company has decided to use a petty cash fund. Transactions involving this fund in
1999 follow:

June 4   Set up a petty cash fund of $225.

22   When the fund had a cash amount of $31.35, the custodian of the fund was
reimbursed for expenditures made, including:

Transportation-in	$82.50
Postage	27.00
Office supplies	81.75

30   The fund was reimbursed to include petty cash items in the financial
statements prepared for the fiscal year ending on this date. The fund had the
following cash and vouchers before reimbursement:

Coins and currency	$174.00
Petty cash vouchers for:	
Employee's IOU	15.00
Postage	27.00
Office supplies	11.10

July 1   The petty cash fund balance is increased to $300.

Required   Prepare journal entries for all of these transactions.

ALTERNATE PROBLEMS

Problem 8–1A
Prepare bank reconciliation
with necessary journal
entry or entries (L.O. 4)

The following June 30, 1999, bank reconciliation pertains to Tiffany Company:

		Cash Account	Bank Statement
Balance, June 30		$29,143.36	$28,644.31
Add: Deposit not credited by bank			942.60
Total			$29,586.91
Less: Outstanding checks:			
No. 724	$ 18.45		
No. 886	15.00		
No. 896	143.55		
No. 897	187.65		
No. 898	78.90		443.55
Adjusted cash balance, June 30		$29,143.36	$29,143.36

Tiffany's July bank statement follows:

Balance, July 1		$28,644.31
Deposits during July		5,441.94 $34,086.25
Canceled checks returned:		
No. 724	$ 18.45	
No. 896	143.55	
No. 897	187.65	
No. 898	78.90	
No. 899	18.86	
No. 900	1,349.55	
No. 902	946.92	
No. 904	44.01	$ 2,787.89
NSF check of Starr Company		139.98 2,927.87
Bank statement balance, July 31		$31,158.38

The cash receipts deposited in July, including receipts of July 31, amounted to $5,178.30. Tiffany wrote these checks in July:

No. 899	$ 18.86
No. 900	1,349.55
No. 901	27.75
No. 902	946.92
No. 903	59.70
No. 904	44.01
No. 905	1,093.50
No. 906	15.00

The cash balance per the ledger on July 31, 1999, was $30,766.37.

Prepare a bank reconciliation as of July 31, 1999, and any necessary journal entry or entries to correct the accounts. *Required*

The following information pertains to Hughes Company as of May 31, 1999:

Problem 8–2A
Prepare bank reconciliation with necessary journal entry or entries (L.O. 4)

1. Balance per bank statement as of May 31, 1999, was $59,410.
2. Balance per Hughes Company's Cash account at May 31, 1999, was $60,904.
3. A late deposit on May 31 did not appear on the bank statement, $4,275.
4. Outstanding checks as of May 31 totaled $7,614.
5. During May, the bank credited Hughes Company with the proceeds, $6,795, of a note which it had collected for the company. Interest revenue was $45 of the total.
6. Bank service and collection charges for May amounted to $18.
7. Comparison of the canceled checks with the check register revealed that one check in the amount as $1,458 had been recorded in the books as $1,539. The check had been issued in payment of an account payable.
8. A review of the deposit slips with the bank statement showed that a deposit for $2,250 of a company with a similar account number had been credited to the Hughes Company account in error.
9. A $270 check received from a customer, R. Petty, was returned with the bank statement marked NSF.
10. During May, the bank paid a $13,500 note of Hughes Company plus interest of $135 and charged it to the company's account per instructions received. Hughes Company had not recorded the payment of this note.
11. An examination of the cash receipts and the deposit tickets revealed that the bookkeeper erroneously recorded a check from a customer, C. Parker, of $1,458 as $1,944.
12. The bank statement showed a credit to the company's account for interest earned on the account balance in May of $450.

a. Prepare a bank reconciliation as of May 31, 1999. *Required*
b. Prepare the journal entry or entries necessary to adjust the accounts as of May 31, 1999.

Problem 8–3A
Prepare journal entries to record establishment and reimbursement of petty cash fund (L.O. 5)

The following transactions pertain to the petty cash fund of Carrington Company during 1999:

Nov. 2   A $450 check is drawn, cashed, and the cash placed in the care of the assistant office manager to be used as a petty cash fund.

Dec 17   The fund is replenished. An analysis of the fund shows:

Coins and currency	$147.40
Petty cash vouchers for:	
Delivery expenses	173.48
Transportation-in	111.12
Postage stamps purchased	15.00

31   The end of the accounting period falls on this date. The fund was not replenished. The fund's contents on this date consist of:

Coins and currency	$352.05
Petty cash vouchers for:	
Delivery expenses	31.65
Postage stamps purchased	36.30
Employee's IOU	30.00

Required   Present journal entries to record these transactions. Use the Cash Short and Over account for any shortage or overage in the fund.

Problem 8–4A
Prepare journal entries to record establishment, reimbursement, and increase of petty cash fund (L.O. 5)

The following transactions relate to the petty cash fund of Jarvis Wrecking Company in 1999:

Apr. 1   The petty cash fund is set up with a $350 cash balance.
19   Because the money in the fund is down to $70.20, the fund is replenished. Petty cash vouchers are as follows:

Flowers for hospitalized employee (miscellaneous expense)	$ 84.38
Postage stamps	135.00
Office supplies	46.71

30   The cash in the fund is $193.07. The fund is replenished to include petty cash payments in this period's financial statements. The petty cash vouchers are for the following:

Transportation-in	$64.12
Office supplies	92.81

May 1   The petty cash fund balance is increased to $400.

Required   Prepare the journal entries to record these transactions.

BEYOND THE NUMBERS—CRITICAL THINKING

Business Decision Case 8–1
Discuss steps to prevent theft (L.O. 1, 3)

During a national emergency, a managerial accountant was called back to active duty with the U.S. Army. An acquaintance of the accountant forged papers and assumed the identity of the accountant. He obtained a position in a small company as the only accountant. Eventually he took over from the manager the functions of approving bills for payment, preparing and signing checks, and almost all other financial duties. On one weekend, he traveled to some neighboring cities and mailed invoices made out to the company for which he worked. On Monday morning, he returned to work and began receiving, approving, and paying the invoices he had prepared. The following weekend he returned to the neighboring cities and cashed and deposited the checks in bank accounts under his own name. After continuing this practice for several months, he withdrew all of the funds and never was heard from again.

Required   Prepare a written list of the steps you would have taken to prevent this theft. Remember that this small company had limited financial resources.

Business Decision Case 8–2
List procedures that would have prevented theft of cash (L.O. 1, 3)

John Billings was set up in business by his father, who purchased the business of an elderly acquaintance wishing to retire. One of the few changes in personnel made by Billings was to install a college classmate as the office manager-bookkeeper-cashier-sales manager. During the course of the year, Billings borrowed money from the bank with his father as cosigner. Although his business seemed profitable, there was a shortage of cash. The company's investments in inventories and receivables grew substantially. Finally, after a year had elapsed, Billings's father employed you, a certified public accountant, to audit the records of his business. You reported that the office manager-bookkeeper-cashier-sales manager had been misappropriating funds and had been using a variety of schemes to cover his actions. More specifically, he had:

1. Pocketed cash receipts from sales and understated the cash register readings at the end of the day or altered the copies of the sales tickets retained.

2. Stolen checks mailed to the company in payment of accounts receivable, credited the proper accounts, and then debited fictitious receivables to keep the records in balance.

3. Issued checks to fictitious suppliers and deposited them in accounts bearing these names with himself as signer of checks drawn on these accounts; the books were kept in balance by debiting the Purchases account.

4. Stolen petty cash funds by drawing false vouchers purporting to cover a variety of expenses incurred.

5. Prepared false sales returns vouchers indicating the return of cash sales to cover further thefts of cash receipts.

For each item in the preceding list, describe in writing at least one feature of good internal control that would have prevented the losses due to dishonesty.

Required

Business Decision Case 8–3*
Describe method used to steal cash; determine amount stolen; prepare correct bank reconciliation; and describe internal control procedures that would have prevented such theft (L.O. 1, 3, 4)

The outstanding checks of Brothers Company at November 30, 1999, were:

No.	229	$1,000
No.	263	1,089
No.	3678	679
No.	3679	804
No.	3680	1,400

During December, Brothers issued checks numbered 3681–3720; and all of these checks cleared the bank except 3719 and 3720 for $963 and $726, respectively. Checks 3678, 3679, and 3680 also cleared the bank.

The bank statement on December 31 showed a balance of $23,944. Service charges amounted to $20, and two checks were returned by the bank, one marked NSF in the amount of $114 and the other marked "No account" in the amount of $2,000.

Brian Askew recently retired as the office manager-cashier-bookkeeper for Brothers Company and was replaced by Fred Hannah. Hannah noted the absence of an internal control structure but was momentarily deterred from embezzling for lack of a scheme of concealment. Finally, he hit upon several schemes. The $2,000 check marked "No account" by the bank is the product of one scheme. Hannah took cash receipts and replaced them with a check drawn on a nonexistent account to make it appear that a customer had given the company a worthless check.

The other scheme was more subtle. Hannah pocketed cash receipts in an amount equal to two unlisted outstanding checks and prepared the following bank reconciliation:

Balance per bank statement, December 31, 1999		$23,944.00
Add: Deposit in transit		2,837.80
		$26,781.80
Less: Outstanding checks:		
No. 3719	$ 963.00	
No. 3720	726.00	1,689.00
Adjusted balance		$25,092.80
Balance, Cash account December 31, 1999		$27,226.80
Less: Worthless check	$2,000.00	
NSF check	114.00	
Service charges	20.00	2,134.00
Adjusted balance, December 31, 1999		$25,092.80

*Note: This challenging problem was not specifically illustrated in the chapter, but it can be worked by applying the principles discussed in the chapter.

Required

a. State the nature of the second scheme hit on by Hannah. How much in total does it appear he has stolen by use of the two schemes together?

b. Prepare a correct bank reconciliation as of December 31, 1999.

c. After your analysis in (a) and (b), describe several procedures that would have defeated Fred Hannah's attempts to misappropriate funds and conceal these actions.

Annual Report Analysis 8–4
Discuss internal control elements (L.O. 1)

In Reader's Digest's 1996 Annual Report, under Report of Management, the chairman and chief executive officer and the executive vice president and chief financial officer stated:

The company maintains a system of internal accounting controls designed to provide reasonable assurance, at reasonable cost, that transactions and events are recorded properly and that assets are safeguarded. The internal control system is supported by written policies and procedures and by the careful selection, training, and supervision of qualified personnel, and is monitored by an internal audit function.

Required

What is the purpose of this statement? To which basic elements of the internal control structure does the statement refer?

Annual Report Analysis 8–5
Calculate the quick ratio (L.O. 6)

Determine the 1996 and 1995 quick ratios for the John H. Harland Company based on its annual report in the annual report booklet. Comment on the results.

Ethics Case—Writing Experience 8–6
Respond regarding the ethics case

After reading the ethics case on page 315, discuss the ethical situation at the City Club Restaurant. Describe the steps the owners could take to end John Blue's wage supplement scheme.

Group Project 8–7
Evaluate internal controls

With a small group of students, visit a large local company to inquire about its internal control structure. Specifically, discover how it protects its assets against theft and waste, ensures compliance with company policies and federal laws, evaluates performance of its personnel, and ensures accurate and reliable operating data and accounting reports. If an internal audit staff exists, inquire about some of its activities. Write a report to your instructor summarizing your findings and be prepared to make a short presentation to the class.

Group Project 8–8
Evaluate controls over petty cash

With one or two other students, locate and visit two companies that maintain petty cash funds. Interview the custodians of those funds to identify the controls that are used to manage those funds. Write a report to your instructor comparing the controls used, pointing out any differences between the control systems and any deficiencies in the systems. Be prepared to make a short presentation to the class.

Group Project 8–9
Perform library research

"Kiting" of bank accounts has been used to conceal shortages in bank accounts. With one or two other students, research this topic in the library. Write a paper to your instructor describing how this technique works and the steps that can be taken to detect it once it occurs and to prevent it in the future.

USING THE INTERNET—A VIEW OF THE REAL WORLD

Internet Project 8–10
Learn about internal control department

Visit the following site:

http://www.aetna.com/audit/

Aetna is the 42nd largest company on the Fortune 500 list and is one of the world's largest insurance and financial services. Browse around this site to learn about Aetna's internal control department and its approach to their work. Then write a memo to your instructor summarizing what you learned.

Internet Project 8–11
Investigate EDGAR

Visit the Securities and Exchange website and find the EDGAR database at:

http://www.sec.gov/edgarhp.htm

EDGAR stands for the Electronic Data Gathering, Analysis, and Retrieval system. What is its purpose? What kinds of information can be found at this site? Select a company of your choice and search the EDGAR database for information on that company. Write a report to your instructor summarizing your findings.

ANSWERS TO SELF-TEST

TRUE-FALSE

1. **False.** Postdated checks are not included as cash.

2. **True.** A company should make sure that enough cash is available to pay bills as they come due.

3. **False.** The cash balance on a bank statement is not usually the same as the cash balance in the depositor's books because of deposits in transit, outstanding checks, and bank service charges.

4. **False.** A deposit in transit is one of the items that has been correctly recorded as a debit to the Cash account of the depositor and will be recorded as a deposit by the bank after the bank employees open the night deposit chute.

5. **False.** For convenience, a company may use a petty cash fund for small amounts of cash payments such as delivery charges or postage stamps.

MULTIPLE-CHOICE

1. **d.** An effective internal control structure does not necessarily guarantee a certain level of profits.

2. **a.**

Balance per bank statement	$1,951.20
Add: Deposits in transit	271.20
Less: Outstanding checks	(427.80)
Adjusted balance	$1,794.60
Balance per ledger	$1,869.60
Less: NSF check	(61.20)
Service charges	(13.80)
Adjusted balance	$1,794.60

3. **d.** Deposits in transit have been recorded in the company's accounting records but have not yet been recorded in the bank's records.

4. **b.** The entry to record bank service charges on the books is:

Bank Service Charge Expense	13.80	
Cash		13.80

5. **d.** The entry to replenish the petty cash fund has a credit to Cash, not Petty Cash.

Postage Expense	xxx	
Cash		xxx

9

RECEIVABLES AND PAYABLES

Much of the growth of business in recent years is due to the immense expansion of credit. Managers of companies have learned that by granting customers the privilege of *charging* their purchases, sales and profits increase. Using credit is not only a convenient way to make purchases but also the only way many people can own high-priced items such as automobiles.

This chapter discusses receivables and payables. For a company, a **receivable** is any sum of money due to be paid to that company from any party for any reason. Similarly, a **payable** describes any sum of money to be paid by that company to any party for any reason.

Primarily, receivables arise from the sale of goods and services. The two types of receivables are accounts receivable, which companies offer for short-term credit with no interest charge; and notes receivable, which companies sometimes extend for both short- and long-term credit with an interest charge. We pay particular attention to accounting for uncollectible accounts receivable.

Like their customers, companies use credit, which they show as accounts payable or notes payable. Accounts payable normally result from the purchase of goods or services and do not carry an interest charge. Short-term notes payable carry an interest charge and may arise from the same transactions as accounts payable, but they can also result from borrowing money from a bank or other institution. Chapter 4 identified accounts payable and short-term notes payable as current liabilities. A company also incurs other current liabilities, including payables such as sales tax payable, estimated product warranty payable, and certain liabilities that are contingent on the occurrence of future events. Long-term notes payable usually result from borrowing money from a bank or other institution to finance the acquisition of plant assets. As you study this chapter and learn how important credit is to our economy, you will realize that credit in some form will probably always be with us.

ACCOUNTS RECEIVABLE

In Chapter 3, you learned that most companies use the accrual basis of accounting since it better reflects the actual results of the operations of a business. Under the accrual basis, a merchandising company that extends credit records revenue when it makes a sale because at this time it has earned and realized the revenue. The company has earned the revenue because it has completed the seller's part of the sales contract by delivering the goods. The company has realized the revenue because it has received the customer's promise to pay in exchange for the goods. This promise to pay by the customer is an account receivable to the seller. Accounts receivable are amounts that customers owe a company for goods sold and services rendered on account. Frequently, these receivables resulting from credit sales of goods and services are called **trade receivables**.

When a company sells goods on account, customers do not sign formal, written promises to pay, but they agree to abide by the company's customary credit terms. However, customers may sign a sales invoice to acknowledge purchase of goods. Payment terms for sales on account typically run from 30 to 60 days. Companies usually do not charge interest on amounts owed, except on some past-due amounts.

Because customers do not always keep their promises to pay, companies must provide for these uncollectible accounts in their records. Companies use two methods for handling uncollectible accounts. The allowance method provides in advance for uncollectible accounts. The direct write-off method recognizes bad accounts as an expense at the point when judged to be uncollectible and is the required method for federal income tax purposes. However, since the allowance method represents the accrual basis of accounting and is the accepted method to record uncollectible accounts for financial accounting purposes, we only discuss and illustrate the allowance method in this text.

Even though companies carefully screen credit customers, they cannot eliminate all uncollectible accounts. Companies expect some of their accounts to become uncollectible, but they do not know which ones. The matching principle requires deducting expenses incurred in producing revenues from those revenues during the accounting period. The allowance method of recording uncollectible accounts adheres to this principle by recognizing the uncollectible accounts expense in advance of identifying *specific accounts* as being uncollectible. The required entry has some similarity to the depreciation entry in Chapter 3 because it debits an expense and credits an allowance (contra asset). The purpose of the entry is to make the income statement fairly present the proper expense and the balance sheet fairly present the asset. **Uncollectible accounts expense** (also called *doubtful accounts expense* or **bad debts expense**) is an operating expense that a business incurs when it sells on credit. We classify uncollectible accounts expense as a selling expense because it results from credit sales. Other accountants might classify it as an administrative expense because the credit department has an important role in setting credit terms.

To adhere to the matching principle, companies must match the uncollectible accounts expense against the revenues it generates. Thus, an uncollectible account arising from a sale made in 1999 is a 1999 expense even though this treatment requires the use of estimates. Estimates are necessary because the company sometimes cannot determine until 2000 or later which 1999 customer accounts will become uncollectible.

RECORDING THE UNCOLLECTIBLE ACCOUNTS ADJUSTMENT   A company that estimates uncollectible accounts makes an adjusting entry at the end of each accounting period. It debits Uncollectible Accounts Expense, thus recording the operating expense in the proper period. The credit is to an account called *Allowance for Uncollectible Accounts*.

(*concluded*)

6. Account for borrowing money using an interest-bearing note versus a noninterest-bearing note.

7. Analyze and use the financial results—accounts receivable turnover and the number of days' sales in accounts receivable.

Note to the Student
How many credit cards do you use? Which type? What form of credit do you use to purchase a car? What form of credit would you use to purchase a CD player?

The Allowance Method for Recording Uncollectible Accounts

Objective 1
Account for uncollectible accounts receivable under the allowance method.

Note to the Student
Why would a company sell for credit and risk uncollectible expenses?
Answer: The profit a company makes by granting credit is greater than the cost of granting credit—uncollectible accounts expense.

Note to the Student

Accounts
receivable   −   Allowance for uncollectible accounts
= Net realizable value
This formula reflects what management expects to collect on its total accounts receivable.

As a contra account to the Accounts Receivable account, the **Allowance for Uncollectible Accounts** (also called *Allowance for Doubtful Accounts* or *Allowance for Bad Debts*) reduces accounts receivable to their net realizable value. **Net realizable value** is the amount the company expects to collect from accounts receivable. When the firm makes the uncollectible accounts adjusting entry, it does not know which specific accounts will become uncollectible. Thus, the company cannot enter credits in either the Accounts Receivable control account or the customers' accounts receivable subsidiary ledger accounts. If only one or the other were credited, the Accounts Receivable control account balance would not agree with the total of the balances in the accounts receivable subsidiary ledger. Without crediting the Accounts Receivable control account, the allowance account lets the company show that some of its accounts receivable are probably uncollectible.

To illustrate the adjusting entry for uncollectible accounts, assume a company has $100,000 of accounts receivable and estimates its uncollectible accounts expense for a given year at $4,000. The required year-end adjusting entry is:

Dec.	31	Uncollectible Accounts Expense.	4,000	
		Allowance for Uncollectible Accounts		4,000
		To record estimated uncollectible accounts.		

The debit to Uncollectible Accounts Expense brings about a matching of expenses and revenues on the income statement; uncollectible accounts expense is matched against the revenues of the accounting period. The credit to Allowance for Uncollectible Accounts reduces accounts receivable to their net realizable value on the balance sheet. When the books are closed, the firm closes Uncollectible Accounts Expense to Income Summary. It reports the allowance on the balance sheet as a deduction from accounts receivable as follows:

BRICE COMPANY
Balance Sheet
December 31, 1999
Assets

Current assets:		
Cash		$21,200
Accounts receivable	$100,000	
Less: Allowance for uncollectible accounts	4,000	96,000

ESTIMATING UNCOLLECTIBLE ACCOUNTS   Accountants use two basic methods to estimate uncollectible accounts for a period. The first method—percentage-of-sales method—focuses on the income statement and the relationship of uncollectible accounts to sales. The second method—percentage-of-receivables method—focuses on the balance sheet and the relationship of the allowance for uncollectible accounts to accounts receivable. Either of these estimation methods is acceptable, and over time their results are similar. However, some accountants claim the percentage-of-sales method does a better job of matching expenses with revenues.

Percentage-of-Sales Method   The **percentage-of-sales method** estimates uncollectible accounts from the credit sales of a given period. In theory, the method is based on a percentage of prior years' actual uncollectible accounts to prior years' credit sales. When cash sales are small or make up a fairly constant percentage of total sales, firms base the calculation on total net sales. Since at least one of these conditions is usually met, companies commonly use total net sales rather than credit sales. The formula to determine the amount of the entry is:

$$\text{Amount of journal entry for uncollectible accounts} = \frac{\text{Net sales}}{\text{(total or credit)}} \times \frac{\text{Percentage estimated as uncollectible}}{}$$

To illustrate, assume that Rankin Company's uncollectible accounts from 1997 sales were 1.1% of total net sales. A similar calculation for 1998 showed an uncollectible account percentage of 0.9%. The average for the two years is 1% [(1.1 + 0.9) ÷ 2]. Rankin does not expect 1999 to differ from the previous two years. Total net sales for 1999 were $500,000; receivables at year-end were $100,000; and the Allowance for Uncollectible Accounts had a zero balance. Rankin would make the following adjusting entry for 1999:

Dec.	31	Uncollectible Accounts Expense.	5,000	
		Allowance for Uncollectible Accounts		5,000
		To record estimated uncollectible accounts ($500,000 × 0.01).		

Using T-accounts, Rankin would show:

Uncollectible Accounts Expense		Allowance for Uncollectible Accounts	
Dec. 31 Adjustment	5,000	Bal. before adjustment	–0–
		Dec. 31 Adjustment	5,000
		Bal. after adjustment	5,000

Rankin reports Uncollectible Accounts Expense on the income statement. It reports the accounts receivable less the allowance among current assets in the balance sheet as follows:

Accounts receivable $100,000
Less: Allowance for uncollectible accounts 5,000 $95,000

Or Rankin's balance sheet could show:

Accounts receivable (less estimated
uncollectible accounts, $5,000) $95,000

On the income statement, Rankin would match the uncollectible accounts expense against sales revenues in the period. We would classify this expense as a selling expense since it is a normal consequence of selling on credit.

The Allowance for Uncollectible Accounts account usually has either a debit or credit balance before the year-end adjustment. Under the percentage-of-sales method, the company ignores any existing balance in the allowance when calculating the amount of the year-end adjustment (except that the allowance account must have a credit balance after adjustment).

For example, assume Rankin's allowance account had a $300 credit balance before adjustment. The adjusting entry would still be for $5,000. However, the balance sheet would show $100,000 accounts receivable less a $5,300 allowance for uncollectible accounts, resulting in net receivables of $94,700. On the income statement, Uncollectible Accounts Expense would still be 1% of total net sales, or $5,000.

In applying the percentage-of-sales method, companies annually review the percentage of uncollectible accounts that resulted from the previous year's sales. If the percentage rate is still valid, the company makes no change. However, if the situation has changed significantly, the company increases or decreases the percentage rate to reflect the changed condition. For example, in periods of recession and high unemployment, a firm may increase the percentage rate to reflect the customers' decreased ability to pay. However, if the company adopts a more stringent credit policy, it may have to decrease the percentage rate because the company would expect fewer uncollectible accounts.

Percentage-of-Receivables Method   The **percentage-of-receivables method** estimates uncollectible accounts by determining the desired size of the Allowance for Uncollectible Accounts. Rankin would multiply the ending balance in Accounts Receivable by a rate (or rates) based on its uncollectible accounts experience. In the

Note to the Student
Under the percentage-of-receivables method, we focus on the valuation of the receivables on the balance sheet. Our goal is to accurately reflect the net realizable value of receivables.

percentage-of-receivables method, the company may use either an overall rate or a different rate for each age category of receivables.

To calculate the amount of the entry for uncollectible accounts under the percentage-of-receivables method using an overall rate, Rankin would use:

$$
\begin{pmatrix} \text{Amount of} \\ \text{entry for} \\ \text{uncollectible} \\ \text{accounts} \end{pmatrix} = \begin{pmatrix} \text{Accounts} \\ \text{Receivable} \\ \text{ending} \\ \text{balance} \end{pmatrix} \times \begin{pmatrix} \text{Percentage} \\ \text{estimated as} \\ \text{uncollectible} \end{pmatrix} - \begin{pmatrix} \text{Existing credit} \\ \text{balance in} \\ \text{Allowance for} \\ \text{Uncollectible} \\ \text{Accounts or} \end{pmatrix} + \begin{pmatrix} \text{Existing debit} \\ \text{balance in} \\ \text{Allowance for} \\ \text{Uncollectible} \\ \text{Accounts} \end{pmatrix}
$$

Using the same information as before, Rankin makes an estimate of uncollectible accounts at the end of 1999. The balance of accounts receivable is $100,000, and the allowance account has no balance. If Rankin estimates that 6% of the receivables will be uncollectible, the adjusting entry would be:

Dec.	31	Uncollectible Accounts Expense.	6,000	
		Allowance for Uncollectible Accounts		6,000
		To record estimated uncollectible accounts ($100,000 × 0.06).		

Using T-accounts, Rankin would show:

Uncollectible Accounts Expense		Allowance for Uncollectible Accounts	
Dec. 31 Adjustment 6,000		Bal. before adjustment –0– Dec. 31 Adjustment 6,000	
		Bal. after adjustment 6,000	

If Rankin had a $300 credit balance in the allowance account before adjustment, the entry would be the same, except that the amount would be $5,700. The difference in amounts arises because management wants the allowance account to contain a credit balance equal to 6% of the outstanding receivables when presenting the two accounts on the balance sheet. The calculation of the necessary adjustment is [($100,000 × 0.06) − $300] = $5,700. Thus, under the percentage-of-receivables method, firms consider any existing balance in the allowance account when adjusting for uncollectible accounts. Using T-accounts, Rankin would show:

Uncollectible Accounts Expense		Allowance for Uncollectible Accounts	
Dec. 31 Adjustment 5,700		Bal. before adjustment 300 Dec. 31 Adjustment 5,700	
		Bal. after adjustment 6,000	

As another example, suppose that Rankin had a $300 debit balance in the allowance account before adjustment. Then, a credit of $6,300 would be necessary to get the balance to the required $6,000 credit balance. The calculation of the necessary adjustment is [($100,000 × 0.06) + $300] = $6,300. Using T-accounts, Rankin would show:

Reinforcing Problem
E9–1 Prepare journal entries to record uncollectible accounts expense.

Uncollectible Accounts Expense		Allowance for Uncollectible Accounts	
Dec. 31 Adjustment 6,300		Bal. before adjustment 300	Dec. 31 Adjustment 6,300
			Bal. after adjustment 6,000

No matter what the preadjustment allowance account balance is, when using the percentage-of-receivables method, Rankin adjusts the Allowance for Uncollectible Accounts so that it has a credit balance of $6,000—equal to 6% of its $100,000 in Accounts Receivable. The desired $6,000 ending credit balance in the Allowance for Uncollectible Accounts serves as a "target" in making the adjustment.

So far, we have used one uncollectibility rate for all accounts receivable, regardless of their age. However, some companies use a different percentage for each age category of accounts receivable. When accountants decide to use a different rate for each age category of receivables, they prepare an aging schedule. An **aging schedule** classifies accounts receivable according to how long they have been outstanding and uses a different uncollectibility percentage rate for each age category. Companies base these percentages on experience. In Illustration 9.1, the aging schedule shows that the older the receivable, the less likely the company is to collect it.

Classifying accounts receivable according to age often gives the company a better basis for estimating the total amount of uncollectible accounts. For example, based on experience, a company can expect only 1% of the accounts not yet due (sales made less than 30 days before the end of the accounting period) to be uncollectible. At the other extreme, a company can expect 50% of all accounts over 90 days past due to be uncollectible. For each age category, the firm multiplies the accounts receivable by the percentage estimated as uncollectible to find the estimated amount uncollectible. The sum of the estimated amounts for all categories yields the total estimated amount uncollectible and is the desired credit balance (the target) in the Allowance for Uncollectible Accounts.

Since the aging schedule approach is an alternative under the percentage-of-receivables method, the balance in the allowance account before adjustment affects the year-end adjusting entry amount recorded for uncollectible accounts. For example, the schedule in Illustration 9.1 shows that $24,400 is needed as the ending credit balance in the allowance account. If the allowance account has a $5,000 credit balance before adjustment, the adjustment would be for $19,400.

The information in an aging schedule also is useful to management for other purposes. Analysis of collection patterns of accounts receivable may suggest the need for changes in credit policies or for added financing. For example, if the age of many customer balances has increased to 61–90 days past due, collection efforts may have to be strengthened. Or, the company may have to find other sources of cash to pay its debts within the discount period. Preparation of an aging schedule may also help identify certain accounts that should be written off as uncollectible.

BUSINESS INSIGHT   According to the Fair Debt Collection Practices Act, collection agencies can call persons only between 8 A.M. and 9 P.M., and cannot use foul language. Agencies can call employers only if the employers allow such calls. And, they can threaten to sue only if they really intend to do so.

AN ACCOUNTING PERSPECTIVE

WRITE-OFF OF RECEIVABLES   As time passes and a firm considers a specific customer's account to be uncollectible, it writes that account off. It debits the Allowance for Uncollectible Accounts. The credit is to the Accounts Receivable control account in the general ledger and to the customer's account in the accounts receivable subsidiary ledger. For example, assume Smith's $750 account has been determined to be uncollectible. The entry to write off this account is:

Allowance for Uncollectible Accounts	750	
Accounts Receivable—Smith		750
To write off Smith's account as uncollectible.		

The credit balance in Allowance for Uncollectible Accounts before making this entry represented potential uncollectible accounts not yet specifically identified. Debiting the allowance account and crediting Accounts Receivable shows that the

ILLUSTRATION 9.1
Accounts Receivable
Aging Schedule

Balance in the Accounts Receivable account in the general ledger

Desired credit balance in the Allowance for Uncollectible Accounts

DARCY COMPANY
Accounts Receivable Aging Schedule
December 31, 1999

Customer	Accounts Receivable Balance	Not Yet Due	Days Past Due			
			1–30	31–60	61–90	Over 90
X	$ 5,000					$ 5,000
Y	14,000		$ 12,000	$2,000		
Z	400				$200	200
All others	808,600	$560,000	240,000	2,000	600	6,000
	$828,000	$560,000	$252,000	$4,000	$800	$11,200
Percentage estimated as uncollectible		1%	5%	10%	25%	50%
Estimated amount uncollectible	$ 24,400	$ 5,600	$ 12,600	$ 400	$200	$ 5,600

firm has identified Smith's account as uncollectible. Notice that the debit in the entry to write off an account receivable does not involve recording an expense. The company recognized the uncollectible accounts expense in the same accounting period as the sale. If Smith's $750 uncollectible account were recorded in Uncollectible Accounts Expense again, it would be counted as an expense twice.

A write-off does not affect the net realizable value of accounts receivable. For example, suppose that Amos Company has total accounts receivable of $50,000 and an allowance of $3,000 before the previous entry; the net realizable value of the accounts receivable is $47,000. After posting that entry, accounts receivable are $49,250, and the allowance is $2,250; net realizable value is still $47,000, as shown here:

	Before Write-Off	Entry for Write-Off	After Write-Off
Accounts receivable	$50,000 Dr.	$750 Cr.	$49,250 Dr.
Allowance for uncollectible accounts	3,000 Cr.	750 Dr.	2,250 Cr.
Net realizable value	$47,000		$47,000

You might wonder how the allowance account can develop a debit balance before adjustment. To explain this, assume that Jenkins Company began business on January 1, 1998, and decided to use the allowance method and make the adjusting entry for uncollectible accounts only at year-end. Thus, the allowance account would not have any balance at the beginning of 1998. If the company wrote off any uncollectible accounts during 1998, it would debit Allowance for Uncollectible Accounts and cause a debit balance in that account. At the end of 1998, the company would debit Uncollectible Accounts Expense and credit Allowance for Uncollectible Accounts. This adjusting entry would cause the allowance account to have a credit balance. During 1999, the company would again begin debiting the allowance account for any write-offs of uncollectible accounts. Even if the adjustment at the end of 1998 was adequate to cover all accounts receivable existing at that time that would later become uncollectible, some accounts receivable from 1999 sales may be written off before the end of 1999. If so, the allowance account would again develop a debit balance before the end-of-year 1999 adjustment.

UNCOLLECTIBLE ACCOUNTS RECOVERED Sometimes companies collect accounts previously considered to be uncollectible after the accounts have been written off. A

A BROADER
PERSPECTIVE
—
GECS
Allowance for
Losses on
Financing
Receivables

GECS allowance for losses on financing receivables represented 2.63% of total financing receivables at year-end 1995 and 1994. The allowance for small-balance receivables is determined principally on the basis of actual experience during the preceding three years. Further allowances are provided to reflect management's judgment of additional loss potential. For other receivables, principally the larger loans and leases, the allowance for losses is determined primarily on the basis of management's judgment of net loss potential, including specific allowances for known troubled accounts. The table below shows the activity in the allowance for losses on financing receivables during each of the last three years.

All accounts or portions thereof deemed to be uncollectible or to require an excessive collection cost are written off to the allowance for losses. Small-balance accounts are progressively written down (from 10% when more than three months delinquent to 100% when 9–12 months delinquent) to record the balances at estimated realizable value. If at any time during that period an account is judged to be uncollectible, such as in the case of a bankruptcy, the uncollectible balance is written off. Large-balance accounts are reviewed at least quarterly, and those accounts with amounts that are judged to be uncollectible are written down to estimated realizable value.

(In millions)	1995	1994	1993
Balance at January 1	$2,062	$1,730	$1,607
Provisions charged to operations	1,117	873	987
Net transfers related to companies acquired or sold	217	199	126
Amounts written off—net	(877)	(740)	(990)
Balance at December 31	$2,519	$2,062	$1,730

Source: General Electric Company, *1995 Annual Report*, p. 49.

company usually learns that an account has been written off erroneously when it receives payment. Then the company reverses the original write-off entry and reinstates the account by debiting Accounts Receivable and crediting Allowance for Uncollectible Accounts for the amount received. It posts the debit to both the general ledger account and to the customer's accounts receivable subsidiary ledger account. The firm also records the amount received as a debit to Cash and a credit to Accounts Receivable. And it posts the credit to both the general ledger and to the customer's accounts receivable subsidiary ledger account.

To illustrate, assume that on May 17 a company received a $750 check from Smith in payment of the account previously written off. The two required journal entries are:

May	17	Accounts Receivable—Smith	750	
		Allowance for Uncollectible Accounts		750
		To reverse original write-off of Smith's account.		
	17	Cash	750	
		Accounts Receivable—Smith		750
		To record collection of account.		

The debit and credit to Accounts Receivable—Smith on the same date is to show in Smith's subsidiary ledger account that he did eventually pay the amount due. As a result, the company may decide to sell to him in the future.

When a company collects part of a previously written off account, the usual procedure is to reinstate only that portion actually collected, unless evidence indicates the amount will be collected in full. If a company expects full payment, it reinstates the entire amount of the account.

Because of the problems companies have with uncollectible accounts when they offer customers credit, many now allow customers to use bank or external credit cards. This policy relieves the company of the headaches of collecting overdue accounts.

AN ACCOUNTING
PERSPECTIVE
———

USES OF TECHNOLOGY   Auditors use *expert systems* to review a client's internal control structure and to test the reasonableness of a client's Allowance for Uncollectible Accounts balance. The expert system reaches conclusions based on rules and information programmed into the expert system software. The rules are modeled on the mental processes that a human expert would use in addressing the situation. In the medical field, for instance, the rules constituting the expert system are derived from modeling the diagnostic decision processes of the foremost experts in a given area of medicine. A physician can input information from a remote location regarding the symptoms of a certain patient, and the expert system will provide a probable diagnosis based on the expert model. In a similar fashion, an accountant can feed client information into the expert system and receive an evaluation as to the appropriateness of the account balance or internal control structure.

Credit Cards

Objective 2
Record credit card sales and collections.

Credit cards are either nonbank (American Express and Diners Club) or bank (VISA and MasterCard) charge cards that customers use to purchase goods and services. For some businesses, uncollectible account losses and other costs of extending credit are a burden. By paying a service charge of 2% to 8%, businesses pass these costs on to banks and agencies issuing national credit cards. The banks and credit card agencies then absorb the uncollectible accounts and costs of extending credit and maintaining records.

Usually, banks and agencies issue credit cards to approved credit applicants for an annual fee. When a business agrees to honor these credit cards, it also agrees to pay the percentage fee charged by the bank or credit agency.

When making a credit card sale, the seller checks to see if the customer's card has been canceled and requests approval if the sale exceeds a prescribed amount, such as $50. This procedure allows the seller to avoid accepting lost, stolen, or canceled cards. Also, this policy protects the credit agency from sales causing customers to exceed their established credit limits.

The seller's accounting procedures for credit card sales differ depending on whether the business accepts a nonbank or a bank credit card. To illustrate the entries for the use of *nonbank* credit cards (such as American Express or Diners Club), assume that a restaurant has Diners Club invoices amounting to $1,400 at the end of a day. The Diners Club charges the restaurant a 5% service charge. The restaurant uses the **Credit Card Expense account** to record the credit card agency's service charge and makes the following entry:

Reinforcing Problem
E9–4 Record use of nonbank and bank credit cards.

Accounts Receivable—Diners Club	1,330	
Credit Card Expense	70	
Sales		1,400
To record credit card sales.		

The restaurant mails the invoices to Diners Club. Sometime later, the restaurant receives payment from Diners Club and makes the following entry:

Note to the Student
Why would a company accept credit cards as a means of payment if it costs the company 2% to 8% of the sales revenue?
Answer: To encourage more immediate purchases from buyers and to ensure payment from the sales. Also, a company can avoid bad debts and collection costs.

Cash	1,330	
Accounts Receivable—Diners Club		1,330
To record remittance from Diners Club.		

To illustrate the accounting entries for the use of *bank* credit cards (such as VISA or MasterCard), assume that a retailer has made sales of $1,000 for which VISA cards were accepted and the service charge is $50 (which is 5% of sales). VISA sales are treated as cash sales because the receipt of cash is certain. The retailer deposits the credit card sales invoices in its VISA checking account at a bank just as it deposits checks in its regular checking account. The entry to record this deposit is:

Cash	950	
Credit Card Expense	50	
Sales		1,000
To record VISA credit card sales.		

BUSINESS INSIGHT   Recent innovations in credit cards include picture IDs on cards to reduce theft, credits toward purchases of new automobiles (Ford Citibank and General Motors cards), credit toward free trips on airlines, and cash rebates on all purchases. Discover Card remits 1% of all charges back to credit card holders at the end of the year. Also some credit card companies have reduced interest rates on unpaid balances and have eliminated the annual fee.

AN ACCOUNTING PERSPECTIVE

Just as every company must have current assets such as cash and accounts receivable to operate, every company incurs current liabilities in conducting its operations. Corporations (IBM and General Motors), partnerships (CPA firms), and single proprietorships (corner grocery stores) all have one thing in common—they have liabilities. The next section discusses some of the current liabilities companies incur.

USES OF TECHNOLOGY   To find your way around on the Internet, you may want to use a search engine such as **Yahoo** (other leaders include Alta Vista, Infoseek, Lycos, and Excite). For instance, the website for Yahoo is:

http://www.yahoo.com

You can use this site to search the yellow pages in any city (e.g., companies or CPA firms in a given city), locate the address and phone number for any person in any city (unless they have an unlisted phone number), city maps, today's news, stock quotes, and other information. You can also type in a key word or words to search for information relating to that topic. The other search engines work in about the same way.

AN ACCOUNTING PERSPECTIVE

CURRENT LIABILITIES

Liabilities result from some past transaction and are obligations to pay cash, provide services, or deliver goods at some future time. This definition includes each of the liabilities discussed in previous chapters and the new liabilities presented in this chapter. The balance sheet divides liabilities into current liabilities and long-term liabilities. **Current liabilities** are obligations that (1) are payable within one year or one operating cycle, whichever is longer, or (2) will be paid out of current assets or create other current liabilities. **Long-term liabilities** are obligations that do not qualify as current liabilities. This chapter focuses on current liabilities and Chapter 15 describes long-term liabilities.

Objective 3
Define liabilities, current liabilities, and long-term liabilities.

Note the definition of a current liability uses the term *operating cycle*. An **operating cycle** (or cash cycle) is the time it takes to begin with cash, buy necessary items to produce revenues (such as materials, supplies, labor, and/or finished goods), sell goods or services, and receive cash by collecting the resulting receivables. For most companies, this period is no longer than a few months. Service companies generally have the shortest operating cycle, since they have no cash tied up in inventory. Manufacturing companies generally have the longest cycle because their cash is tied up in inventory accounts and in accounts receivable before coming back. Even for manufacturing companies, the cycle is generally less than one year. Thus, as a practical matter, current liabilities are due in one year or less, and long-term liabilities are due after one year from the balance sheet date.

The operating cycles for various businesses follow:

Type of Business	Operating Cycle
Service company selling for cash only	Instantaneous
Service company selling on credit	Cash → Accounts receivable → Cash
Merchandising company selling for cash	Cash → Inventory → Cash
Merchandising company selling on credit	Cash → Inventory → Accounts receivable → Cash
Manufacturing company selling on credit	Cash → Materials inventory → Work in process inventory → Finished goods inventory → Accounts receivable → Cash

Objective 4
Define and account for clearly determinable, estimated, and contingent liabilities.

Current liabilities fall into these three groups:

1. **Clearly determinable liabilities.** The existence of the liability and its amount are certain. Examples include most of the liabilities discussed previously, such as accounts payable, notes payable, interest payable, unearned delivery fees, and wages payable. Sales tax payable, federal excise tax payable, current portions of long-term debt, and payroll liabilities are other examples.

2. **Estimated liabilities.** The existence of the liability is certain, but its amount only can be *estimated*. An example is estimated product warranty payable.

3. **Contingent liabilities.** The existence of the liability is uncertain and usually the amount is uncertain because contingent liabilities depend (or are *contingent*) on some future event occurring or not occurring. Examples include liabilities arising from lawsuits, discounted notes receivable, income tax disputes, penalties that may be assessed because of some past action, and failure of another party to pay a debt that a company has guaranteed.

The following table summarizes the characteristics of current liabilities:

Type of Liability	Is the Existence Certain?	Is the Amount Certain?
Clearly determinable liabilities	Yes	Yes
Estimated liabilities	Yes	No
Contingent liabilities	No	No

Clearly Determinable Liabilities

Clearly determinable liabilities have clearly determinable amounts. In this section, we describe liabilities not previously discussed that are clearly determinable—sales tax payable, federal excise tax payable, current portions of long-term debt, and payroll liabilities. Later in this chapter, we discuss clearly determinable liabilities such as notes payable.

SALES TAX PAYABLE   Many states have a state sales tax on items purchased by consumers. The company selling the product is responsible for collecting the sales tax from customers. When the company collects the taxes, the debit is to Cash and the credit is to Sales Tax Payable. Periodically, the company pays the sales taxes collected to the state. At that time, the debit is to Sales Tax Payable and the credit is to Cash.

To illustrate, assume that a company sells merchandise in a state that has a 6% sales tax. If it sells goods with a sales price of $1,000 on credit, the company makes this entry:

Accounts Receivable.	1,060	
Sales		1,000
Sales Tax Payable		60
To record sales and sales tax payable.		

Real World Example
Comingling of sales taxes collected with sales revenue can lead to serious problems. When cash inflow is lean, often companies use sales taxes collected to pay business expenses, making sales taxes collected unavailable on the tax payment date. Taxing authorities take vigorous enforcement and collection action against this practice.

Now assume that sales for the entire period are $100,000 and that $6,000 is in the Sales Tax Payable account when the company remits the funds to the state taxing agency. The following entry shows the payment to the state:

Sales Tax Payable	6,000	
Cash		6,000
To record the payment to the state for sales taxes collected from customers.		

Reinforcing Problem
E9–5 Determine sales revenue and sales tax payable.

An alternative method of recording sales taxes payable is to include these taxes in the credit to Sales. For instance, the previous company could record sales as follows:

Accounts Receivable.	1,060	
Sales		1,060

When recording sales taxes in the same account as sales revenue, the firm must separate the sales tax from sales revenue at the end of the accounting period. To make this separation, it adds the sales tax rate to 100% and divides this percentage into recorded sales revenue. For instance, assume that total recorded sales revenues for an accounting period are $10,600, and the sales tax rate is 6%. To find the sales revenue, use the following formula:

$$\text{Sales} = \frac{\text{Amount recorded in Sales account}}{100\% + \text{Sales tax rate}}$$

$$= \frac{\$10,600}{106\%} = \$10,000$$

The sales revenue is $10,000 for the period. Sales tax is equal to the recorded sales revenue of $10,600 less actual sales revenue of $10,000, or $600.

FEDERAL EXCISE TAX PAYABLE Consumers pay federal excise tax on some goods, such as alcoholic beverages, tobacco, gasoline, cosmetics, tires, and luxury automobiles. The 1990 federal budget compromise increased the tax on many of these items. Some of these increases have since been eliminated or are scheduled to be phased out. The entries a company makes when selling goods subject to the federal excise tax are similar to those made for sales taxes payable. For example, assume that the Dixon Jewelry Store sells a diamond ring to a young couple for $2,000. The sale is subject to a 6% sales tax and a 10% federal excise tax. The entry to record the sale is:

Accounts Receivable	2,320	
Sales		2,000
Sales Tax Payable		120
Federal Excise Tax Payable		200
To record the sale of a diamond ring.		

The company records the remittance of the taxes to the federal taxing agency by debiting Federal Excise Tax Payable and crediting Cash.

CURRENT PORTIONS OF LONG-TERM DEBT Accountants move any portion of long-term debt that becomes due within the next year to the current liability section of the balance sheet. For instance, assume a company signed a series of 10 individual notes payable for $10,000 each; beginning in the 6th year, one comes due each year through the 15th year. Beginning in the 5th year, an accountant would move a $10,000 note from the long-term liability category to the current liability category on the balance sheet. The current portion would then be paid within one year.

USES OF TECHNOLOGY Many companies use service bureaus to process their payrolls because these bureaus keep up to date on rates, bases, and changes in the laws affecting payroll. Companies can either send their data by modem or have the service bureaus pick up time sheets and other data. Managers instruct service bureaus either to print the payroll checks or to transfer data by modem back to the company, so it can print the checks.

AN ACCOUNTING PERSPECTIVE

PAYROLL LIABILITIES In most business organizations, accounting for payroll is particularly important because (1) payrolls often are the largest expense that a company incurs, (2) both federal and state governments require maintaining detailed payroll records, and (3) companies must file regular payroll reports with state and federal governments and remit amounts withheld or otherwise due. Payroll liabilities include taxes and other amounts withheld from employees' paychecks and taxes paid by employers.

Employers normally withhold amounts from employees' paychecks for federal income taxes; state income taxes; FICA (social security) taxes; and other items such as union dues, medical insurance premiums, life insurance premiums, pension plans, and pledges to charities. Assume that a company had a payroll of $35,000 for the month of April 1999. The company withheld the following amounts from the employees' pay: federal income taxes, $4,100; state income taxes, $360; FICA taxes, $2,678; and medical insurance premiums, $940. This entry records the payroll:

1999					
April	30	Salaries Expense	35,000	
		Employees' Federal Income Taxes Payable		4,100
		Employees' State Income Taxes Payable		360
		FICA Taxes Payable		2,678
		Employees' Medical Insurance Premiums Payable		940
		Salaries Payable.		26,922
		To record the payroll for the month ending April 30.		

All accounts credited in the entry are current liabilities and will be reported on the balance sheet if not paid prior to the preparation of financial statements. When these liabilities are paid, the employer debits each one and credits Cash.

Employers normally record payroll taxes at the same time as the payroll to which they relate. Assume the payroll taxes an employer pays for April are FICA taxes, $2,678; state unemployment taxes, $1,890; and federal unemployment taxes, $280. The entry to record these payroll taxes would be:

1999					
April	30	Payroll Taxes Expense	4,848	
		FICA Taxes Payable		2,678
		State Unemployment Taxes Payable		1,890
		Federal Unemployment Taxes Payable		280
		To record employer's payroll taxes.		

These amounts are in addition to the amounts withheld from employees' paychecks. The credit to FICA Taxes Payable is equal to the amount withheld from the employees' paychecks. The company can credit both its own and the employees' FICA taxes to the same liability account, since both are payable at the same time to the same agency. When these liabilities are paid, the employer debits each of the liability accounts and credits Cash.

AN ACCOUNTING PERSPECTIVE	**USES OF TECHNOLOGY** One of the basic components in accounting software packages is the payroll module. As long as companies update this module each time rates, bases, or laws change, they can calculate withholdings, print payroll checks, and complete reporting forms for taxing agencies. In addition to calculating the employer's payroll taxes, this software maintains all accounting payroll records.

Estimated Liabilities

Managers of companies that have estimated liabilities know these liabilities exist but can only estimate the amount. The primary accounting problem is to estimate a reasonable liability as of the balance sheet date. An example of an estimated liability is product warranty payable.

ESTIMATED PRODUCT WARRANTY PAYABLE   When companies sell products such as computers, often they must guarantee against defects by placing a warranty on their products. When defects occur, the company is obligated to reimburse the customer or repair the product. For many products, companies can predict the number of defects based on experience. To provide for a proper matching of revenues and expenses, the accountant estimates the warranty expense resulting from an accounting period's sales. The debit is to Product Warranty Expense and the credit to Estimated Product Warranty Payable.

To illustrate, assume that a company sells personal computers and warrants all parts for one year. The average price per computer is $1,500, and the company sells 1,000 computers in 1999. The company expects 10% of the computers to develop defective parts within one year. By the end of 1999, customers have returned 40 computers sold that year for repairs, and the repairs on those 40 computers have been recorded. The estimated average cost of warranty repairs per defective computer is $150. To arrive at a reasonable estimate of product warranty expense, the accountant makes the following calculation:

Number of computers sold	1,000
Percent estimated to develop defects	× 10%
Total estimated defective computers	100
Deduct computers returned as defective to date	40
Estimated additional number to become defective during warranty period	60
Estimated average warranty repair cost per computer	×$ 150
Estimated product warranty payable	$9,000

The entry made at the end of the accounting period is:

Product Warranty Expense	9,000	
Estimated Product Warranty Payable		9,000
To record estimated product warranty expense.		

When a customer returns one of the computers purchased in 1999 for repair work in 2000 (during the warranty period), the company debits the cost of the repairs to Estimated Product Warranty Payable. For instance, assume that Evan Holman returns his computer for repairs within the warranty period. The repair cost includes parts, $40, and labor, $160. The company makes the following entry:

Estimated Product Warranty Payable	200	
Repair Parts Inventory		40
Wages Payable		160
To record replacement of parts under warranty.		

BUSINESS INSIGHT   Another estimated liability that is quite common relates to clean-up costs for industrial pollution. One company had the following note in its recent financial statements:

In the past, the Company treated hazardous waste at its chemical facilities. Testing of the ground waters in the areas of the treatment impoundments at these facilities disclosed the presence of certain contaminants. In compliance with environmental regulations, the Company developed a plan that will prevent further contamination, provide for remedial action to remove the present contaminants, and establish a monitoring program to monitor ground water conditions in the future. A similar plan has been developed for a site previously used as a metal pickling facility. Estimated future costs of $2,860,000 have been accrued in the accompanying financial statements . . . to complete the procedures required under these plans.

AN ACCOUNTING PERSPECTIVE

Contingent Liabilities

When liabilities are contingent, the company usually is not sure that the liability exists and is uncertain about the amount. *FASB Statement No. 5* defines a contingency as "an existing condition, situation, or set of circumstances involving uncertainty as to possible gain or loss to an enterprise that will ultimately be resolved when one or more future events occur or fail to occur."[1]

According to *FASB Statement No. 5,* if the liability is probable and the amount can be reasonably estimated, companies should record contingent liabilities in the accounts. However, since most contingent liabilities may not occur and the amount

Reinforcing Problem
E9–6 Answer questions regarding note in financial statements.

[1]FASB, *Statement of Financial Accounting Standards No. 5,* "Accounting for Contingencies" (Stamford, Conn., 1975). Copyright © by Financial Accounting Standards Board, High Ridge Park, Stamford, Connecticut 06905, USA.

often cannot be reasonably estimated, the accountant usually does not record them in the accounts. Instead, firms typically disclose these contingent liabilities in notes to their financial statements.

Many contingent liabilities arise as the result of lawsuits. In fact, 366 of the 600 companies contacted in the AICPA's annual survey of accounting practices reported contingent liabilities resulting from litigation.[2]

The following two examples from annual reports are typical of the disclosures made in notes to the financial statements. Be aware that just because a suit is brought, the company being sued is not necessarily guilty. One company included the following note in its annual report to describe its contingent liability regarding various lawsuits against the company:

Contingent Liabilities:

Various lawsuits and claims, including those involving ordinary routine litigation incidental to its business, to which the Company is a party, are pending, or have been asserted, against the Company. In addition, the Company was advised . . . that the United States Environmental Protection Agency had determined the existence of PCBs in a river and harbor near Sheboygan, Wisconsin, and that the Company, as well as others, allegedly contributed to that contamination. It is not presently possible to determine with certainty what corrective action, if any, will be required, what portion of any costs thereof will be attributable to the Company, or whether all or any portion of such costs will be covered by insurance or will be recoverable from others. Although the outcome of these matters cannot be predicted with certainty, and some of them may be disposed of unfavorably to the Company, management has no reason to believe that their disposition will have a materially adverse effect on the consolidated financial position of the Company.

Another company dismissed an employee and included the following note to disclose the contingent liability resulting from the ensuing litigation:

Contingencies:

. . . A jury awarded $5.2 million to a former employee of the Company for an alleged breach of contract and wrongful termination of employment. The Company has appealed the judgment on the basis of errors in the judge's instructions to the jury and insufficiency of evidence to support the amount of the jury's award. The Company is vigorously pursuing the appeal.

The Company and its subsidiaries are also involved in various other litigation arising in the ordinary course of business.

Since it presently is not possible to determine the outcome of these matters, no provision has been made in the financial statements for their ultimate resolution. The resolution of the appeal of the jury award could have a significant effect on the Company's earnings in the year that a determination is made; however, in management's opinion, the final resolution of all legal matters will not have a material adverse effect on the Company's financial position.

Contingent liabilities may also arise from discounted notes receivable, income tax disputes, penalties that may be assessed because of some past action, and failure of another party to pay a debt that a company has guaranteed.

The remainder of this chapter discusses notes receivable and notes payable. Business transactions often involve one party giving another party a note.

NOTES RECEIVABLE AND NOTES PAYABLE

Objective 5
Account for notes receivable and payable, including calculation of interest.

A note (also called a **promissory note**) is an unconditional written promise by a borrower (**maker**) to pay a definite sum of money to the lender (**payee**) on demand or on a specific date. On the balance sheet of the lender (payee), a note is a receivable; on the balance sheet of the borrower (maker), a note is a payable. Since the note is usually negotiable, the payee may transfer it to another party, who then receives payment from the maker. Look at the promissory note in Illustration 9.2.

Real World Example
McDonnell Douglas reported a contingent liability in notes to its financial statements for the year ended December 31, 1995, as follows:

The Company believes any amounts paid in excess of the accrued liability will not have a material effect on its earnings, cash flow, or financial position.

A number of legal proceedings and claims are pending or have been asserted against the Company, including legal proceedings and claims relating to alleged injuries to persons associated with the disposal of hazardous substances. A substantial portion of such legal proceedings and claims is covered by insurance. The Company believes that the final outcome of such proceedings and claims will not have a material adverse effect on its earnings, cash flow, or financial position.

---

[2]AICPA, *Accounting Trends & Techniques* (New York, 1993), p. 57.

ILLUSTRATION 9.2 Promissory Note

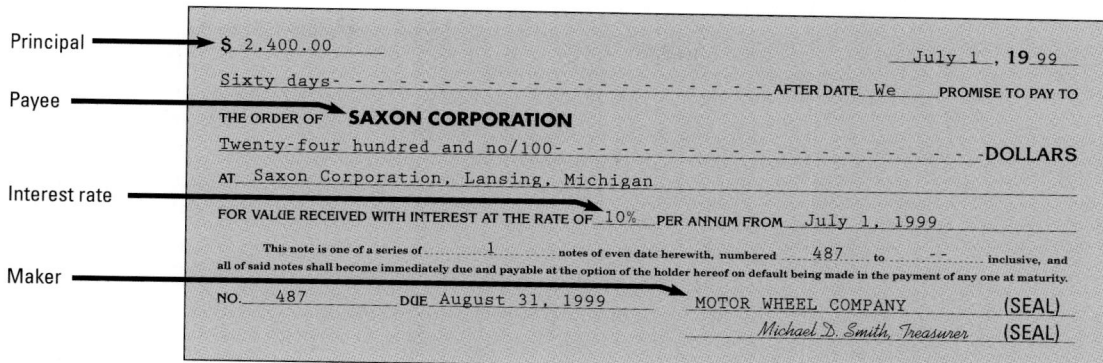

A customer may give a note to a business for an amount due on an account receivable or for the sale of a large item such as a refrigerator. Also, a business may give a note to a supplier in exchange for merchandise to sell or to a bank or an individual for a loan. Thus, a company may have notes receivable or notes payable arising from transactions with customers, suppliers, banks, or individuals.

Companies usually do not establish a subsidiary ledger for notes. Instead, they maintain a file of the actual notes receivable and copies of notes payable.

Interest Calculation

Most promissory notes have an explicit interest charge. **Interest** is the fee charged for use of money over a period. To the maker of the note, or borrower, interest is an expense; to the payee of the note, or lender, interest is a revenue. A borrower incurs interest expense; a lender earns interest revenue. For convenience, bankers sometimes calculate interest on a 360-day year; we calculate it on that basis in this text. (Some companies use a 365-day year.)

The basic formula for computing interest is:

$$\text{Interest} = \text{Principal} \times \text{Rate} \times \text{Time, or } I = P \times R \times T$$

Principal is the face value of the note. The **rate** is the stated interest rate on the note; interest rates are generally stated on an annual basis. **Time,** which is the amount of time the note is to run, can be either days or months.

To show how to calculate interest, assume a company borrowed $20,000 from a bank. The note has a principal (face value) of $20,000, an annual interest rate of 10%, and a life of 90 days. The interest calculation is:

$$\text{Interest} = \$20,000 \times 0.10 \times {}^{90}\!/_{360}$$
$$\text{Interest} = \$500$$

Note that in this calculation we expressed the time period as a fraction of a 360-day year because the interest rate is an annual rate.

Determination of Maturity Date

The **maturity date** is the date on which a note becomes due and must be paid. Sometimes notes require monthly installments (or payments) but usually all of the principal and interest must be paid at the same time as in Illustration 9.2. The wording in the note expresses the maturity date and determines when the note is to be paid. A note falling due on a Sunday or a holiday is due on the next business day. Examples of the maturity date wording are:

1. *On demand.* "On demand, I promise to pay . . ." When the maturity date is on demand, it is at the option of the holder and cannot be computed. The holder is the payee, or another person who legally acquired the note from the payee.

Reinforcing Problem
E9–7 Determine maturity dates on several notes.

2. *On a stated date.* "On July 18, 1999, I promise to pay . . ." When the maturity date is designated, computing the maturity date is not necessary.

3. *At the end of a stated period.*

 a. "One year after date, I promise to pay . . ." When the maturity is expressed in years, the note matures on the same day of the same month as the date of the note in the year of maturity.

 b. "Four months after date, I promise to pay . . ." When the maturity is expressed in months, the note matures on the same date in the month of maturity. For example, one month from July 18, 1999, is August 18, 1999, and two months from July 18, 1999, is September 18, 1999. If a note is issued on the last day of a month and the month of maturity has fewer days than the month of issuance, the note matures on the last day of the month of maturity. A one-month note dated January 31, 1999, matures on February 28, 1999.

 c. "Ninety days after date, I promise to pay . . ." When the maturity is expressed in days, the exact number of days must be counted. The first day (date of origin) is omitted, and the last day (maturity date) is included in the count. For example, a 90-day note dated October 19, 1999, matures on January 17, 2000, as shown here:

Life of note (days)	90 days
Days remaining in October not counting date of origin of note:	
Days to count in October (31 − 19) 12	
Total days in November 30	
Total days in December 31	73
Maturity date in January	17 days

Accounting for Notes in Normal Business Transactions

Sometimes a company receives a note when it sells high-priced merchandise; more often, a note results from the conversion of an overdue account receivable. When a customer does not pay an account receivable that is due, the company (creditor) may insist that the customer (debtor) give a note in place of the account receivable. This action allows the customer more time to pay the balance due, and the company earns interest on the balance until paid. Also, the company may be able to sell the note to a bank or other financial institution.

To illustrate the conversion of an account receivable to a note, assume that Price Company (maker) had purchased $18,000 of merchandise on August 1 from Cooper Company (payee) on account. The normal credit period has elapsed, and Price cannot pay the invoice. Cooper agrees to accept Price's $18,000, 15%, 90-day note dated September 1 to settle Price's open account. Assuming Price paid the note at maturity and both Cooper and Price have a December 31 year-end, the entries on the books of the payee and the maker are:

Reinforcing Problem
E9–8 Prepare entries for a note.

Cooper Company, Payee

Aug.	1	Accounts Receivable—Price Company	18,000	
		Sales		18,000
		To record sale of merchandise on account.		
Sept.	1	Notes Receivable	18,000	
		Accounts Receivable—Price Company		18,000
		To record exchange of note from Price Company for open account.		
Nov.	30	Cash	18,675	
		Notes Receivable		18,000
		Interest Revenue ($18,000 × 0.15 × 90/360)		675
		To record receipt of Price Company note principal and interest.		

Price Company, Maker

Aug.	1	Purchases	18,000	
		Accounts Payable—Cooper Company		18,000
		To record purchase of merchandise on account.		
Sept.	1	Accounts Payable—Cooper Company	18,000	
		Notes Payable		18,000
		To record exchange of note to Cooper Company for open account.		
Nov.	30	Notes Payable	18,000	
		Interest Expense ($18,000 \times 0.15 \times {}^{90}/_{360}$)	675	
		Cash		18,675
		To record payment of note principal and interest.		

The $18,675 paid by Price to Cooper is called the *maturity value of the note.* **Maturity value** is the amount that the maker must pay on a note on its maturity date; typically, it includes principal and accrued interest, if any.

Sometimes the maker of a note does not pay the note when it becomes due. The next section describes how to record a note not paid at maturity.

A **dishonored note** is a note that the maker failed to pay at maturity. Since the note has matured, the holder or payee removes the note from Notes Receivable and records the amount due in Accounts Receivable (or Dishonored Notes Receivable).

At the maturity date of a note, the maker should pay the principal plus interest. If the interest has not been accrued in the accounting records, the maker of a dishonored note should record interest expense for the life of the note by debiting Interest Expense and crediting Interest Payable. The payee should record the interest earned and remove the note from its Notes Receivable account. Thus, the payee of the note should debit Accounts Receivable for the maturity value of the note and credit Notes Receivable for the note's face value and Interest Revenue for the interest. After these entries have been posted, the full liability on the note—principal plus interest—is included in the records of both parties. Interest continues to accrue on the note until it is paid, replaced by a new note, or written off as uncollectible. To illustrate, assume that Price did not pay the note at maturity. The entries on each party's books are:

Dishonored Notes

Cooper Company, Payee

Nov.	30	Accounts Receivable—Price Company	18,675	
		Notes Receivable		18,000
		Interest Revenue		675
		To record dishonor of Price Company note.		

Reinforcing Problem
E9–9 Prepare entries when maker defaults.

Price Company, Maker

Nov.	30	Interest Expense	675	
		Interest Payable.		675
		To record interest on note payable.		

When unable to pay a note at maturity, sometimes the maker pays the interest on the original note or includes the interest in the face value of a new note that replaces the old note. Both parties account for the new note in the same manner as the old note. However, if it later becomes clear that the maker of a dishonored note will never pay, the payee writes off the account with a debit to Uncollectible Accounts Expense (or to an account with a title such as Loss on Dishonored Notes) and a credit to Accounts Receivable. The debit should be to the Allowance for Uncollectible Accounts if the payee made an annual provision for uncollectible notes receivable.

Renewal of Notes

Assume that Price Company pays the interest at the maturity date and issues a new 15%, 90-day note for $18,000. The entries on both sets of books would be:

Cooper Company, Payee			**Price Company, Maker**		
Cash	675		Interest Expense	675	
Interest Revenue . . .		675	Cash		675
To record the receipt of interest on Price Company note.			To record the payment of interest on note to Cooper Company.		
(Optional entry)			(Optional entry)		
Notes Receivable	18,000		Notes Payable	18,000	
Notes Receivable . .		18,000	Notes Payable		18,000
To replace old 15%, 90-day note from Price Company with new 15%, 90-day note.			To replace old 15%, 90-day note to Cooper Company with new 15%, 90-day note.		

Although the second entry on each set of books has no effect on the existing account balances, it indicates that the old note was renewed (or replaced). Both parties substitute the new note, or a copy, for the old note in a file of notes.

Now assume that Price Company does not pay the interest at the maturity date but instead includes the interest in the face value of the new note. The entries on both sets of books would be:

Cooper Company, Payee			**Price Company, Maker**		
Notes Receivable	18,675		Interest Expense	675	
Interest Revenue . . .		675	Notes Payable	18,000	
Notes Receivable . .		18,000	Notes Payable		18,675
To record the replacement of the old Price Company $18,000, 15%, 90-day note with a new $18,675, 15%, 90-day note.			To record the replacement of the old $18,000, 15%, 90-day note to Cooper Company with a new $18,675, 15%, 90-day note.		

Accruing Interest

On an interest-bearing note, even though interest accrues, or accumulates, on a day-to-day basis, usually both parties record it only at the note's maturity date. If the note is outstanding at the end of an accounting period, however, the time period of the interest overlaps the end of the accounting period and requires an adjusting entry at the end of the accounting period. Both the payee and maker of the note must make an adjusting entry to record the accrued interest and report the proper assets and revenues for the payee and the proper liabilities and expenses for the maker. Failure to record accrued interest understates the payee's assets and revenues by the amount of the interest earned but not collected and understates the maker's expenses and liabilities by the interest expense incurred but not yet paid.

PAYEE'S BOOKS To illustrate how to record accrued interest on the payee's books, assume that the payee, Cooper Company, has a fiscal year ending on October 31 instead of December 31. On October 31, Cooper would make the following adjusting entry relating to the Price Company note:

Oct.	31	Interest Receivable		450	
		Interest Revenue ($18,000 × 0.15 × $^{60}/_{360}$)			450
		To record interest earned on Price Company note for the period September 1 through October 31.			

The **Interest Receivable account** shows the interest earned but not yet collected. Interest receivable is a current asset in the balance sheet because the interest will be collected in 30 days. The interest revenue appears in the income statement. When Price pays the note on November 30, Cooper makes the following entry to record the collection of the note's principal and interest:

Nov.	30	Cash	18,675	
		Notes Receivable		18,000
		Interest Receivable		450
		Interest Revenue		225
		To record collection of Price Company note and interest.		

Note that the entry credits the Interest Receivable account for the $450 interest accrued from September 1 through October 31, which was debited to the account in the previous entry, and credits Interest Revenue for the $225 interest earned in November.

MAKER'S BOOKS   Assume Price Company's accounting year also ends on October 31 instead of December 31. Price's accounting records would be incomplete unless the company makes an adjusting entry to record the liability owed for the accrued interest on the note it gave to Cooper Company. The required entry is:

Oct.	31	Interest Expense ($18,000 × 0.15 × $^{60}/_{360}$)	450	
		Interest Payable.		450
		To record accrued interest on note to Cooper Company for the period September 1 through October 31.		

The **Interest Payable account**, which shows the interest expense incurred but not yet paid, is a current liability in the balance sheet because the interest will be paid in 30 days. Interest expense appears in the income statement. When the note is paid, Price makes the following entry:

Nov.	30	Notes Payable	18,000	
		Interest Payable.	450	
		Interest Expense	225	
		Cash		18,675
		To record payment of principal and interest on note to Cooper Company.		

In this illustration, Cooper's financial position made it possible for the company to *carry* the Price note to the maturity date. Alternatively, Cooper could have sold, or discounted, the note to receive the proceeds before the maturity date. This topic is reserved for a more advanced text.

SHORT-TERM FINANCING THROUGH NOTES PAYABLE

A company sometimes needs short-term financing. This situation may occur when (1) the company's cash receipts are delayed because of lenient credit terms granted customers, or (2) the company needs cash to finance the buildup of seasonal inventories, such as before Christmas. To secure short-term financing, companies issue interest-bearing or noninterest-bearing notes.

Objective 6
Account for borrowing money using an interest-bearing note versus a noninterest-bearing note.

INTEREST-BEARING NOTES   To receive short-term financing, a company may issue an interest-bearing note to a bank. An interest-bearing note specifies the interest rate charged on the principal borrowed. The company receives from the bank the principal borrowed; when the note matures, the company pays the bank the principal plus the interest.

Accounting for an interest-bearing note is simple. For example, assume the company's accounting year ends on December 31. Needham Company issued a $10,000, 90-day, 9% note on December 1, 1998. The following entries would record the loan, the accrual of interest on December 31, 1998, and its payment on March 1, 1999:

1998					
Dec.	1	Cash	10,000	
		Notes Payable		10,000
		To record 90-day bank loan.		
	31	Interest Expense	75	
		Interest Payable		75
		To record accrued interest on a note payable at year-end ($10,000 × 0.09 × 30/360).		
1999				
Mar.	1	Notes Payable	10,000	
		Interest Expense ($10,000 × 0.09 × 60/360)	150	
		Interest Payable	75	
		Cash		10,225
		To record principal and interest paid on bank loan.		

NONINTEREST-BEARING NOTES (DISCOUNTING NOTES PAYABLE)   A company may also issue a noninterest-bearing note to receive short-term financing from a bank. A noninterest-bearing note does not have a stated interest rate applied to the face value of the note. Instead, the note is drawn for a maturity amount less a bank discount; the borrower receives the proceeds. A **bank discount** is the difference between the maturity value of the note and the cash proceeds given to the borrower. The **cash proceeds** are equal to the maturity amount of a note less the bank discount. This entire process is called **discounting a note payable.** The purpose of this process is to introduce interest into what appears to be a noninterest-bearing note. The meaning of *discounting* here is to deduct interest in advance.

Because interest is related to time, the bank discount is not interest on the date the loan is made; however, it becomes interest expense to the company and interest revenue to the bank as time passes. To illustrate, assume that on December 1, 1998, Needham Company presented its $10,000, 90-day, noninterest-bearing note to the bank, which discounted the note at 9%. The discount is $225 ($10,000 × 0.09 × 90/360), and the proceeds to Needham are $9,775. The entry required on the date of the note's issue is:

1998					
Dec.	1	Cash	9,775	
		Discount on Notes Payable	225	
		Notes Payable		10,000
		Issued 90-day note to bank.		

Needham credits Notes Payable for the face value of the note. **Discount on Notes Payable** is a contra account used to reduce Notes Payable from face value to the net amount of the debt. The balance in the Discount on Notes Payable account appears on the balance sheet as a deduction from the balance in the Notes Payable account.

Over time, the discount becomes interest expense. If Needham paid the note before the end of the fiscal year, it would charge the entire $225 discount to Interest Expense and credit Discount on Notes Payable. However, if Needham's fiscal year ended on December 31, an adjusting entry would be required as follows:

1998					
Dec.	31	Interest Expense	75	
		Discount on Notes Payable		75
		To record accrued interest on a note payable at year-end.		

ILLUSTRATION 9.3 Comparison between Interest-Bearing Notes and Noninterest-Bearing Notes

Interest-Bearing Notes				Noninterest-Bearing Notes			
1998 Dec.	1	Cash	10,000	1998 Dec.	1	Cash	9,775
		Notes Payable	10,000			Discount on Notes Payable	225
		To record 90-day bank loan.				Notes Payable	10,000
						To record 90-day bank loan.	
	31	Interest Expense	75		31	Interest Expense	75
		Interest Payable	75			Discount on Notes Payable	75
		To record accrued interest on a note payable at year-end.				To record accrued interest on a note payable at year-end.	
1999 Mar.	1	Notes Payable	10,000	1999 Mar.	1	Notes Payable	10,000
		Interest Expense	150			Interest Expense	150
		Interest Payable	75			Cash	10,000
		Cash	10,225			Discount on Notes Payable	150
		To record note principal and interest payment.				To record note payment and interest expense.	

This entry records the interest expense incurred by Needham for the 30 days the note has been outstanding. The expense can be calculated as $10,000 \times 0.09 \times {}^{30}/_{360}$, or ${}^{30}/_{90} \times \$225$. Notice that for entries involving discounted notes payable, no separate Interest Payable account is needed. The Notes Payable account already contains the total liability that will be paid at maturity, $10,000. From the date the proceeds are given to the borrower to the maturity date, the liability grows by reducing the balance in the Discount on Notes Payable contra account. Thus, the current liability section of the December 31, 1998, balance sheet would show:

```
Current liabilities:
    Notes payable . . . . . . . . . . . . . $10,000
    Less: Discount on notes payable . . . .    150    $9,850
```

When the note is paid at maturity, the entry is:

1999 Mar.	1	Notes Payable	10,000	
		Interest Expense	150	
		Cash		10,000
		Discount on Notes Payable		150
		To record note payment and interest expense.		

Reinforcing Problem
E9–11 Prepare entries at maturity date.

The T-accounts for Discount on Notes Payable and for Interest Expense appear as follows:

Discount on Notes Payable				Interest Expense			
1998 Dec. 1	225	1998 Dec. 31	75	1998 Dec. 31	75	1998 Dec. 31 To close	75
Dec. 31 Balance	150	1999 Mar. 1	150	1999 Mar. 1	150		

Reinforcing Problem
E9–10 Prepare entries for noninterest-bearing note and interest-bearing note.

In Illustration 9.3, we compare the journal entries for interest-bearing notes and noninterest-bearing notes used by Needham Company.

ANALYZING AND USING THE FINANCIAL RESULTS—ACCOUNTS RECEIVABLE TURNOVER AND NUMBER OF DAYS' SALES IN ACCOUNTS RECEIVABLE

Objective 7
Analyze and use the financial results—accounts receivable turnover and the number of days' sales in accounts receivable.

Reinforcing Problem
E9–12 Calculate the accounts receivable turnover and the number of days' sales in accounts receivable for AT&T.

Accounts receivable turnover is the number of times per year that the average amount of accounts receivable is collected. To calculate this ratio divide net credit sales, or net sales, by the average net accounts receivable (accounts receivable after deducting the allowance for uncollectible accounts):

$$\text{Accounts receivable turnover} = \frac{\text{Net credit sales (or net sales)}}{\text{Average net accounts receivable}}$$

Ideally, average net accounts receivable should represent weekly or monthly averages; often, however, beginning and end-of-year averages are the only amounts available to users outside the company. Although analysts should use net credit sales, frequently net credit sales are not known to those outside the company. Instead, they use net sales in the numerator.

Generally, the faster firms collect accounts receivable, the better. A company with a high accounts receivable turnover ties up a smaller proportion of its funds in accounts receivable than a company with a low turnover. Both the company's credit terms and collection policies affect turnover. For instance, a company with credit terms of 2/10, n/30 would expect a higher turnover than a company with terms of n/60. Also, a company that aggressively pursues overdue accounts receivable has a higher turnover of accounts receivable than one that does not.

Using their 1995 annual reports, we calculated these accounts receivable turnovers for the following companies:

Company	Net Sales (millions)	Accounts Receivable Average Net	Accounts Receivable Turnover
Continental Airlines	$ 5,825	$ 364	16.00
Dow Chemical Company	20,200	3,044	6.64
International Paper	19,797	2,406	8.23
J. C. Penney Company, Inc.	21,419	5,183	4.13
Kimberly-Clark Corporation	13,789	1,573	8.77

Continental Airlines
is a major U.S. airline serving many U.S. and foreign destinations with over 300 aircraft in its fleet.

Dow Chemical Company
is the fifth largest chemical company in the world. The company operates in 30 countries and employs about 40,000 people.

International Paper
is a worldwide producer of paper, packaging, and forest products, all complemented by related specialty products and an extensive distribution system. The company operates facilities in 31 countries.

J. C. Penney Company, Inc.
is one of the nation's largest retail companies. The company operates slightly more than 1,200 retail stores and slightly more than 500 drug stores.

We calculate the **number of days' sales in accounts receivable** (also called the *average collection period for accounts receivable*) as follows:

$$\frac{\text{Number of days' sales in}}{\text{accounts receivable}} = \frac{\text{Number of days in year (365)}}{\text{Accounts receivable turnover}}$$

This ratio measures the average liquidity of accounts receivable and gives an indication of their quality. The faster a firm collects receivables, the more liquid (the closer to being cash) they are and the higher their quality. The longer accounts receivable remain outstanding, the greater the probability they never will be collected. As the time period increases, so does the probability that customers will declare bankruptcy or go out of business.

Based on 365 days, we calculated the number of days' sales for each of these companies in 1995:

Company	Accounts Receivable Turnover	Accounts Receivable Number of Day's Sales in
Continental Airlines	16.00	22.8
Dow Chemical Company	6.64	55.0
International Paper	8.23	44.3
J. C. Penney Company, Inc.	4.13	88.4
Kimberly-Clark Corporation	8.77	41.6

These companies have collection periods ranging from 22.8 to 88.4 days. Assuming credit terms of 2/10, n/30, one would expect the average collection period to be under 30 days. If customers do not pay within 10 days and take the discount offered, they incur an annual interest rate of 36.5% on these funds. (They lose a 2% discount and get to use the funds another 20 days, which is equivalent to an annual rate of 36.5%.) Possibly, some of these five companies had more lenient discount terms such as 2/20, n/60 or 2/10/EOM, n/60.

Having studied receivables and payables in this chapter, you will study plant assets in the next chapter. These long-term assets include land and depreciable assets such as buildings, machinery, and equipment.

Kimberly-Clark manufactures and markets a wide range of paper and lumber products for personal, business, and industrial uses.

Understanding the Learning Objectives

- Companies use two methods to account for uncollectible accounts receivable: the allowance method, which provides in advance for uncollectible accounts; and the direct write-off method, which recognizes uncollectible accounts as an expense when judged uncollectible. The allowance method is the preferred method and is the only method discussed and illustrated in this text.

- The two basic methods for estimating uncollectible accounts under the allowance method are the percentage-of-sales method and the percentage-of-receivables method.

- The percentage-of-sales method focuses attention on the income statement and the relationship of uncollectible accounts to sales. The debit to Uncollectible Accounts Expense is a certain percent of credit sales or total net sales.

- The percentage-of-receivables method focuses attention on the balance sheet and the relationship of the allowance for uncollectible accounts to accounts receivable. The credit to the Allowance for Uncollectible Accounts is the amount necessary to bring that account up to a certain percentage of the Accounts Receivable balance. Either one overall percentage or an aging schedule may be used.

Objective 1
Account for uncollectible accounts receivable under the allowance method.

- Credit cards are charge cards used by customers to charge purchases of goods and services. These cards are of two types—nonbank credit cards (such as American Express) and bank credit cards (such as VISA).

- The sale is recorded at the gross amount of the sale, and the cash or receivable is recorded at the net amount the company will receive.

Objective 2
Record credit card sales and collections.

- Liabilities result from some past transaction and are obligations to pay cash, provide services, or deliver goods at some time in the future.

- Current liabilities are obligations that (1) are payable within one year or one operating cycle, whichever is longer, or (2) will be paid out of current assets or create other current liabilities.

- Long-term liabilities are obligations that do not qualify as current liabilities.

Objective 3
Define liabilities, current liabilities, and long-term liabilities.

- Clearly determinable liabilities are those for which the existence of the liability and its amount are certain. An example is accounts payable.

- Estimated liabilities are those for which the existence of the liability is certain, but its amount can only be estimated. An example is estimated product warranty payable.

- Contingent liabilities are those for which the existence, and usually the amount, are uncertain because these liabilities depend (or are contingent) on some future event occurring or not occurring. An example is a liability arising from a lawsuit.

Objective 4
Define and account for clearly determinable, estimated, and contingent liabilities.

- A promissory note is an unconditional written promise by a borrower (maker) to pay the lender (payee) or someone else who legally acquired the note a certain sum of money on demand or at a definite time.

- Interest is the fee charged for the use of money through time. Interest = Principal × Rate of interest × Time.

Objective 5
Account for notes receivable and payable, including calculation of interest.

- Companies sometimes need short-term financing. Short-term financing may be secured by issuing interest-bearing notes or by issuing noninterest-bearing notes.

- An interest-bearing note specifies the interest rate that will be charged on the principal borrowed.

- A noninterest-bearing note does not have a stated interest rate applied to the face value of the note.

Objective 6
Account for borrowing money using an interest-bearing note versus a noninterest-bearing note.

- Calculate accounts receivable turnover by dividing net credit sales, or net sales, by average net accounts receivable.
- Calculate the number of days' sales in accounts receivable (or average collection period) by dividing the number of days in the year by the accounts receivable turnover.
- Together, these ratios show the liquidity of accounts receivable and give some indication of their quality. Generally, the higher the accounts receivable turnover, the better; and the shorter the average collection period, the better.

DEMONSTRATION PROBLEM 9–A

a. Prepare the journal entries for the following transactions:
  (1) As of the end of 1999, Post Company estimates its uncollectible accounts expense to be 1% of sales. Sales in 1999 were $1,125,000.
  (2) On January 15, 2000, the company decided that the account for John Nunn in the amount of $750 was uncollectible.
  (3) On February 12, 2000, John Nunn's check for $750 arrived.

b. Prepare the journal entries in the records of Lyle Company for the following:
  (1) On June 15, 1999, Lyle Company received a $22,500, 90-day, 12% note dated June 15, 1999, from Stone Company in payment of its account.
  (2) Assume that Stone Company did not pay the note at maturity. Lyle Company decided that the note was uncollectible.

SOLUTION TO DEMONSTRATION PROBLEM 9–A

a.

(1)	1999 Dec.	31	Uncollectible Accounts Expense.	11,250	
			Allowance for Uncollectible Accounts		11,250
			To record estimated uncollectible accounts for the year.		
(2)	2000 Jan.	15	Allowance for Uncollectible Accounts	750	
			Accounts Receivable—John Nunn		750
			To write off the account of John Nunn as uncollectible.		
(3)	Feb.	12	Accounts Receivable—John Nunn	750	
			Allowance for Uncollectible Accounts		750
			To correct the write-off of John Nunn's account on January 15.		
		12	Cash.	750	
			Accounts Receivable—John Nunn		750
			To record the collection of John Nunn's account receivable.		

b.

(1)	1999 June	15	Notes Receivable	22,500	
			Accounts Receivable—Stone Company		22,500
			To record receipt of a note from Stone Company.		
(2)	Sept.	13	Accounts Receivable—Stone Company	23,175	
			Notes Receivable		22,500
			Interest Revenue		675
			To record the default of the Stone Company note of $22,500. Interest revenue was $675.		
		13	Allowance for Uncollectible Accounts*	23,175	
			Accounts Receivable—Stone Company		23,175
			To write off the Stone Company note as uncollectible.		

*This debit assumes that Notes Receivable were taken into consideration when an allowance was established. If not, the debit should be to Loss from Dishonored Notes Receivable.

DEMONSTRATION PROBLEM 9–B

a. Prepare the entries on the books of Cromwell Company assuming the company borrowed $10,000 at 7% from First National Bank and signed a 60-day noninterest-bearing note payable on December 1, 1998, accrued interest on December 31, 1998, and paid the debt on the maturity date.

b. Prepare the entries on the books of Cromwell Company assuming it purchased equipment from Jones Company for $5,000 and signed a 30-day, 9% interest-bearing note payable on February 24, 1999. Cromwell paid the note on its maturity date.

SOLUTION TO DEMONSTRATION PROBLEM 9–B

a.

1998				
Dec.	1	Cash	9,883.33	
		Bank Discount ($10,000 × 0.07 × 60/360)	116.67	
		Notes Payable		10,000.00
	31	Interest Expense	58.33	
		Bank Discount		58.33
		($10,000 × 0.07 × 30/360).		
1999				
Jan.	30	Notes Payable	10,000.00	
		Interest Expense	58.33	
		Bank Discount		58.33
		Cash		10,000.00

b.

1999				
Feb.	24	Equipment	5,000.00	
		Notes Payable		5,000.00
Mar.	26	Notes Payable	5,000.00	
		Interest Expense	37.50	
		Cash		5,037.50
		($5,000 × 0.09 × 30/360). = $37.50.		

NEW TERMS

Accounts receivable turnover Net credit sales (or net sales) divided by average net accounts receivable. *352*

Aging schedule A means of classifying accounts receivable according to their age; used to determine the necessary balance in an Allowance for Uncollectible Accounts. A different uncollectibility percentage rate is used for each age category. *335*

Allowance for Uncollectible Accounts A contra-asset account to the Accounts Receivable account; it reduces accounts receivable to their net realizable value. Also called *Allowance for Doubtful Accounts* or *Allowance for Bad Debts*. *332*

Bad debts expense See Uncollectible accounts expense.

Bank discount The difference between the maturity value of a note and the actual amount—the note's proceeds—given to the borrower. *350*

Cash proceeds The maturity amount of a note less the bank discount. *350*

Clearly determinable liabilities Liabilities whose existence and amount are certain. Examples include accounts payable, notes payable, interest payable, unearned delivery fees, wages payable, sales tax payable, federal excise tax payable, current portions of long-term debt, and various payroll liabilities. *340*

Contingent liabilities Liabilities whose existence is uncertain. Their amount is also usually uncertain. Both their existence and amount depend on some future event that may or may not occur. Examples include liabilities arising from lawsuits, discounted notes receivable, income tax disputes, penalties that may be assessed because of some past action, and failure of another party to pay a debt that a company has guaranteed. *340*

Credit Card Expense account Used to record credit card agency's service charges for services rendered in processing credit card sales. *338*

Credit cards Nonbank charge cards (American Express and Diners Club) and bank charge cards (VISA and

MasterCard) that customers use to charge their purchases of goods and services. *338*

Current liabilities   Obligations that (1) are payable within one year or one operating cycle, whichever is longer, or (2) will be paid out of current assets or result in the creation of other current liabilities. *339*

Discount on Notes Payable   A contra account used to reduce Notes Payable from face value to the net amount of the debt. *350*

Discounting a note payable   The act of borrowing on a noninterest-bearing note drawn for a maturity amount, from which a bank discount is deducted, and the proceeds are given to the borrower. *350*

Dishonored note   A note that the maker failed to pay at maturity. *347*

Estimated liabilities   Liabilities whose existence is certain, but whose amount can only be estimated. An example is estimated product warranty payable. *340*

Interest   The fee charged for use of money over a period of time $(I = P \times R \times T)$. *345*

Interest Payable account   An account showing the interest expense incurred but not yet paid; reported as a current liability in the balance sheet. *349*

Interest Receivable account   An account showing the interest earned but not yet collected; reported as a current asset in the balance sheet. *349*

Liabilities   Obligations that result from some past transaction and are obligations to pay cash, perform services, or deliver goods at some time in the future. *339*

Long-term liabilities   Obligations that do not qualify as current liabilities. *339*

Maker (of a note)   The party who prepares a note and is responsible for paying the note at maturity. *344*

Maturity date   The date on which a note becomes due and must be paid. *345*

Maturity value   The amount that the maker must pay on the note on its maturity date. *347*

Net realizable value   The amount the company expects to collect from accounts receivable. *332*

Number of days' sales in accounts receivable   The number of days in a year (365) divided by the accounts receivable turnover. *352*

Operating cycle   The time it takes to start with cash, buy necessary items to produce revenues (such as materials, supplies, labor, and/or finished goods), sell goods or services, and receive cash by collecting the resulting receivables. *339*

Payable   Any sum of money due to be paid by a company to any party for any reason. *330*

Payee (of a note)   The party who receives a note and will be paid cash at maturity. *344*

Percentage-of-receivables method   A method for determining the desired size of the Allowance for Uncollectible Accounts by basing the calculation on the Accounts Receivable balance at the end of the period. *333*

Percentage-of-sales method   A method of estimating the uncollectible accounts from the sales of a given period's total net credit sales or net sales. *332*

Principal (of a note)   The face value of a note. *345*

Promissory note   An unconditional written promise by a borrower (maker) to pay a definite sum of money to the lender (payee) on demand or at a specific date. *344*

Rate (of a note)   The stated interest rate on the note. *345*

Receivable   Any sum of money due to be paid to a company from any party for any reason. *330*

Time (of a note)   The amount of time the note is to run; can be expressed in days, months, or years. *345*

Trade receivables   Amounts customers owe a company for goods sold or services rendered on account. Also called *accounts receivable* or *trade accounts receivable*. *331*

Uncollectible accounts expense   An operating expense that a business incurs when it sells on credit; also called *doubtful accounts expense* or *bad debts expense*. *331*

Self Test

True-False

Indicate whether each of the following statements is true or false.

1. The percentage-of-sales method estimates the uncollectible accounts from the ending balance in Accounts Receivable.

2. Under the allowance method, uncollectible accounts expense is recognized when a specific customer's account is written off.

3. Bank credit card sales are treated as cash sales because the receipt of cash is certain.

4. Liabilities result from some future transaction.

5. Current liabilities are classified as clearly determinable, estimated, and contingent.

6. A dishonored note is removed from Notes Receivable, and the total amount due is recorded in Accounts Receivable.

7. When an interest-bearing note is given to a bank when taking out a loan, the difference between the cash proceeds and the maturity amount is debited to Discount on Notes Payable.

MULTIPLE-CHOICE

Select the best answer for each of the following questions.

1. Which of the following statements is false?
   a. Any existing balance in the Allowance for Uncollectible Accounts is ignored in calculating the uncollectible accounts expense under the percentage-of-sales method except that the allowance account must have a credit balance after adjustment.
   b. The percentage-of-receivables method may use either an overall rate or a different rate for each age category.
   c. The Allowance for Uncollectible Accounts reduces accounts receivable to their net realizable value.
   d. A write-off of an account reduces the net amount shown for accounts receivable on the balance sheet.
   e. None of the above.

2. Hunt Company estimates uncollectible accounts using the percentage-of-receivables method and expects that 5% of outstanding receivables will be uncollectible for 1999. The balance in Accounts Receivable is $200,000, and the allowance account has a $3,000 credit balance before adjustment at year-end. The uncollectible accounts expense for 1999 will be:
   a. $7,000.
   b. $10,000.
   c. $13,000.
   d. $9,850.
   e. None of the above.

3. Which type of company typically has the longest operating cycle?
   a. Service company.
   b. Merchandising company.
   c. Manufacturing company.
   d. All equal.

4. Maxwell Company records its sales taxes in the same account as sales revenues. The sales tax rate is 6%. At the end of the current period, the Sales account has a balance of $265,000. The amount of sales tax payable is:
   a. $12,000.
   b. $15,000.
   c. $15,900.
   d. $18,000.

5. Dawson Company sells fax machines. During 1999, the company sold 2,000 fax machines. The company estimates that 5% of the machines require repairs under warranty. To date, 30 machines have been repaired. The estimated average cost of warranty repairs per defective fax machine is $200. The required amount of the adjusting entry to record estimated product warranty payable is:
   a. $400,000.
   b. $6,000.
   c. $14,000.
   d. $–0–.

6. To compute interest on a promissory note, all of the following elements must be known except:
   a. The face value of the note.
   b. The stated interest rate.
   c. The name of the payee.
   d. The life of the note.
   e. None of the above.

7. Keats Company issued its own $10,000, 90-day, noninterest-bearing note to a bank. If the note is discounted at 10%, the proceeds to Keats are:
   a. $10,000.
   b. $9,000.
   c. $9,750.
   d. $10,250.
   e. None of the above.

Now turn to page 364 to check your answers.

QUESTIONS

1. In view of the difficulty in estimating future events, would you recommend that accountants wait until collections are made from customers before recording sales revenue? Should they wait until known accounts prove to be uncollectible before charging an expense account?

2. The credit manager of a company has established a policy of seeking to completely eliminate all losses from uncollectible accounts. Is this policy a desirable objective for a company? Explain.

3. What are the two major purposes of establishing an allowance for uncollectible accounts?

4. In view of the fact that it is impossible to estimate the exact amount of uncollectible accounts receivable for any one year in advance, what exactly does the Allowance for Uncollectible Accounts account contain after a number of years?

5. What must be considered before adjusting the allowance for uncollectible accounts under the percentage-of-receivables method?

6. How might information in an aging schedule prove useful to management for purposes other than estimating the size of the required allowance for uncollectible accounts?

7. For a company using the allowance method of accounting for uncollectible accounts, which of the following directly affects its reported net income: (1) the establishment of the allowance, (2) the writing off of a specific account, or (3) the recovery of an account previously written off as uncollectible?

8. Why might a retailer agree to sell by credit card when such a substantial discount is taken by the credit card agency in paying the retailer?

9. Define liabilities, current liabilities, and long-term liabilities.

10. What is an operating cycle? Which type of company is likely to have the shortest operating cycle, and which is likely to have the longest operating cycle? Why?

11. Describe the differences between clearly determinable, estimated, and contingent liabilities. Give one or more examples of each type.

12. In what instances might a company acquire notes receivable?

13. How is the maturity value of a note calculated?

14. What is a dishonored note receivable and how is it reported in the balance sheet?

15. Under what circumstances does the account Discount on Notes Payable arise? How is it reported in the financial statements? Explain why.

16. **Real World Question** Refer to "A Broader Perspective" on page 337. What factors are taken into account by the General Electric Company in determining the adjusting entry to establish the desired balance in the Allowance for Uncollectible Accounts?

17. **Real World Question** Refer to "A Broader Perspective" on page 337. Explain how the General Electric Company writes off uncollectible accounts.

18. **Real World Question** Refer to the annual reports of The Coca-Cola Company and Maytag Corporation in the annual report booklet. Determine the percentage of accounts receivable on December 31, 1996, that each of the companies estimates will be uncollectible (round to the nearest whole percent).

EXERCISES

Exercise 9–1
Prepare journal entries to record uncollectible accounts expense (L.O. 1)

The accounts of Stackhouse Company as of December 31, 1999, show Accounts Receivable, $190,000; Allowance for Uncollectible Accounts, $950 (credit balance); Sales, $920,000; and Sales Returns and Allowances, $12,000. Prepare journal entries to adjust for possible uncollectible accounts under each of the following assumptions:

a. Uncollectible accounts are estimated at 1% of net sales.

b. The allowance is to be increased to 3% of accounts receivable.

Exercise 9–2
Use aging schedule to estimate Allowance for Uncollectible Accounts (L.O. 1)

Compute the required balance of the Allowance for Uncollectible Accounts for the following receivables:

Accounts Receivable	Age (months)	Probability of Collection
$180,000	Less than 1	95%
90,000	1–3	85
39,000	3–6	75
12,000	6–9	35
2,250	9–12	10

Exercise 9–3
Record write-off and subsequent recovery of account (L.O. 1)

On April 1, 1998, Kelley Company, which uses the allowance method of accounting for uncollectible accounts, wrote off Bob Dyer's $400 account. On December 14, 1998, the company received a check in that amount from Dyer marked "in full payment of account." Prepare the necessary entries.

Exercise 9–4
Record use of nonbank and bank credit cards (L.O. 2)

Jamestown Furniture Mart, Inc., sold $80,000 of furniture in May to customers who used their Carte Blanche credit cards. Such sales are subject to a 3% discount by Carte Blanche (a nonbank credit card),

a. Prepare journal entries to record the sales and the subsequent receipt of cash from the credit card company.

b. Do the same as requirement **a,** but assume the credit cards used were VISA cards (a bank credit card).

Exercise 9–5
Determine sales revenue and sales tax payable (L.O. 4)

Dunwoody Discount Toys, Inc., sells merchandise in a state that has a 5% sales tax. Rather than record sales taxes collected in a separate account, the company records both the sales revenue and the sales taxes in the Sales account. At the end of the first quarter of operations, when it is time to remit the sales taxes to the state taxing agency, the company has $420,000 in the Sales account. Determine the correct amount of sales revenue and the amount of sales tax payable.

Exercise 9–6
Answer questions regarding note in financial statements (L.O. 3, 4)

Assume the following note appeared in the annual report of a company:

In 1998, two small retail customers filed separate suits against the company alleging misrepresentation, breach of contract, conspiracy to violate federal laws, and state antitrust violations arising out of their purchase of retail grocery stores through the company from a third party. Damages sought range up to $10 million in each suit for actual and treble damages and punitive damages of $2 million in one suit and $10 million in the other. The company is vigorously defending the actions and management believes there will be no adverse financial effect.

What kind of liability is being reported? Why is it classified this way? Do you think it is possible to calculate a dollar amount for this obligation? How much would the company have to pay if it lost the suit and had to pay the full amount?

Determine the maturity date for each of the following notes:

Issue Date	Life
January 13, 1999	30 days
January 31, 1999	90 days
June 4, 1999	1 year
December 2, 1999	1 month

Exercise 9–7
Determine maturity dates on several notes (L.O. 5)

Crawford, Inc., gave a $20,000, 120-day, 12% note to Dunston, Inc., in exchange for merchandise. Crawford uses periodic inventory procedure. Prepare journal entries to record the issuance of the note and the entries needed at maturity for both parties, assuming payment is made.

Exercise 9–8
Prepare entries for a note (L.O. 5)

Based on the facts in the previous exercise, prepare the entries that Crawford, Inc., and Dunston, Inc., would make at the maturity date, assuming Crawford defaults.

Exercise 9–9
Prepare entries when maker defaults (L.O. 5)

John Wood is negotiating a bank loan for his company, Wood, Inc., of $16,000 for 90 days. The bank's current interest rate is 10%. Prepare Wood's entries to record the loan under each of the following assumptions:

a. Wood signs a note for $16,000. Interest is deducted in calculating the proceeds turned over to him.

b. Wood signs a note for $16,000 and receives that amount. Interest is to be paid at maturity.

Exercise 9–10
Prepare entries for noninterest-bearing note and interest-bearing note (L.O. 6)

Based on the previous exercise, prepare the entry or entries that would be made at maturity date for each alternative, assuming the loan is paid before the end of the accounting period.

Exercise 9–11
Prepare entries at maturity date (L.O. 6)

AT&T provides communication services and products, as well as network equipment and computer systems, to businesses, consumers, communications services providers, and government agencies. The following amounts were included in its 1995 annual report:

	(Millions)
Net sales	$79,609
Receivables, net, 12/31/95	29,275
Receivables, net, 12/31/94	28,623

Calculate the accounts receivable turnover and the number of days' sales in accounts receivable. Use net sales instead of net credit sales in the calculation. Comment on the results.

Exercise 9–12
Calculate the accounts receivable turnover and the number of days' sales in accounts receivable for AT&T (L.O. 7)

PROBLEMS

The following selected accounts are for Keystone, Inc., a name brand shoe wholesale store, as of December 31, 1998. Prior to closing the accounts and making allowance for uncollectible accounts entries, the $5,000 account of Morgan Company is to be written off (this was a credit sale of February 12, 1998).

Accounts receivable	$ 360,000
Allowance for uncollectible accounts (credit)	6,000
Sales	1,680,000
Sales returns and allowances	30,000

Problem 9–1
Write off uncollectible account, record expense under alternative methods of estimation (L.O. 1)

a. Prepare journal entries to record all of these transactions and the uncollectible accounts expense for the period. Assume the estimated expense is 2% of net sales.

b. Give the entry to record the estimated expense for the period if the allowance account is to be adjusted to 5% of outstanding receivables instead of as in **a.**

Required

Problem 9–2
Record use of bank and nonbank credit cards
(L.O. 2)

The cash register at Frank's Restaurant at the close of business showed cash sales of $7,500 and credit card sales of $10,000 ($6,000 VISA and $4,000 American Express). The VISA (bank credit card) invoices were discounted 5% when they were deposited. The American Express (nonbank credit card) charges were mailed to the company and were subject to a 5% service charge. A few days later, Frank received a check for the net amount of the American Express credit card charges.

Required   Prepare journal entries for all of these transactions.

Problem 9–3
Prepare journal entries for sales and excise taxes
(L.O. 4)

Beacham Hardware, Inc., sells merchandise in a state that has a 6% sales tax. On July 1, 1999, it sold goods with a sales price of $20,000 on credit. Sales taxes collected are recorded in a separate account. Assume that sales for the entire month were $400,000. On July 31, 1999, the company remitted the sales taxes collected to the state taxing agency.

Required   a.   Prepare the general journal entries to record the July 1 sales revenue and sales tax payable. Also prepare the entry to show the remittance of the taxes on July 31.

b.   Now assume that the merchandise sold also is subject to federal excise taxes of 10% in addition to the 6% sales tax. The company remitted the federal excise taxes collected to the proper agency on July 31. Show the entries on July 1 and July 31.

Problem 9–4
Prepare journal entries for product warranty (L.O. 4)

Quick Wheels, Inc., sells racing bicycles and warrants all parts for one year. The average price per bicycle is $560, and the company sold 4,000 in 1998. The company expects 20% of the bicycles to develop defective parts within one year of sale. The estimated average cost of warranty repairs per defective bicycle is $40. By the end of the year, 500 bicycles sold that year had been returned and repaired under warranty. On January 2, 1999, a customer returned a bicycle purchased in 1998 for repairs under warranty. The repairs were made on January 3. The cost of the repairs included parts, $25, and labor, $15.

Required   a.   Calculate the amount of the estimated product warranty payable.

b.   Prepare the entry to record the estimated product warranty payable on December 31, 1998.

c.   Prepare the entry to record the repairs made on January 3, 1999.

Problem 9–5
Prepare entries to record a number of note transactions, discounting of a note payable, adjusting entries for interest, and payment of notes
(L.O. 5, 6)

Vance Commercial Properties, Inc., has an accounting period of one year, ending on July 31. On July 1, 1998, the balances of certain ledger accounts are Notes Receivable, $654,000; and Notes Payable, $900,000. A schedule of the notes receivable is as follows:

Face Amount	Maker	Date of Note	Life	Interest Rate
$270,000	Parker Co.	5/15/98	60 days	12%
120,000	Dot Co.	5/31/98	60	12
264,000	Fixx Co.	6/15/98	30	10
$654,000				

The note payable is a 60-day bank loan dated May 20, 1998. Notes Payable—Discount was debited for the discount of $6,000. Following are the company's transactions during July:

July   1   Vance Commercial Properties, Inc., discounted its own $90,000, 60-day, noninterest-bearing note at Key Bank. The discount rate is 10%, and the note was dated today.

3   Received a 20-day, 12% note, dated today, from Sox Company in settlement of an account receivable of $36,000.

6   Purchased merchandise from Link Company, $288,000, and issued a 60-day, 12% note, dated today, for the purchase.

8   Sold merchandise to Fan Company, $360,000. A 30-day, 12% note, dated today, is received to cover the sale.

14   Received payment on the Parker Company note dated June 15, 1998.

15   Fixx Company sent a $120,000, 30-day, 12% note, dated today, and a check to cover the part of the old note not covered by the new note, *plus* all interest expense incurred on the prior note.

19   The note payable dated May 20, 1998, was paid in full.

    23   Sox Company dishonored its note of July 3 and sent a check for the interest on the dishonored note and a new 30-day, 12% note dated July 23, 1998.

    30   The Dot Company note dated May 31, 1998, was paid with interest in full.

Prepare dated journal entries for these transactions and necessary July 31 adjusting entries.

Required

On November 1, 1999, Grand Strand Property Management, Inc., discounted its own $50,000, 180-day, noninterest-bearing note at its bank at 18%. The note was paid on its maturity date. The company uses a calendar-year accounting period.

Problem 9–6
Account for discounted note payable (L.O. 6)

Prepare dated journal entries to record *(a)* the discounting of the note, *(b)* the year-end adjustment, and *(c)* the payment of the note.

Required

ALTERNATE PROBLEMS

As of December 31, 1998, Fargo Company's accounts prior to adjustment show:

Problem 9–1A
Write off uncollectible account, record expense under alternative methods of estimation (L.O. 1)

Accounts receivable	$ 40,000
Allowance for uncollectible accounts (credit balance)	750
Sales	250,000

Fargo Company estimates uncollectible accounts at 1% of sales.

    On February 23, 1999, the account of Dan Hall in the amount of $300 was considered uncollectible and written off. On August 12, 1999, Hall remitted $200 and indicated that he intends to pay the balance due as soon as possible. By December 31, 1999, no further remittance had been received from Hall and no further remittance was expected.

a.   Prepare journal entries to record all of these transactions and adjusting entries.

b.   Give the entry necessary as of December 31, 1998, if Fargo Company estimated its uncollectible accounts at 8% of outstanding receivables rather than at 1% of sales.

Required

At the close of business, Jim's Restaurant had credit card sales of $12,000. Of this amount, $4,000 were VISA (bank credit card) sales invoices, which can be deposited in a bank for immediate credit, less a discount of 3%. The balance of $8,000 consisted of American Express (nonbank credit card) charges, subject to a 5% service charge. These invoices were mailed to American Express. Shortly thereafter, a check was received.

Problem 9–2A
Record use of bank and nonbank credit cards (L.O. 2)

Prepare journal entries for all these transactions.

Required

Ruiz Company sells merchandise in a state that has a 5% sales tax. On January 2, 1999, Ruiz sold goods with a sales price of $80,000 on credit. Sales taxes collected are recorded in a separate account. Assume that sales for the entire month were $900,000. On January 31, 1999, the company remitted the sales taxes collected to the state taxing agency.

Problem 9–3A
Prepare journal entries for sales and excise taxes (L.O. 4)

a.   Prepare the general journal entries to record the January 2 sales revenue. Also prepare the entry to show the remittance of the taxes on January 31.

b.   Now assume that the merchandise sold on January 2 also is subject to federal excise taxes of 12%. The federal excise taxes collected are remitted to the proper agency on January 31. Show the entries on January 2 and January 31.

Required

Honest Tim's Auto Company sells used cars and warrants all parts for one year. The average price per car is $10,000, and the company sold 900 in 1998. The company expects 30% of the cars to develop defective parts within one year of sale. The estimated average cost of warranty repairs per defective car is $600. By the end of the year, 80 cars sold that year had been returned and repaired under warranty. On January 4, 1999, a customer returned a car purchased in 1998 for repairs under warranty. The repairs were made on January 8. The cost of the repairs included parts, $400, and labor, $210.

Problem 9–4A
Prepare journal entries for product warranty (L.O. 4)

a.   Calculate the amount of the estimated product warranty payable.

b.   Prepare the entry to record the estimated product warranty payable on December 31, 1998.

c.   Prepare the entry to record the repairs made on January 8, 1999.

Required

Problem 9–5A
Prepare entries to record a number of note transactions, adjusting entries for interest, and entries for payment of notes (L.O. 5)

Celoron Power Boat Company is in the power boat manufacturing business. As of September 1, the balance in its Notes Receivable account is $256,000. The balance in Dishonored Notes Receivable is $60,660 (includes the interest of $600 and the protest fee of $60). A schedule of the notes (including the dishonored note) is as follows:

Face Amount	Maker	Date of Note	Life	Interest Rate	Comments
$100,000	C. Glass Co.	6/1/96	120 days	12%	
72,000	A. Lamp Co.	6/15/96	90	8	
84,000	C. Wall Co.	7/1/96	90	10	
60,000	N. Case Co.	7/1/96	60	6	Dishonored, interest, $600; protest fee, $60.
$316,000					

Following are Celoron Power Boat Company's transactions for September:

Sept. 10 Received $36,660 from N. Case Company as full settlement of the amount due from it. The company does not charge losses on notes to the Allowance for Uncollectible Accounts account.

? The A. Lamp Company note was collected when due.

? The C. Glass Company note was not paid at maturity.

? C. Wall Company paid its note at maturity.

30 Received a new 60-day, 12% note from C. Glass Company for the total balance due on the dishonored note. The note was dated as of the maturity date of the dishonored note. Celoron Power Boat Company accepted the note in good faith.

Required   Prepare dated journal entries for these transactions.

Problem 9–6A
Account for discounted note payable (L.O. 6)

Premium Office Equipment, Inc., discounted its own $30,000, noninterest-bearing, 180-day note on November 16, 1998, at Niagara County Bank at a discount rate of 12%.

Required   Prepare dated journal entries for:

a. The original discounting on November 16.

b. The adjustment required at the end of the company's calendar-year accounting period.

c. Payment at maturity.

BEYOND THE NUMBERS—CRITICAL THINKING

Business Decision Case 9–1
Compare costs of maintaining own accounts receivable with costs of allowing the use of credit cards; identify other factors to consider (L.O. 1, 3)

Sally Stillwagon owns a hardware store; she sells items for cash and on account. During 1998, which seemed to be a typical year, some of her company's operating data and other data were as follows:

Sales:	
For cash	$1,200,000
On credit	2,200,000
Cost of obtaining credit reports on customers	3,600
Cost incurred in paying a part-time bookkeeper to keep the accounts receivable subsidiary ledger up to date	12,000
Cost associated with preparing and mailing invoices to customers and other collection activities	18,000
Uncollectible accounts expense	45,000
Average outstanding accounts receivable balance (on which Stillwagon estimates she could have earned 10% if it had been invested in other assets)	180,000

A national credit card agency has tried to convince Stillwagon that instead of carrying her own accounts receivable, she should accept only the agency's credit card for sales on credit. The agency would pay her two days after she submits sales charges, deducting 6% from the amount and paying her 94%.

Required   a. Using the data given, prepare an analysis showing whether or not Stillwagon would benefit from switching to the credit card method of selling on credit.

b. What other factors should she take into consideration?

Jim Perry operates a large fruit and vegetable stand on the outskirts of a city. In a typical year he sells $600,000 of goods to regular customers. His sales are 40% for cash and 60% on credit. He carries all of the credit himself. Only after a customer has a $300 unpaid balance on which no payments have been made for two months does he refuse that customer credit for future purchases. His income before taxes is approximately $95,000. The total of uncollectible accounts for a given year is about 10% of credit sales, or $48,000.

You are one of Perry's regular customers. He knows that you are taking a college course in accounting and has asked you to tell him your opinion of several alternatives recommended to him to reduce or eliminate the $48,000 per year uncollectible accounts expense. The alternatives are as follows:

1. Do not sell on credit.
2. Sell on credit by national credit card only.
3. Allow customers to charge only until their account balances reach $50.
4. Allow a bill collector to go after uncollectible accounts and keep half of the amount collected.

Write a report for Perry about the advisability of following any of these alternatives.

Refer to the annual reports of The Coca-Cola Company, Maytag Corporation, The Limited, Inc., and John H. Harland Company in the annual report booklet. For the most recent year shown, calculate accounts receivable turnover and the number of days' sales in accounts receivable for each company and prepare a written comment on the results.

In groups of two or three students, write a two-page, double-spaced paper on one of the following topics:

Which is better—the percentage-of-sales method or the percentage-of-receivables method?

Why not eliminate bad debts by selling only for cash?

Why allow customers to use credit cards when credit card expense is so high?

Should banks be required to use 365 days instead of 360 days in interest calculations?

Present your analysis in a convincing manner, without spelling or grammatical errors. This paper should be the result of several drafts and neatly prepared using word processing software. If a computer is not available, type this paper. Include a cover page with the title and authors' names.

"Lapping" of accounts receivable has been used to conceal the fact that payments received on accounts receivable have been "borrowed" and used by an employee for personal use. With one or two other students, research this topic in the library. Write a paper to your instructor describing how this technique works and the steps that can be taken to detect it once it occurs and to prevent it in the future.

In a group of two or three students, visit a fairly large company in your community to investigate the effectiveness of its management of accounts receivable. Inquire about its credit and sales discount policies, collection policies, and how it establishes the amount for the adjusting entry for uncollectible accounts at year-end. Also ask about how it decides to write off accounts as uncollectible. Calculate its accounts receivable turnover and average collection period for each of the last two years. In view of its credit policies, does its collection period seem reasonable?

**Business Decision
Case 9–2**
Evaluate alternative means
of making sales (L.O. 3, 4)

Required

**Annual Report
Analysis 9–3**
Calculate accounts receivable turnover and the
number of days' sales in
accounts receivable for
four real companies and
comment on the results
(L.O. 7)

Group Project 9–4
Write paper on a specific
topic

Group Project 9–5
Perform library research

Group Project 9–6
Evaluate management of
accounts receivable

Using the Internet—A View of the Real World

Internet Project 9–7
Check some mutual funds

Visit the following Internet site:

http://www.networth.galt.com

Click on Morningside Profiles to check out some mutual funds. You might start by clicking on some of the Premier Partners appearing on the screen (e.g., Dreyfus, INVESCO, or Kaufmann funds). Then follow some of the other options available at this site. Write a report to your instructor on your experience, describing some of the things you learned at this site. You may want to pretend that you invested in one or more of these funds for the duration of the quarter or semester and see how your investment would have fared during that period. Many investors with a limited amount to invest can have a diversified portfolio by investing in mutual funds. Thus, they spread their risk by investing in a mutual fund that, in turn, invests in many different companies.

Internet Project 9–8
Learn about financial highlights

Visit Procter & Gamble's site at:

http://www.pg.com

Procter & Gamble markets more than 300 brands to nearly five billion consumers in over 140 countries. Click on any items that deal with financial news, annual report summary, stock quote, and anything else that looks interesting. Write a memo to your instructor summarizing your findings. Include in your memo some of the financial highlights contained in the annual report summary.

Answers to Self Test

True-False

1. **False.** The percentage-of-sales method estimates the uncollectible accounts from the net credit sales or net sales of a given period.
2. **False.** Uncollectible accounts expense is recognized at the end of the accounting period in an adjusting entry.
3. **True.** The retailer deposits the credit card invoices directly in a special checking account.
4. **False.** Liabilities result from a past transaction.
5. **True.** Current liabilities are classified into those three categories.

6. **True.** The note has passed its maturity date and should be removed from the Notes Receivable account. The maturity value plus any protest fee should be debited to Accounts Receivable.
7. **False.** Discount on Notes Payable is recorded when a noninterest-bearing note is issued.

Multiple-Choice

1. **d.** A write-off of an account receivable results in a debit to Allowance for Uncollectible Accounts and a credit to Accounts Receivable for the same amount. The net amount (accounts receivable minus allowance for uncollectible accounts) does not change.
2. **a.** The uncollectible accounts expense for 1999 is computed as follows:

Allowance balance after adjustment
($200,000 × 0.05) $10,000
Balance before adjustment . . . . (3,000)
Uncollectible accounts expense . . . . $ 7,000

3. **c.** Manufacturing companies tend to have the longest operating cycle. They must invest cash in raw materials, convert these raw materials into work in process and then finished goods, sell the items on account, and then collect the accounts receivable.

4. **b.** $265,000 divided by 1.06 = $250,000; $265,000 − $250,000 = $15,000.
5. **c.** 2,000 × 5% = 100 machines expected to be defective. 100 − 30 already returned = 70 more expected to be returned. 70 × $200 = $14,000 estimated product warranty payable.
6. **c.** The name of the payee is not needed to compute interest expense on a promissory note.
7. **c.** The proceeds from a bank are computed as follows:

Discount amount = $10,000 × 0.10 × $90/360$
= $250
Proceeds = $10,000 − $250 = $9,750

10

PROPERTY, PLANT, AND EQUIPMENT

On a classified balance sheet, the asset section contains: (1) current assets; (2) property, plant, and equipment; and (3) other categories such as intangible assets and long-term investments. Previous chapters discussed current assets. This chapter begins a discussion of property, plant, and equipment that is concluded in Chapter 11. Property, plant, and equipment are often called **plant and equipment** or simply *plant assets*. Plant assets are long-lived assets because they are expected to last for more than one year. Long-lived assets consist of tangible assets and intangible assets. **Tangible assets** have physical characteristics that we can see and touch; they include plant assets such as buildings and furniture, and natural resources such as gas and oil. *Intangible assets* have no physical characteristics that we can see and touch but represent exclusive privileges and rights to their owners.

NATURE OF PLANT ASSETS

To be classified as a *plant asset*, an asset must: (1) be tangible, that is, capable of being seen and touched; (2) have a useful service life of more than one year; and (3) be used in business operations rather than held for resale. Common plant assets are buildings, machines, tools, and office equipment. On the balance sheet, these assets appear under the heading "Property, plant, and equipment."

Plant assets include all long-lived tangible assets used to generate the principal revenues of the business. Inventory is a tangible asset but not a plant asset because inventory is usually not long-lived and it is held for sale rather than for use. What represents a plant asset to one company may be inventory to another. For example, a business such as a retail appliance store may classify a delivery truck as a plant asset because the truck is used to deliver merchandise. A business such as a truck dealership would classify the same delivery truck as inventory because the truck is held for sale. Also, land held for speculation or not yet put into service is a long-term investment rather than a plant asset because the land is not being used by the business.

Objective 1
List the characteristics of plant assets and identify the costs of acquiring plant assets.

Real World Example
In many business entities, plant assets represent the major portion of the total assets of the business. Duracell's balance sheets for the calendar years ended June 30, 1996 and 1995, show plant asset totals of $926 million and $811.8 million, respectively.

However, standby equipment used only in peak or emergency periods is a plant asset because it is used in the operations of the business.

Accountants view plant assets as a collection of *service potentials* that are consumed over a long time. For example, over several years, a delivery truck may provide 100,000 miles of delivery services to an appliance business. A new building may provide 40 years of shelter, while a machine may perform a particular operation on 400,000 parts. In each instance, purchase of the plant asset actually represents the advance payment or prepayment for expected services. Plant asset costs are a form of prepaid expense. As with short-term prepayments, the accountant must allocate the cost of these services to the accounting periods benefited.

Accounting for plant assets involves the following four steps:

1. Record the acquisition cost of the asset.
2. Record the allocation of the asset's original cost to periods of its useful life through depreciation.
3. Record subsequent expenditures on the asset.
4. Account for the disposal of the asset.

In Illustration 10.1, note how the asset's life begins with its procurement and the recording of its acquisition cost, which is usually in the form of a dollar purchase. Then, as the asset provides services through time, accountants record the asset's depreciation and any subsequent expenditures related to the asset. Finally, accountants record the disposal of the asset. We discuss the first three steps in this chapter and the disposal of an asset in Chapter 11. The last section in this chapter explains how accountants use subsidiary ledgers to control assets.

Remember that in recording the life history of an asset, accountants match expenses related to the asset with the revenues generated by it. Because measuring the periodic expense of plant assets affects net income, accounting for property, plant, and equipment is important to financial statement users.

INITIAL RECORDING OF PLANT ASSETS

When a company acquires a plant asset, accountants record the asset at the cost of acquisition (historical cost). This cost is objective, verifiable, and the best measure of an asset's fair market value at the time of purchase. Even if the market value of the asset changes over time, accountants continue to report the acquisition cost in the asset account in subsequent periods.

The **acquisition cost** of a plant asset is the amount of cash or cash equivalents given up to acquire and place the asset in operating condition at its proper location. Thus, cost includes all normal, reasonable, and necessary expenditures to obtain the asset and get it ready for use. Acquisition cost also includes the repair and reconditioning costs for used or damaged assets. Unnecessary costs (such as traffic tickets or fines) that must be paid as a result of hauling machinery to a new plant are not part of the acquisition cost of the asset.

The next sections discuss which costs are capitalized (debited to an asset account) for: (1) land and land improvements; (2) buildings; (3) group purchases of assets; (4) machinery and other equipment; (5) self-constructed assets; (6) noncash acquisitions; and (7) gifts of plant assets.

Land and Land Improvements

Reinforcing Problem
E10–1 Determine cost of land.

The cost of land includes its purchase price and other costs such as option cost, real estate commissions, title search and title transfer fees, and title insurance premiums. Also included are an existing mortgage note or unpaid taxes (back taxes) assumed by the purchaser; costs of surveying, clearing, and grading; and local assessments for sidewalks, streets, sewers, and water mains. Sometimes land purchased as a building site contains an unusable building that must be removed. Then, the accountant debits the entire purchase price to Land, including the cost of removing the building less any cash received from the sale of salvaged items while the land is being readied for use.

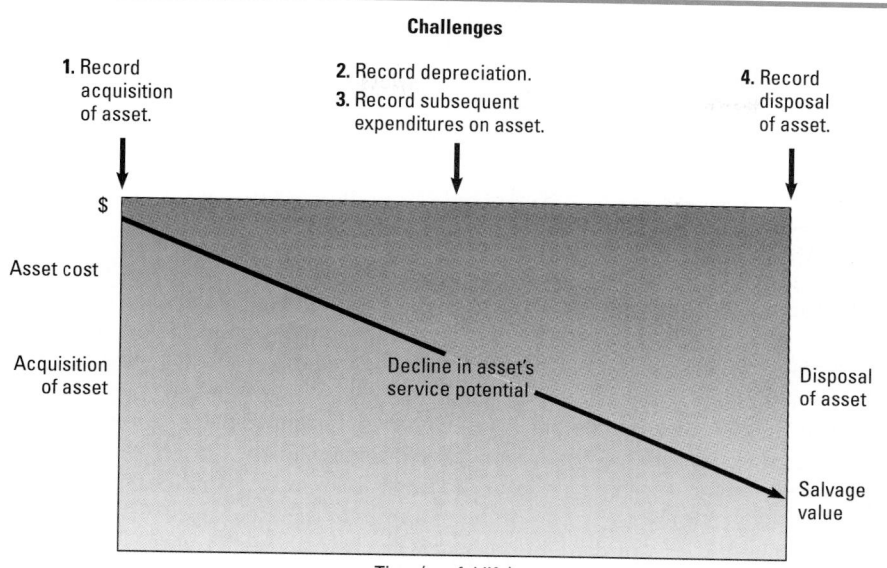

Challenges

1. Record acquisition of asset.

2. Record depreciation.
3. Record subsequent expenditures on asset.

4. Record disposal of asset.

$

Asset cost

Acquisition of asset

Decline in asset's service potential

Disposal of asset

Salvage value

Time (useful life)

ILLUSTRATION 10.1
Recording the Life History of a Depreciable Asset

To illustrate, assume that Spivey Company purchased an old farm on the outskirts of San Diego, California, as a factory site. The company paid $225,000 for the property. In addition, the company agreed to pay unpaid property taxes from previous periods (called *back taxes*) of $12,000. Attorneys' fees and other legal costs relating to the purchase of the farm totaled $1,800. Spivey demolished (razed) the farm buildings at a cost of $18,000. The company salvaged some of the structural pieces of the building and sold them for $3,000. Because the firm was constructing a new building at the site, the city assessed Spivey Company $9,000 for water mains, sewers, and street paving. Spivey computed the cost of the land as follows:

	Land
Cost of factory site	$225,000
Back taxes	12,000
Attorneys' fees and other legal costs	1,800
Demolition	18,000
Sale of salvaged parts	(3,000)
City assessment	9,000
	$262,800

Accountants assigned all costs relating to the farm purchase and razing of the old buildings to the Land account because the old buildings purchased with the land were not usable. The real goal was to purchase the land, but the land was not available without the buildings.

Land is considered to have an unlimited life and is therefore not depreciable. However, **land improvements,** including driveways, temporary landscaping, parking lots, fences, lighting systems, and sprinkler systems, are attachments to the land. They have limited lives and therefore are depreciable. Owners record depreciable land improvements in a separate account called Land Improvements. They record the cost of permanent landscaping, including leveling and grading, in the Land account.

Buildings

When a business buys a building, its cost includes the purchase price, repair and remodeling costs, unpaid taxes assumed by the purchaser, legal costs, and real estate commissions paid.

Determining the cost of constructing a new building is often more difficult. Usually this cost includes architect's fees; building permits; payments to contractors; and the cost of digging the foundation. Also included are labor and materials to build the building; salaries of officers supervising the construction; and insurance, taxes, and interest during the construction period. Any miscellaneous amounts earned from the building during construction reduce the cost of the building. For example, an owner who could rent out a small completed portion during construction of the remainder of the building, would credit the rental proceeds to the Buildings account rather than to a revenue account.

Group Purchases of Assets

Reinforcing Problem
E10–2 Determine cost of land and building when acquired together.

Sometimes a company buys land and other assets for a lump sum. When land and buildings purchased together are to be used, the firm divides the total cost and establishes separate ledger accounts for land and for buildings. This division of cost establishes the proper balances in the appropriate accounts. This is especially important later because the depreciation recorded on the buildings affects reported income, while no depreciation is taken on the land.

Returning to our example of Spivey Company, suppose one of the farm buildings was going to be remodeled for use by the company. Then, Spivey would determine what portion of the purchase price of the farm, back taxes, and legal fees ($225,000 + $12,000 + $1,800 = $238,800) it could assign to the buildings and what portion to the land. (The net cost of demolition would not be incurred, and the city assessment would be incurred at a later time.) Spivey would assign the $238,800 to the land and the buildings on the basis of their appraised values. For example, assume that the land was appraised at $162,000 and the buildings at $108,000. Spivey would determine the cost assignable to each of these plant assets as follows:

Asset	Appraised Value	Percent of Total Value
Land	$162,000	60% (162/270)
Buildings . . .	108,000	40 (108/270)
	$270,000	100% (270/270)

	Percent of Total Value	×	Purchase Price	=	Cost Assigned
Land	60%	×	$238,800*	=	$143,280
Buildings	40	×	238,800	=	95,520
					$238,800

* The purchase price is the sum of the cash price, back taxes, and legal fees.

The journal entry to record the purchase of the land and buildings would be:

Land	143,280	
Buildings	95,520	
Cash		238,800
To record purchase of land and buildings.		

When the city eventually assessed the charges for the water mains, sewers, and street paving, the company would still debit these costs to the Land account as in the previous example.

Machinery and Other Equipment

Reinforcing Problem
E10–3 Determine cost of a machine.

Often companies purchase machinery or other equipment such as delivery or office equipment. Its cost includes the seller's *net* invoice price (whether the discount is taken or not), transportation charges incurred, insurance in transit, cost of installation, costs of accessories, and testing and break-in costs. Also included are other costs needed to put the machine or equipment in operating condition in its intended location. The cost of machinery does not include removing and disposing of a replaced, old machine that has been used in operations. Such costs are part of the gain or loss on disposal of the old machine, as discussed in Chapter 11.

To illustrate, assume that Clark Company purchased new equipment to replace equipment that it has used for five years. The company paid a net purchase price of $150,000, brokerage fees of $5,000, legal fees of $2,000, and freight and insurance in transit of $3,000. In addition, the company paid $1,500 to remove old equipment and $2,000 to install new equipment. Clark would compute the cost of new equipment as follows:

Net purchase price	$150,000
Brokerage fees	5,000
Legal fees	2,000
Freight and insurance in transit	3,000
Installation costs	2,000
Total cost	$162,000

Self-Constructed Assets

If a company builds a plant asset for its own use, the cost includes all materials and labor directly traceable to construction of the asset. Also included in the cost of the asset are interest costs related to the asset and amounts paid for utilities (such as heat, light, and power) and for supplies used during construction. To determine how much of these indirect costs to capitalize, the company compares utility and supply costs during the construction period with those costs in a period when no construction occurred. The firm records the increase as part of the asset's cost. For example, assume a company normally incurred a $600 utility bill for June. This year, the company constructed a machine during June, and the utility bill was $975. Thus, it records the $375 increase as part of the machine's cost.

To illustrate further, assume that Tanner Company needed a new die-casting machine and received a quote from Smith Company for $23,000, plus $1,000 freight costs. Tanner decided to build the machine rather than buy it. The company incurred the following costs to build the machine: materials, $4,000; labor, $13,000; and indirect services of heat, power, and supplies, $3,000. Tanner would record the machine at its cost of $20,000 ($4,000 + $13,000 + $3,000) rather than $24,000, the purchase price of the machine. The $20,000 is the cost of the resources given up to construct the machine. Also, recording the machine at $24,000 would require Tanner to recognize a gain on construction of the assets. Accountants do not subscribe to the idea that a business can earn revenue (or realize a gain), and therefore net income, by dealing with itself.

You can apply the general guidelines we have just discussed to other plant assets, such as furniture and fixtures. The accounting methods are the same.

Noncash Acquisitions

When a plant asset is purchased for cash, its acquisition cost is simply the agreed on cash price. However, when a business acquires plant assets in exchange for other noncash assets (shares of stock, a customer's note, or a tract of land) or as gifts, it is more difficult to establish a cash price. This section discusses three possible asset valuation bases.

Reinforcing Problem
E10–4 Determine cost of machine in noncash acquisition.

FAIR MARKET VALUE   **Fair market value** is the price received for an item sold in the normal course of business (not at a forced liquidation sale). Accountants record noncash exchange transactions at fair market value.

The general rule on noncash exchanges is to value the noncash asset received at its fair market value or the fair market value of what was given up, whichever is more clearly evident. The reason for not using the book value of the old asset to value the new asset is that the asset being given up is often carried in the accounting records at historical cost or book value. Neither amount may adequately represent the actual fair market value of either asset. Therefore, if the fair market value of one asset is clearly evident, a firm should record this amount for the new asset at the time of the exchange.

APPRAISED VALUE   Sometimes, neither of the items exchanged has a clearly determinable fair market value. Then, accountants record exchanges of items at their appraised values as determined by a professional appraiser. An **appraised value** is an expert's opinion of an item's fair market price if the item were sold. Appraisals are used often to value works of art, rare books, and antiques.

BOOK VALUE   The **book value** of an asset is its recorded cost less accumulated depreciation. An old asset's book value is usually not a valid indication of the new asset's fair market value. If a better basis is not available, however, a firm could use the book value of the old asset.

Gifts of Plant Assets

Occasionally, a company receives an asset without giving up anything for it. For example, to attract industry to an area and provide jobs for local residents, a city may give a company a tract of land on which to build a factory. Although such a gift costs the recipient company nothing, it usually records the asset (land) at its fair market value. Accountants record gifts of plant assets at fair market value to provide information on all assets owned by the company. Omitting some assets may make information provided misleading. They would credit assets received as gifts to a stockholders' equity account titled Paid-in Capital—Donations.

AN ACCOUNTING PERSPECTIVE

USE OF TECHNOLOGY   How can CPA firms sell services on the Web other than by advertising their services? Ernst & Young has developed a website for consulting clients in which they charge an annual fixed fee (about $6,000) for clients to obtain advice from the firm's consultants. The site is secure in that it can only be accessed by those who have paid the fee. The subscribers type in their questions on any business topic and get a response from an expert within two working days. Another firm, Coopers & Lybrand, has an on-line service for tax professionals to seek advice. The other large accounting firms undoubtedly have developed or are developing secure websites for providing similar types of services.

DEPRECIATION OF PLANT ASSETS

Companies record depreciation on all plant assets except land. Since the amount of depreciation may be relatively large, depreciation expense is often a significant factor in determining net income. For this reason, most financial statement users are interested in the amount of, and the methods used to compute, a company's depreciation expense.

Depreciation is the amount of plant asset cost allocated to each accounting period benefiting from the plant asset's use. Depreciation is a *process of allocation*, not valuation. Eventually, all assets except land wear out or become so inadequate or outmoded that they are sold or discarded; therefore, firms must record depreciation on every plant asset except land. They record depreciation even when the market value of a plant asset temporarily rises above its original cost because eventually the asset is no longer useful to its current owner.

Major causes of depreciation are (1) physical deterioration, (2) inadequacy for future needs, and (3) obsolescence. **Physical deterioration** results from the use of the asset—wear and tear—and the action of the elements. For example, an automobile may have to be replaced after a time because its body rusted out. The **inadequacy** of a plant asset is its inability to produce enough products or provide enough services to meet current demands. For example, an airline cannot provide air service for 125 passengers using a plane that seats 90. The **obsolescence** of an asset is its decline in usefulness brought about by inventions and technological progress. For example, the development of the xerographic process of reproducing printed matter rendered almost all previous methods of duplication obsolete.

The use of a plant asset in business operations transforms a plant asset cost into an operating expense. Depreciation, then, is an operating expense resulting from the use of a depreciable plant asset. Because depreciation expense does not require a current cash outlay, it is often called a *noncash expense*. The purchaser gave up cash in the period when the asset was acquired, not during the periods when depreciation expense is recorded.

Note to the Student
Depreciation is a device for matching expense against revenue, not a valuation process nor a fund of cash for replacing assets. Once residual (salvage) value and useful life have been estimated, the company selects a method of depreciation.

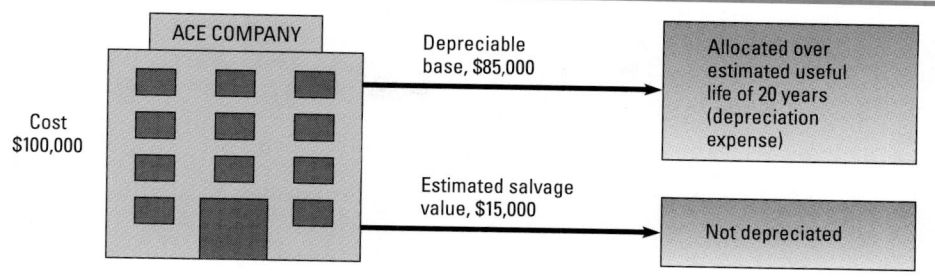

ILLUSTRATION 10.2
Factors Affecting
Depreciation

To compute depreciation expense, accountants consider four major factors:

Factors Affecting Depreciation

1. Cost of the asset.

2. Estimated salvage value of the asset. **Salvage value** (or *scrap value*) is the amount of money the company expects to recover, less disposal costs, on the date a plant asset is scrapped, sold, or traded in.

3. Estimated useful life of the asset. **Useful life** refers to the time the company owning the asset intends to use it; useful life is not necessarily the same as either economic life or physical life. The economic life of a car may be 7 years and its physical life may be 10 years, but if a company has a policy of trading cars every 3 years, the useful life for depreciation purposes is 3 years. Various firms express useful life in years, months, working hours, or units of production. Obsolescence also affects useful life. For example, a machine capable of producing units for 20 years, may be expected to be obsolete in 6 years. Thus, its estimated useful life is 6 years—not 20. Another example, on TV you may have seen a demolition crew setting off explosives in a huge building (e.g., The Dunes Hotel and Casino in Las Vegas) and wondering why the owners decided to destroy what looked like a perfectly good building. The building was destroyed because it had reached the end of its economic life. The land on which the building stood could be put to better use, possibly by constructing a new building.

4. Depreciation method used in depreciating the asset. We describe the four common depreciation methods in the next section.

Objective 2
List the four major factors affecting depreciation expense.

In Illustration 10.2, note the relationship among these factors. Assume Ace Company purchased an office building for $100,000. The building has an estimated salvage value of $15,000 and a useful life of 20 years. The depreciable cost of the building is $85,000 (cost less estimated salvage value). Ace would allocate this depreciable base over the useful life of the building using the proper depreciation method under the circumstances.

Today, companies can use many different methods to calculate depreciation on assets.[1] This section discusses and illustrates the most common methods—straight-line, units-of-production, and two accelerated depreciation methods (sum-of-the-years' digits and double-declining-balance).

Depreciation Methods

As is true for inventory methods, normally a company is free to adopt the most appropriate depreciation method for its business operations. According to accounting theory, companies should use a depreciation method that reflects most closely their underlying economic circumstances. Thus, companies should adopt the depreciation method that allocates plant asset cost to accounting periods according to the benefits received from the use of the asset. Illustration 10.3 shows the frequency of use of these methods for 600 companies. You can see that most companies use the straight-line method for financial reporting purposes. Note that some companies use

Objective 3
Describe the various methods of calculating depreciation expense.

---

[1]Because depreciation expense is an estimate, calculations may be rounded to the nearest dollar.

ILLUSTRATION 10.3
Depreciation Methods
Used

	Number of Companies			
Method	**1995**	**1994**	**1993**	**1992**
Straight line	572	573	570	564
Declining balance	27	27	26	26
Sum of the years' digits	12	9	9	12
Accelerated method—not specified	49	49	56	62
Units of production	38	49	46	47
Other	11	11	9	5

Source: Based on American Institute of Certified Public Accountants, *Accounting Trends & Techniques* (New York: AICPA, 1996), p. 357.

one method for certain assets and another method for other assets. In practice, measuring the benefits from the use of a plant asset is impractical and often not possible. As a result, a depreciation method must meet only one standard: the depreciation method must allocate plant asset cost to accounting periods in a systematic and rational manner. The following four methods meet this requirement.

AN ACCOUNTING PERSPECTIVE

BUSINESS INSIGHT   Regardless of the method or methods of depreciation chosen, companies must disclose their depreciation methods in the footnotes to their financial statements. They include this information in the first footnote, which summarizes significant accounting policies.

The disclosure is generally straightforward: Sears, Roebuck & Co. operates department stores, paint and hardware stores, auto supply stores, and eyewear stores. Its annual report states simply that "depreciation is provided principally by the straight-line method." Companies may use different depreciation methods for different assets. General Electric Company is a highly diversified multinational corporation that develops, manufactures, and markets aerospace products, major appliances, industrial products, and high-performance engineered plastics. It uses an accelerated method for most of its property, plant, and equipment; however, it depreciates some assets on a straight-line basis, while the company's mining properties are depreciated under the units-of-production method.

In the illustrations of the four depreciation methods that follow, we assume the following: On January 1, 1999, a company purchased a machine for $54,000 with an estimated useful life of 10 years, or 50,000 units of output, and an estimated salvage value of $4,000.

STRAIGHT-LINE METHOD   **Straight-line depreciation** has been the most widely used depreciation method in the United States for many years because, as you saw in Chapter 3, it is easily applied. To apply the straight-line method, a firm charges an equal amount of plant asset cost to each accounting period. The formula for calculating depreciation under the straight-line method is:

$$\frac{\text{Depreciation}}{\text{per period}} = \frac{\text{Asset cost} - \text{Estimated salvage value}}{\text{Number of accounting periods in estimated useful life}}$$

Using our example of a machine purchased for $54,000, the depreciation is:

$$\frac{\$54,000 - \$4,000}{10 \text{ years}} = \$5,000 \text{ per year}$$

In Illustration 10.4, we present a schedule of annual depreciation entries, cumulative balances in the accumulated depreciation account, and the book (or carrying) values of the $54,000 machine.

Using the straight-line method for assets is appropriate where (1) time rather than obsolescence is the major factor limiting the asset's life and (2) the asset produces relatively constant amounts of periodic services. Assets that possess these features include items such as pipelines, fencing, and storage tanks.

End of Year	Depreciation Expense Dr.; Accumulated Depreciation Cr.	Total Accumulated Depreciation	Book Value
			$54,000
1	$ 5,000	$ 5,000	49,000
2	5,000	10,000	44,000
3	5,000	15,000	39,000
4	5,000	20,000	34,000
5	5,000	25,000	29,000
6	5,000	30,000	24,000
7	5,000	35,000	19,000
8	5,000	40,000	14,000
9	5,000	45,000	9,000
10	5,000	50,000	4,000*
	$50,000		

* Estimated salvage value.

ILLUSTRATION 10.4
Straight-Line
Depreciation Schedule

Reinforcing Problem
E10–5 Record cost of office equipment, depreciation, and repairs expense.

UNITS-OF-PRODUCTION (OUTPUT) METHOD The **units-of-production depreciation** method assigns an equal amount of depreciation to each unit of product manufactured or service rendered by an asset. Since this method of depreciation is based on physical output, firms apply it in situations where usage rather than obsolescence leads to the demise of the asset. Under this method, you would compute the depreciation charge per unit of output. Then, multiply this figure by the number of units of goods or services produced during the accounting period to find the period's depreciation expense. The formula is:

$$\frac{\text{Depreciation}}{\text{per unit}} = \frac{\text{Asset cost} - \text{Estimated salvage value}}{\text{Estimated total units of production (or service) during useful life of asset}}$$

$$\frac{\text{Depreciation}}{\text{per period}} = \frac{\text{Depreciation}}{\text{per unit}} \times \frac{\text{Number of units of goods}}{\text{or services produced}}$$

You would determine the depreciation charge for the $54,000 machine as:

$$\frac{\$54,000 - \$4,000}{50,000 \text{ units}} = \$1 \text{ per unit}$$

If the machine produced 1,000 units in 1999 and 2,500 units in 2000, depreciation expense for those years would be $1,000 and $2,500, respectively.

ACCELERATED DEPRECIATION METHODS Accelerated depreciation methods record higher amounts of depreciation during the early years of an asset's life and lower amounts in the asset's later years. A business might choose an accelerated depreciation method for the following reasons:

1. The value of the benefits received from the asset decline with age (for example, office buildings).
2. The asset is a high-technology asset subject to rapid obsolescence (for example, computers).
3. Repairs increase substantially in the asset's later years; under this method, the depreciation and repairs together remain fairly constant over the asset's life (for example, automobiles).

The two most common accelerated methods of depreciation are the *sum-of-the-years'-digits (SOYD)* method and the *double-declining-balance (DDB)* method.

Sum-of-the-Years'-Digits Method The **sum-of-the-years'-digits (SOYD)** method adds the consecutive digits for each year of an asset's estimated life together and uses

ILLUSTRATION 10.5
Sum-of-the-Years'-Digits
Depreciation Schedule

End of Year		Depreciation Expense Dr.; Accumulated Depreciation Cr.	Total Accumulated Depreciation	Book Value
				$54,000
1.	$50,000* × ¹⁰⁄₅₅.	$ 9,091	$ 9,091	44,909
2.	$50,000 × ⁹⁄₅₅.	8,182	17,273	36,727
3.	$50,000 × ⁸⁄₅₅.	7,273	24,546	29,454
4.	$50,000 × ⁷⁄₅₅.	6,364	30,910	23,090
5.	$50,000 × ⁶⁄₅₅.	5,455	36,365	17,635
6.	$50,000 × ⁵⁄₅₅.	4,545	40,910	13,090
7.	$50,000 × ⁴⁄₅₅.	3,636	44,546	9,454
8.	$50,000 × ³⁄₅₅.	2,727	47,273	6,727
9.	$50,000 × ²⁄₅₅.	1,818	49,091	4,909
10.	$50,000 × ¹⁄₅₅.	909	50,000	4,000
		$50,000		

* $54,000 cost − $4,000 salvage value.

that as the denominator of a fraction. The numerator is the years of useful life remaining at the *beginning* of the accounting period. To compute that period's depreciation expense, you would multiply this fraction by the asset cost less the estimated salvage value. The formula is:

$$\frac{\text{Depreciation}}{\text{per period}} = \frac{\begin{array}{c}\text{Number of years of useful}\\\text{life remaining at beginning}\\\text{of accounting period}\end{array}}{\text{SOYD}} \times \left(\begin{array}{cc}\text{Asset} & \text{Estimated}\\\text{cost} & \text{salvage value}\end{array}\right)$$

The years are totaled to find SOYD. For an asset with a 10-year useful life, SOYD = 10 + 9 + 8 + 7 + 6 + 5 + 4 + 3 + 2 + 1 = 55. Alternatively, rather than adding the digits for all years together, you can use this formula to find the SOYD for any given number of periods:

$$\text{SOYD} = \frac{n(n + 1)}{2}$$

where n is the number of periods in the asset's useful life. Thus, SOYD for an asset with a 10-year useful life is:

$$\text{SOYD} = \frac{10(10 + 1)}{2} = 55$$

To apply the SOYD method to the $54,000 machine, you would determine that at the beginning of year 1 (1999), the machine has 10 years of useful life remaining. Then, using the formula, compute the first year's depreciation as ¹⁰⁄₅₅ times $50,000 (the $54,000 cost less the $4,000 salvage value). The depreciation for the first year is $9,091 (see Illustration 10.5). Note that the fraction gets smaller every year, resulting in a declining depreciation charge for each successive year.

Double-Declining-Balance Method   To apply the **double-declining-balance (DDB)** method of computing periodic depreciation charges you begin by calculating the straight-line depreciation rate. To do this, divide 100% by the number of years of useful life of the asset. Then, multiply this rate by 2. Next, apply the resulting double-declining rate to the declining book value of the asset. Ignore salvage value in making the calculations. At the point where book value is equal to the salvage value, no more depreciation is taken. The formula for DDB depreciation is:

$$\frac{\text{Depreciation}}{\text{per period}} = \left(2 \times \frac{\text{Straight-line}}{\text{rate}}\right) \times \left(\begin{array}{cc}\text{Asset} & \text{Accumulated}\\\text{cost} & \text{depreciation}\end{array}\right)$$

End of Year	Depreciation Expense Dr.; Accumulated Depreciation Cr.	Total Accumulated Depreciation	Book Value
			$54,000
1. (20% of $54,000)	$10,800	$10,800	43,200
2. (20% of $43,200)	8,640	19,440	34,560
3. (20% of $34,560)	6,912	26,352	27,648
4. (20% of $27,648)	5,530	31,882	22,118
5. (20% of $22,118)	4,424	36,306	17,694
6. (20% of $17,694)	3,539	39,845	14,155
7. (20% of $14,155)	2,831	42,676	11,324
8. (20% of $11,324)	2,265	44,941	9,059
9. (20% of $9,059)	1,812	46,753	7,247
10. (20% of $7,247)	1,449*	48,202	5,798

ILLUSTRATION 10.6 Double-Declining-Balance (DDB) Depreciation Schedule

* This amount could be $3,247 to reduce the book value to the estimated salvage value of $4,000. Then, accumulated depreciation would be $50,000.

ILLUSTRATION 10.7 Summary of Depreciation Methods

Method	Base	Calculation
Straight line	Asset cost − Estimated salvage value	Base ÷ Number of accounting periods in estimated useful life
Units of production	Asset cost − Estimated salvage value	(Base ÷ Estimated total units of production) × Units produced this period
Sum of the years' digits	Asset cost − Estimated salvage value	Base × $\frac{\text{Number of years of useful life remaining at beginning of accounting period}}{\text{SOYD}}$
Double-declining balance	Asset cost − Accumulated depreciation	Base × (2 × Straight-line rate)

Look at the calculations for the $54,000 machine using the DDB method in Illustration 10.6. The straight-line rate is 10% (100%/10 years), which, when doubled, yields a DDB rate of 20%. (Expressed as fractions, the straight-line rate is $\frac{1}{10}$, and the DDB rate is $\frac{2}{10}$.) Since at the beginning of year 1 no accumulated depreciation has been recorded, cost is the basis of the calculation. In each of the following years, book value is the basis of the calculation at the beginning of the year.

In the 10th year, you could increase depreciation to $3,247 if the asset is to be retired and its salvage value is still $4,000. This higher depreciation amount for the last year ($3,247) would reduce the book value of $7,247 down to the salvage value of $4,000. If an asset is continued in service, depreciation should only be recorded until the asset's book value equals its estimated salvage value.

For a summary of the four depreciation methods, see Illustration 10.7.

In Illustration 10.8, we compare three of the depreciation methods just discussed—straight line, sum of the years' digits, and double-declining balance—using the same example of a machine purchased on January 1, 1999, for $54,000. The machine has an estimated useful life of 10 years and an estimated salvage value of $4,000.

Real World Example

The use of depreciation methods in 1995:

Straight line	95.3%
Declining balance	4.5%
Sum of the years' digits	2%
Accelerated method—not specified	8.2%
Units of production	6.3%
Other	1.8%

Adds up to more than 100% because some companies use more than one method.

Source: Based on American Institute of Certified Public Accountants, *Accounting Trends & Techniques* (New York: AICPA, 1996), p. 357.

USES OF TECHNOLOGY Corporations are subject to corporate income taxes. Also, CPA firms hire many tax professionals to address the tax matters of their clients. If you have an interest in taxes and if your Internet browser is Microsoft Explorer 3.0 or Netscape Navigator 2.01 or higher, you may want to visit the following website to learn more about taxes:

http://www.taxcast.com

This site was created by the CPA firm, Ernst & Young, and has many interesting features. For instance, you can see highlights of what is new in the world of tax, it lists the best tax sites on the World Wide Web, it even gives current stock quotes and other investment information and contains much more information.

AN ACCOUNTING PERSPECTIVE

ILLUSTRATION 10.8

Comparison of Straight-Line, Sum-of-the-Years'-Digits, and Double-Declining-Balance Depreciation Methods

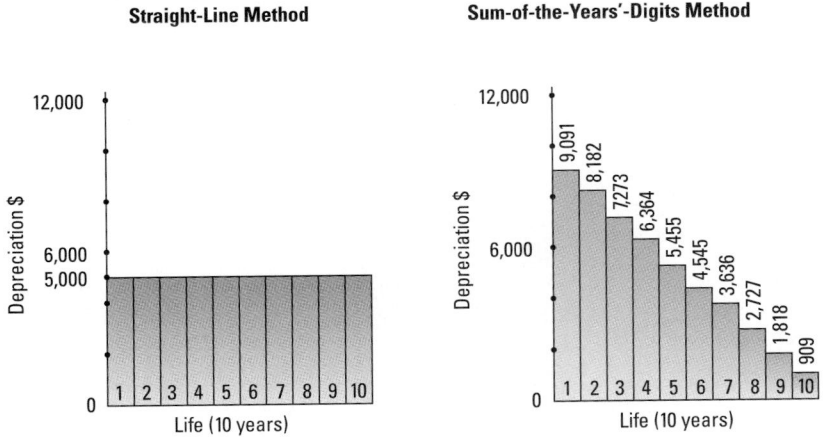

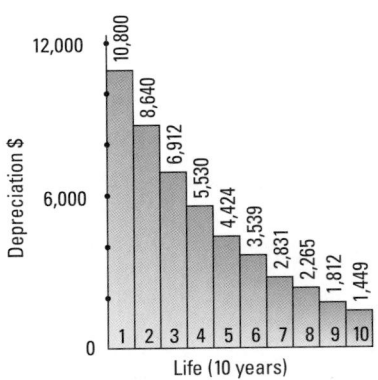

Double-Declining-Balance Method

Partial-Year Depreciation

Reinforcing Problems

E10–6 Compute annual depreciation for two years under each of the four different depreciation methods.
E10–7 Determine information concerning machinery.
E10–8 Compute depreciation under SOYD and DDB methods.
E10–9 Compute DDB depreciation.

So far we have assumed that the assets were put into service at the beginning of an accounting period and ignored the fact that often assets are put into service *during* an accounting period. When assets are acquired during an accounting period, the first recording of depreciation is for a partial year. Normally, firms calculate the depreciation for the partial year to the nearest full month the asset was in service. For example, they treat an asset purchased on or before the 15th day of the month as if it were purchased on the 1st day of the month. And they treat an asset purchased after the 15th of the month as if it were acquired on the 1st day of the following month.

To illustrate how to calculate partial-year depreciation for each of the four depreciation methods, we use a machine purchased for $7,600 on September 1, 1999, with an estimated salvage value of $400, an estimated useful life of five years, and an estimated total units of production of 25,000 units.

STRAIGHT-LINE METHOD   Partial-year depreciation calculations for the straight-line depreciation method are relatively easy. Begin by finding the 12-month charge by the normal computation explained earlier. Then, multiply this annual amount by the fraction of the year for which the asset was in use. For example, for the $7,600 machine purchased September 1, 1999 (estimated salvage value, $400; and estimated useful life, five years), the annual straight-line depreciation is [($7,600 − $400)/5 years] = $1,440. The machine would operate for four months prior to the end of the accounting year, December 31, or one-third of a year. The 1999 depreciation is ($1,440 × ⅓) = $480.

UNITS-OF-PRODUCTION METHOD   The units-of-production method requires no unusual computations to record depreciation for a partial year. To compute the partial-year depreciation, multiply the depreciation charge per unit by the units produced. The charge for a partial year would be less than for a full year because fewer units of goods or services are produced.

SUM-OF-THE-YEARS'-DIGITS METHOD   Under the SOYD method, computing partial-year depreciation is more complex. Problems occur because the 12 months for which depreciation is computed using the SOYD fraction do not correspond with the 12 months for which the financial statements are being prepared. For example, the depreciation recorded in 1999 on the $7,600 asset is for the last four months of 1999, which is the first one-third of the first year of the asset's life. You would compute the depreciation for the four months of 1999 as ($7,600 − $400) × ⁵⁄₁₅ × ⅓; thus, depreciation is $800. In 2000, the depreciation recorded is $2,240, computed as follows:

For the first two-thirds of the year:	($7,200 × ⁵⁄₁₅ × ⅔) = $1,600
For the last one-third of the year:	($7,200 × ⁴⁄₁₅ × ⅓) = 640
Total depreciation expense for 2000	$2,240

With the SOYD method, you compute annual depreciation charges in this same way throughout the asset's life:

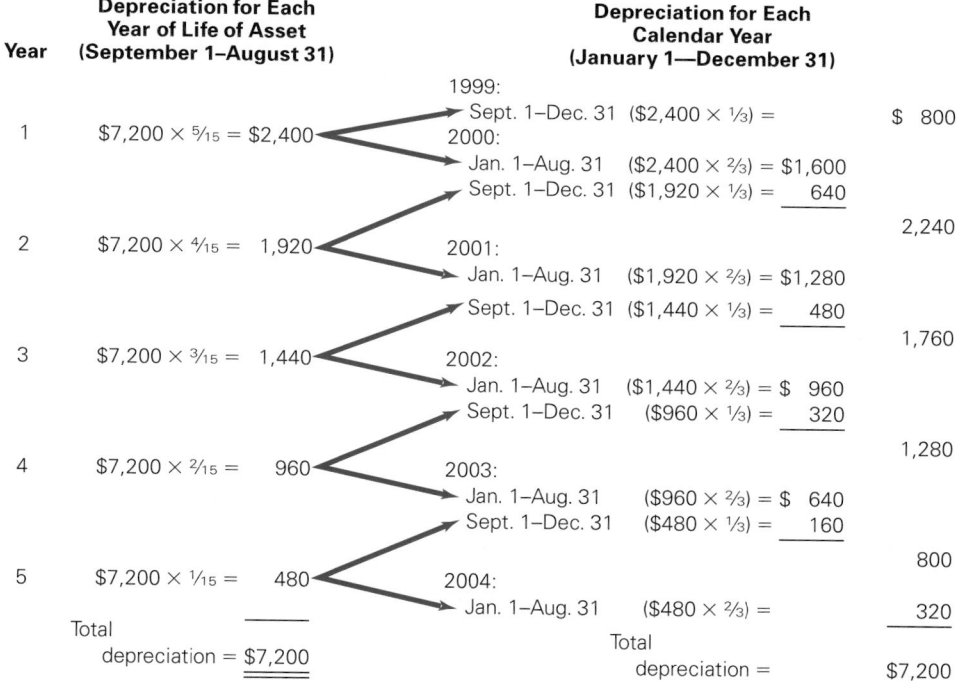

DOUBLE-DECLINING-BALANCE METHOD   Under the double-declining-balance method, it is relatively easy to determine depreciation for a partial year and then for subsequent full years. For the partial year, simply multiply the fixed rate times the cost of the asset times the fraction of the partial year. For example, DDB depreciation on the $7,600 asset for 1999 is ($7,600 × 0.4 × ⅓) = $1,013. For subsequent years, compute the depreciation using the regular procedure of multiplying the book value at the beginning of the period by the fixed rate. The 2000 depreciation would be $[(\$7,600 - \$1,013) \times 0.4] = \$2,635$.

AN ACCOUNTING PERSPECTIVE

USES OF TECHNOLOGY   Most companies report property, plant, and equipment as one amount in the balance sheet in their annual report; however, that account is made up of many items. Computers and accounting software have simplified recordkeeping for all of a company's depreciable assets. When depreciable plant assets are purchased, employees enter in the computer the cost, estimated useful life, and estimated salvage value of the assets. In addition, they enter the method of depreciation that the company decides to use on the assets. After processing this information, the computer calculates the company's depreciation expense and accumulates depreciation for each type of asset and each individual asset (e.g., a machine).

Changes in Estimates

Note to the Student
Remember that depreciation is an estimate. Revising the estimates used in determining depreciation affects future but not past periods.

Reinforcing Problems
E10–10 Compute depreciation before and after revision of expected life and salvage value.
E10–11 Allocate periodic depreciation to building and expense.
E10–12 Compute straight-line depreciation given changes in estimated life and salvage value.

After depreciating an asset down to its estimated salvage value, a firm records no more depreciation on the asset even if continuing to use it. At times, a firm finds the estimated useful life of an asset or its estimated salvage value is incorrect before the asset is depreciated down to its estimated salvage value; then, it computes revised depreciation charges for the remaining useful life. These revised charges do not correct past depreciation taken; they merely compensate for past incorrect charges through changed expense amounts in current and future periods. To compute the new depreciation charge per period, divide the book value less the newly estimated salvage value by the estimated periods of useful life remaining.

For example, assume that a machine cost $30,000, has an estimated salvage value of $3,000, and originally had an estimated useful life of eight years. At the end of the fourth year of the machine's life, the balance in its accumulated depreciation account (assuming use of the straight-line method) was $(\$30,000 - \$3,000) \times \frac{4}{8} = \$13,500$. At the beginning of the fifth year, a manager estimates that the asset will last six more years. The newly estimated salvage value is $2,700. To determine the revised depreciation per period:

Original cost	$30,000
Less: Accumulated depreciation at the end of 4th year	13,500
Book value at the beginning of 5th year	$16,500
Less: revised salvage value	2,700
Remaining depreciable base	$13,800
Revised depreciation per period: $13,800/6	$ 2,300

Had this company used the units-of-production method, its revision of the life estimate would have been in units. Thus, to determine depreciation expense, compute a new per-unit depreciation charge by dividing book value less revised salvage value by the estimated remaining units of production. Multiply this per unit charge by the periodic production to determine depreciation expense.

Using the double-declining-balance method, the book value at the beginning of year 5 would be $9,492.19 (cost of $30,000 less accumulated depreciation of $20,507.81). Depreciation expense for year 5 would be twice the new straight-line rate times book value. The straight-line rate is 100%/6 = 16.67%. So twice the straight-line rate is 33.33%, or ⅓. Thus, ⅓ × $9,492.19 = $3,164.06.

Under the sum-of-the-years'-digits method, you must calculate a new fraction. The sum-of-the-years'-digits is now 6 + 5 + 4 + 3 + 2 + 1 = 21. The fraction for year 5 is ⁶⁄₂₁. To compute depreciation under the sum-of-the-years'-digits method:

Book value at the beginning of 5th year	$10,500.00
Revised salvage value	2,700.00
Remaining depreciable base	$ 7,800.00
Depreciation expense for year 5: $7,800 × ⁶⁄₂₁	$ 2,228.57

ILLUSTRATION 10.9
Partial Balance Sheet

REED COMPANY
Partial Balance Sheet
June 30, 1999

Property, plant, and equipment:

Land		$30,000
Buildings	$75,000	
Less: Accumulated depreciation	45,000	30,000
Equipment	$ 9,000	
Less: Accumulated depreciation	1,500	7,500
Total property, plant, and equipment		$67,500

AN ACCOUNTING PERSPECTIVE

BUSINESS INSIGHT   In their financial statements, companies often provide one amount for property, plant, and equipment that is net of accumulated depreciation. Nonetheless, notes (footnotes) actually provide the additional information regarding the separate types of assets. Perkin-Elmer Corporation is a world leader in the development, manufacturing, and distribution of analytical instrumentation and the life science systems used in environmental technology, pharmaceuticals, biotechnology, chemicals, plastics, food, agriculture, and scientific research. For instance, its June 30, 1996, balance sheet showed property, plant, and equipment, net, equal to $148,008,000. In a note to the financial statements (slightly modified to clarify), management explained this amount as follows:

Property, Plant, and Equipment and Depreciation   Property, plant, and equipment are stated at cost and consisted of the following:

(Dollar amounts in millions)	**1996**	**1995**
Land	$ 22.4	$ 24.1
Buildings and leasehold improvements	133.0	132.9
Machinery and equipment	213.1	205.3
Property, plant, and equipment, at cost	$368.5	$362.3
Accumulated depreciation and amortization	220.5	206.9
Property, plant, and equipment, net	$148.0	$155.4

Depreciation and Financial Reporting

APB Opinion No. 12 requires that companies separately disclose the methods of depreciation they use and the amount of depreciation expense for the period in the body of the income statement or in the notes to the financial statements. Major classes of plant assets and their related accumulated depreciation amounts are reported as shown in Illustration 10.9.

Showing cost less accumulated depreciation in the balance sheet gives statement users a better understanding of the percentages of a company's plant assets that have been used up than reporting only the book value (remaining undepreciated cost) of the assets. For example, reporting buildings at $75,000 less $45,000 of accumulated depreciation, resulting in a net amount of $30,000, is quite different from merely reporting buildings at $30,000. In the first case, the statement user can see that the assets are about 60% used up. In the latter case, the statement user has no way of knowing whether the assets are new or old.

A MISCONCEPTION   Some mistaken financial statement users believe that accumulated depreciation represents cash available for replacing old plant assets with new assets. However, the accumulated depreciation account balance does not represent cash; accumulated depreciation simply shows how much of an asset's cost has been charged to expense. Companies use the plant asset and its contra account, accumulated depreciation, so that data on the total original acquisition cost and accumulated depreciation are readily available to meet reporting requirements.

COSTS OR MARKET VALUES IN THE BALANCE SHEET   In the balance sheet, firms report plant assets at original cost less accumulated depreciation. One of the

A BROADER PERSPECTIVE

Anthony Industries, Inc.

The information below is from the Anthony Industries, Inc., 1995 annual report.

(Dollars in thousands)	1995	1994
Total current assets . . .	$300,455	$226,474
Property, Plant and Equipment		
Land and land improvements . .	1,704	1,426
Buildings and leasehold improvements	28,963	26,161
Machinery and equipment	103,434	91,294
Construction in progress	5,605	3,851
	$139,706	$122,732
Less allowance for depreciation and amortization	82,599	73,640
Total plant assets	$ 57,107	$ 49,092
Other Assets		
Inangibles, principally goodwill, net	14,108	12,197
Net assets of discontinued operations	8,650	10,207
Other	4,103	3,566
Total other assets	$ 26,861	$ 25,970
Total Assets	**$384,423**	**$301,536**

NOTES TO CONSOLIDATED FINANCIAL STATEMENTS

Note 1 (In Part): Summary of Significant Accounting Policies

Property, Plant and Equipment
Property, plant and equipment is recorded at cost. Depreciation is provided on the straight-line method based upon the estimated useful lives of the assets. Repairs and maintenance of $7,270,000, $6,020,000 and $5,438,000 in 1995, 1994, and 1993, respectively, were expensed as incurred.

Source: Based on American Institute of Certified Public Accountants, *Accounting Trends & Techniques* (New York: AICPA, 1996), p. 177.

justifications for reporting the remaining undepreciated costs of the asset rather than market values is the going-concern concept. As you recall from Chapter 5, the going-concern concept assumes that the company will remain in business indefinitely, which implies the company will use its plant assets rather than sell them. Generally, analysts do not consider market values relevant for plant assets in primary financial statements, although they may be reported in supplemental statements.

SUBSEQUENT EXPENDITURES (CAPITAL AND REVENUE) ON ASSETS

Objective 4
Distinguish between capital and revenue expenditures for plant assets.

Companies often spend additional funds on plant assets that have been in use for some time. They debit these expenditures to: (1) an asset account; (2) an accumulated depreciation account; or (3) an expense account.

Expenditures debited to an asset account or to an accumulated depreciation account are **capital expenditures.** Capital expenditures increase the book value of plant assets. **Revenue expenditures,** on the other hand, do not qualify as capital expenditures because they help to generate the current period's revenues rather than future periods' revenues. As a result, companies expense these revenue expenditures immediately and report them in the income statement as expenses.

Expenditures Capitalized in Asset Accounts

Betterments or **improvements** to existing plant assets are capital expenditures because they increase the *quality* of services obtained from the asset. Because betterments or improvements add to the service-rendering ability of assets, firms charge them to the asset accounts. For example, installing an air conditioner in an automobile that did not previously have one is a betterment. The debit for such an expenditure is to the asset account, Automobiles.

Occasionally, expenditures made on plant assets extend the *quantity* of services *beyond the original estimate* but do not improve the quality of the services. Since these expenditures benefit an increased number of future periods, accountants capitalize rather than expense them. However, since there is no visible, tangible addition to, or improvement in, the quality of services, they charge the expenditures to the accumulated depreciation account, thus reducing the credit balance in that account. Such expenditures cancel a part of the existing accumulated depreciation; firms often call them **extraordinary repairs.**

To illustrate, assume that after operating a press for four years, a company spent $5,000 to recondition the press. The reconditioning increased the machine's life to 14 years instead of the original estimate of 10 years. The journal entry to record the extraordinary repair is:

Accumulated Depreciation—Machinery	5,000	
Cash (or Accounts Payable)		5,000
To record the cost of reconditioning a press.		

Note to the Student

Capital and revenue expenditures should be distinguished, so that revenues and expenses can be properly matched.

Originally, the press cost $40,000, had an estimated useful life of 10 years, and had no estimated salvage value. At the end of the fourth year, the balance in its accumulated depreciation account under the straight-line method is [($40,000 ÷ 10) × 4] = $16,000. After debiting the $5,000 spent to recondition the press to the accumulated depreciation account, the balances in the asset account and its related accumulated depreciation account are as shown in the last column:

	Before Extraordinary Repair	After Extraordinary Repair
Press	$40,000	$40,000
Accumulated depreciation	16,000	11,000
Book value (end of four years)	$24,000	$29,000

In effect, the expenditure increases the carrying amount (book value) of the asset by reducing its contra account, accumulated depreciation. Under the straight-line method, we would divide the new book value of the press, $29,000, equally among the 10 remaining years in amounts of $2,900 per year (assuming that the estimated salvage value is still zero).

As a practical matter, expenditures for major repairs not extending the asset's life are sometimes charged to accumulated depreciation. This avoids distorting net income by expensing these expenditures in the year incurred. Then, firms calculate a revised depreciation expense, and spread the cost of major repairs over a number of years. This treatment is not theoretically correct.

To illustrate, assume the same facts as in the previous example except that the $5,000 expenditure did not extend the life of the asset. Because of the size of this expenditure, the company still charges it to accumulated depreciation. Now, it would spread the $29,000 remaining book value over the remaining six years of the life of the press. Under the straight-line method, annual depreciation would then be ($29,000 ÷ 6) = $4,833.

Accountants treat as expenses those recurring and/or minor expenditures that neither add to the asset's service-rendering quality nor extend its quantity of services beyond its original estimated useful life. Thus, firms immediately expense regular maintenance (lubricating a machine) and ordinary repairs (replacing a broken fan belt on an automobile) as revenue expenditures. For example, a company that spends $190 to repair a machine after using it for some time, debits Maintenance Expense or Repairs Expense.

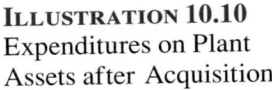

ILLUSTRATION 10.10
Expenditures on Plant
Assets after Acquisition

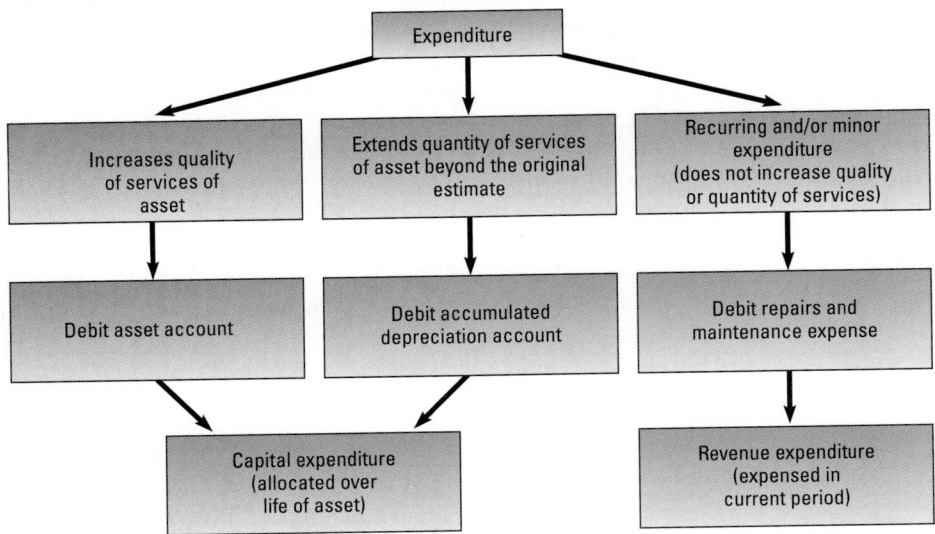

LOW-COST ITEMS   Most businesses purchase **low-cost items** that provide years of service, such as paperweights, hammers, wrenches, and drills. Because of the small dollar amounts involved, it is impractical to use the ordinary depreciation methods for such assets, and it is often costly to maintain records of individual items. Also, the effect of low-cost items on the financial statements is not significant. Accordingly, it is more efficient to record the items as expenses when they are purchased. For instance, many companies charge any expenditure less than an arbitrary minimum, say, $100, to expense regardless of its impact on the asset's useful life. This practice of accounting for such low unit cost items as expenses is an example of the modifying convention of materiality that was discussed in Chapter 5. In Illustration 10.10, we summarize expenditures on plant assets after acquisition.

Errors in Classification

Reinforcing Problems
E10–14 Compute error in net income when installation and freight costs are expensed.
E10–15 Determine the effect of an error in classification.

In practice, it is difficult to decide whether to debit an expenditure to the asset account or to the accumulated depreciation account. For example, some expenditures seem to affect both the quality and quantity of services. Even if the wrong account were debited for the expenditure, the book value of the plant asset at that point would be the same amount it would have been if the correct account had been debited. However, both the asset and accumulated depreciation accounts would be misstated.

As an example of the effect of misstated asset and accumulated depreciation accounts, assume Watson Company had an asset that had originally cost $15,000 and had been depreciated to a book value of $6,000 at the beginning of 1999. At that time, Watson estimated the equipment had a remaining useful life of two years. The company spent $4,000 in early January 1999 to install a new motor in the equipment. This motor extended the useful life of the asset four years beyond the original estimate. Since the expenditure extended the life, the firm should capitalize it by a debit to the accumulated depreciation account. We show the calculations for depreciation expense if the entry was made correctly and if the expenditure had been improperly charged (debited) to the asset account in Illustration 10.11.

If an expenditure that should be expensed is capitalized, the effects are more significant. Assume now that $6,000 in repairs expense is incurred for a plant asset that originally cost $40,000 and had a useful life of four years and no estimated salvage value. This asset had been depreciated using the straight-line method for one year and had a book value of $30,000 ($40,000 cost—$10,000 first-year depreciation) at the beginning of 1999. The company capitalized the $6,000 that should have been charged to repairs expense in 1999. The charge for depreciation should have remained

	January 1, 1999	After Expenditure Entry	
		Correct	Incorrect
Cost	$15,000	$15,000	$19,000†
Accumulated depreciation	9,000	5,000*	9,000
Book value	$ 6,000	$10,000	$10,000
Remaining life	2 years	6 years	6 years
Depreciation expense per year	$ 3,000	$ 1,667	$ 1,667

* ($9,000 − $4,000).
† ($15,000 + $4,000).

ILLUSTRATION 10.11
Expenditure Extending Plant Asset Life

	1999	
	Correctly Expensing	Incorrectly Capitalizing
Depreciation expense	$10,000	$12,000
Repair expense	6,000	–0–
Net income overstated by $4,000, which affects retained earnings . . .	$16,000	$12,000
Asset cost	$40,000	$46,000
Accumulated depreciation	20,000	22,000
Book value	$20,000	$24,000

	2000	
	Correctly Expensing	Incorrectly Capitalizing
Depreciation expense	$10,000	$12,000
Repair expense	–0–	–0–
Net income understated by $2,000, which affects retained earnings . . .	$10,000	$12,000
Asset cost	$40,000	$46,000
Accumulated depreciation	30,000	34,000
Book value	$10,000	$12,000

ILLUSTRATION 10.12
Effect of Revenue Expenditure Treated as Capital Expenditure

at $10,000 for each of the next three years. With the incorrect entry, however, depreciation increases.

Regardless of whether the repair was debited to the asset account or the accumulated depreciation account, the firm would change the depreciation expense amount to $12,000 for each of the next three years [($30,000 book value + $6,000 repairs expense) ÷ 3 more years of useful life]. These errors would cause net income for the year 1999 to be overstated $4,000: (1) repairs expense is understated by $6,000, causing income to be overstated by $6,000; and (2) depreciation expense is overstated by $2,000, causing income to be understated by $2,000. In 2000, the overstatement of depreciation by $2,000 would cause 2000 income to be understated by $2,000.

Note that the $6,000 recording error affects more than just the expense accounts and net income. Plant asset and Retained Earnings accounts on the balance sheet also reflect the impact of this error. To see the effect of incorrectly capitalizing the $6,000 to the asset account rather than correctly expensing it, look at Illustration 10.12.

SUBSIDIARY RECORDS USED TO CONTROL PLANT ASSETS

Most companies maintain formal records (ranging from handwritten documents to computer tapes) to ensure control over their plant assets. These records include an asset account and a related accumulated depreciation account in the general ledger for *each* major class of depreciable plant assets, such as buildings, factory machinery, office equipment, delivery equipment, and store equipment.

Objective 5
Describe the subsidiary records used to control plant assets.

ILLUSTRATION 10.13
Detailed Record of a
Specific Plant Asset

Item IBM 486 SX/33

Id. No. Z-43806

Location Rm. 403, Adm. bldg.

Date acquired Jan. 1, 1998

Cost $3,000

Estimated salvage value $200

Estimated useful life   4 yrs.

Depreciation per year $700

Accumulated depreciation:

    12/31/98 $ 700

    12/31/99   1,400

    12/31/00

    12/31/01

Insurance coverage:

  United Ins. Co.

  Pol. No. 0052-61481-24

  Amt. $3,000

Repairs:

  6/13/99 $140

Disposal date _____

Gain or loss _____

Because the general ledger account has no room for detailed information about each item in a major class of depreciable plant assets, many companies use plant asset subsidiary ledgers. Subsidiary ledgers for Accounts Receivable and Accounts Payable were explained briefly in **An Accounting Perspective** in Chapter 4 on page 145. A company may also use subsidiary ledgers for plant assets. For instance, assume a company has a general ledger account for office furniture. The subsidiary ledger for office furniture might contain four separate accounts entitled: Desks, Chairs, File Cabinets and Bookshelves. Alternatively, a company could even have a separate subsidiary account for each piece of furniture. The total of all the subsidiary account balances must equal the total of the general ledger "control" account for Office Furniture at the end of the accounting period. Each general ledger account for each class of depreciable asset, such as Buildings, Delivery Equipment, and so on, could have a subsidiary ledger backing it up and showing information such as the description, cost, and purchase date for each asset. These subsidiary ledgers and detailed records provide more information and allow the company to maintain better control over plant and equipment.

When they are kept for each major class of plant and equipment, a company may have subsidiary ledgers for factory machinery, office equipment, and other classes of depreciable plant assets. Then there may be an additional subsidiary ledger for each type of asset within each category. For example, the subsidiary office equipment ledger may contain accounts for microcomputers, printers, fax machines, copying machines, and so on. Companies also keep a detailed record for each item represented in a subsidiary ledger account. For example, there may be a separate detailed record for each microcomputer represented in the Microcomputer subsidiary ledger account. Each detailed record should include a description of the asset, identification or serial number, location of the asset, date of acquisition, cost, estimated salvage value, estimated useful life, annual depreciation, accumulated depreciation, insurance coverage, repairs, date of disposal, and gain or loss on final disposal of the asset. Note the detailed record for one particular microcomputer as of December 31, 1999, in Illustration 10.13.

To enhance control over plant and equipment, companies stencil on or attach the identification or serial number to each asset. Periodically, firms must take a physical inventory to determine whether all items in the accounting records actually exist, whether they are located where they should be, and whether they are still being used. A company that does not use detailed records and identification numbers or take physical inventories finds it difficult to determine whether assets have been discarded or stolen.

The general ledger control account balance for each major class of plant and equipment should equal the total of the amounts in the subsidiary ledger accounts for

JOHNSON & JOHNSON AND SUBSIDIARIES
Consolidated Balance Sheet
At December 31, 1995 and January 1, 1994 (Dollars in Millions)

ILLUSTRATION 10.14

Johnson & Johnson
Johnson & Johnson develops, manufactures, and sells toiletries, hygienic products, nonprescription drugs, pharmaceutical products, and professional products such as sutures, surgical instruments, and diagnostic products.

Assets	1995	1994
Current assets		
Cash and cash equivalents	$ 1,201	$ 636
Marketable securities, at cost	163	68
Accounts receivable, trade, less allowances $258 (1994, $200)	2,903	2,601
Inventories	2,276	2,161
Deferred taxes on income	717	582
Prepaid expenses and other receivables	678	632
Total current assets	$ 7,938	$ 6,680
Marketable securities, non-current, at cost	338	354
Property, plant and equipment, net	5,196	4,910
Intangible assets, net	2,950	2,403
Deferred taxes on income	307	262
Other assets	1,144	1,059
Total assets	$17,873	$15,668
Net operating earnings	$ 3,345	$ 2,763

that class of plant assets. Also, the totals in the detailed records for a specific subsidiary ledger account (such as Microcomputers) should equal the balance of that account. Each time a plant asset is acquired, exchanged, or disposed of, the firm posts an entry to both a general ledger control account and the appropriate subsidiary ledger account. It also updates the detailed record for the items affected.

ANALYZING AND USING THE FINANCIAL RESULTS—RATE OF RETURN ON OPERATING ASSETS

Analyzing the ratios of income statement and balance sheet items from one year to the next can reveal important trends. Management uses these ratios to measure performance by establishing targets and evaluating results. As an example, look at Illustration 10.14 taken from the 1995 annual report of Johnson & Johnson. Analysts use these figures to calculate the ratios and to explain the importance of this information to management and investors.

Objective 6
Analyze and use the financial results—rate of return on operating assets.

To determine the **rate of return on operating assets** for Johnson & Johnson for 1994 and 1995, use the following formula:

$$\text{Rate of return on operating assets} = \frac{\text{Net operating income}}{\text{Operating assets}}$$

1994: $2,763,000/$15,668,000 = 17.63%

1995: $3,345,000/$17,873,000 = 18.72%

Net operating income is also called net operating earnings or income before interest and taxes. In calculating Johnson & Johnson's ratio, we have assumed that all assets are operating assets used in producing operating revenues.

This ratio measures the profitability of the company in carrying out its primary business function. For Johnson & Johnson, these figures indicate a slight increase in the earning power of the company in 1995. Net operating income increased more than proportionately compared to the increase in operating assets. Perhaps this performance justifies the increase in operating assets.

In this chapter, you learned how to account for the acquisition of plant assets and depreciation. The next chapter discusses how to record the disposal of plant assets and how to account for natural resources and intangible assets.

UNDERSTANDING THE LEARNING OBJECTIVES

Objective 1
List the characteristics of plant assets and identify the costs of acquiring plant assets.

- To be classified as a plant asset, an asset must: (1) be tangible; (2) have a useful service life of more than one year; and (3) be used in business operations rather than held for resale.
- In accounting for plant assets, accountants must:
  1. Record the acquisition cost of the asset.
  2. Record the allocation of the asset's original cost to periods of its useful life through depreciation.
  3. Record subsequent expenditures on the asset.
  4. Account for the disposal of the asset.

Objective 2
List the four major factors affecting depreciation expense.

- Accountants consider four major factors in computing depreciation: (1) cost of the asset; (2) estimated salvage value of the asset; (3) estimated useful life of the asset; and (4) depreciation method to use in depreciating the asset.

Objective 3
Describe the various methods of calculating depreciation expense.

- **Straight-line method:** Assigns an equal amount of depreciation to each period. The formula for calculating straight-line depreciation is:

$$\frac{\text{Depreciation}}{\text{per period}} = \frac{\text{Asset cost} - \text{Estimated salvage value}}{\substack{\text{Number of accounting periods} \\ \text{in estimated useful life}}}$$

- **Units-of-production method:** Assigns an equal amount of depreciation to each unit of product manufactured by an asset. The units-of-production depreciation formulas are:

$$\frac{\text{Depreciation}}{\text{per period}} = \frac{\text{Asset cost} - \text{Estimated salvage value}}{\substack{\text{Estimated total units of production (or service)} \\ \text{during useful life of asset}}}$$

$$\frac{\text{Depreciation}}{\text{per period}} = \frac{\text{Depreciation}}{\text{per unit}} \times \substack{\text{Number of units of goods} \\ \text{or services produced}}$$

- **Sum-of-the-years'-digits (SOYD) method:** SOYD is an accelerated depreciation method. The SOYD depreciation formulas are:

$$\frac{\text{Depreciation}}{\text{per period}} = \frac{\substack{\text{Number of years} \\ \text{of useful life} \\ \text{remaining at beginning} \\ \text{of accounting period}}}{\text{SOYD}} \times \left(\substack{\text{Asset} \\ \text{cost}} - \substack{\text{Estimated} \\ \text{salvage value}} \right)$$

$$\text{Sum-of-the-years'-digits (SOYD)} = \frac{n(n+1)}{2}$$

- **Double-declining-balance method:** DDB is an accelerated depreciation method. Salvage value is ignored in making annual calculations. The formula for DDB depreciation is:

$$\frac{\text{Depreciation}}{\text{per period}} = (2 \times \text{Straight-line rate}) \times \left(\substack{\text{Asset} \\ \text{cost}} + \substack{\text{Accumulated} \\ \text{depreciation}} \right)$$

Objective 4
Distinguish between capital and revenue expenditures for plant assets.

- Capital expenditures are debited to an asset account or an accumulated depreciation account and increase the book value of plant assets. Expenditures that increase the quality of services or extend the quantity of services beyond the original estimate are capital expenditures.
- Revenue expenditures are expensed immediately and reported in the income statement as expenses. Recurring and or minor expenditures that neither add to the asset's quality of service-rendering abilities nor extend its quantity of services beyond the asset's original estimated useful life are expenses.

- Plant asset subsidiary ledgers contain detailed information that cannot be maintained in the general ledger account about each item in a major class of depreciable plant assets.

- Control over plant and equipment is enhanced by plant asset subsidiary ledgers and other detailed records. Information in a detailed record may include a description of the asset, identification or serial number, location of the asset, date of acquisition, cost, estimated salvage value, estimated useful life, annual depreciation, accumulated depreciation, insurance coverage, repairs, date of disposal, and gain or loss on final disposal of the asset. A periodic physical inventory should be taken to determine whether items in accounting records actually exist and are still being used at the proper location.

- To calculate the rate of return on operating assets, divide net operating income by operating assets. This ratio helps management determine how effectively it used assets to produce a profit.

Objective 5
Describe the subsidiary records used to control plant assets.

Objective 6
Analyze and use the financial results—rate of return on operating assets.

DEMONSTRATION PROBLEM 10–A

Cleveland Company purchased a 2-square-mile farm under the following terms: cash paid, $486,000; mortgage note assumed, $240,000; and accrued interest on mortgage note assumed, $6,000. The company paid $55,200 for brokerage and legal services to acquire the property and secure clear title. Cleveland planned to subdivide the property into residential lots and to construct homes on these lots. Clearing and leveling costs of $21,600 were paid. Crops on the land were sold for $14,400. A house on the land, to be moved by the buyer of the house, was sold for $5,040. The other buildings were torn down at a cost of $9,600, and salvaged material was sold for $10,080.

Approximately 6 acres of the land were deeded to the township for roads, and another 10 acres were deeded to the local school district as the site for a future school. After the subdivision was completed, this land would have an approximate value of $7,680 per acre. The company secured a total of 1,200 salable lots from the remaining land.

Present a schedule showing in detail the composition of the cost of the 1,200 salable lots. *Required*

SOLUTION TO DEMONSTRATION PROBLEM 10–A

CLEVELAND COMPANY
Schedule of Cost of 1,200 Residential Lots

Costs incurred:		
Cash paid	$486,000	
Mortgage note assumed	240,000	
Interest accrued on mortgage note assumed	6,000	
Broker and legal services	55,200	
Clearing and leveling costs	21,600	
Tearing down costs	9,600	$818,400
Less proceeds from sale of:		
Crops	$ 14,400	
House	5,040	
Salvaged materials	10,080	29,520
Net cost of land to be subdivided into 1,200 lots		$788,880

DEMONSTRATION PROBLEM 10–B

Calvin Company acquired and put into use a machine on January 1, 1999, at a total cost of $45,000. The machine was estimated to have a useful life of 10 years and a salvage value of $5,000. It was also estimated that the machine would produce one million units of product during its life. The machine produced 90,000 units in 1999 and 125,000 units in 2000.

Required Compute the amounts of depreciation to be recorded in 1999 and 2000 under each of the following:

a. Straight-line method.

b. Units-of-production method.

c. Sum-of-the-years'-digits method.

d. Double-declining-balance method.

e. Assume 30,000 units were produced in the first quarter of 1999. Compute depreciation for this quarter under each of the four methods.

SOLUTION TO DEMONSTRATION PROBLEM 10–B

a. Straight-line method:

1999: ($45,000 − $5,000)/10 = $4,000

2000: ($45,000 − $5,000)/10 = $4,000

b. Units-of-production method:

1999: [($45,000 − $5,000)/1,000,000] × 90,000 = $3,600

2000: [($45,000 − $5,000)/1,000,000] × 125,000 = $5,000

c. Sum-of-the-years'-digits method:

1999: ($45,000 − $5,000) × $^{10}/_{55}$ = $7,272.73

2000: ($45,000 − $5,000) × $^{9}/_{55}$ = $6,545.45

d. Double-declining-balance method:

1999: $45,000 × 20% = $9,000

2000: ($45,000 − $9,000) × 20% = $7,200

e. Straight-line: ($45,000 − $5,000)/10 × ¼ = $1,000

Units-of-production: (30,000 × $0.04) = $1,200

Sum-of-the-years'-digits: ($45,000 − $5,000) × $^{8}/_{55}$ × ¼ = $1,454.55

Double-declining-balance:

($45,000 − $9,000 − $7,200) × 0.2 × ¼ = $1,440

NEW TERMS

Accelerated depreciation methods   Record higher amounts of depreciation during the early years of an asset's life and lower amounts in later years.   *373*

Acquisition cost   Amount of cash and/or cash equivalents given up to acquire a plant asset and place it in operating condition at its proper location.   *366*

Appraised value   An expert's opinion as to what an item's market price would be if the item were sold.   *369*

Betterments (improvements)   Capital expenditures that are properly charged to asset accounts because they add to the service-rendering ability of the assets; they increase the quality of services obtained from an asset.   *380*

Book value   An asset's recorded cost less its accumulated depreciation.   *370*

Capital expenditures   Expenditures debited to an asset account or to an accumulated depreciation account.   *380*

Depreciation   The amount of plant asset cost allocated to each accounting period benefiting from the plant asset's use (*370*). The **straight-line depreciation** method charges an equal amount of plant asset cost to each period (*372*). The **units-of-production depreciation** method assigns an equal amount of depreciation for each unit of product manufactured or service rendered by an asset (*373*). The **sum-of-the-years'-digits (SOYD)** (*373*) and the **double-declining-balance (DDB)** (*374*) methods assign decreasing amounts of depreciation to successive periods of time.

Double-declining-balance (DDB) depreciation   See *depreciation*.

Extraordinary repairs   Expenditures that cancel a part of the existing accumulated depreciation because they increase the quantity of services expected from an asset.   *381*

Fair market value The price that would be received for an item being sold in the normal course of business (not at a forced liquidation sale). *369*

Inadequacy The inability of a plant asset to produce enough products or provide enough services to meet current demands. *370*

Land improvements Attachments to land, such as driveways, landscaping, parking lots, fences, lighting systems, and sprinkler systems, that have limited lives and therefore are depreciable. *367*

Low-cost items Items that provide years of service at a relatively low unit cost, such as hammers, paperweights, and drills. *382*

Obsolescence Decline in usefulness of an asset brought about by inventions and technological progress. *370*

Physical deterioration Results from use of the asset—wear and tear—and the action of the elements. *370*

Plant and equipment A shorter title for property, plant, and equipment; also called *plant assets*. Included are land and manufactured or constructed assets such as buildings, machinery, vehicles, and furniture. *365*

Rate of return on operating assets Net operating income/Operating assets. This ratio helps management determine how effectively it used assets to produce a profit. *385*

Revenue expenditures Expenditures (on a plant asset) that are immediately expensed. *380*

Salvage value The amount of money the company expects to recover, less disposal costs, on the date a plant asset is scrapped, sold, or traded in. Also called *scrap value* or *residual value*. *371*

Straight-line depreciation See *depreciation*.

Sum-of-the-years'-digits (SOYD) depreciation See *depreciation*.

Tangible assets Assets that we can see and touch such as land, buildings, and equipment. *365*

Units-of-production depreciation See *depreciation*.

Useful life Refers to the length of time the company owning the asset intends to use it. *371*

Self-Test

True-False

Indicate whether each of the following statements is true or false.

1. The cost of land includes its purchase price and other related costs, including the cost of removing an old unusable building that is on the land.

2. Depreciation is the process of valuation of an asset to arrive at its market value.

3. The purpose of depreciation accounting is to provide the cash required to replace plant assets.

4. Expenditures made on plant assets that increase the quality of services are debited to the accumulated depreciation account.

5. Plant asset subsidiary ledgers are used to increase control over plant assets.

Multiple-Choice

Select the best answer for each of the following questions.

1. On January 1, 1999, Jackson Company purchased equipment for $400,000, and installation and testing costs totaled $40,000. The equipment has an estimated useful life of 10 years and an estimated salvage value of $40,000. If Jackson uses the straight-line depreciation method, the depreciation expense for 1999 is:
   a. $36,000.
   b. $40,000.
   c. $44,000.
   d. $80,000.
   e. $88,000.

2. In Question 1, if the equipment were purchased on July 1, 1999, and Jackson used the double-declining-balance method, the depreciation expense for 1999 would be:
   a. $88,000.
   b. $72,000.
   c. $36,000.
   d. $44,000.
   e. $40,000.

3. In Question 1, if Jackson acquired the asset on January 1, 1999, and uses the sum-of-the-years'-digits method, the depreciation expense for 1999 is:
   a. $72,727.
   b. $80,000.
   c. $65,454.
   d. $7,272.
   e. $8,000.

4. Hatfield Company purchased a computer on January 2, 1997, for $10,000. The computer had an estimated salvage value of $3,000 and an estimated useful life of five years. At the beginning of 1999, the estimated salvage value changed to $1,000, and the computer is expected to have a remaining useful life of two years. Using the straight-line method, the depreciation expense for 1999 is:
   a. $1,400.
   b. $1,750.
   c. $2,250.
   d. $1,800.
   e. $3,100.

5. The result of recording a capital expenditure as a revenue expenditure is an:
   a. Overstatement of current year's expense.
   b. Understatement of current year's expense.
   c. Understatement of subsequent year's net income.
   d. Overstatement of current year's net income.
   e. None of the above.

Now turn to page 398 to check your answers.

QUESTIONS

1. What is the main distinction between inventory and a plant asset?

2. Which of the following items are properly classifiable as plant assets on the balance sheet?
   a. Advertising that will appear in the future to inform the public about new energy-saving programs at a manufacturing plant.
   b. A truck acquired by a manufacturing company to be used to deliver the company's products to wholesalers.
   c. An automobile acquired by an insurance company to be used by one of its salespersons.
   d. Adding machines acquired by an office supply company to be sold to customers.
   e. The cost of constructing and paving a driveway that has an estimated useful life of 10 years.

3. In general terms, what does the cost of a plant asset include?

4. In what way does the purchase of a plant asset resemble the prepayment of an expense?

5. Brown Company purchased an old farm with a vacant building as a factory site for $1,040,000. Brown decided to use the building in its operations. How should Brown allocate the purchase price between the land and the building? How should this purchase be handled if the building is to be torn down?

6. Describe how a company may determine the cost of a self-constructed asset.

7. In any exchange of noncash assets, the accountant's task is to find the most appropriate valuation for the asset received. What is the general rule for determining the most appropriate valuation in such a situation?

8. Why should periodic depreciation be recorded on all plant assets except land?

9. Define the terms *inadequacy* and *obsolescence* as used in accounting for depreciable plant assets.

10. What four factors must be known to compute depreciation on a plant asset? How *objective* is the calculation of depreciation?

11. A friend, Mindy Jacobs, tells you her car depreciated $5,000 last year. Explain whether her concept of depreciation is the same as the accountant's concept.

12. What does the term *accelerated depreciation* mean? Give an example showing how depreciation is accelerated.

13. Provide a theoretical reason to support using an accelerated depreciation method.

14. If a machine has an estimated useful life of nine years, what will be the total digits to use in calculating depreciation under the sum-of-the-years'-digits method? How is this figure used in the depreciation calculation?

15. Nancy Company purchased a machine that originally had an estimated eight years of useful life. At the end of the third year, Nancy determined that the machine would last only three more years. Does this revision affect past depreciation taken?

16. What does the balance in the accumulated depreciation account represent? Does this balance represent cash that can be used to replace the related plant asset when it is completely depreciated?

17. What is the justification for reporting plant assets on the balance sheet at undepreciated cost (book value) rather than market value?

18. Distinguish between *capital expenditures* and *revenue expenditures*.

19. For each of the following, state whether the expenditure made should be charged to an expense, an asset, or an accumulated depreciation account:
   a. Cost of installing air-conditioning equipment in a building that was not air conditioned.
   b. Painting of an owned factory building every other year.
   c. Cost of replacing the roof on a 10-year-old building that was purchased new and has an estimated total life of 40 years. The expenditure did not extend the life of the asset beyond the original estimate.
   d. Cost of repairing an electric motor. The expenditure extended the estimated useful life beyond the original estimate.

20. Indicate which type of account (asset, accumulated depreciation, or expense) would be debited for each of the following expenditures:
   a. Painting an office building at a cost of $1,000. The building is painted every year.
   b. Adding on a new plant wing at a cost of $24,000,000.
   c. Expanding a paved parking lot at a cost of $144,000.
   d. Replacing a stairway with an escalator at a cost of $20,000.
   e. Replacing the transmission in an automobile at a cost of $1,600, thus extending its useful life two years beyond the original estimate.
   f. Replacing a broken fan belt at a cost of $600.

21. How do subsidiary records provide control over a company's plant assets?

22. What advantages can accrue to a company that maintains plant asset subsidiary records?

The Coca-Cola Company

23. **Real World Question** From the consolidated balance sheet of The Coca-Cola Company in the annual report booklet, identify the 1996 gross property, plant, and equipment and the net property, plant, and equipment.

What percentage of the depreciable assets have been depreciated? Are the assets almost completely depreciated?

MAYTAG

24. **Real World Question** Based on the financial statements of Maytag Corporation contained in the annual report booklet, what was the 1996 ending balance in the Land account? Did the company acquire any of these assets in 1996?

THE LIMITED, INC.

25. **Real World Question** Based on the financial statements and the notes to those statements of The Limited,

Inc., contained in the annual report booklet, what was the 1996 ending net property and equipment balance? Did the company acquire any of these assets in 1996? What depreciation method did the company use?

HARLAND

26. **Real World Question** Based on the financial statements and the notes of John H. Harland Company contained in the annual report booklet, what was the 1996 ending balance of accumulated depreciation and amortization? Did the company acquire any of these assets in 1996? What depreciation methods did the company use?

EXERCISES

Stephon Company paid $640,000 cash for a tract of land on which it plans to erect a new warehouse, and paid $8,000 in legal fees related to the purchase. Stephon also agreed to assume responsibility for $25,600 of unpaid taxes on the property. The company incurred a cost of $28,800 to remove an old apartment building from the land. Prepare a schedule showing the cost of the land acquired.

Exercise 10–1
Determine cost of land
(L.O. 1)

Laural Company paid $840,000 cash for real property consisting of a tract of land and a building. The company intended to remodel and use the old building. To allocate the cost of the property acquired, Laural had the property appraised. The appraised values were as follows: land, $576,000, and office building, $384,000. The cost of clearing the land was $18,000. The building was remodeled at a cost of $76,800. The cost of a new identical office building was estimated to be $432,000. Prepare a schedule showing the cost of the assets acquired.

Exercise 10–2
Determine cost of land and building when acquired together (L.O. 1)

Fine Company purchased a heavy machine to be used in its factory for $720,000, less a 2% cash discount. The company paid a fine of $3,600 because an employee hauled the machine over city streets without securing the required permits. The machine was installed at a cost of $21,600, and testing costs of $7,200 were incurred to place the machine in operation. Prepare a schedule showing the recorded cost of the machine.

Exercise 10–3
Determine cost of a machine (L.O. 1)

A machine is acquired in exchange for 50 shares of Marley Corporation capital stock. The stock recently traded at $400 per share. The machine cost $30,000 three years ago. At what amount should the machine be recorded?

Exercise 10–4
Determine cost of machine in noncash acquisition (L.O. 1)

Keely Company purchased some office furniture for $29,760 cash on March 1, 1998. It also paid $480 cash for freight costs incurred. The furniture is being depreciated over four years under the straight-line method, assuming a salvage value of $1,440. The company employs a calendar-year accounting period. On July 1, 1999, it spent $192 to refinish the furniture. Prepare journal entries for the Keely Company to record all of the data, including the annual depreciation adjustments through 1999.

Exercise 10–5
Record cost of office equipment, depreciation, and repairs expense (L.O. 1, 3, 4)

On January 2, 1998, a new machine was acquired for $900,000. The machine has an estimated salvage value of $100,000 and an estimated useful life of 10 years. The machine is expected to produce a total of 500,000 units of product throughout its useful life. Compute depreciation for 1998 and 1999 using each of the following methods:

a. Straight line.

b. Units of production (assume 30,000 and 60,000 units were produced in 1998 and 1999, respectively).

c. Sum of the years' digits.

d. Double-declining balance.

Exercise 10–6
Compute annual depreciation for two years under each of four different depreciation methods (L.O. 3)

Exercise 10–7
Determine information concerning machinery (L.O. 3)

Terrill Company finds its records are incomplete concerning a piece of machinery used in its plant. According to the company records, the machinery has an estimated useful life of 10 years and an estimated salvage value of $24,000. It has recorded $12,000 in depreciation each year using the straight-line method. If the accumulated depreciation account shows a balance of $72,000, what is the original cost of the machinery and how many years remain to be depreciated?

Exercise 10–8
Compute depreciation under SOYD and DDB methods (L.O. 3)

Katherine Company purchased a machine on April 1, 1998, for $72,000. The machine has an estimated useful life of five years with no expected salvage value. The company's accounting year ends on December 31.

Compute the depreciation expense for 1998 and 1999 under (a) the sum-of-the-years'-digits method and (b) the double-declining-balance method.

Exercise 10–9
Compute DDB depreciation (L.O. 3)

Australia Company purchased a machine for $3,200 and incurred installation costs of $800. The estimated salvage value of the machine is $200. The machine has an estimated useful life of four years. Compute the annual depreciation charges for this machine under the double-declining-balance method.

Exercise 10–10
Compute depreciation before and after revision of expected life and salvage value (L.O. 3)

Regal Company acquired a delivery truck on January 2, 1998, for $107,200. The truck had an estimated salvage value of $4,800 and an estimated useful life of eight years. At the beginning of 2001, a revised estimate shows that the truck has a remaining useful life of six years. The estimated salvage value changed to $1,600.

Compute the depreciation charge for 1998 and the revised depreciation charge for 2001 using the straight-line method.

Exercise 10–11
Allocate periodic depreciation to building and to expense (L.O. 3)

Assume that the truck described in Exercise 10–10 was used 40% of the time in 1999 to haul materials used in the construction of a building by Regal Company for its own use. (Remember that 1999 is before the revision was made on estimated life.) During the remaining time, Regal used the truck to deliver merchandise to its customers.

Prepare the journal entry to record straight-line depreciation on the truck for 1999.

Exercise 10–12
Compute straight-line depreciation given changes in estimated life and salvage value (L.O. 3)

Vineland Company purchased a computer for $60,000 and placed it in operation on January 2, 1997. Depreciation was recorded for 1997 and 1998 using the straight-line method, a six-year life, and an expected salvage value of $2,400. The introduction of a new model of this computer in 1999 caused the company to revise its estimate of useful life to a total of four years and to reduce the estimated salvage value to zero.

Compute the depreciation expense on the computer for 1999.

Exercise 10–13
Compute straight-line depreciation after major overhaul (L.O. 3, 4)

On January 2, 1998, a company purchased and placed in operation a new machine at a total cost of $60,000. Depreciation was recorded on the machine for 1998 and 1999 under the straight-line method using an estimated useful life of five years and no expected salvage value. Early in 2000, the machine was overhauled at a cost of $20,000. The estimated useful life of the machine was revised upward to a total of seven years.

Compute the depreciation expense on the machine for 2000.

Exercise 10–14
Compute error in net income when installation and freight costs are expensed (L.O. 4)

Lasky Company purchased a machine on January 3, 1998, at a cost of $50,000. It debited freight and installation charges of $10,000 to Repairs Expense. It recorded straight-line depreciation on the machine in 1998 and 1999 using an estimated life of 10 years and no expected salvage value.

Compute the amount of the error in net income for 1998 and 1999, and state whether net income is understated or overstated.

Exercise 10–15
Determine the effect of an error in classification (L.O. 4)

Bragg Company owns a plant asset that originally cost $240,000 in 1995. The asset has been depreciated for three years assuming an eight-year useful life and no salvage value. During 1998, Bragg incorrectly capitalized $120,000 in repairs on the plant asset rather than expensing them. Describe the impact of this error on the asset's cost and Bragg's net income over the next five years.

Problems

Problem 10–1
Determine cost of machine (L.O. 1)

Brite Company purchased a machine that had an invoice price of $400,000 excluding sales tax. Terms were net 30. A 4% sales tax was levied on the sale. The company incurred and paid freight costs of $10,000. Special electrical connections were run to the machine at a cost of $14,000 and a special reinforced base for the machine was built at a cost of $18,000. The machine was dropped and damaged while being mounted on this base. Repairs cost $4,000. Raw materials with a cost of $1,000 were consumed in testing the machine. Safety guards were installed on the machine at a cost of $1,400, and the machine was placed in operation. In addition, $500 of costs were incurred in removing an old machine.

Prepare a schedule showing the amount at which the machine should be recorded in Brite Company's account.

Required

Problem 10–2
Determine cost of land
(L.O. 1)

Maxwell Company purchased 2 square miles of farmland under the following terms: $968,000 cash; and liability assumed on mortgage note of $320,000 and interest accrued on mortgage note assumed, $12,800. The company paid $67,200 of legal and brokerage fees and also paid $3,200 for a title search on the property.

    The company planned to use the land as a site for a new office building and a new factory. Maxwell paid clearing and leveling costs of $28,800. It sold crops on the land for $7,360 and sold one of the houses on the property for $19,200. The other buildings were torn down at a cost of $14,400; sale of salvaged materials yielded cash proceeds of $13,600. Approximately 1% of the land acquired was deeded to the county for roads. The cost of excavating a basement for the office building amounted to $9,120.

Prepare a schedule showing the amount at which the land should be carried on Maxwell Company's books.

Required

Problem 10–3
Determine cost of truck; prepare entry for depreciation under DDB and for straight-line depreciation assuming change in estimated life (L.O. 1, 3)

Dawson Towing Company purchased a used panel truck for $28,800 cash. The next day the company's name and business were painted on the truck at a total cost of $1,488. The truck was then given a minor overhaul at a cost of $192, and new "super" tires were mounted on the truck at a cost of $1,920, less a trade-in allowance of $240 for the old tires. The truck was placed in service on April 1, 1998, at which time it had an estimated useful life of five years and a salvage value of $3,360.

Required

a. Prepare a schedule showing the cost to be recorded for the truck.
b. Prepare the journal entry to record depreciation at the end of the calendar-year accounting period, December 31, 1998. Use the double-declining-balance method.
c. Assume that the straight-line depreciation method has been used. At the beginning of 2001 it is estimated the truck will last another four years. The estimated salvage value changed to $1,920. Prepare the entry to record depreciation for 2001.

Problem 10–4
Compute cost of land, land improvements, building, and machinery; prepare entry to correct the accounts (L.O. 1, 4)

You are the new controller for Jayson Company, which began operations on October 1, 1998, after a start-up period that ran from the middle of 1997. While reviewing the accounts, you find an account entitled "Fixed Assets," which contains the following items:

Cash paid to previous owner of land and old building	$ 192,000
Cash given to construction company as partial payment for the new building	72,000
Legal and title search fees	2,400
Real estate commission	14,400
Cost of demolishing old building	16,800
Cost of leveling and grading	9,600
Architect's fee (90% building and 10% improvements)	36,000
Cost of excavating (digging) basement for new building	21,600
Cash paid to construction company for new building	288,000
Repair damage done by vandals	7,200
Sprinkler system for lawn	31,200
Lighting system for parking lot	40,800
Paving of parking lot	60,000
Net invoice price of machinery	1,152,000
Freight cost incurred on machinery	50,400
Installation and testing of machinery	19,200
Medical bill paid for employee injured in installing machinery	3,600
Landscaping (permanent)	38,400
Repair damage to building in installation of machinery	4,800
Special assessment paid to city for water mains and sewer line	45,600
Account balance	$2,106,000

In addition, you discover that cash receipts of $1,200 from selling materials salvaged from the old building were credited to Miscellaneous Revenues in 1998. Digging deeper, you find that the plant manager spent all of his time for the first nine months of 1998 supervising installation of land improvements (10%), building construction (40%), and installation of machinery (50%). The plant manager's nine-month salary of $108,000 was debited to Officers' Salaries Expense.

Required **a.** List all items on a form containing columns for Land, Land Improvements, Building, and Machinery. Sort the items into the appropriate columns, omitting those items not properly included as an element of asset cost. Show negative amounts in parentheses. Total your columns.

b. Prepare one compound journal entry to reclassify and adjust the accounts and to eliminate the Fixed Assets account. Do not attempt to record depreciation for the partial year.

Problem 10–5
Compute depreciation for first year under each of four different depreciation methods (L.O. 3)

Land Company acquired and put into use a machine on January 1, 1998, at a cash cost of $120,000 and immediately spent $5,000 to install it. The machine had an estimated useful life of eight years and an estimated salvage value of $15,000 at the end of this time. It was further estimated that the machine would produce 500,000 units of product during its life. In the first year, the machine produced 100,000 units.

Required Prepare journal entries to record depreciation to the nearest dollar for 1998, using:

a. Straight-line method.

b. Units-of-production method.

c. Sum-of-the-years'-digits method.

d. Double-declining-balance method.

Problem 10–6
Compute depreciation for two years using three depreciation methods; partial-year depreciation used first year (L.O. 3)

Crawford Company paid $60,000 for a machine on April 1, 1998, and placed it in use on that same date. The machine has an estimated life of 10 years and an estimated salvage value of $10,000.

Required Compute the amount of depreciation to the nearest dollar the company should record on this asset for the years ending December 31, 1998, and 1999, under each of the following methods:

a. Straight-line.

b. Sum-of-the-years'-digits.

c. Double-declining-balance.

ALTERNATE PROBLEMS

Problem 10–1A
Determine cost of machine (L.O. 1)

Bolt Company purchased a machine for use in its operations that had an invoice price of $80,000 excluding sales tax. A 4% sales tax was levied on the sale. Terms were net 30. The company estimated the total cost of hauling the machine from the dealer's warehouse to the company's plant at $5,600, which did not include a fine of $1,600 for failure to secure the necessary permits to use city streets in transporting the machine. In delivering the machine to its plant, a Bolt employee damaged the truck used; repairs cost $3,600. The machine was also slightly damaged with repair costs amounting to $1,600.

Bolt incurred installation costs of $32,000 that included the $4,000 cost of shoring up the floor under the machine. Testing costs amounted to $2,400. Safety guards were installed on the machine at a cost of $640, and the machine was placed in operation.

Required Prepare a schedule showing the amount at which the machine should be recorded in Bolt's accounts.

Pressler Company planned to erect a new factory building and a new office building in Atlanta, Georgia. A report on a suitable site showed an appraised value of $180,000 for land and orchard and $120,000 for a building.

After considerable negotiation, the company and the owner reached the following agreement: Pressler Company was to pay $216,000 in cash, assume a $90,000 mortgage note on the property, assume the interest of $1,920 accrued on the mortgage note, and assume unpaid property taxes of $13,200. Pressler Company paid $18,000 cash for brokerage and legal services in acquiring the property.

Shortly after acquisition of the property, Pressler Company sold the fruit on the trees for $2,640, remodeled the building into an office building at a cost of $38,400, and removed the trees from the land at a cost of $9,000. Construction of the factory building was to begin in a week.

Prepare schedules showing the proper valuation of the assets acquired by Pressler Company.

Problem 10–2A
Determine cost of land and building (L.O. 1)

Required

Timothy Company acquired and placed into use a heavy factory machine on October 1, 1998. The machine had an invoice price of $360,000, but the company received a 3% cash discount by paying the bill on the date of acquisition. An employee of Timothy Company hauled the machine down a city street without a permit. As a result, the company had to pay a $1,500 fine. Installation and testing costs totaled $35,800. The machine is estimated to have a $35,000 salvage value and a seven-year useful life. (A fraction should be used for the DDB calculation rather than a percentage.)

a. Prepare the journal entry to record the acquisition of the machine.

b. Prepare the journal entry to record depreciation for 1998 under the double-declining-balance method.

c. Assume Timothy Company used the straight-line depreciation method. At the beginning of 2001, it estimated the machine will last another six years. Prepare the journal entry to record depreciation for 2001. The estimated salvage value would not change.

Problem 10–3A
Prepare entry for acquisition of machine, for depreciation under DDB, and for straight-line depreciation assuming a change in estimated life (L.O. 1, 3)

Required

Peach Company has the following entries in its Building account:

Debits

1998
May 5 Cost of land and building purchased $200,000
     5 Broker fees incident to purchase of land and building 12,000
1999
Jan. 3 Contract price of new wing added to south end 84,000
     15 Cost of new machinery, estimated life 10 years 160,000
June 10 Real estate taxes for six months ended 6/30/99   3,600
Aug. 10 Cost of building parking lot for employees in back of building.   4,960
Sept. 6 Replacement of windows broken in August   160
Oct. 10 Repairs due to regular usage   2,240

Credits

1998
May 24 Transfer to Land account, per allocation of purchase cost authorized in
            minutes of board of directors 32,000
1999
Jan. 5 Proceeds from lease of second floor for six months ended 12/31/98   8,000

Problem 10–4A
Compute cost of land, land improvements, building, and machinery; prepare entry to correct the accounts (L.O. 1, 4)

Peach acquired the original property on May 5, 1998. Orange immediately engaged a contractor to construct a new wing on the south end of the building. While the new wing was being constructed, the company leased the second floor as temporary warehouse space to Kellett Company. During this period (July 1 to December 31, 1998), the company installed new machinery costing $160,000 on the first floor of the building. Regular operations began on January 2, 1999.

a. Compute the correct balance for the Buildings account as of December 31, 1999. The company employs a calendar-year accounting period.

b. Prepare the necessary journal entries to correct the records of Peach Company at December 31, 1999. No depreciation entries are required.

Required

Problem 10–5A
Compute depreciation for first year under each of four different depreciation methods (L.O. 3)

Cardine Company acquired and placed into use equipment on January 2, 1998, at a cash cost of $935,000. Transportation charges amounted to $7,500, and installation and testing costs totaled $55,000.

The equipment was estimated to have a useful life of nine years and a salvage value of $37,500 at the end of its life. It was further estimated that the equipment would be used in the production of 1,920,000 units of product during its life. During 1998, 426,000 units of product were produced.

Required   Compute the depreciation to the nearest dollar for the year ended December 31, 1998, using:

a. Straight-line method.

b. Units-of-production method.

c. Sum-of-the-years'-digits method.

d. Double-declining-balance method (use a fraction rather than a percentage).

Problem 10–6A
Compute depreciation for two years using three depreciation methods; partial-year depreciation used first year (L.O. 3)

Goodrich Company purchased a machine on October 1, 1998, for $100,000. The machine has an estimated salvage value of $30,000 and an estimated useful life of eight years.

Required   Compute to the nearest dollar the amount of depreciation Goodrich should record on the machine for the years ending December 31, 1998, and 1999, under each of the following methods:

a. Straight-line.

b. Sum-of-the-years'-digits.

c. Double-declining-balance.

BEYOND THE NUMBERS—CRITICAL THINKING

Business Decision Case 10–1
Compute correct cost of land, buildings, and land improvements; compute depreciation; prepare entry to correct the accounts (L.O. 1, 3)

You are a new staff auditor assigned to audit Cray Company's Buildings account. You determine that Cray Company made the following entries in its Buildings account in 1998:

Debits

1998			
Jan.	2	Cost of land and old buildings purchased.	$ 720,000
	2	Legal fees incident to purchase.	9,600
	2	Fee for title search	1,200
	12	Cost of demolishing old buildings on land	19,200
June	16	Cost of insurance during construction of new building	4,800
July	30	Payment to contractor on completion of new building	1,080,000
Aug.	5	Architect's fees for design of new building	48,000
Sept.	15	City assessment for sewers and sidewalks (considered permanent)	16,800
Oct.	6	Cost of landscaping (considered permanent)	9,600
Nov.	1	Cost of driveways and parking lots	60,000

Credit

Jan.	15	Proceeds received upon sale of salvaged materials from old buildings	4,800

In addition to the entries in the account, you obtained the following information in your interview with the accountant in charge of the Buildings account:

1. The company began using the new building on September 1, 1998. The building is estimated to have a 40-year useful life and no salvage value.

2. The company began using the driveways and parking lots on November 1, 1998. The driveways and parking lots have an estimated 10-year useful life and no salvage value.

3. The company uses the straight-line depreciation method to depreciate all of its plant assets.

Using all of this information, do the following:

a.   Prepare a schedule that shows the separate cost of land, buildings, and land improvements.

b.   Compute the amount of depreciation expense for 1998.

c.   Complete the journal entries required to correct the accounts at December 31, 1998. Assume that closing entries have not been made.

d.   Write a brief statement describing to management why depreciation must be recorded and how recording depreciation affects net income.

On October 1, 1999, Besler Company acquired and placed into use new equipment costing $504,000. The equipment has an estimated useful life of five years and an estimated salvage value of $24,000. Besler estimates that the equipment will produce 2 million units of product during its life. In the last quarter of 1999, the equipment produced 120,000 units of product. As the company's accountant, management has asked you to do the following:

a.   Compute the depreciation for the last quarter of 1999, using each of the following methods:
   1.   Straight-line.
   2.   Units-of-production.
   3.   Sum-of-the-years'-digits.
   4.   Double-declining-balance.

b.   Prepare a written report describing the conditions in which each of these four methods would be most appropriate.

Business Decision Case 10–2
Compute partial-year depreciation under each of four different methods; cite circumstances in which each of the different methods seems most appropriate (L.O. 2, 3)

The notes to the financial statements of Anthony Industries, Inc., in "A Broader Perspective" on page 380, stated that substantially all fixed assets are depreciated using the straight-line method. Explain why the straight-line method of depreciation may be appropriate for this company.

Business Decision Case 10–3
Discuss why staight-line depreciation method may be appropriate (L.O. 3)

Discuss the meaning of rate of return on operating assets, its elements, and what it means to investors and management.

Calculate the rate of return on operating assets for the four companies in the annual report booklet for the two most recent years. Assume all assets are operating assets. Comment on the results.

Business Decision Case 10–4
Discuss the rate of return on operating assets and calculate the ratio for four actual companies (L.O. 6)

The following footnote excerpted from the 1996 annual report of John H. Harland Company describes the company's accounting policies for property, plant, and equipment:

Property, plant, and equipment are carried at cost. Depreciation of buildings is computed primarily by the declining balance method. Depreciation of equipment, furniture and fixtures is calculated by the straight-line or sum-of-the-years'-digits methods. Accelerated methods are used for income tax purposes for all property where it is allowed.

Annual Report Analysis 10–5
Determine the number of depreciation methods used. Cite the advantages of each method (L.O. 3)

a.   How many different depreciation methods are used by John H. Harland Company? Does this practice conform with generally accepted accounting principles?

b.   Discuss why management might select each of these methods to depreciate plant assets.

Required

In a group of two or three students, visit a large company in your community and inquire about the subsidiary records it maintains to establish accounting control over its plant assets. Also inquire about physical controls used to protect its equipment that is movable, such as computers, copy machines, and so on. Write a report to your instructor summarizing your findings and be prepared to give a short report to your class.

Group Project 10–6
Describe plant asset records

Group Project 10–7
Determine why certain depreciation methods were used

With a team of two or three students, visit two companies in your community to inquire about why they use certain depreciation methods. Try to locate companies that use several depreciation methods in accounting for various depreciable fixed assets. Interview those who made the decision as to methods to use to find out the reasons for their choices. Write a report to your instructor summarizing your findings.

Group Project 10–8
Determine decision rules for subsequent expenditures

In a small group of students, visit a large company in your community to determine how it decides to account for expenditures on fixed assets made after the assets have been in use for some time. In other words, how does it decide whether to debit the asset account, the accumulated depreciation account, or an expense account? What role does materiality play in the decision? Evaluate the reasonableness of the decision model used. Write a report to your instructor summarizing your findings and be prepared to make a short presentation to your class.

USING THE INTERNET—A VIEW OF THE REAL WORLD

Internet Project 10–9
Investigate careers in accounting

Visit the Becker CPA Review site at:
http://www.beckercpa/careers.htm
Study the descriptions of accounting careers at this site. Identify the major types of employers. Identify the types of public accounting firms. Describe the types of services provided by these firms. Make note of any other interesting information at this site. Write a report to your instructor summarizing your findings. Be prepared to make a short presentation to the class.

Internet Project 10–10
Investigate a fixed asset system

Visit the Best Software website at:
http://www.bestsoftware.com
Click on "Fixed Asset Management Systems." Investigate what types of information the system tracks on a particular fixed asset, such as an automobile. Why might a company buy this software and how much does it cost? Study any other aspect of the information that looks interesting. Write a report to your instructor summarizing your findings.

ANSWERS TO SELF-TEST

TRUE-FALSE

1. **True.** The cost of land includes all normal, reasonable, and necessary expenditures to obtain the land and get it ready for use.

2. **False.** Depreciation is a process of allocation, not valuation, and the book value of an asset has little to do with its market value.

3. **False.** Depreciation accounting does not provide funds required to replace plant assets. Instead, accumulated depreciation simply shows how much of an asset's cost has been charged to expense since the asset was acquired.

4. **False.** Expenditures that improve the quality of services are charged to the asset account.

5. **True.** Plant asset subsidiary ledgers provide detailed information that the general ledger account cannot provide and thus give better control over plant assets.

MULTIPLE-CHOICE

1. **b.** The depreciation expense for 1999 using the straight-line method is computed as follows:

$$(\$440,000 - \$40,000)/10 = \$40,000$$

2. **d.** $\text{Double-declining balance rate} = 2 \times (100\%/10)$
$= 20\%$

$\text{Depreciation expense for 1999} = (20\% \times \$440,000) \times {}^{6}/_{12}$
$= \$44,000$

3. **a.** $\text{SOYD} = \dfrac{10(10 + 1)}{2} = 55$

$\text{Depreciation expense} = \dfrac{10}{55} \times (\$440,000 - \$40,000)$
$= \$72,727$

4. **e.** At the beginning of 1999, the balance of accumulated depreciation is $2,800 (annual depreciation of $1,400 × 2) and book value is $7,200, or ($10,000 − $2,800). The revised annual depreciation expense is $3,100, or [($7,200 − $1,000)/2].

5. **a.** The error in recording a capital expenditure as a revenue expenditure results in an overstatement of current year's expense, as well as an understatement of current year's net income.

11

PLANT ASSET DISPOSALS, NATURAL RESOURCES, AND INTANGIBLE ASSETS

Your study of long-term assets—plant assets, natural resources, and intangible assets—began in Chapter 10, which focused on determining plant asset cost, computing depreciation, and distinguishing between capital and revenue expenditures. This chapter begins by discussing the disposal of plant assets. The next topic is accounting for natural resources such as ores, minerals, oil and gas, and timber. The final topic is accounting for intangible assets such as patents, copyrights, franchises, trademarks and trade names, leases, and goodwill.

Note that accounting for all the long-term assets discussed in these chapters is basically the same. A company that purchases a long-term asset records it at cost. As the company receives benefits from the asset and its future service potential decreases, the accountant transfers the cost from an asset account to an expense account. Finally, the asset is sold, retired, or traded in on a new asset. Because the lives of long-term assets can extend for many years, the methods accountants use in reporting such assets can have a dramatic effect on the financial statements of many accounting periods.

DISPOSAL OF PLANT ASSETS

All plant assets except land eventually wear out or become inadequate or obsolete and must be sold, retired, or traded for new assets. When disposing of a plant asset, a company must remove both the asset's cost and accumulated depreciation from the accounts. Overall, then, all plant asset disposals have the following steps in common:

1. Bring the asset's depreciation up to date.
2. Record the disposal by:
   a. Writing off the asset's cost.
   b. Writing off the accumulated depreciation.

LEARNING OBJECTIVES

After studying this chapter, you should be able to:

1. Calculate and prepare entries for the sale, retirement, and destruction of plant assets.

2. Describe and record exchanges of dissimilar and similar plant assets.

3. Determine the periodic depletion cost of a natural resource and calculate depreciation of plant assets located on extractive industry property.

(continued)

(concluded)

4. Prepare entries for the acquisition and amortization of intangible assets.

5. Analyze and use the financial results—total assets turnover.

c. Recording any consideration (usually cash) received or paid or to be received or paid.
d. Recording the gain or loss, if any.

As you study this section, remember these common procedures accountants use to record the disposal of plant assets. In the paragraphs that follow, we discuss accounting for the (1) sale of plant assets, (2) retirement of plant assets without sale, (3) destruction of plant assets, (4) exchange of plant assets, and (5) cost of dismantling and removing plant assets.

Sale of Plant Assets

Companies frequently dispose of plant assets by selling them. By comparing an asset's book value (cost less accumulated depreciation) with its selling price (or net amount realized if there are selling expenses), the company may show either a gain or loss. If the sales price is greater than the asset's book value, the company shows a gain. If the sales price is less than the asset's book value, the company shows a loss. Of course, when the sales price equals the asset's book value, no gain or loss occurs.

To illustrate accounting for the sale of a plant asset, assume that a company sells equipment costing $45,000 with accumulated depreciation of $14,000 for $35,000. The firm realizes a gain of $4,000:

Objective 1
Calculate and prepare entries for the sale, retirement, and destruction of plant assets.

Equipment cost	$45,000
Accumulated depreciation	14,000
Book value	$31,000
Sales price	35,000
Gain realized	$ 4,000

The journal entry to record the sale is:

Cash	35,000	
Accumulated Depreciation—Equipment	14,000	
Equipment		45,000
Gain on Disposal of Plant Assets		4,000
To record sale of equipment at a price greater than book value.		

If on the other hand, the company sells the equipment for $28,000, it realizes a loss of $3,000 ($31,000 book value − $28,000 sales price). The journal entry to record the sale is:

Cash	28,000	
Accumulated Depreciation—Equipment	14,000	
Loss from Disposal of Plant Assets	3,000	
Equipment		45,000
To record sale of equipment at a price less than book value.		

If a firm sells the equipment for $31,000, no gain or loss occurs. The journal entry to record the sale is:

Cash	31,000	
Accumulated Depreciation—Equipment	14,000	
Equipment		45,000
To record sale of equipment at a price equal to book value.		

Reinforcing Problems
E11–1 Record sale of equipment; account for removal costs.
E11–2 Update depreciation and record sale of truck.
E11–3 Record the destruction of machinery by fire—uninsured and insured.

Note to the Student
Remember the importance of recording the depreciation of a plant asset up to the date of sale or disposal.

ACCOUNTING FOR DEPRECIATION TO DATE OF DISPOSAL When selling or otherwise disposing of a plant asset, a firm must record the depreciation up to the date of sale or disposal. For example, if it sold an asset on April 1 and last recorded depreciation on December 31, the company should record depreciation for three months (January 1–April 1). When depreciation is not recorded for the three months, operating expenses for that period are understated, and the gain on the sale of the asset is understated or the loss overstated.

To illustrate, assume that on August 1, 2000, Ray Company sold a machine for $1,500. When purchased on January 2, 1992, the machine cost $12,000; Ray was depreciating it at the straight-line rate of 10% per year. As of December 31, 1999, after closing entries were made, the machine's accumulated depreciation account had a balance of $9,600. Before determining a gain or loss and before making an entry to record the sale, the firm must make the following entry to record depreciation for the seven months ended July 31, 2000:

July	31	Depreciation Expense—Machinery	700	
		Accumulated Depreciation—Machinery		700
		To record depreciation for seven months		
		($12,000 × 0.10 × 7/12).		

An accountant would compute the $200 loss on the sale as follows:

Machine cost	$12,000
Accumulated depreciation ($9,600 + $700)	10,300
Book value	$ 1,700
Sales price	1,500
Loss realized	$ 200

The journal entry to record the sale is:

Cash	1,500	
Accumulated Depreciation—Machinery	10,300	
Loss from Disposal of Plant Assets	200	
Machinery		12,000
To record sale of machinery at a price less than book value.		

When retiring a plant asset from service, a company removes the asset's cost and accumulated depreciation from its plant asset accounts. For example, Hayes Company would make the following journal entry when it retired a fully depreciated machine that cost $15,000 and had no salvage value:

Retirement of Plant Assets without Sale

Accumulated Depreciation—Machinery	15,000	
Machinery		15,000
To record the retirement of a fully depreciated machine.		

Occasionally, a company continues to use a plant asset after it has been fully depreciated. In such a case, the firm should not remove the asset's cost and accumulated depreciation from the accounts until the asset is sold, traded, or retired from service. Of course, the company cannot record more depreciation on a fully depreciated asset because total depreciation expense taken on an asset may not exceed its cost.

Sometimes a business retires or discards a plant asset before fully depreciating it. When selling the asset as scrap (even if not immediately), the firm removes its cost and accumulated depreciation from the asset and accumulated depreciation accounts. In addition, the accountant records its estimated salvage value in a Salvaged Materials account and recognizes a gain or loss on disposal. To illustrate, assume that a firm retires a machine with a $10,000 original cost and $7,500 of accumulated depreciation. If the machine's estimated salvage value is $500, the following entry is required:

Salvaged Materials	500	
Accumulated Depreciation—Machinery	7,500	
Loss from Disposal of Plant Assets	2,000	
Machinery		10,000
To record retirement of machinery, which will be sold for scrap at a later time.		

Destruction of Plant Assets

Sometimes accidents, fires, floods, and storms wreck or destroy plant assets, causing companies to incur losses. For example, assume that fire completely destroyed an *uninsured* building costing $40,000 with up-to-date accumulated depreciation of $12,000. The journal entry is:

Fire Loss	28,000	
Accumulated Depreciation—Buildings	12,000	
Buildings		40,000
To record fire loss.		

If the building was *insured,* the company would debit only the amount of the fire loss exceeding the amount to be recovered from the insurance company to the Fire Loss account. To illustrate, assume the company partially insured the building and will recover $22,000 from the insurance company. The journal entry is:

Receivable from Insurance Company	22,000	
Fire Loss	6,000	
Accumulated Depreciation—Buildings	12,000	
Buildings		40,000
To record fire loss and amount recoverable from insurance company.		

Exchanges of Plant Assets (Nonmonetary Assets)

Nonmonetary assets are those whose price may change over time, such as inventories, property, plant, and equipment. In accounting for the exchange of nonmonetary assets, ordinarily firms base the recorded amount on the fair market value of the asset given up or the fair market value of the asset received, whichever is more clearly evident. If a gain or loss results from the exchange, companies always recognize the loss. They may or may not recognize the gain, depending on whether the asset exchanged is similar or dissimilar to the asset received.

Similar assets are those of the same general type, that perform the same function, or that are employed in the same line of business. Examples of the exchange of similar assets include exchanging a building for another building, a delivery truck for another delivery truck, and equipment for other equipment. Conversely, examples of the exchange of dissimilar assets include exchanging a building for land or equipment for inventory.

In general, companies recognize losses on nonmonetary assets regardless of whether the assets are similar or dissimilar. They recognize gains if the assets are dissimilar in nature because the earnings process related to those assets is considered to be completed. With one exception, firms defer gains on the exchange of similar nonmonetary assets. The exception occurs when they receive monetary consideration in addition to the similar asset. Companies recognize a partial gain when they receive cash along with an asset. Because the specific details of monetary consideration are reserved for an intermediate accounting text, assume in the examples given that cash has been paid, not received. Compute both gains and losses on the disposal of nonmonetary assets by comparing the book value of the asset given up with the fair market value of the asset given up.

EXCHANGES OF DISSIMILAR PLANT ASSETS Sometimes firms trade a machine for a dissimilar plant asset such as a truck. For exchanges of dissimilar plant assets, accountants record the new asset at the fair market value of the asset received or the asset(s) given up, whichever is more clearly evident.[1] When the cash price of the new asset is stated, they use the cash price to record the new asset. If the cash price is not stated, they assume the fair market value of the old asset plus any cash paid is the cash price and use it to record the new asset. Thus, accountants would normally record the asset received at either (1) the stated cash price of the new asset or (2) a known fair market value of the asset given up plus any cash paid.

Debiting accumulated depreciation and crediting the old asset removes the book value of the old asset from the accounts. The firm credits the Cash account for any amount paid. If the amount at which the new asset is recorded exceeds the book value of the old asset plus any cash paid, a company records a gain to balance the journal entry. If the situation is reversed, it records a loss to balance the journal entry.

To illustrate such an exchange, assume a factory exchanges an old machine for a new delivery truck. The machine cost $45,000 and had an up-to-date accumulated depreciation balance of $38,000. The truck had a $55,000 cash price and was acquired by trading in the machine with a fair value of $3,000 and paying $52,000 cash. The journal entry to record the exchange is:

Trucks	55,000	
Accumulated Depreciation—Machinery	38,000	
Loss from Disposal of Plant Assets	4,000	
Machinery		45,000
Cash		52,000
To record loss on exchange of dissimilar plant assets.		

Another way to compute the $4,000 loss on the exchange is to use the book value of the old asset less the fair market value of the old asset. The calculation is as follows:

Machine cost	$45,000
Accumulated depreciation	38,000
Book value	$ 7,000
Fair market value of old asset (trade-in allowance)	3,000
Loss realized	$ 4,000

To illustrate the recognition of a gain from an exchange of dissimilar plant assets, assume that the fair market value of the machine was $9,000 instead of $3,000, and that only $46,000 was paid in cash. The journal entry to record the exchange would be:

Trucks	55,000	
Accumulated Depreciation—Machinery	38,000	
Machinery		45,000
Cash		46,000
Gain on Disposal of Plant Assets		2,000
To record gain on exchange of dissimilar plant assets.		

Another way to compute the gain of $2,000 on the exchange is to use the fair market value of the old asset less the book value of the old asset. The calculation is as follows:

Machine cost	$45,000
Accumulated depreciation	38,000
Book value	$ 7,000
Fair market value of old asset (trade-in allowance)	9,000
Gain realized	$ 2,000

Objective 2
Describe and record exchanges of dissimilar and similar plant assets.

---

[1]APB, *APB Opinion No. 29*, "Accounting for Nonmonetary Transactions" (New York: AICPA, May 1973), par. 16.

Remember, companies always recognize both gains and losses on exchanges of dissimilar plant assets. They do not recognize gains on exchanges of similar plant assets.

EXCHANGES OF SIMILAR PLANT ASSETS   Often firms exchange plant assets such as automobiles, trucks, and office equipment by trading the old asset for a similar new one. When such an exchange occurs, the company receives a trade-in allowance for the old asset, and pays the balance in cash.[2] Usually, the cash price of the new asset is stated. If not, accountants assume the cash price is the fair market value of the old asset plus the cash paid.

When similar assets are exchanged, we must modify the general rule that new assets are recorded at the fair market value of what is given up or received. Thus, companies record the new asset at (1) the cash price of the asset received or (2) the book value of the old asset plus the cash paid, whichever is lower. When applying this rule to exchanges of similar assets, firms recognize losses, but not gains.

To illustrate the accounting for exchanges of similar plant assets, assume that a delivery service exchanged $50,000 cash and truck No. 1—which cost $45,000, had $38,000 of up-to-date accumulated depreciation, and had a $5,000 fair market value—for truck No. 2. The new truck has a cash price (fair market value) of $55,000. The delivery service realized a loss of $2,000 on the exchange.

Cost of truck No. 1	$45,000
Accumulated depreciation	38,000
Book value	$ 7,000
Fair market value of old asset (trade-in allowance)	5,000
Loss on exchange of plant assets	$ 2,000

The journal entry to record the exchange is:

Trucks (cost of No. 2)	55,000	
Accumulated Depreciation—Trucks	38,000	
Loss from Disposal of Plant Assets	2,000	
Trucks (cost of No. 1)		45,000
Cash		50,000
To record loss on exchange of similar plant assets.		

Note that firms record exchanges of similar plant assets just like exchanges of dissimilar plant assets when a *loss* occurs from the exchange.

Accounting for any gain resulting from exchanges of similar plant assets is different than accounting for a gain resulting from exchanges of dissimilar plant assets. To illustrate, assume that in the preceding example, the delivery service gave truck No. 1 (now with a fair market value of $9,000) and $46,000 cash in exchange for truck No. 2. The gain on the exchange is $2,000:

Cost of truck No. 1	$45,000
Accumulated depreciation	38,000
Book value	$ 7,000
Fair market value of old asset (trade-in allowance)	9,000
Gain indicated	$ 2,000

When a firm exchanges similar assets, it does not recognize a gain. It records the new asset at book value of the old asset ($7,000) plus cash paid ($46,000). The company deducts the gain from the cost of the new asset ($55,000). Thus, the cost

---

[2]Trade-in allowance is sometimes expressed as the difference between *list* price and cash paid, but we choose to define it as the difference between *cash* price and cash paid because this latter definition seems to agree with current practice for exchange transactions.

basis of the new delivery truck is equal to $55,000 less the $2,000 gain, or $53,000. The delivery service uses this $53,000 cost basis in recording depreciation on the truck and determining any gain or loss on its disposal.

Book value of old truck (No. 1)	$ 7,000
Cash paid	46,000
Cost of new truck (No. 2)	$53,000
Fair market value of new truck (No. 2)	$55,000 (equal)
Less: Gain indicated	2,000
Cost of new truck (No. 2)	$53,000

The journal entry to record the exchange is:

Trucks (cost of No. 2)	53,000	
Accumulated Depreciation—Trucks	38,000	
Trucks (cost of No. 1)		45,000
Cash		46,000
To record exchange of similar plant assets.		

The justification used by the Accounting Principles Board for not recognizing gains on exchanges of similar plant assets is that "revenue should not be recognized merely because one productive asset is substituted for a similar productive asset but rather should be considered to flow from the production and sale of the goods or services to which the substituted productive asset is committed."[3] In effect, firms would realize the gain on an exchange of similar plant assets in future accounting periods as increased net income resulting from smaller depreciation charges on the newly acquired asset. In the preceding example, annual depreciation expense is less if it is based on the truck's $53,000 cost basis than if it is based on the truck's $55,000 cash price. Thus, future net income per year will be larger.

In Illustration 11.1, we summarize the rules for recording plant asset exchanges.

Note to the Student
Why do accountants not recognize a gain on an exchange of a similar asset?
Answer: 1. Accountants substituted one plant asset for another plant asset with a similar production function. 2. By postponing the recognition of the gain, they are applying the conservatism principle.

Reinforcing Problems
E11–4 Record exchange of automobiles.
E11–5 Record variety of cases involving sale, retirement, or exchange of equipment.

USES OF TECHNOLOGY Although sophisticated computer systems automatically compute the gain or loss on the disposal of assets, such programs depend on human input. If an error was made in inputting the type of disposal or exchange or if the life of the asset was estimated inaccurately, the calculated gain or loss would be incorrect.

AN ACCOUNTING PERSPECTIVE

Removal Costs

Companies incur removal costs when dismantling and removing old plant assets. They deduct these costs from salvage proceeds to determine the asset's net salvage value. (The removal costs could be greater than the salvage proceeds.) Accountants associate removal costs with the old asset, not the new asset acquired as a replacement.

The next section discusses natural resources. Note the underlying accounting principle of matching the expenses with the revenues earned in that same accounting period.

NATURAL RESOURCES

Resources supplied by nature, such as ore deposits, mineral deposits, oil reserves, gas deposits, and timber stands, are **natural resources** or **wasting assets.** Natural resources represent inventories of raw materials that can be consumed (exhausted) through extraction or removal from their natural setting (e.g., removing oil from the ground).

Real World Example
Georgia-Pacific Corporation depletes its investment in timber based on the total timber that will be available during the estimated growth cycle.

---

[3]*APB Opinion No. 29*, par. 16.

ILLUSTRATION 11.1
Summary of Rules for
Recording Exchanges
of Plant Assets

	Dissimilar Assets	Similar Assets	
Recognize Gains?	Yes	No	
Recognize Losses?	Yes	Yes	
Record New Asset at:	Cash price of new asset **or** fair market value of old asset plus cash paid	**If loss:** Cash price of new asset **or** fair market value of old asset plus cash paid	**If gain:** Book value of old asset plus cash paid

On the balance sheet, we classify natural resources as a separate group among noncurrent assets under headings such as "Timber stands" and "Oil reserves." Typically, we record natural resources at their cost of acquisition plus exploration and development costs; on the balance sheet, we report them at total cost less accumulated depletion. (Accumulated depletion is similar to the accumulated depreciation used for plant assets.) When analyzing the financial condition of companies owning natural resources, exercise caution because the historical costs reported for the natural resources may be only a small fraction of their current value.

AN ACCOUNTING PERSPECTIVE
—

BUSINESS INSIGHT   Union Texas Petroleum Corporation is engaged in oil and gas exploration and production overseas and has petrochemical interests in the United States. Oil and gas reserves cannot be measured exactly. In notes to their financial statements, Union Texas states that the reliability of reserve estimates at any time depends on both the quality and quantity of the technical and economic data, the production performance of the reservoirs, and extensive engineering judgment. Consequently, as additional data become available during the producing life of a reservoir, the company revises its reserve estimates.

Depletion

Depletion is the exhaustion that results from the physical removal of a part of a natural resource. In each accounting period, the depletion recognized is an estimate of the cost of the natural resource that was removed from its natural setting during the period. To record depletion, debit a Depletion account and credit an Accumulated Depletion account, which is a contra account to the natural resource asset account.

By crediting the Accumulated Depletion account instead of the asset account, we continue to report the original cost of the entire natural resource on the financial statements. Thus, statement users can see the percentage of the resource that has been removed. To determine the total cost of the resource available, we combine this depletion cost with other extraction, mining, or removal costs. We can assign this total cost to either the cost of natural resources sold or the inventory of the natural resource still on hand. Thus, we could expense all, some, or none of the depletion and removal costs recognized in an accounting period, depending on the portion sold. If all of the resource is sold, we expense all of the depletion and removal costs. The cost of any portion not yet sold is part of the cost of inventory.

Objective 3
Determine the periodic depletion cost of a natural resource and calculate depreciation of plant assets located on extractive industry property.

COMPUTING PERIODIC DEPLETION COST   To compute depletion charges, companies usually use the units-of-production method. They divide total cost by the estimated number of units—tons, barrels, or board feet—that can be economically extracted from the property. This calculation provides a per-unit depletion cost. For example, assume that in 1999 a company paid $650,000 for a tract of land containing ore deposits. The company spent $100,000 in exploration costs. The results indicated that approximately 900,000 tons of ore can be removed economically from the land, after which the land will be worth $50,000. The company incurred costs of $200,000 to develop the site, including the cost of running power lines and building roads. Total cost subject to depletion is the net cost assignable to the natural resource plus the exploration and development costs. When the property is purchased, a journal entry assigns the purchase price to the two assets purchased—the natural resource and the land. The entry would be:

Land	50,000	
Ore Deposits	600,000	
Cash		650,000
To record purchase of land and mine.		

After the purchase, an entry debits all costs to develop the site (including exploration) to the natural resource account. The entry would be:

Ore Deposits ($100,000 + $200,000)	300,000	
Cash		300,000
To record costs of exploration and development.		

The formula for finding depletion cost per unit is:

$$\text{Depletion cost per unit} = \frac{\text{Cost of site} - \text{Residual value of land (if owned)} + \text{Costs to develop site}}{\text{Estimated number of units that can be economically extracted}}$$

In some instances, companies buy only the right to extract the natural resource from someone else's land. *When the land is not purchased, its residual value is irrelevant and should be ignored.* If there is an obligation to restore the land to a usable condition, the firm adds these estimated restoration costs to the costs to develop the site.

In the example where the land was purchased, the total costs of the mineral deposits equal the cost of the site ($650,000) minus the residual value of land ($50,000) plus costs to develop the site ($300,000), or a total of $900,000. The unit (per ton) depletion charge is $1 (or $900,000/900,000 tons).

The formula to compute the depletion cost of a period is:

$$\text{Depletion cost of a period} = \text{Depletion cost per unit} \times \text{Number of units extracted during period}$$

In this example, if 100,000 tons are mined in 1999, this entry records the depletion cost of $100,000 ($1 × 100,000) for the period:

Depletion	100,000	
Accumulated Depletion—Ore Deposits[4]		100,000
To record depletion for 1999.		

The Depletion account contains the "in the ground" cost of the ore or natural resource mined. Combined with other extractive costs, this cost determines the total cost of the ore mined. To illustrate, assume that in addition to the $100,000 depletion cost, mining labor costs totaled $320,000, and other mining costs, such as depreciation, property taxes, power, and supplies, totaled $60,000. If 80,000 tons were sold

---

[4]Instead of crediting the accumulated depletion account, the Ore Deposits account could have been credited directly. But for reasons indicated earlier, the credit is usually to an accumulated depletion account.

and 20,000 remained on hand at the end of the period, the firm would allocate total cost of $480,000 as follows:

Note to the Student

Notice that the cost per ton is the same for the ore sold and the ore in ending inventory. Remember that depletion costs, labor costs, and other mining costs are included in both computations.

Reinforcing Problems

E11–6 Compute depletion cost per ton.
E11–7 Determine depletion cost and expense.

Depletion cost	$100,000
Mining labor costs	320,000
Other mining costs	60,000
Total cost of 100,000 tons mined ($4.80 per ton)	$480,000
Less: Ore inventory (20,000 tons at $4.80)	96,000
Cost of ore sold (80,000 tons at $4.80)	$384,000

Note that the average cost per ton to mine 100,000 tons was $4.80 (or $480,000/100,000). The income statement would show cost of ore sold of $384,000. The mining company does not report depletion separately as an expense because depletion is included in cost of ore sold. The balance sheet would show inventory of ore on hand (a current asset) at $96,000 (or $4.80 × 20,000). Also, it would report the cost less accumulated depletion of the natural resource as follows:

Ore deposits	$900,000	
Less: Accumulated depletion	100,000	$800,000

Another method of calculating depletion cost is the percentage of revenue method. Because firms use this method only for income tax purposes and not for financial statements, we do not discuss it in this text.

Depreciation of Plant Assets Located on Extractive Industry Property

Companies depreciate plant assets erected on extractive industry property the same as other depreciable assets. If such assets will be abandoned when the natural resource is exhausted, they depreciate these assets over the shorter of the (a) physical life of the asset or (b) life of the natural resource. In many cases, firms compute periodic depreciation charges using the units-of-production method. Using this method matches the life of the plant asset with the life of the natural resource. This method is recommended where the *physical* life of the plant asset equals or exceeds the resource's life but its *useful* life is limited to the life of the natural resource.

Assume a mining company acquires mining property with a building it plans to use only in the mining operations. Also assume that the firm uses the units-of-production method for computing building depreciation. Relevant facts are:

Building cost	$310,000
Estimated physical life of building	20 years
Estimated salvage value of building (after mine is exhausted)	$ 10,000
Capacity of mine	1,000,000 tons
Expected life of mine	10 years

Because the life of the mine (10 years or 1,000,000 tons) is shorter than the life of the building (20 years), the building should be depreciated over the life of the mine. The basis of the depreciation charge is tons of ore rather than years because the mine's life could be longer or shorter than 10 years, depending on how rapidly the ore is removed.

Suppose that during the first year of operations, workers extracted 150,000 tons of ore. Building depreciation for the first year is $45,000, computed as follows:

$$\text{Depreciation per unit} = \frac{\text{Asset cost} - \text{Estimated salvage value}}{\begin{array}{c}\text{Total tons of ore in mine that}\\\text{can be economically extracted}\end{array}}$$

$$= \frac{\$310,000 - \$10,000}{1,000,000 \text{ tons}} = \$0.30 \text{ per ton}$$

$$\text{Depreciation for year} = \text{Depreciation per unit} \times \text{Units extracted}$$

$$= \$0.30 \text{ per ton} \times 150,000 \text{ tons} = \$45,000$$

On the income statement, depreciation on the building appears as part of the cost of ore sold and is carried as part of inventory cost for ore not sold during the period. On the balance sheet, accumulated depreciation on the building appears with the related asset account.

Plant assets and natural resources are tangible assets used by a company to produce revenues. A company also may acquire intangible assets to assist in producing revenues.

Reinforcing Problem
E11–8 Compute depreciation charge of a plant asset used for mining purposes.

INTANGIBLE ASSETS

Although they have no physical characteristics, **intangible assets** have value because of the advantages or exclusive privileges and rights they provide to a business. Intangible assets generally arise from two sources: (1) exclusive privileges granted by governmental authority or by legal contract, such as patents, copyrights, franchises, trademarks and trade names, and leases; and (2) superior entrepreneurial capacity or management know-how and customer loyalty, which is called *goodwill*.

All intangible assets are nonphysical, but not all nonphysical assets are intangibles. For example, accounts receivable and prepaid expenses are nonphysical, yet classified as current assets rather than intangible assets. Intangible assets are generally both nonphysical and noncurrent; they appear in a separate long-term section of the balance sheet entitled "Intangible assets."

Initially, firms record intangible assets at cost like most other assets. However, computing an intangible asset's acquisition cost differs from computing a plant asset's acquisition cost. Firms may include only outright purchase costs in the acquisition cost of an intangible asset; *the acquisition cost does not include cost of internal development or self-creation of the asset.* If an intangible asset is internally generated in its entirety, none of its costs are capitalized. Therefore, some companies have extremely valuable assets that may not even be recorded in their asset accounts. To explain the reasons for this practice, we discuss the history of accounting for research and development costs next.

Research and development (R&D) costs are costs incurred in a planned search for new knowledge and in translating such knowledge into new products or processes. Prior to 1975, businesses often capitalized research and development costs as intangible assets when future benefits were expected from their incurrence. Due to the difficulty of determining the costs applicable to future benefits, many companies expensed all such costs as incurred. Other companies capitalized those costs that related to proven products and expensed the rest as incurred.

As a result of these varied accounting practices, in 1974 the Financial Accounting Standards Board in *Statement No. 2* ruled that firms must expense all research and development costs when incurred, unless they were directly reimbursable by government agencies and others. Immediate expensing is justified on the grounds that (1) the amount of costs applicable to the future cannot be measured with any high degree of precision; (2) doubt exists as to whether any future benefits will be received; and (3) even if benefits are expected, they cannot be measured. Thus, research and development costs no longer appear as intangible assets on the balance sheet. The Board applies the same line of reasoning to other costs associated with internally generated intangible assets, such as the internal costs of developing a patent.

Acquisition of Intangible Assets

Objective 4
Prepare entries for the acquisition and amortization of intangible assets.

Note to the Student
The acquisition cost includes only outright costs such as the legal costs of an intangible asset. The acquisition cost does not include the cost of internal development of self-created assets.

Amortization is the systematic write-off of the cost of an intangible asset to expense. A portion of an intangible asset's cost is allocated to each accounting period in the economic (useful) life of the asset. All intangible assets are subject to amortization, which is similar to plant asset depreciation. Generally, we record amortization by debiting Amortization Expense and crediting the intangible asset account. An accumulated amortization account could record amortization. However, the information

Amortization of Intangible Assets

gained from such accounting would not be significant because normally intangibles do not account for as many total asset dollars as do plant assets.

Intangibles should be amortized over the shorter of (1) their economic life, (2) their legal life, or (3) 40 years. In *APB Opinion No. 17,* the Accounting Principles Board requires an intangible asset acquired after October 31, 1970, to be amortized over a period not to exceed 40 years. Straight-line amortization must be used unless another method of amortization (such as units-of-production) can be shown to be superior. We calculate straight-line amortization in the same way as straight-line depreciation for plant assets.

Patents

A **patent** is a right granted by the federal government. This exclusive right enables the owner to manufacture, sell, lease, or otherwise benefit from an invention for a limited period. The value of a patent lies in its ability to produce revenue. Patents have a legal life of 17 years. Protection for the patent owner begins at the time of patent application and lasts for 17 years from the date the patent is granted.

When purchasing a patent, a company records it in the Patents account at cost. The firm also debits the Patents account for the cost of the first successful defense of the patent in lawsuits (assuming an outside law firm was hired rather than using internal legal staff). Such a lawsuit establishes the validity of the patent and thereby increases its service potential. In addition, the firm debits the cost of any competing patents purchased to ensure the revenue-generating capability of its own patent to the Patents account.

The firm would amortize the cost of a purchased patent over the shorter of 17 years (or remaining legal life) or its estimated useful life. If a patent cost $40,000 and has a useful life of 10 years, the journal entries to record the patent and periodic amortization are:

Patents	40,000	
Cash		40,000
To record purchase of patent.		
Patent Amortization Expense	4,000	
Patents		4,000
To record annual patent amortization.		

Reinforcing Problem
E11–9 Determine patent cost and periodic amortization.

For a patent that becomes worthless before it is fully amortized, the company expenses the unamortized balance in the Patents account.

As noted earlier, all R&D costs incurred in the internal development of a product, process, or idea that is later patented must be expensed, rather than capitalized. In the previous example, the company amortized the cost of the purchased patent over its useful life of 10 years. If the patent had been the result of an internally generated product or process, the firm would have expensed its cost of $40,000 as incurred, in accordance with *Statement No. 2* of the Financial Accounting Standards Board.

Copyrights

Real World Example
Mattel, Inc., holds the copyright for Barbie dolls and has successfully defended this copyright against infringement by other companies.

A **copyright** is an exclusive right granted by the federal government giving protection against the illegal reproduction by others of the creator's written works, designs, and literary productions. The copyright period is for the life of the creator plus 50 years. Most publications have a limited life; a creator may charge the cost of the copyright to expense on a straight-line basis over the life of the first edition published or based on projections of the copies to be sold per year.

Franchises

A **franchise** is a contract between two parties granting the franchisee (the purchaser of the franchise) certain rights and privileges ranging from name identification to complete monopoly of service. In many instances, both parties are private businesses. For example, an individual who wishes to open a hamburger restaurant may purchase a McDonald's franchise; the two parties involved are the individual business owner and McDonald's Corporation. This franchise would allow the business owner to use the McDonald's name and golden arch, and would provide the owner with advertising and many other benefits. The legal life of a franchise may be limited by contract.

The parties involved in a franchise arrangement are not always private businesses. A government agency may grant a franchise to a private company. A city may give a franchise to a utility company, giving the utility company the exclusive right to provide service to a particular area.

In addition to providing benefits, a franchise usually places certain restrictions on the franchisee. These restrictions generally are related to rates or prices charged; also they may be in regard to product quality or to the particular supplier from whom supplies and inventory items must be purchased.

If periodic payments to the grantor of the franchise are required, the franchisee debits them to a Franchise Expense account. If a lump-sum payment is made to obtain the franchise, the franchisee records the cost in an asset account entitled Franchise and amortizes it over the shorter of the legal life (if limited by contract), the economic life of the franchise, or 40 years.

Reinforcing Problem
E11–10 Record franchise; record accrued franchise fees and franchise amortization.

BUSINESS INSIGHT   Procter & Gamble markets more than 300 brands of products. Examples include Tide, Ariel, Pantene Pro-V, Pringles, and Oil of Olay. On June 30, 1996, the total assets of Procter & Gamble were $27,730 million, $5,270 million of which consisted of goodwill and other intangible assets, including trademarks. Accumulated amortization amounted to $989 million.

AN ACCOUNTING PERSPECTIVE

A **trademark** is a symbol, design, or logo used in conjunction with a particular product or company. A **trade name** is a brand name under which a product is sold or a company does business. Often trademarks and trade names are extremely valuable to a company, but if they have been internally developed, they have no recorded asset cost. However, when a business purchases such items from an external source, it records them at cost and amortizes them over their economic life or 40 years, whichever is shorter.

A **lease** is a contract to rent property. The property owner is the grantor of the lease and is the *lessor*. The person or company obtaining rights to possess and use the property is the *lessee*. The rights granted under the lease are a **leasehold.** The accounting for a lease depends on whether it is a capital lease or an operating lease.

CAPITAL LEASES   A **capital lease** transfers to the lessee virtually all rewards and risks that accompany ownership of property. A lease is a capital lease if, among other provisions, it (1) transfers ownership of the leased property to the lessee at the end of the lease term or (2) contains a bargain purchase option that permits the lessee to buy the property at a price significantly below fair market value at the end of the lease term.

A capital lease is a means of financing property acquisitions; it has the same economic impact as a purchase made on an installment plan. Thus, the lessee in a capital lease must record the leased property as an asset and the lease obligation as a liability. Because a capital lease is an asset, the lessee depreciates the leased property over its useful life. The lessee records part of each lease payment as interest expense and the balance as a payment on the lease liability.

The proper accounting for capital leases for both lessees and lessors has been an extremely difficult problem. We leave further discussion of capital leases for an intermediate accounting text.

OPERATING LEASES   A lease that does not qualify as a capital lease is an **operating lease.** A one-year lease on an apartment and a week's rental of an automobile are examples of operating leases. Such leases make no attempt to transfer any of the rewards and risks of ownership to the lessee. As a result, there may be no recordable transaction when a lease is signed.

Trademarks; Trade Names

Real World Example
McDonald's and its golden arches are familiar to us all. McDonald's is the company's trade name and the golden arches, its trademark.

Leases

Reinforcing Problem
E11–11 Record leasehold; record rent accrued and leasehold amortization.

In some situations, the lease may call for an immediate cash payment that must be recorded. Assume that a business signed a lease requiring the immediate payment of the annual rent of $15,000 for each of the first and fifth years of a five-year lease. The lessee would record the payment as follows:

Prepaid Rent	15,000	
Leasehold	15,000	
Cash		30,000
To record first and fifth years' rent on a five-year lease.		

Since the Leasehold account is actually a long-term prepaid rent account for the fifth year's annual rent, it is an intangible asset until the beginning of the fifth year. Then the Leasehold account becomes a current asset and may be transferred into a Prepaid Rent account. Accounting for the balance in the Leasehold account depends on the terms of the lease. In the previous example, the firm would charge the $15,000 in the Leasehold account to expense over the fifth year only. It would charge the balance in Prepaid Rent to expense in the first year. Thus, assuming the lease year and fiscal year coincide, the entry for the first year is:

Rent Expense	15,000	
Prepaid Rent		15,000
To record rent expense.		

The entry in the fifth year is:

Rent Expense	15,000	
Leasehold		15,000
To record rent expense.		

The accounting for the second, third, and fourth years would be the same as for the first year. The lessee records the rent in Prepaid Rent when paid in advance for the year and then expenses it. As stated above, the lessee may transfer the amount in the Leasehold account to Prepaid Rent at the beginning of the fifth year by debiting Prepaid Rent and crediting Leasehold. If this entry was made, the previous entry would have credited Prepaid Rent.

In some cases, when a lease is signed, the lump-sum payment does not cover a specific year's rent. The lessee debits this payment to the Leasehold account and amortizes it over the life of the lease. The straight-line method is required unless another method can be shown to be superior. Assume the $15,000 rent for the fifth year in the example was, instead, a lump-sum payment on the lease in addition to the annual rent payments. An annual adjusting entry to amortize the $15,000 over five years would read:

Rent Expense	3,000	
Leasehold		3,000
To amortize leasehold.		

In this example, the annual rental expense is $18,000: $15,000 annual cash rent plus $3,000 amortization of leasehold ($15,000/5).

The lessee may base periodic rent on current-year sales or usage rather than being a constant amount. For example, if a lease called for rent equal to 5% of current-year sales and sales were $400,000 in 1999, the rent for 1999 would be $20,000. The rent would either be paid or an adjusting entry would be made at the end of the year.

Leasehold Improvements

A leasehold improvement is any physical alteration made by the lessee to the leased property in which benefits are expected beyond the current accounting period. Leasehold improvements made by a lessee usually become the property of the lessor after the lease has expired. However, since leasehold improvements are an asset of the lessee during the lease period, the lessee debits them to a Leasehold Improvements account.

The lessee then amortizes the leasehold improvements to expense over the period benefited by the improvements. The amortization period for leasehold improvements should be the shorter of the life of the improvements or the life of the lease. If the lease can (and probably will) be renewed at the option of the lessee, the life of the lease should include the option period.

As an illustration, assume that on January 2, 1999, Wolf Company leases a building for 20 years under a nonrenewable lease at an annual rental of $20,000, payable on each December 31. Wolf immediately incurs a cost of $80,000 for improvements to the building, such as interior walls for office separation, ceiling fans, and recessed lighting. The improvements have an estimated life of 30 years. The company should amortize the $80,000 over the 20-year lease period, since that period is shorter than the life of the improvements, and Wolf cannot use the improvements beyond the life of the lease. If only annual financial statements are prepared, the following journal entry properly records the rental expense for the year ended December 31, 1999:

Rent Expense (or Leasehold Improvement Expense)	4,000	
Leasehold Improvements		4,000
To record amortization of leasehold improvement.		
Rent Expense	20,000	
Cash		20,000
To record annual rent.		

Thus, the total cost to rent the building each year equals the $20,000 cash rent plus the amortization of the leasehold improvements.

Although leaseholds are intangible assets, leaseholds and leasehold improvements sometimes appear in the property, plant, and equipment section of the balance sheet.

Goodwill

In accounting, **goodwill** is an intangible value attached to a company resulting mainly from the company's management skill or know-how and a favorable reputation with customers. A company's value may be greater than the total of the fair market value of its tangible and identifiable intangible assets. This greater value means that the company generates an above-average income on each dollar invested in the business. Thus, proof of a company's goodwill is its ability to generate superior earnings or income.

A Goodwill account appears in the accounting records only if goodwill has been purchased. A company cannot purchase goodwill by itself; it must buy an entire business or a part of a business to obtain the accompanying intangible asset, goodwill.

To illustrate, assume that Lenox Company purchased all of Martin Company's assets for $700,000. Lenox also agreed to assume responsibility for a $350,000 mortgage note payable owed by Martin. Goodwill is the difference between the amount paid for the business including the debt assumed ($700,000 + $350,000 = $1,050,000) and the fair market value of the assets purchased. Notice that Lenox would use the fair market value of the assets rather than book value to determine the amount of goodwill. The following computation is for the goodwill purchased by Lenox:

Note to the Student
Goodwill can only be recorded when a business or a part of a business has been purchased. Goodwill cannot be purchased separately nor can it be generated internally.

Cash paid		$ 700,000
Mortgage note payable assumed		350,000
Total price paid		$1,050,000
Less fair market values of individually		
identifiable assets:		
Accounts receivable	$ 95,000	
Merchandise inventory	100,000	
Land	240,000	
Buildings	275,000	
Equipment	200,000	
Patents	65,000	975,000
Goodwill		$ 75,000

The $75,000 is the goodwill Lenox records as an intangible asset; it records all of the other assets at their fair market values, and the liability at the amount due. Specific reasons for a company's goodwill include a good reputation, customer loyalty, superior product design, unrecorded intangible assets (because they were developed internally), and superior human resources. Since these positive factors are not individually quantifiable, when grouped together they constitute *goodwill*. The journal entry to record the purchase is:

Accounts Receivable	95,000	
Merchandise Inventory	100,000	
Land	240,000	
Buildings	275,000	
Equipment	200,000	
Patents	65,000	
Goodwill	75,000	
Cash		700,000
Mortgage Note Payable		350,000
To record the purchase of Martin Company's assets and assumption of mortgage note payable.		

Reinforcing Problem
E11–12 Determine the amount of goodwill.

As with all other intangibles, Lenox must amortize goodwill. No legal life exists for goodwill, nor can anyone accurately determine the useful life of goodwill. If, for example, the new owner made substantial changes in the method of doing business, goodwill that existed at the purchase date could rapidly disappear. Therefore, current accounting practice requires the amortization of goodwill over a period not to exceed 40 years. This requirement is necessary because the value of purchased goodwill eventually disappears. Even though it generates other goodwill in its place, the organization cannot record internally created goodwill any more than it can any other internally generated intangible assets. The entry to amortize the $75,000 goodwill over a 40-year period is:

Goodwill Amortization Expense	1,875	
Goodwill		1,875
To amortize goodwill ($75,000/40 years).		

Reporting Amortization

In Illustration 11.2, we show how often a group of representative companies amortized intangible assets for the years 1992–1995.

Amortization expense for most intangible assets discussed in this chapter appears among the operating expenses on the income statement. The account titles are all of this type: "Amortization of Goodwill (or Patents, Copyrights, Franchises, Leaseholds) Expense." Often companies report periodic amortization of leaseholds and leasehold improvements as rent expense. The 1993 tax law allows straight-line amortization over 15 years for many intangible assets (including goodwill) if they were acquired after August 10, 1993. Prior to 1993, goodwill could not be amortized for tax purposes, while several other intangible assets could be amortized.

The following intangible asset note and General Mills' reporting of amortization appeared in its 1996 annual report:

Note 1D. *Intangible Assets.* Goodwill represents the difference between purchase prices of acquired companies and the related fair values of new assets acquired and accounted for by the purchase method of accounting. Goodwill is amortized on a straight-basis over 40 years or less.

Intangible assets include an amount that offsets a minimum liability recorded for a pension plan with assets less than accumulated benefits as required by Financial Accounting Standard No. 87.

The costs of patents, copyrights and other intangible assets are amortized evenly over their estimated useful lives.

Assets Being Amortized	Number of Companies			
	1995	1994	1993	1992
Goodwill recognized in a business combination	402	395	385	383
Patents, patent rights	72	62	69	62
Trademarks, brand names, copyrights	57	52	51	50
Noncompete covenants	24	27	26	21
Licenses, franchises, memberships	24	19	19	17
Technology	14	15	15	13
Customer lists	15	13	9	13
Other—described	42	40	32	29

Source: Based on American Institute of Certified Public Accountants, *Accounting Trends & Techniques* (New York: AICPA, 1993), p. 196.

ILLUSTRATION 11.2
Intangible Assets Held by a Group of Representative Companies

Intangible Asset	Amortized over Shorter of		
	Useful Life	Legal Life	Maximum Life (years)
Patents	?	17 years	40
Copyrights	?	Life of creator plus 50 years	40
Franchises	?	No limit (unless limited by contract)	40
Trademarks; trade names	?	No limit	40
Leasehold improvements	?	Life of lease	40
Goodwill	?	No limit	40

ILLUSTRATION 11.3
Rules for Amortization of Intangible Assets

REED COMPANY
Partial Balance Sheet
June 30, 1999

Property, plant, and equipment:			
Land		$ 30,000	
Buildings	$75,000		
Less: Accumulated depreciation	45,000	30,000	
Equipment	$ 9,000		
Less: Accumulated depreciation	1,500	7,500	
Total property, plant, and equipment			$ 67,500
Natural resources:			
Mineral deposits		$300,000	
Less: Accumulated depletion		100,000	
Total natural resources			$200,000
Intangible assets:			
Patents		$ 10,000	
Goodwill		20,000	
Total intangible assets			$ 30,000

ILLUSTRATION 11.4
Partial Balance Sheet

The Audit Committee of the Board of Directors annually reviews goodwill and other intangibles. At its meeting on April 22, 1996, the Board of Director affirmed that the remaining amounts of these assets have continuing value.

In Illustration 11.3, we summarize the amortization rules for intangible assets.

Look at Illustration 11.4, a partial balance sheet for Reed Company. Unlike plant assets or natural resources, intangible assets usually are a net amount in the balance sheet.

Balance Sheet Presentation

Analyzing and Using The Financial Results—Total Assets Turnover

Objective 5
Analyze and use the
financial results—total
assets turnover.

In determining the productivity of assets, management may compare one year's assets turnover ratio to a previous year's. **Total assets turnover** shows the relationship between the dollar volume of sales and the average total assets used in the business. To calculate this ratio:

$$\text{Total assets turnover} = \frac{\text{Net sales}}{\text{Average total assets}}$$

This ratio indicates the efficiency with which a company uses its assets to generate sales. When the ratio is low relative to industry standards or the company's ratio in previous years, it could indicate an overinvestment in assets, a slow year in sales, or both. Thus, if the ratio is relatively low and there was no significant decrease in sales during the current year, management should identify and dispose of any inefficient equipment.

CompUSA
is a retailer for personal computers and related products and services.

The Procter & Gamble Company
markets more than 300 brands. Examples include Tide, Ariel, Pantene Pro-V, Pringles, and Oil of Olay.

Tyco International
manufactures many products including steel, fiber optic telecommunications cables, and circuit boards for mobile phones.

Duracell
is a leading manufacturer and marketer of batteries.

Kimball International, Inc.
manufactures and markets a broad range of diversified consumer durable products including furniture and electronics.

The total assets turnover in 1996 for several actual companies was as follows:

| Company | Net Sales ($ thousands) | Total Assets ($ thousands) | | | Turnover |
		Beginning of Year	End of Year	Average	
CompUSA	$ 3,829,786	$ 641,329	$ 909,337	$ 775,333	493.95%
Procter & Gamble . . .	35,284,000	28,125,000	27,730,000	27,927,500	126.34%
Tyco International . . .	5,089,828	3,381,461	3,953,936	3,667,699	138.77%
Duracell	2,289,600	2,419,800	2,728,500	2,574,150	88.95%
Kimball International . .	923,636	497,086	538,225	517,656	178.43%

These five companies compete in very different industries. However, they are all manufacturers. To see if each of these companies is performing above standard, management should compare its company's percentage to the industry's standard. In addition, calculating this ratio over approximately five years would help management see any trends indicating problems or confirm successful asset management.

This chapter concludes your study of accounting for long-term assets. In Chapter 12, you learn about classes of capital stock.

Understanding the Learning Objectives

Objective 1
Calculate and prepare entries for the sale, retirement, and destruction of plant assets.

- By comparing an asset's book value (cost less up-to-date accumulated depreciation) with its sales price, the company may show either a gain or a loss. If sales price is greater than book value, the company shows a gain. If sales price is less than book value, the company shows a loss. If sales price equals book value, no gain or loss results.

- When a plant asset is retired from service, the asset's cost and accumulated depreciation must be removed from the plant asset accounts.

- Plant assets are sometimes wrecked in accidents or destroyed by fire, flood, storm, and other causes. If the asset was not insured, the loss is equal to the book value. If the asset was insured, only the amount of the loss exceeding the amount to be recovered from the insurance company would be debited to a loss account.

Objective 2
Describe and record exchanges of dissimilar and similar plant assets.

- In exchanges of dissimilar assets, the firm records the asset received at either (1) the stated cash price of the new asset or (if the cash price is not stated) (2) the known fair market value of the asset given up plus any cash paid.

- In exchanges of similar assets, the firm records the new asset at (1) the cash price of the asset received or (2) the book value of the old asset plus the cash paid, whichever is lower.

In 1992, prior to the tax law change permitting the amortization of goodwill for tax purposes, ABC Corporation acquired XYZ Company for $10,000,000 cash. ABC acquired the following assets:

Accounts receivable. $80,000

	Old Book Value	Fair Market Value
Merchandise inventory . .	$ 200,000	$ 300,000
Buildings	3,000,000	4,000,000
Land	1,000,000	3,000,000
Equipment	500,000	700,000

An experienced appraiser with an excellent reputation established the fair market values of the assets. ABC also assumed the liability for paying XYZ's $50,000 of accounts payable.

John Gilbert, ABC's accountant, prepared the following journal entry to record the purchase:

Accounts Receivable	80,000	
Merchandise Inventory . . .	300,000	
Buildings	4,000,000	
Land	3,000,000	
Equipment	700,000	
Goodwill	1,970,000	
Accounts Payable . . .		50,000
Cash		10,000,000
To record the purchase of XYZ Company.		

In explaining the entry to ABC's president, Gilbert said that the assets had to be recorded at their fair market values. He also stated that the goodwill had to be amortized over a period not to exceed 40 years for accounting purposes, but that the goodwill could not be amortized for tax purposes.

The president reacted with, "It's not fair that we are prohibited from amortizing goodwill for tax purposes when it is a part of the cost of the purchase. Besides, appraisals are very inexact, and maybe some of our other assets are worth more than the one appraiser indicated. I want you to reduce goodwill down to $470,000 and assign the other $1,500,000 to the buildings and equipment. Then, we can benefit from the depreciation on these assets. If I need to find an appraiser who will support the new allocations, I will."

When Gilbert protested, the president stated, "If you are going to have a future with us, you need to be a team player. We just can't afford to lose those tax deductions." Gilbert feared that if he did not go along, he would soon be unemployed.

AN ETHICAL PERSPECTIVE
—
ABC Corporation

- Depletion charges usually are computed by the units-of-production method. Total cost is divided by the estimated number of units that are economically extractable from the property. This calculation provides a per unit depletion cost that is multiplied by the units extracted each year to obtain the depletion cost for that year.

- Depreciable assets located on extractive industry property should be depreciated over the shorter of the (1) physical life of the asset or (2) life of the natural resource. The periodic depreciation charges usually are computed using the units-of-production method. Using this method matches the life of the plant asset with the life of the natural resource.

- Only outright purchase costs are included in the acquisition cost of an intangible asset. If an intangible asset is internally generated, its cost is immediately expensed.

- Intangibles should be amortized over the shorter of (1) their economic life, (2) their legal life, or (3) 40 years. Straight-line amortization must be used unless another method can be shown to be superior.

- Total assets turnover = $\dfrac{\text{Net sales}}{\text{Average total assets}}$

- This ratio indicates the efficiency with which a company uses its assets to generate sales.

Objective 3
Determine the periodic depletion cost of a natural resource and calculate depreciation of plant assets located on extractive industry property.

Objective 4
Prepare entries for the acquisition and amortization of intangible assets.

Objective 5
Analyze and use the financial results—total assets turnover.

DEMONSTRATION PROBLEM 11–A

On January 2, 1996, Darton Company purchased a machine for $36,000 cash. The machine has an estimated useful life of six years and an estimated salvage value of $1,800. Darton uses the straight-line method of depreciation.

a. Compute the book value of the machine as of July 1, 1999.

Required

b. Assume the machine was disposed of on July 1, 1999. Prepare the journal entries to record the disposal of the machine under each of the following unrelated assumptions:
(1) The machine was sold for $12,000 cash.
(2) The machine was sold for $18,000 cash.
(3) The machine and $24,000 cash were exchanged for a new machine that had a cash price of $39,000.
(4) The machine was completely destroyed by fire. Darton expects to recover cash of $10,800 from the insurance company.

SOLUTION TO DEMONSTRATION PROBLEM 11–A

a.

DARTON COMPANY
Schedule to Compute Book Value
July 1, 1999

Cost	$36,000
Less accumulated depreciation:	
$\dfrac{\$36{,}000 - \$1{,}800}{6 \text{ years}} = \$5{,}700$ per year	
$5,700 × 3½ years = $19,950	19,950
Book value	$16,050

b. (1)

Cash	12,000	
Accumulated Depreciation—Machinery	19,950	
Loss from Disposal of Plant Assets	4,050	
Machinery		36,000
To record sale of machinery at a loss.		

(2)

Cash	18,000	
Accumulated Depreciation—Machinery	19,950	
Machinery		36,000
Gain on Disposal of Plant Assets		1,950
To record sale of machinery at a gain.		

(3)

Machinery (new)	39,000	
Accumulated Depreciation—Machinery	19,950	
Loss from Disposal of Plant Assets	1,050	
Machinery (old)		36,000
Cash		24,000
To record exchange of machines.		

(4)

Receivable from Insurance Company	10,800	
Accumulated Depreciation—Machinery	19,950	
Fire Loss	5,250	
Machinery		36,000
To record loss of machinery.		

DEMONSTRATION PROBLEM 11–B

Howard Company acquired on January 1, 1999, a tract of property containing timber at a cost of $8,000,000. After the timber is removed, the land will be worth about $3,200,000 and will be sold to another party. Costs of developing the site were $800,000. A building was erected at a cost of $160,000. The building had an estimated physical life of 20 years and will have an estimated salvage value of $80,000 when the timber is gone. It was expected that 50,000,000 board feet of timber can be economically cut. During the first year, 16,000,000 board feet were cut. Howard uses the units-of-production basis to depreciate the building.

Required   Prepare the entries to record:

a. The acquisition of the property.

b. The development costs.

c. Depletion cost for the first year.

d. Depreciation on the building for the first year.

SOLUTION TO DEMONSTRATION PROBLEM 11–B

a.

Land	3,200,000	
Timber Stands	4,800,000	
Cash		8,000,000
To record purchase of land and timber.		

b.

Timber Stands	800,000	
Cash		800,000
To record costs of development of the site.		

c.

Depletion	1,792,000	
Accumulated Depletion—Timber Stands		1,792,000
To record depletion for 1999:		
($4,800,000 + $800,000)/50,000,000 = $0.112 per board foot.		
$0.112 × 16,000,000 = $1,792,000.		

d.

Depreciation Expense—Buildings	25,600	
Accumulated Depreciation—Buildings		25,600
To record depreciation expense:		

$$\frac{\$160,000 - \$80,000}{50,000,000 \text{ board feet}} = \$0.0016 \text{ per board foot.}$$

$0.0016 × 16,000,000 = $25,600.

DEMONSTRATION PROBLEM 11–C

On January 2, 1999, Bedford Company purchased a 10-year sublease on a warehouse for $30,000. Bedford will also pay annual rent of $6,000. Bedford immediately incurred costs of $20,000 for improvements to the warehouse, such as lighting fixtures, replacement of a ceiling, heating system, and loading dock. The improvements have an estimated life of 12 years and no residual value.

Prepare the entries to record: *Required*

a. The payment for the sublease on a warehouse.

b. The rent payment for the first year.

c. The payment for the improvements.

d. Amortization of the leasehold for the first year.

e. Amortization of the leasehold improvements for the first year.

SOLUTION TO DEMONSTRATION PROBLEM 11–C

a.

Leasehold	30,000	
Cash		30,000
To record purchase of sublease on warehouse.		

b.

Rent Expense	6,000	
Cash		6,000
To record annual rent payment.		

c.

Leasehold Improvements	20,000	
Cash		20,000
To record payment for leasehold improvements.		

d.	Rent Expense		3,000	
	Leasehold			3,000

To record leasehold amortization for 1999:

$$\text{Annual amortization} = \frac{\$30,000}{10 \text{ years}}$$
$$= \$3,000$$

e.	Rent Expense		2,000	
	Leasehold Improvements			2,000

To amortize leasehold improvements:

$$\text{Annual amortization} = \frac{\$20,000}{10 \text{ years}}$$
$$= \$2,000$$

New Terms

Amortization The term used to describe the systematic write-off of the cost of an intangible asset to expense. *409*

Capital lease A lease that transfers to the lessee virtually all of the rewards and risks that accompany ownership of property. *411*

Copyright An exclusive right granted by the federal government giving protection against the illegal reproduction by others of the creator's written works, designs, and literary productions. *410*

Depletion The exhaustion of a natural resource; an estimate of the cost of the resource that was removed from its natural setting during the period. *406*

Franchise A contract between two parties granting the franchisee (the purchaser of the franchise) certain rights and privileges ranging from name identification to complete monopoly of service. *410*

Goodwill An intangible value attached to a company resulting mainly from the company's management skill or know-how and a favorable reputation with customers. Evidenced by the ability to generate an above-average rate of income on each dollar invested in the business. *413*

Intangible assets Items that have no physical characteristics but are of value because of the advantages or exclusive privileges and rights they provide to a business. *409*

Lease A contract to rent property. Grantor of the lease is the **lessor**; the party obtaining the rights to possess and use property is the **lessee**. *411*

Leasehold The rights granted under a lease. *411*

Leasehold improvement Any physical alteration made by the lessee to the leased property in which benefits are expected beyond the current accounting period. *412*

Natural resources Resources supplied by nature, such as ore deposits, mineral deposits, oil reserves, gas deposits, and timber stands supplied by nature. *405*

Operating lease A lease that does not qualify as a capital lease. *411*

Patent A right granted by the federal government giving the owner the exclusive right to manufacture, sell, lease, or otherwise benefit from an invention for a limited period. *410*

Research and development (R&D) costs Costs incurred in a planned search for new knowledge and in translating such knowledge into a new product or process. *409*

Total assets turnover Equal to Net sales/Average total assets. This ratio indicates the efficiency with which a company uses its assets to generate sales. *416*

Trademark A symbol, design, or logo used in conjunction with a particular product or company. *411*

Trade name A brand name under which a product is sold or a company does business. *411*

Wasting assets See *Natural resources.*

Self-Test

True-False

Indicate whether each of the following statements is true or false.

1. When a plant asset is still being used after it has been fully depreciated, depreciation can be taken in excess of its cost.

2. In an exchange of dissimilar assets, the new asset is recorded at the fair market value of the asset received or the fair market value of the asset given up plus cash paid, whichever is more clearly evident.

3. In calculating depletion, the residual value of acquired land containing an ore deposit is included in total costs subject to depletion.

4. All recorded intangible assets are subject to amortization.

MULTIPLE-CHOICE

Select the best answer for each of the following questions.

1. When a fully depreciated asset is still in use:
   a. Prior years' depreciation should be adjusted.
   b. The cost should be adjusted to market value.
   c. Part of the depreciation should be reversed.
   d. The cost and accumulated depreciation should remain in the ledger and no more depreciation should be taken.
   e. It should be written off the books.

2. A truck costing $45,000 and having an estimated salvage value of $4,500 and an original life of five years is exchanged for a new truck. The cash price of the new truck is $57,000, and a trade-in allowance of $22,500 is received. The old truck has been depreciated for three years using the straight-line method. The new truck would be recorded at:
   a. $55,200.
   b. $57,000.
   c. $34,500.
   d. $43,200.
   e. None of the above.

3. Land containing a mine having an estimated 1,000,000 tons of economically extractable ore is purchased for $375,000. After the ore deposit is removed, the land will be worth $75,000. If 100,000 tons of ore are mined and sold during the first year, the depletion cost charged to expense for the year is:
   a. $300,000.
   b. $37,500.
   c. $30,000.
   d. $375,000.
   e. None of the above.

4. Bren Company purchased a patent for $36,000. The patent is expected to have value for 10 years even though its legal life is 17 years. The amortization for the first year is:
   a. $36,000.
   b. $3,600.
   c. $2,118.
   d. $3,240.
   e. None of the above.

Now turn to page 429 to check your answers.

QUESTIONS

1. When depreciable plant assets are sold for cash, how is the gain or loss measured?

2. A plant asset that cost $27,000 and has a related accumulated depreciation account balance of $27,000 is still being used in business operations. Would it be appropriate to continue recording depreciation on this asset? Explain. When should the asset's cost and accumulated depreciation be removed from the accounting records?

3. A machine and $22,500 cash were exchanged for a delivery truck. How should the cost basis of the delivery truck be measured?

4. A plant asset was exchanged for a new asset of a similar type. How is the cost of the new asset determined?

5. When similar assets are exchanged, a resulting gain is not recognized. Justify this.

6. What is the proper accounting treatment for the costs of removing or dismantling a company's old plant assets?

7. a. Distinguish between depreciation, depletion, and amortization. Name two assets that are subject to depreciation, to depletion, and to amortization.
   b. Distinguish between tangible and intangible assets, and classify the assets named in part (a) accordingly.

8. A building with an estimated physical life of 40 years was constructed at the site of a coal mine. The coal mine is expected to be completely exhausted within 20 years. Over what length of time should the building be depreciated, assuming the building will be abandoned after all the coal has been extracted?

9. What are the characteristics of intangible assets? Give an example of an asset that has no physical existence but is not classified as an intangible asset.

10. What reasons justify the immediate expensing of most research and development costs?

11. Over what length of time should intangible assets be amortized?

12. Should costs incurred on internally generated intangible assets be capitalized in asset accounts?

13. Describe the typical accounting for a patent.

14. During 1999, Hardy Company incurred $123,000 of research and development costs in its laboratory to develop a patent that was granted on December 29, 1999. Legal fees (outside counsel) and other costs associated with registration of the patent totaled $22,800. What amount should be recorded as a patent on December 29, 1999?

15. What is a capital lease? What features may characterize a capital lease?

16. What is the difference between a leasehold (under an operating lease contract) and a leasehold improvement? Is there any difference in the accounting procedures applicable to each?

17. Walt Company leased a tract of land for 40 years at an agreed annual rental fee of $18,000. The effective date of the lease was July 1, 1998. During the last six months of 1998, Walt constructed a building on the land at a cost of $450,000. The building was placed in operation on January 2, 1999, at which time it was estimated to have a physical life of 50 years. Over what period should the building be depreciated? Why?

18. You note that a certain store seems to have a steady stream of regular customers, a favorable location, courteous employees, high-quality merchandise, and a reputation for fairness in dealing with customers, employees, and suppliers. Does it follow automatically

that this business should have goodwill recorded as an asset? Explain.

percentage did the intangible assets balance represent of the 1995 and 1996 total assets?

The Coca-Cola Company

MAYTAG

19. Real World Question From the consolidated balance sheet of The Coca-Cola Company in the annual report booklet, identify the 1996 intangible assets ending balance. What percentage increase does this amount represent over the 1995 ending balance and what

20. Real World Question Based on the financial statements of Maytag Corporation contained in the annual report booklet, what was the 1996 allowance for amortization of intangibles? What percentage change does this represent from the preceding year?

EXERCISES

Exercise 11–1
Record sale of equipment; account for removal costs (L.O. 1)

Plant equipment originally costing $32,400, on which $21,600 of up-to-date depreciation has been accumulated, was sold for $8,100.

a.   Prepare the journal entry to record the sale.

b.   Prepare the entry to record the sale of the equipment if $90 of removal costs were incurred to allow the equipment to be moved.

Exercise 11–2
Update depreciation and record sale of truck (L.O. 1)

On August 31, 1998, Hutch Company sold a truck for $6,900 cash. The truck was acquired on January 1, 1995, at a cost of $17,400. Depreciation of $10,800 on the truck has been recorded through December 31, 1997, using the straight-line method, four-year expected useful life, and an expected salvage value of $3,000.

Prepare the journal entries to update the depreciation on the truck on August 31, 1998, and to record the sale of the truck.

Exercise 11–3
Record the destruction of machinery by fire—uninsured and insured asset (L.O. 1)

A machine costing $120,000, on which $90,000 of up-to-date depreciation has been accumulated, was completely destroyed by fire. What journal entry should record the machine's destruction and the resulting fire loss under each of the following unrelated assumptions?

a.   The machine was not insured.

b.   The machine was insured, and it is estimated that $22,500 will be recovered from the insurance company.

Exercise 11–4
Record exchange of automobiles (L.O. 2)

Kale Company owned an automobile acquired on January 1, 1996, at a cash cost of $35,100; at that time, the automobile was estimated to have a useful life of four years and a $2,700 salvage value. Depreciation has been recorded through December 31, 1998, on a straight-line basis. On January 1, 1999, the automobile was traded for a new automobile. The old automobile had a fair market value (trade-in allowance) of $6,750. Cash of $31,050 was paid.

Prepare the journal entry to record the trade-in under generally accepted accounting principles.

Exercise 11–5
Record variety of cases involving sale, retirement, or exchange of equipment (L.O. 1, 2)

Equipment costing $330,000, on which $225,000 of up-to-date accumulated depreciation has been recorded, was disposed of on January 2, 1998. What journal entries are required to record the equipment's disposal under each of the following unrelated assumptions?

a.   The equipment was sold for $120,000 cash.

b.   The equipment was sold for $87,000 cash.

c.   The equipment was retired from service and hauled to the junkyard. No material was salvaged.

d.   The equipment was exchanged for similar equipment having a cash price of $450,000. A trade-in allowance of $150,000 from the cash price was received, and the balance was paid in cash.

e.   The equipment was exchanged for similar equipment having a cash price of $450,000. A trade-in allowance of $75,000 was received, and the balance was paid in cash.

Exercise 11–6
Compute depletion cost per ton (L.O. 3)

Nola Mining Company purchased a tract of land containing ore for $630,000. After spending $90,000 in exploration costs, the company determined that 600,000 tons of ore existed on the tract but only 500,000 tons could be economically removed. No other costs were incurred. When the company finishes with the tract, it estimates the land will be worth $180,000. Determine the depletion cost per ton.

Boyd Company paid $7,200,000 for the right to extract all of the mineral-bearing ore, estimated at 10 million tons, that can be economically extracted from a certain tract of land. During the first year, Boyd Company extracted 1,000,000 tons of the ore and sold 800,000 tons. What part of the $7,200,000 should be charged to expense during the first year?

Exercise 11–7
Determine depletion cost and expense (L.O. 3)

The Slate Mining Company acquired a tract of land for mining purposes and erected a building on-site at a cost of $675,000 and having no salvage value. Though the building has a useful life of 10 years, the mining operations are expected to last only 6 years. The company has determined that 800,000 tons of ore exist on the tract but only 600,000 tons can be economically removed. If 100,000 tons of ore are extracted in the first year of operations, what is the appropriate depreciation charge using the units-of-production method?

Exercise 11–8
Compute depreciation charge on plant asset used for mining purposes (L.O. 3)

Talse Company purchased a patent on January 1, 1984, at a total cost of $61,200. In January 1995, the company hired an outside law firm and successfully defended the patent in a lawsuit. The legal fees amounted to $13,500. What will be the amount of patent cost amortized in 1998? (The useful life of the patent is the same as its legal life—17 years.)

Exercise 11–9
Determine patent cost and periodic amortization (L.O. 4)

Don Jackson paid Hungry Hannah's Hamburgers $54,000 for the right to operate a fast-food restaurant in Thomasville under the Hungry Hannah's name. Jackson also agreed to pay an operating fee of 0.5% of sales for advertising and other services rendered by Hungry Hannah's. Jackson began operations on January 2, 1998. Sales for 1998 amounted to $540,000.

Give the entries to record the payment of the $54,000 and to record expenses incurred relating to the right to use the Hungry Hannah's name.

Exercise 11–10
Record franchise; record accrued franchise fees and franchise amortization (L.O. 4)

Lem Company leased the first three floors in a building under an operating lease contract for a 10-year period beginning January 1, 1998. The company paid $240,000 in cash (not representing a specific period's rent) and agreed to make annual payments equal to 1% of the first $1,500,000 of sales and 0.5% of all sales over $1,500,000. Sales for 1998 amounted to $4,500,000. Payment of the annual amount will be made in January 1999.

Prepare journal entries to record the cash payment of January 1, 1998, and the proper expense to be recognized for the use of the space in the leased building for 1998.

Exercise 11–11
Record leasehold; record rent accrued and leasehold amortization (L.O. 4)

Rye Company purchased all of the assets of Shef Company for $900,000. Rye Company also agreed to assume responsibility for Shef Company's liabilities of $90,000. The fair market value of the assets acquired was $810,000. How much goodwill should be recorded in this transaction? Give the journal entry to record this transaction.

Exercise 11–12
Determine the amount of goodwill (L.O. 4)

PROBLEMS

Ray, Inc., purchased a new 1999 model automobile on December 31, 1999. The cash price of the new automobile was $28,080, from which Ray received a trade-in allowance of $4,320 for a 1997 model traded in. The 1997 model had been acquired on January 1, 1997, at a cost of $20,700. Depreciation has been recorded on the 1997 model through December 31, 1998, using the straight-line method, an expected four-year useful life, and an expected salvage value of $2,700.

Problem 11–1
Update depreciation and record exchange of automobiles (L.O. 2)

a.   Record depreciation expense for 1999.
b.   Prepare the journal entries needed to record the exchange of automobiles.

Required

On January 1, 1996, Wood Company purchased a truck for $43,200 cash. The truck has an estimated useful life of six years and an expected salvage value of $5,400. Depreciation on the truck was computed using the straight-line method.

Problem 11–2
Update depreciation and record six cases of asset disposal (L.O. 1, 2)

a.   Prepare a schedule showing the computation of the book value of the truck on December 31, 1998.
b.   Prepare the journal entry to record depreciation for the six months ended June 30, 1999.
c.   Prepare journal entries to record the disposal of the truck on June 30, 1999, under each of the following unrelated assumptions:
   (1)   The truck was sold for $3,600 cash.
   (2)   The truck was sold for $25,200 cash.
   (3)   The truck was scrapped. Used parts valued at $6,660 were salvaged.

Required

(4) The truck (which has a fair market value of $10,800) and $32,400 of cash were exchanged for a used back hoe that did not have a known market value.

(5) The truck and $29,700 cash were exchanged for another truck that had a cash price of $51,300.

(6) The truck was stolen July 1, and insurance proceeds of $7,560 were expected.

Problem 11–3
Update depreciation and record exchange of plant asset for similar asset (L.O. 2)

Kine Company purchased a new Model II computer October 1, 1998. Cash price of the new computer was $24,960; Jackson received a trade-in allowance of $9,300 from the cash price for a Model I computer. The old computer was acquired on January 1, 1996, at a cost of $23,040. Depreciation has been recorded through December 31, 1997, on a straight-line basis, with an estimated useful life of four years and $3,840 expected salvage value.

Required   Prepare the journal entries to record the exchange.

Problem 11–4
Record leasehold amortization; record depreciation and trade-in (L.O. 2, 4)

On July 1, 1998, Morgan Company had the following balances in some of its accounts:

	Asset	Accumulated Depreciation
Land	$ 672,000	
Leasehold	252,000	
Buildings	3,151,680	$369,768
Equipment	1,370,880	436,800
Trucks	238,560	71,652

Additional data

1. The leasehold covers a plot of ground leased on July 1, 1993, for a period of 25 years under an operating lease.

2. The office building is on the leased land and was completed on July 1, 1994, at a cost of $967,680; its physical life is set at 40 years. The factory building is on the owned land and was completed on July 1, 1993, at a cost of $2,184,000; its life is also set at 40 years with no expected salvage value.

3. The equipment has a 15-year useful life with no expected salvage value.

4. The company owns three trucks—A, B, and C. Truck A, purchased on July 1, 1996, at a cost of $53,760, had an expected useful life of three years and a salvage value of $3,360. Truck B, purchased on January 2, 1997, at a cost of $84,000, had an expected life of four years and an estimated salvage value of $6,720. Truck C, purchased on January 2, 1998, at a cost of $100,800, had an expected life of five years and an estimated salvage value of $10,080.

The following transactions occurred in the fiscal year ended June 30, 1999:

1998
July 1   Rent for July 1, 1998, through June 30, 1999, on leased land was paid, $31,920.

Oct. 1   Truck A was traded in on truck D. Cash price of the new truck was $107,520. Cash of $90,720 was paid. Truck D has an expected life of four years and a salvage value of $5,880.

1999
Feb. 2   Truck B was sold for $47,040 cash.

June 1   Truck C was completely demolished in an accident. The truck was not insured.

Required   Prepare journal entries to record these transactions and the necessary June 30, 1999, adjusting entries. Use the straight-line depreciation method.

Problem 11–5
Determine depletion for period and depreciation on building and mining equipment; compute average cost per ton of ore mined (L.O. 3)

In December 1997, Brown Company acquired a mine for $2,700,000. The mine contained an estimated 10 million tons of ore. It was also estimated that the land would have a value of $240,000 when the mine was exhausted and that only 4 million tons of ore could be economically extracted. A building was erected on the property at a cost of $360,000. The building had an estimated useful life of 35 years and no salvage value. Specialized mining equipment was installed at a cost of $495,000. This equipment had an estimated useful life of seven years and an estimated $33,000 salvage value. The company began operating on January 1, 1998, and put all of its assets into use on that date. During the year ended December 31, 1998, 400,000 tons of ore were extracted. The company decided to use the units-of-production method to record depreciation on the building and the straight-line method to record depreciation on the equipment.

Prepare journal entries to record the depletion and depreciation charges for the year ended December 31, 1998. Show calculations.

Required

Trask Company purchased a patent for $108,000 on January 2, 1998. The patent was estimated to have a useful life of 10 years. The $108,000 cost was properly charged to an asset account and amortized in 1998. On January 1, 1999, the company incurred legal and court costs of $32,400 in a successful defense of the patent in a lawsuit. The legal work was performed by an outside law firm.

Problem 11–6
Record cost and amortization of patent (L.O. 4)

a. Compute the patent amortization expense for 1998 and give the entry to record it.

b. Compute the patent amortization expense for 1999 and give the entry to record it.

Required

Selected transactions and other data for Grant Company:

Problem 11–7
Record amortization expense for a variety of intangible assets (L.O. 4)

a. The company purchased a patent in early January 1995 for $144,000 and began amortizing it over 10 years. In early January 1997, the company hired an outside law firm and successfully defended the patent in an infringement suit at a cost of $38,400.

b. Research and development costs incurred in 1997 of $43,200 were expected to provide benefits over the three succeeding years.

c. On January 2, 1998, the company rented space in a warehouse for five years at an annual fee of $9,600. Rent for the first and last years was paid in advance.

d. A total of $96,000 was spent uniformly throughout 1998 by the company in promoting its lesser known trademark, which is expected to have an indefinite life.

e. In January 1996, the company purchased all of the assets and assumed all of the liabilities of another company, paying $192,000 more than the fair market value of all identifiable assets acquired, less the liabilities assumed. The company expects the benefits for which it paid the $192,000 to last 10 years.

For each of these unrelated transactions, prepare journal entries to record only those entries required for 1998. Note any items that do not require an entry in 1998.

Required

ALTERNATE PROBLEMS

Orr Company traded in an automobile that cost $18,000 and on which $15,000 of up-to-date depreciation has been recorded for a new automobile with a cash price of $34,500. The company received a trade-in allowance (its fair value) for the old automobile of $2,100 and paid the balance in cash.

Problem 11–1A
Record exchange of automobiles (L.O. 2)

Record the exchange of automobiles.

Required

On January 2, 1996, Blake Company purchased a delivery truck for $78,750 cash. The truck has an estimated useful life of six years and an estimated salvage value of $6,750. The straight-line method of depreciation is being used.

Problem 11–2A
Update depreciation and record six cases of asset disposal (L.O. 1, 2)

Required

a. Prepare a schedule showing the computation of the book value of the truck on December 31, 1998.

b. Assume the truck is to be disposed of on July 1, 1999. Prepare the journal entry to record depreciation for the six months ended June 30, 1999.

c. Prepare the journal entries to record the disposal of the truck on July 1, 1999, under each of the following unrelated assumptions:
   1. The truck was sold for $26,250 cash.
   2. The truck was sold for $48,000 cash.
   3. The truck was retired from service, and it is expected that $20,625 will be received from the sale of salvaged materials.
   4. The truck and $60,000 cash were exchanged for office equipment that had a cash price of $105,000.
   5. The truck and $67,500 cash were exchanged for a new delivery truck that had a cash price of $112,500.
   6. The truck was completely destroyed in an accident. Cash of $25,500 is expected to be recovered from the insurance company.

Problem 11–3A
Update depreciation and
record exchange of plant
asset for similar asset
(L.O. 2)

Eagle Moving Company purchased a new moving van on October 1, 1998. The cash price of the new van was $33,750, and the company received a trade-in allowance of $5,600 for a 1996 model. The balance was paid in cash. The 1996 model had been acquired on January 1, 1996, at a cost of $22,500. Depreciation has been recorded through December 31, 1997, on a straight-line basis, with three years of expected useful life and no expected salvage value.

Required

Prepare journal entries to update the depreciation and to record the exchange of the moving vans.

Problem 11–4A
Record leasehold amortization; record depreciation
and trade-in (L.O. 2, 4)

On January 1, 1998, Moyer Company had the following balances in some of its accounts:

	Asset	Accumulated Depreciation
Land	$ 624,000	
Leasehold	780,000	
Buildings	3,425,760	$ 286,650
Equipment	2,995,200	1,389,960
Trucks	449,280	158,790

Additional data

1. The leasehold covers a plot of ground leased on January 1, 1994, for a period of 20 years.

2. Building No. 1 is on the owned land and was completed on July 1, 1997, at a cost of $1,965,600; its life is set at 40 years with no salvage value. Building No. 2 is on the leased land and was completed on July 1, 1994, at a cost of $1,460,160; its life is also set at 40 years with no expected salvage value.

3. The equipment had an expected useful life of eight years with no estimated salvage value.

4. Truck A, purchased on January 1, 1996, at a cost of $149,760, had an expected useful life of 2½ years and a salvage value of $9,360. Truck B, purchased on July 1, 1996, at a cost of $131,040, had an expected life of two years and an estimated salvage value of $21,840. Truck C, purchased on July 1, 1997, at a cost of $168,480, had an expected life of three years and an estimated salvage value of $21,060.

The following transactions occurred in 1998:

Jan. 2 Rent for 1998 on leased land was paid, $87,360.

April 1 Truck B was traded in for truck D. The cash price of the new truck was $149,760. A trade-in allowance of $28,080 was granted from the cash price. The balance was paid in cash. Truck D has an expected life of 2½ years and an estimated salvage value of $9,360.

1 Truck A was sold for $28,080 cash.

Required

Prepare journal entries to record the 1998 transactions and the necessary December 31, 1998, adjusting entries, assuming a calendar-year accounting period. Use the straight-line depreciation method.

Problem 11–5A
Determine depletion for
period and depreciation
on mining equipment;
compute average cost per
ton of ore mined (L.O. 3)

On January 2, 1998, York Mining Company acquired land with ore deposits at a cash cost of $1,800,000. Exploration and development costs amounted to $192,000. The residual value of the land is expected to be $360,000. The ore deposits contain an estimated 6 million tons. Present technology will allow the economical extraction of only 85% of the total deposit. Machinery, equipment, and temporary sheds were installed at a cost of $255,000. The assets will have no further value to the company when the ore body is exhausted; they have a physical life of 12 years. In 1998, 200,000 tons of ore were extracted. The company expects the mine to be exhausted in 10 years, with sharp variations in annual production.

Required

a. Compute the depletion charge for 1998. Round to the nearest cent.

b. Compute the depreciation charge for 1998 under the units-of-production method.

c. If all other mining costs, except depletion, amounted to $1,260,000, what was the average cost per ton mined in 1998? (The depreciation calculated in **b** is included in the $1,260,000.)

East Company spent $249,900 to purchase a patent on January 2, 1998. Management assumes that the patent will be useful during its full legal life. In January 1999, the company hired an outside law firm and successfully defended the patent in a lawsuit at a cost of $48,000. Also, in January 1999, the company paid $72,000 to obtain patents that could, if used by competitors, make the earlier East patent useless. The purchased patents will never be used.

Give the entries for 1998 and 1999 to record the information relating to the patents.

Following are selected transactions and other data relating to Long Company for the year ended December 31, 1998.

a. The company rented the second floor of a building for five years on January 2, 1998, and paid the annual rent of $18,000 for the first and fifth years in advance.

b. In 1997, the company incurred legal fees of $54,000 paid to an outside law firm in applying for a patent and paid a fee of $18,000 to a former employee who conceived a device that substantially reduced the cost of manufacturing one of the company's products. The patent on the device has a market value of $540,000 and is expected to be useful for 10 years.

c. In 1997, the company entered into a 10-year operating lease on several floors of a building, paying $36,000 in cash immediately and agreeing to pay $18,000 at the end of each of the 10 years of life in the lease. The company then incurred costs of $72,000 to install partitions, shelving, and fixtures. These items would normally last 25 years.

d. The company spent $21,600 promoting a trademark in a manner that it believed enhanced the value of the trademark considerably. The trademark has an indefinite life.

e. The company incurred costs amounting to $180,000 in 1997 and $234,000 in 1998 for research and development of new products that are expected to enhance the company's revenues for at least five years.

f. The company paid $180,000 to the author of a book that the company published on July 2, 1998. Sales of the book are expected to be made over a two-year period from that date.

For each of the situations just described, prepare only the journal entries to record the expense applicable to 1998.

Problem 11–6A
Record cost and amortization of patent (L.O. 4)

Required

Problem 11–7A
Record amortization expense for a variety of intangible assets (L.O. 4)

Required

BEYOND THE NUMBERS–CRITICAL THINKING

During your audit examination of the Shirley Company's Plant, Property, and Equipment accounts, the following transaction came to your attention. On January 2, 1998, machine A was exchanged for machine B. Shirley Company acquired machine A for $90,000 on January 2, 1996. Machine A had an estimated useful life of four years and no salvage value, and the machine was depreciated on the straight-line basis. Machine B had a cash price of $108,000. In addition to machine A, cash of $30,000 was given up in the exchange. Machine B has an estimated useful life of five years and no salvage value, and the machine is being depreciated using the straight-line method. Upon further analysis, you discovered that the company recorded the transaction as an exchange of dissimilar assets instead of an exchange of similar assets. You must now determine the following:

a. What journal entry did the Shirley Company make when it recorded the exchange of machines? (Show computations.)

b. What journal entry should the Shirley Company have made to record the exchange of machines?

c. Assume the error was discovered on December 31, 1999, before adjusting journal entries have been made. What journal entries should be made to correct the accounting records? (Adjustments of prior years' net income because of errors should be debited or credited to Retained Earnings.) What adjusting journal entry should be made to record depreciation for 1999? (Ignore income taxes.)

d. What effect did the error have on reported net income for 1998? (Ignore income taxes.)

e. How should machine B be reported on the December 31, 1999, balance sheet?

Business Decision Case 11–1
Record exchange of similar assets; adjust accounts for errors in accounting for depreciable assets (L.O. 2)

Business Decision Case 11–2
Record purchase of two businesses and explain differences between the two; advise client as to which company should be purchased (L.O. 4)

Currently, many corporations are looking for acquisition opportunities. Tyre, Inc., is trying to decide whether to buy Amite Company or Beauman Company. Tyre, Inc., has hired you as a consultant to analyze the two companies' financial information and to determine the more advantageous acquisition. Your review of the companies' books has revealed that both Amite and Beauman have assets with the following book values and fair market values:

	Book Value	Fair Market Value
Accounts receivable	$150,000	$ 150,000
Inventories	450,000	750,000
Land	375,000	675,000
Buildings	450,000	1,050,000
Equipment	180,000	300,000
Patents	120,000	150,000

Liabilities assumed on the purchase of either company include accounts payable, $300,000, and notes payable, $75,000.

The only difference between the companies is that Amite has net income that is about average for the industry, while Beauman's net income is greatly above average for the industry.

Required

Top-level management at Tyre, Inc., has asked you to respond in writing to the following possible situations:

a. Assume Tyre, Inc., can buy Amite Company for $2,700,000 or Beauman Company for $3,450,000. Prepare the journal entries to record the acquisition of Amite Company and Beauman Company. What accounts for the difference between the purchase price of the two companies?

b. Assume Tyre, Inc, can buy either company for $2,700,000. Write a report for Tyre, Inc., advising which company to buy.

Annual Report Analysis 11–3
Calculate and discuss total assets turnover (L.O. 5)

The mission of Rational Software Corporation is to ensure the success of customers constructing the software systems that they depend on.

Using the following excerpt from Rational Software's 1996 annual report, calculate the firm's total assets turnover for 1995 and 1996. (Amounts are in $ thousands.)

	1996	1995	1994
Net sales	$91,107	$72,899	$70,343
Total assets	$85,674	$38,000	$39,343

In a written report, discuss the meaning of the total assets turnover ratio and what the ratio means to management and investors. Use the total assets turnover ratios you computed for Rational Software as an example in your report.

Ethics Case 11–4
Answer questions regarding ethics case

Based on the situation described in the ethics case on page 417 regarding ABC Corporation, respond in writing to the following questions.

a. Depending on his actions, what are the possible consequences for John Gilbert in this situation?

b. Assuming that the president cannot find another appraiser to support the new allocations, what would you do if you were Gilbert?

c. If the president can find a reputable appraiser to support these new allocations, what would you do if you were Gilbert?

Group Project 11–5
Make intangible assets presentation

In teams of two or three students, find a recent annual report that includes intangible assets on the balance sheet. Select one member of each team to give an informal presentation discussing intangible asset disclosures on the face of the statements and in the notes to the financial statements. All members should be prepared to discuss intangible asset disclosures from their annual report in detail.

Group Project 11–6
Perform library project on accounting for research and development costs

In a group of one or two other students, go to the library and locate *Statement of Financial Accounting Standards No. 2,* "Accounting for Research and Development Costs," published by the Financial Accounting Standards Board. Write a report to your instructor giving the highlights of the standard. For instance, what alternatives were considered and why did the board conclude that all research and development costs should be expensed when incurred?

In a group of one or two other students, go to the library and locate *Statement of Financial Accounting Standards No. 121,* "Accounting for the Impairment of Long-Lived Assets and for Long-Lived Assets to Be Disposed Of," published by the Financial Accounting Standards Board. Write a report to your instructor giving the highlights of the standard. For instance, what does "impairment" mean and what are its causes? How can one determine that impairment of an asset has possibly occurred? Also review some of the background information as to why this was important enough for the FASB to act.

Group Project 11–7
Perform library project on accounting for the impairment of long-lived assets

USING THE INTERNET—A VIEW OF THE REAL WORLD

Visit the Accounting News Network at Microsoft's website:
http://www.microsoft.com/smallbiz/ann/
Click on each icon to investigate the information available at this site. Browse any of the areas that look interesting. How would accounting practitioners make good use of this site? In a report to your instructor, summarize the features available at this site.

Internet Project 11–8
Check out Microsoft's Accounting News Network

Visit the Small Business Administration site at:
http://www.sba.gov
Suppose you wanted to start a small business. What helpful information would you find at this site? Would this site provide information on how to finance the business? Browse around this site to see what it offers. Then write a report to your instructor summarizing the types of helpful information this site provides.

Internet Project 11–9
Investigate the Small Business Administration site

ANSWERS TO SELF-TEST

TRUE-FALSE

1. **False.** No more depreciation can be taken on a fully depreciated plant asset.
2. **True.** The new asset is recorded at the fair market value of the asset received or given up, whichever is more clearly evident.
3. **False.** The residual value of land should be deducted from total costs subject to depletion.
4. **True.** All recorded intangible assets should be amortized over their economic life, their legal life, or 40 years, whichever is shorter.

MULTIPLE-CHOICE

1. **d.** The cost and accumulated depreciation should not be removed from the accounts until the disposal of the asset.
2. **a.** On the date of exchange, the book value of the old truck is $20,700 ($45,000 minus accumulated depreciation of $24,300). The trade-in allowance of $22,500 indicates a gain on exchange of $1,800. In an exchange of similar assets, a gain is not recognized, but reduces the cost of a new asset. Therefore, the cost of the new truck is $55,200 ($57,000 minus $1,800), and no gain is recognized.

3. **c.** The depletion charge for the first year is:

$$\text{Depletion charge per ton} = (\$375,000 - \$75,000)/1,000,000$$
$$= \$0.30$$

$$\text{Depletion charge for the year} = \$0.30 \times 100,000$$
$$= \$30,000$$

Since all of the ore that was extracted was sold, all of the $30,000 is expensed as cost of ore sold.

4. **b.** The patent is amortized over 10 years:

$$\text{Annual amortization expense} = \$36,000/10$$
$$= \$3,600$$

IV

SOURCES OF EQUITY CAPITAL FOR MANAGEMENT'S USE IN PRODUCING REVENUES

A MANAGER'S PERSPECTIVE

Judy Knighten
Senior Sales Development Manager
The Coca-Cola Company

I call on retailers such as grocery stores and convenience stores based in Atlanta that are serviced by multiple Coca-Cola bottlers. Since our bottlers are all independent of The Coca-Cola Company, my primary responsibilities revolve around coordinating sales between the bottlers and the retail accounts.

I work with my accounts and Coca-Cola bottlers to develop marketing programs that will drive sales of Coca-Cola products. Profitability analyses are used to determine the effectiveness of our sales programs.

I also manage a budget and ensure the budget is allocated properly to the bottlers. If I don't understand the accounting functions, I can't effectively work with the finance group to ensure a reasonable budget is allocated for my accounts. Companies are bottom-line oriented these days, so you have to understand how the numbers are determined and what they mean in order to get the resources you need to achieve your objectives.

It's also important to understand how a profit-and-loss statement is used to make decisions, or I could actually end up losing money. For example, if I don't understand the systems my retail accounts are using to account for inventory, I won't be able to put together the most effective plan for them, and I could potentially lose business.

My top three objectives as a sales manager are based on sales in the Atlanta market. In order to be an effective sales manager, I need to understand basic financial information so I can make sound business decisions that will meet my objective of growing sales for both our retail partners and Coca-Cola bottlers.

12

STOCKHOLDERS' EQUITY
CLASSES OF CAPITAL STOCK

In this chapter, you study the corporate form of business organization in greater detail than in preceding chapters. Although corporations are fewer in number than single proprietorships and partnerships, corporations possess the bulk of our business capital and currently supply us with most of our goods and services.

This chapter discusses the advantages and disadvantages of the corporation, how to form and direct a corporation, and some of the unique situations encountered in accounting for and reporting on the different classes of capital stock.

THE CORPORATION

A **corporation** is an entity recognized by law as possessing an existence separate and distinct from its owners; that is, it is a separate legal entity. Endowed with many of the rights and obligations possessed by a person, a corporation can enter into contracts in its own name; buy, sell, or hold property; borrow money; hire and fire employees; and sue and be sued.

Corporations have a remarkable ability to obtain the huge amounts of capital necessary for large-scale business operations. Corporations acquire their capital by issuing **shares of stock;** these are the units into which corporations divide their ownership. Investors buy shares of stock in a corporation for two basic reasons. First, investors expect the value of their shares to increase over time so that the stock may be sold in the future at a profit. Second, while investors hold stock, they expect the corporation to pay them dividends (usually in cash) in return for using their money. Chapter 13 discusses the various kinds of dividends and their accounting treatment.

Advantages of the Corporate Form of Business

Corporations have many advantages over single proprietorships and partnerships. The major advantages a corporation has over a single proprietorship are the same advantages a partnership has over a single proprietorship. Although corporations have more

LEARNING OBJECTIVES

After studying this chapter, you should be able to:

1. State the advantages and disadvantages of the corporate form of business.

2. List the values commonly associated with capital stock and give their definitions.

3. List the various kinds of stock and describe the differences between them.

4. Present in proper form the stockholders' equity section of a balance sheet.

5. Account for the issuances of stock for cash and other assets.

(continued)

433

(concluded)

6. Determine book values of both preferred and common stock.

7. Analyze and use the financial results--return on average common stockholders' equity.

Objective 1
State the advantages and disadvantages of the corporate form of business.

Real World Example
In the early 1990s, there were more than 3.5 million corporations in the United States out of a total of over 18 million enterprises. Corporate total revenues were in excess of $9 trillion. This represented 90% of the total revenues generated in the nation. Source: U.S. Bureau of Census, *Statistical Abstract of the United States* (Washington, D.C.: U.S. Government Printing Office, 1991), p. 525.

owners than partnerships, both have a broader base for investment, risk, responsibilities, and talent than do single proprietorships. Since corporations are more comparable to partnerships than to single proprietorships, the following discussion of advantages contrasts the partnership with the corporation.

1. **Easy transfer of ownership.** In a partnership, a partner cannot transfer ownership in the business to another person if the other partners do not want the new person involved in the partnership. In a publicly held (owned by many stockholders) corporation, shares of stock are traded on a stock exchange between unknown parties; one owner usually cannot dictate to whom another owner can or cannot sell shares.

2. **Limited liability.** Each partner in a partnership is personally responsible for all the debts of the business. In a corporation, the stockholders are not personally responsible for its debts; the maximum amount a stockholder can lose is the amount of his or her investment. However, when a small, closely held corporation (owned by only a few stockholders) borrows money, banks and lending institutions often require an officer of the small corporation to sign the loan agreement. Then, the officer has to repay the loan if the corporation does not.

3. **Continuous existence of the entity.** In a partnership, many circumstances, such as the death of a partner, can terminate the business entity. These same circumstances have no effect on a corporation because it is a legal entity, separate and distinct from its owners.

4. **Easy capital generation.** The easy transfer of ownership and the limited liability of stockholders are attractive features to potential investors. Thus, it is relatively easy for a corporation to raise capital by issuing shares of stock to many investors. Corporations with thousands of stockholders are not uncommon.

5. **Professional management.** Generally, the partners in a partnership are also the managers of that business, regardless of whether they have the necessary expertise to manage a business. In a publicly held corporation, most of the owners (stockholders) do not participate in the day-to-day operations and management of the entity. They hire professionals to run the business on a daily basis.

6. **Separation of owners and entity.** Since the corporation is a separate legal entity, the owners do not have the power to bind the corporation to business contracts. This feature eliminates the potential problem of mutual agency that exists between partners in a partnership. In a corporation, one stockholder cannot jeopardize other stockholders through poor decision making.

Disadvantages of the Corporate Form of Business

Note to the Student
How do income tax laws for regular corporations differ from partnership and proprietorship income tax laws? *Answer:* A regular corporation pays income tax on its net income. Then its stockholders pay taxes on dividends received. Partnerships and proprietorships pay no tax on their business income. Their net income becomes the taxable income of the owners.

The corporate form of business has the following disadvantages:

1. **Double taxation.** Because a corporation is a separate legal entity, its net income is subject to double taxation. The corporation pays a tax on its income, and stockholders pay a tax on corporate income received as dividends.

2. **Government regulation.** Because corporations are created by law, they are subject to greater regulation and control than single proprietorships and partnerships.

3. **Entrenched, inefficient management.** A corporation may be burdened with an inefficient management that remains in control by using corporate funds to solicit the needed stockholder votes to back its positions. Stockholders scattered across the country, who individually own only small portions of a corporation's stock, find it difficult to organize and oppose existing management.

4. **Limited ability to raise creditor capital.** The limited liability of stockholders makes a corporation an attractive means for accumulating stockholder capital. At the same time, this limited liability feature restrains the amount of creditor capital a corporation can amass because creditors cannot look to stockholders to pay the debts of a corporation. Thus, beyond a certain point, creditors do not

lend some corporations money without the personal guarantee of a stockholder or officer of the corporation to repay the loan if the corporation does not.

Corporations are chartered by the state. Each state has a corporation act that permits the formation of corporations by qualified persons. **Incorporators** are persons seeking to bring a corporation into existence. Most state corporation laws require a minimum of three incorporators, each of whom must be of legal age, and a majority of whom must be citizens of the United States. **Incorporating**

The laws of each state view a corporation organized in that state as a **domestic corporation** and a corporation organized in any other state as a **foreign corporation.** If a corporation intends to conduct business solely within one state, it normally seeks incorporation in that state because most state laws are not as severe for domestic corporations as for foreign corporations. Corporations conducting interstate business usually incorporate in the state that has laws most advantageous to the corporation being formed. Important considerations in choosing a state are the powers granted to the corporation, the taxes levied, the defenses permitted against hostile takeover attempts by others, and the reports required by the state.

Once incorporators agree on the state in which to incorporate, they apply for a corporate charter. A **corporate charter** is a contract between the state and the incorporators, and their successors, granting the corporation its legal existence. The application for the corporation's charter is called the **articles of incorporation.** **Articles of Incorporation**

After supplying the information requested in the incorporation application form, incorporators file the articles with the proper office in the state of incorporation. Each state requires different information in the articles of incorporation, but most states ask for the following:

1. Name of corporation.
2. Location of principal offices.
3. Purposes of business.
4. Number of shares of stock authorized, class or classes of shares, and voting and dividend rights of each class of shares.
5. Value of assets paid in by the incorporators (the stockholders who organize the corporation).
6. Limitations on authority of the management and owners of the corporation.

On approving the articles, the state office (frequently the secretary of state's office) grants the charter and creates the corporation.

As soon as the corporation obtains the charter, it is authorized to operate its business. The incorporators call the first meeting of the stockholders. Two of the purposes of this meeting are to elect a board of directors and to adopt the bylaws of the corporation. **Bylaws**

The **bylaws** are a set of rules or regulations adopted by the board of directors of a corporation to govern the conduct of corporate affairs. The bylaws must be in agreement with the laws of the state and the policies and purposes in the corporate charter. The bylaws contain, along with other information, provisions for: (1) the place, date, and manner of calling the annual stockholders' meeting; (2) the number of directors and the method for electing them; (3) the duties and powers of the directors; and (4) the method for selecting officers of the corporation.

Organization costs are the costs of organizing a corporation, such as state incorporation fees and legal fees applicable to incorporation. The firm debits these costs to an account called *Organization Costs.* The Organization Costs account is an asset because the costs yield benefits over the life of the corporation; if the fees had not been paid, no corporate entity would exist. Since the account is classified on the **Organization Costs**

balance sheet as an intangible asset, it is amortized over a period not to exceed 40 years. Most organizations write off these costs fairly rapidly because they are small in amount.

As an illustration, assume that De-Leed Corporation pays state incorporation fees of $10,000 and attorney's fees of $5,000 for services rendered related to the acquisition of a charter with the state. The entry to record these costs is:

Organization Costs	15,000	
Cash		15,000
To record costs incurred in organizing corporation.		

Assuming the corporation amortizes the organization costs over a 10-year period, this entry records amortization at the end of the year:

Amortization Expense—Organization Costs	1,500	
Organization Costs		1,500
To record organization costs amortization expense.		
(15,000/10 years = $1,500).		

Directing the Corporation

Management of the corporation is through the delegation of authority from the stockholders to the directors to the officers, as shown in the organization chart in Illustration 12.1. The stockholders elect the board of directors. The board of directors formulates the broad policies of the company and selects the principal officers, who execute the policies.

STOCKHOLDERS   Stockholders do not have the right to participate actively in the management of the business unless they serve as directors and/or officers. However, stockholders do have certain basic rights, including the right to (1) dispose of their shares, (2) buy additional newly issued shares in a proportion equal to the percentage of shares they already own (called the **preemptive right),** (3) share in dividends when declared, (4) share in assets in case of liquidation, and (5) participate in management indirectly by voting at the stockholders' meeting.

The preemptive right allows stockholders to maintain their percentage of ownership in a corporation when additional shares are issued. For example, assume Joe Thornton owns 10% of the outstanding shares of Corporation X. When Corporation X decides to issue 1,000 additional shares of stock, Joe Thornton has the right to buy 100 (10%) of the new shares. Should he decide to do so, he maintains his 10% interest in the corporation. If he does not wish to exercise his preemptive right, the corporation may sell the shares to others.[1]

Normally, companies hold stockholders' meetings annually. At the annual stockholders' meeting, stockholders indirectly share in management by voting on such issues as changing the charter, increasing the number of authorized shares of stock to be issued, approving pension plans, selecting the independent auditor, and other related matters.

At stockholders' meetings, each stockholder is entitled to one vote for each share of voting stock held. Stockholders who do not personally attend the stockholders' meeting may vote by proxy. A **proxy** is a legal document signed by a stockholder, giving a designated person the authority to vote the stockholder's shares at a stockholders' meeting.

BOARD OF DIRECTORS   Elected by the stockholders, the **board of directors** is primarily responsible for formulating policies for the corporation. The board appoints administrative officers and delegates to them the execution of the policies established by the board. The board's more specific duties include: (1) authorizing contracts, (2) declaring dividends, (3) establishing executive salaries, and (4) granting authorization

---

[1]Some corporations have eliminated the preemptive right because the preemptive right makes it difficult to issue large blocks of stock to the stockholders of another corporation to acquire that corporation.

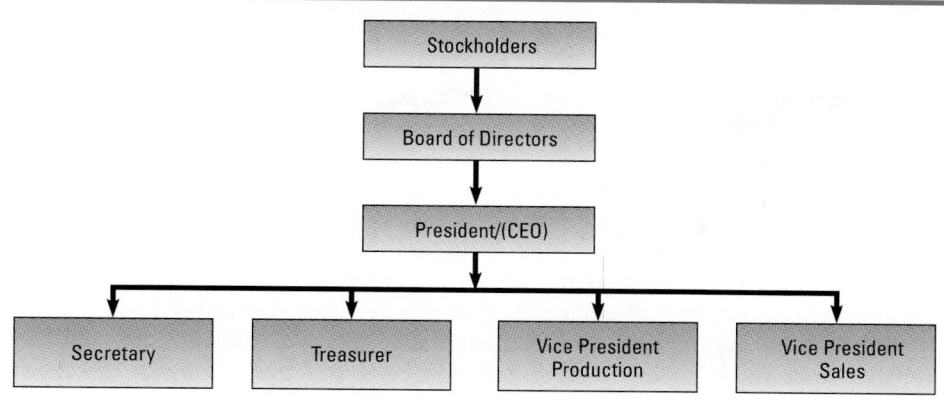

ILLUSTRATION 12.1
Typical Corporation's
Organization Chart

to borrow money. The decisions of the board are recorded in the minutes of its meetings. The minutes are an important source of information to an independent auditor, since they may serve as notice to record transactions (such as a dividend declaration) or to identify certain future transactions (such as a large loan).

CORPORATE OFFICERS A corporation's bylaws usually specify the titles and duties of the officers of a corporation. The number of officers and their exact titles vary from corporation to corporation, but most have a president, several vice presidents, a secretary, a treasurer, and a controller.

The president is the chief executive officer (CEO) of the corporation. He or she is empowered by the bylaws to hire all necessary employees except those appointed by the board of directors.

Most corporations have more than one vice president. Each vice president is responsible for one particular corporate operation, such as sales, engineering, or production. The corporate secretary maintains the official records of the company and records the proceedings of meetings of stockholders and directors. The treasurer is accountable for corporate funds and may supervise the accounting function within the company. A controller carries out the accounting function. The controller usually reports to the treasurer of the corporation.

Real World Example
On September 14, 1993, *The Wall Street Journal* reported that IBM's chairman created an executive committee to coordinate the company's activities. He told company employees the new unit would ensure that IBM's business could "work in a cohesive and responsive way."

DOCUMENTS, BOOKS, AND RECORDS RELATING TO CAPITAL STOCK

Capital stock consists of transferable units of ownership in a corporation. Each unit of ownership is called a *share of stock*. Typically, traders sell between 100 and 400 million shares of corporate capital stock every business day on stock exchanges, such as the New York Stock Exchange and the American Stock Exchange, and on the over-the-counter market. These sales (or *trades*) seldom involve the corporation issuing the stock as a party to the exchange. Existing stockholders sell their shares to other individual or institutional investors. The physical transfer of the stock certificates follows these trades.

A **stock certificate** is a printed or engraved document serving as evidence that the holder owns a certain number of shares of capital stock. When selling shares of stock, the stockholder signs over the stock certificate to the new owner, who presents it to the issuing corporation. When the old certificate arrives, the issuing corporation cancels the certificate and attaches it to its corresponding stub in the stock certificate book. The issuer prepares a new certificate for the new owner. To determine the number of shares of stock outstanding at any time, the issuer sums the shares shown on the open stubs (stubs without certificates attached) in the stock certificate book.

Among the more important records maintained by a corporation is the stockholders' ledger. The **stockholders' ledger** contains a group of subsidiary accounts showing the number of shares of stock currently held by *each* stockholder. Since the ledger

Stockholders' Ledger

contains an account for *each* stockholder, in a large corporation this ledger may have more than a million individual accounts. Each stockholder's account shows the number of shares currently or previously owned, their certificate numbers, and the dates on which shares were acquired or sold. Entries are made in the number of shares rather than in dollars.

The stockholders' ledger and the stock certificate book contain the same information, but the stockholders' ledger summarizes it alphabetically by stockholder. Since a stockholder may own a dozen or more certificates, each representing a number of shares, this summary enables a corporation to (1) determine the number of shares a stockholder is entitled to vote at a stockholders' meeting and (2) prepare one dividend check per stockholder rather than one per stock certificate.

Many large corporations with actively traded shares turn the task of maintaining reliable stock records over to an outside *stock-transfer agent* and a *stock registrar*. The **stock-transfer agent,** usually a bank or trust company, transfers stock between buyers and sellers for a corporation. The stock-transfer agent cancels the certificates covering shares sold, issues new stock certificates, and makes appropriate entries in the stockholders' ledger. It sends new certificates to the **stock registrar,** typically another bank, that maintains separate records of the shares outstanding. This control system makes it difficult for a corporate employee to issue stock certificates fraudulently and steal the proceeds.

The Minutes Book

The **minutes book,** kept by the secretary of the corporation, is (1) a record book of the actions taken at stockholders' and board of directors' meetings and (2) the written authorization for many actions taken by corporate officers. Remember that all actions taken by the board of directors and the stockholders must be in accordance with the provisions in the corporate charter and the bylaws. The minutes book contains a variety of data, including:

1. A copy of the corporate charter.
2. A copy of the bylaws.
3. Dividends declared by the board of directors.
4. Authorization for the acquisition of major assets.
5. Authorization for borrowing.
6. Authorization for increases or decreases in capital stock.

PAR VALUE AND NO-PAR CAPITAL STOCK

Par Value Stock

Objective 2
List the values commonly associated with capital stock and give their definitions.

Many times, companies issue par value stock. **Par value** is an arbitrary amount assigned to each share of a given class of stock and printed on the stock certificate. *Par value per share is no indication of the amount for which the stock sells;* it is simply the amount per share credited to the capital stock account for each share issued. Also, the total par value of all issued stock often constitutes the legal capital of the corporation. The concept of legal capital protects creditors from losses. **Legal capital,** or **stated capital,** is an amount prescribed by law (usually the par value or stated value of shares issued) below which a corporation may not reduce stockholders' equity through declaration of dividends or other payments to stockholders. Stated value relates to no-par stock and is explained below. Legal capital does not guarantee that a company can pay its debts, but it does keep a company from compensating owners to the detriment of creditors. The formula for determining legal capital is:

$$\text{Legal Capital} = \text{Shares issued} \times \text{Par or Stated Value}$$

No-Par Stock

In 1912, the state of New York first enacted laws permitting the issuance of **no-par stock (stock without par value).** Many other states have passed similar, but not uniform, legislation.

A corporation might issue no-par stock for two reasons. One reason is to avoid confusion. The use of a par value may confuse some investors because the par value usually does not conform to the market value. Issuing a stock with no par value avoids this source of confusion.

A second reason is related to state laws regarding the original issue price per share. A **discount on capital stock** is the amount by which the shares' par value exceeds their issue price. Thus, if stock with a par value of $100 is issued at $80, the discount is $20. Most states do not permit the original issuance of stock at a discount. Only Maryland, Georgia, and California allow its issuance. The original purchasers of the shares are contingently liable for the discount unless they have transferred (by contract) the discount liability to subsequent holders. If the contingent liability has been transferred, the present stockholders are contingently liable to creditors for the difference between par value and issue price. Although this contingent liability seldom becomes an actual liability, the issuance of no-par stock avoids such a possibility.

Note to the Student
Companies regard capital stock as the permanent capital of the business. Often we refer to it as the *legal capital*. In effect, it is an amount for the protection of creditors because it cannot be paid out to shareholders until all creditors' claims have been satisfied.

No-Par Stock with a Stated Value

The board of directors of a corporation issuing no-par stock may assign a stated value to each share of capital stock. **Stated value** is an arbitrary amount assigned by the board to each share of a given class of no-par stock. The board may set this stated value, like par value, at any amount, although some state statutes specify a minimum amount, such as $5 per share. If not specified by applicable state law, the board may establish stated value either before or after the shares are issued.

Other Values Commonly Associated with Capital Stock

Market Value

Market value is the price of shares of capital stock bought and sold by investors in the market; it is the value of greatest interest to investors. Market price is directly affected by (1) all the factors that influence general economic conditions, (2) investors' expectations concerning the corporation, and (3) the corporation's earnings.

Book Value

Book value per share is the amount per share that each stockholder would receive if the corporation were liquidated without incurring any further expenses and if assets were sold and liabilities liquidated at their recorded amounts. A later section discusses book value per share in greater detail.

Liquidation Value

Liquidation value is the amount a stockholder would receive if a corporation discontinued operations and liquidated by selling its assets, paying its liabilities, and distributing the remaining cash among the stockholders. Since the assets might be sold for more or less than the amounts at which they are recorded in the corporation's accounts, liquidation value may be more or less than book value. If only one class of capital stock is outstanding, each stockholder would receive, per share, the amount obtained by dividing the remaining cash by the number of outstanding shares. If two or more classes of stock are outstanding, liquidation value depends on the rights of the various classes.

Redemption Value

A corporation issues certain capital stock with the stipulation that it has the right to redeem it. **Redemption value** is the price per share at which a corporation may call in (or redeem) its capital stock for retirement.

Capital Stock Authorized and Outstanding

Objective 3
List the various kinds of stock and describe the differences between them.

The corporate charter states the number of shares and the par value, if any, per share of each class of stock that the corporation is permitted to issue. **Capital stock authorized** is the number of shares of stock that a corporation is entitled to issue as designated in its charter.

A corporation might not issue all of its authorized stock immediately; it might hold some stock for future issuance when additional funds are needed. If all authorized stock has been issued and more funds are needed, the state of incorporation must consent to an increase in authorized shares.

Note to the Student
Differentiate between *authorized shares* and *outstanding shares*.

The authorization to issue stock does not trigger a journal entry. Instead, companies note the authorization in the capital stock account in the ledger (and often in the general journal) as a reminder of the number of shares authorized. **Capital stock issued** is the number of shares of stock sold and issued to stockholders.

Capital stock outstanding is the number of authorized shares of stock issued and currently held by stockholders. The total ownership of a corporation rests with the holders of the capital stock outstanding. For example, when a corporation authorized to issue 10,000 shares of capital stock has issued only 8,000 shares, the holders of the 8,000 shares own 100% of the corporation.

Each outstanding share of stock of a given class carries rights and privileges identical to any other outstanding share of that class. Shares authorized but not yet issued are referred to as **unissued shares** (the previous example had 2,000 unissued shares). No rights or privileges are attached to these shares until they are issued; they are not entitled to dividends, nor can they be voted at stockholders' meetings.

The number of shares issued and the number of shares outstanding may be different. Issued stock has been issued at some time, while outstanding shares are currently held by stockholders. All outstanding stock is issued stock, but the reverse is not necessarily true. The difference is due to shares returned to the corporation by stockholders; it is called *treasury stock*. Chapter 13 discusses treasury stock.

AN ACCOUNTING PERSPECTIVE

BUSINESS INSIGHT   SCI Systems, Inc., designs, manufactures, and distributes electronic products for a wide variety of industries. The following illustration is adapted from the company's balance sheet. The stockholders' equity section shows the actual number of shares of common stock authorized and outstanding and shows the dollar amounts in thousands:

	June 30,	
	1996	**1995**
Common Stock, $.10 par value: authorized 100,000,000 shares; issued 29,621,895 shares in 1996 and 27,465,675 shares in 1995	$2,962	$2,747

CLASSES OF CAPITAL STOCK

A corporation may issue two basic classes or types of capital stock—common and preferred.

Common Stock

If a corporation issues only one class of stock, this stock is *common stock*. All of the stockholders enjoy equal rights. **Common stock** is usually the *residual equity* in the corporation. This term means that all other claims against the corporation rank ahead of the claims of the common stockholder.

Preferred Stock

Preferred stock is a class of capital stock that carries certain features or rights not carried by common stock. Within the basic class of preferred stock, a company may have several specific classes of preferred stock, each with different dividend rates or other features.

Companies issue preferred stock to avoid: (1) using bonds with fixed interest charges that must be paid regardless of the amount of net income; (2) issuing so many additional shares of common stock that earnings per share are less in the current year than in prior years; and (3) diluting the common stockholders' control of the corporation, since preferred stockholders usually have no voting rights.

Unlike common stock, which has no set maximum or minimum dividend, the dividend return on preferred stock is usually stated at an amount per share or as a percentage of par value. Therefore, the firm fixes the dividend per share. Illustration 12.2 shows the various classes and combinations of capital stock outstanding for a sample of 600 companies.

	1995	**1994**	**1993**	**1992**
Common stock with:				
No preferred stock	457	448	438	450
One class of preferred stock	115	118	127	112
Two classes of preferred stock	24	28	29	31
Three or more classes of preferred stock	4	6	6	7
Total companies	600	600	600	600
Companies included above with two or				
more classes of common stock	58	59	61	54

ILLUSTRATION 12.2
Capital Structures

Source: Based on American Institute of Certified Public Accountants, *Accounting Trends & Techniques* (New York: AICPA, 1996), p. 256.

TYPES OF PREFERRED STOCK

When a corporation issues both preferred and common stock, the preferred stock may be:

1. Preferred as to dividends. It may be noncumulative or cumulative.
2. Preferred as to assets in the event of liquidation.
3. Convertible or nonconvertible.
4. Callable.

A **dividend** is a distribution of assets (usually cash) that represents a withdrawal of earnings by the owners. Dividends are normally paid in cash.

Stock preferred as to dividends means that the preferred stockholders receive a specified dividend per share before common stockholders receive any dividends. A **dividend on preferred stock** is the amount paid to preferred stockholders as a return for the use of their money. For no-par preferred stock, the dividend is a specific dollar amount per share per year, such as $4.40. For par value preferred stock, the dividend is usually stated as a percentage of the par value, such as 8% of par value; occasionally, it is a specific dollar amount per share. Most preferred stock has a par value.

Usually, stockholders receive dividends on preferred stock quarterly. Such dividends—in full or in part—must be declared by the board of directors before being paid. In some states, corporations can declare preferred stock dividends only if they have retained earnings (income that has been retained in the business) at least equal to the dividend declared.

NONCUMULATIVE PREFERRED STOCK Noncumulative preferred stock is preferred stock on which the right to receive a dividend expires whenever the dividend is not declared. When noncumulative preferred stock is outstanding, a dividend omitted or not paid in any one year need not be paid in any future year. Because omitted dividends are lost forever, noncumulative preferred stocks are not attractive to investors and are rarely issued.

CUMULATIVE PREFERRED STOCK Cumulative preferred stock is preferred stock for which the right to receive a basic dividend, usually each quarter, accumulates if the dividend is not paid. Companies must pay unpaid cumulative preferred dividends before paying any dividends on the common stock. For example, assume a company has cumulative, $10 par value, 10% preferred stock outstanding of $100,000, common stock outstanding of $100,000, and retained earnings of $30,000. It has paid no dividends for two years. The company would pay the preferred stockholders dividends of $20,000 ($10,000 per year times two years) before paying any dividends to the common stockholders.

Dividends in arrears are cumulative unpaid dividends, including the quarterly dividends not declared for the current year. Dividends in arrears never appear as a liability of the corporation because they are not a legal liability until declared by the

Stock Preferred as to Dividends

Reinforcing Problem
E12–1 Determine dividends for common and noncumulative preferred stock.

Note to the Student
The term *cumulative* means that unpaid dividends in a given year carry over and must be paid to preferred stockholders before common stockholders receive any distributions.

Reinforcing Problem
E12–2 Determine dividends for common and cumulative preferred stock.

Note to the Student
Dividends in arrears on cumulative preferred stock are not a liability until declared by the board of directors.

board of directors. However, since the amount of dividends in arrears may influence the decisions of users of a corporation's financial statements, firms disclose such dividends in a footnote. An appropriate footnote might read: "Dividends in the amount of $20,000, representing two years' dividends on the company's 10%, cumulative preferred stock, were in arrears as of December 31, 1999."

Stock Preferred as to Assets

Most preferred stocks are preferred as to assets in the event of liquidation of the corporation. **Stock preferred as to assets** is preferred stock that receives special treatment in liquidation. Preferred stockholders receive the par value (or a larger stipulated liquidation value) per share before any assets are distributed to common stockholders. A corporation's cumulative preferred dividends in arrears at liquidation are payable even if there are not enough accumulated earnings to cover the dividends. Also, the cumulative dividend for the current year is payable. Stock may be preferred as to assets, dividends, or both.

Convertible Preferred Stock

Note to the Student
Companies record no gain or loss when preferred stock is converted to common stock. The par value plus additional paid-in capital in excess of par or stated value on the preferred stock determines the issue price of the common stock.

Convertible preferred stock is preferred stock that is convertible into common stock of the issuing corporation. Many preferred stocks do not carry this special feature; they are nonconvertible. Holders of convertible preferred stock shares may exchange them, at their option, for a certain number of shares of common stock of the same corporation.

Investors find convertible preferred stock attractive for two reasons: First, there is a greater probability that the dividends on the preferred stock will be paid (as compared to dividends on common shares). Second, the conversion privilege may be the source of substantial price appreciation. To illustrate this latter feature, assume that Olsen Company issued 1,000 shares of 6%, $100 par value convertible preferred stock at $100 per share. The stock is convertible at any time into four shares of Olsen $10 par value common stock, which has a current market value of $20 per share. In the next several years, the company reported much higher net income and increased the dividend on the common stock from $1 to $2 per share. Assume that the common stock now sells at $40 per share. The preferred stockholders can: (1) convert each share of preferred stock into four shares of common stock and increase the annual dividend they receive from $6 to $8; (2) sell their preferred stock at a substantial gain, since it sells in the market at approximately $160 per share, the market value of the four shares of common stock into which it is convertible; or (3) continue to hold their preferred shares in the expectation of realizing an even larger gain at a later date.

If all 1,000 shares of $100 par value Olsen Company preferred stock are converted into 4,000 shares of $10 par value common stock, the entry is:

Preferred Stock	100,000	
Common Stock		40,000
Paid-In Capital in Excess of Par Value—Common		60,000
To record the conversion of preferred stock into common stock.		

AN ACCOUNTING PERSPECTIVE

BUSINESS INSIGHT   In the early 1970s, only about 10% of undergraduate degrees in accounting were awarded to women. This percentage increased steadily, and by the mid-1980s approximately half of all undergraduate accounting degrees were earned by women. By 1996, the rate increased to slightly more than half. This rate is more than twice the rate in the medical and legal professions. For more information see "Accounting's Big Gender Switch," *Business Week*, January 20, 1997, p. 20.

Callable Preferred Stock

Most preferred stocks are callable at the option of the issuing corporation. **Callable preferred stock** means that the corporation can inform nonconvertible preferred stockholders that they must surrender their stock to the company. Also, convertible preferred stockholders must either surrender their stock or convert it to common shares.

Preferred shares are usually callable at par value plus a small premium of 3 or 4% of the par value of the stock. This **call premium** is the difference between the amount at which a corporation calls its preferred stock for redemption and the par value of the stock.

An issuing corporation may force conversion of convertible preferred stock by calling in the preferred stock for redemption. Stockholders who do not want to surrender their stock have to convert it to common shares. When preferred stockholders surrender their stock, the corporation pays these stockholders par value plus the call premium, any dividends in arrears from past years, and a prorated portion of the current period's dividend. If the market value of common shares into which the preferred stock could be converted is higher than the amount the stockholders would receive in redemption, they should convert their preferred shares to common shares. For instance, assume that a stockholder owns 1,000 shares of convertible preferred stock. Each share is callable at $104 per share, convertible to two common shares (currently selling at $62 per share), and entitled to $10 of unpaid dividends. If the issuing corporation calls in its preferred stock, it would give the stockholder either (1) $114,000 [($104 + $10) × 1,000] if the shares are surrendered or (2) common shares worth $124,000 ($62 × 2,000) if the shares are converted. Obviously, the stockholder should convert these preferred shares to common shares.

Why would a corporation call in its preferred stock? Corporations call in preferred stock for many reasons: (1) the outstanding preferred stock may require a 12% annual dividend at a time when the company can secure capital to retire the stock by issuing a new 8% preferred stock; (2) the issuing company may have been sufficiently profitable to retire the preferred stock out of earnings; or (3) the company may wish to force conversion of its convertible preferred stock because the cash dividend on the equivalent common shares is less than the dividend on the preferred shares.

BALANCE SHEET PRESENTATION OF STOCK

The stockholders' equity section of a corporation's balance sheet contains two main elements: paid-in capital and retained earnings. **Paid-in capital** is the part of stockholders' equity that normally results from cash or other assets invested by owners. Paid-in capital also results from services performed for the corporation in exchange for capital stock and from certain other transactions discussed in Chapter 13. As stated earlier, **retained earnings** is the part of stockholders' equity resulting from accumulated net income, reduced by dividends and net losses. Net income increases the Retained Earnings account balance and net losses decrease it. In addition, dividends declared to stockholders decrease Retained Earnings. Since Retained Earnings is a stockholders' equity account and represents accumulated net income retained by the company, it normally has a credit balance. We discuss retained earnings in more detail in Chapter 13.

The following illustration shows the proper financial reporting for preferred and common stock. Assume that a corporation is authorized to issue 10,000 shares of $100 par value, 6%, cumulative, convertible preferred stock (five common for one preferred), all of which have been issued and are outstanding; and 200,000 shares of $10 par value common stock, of which 80,000 shares are issued and outstanding. The stockholders' equity section of the balance sheet (assuming $450,000 of retained earnings) is:

Objective 4
Present in proper form the stockholders' equity section of a balance sheet.

Stockholders' equity:

Paid-in capital:		
Preferred stock—$100 par value, 6%, cumulative, convertible (5 common for 1 preferred); authorized, issued, and outstanding, 10,000 shares	$1,000,000	
Common stock—$10 par value; authorized, 200,000 shares; issued and outstanding, 80,000 shares	800,000	
Total paid-in capital		$1,800,000
Retained earnings		450,000
Total stockholders' equity		$2,250,000

Note to the Student
Note that a corporation's equity consists of two major components: stockholder investments (paid-in capital) and retained earnings.

Notice that the balance sheet lists preferred stock before common stock because the preferred stock is preferred as to dividends, assets, or both. The company discloses the conversion rate in a parenthetical note within the description of preferred stock or in a footnote.

| **AN ACCOUNTING PERSPECTIVE** | **BUSINESS INSIGHT**   Coca-Cola Enterprises Incorporated is the world's largest bottler of Coca-Cola products. Its 1995 annual report provided the following presentation of preferred stock in the stockholders' equity section of its balance sheet: |

	1995
Preferred stock, $35 stated value—1,000,000 shares authorized and issued	$35M

STOCK ISSUANCES FOR CASH

Issuance of Par Value Stock for Cash

Objective 5
Account for the issuances of stock for cash and other assets.

Each share of common or preferred capital stock either has a par value or lacks one. The corporation's charter determines the par value printed on the stock certificates issued. Par value may be any amount—1 cent, 10 cents, 16⅔ cents, $1, $5, or $100. Low par values of $10 or less are common in our economy.

As previously mentioned, par value gives no clue as to the stock's market value. Shares with a par value of $5 have traded (sold) in the market for more than $600, and many $100 par value preferred stocks have traded for considerably less than par. Par value is not even a reliable indicator of the price at which shares can be issued. New corporations can issue shares at prices well in excess of par value or for less than par value if state laws permit. Par value gives the accountant a constant amount at which to record capital stock issuances in the capital stock accounts. As stated earlier, the total par value of all issued shares is generally the legal capital of the corporation.

To illustrate the issuance of stock for cash, assume a company issues 10,000 authorized shares of $20 par value common stock at $22 per share. The following entry records the issuance:

Cash	220,000	
Common Stock		200,000
Paid-In Capital in Excess of Par Value—Common		20,000
To record the issuance of 10,000 shares of stock for cash.		

Notice that the credit to the Common Stock account is the par value ($20) times the number of shares issued. The accountant credits the excess over par value ($20,000) to Paid-In Capital in Excess of Par Value; it is part of the paid-in capital contributed by the stockholders. Thus, **paid-in capital in excess of par (or stated) value** represents capital contributed to a corporation in addition to that assigned to the shares issued and recorded in capital stock accounts. The paid-in capital section of the balance sheet appears as follows:

Paid-in capital:		
Common stock—par value, $20; 10,000 shares authorized, issued, and outstanding . .	$200,000	
Paid-in capital in excess of par value—common	20,000	
Total paid-in capital	$220,000	

Issuance of No-Par, Stated Value Stock for Cash

When it issues no-par stock with a stated value, a company carries the shares in the capital stock account at the stated value. Any amounts received in excess of the stated value per share represent a part of the paid-in capital of the corporation and the company credits them to Paid-In Capital in Excess of Stated Value. The legal capital of a corporation issuing no-par shares with a stated value is usually equal to the total stated value of the shares issued.

To illustrate, assume that the DeWitt Corporation, which is authorized to issue 10,000 shares of common stock without par value, assigns a stated value of $20 per share to its stock. DeWitt issues the 10,000 authorized shares for cash at $22 per share. The entry to record this transaction is:

```
Cash  . . . . . . . . . . . . . . . . . . . . . . . . . . . . . . . . .   220,000
    Common Stock  . . . . . . . . . . . . . . . . . . . . . . . . . . .              200,000
    Paid-In Capital in Excess of Stated Value—Common  . . . . . . . . . . .           20,000
    To record issuance of 10,000 shares for cash.
```

The paid-in capital section of the balance sheet appears as follows:

Paid-in capital:
  Common stock—without par value; stated value, $20; 10,000 shares authorized,
    issued, and outstanding $200,000
  Paid-in capital in excess of stated value—common   20,000
      Total paid-in capital $220,000

DeWitt carries the $20,000 received over and above the stated value of $200,000 permanently as paid-in capital because it is a part of the capital originally contributed by the stockholders. However, the legal capital of the DeWitt Corporation is $200,000.

A corporation that issues no-par stock without a stated value credits the entire amount received to the capital stock account. For instance, consider the DeWitt Corporation's issuance of no-par stock. If no stated value had been assigned, the entry would have been as follows:

Issuance of No-Par Stock without a Stated Value for Cash

```
Cash  . . . . . . . . . . . . . . . . . . . . . . . . . . . . . . . . .   220,000
    Common Stock  . . . . . . . . . . . . . . . . . . . . . . . . . . .              220,000
    To record the issuance of 10,000 shares for cash.
```

Since the company may issue shares at different times and at differing amounts, its credits to the capital stock account are not uniform amounts per share. This contrasts with issuing par value shares or shares with a stated value.

To continue our example, the paid-in capital section of the company's balance sheet would be as follows:

Paid-in capital:
  Common stock—without par or stated value; 10,000 shares authorized,
    issued, and outstanding $220,000
      Total paid-in capital $220,000

The actual capital contributed by stockholders is $220,000. In some states, the entire amount received for shares without par or stated value is the amount of legal capital. The legal capital in this example would then be equal to $220,000.

CAPITAL STOCK ISSUED FOR PROPERTY OR SERVICES

When issuing capital stock for property or services, companies must determine the dollar amount of the exchange. Accountants generally record the transaction at the fair value of (1) the property or services received or (2) the stock issued, whichever is more clearly evident.

To illustrate, assume that the owners of a tract of land deeded it to a corporation in exchange for 1,000 shares of $12 par value common stock. The firm can only estimate the fair market value of the land. At the time of the exchange, the stock has an established total market value of $14,000. The required entry is:

```
Land  . . . . . . . . . . . . . . . . . . . . . . . . . . . . . . . . .    14,000
    Common Stock  . . . . . . . . . . . . . . . . . . . . . . . . . . .               12,000
    Paid-In Capital in Excess of Par Value—Common  . . . . . . . . . . . .             2,000
    To record the receipt of land for capital stock.
```

As another example, assume a firm issues 100 shares of common stock with a par value of $40 per share in exchange for legal services received in organizing as a corporation. No shares have been traded recently, so there is no established market

Reinforcing Problems
E12–3 Journalize stock issuance.
E12–4 Prepare entries for stock issuance.

Note to the Student
Companies do not record paid-in capital received in excess of par as a gain or revenue. Revenues arise from the sale of goods or services. Corporate paid-in capital is part of stockholders' equity.

Note to the Student
Corporations do not make journal entries when investors buy stock from each other in the marketplace; instead, they register the names of the new holders of the stock.

Reinforcing Problems
E12–5 Journalize stock issuance for property.
E12–6 Journalize stock issuance to satisfy liability.
E12–7 Journalize stock issuance for legal services.

value. The attorney previously agreed to a price of $5,000 for these legal services but decided to accept stock in lieu of cash. In this example, the correct entry is:

Organization Costs	5,000	
Common Stock		4,000
Paid-In Capital in Excess of Par Value—Common		1,000
To record the receipt of legal services for capital stock.		

Note to the Student

All intangible assets must be amortized over a period not to exceed 40 years.

The company should value the services at the price previously agreed on since that value is more clearly evident than the market value of the shares. It should debit an intangible asset account because these services benefit the corporation throughout its entire life. The company credits the amount by which the value of the services received exceeds the par value of the shares issued to a Paid-In Capital in Excess of Par Value—Common account.

BALANCE SHEET PRESENTATION OF PAID-IN CAPITAL IN EXCESS OF PAR (OR STATED) VALUE—COMMON OR PREFERRED

Accountants credit amounts received in excess of the par or stated value of shares to a Paid-In Capital in Excess of Par (or Stated) Value—Common (or Preferred) account. They carry the amounts received in excess of par or stated value in separate accounts for each class of stock issued. Using the following assumed data, the stockholders' equity section of the balance sheet of a company with both preferred and common stock outstanding would appear as follows:

Stockholders' equity:			
Paid-in capital:			
Preferred stock—$100 par value, 6% cumulative;			
1,000 shares authorized, issued, and			
outstanding	$100,000		
Common stock—without par value, stated value			
$5; 100,000 shares authorized, 80,000			
shares issued and outstanding	400,000	$500,000	
Paid-in capital in excess of par (or stated) value:			
From preferred stock issuances	$ 5,000		
From common stock issuances	20,000	25,000	
Total paid-in capital			$525,000
Retained earnings			200,000
Total stockholders' equity			$725,000

BOOK VALUE

Objective 6

Determine book values of both preferred and common stock.

The total book value of a corporation's outstanding shares is equal to its recorded net asset value—that is, assets minus liabilities. Quite simply, the amount of net assets is equal to stockholders' equity. When only common stock is outstanding, companies compute the **book value per share** by dividing total stockholders' equity by the number of common shares outstanding. In calculating book value, they assume that (1) the corporation could be liquidated without incurring any further expenses, (2) the assets could be sold at their recorded amounts, and (3) the liabilities could be satisfied at their recorded amounts. Assume the stockholders' equity of a corporation is as follows:

Stockholders' equity:		
Paid-in capital:		
Common stock—without par value, stated value $10; authorized,		
20,000 shares; issued and outstanding, 15,000 shares	$150,000	
Paid-in capital in excess of stated value	10,000	
Total paid-in capital		$160,000
Retained earnings		50,000
Total stockholders' equity		$210,000

To determine the book value per share of the stock:

Total stockholders' equity . . .	$210,000
Total shares outstanding	÷15,000
Book value per share	$ 14

Reinforcing Problem
E12–8 Compute the book value and average price of common stock.

When two or more classes of capital stock are outstanding, the computation of book value per share is more complex. The book value for each share of stock depends on the rights of the preferred stockholders. Preferred stockholders typically are entitled to a specified liquidation value per share, plus cumulative dividends in arrears, since most preferred stocks are preferred as to assets and are cumulative. In each case, the specific provisions in the preferred stock contract govern. To illustrate, assume the Celoron Corporation's stockholders' equity is as follows:

Stockholders' equity:
Paid-in capital:

Preferred stock—$100 par value, 6% cumulative; 5,000 shares authorized, issued, and outstanding		$ 500,000
Common stock—$10 par value, 200,000 shares authorized, issued, and outstanding		2,000,000
Paid-in capital in excess of par value—preferred		200,000
Total paid-in capital		$2,700,000
Retained earnings		400,000
Total stockholders' equity		$3,100,000

The preferred stock is 6%, cumulative. It is preferred as to dividends and as to assets in liquidation to the extent of the liquidation value of $100 per share, plus any cumulative dividends on the preferred stock. Dividends for four years (including the current year) are unpaid. You would calculate the book values of each class of stock as follows:

	Total	Per Share
Total stockholders' equity	$3,100,000	
Book value of preferred stock (5,000 shares):		
Liquidation value (5,000 shares × $100) $500,000		
Dividends (4 years at $30,000) 120,000	620,000	$124.00*
Book value of common stock (200,000 shares)	$2,480,000	12.40†

* $620,000 ÷ 5,000 shares.
† $2,480,000 ÷ 200,000 shares.

Notice that Celoron did not assign the paid-in capital in excess of par value—preferred to the preferred stock in determining the book values. Celoron assigned only the liquidation value and cumulative dividends on the preferred stock to the preferred stock.

Assume now that the features attached to the preferred stock are the same except that the preferred stockholders have the right to receive $103 per share in liquidation. The book values of each class of stock would be:

	Total	Per Share
Total stockholders' equity	$3,100,000	
Book value of preferred stock (5,000 shares):		
Liquidation value (5,000 shares × $103) $515,000		
Dividends (4 years at $30,000) 120,000	635,000	$127.00
Book value of common stock (200,000 shares)	$2,465,000	12.33

Book value rarely equals market value of a stock because many of the assets have changed in value due to inflation. Thus, the market prices of the shares of many corporations traded regularly are different from their book values.

Real World Example
There are two-thirds as many mutual funds as there are stocks listed on the New York Stock Exchange. More money is invested in these mutual funds than all the gold in Fort Knox and the New York Fed combined. There are more people in mutual funds than there are homes with personal computers. "Time for Straight Talk from Mutual Funds," *The Wall Street Journal,* Thursday, January 9, 1997.

Note to the Student
There is not necessarily any direct relationship between book value and the market price of stock.

AN ACCOUNTING PERSPECTIVE

BUSINES INSIGHT   *The Wall Street Journal* publishes the New York Stock Exchange (NYSE) Composite Transactions each Monday through Friday except when the exchange is closed. For each stock listed on the NYSE, it lists the following data. We use data for the Kellogg Company, which produces ready-to-eat cereals and other food products, as recently reported in *The Wall Street Journal* as an example:

52 Weeks											
Hi	Lo	Stock	Sym	Div	Yld %	PE	Vol 100s	Hi	Lo	Close	Net Chg
80⅝	64¾	Kellogg	K	1.68	2.5	33	3838	67⅜	66	67⅛	−⅛

The first two columns show the high and low price over the preceding 52 weeks plus the current week. The next two columns show the company name (Kellogg) and the NYSE's symbol (K) for that company. The Div column is the annual dividend based on the last quarterly, semiannual, or annual declaration. Yield % is calculated as dividends paid divided by the current market price. The PE ratio is the closing market price divided by the total earnings per share for the most recent four quarters. The Vol 100s column shows the unofficial daily total of shares traded, quoted in hundreds. Thus, 383,800 shares of Kellogg's were traded that day. The next two columns show the high and low price for that day. The next to last column shows the closing price for that day. The final column shows the change in the closing price as compared to the closing price of the preceding day.

ANALYZING AND USING THE FINANCIAL RESULTS—RETURN ON AVERAGE COMMON STOCKHOLDERS' EQUITY

Objective 7
Analyze and use the financial results—return on average common stockholders' equity.

Stockholders' equity is particularly important to managers, creditors, and investors in determining the return on equity, which is the return on average common stockholders' equity.

The **return on average common stockholders' equity** measures what a given company earned for its common stockholders from all sources as a percentage of the common stockholders' investment. From the common stockholders' point of view, it is an important measure of the income-producing ability of the company. The ratio's formula is:

$$\text{Return on average common stockholders' equity} = \frac{\text{Net income available to common stockholders}}{\text{Average common stockholders' equity}}$$

If preferred stock is outstanding, the numerator is net income minus the annual dividend on preferred stock, and the denominator is the average total book value of common stock. If no preferred stock is outstanding, the numerator is net income, and the denominator is average stockholders' equity.

Procter & Gamble
Procter & Gamble markets more than 300 brands. Examples include Tide, Ariel, Pantene Pro-V, Always, Pringles, and Oil of Olay.

The Procter & Gamble Company reported the following information in its 1996 financial statements ($ millions):

	1996
Net earnings	$ 3,046
Stockholders' equity, beginning . . .	10,589
Stockholders' equity, ending	11,722

The return on average common stockholders' equity for Procter & Gamble is 27.3%, or $3,046/[($10,589 + $11,722)/2]. Investors view any increase from year to year as favorable and any decrease as unfavorable.

Since the stock market is frequently referred to as an economic indicator, the knowledge you now have on corporate stock issuances should help you relate to stocks traded in the market. Chapter 13 continues the discussion of paid-in capital and also discusses treasury stock, retained earnings, and dividends.

Joe Morrison is the controller for Belex Corporation. He is involved in a discussion with other members of management concerning how to get rid of some potentially harmful toxic waste materials that are a by-product of the company's manufacturing process.

There are two alternative methods of disposing of the materials. The first alternative is to bury the waste in steel drums on a tract of land adjacent to the factory building. There is currently no legal prohibition against doing this. The cost of disposing of the materials in this way is estimated to be $50,000 per year. The best estimate is that the steel drums would not leak for at least 50 years, but probably would begin leaking after that time. The second alternative is to seal the materials in lead drums that would be disposed of at sea by a waste management company. The cost of this alternative is estimated to be $400,000 per year. The federal government has certified this method as the preferred method of disposal. The best estimate is that the lead drums would never rupture or leak.

Belex Corporation has seen some tough economic times. The company suffered losses until last year, when it showed a profit of $750,000 as a result of a new manufacturing project. So far, the waste materials from that project have been accumulating in two large vats on the company's land. However, these vats are almost full, so soon management must decide how to dispose of the materials.

One group of managers is arguing in favor of the first alternative because it is legally permissible and results in annual profits of about $700,000. They point out that using the second alternative would reduce profits to about $350,000 per year and cut managers' bonuses in half. They also claim that some of their competitors are now using the first alternative, and to use the second alternative would place the company at a serious competitive disadvantage.

Another group of managers argues that the second alternative is the only safe alternative to pursue. They claim that when the steel drums start leaking they will contaminate the ground water and could cause serious health problems. When this contamination occurs, the company will lose public support and may even have to pay for the cleanup. The cost of that cleanup could run into the millions.

AN ETHICAL PERSPECTIVE
___

Belex Corporation

UNDERSTANDING THE LEARNING OBJECTIVES

- Advantages:
  1. Easy transfer of ownership.
  2. Limited liability.
  3. Continuous existence of the entity.
  4. Easy capital generation.
  5. Professional management.
  6. Separation of owners and entity.
- Disadvantages:
  1. Double taxation.
  2. Government regulation.
  3. Entrenched, inefficient management.
  4. Limited ability to raise creditor capital.

Objective 1
State the advantages and disadvantages of the corporate form of business.

- Par value—an arbitrary amount assigned to each share of a given class of stock and printed on the stock certificate.
- Stated value—an arbitrary amount assigned by the board of directors to each share of a given class of no-par stock.
- Market value—the price at which shares of capital stock are bought and sold in the market.
- Book value—the amount per share that each stockholder would receive if the corporation were liquidated without incurring any further expenses and if assets were sold and liabilities liquidated at their recorded amounts.
- Liquidation value—the amount a stockholder would receive if a corporation discontinues operations, pays its liabilities, and distributes the remaining cash among the stockholders.
- Redemption value—the price per share at which a corporation may call in (redeem) its capital stock for retirement.

Objective 2
List the values commonly associated with capital stock and give their definitions.

- Capital stock authorized—the number of shares of stock that a corporation is entitled to issue as designated in its charter.
- Capital stock issued—the number of shares of stock that have been sold and issued to stockholders.

Objective 3
List the various kinds of stock and describe the differences between them.

- Capital stock outstanding—the number of authorized shares of stock that have been issued and that are still currently held by stockholders.
- Two basic classes of capital stock:
  1. Common stock—represents the residual equity.
  2. Preferred stock—may be preferred as to dividends and/or assets. Also may be cumulative and/or callable.
- If the company has paid-in capital in excess of par value, the proper form would be:

Objective 4
Present in proper form the stockholders' equity section of a balance sheet.

Stockholders' equity:

Paid-in capital:			
Preferred stock—$100 par value, 6% cumulative; 1,000 shares authorized, issued, and outstanding		$100,000	
Common stock—without par value, stated value $5; 100,000 shares authorized, 80,000 shares issued and outstanding		400,000	$500,000
Paid-in capital in excess of par (or stated) value:			
From preferred stock issuances		$ 5,000	
From common stock issuances		20,000	25,000
Total paid-in capital			$525,000
Retained earnings			200,000
Total stockholders' equity			$725,000

Objective 5
Account for the issuances of stock for cash and for other assets.

The following examples illustrate the issuance for cash of: (1) stock with a par value, (2) no-par value stock with a stated value, and (3) no-par value stock without a stated value.

- Issuance of par value stock for cash—10,000 shares of $20 par value common stock issued for $22 per share.

Cash	220,000	
Common Stock		200,000
Paid-In Capital in Excess of Par Value—Common		20,000

- Issuance of no-par, stated value stock for cash—10,000 shares (no-par value) with $20 per share stated value issued for $22 per share.

Cash	220,000	
Common Stock		200,000
Paid-In Capital in Excess of Stated Value—Common		20,000

- Issuance of no-par stock without a stated value for cash—10,000 shares (no-par value) issued at $22 per share.

Cash	220,000	
Common Stock		220,000

Objective 6
Determine book values of both preferred and common stock.

- *Example:* A corporation has 200,000 shares of common stock and 5,000 shares of preferred stock outstanding. Preferred stock is 6% and cumulative. It is preferred as to dividends and as to assets in liquidation to the extent of the liquidation value of $100 per share, plus any cumulative dividends on the preferred stock. Dividends for three years are unpaid. Total stockholders' equity is $4,100,000. Calculations are as follows:

		Total	Per Share
Total stockholders' equity		$4,100,000	
Book value of preferred stock (5,000 shares):			
Liquidation value (5,000 shares × $100)	$500,000		
Dividends (3 years at $30,000)	90,000	590,000	$118.00
Book value of common stock (200,000 shares)		$3,510,000	17.55

Objective 7
Analyze and use the financial results—return on average common stockholders' equity.

- The return on average common stockholders' equity equals net income available to common stockholders divided by average common stockholders' equity.
- The return on average common stockholders' equity is an important measure of the income-producing ability of the company.

DEMONSTRATION PROBLEM 12–A

Violet Company has paid all required preferred dividends through December 31, 1993. Its outstanding stock consists of 10,000 shares of $125 par value common stock and 4,000 shares of 6%, $125 par value preferred stock. During five successive years, the company's dividend declarations were as follows:

1994	$85,000
1995	52,500
1996	7,500
1997	15,000
1998	67,500

Compute the amount of dividends that would have been paid to each class of stock in each of the last five years assuming the preferred stock is: *Required*

a. Cumulative.
b. Noncumulative.

SOLUTION TO DEMONSTRATION PROBLEM 12–A

VIOLET COMPANY

Year	Dividends to	Assumptions a	b
1994	Preferred	$30,000*	$30,000
	Common	55,000	55,000
1995	Preferred	30,000	30,000
	Common	22,500	22,500
1996	Preferred	7,500	7,500
	Common	–0–	–0–
1997	Preferred	15,000	15,000
	Common	–0–	–0–
1998	Preferred	67,500†	30,000‡
	Common	–0–	37,500

* 4,000 shares × $125 × 0.06 = $30,000.

† $30,000 + $22,500 preferred dividend missed in 1996 + $15,000 preferred dividend missed in 1997.

‡ Only the basic $30,000 dividend is paid because the stock is noncumulative.

DEMONSTRATION PROBLEM 12–B

Terrier Company has been authorized to issue 100,000 shares of $6 par value common stock and 1,000 shares of 14%, cumulative, preferred stock with a par value of $12.

a. Prepare the entries for the following transactions that all took place in June 1998:   *Required*

    (1) 50,000 shares of common stock are issued for cash at $24 per share.
    (2) 750 shares of preferred stock are issued for cash at $18 per share.
    (3) 1,000 shares of common stock are issued in exchange for legal services received in the incorporation process. The fair market value of the legal services is $9,000.

b. Prepare the paid-in capital section of Terrier's balance sheet as of June 30, 1998.

SOLUTION TO DEMONSTRATION PROBLEM 12–B

a. (1)	Cash	1,200,000	
	Common Stock		300,000
	Paid-In Capital in Excess of Par Value—Common Stock		900,000
	To record issuance of 50,000 shares at $24 per share.		

(2)	Cash	13,500	
	Preferred Stock		9,000
	Paid-In Capital in Excess of Par Value—Preferred		4,500
	To record the issuance of 750 shares for cash, at $18 per share.		

(3)	Organization Costs	9,000	
	Common Stock		6,000
	Paid-In Capital in Excess of Par Value—Common		3,000
	To record issuance of 1,000 shares in exchange for legal services.		

b.

TERRIER COMPANY
Partial Balance Sheet
June 30, 1998

Paid-in capital:
Preferred stock—$12 par value, 14% cumulative; 1,000 shares
authorized; issued and outstanding, 750 shares . . . . $ 9,000
Common stock—$6 par value per share; 100,000 shares authorized;
issued and outstanding, 51,000 shares . . . . 306,000 $ 315,000

Paid-in capital in excess of par value:
From preferred stock issuances . . . . $ 4,500
From common stock issuances 903,000   907,500

Total paid-in capital $1,222,500

NEW TERMS

Articles of incorporation   The application for the corporation's charter. *435*

Board of directors   Elected by the stockholders to have primary responsibility for formulating policies for the corporation. The board also authorizes contracts, declares dividends, establishes executive salaries, and grants authorization to borrow money. *436*

Book value per share   Stockholders' equity per share; the amount per share each stockholder would receive if the corporation were liquidated without incurring any further expenses and if assets were sold and liabilities liquidated at their recorded amounts. *439, 446*

Bylaws   A set of rules or regulations adopted by the board of directors of a corporation to govern the conduct of corporate affairs. The bylaws must be in agreement with the laws of the state and the policies and purposes in the corporate charter. *435*

Callable preferred stock   If the stock is nonconvertible, it must be surrendered to the company when the holder is requested to do so. If the stock is convertible, it may be either surrendered or converted into common shares when called. *442*

Call premium (on preferred stock)   The difference between the amount at which a corporation calls its preferred stock for redemption and the par value of the stock. *442*

Capital stock   Transferable units of ownership in a corporation. *437*

Capital stock authorized   The number of shares of stock that a corporation is entitled to issue as designated in its charter. *439*

Capital stock issued   The number of shares of stock that have been sold and issued to stockholders. *440*

Capital stock outstanding   The number of shares of authorized stock issued and currently held by stockholders. *440*

Common stock   Shares of stock representing the residual equity in the corporation. If only one class of stock is issued, it is known as *common stock*. All other claims rank ahead of common stockholders' claims. *440*

Convertible preferred stock   Preferred stock that is convertible into common stock of the issuing corporation. *442*

Corporate charter   The contract between the state and the incorporators of a corporation, and their successors, granting the corporation its legal existence. *435*

Corporation   An entity recognized by law as possessing an existence separate and distinct from its owners; that is, it is a separate legal entity. A corporation is granted many of the rights, and placed under many of the obligations, of a natural person. In any given state, all corporations organized under the laws of that state are **domestic corporations;** all others are **foreign corporations.** *433*

Cumulative preferred stock   Preferred stock for which the right to receive a basic dividend accumulates if any dividends have not been paid; unpaid cumulative preferred dividends must be paid before any dividends can be paid on the common stock. *441*

Discount on capital stock   The amount by which the par value of shares issued exceeds their issue price. The original issuance of shares at a discount is illegal in most states. *439*

Dividend   A distribution of assets (usually cash) that represents a withdrawal of earnings by the owners. *441*

Dividend on preferred stock   The amount paid to preferred stockholders as a return for the use of their money; usually a fixed or stated amount expressed in dollars per share or as a percentage of par value per share.   *441*

Dividends in arrears   Cumulative unpaid dividends, including quarterly dividends not declared for the current year.   *441*

Domestic corporation   See *corporation*.

Foreign corporation   See *corporation*.

Incorporators   Persons seeking to bring a corporation into existence.   *435*

Legal capital (stated capital)   An amount prescribed by law (usually the par value or stated value of shares issued) below which a corporation may not reduce stockholders' equity through the declaration of dividends or other payments to stockholders.   *438*

Liquidation value   The amount a stockholder will receive if a corporation discontinues operations and liquidates by selling its assets, paying its liabilities, and distributing the remaining cash among the stockholders.   *439*

Market value   The price at which shares of capital stock are bought and sold in the market.   *439*

Minutes book   The record book in which actions taken at stockholders' and board of directors' meetings are recorded; the written authorization for many actions taken by corporate officers.   *438*

Noncumulative preferred stock   Preferred stock on which the right to receive a dividend expires if the dividend is not declared.   *441*

No-par stock   Capital stock without par value, to which a stated value may or may not be assigned.   *438*

Organization costs   Costs of organizing a corporation, such as incorporation fees and legal fees applicable to incorporation.   *435*

Paid-in capital   Amount of stockholders' equity that normally results from the cash or other assets invested by owners; it may also result from services provided for shares of stock and certain other transactions.   *443*

Paid-in capital in excess of par (or stated) value—common or preferred   Capital contributed to a corporation in addition to that assigned to the shares issued and recorded in capital stock accounts.   *444*

Par value   An arbitrary amount assigned to each share of a given class of stock and printed on the stock certificate.   *438*

Preemptive right   The right of stockholders to buy additional shares in a proportion equal to the percentage of shares already owned.   *436*

Preferred stock   Capital stock that carries certain features or rights not carried by common stock. Preferred

stock may be preferred as to dividends, as to assets, or as to both dividends and assets. Preferred stock may be callable and/or convertible and may be cumulative or noncumulative.   *440*

Proxy   A legal document signed by a stockholder, giving another person the authority to vote the stockholder's shares at a stockholders' meeting.   *436*

Redemption value   The price per share at which a corporation may call in (or redeem) its capital stock for retirement.   *439*

Retained earnings   The part of stockholders' equity resulting from net income, reduced by dividends and net losses.   *443*

Return on average common stockholders' equity   A measure of the income-producing ability of the company. It is the ratio of net income available to common stockholders divided by average common stockholders' equity.   *448*

Shares of stock   Units of ownership in a corporation.   *433*

Stated value   An arbitrary amount assigned by the board of directors to each share of a given class of no-par stock.   *439*

Stock certificate   A printed or engraved document serving as evidence that the holder owns a certain number of shares of capital stock.   *437*

Stockholders' ledger   Contains a group of subsidiary accounts showing the number of shares of stock currently held by each stockholder.   *437*

Stock preferred as to assets   Means that in liquidation, the preferred stockholders are entitled to receive the par value (or a larger stipulated liquidation value) per share before any assets may be distributed to common stockholders.   *442*

Stock preferred as to dividends   Means that the preferred stockholders are entitled to receive a specified dividend per share before any dividend on common stock is paid.   *441*

Stock registrar   Typically, a bank that maintains records of the shares outstanding for a company.   *438*

Stock-transfer agent   Typically, a bank or trust company employed by a corporation to transfer stock between buyers and sellers.   *438*

Stock without par value   See *no-par stock*.

Unissued shares   Capital stock authorized but not yet issued.   *440*

Self-Test

True-False

Indicate whether each of the following statements is true or false.

1.   A person may favor the corporate form of organization for a risky business enterprise primarily because a corporation's shares can be easily transferred.

2.   In the event of corporate liquidation, stockholders whose stock is preferred as to assets are entitled to receive the par value of their shares before any amounts are distributed to creditors or common stockholders.

3. The par value of a share of capital stock is no indication of the market value or book value of the share of stock.

4. When 10,000 shares of $20 par value common stock are issued in payment for a parcel of land with a fair market value of $300,000, the Common Stock account is credited for $200,000, and the Paid-In Capital in Excess of Par Value—Common account is credited for $100,000.

MULTIPLE-CHOICE

Select the best answer for each of the following questions.

1. Which of the following is not an advantage of the corporate form of organization?
   a. Continuous existence of the entity.
   b. Limited liability of stockholders.
   c. Government regulation.
   d. Easy transfer of ownership.

2. An arbitrary amount assigned by the board of directors to each share of a given class of no-par stock is:
   a. Quasi-par value.
   b. Stated value.
   c. Redemption value.
   d. Liquidation value.

3. Preferred stock that has dividends in arrears is:
   a. Noncumulative preferred stock.
   b. Noncumulative and callable preferred stock.
   c. Noncumulative and convertible preferred stock.
   d. Cumulative preferred stock.

4. Quinn Corporation issued 10,000 shares of $20 par value common stock at $50 per share. The amount that would be credited to Paid-In Capital in Excess of Par Value—Common is:
   a. $200,000.　　　 d. $700,000.
   b. $300,000.　　　 e. None of the above.
   c. $500,000.

5. You are given the following information: Capital Stock, $80,000 ($80 par); Paid-In Capital in Excess of Par Value—Common, $200,000; and Retained Earnings, $400,000. Assuming only one class of stock, the book value per share is:
   a. $680.　　　 d. $400.
   b. $280.　　　 e. None of the above.
   c. $80.

Now turn to page 462 to check your answers.

QUESTIONS

1. Cite the major advantages of the corporate form of business organization and indicate why each is considered an advantage.

2. What is meant by the statement that corporate income is subject to double taxation? Cite several other disadvantages of the corporate form of organization.

3. Why is Organization Expense not a good title for the account that records the costs of organizing a corporation? Could you justify leaving the balance of an Organization Costs account intact throughout the life of a corporation?

4. What are the basic rights associated with a share of capital stock if there is only one class of stock outstanding?

5. Explain the purpose or function of: *(a)* the stockholders' ledger, *(b)* the minutes book, *(c)* the stock-transfer agent, and *(d)* the stock registrar.

6. What are the differences between par value stock and stock with no-par value?

7. Corporate capital stock is seldom issued for less than par value. Give two reasons why this statement is true.

8. Explain the terms *liquidation value* and *redemption value*.

9. What are the meanings of the terms *stock preferred as to dividends* and *stock preferred as to assets?*

10. What do the terms *cumulative* and *noncumulative* mean in regard to preferred stock?

11. What are *dividends in arrears,* and how should they be disclosed in the financial statements?

12. A corporation has 1,000 shares of 8%, $200 par value, cumulative, preferred stock outstanding. Dividends on this stock have not been declared for three years. Is the corporation legally liable to its preferred stockholders for these dividends? How should this fact be shown in the balance sheet, if at all?

13. Explain why a corporation might issue a preferred stock that is both convertible into common stock and callable.

14. Explain the nature of the account entitled Paid-In Capital in Excess of Par Value. Under what circumstances is this account credited?

15. Blake Corporation issued 5,000 shares of $100 par value common stock at $120 per share. What is the legal capital of Blake Corporation, and why is the amount of legal capital important?

16. What is the general approach of the accountant in determining the dollar amount at which to record the issuance of capital stock for services or property other than cash?

17. What assumptions are made in determining book value?

18. Assuming there is no preferred stock outstanding, how can the book value per share of common stock be determined? Of what significance is the book value per share? What is the relationship of book value per share to market value per share?

MAYTAG

19. **Real World Question** Based on the financial statements of Maytag Corporation contained in the annual report booklet, what was the number of shares of common stock authorized?

THE LIMITED, INC.

20. **Real World Question** Based on the financial statements of The Limited, Inc., contained in the annual report booklet, what was the 1996 ending paid-in capital?

HARLAND

21. **Real World Question** Based on the financial statements of John H. Harland Company contained in the annual report booklet, what was the 1996 ending number of shares of common stock issued?

EXERCISES

Winters Corporation has outstanding 1,000 shares of noncumulative preferred stock and 2,000 shares of common stock. The preferred stock is entitled to an annual dividend of $100 per share before dividends are declared on common stock. What are the total dividends received by each class of stock if Winters Corporation distributes $280,000 in dividends in 1999?

Exercise 12–1
Determine dividends for common and noncumulative preferred stock (L.O. 3)

Zeff Corporation has 2,000 shares outstanding of cumulative preferred stock and 6,000 shares of common stock. The preferred stock is entitled to an annual dividend of $18 per share before dividends are declared on common stock. No preferred dividends were paid for last year and the current year. What are the total dividends received by each class of stock if Zeff Corporation distributes $108,000 in dividends?

Exercise 12–2
Determine dividends for common and cumulative preferred stock (L.O. 3)

Gordon Company issued 10,000 shares of common stock for $1,120,000 cash. The common stock has a par value of $100 per share. Give the journal entry for the stock issuance.

Exercise 12–3
Journalize stock issuance (L.O. 5)

Thore Company issued 30,000 shares of $20 par value common stock for $680,000. What is the journal entry for this transaction? What would the journal entry be if the common stock had no-par or stated value?

Exercise 12–4
Prepare entries for stock issuance (L.O. 5)

Li & Tu, Inc., needed land for a plant site. It issued 100 shares of $480 par value common stock to the incorporators of their corporation in exchange for land, which cost $56,000 one year ago. Experienced appraisers recently valued the land at $72,000. What journal entry would be appropriate to record the acquisition of the land?

Exercise 12–5
Journalize stock issuance for property (L.O. 5)

Smart Corporation owes a trade creditor $30,000 on open account which the corporation does not have sufficient cash to pay. The trade creditor suggests that Smart Corporation issue to him 750 shares of the $24 par value common stock, which is currently selling on the market at $40. Present the entry or entries that should be made on Smart Corporation's books.

Exercise 12–6
Journalize stock issuance to satisfy liability (L.O. 5)

Why would a law firm ever consider accepting stock of a new corporation having a total par value of $320,000 as payment in full of a $480,000 bill for legal services rendered? If such a transaction occurred, give the journal entry the issuing company would make on its books.

Exercise 12–7
Journalize stock issuance for legal services (L.O. 5)

The stockholders' equity section of Graf Company's balance sheet is as follows:

Exercise 12–8
Compute the book value and average price of common stock (L.O. 6)

Stockholders' equity:
  Paid-in capital:
    Common stock—without par value, $12 stated value;
      authorized 100,000 shares; issued and
      outstanding, 70,000 shares $840,000
    Paid-in capital in excess of stated value 340,000
      Total paid-in capital $1,180,000
  Retained earnings 80,000
      Total stockholders' equity $1,260,000

Compute the average price at which the 70,000 issued shares of common stock were sold. Compute the book value per share of common stock.

PROBLEMS

Problem 12–1
Determine dividends for common stock and cumulative and noncumulative preferred stock (L.O. 3)

On January 1, 1994, the retained earnings of Quigley Company were $432,000. Net income for the succeeding five years was as follows:

1994	$288,000
1995	216,000
1996	4,800
1997	48,000
1998	264,000

The outstanding capital stock of the corporation consisted of 2,000 shares of preferred stock with a par value of $480 per share that pays a dividend of $19.20 per year and 8,000 shares of no-par common stock with a stated value of $240 per share. No dividends were in arrears as of January 1, 1994.

Required

Prepare schedules showing how the net income for these five years was distributed to the two classes of stock if in each of the years the entire current net income was distributed as dividends and the preferred stock was:

a. Cumulative.

b. Noncumulative.

Problem 12–2
Journalize stock issuances for cash, services (organization costs), and property; prepare resulting balance sheet (L.O. 5)

On January 1, 1998, Cowling Company was authorized to issue 500,000 shares of $5 par value common stock. It then completed the following transactions:

1998
Jan. 14   Issued 90,000 shares of common stock at $24 per share for cash.
    29   Gave the promoters of the corporation 50,000 shares of common stock for their services in organizing the company. The board of directors valued these services at $620,000.
Feb. 19   Exchanged 100,000 shares of common stock for the following assets at the indicated fair market values:

Equipment	$180,000
Building	440,000
Land	600,000

Required

a. Prepare general journal entries to record the transactions.

b. Prepare the balance sheet of the company as of March 1, 1998.

Problem 12–3
Post transactions; prepare balance sheets for par value stock, stated value stock, and no-par or stated value stock (L.O. 2, 4, 5)

On July 3, 1998, Barr Company was authorized to issue 15,000 shares of common stock; 3,000 shares were issued immediately to the incorporators of the company for cash at $320 per share. On July 5 of that year, an additional 300 shares were issued to the incorporators for services rendered in organizing the company. The board valued these services at $96,000. On July 6, 1998, legal and printing costs of $12,000 were paid. These costs related to securing the corporate charter and the stock certificates.

Required

a. Set up T-accounts and post these transactions. Then prepare the balance sheet of the Barr Company as of the close of July 10, 1998, assuming the authorized stock has a $160 par value.

b. Repeat (a) for the T-accounts involving stockholders' equity, assuming the stock is no-par stock with a $240 stated value. Prepare the stockholders' equity section of the balance sheet.

c. Repeat (a) for the T-accounts involving stockholders' equity, assuming the stock is no-par stock with no stated value. Prepare the stockholders' equity section of the balance sheet.

Problem 12–4
Journalize stock transactions, including conversions; prepare stockholders' equity section (L.O. 3–5)

Tempo Company received its charter on April 1, 1998, authorizing it to issue: (1) 10,000 shares of $400 par value, $32 cumulative, convertible preferred stock; (2) 10,000 shares of $12 cumulative no-par preferred stock having a stated value of $20 per share and a liquidation value of $100 per share; and (3) 100,000 shares of no-par common stock without a stated value.

On April 2, incorporators of the corporation acquired 50,000 shares of the common stock for cash at $80 per share, and 200 shares were issued to an attorney for services rendered in organizing the corporation. On April 3, the company issued all of its authorized shares of $32 convertible preferred stock for land valued at $1,600,000 and a building valued at $4,800,000. The property was subject to a mortgage of $2,400,000. On April 8, the company issued 5,000 shares of the $12 preferred stock in exchange for a patent valued at $1,040,000. On April 10, the company issued 1,000 shares of common stock for cash at $80 per share.

a. Prepare general journal entries for these transactions.

b. Prepare the stockholders' equity section of the April 30, 1998, balance sheet. Assume retained earnings were $80,000.

c. Assume that each share of the $32 convertible preferred stock is convertible into six shares of common stock and that one-half of the preferred is converted on September 1, 1998. Give the required journal entry.

Required

Kane Company issued all of its 5,000 shares of authorized preferred stock on January 1, 1997, at $100 per share. The preferred stock is no-par stock, has a stated value of $5 per share, is entitled to a cumulative basic preference dividend of $6 per share, is callable at $110 beginning in 2002, and is entitled to $100 per share in liquidation plus cumulative dividends. On this same date, Kane also issued 10,000 authorized shares of no-par common stock with a $10 stated value at $50 per share.

On December 31, 1998, the end of its second year of operations, the company's retained earnings amounted to $160,000. No dividends have been declared or paid on either class of stock since the date of issue.

a. Prepare the stockholders' equity section of Kane Company's December 31, 1998, balance sheet.

b. Compute the book value in total and per share of each class of stock as of December 31, 1998.

c. If $110,000 of dividends are to be declared as of December 31, 1998, compute the amount payable to each class of stock.

Problem 12–5
Prepare stockholders' equity section; determine book values of stock; and determine dividends for each class of stock (L.O. 3, 6)

Required

The stockholders' equity sections from three different corporations' balance sheets follow.

Problem 12–6
Determine book value for each class of stock (L.O. 6)

1. Stockholders' equity:

Paid-in capital:
Preferred stock—7% cumulative, $240 par value,
500 shares authorized, issued, and outstanding . . . . . $ 120,000
Common stock—$48 par value, 10,000 shares
authorized, issued, and outstanding   480,000

Total paid-in capital	$ 600,000
Retained earnings	422,400
Total stockholders' equity	$ 1,022,400

(All dividends have been paid.)

2. Stockholders' equity:

Paid-in capital:
Preferred stock—6% cumulative, $80 par value,
10,000 shares authorized, issued, and outstanding . . . . $ 800,000
Common stock—$240 par value, 30,000 shares
authorized, issued, and outstanding   7,200,000

Total paid-in capital	$ 8,000,000
Retained earnings	88,000
Total stockholders' equity	$ 8,088,000

(The current year's dividends have not been paid.)

3. Stockholders' equity:

Paid-in capital:
Preferred stock—7% cumulative, $480 par value,
10,000 shares authorized, issued, and outstanding . . . . $ 4,800,000
Common stock—$240 par value, 50,000 shares
authorized, issued, and outstanding   12,000,000

Total paid-in capital	$16,800,000
Retained earnings (deficit)	(1,872,000)
Total stockholders' equity	$14,928,000

(Dividends have not been paid for 2 previous years or the current year.)

Required   Compute the book values per share of the preferred and common stock of each corporation assuming that in a liquidation the preferred stock receives par value plus dividends in arrears.

Problem 12–7
Compute book values of a stockholder's preferred and common stock (L.O. 6)

Mendell, Inc., is a corporation in which all of the outstanding preferred and common stock is held by the four Lehman brothers. The brothers have an agreement stating that the remaining brothers will, upon the death of a brother, purchase from the estate his holdings of stock in the company at book value.

The stockholders' equity section of the balance sheet for the company on December 31, 1998, the date of the death of James Lehman, shows:

Stockholders' equity:
Paid-in capital:		
Preferred stock—6%; $320 par value; $320 liquidation value;		
4,000 shares authorized, issued, and outstanding		$1,280,000
Paid-in capital in excess of par—preferred		64,000
Common stock—without par value, $16 stated value,		
60,000 shares authorized, issued, and outstanding		960,000
Paid-in capital in excess of par—common		960,000
Total paid-in capital		$3,264,000
Retained earnings		128,000
Total stockholders' equity		$3,392,000

No dividends have been paid for the last year on the preferred stock, which is cumulative. At the time of his death, James Lehman held 2,000 shares of preferred stock and 10,000 shares of common stock of the company.

Required   **a.** Compute the book value of the preferred stock.

b. Compute the book value of the common stock.

c. Compute the amount the remaining brothers must pay to the estate of James Lehman for the preferred and common stock that he held at the time of his death.

ALTERNATE PROBLEMS

Problem 12–1A
Determine dividends for common stock and cumulative and noncumulative preferred stock (L.O. 3)

The outstanding capital stock of Robbins Corporation consisted of 3,000 shares of 10% preferred stock, $250 par value, and 30,000 shares of no-par common stock with a stated value of $250. The preferred was issued at $412, the common at $480 per share. On January 1, 1994, the retained earnings of the company were $250,000. During the succeeding five years, net income was as follows:

1994	$767,500
1995	510,000
1996	48,000
1997	160,000
1998	662,500

No dividends were in arrears as of January 1, 1994, and during the five years 1994–98, the board of directors declared dividends in each year equal to net income of the year.

Required   Prepare a schedule showing the dividends declared each year on each class of stock assuming the preferred stock is:

a. Cumulative.

b. Noncumulative.

Problem 12–2A
Journalize stock issuances for cash, services (organization costs), and property; prepare resulting balance sheet (L.O. 5)

On December 27, 1997, Glade Company was authorized to issue 250,000 shares of $24 par value common stock. It then completed the following transactions:

1998
Jan. 14   Issued 45,000 shares of common stock at $30 per share for cash.
    29   Gave the promoters of the corporation 25,000 shares of common stock for their services in organizing the company. The board of directors valued these services at $744,000.
Feb. 19   Exchanged 50,000 shares of common stock for the following assets at the indicated fair market values:

Land	$216,000
Building	528,000
Machinery	720,000

a. Prepare general journal entries to record the transactions.

b. Prepare the balance sheet of the company as of March 1, 1998.

Required

In the corporate charter that it received on May 1, 1998, Norris Company was authorized to issue 15,000 shares of common stock. The company issued 1,000 shares immediately for $82 per share, cash.

    On July 2, the company issued 100 shares of stock to a lawyer to satisfy a $8,400 bill for legal services rendered in organizing the corporation.

    On July 5, the company issued 1,000 shares to the principal promoter of the corporation in exchange for a patent. Another 200 shares were issued to this same person for costs incurred and services rendered in bringing the corporation into existence. The market value of the stock was $84 per share.

Problem 12–3A
Post transactions; prepare balance sheets for par value stock, stated value stock, and no-par or stated value stock (L.O. 2, 4, 5)

a. Set up T-accounts, and post these transactions. Then prepare a balance sheet for the Norris Company as of July 5, 1998, assuming the authorized stock has a par value of $75 per share.

b. Repeat part **(a)** for the stockholders' equity accounts, and prepare the stockholders' equity section of the July 5 balance sheet assuming the stock authorized has no par value but has a $30 per share stated value.

c. Repeat part **(a)** for the stockholders' equity accounts assuming the stock authorized has neither par nor stated value. Prepare the stockholders' equity section of the balance sheet.

Required

On May 1, 1998, Farmington Company received a charter that authorized it to issue:

1. 4,000 shares of no-par preferred stock to which a stated value of $12 per share is assigned. The stock is entitled to a cumulative dividend of $9.60, convertible into two shares of common stock, callable at $208, and entitled to $200 per share in liquidation.

2. 1,500 shares of $400 par value, $20 cumulative preferred stock, which is callable at $420 and entitled to $412 in liquidation.

3. 60,000 shares of no-par common stock to which a stated value of $40 is assigned.

Problem 12–4A
Journalize stock issuances for cash, property, and services; and prepare resulting stockholders' equity section (L.O. 5)

May 1 All of the $9.60 cumulative preferred was issued at $204 per share, cash.
      2 All of the $20 cumulative preferred was exchanged for merchandise inventory, land, and buildings valued at $128,000, $160,000, and $425,000, respectively.
      3 Cash of $15,000 was paid to reimburse promoters for costs incurred for accounting, legal, and printing services. In addition, 1,000 shares of common stock were issued to the promoters for their services. The value of all of the services (including those paid in cash) was $55,000.

Transactions

a. Prepare journal entries for these transactions.

b. Assume that retained earnings were $200,000. Prepare the stockholders' equity section of the May 31, 1998, balance sheet.

Required

On January 2, 1997, the King Company received its charter. It issued all of its authorized 3,000 shares of no-par preferred stock at $104 and all of its 12,000 authorized shares of no-par common stock at $40 per share. The preferred stock has a stated value of $50 per share, is entitled to a basic cumulative dividend of $6 per share, is callable at $106 beginning in 1999, and is entitled to $100 per share plus cumulative dividends in the event of liquidation. The common stock has a stated value of $10 per share.

    On December 31, 1998, the end of the second year of operations, retained earnings were $90,000. No dividends have been declared or paid on either class of stock.

Problem 12–5A
Prepare stockholders' equity section; determine book values of stock; and determine dividends for each class of stock (L.O. 3, 6)

a. Prepare the stockholders' equity section of King Company's December 31, 1998, balance sheet.

b. Compute the book value of each class of stock.

c. If $42,000 of dividends were declared as of December 31, 1998, compute the amount paid to each class of stock.

Required

Problem 12–6A
Compute total market value for common stock; compute book value of common and preferred stock (L.O. 6)

The common stock of Lang Corporation is selling on a stock exchange for $90 per share. The stockholders' equity of the corporation at December 31, 1998, consists of:

Stockholders' equity:

Paid-in capital:		
Preferred stock–9% cumulative, $120 par value, $120 liquidation value, 3,000 shares authorized, issued, and outstanding	$ 360,000	
Common stock–$72 par value, 30,000 shares authorized, issued, and outstanding	2,160,000	
Total paid-in capital		$2,520,000
Retained earnings		354,600
Total stockholders' equity		$2,874,600

Assume that in liquidation the preferred stock is entitled to par value plus cumulative unpaid dividends.

Required
a. What is the total market value of all of the corporation's common stock?
b. If all dividends have been paid on the preferred stock as of December 31, 1998, what are the book values of the preferred stock and the common stock?
c. If two years' dividends were due on the preferred stock as of December 31, 1998, what are the book values of the preferred stock and common stock?

Problem 12–7A
Compute book values of a stockholder's preferred and common stock (L.O. 6)

Haft Corporation has an agreement with each of its 15 preferred and 30 common stockholders that in the event of the death of a stockholder, it will purchase at book value from the stockholder's estate or heirs the shares of Haft Corporation stock held by the deceased at the time of death. The book value is to be computed in accordance with generally accepted accounting principles.

Following is the stockholders' equity section of the Haft Corporation's December 31, 1998, balance sheet.

Stockholders' equity:

Paid-in capital:		
Preferred stock—without par value, $50 stated value, $15 cumulative; 3,000 shares authorized, issued, and outstanding	$ 150,000	
Common stock—$62.50 par value, 60,000 shares authorized, issued, and outstanding	3,750,000	
Paid-in capital in excess of stated value—preferred	840,000	
Paid-in capital in excess of par value—common	30,000	
Total paid-in capital		$4,770,000
Retained earnings		1,800,000
Total stockholders' equity		$6,570,000

The preferred stock is cumulative and entitled to $300 per share plus cumulative dividends in liquidation. No dividends have been paid for 1½ years.

A stockholder who owned 100 shares of preferred stock and 1,000 shares of common stock died on December 31, 1998. You have been employed by the stockholder's executor to compute the book value of each class of stock and to determine the price to be paid for the stock held by her late husband.

Required
Prepare a schedule showing the computation of the amount to be paid for the deceased stockholder's preferred and common stock.

BEYOND THE NUMBERS—CRITICAL THINKING

Business Decision Case 12–1
Compute dividends on preferred stock and common stock and determine their relationship to stock prices (L.O. 3)

Rudd Company and Clay Company have extremely stable net income amounts of $4,800,000 and $3,200,000, respectively. Both companies distribute all their net income as dividends each year. Rudd Company has 100,000 shares of $80 par value, 6% preferred stock, and 500,000 shares of $8 par value common stock outstanding. Clay Company has 50,000 shares of $40 par value, 8% preferred stock, and 400,000 shares of $8 par value common stock outstanding. Both preferred stocks are cumulative.

a.   Compute the annual dividend per share of preferred stock and per share of common stock for each company.

b.   Based solely on the preceding information, which common stock would you predict to have the higher market price per share? Why?

c.   Which company's stock would you buy? Why?

Required

Jesse Waltrip recently inherited $480,000 cash that he wishes to invest in the common stock of either the West Corporation or the East Corporation. Both corporations have manufactured the same types of products for five years. The stockholders' equity sections of the two corporations' latest balance sheets follow:

Business Decision Case 12–2
Determine book values and their relationship to investment decisions (L.O. 6)

WEST CORPORATION

Stockholders' equity:

Paid-in capital:
Common stock—$125 par value, 30,000 shares authorized,

issued, and outstanding	$3,750,000
Retained earnings	3,450,000
Total stockholders' equity	$7,200,000

EAST CORPORATION

Stockholders' equity:

Paid-in capital:
Preferred stock–8%, $500 par value, cumulative 4,000 shares

authorized, issued, and outstanding	$2,000,000	
Common stock–$125 par value, 40,000 shares authorized,		
issued, and outstanding	5,000,000	
Total paid-in capital		$7,000,000
Retained earnings		560,000
Total stockholders' equity		$7,560,000

The West Corporation has paid a cash dividend of $6 per share each year since its creation; its common stock is currently selling for $590 per share. The East Corporation's common stock is currently selling for $480 per share. The current year's dividend and three prior years' dividends on the preferred stock are in arrears. The preferred stock has a liquidation value of $600 per share.

Required

a.   What is the book value per share of the West Corporation common stock and the East Corporation common stock? Is book value the major determinant of market value of the stock?

b.   Based solely on the previous information, which investment would you recommend to Waltrip? Why?

Refer to the 1996 consolidated balance sheet of The Coca-Cola Company in the annual report booklet. In the shareholders' equity section, determine the price paid per share of common stock upon original issuance. Assume that the capital surplus represents additional paid-in capital from the issuance of common stock.

Determine the 1996 return on average common stockholders' equity for each of the companies in the annual report booklet. Explain in writing why this information is important to managers, investors, and creditors.

Annual Report Analysis 12–3
Determine original issuance price of common stock (L.O. 4)
Determine return on average common stockholders' equity (L.O. 7)

Refer to the ethics case concerning Joe Morrison on page 449 to answer the following questions:

Ethics Case 12–4
Answer questions regarding the ethics case

a.   Which alternative would benefit the company and its management over the next several years?

b.   Which alternative would benefit society?

c.   If you were Morrison, which side of the argument would you take?

Group Project 12–5
Calculate return on average common stockholders' equity and make investment decision

In teams of two or three students, examine the annual reports of three companies and calculate each company's return on common shareholders' equity for the most recent two years. At least two years are needed to observe any changes. As a team, decide in which of the three companies you would invest. Appoint a spokesperson for the team to explain to the class which company the team would invest in and why.

Group Project 12–6
Examine annual reports of companies with preferred stock

In a team of two or three students, locate the annual reports of three companies that have preferred stock in their stockholders' equity section. Determine the features of the preferred stock. Analyze the data in the annual report to determine whether dividends have been paid on the preferred stock each year. Are there dividends in arrears? Write a report to your instructor summarizing your findings. Also be prepared to make a short presentation to the class.

Group Project 12–7
Investigate incorporation laws of your state

In a group of one or two students, contact state officials and/or consult library resources to inquire about the incorporation laws in your state. Determine your state laws regarding the issuance of stock at an amount below par value, how legal capital is determined, and the requirements and government fees for incorporating a company in your state. Write a report to your instructor summarizing the results of your investigation and be prepared to make a short presentation to your class.

Using the Internet—A View of the Real World

Internet Project 12–8
Investigate a consolidated statement of stockholders' equity

Visit the following website for Macromedia:
http://www.macromedia.com
Pursue choices on the screen until you locate the consolidated statement of stockholders' equity. You will probably go down some "false paths" to get to this financial statement, but you can get there. This experience is all part of learning to use the Internet. Note the changes that have occurred in the Common Stock, Additional Paid-In Capital, and Retained Earnings accounts. Check out the notes to the financial statements for further information. Write a memo to your instructor summarizing your findings.

Internet Project 12–9
Investigate a consolidated statement of stockholders' equity

Visit the following website for Gartner Group:
http://www.gartner.com
Pursue choices on the screen until you locate the consolidated statement of stockholders' equity. You will probably go down some "false paths" to get to this financial statement, but you can get there. This experience is all part of learning to use the Internet. Trace the changes that have occurred in the last three years in the Common Stock account. Check out the notes to the financial statements for further information. Write a memo to your instructor summarizing your findings.

Answers to Self-Test

True-False

1. **False.** This is not the primary reason a person may prefer the corporate form of business organization in a situation involving considerable risk. The primary reason is that stockholders can lose only the amount of capital they have invested in a corporation.

2. **False.** The claims of the creditors rank ahead of the claims of the stockholders, even those stockholders whose stock is preferred as to assets.

3. **True.** Par value is simply the amount per share that is credited to the Capital Stock account for each share issued and is no indication of the market value or the book value of the stock.

4. **True.** When capital stock is issued for property or services, the transaction is recorded at the fair market value of (1) the property or services received or (2) the stock issued, whichever is more clearly evident.

Multiple-Choice

1. **c.** This feature of corporations is one of the disadvantages of the corporate form of organization.

2. **b.** Stated value is an arbitrary amount assigned by the board of directors to each share of capital stock without a par value.

3. **d.** Dividends in arrears are cumulative unpaid dividends. Only cumulative preferred stock has dividends in arrears.

4. **b.** The amount credited to the Paid-In Capital in Excess of Par Value—Common is computed as follows:

$$10{,}000 \text{ shares} \times (\$50 - \$20) = \$300{,}000$$

5. **a.** The book value of common stock is computed as follows:

Total book value of stockholders' equity ($80,000 + $200,000 + $400,000)	$680,000
Total shares	÷1,000
Book value per share	$ 680

13

CORPORATIONS
PAID-IN CAPITAL, RETAINED EARNINGS, DIVIDENDS, AND TREASURY STOCK

As owners of a corporation, stockholders provide much of the capital for its activities. On the balance sheet, we show the stockholders' capital investment in the corporation as paid-in capital under stockholders' equity. Also included in stockholders' equity is the capital accumulated through the retention of corporate earnings (retained earnings). Paid-in capital is a relatively permanent portion of stockholders' equity; the retained earnings balance is a relatively temporary portion of corporate capital and is the source of stockholders' dividends.

The preceding chapter discussed the paid-in capital obtained by issuing shares of stock for cash, property, or services. This chapter describes additional sources of paid-in capital and items affecting retained earnings.

PAID-IN (OR CONTRIBUTED) CAPITAL

As you have learned in the preceding chapter, **paid-in capital,** or **contributed capital,** refers to all of the contributed capital of a corporation, including the capital carried in the capital stock accounts. The general ledger does not contain an account titled "Paid-In Capital." Instead, paid-in capital is a category, and companies establish a separate account for each source of paid-in capital.

In Illustration 13.1, we summarize several sources of stockholders' equity and list general ledger account titles used to record increases and decreases in capital from each of these sources. Chapter 12 discussed some of these general ledger accounts. This chapter discusses other general ledger accounts that record sources of stockholders' equity.

The stockholders' equity section of a balance sheet shows the different sources of the corporation's paid-in capital because these sources are important information. For example, these additional sources may be from stock dividends, treasury stock transactions, or donations.

LEARNING OBJECTIVES

After studying this chapter, you should be able to:

1. Identify the different sources of paid-in capital and describe how to present them on a balance sheet.

2. Account for a cash dividend, a stock dividend, a stock split, and a retained earnings appropriation.

3. Account for the acquisition and reissuance of treasury stock.

4. Describe the proper accounting treatment of discontinued operations, extraordinary items, and changes in accounting principle.

(continued)

Sources of Stockholders' Equity	Illustrative General Ledger Account Titles	

I. Capital paid in (or contributed).
  A. For, or assigned to, shares:
    1. Issued to the extent of par or stated value or the amount received for shares without par or stated value.
    2. To be distributed as a stock dividend.
    3. In addition to par or stated value:
      a. In excess of par.
 	
      b. In excess of stated value.
 	
      c. Resulting from declaration of stock dividends.
      d. Resulting from reissue of treasury stock at a price above its acquisition price.
  B. Donations (gifts), whether from stockholders or from others.
II. Capital accumulated by retention of earnings (retained earnings).
  A. Appropriated retained earnings.
  B. Free and unappropriated retained earnings.
	Common Stock
	5% Preferred Stock
	
	Stock Dividend Distributable—Common (Preferred)
	
	Paid-In Capital in Excess of Par Value—Common (Preferred)
	Paid-In Capital in Excess of Stated Value—Common (Preferred)
	Paid-In Capital—Stock Dividends
	
	Paid-In Capital—Common (Preferred) Treasury Stock Transactions
	
	Paid-In Capital—Donations
	
	Appropriation per Loan Agreement
	Retained Earnings (Unappropriated)
		ILLUSTRATION 13.1
		Sources of Stockholders' Equity

Paid-In Capital—Stock Dividends

When it declares a stock dividend, a corporation distributes additional shares of stock (instead of cash) to its present stockholders. A later section discusses and illustrates how the issuance of a stock dividend results in a credit to a Paid-In Capital—Stock Dividends account.

Paid-In Capital—Treasury Stock Transactions

Another source of capital is treasury stock transactions. **Treasury stock** is the corporation's own stock, either preferred or common, that it has issued and reacquired. It is legally available for reissuance. By reacquiring shares of its own outstanding capital stock at one price and later reissuing them at a higher price, a corporation can increase its capital by the difference between the two prices. If the reissue price is *less* than acquisition cost, however, corporate capital decreases. We discuss treasury stock transactions at length later in this chapter.

Paid-In Capital—Donations

Occasionally, a corporation receives a gift of assets, such as a $500,000 building. These donated gifts increase stockholders' equity and are called **donated capital.** The entry to record the gift of a $500,000 building is a debit to Buildings and a credit to Paid-In Capital—Donations. Accountants would make this entry in the amount of the $500,000 fair market value of the gift when received.

RETAINED EARNINGS

The **retained earnings** portion of stockholders' equity typically results from accumulated earnings, reduced by net losses and dividends. Like paid-in capital, retained earnings is a source of assets received by a corporation. Paid-in capital is the actual investment by the stockholders; retained earnings is the investment by the stockholders through earnings not yet withdrawn.

(concluded)

5. Define prior period adjustments and show their proper presentation in the financial statements.

6. Analyze and use the financial results—earnings per share and price-earnings ratio.

Objective 1
Identify the different sources of paid-in capital and describe how to present them on a balance sheet.

The balance in the corporation's Retained Earnings account is the corporation's net income, less net losses, from the date the corporation began to the present, less the sum of dividends paid during this period. Net income increases Retained Earnings, while net losses and dividends decrease Retained Earnings in any given year. Thus, the balance in Retained Earnings represents the corporation's accumulated net income not distributed to stockholders.

When the Retained Earnings account has a debit balance, a **deficit** exists. A company indicates a deficit by listing retained earnings with a negative amount in the stockholders' equity section of the balance sheet. The firm need not change the title of the general ledger account even though it contains a debit balance. The most common credits and debits made to Retained Earnings are for income (or losses) and dividends. Occasionally, accountants make other entries to the Retained Earnings account. We discuss some of these entries later in the chapter.

PAID-IN CAPITAL AND RETAINED EARNINGS ON THE BALANCE SHEET

The following stockholders' equity section of a balance sheet presents the various sources of capital in proper form:

Stockholders' equity:

Paid-in capital:		
Preferred stock—6%, $100 par value; authorized, issued, and outstanding, 4,000 shares	$ 400,000	
Common stock—no-par value, $5 stated value; authorized, issued, and outstanding, 400,000 shares	2,000,000	$2,400,000
Paid-in capital—		
From preferred stock issuances*	$ 40,000	
From donations	10,000	50,000
Total paid-in capital		$2,450,000
Retained earnings		500,000
Total stockholders' equity		$2,950,000

*This label is not the exact account title but is representative of the descriptions used on balance sheets. The exact account title could be used, but shorter descriptions are often shown.

In their highly condensed, published balance sheets, companies often omit the details regarding the sources of the paid-in capital in excess of par or stated value and replace them by a single item, such as:

Paid-in capital in excess of par (or stated) value $50,000

DIVIDENDS

Objective 2
Account for a cash dividend, a stock dividend, a stock split, and a retained earnings appropriation.

Dividends are distributions of earnings by a corporation to its stockholders. Usually the corporation pays dividends in cash, but it may distribute additional shares of the corporation's own capital stock as dividends. Occasionally, a company pays dividends in merchandise or other assets. Since dividends are the means whereby the owners of a corporation share in its earnings, accountants charge them against retained earnings.

Before dividends can be paid, the board of directors must declare them so they can be recorded in the corporation's minutes book. Three dividend dates are significant:

1. **Date of declaration.** The date of declaration indicates when the board of directors approved a motion declaring that dividends should be paid. The board action creates the liability for dividends payable (or stock dividends distributable for stock dividends).

2. **Date of record.** The board of directors establishes the date of record; it determines which stockholders receive dividends. The corporation's records (the stockholders' ledger) determine its stockholders as of the date of record.

3. **Date of payment.** The date of payment indicates when the corporation will pay dividends to the stockholders.

To illustrate how these three dates relate to an actual situation, assume the board of directors of the Allen Corporation declared a cash dividend on May 5, 1999 (date of declaration). The cash dividend declared is $1.25 per share to stockholders of record on July 1, 1999 (date of record), payable on July 10 (date of payment). Because financial transactions occur on both the date of declaration (a liability is incurred) and on the date of payment (cash is paid), journal entries record the transactions on both of these dates. No journal entry is required on the date of record.

Illustration 13.2 shows the frequencies of dividend payments made by a sample of representative companies for the years 1992–95. Note that cash dividends are far more numerous than stock dividends or dividends in kind (paid in merchandise or other assets).

USES OF TECHNOLOGY After original issuance, investors may trade the stock of a company on secondary markets, such as the New York Stock Exchange. The company makes no entry on its books for these outside trades after issuance. Often, a company uses a spreadsheet or database program to note trades between shareholders. These computer programs can print a report on the date of record. This information allows a company that declares a dividend to be certain the money or stock goes to the stockholders who own the stock on the date of record rather than to the stockholders who originally purchased the stock.

AN ACCOUNTING PERSPECTIVE

Cash Dividends

Cash dividends are cash distributions of accumulated earnings by a corporation to its stockholders. To illustrate the entries for cash dividends, consider the following example. On January 21, 1999, a corporation's board of directors declared a 2% quarterly cash dividend on $100,000 of outstanding preferred stock. This dividend is one-fourth of the annual dividend on 1,000 shares of $100 par value, 8% preferred stock. The dividend will be paid on March 1, 1999, to stockholders of record on February 5, 1999. An entry is not needed on the date of record; however, the entries at the declaration and payment dates are as follows:

Real World Example
On November 18, 1993, Pepsico, Inc., declared a $.16 per share quarterly cash dividend, payable on January 1, 1994, to stockholders of record on December 10, 1993.

1999					
Jan.	21	Retained Earnings.	2,000	
		Dividends Payable.		2,000
		Dividends declared: 2% on $100,000 of outstanding preferred stock, payable March 1, 1999, to stockholders of record on February 5, 1999.		
Mar.	1	Dividends Payable.	2,000	
		Cash		2,000
		Paid the dividend declared on January 21, 1999.		

Often a cash dividend is stated as so many dollars per share. For instance, the quarterly dividend could have been stated as $2 per share. When they declare a cash dividend, some companies debit a Dividends account instead of Retained Earnings. (Both methods are acceptable.) The Dividends account is then closed to Retained Earnings at the end of the fiscal year.

Once a cash dividend is declared and notice of the dividend is given to stockholders, a company generally cannot rescind it unless all stockholders agree to such action.[1] Thus, the credit balance in the Dividends Payable account appears as a current liability on the balance sheet.

Reinforcing Problem
E13–2 Prepare journal entries for cash dividends.

---

[1]Stockholders might agree to rescind (cancel) a dividend already declared if the company is in difficult financial circumstances and needs to retain cash to pay bills or acquire assets to continue operations.

ILLUSTRATION 13.2
Types of Dividends

	Number of Companies			
	1995	**1994**	**1993**	**1992**
Cash Dividends Paid to Common Stock Shareholders				
Per share amount disclosed in retained earnings statements	276	278	283	290
Per share amount not disclosed in retained earnings statements	168	159	161	162
Total	444	437	444	452
Cash Dividends Paid to Preferred Stock Shareholders				
Per share amount disclosed in retained earnings statements	49	45	51	47
Per share amount not disclosed in retained earnings statements	84	91	87	83
Total	133	136	138	130
Dividends Paid by Pooled Companies	3	2	—	1
Stock dividends	11	8	12	10
Dividends in kind	14	8	11	12
Stock purchase rights	10	3	4	2

Source: Based on American Institute of Certified Public Accountants, *Accounting Trends & Techniques* (New York: AICPA, 1996), p. 401.

AN ACCOUNTING PERSPECTIVE

BUSINESS INSIGHT   Fleetwood Enterprises, Inc., is the nation's leading producer of manufactured housing and recreational vehicles. Often investors believe a company that pays dividends is doing well. Therefore, companies try to maintain a record of paying dividends, as Fleetwood noted in its 1996 annual report.

Shareholder Dividend Increased for 14th Consecutive Year. At the June 1996 meeting, the board of directors approved a 7 percent increase in the shareholder dividend to an annual rate of 64 cents per share. This action, which is consistent with the Company's objective of long-term dividend growth, reflects the Company's solid financial position and excellent prospects for future earnings growth.

A company that lacks sufficient cash for a cash dividend may declare a stock dividend to satisfy its shareholders. Note that in the long run it may be more beneficial to the company and the shareholders to reinvest the capital in the business rather than paying a cash dividend. If so, the company would be more profitable and the shareholders would be rewarded with a higher stock price in the future.

Stock Dividends

Stock dividends are payable in additional shares of the declaring corporation's capital stock. When declaring stock dividends, companies issue additional shares of the same class of stock as that held by the stockholders.

Corporations usually account for stock dividends by transferring a sum from retained earnings to permanent paid-in capital. The amount transferred for stock dividends depends on the size of the stock dividend. For stock dividends, most states permit corporations to debit Retained Earnings or any paid-in capital accounts other than those representing legal capital. In most circumstances, however, they debit Retained Earnings when a stock dividend is declared.

Stock dividends have no effect on the total amount of stockholders' equity or on net assets. They merely decrease retained earnings and increase paid-in capital by an equal amount. Immediately after the distribution of a stock dividend, each share of similar stock has a lower book value per share. This decrease occurs because more shares are outstanding with no increase in total stockholders' equity.

Stock dividends do not affect the individual stockholder's percentage of ownership in the corporation. For example, a stockholder who owns 1,000 shares in a corporation having 100,000 shares of stock outstanding, owns 1% of the outstanding shares. After a 10% stock dividend, the stockholder still owns 1% of the outstanding shares—1,100 of the 110,000 outstanding shares.

A corporation might declare a stock dividend for several reasons:

1. Retained earnings may have become large relative to total stockholders' equity, so the corporation may desire a larger permanent capitalization.

2. The market price of the stock may have risen above a desirable trading range. A stock dividend generally reduces the per share market value of the company's stock.

3. The board of directors of a corporation may wish to have more stockholders (who might then buy its products) and eventually increase their number by increasing the number of shares outstanding. Some of the stockholders receiving the stock dividend are likely to sell the shares to other persons.

4. Stock dividends may silence stockholders' demands for cash dividends from a corporation that does not have sufficient cash to pay cash dividends.

The percentage of shares issued determines whether a stock dividend is a small stock dividend or a large stock dividend. Firms use different accounting treatments for each category.

RECORDING SMALL STOCK DIVIDENDS   A stock dividend of less than 20 to 25% of the outstanding shares is a small stock dividend and has little effect on the market value (quoted market price) of the shares. Thus, the firm accounts for the dividend at the current market value of the outstanding shares.

Assume a corporation is authorized to issue 20,000 shares of $100 par value common stock, of which 8,000 shares are outstanding. Its board of directors declares a 10% stock dividend (800 shares). The quoted market price of the stock is $125 per share immediately before the stock dividend is announced. Since the distribution is less than 20 to 25% of the outstanding shares, the dividend is accounted for at market value. The entry for the declaration of the stock dividend on August 10, 1999, is:

Aug.	10	Retained Earnings (or Stock Dividends) (800 shares × $125)	100,000	
		Stock Dividend Distributable—Common		
		(800 shares × $100).		80,000
		Paid-In Capital—Stock Dividends		
		(800 shares × $25)		20,000
		To record the declaration of a 10% stock dividend; shares to be distributed on September 20, 1999, to stockholders of record on August 31, 1999.		

This entry records the issuance of the shares:

Sept.	20	Stock Dividend Distributable—Common	80,000	
		Common Stock		80,000
		To record the distribution of 800 shares of common stock as authorized in stock dividend declared on August 10, 1999.		

The **Stock Dividend Distributable—Common account** is a stockholders' equity (paid-in capital) account credited for the par or stated value of the shares distributable when recording the declaration of a stock dividend. Since a stock dividend distributable is not to be paid with assets, it is not a liability. When a balance sheet is prepared between the date the 10% dividend is declared and the date the shares are issued, the proper statement presentation of the effects of the stock dividend is:

Stockholders' equity:
Paid-in capital:		
Common stock—$100 par value; authorized, 20,000 shares; issued		
and outstanding, 8,000 shares	$800,000	
Stock dividend distributable on September 20, 1999, 800 shares at		
par value	80,000	
Total par value of shares issued and to be issued	$880,000	
Paid-in capital from stock dividends	20,000	
Total paid-in capital		$ 900,000
Retained earnings		150,000
Total stockholders' equity		$1,050,000

Reinforcing Problems
P13–2 and P13–2A Prepare journal entries for cash dividend and small stock dividend.

Suppose, on the other hand, that the common stock in the preceding example is no-par stock and has a stated value of $50 per share. The entry to record the declaration of the stock dividend (when the market value is $125) is:

Retained Earnings (800 shares × $125)	100,000	
Stock Dividend Distributable—Common		
(800 shares × $50)		40,000
Paid-In Capital—Stock Dividends (800 shares × $75)		60,000
To record the declaration of a stock dividend.		

The entry to record the issuance of the stock dividend is:

Stock Dividend Distributable—Common	40,000	
Common Stock		40,000
To record the issuance of the stock dividend.		

RECORDING LARGE STOCK DIVIDENDS   A stock dividend of more than 20 to 25% of the outstanding shares is a large stock dividend. Since one purpose of a large stock dividend is to reduce the market value of the stock so the shares can be traded more easily, firms do not use the current market value of the stock in the entry. They account for such dividends at their par or stated value rather than at their current market value. The laws of the state of incorporation or the board of directors establish the amounts for stocks without par or stated value.

To illustrate the treatment of a stock dividend of more than 20 to 25%, assume X Corporation has been authorized to issue 10,000 shares of $10 par value common stock, of which 5,000 shares are outstanding. X Corporation declared a 30% stock dividend (1,500 shares) on September 20, 1999, to be issued on October 15, 1999. The required entries are:

Sept.	20	Retained Earnings (or Stock Dividends) (1,500 shares × $10)	15,000	
		Stock Dividend Distributable—Common		15,000
		To declare a 30% stock dividend.		
Oct.	15	Stock Dividend Distributable—Common	15,000	
		Common Stock		15,000
		To issue the 30% stock dividend.		

Note to the Student
Accountants capitalize small stock dividends at the current market price, while they capitalize large stock dividends at par or stated value.

Reinforcing Problem
E13–4 Prepare journal entry for small stock dividend and discuss large stock dividend.

Note that although firms account for the small stock dividend at current market value, they account for the 30% stock dividend at par value (1,500 shares × $10 = $15,000). Because of the differences in accounting for large and small stock dividends, accountants must determine the relative size of the stock dividend before making any journal entries.

To see the effect of small and large stock dividends on stockholders' equity, look at Illustration 13.3.

Stock Splits

Real World Example
On February 13, 1997, Campbell Soup Company declared a 2-for-1 stock split payable to stockholders of record on February 24, 1997.

A **stock split** is a distribution of 100% or more of additional shares of the issuing corporation's stock accompanied by a corresponding reduction in the par value per share. The corporation receives no assets in this transaction. A stock split causes a large reduction in the market price per share of the outstanding stock. A two-for-one split doubles the number of shares outstanding, a three-for-one split triples the number of shares, and so on. The split reduces the par value per share at the same time so that the total dollar amount credited to Common Stock remains the same. For instance, a two-for-one split halves the par value per share.[2] If the corporation issues 100% more stock without a reduction in the par value per share, the transaction is a 100% stock dividend rather than a two-for-one stock split.

---

[2]If a corporation *reduces* the par value of its stock without issuing more shares, say, from $100 to $60 per share, then $40 per share must be removed from the appropriate capital stock account and credited to Paid-In Capital—Recapitalization. Further discussion of this process, called *recapitalization*, is beyond the scope of this text.

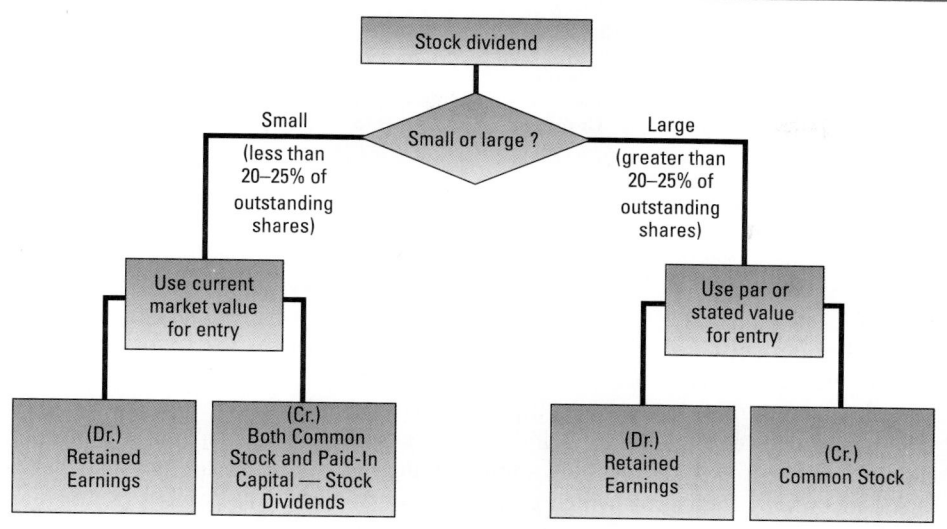

ILLUSTRATION 13.3
Stock Dividends

The entry to record a stock split depends on the particular circumstances. Usually, firms change only the number of shares outstanding and the par or stated value in the records. (The number of shares authorized may also change.) Thus, they would record a two-for-one stock split in which the par value of the shares decreases from $20 to $10 as follows:

Common Stock—$20 par value	100,000	
Common Stock—$10 par value		100,000
To record a two-for-one stock split; 5,000 shares of $20 par value common stock were replaced by 10,000 shares of $10 par value common stock.		

In Illustration 13.4, we summarize the effects of stock dividends and stock splits. Stock dividends and stock splits have no effect on the total amount of stockholders' equity. In addition, stock splits have no effect on the total amount of paid-in capital or retained earnings. They merely increase the number of shares outstanding and decrease the par value per share. Stock dividends increase paid-in capital and decrease retained earnings by equal amounts.

Reinforcing Problem
E13–5 Prepare journal entries for stock split and small stock dividend.

Legality of Dividends

The preceding chapter discussed how corporate laws differ regarding the legality of a dividend. State law establishes the *legal* or *stated capital* of a corporation as that portion of the stockholders' equity that must be maintained intact, unimpaired by dividend declarations or other distributions to stockholders. The legal capital often equals the par or stated value of the shares issued or a minimum price per share issued.

The objective of these state corporate laws is to protect the corporation's creditors, whose claims have priority over those of the corporation's stockholders. To illustrate the significance of the legal capital concept, assume a corporation in severe financial difficulty is about to go out of business. If there were no legal capital restrictions on dividends, the stockholders of that corporation might pay themselves a cash dividend or have the corporation buy back their stock, leaving no funds available for the corporation's creditors.

The board of directors of a corporation possesses sole power to declare dividends. The legality of a dividend generally depends on the amount of retained earnings available for dividends—not on the net income of any one period. Firms can pay dividends in periods in which they incurred losses, provided retained earnings and the cash position justify the dividend. And in some states, companies can declare dividends from current earnings despite an accumulated deficit. The financial advisability of declaring a dividend depends on the cash position of the corporation.

ILLUSTRATION 13.4   Summary of Effects of Stock Dividends and Stock Splits

	Total Stockholders' Equity	Common Stock	Paid-In Capital— Common	Retained Earnings	Number of Shares Outstanding	Par Value per Share
Stock dividends:						
Small	No effect	Increases	Increases*	Decreases	Increases	No effect
Large	No effect	Increases	No effect	Decreases	Increases	No effect
Stock splits	No effect	No effect	No effect	No effect	Increases	Decreases

*Assuming current market value is greater than par value.

Liquidating Dividends

Normally, dividends are reductions of retained earnings since they are distributions of the corporation's net income. However, dividends may be distributions of contributed capital. These dividends are called **liquidating dividends.**

Accountants debit liquidating dividends to a paid-in capital account. Corporations should disclose to stockholders the source of any dividends that are not distributions of net income by indicating which paid-in capital account was debited as a result of the dividend. The legality of paying liquidating dividends depends on the source of the paid-in capital and the laws of the state of incorporation.

AN ACCOUNTING PERSPECTIVE
—

BUSINESS INSIGHT   The Private Securities Litigation Reform Act, passed in 1996, seeks to protect investors against white-collar crime. Auditors are required by this law to become more aggressive in looking for fraud in companies they audit. Risk factors that might encourage management to engage in fraudulent activities include weak internal controls, an aggressive effort to drive up the stock price by reporting higher earnings, and/or executive bonuses or stock options based on earnings. A strong company code of ethics and an effective internal control structure can help deter fraud from occurring.

RETAINED EARNINGS APPROPRIATIONS

The amount of retained earnings that a corporation may pay as cash dividends may be less than total retained earnings for several contractual or voluntary reasons. These contractual or voluntary restrictions or limitations on retained earnings are **retained earnings appropriations.** For example, a loan contract may state that part of a corporation's $100,000 of retained earnings is not available for cash dividends until the loan is paid. Or a board of directors may decide to use assets resulting from net income for plant expansion rather than for cash dividends. An example of a voluntary restriction was General Electric's annual report statement that cash dividends were limited "to support enhanced productive capability and to provide adequate financial resources for internal and external growth opportunities."

Companies formally record retained earnings appropriations by transferring amounts from Retained Earnings to accounts such as "Appropriation for Loan Agreement" or "Retained Earnings Appropriated for Plant Expansion." Even though some refer to retained earnings appropriations as *retained earnings reserves,* using the term *reserves* is discouraged.

Other reasons for appropriations of retained earnings include pending litigation, debt retirement, and contingencies in general. Such appropriations do not reduce total retained earnings. They merely disclose to balance sheet readers that a portion of retained earnings is not available for cash dividends. Thus, recording these appropriations guarantees that the corporation limits its outflow of cash dividends while repaying a loan, expanding a plant, or taking on some other costly endeavor. *Recording retained earnings appropriations does not involve the setting aside of cash for the indicated purpose; it merely divides retained earnings into two parts—appropriated retained earnings and unappropriated retained earnings.* The establishment of a separate fund would require a specific directive from the board of directors. The only entry required to record the appropriation of $25,000 of retained earnings to fulfill the provisions in a loan agreement is:

Retained Earnings	25,000	
Appropriation per Loan Agreement		25,000
To record restriction on retained earnings.		

Reinforcing Problem
E13–6 Prepare journal entry for appropriation of retained earnings and explain.

When the retained earnings appropriation has served its purpose of restricting dividends and the loan has been repaid, the board of directors may decide to return the appropriation intact to Retained Earnings. The entry to do this is:

Appropriation per Loan Agreement	25,000	
Retained Earnings		25,000
To return balance in Appropriation per Loan Agreement account to Retained Earnings.		

On the balance sheet, retained earnings appropriations appear in the stockholders' equity section as follows:

Retained Earnings Appropriations on the Balance Sheet

Reinforcing Problem
E13–1 Prepare stockholders' equity section of balance sheet.

Stockholders' equity:

Paid-in capital:		
Preferred stock—8%, $50 par value; 500 shares authorized, issued, and		
outstanding	$25,000	
Common stock—$5 par value; 10,000 shares authorized, issued, and		
outstanding	50,000	
Total paid-in capital		$ 75,000
Retained earnings:		
Appropriated:		
Per loan agreement	$25,000	
Unappropriated	20,000	
Total retained earnings		45,000
Total stockholders' equity		$120,000

Note that a retained earnings appropriation does not reduce either stockholders' equity or total retained earnings but merely earmarks (restricts) a portion of retained earnings for a specific reason.

The formal practice of recording and reporting retained earnings appropriations is decreasing. Footnote explanations such as the following are replacing these appropriations:

Note 7. Retained earnings restrictions. According to the provisions in the loan agreement, retained earnings available for dividends are limited to $20,000.

Such footnotes appear after the formal financial statements in "Notes to Financial Statements." The Retained Earnings account on the balance sheet would be referenced as follows: "Retained Earnings (see note 7) . . . $45,000."

Changes in the composition of retained earnings reveal important information about a corporation to financial statement users. A separate formal statement—the *statement of retained earnings*—discloses such changes.

STATEMENT OF RETAINED EARNINGS

A **statement of retained earnings** is a formal statement showing the items causing changes in unappropriated and appropriated retained earnings during a stated period of time. Changes in unappropriated retained earnings usually consist of the addition of net income (or deduction of net loss) and the deduction of dividends and appropriations. Changes in appropriated retained earnings consist of increases or decreases in appropriations.

ILLUSTRATION 13.5
Statement of Retained
Earnings

WARD CORPORATION
Statement of Retained Earnings
For Year Ended December 31, 1999

Unappropriated retained earnings:		
January 1, 1999, balance		$180,000
Add: Net income		80,000
		$260,000
Less: Dividends	$15,000	
Appropriation for plant expansion	35,000	50,000
Unappropriated retained earnings, December 31, 1999		$210,000
Appropriated retained earnings:		
Appropriation for plant expansion, January 1, 1999, balance	$25,000	
Add: Increase in 1999	35,000	$ 60,000
Appropriation for contract obligation, January 1, 1999, balance		20,000
Appropriated retained earnings, December 31, 1999		$ 80,000
Total retained earnings, December 31, 1999		$290,000

Note Ward Corporation's statement of retained earnings in Illustration 13.5. The only new appropriation during 1999 was an additional $35,000 for plant expansion. Ward added this new $35,000 to the $25,000 beginning balance in that account and subtracted that amount from unappropriated retained earnings. An alternative to the statement of retained earnings is the statement of stockholders' equity.

STATEMENT OF STOCKHOLDERS' EQUITY

Most corporations include four financial statements in their annual reports: a balance sheet, an income statement, a statement of stockholders' equity (in place of a statement of retained earnings), and a statement of cash flows (discussed in Chapter 16). A **statement of stockholders' equity** is a summary of the transactions affecting the accounts in the stockholders' equity section of the balance sheet during a stated period. These transactions include activities affecting both paid-in capital and retained earnings accounts. Thus, the statement of stockholders' equity includes the information contained in a statement of retained earnings plus some additional information. The columns in the statement of stockholders' equity reflect the major account titles within the stockholders' equity section: the types of stock issued and outstanding, paid-in capital in excess of par (or stated) value, retained earnings, and treasury stock. Each row indicates the effects of major transactions affecting one or more stockholders' equity accounts.

Look at Illustration 13.6, a statement of stockholders' equity. The first row indicates the beginning balances of each account in the stockholders' equity section. This summary shows that Larkin Corporation issued 10,000 shares of common stock, declared a 5% stock dividend on common stock, repurchased 1,200 shares of treasury stock, earned net income of $185,000, and paid cash dividends on both its preferred and common stock. After the transactions' effects are indicated within each row, Larkin added or subtracted each column's components to determine the ending balance in each stockholders' equity account.

TREASURY STOCK

Objective 3
Account for the acquisition and reissuance of treasury stock.

Treasury stock is the corporation's own capital stock that it has issued and then reacquired; this stock has not been canceled and is legally available for reissuance. Because it has been issued, we cannot classify treasury stock as unissued stock.

Recall that when a corporation has additional authorized shares of stock that are to be issued after the date of original issue, in most states the preemptive right requires offering these additional shares first to existing stockholders on a pro rata

ILLUSTRATION 13.6   Statement of Stockholders' Equity

LARKIN CORPORATION
Statement of Stockholders' Equity
For the Year Ended December 31, 1999

	$50 Par, Value, 6% Preferred Stock	$20 Par Value Common Stock	Paid-In Capital in Excess of Par Value	Retained Earnings	Treasury Stock	Total
Balance, January 1, 1999	$250,000	$300,000	$200,000	$500,000	$(42,000)	$1,208,000
Issuance of 10,000 shares of common stock		200,000	100,000			300,000
5% stock dividend on common stock, 1,250 shares . .		25,000	27,500	(52,500)		–0–
Purchase of 1,200 shares of treasury stock					(48,000)	(48,000)
Net income				185,000		185,000
Cash dividends:						
Preferred stock				(15,000)		(15,000)
Common stock				(25,000)		(25,000)
Balance, December 31, 1999	$250,000	$525,000	$327,500	$592,500	$(90,000)	$1,605,000

basis. However, firms may reissue treasury stock without violating the preemptive right provisions of state laws; that is, treasury stock does not have to be offered to current stockholders on a pro rata basis.

A corporation may reacquire its own capital stock as treasury stock to: (1) cancel and retire the stock; (2) reissue the stock later at a higher price; (3) reduce the shares outstanding and thereby increase earnings per share; or (4) issue the stock to employees. If the intent of reacquisition is cancellation and retirement, the treasury shares exist only until they are retired and canceled by a formal reduction of corporate capital.

For dividend or voting purposes, most state laws consider treasury stock as issued but not outstanding, since the shares are no longer in the possession of stockholders. Also, accountants do not consider treasury shares outstanding in calculating earnings per share. However, they generally consider treasury shares outstanding for purposes of determining legal capital, which includes outstanding shares plus treasury shares.

In states that consider treasury stock as part of legal capital, the cost of treasury stock may not exceed the retained earnings at the date the shares are reacquired. This regulation protects creditors by preventing the corporation in financial difficulty from using funds to purchase its own stock instead of paying its debts. Thus, if a corporation is subject to such a law (as is assumed in this text), the retained earnings available for dividends must exceed the cost of the treasury shares on hand.

Real World Example
At March 1, 1997, Pier 1 Imports, Inc., reported a balance of $5,437,000 in its Treasury Stock account.

Acquisition and Reissuance of Treasury Stock

When firms reacquire treasury stock, they record the stock at cost as a debit in a stockholders' equity account called *Treasury Stock*.[3] They credit reissuances to the Treasury Stock account at the cost of acquisition. Thus, the Treasury Stock account is debited at cost when shares are acquired and credited at cost when these shares are sold. Any excess of the reissue price over cost represents additional paid-in capital and is credited to **Paid-In Capital—Common (Preferred) Treasury Stock Transactions.**

To illustrate, assume that on February 18, 1999, the Hillside Corporation reacquired 100 shares of its outstanding common stock for $55 each. (The company's stockholders' equity consisted solely of common stock and retained earnings.) On April 18, 1999, the company reissued 30 shares for $58 each. The entries to record these events are:

---

[3]Another acceptable method of accounting for treasury stock transactions is the par value method. We leave further discussion of the par value method to intermediate accounting texts.

1999				
Feb.	18	Treasury Stock—Common (100 shares × $55)	5,500	
		Cash		5,500
		Acquired 100 shares of treasury stock at $55.		
Apr.	18	Cash (30 shares × $58)	1,740	
		Treasury Stock—Common (30 shares × $55)		1,650
		Paid-In Capital—Common Treasury Stock Transactions		90
		Reissued 30 shares of treasury stock at $58; cost is $55 per share.		

When the reissue price of subsequent shares is less than the acquisition price, firms debit the difference between cost and reissue price to Paid-In Capital—Common Treasury Stock Transactions. This account, however, never develops a debit balance. By definition, no paid-in capital account can have a debit balance. If Hillside reissued an additional 20 shares at $52 per share on June 12, 1999, the entry would be:

June	12	Cash (20 shares × $52)	1,040	
		Paid-In Capital—Common Treasury Stock Transactions	60	
		Treasury Stock—Common (20 shares × $55)		1,100
		Reissued 20 shares of treasury stock at $52; cost is $55 per share.		

At this point, the credit balance in the Paid-In Capital—Common Treasury Stock Transactions account would be $30. If the remaining 50 shares are reissued on July 16, 1999, for $53 per share, the entry would be:

July	16	Cash (50 shares × $53)	2,650	
		Paid-In Capital—Common Treasury Stock Transactions	30	
		Retained Earnings.	70	
		Treasury Stock—Common (50 shares × $55)		2,750
		Reissued 50 shares of treasury stock at $53; cost is $55 per share.		

Notice that Hillside has exhausted the Paid-In Capital—Common Treasury Stock Transactions account credit balance. If more than $30 is debited to that account, it would develop a debit balance. Thus, the remaining $70 of the excess of cost over reissue price is a special distribution to the stockholders involved and is debited to the Retained Earnings account.

Sometimes stockholders donate stock to a corporation. Since donated treasury shares have no cost to the corporation, accountants make only a memo entry when the shares are received.[4] The only formal entry required is to debit Cash and credit the Paid-In Capital—Donations account when the stock is reissued. For example, if donated treasury stock is sold for $5,000, the entry would be:

Reinforcing Problems
E13–7 Prepare journal entries for reacquisition and reissuance of treasury stock.
E13–8 Prepare journal entry(ies) for reissuance of donated stock.
E13–3 Prepare journal entries for cash dividend when treasury stock is held.

Cash	5,000	
Paid-In Capital—Donations		5,000
To record the sale of donated treasury stock.		

Treasury Stock on the Balance Sheet

When treasury stock is held on a balance sheet date, it customarily appears at cost, as a deduction from the sum of total paid-in capital and retained earnings, as follows:

Stockholders' equity:

Paid-in capital:		
Common stock—$10 par value; authorized and issued, 20,000 shares, of which 2,000 shares are in the treasury	$200,000	
Retained earnings (including $22,000 restricted by acquisition of treasury stock)	80,000	
Total paid-in capital and retained earnings		$280,000
Less: Treasury stock at cost, 2,000 shares		22,000
Total stockholders' equity		$258,000

---

[4]The method illustrated here is called the *memo* method. Other acceptable methods of accounting for donated stock are the *cost* method and *par value* method. Intermediate accounting texts discuss these latter two methods.

HYPOTHETICAL CORPORATION
Partial Balance Sheet
December 31, 1999

ILLUSTRATION 13.7
Stockholders' Equity
Section of the Balance
Sheet

Stockholders' equity:

Paid-in capital:

Preferred stock—8%, $100 par value; 2,000 shares authorized, issued, and outstanding			$ 200,000
Common stock—$10 par value; authorized, 100,000 shares; issued, 80,000 shares of which 1,000 are held in the treasury		$800,000	
Stock dividend distributable on common stock on January 15, 2000, 7,900 shares		79,000	879,000
Paid-in capital—			
From common stock issuances	$ 40,000		
From stock dividends	60,000		
From treasury stock transactions	30,000		
From donations	50,000	180,000	
Total paid-in capital			$1,259,000
Retained earnings:			
Appropriated:			
Per loan agreement		$250,000	
Unappropriated (restricted to the extent of $20,000, the cost of treasury shares held)		150,000	
Total retained earnings			400,000
Total paid-in capital and retained earnings			$1,659,000
Less: Treasury stock, common, 1,000 shares at cost			20,000
Total stockholders' equity			$1,639,000

Reinforcing Problem
E13–1 Prepare stockholders' equity section of balance sheet.

BUSINESS INSIGHT   General Mills is a leading producer of ready-to-eat cereals, desserts and baking mixes, snack products, and dinner and side dish mixes. Popular brand names include Hamburger Helper, Betty Crocker, and Yoplait. For 1996 and 1995, General Mills reported common stock in the treasury (treasury stock) of 45,200,000 and 46,300,000 shares, respectively. General Mills deducted the cost of these shares in the stockholders' equity section of the balance sheet.

AN ACCOUNTING PERSPECTIVE

To summarize much of what we have discussed in Chapters 12 and 13, we present the stockholders' equity section of the balance sheet in Illustration 13.7. This partial balance sheet shows: (1) the amount of capital assigned to shares outstanding; (2) the capital contributed for outstanding shares in addition to that assigned to the shares; (3) other forms of paid-in capital; and (4) retained earnings, appropriated and unappropriated.

Stockholders' Equity on the Balance Sheet

NET INCOME INCLUSIONS AND EXCLUSIONS

Accounting has long faced the problem of what to include in the net income reported for a period. Should net income include only the revenues and expenses related to normal operations? Or should it include the results of discontinued operations and unusual, nonrecurring gains and losses? And further, should the determination of net income for 1999, for example, include an item that can be clearly associated with a prior year, such as additional federal income taxes for 1998? Or should such items, including corrections of errors, be carried directly to retained earnings? How are the effects of making a change in accounting principle (like a change in depreciation methods) to be reported?

APB Opinion No. 9 (December 1966) sought to provide answers to some of these questions. The *Opinion* directed that unusual and nonrecurring items having an earnings or loss effect are extraordinary items (reported in the income statement) or prior

Objective 4
Describe the proper accounting treatment of discontinued operations, extraordinary items, and changes in accounting principle.

ILLUSTRATION 13.8   Income Statement

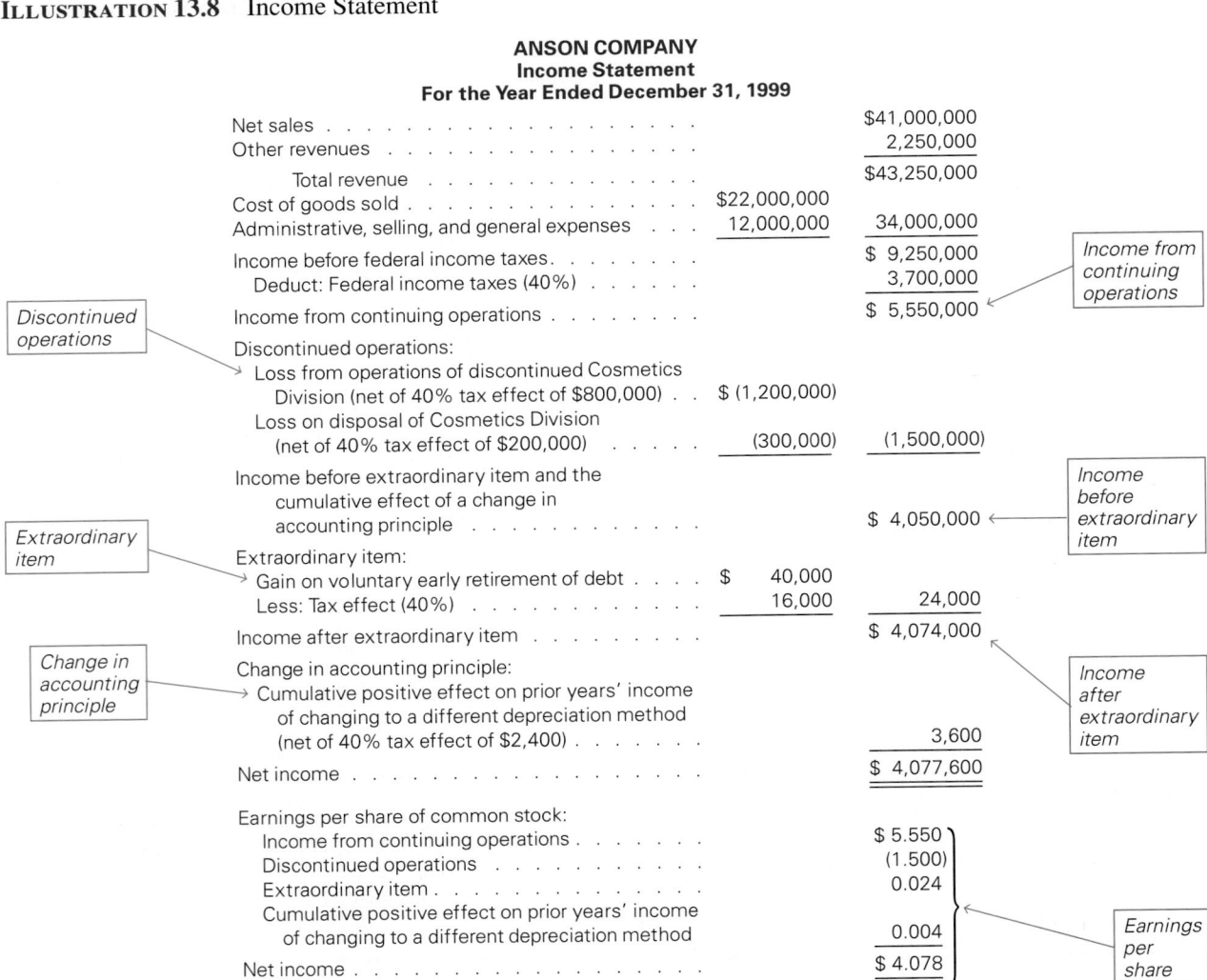

ANSON COMPANY
Income Statement
For the Year Ended December 31, 1999

Net sales		$41,000,000
Other revenues		2,250,000
Total revenue		$43,250,000
Cost of goods sold	$22,000,000	
Administrative, selling, and general expenses . . .	12,000,000	34,000,000
Income before federal income taxes.		$ 9,250,000
Deduct: Federal income taxes (40%)		3,700,000
Income from continuing operations		$ 5,550,000

Discontinued operations

Income from continuing operations

Discontinued operations:		
Loss from operations of discontinued Cosmetics Division (net of 40% tax effect of $800,000) . .	$ (1,200,000)	
Loss on disposal of Cosmetics Division (net of 40% tax effect of $200,000)	(300,000)	(1,500,000)
Income before extraordinary item and the cumulative effect of a change in accounting principle		$ 4,050,000

Income before extraordinary item

Extraordinary item

Extraordinary item:		
Gain on voluntary early retirement of debt	$ 40,000	
Less: Tax effect (40%)	16,000	24,000
Income after extraordinary item		$ 4,074,000

Change in accounting principle

Income after extraordinary item

Change in accounting principle:		
Cumulative positive effect on prior years' income of changing to a different depreciation method (net of 40% tax effect of $2,400)		3,600
Net income		$ 4,077,600

Earnings per share of common stock:	
Income from continuing operations	$ 5.550
Discontinued operations	(1.500)
Extraordinary item	0.024
Cumulative positive effect on prior years' income of changing to a different depreciation method	0.004
Net income	$ 4.078

Earnings per share

period adjustments (reported in the statement of retained earnings). Extraordinary items are reported separately after net income from regular continuing activities.

In Illustrations 13.8 and 13.10 (p. 482), we show the reporting of discontinued operations, extraordinary items, changes in accounting principle, and prior period adjustments. For Illustrations 13.8 and 13.10, assume that the Anson Company has 1,000,000 shares of common stock outstanding and the company's earnings are taxed at 40%. Also, assume the following:

1. Anson sold its Cosmetics Division on August 1, 1999, at a loss of $500,000. The net operating loss of that division through July 31, 1999, was $2,000,000.

2. Anson had a taxable gain in 1999 of $40,000 from voluntary early retirement of debt (extraordinary item).

3. Anson changed depreciation methods in 1999 (change in accounting principle), and the cumulative effect of the changes was a $6,000 decrease in prior years' depreciation expense.

4. In 1999, Anson discovered that the $200,000 cost of land acquired in 1998 had been expensed for both financial accounting and tax purposes. A prior period adjustment was made in 1999.

Next, we explain the effects of these assumptions in greater detail.

A **discontinued operation** occurs when a business sells a segment (usually an unprofitable department or division) to another company or abandons it. When a company discontinues a segment, it shows the relevant information in a special section of the income statement immediately after income from continuing operations and before extraordinary items. Two items of information appear:

1. The income or loss (net of tax effect) from the segment's operations for the portion of the current year before it was discontinued.
2. The gain or loss (net of tax effect) on disposal of the segment.

To illustrate, Anson's sale of its Cosmetics Division on July 31 led to a before-tax loss of $500,000. The after-tax loss was $500,000 × 60% = $300,000. The operating loss before taxes through July 31 was $2,000,000. The after-tax operating loss for that period was $2,000,000 × 60% = $1,200,000. Note this information on the income statement in Illustration 13.8.

Discontinued Operations

Prior to 1973, companies reported a gain or loss as an extraordinary item if it was either unusual in nature or occurred infrequently. As a result, companies were inconsistent in the financial reporting of certain gains and losses. This inconsistency led to the issuance of *APB Opinion No. 30* (September 1973). *Opinion No. 30* redefined **extraordinary items** as those *unusual in nature* and *occurring infrequently*. Note that both conditions must be met—unusual nature and infrequent occurrence. Accountants determine whether an item is unusual and infrequent in light of the environment in which the company operates. Examples of extraordinary items include gains or losses that are the direct result of a major catastrophe (a flood or hurricane where few have occurred before), a confiscation of property by a foreign government, or a prohibition under a newly enacted law. *FASB Statement No. 4* further directs that gains and losses from the voluntary early extinguishment (retirement) of debt are extraordinary items. This treatment applies whether an extinguishment is before maturity, at maturity, or later than maturity.

Extraordinary items are included in the determination of periodic net income, but are disclosed separately (net of their tax effects) in the income statement below "Income from continuing operations." As shown in Illustration 13.8, Anson reported the extraordinary items after reporting the loss from discontinued operations.

Gains or losses related to ordinary business activities are not extraordinary items regardless of their size. For example, material write-downs of uncollectible receivables, obsolete inventories, and intangible assets are not extraordinary items. However, such items may be separately disclosed as part of income from continuing operations.

Extraordinary Items

Note to the Student
Extraordinary items must be both unusual and infrequent. If an asteroid fell on a building, this clearly would be an extraordinary loss.

BUSINESS INSIGHT   Rohr, Inc., is a supplier of nacell and pylon systems, products used in aircraft. One of the most common causes of an extraordinary item is the early extinguishment of debt. In 1995, Rohr prepaid $10.7 million of its notes payable. A premium and certain other expenses associated with the early extinguishment were recorded as an extraordinary item net of tax.

The annual report presentation was:

AN ACCOUNTING PERSPECTIVE

	1995
Loss from Extraordinary Item—Net of Taxes (Note 7)	($1,146)

In Illustration 13.9, note that in a sample of 600 companies for the years 1992–1995, most companies do not report extraordinary items.

Changes in accounting principle can materially alter a company's reported net income and financial position. **Changes in accounting principle** are changes in accounting methods pertaining to such items as inventory and depreciation. Such changes include a change in inventory valuation method from FIFO to LIFO or a change in depreciation method from accelerated to straight-line.

Changes in Accounting Principle

ILLUSTRATION 13.9
Extraordinary Items

	1995	1994	1993	1992
Nature				
Debt extinguishments	53	59	79	60
Operating loss carryforwards	—	—	9	17
Litigation settlements	—	—	1	2
Other	3	—	6	5
Total Extraordinary Items	**56**	**59**	**95**	**84**
Number of Companies				
Presenting extraordinary items	55	59	91	81
Not presenting extraordinary items	545	541	509	519
Total	**600**	**600**	**600**	**600**

Source: Based on American Institute of Certified Public Accountants, *Accounting Trends & Techniques* (New York: AICPA, 1996), p. 390.

According to *APB Opinion No. 20,* a company should consistently apply the same accounting methods from one period to another. However, a company may make a change if the newly adopted method is preferable and if the change is adequately disclosed in the financial statements. In the period in which a company makes a change in accounting principle, it must disclose on the financial statements the nature of the change, its justification, and its effect on net income. Also, the company must show on the income statement for the year of the change (Illustration 13.8) the cumulative effect of the change on prior years' income (net of tax).

As an example of a change in accounting principle, assume that Anson purchased a machine on January 2, 1997, for $30,000. The machine has an estimated useful life of five years with no salvage value. Anson decided to depreciate the machine for financial reporting purposes using the sum-of-the-years'-digits method. At the beginning of 1999, the company decided to change to the straight-line method of depreciation. The cumulative effect of the change in accounting principle is as follows:

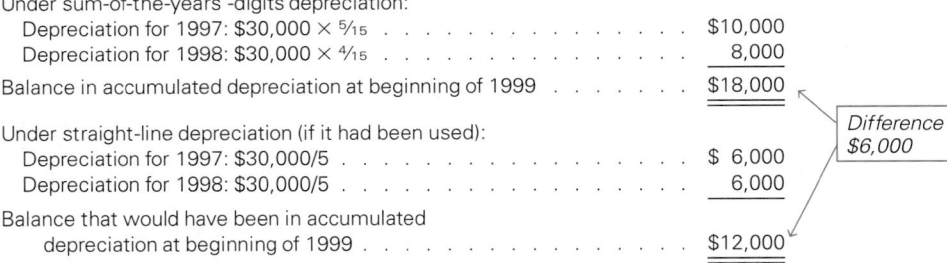

Note to the Student
A change in accounting principle requires that the company show the cumulative effect of the change on the prior year's income. This effect must be reported on the current income statement.

Under sum-of-the-years'-digits depreciation:
Depreciation for 1997: $30,000 × 5/15 . . . . $10,000
Depreciation for 1998: $30,000 × 4/15 8,000
Balance in accumulated depreciation at beginning of 1999 . . . . $18,000

Difference $6,000

Under straight-line depreciation (if it had been used):
Depreciation for 1997: $30,000/5 . . . . $ 6,000
Depreciation for 1998: $30,000/5 6,000
Balance that would have been in accumulated
depreciation at beginning of 1999 . . . . $12,000

The accumulated depreciation account balance would have been $6,000 less under the straight-line method. Also, depreciation expense over the two years would have been $6,000 less. Assume that federal income tax would have been $2,400 more ($6,000 × 0.4). The net effect of the change is $6,000 − $2,400 = $3,600. Therefore, Anson corrects the appropriate account balances by reducing (debiting) the accumulated depreciation account balance by $6,000, crediting an account entitled Cumulative Effect of Change in Accounting Principle for $3,600 (which is closed to Retained Earnings during the normal closing process), and crediting Federal Income Taxes Payable for $2,400. The journal entry would be:

Accumulated Depreciation—Machinery	6,000	
Cumulative Effect of Change in Accounting Principle		3,600
Federal Income Taxes Payable		2,400
To record the effect of changing from sum-of-the-years'-digits depreciation to straight-line depreciation on machinery.		

Ace Chemical Company is a small, privately held manufacturer that has been operating at a profit for years. The current balance in the Cash account is $8 million, and the balance in Retained Earnings is $4 million. The company's plant assets consist of special purpose equipment that can produce only certain chemicals. The company has long-term debt with a principal balance of $10 million. Its officers (all of whom are stockholders) are concerned about the future prospects of the company. Many similar firms have been sued by customers and employees claiming that toxic chemicals produced by the company caused their health problems. No such suits have yet been filed against Ace, but the officers fully expect them to be filed within the next two years.

The company's stock is not listed on a stock exchange, nor has it recently been traded. The officers hold 70% of the stock and estimate that their total stockholdings have a current market value of about $8 million (although its value would be much lower if all the facts were known). They are worried that if suits are filed and the company loses, there will not even be enough remaining assets to satisfy creditors' claims, and the officers' stock would be worthless. Private legal counsel has informed the officers that the company is likely to lose any suits that are filed.

One of the officers suggested that they could at least receive something for their stock by having the company buy half of the shares held by the officers at a total price of $4 million. Another officer asked if such a treasury stock transaction would be legal. The response was that the transaction would be legal because it did not dip into the present legal capital of the company. Retained earnings would be reduced to a zero balance, but would not develop a debit balance as a result of the transaction.

AN ETHICAL PERSPECTIVE
—
Ace Chemical Company

Note the cumulative effect of changing to the straight-line depreciation method appears below "income from continuing operations" in Illustration 13.8 at the after-tax amount of $3,600. Discontinued operations, extraordinary items, and changes in accounting principle are reported in the above order below "income from continuing operations."

cording to *FASB Statement No. 16*, **prior period adjustments** consist almost entirely of corrections of errors in previously published financial statements. Corrections of abnormal, nonrecurring errors that may have been caused by the improper ꞏe of an accounting principle or by mathematical mistakes are prior period adjustments. Normal, recurring corrections and adjustments, which follow inevitably from ꞏe use of estimates in accounting practice, are not treated as prior period adjustments. .so, mistakes corrected in the same year they occur are not prior period adjustments. ꞏꞏ illustrate a prior period adjustment, suppose that Anson purchased land in 1998 at a total cost of $200,000 and recorded this amount in an expense account instead of in the Land account. Discovery of the error on May 1, 1999, after publication of the 1998 financial statements, would require a prior period adjustment. The adjustment would be recorded directly in the Retained Earnings account. Assuming the error had resulted in an $80,000 underpayment of taxes in 1998, the entry to correct the error would be:

Prior Period Adjustments

Objective 5
Define prior period adjustments and show their proper presentation in the financial statements.

May	1	Land	200,000	
		Federal Income Taxes Payable		80,000
		Retained Earnings (or Prior Period Adjustment—Land)		120,000
		To correct an accounting error expensing land.		

Prior period adjustments do not appear on the income statements but in the current-year financial statements as adjustments to the opening balance of retained earnings on the statement of retained earnings (Illustration 13.10).

Most discontinued operations, extraordinary items, changes in accounting principle, and prior period adjustments affect the amount of income taxes a corporation must pay. To report the income tax effect, *FASB Statement No. 96* requires reporting all of

Accounting for Tax Effects

ILLUSTRATION 13.10
Statement of Retained
Earnings

ANSON COMPANY
Statement of Retained Earnings
For the Year Ended December 31, 1999

Retained earnings, January 1, 1999	$5,000,000
Prior period adjustment:	
Correction of error of expensing land (net of tax effect of $80,000)	120,000
Retained earnings, January 1, 1999, as adjusted	$5,120,000
Add: Net income	4,077,600
	$9,197,600
Less: Dividends	500,000
Retained earnings, December 31, 1999	$8,697,600

Prior period adjustment →

Reinforcing Problems
E13–9 Prepare income statement and statement of retained earnings.
E13–10 Prepare statement of retained earnings.

these items *net of their tax effects,* as shown in Illustrations 13.8 and 13.10.[5] **Net-of-tax effect** means that items appear at the dollar amounts remaining after deducting the income tax effects. Thus, the total effect of a discontinued operation, an extraordinary item, a change in accounting principle, or a prior period adjustment appears in one place in the appropriate financial statement. The reference to "Income from continuing operations" on the income statement represents the results of transactions (including income taxes) that are normal for the business and may be expected to recur. Note that the tax effect of an item may appear separately, as it does for the gain on voluntary early retirement of debt in Illustration 13.8. Or the company may mention it parenthetically with only the net amount shown (see loss from discontinued operations and change in accounting principle in Illustration 13.8 and correction of error in Illustration 13.10).

Summary of Illustrative Financial Statements

1. Income from continuing operations of $5,550,000 (Illustration 13.8) is more representative of the continuing earning power of the company than is the net income figure of $4,077,600.
2. Following income, the special items from continuing operations appear at their actual impact on the company—that is, net of their tax effect.
3. EPS is reported both before ($5.550) and after ($4.078) the discontinued operations, extraordinary item, and the cumulative effect of a change in accounting principle (Illustration 13.8).
4. The correction of the $200,000 error adds only $120,000 to retained earnings (Illustration 13.10). This result occurs because the mistake was included in the 1998 tax return and taxes were underpaid by $80,000. In the 1999 return, the $80,000 of taxes would have to be paid.

ANALYZING AND USING THE FINANCIAL RESULTS—EARNINGS PER SHARE AND PRICE-EARNINGS RATIO

Objective 6
Analyze and use the financial results—earnings per share and price-earnings ratio.

A major item of interest to investors and potential investors is how much a company earned during the current year, both in total and for each share of stock outstanding. Firms calculate the earnings per share amount only for the common shares of ownership. They compute **earnings per share (EPS)** as net income available to common stockholders divided by the average number of common shares outstanding during that period. **Income available to common stockholders** is net income less any divi-

---

[5]FASB, *Statement of Financial Accounting Standards No. 96,* "Accounting for Income Taxes" (Stamford. Conn., 1987). Copyright © by the Financial Accounting Standards Board, High Ridge Park, Stamford, Connecticut 06905, U.S.A.

dends on preferred stock. They deduct the regular preferred dividend on cumulative preferred stock (but not a dividend in arrears) whether or not declared; however, they deduct only declared dividends on noncumulative preferred stock.

To illustrate, Sun Microsystems, Incorporated, had 196,690,000 weighted-average common shares outstanding with income available to common shareholders of $476,388,000 during 1996. Sun would compute EPS as follows:

$$EPS = \frac{\text{Income available to common stockholders}}{\text{Weighted-average number of common shares outstanding}}$$

$$= \frac{\$476,388,000}{196,690,000 \text{ shares}}$$

$$= \$2.42 \text{ per share}$$

Sun Microsystems
Sun Microsystems develops core networking technologies used in the Internet and corporate intranets as well as hardware and software.

Firms calculate EPS for each major category on the face of the income statement. In other words, they make an EPS calculation for income from continuing operations, discontinued operations, extraordinary items, changes in accounting principle, and net income. Note in Illustration 13.8 that Anson reports the EPS amounts at the bottom of its income statement.

The **price-earnings ratio** (current market price per share of common stock divided by EPS) provides an index on whether a stock has future high income potential compared to other stocks. Stocks with future high income potential tend to have a high price-earnings ratio.

In the financial highlights of Kimball International, Incorporated's, 1996 annual report, the market price at year-end was $27⅝. Earnings per share were $2.15. Kimball would compute its price-earnings ratio that day as follows:

$$\text{Price-earnings ratio} = \frac{\text{Current market price per share of common stock}}{\text{EPS}}$$

$$= \frac{\$27.625}{\$2.15}$$

$$= 12.85$$

Reinforcing Problems
E13–11 Calculate EPS; present information in income statement format.
E13–12 Calculate EPS; comment on resulting amounts.

Kimball International
Kimball International, Incorporated, manufactures and markets a broad range of diversified consumer durable products including furniture and electronics.

This chapter completes the study of stockholders' equity. In Chapter 14, you learn about stock investments and international accounting.

UNDERSTANDING THE LEARNING OBJECTIVES

- Paid-in capital is presented in the stockholders' equity section of the balance sheet. Each source of paid-in capital is listed separately.
- Sources of paid-in capital are:
  1. Common stock.
  2. Preferred stock.
  3. In excess of par value or stated value (common and preferred).
  4. Stock dividends.
  5. Treasury stock transactions.
  6. Donations.

Objective 1
Identify the different sources of paid-in capital and describe how to present them on a balance sheet.

- Cash dividend of 3% on $100,000 of outstanding common stock: declared on July 1 and paid on September 15.

July	1	Retained Earnings	3,000	
		Dividends Payable		3,000
Sept	15	Dividends Payable	3,000	
		Cash		3,000

Objective 2
Account for a cash dividend, a stock dividend, a stock split, and a retained earnings appropriation.

Ten percent stock dividend on 10,000 shares of common stock outstanding; par value, $100; market value at declaration, $125 per share (declared on January 1 and paid on February 1).

Jan.	1	Retained Earnings (1,000 shares × $125)	125,000	
		Stock Dividend Distributable—Common		
		(1,000 shares × $100).		100,000
		Paid-In Capital—Stock Dividends		
		(1,000 shares × $25)		25,000
Feb.	1	Stock Dividend Distributable—Common	100,000	
		Common Stock.		100,000

- Thirty percent stock dividend on 10,000 shares of common stock outstanding: declared on January 1 and payable on February 1; par value, $100.

Jan.	1	Retained Earnings (3,000 shares × $100)	300,000	
		Stock Dividend Distributable—Common		300,000
Feb.	1	Stock Dividend Distributable—Common	300,000	
		Common Stock.		300,000

- Stock split: 1,000 shares of $50 par value common stock replaced by 2,000 shares of $25 par value common stock.

Common Stock—$50 par value	50,000	
Common Stock—$25 par value		50,000

- Retained earnings appropriation: $75,000 appropriated for plant expansion.

Retained Earnings	75,000	
Retained Earnings Appropriated for Plant Expansion		75,000

Objective 3
Account for the acquisition and reissuance of treasury stock.

- Treasury stock transactions: 100 shares of common stock were reacquired at $100 each and reissued for $105 each.

Treasury Stock—Common (100 shares × $100)	10,000	
Cash		10,000
Cash (100 shares × $105)	10,500	
Treasury Stock—Common (100 shares × $100)		10,000
Paid-In Capital—Common Treasury Stock Transactions		
(100 shares × $5)		500

Objective 4
Describe the proper accounting treatment of discontinued operations, extraordinary items, and changes in accounting principle.

- The income or loss (net of tax effect) from the segment's operations for the portion of the current year before it was discontinued is reported on the income statement below "Income from continuing operations."

- The gain or loss (net of tax effect) on disposal of the segment is also reported in that same section of the income statement.

- Extraordinary items are both unusual in nature and infrequent in occurrence. Extraordinary items appear on the income statement (net-of-tax effect) below "Income from continuing operations."

- In the period in which a change in principle is made, the nature of the change, its justification, and its effect on net income must be disclosed in the financial statements. Also, the cumulative effect of the change on prior years' income (net of tax effect) must be shown on the income statement for the year of the change below "Income from continuing operations."

Objective 5
Define prior period adjustments and show their proper presentation in the financial statements.

- Prior period adjustments consist of errors in previously published financial statements. Prior period adjustments appear (net-of-tax effect) as a correction to the beginning retained earnings balance on the statement of retained earnings.

- EPS equals the income available to common stockholders divided by the weighted-average number of common shares outstanding. Income available to common stockholders is net income less any dividends on preferred stock. EPS provides information on the return of an investment in common stock.

- The price-earnings ratio equals the current market price per share of common stock divided by EPS. The price-earnings ratio indicates whether a stock has a future high income potential as compared to other stocks.

Objective 6
Analyze and use the financial results—earnings per share and price-earnings ratio.

DEMONSTRATION PROBLEM 13–A

Wylie Corporation has outstanding 10,000 shares of $150 par value common stock.

Prepare the entries to record:

Required

a. The declaration of a cash dividend of $1.50 per share.

b. The declaration of a stock dividend of 10% at a time when the market value per share is $185.

c. The declaration of a stock dividend of 40% at a time when the market value per share is $195.

SOLUTION TO DEMONSTRATION PROBLEM 13–A

a.	Retained Earnings (or Dividends)	15,000	
	Dividends Payable		15,000
	To record declaration of a cash dividend.		
b.	Retained Earnings (or Stock Dividends).	185,000	
	(1,000 shares × $185)		
	Stock Dividend Distributable—Common		
	(1,000 shares × $150)		150,000
	Paid-In Capital—Stock Dividends		35,000
	To record declaration of a small stock dividend (10%).		
c.	Retained Earnings (or Stock Dividends) (4,000 shares × $150)	600,000	
	Stock Dividend Distributable—Common		600,000
	To record declaration of a large stock dividend (40%).		

DEMONSTRATION PROBLEM 13–B

Following are selected transactions of Brackett Company:

1. The company reacquired 200 shares of its own $100 par value common stock, previously issued at $105 per share, for $20,600.

2. Fifty of the treasury shares were reissued at $110 per share, cash.

3. Seventy of the treasury shares were reissued at $95 per share, cash.

4. Stockholders of the corporation donated 100 shares of their common stock to the company.

5. The 100 shares of treasury stock received by donation were reissued for $9,000.

Prepare the necessary journal entries to record these transactions.

Required

SOLUTION TO DEMONSTRATION PROBLEM 13–B

1.	Treasury Stock	20,600	
	Cash		20,600
	Acquired 200 shares at $20,600 ($103 per share).		
2.	Cash (50 shares × $110)	5,500	
	Treasury Stock—Common (50 shares × $103)		5,150
	Paid-In Capital—Common Treasury Stock Transactions		350
	Reissued 50 shares at $110 per share; cost is $5,150.		

3.	Cash (70 shares × $95)	6,650	
	Paid-In Capital—Common Treasury Stock Transactions		
	(50 shares × $7)	350	
	Retained Earnings	210	
	Treasury Stock—Common (70 shares × $103)		7,210
	Reissued 70 shares at $95 per share; cost is $7,210.		
4.	Stockholders donated 100 shares of common stock to the company.		
	(Only memo entry is made.)		
5.	Cash	9,000	
	Paid-In Capital—Donations (100 shares × $90)		9,000
	Reissued donated shares at $90 per share.		

DEMONSTRATION PROBLEM 13–C

Selected account balances of Nexis Corporation at December 31, 1999, are:

Common Stock (no par value; 100,000 shares authorized, issued, and outstanding; stated value of $20 per share)	$2,000,000
Retained Earnings	570,000
Dividends Payable (in cash, declared December 15 on preferred stock)	16,000
Preferred Stock (8%, par value $200; 1,000 shares authorized, issued, and outstanding)	200,000
Paid-In Capital from Donation of Plant Site	100,000
Paid-In Capital in Excess of Par Value—Preferred	8,000

Required   Present in good form the stockholders' equity section of the balance sheet.

SOLUTION TO DEMONSTRATION PROBLEM 13–C

NEXIS CORPORATION
Partial Balance Sheet
December 31, 1999

Stockholders' equity:

Paid-in capital:

Preferred stock—8%, par value $200; 1,000 shares authorized, issued, and outstanding	$ 200,000	
Common stock—no par value, stated value of $20 per share; 100,000 shares authorized, issued, and outstanding	2,000,000	
Paid-in capital from donation of plant site	100,000	
Paid-in capital in excess of par value—preferred	8,000	
Total paid-in capital		$2,308,000
Retained earnings		570,000
Total stockholders' equity		$2,878,000

NEW TERMS

Cash dividends   Cash distributions of accumulated earnings by a corporation to its stockholders.   *467*

Changes in accounting principle   Changes in accounting methods pertaining to such items as inventory and depreciation.   *479*

Contributed capital   See *paid-in capital.*

Date of declaration (of dividends)   The date the board of directors takes action in the form of a motion that dividends be paid.   *466*

Date of payment (of dividends)   The date of actual payment of a dividend, or issuance of additional shares for a stock dividend.   *467*

Date of record (of dividends) The date of record established by the board that determines the stockholders who will receive dividends. *466*

Deficit A debit balance in the Retained Earnings account. *466*

Discontinued operation When a segment of a business is sold to another company or is abandoned. *479*

Dividends Distribution of earnings by a corporation to its stockholders. *466*

Dividends (cash) See *cash dividends.*

Dividends (stock) See *stock dividends.*

Donated capital Results from donation of assets to the corporation, which increases stockholders' equity. *465*

Earnings per share (EPS) Earnings to the common stockholders on a per share basis, computed as income available to common stockholders divided by the weighted-average number of common shares outstanding. *482*

Extraordinary items Items both unusual in nature and infrequent in occurrence; reported in the income statement net of their tax effects, if any. *479*

Income available to common stockholders Net income less any dividends on preferred stock. *482*

Liquidating dividends Dividends that are a return of contributed capital, not a distribution chargeable to retained earnings. *472*

Net-of-tax effect Used for discontinued operations, extraordinary items, changes in accounting principle, and prior period adjustments, whereby items are shown at the dollar amounts remaining after deducting the effects of such items on income taxes, if any, payable currently. *482*

Paid-in capital All of the contributed capital of a corporation, including that carried in capital stock accounts. When the words *paid-in capital* are included in the account title, the account contains capital contributed in addition to that assigned to the shares issued and recorded in the capital stock accounts. *464*

Paid-In Capital—Common (Preferred) Treasury Stock Transactions The account credited when treasury stock is reissued for more than its cost; this account is debited to the extent of its credit balance when such shares are reissued at less than cost. *475*

Price-earnings ratio The current market price per share of common stock divided by EPS. *483*

Prior period adjustments Consist almost entirely of corrections of errors in previously published financial statements. Prior period adjustments are reported in the statement of retained earnings net of their tax effects, if any. *481*

Retained earnings That part of stockholders' equity resulting from accumulated earnings; the account to which the results of corporate activity, including prior period adjustments, are carried and to which dividends and certain items resulting from capital transactions are charged. *465*

Retained earnings appropriations Contractual or voluntary restrictions or limitations on retained earnings that reduce the amount of dividends that may be declared. *472*

Statement of retained earnings A formal statement showing the items causing changes in unappropriated and appropriated retained earnings during a stated period of time. *473*

Statement of stockholders' equity A summary of the transactions affecting the accounts in the stockholders' equity section of the balance sheet during a stated period of time. *474*

Stock Dividend Distributable—Common account The stockholders' equity (paid-in capital) account that is credited for the par or stated value of the shares distributable when recording the declaration of a stock dividend. *469*

Stock dividends Dividends that are payable in additional shares of the declaring corporation's capital stock. *468*

Stock split A distribution of 100% or more of additional shares of the issuing corporation's stock, accompanied by a corresponding reduction in the par value per share. The purpose of a stock split is to cause a large reduction in the market price per share of the outstanding stock. *470*

Treasury stock Shares of capital stock issued and reacquired by the issuing corporation; they have not been formally canceled and are available for reissuance. *465*

SELF-TEST

TRUE-FALSE

Indicate whether each of the following statements is true or false.

1. The retained earnings balance of a corporation is part of its paid-in capital.

2. The purchase of treasury stock does not affect stockholders' equity.

3. Dividends are expenses since they decrease stockholders' equity.

4. A stock dividend reduces the retained earnings balance and permanently capitalizes the reduced portion of the retained earnings.

5. A retained earnings appropriation reduces the total stockholders' equity shown on the balance sheet.

6. Heavy frost damage suffered by a Florida citrus grower's orange trees would probably be reported as an extraordinary item.

MULTIPLE-CHOICE

Select the best answer for each of the following questions.

1. Which of the following is not included in paid-in capital?
   a. Common Stock.
   b. Paid-In Capital—Donations.
   c. Stock Dividend Distributable.
   d. Appropriation per Loan Agreement.

2. Bevins Company issued 10,000 shares of $20 par value common stock at $24 per share. Bevins reacquired 1,000 shares of its own stock at a cost of $30 per share. The entry to record the reacquisition is:

   a.
Premium on		
Treasury Stock	10,000	
Treasury Stock	20,000	
Cash		30,000

   b.
Premium on		
Treasury Stock	6,000	
Treasury Stock	24,000	
Cash		30,000

   c.
Treasury Stock	30,000	
Cash		30,000

   d.
Treasury Stock	20,000	
Paid-In Capital—		
Treasury Stock		
Transactions	10,000	
Cash		30,000

3. If the company reissues 500 shares of the treasury stock in (2) for $36 per share, the entry is:

   a.
Cash	18,000	
Treasury Stock		15,000
Paid-In Capital—		
Treasury Stock		
Transactions		3,000

   b.
Cash	18,000	
Treasury Stock		18,000

   c.
Cash	18,000	
Treasury Stock		15,000
Retained Earnings		3,000

   d.
Cash	18,000	
Treasury Stock		10,000
Retained Earnings		8,000

4. Treasury stock should be shown on the balance sheet as a:
   a. Reduction of the corporation's stockholders' equity.
   b. Current asset.
   c. Current liability.
   d. Investment asset.

5. An individual stockholder is entitled to receive any dividends declared on stock owned, provided the stock is held on the:
   a. Date of declaration.
   b. Date of record.
   c. Date of payment.
   d. Last day of a fiscal year.

6. ABC Corporation declared the regular quarterly dividend of $2 per share. ABC had issued 12,000 shares and subsequently reacquired 2,000 shares as treasury stock. What would be the total amount of the dividend?
   a. $24,000.
   b. $28,000.
   c. $20,000.
   d. $4,000.

7. Which item is not reported as a separate line item below income from continuing operations, net of tax effects, in the income statement?
   a. Extraordinary items.
   b. Prior period adjustments.
   c. Discontinued operations.
   d. Changes in accounting principle.

Now turn to page 499 to check your answers.

QUESTIONS

1. What are the two main elements of stockholders' equity in a corporation? Explain the difference between them.

2. Name several sources of paid-in capital. Would it suffice to maintain one account called *Paid-In Capital* for all sources of paid-in capital? Why or why not?

3. Does accounting for treasury stock resemble accounting for an asset? Is treasury stock an asset? If not, where is it properly shown on a balance sheet?

4. What are some possible reasons for a corporation to reacquire its own capital stock as treasury stock?

5. What is the purpose underlying the statutes that provide for restriction of retained earnings in the amount of the cost of treasury stock? Are such statutes for the benefit of stockholders, management, or creditors?

6. What is the effect of each of the following on the total stockholders' equity of a corporation: (*a*) declaration of a cash dividend, (*b*) payment of a cash dividend already declared, (*c*) declaration of a stock dividend, and (*d*) issuance of a stock dividend already declared?

7. The following dates are associated with a cash dividend of $80,000: July 15, July 31, and August 15. Identify each of the three dates, and give the journal entry required on each date, if any.

8. How should a declared but unpaid cash dividend be shown on the balance sheet? How should a declared but unissued stock dividend be shown?

9. On May 8, the board of directors of Park Corporation declared a dividend, payable on June 5, to stockholders of record on May 17. On May 10, James sold his capital stock in Park Corporation directly to Benton for $20,000, endorsing his stock certificate and giving it to Benton. Benton placed the stock certificate in her safe. On May 30, Benton sent the certificate to the transfer agent of Park Corporation for transfer. Who received the dividend? Why?

10. What are the possible reasons for a corporation to declare a stock dividend?

11. Why is a dividend consisting of the distribution of additional shares of the common stock of the declaring corporation not considered income to the recipient stockholders?

12. What is the difference between a small stock dividend and a large stock dividend?

13. What are liquidating dividends?

14. What is the purpose of a retained earnings appropriation?

15. What is a statement of stockholders' equity?

16. Describe a discontinued operation.

17. What are extraordinary items? Where and how are they reported?

18. Give an example of a change in accounting principle. How are the effects of changes in accounting principle reported?

19. What are prior period adjustments? Where and how are they reported?

20. Why are stockholders and potential investors interested in the amount of a corporation's EPS? What does the EPS amount reveal that total earnings do not?

The Coca-Cola Company

21. **Real World Question** From the consolidated statements of share-owners' equity of The Coca-Cola Company in the annual report booklet, identify the 1996 total dollar amount for each of the following items:
 a. Sales to employees exercising stock options.
 b. Purchase of common stock for treasury.
 c. Total cash dividends.
 d. Total stockholders' equity—December 31, 1996.

MAYTAG

22. **Real World Question** Based on the financial statements of Maytag Corporation contained in the annual report booklet, how many shares of treasury stock were on hand as of December 31, 1996?

THE LIMITED, INC.

23. **Real World Question** Based on the financial statements of The Limited, Inc., contained in the annual report booklet, what was the cost of treasury stock as of February 1, 1997?

HARLAND

24. **Real World Question** Based on the financial statements of John H. Harland Company contained in the annual report booklet, how many shares of treasury stock were on hand as of December 31, 1996?

EXERCISES

The December 31, 1998, trial balance of Yamey Corporation had the following account balances:

Common Stock (no-par value; 200,000 shares authorized, issued, and outstanding; stated value of $20 per share)	$4,000,000
Notes Payable (12% due May 1, 1999)	500,000
Retained Earnings, Unappropriated	2,500,000
Dividends Payable in Cash (declared December 15, on preferred stock)	12,000
Appropriation per Loan Agreement	480,000
Preferred Stock (6%, par value $200; 2,000 shares authorized, issued, and outstanding)	400,000
Paid-In Capital in Excess of Stated Value—Common	300,000
Paid-In Capital in Excess of Par Value—Preferred	40,000

Present in proper form the stockholders' equity section of the balance sheet.

Exercise 13–1
Prepare stockholders' equity section of balance sheet (L.O. 1)

Fogg Company has issued all of its authorized 5,000 shares of $400 par value common stock. On February 1, 1998, the board of directors declared a dividend of $12 per share payable on March 15, 1998, to stockholders of record on March 1, 1998. Give the necessary journal entries.

Exercise 13–2
Prepare journal entries for cash dividends (L.O. 2)

The stockholders' equity section of Jay Company's balance sheet on December 31, 1998, shows 100,000 shares of authorized and issued $20 stated value common stock, of which 9,000 shares are held in the treasury. On this date, the board of directors declared a cash dividend of $2 per share payable on January 21, 1999, to stockholders of record on January 10. Give dated journal entries for these.

Exercise 13–3
Prepare journal entries for cash dividend when treasury stock is held (L.O. 2)

Exercise 13–4
Prepare journal entry for small stock dividend and discuss large stock dividend (L.O. 2)

Kevin Company has outstanding 75,000 shares of common stock without par or stated value, which were issued at an average price of $80 per share, and retained earnings of $3,200,000. The current market price of the common stock is $120 per share. Total authorized stock consists of 500,000 shares.

a. Give the required entry to record the declaration of a 10% stock dividend.

b. If, alternatively, the company declared a 30% stock dividend, what additional information would you need before making a journal entry to record the dividend?

Exercise 13–5
Prepare journal entries for stock split and small stock dividend (L.O. 2)

Grant Corporation's stockholders' equity consisted of 60,000 authorized shares of $30 par value common stock, of which 30,000 shares had been issued at par, and retained earnings of $750,000. The company then split its stock, two for one, by changing the par value of the old shares and issuing new $15 par shares.

a. Give the required journal entry to record the stock split.

b. Suppose instead that the company declared and later issued a 10% stock dividend. Give the required journal entries, assuming that the market value on the date of declaration was $40 per share.

Exercise 13–6
Prepare journal entry for appropriation of retained earnings and explain (L.O. 2)

The balance sheet of Willis Company contains the following:

Appropriation per loan agreement $900,000

a. Give the journal entry made to create this account.

b. Explain the reason for the appropriation's existence and its manner of presentation in the balance sheet.

Exercise 13–7
Prepare journal entries for reacquisition and reissuance of treasury stock (L.O. 3)

Kelly Company had outstanding 50,000 shares of $20 stated value common stock, all issued at $24 per share, and had retained earnings of $800,000. The company reacquired 2,000 shares of its stock for cash at book value from the widow of a deceased stockholder.

a. Give the entry to record the reacquisition of the stock.

b. Give the entry to record the subsequent reissuance of this stock at $50 per share.

c. Give the entry required if the stock is instead reissued at $30 per share and there were no prior treasury stock transactions.

Exercise 13–8
Prepare journal entry(ies) for reissuance of donated stock (L.O. 3)

Evan Company received 200 shares of its $200 stated value common stock on December 1, 1998, as a donation from a stockholder. On December 15, 1998, it reissued the stock for $62,400 cash. Give the journal entry or entries necessary for these transactions.

Exercise 13–9
Prepare income statement and statement of retained earnings (L.O. 2, 4)

Vista Company has revenues of $80 million, expenses of $64 million, a tax-deductible earthquake loss (its first such loss) of $4 million, and a tax-deductible loss of $6 million resulting from the voluntary early extinguishment (retirement) of debt. The assumed income tax rate is 40%. The company's beginning-of-the-year retained earnings were $30 million, and a dividend of $2 million was declared.

a. Prepare an income statement for the year.

b. Prepare a statement of retained earnings for the year.

Exercise 13–10
Prepare statement of retained earnings (L.O. 2, 5)

Conner Company had retained earnings of $56,000 as of January 1, 1998. In 1998, Conner Company had sales of $160,000, cost of goods sold of $96,000, and other operating expenses, excluding taxes, of $32,000. In 1998, Conner Company discovered that it had, in error, depreciated land over the last three years resulting in a balance in the accumulated depreciation account of $40,000. The assumed tax rate for Conner Company is 40%. Present in proper form a statement of retained earnings for the year ended December 31, 1998.

Exercise 13–11
Calculate EPS; present information in income statement format (L.O. 6)

The following information relates to Perry Corporation for the year ended December 31, 1998:

Common stock outstanding	75,000 shares
Income from continuing operations	$1,523,200
Loss on discontinued operations (net of tax)	240,000
Extraordinary gain (net of tax)	144,000

Calculate EPS for the year ended December 31, 1998. Present the information in the same format used in the corporation's income statement.

Dean Company had an average number of shares of common stock outstanding of 200,000 in 1998 and 215,000 in 1999. Net income for these two years was as follows:

Exercise 13–12
Calculate EPS; comment on resulting amounts (L.O. 6)

1998	$2,208,000
1999	2,304,000

a. Calculate EPS for the years ended December 31, 1998, and 1999.

b. What might the resulting figures tell a stockholder or a potential investor?

PROBLEMS

The trial balance of Dex Corporation as of December 31, 1998, contains the following selected balances:

Problem 13–1
Present stockholders' equity section of balance sheet (L.O. 1)

Notes Payable (17%, due May 1, 2000)	$4,000,000
Allowance for Uncollectible Accounts	60,000
Common Stock (without par value, $20 stated value; 300,000 shares authorized, issued, and outstanding)	6,000,000
Retained Earnings, Unappropriated	500,000
Dividends Payable (in cash, declared December 15 on preferred stock)	14,000
Appropriation for Pending Litigation	600,000
Preferred Stock (6%, $200 par value; 3,000 shares authorized, issued, and outstanding)	600,000
Paid-In Capital—Donations	400,000
Paid-In Capital in Excess of Par Value—Preferred	10,000

Present the stockholders' equity section of the balance sheet as of December 31, 1998.

Required

The stockholders' equity section of Carson Company's December 31, 1997, balance sheet follows:

Problem 13–2
Prepare journal entries for cash dividend and small stock dividend (L.O. 2)

Stockholders' equity:

Paid-in-capital:		
Common stock—$120 par value; authorized, 2,000 shares; issued and outstanding, 1,000 shares	$120,000	
Paid-in capital in excess of par value	6,000	
Total paid-in capital		$126,000
Retained earnings		48,000
Total stockholders' equity		$174,000

On July 15, 1998, the board of directors declared a cash dividend of $12 per share, which was paid on August 1, 1998. On December 1, 1998, the board declared a stock dividend of 10%, and the shares were issued on December 15, 1998. Market value of the stock was $144 on December 1 and $168 on December 15.

Prepare journal entries for these dividend transactions.

Required

The ledger of Falcone Company includes the following account balances on September 30, 1998:

Problem 13–3
Prepare journal entries for appropriations of retained earnings (L.O. 2)

Appropriation for Contingencies	$210,000
Appropriation for Plant Expansion	392,000
Retained Earnings, Unappropriated	700,000

During October 1998, the company took action to:

1. Increase the appropriation for contingencies by $60,000.
2. Decrease the appropriation for plant expansion by $160,000.
3. Establish an appropriation per loan agreement, with an annual increase of $48,000.
4. Declare a cash dividend of $140,000.

Prepare the journal entries to record these transactions of Falcone Company.

Required

Following are selected transactions of Taylor Corporation:

Problem 13–4
Prepare journal entries for retained earnings appropriation and small stock dividend (L.O. 2)

1993

Dec. 31 By action of the board of directors, $450,000 of retained earnings was appropriated to provide for future expansion of the company's main building.

(On the last day of each of the next four years, the same action was taken. You need not make entries for these years.)

1998

Jan. 3   Obtained, at a cost of $4,500, a building permit to construct a new wing on the main plant building.

July 30   Paid $1,800,000 to Starke Construction Company for completion of the new wing.

Aug. 4   The board of directors authorized the release of the sum appropriated for expansion of the plant building.

      4   The board of directors declared a 10% common stock dividend on the 25,000 shares of $500 par value common stock outstanding. The market price on this date was $660 per share.

Required   Prepare journal entries to record all of these transactions.

Problem 13–5
Present statement of retained earnings (L.O. 2)

The following information relates to Dahl Corporation for the year 1998:

Net income for the year	$1,680,000
Dividends declared on common stock	235,200
Dividends declared on preferred stock	134,400
Retained earnings, January 1, unappropriated	5,040,000
Appropriation for retirement of bonds	672,000
Balance in "Appropriation for possible loss of a lawsuit," no longer needed on December 31 because of a favorable court decision, is (by directors' order) returned to unappropriated retained earnings	840,000

Required   Prepare a statement of retained earnings for the year ended December 31, 1998.

Problem 13–6
Prepare journal entries for treasury stock transactions and for cash dividends; present stockholders' equity section (L.O. 2, 3)

The stockholders' equity of Acorn Company as of December 31, 1997, consisted of 20,000 shares of authorized, issued, and outstanding $50 par value common stock, paid-in capital in excess of par of $240,000, and retained earnings of $400,000. Following are selected transactions for 1998:

May 1   Acquired 3,000 shares of its own common stock at $100 per share.

June 1   Reissued 500 shares at $120.

    30   Reissued 700 shares at $90.

Oct. 1   Declared a cash dividend of $5 per share.

    31   Paid the cash dividend declared on October 1.

Net income for the year was $80,000. No other transactions affecting retained earnings occurred during the year.

Required   a.   Prepare general journal entries for these transactions.

        b.   Prepare the stockholders' equity section of the December 31, 1998, balance sheet.

Problem 13–7
Prepare journal entries for stock transactions, cash dividend, small stock dividend, and retained earnings appropriation; prepare statement of retained earnings and stockholders' equity section of balance sheet (L.O. 2, 3)

The stockholders' equity section of Sager Company's December 31, 1997, balance sheet follows:

Stockholders' equity:		
Paid-in capital:		
Preferred stock—$60 par value, 5%; authorized, 5,000 shares;		
issued and outstanding, 2,500 shares		$150,000
Common stock—without par or stated value; authorized, 50,000		
shares; issued, 25,000 shares of which 500 are held in treasury		225,000
Paid-in capital in excess of par—preferred		3,000
Total paid-in capital		$378,000
Retained earnings:		
Appropriated:		
For plant expansion	$ 15,000	
Unappropriated (restricted as to dividends to the extent of		
$6,000, the cost of the treasury stock held)	126,000	
Total retained earnings		141,000
Total paid-in capital and retained earnings		$519,000
Less: Treasury stock, common, at cost (500 shares)		6,000
Total stockholders' equity		$513,000

Following are selected transactions that occurred in 1998:

Jan. 13   Cash was received for 550 shares of previously unissued common stock at $13.20.

Feb. 4   A plot of land was accepted as payment in full for 500 shares of common stock, and the stock was issued. Closing market price of the common stock on this date was $12 per share.

Mar. 24   All of the treasury stock was reissued at $14.40 per share.

June 23   The regular semiannual dividend on the preferred stock was declared.

     30   The preferred dividend was paid.

July 3   A 10% stock dividend was declared on the common stock. Market price on this date was $16.80.

     18   The stock dividend shares were issued.

Oct. 4   The company reacquired 105 shares of its common stock at $14.40.

Dec. 18   The regular semiannual dividend on the preferred stock and a $0.24 per share dividend on the common stock were declared.

     31   Both dividends were paid.

     31   An additional appropriation of retained earnings of $3,000 for plant expansion was authorized.

a.   Prepare journal entries to record the 1998 transactions.

b.   Prepare a statement of retained earnings for the year 1998, assuming net income for the year was $25,800.

c.   Prepare the stockholders' equity section of the December 31, 1998, balance sheet.

Required

Selected data of Ace Company for the year ended December 31, 1998, are:

Problem 13–8
Present income statement and statement of retained earnings (L.O. 2, 4, 5)

Sales, net	$1,000,000
Interest expense	90,000
Cash dividends on common stock	150,000
Selling and administrative expenses	245,000
Cash dividends on preferred stock	70,000
Rent revenue	400,000
Cost of goods sold	650,000
Flood loss (has never occurred before)	200,000
Interest revenue	90,000
Other revenue	150,000
Depreciation and maintenance on rental equipment	270,000
Stock dividend on common stock	300,000
Operating income on Plastics Division up to point of sale in 1998	50,000
Gain on disposal of Plastics Division	25,000
Litigation loss (has never occurred before)	400,000
Cumulative positive effect on prior years' income of changing to a different depreciation method	80,000

Assume the applicable federal income tax rate is 40%. All of the preceding items of expense, revenue, and loss are included in the computation of taxable income. The litigation loss resulted from a court award of damages for patent infringement on a product that the company produced and sold in 1994 and 1995, but was discontinued in 1995. In addition, the company discovered that in 1997 it had erroneously charged to expense the $250,000 cost of a tract of land purchased that year and had made the same error on its tax return for 1997. Retained earnings as of January 1, 1998, were $5,600,000. Assume there were 10,000 shares of common stock and 5,000 shares of preferred stock outstanding for the entire year.

Prepare an income statement and a statement of retained earnings for 1998.

Required

ALTERNATE PROBLEMS

The bookkeeper of Hart Company has prepared the following incorrect statement of stockholders' equity for the year ended December 31, 1998:

Problem 13–1A
Prepare stockholders' equity section of balance sheet (L.O. 1)

Stockholders' equity:

Paid-in capital:

Preferred stock—6%, cumulative (8,000 shares)	$1,003,200	
Common stock—50,000 shares	2,856,000	
Total paid-in capital		$3,859,200
Retained earnings		1,636,800
Total stockholders' equity		$5,496,000

The authorized stock consists of 12,000 shares of preferred stock with a $120 par value and 75,000 shares of common stock, $48 par value. The preferred stock was issued on two occasions: (1) 5,000 shares at par, and (2) 3,000 shares at $134.40 per share. The 50,000 shares of common stock were issued at $62.40 per share. Five thousand shares of treasury common stock were reacquired for $264,000. The bookkeeper deducted the cost of the treasury stock from the Common Stock account.

Required   Prepare the correct stockholders' equity section of the balance sheet at December 31, 1998.

Problem 13–2A
Prepare journal entries for cash dividend and small stock dividend (L.O. 2)

The only stockholders' equity items of Jody Company at June 30, 1998, are:

Stockholders' equity:

Paid-in capital:

Common stock—$200 par value, 10,000 shares authorized, 6,000 shares issued and outstanding	$1,200,000	
Paid-in capital in excess of par value	480,000	
Total paid-in capital		$1,680,000
Retained earnings		480,000
Total stockholders' equity		$2,160,000

On August 4, 1998, a 4% cash dividend was declared, payable on September 3. On November 16, a 10% stock dividend was declared. The shares were issued on December 1. The market value of the common stock was $360 per share on November 16 and $354 per share on December 1.

Required   Prepare journal entries for these dividend transactions.

Problem 13–3A
Prepare journal entries for retained earnings appropriation, asset acquisition, and stock dividend (L.O. 2)

Following are selected transactions of White Corporation:

1991
Dec. 31   The board of directors authorized the appropriation of $50,000 of retained earnings to provide for the future acquisition of a new plant site and the construction of a new building. (On the last day of the next six years, the same action was taken. You need not make entries for these six years.)

1996
Jan. 2   Purchased a new plant site for cash, $100,000.

Mar. 29   Entered into a contract for construction of a new building, payment to be made within 30 days following completion.

1998
Feb. 10   Following final inspection and approval of the new building, Dyer Construction Company was paid in full, $500,000.

Mar. 10   The board of directors authorized release of the retained earnings appropriated for the plant site and building.

Apr. 2   A 5% stock dividend on the 100,000 shares of $50 par value common stock outstanding was declared. The market price on this date was $55 per share.

Required   Prepare journal entries for all of these transactions.

Problem 13–4A
Present statement of retained earnings (L.O. 2)

Following are selected data of Kane Corporation at December 31, 1998:

Net income for the year	$512,000
Dividends declared on preferred stock	72,000
Retained earnings appropriated during the year for future plant expansion	240,000
Dividends declared on common stock	64,000
Retained earnings, January 1, unappropriated	720,000
Directors ordered that the balance in the "Appropriation per loan agreement," related to a loan repaid on March 31, 1998, be returned to unappropriated retained earnings	480,000

Prepare a statement of retained earnings for the year ended December 31, 1998.

The stockholders' equity of Sayers Company at January 1, 1998, is as follows:

Common stock—no-par value, stated value of $20;	
100,000 shares authorized, 60,000 shares issued	$1,200,000
Paid-in capital in excess of stated value.	200,000
Appropriation per loan agreement	75,200
Unappropriated retained earnings	424,000
Treasury stock (3,000 shares at cost)	(72,000)

During 1998, the following transactions occurred in the order listed:

1. Issued 10,000 shares of stock for $368,000.
2. Declared a 4% stock dividend when the market price was $48 per share.
3. Sold 1,000 shares of treasury stock for $43,200.
4. Issued stock certificates for the stock dividend declared in transaction 2.
5. Bought 2,000 shares of treasury stock for $67,200.
6. Increased the appropriation by $43,200 per loan agreement.

Prepare journal entries as necessary for these transactions.

The stockholders' equity of Briar Company on December 31, 1997, consisted of 1,000 authorized, issued, and outstanding shares of $72 cumulative preferred stock, stated value $240 per share, which were originally issued at $1,192 per share; 100,000 shares authorized, issued, and outstanding of no-par, $160 stated value common stock, which were originally issued at $160; and retained earnings of $1,120,000. Following are selected transactions and other data relating to 1998. No previous treasury stock transactions had occurred.

1. The company reacquired 2,000 shares of its common stock at $336.
2. One thousand of the treasury shares were reissued at $288.
3. Stockholders donated 1,000 shares of common stock to the company. These shares were immediately reissued at $256 to provide working capital.
4. The first quarter's dividend of $18 per share was declared and paid on the preferred stock. No other dividends were declared or paid during 1998.

The company suffered a net loss of $224,000 for the year 1998.

a. Prepare journal entries for the preceding numbered transactions.
b. Prepare the stockholders' equity section of the December 31, 1998, balance sheet.

The following stockholders' equity section is from Bell Company's October 31, 1997, balance sheet:

Stockholders' equity:

Paid-in capital:		
Preferred stock—$60 par value, 6%; 1,000 shares authorized;		
350 shares issued and outstanding	$ 21,000	
Common stock—$6 par value; 100,000 shares authorized;		
40,000 shares issued and outstanding	240,000	
Paid-in capital from donation of plant site	15,000	
Total paid-in capital		$276,000
Retained earnings:		
Appropriated:		
Appropriation for contingencies	$ 12,000	
Unappropriated	33,300	
Total retained earnings		45,300
Total stockholders' equity		$321,300

During the ensuing fiscal year, Bell Company entered into the following transactions:

1. The appropriation of $12,000 of retained earnings had been authorized in October 1997 because of the likelihood of an unfavorable court decision in a pending lawsuit. The suit was brought by a customer seeking damages for the company's alleged breach of a contract to supply the customer with certain products at stated prices in 1996. The suit was concluded on March 6, 1998, with a court order directing the company to pay

Required

Problem 13–5A
Prepare journal entries for stock dividend, treasury stock transactions, and retained earnings appropriation (L.O. 2, 3)

Required

Problem 13–6A
Prepare journal entries for treasury stock transactions and for cash dividend; present stockholders' equity section of balance sheet (L.O. 2, 3)

Required

Problem 13–7A
Prepare journal entries to close retained earnings appropriation and for treasury stock transactions and cash dividends; present statement of retained earnings and stockholders' equity section of balance sheet (L.O. 2, 3)

$10,500 in damages. These damages were not deductible in determining the income tax liability. The board ordered the damages paid and the appropriation closed. The loss does not qualify as an extraordinary item.

2. The company acquired 1,000 shares of its own common stock at $9 in May 1998. On June 30, it reissued 500 of these shares at $7.20.

3. Dividends declared and paid during the year were 6% on preferred stock and 18 cents per share on common stock. Both dividends were declared on September 1 and paid on September 30, 1998.

For the fiscal year, the company had net income after income taxes of $11,400, excluding the loss of the lawsuit.

Required
a. Prepare journal entries for the preceding numbered transactions.
b. Prepare a statement of retained earnings for the year ended October 31, 1998.
c. Prepare the stockholders' equity section of the October 31, 1998, balance sheet.

Problem 13–8A
Present income statement and statement of retained earnings (L.O. 2, 4, 5)

Selected data for Brinks Company for 1998 are given below:

Common stock—$20 par value	$2,000,000
Sales, net	1,740,000
Selling and administrative expenses	320,000
Cash dividends declared and paid	120,000
Cost of goods sold	800,000
Depreciation expense	120,000
Interest revenue	20,000
Loss on write-down of obsolete inventory	40,000
Retained earnings (as of 12/31/97)	2,000,000
Operating loss on Candy Division up to point of sale in 1998	40,000
Loss on disposal of Candy Division	200,000
Earthquake loss	96,000
Cumulative negative effect on prior years' income of changing from straight-line to an accelerated method of computing depreciation	64,000

Assume the applicable federal income tax rate is 40%. All of the items of expense, revenue, and loss are included in the computation of taxable income. The earthquake loss resulted from the first earthquake experienced at the company's location. In addition, the company discovered that in 1997 it had erroneously charged to expense the $160,000 cost of a tract of land purchased that year and had made the same error on its tax return for 1997.

Required
a. Prepare an income statement for the year ended December 31, 1998.
b. Prepare a statement of retained earnings for the year ended December 31, 1998.

BEYOND THE NUMBERS—CRITICAL THINKING

Business Decision Case 13–1
Determine amount of dividends received and effect on stock prices (L.O. 2)

The stockholders' equity section of the Bates Corporation's balance sheet for June 30, 1998, follows:

Stockholders' equity:
Paid-in capital:		
Common stock—$20 par value; authorized 200,000 shares; issued and outstanding 80,000 shares	$1,600,000	
Paid-in capital in excess of par value	960,000	
Total paid-in capital		$2,560,000
Retained earnings		1,520,000
Total stockholders' equity		$4,080,000

On July 1, 1998, the corporation's directors declared a 10% stock dividend distributable on August 2 to stockholders of record on July 16. On November 1, 1998, the directors voted a $2.40 per share annual cash dividend payable on December 2 to stockholders of record on November 16. For four years prior to 1998, the corporation had paid an annual cash dividend of $2.52.

As of July 1, 1998, Bob Jones owned 8,000 shares of Bates Corporation's common stock, which he had purchased four years earlier. The market value of his stock was $48 per share on July 1, 1998, and $43.64 per share on July 16, 1998.

a. What amount of cash dividends will Jones receive in 1998? How does this amount differ from the amount of cash dividends Jones received in the previous four years?

b. Jones has asked you, his CPA, to explain why the price of the stock dropped from $48 to $43.64 on July 16, 1998. Write a memo to Jones explaining your answer.

c. Do you think Jones is better off as a result of the stock dividend and the $2.40 cash dividend than he would have been if he had just received the $2.52 cash dividend? Write a memo to Jones explaining your answer.

Required

The following journal entries are for Keel Corporation:

Business Decision Case 13–2
Analyze journal entries for impropriety and make subsequent corrections (L.O. 2, 3)

1.	Retained Earnings	12,000	
	Reserve for Uncollectible Accounts		12,000
	To record the adjusting entry for uncollectible accounts.		

2.	Retained Earnings	48,000	
	Reserve for Depreciation		48,000
	To record depreciation expense.		

3.	Retained Earnings	120,000	
	Appropriation for Plant Expansion		120,000
	To record retained earnings appropriation.		

4.	Retained Earnings	8,000	
	Stock Dividend Distributable—Common		8,000
	To record 10% stock dividend declaration (100 shares to be distributed—$80 par value, $120 market value).		

5.	Stock Dividend Distributable—Common	8,000	
	Common Stock		8,000
	To record distribution of stock dividend.		

6.	Treasury Stock	32,000	
	Cash		32,000
	To record acquisition of 200 shares of $80 par value common stock at $160 per share.		

7.	Cash	17,600	
	Treasury Stock		17,600
	To record sale of 100 treasury shares at $176 per share.		

8.	Cash	6,800	
	Treasury Stock		6,800
	To record sale of 50 treasury shares at $136 per share.		

9.	Common Stock	16,000	
	Dividends Payable		16,000
	To record declaration of cash dividend.		

10.	Dividends Payable	16,000	
	Cash		16,000
	To record payment of cash dividend.		

The management of Keel Corporation has asked you, a CPA, to analyze these journal entries and decide whether each is correct. The explanations are all correct. Wherever a journal entry is incorrect, prepare the journal entry that should have been made.

Required

Annual Report Analysis 13–3
Determine the number of shares of common stock issued and the cost of treasury stock. Compute EPS. (L.O. 3, 7)

Refer to the financial statements of The Coca-Cola Company in the annual report booklet. Note 11 discusses the treasury stock transactions during the 1996 fiscal period.

Required

a. Based on the information in the balance sheet and the note, determine the number of common shares issued and outstanding; and the average cost of treasury stock shares on hand at the end of 1996 and 1995, as shown on the balance sheets.

b. In writing, discuss what reasons Coca-Cola might have to acquire treasury stock.

c. Find Coca-Cola's EPS listed in its annual report. If the common stock's market price at December 31, 1996, was $52.63, what was the price-earnings ratio?

Ethics Case—Writing Experience 13–4
Answer questions based on the ethics case

Based on the ethics case on page 481, answer the following questions concerning Ace Chemical Company in writing:

a. Is this transaction fair to the creditors?

b. Why wouldn't the officers merely declare a $4 million cash dividend? Is the proposed treasury stock transaction fair to the other stockholders?

c. If you were one of the officers, would you feel comfortable in going ahead with this proposed treasury stock transaction?

Group Project 13–5
Library project—Compare features of accounting software packages

In teams of two to three students, go to the library to find articles evaluating accounting software packages. Use a periodicals index such as the *Accounting and Tax Index* or the *Business Periodicals Index* to locate these articles. Compare the cost and features of three accounting software packages. As a team, prepare a memorandum to the manager of a small retail business. Compare and contrast the three accounting software packages so the manager might decide which package to purchase. In the memorandum, cite the sources used in gathering the data and properly reference any direct quotes or paraphrasing. The heading of the memorandum should contain the date, to whom it is written, from whom, and the subject matter.

Group Project 13–6
Library Project—Investigate accounting treatment for gains and losses from extinguishment of debt

With a small group of students, go to the library and locate *Statement of Financial Accounting Standards No. 4,* "Reporting Gains and Losses from Extinguishing of Debt," published by the Financial Accounting Standards Board. Write a report to your instructor giving the highlights of the standard. Why are these gains and losses treated as extraordinary items? Why did the Board act on this topic? Why did one member of the Board dissent?

Group Project 13–7
Study statements of stockholders' equity

With one or two other students, locate the annual reports of three companies and study their statements of stockholders' equity. Determine why the number of common shares outstanding changed (if at all) during the current year. For instance, the number of outstanding shares may have increased due to new issuances, exercise of stock options, conversion of preferred stock, exercise of warrants, stock dividends, and other causes. The number of shares outstanding may have decreased because of repurchases of stock (treasury stock transactions). Write a report to your instructor presenting your findings. Also be prepared to make a short presentation to your class.

Using the Internet—A View of the Real World

Internet Project 13–8
Investigate a consolidated statement of stockholders' equity

Visit the following website for Computer Associates International, Inc.:

http://www.cai.com

Pursue choices on the screen until you locate the consolidated statement of stockholders' equity. You will probably go down some "false paths" to get to this financial statement, but you can get there. This experience is all part of learning to use the Internet. Trace the changes that have occurred in the last three years in the treasury stock account. Identify the causes of the changes. Check out the notes to the financial statements for further information. Write a memo to your instructor summarizing your findings.

Visit the following website for International Paper:

http://www.ipaper.com

Pursue choices on the screen until you locate the consolidated statement of stockholders' equity. You will probably go down some "false paths" to get to this financial statement, but you can get there. This experience is all part of learning to use the Internet. Trace the changes that have occurred in the paid-in capital, retained earnings, and treasury stock accounts for the most recent two years. Identify the causes of the changes. Check out the notes to the financial statements for further information. Write a memo to your instructor summarizing your findings.

Internet Project 13–9
Investigate a consolidated statement of stockholders' equity

ANSWERS TO SELF-TEST

TRUE-FALSE

1. **False.** The paid-in capital of a corporation only includes capital contributed by stockholders or others. Thus, it does not include retained earnings.

2. **False.** The purchase of treasury stock reduces total stockholders' equity.

3. **False.** Dividends are distributions of earnings in the past and are not expenses.

4. **True.** A stock dividend permanently capitalizes a portion of retained earnings by decreasing retained earnings and increasing paid-in capital by an equal amount.

5. **False.** The purpose of a retained earnings appropriation is to disclose that a portion of retained earnings is not available for cash dividends. Thus, such an appropriation does not reduce total stockholders' equity.

6. **False.** Such damage occurs too frequently to be considered nonrecurring.

MULTIPLE-CHOICE

1. **d.** Appropriation per Loan Agreement is part of retained earnings.

2. **c.** When treasury stock is reacquired, the stock is recorded at cost in a debit-balance stockholders' equity account, Treasury Stock.

3. **a.** The excess of the reissue price over the cost of treasury stock is recorded in the Paid-In Capital—Treasury Stock Transactions account.

4. **a.** Treasury stock is customarily shown as a deduction from total stockholders' equity.

5. **b.** The date of record determines who is to receive the dividends.

6. **c.** The total amount of dividends is computed as follows:

Total outstanding shares at declaration:	
(12,000 − 2,000) shares	10,000
Dividend per share	× $2
Total dividend amount	$20,000

7. **b.** Prior period adjustments are shown as adjustments to the opening balance of retained earnings on the statement of retained earnings.

14

STOCK INVESTMENTS
COST, EQUITY, CONSOLIDATIONS;
INTERNATIONAL ACCOUNTING

Often a large company attempts to take over a smaller company by acquiring a controlling interest (more than 50% of the outstanding shares) in that target company. Some of these takeover attempts are friendly (not resisted by the target company), and some are unfriendly (resisted by the target company). If the attempt is successful, the two companies become one business entity for accounting purposes, and consolidated financial statements are prepared. The company that takes over another company is the *parent company;* the company acquired is the *subsidiary company.* This chapter discusses accounting for parent and subsidiary companies.

When a corporation purchases the stock of another corporation, the method of accounting for the stock investment depends on the corporation's motivation for making the investment and the relative size of the investment. A corporation's motivation for purchasing the stock of another company may be as: (1) a short-term investment of excess cash; (2) a long-term investment in a substantial percentage of another company's stock to ensure a supply of a required raw material (for example, when large oil companies invest heavily in, or purchase outright, wildcat oil drilling companies); or (3) a long-term investment for expansion (when a company purchases another profitable company rather than starting a new business operation). On the balance sheet, the first type of investment is a current asset, and the last two types are long-term (noncurrent) investments. As explained in the chapter, the purchaser's level of ownership of the investee company determines whether the investment is accounted for by the cost method or the equity method.

The chapter appendix discusses international accounting. As businesses expand their operations across international borders, accountants must become aware of the accounting challenges this expansion presents.

COST AND EQUITY METHODS

Investors in common stock can use two methods to account for their investments— the cost method or the equity method. Under both methods, they initially record the investment at cost (price paid at acquisition). Under the **cost method,** the investor company does not adjust the investment account balance subsequently for its share of the investee's reported income, losses, and dividends. Instead, the investor company receives dividends and credits them to a Dividends Revenue account. Under the **equity method,** the investor company adjusts the investment account for its share of the investee's reported income, losses, and dividends.

The Accounting Principles Board (the predecessor of the Financial Accounting Standards Board) has identified the circumstances under which each method must be used. This chapter illustrates each of those circumstances. The general rules for determining the appropriate method of accounting follow:

Types of Common Stock Investment	Method of Accounting Required by Accounting Principles Board in Most Cases
All short-term investments	Cost
Long-term investments of:	
Less than 20%:	
If no significant influence	Cost
If significant influence.	Equity
20%–50%	Equity
More than 50%	Cost or equity

ACCOUNTING FOR SHORT-TERM STOCK INVESTMENTS AND FOR LONG-TERM STOCK INVESTMENTS OF LESS THAN 20%

Accountants use the cost method to account for all short-term stock investments. When a company owns less than 50% of the outstanding stock of another company as a long-term investment, the percentage of ownership determines whether to use the cost or equity method. A purchasing company that owns less than 20% of the outstanding stock of the investee company, and does not exercise significant influence over it, uses the cost method. A purchasing company that owns from 20% to 50% of the outstanding stock of the investee company or owns less than 20%, but still exercises significant influence over it, uses the equity method. Thus, firms use the cost method for all short-term stock investments and almost all long-term stock investments of less than 20%. For investments of more than 50%, they use either the cost or equity method because the application of consolidation procedures yields the same result.

Cost Method for Short-Term Investments and for Long-Term Investments of Less Than 20%

When a company purchases stock (equity securities) as an investment, accountants must classify the stock according to management's intent. If management bought the security for the principal purpose of selling it in the near term, the security would be a **trading security.** If the stock will be held for a longer term, it is called an **available-for-sale security.** Trading securities are always current assets. Available-for-sale securities may be either current assets or noncurrent assets, depending on how long management intends to hold them. Each classification is accounted for differently. This topic will be discussed later in this chapter.

Securities can be transferred between classifications; however, there are specific rules that must be met for these transfers to be allowed. These rules will be addressed in intermediate accounting. Under the cost method, investors record stock investments at cost, which is usually the cash paid for the stock. They purchase most stocks from other investors (not the issuing company) through brokers who execute trades in an organized market, such as the New York Stock Exchange. Thus, cost usually consists of the price paid for the shares, plus a broker's commission.

(concluded)

5. Prepare consolidated financial statements through the use of a consolidated statement work sheet.

6. Identify the differences between purchase accounting and pooling of interests accounting.

7. Describe the uses and limitations of consolidated financial statements.

8. Analyze and use the financial results—dividend yield on common stock and payout ratio on common stock.

9. Discuss the differences in international accounting among nations (Appendix).

Objective 1
Report stock investments and distinguish between the cost and equity methods of accounting for stock investments.

Objective 2
Prepare journal entries to account for short-term stock investments and for long-term stock investments of less than 20%.

For example, assume that Brewer Corporation purchased as a near-term investment 1,000 shares of Cowen Company's $10 par value common stock at 14⅛, plus a
$175 broker's commission. Brokers quote stock prices in dollars and fractions of one
dollar; thus, 14⅛ means $14.125 per share. Brewer's entry to record its investment is:

Real World Example
One share of General Motors common stock sold for $32 per share on
January 4, 1993. On February 20,
1997, one share of GM stock sold
for $57¾ per share.

Trading Securities [(1,000 shares × $14.125) + $175 commission]	14,300	
Cash		14,300
Purchased 1,000 shares of Cowen common stock as a near-term investment at 14⅛, plus commission.		

ACCOUNTING FOR CASH DIVIDENDS RECEIVED   Investments in stock provide dividends revenue. As a general rule, investors debit cash dividends to Cash and credit
Dividends Revenue. The only exception to this general rule is when a dividend declared in one accounting period is payable in the next. This exception allows a company to record the revenue in the proper accounting period. Assume that Cowen
declared a $1 per share cash dividend on December 1, 1999, to stockholders of record
as of December 20, payable on January 15, 2000. Brewer should make the following
entry in 1999:

1999				
Dec.	1	Dividends Receivable	1,000	
		Dividends Revenue		1,000
		To record $1 per share cash dividend on Cowen common stock, payable January 15, 2000.		

When collecting the dividend on January 15, Brewer debits Cash and credits
Dividends Receivable:

2000				
Jan.	15	Cash	1,000	
		Dividends Revenue		1,000
		To record the receipt of a cash dividend on Cowen common stock.		

STOCK DIVIDENDS AND STOCK SPLITS   As discussed in Chapter 13, a company
might declare a stock dividend rather than a cash dividend. An investor does not
recognize revenue on receipt of the additional shares from a stock dividend. The
investor merely records the number of additional shares received and reduces the cost
per share for each share held. For example, if Cowen distributed a 10% stock dividend
in February 2000, Brewer, which held 1,000 shares at a cost of $14,300 (or $14.30
per share), would receive another 100 shares and would then hold 1,100 shares at a
cost per share of $13 (computed as $14,300/1,100 shares). Similarly, when a corporation declares a stock split, the investor would note the shares received and the reduction in the cost per share.

Subsequent Valuation of Stock Investments under the Fair Market Value Method

FASB Statement No. 115 (1993) governs the subsequent valuation of **marketable
equity securities** accounted for under the fair market value method.[1] Marketable
refers to the fact that the stocks are readily saleable; equity securities are common and
preferred stocks. The *Statement* also addresses the subsequent valuation of debt securities. The subsequent valuation of debt securities will be addressed in intermediate
accounting classes.

---

[1]*FASB, Statement of Financial Accounting Standards No. 115,* "Accounting for Certain Marketable Securities"
(Stamford, Conn., 1993). Copyright © by the Financial Accounting Standards Board, Stamford, Connecticut 06856,
U.S.A. Quoted (or excerpted) with permission. Copies of the complete document are available from the FASB.

Company	No. of Shares	Cost per Share	Market Price per Share, 12/31/99	Total Cost	Total Market, 12/31/99	Increase/ (Decrease) in Market Value
A	200	$35	$40	$ 7,000	$ 8,000	$ 1,000
B	400	10	15	4,000	6,000	2,000
C	100	90	50	9,000	5,000	(4,000)
				$20,000	$19,000	$(1,000)

ILLUSTRATION 14.1
Stock Portfolio of
Hanson Company

The FASB *Statement* requires that at year-end, companies adjust the carrying value of each of their two portfolios (trading securities and available-for-sale securities) to their fair market value. Fair market value is considered to be the market price of the securities or what a buyer or seller would pay to exchange the securities. An unrealized holding gain or loss will usually result in each portfolio.

TRADING SECURITIES To illustrate the application of the fair market value to trading securities, assume that Hanson Company has the securities shown in Illustration 14.1 in its trading securities portfolio. Applying the fair market value method reveals that the total fair market value of the trading securities portfolio is $1,000 less than its cost. The journal entry required at the end of 1999 is:

1999			
Dec.	31	Unrealized Loss on Trading Securities	1,000	
		Trading Securities		1,000
		To record unrealized loss from market decline of trading securities.		

Note to the Student
Check yesterday's *Wall Street Journal* to determine the current market price of one share of General Motor's stock. Calculate the gain or loss on 100 shares of GM stock, if the shares were purchased on July 1, 1993, at $44 per share and sold at yesterday's market price. When the stock is sold, there is a realized gain or loss.

Reinforcing Problems
E14–1 Prepare entries for trading securities.
E14–2 Prepare entries for trading securities.

Note that the debit is to the Unrealized Loss on Trading Securities account. This loss is *unrealized* because the securities have not been sold. However, **the loss is reported in the income statement as a deduction in arriving at net income.** The credit in the preceding entry is to the Trading Securities account so as to adjust its balance to its fair market value. (An unrealized holding gain would be an addition to net income.)

If Hanson sold investment C on January 1, 2000, the company would receive $5,000 (assuming no change in market values from the previous day). The loss on the sale results from market changes in 1999 rather than in 2000; the fair market value procedure placed that loss in the proper year. The entry for the sale is:

Cash	5,000	
Trading Security—Company C Stock		5,000

No adjustment needs to be made to the unrealized loss account previously debited because the unrealized loss recorded in 1999 has flowed through the income statement and been closed to retained earnings through the closing process.

AVAILABLE-FOR-SALE SECURITIES Assume a marketable equity security that management does not intend to sell in the near term has a cost of $32,000 and a current market value on December 31, 1999, of $31,000. The treatment of the loss depends on whether it results from a temporary decline in market value of the stock or a permanent decline in the value. Assume first that the loss is related to a "temporary" decline in the market value of the stock. The required entry is:

1999			
Dec.	31	Unrealized Loss on Available-for-Sale Securities	1,000	
		Available-for-Sale Securities		1,000
		To record unrealized losses from market decline of available-for-sale securities.		

These accounts would appear on the balance sheet as follows:

HANSON COMPANY
Partial Balance Sheet
December 31, 1999

Investments (or Current Assets):*	
Available-for-sale securities	$ 31,000
Stockholders' equity:	
Capital stock	$xxx,xxx
Additional paid-in capital	x,xxx
Total paid-in capital	$xxx,xxx
Less: Unrealized loss on available-for-sale securities . . .	1,000
	$xxx,xxx
Retained earnings	xx,xxx
Total stockholders' equity	$xxx,xxx

* Depending on the length of time management intends to hold the securities.

Note that the unrealized loss for available-for-sale securities appears in the balance sheet as a separate negative component of stockholders' equity rather than in the income statement (as it does for trading securities). An unrealized gain would be shown as a separate positive component of stockholders' equity. An unrealized loss or gain on available-for-sale securities is **not** included in the determination of net income because it is not expected to be realized in the near future. These securities will probably not be sold soon.

The sale of an available-for-sale security results in a realized gain or loss and is reported on the income statement for the period. Any unrealized gain or loss on the balance sheet must be recognized at that time. Assume the stock discussed above is sold on January 1, 2000, for $31,000 (assuming no change in market value from the previous day) after the company had held the stock for three years. The entries to record this sale are:

2000				
Jan.	1	Realized Loss on Available-for-Sale Securities	1,000	
		Unrealized Loss on Available-for-Sale Securities		1,000
		Cash	31,000	
		Available-for-Sale Securities		31,000

The account debited in the first entry shows that the unrealized loss has been realized with the sale of the security; the amount is reported in the income statement. The second entry writes off the security and records the cash received and is similar to the entry for the sale of trading securities.

Reinforcing Problem
E14–3 Apply fair market value method to marketable equity securities

A loss on an individual available-for-sale security that is considered to be "permanent" is recorded as a realized loss and deducted in determining net income. The entry to record a permanent loss of $1,400 reads:

Realized Loss on Available-for-Sale Securities	1,400	
Available-for-Sale Securities		1,400
To record loss in value of available-for-sale securities.		

Note to the Student
If a loss on an available-for-sale security is considered to be permanent, the loss is *realized* even though the security has not been sold. As a realized loss, it appears in the income statement.

No part of the $1,400 loss is subject to reversal if the market price of the stock recovers. The stock's reduced value is now its "cost." When this stock is later sold, the sale will be treated in the same manner as trading securities. The loss or gain has already been recognized on the income statement. Therefore, the entry would simply record the cash received and write off the security sold for its fair market value. If the market value of the security has fluctuated since the last time the account had been adjusted (end of the year), then an additional gain or loss may have to be recorded to account for this fluctuation.

THE EQUITY METHOD FOR LONG-TERM INVESTMENTS OF BETWEEN 20% AND 50%

When a company (the **investor**) purchases between 20% and 50% of the outstanding stock of another company (the **investee**) as a long-term investment, the purchasing company is said to have significant influence over the investee company. In certain cases, a company may have significant influence even when its investment is less than 20%. In either situation, the investor must account for the investment under the equity method.

Objective 3
Prepare journal entries to account for long-term stock investments of 20% to 50%.

When using the **equity method** in accounting for stock investments, the investor company must recognize its share of the investee company's income, regardless of whether or not it receives dividends. The logic behind this treatment is that the investor company may exercise influence over the declaration of dividends and thereby manipulate its own income by influencing the investee's decision to declare (or not declare) dividends.

Thus, when the investee reports income or losses, the investor company must recognize its share of the investee's income or losses. For example, assume that Tone Company (the investor) owns 30% of Dutch Company (the investee) and Dutch reports $50,000 net income in the current year. Under the equity method, Tone makes the following entry as of the end of 1999:

Investment in Dutch Company	15,000	
Income from Dutch Company ($50,000 × 0.30)		15,000
To recognize 30% of Dutch Company's net income.		

The $15,000 income from Dutch would be reported on Tone's 1999 income statement. The investment account is also increased by $15,000.

If the investee incurs a loss, the investor company debits a loss account and credits the investment account for the investor's share of the loss. For example, assume Dutch incurs a loss of $10,000 in 2000. Since it still owns 30% of Dutch, Tone records its share of the loss as follows:

Loss from Dutch Company ($10,000 × 0.30)	3,000	
Investment in Dutch Company		3,000
To record 30% of Dutch Company's loss.		

Tone would report the $3,000 loss on its 2000 income statement. The $3,000 credit reduces Tone's equity in the investee. Furthermore, because dividends are a distribution of income to the owners of the corporation, if Dutch declares and pays $20,000 in dividends, this entry would also be required for Tone:

Cash	6,000	
Investment in Dutch Company ($20,000 × 0.30)		6,000
To record receipt of 30% of dividends paid by Dutch Company.		

Reinforcing Problem
E14–4 Prepare equity method entries for an investment.

Under the equity method just illustrated, the Investment in Dutch Company account always reflects Tone's 30% interest in the net assets of Dutch.

REPORTING FOR STOCK INVESTMENTS OF MORE THAN 50%

In recent years, many companies have expanded by purchasing a major portion, or all, of another company's outstanding voting stock. The purpose of such acquisitions ranges from ensuring a source of raw materials (such as oil), to desiring to enter into a new industry, or seeking income on the investment. Both corporations remain separate legal entities, regardless of the investment purpose. In this section, you learn how to account for business combinations.

Parent and Subsidiary Corporations

Objective 4
Describe the nature of parent and subsidiary corporations.

Real World Example
PepsiCo is a parent company; its subsidiaries include Taco Bell, KFC, and Pizza Hut.

As stated in the introduction to this chapter, a corporation that owns more than 50% of the outstanding voting common stock of another corporation is the **parent company.** The corporation acquired and controlled by the parent company is the **subsidiary company.**

A parent company and its subsidiaries maintain their own accounting records and prepare their own financial statements. However, since a central management controls the parent and its subsidiaries and they are related to each other, the parent company usually must prepare one set of financial statements. These statements, called **consolidated statements,** consolidate the parent's financial statement amounts with its subsidiaries' and show the parent and its subsidiaries as a single enterprise.

According to *FASB Statement No. 94,* consolidated statements must be prepared (1) when one company owns more than 50% of the outstanding voting common stock of another company, and (2) unless control is likely to be temporary or if it does not rest with the majority owner (e.g., the company is in legal reorganization or bankruptcy).[2] Thus, almost all subsidiaries must be included in the consolidated financial statements under *FASB Statement No. 94.* Previously, the consolidated statements did not include subsidiaries in markedly dissimilar businesses than those of the parents.

AN ACCOUNTING PERSPECTIVE

BUSINESS INSIGHT Procter & Gamble markets more than 300 brands. Examples include Tide, Ariel, Pantene Pro-V, Pringles, and Oil of Olay. The company's 1996 annual report includes the following information about presentation of subsidiaries and equity investments:

The consolidated financial statements include The Procter & Gamble Company and its controlled subsidiaries (the Company). Investments in companies that are at least 20% to 50% owned and over which the Company exerts significant influence but does not control the financial and operating decisions are accounted for by the equity method.

Eliminations

Financial transactions involving a parent and one of its subsidiaries or between two of its subsidiaries are **intercompany transactions.** In preparing consolidated financial statements, parent companies eliminate the effects of intercompany transactions by making **elimination entries.** Elimination entries allow the presentation of all account balances as if the parent and its subsidiaries were a single economic enterprise. *Elimination entries appear only on a consolidated statement work sheet, not in the accounting records of the parent or subsidiaries.* After elimination entries are prepared, the parent totals the amounts remaining for each account of the work sheet and prepares the consolidated financial statements.

To illustrate the need for elimination entries, assume Y Company formed the Z Company, receiving all of Z Company's $100,000 par value common stock for $100,000 cash. If the stock of an existing company had been acquired, it would have been purchased from that company's stockholders. The parent records the following entry on its books:

---

[2] FASB, *Statement of Financial Accounting Standards No. 94,* "Consolidation of All Majority-Owned Subsidiaries" (Stamford, Conn., 1987), p. 5. Copyright © by the Financial Accounting Standards Board, High Ridge Park, Stamford, Connecticut 06905, U.S.A.

Investment in Z Company	100,000	
Cash		100,000
To record an investment in Z Company. Purchased 100% of Z Company stock.		

Z Company, the subsidiary, records the following entry on its books:

Cash	100,000	
Common Stock		100,000
To record issuance of all of the common stock to Y Company.		

An elimination entry can offset the parent company's subsidiary investment account against the stockholders' equity accounts of the subsidiary. On the consolidated statements work sheet, the required elimination is:

| Common Stock (Z Company) | 100,000 | |
| Investment in Z Company | | 100,000 |

This elimination is required because the parent company's investment in the stock of the subsidiary actually represents an equity interest in the net assets of the subsidiary. Unless the investment is eliminated, the same resources appear twice on the consolidated balance sheet—first as the investment account of the parent and second as the assets of the subsidiary. By eliminating Z Company's common stock, the parent avoids double counting stockholders' equity. Viewing the two companies as if they were one, the Z Company common stock is really not outstanding; it is held within the consolidated group.

Consolidated financial statements present financial data as though the companies were a single entity. Since no entity can owe an amount to itself or be due an amount from itself, Z Company must eliminate intercompany receivables and payables (amounts owed to and due from companies within the consolidated group) during the preparation of consolidated financial statements. For example, assume the parent company purchased $5,000 of bonds issued by its subsidiary company. Because no debt is owed to or due from any entity outside the consolidated enterprise, Y Company would eliminate those balances by an entry like the following that offsets the Investment in Bonds against the Bonds Payable:

Bonds Payable (subsidiary company)	5,000	
Investment in Bonds (parent company)		5,000
To eliminate intercompany bonds and bond investment.		

When preparing consolidated statements, the parent would similarly eliminate other intercompany balances.

CONSOLIDATED BALANCE SHEET AT TIME OF ACQUISITION

A parent company may acquire a subsidiary at its book value or at a cost above or below book value. Also, the parent may acquire 100% of the outstanding voting common stock of the subsidiary or some lesser percentage exceeding 50%.

To consolidate its assets and liabilities with those of its subsidiaries, a parent company prepares a consolidated statement work sheet similar to the one in Illustration 14.2. A **consolidated statement work sheet** is an informal record on which elimination entries are made for the purpose of showing account balances as if the parent and its subsidiaries were a single economic enterprise. The first two columns of the work sheet show assets, liabilities, and stockholders' equity of the parent and subsidiary as they appear on each corporation's balance sheet. The pair of columns labeled Eliminations allows intercompany items to be offset and consequently eliminated from the consolidated statement. The final column shows the amounts that will appear on the consolidated balance sheet.

Acquisition of Subsidiary at Book Value

Objective 5
Prepare consolidated financial statements through the use of a consolidated statement work sheet.

ILLUSTRATION 14.2
Consolidated Balance
Sheet Work Sheet (stock
acquired at book value)

P COMPANY AND SUBSIDIARY S COMPANY
Work Sheet for Consolidated Balance Sheet
January 1, 1999 (date of acquisition)

	P Company	S Company	Eliminations Debit	Eliminations Credit	Consolidated Amounts
Assets					
Cash	26,000	12,000			38,000
Notes receivable	5,000			(2) 5,000	
Accounts receivable, net	24,000	15,000			39,000
Merchandise inventory	35,000	30,000			65,000
Investment in S Company	106,000			(1) 106,000	
Equipment, net	41,000	15,000			56,000
Buildings, net	65,000	35,000			100,000
Land	20,000	10,000			30,000
	322,000	117,000			328,000
Liabilities and Stockholders' Equity					
Accounts payable	18,000	6,000			24,000
Notes payable		5,000	(2) 5,000		
Common stock	250,000	100,000	(1) 100,000		250,000
Paid-in capital in excess					
of par value—common		4,000	(1) 4,000		–0–
Retained earnings	54,000	2,000	(1) 2,000		54,000
	322,000	117,000	111,000	111,000	328,000

The work sheet in Illustration 14.2 consolidates the accounts of P Company and its subsidiary, S Company, on January 1, 1999. P Company acquired S Company on January 1, 1999, by purchasing all of its outstanding voting common stock for $106,000 cash, which was the book value of the stock. Book value is equal to stock-holders' equity, or net assets (assets minus liabilities). Thus, common stock ($100,000), paid-in capital in excess of par value—common ($4,000), and retained earnings ($2,000) equal $106,000. When P Company acquired the S Company stock, P Company made the following entry in its books:

Investment in S Company	106,000	
Cash		106,000
To record investment in S Company.		

The Investment in S Company account appears as an asset on P Company's balance sheet. By buying the subsidiary's stock, the parent acquired a 100% equity, or ownership, interest in the subsidiary's net assets. Thus, if both the investment account and the subsidiary's assets appear on the consolidated balance sheet, the same resources would be counted twice. The Common Stock and Retained Earnings accounts of the subsidiary also represent an equity interest in the subsidiary's assets. Therefore, P's investment in S Company must be offset against S Company's stock-holders' equity accounts so that the subsidiary's assets and the ownership interest in these assets appear only once on the consolidated balance sheet. P Company accomplishes this elimination by entry *1* under Eliminations on the work sheet. The entry debits S Company's Common Stock for $100,000, Paid-In Capital in Excess of Par

Value—Common for $4,000, and Retained Earnings for $2,000 and credits Investment in S Company for $106,000. In journal entry form, the elimination entry made only on the consolidated work sheet is:

Common Stock	100,000	
Paid-In Capital in Excess of Par Value—Common	4,000	
Retained Earnings	2,000	
Investment in S Company		106,000
To eliminate investment account and subsidiary stockholders' equity.		

Entry *2* eliminates the effect of an intercompany debt. On the date it acquired S Company, P Company loaned S Company $5,000. The loan is a $5,000 note receivable on P's books and a $5,000 note payable on S's books. If the elimination entry is not made on the work sheet, the consolidated balance sheet would show $5,000 owed to the consolidated enterprise by itself. From the viewpoint of the consolidated equity, neither an asset nor a liability exists. Therefore, entry *2* on the work sheet eliminates both the asset and liability. The entry debits Notes Payable and credits Notes Receivable for $5,000. In general journal form, entry *2* is:

Notes Payable	5,000	
Notes Receivable		5,000
To eliminate intercompany payable and receivable.		

Note that P Company makes elimination entries only on the consolidated statement work sheet; no elimination entries appear in the accounting records of either P Company or S Company. P Company uses the final work sheet column to prepare the consolidated balance sheet.

Reinforcing Problem
E14–5 Record investment at book value and elimination entry as of acquisition date.

USES OF TECHNOLOGY Computer applications have greatly simplified the preparation of consolidated work sheets. Spreadsheet programs in particular expedite the process of constructing consolidated financial statements.

AN ACCOUNTING PERSPECTIVE

In the previous example, P Company acquired 100% of S Company at a cost equal to book value. In some cases, firms acquire subsidiaries at a cost greater than or less than book value. For example, assume P Company purchased 100% of S Company's outstanding voting common stock for $125,000 (instead of $106,000). The book value of this stock is $106,000. Cost exceeds book value by $19,000. P Company's management may have paid more than book value because (1) the subsidiary's earnings prospects justify paying a price greater than book value or (2) the total fair market value of the subsidiary's assets exceeds their total book value.

According to the Accounting Principles Board (*APB Opinion No. 16*), where cost exceeds book value because of expected above-average earnings, the investor labels the excess *goodwill* on the consolidated balance sheet. **Goodwill** is an intangible value attached to a business primarily due to above-average earnings prospects (as discussed in Chapter 11). On the other hand, if the excess is attributable to the belief that assets of the subsidiary are undervalued, then the investor increases the asset values on the consolidated balance sheet to the extent of the excess.[3] In Illustration 14.3, $4,000 is due to the undervaluation of land owned by the company, and the remaining $15,000 of the excess of cost over book value is due to expected above-average earnings. As a result, P Company adds $4,000 of the $19,000 excess to Land, and identifies the other $15,000 as Goodwill on the work sheet (Illustration 14.3) and on the balance sheet (Illustration 14.4).

Acquisition of Subsidiary at a Cost above or below Book Value

Note to the Student
Goodwill is the excess over fair market value of the net assets of the subsidiary. Net assets are total assets less total liabilities, or total stockholders' equity. Thus, a company that pays more than the fair market value of the net assets creates an intangible asset called goodwill on its books but not on the subsidiary's books.

---

[3] *APB Accounting Principles* (Chicago: Commerce Clearing House, Inc., 1973), vol. II, p. 6655.

ILLUSTRATION 14.3
Consolidated Balance
Sheet Work Sheet (stock
acquired at more than
book value)

P COMPANY AND SUBSIDIARY S COMPANY
Work Sheet for Consolidated Balance Sheet
January 1, 1999 (date of acquisition)

	P Company	S Company	Eliminations Debit	Eliminations Credit	Consolidated Amounts
Assets					
Cash	7,000	12,000			19,000
Notes receivable	5,000			(2) 5,000	
Accounts receivable, net	24,000	15,000			39,000
Merchandise inventory	35,000	30,000			65,000
Investment in S Company	125,000			(1) 125,000	
Equipment, net	41,000	15,000			56,000
Buildings, net	65,000	35,000			100,000
Land	20,000	10,000	(1) 4,000		34,000
Goodwill			(1) 15,000		15,000
	322,000	117,000			328,000
Liabilities and Stockholders' Equity					
Accounts payable	18,000	6,000			24,000
Notes payable		5,000	(2) 5,000		
Common stock	250,000	100,000	(1) 100,000		250,000
Paid-in capital in excess					
of par value—common		4,000	(1) 4,000		–0–
Retained earnings	54,000	2,000	(1) 2,000		54,000
	322,000	117,000	130,000	130,000	328,000

P Company establishes Goodwill as part of the first elimination entry. Elimination entry *1* in Illustration 14.3 involves debits to the subsidiary's Common Stock for $100,000, Paid-In Capital in Excess of Par Value—Common for $4,000, Retained Earnings for $2,000, Land for $4,000, and Goodwill for $15,000, and a credit to Investment in S Company for $125,000. In journal form, entry *1* is:

```
Common Stock . . . . . . . . . . . . . . . . . . . . . . . . . . . . .   100,000
Paid-In Capital in Excess of Par Value—Common  . . . . . . . . . . . .     4,000
Retained Earnings . . . . . . . . . . . . . . . . . . . . . . . . . . .     2,000
Land  . . . . . . . . . . . . . . . . . . . . . . . . . . . . . . . . .     4,000
Goodwill . . . . . . . . . . . . . . . . . . . . . . . . . . . . . . . .   15,000
    Investment in S Company  . . . . . . . . . . . . . . . . . . . . . .            125,000
  To eliminate investment and subsidiary stockholders' equity and to
  establish increased value of land and goodwill.
```

Entry *2* is the same as elimination entry *2* in Illustration 14.2. Entry *2* eliminates the intercompany loan by debiting Notes Payable and crediting Notes Receivable for $5,000.

After these elimination entries are made, the company consolidates and extends the remaining amounts to the Consolidated Amounts column. It uses the amounts in this column to prepare the consolidated balance sheet in Illustration 14.4. Notice that the firm carries the $15,000 debit to Goodwill to the Consolidated Amounts column and lists it as an asset in the consolidated balance sheet.

As noted earlier, a company may purchase all or part of another company at more than book value and create goodwill on the consolidated balance sheet. The Account-

P COMPANY AND SUBSIDIARY S COMPANY
Consolidated Balance Sheet
January 1, 1999

Assets

Current assets:

Cash	$ 19,000	
Accounts receivable, net	39,000	
Merchandise inventory	65,000	
Total current assets		$123,000

Property, plant, and equipment:

Equipment, net	$ 56,000	
Buildings, net	100,000	
Land	34,000	
Total property, plant, and equipment		190,000
Goodwill		15,000
Total assets		$328,000

Liabilities and Stockholders' Equity

Current liabilities:

Accounts payable		$ 24,000

Stockholders' equity:

Common stock	$250,000	
Retained earnings	54,000	
Total stockholders' equity		304,000
Total liabilities and stockholders' equity		$328,000

ILLUSTRATION 14.4
Consolidated Balance
Sheet

ing Principles Board, in *APB Opinion No. 17,* requires that all goodwill be amortized over a period not to exceed 40 years. This amortization is necessary under the cost and equity methods. We leave a discussion of this topic to a more advanced text.

Under some circumstances, a parent company may pay less than book value of the subsidiary's net assets. In such cases, it is highly unlikely that a bargain purchase has been made. The most logical explanation is that some of the subsidiary's assets are overvalued. The Accounting Principles Board requires that firms use the excess of book value over cost to reduce proportionately the value of the noncurrent assets acquired (except long-term investments in marketable securities). If noncurrent assets are reduced to zero, the remaining dollar amount is a deferred credit entitled, Excess of Fair Value Over Cost of Assets Acquired. This deferred credit is amortized over a period not to exceed 40 years, thus increasing net income each year during the amortization period.[4]

Sometimes a parent company acquires less than 100% of the outstanding voting common stock of a subsidiary. For example, assume P Company acquired 80% of S Company's outstanding voting common stock. P Company is the majority stockholder, but another group of stockholders owns the remaining 20% of the stock. Stockholders who own less than 50% of a subsidiary's outstanding voting common stock are *minority stockholders,* and their claim or interest in the subsidiary is the **minority interest.** Minority stockholders have an interest in the subsidiary's net assets and share the subsidiary's income or loss with the parent company.

Look at Illustration 14.5, which shows the elimination entries required when P Company purchases 80% of S Company's stock for $90,000. The book value of the stock acquired by P Company is $84,800 (80% of $106,000). Assuming no assets are undervalued, P Company attributes the excess of cost ($90,000) over book value ($84,800) of $5,200 to S Company's above-average earnings prospects (goodwill).

**Acquisition of Less
Than 100% of a
Subsidiary**

---

[4] Ibid., p. 6655.

ILLUSTRATION 14.5
Consolidated Balance
Sheet Work Sheet (80%
of stock acquired at more
than book value)

P COMPANY AND SUBSIDIARY S COMPANY
Work Sheet for Consolidated Balance Sheet
January 1, 1999 (date of acquisition)

	P Company	S Company	Eliminations Debit	Eliminations Credit	Consolidated Amounts
Assets					
Cash	42,000	12,000			54,000
Notes receivable	5,000			(2) 5,000	
Accounts receivable, net	24,000	15,000			39,000
Merchandise inventory	35,000	30,000			65,000
Investment in S Company	90,000			(1) 90,000	
Equipment, net	41,000	15,000			56,000
Buildings, net	65,000	35,000			100,000
Land	20,000	10,000			30,000
Goodwill			(1) 5,200		5,200
	322,000	117,000			349,200
Liabilities and Stockholders' Equity					
Accounts payable	18,000	6,000			24,000
Notes payable		5,000	(2) 5,000		
Common stock	250,000	100,000	(1) 100,000		250,000
Paid-in capital in excess					
of par value—common		4,000	(1) 4,000		–0–
Retained earnings	54,000	2,000	(1) 2,000		54,000
Minority interest				(1) 21,200	21,200
	322,000	117,000	116,200	116,200	349,200

Elimination entry *1* eliminates S Company's stockholders' equity by debiting Common Stock for $100,000, Paid-In Capital in Excess of Par Value—Common for $4,000, and Retained Earnings for $2,000. To establish minority interest, it credits a Minority Interest account for $21,200 (20% of $106,000). P Company eliminates the investment account by crediting Investment in S Company for $90,000. The $5,200 debited to Goodwill makes the debits equal the credits. In journal form, the elimination entry *1* is:

Reinforcing Problems
E14–6 Determine amount of goodwill.
E14–7 Record investment at more than book value and elimination entry as of acquisition date.
E14–8 Compute difference between cost and book value of common stock investments.
E14–9 Compute book value, difference between cost and book value, and minority interest of an investment.

Common Stock	100,000	
Paid-In Capital in Excess of Par Value—Common	4,000	
Retained Earnings	2,000	
Goodwill	5,200	
Investment in S Company		90,000
Minority Interest		21,200

To eliminate investment and subsidiary stockholders' equity and to establish minority interest and goodwill.

Elimination entry *2* is the same as shown in Illustration 14.2. The entry eliminates intercompany debt by debiting Notes Payable and crediting Notes Receivable for $5,000.

On the consolidated balance sheet (Illustration 14.6), minority interest appears between the liabilities and stockholders' equity sections.

P COMPANY AND SUBSIDIARY S COMPANY
Consolidated Balance Sheet
January 1, 1999

Assets

Current assets:

Cash	$ 54,000	
Accounts receivable, net	39,000	
Merchandise inventory	65,000	
Total current assets		$158,000

Property, plant, and equipment:

Equipment, net	$ 56,000	
Buildings, net	100,000	
Land	30,000	
Total property, plant, and equipment		186,000
Goodwill		5,200
Total assets		$349,200

Liabilities and Stockholders' Equity

Liabilities:

Accounts payable		$ 24,000
Minority interest		21,200

Stockholders' equity:

Common stock	$250,000	
Retained earnings	54,000	
Total stockholders' equity		304,000
Total liabilities and stockholders' equity		$349,200

ILLUSTRATION 14.6
Consolidated Balance Sheet

ACCOUNTING FOR INCOME, LOSSES, AND DIVIDENDS OF A SUBSIDIARY

When a subsidiary is operating profitably, its net assets and retained earnings increase. The subsidiary pays dividends to both the parent company and minority stockholders. The subsidiary records all transactions in its accounting records in a normal manner.

As noted earlier, two different methods used by an investor to account for investments in common stock are the cost and equity methods. A parent company may use either the cost or equity method of accounting for its investment in a consolidated subsidiary. This choice is allowed because the investment account is eliminated during the consolidation process; therefore, the results are identical after consolidation. To illustrate the consolidation process at a date after acquisition, we assume the parent company uses the equity method.

CONSOLIDATED FINANCIAL STATEMENTS AT A DATE AFTER ACQUISITION

Under the equity method, the investment account on the parent company's books increases and decreases as the parent records its share of the income, losses, and dividends reported by the subsidiary. Thus, the balance in the investment account differs after acquisition from its balance on the date of acquisition. Consequently, the amounts eliminated on the consolidated statements work sheet differ from year to year. As an illustration, assume the following facts:

1. P Company acquired 100% of the outstanding voting common stock of S Company on January 1, 1999. P Company paid $121,000 for stockholders' equity totaling $106,000. The excess of cost over book value is attributable to (*a*) an undervaluation of land amounting to $4,000 and (*b*) the remainder to S Company's above-average earnings prospects.

2. During 1999, S Company earned $20,000 from operations.

3. On December 31, 1999, S Company paid a cash dividend of $8,000.
4. S Company owes P Company $5,000 on a note at December 31.
5. Including its share (100%) of S Company's income, P Company earned $31,000 during 1999.
6. P Company paid a cash dividend of $10,000 during December 1999.
7. P Company uses the equity method of accounting for its investment in S Company.

The financial statements for the two companies as of December 31, 1999, are in the first two columns of Illustration 14.7.

The work sheet shown in Illustration 14.7 allows us to prepare a consolidated income statement, statement of retained earnings, and balance sheet. Notice that in Illustration 14.7, P Company has a balance of $20,000 in its Income of S Company account and a balance of $133,000 in its Investment in S Company account. These balances are the result of the following journal entries made by P Company in 1999:

1999 Jan.	1	Investment in S Company	121,000	
		Cash		121,000
		To record 100% investment in subsidiary.		
Dec.	31	Investment in S Company	20,000	
		Income of S Company		20,000
		To record income of subsidiary.		
	31	Cash	8,000	
		Investment in S Company		8,000
		To record dividends received from subsidiary.		

The explanations for the elimination entries on the work sheet in Illustration 14.7 are as follows:

Entry 1: During the year, S Company earned $20,000. P Company increased its investment account balance by $20,000. Entry 1 on the work sheet eliminates the subsidiary's income from the Investment in S Company account and the Income of S Company account ($20,000). This entry reverses the entry made on the books of P Company to recognize the parent's share of the subsidiary's income (the first December 31 journal entry).

Entry 2: When S Company paid its cash dividend, P Company debited Cash and credited the investment account for $8,000 (the second December 31 journal entry). Entry 2 restores the investment account to its balance before the dividends from S Company were deducted. That is, P Company debits its investment account and credits S Company's dividends account for $8,000. On a consolidated basis, a company cannot pay a dividend to itself.

Entry 3: Entry 3 eliminates the original investment account balance ($121,000) and the subsidiary's stockholders' equity accounts as of the date of acquisition (retained earnings of $6,000 and common stock of $100,000). The entry also establishes goodwill of $11,000 and increases land by $4,000 to account for the excess of acquisition cost over book value.

Entry 4: Entry 4 eliminates the intercompany debt of $5,000.

After the first three entries have been made, the investment account contains a zero balance from the viewpoint of the consolidated entity.

After making the eliminations, P Company combines the corresponding amounts and places them in the Consolidated Amounts column. Notice that certain totals in the first two columns do not add across to the total in the Consolidated Amounts column. For instance, consolidated net income is $31,000, not $31,000 plus $20,000. The firm carries the net income row in the Income Statement section forward to the net income

Reinforcing Problem
E14–10 Compute investment account balance at year-end and minority interest at beginning and end of year.

P COMPANY AND SUBSIDIARY S COMPANY
Work Sheet for Consolidated Financial Statements
December 31, 1999

ILLUSTRATION 14.7
Consolidated Work
Sheet One Year after
Acquisition

	P Company	S Company	Eliminations Debit	Eliminations Credit	Consolidated Amounts
Income Statement					
Revenue from sales	397,000	303,000			700,000
Income of S Company	20,000		(1) 20,000		
Cost of goods sold	(250,000)	(180,000)			(430,000)
Expenses (excluding depreciation and taxes)	(100,000)	(80,000)			(180,000)
Depreciation expense	(7,400)	(5,000)			(12,400)
Federal income tax expense	(28,600)	(18,000)			(46,600)
Net income, carried forward	31,000	20,000			31,000*
Statement of Retained Earnings					
Retained earnings— January 1:					
P Company	54,000				54,000
S Company		6,000	(3) 6,000		
Net income— brought forward	31,000	20,000			31,000*
	85,000	26,000			85,000*
Dividends:					
P Company	(10,000)				(10,000)
S Company		(8,000)		(2) 8,000	
Retained earnings—Dec. 31—carried forward	75,000	18,000			75,000*
Balance Sheet Assets					
Cash	38,000	16,000			54,000
Notes receivable	5,000			(4) 5,000	
Accounts receivable, net	25,000	18,000			43,000
Merchandise inventory	40,000	36,000			76,000
Investment in S Company	133,000		(2) 8,000	(3) 121,000	
				(1) 20,000	
Equipment, net	36,900	12,000			48,900
Buildings, net	61,700	33,000			94,700
Land	20,000	10,000	(3) 4,000		34,000
Goodwill			(3) 11,000		11,000
	359,600	125,000			361,600*
Liabilities and Stockholders' Equity					
Accounts payable	19,600	2,000			21,600
Notes payable	15,000	5,000	(4) 5,000		15,000
Common stock	250,000	100,000	(3) 100,000		250,000
Retained earnings— brought forward	75,000	18,000			75,000*
	359,600	125,000	154,000	154,000	361,600*

*Totals are determined vertically, not horizontally

row in the Statement of Retained Earnings section. Likewise, it carries the ending retained earnings row in the Statement of Retained Earnings section forward to the retained earnings row in the Balance Sheet section. P Company uses the final work sheet column to prepare the consolidated income statement (Illustration 14.8), the consolidated statement of retained earnings (Illustration 14.9), and the consolidated balance sheet (Illustration 14.10).[5] We ignore the amortization of goodwill in the illustration.

PURCHASE VERSUS POOLING OF INTERESTS

Objective 6
Identify the differences between purchase accounting and pooling of interests accounting.

In the illustrations in this chapter, we have assumed that the parent company acquired the subsidiary's common stock in exchange for cash. The acquiring company could also have used assets other than cash in the exchange. This transaction—the exchange of cash or other assets for the common stock of another company—is a **purchase.** When assets other than cash are used, the cost of the acquired company's stock is the fair market value of the assets given up or of the stock received, whichever can be more clearly and objectively determined.

A company can also acquire the common stock of another company by issuing its own common stock in exchange for the other company's common stock. When such an exchange occurs, the stockholders of both companies maintain a joint ownership interest in the combined company. Such a business combination involving the issuance of common stock in exchange for common stock is a **pooling of interests** if it meets all the criteria cited in *APB Opinion No. 16.* When a combination resulting from an exchange of stock does not qualify as a pooling of interests, we record it as a purchase.

The purchase and pooling of interests methods are not alternatives that can be applied to the same situation. Given the circumstances surrounding a particular business combination, only one of the two methods—purchase or pooling of interests—is appropriate. *APB Opinion No. 16* specifies that 12 conditions must be met before a business combination can be classified as a pooling of interests. For example, two of these conditions are (1) the combination must be completed in one transaction or be completed within one year in accordance with a specific plan, and (2) one corporation must issue only its common stock (no cash or other assets) in exchange for 90% or more of the voting common stock of another company. If all 12 conditions specified by the APB are met, companies can account for the resulting business combination as a pooling of interests. Otherwise, they must use the purchase method to account for the combination.

When using the pooling of interests method, the parent company records its investment at the book value of the subsidiary's net assets (assets minus liabilities). Since the investment is recorded at the book value, there can be no goodwill or changes in asset valuations from consolidation. The subsidiary's retained earnings at the date of acquisition become a part of the consolidated retained earnings, whereas under the purchase method they do not. Also, the pooling of interests method includes all subsidiary income for the year of acquisition in the consolidated net income. The purchase method includes in consolidated net income only that portion of the subsidiary's income that arises after the date of acquisition.

It is apparent that these two methods lead to significant differences in financial statement amounts. For instance, the purchase method uses any excess of investment cost over the book value of the ownership interest acquired to increase the value of any assets that are undervalued or that must be recognized as goodwill from consolidation. On the other hand, under the pooling of interests method, book value—rather than cost—is the amount of the investment. Thus, whenever cost exceeds book value, the purchase method records either more depreciation or more amortization than the

---

[5] The annual report booklet shows consolidated financial statements for actual corporations.

ILLUSTRATION 14.8
Consolidated Income
Statement

P COMPANY AND SUBSIDIARY S COMPANY
Consolidated Income Statement
For the Year Ended December 31, 1999

Revenue from sales		$700,000
Cost of goods sold		430,000
Gross margin		$270,000
Expenses (excluding depreciation and taxes)	$180,000	
Depreciation expense	12,400	
Federal income tax expense	46,600	239,000
Net income		$ 31,000

ILLUSTRATION 14.8
Consolidated Income
Statement

P COMPANY AND SUBSIDIARY S COMPANY
Consolidated Statement of Retained Earnings
For the Year Ended December 31, 1999

Retained earnings, January 1, 1999	$54,000
Net income	31,000
Subtotal	$85,000
Dividends	10,000
Retained earnings, December 31, 1999	$75,000

ILLUSTRATION 14.9
Consolidated Statement
of Retained Earnings

P COMPANY AND SUBSIDIARY S COMPANY
Consolidated Balance Sheet
January 1, 1999

Assets

Current assets:		
Cash	$ 54,000	
Accounts receivable, net	43,000	
Merchandise inventory	76,000	
Total current assets		$173,000
Property, plant, and equipment:		
Equipment, net	$ 48,900	
Buildings, net	94,700	
Land	34,000	
Total property, plant, and equipment		177,600
Goodwill		11,000
Total assets		$361,600

Liabilities and Stockholders' Equity

Current liabilities:		
Accounts payable	$ 21,600	
Notes payable	15,000	
Total liabilities		$ 36,600
Stockholders' equity:		
Common stock	$250,000	
Retained earnings	75,000	
Total stockholders' equity		325,000
Total liabilities and stockholders' equity		$361,600

ILLUSTRATION 14.10
Consolidated Balance
Sheet (one year after
acquisition)

pooling of interests method. Also, consolidated net income is smaller under the purchase method than under the pooling of interests method.

In Illustration 14.11, we show the number of business combinations involving the two methods that occurred in a sample of representative companies for the years 1992–1995. The companies used the purchase method much more extensively than the pooling of interests method.

ILLUSTRATION 14.11
Business Combinations

	1995	1994	1993	1992
Pooling of interests				
Prior year financial statements restated	19	7	11	7
Prior year financial statements not restated . . .	13	12	10	10
Total	**32**	**19**	**21**	**17**
Purchase method	**244**	**215**	**200**	**182**

Source: Based on American Institute of Certified Public Accountants, *Accounting Trends & Techniques* (New York: AICPA, 1996), p. 57.

USES AND LIMITATIONS OF CONSOLIDATED STATEMENTS

Objective 7
Describe the uses and limitations of consolidated financial statements.

Real World Example
Colgate-Palmolive Company reported consolidated net income of $635 million for the 1996 fiscal year.

Consolidated financial statements are of primary importance to stockholders, managers, and directors of the parent company. The parent company benefits from the income and other financial strengths of the subsidiary. Likewise, the parent company suffers from a subsidiary's losses and other financial weaknesses.

Consolidated financial statements are of limited use to the creditors and minority stockholders of the subsidiary. The subsidiary's creditors have a claim against the subsidiary alone; they cannot look to the parent company for payment. Minority stockholders in the subsidiary do not benefit or suffer from the parent company's operations. These minority stockholders benefit from the subsidiary's income and financial strengths; they suffer from the subsidiary's losses and financial weaknesses. Thus, the subsidiary's creditors and minority stockholders are more interested in the subsidiary's individual financial statements than in the consolidated statements. Because of these factors, annual reports always include the financial statements of the consolidated entity, and sometimes include the financial statements of certain subsidiary companies alone, but never include the parent company's financial statements alone.

ANALYZING AND USING THE FINANCIAL RESULTS—DIVIDEND YIELD ON COMMON STOCK AND PAYOUT RATIOS

Objective 8
Analyze and use the financial results—dividend yield on common stock and payout ratio on common stock.

Tyco International
Tyco International manufactures many products including steel, fiber optic telecommunications cables, and circuit boards for mobile phones.

Investors often search for stock that fulfills their needs. To locate this stock, potential stockholders may use the dividend yield on common stock ratio or the payout ratio on common stock. To demonstrate these ratios, consider the 1996 annual report of Tyco International.

	1996	1995
Dividend per share of common stock . . .	$ 0.20	$ 0.20
Current market price per share	35.13	25.50
Earnings per share	2.03	1.42

Investors use the **dividend yield on common stock ratio** as a tool to compare stocks. Some investors favor stocks with a high dividend yield ratio and a high payout ratio. Other investors would rather have the corporation retain more of the funds and use them to attempt to increase future earnings and the market price of the stock. The formula for the dividend yield on common stock ratio is:

$$\text{Dividend yield on common stock ratio} = \frac{\text{Dividend per share of common stock}}{\text{Current market price per share}}$$

For Tyco, the dividend yield on common stock ratios are:

1996: $0.20/$35.13 = .57%
1995: $0.20/$25.50 = .78%

To determine the relevance of this ratio, an investor compares these numbers to ratios calculated on other stocks.

Investors calculate the **payout ratio on common stock** as follows:

$$\text{Payout ratio on common stock} = \frac{\text{Dividend per share of common stock}}{\text{Earnings per share (EPS)}}$$

This ratio indicates whether a company pays out a large percentage of earnings as dividends or reinvests most of its earnings. When computing the payout ratio, remember that negative earnings per share result in an invalid calculation. Tyco's payout ratios are:

$$1996: \ \$0.20/\$2.03 = \ 9.85\%$$
$$1995: \ \$0.20/\$1.42 = 14.08\%$$

Now that you have studied consolidated financial statements, you should realize the importance of presenting a complete picture of the business operations of a company. In Chapter 15 you learn about long-term financing, its advantages and disadvantages, and how bonds differ from stocks.

UNDERSTANDING THE LEARNING OBJECTIVES

- Under the cost method, the investor company records its investment at the price paid at acquisition and does not adjust the investment account balance subsequently. The cost method is used for all short-term investments, long-term investments of less than 20% where the purchasing company does not exercise significant influence over the investee company, and may be used for long-term investments of more than 50%.

- Under the equity method, the investment is also initially recorded at acquisition price but is then adjusted periodically for the investor company's share of the investee's reported income, losses, and dividends. The equity method is used for all long-term investments of between 20% and 50% and may be used for investments of more than 50%. This method is also used for investments of less than 20% if the purchasing company exercises significant influence over the investee company.

Objective 1
Report stock investments and distinguish between the cost and equity methods of accounting for stock investments.

- Under the cost method, the initial investment is debited to either Trading Securities or Available-for-Sale Securities, depending on whether the investment is a near-term or longer-term investment.

- At the end of each accounting period, the company must adjust the carrying value of each investment. The fair market value method is applied independently to each of these portfolios.

- Under the cost method, dividends received are credited to Dividend Revenue.

- Under the equity method, the initial investment is debited to an Investment in (Company Name) account. Income, losses, and dividends result in increases or decreases to the investment account.

Objective 2
Prepare journal entries to account for short-term stock investments and for long-term stock investments of less than 20%.

- The equity method must be used for long-term investments of 20% to 50% and for long-term investments of less than 20% where significant influence is present.

- The initial investment is debited to an Investment in (Company Name) account. The purchasing company's share of the investee's income is debited to the investment account, and the purchaser's share of the investee's losses and dividends is credited to the investment account as they are reported by the investee.

Objective 3
Prepare journal entries to account for long-term investments of 20% to 50%.

- A corporation that owns more than 50% of the outstanding voting common stock of another corporation is called the *parent company.*

- The corporation acquired and controlled by the parent company is known as the *subsidiary company.*

- A parent company and its subsidiaries maintain their own accounting records and prepare their own financial statements, but the parent company must also prepare consolidated financial statements. The consolidated financial statements consolidate the financial results of the parent and subsidiaries as a single enterprise.

Objective 4
Describe the nature of parent and subsidiary corporations.

- Consolidated financial statements must be prepared (1) when one company owns more than 50% of the outstanding voting stock of another company and (2) unless control is likely to be temporary or if it does not rest with the majority owner.

- In preparing consolidated financial statements, the effects of intercompany transactions must be eliminated by making elimination entries. Elimination entries are made only on a consolidated statement work sheet, not in the accounting records of either company.

- One elimination entry offsets the parent company's subsidiary investment account against the stockholders' equity accounts of the subsidiary. Intercompany receivables and payables also must be eliminated.

<table>
<tr><td>

Objective 5
Prepare consolidated financial statements through the use of a consolidated statement work sheet.

</td><td>

- A consolidated financial statements work sheet is an informal record in which elimination entries are made for the purpose of showing account balances as if the parent and its subsidiaries were a single economic enterprise.
- A consolidated balance sheet work sheet is prepared at the time of acquisition. The first two columns of the work sheet show assets, liabilities, and stockholders' equity of the parent and subsidiary as they appear on each corporation's individual balance sheet. The next pair of columns shows the eliminations. The final column shows the amounts that appear on the consolidated balance sheet.
- A consolidated work sheet is prepared at various dates after acquisition. The first two columns show the income statements, statements of retained earnings, and balance sheets of the parent and subsidiary. The next pair of columns shows the eliminations. The final column shows the amounts that appear in the consolidated financial statements.

</td></tr>
<tr><td>

Objective 6
Identify the differences between purchase accounting and pooling of interests accounting.

</td><td>

- The exchange of cash or other assets for the common stock of another company is called a *purchase*. Any other combination that does not qualify as a pooling of interests must be accounted for as a purchase.
- When a company exchanges some of its own common stock for all or some of the other company's common stock, the business combination is classified as a pooling of interests (if certain other criteria are met). If a combination results from an exchange of stock but does not qualify as a pooling of interests, it must be recorded as a purchase.
- When the purchase method is used, the parent company's investment is recorded at cost, which may be greater than or less than book value. When the pooling of interests method is used, the parent company's investment is recorded at the book value of the subsidiary's net assets.

</td></tr>
<tr><td>

Objective 7
Describe the uses and limitations of consolidated financial statements.

</td><td>

- Consolidated financial statements are of primary importance to stockholders, managers, and directors of the parent company. On the other hand, consolidated financial statements are of limited use to the creditors and minority stockholders of the subsidiary.

</td></tr>
<tr><td>

Objective 8
Analyze and use the financial results—dividend yield on common stock and payout ratio on common stock.

</td><td>

- $$\text{Dividend yield on common stock ratio} = \frac{\text{Dividend per share of common stock}}{\text{Current market price per share}}$$
- This ratio helps investors to compare stocks.
- $$\text{Payout ratio on common stock} = \frac{\text{Dividend per share of common stock}}{\text{Earnings per share (EPS)}}$$
- This ratio indicates whether a company pays out a large percentage of earnings as dividends or reinvests most of its earnings.

</td></tr>
<tr><td>

Objective 9
Discuss the differences in international accounting among nations (appendix).

</td><td>

- Accounting principles differ among nations because they were developed independently.
- There have been attempts at harmonizing accounting principles throughout the world.
- Differences in accounting principles exist between nations regarding foreign currency translation, inventory cost, and the effects of changing prices.

</td></tr>
</table>

APPENDIX	# INTERNATIONAL ACCOUNTING*
Objective 9 Discuss the differences in international accounting among nations.	In today's world, we do not find it surprising to discover a British bank in Atlanta, Coca-Cola in Paris, and French airplanes in Zaire. German automobile parts assembled in Spain are sold in the United States. Japan buys oil from Saudi Arabia and sells cameras in Italy. Russian livestock eat American grain, and the British sip tea from Sri Lanka and China. Business has become truly international, but accounting, often described as the language of business, does not cross borders easily.

---

*The authors are indebted to Paul A. Pacter, CPA, Director of Research of IASC in London, United Kingdom, for making suggestions on this section of our text.

WHY ACCOUNTING PRINCIPLES AND PRACTICES DIFFER AMONG NATIONS

Accounting principles and reporting practices differ from country to country, and international decision making is made more difficult by the lack of a common communication system. However, since business is practiced at an international level, accounting must find a way to provide its services at that level.

Other accounting differences stem from the various legal or political systems of nations. In centrally controlled economies, for instance, the state owns all or most of the property. It makes little sense to prescribe full disclosure of accounting procedures to protect investors when little or no private ownership of property exists. In these nations with centrally controlled economies, an accounting profession is virtually nonexistent. One of the great challenges for Western nations over the next few decades will be to assist the nations of Eastern Europe to build an accounting profession to serve the companies that evolve under their new market-oriented economies. Some of these countries standardize their accounting methods and incorporate them into law.

In some market-oriented economies, such as the United States, Canada, Australia, and the United Kingdom, the development of accounting principles and reporting practices is left mainly to the private sector. Where uniformity exists, it occurs more by general agreement or consensus of interested parties than by governmental decree. In others, such as Japan, Germany, and France, tax law or government regulations drive financial reporting. The requirement in many countries that the financial statements must conform to tax returns contributes to diversity in accounting practices among countries.

The degree of development of the accounting profession and the general level of education of a country also influence accounting practices and procedures. Nations that lack a well-organized accounting profession may adopt, almost in total, the accounting methods of other countries. Commonwealth countries, for example, tend to follow British accounting standards; the former French colonies of Africa use French systems; Bermuda follows Canadian pronouncements; and the influence of the United States is widespread. At the same time, levels of expertise vary. In countries that have little knowledge or understanding of statistics, nothing is gained by advocating statistical accounting and auditing techniques. Accounting systems designed for electronic data processing are not helpful in countries where few or no businesses use computers.

Even in advanced countries, genuine differences of opinion exist regarding accounting theory and appropriate accounting methods. American standards, for example, require the periodic amortization of goodwill to expense, but British and Dutch standards do not. The lack of agreement on the objectives of financial statements and the lack of any effort in most countries to articulate objectives also contributes to diversity. Accounting methods also differ within nations. Most countries, including the United States, permit several depreciation methods and two or more inventory costing methods.

ATTEMPTED HARMONIZATION OF ACCOUNTING PRACTICES

The question arises as to whether financial statements that reflect the economic and social environment of, say, France can also be useful to a potential American investor. Can some of the differences between French and American accounting be eliminated or at least explained so that French and American investors understand each other's financial reports and find them useful when they make decisions?

With the increase in international business, there is a need for harmonization of accounting principles around the world. The two main organizations involved in the move toward international accounting standards are the International Organization of Securities Commissioners (IOSCO) and the International Accounting Standards Committee (IASC). These organizations study the information needs and accounting and reporting practices of different nations.

IOSCO, founded in 1983, is an organization representing capital market regulators worldwide. IOSCO consists of 134 member securities regulatory agencies around the world. The objectives of IOSCO are (1) securing better market regulation, (2) exchanging information to promote market development, (3) setting principles for and monitoring international transactions, and (4) facilitating cooperation among member nations in order to obtain market integrity. IOSCO has no inherent authority; it recommends courses of action that each member national regulator attempts to carry out.

A BROADER PERSPECTIVE

Reuters: Summary of Differences between U.K. and U.S. GAAP

Author's Note: We believe the following summary of the differences between U.K. and U.S. GAAP are still valid in the late 1990s.

Accounting principles

These consolidated financial statements have been prepared in accordance with U.K. GAAP, which differ in certain significant respects from U.S. GAAP. A description of the relevant accounting principles which differ materially is given below.

Goodwill and other intangibles

Under U.K. GAAP, purchased goodwill arising after ascribing fair values to all assets acquired, other than separate intangible assets, may be written off against reserves. Under U.S. GAAP, fair values are ascribed to all assets including separate intangibles. For the purpose of the U.S. GAAP adjustments included in notes 35–37, the intangible assets and the resultant goodwill are being amortised to income over their estimated lives, not exceeding 20 years.

Software development costs

Under U.K. GAAP, costs of developing computer software products are expensed in the year in which they are incurred. Under U.S. GAAP, the costs of developing computer software products subsequent to establishing technical feasibility are capitalised. The amortisation of the capitalised costs is based on the estimated useful economic lives of the products involved or on estimated future revenues if greater.

Employee costs

In 1992, Reuters changed its method of accounting under U.K. GAAP for its U.S. post-retirement health care plan from a cash to an accruals basis. The new method is consistent with the U.S. *Statement of Financial Accounting Standard (FAS) Number 106.* Under U.K. GAAP, Reuters has recorded the previously unrecognised obligation of £3.6 million (net of £1.8 million tax) as a prior year adjustment, whereas under U.S. GAAP the amount has been written off in 1992 as a cumulative change in accounting principle.

Since 1990, options have been granted under Reuters save as you earn plans at a 20% discount which renders the grants "compensatory" as defined in *Opinion 25* of the U.S. Accounting Principles Board. Under U.K. GAAP, the related share issues are recorded at their discounted price when the options are exercised. Under U.S. GAAP the discount is regarded as employee compensation and is accrued over the five-year vesting period of the grants.

Taxes on income

Under U.K. GAAP, deferred taxes are accounted for to the extent that it is considered probable that a liability or asset will crystallise in the foreseeable future. Under U.S. GAAP, in accordance with *FAS 109,* deferred taxes are accounted for on all timing differences, including those arising from the U.S. GAAP adjustments and a valuation allowance is established in respect of those deferred tax assets where it is more likely than not that some portion will not be realised. Effective 1 January 1992, Reuters has implemented *FAS 109* in its U.S. GAAP disclosures, having previously applied *FAS 96* in 1991 and 1990. The different approaches for deferred tax enshrined in *FAS 109, FAS 96* and the U.K. *Statement of Standard Accounting Practice Number 15* have not led to any GAAP adjustments in 1992.

Dividends

Under U.K. GAAP, dividends are provided for in the year in respect of which they are declared or proposed. Under U.S. GAAP, dividends and the related advance corporation tax are given effect only in the period in which dividends are formally declared.

Source: Reuters *1992 Annual Report.*

The IASC is making significant contributions to the development of international accounting standards. That organization, a London-based committee formed in 1973, includes 119 professional accountancy bodies in 86 countries. IASC is currently headed by a board including representatives of 13 countries: Australia, Canada, France, Germany, India, Japan, Malaysia, Mexico, Netherlands, the Nordic countries, South Africa, United Kingdom, and United States. The board also consists of three other organizations—the International Association of Financial Executives Institute, the International Coordinating Committee of Financial Analysts Association, and the Federation of Swiss Industrial Holding Companies.

The objectives of the IASC are (1) to develop international accounting standards that meet the need for accounting and disclosure by capital markets and the international business community and which are acceptable for use in the financial statements of all holders of equity and debt securities; (2) to work for greater comparability between national accounting standards and IAS and the removal of existing differences; and (3) to promote the use of International Accounting Standards (IAS) in the financial statements of all business enterprises. Over 31 international accounting standards have been issued during the last 24 years.

The IASC selects a topic for study from lists of problems submitted by the profession all over the world. After research and discussion by special committees, the IASC issues an exposure draft of a proposed standard for consideration by the profession and the business and financial communities. After due process, the IASC issues the final international accounting standard. To date, it has issued approximately 33 standards on topics as varied as "Disclosure of Accounting Policies" (*IAS 1*), "Depreciation Accounting" (*IAS 4*), "Statement of Changes in Financial Position" (*IAS 7*), and "Revenue Recognition" (*IAS 18*). Setting international standards is not easy. If the standards are too detailed or rigid, the flexibility needed to reflect different national environments is lost. On the other hand, if pronouncements are vague and allow too many alternative methods, there is little point in setting international standards.

For many years, the IASC has attempted to obtain IOSCO's support for the standards it has developed. IOSCO's support for the work of IASC is vital since the decision to require, accept, or disallow issuers from using international accounting standards when filing financial statements to list securities in a given country rests with each regulatory agency, not with the IASC. If the IASC obtains IOSCO's acceptance of its IAS's, foreign companies seeking a listing in a U.S. securities market would no longer have to undergo the process of reconciling their financial statements to U.S. generally accepted accounting principles (GAAP).

The IASC addressed the importance of the international harmonization of cash flow statements with *IAS 7,* "Cash Flow Statements." If accepted and complied with on a global basis, the harmonization of cash flow statements will have a significant effect on the use of cross-border offerings for companies seeking global financing. A prospective finance-seeking company would be able to generate a cash flow statement that is accepted in all foreign markets. A cash flow statement that complies with *IAS 7* would not require modification or the inclusion of additional data and would greatly simplify cross-border offerings and any future reporting by foreign investors, thus encouraging global financing.[6]

One major problem is obtaining compliance with these standards. There is no organization, nor is there likely to be an organization, to ensure compliance with international standards. Adoption is left to national standard-setting bodies or legislatures, which may or may not adopt a recommended international standard. Generally, members commit themselves to support the objectives of the international body. The members promise to use their best endeavors to see that international standards are formally adopted by local professional accountancy bodies; by government departments or other authorities that control the securities markets; and by the industrial, business, and financial communities of their respective countries.

In July 1995, the IASC and IOSCO agreed to develop a joint work program which would result in a comprehensive core set of 16 standards that would allow for cross-border capital raising and listing purposes in all global markets. The agreement is that the IASC must complete an ambitious work program designed to ensure that International Accounting Standards will comprise a comprehensive set of rules acceptable to IOSCO by summer of 1999. As a result of the strong demand for early competition, IASC has set for itself a deadline of March 1998.

The Financial Accounting Standards Board (FASB), which is not a member of the IASC, fully and actively supports the internationalization of accounting standards. FASB joined with the IASC to promote greater comparability of accounting standards as well as financial reporting. In order to obtain harmonization, the FASB and the IASC have attempted to understand the various differences between international accounting standards and generally accepted accounting standards. The FASB believes that international accounting standards should meet the need for both the comparability and high quality of financial information.[7]

U.S. GAAP and IASC standards have several similarities as well as differences. Many of these similarities between the two are obtained through the existence of alternatives or absence of implementation guidance within the standards. Although IASC standards may be too broad compared to that of U.S. GAAP, the IASC standards may be more effective in another country. The allowance of this alternative method allows countries to adapt the standard to that of their own country. While IASC standards allow for this alternative method, U.S. GAAP generally provides a set standard as well as a detailed guidance.

---

[6] *IASC Insight,* December 1993, p. 4.

[7] This discussion is based on a book titled, *The IASC-US Comparison Project: A Report on the Similarities and Differences between IASC Standards and U.S. GAAP* by FASB, 1996.

Once IOSCO is satisfied with the IASC's completed standards, the SEC must then consider whether or not to adopt these standards in the United States. This would allow foreign countries that wish to list their securities in the United States to do so using U.S. GAAP or international accounting standards. The SEC has stated that three elements must exist in order for the SEC to be able to accept the use of IASC's standards for cross-border listings in the United States. These are that the core standards must constitute a comprehensive generally accepted basis of accounting, be of high quality, and be rigorously interpreted and applied.

The general movement toward international harmonization of accounting standards is increasing in other areas of society. The accounting profession, national standard-setting bodies, universities, academic societies, and multinational corporations have all shown an increased interest in international accounting problems in recent years. The AICPA has an International Practice Division as a formal part of its organization. The American Accounting Association officially established an International Accounting section in 1976 and has approximately one dozen international accounting organizations as associate members. The University of Lancaster (England) and the University of Illinois have international accounting research centers that support research studies and conduct international conferences and seminars. Georgia State University received a Deloitte & Touche LLP grant to internationalize its accounting curriculum. Many universities currently offer courses in international business and accounting.

All this activity helps increase the flow of information and our understanding of the accounting and reporting practices in other parts of the world. Greater understanding improves the likelihood that unnecessary differences will be eliminated and enhances the general acceptance of international standards.

The remainder of this appendix gives examples of the accounting methods used in different countries and of the concepts that underlie them to illustrate the difficulty of achieving international harmonization.

FOREIGN CURRENCY TRANSLATION

Foreign currency translation is probably the most common problem in an international business environment. Foreign currency translation has two main components: accounting for transactions in a foreign currency and translating the financial statements of foreign enterprises into a different, common currency. This topic is presented here to give you an idea of the complexity of the harmonization effort.

Accounting for Transactions in a Foreign Currency

Suppose an American automobile dealership imports vehicles from Japan and promises to pay for them in yen 90 days after receiving them. If no change in the dollar-yen exchange rate occurs between the date the goods are received and the date the invoice is paid, no problem exists. The importer records both the purchase and the payment at the same dollar value based on the dollar/yen exchange rate at date of purchase. But if the yen appreciates against the dollar during the 90-day period, the importer must pay more dollars for the yen needed on the settlement date.[8] Which exchange rate should the importer use to record the purchase of the vehicles—the rate in effect on the purchase date or on the payment date?

One approach to the problem is to regard the purchase of the automobiles and settlement of the invoice as two separate transactions and record them at two different exchange rates. The difference between the amount recorded in Accounts Payable on the purchase date and the amount of cash paid on the settlement date is considered an exchange gain or loss. This approach is known as the *time-of-transaction method* and is the method recommended in the IASC's *Statement No. 21,* "Accounting for the Effects of Changes in Foreign Exchange Rates," issued in July 1983.

Another approach, the time-of-settlement method, regards the transaction and its settlement as a single event. This method regards the amount recorded on the purchase date as an estimate of the settlement amount. It accounts for any fluctuations in the exchange rate between the purchase date and the settlement date as part of the transaction and not as a separate gain or loss. Consequently, it does not recognize the effect on earnings until the purchased items are sold and the dollar cost of inventory is adjusted.

---

[8] This example ignores the possibility that the importer might obtain a forward exchange contract, a discussion of which is beyond the scope of this text.

Although the time-of-transaction method is widely used, the treatment of resulting exchange gains and losses is not uniform. If the gains or losses are realized (that is, if settlement is made within the same accounting period as the purchase), most countries recognize the gains and losses in the income statement for that period. If the **exchange gains or losses** are unrealized—that is, if they result from translating accounts payable (or accounts receivable for the vendor) at the balance sheet date—the treatment varies. In the United States, under the provision of FASB *Statement No. 52,* we recognize both realized and unrealized transaction gains and losses in earnings of the period in which the exchange rate changes.

Companies translate the financial statements of foreign subsidiaries into a single common unit of measurement, such as the dollar, for purposes of consolidation. Considerable argument has arisen in recent years regarding the correct way to make this translation. That is, which exchange rate should a firm use to translate items in the foreign subsidiary's balance sheet and income statement, and what treatment is appropriate for any resulting exchange gains and losses? Items translated at the historical rate cannot result in exchange gains or losses. However, items translated at the exchange rate in effect on the balance sheet date (the **current rate**) can result in exchange gains and losses if the current rate differs from the rate in effect when those items were recorded (the historical rate). If the current rate is used, a related question arises: Should the resulting exchange gains or losses be recognized immediately in income or deferred in some way?

Translating Financial Statements

The methods used to translate financial statements fall basically into two groups: translation of all items at the current rate and translation of some items at the current rate and others at the historical rates. The two groups are based on different concepts of both consolidation and international business.

THE CURRENT-RATE APPROACH The **current-rate or closing-rate approach** translates all assets and liabilities at the current rate, the exchange rate in effect on the balance sheet date. The main advantage of this method is its simplicity; it treats all items uniformly. The approach treats a foreign subsidiary as a unit separate from the domestic parent company. It considers the subsidiary's assets as being acquired largely out of local borrowing. Multinational groups, therefore, consist of entities that operate independently but contribute to a central fund of resources. Consequently, in consolidation, stockholders of the parent company are interested primarily in the parent company's net investment in the foreign subsidiary.

THE CURRENT/HISTORICAL-RATES APPROACH The **current/historical-rates approach** regards the parent company and its foreign subsidiaries as a single business undertaking. Assets owned by a foreign subsidiary are indistinguishable from assets owned by the parent company. Therefore, parent companies reflect foreign assets in consolidated statements in the same way that they report their similar assets, that is, at historical cost in the parent company's currency.

Firms commonly use three translation methods under this approach. The **current-noncurrent method** translates current assets and current liabilities at the current rate—the rate in effect on the balance sheet date—while noncurrent items are translated at their respective historical rates. The **historical rate** is the rate in effect when an asset or liability is originally recorded. The **monetary-nonmonetary method** uses the current rate for monetary assets and liabilities—that is, for those that have a fixed, nominal value in terms of the foreign currency—while historical rates are applied to nonmonetary items. The **temporal method** is a variation of the monetary-nonmonetary method. This method translates cash, receivables and payables, and other assets and liabilities carried at current prices (for example, marketable securities carried at current fair market value) at the current rate of exchange. This method translates all other assets and liabilities at historical rates.

IASC's *Statement No. 21,* "Accounting for the Effects of Changes in Foreign Exchange Rates," and FASB *Statement 52* both have a similar basic approach to foreign currency translation.[9] Although these similarities exist, there are important differences in the requirements of these two standards.

IAS 21 does not deal with the accounting issues for forward exchange contracts and hedging transactions, while FASB *Statement No. 52* requires a treatment.[10] When dealing with

---

[9] FASB, *Statement No. 52,* "Foreign Currency Translation" (Stamford, Conn., 1981).

[10]This discussion is based on a book titled, *The IASC-U.S. Comparison Project: A Report on the Similarities and Differences between IASC Standards and U.S. GAAP* by FASB, 1996.

a foreign entity with a highly inflationary economy, *IAS 21* allows the financial statements to be restated. This is done in accordance with *IAS 29*, "Financial Reporting for Hyperinflationary Economies," which permits restatement before translating into the reporting currency. Under *Statement No. 52*, the foreign subsidiary's current financial statements are remeasured under the reporting currency as if it were the functional currency.

IAS 21 permits alternatives that are not allowed under FASB *Statement 52*. These alternatives include losses on a liability for acquisition of assets in a foreign currency and translating goodwill and fair value adjustments to assets and liabilities after purchasing a foreign entity.

FASB *Statement No. 52* does not permit the immediate recognition of translation gains and losses in income in the United States. Instead, parent companies report them separately and accumulate them in a separate component of stockholders' equity until they sell or liquidate their investment in the foreign subsidiary. At this time the parent companies report translation gains or losses as part of the gain or loss on the sale or liquidation of the investment.

AN ACCOUNTING PERSPECTIVE	**BUSINESS INSIGHT** Reader's Digest publishes and produces magazines, books, and other home entertainment products. According to its 1996 annual report, the company translated assets and liabilities of non-U.S. subsidiaries at exchange rates in effect at the balance sheet date and revenues and expenses at average rates of exchange in effect during the year. The resulting translation adjustment is reflected as a separate component of stockholders' equity. Foreign currency translation resulted in a negative $1.3 million adjustment to stockholders' equity.

INVENTORIES

Variations in accounting for inventories relate principally to the basis for determining cost and whether cost, once determined, should be increased or decreased to reflect the fair market value of the inventories.

Determination of Cost

Although some countries occasionally use other methods, the three principal bases for determining inventory cost are first-in, first-out (FIFO); last-in, first-out (LIFO); and average cost. The most frequently used methods are FIFO and average cost. The two supporting standards for the accounting treatment of inventory are *IAS 2*, "Inventories," and *Accounting Research Bulletins No. 43*, Chapter 4, "Inventory Pricing." Each of these standards provides specific guidance for accounting for inventories of manufacturing and retail enterprises. *IAS 2* also provides a section for service providers with inventory. IASC's *Statement No. 2* supports the preference of the majority of countries and recommends the use of FIFO or average cost. An entity that chooses to use LIFO must disclose either the lower of FIFO or weighted-average method and the net realizable value, or the lower of the current balance sheet date and the net realizable value.[11]

ACCOUNTING FOR THE EFFECTS OF CHANGING PRICES

The final example of international differences illustrates an opportunity for international harmonization that is almost unique. Accounting for the effects of changing prices is a relatively recent development, so it may be possible to achieve a general international approach to the problem before national practices become too varied and too entrenched.

The FASB, in *Statement No. 33*, required two methods: general price-level (constant-dollar) accounting and current-cost accounting. However, *Statement No. 82* eliminated the requirement to use the first of these methods. The first approach attempts to reflect the effects of changes in general purchasing power on historical-cost financial statements, while the second is concerned with the impact of specific price changes. FASB *Statement No. 89* made reporting the effects of inflation completely optional.

---

[11]This discussion is based on a book titled, *The IASC-US Comparison Project: A Report on the Similarities and Differences between IASC Standards and U.S. GAAP* by FASB, 1996.

A number of countries are concerned about the loss of relevance of historical-cost financial reporting in inflationary environments, and several have adopted one of the two standard approaches—constant dollar or current cost. Some countries, usually those with the longest history of severe inflation, have issued standards that are mandatory for all enterprises, or at least for large or publicly held entities. In other countries, the accounting profession recommends, but does not prescribe, a form of inflation-adjusted statements, usually as supplementary information. Few countries, however, are prepared to abandon the present system based on historical cost and nominal units of currency for their primary financial statements, at least until decision makers have had sufficient experience with inflation accounting to give an opinion on its utility. Exceptions to this view are Argentina, Brazil, and Chile, which have had high rates of inflation, which now require incorporation of general-price-level accounting in the primary financial statements of all enterprises.

The United Kingdom's standard, until it was withdrawn, prescribed the provision of current-cost information either in the primary financial statements or as supplementary statements or additional information. New Zealand requires a supplementary income statement and balance sheet on a current-cost basis. Australia and South Africa recommend, but do not yet require, similar supplementary current-cost statements. Germany recommends the incorporation of current-cost information in notes to the historical-cost financial statements; while in the Netherlands, some companies prepare the primary statements on a current-cost basis, and some provide only supplementary information.

The fact that the accountancy bodies of various nations are adopting neither a uniform approach nor a uniform application of any approach, even with something as relatively new as accounting for changing prices, highlights the difficulty of achieving international harmonization of accounting standards. Adoption of different approaches to accounting for changing prices by different countries will make the preparation of consolidated financial statements by multinational corporations especially difficult, while at the same time comparability of the financial reports of companies in different nations will be further reduced. However, even if all countries adopted a similar approach, a major barrier to comparability would still remain: the price indexes used in each country to compute adjustments for price changes are not comparable in composition, accuracy, frequency of publication, or timeliness.

Many accountants are reluctant to see current-cost-adjusted statements replace historical-cost financial statements because they believe historical cost is the most objective basis of valuation. However, business entities may be more likely to favor inflation accounting once they become accustomed to it because of its tax implications—assuming the tax law permits the method. Since inflation accounting generally leads to lower profit figures than those computed on the historical-cost basis, companies have a strong incentive to adopt inflation accounting in those countries where computation of the tax liability is based on reported net income. Governments, on the other hand, could then decide to prohibit the use of inflation accounting for tax purposes when a decline in tax revenues becomes apparent.

The current trend in the use of approaches to accounting for changing prices appears to be toward current-cost accounting and away from general-price-level accounting. Some suggest that, of the two approaches, governments prefer current-cost accounting, and this preference may influence the decisions of the accounting profession in some countries. As one British writer has pointed out:

No government wants to have the effects of its currency debasement measured by anyone—certainly not by every business enterprise in the country. Much better to point the finger at all those individual prices moving around because of the machinations of big business, big labour and big aliens.[12]

Whether current-cost accounting will become common practice or whether some combination of current-cost and general-price-level accounting will gain favor should depend on the usefulness to decision makers of the information provided by each approach. One thing is clear: When inflation again becomes a problem, more countries will adopt some form of inflation accounting. The opportunity to achieve a higher level of international harmonization while national standards are still at the development stage should not be missed.

We have attempted in these few pages to provide a broad and general picture of the variety of accounting principles and reporting practices that exist across the world. Articulation among countries is a challenging problem—and one that will receive increasing attention in the years to come.

---

[12]P. H. Lyons, "Farewell to Historical Costs?" *CA Magazine,* February 1976, p. 23.

SELECTED BIBLIOGRAPHY

The following sources can provide additional information about international accounting:

Arthur Andersen & Co. (London). *European Review,* nos. 1–5 (January 1981–May 1982).

Choi, Frederick D. S., and Richard M. Levich. "Behavioral Effects of International Accounting Diversity." *Accounting Horizons* 5, no. 2 (June 1991), pp. 1–13.

Choi, Frederick D. S., and Gerhard G. Mueller. *An Introduction to Multinational Accounting.* Englewood Cliffs, N.J.: Prentice Hall, 1984.

Cohen, Jeffery R.; Lanie W. Pant; and David J. Sharp. "Culture-Based Ethical Conflicts Confronting Multinational Accounting Firms," *Accounting Horizons* 7, no. 3 (September 1993), pp. 1–13.

FASB. *The IASC-U.S. Comparison Project: A Report on the Similarities and Differences between IASC Standards and U.S. GAAP* (1996).

Gaudy, Lisa A. "German and Japanese Annual Reports Lack Sufficient Information." *Corporate Accounting International,* no. 1 (November 1989), pp. 14–15.

Gray, Sidney J., and Clare B. Robert. "East-West Accounting Issues: A New Agenda." *Accounting Horizons* 5, no. 1 (March 1991), pp. 42–50.

Hauworth, William P., II. "A Comparison of Various International Proposals on Inflation Accounting: A Practitioner's View." Monograph, 1980.

Hobson, D. "International Harmonization." *Public Finance and Accountancy* (May 1983), pp. 34–36.

Horner, Lawrence D. "Efficient Markets and Universal Standards." *Chief Executive* (Winter 1985), p. 38.

London, David Aron. "Soviets Begin to Westernize Accounting Standards with East-West Joint Ventures." *Corporate Accounting International,* no. 1 (November 1989), pp. 6–7.

O'Carroll, Anne. "IASC's Goodwill Proposal Draws Much Negative Criticism." *Corporate Accounting International,* no. 1 (November 1989), pp. 8–9.

Purvis, S. E. C.; Helen Gernon; and Michael A. Diamond. "The IASC and Its Comparability Project: Prerequisite for Success." *Accounting Horizons* 5, no. 2 (June 1991), pp. 25–44.

Smith, Bradford E. "Red Revolution Jostles World Rule Makers." *Accounting Today* (January 22, 1990), p. 12.

Stamp, Edward, and Maurice Moonitz. "International Auditing Standards—Parts I and II." *The CPA Journal* LII, nos. 6 and 7 (June–July 1982).

DEMONSTRATION PROBLEM 14–A

Following are selected transactions and other data for Kelly Company for 1999:

Mar. 21 Purchased 600 shares of Sly Company common stock at $48.75 per share, plus a $450 broker's commission. Also purchased 100 shares of Rob Company common stock at $225 per share, plus a $376 broker's commission. Both investments are expected to be temporary.

June 2 Received cash dividends of $1.50 per share on the Sly common shares and $3 per share on the Rob common shares.

Aug. 12 Received shares representing a 100% stock dividend on the Rob shares.

30 Sold 100 shares of Rob common stock at $120 per share, less a $360 broker's commission.

Sept. 15 Received shares representing a 10% stock dividend on the Sly common stock. Market price today was $52.50 per share.

Dec. 31 Per share market values for the two investments in common stock are Sly, $45.75, and Rob, $106.50. Both investments are considered temporary.

Required Prepare journal entries to record these transactions and the necessary adjustments for a December 31 closing.

SOLUTION TO DEMONSTRATION PROBLEM 14–A

KELLY COMPANY
GENERAL JOURNAL

1999				
Mar.	21	Trading Securities	52,576	
		Cash		52,576
		To record purchase of 600 shares of Sly common stock for $29,700 and 100 shares of Rob common stock for $22,876.		
June	2	Cash	1,200	
		Dividend Revenue		1,200
		To record cash dividends: $900 Sly, and $300 Rob.		
Aug.	12	Received 100 shares of Rob common stock as a 100% stock dividend. The new cost per share is $22,876 ÷ 200 shares = $114.38.		
	30	Cash	11,640	
		Trading Securities		11,438
		Gain on Sales of Trading Securities		202
		To record sale of trading securities: proceeds = $12,000 − $360; cost = $114.38 × 100 shares.		
Sept.	15	Received 60 shares of Sly common stock as a 10% stock dividend. New cost per share is $29,700 ÷ 660 shares = $45.		
Dec.	31	Unrealized Loss on Trading Securities	293	
		Trading Securities		293
		To write trading securities down to market value:		

	Cost	Market	Inc. (Dec.) in Market Value
Sly common stock	$29,700	$30,195*	$ 495
Rob common stock	11,438	10,650†	(788)
Total	$41,138	$40,845	$(293)

* $45.75 × 660 shares = $30,195.
† $106.50 × 100 shares = $10,650.

DEMONSTRATION PROBLEM 14–B

Lanford Company acquired all of the outstanding voting common stock of Casey Company on January 2, 1999, for $300,000 cash. After the close of business on the date of acquisition, the balance sheets for the two companies were as follows:

	Lanford Company	Casey Company
Assets		
Cash	$ 75,000	$ 30,000
Accounts receivable, net	90,000	37,500
Notes receivable	15,000	7,500
Merchandise inventory	112,500	45,000
Investment in Casey Company	300,000	
Investment in bonds		30,000
Plant and equipment, net	303,000	195,000
Total assets	$895,500	$345,000
Liabilities and Stockholders' Equity		
Accounts payable	$ 75,000	$ 45,000
Notes payable	22,500	15,000
Bonds payable	225,000	
Common stock—$7.50 par value	300,000	150,000
Paid-in capital in excess of par value—common		60,000
Retained earnings	273,000	75,000
Total liabilities and stockholders' equity	$895,500	$345,000

On January 2, 1999, Casey Company borrowed $15,000 from Lanford Company by giving a note. On that same day, Casey Company purchased $30,000 of Lanford Company's bonds. The excess of cost over book value is attributable to Casey Company's above-average earnings prospects.

Required   Prepare a work sheet for a consolidated balance sheet on the date of acquisition.

SOLUTION TO DEMONSTRATION PROBLEM 14–B

LANFORD COMPANY AND SUBSIDIARY CASEY COMPANY
Work Sheet for Consolidated Balance Sheet
January 2, 1999 (date of acquisition)

	Lanford Company	Casey Company	Eliminations Debit	Eliminations Credit	Consolidated Amounts
Assets					
Cash	75,000	30,000			105,000
Accounts receivable, net	90,000	37,500			127,500
Notes receivable	15,000	7,500		*(2)* 15,000	7,500
Merchandise inventory	112,500	45,000			157,500
Investment in Casey Co.	300,000			*(1)* 300,000	–0–
Investment in bonds		30,000		*(3)* 30,000	–0–
Plant and equipment, net	303,000	195,000			498,000
Goodwill			*(1)* 15,000		15,000
	895,500	345,000			910,500
Liabilities and Stockholders' Equity					
Accounts payable	75,000	45,000			120,000
Notes payable	22,500	15,000	*(2)* 15,000		22,500
Bonds payable	225,000		*(3)* 30,000		195,000
Common stock—$7.50 par	300,000	150,000	*(1)* 150,000		300,000
Paid-in capital in excess of par value—common		60,000	*(1)* 60,000		–0–
Retained earnings	273,000	75,000	*(1)* 75,000		273,000
	895,500	345,000	345,000	345,000	910,500

NEW TERMS

Available-for-sale securities   Securities purchased that will be held for longer than the near term.   *501*

Consolidated statements   The financial statements that result from consolidating the parent's financial statement amounts with those of its subsidiaries (after certain eliminations have been made). The consolidated statements reflect the financial position and results of operations of a single economic enterprise.   *506*

Consolidated statement work sheet   An informal record on which elimination entries are made to show account balances as if the parent and its subsidiaries were a single economic enterprise.   *507*

Cost method   A method of accounting for stock investments in which the investor company does not adjust the investment account balance for its share of the investee's

reported income, losses, and dividends. Dividends received are credited to Dividends Revenue.   *501*

Current/historical-rates approach   Regards the parent company and its foreign subsidiaries as a single business undertaking. All assets are shown at historical cost in the parent company's currency.   *525*

Current-noncurrent method   Translates current assets and current liabilities at the current rate and noncurrent items at their historical rates.   *525*

Current rate   Exchange rate in effect on the balance sheet date.   *525*

Current-rate or closing-rate approach   The current-rate or closing-rate method translates all assets and liabilities at the current rate, the exchange rate in effect on the balance sheet date.   *525*

Dividend yield on common stock ratio   Equal to dividend per share of common stock divided by the current market price per share. Investors use this ratio to compare stocks.   *518*

Elimination entries   Entries made on a consolidated statement work sheet to remove certain intercompany items and transactions. Elimination entries allow the presentation of all account balances as if the parent and its subsidiaries were a single economic enterprise.   *506*

Equity method   A method of accounting for stock investments where the investment account is adjusted periodically for the investor company's share of the investee's income, losses, and dividends as they are reported by the investee.   *501, 505*

Exchange gains or losses (time-of-transaction method)   The difference between the amount recorded in Accounts Payable on the purchase date and amount of cash paid on the settlement date.   *525*

Goodwill   An intangible value attached to a business primarily due to above-average earnings prospects.   *509*

Historical rate   The exchange rate in effect when an asset or liability is originally recorded.   *525*

Intercompany transactions   Financial transactions involving a parent and one of its subsidiaries or between two of the subsidiaries.   *506*

Investee   A company that has 20% to 50% of its stock purchased by another company (the investor) as a long-term investment.   *505*

Investor   A company that purchases 20% to 50% of another company (the investee) as a long-term investment.   *505*

Marketable equity securities   Readily saleable common and preferred stocks of other companies.   *502*

Minority interest   The claim or interest of the stockholders who own less than 50% of a subsidiary's outstanding voting common stock. The minority stockholders have an interest in the subsidiary's net assets and share the subsidiary's earnings with the parent company.   *511*

Monetary-nonmonetary method   Translates monetary assets and liabilities at the current rate and nonmonetary items at their historical rates.   *525*

Parent company   A corporation that owns more than 50% of the outstanding voting common stock of another corporation.   *506*

Payout ratio on common stock   Calculated by dividing dividend per share of common stock by earnings per share (EPS). The ratio indicates whether a company pays out a large percentage of earnings as dividends or reinvests most of its earnings.   *518*

Pooling of interests   A business combination that meets certain criteria specified in *APB Opinion No. 16,* including the issuance of common stock in exchange for common stock.   *516*

Purchase   A transaction in which one company issues cash or other assets to acquire common stock of another company. Also, any combination that does not qualify as a pooling of interests.   *516*

Subsidiary company   A corporation acquired and controlled by a parent corporation; control is established by ownership of more than 50% of the subsidiary's outstanding voting common stock.   *506*

Temporal method   Cash, receivables and payables, and other assets and liabilities carried at current prices are translated at the current rate of exchange. All other assets and liabilities are translated at historical rates.   *525*

Trading securities   Securities bought principally for sale in the near term.   *501*

SELF-TEST

TRUE-FALSE

Indicate whether each of the following statements is true or false.

1. Under the cost method, the investment account is adjusted when dividends are received.

2. The cost method should be used when a corporation makes a long-term investment of less than 20%, and there is no significant control.

3. In a stock split, the investor does not recognize revenue, but reduces the cost per share of stock.

4. Trading securities and available-for-sale securities should be grouped separately in applying the fair market value rules.

5. When making elimination entries, the entries are made only on the consolidated statements work sheet and not on the accounting records of the parent and subsidiary.

6. (*Based on appendix*) Pronouncements issued by the International Accounting Standards Committee (IASC) must be followed by member nations.

MULTIPLE-CHOICE

Select the best answer for each of the following questions.

1. In which of the following cases is the investor company limited to use of the equity method in accounting for its stock investments?
   a. Short-term investments.
   b. Long-term investments of less than 20%.
   c. Long-term investments of 20%–50%.
   d. Long-term investments of more than 50%.

2. Under the equity method, which of the following is true?
   a. Dividends received reduce the investment account.
   b. Dividends received increase the investment account.
   c. The investor's share of net income decreases the investment account.
   d. The investor's share of net loss increases the investment account.

3. When the fair market value rules are followed, which of the following is true when the market value of the stocks in the Trading Securities account falls below their cost?
    a. The Unrealized Losses on Trading Securities account is credited.
    b. The Recovery of Market Value of Trading Securities account is credited.
    c. The Allowance for Market Decline of Current Marketable Equity Securities is debited.
    d. The Unrealized Loss on Trading Securities is debited.

4. Under the equity method, the investment account always reflects only the:
    a. Dividends paid by the investee corporation.
    b. Investor's interest in the net assets of the investee.
    c. Investor's share of net income.
    d. Historical cost of the investment.

5. The excess of cost over the book value of an investment that is due to expected above-average earnings is labeled on the consolidated balance sheet as:

a. Goodwill.
b. Common stock.
c. Retained earnings.
d. Loss on investment.

6. (*Based on appendix*) Which of the following statements is true regarding the environment of international accounting?
    a. More and more nations are switching to a market-oriented economy.
    b. The accounting practices around the world are almost completely harmonized.
    c. The other nations of the world are willing to accept accounting methods used in the United States as the best methods to use in their own countries.
    d. The topic of international accounting is becoming less and less relevant over time.

Now turn to page 541 to check your answers.

QUESTIONS

1. For what reasons do corporations purchase the stock of other corporations?

2. Explain how marketable securities should be classified in the balance sheet.

3. Describe the valuation bases used for marketable equity securities.

4. Under what circumstances is the equity method used to account for stock investments?

5. Explain briefly the accounting for stock dividends and stock splits from the investor's point of view.

6. Of what significance is par value to the investing corporation?

7. What is the purpose of preparing consolidated financial statements?

8. Under what circumstances must consolidated financial statements be prepared?

9. Why is it necessary to make elimination entries on the consolidated statement work sheet? Are these elimination entries also posted to the accounts of the parent and subsidiary? Why or why not?

10. Why might a corporation pay an amount in excess of the book value for a subsidiary's stock? Why might it pay an amount less than the book value of the subsidiary's stock?

11. The item *Minority interest* often appears as one amount in the consolidated balance sheet. What does this item represent?

12. How do a subsidiary's earnings, losses, and dividends affect the investment account of the parent when the equity method of accounting is used?

13. When must each of the following methods be used to account for a business combination?
    a. Purchase.
    b. Pooling of interests.

14. List three differences between the purchase and pooling of interests methods of accounting for business combinations.

15. Why are consolidated financial statements of limited usefulness to the creditors and minority stockholders of a subsidiary?

16. Distinguish between a purchase and a pooling of interests.

17. (*Based on appendix*) Why do differences exist in accounting standards and practices from nation to nation?

18. (*Based on appendix*) How successful have efforts at harmonization been to date?

The Coca-Cola Company

19. **Real World Question.** Based on the financial statements of The Coca-Cola Company contained in the annual report booklet, what was the 1996 Investment in Coca-Cola Enterprises, Inc., balance? According to Note 2, what percentage of Coca-Cola Enterprises, Inc., does The Coca-Cola Company own? What method of accounting (cost or equity) does The Coca-Cola Company use for its investment? Why did its investment change from 1995 to 1996?

HARLAND

20. **Real World Question.** Based on the financial statements of John H. Harland Company contained in the annual report booklet, what was the 1996 ending long-term investment balance? What was the net change from 1995?

EXERCISES

On July 1, 1999, Tam Company purchased 200 shares of Del Company capital stock as a temporary investment (trading securities) at $676.80 per share plus a commission of $720. On July 15, a 10% stock dividend was received. Tam received a cash dividend of $3.60 per share on August 12, 1999. On November 1, Tam sold all of the shares for $835.20 per share, less a commission of $720. Prepare entries to record all of these transactions in Tam Company's accounts.

Exercise 14–1
Prepare entries for trading securities (L.O. 2)

Key Company purchased 200 shares of Franklin Company stock at a total cost of $7,560 on July 1, 1999. At the end of the accounting year (December 31, 1999), the market value for these shares was $6,840. By December 31, 2000, the market value had risen to $7,920. This stock is the only marketable equity security that Key Company owns. The company classifies the securities as trading securities. Give the entries necessary at the date of purchase and at December 31, 1999, and 2000.

Exercise 14–2
Prepare entries for trading securities (L.O. 2)

Corbit Company has marketable equity securities that have a fair market value at year-end that is $13,440 below their cost. Give the required entry if:

Exercise 14–3
Apply fair market value method to marketable equity securities (L.O. 2)

a. The securities are current assets classified as trading securities.

b. The securities are noncurrent assets classified as available-for-sale securities, and the loss is considered to be temporary.

c. The securities are noncurrent assets classified as available-for-sale securities, and the loss is considered to be permanent.

State where each of the accounts debited in **a, b,** and **c** would be reported in the financial statements.

Ruiz Company owns 75% of Sim Company's outstanding common stock and uses the equity method of accounting. Sim Company reported net income of $702,000 for 1999. On December 31, 1999, Sim Company paid a cash dividend of $189,000. In 2000, Sim Company incurred a net loss of $125,000. Prepare entries to reflect these events on Ruiz Company's books.

Exercise 14–4
Prepare equity method entries for an investment (L.O. 1, 3)

On February 1, 1999, Larkin Company acquired 100% of the outstanding voting common stock of TRD Company for $8,400,000 cash. The stockholders' equity of the TRD Company consisted of common stock, $6,720,000, and retained earnings, $1,680,000. Prepare (a) the entry to record the investment in TRD Company and (b) the elimination entry on the work sheet used to prepare a consolidated balance sheet as of the date of acquisition.

Exercise 14–5
Record investment at book value and elimination entry as of acquisition date (L.O. 5)

Given the facts in Exercise 14–5, how much would be recorded as goodwill in each of the following instances? The same amount was paid, but the parent company acquired a—

Exercise 14–6
Determine amount of goodwill (L.O. 5)

a. 90% interest.

b. 70% interest.

c. 55% interest.

Heidi Corporation acquired, for cash, 80% of the outstanding voting common stock of Sumpter Company. After the close of business on the date of acquisition, Sumpter Company's stockholders' equity consisted of common stock, $5,880,000, and retained earnings, $2,184,000. The cost of the investment exceeded the book value by $302,400 and was attributable to above-average earnings prospects. Prepare (a) the entry to record the investment in Sumpter Company and (b) the elimination entry on the work sheet used to prepare consolidated financial statements as of the date of acquisition.

Exercise 14–7
Record investment at more than book value and elimination entry as of acquisition date (L.O. 5)

On January 1, 1998, Company J acquired 85% of the outstanding voting common stock of Company K. On that date, Company K's stockholders' equity consisted of:

Exercise 14–8
Compute difference between cost and book value of common stock investments (L.O. 5)

Stockholders' equity:
Paid-in capital:
Common stock, $90 par; 30,000 shares authorized,
   issued, and outstanding $2,700,000
Retained earnings 675,000
   Total stockholders' equity $3,375,000

Compute the difference between cost and book value in each of the following cases:

a. Company J pays $2,868,750 cash for its interest in Company K.

b. Company J pays $3,375,000 cash for its interest in Company K.

c. Company J pays $2,610,000 cash for its interest in Company K.

Exercise 14–9
Compute book value, difference between cost and book value, and minority interest of an investment (L.O. 5)

The January 1, 1999, stockholders' equity section of Saye Company's balance sheet follows:

Stockholders' equity:

Paid-in capital:	
Common stock—$144 par value: authorized, 200,000 shares;	
issued and outstanding, 150,000 shares	$21,600,000
Paid-in capital in excess of par value	3,600,000
Total paid-in capital	$25,200,000
Retained earnings	2,160,000
Total stockholders' equity	$27,360,000

Ninety percent of Saye Company's outstanding voting common stock was acquired by Tim Company on January 1, 2000, for $24,048,000. Compute (*a*) the book value of the investment, (*b*) the difference between cost and book value, and (*c*) the minority interest.

Exercise 14–10
Compute investment account balance at year-end and minority interest at beginning and end of year (L.O. 2, 5)

Company S purchased 90% of Company T's outstanding voting common stock on January 2, 1999. The investment is accounted for under the equity method. Company S paid $2,790,000 for its proportionate equity of $2,430,000. The difference was due to undervalued land owned by Company T. Company T earned $324,000 during 1999 and paid cash dividends of $108,000.

a. Compute the balance in the investment account on December 31, 1999.

b. Compute the amount of the minority interest on (1) January 2, 1999, and (2) December 31, 1999.

PROBLEMS

Problem 14–1
Prepare entries for available-for-sale securities (L.O. 1, 3)

On September 1, 1999, Ramsey Company purchased the following relatively long-term investments classified as available-for-sale securities:

1. Two thousand shares of Lacey Company capital stock at $439.20 plus broker's commission of $5,760.

2. One thousand shares of Membrow Company capital stock at $705.60 plus broker's commission of $5,040.

Cash dividends of $18.00 per share on the Lacey capital stock and $14.40 per share on the Membrow capital stock were received on December 7 and December 10, respectively.

On December 31, 1999, per share market values are Lacey, $460.80; and Membrow, $655.20.

Required a. Prepare journal entries to record these transactions.

b. Prepare the necessary adjusting entry(ies) at December 31, 1999, to adjust the carrying values assuming that market price changes are believed to be temporary. Where would the accounts appear in the financial statements?

Problem 14–2
Prepare entries for trading securities (L.O. 1, 2)

Kress, Inc., purchased on July 2, 1999, 240 shares of Baker Company $180 par value common stock as a temporary investment at $288 per share, plus a broker's commission of $432.

On July 15, 1999, a cash dividend of $7.20 per share was received. On September 15, 1999, Baker Company split its $180 par value common shares two for one.

On November 2, 1999, Kress sold 200 shares of Baker common stock at $180, less a broker's commission of $288.

Required a. Prepare journal entries to record all of the above transactions.

b. How would you recommend that the remaining shares be classified in the December 31, 1999, balance sheet if still held at that date?

c. Assume the remaining shares were considered current assets classified as trading securities at the end of 1999, at which time their market value was $128 per share. Prepare any necessary adjusting entries for the end of 1999.

Prime Company acquired 90% of the outstanding voting common stock of Orr Company on January 1, 1999, for $7,560,000 cash. Prime Company uses the equity method. During 1999, Orr reported $1,512,000 of net income and paid $504,000 in cash dividends. The stockholders' equity section of the December 31, 1998, balance sheet for Orr follows:

Problem 14–3
Prepare equity method entries for an investment and eliminating entries for consolidated work sheet (L.O. 1, 3, 5)

Stockholders' equity:

Paid-in capital:	
Common stock—$21.00 par	$6,720,000
Retained earnings	1,680,000
Total stockholders' equity	$8,400,000

a. Prepare general journal entries to record the investment and the effect of Orr's earnings and dividends on Prime Company's accounts.

Required

b. Prepare the elimination entry that would be made on the work sheet for a consolidated balance sheet as of the date of acquisition.

Codd Company acquired 70% of the outstanding voting common stock of Snow Company for $8,568,000 on January 1, 1999. The investment is accounted for under the equity method. During the years 1999–2001, Snow Company reported the following:

Problem 14–4
Prepare equity method entries for an investment (L.O. 1, 3, 5)

	Net Income (loss)	Dividends Paid
1999	$1,454,880	$871,920
2000	372,960	223,440
2001	(23,520)	55,860

a. Prepare general journal entries to record the investment and the effect of the subsidiary's income, losses, and dividends on Codd Company's accounts.

Required

b. Compute the investment account balance on December 31, 2001.

Maple Company acquired all of the outstanding voting common stock of Dodd Company on January 2, 1999, for $4,320,000. On the date of acquisition, the balance sheets for the two companies were as follows:

Problem 14–5
Prepare work sheet and consolidated balance sheet at acquisition (L.O. 5)

	Maple Company	Dodd Company
Assets		
Cash	$ 900,000	$ 270,000
Accounts receivable, net	432,000	360,000
Notes receivable	180,000	108,000
Merchandise inventory	1,368,000	864,000
Investment in Dodd Company	4,320,000	
Equipment, net	1,224,000	738,000
Buildings, net	3,330,000	1,656,000
Land	1,404,000	450,000
Total assets	$13,158,000	$4,446,000
Liabilities and Stockholders' Equity		
Accounts payable	$ 792,000	$ 360,000
Notes payable	216,000	252,000
Common stock—$120 par value	9,540,000	3,564,000
Retained earnings	2,610,000	270,000
Total liabilities and stockholders' equity	$13,158,000	$4,446,000

The management of Maple Company thinks that the Dodd Company's land is undervalued by $162,000. The remainder of the excess of cost over book value is due to superior earnings potential.

On the date of acquisition, Dodd Company borrowed $180,000 from Maple Company by giving a note.

a. Prepare a work sheet for a consolidated balance sheet as of the date of acquisition.

Required

b. Prepare a consolidated balance sheet for January 2, 1999.

Problem 14–6
Prepare work sheet for consolidated financial statements (L.O. 5)

Refer back to Problem 14–5. Maple Company uses the equity method. Assume the following amounts are taken from the adjusted trial balances of Maple Company and Dodd Company on December 31, 1999:

	Maple Company	Dodd Company
Debit Balance Accounts		
Cash	$ 864,000	$ 364,296
Accounts receivable, net	553,536	414,000
Notes receivable	342,000	90,000
Merchandise inventory, December 31	1,530,000	1,008,000
Investment in Dodd Company	4,519,356	
Equipment, net	1,147,500	691,860
Buildings, net	3,163,500	1,573,200
Land	1,404,000	450,000
Cost of goods sold	8,064,000	2,160,000
Expenses (excluding depreciation and taxes) . . .	2,160,000	810,000
Depreciation expense	243,000	128,940
Income tax expense	569,664	123,504
Dividends	477,000	178,200
Total of the accounts with debit balances	$25,037,556	$7,992,000
Credit Balance Accounts		
Accounts payable	$ 720,000	$ 378,000
Notes payable	270,000	180,000
Common stock—$90 par value	9,540,000	3,564,000
Retained earnings	2,610,000	270,000
Revenue from sales	11,520,000	3,600,000
Income of Dodd Company	377,556	
Total of the accounts with credit balances	$25,037,556	$7,992,000

There is no intercompany debt at the end of the year.

Required

Prepare a work sheet for consolidated financial statements on December 31, 1999. Ignore the amortization of goodwill.

Problem 14–7
Prepare consolidated income statement, statement of retained earnings, and balance sheet (L.O. 5)

Using the work sheet from Problem 14–6, prepare the following items:

a.	Consolidated income statement for the year ended December 31, 1999.
b.	Consolidated statement of retained earnings for the year ended December 31, 1999.
c.	Consolidated balance sheet for December 31, 1999.

Problem 14–8
Answer fill-in-the-blank questions regarding international accounting (based on appendix) (L.O. 8)

Supply the missing word(s) in the following statements:

a.	Accounting must reflect the national _____ and _____ environment in which it is practiced.
b.	Other accounting differences among nations stem from the legal or _____ differences.
c.	Commonwealth nations tend to adopt _____ accounting standards.
d.	Several organizations are working to achieve greater understanding and _____ of accounting principles.
e.	Ultimately, the success of international pronouncements depends on the willingness of the nations to _____ them.
f.	_____ _____ translation is probably the most common problem in an international business environment.

Alternate Problems

Problem 14–1A
Prepare entries for trading securities (L.O. 1, 2)

Paris Company acquired on July 15, 1999, 400 shares of Rome Company $720 par value capital stock at $698.40 per share plus a broker's commission of $1,728. On August 1, 1999, Paris Company received a cash dividend of $8.64 per share. On November 3, 1999, it sold 200 of these shares at $756 per share less a broker's commission of $1,152. On December 1, 1999, Rome Company issued shares comprising a 100% stock dividend declared on its capital stock on November 18.

On December 31, 1999, the end of Paris Company's calendar-year accounting period, the market quotation for Rome Company's common stock was $331.20 per share. The decline was considered to be temporary.

a. Prepare journal entries to record all of these data assuming the securities are considered temporary investments classified as trading securities. Where should the accounts in the last entry appear in the financial statements?

b. Assume Rome Company has become a major customer so the shares are held for long-term affiliation purposes. Indicate how the investment should be shown in the balance sheet.

On October 17, 1999, Strong Company purchased the following common stocks (all trading securities) at the indicated per share prices that included commissions:

Problem 14–2A
Prepare entries for trading securities; compare entries to those for available-for-sale securities (L.O. 1, 2)

600 shares of X Company common stock @ $216	$129,600
1,000 shares of Y Company common stock @ $144 . . .	144,000
1,600 shares of Z Company common stock @ $72	115,200
	$388,800

On December 31, 1999, the market prices per share of the above common stocks were X, $223.20; Y, $136.80; and Z, $54.

Summarized, the cash dividends per share received in 2000 were X, $14.40; Y, $7.20; and Z, $5.40.

On December 31, 2000, the per share market prices were X, $252.80; Y, $115.20; and Z, $72.

All of these changes in market prices are considered temporary.

Required

a. Prepare journal entries for all of these transactions, including calendar year-end adjusting entries, assuming the shares of common stock acquired are considered trading securities.

b. If the securities acquired are considered available-for-sale securities, how would the entries made in **a** differ?

c. For both parts **a** and **b,** give the descriptions (titles) and the dollar amounts of the items that would appear in the income statements for 1999 and 2000.

On January 1, 1999, Long Company acquired 80% of the outstanding voting common stock of Fall Company for $4,032,000 cash. Long Company uses the equity method. During 1999, Fall reported $672,000 of net income and paid $288,000 in dividends. The stockholders' equity section of the December 31, 1998, balance sheet for Fall follows:

Problem 14–3A
Prepare equity method entries for an investment and eliminating entries for consolidated statements work sheet (L.O. 1, 3, 5)

Stockholders' equity:	
Paid-in capital:	
Common stock—$42 par	$4,200,000
Retained earnings	840,000
Total stockholders' equity	$5,040,000

Required

a. Prepare the general journal entries to record the investment and the effect of Fall's income and dividends on Long Company's accounts.

b. Prepare the elimination entry that would be made on the work sheet for a consolidated balance sheet as of the date of acquisition.

Pearson Company acquired 75% of the outstanding voting common stock of Frost Company for $1,444,800 cash on January 1, 1999. The investment is accounted for under the equity method. During 1999, 2000, and 2001, Frost Company reported the following:

Problem 14–4A
Prepare equity method entries for an investment (L.O. 1, 3, 5)

	Net Income (loss)	Dividends Paid
1999	$357,840	$290,640
2000	(45,360)	–0–
2001	108,360	72,240

Required

a. Prepare general journal entries to record the investment and the effect of the subsidiary's income, losses, and dividends on Pearson Company's accounts.

b. Compute the balance in the investment account on December 31, 2001.

Problem 14–5A
Prepare work sheet
and consolidated balance
sheet at acquisition (L.O. 5)

Cord Company acquired 100% of the outstanding voting common stock of Thorpe Company on January 2, 1999, for $2,700,000. At the end of business on the date of acquisition, the balance sheets for the two companies were as follows:

	Cord Company	Thorpe Company
Assets		
Cash	$ 315,000	$ 180,000
Accounts receivable, net	234,000	144,000
Notes receivable	360,000	90,000
Merchandise inventory	495,000	234,000
Investment in Thorpe Company	2,700,000	
Equipment, net	648,000	450,000
Buildings, net	1,890,000	990,000
Land	765,000	405,000
Total assets	$7,407,000	$2,493,000
Liabilities and Stockholders' Equity		
Accounts payable	$ 117,000	$ 135,000
Notes payable	90,000	108,000
Common stock—$45 par value	5,400,000	1,800,000
Retained earnings	1,800,000	450,000
Total liabilities and stockholders' equity	$7,407,000	$2,493,000

The excess of cost over book value is attributable to the above-average earnings prospects of Thorpe Company. On the date of acquisition, Thorpe Company borrowed $72,000 from Cord Company by giving a note.

Required

a. Prepare a work sheet for a consolidated balance sheet as of the date of acquisition.

b. Prepare a consolidated balance sheet for January 2, 1999.

Problem 14–6A
Prepare work sheet for
consolidated financial
statements (L.O. 5)

Refer to Problem 14–5A. Cord Company uses the equity method. Assume the following are from the adjusted trial balances of Cord Company and Thorpe Company on December 31, 1999:

	Cord Company	Thorpe Company
Debit Balance Accounts		
Cash	$ 351,000	$ 315,000
Accounts receivable, net	378,000	180,000
Notes receivable	315,000	45,000
Merchandise inventory, December 31	495,000	287,100
Investment in Thorpe Company	2,790,000	
Equipment, net	615,600	427,500
Buildings, net	1,814,400	950,400
Land	765,000	405,000
Cost of goods sold	1,800,000	630,000
Expenses (excluding depreciation and taxes)	720,000	270,900
Depreciation expense	108,000	62,100
Income tax expense	585,000	189,000
Dividends	540,000	108,000
Total of the accounts with debit balances	$11,277,000	$3,870,000
Credit Balance Accounts		
Accounts payable	$ 135,000	$ 180,000
Notes payable	144,000	90,000
Common stock—$45 par value	5,400,000	1,800,000
Retained earnings—January 1	1,800,000	450,000
Revenue from sales	3,600,000	1,350,000
Income of Thorpe Company	198,000	
Total of the accounts with credit balances	$11,277,000	$3,870,000

There is no intercompany debt at the end of the year.

Prepare a work sheet for consolidated financial statements on December 31, 1999. Ignore the amortization of goodwill.

Required

Using the work sheet from Problem 14–6A, prepare the following items:

a. Consolidated income statement for the year ended December 31, 1999.

b. Consolidated statement of retained earnings for the year ended December 31, 1999.

c. Consolidated balance sheet for December 31, 1999.

Problem 14–7A
Prepare consolidated income statement, statement of retained earnings, and balance sheet (L.O. 5)

Select the best answer to each of the following questions:

Problem 14–8A
Answer multiple-choice questions regarding international accounting (based on appendix) (L.O. 8)

1. Methods used to account for transactions between companies in different nations when goods are received on one date and the invoice is paid on another date include:
   a. Time-of-transaction method.
   b. Time-of-settlement method.
   c. Current-rate method.
   d. **a** and **b** are correct.

2. Which of the following statements is false regarding translating the financial statements of foreign subsidiaries?
   a. Under the *current-rate approach*, all assets and liabilities are translated at the exchange rate in effect on the balance sheet date.
   b. Under the *current-noncurrent method*, current assets and current liabilities are translated at the current rate, and noncurrent items are translated at their historical rates.
   c. Under the *monetary-nonmonetary* method, nonmonetary assets and liabilities are translated at their historical rate.
   d. The nations of the world now have settled on the current-rate method.

3. Variations between nations in accounting for inventories include all *except* which of the following?
   a. The basis for determining cost.
   b. Whether cost should be increased or decreased to reflect changes in market value.
   c. Whether inventories should be written down to an amount below both cost and market.
   d. Whether standard costs should be used.

4. In accounting for the effects of inflation, the approach that seems to be favored by most nations that have adopted an approach is:
   a. Current cost.
   b. Constant dollar (general price-level) adjusted statements.
   c. A combination of **a** and **b** in one set of financial statements.
   d. Both **a** and **b** as two sets of financial statements.

BEYOND THE NUMBERS—CRITICAL THINKING

You are the CPA engaged to audit the records of Quigley Company. You find that your client has a portfolio of marketable equity securities that has a total market value of $300,000 less than the total cost of the portfolio. You ask the vice president for finance if the client expects to sell these securities in the coming year. He answers that he doesn't know. The securities will be sold if additional cash is needed to finance operations. When you ask for a cash forecast, you are told that a forecast has been prepared that covers the next year. It indicates no need to sell the marketable securities.

Business Decision Case 14–1
Classify a portfolio of marketable equity securities as current or noncurrent investments (L.O. 1)

Write a brief statement in which you explain how you would classify the client's portfolio of marketable securities in the balance sheet. Does it really make any difference whether the securities are classified as trading securities or available-for-sale securities? Explain.

Required

**Business Decision
Case 14–2**
Prepare a consolidated
balance sheet at acquisition
(L.O. 5)

On January 2, 1999, Brown Company acquired 60% of the voting common stock of Cobb Company for $720,000 cash. The excess of cost over book value was due to above-average earnings prospects. Brown has hired you to help it prepare consolidated financial statements and has already collected the following information for both companies as of January 2, 1999:

	Brown Company	Cobb Company
Assets		
Cash	$ 72,000	$ 54,000
Accounts receivable, net	108,000	126,000
Merchandise inventory	288,000	216,000
Investment in Cobb Company	720,000	
Plant and equipment, net	936,000	738,000
Total assets	$2,124,000	$1,134,000
Liabilities and Stockholders' Equity		
Accounts payable	$ 144,000	$ 54,000
Common stock	1,440,000	720,000
Retained earnings	540,000	360,000
Total liabilities and stockholders' equity	$2,124,000	$1,134,000

Required

a. Brown believes that consolidated financial statements can be prepared simply by adding together the amounts in the two individual columns. Is this correct? If not, why not?

b. Prepare a consolidated balance sheet for the date of acquisition without preparing a consolidated statement work sheet.

**Business Decision
Case 14–3**
Compute the dividend yield
on common stock and the
payout ratios. Analyze
ratios (L.O. 8)

International Flavors & Fragrances, Inc., is the leading creator and manufacturer of flavors and fragrances used by others to impart or improve flavor or fragrance in a wide variety of consumer products.

Use the following excerpt from International Flavors & Fragrances Inc.'s 1995 annual report to calculate the dividend yield on common stock and the payout ratios. Then comment on the results.

	1995	1994	1993
Earnings per share	$ 2.24	$ 2.03	$ 1.78
Dividends per share ($)	1.24	1.08	1.00
Stock price per common share ($)	48.00	46.25	39.38

**Annual Report
Analysis 14–4**
Determine effect of differences between U.K. GAAP
and U.S. GAAP on net
income (Appendix)

Refer to the Reuters's annual report excerpt in "A Broader Perspective" on page 522. In writing, explain how the differences between the U.K. and the U.S. GAAP would affect Reuters's net income.

Group Project 14–5
Determine gain or loss on
short-term investments

In teams of two or three students, select three companies you believe may be profitable short-term investments. Determine the current market prices for those companies' stocks from today's newspaper and the market prices six months ago. Calculate the gain or loss that your team would have recorded if it had purchased 500 shares of each company's stock six months ago and sold all of the shares today. Write a short memo to your instructor describing why you selected those companies and why you believe the market prices of their stocks increased or decreased. Also, be prepared to describe your analysis to the class.

Group Project 14–6
Library Project—Investi-
gate consolidation standard

With one or two other students, go to the library and locate *Statement of Financial Standards No. 94*, "Consolidation of All Majority-Owned Subsidiaries," published by the Financial Accounting Standard Board. In a report to your instructor answer questions such as: What does the standard require? Why did the FASB act on this topic? Why are "nonhomogeneous" subsidiaries included in the consolidated group? Why did one of the Board members dissent from the statement? Describe some of the important background on this topic as given in the statement.

In a small group of students, locate the annual reports of three companies with investments in other companies. Compare the accounting and reporting for the investments by the three companies. For instance, by reading the notes to the financial statements, try to determine whether they account for the investments using the cost or equity methods. Is there goodwill on the balance sheets? How much of the goodwill is amortized for each of the last two years? What else can you determine about the investments? Write a report to your instructor summarizing your findings.

Group Project 14–7
Analyze annual reports of companies with investments in other companies

Using the Internet—A View of the Real World

Visit the following website for General Electric Company:
http://www.ge.com
Pursue choices on the screen until you locate the consolidated balance sheet. You will probably go down some "false paths" to get to this financial statement, but you can get there. This experience is all part of learning to use the Internet. Check to see if there is a minority interest listed on the consolidated balance sheet. Check out the notes to the financial statements for further information. Browse around the site for any other interesting information concerning the company. Write a memo to your instructor summarizing your findings.

Internet Project 14–8
Investigate a consolidated balance sheet

Visit the following website for the European Accounting Association:
http://www.bham.ac.uk/business/eaacong.html
Browse around this site for any interesting information regarding the activities and programs of the organization. With calls for increased cooperation among nations in further harmonizing international accounting standards, we should know more about accounting activities in foreign nations. Write a report to your instructor on what you learned about the European

Internet Project 14–9
Visit a foreign website

Answers to Self-Test

True-False

1. **False.** Under the cost method of accounting for stock investments, the Dividend Revenue account, rather than the investment account, is adjusted.

2. **True.** For long-term investments of less than 20%, the cost method should be used.

3. **True.** Revenue is not recognized when there is a stock split. The new number of shares is recorded, and the cost per share is reduced.

4. **True.** Trading securities should be considered separately from available-for-sale securities in applying the fair market value method.

5. **True.** Eliminating entries are not made on the accounting records of the parent and subsidiary. Only the work sheet is affected by elimination entries made during consolidation.

6. **False.** The IASC can only recommend specific practices and procedures for adoption by member nations.

Multiple-Choice

1. **c.** The Accounting Principles Board has said that investors must use the equity method when accounting for long-term investments of 20% to 50%.

2. **a.** Under the equity method, dividends received reduce the investment account; the other choices are not true.

3. **d.** If the market value of securities falls below their cost, an unrealized loss account is debited.

4. **b.** Under the equity method, the investment account always reflects the investor's interest in the net assets of the investee.

5. **a.** If cost is greater than the book value of an investment because of expected above-average earnings, *APB Opinion No. 16* tells us that the excess cost should be labeled goodwill.

6. **a.** The move from communism toward democracy is causing East European nations and certain other nations to pursue market-oriented economies.

15

LONG-TERM FINANCING
BONDS

LEARNING OBJECTIVES

After studying this chapter, you should be able to:

1. Describe the features of bonds and tell how bonds differ from shares of stock.

2. List the advantages and disadvantages of financing with long-term debt and prepare examples showing how to employ financial leverage.

3. Prepare journal entries for bonds issued at face value.

4. Explain how interest rates affect bond prices and what causes a bond to sell at a premium or a discount.

(continued)

In previous chapters, you learned that corporations obtain cash for recurring business operations from stock issuances, profitable operations, and short-term borrowing (current liabilities). However, when situations arise that require large amounts of cash, such as the purchase of a building, corporations also raise cash from long-term borrowing, that is, by issuing bonds. The issuing of bonds results in a Bonds Payable account.

BONDS PAYABLE

A **bond** is a long-term debt, or liability, owed by its issuer. Physical evidence of the debt lies in a negotiable *bond certificate.* In contrast to long-term notes, which usually mature in 10 years or less, bond maturities often run for 20 years or more.

Generally, a bond issue consists of a large number of $1,000 bonds rather than one large bond. For example, a company seeking to borrow $100,000 would issue one hundred $1,000 bonds rather than one $100,000 bond. This practice enables investors with less cash to invest to purchase some of the bonds.

Bonds derive their value primarily from two promises made by the borrower to the lender or bondholder. The borrower promises to pay (1) the **face value** or principal amount of the bond on a specific maturity date in the future and (2) periodic interest at a specified rate on face value at stated dates, usually semiannually, until the maturity date.

Large companies often have numerous long-term notes and bond issues outstanding at any one time. The various issues generally have different stated interest rates and mature at different points in the future. Companies present this information in the footnotes to their financial statements. Illustration 15.1 shows a portion of the long-term borrowings footnote from Dow Chemical Company's 1995 annual report. Promissory notes, debenture bonds, and foreign bonds are shown, with their amounts, maturity dates, and interest rates.

Promissory Notes and Debentures at December 31, 1995

	(Millions)	
	1995	**1994**
4.63%, final maturity 1995	$ —	$ 150
8.25%, final maturity 1996	150	150
5.75%, final maturity 1997	197	200
5.75%, final maturity 2001	—	15
7.38%, final maturity 2002	145	150
9.35%, final maturity 2002	194	200
7.13%, final maturity 2003	148	150
8.63%, final maturity 2006	187	200
8.55%, final maturity 2009	140	150
9.00%, final maturity 2010	125	150
9.20%, final maturity 2010	193	200
6.85%, final maturity 2013	138	150
7.13%, final maturity 2015	—	24
9.00%, final maturity 2021	219	300
8.85%, final maturity 2021	188	200
8.70%, final maturity 2022	96	138
7.38%, final maturity 2023	150	150
Subtotal	$2,270	$2,677

Foreign Bonds at December 31, 1995

	(Millions)	
	1995	**1994**
6.75%, final maturity 1995, German mark	$ —	$ 194
5.63%, final maturity 1996, German mark	209	194
10.87%, final maturity 1997, British pound sterling	345	374
4.00%, final maturity 1998, Japanese yen	194	201
4.75%, final maturity 1999, Swiss franc	173	152
4.63%, final maturity 2000, Swiss franc	130	114
6.38%, final maturity 2001, Japanese yen	242	251
Subtotal	$1,293	$1,480

ILLUSTRATION 15.1
Dow Chemical Company's Long-Term Notes and Bonds (in millions)

Dow Chemical Company
Dow Chemical Company is the fifth largest chemical company in the world, with annual sales of more than $20 billion.

Comparison with Stock

A bond differs from a share of stock in several ways:

1. A bond is a debt or liability of the issuer, while a share of stock is a unit of ownership.
2. A bond has a maturity date when it must be paid. A share of stock does not mature; stock remains outstanding indefinitely unless the company decides to retire it.
3. Most bonds require stated periodic interest payments by the company. In contrast, dividends to stockholders are payable only when declared; even preferred dividends need not be paid in a particular period if the board of directors so decides.
4. Bond interest is deductible by the issuer in computing both net income and taxable income, while dividends are not deductible in either computation.

Selling (Issuing) Bonds

A company seeking to borrow millions of dollars generally is not able to borrow from a single lender. By selling (issuing) bonds to the public, the company secures the necessary funds.

Usually companies sell their bond issues through an investment company or a banker called an **underwriter.** The underwriter performs many tasks for the bond issuer, such as advertising, selling, and delivering the bonds to the purchasers. Often the underwriter guarantees the issuer a fixed price for the bonds, expecting to earn a profit by selling the bonds for more than the fixed price.

(*concluded*)

5. Apply the concept of present value to compute the price of a bond.

6. Prepare journal entries for bonds issued at a discount or a premium.

7. Prepare journal entries for bond redemptions and bond conversions.

8. Describe the ratings used for bonds.

9. Analyze and use the financial results—times interest earned ratio.

10. Explain future value and present value concepts and make required calculations (Appendix).

Objective 1
Describe the features of
bonds and tell how bonds
differ from shares of stock.

Note to the Student
Look in *The Wall Street Journal* for
advertisements for bond issues.

When a company sells bonds to the public, many purchasers buy the bonds. Rather than deal with each purchaser individually, the issuing company appoints a *trustee* to represent the bondholders. The **trustee** usually is a bank or trust company. The main duty of the trustee is to see that the borrower fulfills the provisions of the *bond indenture*. A **bond indenture** is the contract or loan agreement under which the bonds are issued. The indenture deals with matters such as the interest rate, maturity date and maturity amount, possible restrictions on dividends, repayment plans, and other provisions relating to the debt. An issuing company that does not adhere to the bond indenture provisions is in default. Then, the trustee takes action to force the issuer to comply with the indenture.

Characteristics of Bonds

Bonds may differ in some respects; they may be secured or unsecured bonds, registered or unregistered (bearer) bonds, and term or serial bonds. We discuss these differences next.

Certain bond features are matters of legal necessity, such as how a company pays interest and transfers ownership. Such features usually do not affect the issue price of the bonds. Other features, such as convertibility into common stock, are *sweeteners* designed to make the bonds more attractive to potential purchasers. These sweeteners may increase the issue price of a bond.

SECURED BONDS   A **secured bond** is a bond for which a company has pledged specific property to ensure its payment. Mortgage bonds are the most common secured bonds. A **mortgage** is a legal claim (lien) on specific property that gives the bondholder the right to possess the pledged property if the company fails to make required payments.

UNSECURED BONDS   An **unsecured bond** is a **debenture bond,** or simply a *debenture*. A debenture is an unsecured bond backed only by the general creditworthiness of the issuer, not by a lien on any specific property. A financially sound company can issue debentures more easily than a company experiencing financial difficulty.

REGISTERED BONDS   A **registered bond** is a bond with the owner's name on the bond certificate and in the register of bond owners kept by the bond issuer or its agent, the registrar. Bonds may be registered as to principal (or face value of the bond) or as to both principal and interest. Most bonds in our economy are registered as to principal only. For a bond registered as to both principal and interest, the issuer pays the bond interest by check. To transfer ownership of registered bonds, the owner endorses the bond and registers it in the new owner's name. Therefore, owners can easily replace lost or stolen registered bonds.

UNREGISTERED (BEARER) BONDS   An **unregistered (bearer) bond** is the property of its holder or bearer because the owner's name does not appear on the bond certificate or in a separate record. Physical delivery of the bond transfers ownership.

COUPON BONDS   A **coupon bond** is a bond not registered as to interest. Coupon bonds carry detachable coupons for the interest they pay. At the end of each interest period, the owner clips the coupon for the period and presents it to a stated party, usually a bank, for collection.

TERM BONDS AND SERIAL BONDS   A **term bond** matures on the same date as all other bonds in a given bond issue. **Serial bonds** in a given bond issue have maturities spread over several dates. For instance, one-fourth of the bonds may mature on December 31, 2000, another one-fourth on December 31, 2001, and so on.

CALLABLE BONDS   A **callable bond** contains a provision that gives the issuer the right to call (buy back) the bond before its maturity date. The provision is similar to the call provision of some preferred stocks. A company is likely to exercise this call right when its outstanding bonds bear interest at a much higher rate than the company would have to pay if it issued new but similar bonds. The exercise of the call provision normally requires the company to pay the bondholder a call premium of about $30 to $70 per $1,000 bond. A **call premium** is the price paid in excess of face value that the issuer of bonds must pay to redeem (call) bonds before their maturity date.

CONVERTIBLE BONDS   A **convertible bond** is a bond that may be exchanged for shares of stock of the issuing corporation at the bondholder's option. A convertible bond has a stipulated conversion rate of some number of shares for each $1,000 bond. Although any type of bond may be convertible, issuers add this feature to make risky debenture bonds more attractive to investors.

BONDS WITH STOCK WARRANTS   A **stock warrant** allows the bondholder to purchase shares of common stock at a fixed price for a stated period. Warrants issued with long-term debt may be nondetachable or detachable. A bond with *nondetachable warrants* is virtually the same as a convertible bond; the holder must surrender the bond to acquire the common stock. *Detachable warrants* allow bondholders to keep their bonds and still purchase shares of stock through exercise of the warrants.

JUNK BONDS   **Junk bonds** are high-interest rate, high-risk bonds. Many junk bonds issued in the 1980s financed corporate restructurings. These restructurings took the form of management buyouts (called leveraged buyouts or LBOs), hostile takeovers of companies by outside parties, or friendly takeovers of companies by outside parties. In the early 1990s, junk bonds lost favor because many issuers defaulted on their interest payments. Some issuers declared bankruptcy or sought relief from the bondholders by negotiating new debt terms.

BUSINESS INSIGHT   Eastman Chemical Company is an international chemical company with headquarters in Kingsport, Tennessee. The company produces a wide range of plastics, chemicals, and fibers. Eastman is the world leader in polyester plastics for packaging. The following note pertaining to debenture bonds was contained in the company's 1995 annual report.

In first quarter 1994, Eastman issued $1 billion of long-term debt securities and repaid existing borrowings under the Credit Agreement. The issuance included $500 million of 6⅜% notes due 2004 and $500 million of 7¼% debentures due 2024. In second quarter 1994, Eastman issued an additional $200 million of 7⅝% debentures due 2024. The 7⅝% debentures may be redeemed June 15, 2006, at the option of their registered holders, at 100% of the principal amount plus accrued interest to that date.

AN ACCOUNTING PERSPECTIVE

Several advantages come from raising cash by issuing bonds rather than stock. First, the current stockholders do not have to dilute or surrender their control of the company when funds are obtained by borrowing rather than issuing more shares of stock. Second, it may be less expensive to issue debt rather than additional stock because the interest payments made to bondholders are tax deductible while dividends are not. Finally, probably the most important reason to issue bonds is that the use of debt may increase the earnings of stockholders through favorable financial leverage.

Advantages of Issuing Debt

Objective 2
List the advantages and disadvantages of financing with long-term debt and prepare examples showing how to employ financial leverage.

FAVORABLE FINANCIAL LEVERAGE   A company has **favorable financial leverage** when it uses borrowed funds to increase earnings per share (EPS) of common stock. An increase in EPS usually results from earning a higher rate of return than the rate of interest paid for the borrowed money. For example, suppose a company borrowed money at 10% and earned a 15% rate of return. The 5% difference increases earnings.

ILLUSTRATION 15.2
Favorable Financial
Leverage

Note to the Student
Financial leverage results from the difference between the cost of borrowed funds and the rate of return earned with those funds. Favorable financial leverage exists when the rate of return is higher than the cost of the borrowed money.

COMPANIES A AND B CONDENSED STATEMENTS
Balance Sheets
December 31, 1999

	Company A	Company B
Total assets	$20,000,000	$20,000,000
Bonds payable, 10%		$10,000,000
Stockholders' equity (capital stock)	$20,000,000	10,000,000
Total equities	$20,000,000	$20,000,000

Income Statements
For the Year Ended December 31, 1999

	Company A	Company B
Income from operations	$ 4,000,000	$ 4,000,000
Interest expense		1,000,000
Income before federal income taxes	$ 4,000,000	$ 3,000,000
Deduct: Federal income taxes (40%)	1,600,000	1,200,000
Net income	$ 2,400,000	$ 1,800,000
Number of common shares outstanding	2,000,000	1,000,000
Earnings per share (EPS) (Net income ÷ Number of common shares outstanding)	$1.20	$1.80
Rate of return on assets employed (Income from operations ÷ Total assets; both companies $4,000,000/$20,000,000)	20%	20%
Rate of return on stockholders' equity (Net income ÷ Stockholders' equity):		
Company A ($2,400,000/$20,000,000)	12%	
Company B ($1,800,000/$10,000,000)		18%

Illustration 15.2 provides a more comprehensive example of favorable financial leverage. The two companies in the illustration are identical in every respect except in the way they are financed. Company A issued only capital stock, while Company B issued equal amounts of 10% bonds and capital stock. Both companies have $20,000,000 of assets, and both earned $4,000,000 of income from operations. If we divide income from operations by assets ($4,000,000 ÷ $20,000,000), we see that both companies earned 20% on assets employed. Yet B's stockholders fared far better than A's. The ratio of net income to stockholders' equity is 18% for B, while it is only 12% for A.

Assume that both companies issued their stock at the beginning of 1999 at $10 per share. B's $1.80 EPS are 50% greater than A's $1.20 EPS. This EPS difference probably would cause B's shares to sell at a substantially higher market price than A's shares. B's larger EPS would also allow a larger dividend on B's shares.

Company B in Illustration 15.2 is employing financial leverage, or **trading on the equity.** The company is using its stockholders' equity as a basis for securing funds on which it pays a fixed return. Company B expects to earn more from the use of such funds than their fixed after-tax cost. As a result, Company B increases its rate of return on stockholders' equity and EPS.[1]

Disadvantages of Issuing Debt

Several disadvantages accompany the use of debt financing. First, the borrower has a fixed interest payment that must be met each period to avoid default. Second, use of debt also reduces a company's ability to withstand a major loss. For example, assume that instead of having net income, both Company A and Company B in Illustration 15.2 sustain a net loss in 1999 of $11,000,000. At the end of 1999, Company A will still have $9,000,000 of stockholders' equity and can continue operations with a

---

[1]Issuing bonds is only one method of using leverage. Other methods of using financial leverage include issuing preferred stock or long-term notes.

chance of recovery. Company B, on the other hand, would have negative stockholders' equity of $1,000,000 and the bondholders could force the company to liquidate if B could not make interest payments as they came due. The result of sustaining the loss by the two companies is as follows:

COMPANIES A AND B
Partial Balance Sheets
December 31, 1999

	Company A	Company B
Stockholders' equity:		
Paid-in capital:		
Common stock	$ 20,000,000	$ 10,000,000
Retained earnings	(11,000,000)	(11,000,000)
Total stockholders' equity	$ 9,000,000	$ (1,000,000)

A third disadvantage of debt financing is that it also causes a company to experience unfavorable financial leverage when income from operations falls below a certain level. **Unfavorable financial leverage** results when the cost of borrowed funds exceeds the revenue they generate; it is the reverse of *favorable financial leverage*. In the previous example, if income from operations fell to $1,000,000, the rates of return on stockholders' equity would be 3% for A and zero for B, as shown in this schedule:

COMPANIES A AND B
Income Statements
For the Year Ended December 31, 1999

	Company A	Company B
Income from operations	$1,000,000	$1,000,000
Interest expense		1,000,000
Income before federal income taxes	$1,000,000	$ –0–
Deduct: Federal income taxes (40%)	400,000	–0–
Net income	$ 600,000	$ –0–
Rate of return on stockholders' equity:		
Company A ($600,000/$20,000,000)	3%	
Company B ($0/$10,000,000)		0%

The fourth disadvantage of issuing debt is that loan agreements often require maintaining a certain amount of working capital (Current assets − Current liabilities) and place limitations on dividends and additional borrowings.

Reinforcing Problem
BDC15–1 Analyze two financing proposals; decide whether investment should be made.

Accounting for Bonds Issued at Face Value

When a company issues bonds, it incurs a long-term liability on which periodic interest payments must be made, usually twice a year. If interest dates fall on other than balance sheet dates, the company must accrue interest in the proper periods. The following examples illustrate the accounting for bonds issued at face value on an interest date and issued at face value between interest dates.

BONDS ISSUED AT FACE VALUE ON AN INTEREST DATE Valley Company's accounting year ends on December 31. On December 31, 1999, Valley issued 10-year, 12% bonds with a $100,000 face value, for $100,000. The bonds are dated December 31, 1999, call for semiannual interest payments on June 30 and December 31, and mature on December 31, 2009. Valley made the required interest and principal payments when due. The entries for the 10 years are as follows:

Objective 3
Prepare journal entries for bonds issued at face value.

On December 31, 1999, the date of issuance, the entry is:

1999					
Dec.	31	Cash		100,000	
		Bonds Payable			100,000
		To record bonds issued at face value.			

On each June 30 and December 31 for 10 years, beginning June 30, 2000 (ending June 30, 2009), the entry would be:

Each year June and Dec.	30 31	Bond Interest Expense ($100,000 × 0.12 × ½) . . . . Cash . . . . To record periodic interest payment.	6,000	6,000

On December 31, 2009, the maturity date, the entry would be:

2009 Dec.	31	Bond Interest Expense. . . . . Bonds Payable . . . . Cash . . . . To record final interest and bond redemption payment.	6,000 100,000	106,000

Note that Valley does not need adjusting entries because the interest payment date falls on the last day of the accounting period. The income statement for each of the 10 years 2000–2009 would show Bond Interest Expense of $12,000 ($6,000 × 2); the balance sheet at the end of each of the years 1999–2007 would report bonds payable of $100,000 in long-term liabilities. At the end of 2008, Valley would reclassify the bonds as a current liability because they will be paid within the next year.

The real world is more complicated. For example, assume the Valley bonds were dated October 31, 1999, issued on that same date, and pay interest each April 30 and October 31. Valley must make an adjusting entry on December 31 to accrue interest for November and December. That entry would be:

1999 Dec.	31	Bond Interest Expense ($100,000 × 0.12 × 2/12) . . . . Bond Interest Payable . . . . To accrue two months' interest expense.	2,000	2,000

The April 30, 2000, entry would be:

2000 Apr.	30	Bond Interest Expense ($100,000 × 0.12 × 4/12) . . . . Bond Interest Payable . . . . Cash . . . . To record semiannual interest payment.	4,000 2,000	6,000

The October 31, 2000, entry would be:

2000 Oct.	31	Bond Interest Expense. . . . . Cash . . . . To record semiannual interest payment.	6,000	6,000

Each year Valley would make similar entries for the semiannual payments and the year-end accrued interest. The firm would report the $2,000 Bond Interest Payable as a current liability on the December 31 balance sheet for each year.

Bonds Issued at Face Value between Interest Dates   Companies do not always issue bonds on the date they start to bear interest. Regardless of when the bonds are physically issued, interest starts to accrue from the most recent interest date. Firms report bonds to be selling at a stated price "plus accrued interest." The issuer must pay holders of the bonds a full six months' interest at each interest date.

Thus, investors purchasing bonds after the bonds begin to accrue interest must pay the seller for the unearned interest accrued since the preceding interest date. The bondholders are reimbursed for this accrued interest when they receive their first six months' interest check.

Using the facts for the Valley bonds dated December 31, 1999, suppose Valley issued its bonds on May 31, 2000, instead of on December 31, 1999. The entry required is:

2000					
May	31	Cash	105,000	
		Bonds Payable		100,000
		Bond Interest Payable ($100,000 × 0.12 × 5/12)		5,000
		To record bonds issued at face value plus accrued interest.		

This entry records the $5,000 received for the accrued interest as a debit to Cash and a credit to Bond Interest Payable.

The entry required on June 30, 2000, when the full six months' interest is paid, is:

2000					
June	30	Bond Interest Expense ($100,000 × 0.12 × 1/12)	1,000	
		Bond Interest Payable	5,000	
		Cash		6,000
		To record bond interest payment.		

This entry records $1,000 interest expense on the $100,000 of bonds that were outstanding for one month. Valley collected $5,000 from the bondholders on May 31 as accrued interest and is now returning it to them.

Reinforcing Problem
E15–1 Record issuances of bonds at face value, adjusting entry, and payment of interest.

BOND PRICES AND INTEREST RATES

The price of a bond issue often differs from its face value. The amount a bond sells for above face value is a **premium.** The amount a bond sells for below face value is a **discount.** A difference between face value and issue price exists whenever the market rate of interest for similar bonds differs from the contract rate of interest on the bonds. The **market interest rate** (also called the effective rate or yield) is the minimum rate of interest that investors accept on bonds of a particular risk category. The higher the risk category, the higher the minimum rate of interest that investors accept. The **contract rate of interest** is also called the *stated, coupon,* or *nominal rate.* Firms state this rate in the bond indenture, print it on the face of each bond, and use it to determine the amount of cash paid each interest period. The market rate fluctuates from day to day, responding to factors such as the interest rate the Federal Reserve Board charges banks to borrow from it; government actions to finance the national debt; and the supply of, and demand for, money.

Market and contract rates of interest are likely to differ. Issuers must set the contract rate before the bonds are actually sold to allow time for such activities as printing the bonds. Assume, for instance, that the contract rate for a bond issue is set at 12%. If the market rate is equal to the contract rate, the bonds will sell at their face value. However, by the time the bonds are sold, the market rate could be higher or lower than the contract rate. As shown in Illustration 15.3, if the market rate is lower than the contract rate, the bonds will sell for more than their face value. Thus, if the market rate is 10% and the contract rate is 12%, the bonds will sell at a premium as the result of investors bidding up their price. However, if the market rate is higher than the contract rate, the bonds will sell for less than their face value. Thus, if the market rate is 14% and the contract rate is 12%, the bonds will sell at a discount. Investors are not interested in bonds bearing a contract rate less than the market rate

Objective 4
Explain how interest rates affect bond prices and what causes a bond to sell at a premium or a discount.

Note to the Student
In *The Wall Street Journal,* examine the details concerning several different corporate bonds.

Real-World Example
AT&T has a bond due in 2024. The contract rate is 8⅛% and the market rate was 7.4% on the date of issue. Since the contract rate is higher than the market rate, the bond sold at $110, 10% over its face value.

ILLUSTRATION 15.3
Bond Premiums and
Discounts

	Market Rate	Contract Rate
Bonds sell at a *premium* if Market rate < Contract rate	10%	12%
Bonds sell at *face value* if Market rate = Contract rate	12%	12%
Bonds sell at a *discount* if Market rate > Contract rate	14%	12%

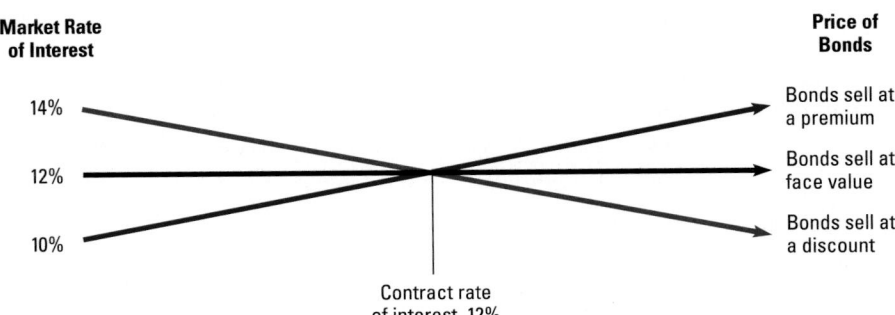

Real World Example
The Wall Street Journal of Friday, June 27, 1997, reported that "The 30-year bellwether Treasury Bond fell 17/32 point, or $5.3125 per $1,000 bond, as the yield rate rose to 6.77%." Thus, when bond prices fall, their yield rates rise.

unless the price is reduced. Selling bonds at a premium or a discount allows the purchasers of the bonds to earn the market rate of interest on their investment.

Computing Bond Prices

Objective 5
Apply the concept of present value to compute the price of a bond.

Computing long-term bond prices involves finding **present values** using compound interest. The appendix to this chapter explains the concepts of future value and present value. If you do not understand the present value concept, read the appendix before continuing with this section.

Buyers and sellers negotiate a price that yields the going rate of interest for bonds of a particular risk class. The price investors pay for a given bond issue is equal to the present value of the bonds. To compute present value, we discount the promised cash flows from the bonds—principal and interest—using the market, or effective, rate. We use the market rate because the bonds must yield at least this rate or investors are attracted to alternative investments. The life of the bonds is stated in interest (compounding) periods. The interest rate is the effective rate per interest period, which is found by dividing the annual rate by the number of times interest is paid per year. For example, if the annual rate is 12%, the semiannual rate would be 6%.

Issuers usually quote bond prices as percentages of face value—100 means 100% of face value, 97 means 97% of face value, and 103 means 103% of face value. For example, one hundred $1,000 face value bonds issued at 103 have a price of $103,000. Regardless of the issue price, at maturity the issuer of the bonds must pay the investor(s) the face value of the bonds.

BONDS ISSUED AT FACE VALUE   The following example illustrates the specific steps in computing the price of bonds. Assume Carr Company issues 12% bonds with a $100,000 face value to yield 12%. Dated and issued on June 30, 1999, the bonds call for semiannual interest payments on June 30 and December 31 and mature on June 30, 2002.[2] The bonds would sell at face value because they offer 12% and investors

---

[2]Bonds do not normally mature in such a short time; we use a three-year life for illustrative purposes only.

seek 12%. Potential purchasers have no reason to offer a premium or demand a discount. One way to prove the bonds would be sold at face value is by showing that their present value is $100,000:

	Cash Flow	Present Value × Factor =	Present Value
Principal of $100,000 due in six interest periods multiplied by present value factor for 6% from Table A.3 of the Appendix (end of text)	$100,000 × 0.70496 =		$ 70,496
Interest of $6,000 due at end of each of six interest periods multiplied by present value factor for 6% from Table A.4 of the Appendix (end of text)	6,000 × 4.91732 =		29,504
Total price (present value)			$100,000

According to this schedule, investors who seek an effective rate of 6% per six-month period should pay $100,000 for these bonds. Notice that the same number of interest periods and semiannual interest rates occur in discounting both the principal and interest payments to their present values. The entry to record the sale of these bonds on June 30, 1999, debits Cash and credits Bonds Payable for $100,000.

BUSINESS INSIGHT   Some persons estimate that Social Security will be broke by the year 2025 unless changes are made. Therefore, you may want to set aside funds during your working career to provide for retirement.

Over the last 60 years, the inflation rate has averaged about 3% per year, treasury bills have averaged a little under 4% per year, corporate bonds have averaged about a little over 5% per year, and stocks have averaged a little over 10% per year. Using the tables at the end of the text we can determine how much you would have at age 65 if you invested $2,000 each year for 45 years in treasury bills, corporate bonds, or stocks, beginning at age 20.

To do this calculation for treasury bills, for instance, we would first use Table A.2 to determine the future value of an annuity of $2,000 for 30 periods at 4% ($2,000 × 56.08494 = $112,170). (We would have used 45 periods, but the table only went up to 30 periods.) Then we would use Table A.1 to find the value of this lump sum of $112,170 for another 15 years at 4% ($112,170 × 1.80094 = $202,011). Then we cannot forget that we have another 15 years of $2,000 annuity to consider. Thus, we go back to Table A.2 and calculate the future value of an annuity of $2,000 for 15 periods at 4% ($2,000 × 20.02359 = $40,047). Then we add the $202,011 and the $40,047 to get the total future value of $242,058. (You would have invested $2,000 × 45 years = $90,000.) Would you be pleased? Not when you see what you could have had at age 65 if you invested in stocks.

If you had invested in corporate bonds at 5%, you would have $319,401. However, if you had invested in stocks at 10%, you would have $1,437,810 at age 65. Can you use the tables in the back of the text to verify these amounts?

AN ACCOUNTING PERSPECTIVE

BONDS ISSUED AT A DISCOUNT   Assume the $100,000, 12% Carr bonds are sold to yield a current market rate of 14% annual interest, or 7% per semiannual period. Carr computes the present value (selling price) of the bonds as follows:

	Cash Flow	Present Value × Factor =	Present Value
Principal of $100,000 due in six interest periods multiplied by present value factor for 7% from Table A.3, Appendix (end of text)	$100,000 × 0.66634 =		$66,634
Interest of $6,000 due at end of each of six interest periods multiplied by present value factor for 7% from Table A.4, Appendix (end of text)	6,000 × 4.76654 =		28,599
Total price (present value)			$95,233

Objective 6
Prepare journal entries for
bonds issued at a discount
or a premium.

Reinforcing Problem
E15–2 Compute bond interest
expense; show how bond price was
determined.

Note that in computing the present value of the bonds, Carr uses the actual $6,000 cash interest payment that will be made each period. The amount of cash the company pays as interest does not depend on the market interest rate. However, the market rate per semiannual period—7%—does change, and Carr uses this new rate to find interest factors in the tables.

The journal entry to record issuance of the bonds is:

1999				
June	30	Cash	95,233	
		Discount on Bonds Payable.	4,767	
		Bonds Payable		100,000
		To record bonds issued at a discount.		

In recording the bond issue, Carr credits Bonds Payable for the face value of the debt. The company debits the difference between face value and price received to Discount on Bonds Payable, a contra account to Bonds Payable. Carr reports the bonds payable and discount on bonds payable in the balance sheet as follows:

Long-term liabilities:
    Bonds payable, 12%, due June 30, 2000 . . . . $100,000
        Less: Discount on bonds payable 4,767 $95,233

The $95,233 is the carrying value, or *net liability*, of the bonds. **Carrying value** is the face value of the bonds minus any unamortized discount or plus any unamortized premium. The next section discusses unamortized premium on bonds payable.

BONDS ISSUED AT A PREMIUM   Assume that Carr issued the $100,000 face value of 12% bonds to yield a current market rate of 10%. The bonds would sell at a premium calculated as follows:

	Cash Flow	Present Value × Factor =	Present Value
Principal of $100,000 due in six interest periods multiplied by present value factor for 5% from Table A.3, Appendix (end of text)	$100,000 × 0.74622 =		$ 74,622
Interest of $6,000 due at end of each of six interest periods multiplied by present value factor for 5% from Table A.4, Appendix (end of text)	6,000 × 5.07569 =		30,454
Total price (present value)			$105,076

The journal entry to record the issuance of the bonds is:

1999				
June	30	Cash	105,076	
		Bonds Payable		100,000
		Premium on Bonds Payable.		5,076
		To record bonds issued at a premium.		

The carrying value of these bonds at issuance is $105,076, consisting of the face value of $100,000 and the premium of $5,076. The premium is an adjunct account shown on the balance sheet as an addition to bonds payable as follows:

Long-term liabilities:
    Bonds payable, 12%, due June 30, 2002 . . . . $100,000
        Add: Premium on bonds payable 5,076 $105,076

When a company issues bonds at a premium or discount, the amount of bond interest expense recorded each period differs from bond interest payments. A discount increases and a premium decreases the amount of interest expense. For example, if Carr issues bonds with a face value of $100,000 for $95,233, the total interest cost of borrowing would be $40,767: $36,000 (which is six payments of $6,000) plus the discount of $4,767. If the bonds had been issued at $105,076, the total interest cost of borrowing would be $30,924: $36,000 less the premium of $5,076. The $4,767 discount or $5,076 premium must be allocated or charged to the six periods that benefit from the use of borrowed money. Two methods are available for amortizing a discount or premium on bonds—the straight-line method and the effective interest rate method.

The straight-line method records interest expense at a *constant amount;* the effective interest rate method records interest expense at a *constant rate. APB Opinion No. 21* states that the straight-line method may be used only when it does not differ materially from the effective interest rate method. In many cases, the differences are not material.

Discount/Premium Amortization

BUSINESS INSIGHT   U.S. government bonds have traditionally offered a fixed rate of interest. In early 1997, the U.S. Treasury was scheduled to begin offering inflation-indexed bonds. The amount of interest on these bonds is tied to the officially reported rate of inflation. The bonds pay interest every six months, and the interest is based on the inflation-adjusted value of the principal. These bonds are designed to protect purchasers against purchasing power loss due to inflation. At that time, there was some concern by investors that the government had been considering calculating the official rate of inflation differently than in the past in such a way that it would lower the annual increase as compared to the then present method of calculation. This change in calculation, if adopted, would lower the amount of interest earned on these bonds. However, there were some assurances that for this purpose the official rate of inflation would be calculated the "old way."

AN ACCOUNTING PERSPECTIVE

THE STRAIGHT-LINE METHOD   The **straight-line method of amortization** allocates an equal amount of discount or premium to each month the bonds are outstanding. The issuer calculates the amount by dividing the discount or premium by the total number of months from the date of issuance to the maturity date. For example, if it sells $100,000 face value bonds for $95,233, Carr would charge the $4,767 discount to interest expense at a rate of $132.42 per month (equal to $4,767/36). Total discount amortization for six months would be $794.52, computed as follows: $132.42 × 6. Interest expense for each six-month period then would be $6,794.52, calculated as follows: $6,000 + ($132.42 × 6). The entry to record the expense on December 31, 1999, would be:

1999				
Dec.	31	Bond Interest Expense	6,794.52	
		Cash		6,000.00
		Discount on Bonds Payable ($132.42 × 6)		794.52
		To record interest payment and discount amortization.		

Reinforcing Problem
E15–3 Calculate interest using straight-line amortization.

By the maturity date, all of the discount would have been amortized.

To illustrate the straight-line method applied to a premium, recall that earlier Carr sold its $100,000 face value bonds for $105,076. Carr would amortize the $5,076 premium on these bonds at a rate of $141 per month, equal to $5,076/36. The entry for the first period's semiannual interest expense on bonds sold at a premium is:

1999				
Dec.	31	Bond Interest Expense.	5,154	
		Premium on Bonds Payable ($141 × 6).	846	
		Cash		6,000
		To record interest payment and premium amortization.		

By the maturity date, all of the premium would have been amortized.

THE EFFECTIVE INTEREST RATE METHOD *APB Opinion No. 21* recommends an amortization procedure called the **effective interest rate method,** or simply the **interest method.** Under the interest method, interest expense for any interest period is equal to the effective (market) rate of interest on the date of issuance times the carrying value of the bonds at the beginning of that interest period. Using the Carr example of 12% bonds with a face value of $100,000 sold to yield 14%, the carrying value at the beginning of the first interest period is the selling price of $95,233. Carr would record the interest expense for the first semiannual period as follows:

1999				
Dec.	31	Bond Interest Expense ($95,233 × 0.14 × ½).	6,666	
		Cash ($100,000 × 0.12 × ½).		6,000
		Discount on Bonds Payable.		666
		To record discount amortization and interest payment.		

Note that interest expense is the carrying value times the effective interest rate. The cash payment is the face value times the contract rate. The discount amortized for the period is the difference between the two amounts.

After the preceding entry, the carrying value of the bonds is $95,899, or $95,233 + $666. Carr reduced the balance in the Discount on Bonds Payable account by $666 to $4,101, or $4,767 − $666. Assuming the accounting year ends on December 31, the entry to record the payment of interest for the second semiannual period on June 30, 2000, is:

2000				
June	30	Bond Interest Expense ($95,899 × 0.14 × ½).	6,713	
		Cash ($100,000 × 0.12 × ½).		6,000
		Discount on Bonds Payable.		713
		To record discount amortization and interest payment.		

Carr can also apply the effective interest rate method to premium amortization. If the Carr bonds had been issued at $105,076 to yield 10%, the premium would be $5,076. The firm calculates interest expense in the same manner as for bonds sold at a discount. However, the entry would differ somewhat, showing a debit to the premium account. The entry for the first interest period is:

Reinforcing Problem
E15–4 Prepare entry to record interest payment.

1999				
Dec.	31	Bond Interest Expense ($105,076 × 0.10 × ½)	5,254	
		Premium on Bonds Payable	746	
		Cash ($100,000 × 0.12 × ½)		6,000
		To record interest payment and premium amortization.		

After the first entry, the carrying value of the bonds is $104,330, or $105,076 − $746. The premium account now carries a balance of $4,330, or $5,076 − $746. The entry for the second interest period is:

2000				
June	30	Bond Interest Expense ($104,330 × 0.10 × ½)	5,216*	
		Premium on Bonds Payable	784	
		Cash ($100,000 × 0.12 × ½)		6,000
		To record interest payment and premium amortization.		

*Rounded down.

BUSINESS INSIGHT   The differences between the straight-line method and effective interest method for amortizing a bond discount can be seen in the following graphic. The carrying values (CV) start at the same point and end at the same point under both methods. The total interest expense is the same under both methods. However, the interest expense and amortization of bond discount are at a constant **amount** each period under the straight-line method, and they are at a constant **rate** under the effective interest rate method.

AN ACCOUNTING PERSPECTIVE

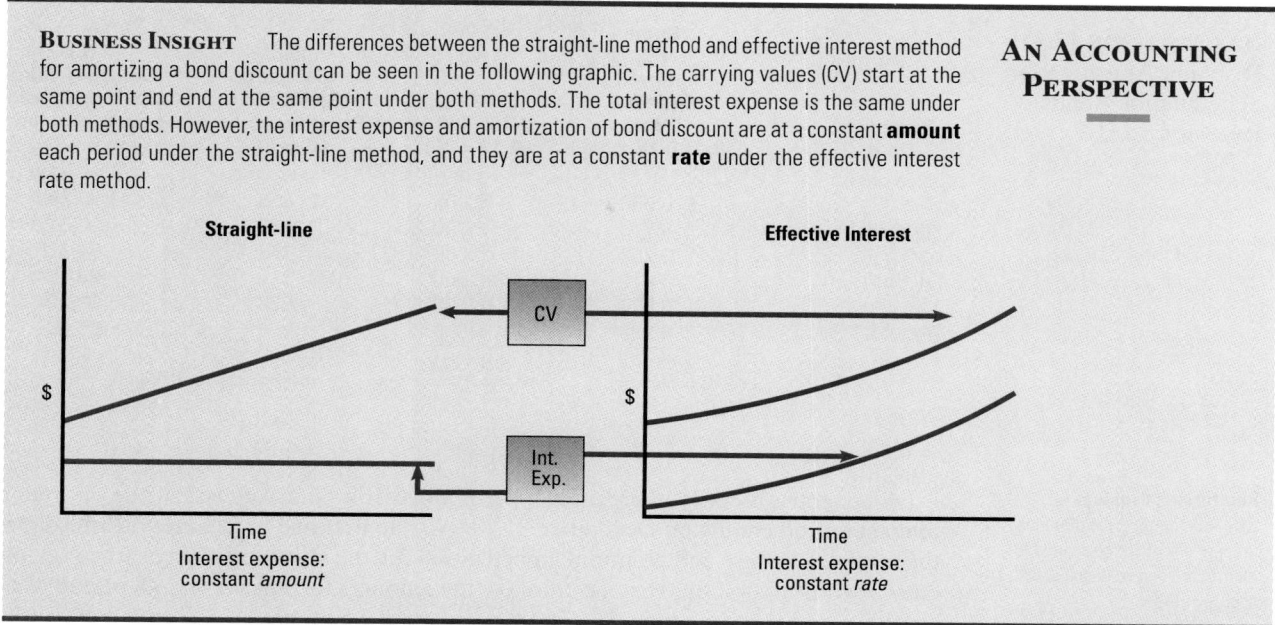

DISCOUNT AND PREMIUM AMORTIZATION SCHEDULES

A discount amortization schedule (Illustration 15.4) and a premium amortization schedule (Illustration 15.5) aid in preparing entries for interest expense. Usually, companies prepare such schedules when they first issue bonds, often using computer programs designed for this purpose. The companies then refer to the schedules whenever they make journal entries to record interest. Note that in each period the amount of interest expense changes; interest expense gets larger when a discount is involved and smaller when a premium is involved. This fluctuation occurs because the carrying value to which a constant interest rate is applied changes each interest payment date. With a discount, carrying value increases; with a premium, it decreases. However, the actual cash paid as interest is always a constant amount determined by multiplying the bond's face value by the contract rate.

Recall that the issue price was $95,233 for the discount situation and $105,076 for the premium situation. The total interest expense of $40,767 for the discount situation in Illustration 15.4 is equal to $36,000 (which is six $6,000 payments) plus the $4,767 discount. This amount agrees with the earlier computation of total interest expense. In Illustration 15.5, total interest expense in the premium situation is $30,924, or $36,000 (which is six $6,000 payments) less the $5,076 premium. In both illustrations, at the maturity date the carrying value of the bonds is equal to the face value because the discount or premium has been fully amortized.

ADJUSTING ENTRY FOR PARTIAL PERIOD

Illustrations 15.4 and 15.5 also would be helpful if Carr must accrue interest for a partial period. Instead of a calendar-year accounting period, assume the fiscal year of the bond issuer ends on August 31. Using the information provided in the premium amortization schedule (Illustration 15.5), the adjusting entry needed on August 31, 1999, is:

1999				
Aug.	31	Bond Interest Expense ($5,254 × $\frac{2}{6}$)	1,751	
		Premium on Bonds Payable ($746 × $\frac{2}{6}$)	249	
		Bond Interest Payable ($6,000 × $\frac{2}{6}$)		2,000
		To record two months' accrued interest.		

ILLUSTRATION 15.4
Discount Amortization
Schedule for Bonds
Payable

(A) Interest Payment Date	Bond (B) Interest Expense Debit (E × 0.14 × ½)	(C) Cash Credit ($100,000 × 0.12 × ½)	(D) Discount on Bonds Payable Credit (B − C)	(E) Carrying Value of Bonds Payable (previous balance in E + D)
Issue price				$ 95,233
12/31/99	$ 6,666	$ 6,000	$ 666	95,899
6/30/00	6,713	6,000	713	96,612
12/31/00	6,763	6,000	763	97,375
6/30/01	6,816	6,000	816	98,191
12/31/01	6,873	6,000	873	99,064
6/30/02	6,936*	6,000	936	100,000
	$40,767	$36,000	$4,767	

*Includes rounding difference.

Reinforcing Problem
P15–4 Compute price of bonds, prepare amortization schedule, journalize bond issuance, and accrue interest.

This entry records interest for two months, July and August, of the six-month interest period ending on December 31, 1999. The first line of Illustration 15.5 shows the interest expense and premium amortization for the six months. Thus, the previous entry records two-sixths (or one-third) of the amounts for this six-month period. Carr would record the remaining four months' interest when making the first payment on December 31, 1999. That entry reads:

1999 Dec.	31	Bond Interest Payable	2,000	
		Bond Interest Expense ($5,254 × 4/6)	3,503	
		Premium on Bonds Payable ($746 × 4/6)	497	
		Cash		6,000
		To record four months' interest expense and semiannual interest payment.		

During the remaining life of the bonds, Carr would make similar entries for August 31 and December 31. The amounts would differ, however, because Carr uses the interest method of accounting for bond interest. The entry for each June 30 would be as indicated in Illustration 15.5.

REDEEMING BONDS PAYABLE

Objective 7
Prepare journal entries for bond redemptions and bond conversions.

Bonds may be (1) paid at maturity, (2) called, or (3) purchased in the market and retired. Bonds may also be retired by being converted into stock. Each action is either a redemption of bonds or the extinguishment of debt. A company that pays its bonds at maturity would have already amortized any related discount or premium and paid the last interest payment. The only entry required at maturity would debit Bonds Payable and credit Cash for the face amount of the bonds as follows:

2002 June	30	Bonds Payable	100,000	
		Cash		100,000
		To pay bonds on maturity date.		

Reinforcing Problems
E15–5 Record call of bonds and payment of interest.
E15–6 Record accrued interest and purchase and retirement of bonds.

An issuer may redeem some or all of its outstanding bonds before maturity by calling them. The issuer may also purchase bonds in the market and retire them. In either case, the accounting is the same. Assume that on January 1, 2001, Carr calls bonds totaling $10,000 of the $100,000 face value bonds in Illustration 15.5 at 103, or $10,300. Even though accrued interest would be added to the price, assume that the interest due on this date has been paid. A look at the last column on the line dated 12/31/00 in Illustration 15.5 reveals that the carrying value of the bonds is $102,723,

(A) Interest Payment Date	(B) Bond Interest Expense Debit (E × 0.10 × ½)	(C) Cash Credit ($100,000 × 0.12 × ½)	(D) Premium on Bonds Payable Debit (C − B)	(E) Carrying Value of Bonds Payable (previous balance in E − D)
Issue price				$105,076
12/31/99	$ 5,254	$ 6,000	$ 746	104,330
6/30/00	5,216*	6,000	784	103,546
12/31/00	5,177	6,000	823	102,723
6/30/01	5,136	6,000	864	101,859
12/31/01	5,093	6,000	907	100,952
6/30/02	5,048	6,000	952	100,000
	$30,924	$36,000	$5,076	

ILLUSTRATION 15.5
Premium Amortization Schedule for Bonds Payable

*Rounded down.

which consists of Bonds Payable of $100,000 and Premium on Bonds Payable of $2,723. Since 10% of the bond issue is being redeemed, Carr must remove 10% from each of these two accounts. The firm incurs a loss for the excess of the price paid for the bonds, $10,300, over their carrying value, $10,272. The required entry is:

2001 Jan.	1	Bonds Payable	10,000	
		Premium on Bonds Payable ($2,723 ÷ 10)	272	
		Loss on Bond Redemption ($10,272 − $10,300).	28	
		Cash		10,300
		To record bonds redeemed.		

According to *FASB Statement No. 4,* gains and losses from *voluntary early* retirement of bonds are extraordinary items, if material. We report such gains and losses in the income statement, net of their tax effects, as described in Chapter 13.

Serial Bonds

To avoid the burden of redeeming an entire bond issue at one time, companies sometimes issue **serial bonds** that mature over several dates. Assume that on June 30, 1994, Jasper Company issued $100,000 face value, 12% serial bonds at 100. Interest is payable each year on June 30 and December 31. A total of $20,000 of the bonds mature each year starting on June 30, 1999. Jasper has a calendar-year accounting period. Entries required for 1999 for interest expense and maturing debt are:

Reinforcing Problem
P15–6A Record serial bond transactions, and show financial reporting.

1999 June	30	Bond Interest Expense ($100,000 × 0.12 × ½)	6,000	
		Cash		6,000
		To record interest payment.		
	30	Serial Bonds Payable	20,000	
		Cash		20,000
		To record retirement of serial debt.		
Dec.	31	Bond Interest Expense ($80,000 × 0.12 × ½).	4,800	
		Cash		4,800
		To record payment of semiannual interest expense.		

Note that Jasper calculates the interest expense for the last six months of 1999 only on the remaining outstanding debt ($100,000 original issue less the $20,000 that matured on June 30, 1999). Each year after the bonds maturing that year are retired, interest expense decreases proportionately. Jasper reports the $20,000 amount maturing the next year as a current liability on each year-end balance sheet. The remaining debt is a long-term liability.

Bond Redemption or Sinking Funds

Naturally, bond investors are concerned about the safety of their investments. They fear the company may default on paying the entire principal at the maturity date. This concern has led to provisions in some bond indentures that require companies to make periodic payments to a **bond redemption fund,** often called a **sinking fund.** The fund trustee uses these payments to redeem a stated amount of bonds annually and pay the accrued bond interest. The trustee determines which bonds to call and uses the cash deposited in the fund only to redeem these bonds and pay their accrued interest.

To illustrate, assume Hand Company has 12% coupon bonds outstanding that pay interest on March 31 and September 30 and were issued at face value. The bond indenture requires that Hand pay a trustee $53,000 each September 30. The entry for the payment to the trustee is:

Sept.	30	Sinking Fund	53,000	
		Cash		53,000
		To record payment to trustee of required deposit.		

The trustee calls $50,000 of bonds, pays for the bonds and accrued interest, and notifies Hand. The trustee also bills Hand for its fee and expenses incurred of $325. Assuming no interest has been recorded on these bonds for the period ended September 30, the entries are:

Reinforcing Problem
E15–7 Record sinking fund transactions.

Sept.	30	Bonds Payable	50,000	
		Bond Interest Expense	3,000	
		Sinking Fund		53,000
		To record bond redemption and interest paid by trustee.		
	30	Sinking Fund Expense	325	
		Cash		325
		To record trustee fee and expenses.		

If a balance exists in the Sinking Fund account at year-end, Hand includes it in a category labeled Investments or Other Assets on the balance sheet. Hand would describe the $50,000 of bonds that must be retired during the coming year as "Current maturity of long-term debt" and report it as a current liability on the balance sheet.

The existence of a sinking fund does not necessarily mean that the company has created a retained earnings appropriation entitled "Appropriation for Bonded Indebtedness." A sinking fund usually is contractual (required by the bond indenture), and an appropriation of retained earnings is simply an announcement by the board of directors that dividend payments will be limited over the term of the bonds. The former requires cash to be paid in to a trustee, and the latter restricts retained earnings available for dividends to stockholders. Also, even if the indenture does not require a sinking fund, the corporation may decide to (1) pay into a sinking fund and not appropriate retained earnings, (2) appropriate retained earnings and not pay into a sinking fund, (3) do neither, or (4) do both.

Convertible Bonds

A company may add to the attractiveness of its bonds by giving the bondholders the option to convert the bonds to shares of the issuer's common stock. In accounting for the conversions of **convertible bonds,** a company treats the carrying value of bonds surrendered as the capital contributed for shares issued.

Suppose a company has $10,000 face value of bonds outstanding. Each $1,000 bond is convertible into 50 shares of the issuer's $10 par value common stock. On May 1, when the carrying value of the bonds was $9,800, investors presented all of the bonds for conversion. The entry required is:

May	1	Bonds Payable	10,000	
		Discount on Bonds Payable.		200
		Common Stock ($10,000 ÷ $1,000 = 10 bonds;		
		10 bonds × 50 shares × $10 par)		5,000
		Paid-In Capital in Excess of Par Value—Common		4,800
		To record bonds converted to common stock.		

Reinforcing Problem
E15–8 Record conversion of bonds into capital stock.

The entry eliminates the $9,800 book value of the bonds from the accounts by debiting Bonds Payable for $10,000 and crediting Discount on Bonds Payable for $200. It credits Common Stock for the par value of the 500 shares issued (500 shares × $10 par). The excess amount ($4,800) is credited to Paid-In Capital in Excess of Par Value—Common.

BUSINESS INSIGHT   The Securities and Exchange Commission took action to protect the public against abusive telemarketing calls from sellers of municipal bonds. The residence of any person can only be called between 8 A.M. and 9 P.M., without their prior consent. Callers must clearly disclose the purpose of the call. Also, a centralized "Do-not-call" list of people who do not wish to receive solicitations must be maintained and honored.

Source: "SEC Approves Rule Governing Calls From Muni-Bond Sellers to Investors," *The Wall Street Journal,* Friday, December 27, 1996, p. A2.

AN ACCOUNTING PERSPECTIVE

The two leading bond rating services are Moody's Investors Service and Standard & Poor's Corporation. The bonds are rated as to their riskiness. The ratings used by these services are:

Bond Rating Services

Objective 8
Describe the ratings used for bonds.

	Moody's	Standard & Poor's
Highest quality to upper medium	Aaa	AAA
	Aa	AA
	A	A
Medium to speculative	Baa	BBB
	Ba	BB
	B	B
Poor to lowest quality	Caa	CCC
	Ca	CC
	C	C
In default, value is questionable		DDD
		DD
		D

Normally, Moody's rates junk bonds at Ba or below and Standard & Poor's at BB or below. As a company's prospects change over time, the ratings of its outstanding bonds change because of the higher or lower probability that the company can pay the interest and principal on the bonds when due. A severe recession may cause many companies' bond ratings to decline.

Real World Example
In *The Wall Street Journal* of June 27, 1997, RJR Nabisco had a Baa/ BBB bond rating, and Xerox Credit Corporation had an A/A bond rating.

Bond prices appear regularly in certain newspapers. For instance, *The Wall Street Journal* recently quoted IBM's bonds as follows:

Issue	Coupon	Maturity	Yield	Price	Change
IBM	7¼	2002	7.0	103¼	−¾

The bonds carry a coupon rate of 7¼%. The bonds mature in 2002. The current price is $103¼ per hundred, or $1,032.50 for a $1,000 bond. The price the preceding day was $104¼, since the change was −¾. The current price yields a return to investors of 7.0%. As the market rate of interest changes from day to day, the market price of the bonds varies inversely. Thus, if the market rate of interest increases, the market price of bonds decreases, and vice versa.

AN ACCOUNTING PERSPECTIVE
—

BUSINESS INSIGHT   Companies sometimes invest in the bonds of other companies. According to *FASB Statement No. 115* (covered in Chapter 14), investments in these bonds fall into three categories— trading securities, available-for-sale securities, or held-to-maturity securities. The bonds would be classified as trading securities if they were acquired principally for the purpose of selling them in the near future. If the bonds were to be held for a longer period of time, but not until maturity, they would be classified as available-for-sale securities. Bonds that will be held to maturity are classified as held-to-maturity securities. All trading securities are current assets. Available-for-sale securities are either current assets or long-term assets, depending on how long management intends to hold them. Discounts and premiums on bonds classified as trading and available-for-sale securities are not amortized because management does not know how long they will be held. Held-to-maturity securities are long-term assets. Discounts and premiums on bonds classified as held-to-maturity securities are amortized by the holder of the bonds in the same manner as for the issuer of the bonds. Further discussion of investments in bonds is reserved for an intermediate accounting course.

ANALYZING AND USING THE FINANCIAL RESULTS—TIMES INTEREST EARNED RATIO

Objective 9
Analyze and use the financial results—times interest earned ratio.

Reinforcing Problem
E15–9 Calculate times interest earned ratios for a company and comment.

The **times interest earned ratio** (or *interest coverage ratio*) indicates the ability of a company to meet required interest payments when due. We calculate the ratio as follows:

$$\text{Times interest earned ratio} = \frac{\text{Income before interest and taxes (IBIT)}}{\text{Interest expense}}$$

Income before interest and taxes (IBIT), also called "earnings before interest and taxes (EBIT)," is the numerator because there would be no income taxes if interest expense is equal to or greater than IBIT. To find IBIT when the income statement is not complex, take net income and add back interest expense and taxes. However, in complex situations, when there are discontinued operations, changes in accounting principle, extraordinary items, interest revenue, and/or other similar items, analysts often use "operating income" to represent IBIT. The higher the ratio, the more comfortable creditors feel about receiving interest payments in the future.

The times interest earned ratios for 1995 for several companies (described in footnotes to the table) were as follows:

Company	Earnings Before Interest and Taxes (Millions)	Interest Expense (Millions)	Times Interest Earned Ratio
Ford Motor Company[a]	$12,963	$9,424	1.38
Procter & Gamble Company[b]	5,153	484	10.65
J. P. Morgan & Co., Inc.[c]	9,840	7,934	1.24
Sun Microsystems, Inc.[d]	718	9	79.78
Hewlett-Packard Company[e]	3,838	206	18.63

[a]Ford Motor Company is the world's largest producer of trucks and the second largest producer of cars and trucks combined.
[b]Procter & Gamble markets more than 300 brands to nearly five billion customers in over 140 countries.
[c]J. P. Morgan & Co., Inc., is a global banking firm that serves clients with complex financial needs.
[d]Sun Microsystems, Inc., was founded in 1982 and has emerged as a global leader in enterprise network computing.
[e]Hewlett-Packard Company designs, manufactures, and services products and systems for measurement, computation, and communications.

You can see from these data that a great deal of variability exists in the times interest earned ratios for real companies. To judge the ability of companies to pay bond interest when due, bondholders would carefully examine other financial data as well.

Some companies that issued high-interest junk bonds in the 1980s defaulted on their interest payments and had to declare Chapter 11 bankruptcy or renegotiate payment terms with bondholders in the 1990s. Other companies with high-interest

The Rawlings brothers inherited 300,000 shares (30%) of the common stock of the Rawlings Furniture Company from their father, who had founded the company 55 years earlier. One brother served as president of the company, and the other two brothers served as vice presidents. The company, which produced a line of fine furniture sold nationwide, earned an average of $4 million per year. Located in Jamesville, New York, the company had provided steady employment for approximately 10% of the city's population. The city had benefited from the revenues the company attracted to the area and from the generous gifts provided by the father.

The remainder of the common stock was widely held and was traded in the over-the-counter market. No other stockholder held more than 4% of the stock. The stock had recently traded at $30 per share. The company has $10 million of 10% bonds outstanding, which mature in 15 years.

The brothers enjoyed the money they received from the company, but did not enjoy the work. They also were frustrated by the fact that they did not own a controlling interest (more than 50%) of the company. If they had a controlling interest, they could make important decisions without obtaining the agreement of the other stockholders.

With the assistance of a New York City brokerage house, the brothers decided to pursue a plan that could increase their wealth. The company would offer to buy back shares of common stock at $40 per share. These shares would then be canceled, and the Rawlings brothers would have a controlling interest. The stock buy-back would be financed by issuing 10-year, 14%, high-interest junk bonds. The brokerage house had located some financial institutions willing to buy the bonds. The interest payments on the junk bonds would be $3 million per year. The brothers thought the company could make these payments unless the country entered a recession. If need be, wage increases could be severely restricted or eliminated and the company's pension plan could be terminated. If the junk bonds could be paid at maturity, the brothers would own a controlling interest in what could be an extremely valuable company. If the interest payments could not be met or if the junk bonds were defaulted at maturity, the company could eventually be forced to liquidate. The risks are high, but so are the potential rewards.

If another buyer entered the picture at this point and bid an even higher amount for the stock, the brothers could sell their shares and exit the company. Two of the brothers hoped that another buyer might bid as much as $50 per share so they could sell their shares and pursue other interests. The changes a new buyer might make are unpredictable at this point.

bonds issued new low-interest bonds and used the proceeds to retire the high-interest bonds.

Chapter 16 discusses the fourth major financial statement—the statement of cash flows, which we mentioned in Chapter 1. This statement shows the cash inflows and outflows from operating, investing, and financing activities.

UNDERSTANDING THE LEARNING OBJECTIVES

- A bond is a liability (with a maturity date) that bears interest that is deductible in computing both net income and taxable income.
- A stock is a unit of ownership on which a dividend is paid only if declared, and dividends are not deductible in determining net income or taxable income.
- Bonds may be secured or unsecured, registered or unregistered, callable, and/or convertible.

Objective 1
Describe the features of bonds and tell how bonds differ from shares of stock.

- Advantages include stockholders retaining control of the company, tax deductibility of interest, and possible creation of favorable financial leverage.
- Disadvantages include having to make a fixed interest payment each period, reduction in a company's ability to withstand a major loss, possible limitations on dividends and future borrowings, and possible reduction in earnings per share caused by unfavorable financial leverage.

Objective 2
List the advantages and disadvantages of financing with long-term debt and prepare examples showing how to employ financial leverage.

- If bonds are issued at face value on an interest date, no accrued interest is recorded.
- If bonds are issued between interest dates, accrued interest must be recorded.

Objective 3
Prepare journal entries for bonds issued at face value.

Objective 4
Explain how interest rates affect bond prices and what causes a bond to sell at a premium or a discount.

- If the market rate is lower than the contract rate, bonds sell for more than their face value, and a premium is recorded.
- If the market rate is higher than the contract rate, bonds sell for less than their face value, and a discount is recorded.

Objective 5
Apply the concept of present value to compute the price of a bond.

- The present value of the principal plus the present value of the interest payments is equal to the price of the bond.
- The contract rate of interest is used to determine the amount of future cash interest payments.
- The effective rate of interest is used to discount the future payment of principal and of interest back to the present value.

Objective 6
Prepare journal entries for bonds issued at a discount or a premium.

- When bonds are issued, Cash is debited, and Bonds Payable is credited. For bonds issued at a discount, Discount on Bonds Payable is also debited. For bonds issued at a premium, Premium on Bonds Payable is also credited. For bonds issued between interest dates, Bond Interest Payable is also credited.
- Any premium or discount must be amortized over the period the bonds are outstanding.
- Under the effective interest rate method, interest expense for any period is equal to the effective (market) rate of interest at date of issuance times the carrying value of the bond at the beginning of that interest period.
- Under the straight-line method of amortization, an equal amount of discount or premium is allocated to each month the bonds are outstanding.

Objective 7
Prepare journal entries for bond redemptions and bond conversions.

- When bonds are redeemed before they mature, a loss or gain (an extraordinary item, if material) on bond redemption may occur.
- A bond sinking fund might be required in the bond indenture.
- Bonds may be convertible into shares of stock. The carrying value of the bonds is the capital contributed for shares of stock issued.

Objective 8
Describe the ratings used for bonds.

- Bonds are rated as to their riskiness.
- The two leading bond rating services are Moody's Investors Services and Standard & Poor's Corporation.
- Each of these services has its own rating scale. For instance, the highest rating is Aaa (Moody's) and AAA (Standard & Poor's).

Objective 9
Analyze and use the financial results—times interest earned ratio.

- The times interest earned ratio indicates a company's ability to meet interest payments when due.
- The ratio is equal to income before interest and taxes (IBIT) divided by interest expense.

Objective 10
Explain future value and present value concepts and make required calculations (Appendix).

- The future value of an investment is the amount to which a sum of money invested today will grow in a stated time period at a specified interest rate.
- Present value is the current worth of a future cash receipt and is the reciprocal of future value. To discount future receipts is to bring them back to their present values.

APPENDIX   # FUTURE VALUE AND PRESENT VALUE

Managers apply the concepts of interest, future value, and present value in making business decisions. Therefore, accountants need to understand these concepts to properly record certain business transactions.

THE TIME VALUE OF MONEY

The concept of the *time value of money* stems from the logical reference for a dollar today rather than a dollar at any future date. Most individuals prefer having a dollar today rather than at some future date because (1) the risk exists that the future dollar will never be received; and (2) if the dollar is on hand now, it can be invested, resulting in an increase in total dollars possessed at that future date.

Objective 10
Explain future value and present value concepts and make required calculations.

Most business decisions involve a comparison of cash flows in and out of the company. To be useful in decision making, such comparisons must be in dollars of the same point in time. That is, the dollars held now must be accumulated or rolled forward, or future dollars must be discounted or brought back to the present dollar value, before comparisons are valid. Such comparisons involve future value and present value concepts.

FUTURE VALUE

The **future value or worth** of any investment is the amount to which a sum of money invested today grows during a stated period of time at a specified interest rate. The interest involved may be simple interest or compound interest. **Simple interest** is interest on principal only. For example, $1,000 invested today for two years at 12% simple interest grows to $1,240 since interest is $120 per year. The principal of $1,000, plus 2 × $120, is equal to $1,240. **Compound interest** is interest on principal and on interest of prior periods. For example, $1,000 invested for two years at 12% compounded annually grows to $1,254.40 as follows:

Principal or present value	$1,000.00
Interest, year 1 = $1,000 × 0.12 =	120.00
Value at end of year 1	$1,120.00
Interest, year 2 = $1,120 × 0.12 =	134.40
Value at end of year 2 (future value)	$1,254.40

In Illustration 15.6, we graphically portray these computations of future worth and show how $1,000 grows to $1,254.40 with a 12% interest rate compounded annually. The effect of compounding is $14.40—the interest in the second year that was based on the interest computed for the first year, or $120 × 0.12 = $14.40.

Interest tables ease the task of computing the future worth to which any invested amount will grow at a given rate for a stated period. An example is Table A.1 in the Appendix at the end of this text. To use the Appendix tables, first determine the number of compounding periods involved. A compounding period may be any length of time, such as a day, a month, a quarter, a half-year, or a year, but normally not more than a year. The number of compounding periods is equal to the number of years in the life of the investment times the number of compoundings per year. Five years compounded annually is five periods, five years compounded quarterly is 20 periods, and so on.

Second, determine the interest rate per compounding period. Interest rates are usually quoted in annual terms; in fact, federal law requires statement of the interest rate in annual terms in some situations. Divide the annual rate by the number of compounding periods per year to get the proper rate per period. Only with an annual compounding period will the annual rate be the rate per period. All other cases involve a lower rate. For example, if the annual rate is 12% and interest is compounded monthly, the rate per period (one month) will be 1%.

To use the tables, find the number of periods involved in the Period column. Move across the table to the right, stopping in the column headed by the Interest Rate per Period, which yields a number called a *factor*. The factor shows the amount to which an investment of $1 will grow for the periods and the rate involved. To compute the future worth of the investment, multiply the number of dollars in the given situation by this factor. For example, suppose your parents tell you that they will invest $8,000 at 12% for four years and give you the amount to which this investment grows if you graduate from college in four years. How much will you receive at the end of four years if the interest rate is 12% compounded annually? How much will you receive if the interest rate is 12% compounded quarterly?

To calculate these amounts, look at the end-of-text Appendix, Table A.1. In the intersection of the 4 period row and the 12% column, you find the factor 1.57352. Multiplying this

ILLUSTRATION 15.6
Compound Interest and
Future Value

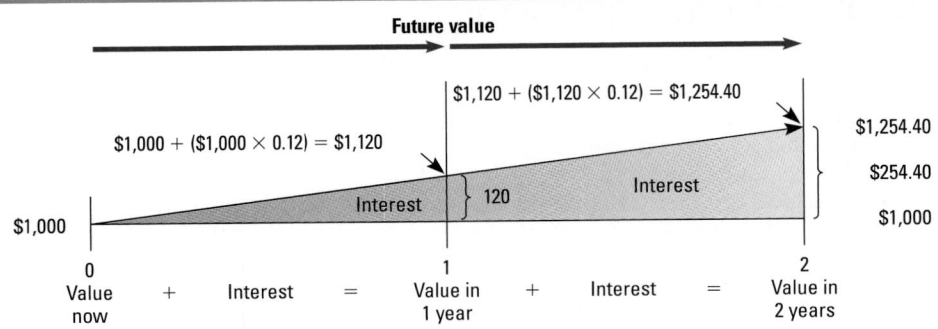

factor by $8,000 yields $12,588.16, the answer to the first question. To answer the second question, look at the intersection of the 16 period row and the 3% column. The factor is 1.60471, and the value of your investment is $12,837.68. The more frequent compounding would add $12,837.68 − $12,588.16 = $249.52 to the value of your investment. The reason for this difference in amounts is that 12% compounded quarterly is a higher rate than 12% compounded annually.

Future Value of an Annuity

An **annuity** is a series of equal cash flows (often called *rents*) spaced equally in time. The semiannual interest payments received on a bond investment are a common example of an annuity. Assume that $100 will be received at the end of each of the next three semiannual periods. The interest rate is 6% per semiannual period. Using Table A.1 in the Appendix, we find the future value of each of the $100 receipts as follows:

> Future value (after three periods) of $100
>   received at the end of the—
> First period: 1.12360 × $100 = $112.36
> Second period: 1.06000 ×   100 =   106.00
> Third period: 1.00000 ×   100 =   100.00
>
> Total future value $318.36

Such a procedure would become quite tedious if the annuity consisted of many receipts. Fortunately, tables are available to calculate the total future value directly. See the Appendix, Table A.2. For the annuity just described, you can identify one single factor by looking at the 3 period row and 6% column. The factor is 3.18360 (the sum of the three factors shown above), and when multiplied by $100, yields $318.36, which is the same answer. In Illustration 15.7, we graphically present the future value of an annuity.

PRESENT VALUE

Present value is the current worth of a future cash receipt and is the reciprocal of future value. In future value, we calculate the future value of a sum of money possessed now. In present value, we calculate the current worth of rights to future cash receipts possessed now. We discount future receipts by bringing them back to their present values.

Reinforcing Problem
E15–10 Determine present value of a lump sum payment (based on appendix).

Assume that you have the right to receive $1,000 in one year. If the appropriate interest rate is 12% compounded annually, what is the present value of this $1,000 future cash receipt? You know that the present value is less than $1,000 because $1,000 due in one year is not worth $1,000 today. You also know that the $1,000 due in one year is equal to some amount, P, plus interest on P at 12% for one year. Thus, $P + 0.12P = \$1,000$, or $1.12P = \$1,000$. Dividing $1,000 by 1.12, you get $892.86; this amount is the present value of your future $1,000. If the $1,000 was due in two years, you would find its present value by dividing $892.86 by 1.12, which equals $797.20. Portrayed graphically, present value looks similar to future value, except for the direction of the arrows (Illustration 15.8).

Table A.3 (end-of-text Appendix) contains present value factors for combinations of a number of periods and interest rates. We use Table A.3 in the same manner as Table A.1. For example, the present value of $1,000 due in four years at 16% compounded annually is

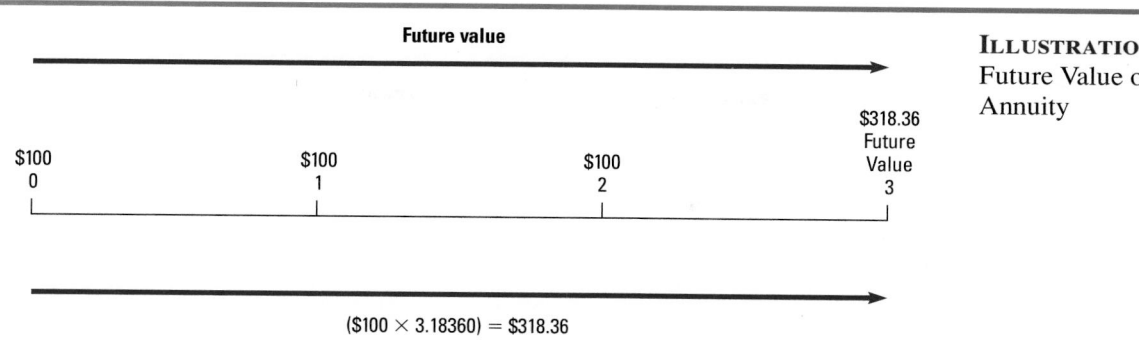

ILLUSTRATION 15.7
Future Value of an
Annuity

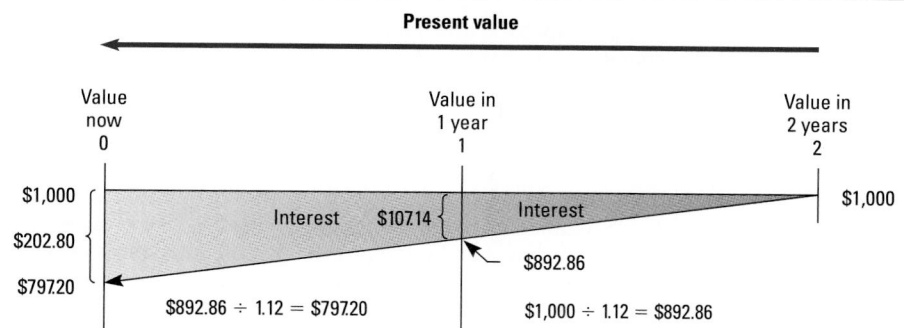

ILLUSTRATION 15.8
Compound Interest and
Present Value

$552.29, computed as $1,000 × 0.55229. The 0.55229 is the present value factor found in the intersection of the 4 period row and the 16% column.

As another example, suppose that you wish to have $4,000 in three years to pay for a vacation in Europe. If your investment increases at a 20% rate compounded quarterly, how much should you invest now? To find the amount, you would use the present value factor found in Table A.3, 12 period row, 5% column. This factor is 0.55684, which means that an investment of about 55½ cents today would grow to $1 in 12 periods at 5% per period. To have $4,000 at the end of three years, you must invest 4,000 times this factor (0.55684), or $2,227.36.

The semiannual interest payments on a bond are a common example of an annuity. As an example of calculating the present value of an annuity, assume that $100 is received at the end of each of the next three semiannual periods. The interest rate is 6% per semiannual period. By using Table A.3 (Appendix), you can find the present value of each of the three $100 payments as follows:

Present Value of an Annuity

Present value of $100 due in:
1 period: 0.94340 × $100 = $ 94.34
2 periods: 0.89000 × 100 =   89.00
3 periods: 0.83962 × 100 =   83.96
Total present value $267.30

Such a procedure could become quite tedious if the annuity consisted of a large number of payments. Fortunately, tables are also available showing the present values of an annuity of $1 per period for varying interest rates and periods. See the end-of-text Appendix, Table A.4. For the annuity just described, you can obtain a single factor from the table to represent the present value of an annuity of $1 per period for three (semiannual) periods at 6% per (semiannual) period. This factor is 2.67301; it is equal to the sum of the present value factors for $1 due in one period, $1 in two periods, and $1 in three periods found in the Appendix, Table

Reinforcing Problems
E15–11 Determine present value for an annuity (based on appendix).
E15–12 Determine present value for lottery winnings (based on appendix).
E15–13 Determine future value of an annuity (based on appendix).

ILLUSTRATION 15.9
Present Value of an
Annuity

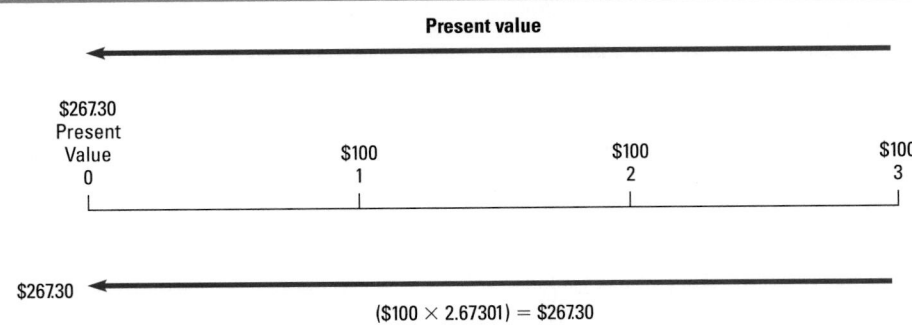

A.3. When this factor is multiplied by $100, the number of dollars in each payment, it yields the present value of the annuity, $267.30. In Illustration 15.9, we graphically present the present value of this annuity and show how to find the present value of the three $100 cash flows by multiplying the $100 by a present value of an annuity factor, 2.67301.

Suppose you won a lottery that awarded you a choice of receiving $10,000 at the end of each of the next five years or $35,000 cash today. You believe you can earn interest on invested cash at 15% per year. Which option should you choose? To answer the question, compute the present value of an annuity of $10,000 per period for five years at 15%. The present value is $33,521.60, or $10,000 × 3.35216. You should accept the immediate payment of $35,000 since it has the larger present value.

DEMONSTRATION PROBLEM

Jackson Company issued $100,000 face value of 15%, 20-year junk bonds on April 30, 1999. The bonds are dated April 30, 1999, call for semiannual interest payments on April 30 and October 31, and are issued to yield 16% (8% per period).

Required   **a.** Compute the amount received for the bonds.

b. Prepare an amortization schedule. Enter data in the schedule for only the first two interest periods. Use the effective interest rate method.

c. Prepare journal entries to record issuance of the bonds, the first six months' interest expense on the bonds, the adjustment needed on December 31, 1999 (assuming Jackson's accounting year ends on that date), and the second six months' interest expense on April 30, 2000.

SOLUTION TO DEMONSTRATION PROBLEM

a.   Price received:
Present value of principal: $100,000 × 0.04603
   (see Appendix, Table A.3, 40 period row, 8% column) . . . . . $ 4,603
Present value of interest: $7,500 × 11.92461
   (see Appendix, Table A.4, 40 period row, 8% column)   89,435
Total $94,038

b.

(A) Interest Payment Date	(B) Bond Interest Expense Debit (E × 0.16 × ½)	(C) Cash Credit ($100,000 × 0.15 × ½)	(D) Discount on Bonds Payable Credit (B − C)	(E) Carrying Value of Bonds Payable (previous balance in E + D)
Issue price				$94,038
10/31/99	$7,523	$7,500	$23	94,061
4/30/00	7,525	7,500	25	94,086

c.

JACKSON COMPANY
GENERAL JOURNAL

1999				
Apr.	30	Cash	94,038	
		Discount on Bonds Payable.	5,962	
		Bonds Payable		100,000
		Issued $100,000 face value of 20-year, 15% bonds to yield 16%.		
Oct.	31	Bond Interest Expense.	7,523	
		Discount on Bonds Payable.		23
		Cash		7,500
		Paid semiannual bond interest expense.		
Dec.	31	Bond Interest Expense ($7,525 × ⅓)	2,508	
		Discount on Bonds Payable.		8
		Bond Interest Payable ($7,500 × ⅓)		2,500
		To record accrual of two months' interest expense.		
2000				
Apr.	30	Bond Interest Payable	2,500	
		Bond Interest Expense ($7,525 × ⅔)	5,017	
		Discount on Bonds Payable.		17
		Cash		7,500
		Paid semiannual bond interest expense.		

NEW TERMS

Annuity   A series of equal cash flows spaced in time.   *564*

Bearer bond   See *unregistered bond.*

Bond   A long-term debt, or liability, owed by its issuer. A *bond certificate,* a negotiable instrument, is the formal, physical evidence of the debt owed.   *542*

Bond indenture   The contract or loan agreement under which bonds are issued.   *544*

Bond redemption (or sinking) fund   A fund used to bring about the gradual redemption of a bond issue.   *558*

Callable bond   A bond that gives the issuer the right to call (buy back) the bond before its maturity date.   *545*

Call premium   The price paid in excess of face value that the issuer of bonds must pay to redeem (call) bonds before their maturity date.   *545*

Carrying value (of bonds)   The face value of bonds minus any unamortized discount or plus any unamortized premium. Sometimes referred to as **net liability** on the bonds.   *552*

Compound interest   Interest calculated on the principal and on interest of prior periods.   *563*

Contract rate of interest   The interest rate printed on the bond certificates and specified on the bond indenture; also called the **stated, coupon,** or **nominal rate.**   *549*

Convertible bond   A bond that may be exchanged for shares of stock of the issuing corporation at the bondholders' option.   *545, 558*

Coupon bond   A bond not registered as to interest; it carries detachable coupons that are to be clipped and presented for payment of interest due.   *544*

Debenture bond   An unsecured bond backed only by the general creditworthiness of its issuer.   *544*

Discount (on bonds)   Amount a bond sells for below its face value.   *549*

Effective interest rate method (interest method)   A procedure for calculating periodic interest expense (or revenue) in which the first period's interest is computed by multiplying the carrying value of bonds payable (bond investments) by the market rate of interest at the issue date. The difference between computed interest expense (revenue) and the interest paid (received), based on the contract rate times face value, is the discount or premium amortized for the period. Computations for subsequent periods are based on the carrying value at the beginning of the period.   *554*

Face value   Principal amount of a bond.   *542*

Favorable financial leverage   An increase in EPS and the rate of return on stockholders' equity resulting from earning a higher rate of return on borrowed funds than the fixed cost of such funds. **Unfavorable financial leverage** results when the cost of borrowed funds exceeds the income they generate, resulting in decreased income to stockholders.   *545, 547*

Future value or worth   The amount to which a sum of money invested today will grow during a stated period of time at a specified interest rate.   *563*

Interest method   See *effective interest rate method.*

Junk bonds   High-interest rate, high-risk bonds; many were issued in the 1980s to finance corporate restructurings.   *545*

Market interest rate   The minimum rate of interest investors will accept on bonds of a particular risk category. Also called **effective rate** or **yield.**   *549*

Mortgage A legal claim (lien) on specific property that gives the bondholder the right to possess the pledged property if the company fails to make required payments. A bond secured by a mortgage is called a **mortgage bond.** *544*

Premium (on bonds) Amount a bond sells for above its face value. *549*

Present value The current worth of a future cash receipt(s); computed by discounting future receipts at a stipulated interest rate. *550, 564*

Registered bond A bond with the owner's name on the bond certificate and in the register of bond owners kept by the bond issuer or its agent, the registrar. *544*

Secured bond A bond for which a company has pledged specific property to ensure its payment. *544*

Serial bonds Bonds in a given bond issue with maturities spread over several dates. *544, 557*

Simple interest Interest on principal only. *563*

Sinking fund See Bond redemption fund.

Stock warrant A right that allows the bondholder to purchase shares of common stock at a fixed price for a stated period of time. Warrants issued with long-term debt may be **detachable** or **nondetachable.** *545*

Straight-line method of amortization A procedure that, when applied to bond discount or premium, allocates an

equal amount of discount or premium to each period in the life of a bond. *553*

Term bond A bond that matures on the same date as all other bonds in a given bond issue. *544*

Times interest earned ratio Income before interest and taxes (IBIT) divided by interest expense. In complex situations, "operating income" is often used to represent IBIT. *560*

Trading on the equity A company using its stockholders' equity as a basis for securing funds on which it pays a fixed return. *546*

Trustee Usually a bank or trust company appointed to represent the bondholders and to enforce the provisions of the bond indenture against the issuer. *544*

Underwriter An investment company or a banker that performs many tasks for the bond issuer in issuing bonds; may also guarantee the issuer a fixed price for the bonds. *543*

Unfavorable financial leverage Results when the cost of borrowed funds exceeds the revenue they generate; it is the reverse of **favorable financial leverage.** *547*

Unregistered (bearer) bond Ownership transfers by physical delivery. *544*

Unsecured bond A **debenture bond,** or simply a **debenture.** *544*

SELF-TEST

TRUE-FALSE

Indicate whether each of the following statements is true or false.

1. An unsecured bond is called a debenture bond.
2. Callable bonds may be called at the option of the holder of the bonds.
3. Favorable financial leverage results when borrowed funds are used to increase earnings per share of common stock.
4. If the market rate of interest exceeds the contract rate, the bonds are issued at a discount.
5. The straight-line method of amortization is the recommended method.

MULTIPLE-CHOICE

Select the best answer for each of the following questions.

1. Harner Company issued $100,000 of 12% bonds on March 1, 1999. The bonds are dated January 1, 1999, and were issued at 96 plus accrued interest. The entry to record the issuance would be:

a.
Cash	98,000	
Discount on Bonds Payable	4,000	
Bonds Payable		100,000
Bond Interest Payable		2,000

b.
Cash	102,000	
Bonds Payable		100,000
Bond Interest Payable		2,000

c.
Cash	96,000	
Discount on Bonds Payable	4,000	
Bonds Payable		100,000

d. None of the above.

2. If the bonds in (1) had been issued at 104, the entry to record the issuance would have been:

a.
Cash	104,000	
Bonds Payable		100,000
Premium on Bonds Payable		4,000

b. | Cash . . . . | 102,000 | |
Bonds Payable		100,000
Bond Interest		
Payable		2,000

c. | Cash . . . . | 106,000 | |
Bonds Payable		100,000
Premium on Bonds		
Payable		4,000
Bond Interest		
Payable		2,000

d. None of the above.

3. On January 1, 1999, the Alvarez Company issued $400,000 face value of 8%, 10-year bonds for cash of $328,298, a price to yield 11%. The bonds pay interest semiannually and mature on January 1, 2009. Using the effective interest rate method, the bond interest expense for the first six months of 1999 would be:
   a. $36,113.

b. $18,056.
c. $32,000.
d. $16,000.

4. If the straight-line amortization method had been used in (3), the interest expense for the first six months would have been:
   a. $39,170.
   b. $32,000.
   c. $18,000.
   d. $19,585.

5. Assume a company has net income of $100,000, income tax expense of $40,000, and interest expense of $20,000. The times interest earned ratio is:
   a. 5 times
   b. 7 times
   c. 8 times
   d. 9 times

Now turn to page 576 to check your answers.

QUESTIONS

1. What are the advantages of obtaining long-term funds by the issuance of bonds rather than additional shares of capital stock? What are the disadvantages?

2. What is a bond indenture? What parties are usually associated with it? Explain why.

3. Explain what is meant by the terms *coupon, callable, convertible,* and *debenture.*

4. What is meant by the term *trading on the equity?*

5. When bonds are issued between interest dates, why should the issuing corporation receive cash equal to the amount of accrued interest (accrued since the preceding interest date) in addition to the issue price of the bonds?

6. Why might it be more accurate to describe a sinking fund as a bond redemption fund?

7. Indicate how each of the following items should be classified in a balance sheet on December 31, 1998.
   a. Cash balance in a sinking fund.

   b. Accrued interest on bonds payable.
   c. Debenture bonds payable due in 2008.
   d. Premium on bonds payable.
   e. First-mortgage bonds payable, due July 1, 1999.
   f. Discount on bonds payable.
   g. First National Bank—Interest account.
   h. Convertible bonds payable due in 2001.

8. Why is the effective interest rate method of computing periodic interest expense considered theoretically preferable to the straight-line method?

9. Why would an investor whose intent is to hold bonds to maturity pay more for the bonds than their face value?

10. Of what use is the times interest earned ratio?

EXERCISES

On September 30, 1999, Domingo's Construction Company issued $120,000 face value of 12%, 10-year bonds dated August 31, 1999, at 100, plus accrued interest. Interest is paid semiannually on February 28 and August 31. Domingo's accounting year ends on December 31. Prepare journal entries to record the issuance of these bonds, the accrual of interest at year-end, and the payment of the first interest coupon.

Exercise 15–1
Record issuance of bonds at face value, adjusting entry, and payment of interest (L.O. 3)

On December 31, 1998, East Lansing Office Equipment Company issued $1,600,000 face value of 8%, 10-year bonds for cash of $1,400,605, a price to yield 10%. The bonds pay interest semiannually and mature on December 31, 2008.

a. State which is higher, the market rate of interest or the contract rate.

b. Compute the bond interest expense for the first six months of 1999, using the interest method.

c. Show how the $1,400,605 price must have been determined.

Exercise 15–2
Compute bond interest expense; show how bond price was determined (L.O. 4–6)

Exercise 15–3
Calculate interest expense using straight-line amortization (L.O. 6)

Compute the annual interest expense on the bonds in Exercise 15–2, assuming the bond discount is amortized using the straight-line method.

Exercise 15–4
Prepare entry to record interest payment (L.O. 6)

After recording the payment of the interest coupon due on June 30, 1999, the accounts of Myrtle Beach Sailboat, Inc., showed Bonds Payable of $300,000 and Premium on Bonds Payable of $10,572. Interest is payable semiannually on June 30 and December 31. The five-year, 12% bonds have a face value of $300,000 and were originally issued to yield 10%. Prepare the journal entry to record the payment of interest on December 31, 1999. Use the interest method. (Round all amounts to the nearest dollar.)

Exercise 15–5
Record call of bonds and payment of interest (L.O. 7)

On June 30, 1999 (a semiannual interest payment date), Holiday Rollerblade Company redeemed all of its $400,000 face value of 10% bonds outstanding by calling them at 106. The bonds were originally issued on June 30, 1995, at 100. Prepare the journal entry to record the payment of the interest and the redemption of the bonds on June 30, 1999.

Exercise 15–6
Record accrued interest and purchase and retirement of bonds (L.O. 7)

On August 31, 1998, as part of the provisions of its bond indenture, Caribbean Cruise Line, Inc., acquired $480,000 of its outstanding bonds on the open market at 96 plus accrued interest. These bonds were originally issued at face value and carry a 12% interest rate, payable semiannually. The bonds are dated November 30, 1987, and pay semiannual interest on May 31 and November 30. Prepare the journal entries required to record the accrual of the interest to the acquisition date on the bonds acquired and the acquisition of the bonds.

Exercise 15–7
Record sinking fund transactions (L.O. 7)

Cleveland Heating Systems, Inc., is required to make a deposit of $18,000 plus semiannual interest expense of $540 on October 31, 1998, to the trustee of its sinking fund so that the trustee can redeem $18,000 of the company's bonds on that date. The bonds were issued at 100. Prepare the journal entries required on October 31 to record the sinking fund deposit, the bond retirement, payment of interest (due on that date), and payment of trustee expenses, assuming the latter is $100.

Exercise 15–8
Record conversion of bonds into capital stock (L.O. 7)

After interest was paid on September 30, 1999, $60,000 face value of Miami Video Rentals, Inc., outstanding bonds were converted into 8,000 shares of the company's $5 par value common stock. Prepare the journal entry to record the conversion, assuming the bonds were issued at 100.

Exercise 15–9
Calculate times interest earned ratios for a company and comment (L.O. 9)

A recent annual report of Wal-Mart Corporation showed the following amounts as of the dates indicated:

	Years Ended January 31		
	1995	**1994**	**1993**
Earnings before interest (and taxes) (millions)	$4,968	$4,208	$3,489
Interest expense (millions)	706	517	323

Calculate the times interest earned ratio for each year and comment on the results.

Exercise 15–10
Determine present value of a lump-sum payment (based on appendix) (L.O. 10)

What is the present value of a lump-sum payment of $20,000 due in five years if the market rate of interest is 10% per year (compounded annually) and the present value of $1 due in five periods at 10% is 0.62092?

Exercise 15–11
Determine present value of an annuity (based on appendix) (L.O. 10)

What is the present value of a series of semiannual payments of $10,000 due at the end of each six months for the next five years if the market rate of interest is 10% per year and the present value of an annuity of $1 for 10 periods at 5% is 7.72173?

Exercise 15–12
Determine present value of lottery winnings (based on appendix) (L.O. 10)

Joe Mordino bought a ticket in the Georgia lottery for $1, hoping to strike it rich. To his amazement, he won $4,000,000. Payment was to be received in equal amounts at the end of each of the next 20 years. Mordino heard from relatives and friends he had not heard from in years. They all wanted to renew their relationship with this new millionaire. Federal and state income taxes were going to be about 40% (36% for federal and 4% for state) on each year's income from the lottery check. The discount rate to use in all present value calculations is 12%.

a. How much will Mordino actually receive after taxes each year?

b. Is Mordino a multimillionaire according to the present value of his cash inflow after taxes?

c. What is the present value of the net amount the state has to pay out? Remember that the state gets part of the money back in the form of taxes.

After Joe Mordino won $4,000,000 in the Georgia lottery, he decided to purchase $10,000 of lottery tickets at the end of each year for the next 20 years. He was hoping to hit the lottery again, but he never did. If the state can earn 12% on ticket revenue received, how much will the annuity of $10,000 from Mordino grow to by the end of 20 years?

Exercise 15–13
Determine future value of an annuity (based on appendix) (L.O. 10)

PROBLEMS

On December 1, 1998, New Jersey Waste Management Company issued $300,000 of 10-year, 9% bonds dated July 1, 1998, at 100. Interest on the bonds is payable semiannually on July 1 and January 1. All of the bonds are registered. The company's accounting period ends on March 31. Quarterly financial statements are prepared.

The company deposits a sum of money sufficient to pay the semiannual interest on the bonds in a special checking account in First National Bank and draws interest payment checks on this account. The deposit is made the day before the checks are drawn.

Problem 15–1
Record issuance of bonds, payment of bonds, payment of interest, and partial period accrual (L.O. 3)

Prepare journal entries to record the issuance of the bonds; the December 31 adjusting entry; the January 1, 1999, interest payment; and the adjusting entry needed on March 31, 1999, to prepare quarterly financial statements.

Required

Safe Toy Company is seeking to issue $800,000 face value of 10%, 20-year bonds. The bonds are dated June 30, 1998, call for semiannual interest payments, and mature on June 30, 2018.

Required

a. Compute the price investors should offer if they seek a yield of 8% on these bonds. Also, compute the first six months' interest assuming the bonds are issued at that price. Use the interest method and calculate all amounts to the nearest dollar.

b. Repeat part **a** assuming investors seek a yield of 12%.

Problem 15–2
Compute two prices on bond issue and first period's interest (L.O. 5, 6)

On July 1, 1998, Tick-Tock Clock Company issued $100,000 face value of 8%, 10-year bonds. These bonds call for semiannual interest payments and mature on July 1, 2008. The company received cash of $87,538, a price that yields 10%.

Required
Assume that the company's fiscal year ends on March 31. Prepare journal entries to record the bond interest expense on January 1, 1999, and the adjustment needed on March 31, 1999, using the interest method. Calculate all amounts to the nearest dollar.

Problem 15–3
Record bond interest expense and accrual for partial period (L.O. 6)

Creative Web Page issued $600,000 face value of 15%, 20-year bonds on October 1, 1999. The bonds are dated October 1, 1999, call for semiannual interest payments on April 1 and October 1, and are issued to yield 16% (8% per period).

Required

a. Compute the amount received for the bonds.

b. Prepare an amortization schedule similar to that in Illustration 15.4. Enter data in the schedule for only the first two interest periods. Use the interest method.

c. Prepare journal entries to record issuance of the bonds, the first six months' interest expense on the bonds, and the adjustment needed on May 31, 2000, assuming Creative Web Page's fiscal year ends on that date.

Problem 15–4
Compute price of bonds, prepare amortization schedule, journalize bond issuance, and accrue interest (L.O. 5, 6)

Problem 15–5
Compute price of bonds;
prepare amortization
schedule; journalize bond
issuance; and record two
interest payments
(L.O. 5, 6)

Goodhew Software Systems, Inc., issued $100,000 face value of 10%, 20-year bonds on July 1, 1998. The bonds are dated July 1, 1998, call for semiannual interest payments on July 1 and January 1, and are issued to yield 12% (6% per period).

Required

a. Compute the amount received for the bonds.

b. Prepare an amortization schedule similar to that in Illustration 15.4. Enter data in the schedule for only the first two interest periods. Use the interest method and calculate all amounts to the nearest dollar.

c. Prepare entries to record the issuance of the bonds, the first six months' interest on the bonds, and the adjustment needed on June 30, 1999, assuming Goodhew's fiscal year ends on that date.

Problem 15–6
Record serial bond
transactions, and show
financial reporting (L.O. 7)

Western Solar Energy Company issued $400,000 of 12% bonds on July 1, 1998, at face value. The bonds are dated July 1, 1998, call for semiannual payments on July 1 and January 1, and mature at the rate of $40,000 per year on July 1, beginning in 2003. The company's accounting period ends on September 30.

Required

a. Prepare journal entries to record the interest expense and payment for the six months ending July 1, 2003; the maturing of the bonds on July 1, 2003; and the adjusting entries needed on September 30, 2003.

b. Show how the bonds would be presented in the company's balance sheet for September 30, 2003.

ALTERNATE PROBLEMS

Problem 15–1A
Record issuance of bonds
and payment of interest
(L.O. 3)

On June 1, 1998, Economy Auto Parts, Inc., issued $180,000 of 10-year, 16% bonds dated April 1, 1998, at 100. Interest on bonds is payable semiannually on presentation of the appropriate coupon. All of the bonds are of $1,000 denomination. The company's accounting period ends on June 30, with semiannual statements prepared on December 31 and June 30. The interest payment dates are April 1 and October 1.

All of the first coupons on the bonds are presented to the company's bank and paid on October 2, 1998. All but two of the second coupons are similarly received and paid on April 1, 1999.

Required

Prepare all necessary journal entries for these transactions through April 1, 1999, including the adjusting entry needed at June 30, 1998.

Problem 15–2A
Compute two prices for
bond issue and first
period's interest (L.O. 5, 6)

Ecological Water Filtration, Inc., is going to issue $400,000 face value of 10%, 15-year bonds. The bonds are dated June 30, 1998, call for semiannual interest payments, and mature on June 30, 2013.

Required

a. Compute the price investors should offer if they seek a yield of 8% on these bonds. Also, compute the first six months' interest, assuming the bonds are issued at this price. Use the interest method and calculate all amounts to the nearest dollar.

b. Repeat part **a,** assuming investors seek a yield of 12%.

Problem 15–3A
Record bond interest
expense payment and
accrual for partial period
(L.O. 6)

On July 1, 1998, South Carolina Table Company issued $600,000 face value of 10%, 10-year bonds. The bonds call for semiannual interest payments and mature on July 1, 2008. The company received cash of $531,180, a price that yields 12%.

Required

Assume that the company's fiscal year ends on March 31. Prepare journal entries (to the nearest dollar) to record the bond interest expense on January 1, 1999, and the adjustment needed on March 31, 1999, using the interest method. Calculate all amounts to the nearest dollar.

Storall Company issued $200,000 face value of 16%, 20-year junk bonds on July 1, 1999. The bonds are dated July 1, 1999, call for semiannual interest payments on July 1 and January 1, and were issued to yield 12% (6% per period).

Required

a. Compute the amount received for the bonds.
b. Prepare an amortization schedule similar to that in Illustration 15.5. Enter data in the schedule for only the first two interest periods. Use the interest method.
c. Prepare journal entries to record issuance of the bonds, the first six months' interest expense on the bonds, and the adjustment needed on May 31, 2000, assuming the company's fiscal year ends on that date.

Problem 15–4A
Compute price of bonds; prepare amortization schedule; journalize bond issuance and interest payment (L.O. 5, 6)

Kelly Furniture Company issued $400,000 face value of 18%, 20-year junk bonds on October 1, 1998. The bonds are dated October 1, 1998, call for semiannual interest payments on April 1 and October 1, and are issued to yield 16% (8% per period).

Required

a. Compute the amount received for the bonds.
b. Prepare an amortization schedule similar to that in Illustration 15.5. Enter data in the schedule for only the first two interest periods. Use the interest method and make all calculations to the nearest dollar.
c. Prepare entries to record the issuance of the bonds, the first six months' interest on the bonds, and the adjustment needed on June 30, 1999, assuming the company's fiscal year ends on that date.

Problem 15–5A
Compute price of bonds; prepare amortization schedule; journalize bond issuance, payment of first period's interest, and accrual of partial period's interest (L.O. 5, 6)

Houston Clothing Company issued $600,000 of 12% serial bonds on July 1, 1998, at face value. The bonds are dated July 1, 1998; call for semiannual interest payments on July 1 and January 1; and mature at the rate of $120,000 per year, with the first maturity date falling on July 1, 2003. The company's accounting period ends on September 30.

Prepare journal entries to record the interest payment of July 1, 2003; the maturing of $120,000 of bonds on July 1, 2003; and the adjusting entry needed on September 30, 2003. Also, show how the bonds would be presented in the company's balance sheet for September 30, 2003.

Problem 15–6A
Record serial bond transactions, and show financial reporting (L.O. 7)

Required

BEYOND THE NUMBERS—CRITICAL THINKING

A company is trying to decide whether to invest $2 million on plant expansion and $1 million to finance a related increase in inventories and accounts receivable. The $3 million expansion is expected to increase business volume substantially. Profit forecasts indicate that income from operations will rise from $1.6 million to $2.4 million. The income tax rate will be about 40%. Net income last year was $918,000. Interest expense on debt now outstanding is $70,000 per year. There are 200,000 shares of common stock currently outstanding.

The $3 million needed can be obtained in two alternative ways:

1. Finance entirely by issuing additional shares of common stock at an expected issue price of $75 per share.
2. Finance two-thirds with bonds, one-third with additional stock. The bonds would have a 20-year life, bear interest at 10%, and sell at face value. The issue price of the stock would be $80 per share.

Should the investment be made? If so, explain which financing plan you would recommend. (Hint: Calculate earnings per share for last year and for future years under each of the alternatives.)

Business Decision Case 15–1
Analyze two financing proposals; decide whether investment should be made (L.O. 2)

Required

An annual report of a company contained the following paragraph in the notes to the financial statements:

The 9⅞% Senior Subordinated Debentures are redeemable at the option of [the company] at 103.635% of the principal amount plus accrued interest if redeemed prior to [a certain date], and at decreasing prices thereafter. Mandatory sinking fund payments of $3,000,000 (which [the company] may increase to $6,000,000 annually) . . . and are intended to retire, at par plus accrued interest, 75% of the issue prior to maturity.

Business Decision Case 15–2
Answer questions regarding annual report (L.O. 7)

Required   Answer the following questions:

a.   What does the term *debentures* mean?

b.   How much is the call premium initially? Does this premium decrease over time?

c.   Under what circumstances might the company want to increase the sinking fund payments?

Business Decision Case 15–3
Answer questions regarding bond yields (L.O. 8)

The April 29, 1994, issue of *The Wall Street Journal* contained a table showing yield comparisons for groups of corporate bonds. The following data have been adapted from the table:

| | Yield Percentage | | | |
| | As of | | 52-week | |
Risk category	4/28	4/27	High	Low
1–10 year maturities:				
High quality	7.08%	6.94%	7.16%	5.32%
Medium quality	7.41	7.26	7.49	5.76
Over 10 year maturities:				
High quality	7.91	7.81	8.06	6.93
Medium quality	8.36	8.25	8.49	7.29
High-yield bonds	10.45	10.48	10.53	9.25

Standard & Poor's ratings were:
High quality   AAA to AA
Medium quality   A to BBB
High yield   BB to C

Required   Prepare written answers to the following questions.

a.   In each column of numbers, why do the yield rates increase from top to bottom?

b.   For the high quality and medium quality bonds, what could account for the increase in the yield rates from 4/27/94 to 4/28/94? Take into consideration the economic events occurring at about that time.

c.   Which risk class of bonds was closest to its 52-week high on 4/28/94? What could have been the cause?

Annual Report Analysis 15–4
Calculate times interest earned ratio for three companies and prepare written comments on results (L.O. 9)

Refer to the annual report booklet and determine the times interest earned ratios for 1996 for The Coca-Cola Company, Maytag Corporation, and The Limited, Inc. Use "operating income" to represent IBIT. Prepare written comments on the results of your analysis.

Annual Report Analysis 15–5
Decide whether to convert or surrender bonds (real world problem) (L.O. 7)

A recent annual report of Emhart Corporation contained the following paragraph in its notes to the financial statements:

The 6¾% convertible subordinated debentures may be converted into shares of common stock at a price of $26.50 per share at any time prior to maturity. They are redeemable at prices decreasing from 105 percent of face amount currently to 100 percent [at a certain future date].

Required   Answer the following questions:

a.   If you held one $1,000 bond, how many shares of stock would you receive if you converted the bond into shares of stock? (Hint: You can use the principal amount of the bond to buy shares of stock at the stated price.)

b.   Assume you held one $1,000 bond and the bond was called by the company at a price of 105% of the face amount. If the current market price per share of the stock was $29, would you convert the bond into shares of stock or would you surrender the bond? Explain.

Refer to "An Ethical Perspective" on page 561. Write out the answers to the following questions:

a. What motivates the brothers to pursue this new strategy?

b. Are the brothers the only ones assuming the risks?

c. How will workers, the city, the holders of the original bond issue, and the other present stockholders be affected if the junk bonds are issued and are then defaulted?

d. How might these parties (stakeholders) be affected if a new buyer outbids the management?

e. What ethical considerations are involved?

Ethics Case—Writing Experience 15–6
Answer questions regarding ethics case

In groups of two or three students, write a two-page, double-spaced paper on one of the following topics:

The Use of Junk Bonds in the 1980s

Why Market Rates of Interest and Prices of Bonds Are Inversely Related

How a Company Can Force Conversion of Callable, Convertible Bonds

How Bond Sinking Funds Work

Group Project 15–7
Write a paper on a specific topic

Do some library research on your topic and properly cite your sources. Make your analysis convincing. Your paper should be neat, contain no spelling or grammatical errors, and be the result of several drafts. Use a word processing program to prepare your paper if possible. Your paper should have a cover page with the title and the authors' names.

In a small group of students, locate *Accounting Principles Board Opinion No. 21* (from a faculty member or from the library) relating to the amortization of premiums and discounts on bonds. Investigate why the Board recommended the effective interest rate method over the straight-line method for amortizing bond premiums and discounts. Which method do you favor and why? Summarize the highlights of the APB *Opinion* and your own opinions in a written report to your instructor.

Group Project 15–8
Investigate why effective interest rate method is favored over straight-line method for amortization of premiums and discounts

With one or two other students, locate the annual reports of three companies with bonds outstanding as part of their long-term debt. You should read the notes to the financial statements to determine the composition of the long-term debt. Identify the bonds (e.g., debentures, serial), their interest rates, and any other information pertaining to them. Compare the bonds outstanding for the three companies. Write a report to your instructor summarizing your findings.

Group Project 15–9
Investigate annual reports of companies with bonds outstanding

USING THE INTERNET—A VIEW OF THE REAL WORLD

Visit the following site for Digital Equipment Corporation:
http://www.dec.com
By following the instructions on the screen, locate the notes to the financial statements and find the one pertaining to long-term debt. In your own words, write a short report to your instructor summarizing the types of long-term debt held by DEC and some of the details of the arrangements with lenders.

Internet Project 15–10
Analyze types of long-term debt

Visit the following website for Eastman Chemical Company:
http://www.eastman.com
Pursue choices on the screen until you locate the financial information. Then investigate long-term borrowings. You will probably go down some "false paths" to get to this financial information, but you can get there. This experience is all part of learning to use the Internet. Check to determine the composition of the long-term borrowings. Check out the notes to the financial statements for further information. Browse around the site for any other interesting information concerning the company. Write a memo to your instructor summarizing your findings.

Internet Project 15–11
Investigate long-term borrowings

ANSWERS TO SELF-TEST

TRUE-FALSE

1. **True.** These unsecured bonds are called debenture bonds and are backed only by the general credit-worthiness of the issuer.

2. **False.** Callable bonds may be called at the option of the issuer.

3. **True.** This statement is the definition of favorable financial leverage. However, unfavorable financial leverage can result when favorable financial leverage was planned. Unfavorable financial leverage will result if income before interest and taxes is much lower than anticipated. Then earnings per share for the common stockholders would be lower than they would have been without the borrowing.

4. **True.** Purchasers will not be willing to pay the face amount if the market rate of interest exceeds the contract rate. By paying less than the face value, purchasers can earn the market rate of interest on the bonds.

5. **False.** The effective interest rate method is the recommended method. The straight-line method may be used only when the results are not materially different from the interest method.

MULTIPLE-CHOICE

1. **a.** The discount of $4,000 must be recorded. Also, the accrued interest must be recognized ($100,000 × 12% × $\frac{2}{12}$ = $2,000).

2. **c.** The premium is $4,000, and the accrued interest is $2,000. Both must be recognized.

3. **b.** The interest is ($328,298 × 0.11 × ½) = $18,056.

4. **d.** The interest would have been ($400,000 × 0.04) + ($71,702/20) = $19,585.

5. **c.** Income before interest and taxes is ($100,000 + $40,000 + $20,000) = $160,000. This total of $160,000 divided by interest of $20,000 = 8 times.

V

Analysis of Financial Statements Using the Statement of Cash Flows

---

A Manager's Perspective

Don Lehman

Principal Accountant

The Coca-Cola Company

After working for three and a half years as a "Big Six" auditor, I moved to The Coca-Cola Company in the corporate finance division, working primarily on the company's external financial reporting. I was project manager for the financial section of the company's Annual Report to Share Owners for two years, and I also coordinated with

the field divisions and the external auditors to implement two of the recently issued accounting standards.

As part of my responsibilities, I work with people from every part of the Company—Marketing, Operations, Legal, Human Resources, etc. I am often a financial division "representative" on committees or task forces. I have found that many of the non-financial people I work with in these situations have a relatively broad knowledge of finance and some knowledge of basic accounting. Many of these people came from accounting backgrounds, and others have sought additional training or education. This working knowledge of accounting is extremely important in getting team assignments completed quickly, because the team members can focus immediately on a solution with the best possible financial impact.

Almost every decision made here, as at most companies, is based on its eventual impact on the company's financial results, so a solid background in accounting and finance is an advantage for persons in non-financial roles who are trying to understand how their actions will be evaluated. The fundamental concepts that define assets, equity, and expenses are crucial to making informed management decisions at every level of every business. While learning all the accounting rules for employee benefits and equity-method investees is not necessary for every student, a good understanding of accounting principles is an essential building-block for your career.

16

ANALYSIS USING THE STATEMENT OF CASH FLOWS

The income statement, statement of stockholders' equity (or statement of retained earnings), and the balance sheet do not answer all the questions raised by users of financial statements. Such questions include: How much cash was generated by the company's operations? How can the Cash account be overdrawn when my accountant said the business was profitable? Why is such a profitable company able to pay only small dividends? How much was spent for new plant and equipment, and where did the company get the cash for the expenditures? How was the company able to pay a dividend when it incurred a net loss for the year?

In this chapter, you will learn about the statement of cash flows, which answers these questions. The statement of cash flows is another major required financial statement; it shows important information not shown directly in the other financial statements.

PURPOSES OF THE STATEMENT OF CASH FLOWS

In November 1987, the Financial Accounting Standards Board issued *Statement of Financial Accounting Standards No. 95,* "Statement of Cash Flows."[1] The *Statement* became effective for annual financial statements for fiscal years ending after July 15, 1988. Thus, the statement of cash flows is now one of the major financial statements issued by a company. The statement of cash flows replaced the statement of changes in financial position, on which *funds* were generally defined as working capital. **Working capital** is equal to current assets minus current liabilities.

The main purpose of the statement of cash flows is to report on the cash receipts and cash disbursements of an entity during an accounting period. Broadly defined, *cash* includes both cash and cash equivalents, such as short-term investments in

LEARNING OBJECTIVES

After studying this chapter, you should be able to:

1. Explain the purposes and uses of the statement of cash flows.

2. Describe the content of the statement of cash flows and where certain items would appear on the statement.

3. Describe how to calculate cash flows from operating activities under both the direct and indirect methods.

(continued)

[1]FASB, *Statement of Financial Accounting Standards No. 95,* "Statement of Cash Flows" (Stamford, Conn., 1987). Copyright by the Financial Accounting Standards Board, High Ridge Park, Stamford, Connecticut 06905. U.S.A. Quoted (or excerpted) with permission. Copies of the complete document are available from the FASB.

Objective 1
Explain the purposes and uses of the statement of cash flows.

Treasury bills, commercial paper, and money market funds. Another purpose of this statement is to report on the entity's investing and financing activities for the period. As shown in Illustration 16.1, the statement of cash flows reports the effects on cash during a period of a company's operating, investing, and financing activities. Firms show the effects of significant investing and financing activities that do not affect cash in a schedule separate from the statement of cash flows.

USES OF THE STATEMENT OF CASH FLOWS

The **statement of cash flows** summarizes the effects on cash of the operating, investing, and financing activities of a company during an accounting period; it reports on past management decisions on such matters as issuance of capital stock or the sale of long-term bonds. This information is available only in bits and pieces from the other financial statements. Since cash flows are vital to a company's financial health, the statement of cash flows provides useful information to management, investors, creditors, and other interested parties.

Management Uses

The statement of cash flows presents the effects on cash of all significant operating, investing, and financing activities. By reviewing the statement, management can see the effects of its past major policy decisions in quantitative form. The statement may show a flow of cash from operating activities large enough to finance all projected capital needs internally rather than having to incur long-term debt or issue additional stock. Alternatively, if the company has been experiencing cash shortages, management can use the statement to determine why such shortages are occurring. Using the statement of cash flows, management may also recommend to the board of directors a reduction in dividends to conserve cash.

Investor and Creditor Uses

The information in a statement of cash flows assists investors, creditors, and others in assessing the following:

1. Enterprise's ability to generate positive future net cash flows.
2. Enterprise's ability to meet its obligations.
3. Enterprise's ability to pay dividends.
4. Enterprise's need for external financing.
5. Reasons for differences between net income and associated cash receipts and payments.
6. Effects on an enterprise's financial position of both its cash and noncash investing and financing transactions during the period (disclosed in a separate schedule).

INFORMATION IN THE STATEMENT OF CASH FLOWS

Objective 2
Describe the content of the statement of cash flows and where certain items would appear on the statement.

The statement of cash flows classifies cash receipts and disbursements as operating, investing, and financing cash flows. Both inflows and outflows are included within each category. Look at Illustration 16.2 to see how activities can be classified to prepare a statement of cash flows.

Operating activities generally include the cash effects (inflows and outflows) of transactions and other events that enter into the determination of net income. *Cash inflows* from operating activities affect items that appear on the income statement and include: (1) cash receipts from sales of goods or services; (2) interest received from making loans; (3) dividends received from investments in equity securities; (4) cash received from the sale of trading securities; and (5) other cash receipts that do not arise from transactions defined as investing or financing activities, such as amounts

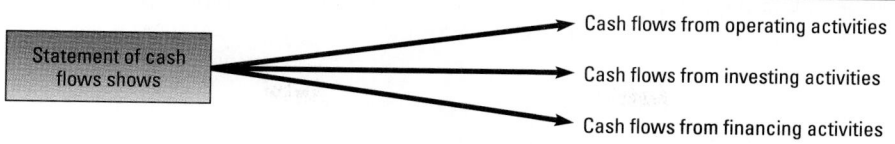

ILLUSTRATION 16.1
Statement of Cash
Flows—Basic Content

Investing and financing activities that do not affect cash are shown in a separate schedule.

Operating activities   Cash effects of transactions and other events that enter into the determination of net income

Cash inflows from:	Cash outflows for:
Sales of goods or services	Merchandise inventory
Interest	Salaries and wages
Dividends	Interest
Sale of trading securities	Purchase of trading securities
Other sources not related to investing or financing activities (e.g., insurance settlements)	Other expenses
	Other items not related to investing or financing activities (e.g., contributions to charities)

Investing activities   Transactions involving the acquisition or disposal of noncurrent assets

Cash inflows from:	Cash outflows for:
Sale of property, plant, and equipment	Purchase of property, plant, and equipment
Sale of available-for-sale and held-to-maturity securities	Purchase of available-for-sale and held-to-maturity securities
Collection of loans	Making of loans

Financing activities   Transactions with creditors and owners

Cash inflows from:	Cash outflows for:
Issuing capital stock	Purchase of treasury stock
Issuing debt (bonds, mortgages, notes, and other short- or long-term borrowing of cash)	Payment of debt (principal only)
	Cash dividends

ILLUSTRATION 16.2
Rules for Classifying
Activities in the
Statement of Cash Flows

received to settle lawsuits, proceeds of certain insurance settlements, and cash refunds from suppliers.

Cash outflows for operating activities affect items that appear on the income statement and include payments: (1) to acquire inventory; (2) to other suppliers and employees for other goods or services; (3) to lenders and other creditors for interest; (4) for purchases of trading securities; and (5) all other cash payments that do not arise from transactions defined as investing or financing activities, such as taxes and payments to settle lawsuits, cash contributions to charities, and cash refunds to customers.

Investing activities generally include transactions involving the acquisition or disposal of noncurrent assets. Thus, *cash inflows* from investing activities include cash received from: (1) the sale of property, plant, and equipment; (2) the sale of available-for-sale and held-to-maturity securities; and (3) the collection of long-term loans made to others. *Cash outflows* for investing activities include cash paid: (1) to purchase property, plant, and equipment; (2) to purchase available-for-sale and held-to-maturity securities; and (3) to make long-term loans to others.

Financing activities generally include the cash effects (inflows and outflows) of transactions and other events involving creditors and owners. *Cash inflows* from financing activities include cash received from issuing capital stock and bonds, mortgages, and notes, and from other short- or long-term borrowing. *Cash outflows* for financing activities include payments of cash dividends or other distributions to owners (including cash paid to purchase treasury stock) and repayments of amounts borrowed. Payment of interest is not included because interest expense appears on the income statement and is, therefore, included in operating activities. Cash payments to

Note to the Student
Cash flows from operating activities consist of items from the income statement converted to a cash basis. Cash flows from investing activities are the cash inflows and outflows resulting from the acquisition and disposal of noncurrent assets. Cash flows from financing activities are generally the cash inflows and outflows resulting from the noncurrent liabilities and equity sections of the balance sheet.

settle accounts payable, wages payable, and income taxes payable are not financing activities. These payments are operating activities.

A Separate Schedule for Significant Noncash Investing and Financing Activities

Reinforcing Problem
E16–1 Report specific items on statement of cash flows.

Information about all material investing and financing activities of an enterprise that do not result in cash receipts or disbursements during the period appear in a separate schedule, rather than in the statement of cash flows. The disclosure may be in narrative form. For instance, assume a company issued a mortgage note to acquire land and buildings. A separate schedule might appear as follows:

Schedule of noncash financing and investing activities:

Mortgage note issued to acquire land and buildings $35,000

AN ACCOUNTING PERSPECTIVE

BUSINESS INSIGHT   In a supplemental schedule of noncash investing and financing activities, Johnson & Johnson reported one item as follows:

Treasury stock issued for employee compensation and stock option
plans, net of cash proceeds . . . . $252 million

The company included the cash proceeds amount from the exercise of stock options ($149 million) in the cash flows from financing activities section of the statement of cash flows.

CASH FLOWS FROM OPERATING ACTIVITIES

Objective 3
Describe how to calculate cash flows from operating activities under both the direct and indirect methods.

Cash flows from operating activities show the net amount of cash received or disbursed during a given period for items that normally appear on the income statement. You can calculate these cash flows using either the direct or indirect method. The **direct method** deducts from cash sales only those operating expenses that *consumed cash*. This method converts each item on the income statement *directly* to a cash basis. Alternatively, the **indirect (addback) method** starts with accrual basis net income and indirectly adjusts net income for items that affected reported net income but did not involve cash.

Note to the Student
The FASB encourages the use of the direct method but permits use of the indirect method. As shown in the chart, only a few companies use the direct method.

The *Statement of Financial Accounting Standards No. 95* encourages use of the direct method but permits use of the indirect method. Companies use the indirect method much more frequently, as shown in the following table. Whenever given a choice between the indirect and direct methods in similar situations, accountants choose the indirect method almost exclusively.

Method of Reporting Cash Flows from Operating Activities

	Number of Companies			
	1995	1994	1993	1992
Indirect method	585	586	585	585
Direct method	15	14	15	15
Total companies presenting statement of cash flows	600	600	600	600

Source: American Institute of Certified Public Accountants, *Accounting Trends & Techniques* (New York: AICPA, 1996), p. 461.

Note to the Student
Even though the indirect method is widely used in practice, studying the direct method is still worthwhile. For example, the insurance industry requires the use of the direct method for statutory reporting and *GASB Statement No. 9* implies a preference for the direct method over the indirect method in reports for governmental entities.

The direct method converts each item on the income statement to a cash basis. For instance, assume that sales are stated at $100,000 on an accrual basis. If accounts receivable increased by $5,000, cash collections from customers would be $95,000, calculated as $100,000 − $5,000. The direct method also converts all remaining items on the income statement to a cash basis, as we will illustrate later.

The indirect method adjusts net income (rather than adjusting individual items in the income statement) for (1) changes in current assets (other than cash) and current liabilities, and (2) items that were included in net income but did not affect cash.

The most common example of an operating expense that does not affect cash is depreciation expense. The journal entry to record depreciation debits an expense account and credits an accumulated depreciation account. This transaction has no effect on cash and, therefore, should not be included when measuring cash from operations. Because accountants deduct depreciation in computing net income, net income understates cash from operations. Under the indirect method, since net income is a starting point in measuring cash flows from operating activities, depreciation expense must be added back to net income.

Consider the following example. Company A had net income for the year of $20,000 after deducting depreciation of $10,000, yielding $30,000 of positive cash flows. Thus, Company A had $30,000 of positive cash flows from operating activities. Company B had a net loss for the year of $4,000 after deducting $10,000 of depreciation. Although Company B experienced a loss, it had $6,000 of positive cash flows from operating activities, as shown here:

	Company A	Company B
Net income (loss)	$20,000	$(4,000)
Add depreciation expense (which did not require use of cash)	10,000	10,000
Positive cash flows from operating activities	$30,000	$ 6,000

Company B's loss would have had to exceed $10,000 to generate negative cash flows from operating activities.

Companies add other expenses and losses back to net income because they do not actually use company cash; they call these addbacks **noncash charges or expenses**. Besides depreciation, the items added back include amounts of depletion that were expensed, amortization of intangible assets such as patents and goodwill, amortization of discount on bonds payable, and losses from disposals of noncurrent assets.

BUSINESS INSIGHT   PSINet, Inc., an Internet-access provider, said it would have a positive cash flow from operations for the first time in early 1997. The company was the first to provide unlimited access to the Internet to consumers at a flat rate of $19.95 per month. However, it was costing about $22 per month per customer to provide the service. The company decided to abandon this market and sell only to the more profitable corporate market. Corporate clients can be charged about $200 per month for dial-up access.

Source: "PSINet Sees Positive Cash Flow in '97; Likely Financial Boost Lifts Shares 24%," *The Wall Street Journal*, Friday, December 27, 1996, p. B11.

AN ACCOUNTING PERSPECTIVE

To illustrate the addback of losses from disposals of noncurrent assets, assume that Quick Company sold a piece of equipment for $6,000. The equipment had cost $10,000 and had accumulated depreciation of $3,000. The journal entry to record the sale is:

Cash	6,000	
Accumulated Depreciation	3,000	
Loss on Sale of Equipment	1,000	
Equipment		10,000
To record disposal of equipment at a loss.		

Quick would show the $6,000 inflow from the sale of the equipment as a cash inflow from investing activities on its statement of cash flows. Although Quick deducted the loss of $1,000 in calculating net income, it recognized the total $6,000 effect on cash (which reflects the $1,000 loss) as resulting from an investing activity. Thus, Quick must add the loss back to net income in converting net income to cash flows from operating activities to avoid double-counting the loss.

Certain revenues and gains included in arriving at net income do not provide cash; these items are **noncash credits or revenues**. Quick should deduct these revenues and gains from net income to compute cash flows from operating activities. Such items include gains from disposals of noncurrent assets, income from investments carried under the equity method, and amortization of premiums on bonds payable.

To illustrate why we deduct the gain on the disposal of a noncurrent asset from net income, assume that Quick sold the equipment just mentioned for $9,000. The journal entry to record the sale is:

Cash	9,000	
Accumulated Depreciation	3,000	
Equipment		10,000
Gain on Sale of Equipment		2,000
To record disposal of equipment at a gain.		

Quick shows the $9,000 inflow from the sale of the equipment on its statement of cash flows as a cash inflow from investing activities. Thus, it has already recognized the total $9,000 effect on cash (including the $2,000 gain) as resulting from an investing activity. Since the $2,000 gain is also included in calculating net income, Quick must deduct the gain in converting net income to cash flows from operating activities to avoid double-counting the gain.

STEPS IN PREPARING STATEMENT OF CASH FLOWS

Objective 4
Prepare a statement of cash flows, under both the direct and indirect methods, showing cash flows from operating activities, investing activities, and financing activities.

Accountants follow specific procedures when preparing a statement of cash flows. We show these procedures using the financial statements and additional data for Welby Company in Illustration 16.3.

After determining the change in cash, the first step in preparing the statement of cash flows is to calculate the cash flows from operating activities, using either the direct or indirect method. The second step is to analyze all of the noncurrent accounts and additional data for changes resulting from investing and financing activities. The third step is to arrange the information gathered in steps 1 and 2 into the proper format for the statement of cash flows.

Step 1: Determining Cash Flows from Operating Activities—Direct Method

The direct method converts the income statement from the accrual basis to the cash basis. Accountants must consider changes in balance sheet accounts that are related to items on the income statement. The accounts involved are all current assets or current liabilities. The following schedule shows which balance sheet accounts are related to the items on Welby's income statement:

Income Statement Items	Related Balance Sheet Items	Cash Flows from Operating Activities
Sales	Accounts Receivable	Cash received from customers
Cost of goods sold	Accounts Payable and Merchandise Inventory	Cash paid for merchandise
Operating expenses and taxes	Accrued Liabilities and Prepaid Expenses	Cash paid for operating expenses

For other income statement items, the relationship is often obvious. For instance, salaries payable relates to salaries expense, federal income tax payable relates to federal income tax expense, prepaid rent relates to rent expense, and so on.

The table below shows how income statement items are affected by the balance sheet accounts:

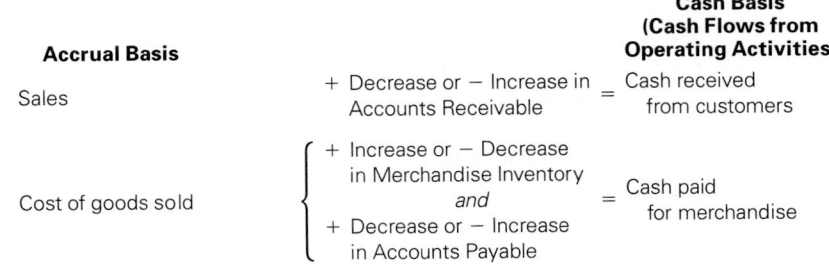

Accrual Basis		Cash Basis (Cash Flows from Operating Activities)
Sales	+ Decrease or − Increase in Accounts Receivable =	Cash received from customers
Cost of goods sold	+ Increase or − Decrease in Merchandise Inventory *and* + Decrease or − Increase in Accounts Payable =	Cash paid for merchandise

ILLUSTRATION 16.3
Financial Statements
and Other Data

WELBY COMPANY
Comparative Balance Sheets
December 31, 1999, and 1998

	1999	1998	Increase/ (Decrease)
Assets			
Cash	$ 21,000	$ 10,000	$11,000
Accounts receivable, net	30,000	20,000	10,000
Merchandise inventory	26,000	30,000	(4,000)
Equipment	70,000	50,000	20,000
Accumulated depreciation—Equipment	(10,000)	(5,000)	(5,000)
Total assets	$137,000	$105,000	$32,000
Liabilities and Stockholders' Equity			
Accounts payable	$ 9,000	$ 15,000	$ (6,000)
Accrued liabilities payable	2,000	–0–	2,000
Common stock ($10 par value)	90,000	60,000	30,000
Retained earnings	36,000	30,000	6,000
Total liabilities and stockholders' equity	$137,000	$105,000	$32,000

WELBY COMPANY
Income Statement
For the Year Ended December 31, 1999

Sales		$140,000
Cost of goods sold		100,000
Gross margin		$ 40,000
Operating expenses		
(other than depreciation)	$25,000	
Depreciation expense	5,000	30,000
Net income		$ 10,000

Additional data
1. Equipment purchased for cash during 1999 amounted to $20,000.
2. Common stock with a par value of $30,000 was issued at par for cash.
3. Cash dividends declared and paid in 1999 totaled $4,000.

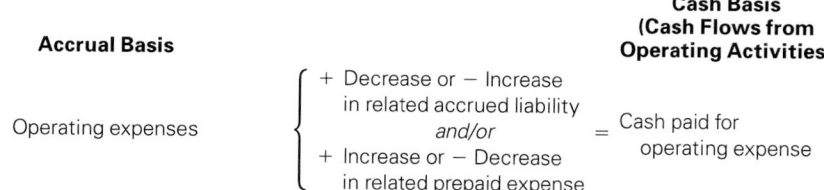

Accrual Basis

Cash Basis (Cash Flows from Operating Activities)

Operating expenses
$$\left\{ \begin{array}{l} + \text{ Decrease or } - \text{ Increase} \\ \text{in related accrued liability} \\ \textit{and/or} \\ + \text{ Increase or } - \text{ Decrease} \\ \text{in related prepaid expense} \end{array} \right\} = \begin{array}{l} \text{Cash paid for} \\ \text{operating expense} \end{array}$$

Noncash operating expenses (such as depreciation expense and amortization expense), revenues, gains, and losses are reduced to zero in the cash basis income statement.

As a general rule, an increase in a current asset (other than cash) decreases cash inflow or increases cash outflow. Thus, when accounts receivable increases, sales revenue on a cash basis decreases (some customers who bought merchandise have not yet paid for it). When inventory increases, cost of goods sold on a cash basis increases (increasing cash outflow). When a prepaid expense increases, the related operating expense on a cash basis increases. (For example, a company not only paid for insurance expense but also paid cash to increase prepaid insurance.) The effect on cash flows is just the opposite for decreases in these other current assets.

An increase in a current liability increases cash inflow or decreases cash outflow. Thus, when accounts payable increases, cost of goods sold on a cash basis decreases (instead of paying cash, the purchase was made on credit). When an accrued liability

ILLUSTRATION 16.4
Working Paper to
Convert Income
Statement from Accrual
Basis to Cash Basis

WELBY COMPANY
Working Paper to Convert Income Statement from Accrual
Basis to Cash Basis
For the Year Ended December 31, 1999

	Accrual Basis		Add	Deduct		Cash Basis (Cash Flows from Operating Activities)
Sales		$140,000		$10,000*		$130,000
Cost of goods sold	$100,000		$6,000†	4,000‡	$102,000	
Operating expenses . . .	25,000			2,000§	23,000	
Depreciation expense . .	5,000			5,000	–0–	
		130,000				125,000
Net income		$ 10,000				$ 5,000

*Increase in Accounts Receivable.
†Decrease in Accounts Payable.
‡Decrease in Merchandise Inventory.
§Increase in Accrued Liabilities Payable.

(such as salaries payable) increases, the related operating expense (salaries expense) on a cash basis decreases. (For example, the company incurred more salaries than it paid.) Decreases in current liabilities have just the opposite effect on cash flows.

Welby Company had no prepaid expenses. The current assets and current liabilities affecting the income statement items changed as follows:

Note to the Student
T-accounts could be used for the conversion from the accrual basis to the cash basis.

	Increase	Decrease
Accounts receivable	$10,000	
Merchandise inventory		$4,000
Accounts payable		6,000
Accrued liabilities payable	2,000	

Reinforcing Problems
E16–2 Calculate the amount of cash paid for merchandise.
E16–3 Show effects of conversion from accrual to cash basis income.

Thus, Welby converted its income statement to a cash basis as shown in Illustration 16.4.

AN ACCOUNTING PERSPECTIVE

BUSINESS PERSPECTIVE   PMT Services, Inc., uses the direct method for determining net cash provided by operating activities. The company is an independent service organization that markets and services electronic credit card authorization and payment systems to small retail, wholesale, and professional businesses located throughout the United States. The cash flows from the operating activities section of its consolidated statement of cash flows was as follows for the years 1994–1996:

	Year ended July 31,		
	1994	**1995**	**1996**
Cash flows from operating activities:			
Net cash received from merchants	$ 19,657,687	$ 34,353,326	$ 67,313,124
Cash paid to vendors and employees	(14,758,040)	(28,467,472)	(49,128,150)
Interest received	22,262	310,136	1,672,714
Interest paid	(268,586)	(198,485)	(505,856)
Income taxes paid	(994,969)	(1,600,405)	(5,630,881)
Net cash provided by operating activities . .	$ 3,658,354	$ 4,397,100	$ 13,720,951

Alternate Step 1: Determining Cash Flows from Operating Activities—Indirect Method

The indirect method makes certain adjustments to convert net income to cash flows from operating activities. Welby must analyze the effects of changes in current accounts (other than cash) on cash. The firm should also take into account noncash items such as depreciation that affected net income but not cash. Welby had only one such item—depreciation expense of $5,000. Applying these adjustments to

Welby's financial statements and other data in Illustration 16.3 yields the following schedule:

Cash flows from operating activities:

Net income	$ 10,000
Adjustments to reconcile net income to net cash provided by operating activities:	
Increase in accounts receivable	(10,000)
Decrease in merchandise inventory	4,000
Decrease in accounts payable	(6,000)
Increase in accrued liabilities payable	2,000
Depreciation expense	5,000
Net cash provided by operating activities . . .	$5,000

Real-World Example
For the year ending December 31, 1996, using the indirect method, General Electric Company reported net cash provided by operating activities of $17,851,000,000.

Notice that both the direct and indirect methods result in $5,000 net cash provided by operating activities.

You can use the following table to make the adjustments to net income for the changes in current assets and current liabilities:

For changes in these current assets and current liabilities:	Make these adjustments to convert accrual basis net income to cash basis net income:	
	Add	**Deduct**
Accounts receivable	Decrease	Increase
Merchandise inventory	Decrease	Increase
Prepaid expenses	Decrease	Increase
Accounts payable	Increase	Decrease
Accrued liabilities payable . . .	Increase	Decrease

Note that you would handle all changes in current asset accounts in a similar manner. All changes in current liability accounts require the opposite treatment of the current asset changes. Use this table in making these adjustments:

For Changes in—	Add the Changes to Net Income	Deduct the Changes from Net Income
Current assets	Decreases	Increases
Current liabilities	Increases	Decreases

In applying the rules in this table, add a decrease in a current asset to net income, and deduct an increase in a current asset from net income. For current liabilities, add increases to net income, and deduct decreases from net income.

Under the indirect method, the amount of cash flows from operating activities is calculated as follows:

Accrual basis net income

+ or − Changes in noncash current asset and current liability accounts

+ Expenses and losses not affecting cash

− Revenues and gains not affecting cash

= Cash flows from operating activities

Reinforcing Problems
E16–4 Compute cash flows from operating activities.
E16–5 Compute cash flows from operating activities.

After analyzing the changes in current accounts for their effect on cash, we examine the noncurrent accounts and additional data. Remember that a change in a noncurrent account usually comes about because cash is received or disbursed.

In the Welby example, we must analyze four noncurrent accounts: Retained Earnings, Equipment, Accumulated Depreciation—Equipment, and Common Stock.

Step 2: Analyzing the Noncurrent Accounts and Additional Data

1. The analysis of the noncurrent accounts can begin with any of the noncurrent accounts; we begin by reviewing the Retained Earnings account. Retained Earnings is the account to which net income or loss for the period was closed.

The $6,000 increase in this account consists of $10,000 of net income less $4,000 of dividends paid.

Retained Earnings

		Beg. bal.	30,000
Dividends	4,000	Net income	10,000
		End. bal.	36,000

The net income amount is in the income statement. We enter both net income and dividends on the statement of cash flows in Illustration 16.5, Part B. The $10,000 net income is the starting figure in determining cash flows from operating activities. Thus, we enter the net income of $10,000 on the statement in the cash flows from operating activities section. The dividends are shown as a deduction in the cash flow from financing activities section.

2. The Equipment account increased by $20,000. The dividends are shown as a deduction in the cash flow from financing activities section. The additional data indicate that $20,000 of equipment was purchased during the period. A purchase of equipment is a deduction in the cash flows from investing activities section.

Reinforcing Problem
E16–6 Indicate treatment of a dividend.

3. The $5,000 increase in the Accumulated Depreciation—Equipment account equals the amount of depreciation expense in the income statement for the period. As shown earlier, because depreciation does not affect cash, under the indirect (addback) method we add it back to net income on the statement of cash flows to convert accrual net income to a cash basis.

4. The $30,000 increase in common stock resulted from the issuance of stock at par value, as disclosed in the additional data (item 2) in Illustration 16.3. An issuance of stock in the statement of cash flows is a positive amount in the cash flows from financing activities section.

Step 3: Arranging Information in the Statement of Cash Flows

After we have analyzed the noncurrent accounts, we can prepare the statement of cash flows from the information generated. Part A of Illustration 16.5 presents the statement of cash flows for Welby using the direct method. Part B shows the statement of cash flows for Welby using the indirect method. The appendix to this chapter shows how a working paper can be used to assist in preparing a statement of cash flows for the Welby Company under the indirect method. However, we believe you will gain a greater conceptual understanding by not using a working paper.

The statement of cash flows has three major sections: cash flows from operating activities, cash flows from investing activities, and cash flows from financing activities. The format in the operating activities section differs for the direct and indirect methods. The direct method adjusts each item in the income statement to a cash basis. The indirect method makes these same adjustments but to net income rather than to each item in the income statement. Both methods eliminate not only the effects of noncash items, such as depreciation, but also gains and losses on sales of plant assets.

Reinforcing Problems
BDC16–1 Prepare a statement of cash flows using the indirect method and answer owner's questions.
BDC16–2 Prepare a schedule showing cash flows from operating activities under the indirect method and decide whether certain goals can be met.

The only item in the cash flows from investing activities section is the cash outflow of $20,000 for the purchase of equipment. In a more complex situation, other items could be included in this category.

Two items are under the cash flows from financing activities section. The issuance of common stock resulted in a cash inflow of $30,000. The payment of dividends resulted in a cash outflow of $4,000.

The last line of the statement is the $11,000 increase in cash for the year. Other examples could result in a decrease in cash for the year.

If the direct method is used, the reconciliation of net income to net cash flows from operating activities (the indirect method) must be shown in a separate schedule. However, if the indirect method is used and the reconciliation is shown in the statement of cash flows, no such separate schedule is required. Possibly this is one of the reasons why so many companies use the indirect method.

ILLUSTRATION 16.5 Statement of Cash Flows—Welby Company

A. Direct Method

WELBY COMPANY
Statement of Cash Flows
For the Year Ended December 31, 1999

Cash flows from operating activities:

Cash received from customers	$ 130,000	
Cash paid for merchandise	(102,000)	
Cash paid for operating expenses	(23,000)	
Net cash provided by operating activities		$ 5,000

Cash flows from investing activities:

Purchase of equipment		(20,000)

Cash flows from financing activities:

Proceeds from issuing common stock	$ 30,000	
Paid cash dividends	(4,000)	
Net cash provided by financing activities		26,000
Net increase (decrease) in cash		$ 11,000

This portion differs between the two versions

This portion is the same in both versions

B. Indirect Method

WELBY COMPANY
Statement of Cash Flows
For the Year Ended December 31, 1999

Cash flows from operating activities:

Net income		$ 10,000
Adjustments to reconcile net income to net cash provided by operating activities:		
Increase in accounts receivable	(10,000)	
Decrease in merchandise inventory	4,000	
Decrease in accounts payable	(6,000)	
Increase in accrued liabilities payable	2,000	
Depreciation expense	5,000	
Net cash provided by operating activities		$ 5,000

Cash flows from investing activities:

Purchase of equipment		(20,000)

Cash flows from financing activities:

Proceeds from issuing common stock	$ 30,000	
Paid cash dividends	(4,000)	
Net cash provided by financing activities		26,000
Net increase (decrease) in cash		$ 11,000

Real-World Example

For the year ending December 31, 1996, Merck & Co., Inc., had net cash provided by operating activities of $6,522,100,000; net cash used by investing activities of ($1,979,300,000); and net cash used by investing activities of ($3,837,300,000).

Reinforcing Problems

E16–7 Compute cash used to purchase plant assets.
E16–8 Prepare statement of cash flows.
E16–9 Report specific items on statement of cash flows.

However, if the indirect method is used, the amount of interest and income taxes paid must be provided in related disclosures, usually immediately below the statement of cash flows. For instance, if Welby Company had paid interest of $200 and income taxes of $8,000, these facts would be reported as follows:

Supplemental cash flow information:	
Interest paid	$ 200
Income taxes paid	8,000

ANALYSIS OF THE STATEMENT OF CASH FLOWS

Objective 5
Analyze a statement of cash flows of a real company.

Business students will benefit throughout their careers from knowing how to analyze a statement of cash flows. We will use the consolidated statement of cash flows from the 1996 Annual Report of the Colgate-Palmolive Company to illustrate the analysis. The company manufactures and markets a wide variety of products in the United States and more than 200 other countries around the world in five core categories—oral care, personal care, household surface care, fabric care, and pet nutrition. Principal global trademarks include Colgate, Palmolive, Mennen, Ajax, Axion, Protex, Kolynos, Soupline, Suavitel, Fab, Fabuloso, and Hill's Science Diet. This same company will be used in the next chapter to illustrate the complete analysis and interpretation of all of the financial statements.

Colgate-Palmolive Company's Consolidated Statements of Cash Flows

Illustration 16.6 shows the consolidated statements of cash flows for the years 1996, 1995, and 1994 for the Colgate-Palmolive Company. We also include portions of Management's Discussion and Analysis of the 1996 statement of cash flows. We will then discuss the statement further, explaining various items and illustrating how the information might be used for decision making.

Management's Discussion and Analysis

The following paragraphs were taken from Colgate-Palmolive's *1996 Annual Report*.

Liquidity and Capital Resources*

Net cash provided by operations increased 13% to $917.4 in 1996 compared with $810.2 in 1995 and $829.4 in 1994. The increase in cash generated by operating activities in 1996 reflects the Company's improved profitability and working capital management. Cash generated from operations was used to fund capital spending, reduce debt levels and increase dividends.

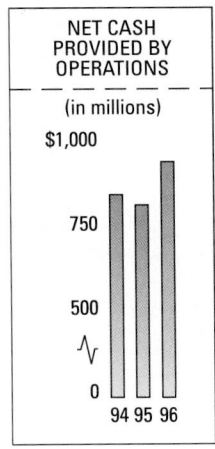

During 1996, long-term debt decreased from $3,029.0 to $2,897.2. The Company continued to focus on enhancing its debt portfolio, resulting in the refinancing of a substantial portion of commercial paper and other short-term borrowings to longer term instruments. In 1996, the Company entered into a $496.3 loan agreement and obtained a $406.0 term loan with foreign commercial banks. In addition, the Company issued $100.0 of notes in a private placement and issued $75.0 of medium-term notes under previously filed shelf registrations.

As of December 31, 1996, $341.9 of domestic and foreign commercial paper was outstanding. These borrowings carry a Standard & Poor's rating of A1 and a Moody's rating of P1. The commercial paper as well as other short-term borrowings are classified as long-term debt at December 31, 1996, as it is the Company's intent and ability to refinance such obligations on a long-term basis. The Company has additional sources of liquidity available in the form of lines of credit maintained with various banks. At December 31, 1996, such unused lines of credit amounted to $1,785.7. In addition, at December 31, 1996, the Company had $697.8 available under previously filed shelf registrations.

During 1995, the Company issued $89.2 of Swiss franc bonds and $71.7 of Luxembourg franc bonds, both of which were immediately swapped into U.S. dollar floating rate debt. In addition, $220.0 of medium-term notes were issued under the shelf registration filed in May 1994. Also in 1995, the Company obtained a $75.0 term note and filed a shelf registration for $700.0 of debt securities.

During 1994, the Company obtained a $50.0 term note and filed a shelf registration for $500.0 of debt securities, of which $208.0 medium-term notes were issued in that year.

*Source: The Colgate-Palmolive Company's 1996 Annual Report, pp. 21–22.

($ Millions)	1996	1995	1994
Operating Activities			
Net income	$ 635.0	$ 172.0	$ 580.2
Adjustments to reconcile net income to net cash provided by operations:			
Restructured operations, net	(105.6)	424.9	(39.1)
Depreciation and amortization	316.3	300.3	235.1
Deferred income taxes and other, net	(23.0)	(62.9)	64.7
Cash effects of changes in:			
Receivables	(15.4)	(44.1)	(50.1)
Inventories	(1.2)	(26.1)	(44.5)
Other current assets	—	(42.4)	(7.8)
Payables and accruals	111.3	88.5	90.9
Net cash provided by operations	917.4	810.2	829.4
Investing Activities			
Capital expenditures	$ (459.0)	$ (431.8)	$ (400.8)
Payment for acquisitions, net of cash acquired	(59.3)	(1,300.4)	(146.4)
Sale of marketable securities and other investments	26.3	6.2	58.4
Other, net	(12.0)	(17.2)	31.1
Net cash used for investing activities	$ (504.0)	$ (1,743.2)	$ (457.7)
Financing Activities			
Principal payments on debt	$ (1,164.6)	$ (17.1)	$ (88.3)
Proceeds from issuance of debt, net	1,077.4	1,220.0	316.4
Proceeds from outside investors	8.5	30.5	15.2
Dividends paid	(296.2)	(276.5)	(246.9)
Purchase of common stock	(27.4)	(9.0)	(357.9)
Proceeds from exercise of stock options and other, net	30.7	28.3	18.5
Net cash (used for) provided by financing activities	$ (371.6)	$ 976.2	$ (343.0)
Effect of exchange rate changes on cash and cash equivalents	$ (2.4)	$ (4.3)	$ (2.9)
Net increase in cash and cash equivalents	$ 39.4	$ 38.9	$ 25.8
Cash and cash equivalents at beginning of year	208.8	169.9	144.1
Cash and cash equivalents at end of year	$ 248.2	$ 208.8	$ 169.9
Supplemental Cash Flow Information			
Income taxes paid	$ 253.7	$ 292.5	$ 261.1
Interest paid	229.1	228.6	96.9
Non-cash consideration in payment for acquisitions	—	48.9	8.0
Principal payments on ESOP debt, guaranteed by the Company	(5.0)	(4.4)	(4.0)

ILLUSTRATION 16.6
Consolidated Statements of Cash Flows for the Colgate-Palmolive Company—Indirect Method

The Company utilizes interest rate agreements and foreign exchange contracts to manage interest rate and foreign currency exposures. The principal objective of such financial derivative contracts is to moderate the effect of fluctuations in interest rates and foreign exchange rates. The Company, as a matter of policy, does not speculate in financial markets and therefore does not hold these contracts for trading purposes. The Company utilizes what are considered straightforward instruments, such as forward foreign exchange contracts and non-leveraged interest rate swaps, to accomplish its objectives. As of December 31, 1996, the Company had $925.9 notional amount of interest rate swaps outstanding converting floating rate debt to fixed rate debt and $285.0 of swaps outstanding converting fixed rate debt to floating.

The ratio of net debt to total capitalization (defined as the ratio of the book values of debt less cash and marketable securities ["net debt"] to net debt plus equity) decreased to 58% during 1996 from 64% in 1995. The decrease is primarily the result of higher Company earnings in 1996 as well as effective working capital management and lower acquisitions than in prior years. The ratio of market debt to market capitalization (defined as above using fair market values) decreased to 17% during 1996 from 23% in 1995. The Company primarily uses market value analyses to evaluate its optimal capitalization.

	1996	1995	1994
Capital Expenditures			
Oral, Personal and Household Care	$413.6	$354.9	$343.1
Pet Nutrition and Other	45.4	76.9	57.7
Total Capital Expenditures	$459.0	$431.8	$400.8
Depreciation and Amortization			
Oral, Personal and Household Care	$286.2	$273.8	$213.0
Pet Nutrition and Other	30.1	26.5	22.1
Total Depreciation and Amortization	$316.3	$300.3	$235.1

Capital expenditures were 5.2% of net sales in both 1996 and 1995 and were 5.3% of net sales in 1994. Capital spending continues to be focused primarily on projects that yield high aftertax returns, thereby reducing the Company's cost structure. Capital expenditures for 1997 are expected to continue at the current rate of approximately 5% of net sales.

Other investing activities in 1996, 1995 and 1994 included strategic acquisitions and equity investments worldwide. During 1996, the Company acquired the Profiden oral care business in Spain, the Seprod fabric care business in Jamaica and other regional brands in the Oral, Personal and Household Care segment. During 1995, the Company acquired Kolynos in Latin America and Odol oral care products in Argentina and made other regional investments. During 1994, the Company acquired the Cibaca toothbrush and toothpaste business in India and several other regional brands across the Oral, Personal and Household Care segment. The aggregate purchase price of all 1996, 1995 and 1994 acquisitions was $38.5, $1,321.9 and $149.8, respectively.

During 1994, the Company repurchased a significant amount of common shares in the open market and private transactions to provide for employee benefit plans and to maintain its targeted capital structure. Aggregate repurchases for the year approximated 6.9 million shares with a total purchase price of $411.1.

Dividend payments were $296.2 in 1996, up from $276.5 in 1995 and $246.9 in 1994. Common stock dividend payments increased to $1.88 per share in 1996 from $1.76 per share in 1995 and $1.54 in 1994. The Series B Preference Stock dividends were declared and paid at the stated rate of $4.88 per share in all three years.

Internally generated cash flows appear to be adequate to support currently planned business operations, acquisitions and capital expenditures. Significant acquisitions, such as the acquisition of Kolynos discussed previously, would require external financing.

The Company is a party to various superfund and other environmental matters and is contingently liable with respect to lawsuits, taxes and other matters arising out of the normal course of business. Management proactively reviews and manages its exposure to, and the impact of, environmental matters. While it is possible that the Company's cash flows and results of operations in particular quarterly or annual periods could be affected by the one-time impacts of the resolution of such contingencies, it is the opinion of management that the ultimate disposition of these matters, to the extent not previously provided for, will not have a material impact on the Company's financial condition or ongoing cash flows and results of operations.

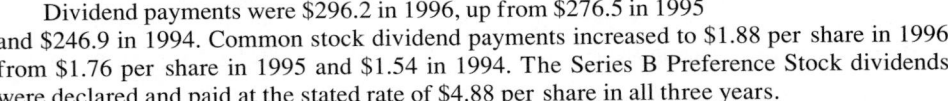

Explanation of Items in Colgate-Palmolive Company's Consolidated Statements of Cash Flows

Refer to Illustration 16.6. First we will discuss the items in the operating activities section of the statement of cash flows, then we will discuss investing activities and financing activities.

OPERATING ACTIVITIES The company used the indirect method of calculating net cash provided by operations. Various adjustments were made to convert accrual based net income to cash basis net income.

The "restructured operations, net" item resulted from the fact that many companies restructured their operations during the 1990s by closing plants and significantly reducing their work forces. Some companies recognized a net loss from restructuring and others recognized a net gain. Apparently, the Colgate-Palmolive Company recognized a net gain in 1996 because it deducted the item from net income

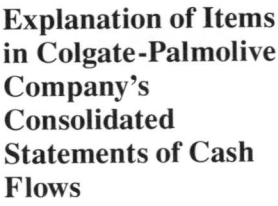

on the statement of cash flows. The actual cash flows from restructuring will occur in a later period.

"Depreciation and amortization" includes depreciation on plant assets and amortization of intangible assets, such as goodwill. Goodwill had been recorded because of using the purchase method (discussed in Chapter 14) to account for the acquisition of other companies and segments of other companies. Depreciation and amortization are noncash charges against revenues and must be added back to net income.

The "deferred income taxes and other, net" item deduction from net income results primarily from the fact that income tax expense on the income statement was lower than the actual income taxes paid in 1996. This phenomenon occurs because of using a different method for tax and accounting purposes for such items as depreciation.

Receivables and inventories increased (causing cash to decrease), while other current assets remained about the same. Payables and accruals increased (causing cash to increase). (These changes are net of any amounts related to acquisitions, dispositions, or amounts that are included elsewhere, such as in "restructured operations, net." The changes described may differ from the amounts derived from only analyzing the balance sheets for the last two years because of certain technical "adjustments" that are beyond the scope of this text.)

INVESTING ACTIVITIES   "Capital expenditures" include the purchase of plant assets, such as new machinery and equipment, to modernize production facilities. Companies, including the Colgate-Palmolive Company, normally select those capital expenditures with the highest rate of return. For instance, if funds are limited (and they normally are) and two capital investments (a machine and a mainframe computer) are being considered, one yielding a 20% return and the other yielding a 25% return, the company will normally select the one with the 25% return.

"Payment for acquisitions, net of cash acquired" shows the amount spent in acquiring other companies and segments of other companies, net of the amount of cash held by those companies and obtained as a part of the acquisition. "Management's Discussion and Analysis" (quoted above) identified some of these acquisitions.

The company sold "marketable securities and other investments." These securities normally consist of stocks, bonds, and other instruments of other companies. For fiscal years beginning after December 15, 1993, marketable securities must be identified as trading securities, available-for-sale securities, or held-to-maturity securities. Trading securities and available-for-sale securities were discussed in some detail in Chapter 14. Held-to-maturity securities were mentioned briefly in Chapter 15. These held-to-maturity securities are debt securities (such as bonds of other companies) that the company has purchased and has both the intent and ability to hold to maturity. As mentioned earlier, the proceeds from sales and purchases of trading securities must be shown as cash flows from operating activities, and the proceeds from sales and purchases of available-for-sale and held-to-maturity securities must be shown as cash flows from investing activities.

FINANCING ACTIVITIES   The company paid off some old debt ($1,164.6 million) and incurred new debt ($1,077.4 million). During the 1990s, many companies have substituted new debt with a low interest rate for old debt with a high interest rate, just as homeowners refinance their homes to lower their interest rate.

The "proceeds from outside investors" resulted from the other participants in the formation of certain businesses in which the Colgate-Palmolive Company holds more than a 50% share.

"Dividends paid" is an item that should be familiar to you. Dividends paid increased each year for the period 1994 through 1996.

The company bought back some of its own stock (treasury stock). Companies often buy back their own shares because they (1) need the shares to issue to employees or officers under stock option plans, (2) want to bolster the market price of the stock, or (3) hope to later sell the stock at a substantially higher price.

"Proceeds from exercise of stock options and other, net" represents the proceeds received from employees and officers who exercised their stock options. Stock options are usually granted to employees to encourage them to work efficiently to increase profitability, which should increase the market price of the stock. Stock options made available to officers are for the same purpose or to attract or retain a talented executive. Normally, an option gives the recipient the right to buy a certain number of shares at a stated price within a given timeframe. For instance, the president of a company may be granted an option to buy 10,000 shares at $40 per share any time after two years from that date and before six years from that date. Assume that the current market price is $38. If the market price of the stock rises to $80 at some time during the option period, the president could buy the shares at $40 and then hold them or sell them at the higher market price. Executives of companies have become multimillionaires by exercising their stock options. The employees and executives of the Colgate-Palmolive Company paid the company between $18.5 million and $30.7 million per year to exercise their stock options during the three-year period. The company resissued some of its treasury stock as a result of the exercise of the stock options.

Use of the Cash Flow Information for Decision Making

Reinforcing Problems

P16–3A Analyze Computer Associates International, Inc.'s 1996 statement of cash flows.

P16–4A Analyze Cabletron Systems, Inc.'s 1996 statement of cash flows.

We will discuss some examples of the ways that the information in the statement of cash flows can be used by management, stockholders, and creditors to make decisions. Each of these parties would use more than the statement of cash flows to perform an analysis of the company's performance, but we will restrict ourselves to the statement of cash flows. The next chapter shows a more complete analysis of the Colgate-Palmolive Company's performance.

MANAGEMENT   Management is the first to see the information contained in the statement of cash flows. You have already read portions of "Management's Discussion and Analysis" concerning the information contained in that statement. Management concluded that the amount of internally generated cash flows (net cash provided by operations) appears adequate to support currently planned business operations, acquisitions, and capital expenditures. Thus, unless the company engages in a significant acquisition it will not have to sell more stock or borrow more funds in the foreseeable future. Also, the company apparently replaced some of its high interest rate debt ($1,164.6 million) with lower interest rate debt ($1,077.4 million). Many companies are doing this same thing in the 1990s to take advantage of the low interest rates available.

STOCKHOLDERS   Stockholders can see that dividend payments ($296.2 million) are comfortably covered by net cash provided by operations ($917.4 million). Stockholders are undoubtedly pleased that the per share dividend rate has increased each year during 1994 through 1996. The company continues to invest in its future by making capital expenditures ($459.0 million) to modernize its productive facilities. The repurchase of its own stock ($27.4 million) decreases the number of shares outstanding, although some of the stock will undoubtedly be reissued in the future as employees and executives exercise their stock options. Any net reduction in the number of shares outstanding will tend to increase earnings per share and help to increase the market price per share in the future. Also, the company may decide to increase dividends per share in the future. These favorable factors might induce present stockholders to retain their stock or even increase their holdings. Potential stockholders might also be attracted to the stock.

CREDITORS   An encouraging factor is the increasing amount of net cash provided by operations in 1996. Also comforting to creditors is the information in Management's Discussion and Analysis that the company has access to $1,785.7 million in lines of credit.

The preceding discussions are merely examples of how the information contained in the statement of cash flows might be analyzed to make decisions. The next section describes three ratios that can provide further analyses of cash flows.

Analyzing and Using the Financial Results— Cash Flow per Share of Common Stock, Cash Flow Margin, and Cash Flow Liquidity Ratios

The information in the statement of cash flows provides a basis for analyzing financial results. However, further analysis is possible through the use of three ratios relating to cash flow: the cash flow per share of common stock, cash flow margin, and cash flow liquidity ratios. The ratios shown below are based on 1996 results for the Colgate-Palmolive Company and 1995 results for the other companies. All dollar amounts are rounded to the nearest million.

Objective 6
Analyze and use the financial results—cash flow per share of common stock, cash flow margin, and cash flow liquidity ratios.

The **cash flow per share of common stock ratio** is equal to the net cash provided by operations divided by the average number of shares of common stock outstanding. This ratio indicates the company's ability to pay dividends and liabilities. The higher the ratio, the greater the ability to pay. The cash flow per share of common stock ratios for the companies were:

Company	Net Cash Provided by Operating Activities (millions)	Average Shares of Common Stock Outstanding* (millions)	Cash Flow per Share
Colgate-Palmolive Company	$ 917	147	$6.24
J. C. Penney, Inc.	1,403	229	6.13
The Walt Disney Company	3,510	571	6.15
General Electric Company	14,946	1,684	8.88

*To determine the average number of shares, add the beginning and ending numbers outstanding and divide by two. No information was available about when new shares were issued.

The **cash flow margin ratio** is equal to net cash provided by operating activities divided by net sales. This ratio is a measure of a company's ability to turn sales revenue into cash. The higher the ratio, the better. The cash flow margin ratios for the companies were:

Company	Net Cash Provided by Operating Activities (millions)	Net Sales (millions)	Cash Flow Margin
Colgate-Palmolive Company	$ 917	8,749	10.48%
J. C. Penney, Inc.	1,403	20,562	6.82
The Walt Disney Company	3,510	12,112	28.98
General Electric Company	14,946	70,028	21.34

The **cash flow liquidity ratio** is equal to the total of cash, marketable securities, and net cash provided by operating activities divided by current liabilities. This ratio is a test of a company's short-term, debt-paying ability. The higher the ratio, the better. The cash flow liquidity ratios for the companies were:

Company	Cash, Marketable Securities, and Net Cash Provided by Operating Activities (millions)	Current Liabilities (millions)	Cash Flow Liquidity Ratio
Colgate-Palmolive Company	$ 1,225	$ 1,904	.64 times
J. C. Penney, Inc.	1,576	4,020	.39 times
The Walt Disney Company	5,453	3,172	1.72 times
General Electric Company	58,836	82,001	.72 times

A BROADER PERSPECTIVE

Johnson & Johnson— Indirect Method

Johnson & Johnson
Johnson & Johnson is the world's largest and most comprehensive manufacturer of health care products serving the consumer, pharmaceutical, and professional markets.

JOHNSON & JOHNSON AND SUBSIDIARIES
Consolidated Statements of Cash Flows
For the Years Ended June 30, 1996, 1995, and 1994
($ millions)

	1996	1995	1994
Cash flows from operating activities			
Net earnings	$ 2,887	$ 2,403	$ 2,006
Adjustments to reconcile net earnings to cash flows:			
Depreciation and amortization of property and intangibles	1,009	857	724
Tax deferrals	(3)	(63)	(66)
Changes in assets and liabilities, net of effects from acquisition of businesses:			
Increase in accounts receivable, less allowances	(306)	(265)	(239)
Increase in inventories	(242)	(9)	(162)
Increase in accounts payable and accrued liabilities	245	617	462
Increase in other current and non-current assets	(40)	(294)	(112)
Increase in other current and non-current liabilities	341	136	362
Net cash flows from operating activities	$ 3,891	$ 3,382	$ 2,975
Cash flows from investing activities			
Additions to property, plant and equipment	$(1,373)	$(1,256)	$ (937)
Proceeds from the disposal of assets	37	465	332
Acquisition of businesses, net of cash acquired	(233)	(154)	(1,932)
Other, principally marketable securities	(123)	(151)	(19)
Net cash used by investing activities	$(1,692)	$(1,096)	$(2,556)
Cash flows from financing activities			
Dividends to shareowners	$ (974)	$ (827)	$ (727)
Repurchase of common stock	(412)	(322)	(185)
Proceeds from short-term debt	282	197	328
Retirement of short-term debt	(128)	(634)	(263)
Proceeds from long-term debt	126	—	960
Retirement of long-term debt	(411)	(260)	(363)
Proceeds from the exercise of stock options	149	112	62
Net cash used by financing activities	$(1,368)	$(1,734)	$ (188)
Effect of exchange rate changes on cash and cash equivalents	$ (21)	$ 13	$ 33
Increase in cash and cash equivalents	$ 810	$ 565	$ 264
Cash and cash equivalents, beginning of year	1,201	636	372
Cash and cash equivalents, end of year	$ 2,011	$ 1,201	$ 636
Supplemental cash flow data			
Cash paid during the year for:			
Interest, net of portion capitalized	$ 113	137	133
Income taxes	1,210	1,071	612
Supplemental schedule of noncash investing and financing activities			
Treasury stock issued for employee compensation and stock option plans, net of cash proceeds	$ 252	$ 212	$ 133
Acquisitions of businesses			
Fair value of assets acquired	$ 237	$ 493	$ 2,279
Fair value of liabilities assumed	(4)	(37)	(347)
	$ 233	$ 456	$ 1,932
Treasury stock issued	—	(302)	—
Net cash payments	$ 233	$ 154	$ 1,932

Source: Johnson & Johnson 1996 Annual Report.

On the first of these measures, General Electric seems to be in the strongest position, although all of the companies are financially sound. On the second measure, Walt Disney and General Electric have the highest cash flow margin ratios. On the third measure, Walt Disney seems to be in the strongest position. However, a more valid comparison on each of these measures would be made if each of these companies was compared with other companies in their industry. Dun & Bradstreet's Industry Norms and Key Business Ratios can be used for this purpose. (This source could also be used for comparisons of ratios in the next chapter.) A complete analysis using the techniques described in the next chapter would provide additional information about the strengths and weaknesses of each of these companies.

UNDERSTANDING THE LEARNING OBJECTIVES

- The statement of cash flows summarizes the effects on cash of the operating, financing, and investing activities of a company during an accounting period.
- Management can see the effects of its past major policy decisions in quantitative form.
- Investors and creditors can assess the entity's ability to generate positive future net cash flows, to meet its obligations, and to pay dividends, and can assess the need for external financing.

Objective 1
Explain the purposes and uses of the statement of cash flows.

- Operating activities generally include the cash effects (inflows and outflows) of transactions and other events that enter into the determination of net income. The cash flows from operating activities can be measured in two ways. The direct method deducts from cash sales only those operating expenses that consumed cash. The indirect method starts with net income and adjusts net income for items that affected reported net income but did not involve cash.
- Investing activities generally include transactions involving the acquisition or disposal of noncurrent assets.
- Financing activities generally include the cash effects (inflows and outflows) of transactions and other events involving creditors and owners.

Objective 2
Describe the content of the statement of cash flows and where certain items would appear on the statement.

- The direct method deducts from cash sales only those operating expenses that consumed cash. The FASB recommends use of the direct method.
- The indirect method starts with accrual basis net income and indirectly adjusts net income for items that affected reported net income but did not involve cash. A large majority of companies use the indirect method.

Objective 3
Describe how to calculate cash flows from operating activities under both the direct and indirect methods.

- The first step is to determine the cash flows from operating activities. Either the direct or indirect method may be used.
- The second step is to analyze all the noncurrent accounts for changes in cash resulting from investing and financing activities.
- The third step is to arrange the information gathered in steps 1 and 2 into the format required for the statement of cash flows.

Objective 4
Prepare a statement of cash flows, under both the direct and indirect methods, showing cash flows from operating activities, investing activities, and financing activities.

- Business students will benefit throughout their careers from knowing how to analyze a statement of cash flows.
- "Management's Discussion and Analysis" in the annual report provides part of the analysis.
- Inspection of the statement of cash flows together with "Management's Discussion and Analysis" will provide the most insight as to the cash flow situation.

Objective 5
Analyze a statement of cash flows of a real company.

- The cash flow per share of common stock ratio tests a company's ability to pay dividends and liabilities and is equal to net cash provided by operating activities divided by the average number of shares of common stock outstanding.
- The cash flow margin ratio measures a company's ability to turn sales revenue into cash and is equal to net cash provided by operating activities divided by net sales.
- The cash flow liquidity ratio tests a company's short-term, debt-paying ability and is equal to the total of cash, marketable securities, and net cash provided by operating activities divided by current liabilities.

Objective 6
Analyze and use the financial results—cash flow per share of common stock, cash flow margin, and cash flow liquidity ratios.

Objective 7
Use a working paper to prepare a statement of cash flows (Appendix).

- A work sheet can be used to assist in preparing a statement of cash flows.
- A company's comparative balance sheets, income statement, and additional data are used to prepare the work sheet.
- The work sheet technique makes the recording of the effects of transactions on cash flows almost a mechanical process.

APPENDIX

USE OF A WORKING PAPER TO PREPARE A STATEMENT OF CASH FLOWS

Objective 7
Use a working paper to prepare a statement of cash flows.

This appendix shows how a work sheet could be used to assist in preparing a statement of cash flows. We use the comparative balance sheets, income statement, and additional data for the Welby Company, shown on page 587, as the basis for this example.

Look at the working paper in Illustration 16.7 for Welby Company, which we use to analyze the transactions and prepare the statement of cash flows. While discussing the steps in preparing the working paper, we describe the items and trace their effects in the entries.

1. Enter the beginning account balances of all balance sheet accounts in the first column and the ending account balances in the fourth column. Notice that the debit items precede the credit items.
2. Total the debits and credits in the first and fourth columns to make sure that debits equal credits in each column.
3. Write "Cash Flows from Operating Activities" immediately below the total of the credit items. Skip sufficient lines for recording adjustments to convert accrual net income to cash flows from operating activities. Then write "Cash Flows from Investing Activities" and allow enough space for those items. Finally, write "Cash Flows from Financing Activities" and allow enough space for those items.
4. Enter entries for analyzing transactions in the second and third columns. The entries serve two functions: (*a*) they explain the change in each account; and (*b*) they classify the changes into operating, investing, and financing activities. We discuss these entries individually in the next section.
5. Total the debits and credits in the second and third columns; they should be equal. You will have one pair of totals for the balance sheet items and another pair for the bottom portion of the working paper. We use the bottom portion of the working paper to prepare the statement of cash flows.

Completing the Working Paper

To complete the working paper in Illustration 16.7, we must analyze the change in each noncash balance sheet account. The focus of this working paper is on cash and every change in cash means a change in a noncash balance sheet account. After we have made the proper entries to analyze all changes in noncash balance sheet accounts, the working paper shows all activities affecting cash flows. The following explanations are keyed to the entry numbers on the working paper:

Entry *0*. In comparing the beginning and ending cash balances, we determine the change in the Cash account during the year is an $11,000 increase. An entry on the working paper debits Cash for $11,000 and credits Increase in Cash for Year near the bottom of the schedule. This *0* entry does not explain the change in cash but is the "target" of the analysis. The entry sets out the change in cash that the statement seeks to explain. No further attention need be paid to cash in completing the working paper.

We now direct our attention toward changes in other balance sheet accounts. These accounts can be dealt with in any order; first, we record the net income for the period and analyze the current assets (other than cash) and the current liabilities. Second, we analyze the changes in the noncurrent accounts.

Entry *1*. The income statement shows a net income for 1999 of $10,000. Entry *1* records the $10,000 as the starting point in measuring cash flows from operating activities and credits Retained Earnings as a partial explanation of the change in that account.

WELBY COMPANY
Working Paper for Statement of Cash Flows
For the Year Ended December 31, 1999

ILLUSTRATION 16.7
Working Paper for
Statement of Cash Flows

	Account Balances 12/31/98	Analysis of Transactions for 1999		Account Balances 12/31/99
		Debit	Credit	
Debits				
Cash	10,000	(0) 11,000		21,000
Accounts Receivable, Net	20,000	(2) 10,000		30,000
Merchandise Inventory	30,000		(3) 4,000	26,000
Equipment	50,000	(7) 20,000		70,000
Totals	110,000			147,000
Credits				
Accumulated Depreciation—Equipment	5,000		(6) 5,000	10,000
Accounts Payable	15,000	(4) 6,000		9,000
Accrued Liabilities Payable	–0–		(5) 2,000	2,000
Common Stock ($10 par value)	60,000		(8) 30,000	90,000
Retained Earnings	30,000	(9) 4,000	(1) 10,000	36,000
Totals	110,000	51,000	51,000	147,000
Cash Flows from Operating Activities:				
Net Income		(1) 10,000		
Increase in Accounts Receivable			(2) 10,000	
Decrease in Merchandise Inventory		(3) 4,000		
Decrease in Accounts Payable			(4) 6,000	
Increase in Accrued Liabilities Payable		(5) 2,000		
Depreciation Expense		(6) 5,000		
Cash Flows from Investing Activities:				
Purchase of Equipment			(7) 20,000	
Cash Flows from Financing Activities:				
Proceeds from Issuing Common Stock		(8) 30,000		
Payment of Cash Dividends			(9) 4,000	
Increase in Cash for Year			(0) 11,000	
		51,000	51,000	

The next task is to analyze changes in current accounts other than Cash. The current accounts of Welby Company are closely related to operations, and their changes are included in converting net income to cash flows from operating activities.

Entry 2. We deduct the $10,000 increase in accounts receivable from net income when converting it to cash flows from operating activities. If accounts receivable increased, sales to customers exceeded cash received from customers. To convert net income to a cash basis, we must deduct the $10,000.

The working paper technique makes the recording of these effects almost mechanical. By debiting Accounts Receivable for $10,000, we increase it from $20,000 to $30,000. If Accounts Receivable is debited, we must credit an item that can be entitled "Increase in Accounts Receivable." We deduct the increase from net income in converting it to cash flows from operating activities.

Entry 3 is virtually a duplicate of entry 2, except it involves merchandise inventory rather than receivables and is a decrease rather than an increase.

Entry 4 records the effect of a decrease in accounts payable on net income in converting it to cash flows from operating activities.

Entry 5 records the effect of an increase in accrued liabilities payable in converting net income to cash flows from operating activities.

Next, we analyze the changes in the noncurrent balance sheet accounts.

Entry 6. We add the $5,000 depreciation back to net income and credit the respective accumulated depreciation account. You can find the depreciation expense (1) on the income statement, or (2) by solving for the credit needed to balance the accumulated depreciation account on the balance sheet.

Accumulated Depreciation—Equipment

		Beg. bal.	5,000
		(6)	5,000
		End. bal.	10,000

Entry 7. We debit the Equipment account and credit "Purchase of Equipment" in the investing activities section for the $20,000 cash spent to acquire new plant assets (equipment).

Entry 8. We show the $30,000 cash received from sale of common stock as a financing activity. The entry also explains the change in the Common Stock account. If stock had been sold for more than its stated value of $50 per share, we would record the excess in a separate Paid-In Capital in Excess of Stated Value account. However, we would report the total amount of cash received from the issuance of common stock as a single figure on the statement of cash flows. Only this total amount received is significant to creditors and other users of the financial statements trying to judge the solvency of the company.

Entry 9. We debit Retained Earnings and credit Payment of Cash Dividends for the $4,000 dividends declared and paid. The entry also completes the following explanation of the change in Retained Earnings. Notice that on the statement of cash flows, the dividends must be paid to be included as a cash outflow from financing activities.

Retained Earnings

(9)	4,000	Beg. bal.	30,000
		(1)	10,000
		End. bal.	36,000

Preparing the Statement of Cash Flows

Using the data in the lower section of the working paper, we would prepare the statement of cash flows under the indirect method shown in Illustration 16.5 (Part B) on page 591.

DEMONSTRATION PROBLEM

The following comparative balance sheets are for Dells Corporation as of June 30, 1999, and June 30, 1998. Also provided is the statement of income and retained earnings for the year ended June 30, 1999, with additional data.

DELLS CORPORATION
Comparative Balance Sheets
June 30, 1999, and 1998

	1999	1998	Increase (Decrease)
Assets			
Current assets:			
Cash	$ 30,000	$ 80,000	$ (50,000)
Accounts receivable, net	160,000	100,000	60,000
Merchandise inventory	100,000	70,000	30,000
Prepaid rent	20,000	10,000	10,000
Total current assets	$310,000	$260,000	$ 50,000
Property, plant, and equipment:			
Equipment	$400,000	$200,000	$200,000
Accumulated depreciation—equipment	(60,000)	(50,000)	(10,000)
Total property, plant, and equipment	$340,000	$150,000	$190,000
Total assets	$650,000	$410,000	$240,000

Liabilities and Stockholders' Equity

Current liabilities:

Accounts payable	$ 50,000	$ 40,000	$ 10,000
Notes payable—bank	–0–	50,000	(50,000)
Salaries payable	10,000	20,000	(10,000)
Federal income taxes payable	30,000	20,000	10,000
Total current liabilities	$ 90,000	$130,000	$ (40,000)

Stockholders' equity:

Common stock, $10 par	$300,000	$100,000	$200,000
Paid-in capital in excess of par	50,000	–0–	50,000
Retained earnings	210,000	180,000	30,000
Total stockholders' equity	$560,000	$280,000	$280,000
Total liabilities and stockholders' equity	$650,000	$410,000	$240,000

DELLS CORPORATION
Statement of Income and Retained Earnings
For the Year Ended June 30, 1999

Sales		$1,000,000
Cost of goods sold	$600,000	
Salaries and wages expense	200,000	
Rent expense	40,000	
Depreciation expense	20,000	
Interest expense	3,000	
Loss on sale of equipment	7,000	870,000
Income before federal income taxes		$ 130,000
Deduct: Federal income taxes		60,000
Net income		$ 70,000
Retained earnings, July 1, 1998		180,000
		$ 250,000
Deduct: Dividends		40,000
Retained earnings, June 30, 1999		$ 210,000

Additional data

1. Equipment with a cost of $20,000, on which $10,000 of depreciation had been recorded, was sold for $3,000 cash. Additional equipment was purchased for $220,000.
2. Stock was issued for $250,000 cash.
3. The $50,000 bank note was paid.

Using the data given for Dells Corporation:

Required

a. Prepare a statement of cash flows—indirect method.
b. Prepare a working paper to convert net income from an accrual basis to a cash basis. Then prepare a partial statement of cash flows—direct method, showing only the cash flows from operating activities section.

SOLUTION TO DEMONSTRATION PROBLEM

a.
DELLS CORPORATION
Statement of Cash Flows—Indirect Method
For the Year Ended June 30, 1999

Cash flows from operating activities:

Net income		$ 70,000
Adjustments to reconcile net income to net cash provided by operating activities:		
Increase in accounts receivable	(60,000)	
Increase in merchandise inventory	(30,000)	
Increase in prepaid rent	(10,000)	
Increase in accounts payable	10,000	
Decrease in salaries payable	(10,000)	
Increase in federal income taxes payable	10,000	
Loss on sale of equipment	7,000	
Depreciation expense	20,000	
Net cash provided by operating activities		$ 7,000

Cash flows from investing activities:

Proceeds from sale of equipment	$ 3,000	
Purchase of equipment	(220,000)	
Net cash used by investing activities		(217,000)

Cash flows from financing activities:

Proceeds from issuing common stock	$ 250,000	
Repayment of bank note	(50,000)	
Dividends paid	(40,000)	
Net cash provided by financing activities		160,000
Net increase (decrease) in cash		$ (50,000)

b.

DELLS CORPORATION
Working Paper to Convert Income Statement
from Accrual Basis to Cash Basis
For the Year Ended June 30, 1999

	Accrual Basis		Add	Deduct	Cash Basis (Cash Flows from Operating Activities)
Sales		$1,000,000		$60,000[a]	$940,000
Cost of goods sold	$600,000		$30,000[b]	10,000[c]	$620,000
Salaries and wages expense	200,000		10,000[d]		210,000
Rent expense	40,000		10,000[e]		50,000
Depreciation expense	20,000			20,000	–0–
Interest expense	3,000				3,000
Loss on sale of equipment . .	7,000			7,000	–0–
Federal income taxes	60,000			10,000[f]	50,000
		930,000			933,000
Net income		$ 70,000			$ 7,000

[a]Increase in Accounts Receivable.
[b]Increase in Merchandise Inventory.
[c]Increase in Accounts Payable.
[d]Decrease in Salaries Payable.
[e]Increase in Prepaid Rent.
[f]Increase in Federal Income Taxes Payable.

DELLS CORPORATION
Partial Statement of Cash Flows—Direct Method
For the Year Ended June 30, 1999

Cash flows from operating activities:

Cash received from customers	$ 940,000	
Cash paid for merchandise	(620,000)	
Salaries and wages paid	(210,000)	
Rent paid	(50,000)	
Interest paid	(3,000)	
Federal income taxes paid	(50,000)	
Net cash provided by operating activities		$7,000

New Terms

Cash flow liquidity ratio   Cash and marketable securities plus net cash provided by operating activities divided by current liabilities.   *597*

Cash flow margin ratio   Net cash provided by operating activities divided by net sales.   *597*

Cash flow per share of common stock ratio   Net cash provided by operating activities divided by the average number of shares of common stock outstanding.   *597*

Cash flows from operating activities   The net amount of cash received or disbursed during a given period on items that normally appear on the income statement.   *584*

Direct method   Deducts from cash sales only those operating expenses that consumed cash.   *584*

Financing activities   Generally include the cash effects of transactions and other events involving creditors and owners. Cash payments made to settle current liabilities such as accounts payable, wages payable, and income taxes payable are not financing activities. These payments are operating activities.   *583*

Indirect method   A method of determining cash flows from operating activities that starts with net income and indirectly adjusts net income for items that do not involve cash. Also called the **addback** method.   *584*

Investing activities   Generally include transactions involving the acquisition or disposal of noncurrent assets. Examples include cash received or paid from the sale or purchase of property, plant, and equipment; available-for-sale and held-to-maturity securities; and loans made to others.   *583*

Noncash charges or expenses   Expenses and losses that are added back to net income because they do not actually use cash of the company. The items added back include amounts of depreciation on plant assets, depletion that was expensed, amortization of intangible assets such as patents

and goodwill, amortization of discount on bonds payable, and losses from disposals of noncurrent assets.   *585*

Noncash credits or revenues   Revenues and gains included in arriving at net income that do not provide cash; examples include gains from disposals of noncurrent assets, income from investments carried under the equity method, and amortization of premium on bonds payable.   *585*

Operating activities   Generally include the cash effects of transactions and other events that enter into the determination of net income.   *582*

Statement of cash flows   A statement that summarizes the effects on cash of the operating, investing, and financing activities of a company during an accounting period. Both inflows and outflows are included in each category. The statement of cash flows must be prepared each time an income statement is prepared.   *582*

Working capital   Equal to current assets minus current liabilities.   *581*

Self-Test

True-False

Indicate whether each of the following statements is true or false.

1. The requirement for a statement of cash flows was preceded by the requirement for the statement of changes in financial position.

2. The statement of cash flows is one of the major financial statements.

3. Investing activities are transactions with creditors and owners.

4. The direct method of calculating cash flows from operations is encouraged by the FASB and is the predominant method used.

5. Issuance of capital stock and the subsequent reacquisition of some of those shares would both be financing activities.

Multiple-Choice

Select the best answer for each of the following questions.

1. Which of the following statements is true?
   a. The direct method of calculating cash flows from operations starts with net income and adjusts for noncash revenues and expenses and changes in current assets and current liabilities.
   b. The indirect method of calculating cash flows from operations adjusts each item in the income statement to a cash basis.
   c. The descriptions in *(a)* and *(b)* should be reversed.
   d. The direct method is easier to use than the indirect method.

2. Investing activities include all of the following except:
   a. Payment of debt.
   b. Collection of loans.
   c. Making of loans.
   d. Sale of available-for-sale and held-to-maturity securities.

3. If sales on an accrual basis are $500,000 and accounts receivable increased by $30,000, the cash received from customers would be:
   a. $500,000.
   b. $470,000.
   c. $530,000.
   d. Cannot be determined.

4. Assume cost of goods sold on an accrual basis is $300,000, accounts payable increased by $20,000, and inventory increased by $50,000. Cash paid for merchandise is:
   a. $370,000.
   b. $230,000.
   c. $270,000.
   d. $330,000.

5. Assume net income was $200,000, depreciation expense was $10,000, accounts receivable increased by $15,000, and accounts payable increased by $5,000. The amount of cash flows from operating activities is:
   a. $200,000.
   b. $180,000.
   c. $210,000.
   d. $190,000.

Now turn to page 624 to check your answers.

QUESTIONS

1. What are the purposes of the statement of cash flows?

2. What are some of the uses of the statement of cash flows?

3. What information is contained in the statement of cash flows?

4. Which activities are generally included in operating activities?

5. Which activities are included in investing activities?

6. Which activities are included in financing activities?

7. Where should significant investing and financing activities that do not involve cash flows be reported?

8. Explain the difference between the direct and indirect methods for computing cash flows from operating activities.

9. What are noncash expenses? How are they treated in computing cash flows from operating activities?

10. Describe the treatment of a gain on the sale of equipment in preparing a statement of cash flows under the indirect method.

11. Depreciation is sometimes referred to as a source of cash. Is it a source of cash? Explain.

12. Why is it unlikely that cash flows from operating activities will be equal to net income for the same period?

13. If the net income for a given period is $25,000, does this mean there is an increase in cash of the same amount? Why or why not?

14. Why might a company have positive cash flows from operating activities even though operating at a net loss?

15. Indicate the type of activity each of the following transactions represents (operating, investing, or financing) and whether it is an inflow or an outflow.
    a. Sold goods.
    b. Purchased building.
    c. Issued capital stock.
    d. Received cash dividends.
    e. Paid cash dividends.
    f. Purchased treasury stock.
    g. Sold available-for-sale securities.
    h. Made a loan.
    i. Paid interest on loan.
    j. Paid bond principal.
    k. Received proceeds of insurance settlement.
    l. Made contribution to charity.

16. Refer to "A Broader Perspective" on page 598. Answer the following questions:
    a. What was the major investing activity in 1996?
    b. Was there a net negative or positive cash flow from investing activities?
    c. Was the positive cash flow from operating activities large enough to pay the cash dividends?

17. **Real World Question** Refer to the annual report booklet. Of the four companies represented, which ones use the direct method of reporting cash flows from operating activities and which ones use the indirect method?

EXERCISES

Exercise 16–1
Report specific items on statement of cash flows
(L.O. 2, 4)

Indicate how the following data should be reported in a statement of cash flows. A company paid $500,000 cash for land. A building was acquired for $2,500,000 by assuming a mortgage on the building.

Exercise 16–2
Calculate the amount of cash paid for merchandise
(L.O. 3)

Cost of goods sold in the income statement for the year ended 1999 was $260,000. The balances in Merchandise Inventory and Accounts Payable were:

	January 1, 1999	December 31, 1999
Merchandise Inventory	$160,000	$180,000
Accounts Payable	44,000	36,000

Calculate the amount of cash paid for merchandise for 1999.

Exercise 16–3
Show effects of conversion from accrual to cash basis income (L.O. 3)

Fill in the following chart, showing how increases and decreases in these accounts affect the conversion of accrual basis income to cash basis income:

	Add	Deduct
Accounts Receivable		
Merchandise Inventory		
Prepaid Expenses		
Accounts Payable		
Accrued Liabilities Payable		

Exercise 16–4
Compute cash flows from operating activities (L.O. 3)

The income statement of a company shows net income of $200,000; merchandise inventory on January 1 was $76,500 and on December 31 was $94,500; accounts payable for merchandise purchases were $57,000 on January 1 and $68,000 on December 31. Compute the cash flows from operating activities under the indirect method.

The operating expenses and taxes (including $80,000 of depreciation) of a company for a given year were $600,000. Net income was $350,000. Prepaid insurance decreased from $18,000 to $14,000 during the year, while wages payable increased from $22,000 to $36,000 during the year. Compute the cash flows from operating activities under the indirect method.

Exercise 16–5
Compute cash flows from operating activities (L.O. 3)

Dividends payable increased by $20,000 during a year in which total dividends declared were $120,000. What amount appears for dividends paid in the statement of cash flows?

Exercise 16–6
Indicate treatment of a dividend (L.O. 2, 4)

Following are balance sheet data for Quality Merchandise, Inc.:

Exercise 16–7
Compute cash used to purchase plant assets (L.O. 2, 4)

	December 31	
	2000	**1999**
Cash	$ 47,000	$ 26,000
Accounts receivable, net	141,000	134,000
Merchandise inventory	83,000	102,000
Prepaid expenses	9,000	11,000
Plant assets (net of accumulated depreciation)	235,000	230,000
Accounts payable	122,000	127,000
Accrued liabilities payable	40,000	41,000
Capital stock	300,000	300,000
Retained earnings	53,000	35,000

Assume that the depreciation recorded in 2000 was $15,000. Compute the cash spent to purchase plant assets, assuming no assets were sold or scrapped in 2000.

Use the data in Exercise 16–7. Assume the net income for 2000 was $24,000, depreciation was $15,000, and dividends declared and paid were $6,000. The company paid interest of $2,000 and income taxes of $14,000. Prepare a statement of cash flows—indirect method. Also prepare any necessary supplemental schedule(s).

Exercise 16–8
Prepare statement of cash flows (L.O. 4)

The following data are from a company's Automobile and the Accumulated Depreciation—Automobile accounts:

Exercise 16–9
Report specific items on statement of cash flows (L.O. 2, 4)

Automobile

Date		Debit	Credit	Balance
Jan. 1	Balance brought forward			16,000
July 1	Traded for new auto		16,000	–0–
	New auto	31,000		31,000

Accumulated Depreciation—Automobile

Date		Debit	Credit	Balance
Jan. 1	Balance brought forward			12,000
July 1	One-half year's depreciation		2,000	14,000
	Auto traded	14,000		–0–
Dec. 31	One-half year's depreciation		4,000	4,000

The old auto was traded for a new one, with the difference in values paid in cash. The income statement for the year shows a loss on the exchange of autos of $1,200.

Indicate the dollar amounts, the descriptions of these amounts, and their exact locations in a statement of cash flows—indirect method.

PROBLEMS

The following income statement and other data are for Kennesaw Auto Glass Specialists, Inc.:

Problem 16–1
Prepare working paper to convert income statement to cash basis; prepare cash flows from operating activities under both methods (L.O. 2, 3)

KENNESAW AUTO GLASS SPECIALISTS, INC.
Income Statement
For the Year Ended December 31, 1999

Sales		$450,000
Cost of goods sold		125,000
Gross margin		$325,000
Operating expenses (other than depreciation)	$60,000	
Depreciation expense	20,000	80,000
Net income		$245,000

Changes in current assets (other than cash) and current liabilities during the year were:

	Increase	Decrease
Accounts receivable	$15,000	
Merchandise inventory		$25,000
Prepaid insurance	8,000	
Accounts payable		15,000
Accrued liabilities payable	4,000	

Depreciation was the only noncash item affecting net income.

Required

a. Prepare a working paper to calculate cash flows from operating activities under the *direct method*.

b. Prepare the cash flows from operating activities section of the statement of cash flows under the *direct method*.

c. Prove that the same cash flows amount is obtained under the indirect method by preparing the cash flows from operating activities section of the statement of cash flows under the *indirect method*. You need not prepare a working paper.

Problem 16–2
Prepare statement of cash flows under the indirect method (L.O. 4)

The following information relates to Dunwoody Nursery & Garden Center, Inc. The company leases a building adjacent to its land.

DUNWOODY NURSERY & GARDEN CENTER, INC.
Comparative Balance Sheets
December 31, 2000 and 1999

	2000	1999
Assets		
Cash	$ 44,500	$ 52,000
Accounts receivable, net	59,000	60,000
Merchandise inventory	175,000	120,000
Equipment	412,500	315,000
Accumulated depreciation—equipment	(120,000)	(105,000)
Land	75,000	15,000
Total assets	$646,000	$457,000
Liabilities and Stockholders' Equity		
Accounts payable	$ 43,750	$ 40,750
Accrued liabilities payable	2,250	3,750
Capital stock—common—$10 par	375,000	300,000
Paid-in capital in excess of par	150,000	75,000
Retained earnings	75,000	37,500
Total liabilities and stockholders' equity	$646,000	$457,000

Additional data

1. Net income was $97,500 for the year.

2. Fully depreciated equipment costing $15,000 was sold for $3,750 (a gain of $3,750), and equipment costing $112,500 was purchased for cash.

3. Depreciation expense for the year was $30,000.

4. Land was purchased, $60,000.

5. An additional 7,500 shares of common stock were issued for cash at $20 per share (total proceeds, $150,000).

6. Cash dividends of $60,000 were declared and paid.

Required   The company paid interest of $6,000 and income taxes of $65,000. Prepare a statement of cash flows under the indirect method. Also prepare any necessary supplemental schedule(s).

Problem 16–3
Analyze PMT Services, Inc.'s statement of cash flows (L.O. 5, 6)

PMT Services, Inc., is an independent service organization that markets and services electronic credit card authorization and payment systems to small retail, wholesale, and professional businesses located throughout the United States. Prior to installing PMT's electronic system, most of these businesses have used manual, paper-based systems to process credit card transactions or have not accepted credit cards at all. As the use of credit cards has significantly expanded, electronic processing has proven more convenient by accelerating customer purchases, lowering processing expenses, and reducing losses from fraudulent cards.

PMT's account portfolio has grown through the purchase of account portfolios as well as through the internal development of accounts using telemarketing and field sales. With approximately 89,500 accounts at July 31, 1996, PMT is one of the largest independent service organizations in the country.

The company's statements of cash flows for the years 1994–1996 follow. Then the relevant portion of Management's Discussion and Analysis of the statement of cash flows is provided.

Consolidated Statement of Cash Flows

	Year Ended July 31,		
	1994	1995	1996
Cash flows from operating activities:			
Net cash received from merchants	$ 19,657,687	$ 34,353,326	$ 67,313,124
Cash paid to vendors and employees	(14,758,040)	(28,467,472)	(49,128,150)
Interest received	22,262	310,136	1,672,714
Interest paid	(268,586)	(198,485)	(505,856)
Income taxes paid	(994,969)	(1,600,405)	(5,630,881)
Net cash provided by operating activities	$ 3,658,354	$ 4,397,100	$ 13,720,951
Cash flows from investing activities:			
Purchase of merchant portfolios	$ (8,415,055)	$(24,576,426)	$ (31,787,725)
Purchase of property and equipment	(1,465,984)	(1,917,395)	(1,777,955)
Net cash used in investing activities	$ (9,881,039)	$(26,493,821)	$ (33,565,680)
Cash flows from financing activities:			
Proceeds from issuance of long-term debt	$ 7,650,000	$ 16,450,000	$ 305,000
Payments on long-term debt	(1,163,170)	(12,828,503)	(16,545,500)
Proceeds from issuance of common stock	—	17,098,894	140,963,115
Payments to repurchase treasury stock	(45,000)	(32,500)	(12,000)
Proceeds from minority shareholder contributions	—	—	120,000
Net cash provided by financing activities	$ 6,441,830	$ 20,687,891	$124,830,615
Net increase (decrease) in cash and cash equivalents	$ 219,145	$ (1,408,830)	$104,985,886
Cash and cash equivalents at beginning of year	1,664,830	1,883,975	475,145
Cash and cash equivalents at end of year	$ 1,883,975	$ 475,145	$105,461,031

Supplemental schedule of noncash activities:

In connection with the purchase of merchant portfolios in fiscal years 1994 and 1995, the Company issued promissory notes totaling $5,061,804 and $80,500, respectively.

The Company recognized a tax benefit of $318,517 for the year ended July 31, 1996 for the excess of the fair market value at the exercise date over that at the award date for stock options exercised.

In connection with the purchase of a merchant portfolio in March 1994, the Company issued 312,500 shares of common stock.

In connection with an agreement between the Company and a processing bank entered into simultaneously with the purchase of a merchant portfolio in March 1994, the Company issued warrants to purchase 120,000 shares of common stock.

Reconciliation of net income to net cash provided by operating activities:			
Net income	$ 2,592,444	$ 3,640,155	$ 8,625,376
Martin Howe fiscal year conversion	—	—	(356,914)
Adjustments:			
Depreciation and amortization expense	1,648,023	3,517,852	7,509,630
Provision for merchant losses	484,993	483,245	654,705
Stock award compensation and other	239,659	241,477	120,395
Deferred income taxes	(453,658)	35,982	(761,705)
Changes in assets and liabilities:			
Accounts receivable	(1,562,961)	(1,459,799)	(2,125,510)
Inventory	(50,235)	(157,087)	(186,289)
Other assets	(1,716,464)	(1,895,097)	(501,353)
Accounts payable	1,557,611	44,106	587,784
Accrued liabilities	975,065	(223,411)	210,064
Deferred revenues	(56,123)	169,677	(55,232)
Net cash provided by operating activities	$ 3,658,354	$ 4,397,100	$ 13,720,951

Management's Discussion and Analysis

Liquidity and Capital Resources*

The Company recognizes as revenue in its statement of income the full discount rate and related fees collected from the merchant. The various costs incurred by the Company, including amounts paid to the card-issuing bank, the processing bank, and the network service provider, are reflected as costs of revenues. In accordance with the Company's contracts with its processing banks, all the funds collection and most of the disbursement function is performed on behalf of the Company by the processing bank. At month end the processing bank collects the total discount rate and related fees from the merchants and disburses to each of the service providers their fees, except disbursements for interchange fees paid to the card-issuing bank are made daily. Shortly after month end, the processing bank disburses to the Company the remainder of the funds collected from the merchant (which represents a significant portion of the Company's gross margin).

Although the Company's revenues reflect the full discount rate and related fees collected, the cash flow statement is prepared using the "direct method" as provided in SFAS 95, "Statement of Cash Flows," and reflects cash received from merchants at the net amount collected as the cash flows received by the Company from processing banks are net of the amounts disbursed to the other parties described above. This presentation follows the actual flow of funds to the Company.

Several factors can alter the profitability to the Company of merchant transactions. Primarily, these include (i) improper use of the card reading terminal by the merchant resulting in higher interchange fees paid to the card-issuing bank, (ii) lower than anticipated average dollar sales of credit card transactions thereby reducing the discount rate collected because many of the transaction costs are fixed, (iii) losses incurred as a result of customer chargebacks (the Company can be required to absorb the full retail purchase amount), (iv) the inability to collect the discount rate because of insufficient funds in the merchant's bank account, (v) merchant fraud and (vi) excessive volume of customer return transactions in which the Company again incurs all costs except interchange fees. Actual losses realized as a result of customer chargebacks, merchant fraud and the Company's inability to collect the discount rate as a result of insufficient merchant funds were approximately $399,000 and $721,000 for fiscal year 1995 and fiscal year 1996, respectively. The Company's actual losses as a percentage of total revenues realized remained consistent from fiscal 1995 to fiscal 1996. Management does not believe that the other factors mentioned above have had a material effect on the Company's profitability.

Working Capital

Cash flow provided by operating activities was $3.7 million in fiscal year 1994 as compared to $4.4 million in fiscal year 1995 and $13.7 million in fiscal year 1996. The increase in cash flow from operating activities resulted from increases in net income for each period which have been achieved principally through purchases of merchant portfolios and internal generation of new merchant accounts. The effect of net income increases is partially offset by increases in working capital needs.

At July 31, 1996, the Company had working capital of $106.7 million, as compared to negative working capital of $634,000 at July 31, 1995. This increase in working capital primarily reflects the net proceeds from the Company's third public offering in April 1996.

Accounts receivable increased $2,670,000 from July 31, 1995 to July 31, 1996. This increase was the result of increases in the number of merchant accounts acquired through purchases of merchant portfolios and, to a lesser extent, the internal generation of new merchant accounts. Additionally, at July 31, 1996, the Company had a current accounts receivable of $1.0 million for the proceeds from a life insurance policy on the Company's former Chief Financial Officer.

Other assets, excluding non-competition agreements and deferred processing costs, at July 31, 1995, increased from July 31, 1994 because of the restricted cash balance of $500,000 required to be maintained in connection with an acquisition. Additionally, in June 1995 when certain acquired merchant accounts were converted to the Company's primary processing bank, the bank required a restricted cash balance of $1.5 million to be maintained for six months. These funds were released to the Company in fiscal year 1996. Additionally, other assets increased as a result of deferred financing costs incurred in fiscal year 1995 as a result of amendments to the Company's credit agreement.

Accounts payable at July 31, 1996 increased $588,000 as compared to July 31, 1995, as a result of increased processing costs related to MHA's increase in merchant accounts. Accrued liabilities increased $621,000 from July 31, 1995, to July 31, 1996, primarily as a result of increased income and state franchise taxes.

Capital Expenditures and Investing Activities

Capital expenditures were approximately $1.8 million for fiscal year 1996 as compared to $1.9 million for fiscal year 1995 and $1.5 million for fiscal year 1994. The increase in capital expenditures was primarily the result of additional expenditures related to the Company's management information system, the purchase of additional credit card terminals, the Company's relocation of its office facilities and the

*Source: PMT Services, Inc.'s 1996 Annual Report, pp. 16–17.

purchase of peripheral equipment for lease to merchants. In addition to the increase in capital expenditures, the Company used $8.4 million, $24.6 million and $31.8 million for the purchase of merchant portfolios in fiscal years 1994, 1995 and 1996, respectively. The Company purchased five merchant portfolios in fiscal 1994, nine merchant portfolios in fiscal year 1995 and five in fiscal year 1996.

Financing Activities

The significant increase in cash provided by financing activities for fiscal year 1995 resulted from the consummation of the Company's initial public offering in August 1994. Cash provided by financing activities for fiscal year 1995 was $20.7 million which reflects the net proceeds of the initial public offering after retirement of the Company's outstanding indebtedness to First Union National Bank of Tennessee and to ABC for the March 1994 ABC purchase. Additionally, the Company issued $15.3 million of long-term debt in connection with three of the nine merchant portfolios purchased in fiscal year 1995.

The cash provided by financing activities for fiscal 1996 reflects the Company's consummation of its second and third public offerings in October 1995 and April 1996, respectively. Net cash provided by financing activities was $124.8 million in fiscal 1996 which reflects the net proceeds from the offerings after retirement of the Company's outstanding bank indebtedness.

Future Capital Needs

Management believes that significant expenditures for the purchase of additional merchant portfolios may be required for the Company to sustain its growth in the future. Management expects to fund such purchases primarily through cash generated from operations and additional bank borrowings. Management believes the combination of these sources will be sufficient to meet the Company's anticipated liquidity needs and its growth plans through fiscal year 1997. The Company, however, may pursue additional expansion opportunities, including purchases of additional merchant portfolios, which may require additional capital, and the Company may incur, from time to time, additional short-term and long-term indebtedness or issue, in public or private transactions, equity or debt securities, the availability and terms of which will depend upon then prevailing market and other conditions.

The Company's revolving credit facility was amended and restated during fiscal year 1995 to increase the line of credit to $17.5 million. The Company repaid all outstanding debt related to this credit facility with the proceeds from its second public offering during fiscal year 1996. The amended agreement expires November 1, 1996 with all amounts then outstanding under the agreement due on November 1, 1996, unless the agreement is extended or the outstanding amounts have been converted to a term loan requiring equal monthly payments for 48 months.

Borrowings under the amended revolving credit facility are used to finance purchases of merchant portfolios and equipment and for working capital purposes. Borrowings are secured by substantially all the Company's assets and life insurance policies on the lives of two of the Company's executive officers.

a. Which method is the company using to determine net cash provided by operating activities?   *Required*

b. Why does the company show the indirect method below the statement of cash flows?

c. What is the trend of net cash provided by operating activities over the three years?

d. How has the company increased its account portfolios?

e. What items of property and equipment were acquired during the three-year period?

f. What was the major source of the huge increase in cash and cash equivalents over the three-year period? How were the proceeds used?

g. How does the company expect to finance future expenditures to acquire additional merchant portfolios?

h. How are amounts secured that are borrowed under the line of credit?

i. Given the following data, calculate the cash flow per share of common stock ratio, the cash flow margin ratio, and the cash flow liquidity ratio. (Round the net cash provided from operating activities to the nearest thousand before you calculate the ratios.) How do the ratios compare with the ones for companies illustrated in the chapter?

	(in thousands)
Average number of shares of common stock outstanding	28,539
Net sales	$149,840
Cash and marketable securities	105,461
Current liabilities	6,862

Problem 16–4
Analyze The Gillette
Company's statement of
cash flows (L.O. 5, 6)

Founded in 1901, The Gillette Company is the world leader in male grooming products, a category that includes blades and razors, shaving preparations and electric shavers. Gillette also holds the number one position worldwide in selected female grooming products, such as wet shaving products and hair epilation devices. The Company is the world's top seller of writing instruments and correction products, toothbrushes and oral care appliances. In addition, the Company is the world leader in alkaline batteries.

Gillette manufacturing operations are conducted at 64 facilities in 27 countries, and products are distributed through wholesalers, retailers, and agents in over 200 countries and territories.

The company's statements of cash flows for the years 1994–1996 follow. Then the relevant portion of Management's Discussion and Analysis of the statement of cash flows is provided.

Consolidated Statement of Cash Flows (Millions of dollars)
Years Ended December 31, 1996, 1995 and 1994

	1996	1995	1994
Operating Activities			
Net income	$ 948.7	$1,069.1	$ 919.1
Adjustments to reconcile net income to net cash provided by operating activities:			
Merger-related costs	283.0	—	—
Depreciation and amortization	381.1	343.5	302.9
Other	—	(2.8)	9.9
Changes in assets and liabilities, net of effects from acquisition of businesses:			
Accounts receivable	(459.1)	(387.2)	(206.4)
Inventories	(104.8)	(118.9)	(108.5)
Accounts payable and accrued liabilities	66.9	91.2	82.2
Other working capital items	(141.6)	20.6	11.0
Other noncurrent assets and liabilities	34.2	31.6	19.1
Net cash provided by operating activities	$ 1,008.4	$1,047.1	$1,029.3
Investing Activities			
Additions to property, plant and equipment	$ (829.7)	$ (593.1)	$ (498.0)
Disposals of property, plant and equipment	40.9	30.6	25.5
Acquisition of businesses, less cash acquired	(299.4)	(276.7)	(25.6)
Other	(6.4)	3.9	19.6
Net cash used in investing activities	$ (1,094.6)	$ (835.3)	$ (478.5)
Financing Activities			
Purchase of treasury stock	$ (11.4)	$ (28.9)	$ (12.3)
Proceeds from exercise of stock option and purchase plans	149.5	83.3	44.8
Decrease in long-term debt	(164.5)	(8.7)	(200.6)
Increase (decrease) in loans payable	577.7	123.3	(48.0)
Dividends paid	(450.8)	(382.2)	(320.4)
Net cash provided by (used in) financing activities	$ 100.5	$ (213.2)	$ (536.5)
Effect of Exchange Rate Changes on Cash	$ (19.0)	$ 4.4	$ (0.4)
Increase (Decrease) in Cash and Cash Equivalents	$ (4.7)	$ 3.0	$ 13.9
Cash and Cash Equivalents at Beginning of Year	81.6	78.6	64.7
Cash and Cash Equivalents at End of Year	$ 76.9	$ 81.6	$ 78.6
Supplemental disclosure of cash paid for:			
Interest	$ 94.0	$ 95.0	$ 91.0
Income taxes	$ 586.1	$ 414.6	$ 303.8
Noncash investing and financing activities:			
Acquisition of businesses			
Fair value of assets acquired	$ 361.4	$ 394.9	$ 19.0
Cash paid	300.1	278.3	25.6
Liabilities assumed	$ 61.3	$ 116.6	$ (6.6)

Management's Discussion and Analysis*
Financial Condition

Since the Gillette merger with Duracell was accomplished through the exchange of stock, with no new debt incurred, the Company's financial condition continued to be strong in 1996. Net debt of the Company increased $422 million during 1996, reflecting spending for the acquisition of businesses in the Company's core categories, particularly the battery business, and increased capital spending.

Net debt (total debt net of associated swaps, less cash and short-term investments) at December 31, 1996, amounted to $2.08 billion, compared with $1.66 billion in 1995 and $1.43 billion in 1994.

After the issuance of shares for the exchange with Duracell shareholders, the Company's market value exceeded $43 billion at the end of 1996, while book equity amounted to $4.49 billion. Stock repurchase programs of Gillette and Duracell were terminated after the merger was announced in 1996.

Net cash provided by operating activities in 1996 was $1.01 billion, compared with $1.05 billion in 1995 and $1.03 billion in 1994. Growth in working capital requirements in all three years reflected the growth in the business. The current ratio of the Company was 1.62 for 1996, compared with ratios of 1.58 for 1995 and 1.66 for 1994.

Capital spending in 1996 amounted to a record $830 million, compared with $593 million in 1995 and $498 million in 1994. Spending in all three years principally reflected significant investments in the blade and razor, Duracell and Braun product segments.

In 1996, the Company spent $300 million for acquisitions, principally in the battery business, compared with $278 million in 1995 and $26 million in 1994. Acquisitions in 1995 and 1994 were in other core business areas.

In December 1996, the Company replaced the revolving credit facilities of Gillette and Duracell with new revolving facilities provided by a syndicate of 19 banks for $400 million, expiring December 1997, and $1.1 billion, expiring December 2001. The Company will continue to use these facilities to provide back-up to its commercial paper program.

The Company generally borrows through the U.S. commercial paper market. At year-end 1996, there was $1.09 billion outstanding under the Gillette and Duracell commercial paper programs, compared with $599 million at the end of 1995 and $510 million at the end of 1994.

Both Moody's and Standard & Poor's reconfirmed the Company's long-term credit ratings in 1996 following the merger announcement. Moody's rates the Company's long-term debt Aa3, while the Standard & Poor's rating is AA−. The commercial paper rating is P1 by Moody's and A1+ by S&P.

Gillette will continue to have capital available for growth through both internally generated funds and substantial credit resources. The Company has substantial unused lines of credit and access to worldwide financial market sources for funds.

*Source: The Gillette Company's 1996 annual report, p. 22.

a. Does the company use the direct or indirect methods of calculating net cash provided by operating activities?   *Required*

b. Did the merger-related costs result in a cash outflow in 1996? Explain.

c. Determine whether each of the current assets (other than cash) and current liabilities increased or decreased during 1996.

d. How is the company expanding its asset base?

e. How much greater is the total market value of the company's outstanding shares of common stock than the book equity (stockholders' equity)?

f. What is the likelihood that the company will be able to pay at least the current level of dividends in the future?

g. Do you expect to see purchases of treasury stock increase or decrease in the future?

h. Given the following data, calculate the cash flow per share of common stock ratio, the cash flow margin ratio, and the cash flow liquidity ratio. (Round the net cash provided by operating activities to the nearest million before you calculate the ratios.) How do the ratios compare with the ones for companies illustrated in the chapter?

		(in millions)
Average number of shares of common stock outstanding	. . . . . .	554
Net sales	. . . .	$9,698
Cash and marketable securities	. . . .	84
Current liabilities	. . . .	2,935

Problem 16–5
Prepare working paper and
statement of cash flows
under the indirect method
(appendix) (L.O. 7)

The following information is from the accounting records of Wescott Office Supplies, Inc.,
for the fiscal years 2000 and 1999:

WESCOTT OFFICE SUPPLIES, INC.
Comparative Balance Sheets
June 30, 2000, and 1999

	2000	1999
Assets		
Cash	$ 66,250	$ 61,000
Accounts receivable, net	84,000	42,000
Merchandise inventory	42,000	48,250
Prepaid expenses	7,875	12,125
Land	94,500	78,750
Buildings	199,500	147,000
Accumulated depreciation—buildings	(31,500)	(26,250)
Equipment	257,250	210,000
Accumulated depreciation—equipment	(78,750)	(63,000)
Total assets	$641,125	$509,875
Liabilities and Stockholders' Equity		
Accounts payable	$ 73,500	$ 47,250
Accrued liabilities payable	50,500	55,750
Five-year note payable	52,500	–0–
Capital stock—$50 par	420,000	367,500
Retained earnings	44,625	39,375
Total liabilities and stockholders' equity	$641,125	$509,875

Additional data

1. Net income for year ended June 30, 2000, was $56,250.
2. Additional land was acquired for cash, $15,750.
3. No equipment or building retirements occurred during the year.
4. Equipment was purchased for cash, $47,250.
5. The five-year note for $52,500 was issued to pay for a building erected on land leased by the company.
6. Stock was issued at par for cash, $52,500.
7. Dividends declared and paid were $51,000.
8. The company paid interest of $10,000 and income taxes of $40,000.

Required

a. Prepare a working paper for a statement of cash flows.
b. Prepare a statement of cash flows under the indirect method. Also prepare any necessary supplemental schedule(s).

ALTERNATE PROBLEMS

Problem 16–1A
Prepare working paper to
convert income statement
to cash basis; prepare cash
flows from operating activities under both methods
(L.O. 2, 3)

The income statement and other data of Dunbar Carpet Outlet, Inc., follow:

DUNBAR CARPET OUTLET, INC.
Income Statement
For the Year Ended December 3, 1999

Sales		$920,000
Cost of goods sold		380,000
Gross margin		$540,000
Operating expenses (other than		
depreciation)	$140,000	
Depreciation expense	40,000	180,000
Net income		$360,000

Changes in current assets (other than cash) and current liabilities during the year were:

	Increase	Decrease
Accounts receivable		$20,000
Merchandise inventory	$16,000	
Prepaid insurance	8,000	
Accounts payable	28,000	
Accrued liabilities payable	4,000	

Depreciation was the only noncash item affecting net income.

a. Prepare a working paper to calculate cash flows from operating activities under the *direct method*.

Required

b. Prepare the cash flows from operating activities section of the statement of cash flows under the *direct method*.

c. Prove that the same cash flows amount will be obtained under the indirect method by preparing the cash flows from operating activities section of the statement of cash flows under the *indirect method*. You need not prepare a working paper.

The following comparative balance sheets and other data are for Cellular Telephone Sales, Inc.:

Problem 16–2A
Prepare statement of cash flows under the indirect method (L.O. 4)

CELLULAR TELEPHONE SALES, INC.
Comparative Balance Sheets
December 31, 2000 and 1999

	2000	1999
Assets		
Cash	$ 76,105	$ 51,000
Accounts receivable, net	26,075	24,250
Merchandise inventory	30,000	35,000
Supplies on hand	1,750	2,550
Prepaid insurance	1,400	1,200
Land	180,000	142,500
Equipment	270,000	300,000
Accumulated depreciation—equipment	(75,000)	(67,500)
Total assets	$510,330	$489,000
Liabilities and Stockholders' Equity		
Accounts payable	$ 45,330	$ 76,300
Salaries payable	4,000	2,000
Accrued liabilities payable	2,000	8,250
Long-term note payable	150,000	150,000
Common stock ($5 par)	185,000	165,000
Paid-in capital in excess of par	32,500	–0–
Retained earnings	91,500	87,450
Total liabilities and stockholders' equity	$510,330	$489,000

1. Land was bought for $37,500 cash. The company intends to build a building on the land. Currently the company leases a building for its operations.

Additional data

2. Equipment costing $50,000 with accumulated depreciation of $30,000 was sold for $23,500 (a gain of $3,500), and equipment costing $20,000 was purchased for cash.

3. Depreciation expense for the year was $37,500.

4. Common stock was issued for $52,500 cash.

5. Dividends declared and paid in 2000 totaled $32,950.

6. Net income was $37,000.

7. The company paid interest of $3,000 and income taxes of $17,000.

Required   Prepare a statement of cash flows under the indirect method. Also prepare any necessary supplemental schedule(s).

Problem 16–3A
Analyze Computer Associates International, Inc.'s 1996 statement of cash flows (L.O. 5, 6)

Computer Associates International, Inc., is the world's largest business software company. The company offers more applications on more kinds of platforms to more kinds of corporations than any other company in the computer industry. The company was founded in 1977 with four employees and has grown to 9,000 employees, 500 products, 100,000 clients, and about 3.5 billion in revenues.

     The company's statements of cash flows for the years 1994 through 1996 follow. Then the relevant portion of Management's Discussion and Analysis of the statement of cash flows is provided.

CONSOLIDATED STATEMENTS OF CASH FLOWS

	Year Ended March 31,		
Operating Activities:	**1996**	**1995**	**1994**
	(In thousands)		
Net (loss) income	$ **(56,354)**	$ 431,904	$ 401,262
Adjustments to reconcile net (loss) income to net cash provided by operating activities:			
Depreciation and amortization	**404,326**	257,699	206,317
Provision for deferred income taxes (benefit)	**(290,070)**	41,669	60,469
Charge for purchased research and development	**1,303,280**	249,300	
Increase in noncurrent installment accounts receivable, net	**(590,407)**	(357,103)	(226,785)
Increase (decrease) in deferred maintenance revenue	**36,990**	(5,352)	(8,064)
Foreign currency transaction (gain) loss—before taxes	**(1,799)**	1,131	10,421
Changes in other operating assets and liabilities, net of effects of acquisitions:			
Increase in trade and installment receivables	**(262,292)**	(59,250)	(30,357)
Other changes in operating assets and liabilities	**75,684**	(70,628)	66,950
Net Cash Provided by Operating Activities	$ **619,358**	$ 489,370	$ 480,213
Investing Activities:			
Acquisitions, primarily purchased software, marketing rights and intangibles	$**(1,787,308)**	$(430,675)	$ (3,923)
Purchases of property and equipment	**(21,296)**	(35,370)	(28,637)
Purchases of marketable securities	**(54,067)**	(145,796)	(169,476)
Sales of marketable securities	**136,356**	193,724	96,405
Increase in capitalized development costs and other	**(15,768)**	(15,552)	(15,471)
Net Cash Used in Investing Activities	$**(1,742,083)**	$(433,669)	$(121,102)
Financing Activities:			
Dividends	**(33,017)**	(32,202)	(23,202)
Purchases of treasury stock	**(30,910)**	(173,283)	(204,699)
Proceeds from borrowings	**1,720,000**	522,000	181,676
Repayments of borrowings	**(569,905)**	(417,404)	(264,225)
Exercise of common stock options and other	**21,110**	15,891	11,611
Net Cash Provided By (Used In) Financing Activities	$ **1,107,278**	$ (84,998)	$(298,839)
(Decrease) Increase In Cash And Cash Equivalents Before Effect of Exchange Rate Changes On Cash	$ **(15,447)**	$ (29,297)	$ 60,272
Effect of exchange rate changes on cash	**(4,593)**	12,749	(6,628)
(Decrease) Increase in Cash and Cash Equivalents	$ **(20,040)**	$ (16,548)	$ 53,644
Cash and Cash Equivalents—Beginning of Year	**116,579**	133,127	79,483
Cash and Cash Equivalents—End of Year	$ **96,539**	$ 116,579	$ 133,127

Management's Discussion and Analysis*

LIQUIDITY AND CAPITAL RESOURCES

Cash from operations for the year ended March 31, 1996 increased by $130 million, or 27%, over the preceding fiscal year. The increase was primarily the result of increased net income, excluding the non-cash charge to earnings for purchased research and development. While absolute accounts receivable balances have increased during fiscal 1996 reflecting the clients' higher propensity to finance licensing fees, collection of billed receivables has reduced the amount of time such receivables are outstanding. Installment, or unbilled, receivables have grown proportionally with revenue and continue to be viewed by the Company both as a competitive advantage when marketing product as well as a beneficial use of the Company's capital. Cash generated from operations and maturities of marketable securities were used to reduce debt drawn as a result of the August 1995 Legent acquisition. The Company's fiscal 1996 open market purchases of its common stock of $31 million was significantly lower than that of the prior year primarily due to concerted efforts to reduce the debt levels associated with the Legent acquisition.

In August 1995, the Company's revolving line of credit was renegotiated from $500 million to $2 billion to fund the $1.8 billion acquisition of Legent. Under the new credit facility, borrowings are subject to interest primarily at the prevailing London interbank rate ("LIBOR") plus a fixed spread dependent on the achievement of certain financial ratios. The agreement provides for a facility fee, also dependent on the achievement of certain financial ratios. The facility calls for the maintenance of certain financial conditions. The Company also has $23 million of unsecured and uncommitted multicurrency lines of credit available. These multicurrency facilities were established to meet any short-term working capital requirements for subsidiaries principally outside the United States. Peak borrowings under all financing arrangements were $1,845 million during fiscal 1996, and the weighted average interest rate for those borrowings was 6.5%. Peak borrowings under credit facilities during fiscal 1995 were $392 million and the weighted average interest rate for these borrowings was 5.3%. At March 31, 1996, approximately $1.4 billion was outstanding under these credit arrangements.

In April 1996, the Company further restructured a portion of its debt by completing a $320 million private placement of debt. The private placement affords the Company several advantages including extending the maturity of its debt, locking in a favorable interest rate and broadening the Company's sources of liquidity.

The Company's capital resource commitment as of March 31, 1996, consisted of lease obligations for office facilities, computer equipment, a mortgage obligation and amounts due resulting from the acquisition of products and companies. The Company intends to meet its capital resource requirements from its available funds. No significant commitments exist for future capital expenditures.

The Company believes that the foregoing sources of liquidity, plus existing cash and marketable securities balances of $201 million as of March 31, 1996, are adequate for its foreseeable operating needs.

The Company purchased approximately 750 thousand shares of its Common Stock under its open market repurchase program during fiscal 1996, bringing the total purchased under this program to approximately 24.5 million shares. An additional 13 million shares is authorized for repurchase. The Company had previously completed a 22.5 million share repurchase program, for a total of 47 million shares. All references to share amounts have been adjusted for the three-for-two stock split effective August 21, 1995.

*Source: Computer Associates International, Inc.'s 1996 Annual Report, p. 20.

Required

a. Explain how the company could have a net loss in 1996 and yet have a positive net cash provided by operating activities.

b. How can management mention increased net income when the company reported a net loss in 1996?

c. What was the reason given by management for the smaller than usual repurchase of its own stock (treasury stock)?

d. How did the company finance the acquisitions made in 1996?

e. How is the interest rate on borrowings determined?

f. What information would normally appear immediately below the statement of cash flows that seems to be missing?

g. Does the amount of cash provided by operating activities seem large enough to continue the present dividend payments?

h. Given the following data, calculate the cash flow per share of common stock ratio, the cash flow margin ratio, and cash flow liquidity ratio.

	(in thousands)
Average number of shares of common stock outstanding	241,512
Net sales	$3,504,629
Cash and marketable securities	201,213
Current liabilities	1,501,477

Problem 16–4A
Analyze Cabletron
Systems, Inc.'s 1996 state-
ment of cash flows
(L.O. 5, 6)

Cabletron develops, manufactures, markets, installs and supports a wide range of standards-based LAN and WAN connectivity hardware and software products. The Company's approach to networking is based on a strategy known as Synthesis, a strategic framework which combines infrastructure products and technologies, automated management tools, and support services to allow users to smoothly migrate from traditional router-based internetworks to switch-based virtual enterprise internetworks. An integral part of Synthesis is the MMAC product family, which includes the MMAC, the Company's wiring closet smart hub, and the MMAC Plus, the Company's modular advanced switching intelligent hub. All of the Company's intelligent networking products are managed by SPECTRUM, Cabletron's sophisticated enterprise-wide network management system. The Company also produces and supports other networking products, such as adapter cards, other interconnection equipment, wiring cables, and file server products, and provides a wide range of networking services. The Company believes that its broad product line and its ability to provide full service enable it to offer its customers "The Complete Networking Solution."

The company's statements of cash flow for the years 1994–1996 follow. Then the relevant portion of Management's Discussion and Analysis of the statement of cash flows is provided.

CONSOLIDATED STATEMENTS OF CASH FLOWS
Years Ended February 29, 1996, and February 28, 1995 and 1994
(in thousands)

	1996	1995	1994
Cash flows from operating activities:			
Net income	**$ 164,418**	$ 161,974	$ 119,218
Adjustments to reconcile net income to net cash provided by operating activities:			
Depreciation and amortization	**32,061**	26,832	17,335
Provision for losses on accounts receivable	**356**	72	1,734
Loss on disposals of property, plant and equipment . . .	**93**	174	113
Deferred taxes	**(38,766)**	(4,434)	(6,151)
Changes in assets and liabilities:			
Accounts receivables	**(55,101)**	(27,698)	(17,707)
Inventories	**(50,483)**	(23,080)	(8,758)
Prepaid expenses and other assets	**(18,844)**	(3,123)	1,211
Accounts payable and accrued expenses	**62,908**	11,336	22,003
Income taxes payable	**3,705**	10,476	(3,924)
Net cash provided by operating activities	**$ 100,347**	$ 152,529	$ 125,074
Cash flows from investing activities:			
Capital expenditures	**$ (65,035)**	$ (63,091)	$ (39,399)
Purchase of available-for-sale securities	**(79,427)**	(71,598)	(30,097)
Purchase of held-to-maturity securities	**(205,852)**	(282,712)	(258,517)
Maturities of marketable securities	**208,922**	323,682	197,406
Net cash used in investing activities	**$(141,392)**	$ (93,719)	$(130,607)
Cash flows from financing activities:			
Repayments of notes receivable from stockholders . . .	**$ 174**	$ 131	$ 66
Repurchase of common stock	**(1,173)**	(13,070)	—
Tax benefit of options exercised	**7,215**	5,712	6,980
Common stock issued to employee stock purchase plan	**3,323**	2,287	1,637
Proceeds from stock option exercise	**16,021**	4,887	7,185
Net cash provided by (used for) financing activities	**$ 25,560**	$ (53)	$ 15,868

Effect of exchange rate changes on cash	**$ 166**	$ 712	$ 161
Net increase (decrease) in cash and cash equivalents	**$ (15,319)**	$ 59,469	$ 10,496
Cash and cash equivalents, beginning of year	**114,032**	54,563	44,067
Cash and cash equivalents, end of year	**$ 98,713**	$ 114,032	$ 54,563
Cash paid during the year for:			
Income taxes	**$ 105,233**	$ 68,420	$ 67,263

Management's Discussion and Analysis*

Net cash provided by operating activities was $100.3 million in fiscal 1996, compared to $152.5 million in fiscal 1995 and $125.1 million in fiscal 1994.

Capital investment for fiscal 1996 of $65.0 million included $9.8 million for building costs of which $3.4 was for the purchase of an engineering building, $21.4 million for engineering computer and computer related software and equipment, $5.5 million for manufacturing and related equipment and $19.0 million for expanding global sales operations. During fiscal 1995, capital expenditures of $63.1 million included approximately $8.2 million for building costs related to expanding manufacturing and distribution capacities and enlarging worldwide sales operations, $12.5 million for manufacturing and manufacturing support equipment and $15.0 million for engineering computer and computer related equipment. Another $15.0 million was spent in support of expanded global sales activities. During fiscal 1994, capital expenditures of $39.4 million included $3.9 million on buildings, $10.1 million on engineering equipment, $7.8 million on manufacturing capacity expansions and $2.0 million to equip new sales offices.

Cash, cash equivalents and marketable securities increased during fiscal 1996 to $407.0 million, from $345.9 million in the prior fiscal year. State and local municipal bonds of approximately $264.2 million, maturing in approximately 1.5 years, were being held by the Company at February 29, 1996.

At February 29, 1996, the Company did not have any short or long term borrowing or any significant financial commitments outstanding, other than those required in the normal course of business.

In the opinion of management, internally generated funds from operations and existing cash, cash equivalents and marketable securities will be adequate to support Cabletron's working capital and capital expenditures requirements for both short and long term needs.

*Source: Cabletron Systems, Inc.'s 1996 Annual Report, pp. 11–12.

Required

a. Which method did the company use in arriving at net cash flows from operating activities?

b. Did current assets other than cash increase or decrease during the year ended February 29, 1996?

c. Did current liabilities increase or decrease during the year ended February 29, 1996?

d. What were the main investing activities during this three-year period?

e. What was the main source of cash from financing activities during the three-year period?

f. Did the company pay any interest expense during the year ended February 19, 1996?

g. Given the following data, calculate the cash flow per share of common stock ratio, the cash flow margin ratio, and the cash flow liquidity ratio. How do these ratios compare with the ratios shown for other companies in the chapter?

	(in thousands)
Average number of shares of common stock outstanding	71,839
Net sales	$1,069,715
Cash and marketable securities	253,540
Current liabilities	164,352

The following comparative balance sheets and other data are for Dayton Tent & Awning Sales, Inc.:

Problem 16–5A
Prepare working paper and statement of cash flows under the indirect method (Appendix) (L.O. 7)

DAYTON TENT & AWNING SALES, INC.
Comparative Balance Sheets
June 30, 2000, and 1999

	2000	1999
Assets		
Cash	$ 441,800	$ 332,600
Accounts receivable, net	750,750	432,900
Merchandise inventory	819,000	850,200
Prepaid insurance	3,900	5,850
Land	312,000	351,000
Buildings	2,184,000	1,209,000
Machinery and tools	858,000	468,000
Accumulated depreciation—machinery and tools	(809,250)	(510,900)
Total assets	$4,560,200	$3,138,650
Liabilities and Stockholders' Equity		
Accounts payable	$ 226,750	$ 275,500
Accrued liabilities payable	185,800	111,700
Bank loans (due in 2002)	56,550	66,300
Mortgage bonds payable	382,200	185,250
Common stock—$100 par	1,755,000	585,000
Paid-in capital in excess of par	58,500	–0–
Retained earnings	1,895,400	1,914,900
Total liabilities and stockholders' equity	$4,560,200	$3,138,650

Additional data

1. Net income for the year was $128,000.
2. Depreciation for the year was $356,850.
3. There was a gain of $7,800 on the sale of land. The land was sold for $46,800.
4. The additional mortgage bonds were issued at face value as partial payment for a building valued at $975,000. The amount of cash paid was $778,050.
5. Machinery and tools were purchased for $448,500 cash.
6. Fully depreciated machinery with a cost of $58,500 was scrapped and written off.
7. Additional common stock was issued at $105 per share. The total proceeds were $1,228,500.
8. Dividends declared and paid were $147,500.
9. A payment was made on the bank loan, $9,750.
10. The company paid interest of $9,000 and income taxes of $75,000.

Required

a. Prepare a working paper for a statement of cash flows.
b. Prepare a statement of cash flows under the indirect method. Also prepare any necessary supplemental schedule(s).

BEYOND THE NUMBERS—CRITICAL THINKING

Business Decision Case 16–1

Prepare a statement of cash flows using the indirect method and answer president's questions (L.O. 1, 2, 4)

National Sports, Inc., is a sports equipment sales company. During 1998, the company replaced $18,000 of its fully depreciated equipment with new equipment costing $23,000. Although a midyear dividend of $5,000 was paid, the company found it necessary to borrow $5,000 from its bank on a two-year note. Further borrowing may be needed since the Cash account is dangerously low at year-end.

Following are the income statement and "cash flow statement," as the company's accountant calls it, for 2000.

NATIONAL SPORTS, INC.
Income Statement
For the Year Ended December 31, 2000

Sales		$195,000
Cost of goods sold	$140,000	
Operating expenses and taxes	49,700	189,700
Net income		$ 5,300

NATIONAL SPORTS, INC.
Cash Flow Statement
For the Year Ended December 31, 2000

Cash received:

From operations:

Net income		$ 5,300
Depreciation		5,000
Total cash from operations		$10,300
Note issued to bank		5,000
Mortgage note issued		16,000
Total funds provided		$31,300

Cash paid:

New equipment	$23,000	
Dividends	5,000	28,000
Increase in cash		$ 3,300

The company's president is very concerned about what he sees in these statements and how it relates to what he knows has actually happened. He turns to you for help. Specifically, he wants to know why the cash flow statement shows an increase in cash of $3,300 when he knows the cash balance decreased from $15,000 to $500 during the year. Also, why is depreciation shown as providing cash?

You believe you can answer the president's questions after receiving the following condensed balance sheet data:

NATIONAL SPORTS, INC.
Comparative Balance Sheets
December 31, 2000, and 1999

	December 31	
	2000	**1999**
Assets		
Current assets:		
Cash	$ 500	$ 15,000
Accounts receivable, net	17,800	13,200
Merchandise inventory	28,500	17,500
Prepaid expenses	700	300
Total current assets	$ 47,500	$ 46,000
Property, plant, and equipment:		
Equipment	$ 40,000	$ 35,000
Accumulated depreciation—equipment	(11,000)	(24,000)
Total property, plant, and equipment	$ 29,000	$ 11,000
Total assets	$ 76,500	$ 57,000
Liabilities and Stockholders' Equity		
Current liabilities:		
Accounts payable	$ 8,700	$ 10,000
Accrued liabilities payable	600	1,100
Total current liabilities	$ 9,300	$ 11,100
Long-term liabilities:		
Notes payable	5,000	–0–
Mortgage note payable	16,000	–0–
Total liabilities	$ 30,300	$ 11,100
Stockholders' equity:		
Common stock	$ 40,000	$ 40,000
Retained earnings	6,200	5,900
Total stockholders' equity	$ 46,200	$ 45,900
Total liabilities and stockholders' equity	$ 76,500	$ 57,000

Prepare a correct statement of cash flows using the indirect method that shows why National *Required* Sports, Inc., is having such a difficult time keeping sufficient cash on hand. Also, answer the president's questions. The company paid interest of $400 and income taxes of $3,000.

Business Decision Case 16–2
Prepare a schedule showing cash flows from operating activities under the indirect method and decide whether certain goals can be met (L.O. 4)

Following are comparative balance sheets for Hardiplank Siding, Inc.:

HARDIPLANK SIDING, INC.
Comparative Balance Sheets
December 31, 2000, and 1999

	2000	1999
Assets		
Cash	$ 80,000	$ 57,500
Accounts receivable, net	60,000	45,000
Merchandise inventory	90,000	52,500
Land	67,500	60,000
Buildings	90,000	90,000
Accumulated depreciation—buildings	(30,000)	(27,000)
Equipment	285,000	225,000
Accumulated depreciation—equipment	(52,500)	(48,000)
Goodwill	120,000	150,000
Total assets	$710,000	$605,000
Liabilities and Stockholders' Equity		
Accounts payable	$ 95,000	$ 65,000
Accrued liabilities payable	30,000	22,500
Capital stock	315,000	300,000
Paid-in capital—stock dividends	75,000	67,500
Paid-in capital—land donations	15,000	–0–
Retained earnings	180,000	150,000
Total liabilities and stockholders' equity	$710,000	$605,000

An analysis of the Retained Earnings account for the year reveals the following:

Balance, January 1, 2000		$150,000
Add: Net income for the year		107,500
		$257,500
Less: Cash dividends	$55,000	
Stock dividends	22,500	77,500
Balance, December 31, 2000		$180,000

Additional data

a. Equipment with a cost of $30,000 on which $27,000 of depreciation had been accumulated was sold during the year at a loss of $1,500. Included in net income is a gain on the sale of land of $9,000.

b. The president of the company has set two goals for 2001: (1) increase cash by $40,000 and (2) increase cash dividends by $35,000. The company's activities in 2001 are expected to be quite similar to those of 2000, and no new fixed assets will be acquired.

Required

Prepare a schedule showing cash flows from operating activities under the indirect method for 2000. Can the company meet its president's goals for 2001? Explain.

Annual Report Analysis 16–3
Decide whether four companies can maintain their current dividends (real world problem) (L.O. 1)

Refer to the annual report booklet. Evaluate the ease with which each of the four companies represented will be able to maintain their dividend payments in the future at 1996 amounts. (Hint: Compare current dividend amounts with net cash provided by operating activities.) Rank the companies in their ability to maintain their dividend payments by dividing their net cash provided by operating activities by their dividends paid.

Annual Report Analysis 16–4
Analyze a company's statement of cash flows and answer questions (L.O. 5)

Refer to "A Broader Perspective" on page 598 and answer the following questions:

a. Over the last three years from which major activities (operations, investing, financing) has Johnson & Johnson received net cash inflows and on which major activities have they spent the funds?

b. What relationship do you see between "Depreciation and amortization of property and intangibles" and "Additions of property, plant, and equipment"?

c. What were the two major sources of cash outflows to stockholders and which was larger?

d. By how much did the investments in marketable securities grow or shrink over the three-year period?

e. By how much did long-term debt grow or shrink over the three-year period?

f. If you were a stockholder, would you feel uncertain or confident that this company will be able to pay future dividends at the same rate as in the past?

g. For what reason or reasons might the company be buying back its own stock?

h. For the latest year, did the current assets (other than cash) and current liabilities go up or down?

i. From the information that is available, does it appear that the company is performing well or poorly?

Refer to the annual report booklet. For each of the four companies—The Coca-Cola Company; Maytag Corporation; The Limited, Inc.; and John H. Harland—calculate the following ratios for 1996:

Annual Report Analysis 16–5
For four real companies, calculate cash flow per share of common stock, cash flow margin, and cash flow liquidity ratios and then comment (L.O. 6)

a. Cash flow per share of common stock ratio. (Look at the Consolidated Statements of Shareholders' Equity or at the Balance Sheet to find the number of outstanding shares of stock.)

b. Cash flow margin ratio.

c. Cash flow liquidity ratio.

Then comment on the results.

In groups of two or three students write a two-page, double-spaced paper on one of the following topics:

Group Project 16–6
Write a paper on a specific topic

Which Is Better, the Direct or Indirect Method (of calculating net cash provided by operating activities)?

Analysis of the Johnson & Johnson Cash Flow Statement (shown in "A Broader Perspective" in this chapter)

Analysis of The Coca-Cola Company's Cash Flow Statement (shown in the annual report booklet)

Your analysis should be convincing and have no spelling or grammatical errors. Your paper should be neat and the result of several drafts. The paper should have a cover page with the title and the authors' names. Use a word processing program if possible.

In a group of one or two other students, go to the library and locate *Statement of Financial Accounting Standards No. 95*, "Statement of Cash Flows," published by the Financial Accounting Standards Board. Write a report to your instructor answering the following questions:

Group Project 16–7
Perform library project on aspects of *Statement of Financial Accounting Standards No. 95*

1. Why did the Board settle on cash flows instead of working capital flows?

2. Why did the Board strongly recommend use of the direct method?

3. Why did some members of the Board dissent from the final statement?

In a group of one or two other students, go to the library and locate *Statement of Financial Accounting Standards No. 95*, "Statement of Cash Flows," published by the Financial Accounting Standards Board. Write a report to your instructor covering the following points:

Group Project 16–8
Perform library project on aspects of *Statement of Financial Accounting Standards No. 95*

1. Describe the controversy over how to treat interest and dividends received.

2. What is the Board's position on reporting cash flow per share? Why did they take that position?

3. What is the Board's position on noncash transactions? Why did they take that position?

USING THE INTERNET—A VIEW OF THE REAL WORLD

Visit the following website for Digital Equipment Corporation:
http://www.dec.com
By following the instructions on the screen, locate the latest statement of cash flows and then print it. Analyze the statement and write a report to your instructor summarizing your analysis.

Internet Project 16–9
Analyze statement of cash flows

Internet Project 16–10
Analyze statement of cash flows

Visit the following website for GTE Corporation:

http://www.GTE.com

By following the information on the screen, locate the latest statement of cash flows and then print it. Analyze the statement and then write a report to your instructor summarizing your analysis.

ANSWERS TO SELF-TEST

TRUE-FALSE

1. **True.** Before July 1988, the statement of changes in financial position was required. This statement emphasized changes in working capital rather than changes in cash.

2. **True.** The statement of cash flows must be published every time an income statement is published.

3. **False.** Investing activities are transactions involving the acquisition or disposal of noncurrent assets. Transactions with creditors and owners are financing activities.

4. **False.** While the direct method is the method encouraged by the FASB, it is not the predominant method in use. In a recent study, only about 3% of the companies surveyed used the direct method.

5. **True.** Both of these transactions are with owners and, therefore, would be financing activities.

MULTIPLE-CHOICE

1. **c.** The descriptions in (a) and (b) would be correct if they were reversed. The indirect method is easier to use, and this characteristic is probably the main reason why it is used by most companies.

2. **a.** Payment of debt is a financing activity because it is a transaction with creditors. All of the others are investing activities because they are transactions involving the acquisition or disposal of noncurrent assets.

3. **b.** Sales of $500,000 minus the increase in accounts receivable of $30,000 = $470,000.

4. **d.** Cost of goods sold of $300,000, less the increase in accounts payable of $20,000, plus the increase in inventory of $50,000 = $330,000.

5. **a.** Net income of $200,000, plus depreciation of $10,000, less the increase in accounts receivable of $15,000, plus the increase in accounts payable of $5,000 = $200,000.

17

ANALYSIS AND INTERPRETATION OF FINANCIAL STATEMENTS

The two primary objectives of every business are solvency and profitability. Solvency is the ability of a company to pay debts as they come due; it is reflected on the company's balance sheet. Profitability is the ability of a company to generate income; it is reflected on the company's income statement. Generally, all those interested in the affairs of a company are especially interested in solvency and profitability.

This chapter discusses several common methods of analyzing and relating the data in financial statements and, as a result, gaining a clear picture of the solvency and profitability of a company. Internally, management analyzes a company's financial statements as do external investors, creditors, and regulatory agencies. Although these users have different immediate goals, their overall objective in financial statement analysis is the same—to make predictions about an organization as an aid in decision making.

OBJECTIVES OF FINANCIAL STATEMENT ANALYSIS

Management's analysis of financial statements primarily relates to parts of the company. Using this approach, management can plan, evaluate, and control operations within the company. Management obtains any information it wants about the company's operations by requesting special-purpose reports. It uses this information to make difficult decisions, such as which employees to lay off and when to expand operations. Our primary focus in this chapter, however, is not on the special reports accountants prepare for management. Rather, it is on the information needs of persons outside the firm.

Investors, creditors, and regulatory agencies generally focus their analysis of financial statements on the company as a whole. Since they cannot request

This chapter uses the following source: Colgate-Palmolive Company, *1996 Annual Report*, Colgate-Palmolive Company, New York, New York, 1996.

special-purpose reports, external users must rely on the general-purpose financial statements that companies publish. These statements include a balance sheet, an income statement, a statement of stockholders' equity, a statement of cash flows, and the explanatory notes that accompany the financial statements.

Objective 1
Describe and explain the objectives of financial statement analysis.

Users of financial statements need to pay particular attention to the explanatory notes, or the financial review, provided by management in annual reports. This integral part of the annual report provides insight into the scope of the business, the results of operations, liquidity and capital resources, new accounting standards, and geographic area data. Moreover, this section provides an economic outlook that an analyst may find very helpful when considering the possible future profitability of the company.

Financial Statement Analysis

Financial statement analysis consists of applying analytical tools and techniques to financial statements and other relevant data to obtain useful information. This information reveals significant relationships between data and trends in those data that assess the company's past performance and current financial position. The information shows the results or consequences of prior management decisions. In addition, analysts use the information to make predictions that may have a direct effect on decisions made by users of financial statements.

Present and potential investors are interested in the future ability of a company to earn profits—its profitability. These investors wish to predict future dividends and changes in the market price of the company's common stock. Since both dividends and price changes are likely to be influenced by earnings, investors may predict earnings. The company's past earnings record is the logical starting point in predicting future earnings.

Some outside parties, such as creditors, are more interested in predicting a company's solvency than its profitability. The **liquidity** of the company affects its short-term solvency. The company's liquidity is its state of possessing liquid assets, such as cash and other assets easily converted to cash. Because companies must pay short-term debts soon, liquid assets must be available for their payment. For example, a bank asked to extend a 90-day loan to a company would want to know the company's projected short-term liquidity. Of course, the company's predicted ability to repay the 90-day loan is likely to be based at least partially on its past ability to pay off debts.

Long-term creditors are interested in a company's long-term solvency, which is usually determined by the relationship of a company's assets to its liabilities. Generally, we consider a company to be solvent when its assets exceed its liabilities so that the company has a positive stockholders' equity. The larger the assets are in relation to the liabilities, the greater the long-term solvency of the company. Thus, the company's assets could shrink significantly before its liabilities would exceed its assets and destroy the company's solvency.

Investors perform several types of analyses on a company's financial statements. All of these analyses rely on comparisons or relationships of data that enhance the utility or practical value of accounting information. For example, knowing that a company's net income last year was $100,000 may or may not, by itself, be useful information. Some usefulness is added when we know that the prior year's net income was $25,000. And even more useful information is gained if we know the amounts of sales and assets of the company. Such comparisons or relationships may be expressed as:

1. Absolute increases and decreases for an item from one period to the next.
2. Percentage increases and decreases for an item from one period to the next.
3. Percentages of single items to an aggregate total.
4. Trend percentages.
5. Ratios.

Earlier chapters have discussed and illustrated many of these analysis techniques. However, in this chapter we apply all of these techniques in analyzing Colgate-Palmolive Company's performance for 1996.

Items 1 and 2 make use of comparative financial statements. **Comparative financial statements** present the same company's financial statements for one or two successive periods in side-by-side columns. The calculation of dollar changes or percentage changes in the statement items or totals is **horizontal analysis.** This analysis detects changes in a company's performance and highlights trends.

Analysts also use vertical analysis of a single financial statement, such as an income statement. **Vertical analysis** (item 3) consists of the study of a single financial statement in which each item is expressed as a *percentage of a significant total.* Vertical analysis is especially helpful in analyzing income statement data such as the percentage of cost of goods sold to sales.

Financial statements that show only percentages and no absolute dollar amounts are **common-size statements.** All percentage figures in a common-size balance sheet are percentages of total assets while all the items in a common-size income statement are percentages of net sales. The use of common-size statements facilitates vertical analysis of a company's financial statements.

Trend percentages (item 4) are similar to horizontal analysis except that comparisons are made to a selected base year or period. Trend percentages are useful for comparing financial statements over several years because they disclose changes and trends occurring through time.

Ratios (item 5) are expressions of logical relationships between items in the financial statements of a single period. Analysts can compute many ratios from the same set of financial statements. A ratio can show a relationship between two items on the same financial statement or between two items on different financial statements (e.g., balance sheet and income statement). The only limiting factor in choosing ratios is the requirement that the items used to construct a ratio have a logical relationship to one another.

SOURCES OF INFORMATION

Financial information about publicly owned corporations can come from different sources such as published reports, government reports, financial service information, business publications, newspapers, and periodicals.

Public corporations must publish annual financial reports. The annual report booklet gives such 1996 data for The Coca-Cola Company; John H. Harland Company; The Limited, Inc.; and Maytag Corporation. The major sections of an annual report are (not necessarily in this order):

1. Consolidated financial statements Consolidated financial statements include a balance sheet containing two years of comparative data; an income statement containing three years of comparative data; a statement of cash flows containing three years of comparative data; and a statement of shareholders' equity containing three years of comparative data. For examples of each statement, refer to the annual report booklet.

2. Notes to consolidated financial statements Notes to consolidated financial statements provide an in-depth look into the numbers contained in the financial statements. The notes usually contain sections on significant accounting policies, long-term debt, leases, stock option plans, etc. These explanations allow stockholders to look beyond the numbers to the events that triggered the dollar amounts recorded in the financial statements.

Published Reports

Objective 2
Describe the sources of information for financial statement analysis.

Chesapeake Corporation
Chesapeake Corporation
is a paper and packaging
company.

3. Letters to stockholders   Most annual reports are introduced with a letter to the stockholders. The letter often includes information about the company's past history, its mission, current year operating results, and the company's future goals. For example, in a recent annual report of the Chesapeake Corporation, the chairman of the board and the president and chief executive officer included in their letter to the stockholders a description of their mission and future company goals, entitled Vision 2000 strategy, as follows:

Mission

Chesapeake's mission is to increase the wealth of our stockholders while fulfilling, with integrity, our responsibilities to our employees, customers, suppliers, the public and the environment.

Vision 2000 Strategy

We will conduct our business in accordance with these goals and principles:

- Maintain high ethical standards
- Be innovative and look beyond the obvious
- Be proactive and strive to be different
- Have respect for people as individuals
    Maintain a clean, safe, injury-free workplace
    Provide the appropriate authority and responsibility to make decisions in a
        decentralized environment
    Utilize the individual talents of our people
    Reward employee innovation, participation and performance
    Achieve a high degree of ownership and commitment
- Continually improve our cost positions and our asset utilization
- Be at least 15 minutes ahead of our competition
- Provide value to our customers through continuous improvement
- Be good stewards of the environment
- Serve our country and communities to the best of our abilities

As the strategy statement indicates, we will manage the company for cash flow and value creation. We are committed to growth, reducing our capital intensity and managing our cyclicality. We have also established financial goals for the year 2000. Our growth target is to have $2 billion in sales by the year 2000. Our profitability target is to achieve an average annual return on equity of 15%. We also will work to control our cyclicality so that our return on equity will not be lower than 10% in any year. The industry in which we participate is the most capital intensive in the United States, and our strategy is intended to achieve a sales to asset ratio of 1.25:1 by the year 2000 while keeping our debt at reasonable levels.

4. Reports of independent accountants   The Securities and Exchange Commission (SEC) requires the financial statements of certain companies to be audited. The report of independent accountants, found at the end of the financial statements, provides assurance that the financial statements prepared by the company have been audited and are free of material misstatements. The report also may include a paragraph highlighting the significant accounting policies that the company has changed recently.

5. Management discussion and analysis   The management discussion and analysis section of the annual report provides management's view of the performance of the company. The analysis is based on the financial statements, the conditions of the industry, and ratios.

Government Reports   Publicly held companies must file detailed annual reports (Form 10–K), quarterly reports (Form 10–Q), and special events reports (Form 8–K) with the Securities and Exchange Commission. These reports are available to the public for a small charge and sometimes contain more detailed information than the published reports.

Financial statement information is often more meaningful when users compare it with industry norms. Two firms that provide information on individual companies and industries are Moody's Investors Service and Standard & Poor's. Dun & Bradstreet Companies, Inc., publishes *Key Business Ratios* and Robert Morris Associates publishes *Annual Statement Studies;* both provide information for specific industries. Standard & Poor's *Industry Surveys* contains background descriptions and the economic outlook for different industries.

Business publications such as *The Wall Street Journal, Barron's, Forbes,* and *Fortune* also report industry financial news. Because financial statement users must be knowledgeable about current developments in business, the information in financial newspapers and periodicals is very valuable to them.

Financial Service Information, Business Publications, Newspapers, and Periodicals

HORIZONTAL ANALYSIS AND VERTICAL ANALYSIS: AN ILLUSTRATION

The comparative financial statements of the Colgate-Palmolive Company will serve as a basis for an example of horizontal analysis and vertical analysis of a balance sheet and a statement of income and retained earnings. Recall that horizontal analysis calculates changes in comparative statement items or totals, whereas vertical analysis consists of a comparison of items on a single financial statement.

Objective 3
Calculate and explain changes in financial statements using horizontal analysis, vertical analysis, and trend analysis.

Imagine that you are a prospective investor interested in Colgate-Palmolive Company. You have acquired the 1996 Annual Report of the company and want to perform some horizontal and vertical analyses of the financial statements.

First, we begin with the balance sheets. Illustration 17.1 shows the comparative balance sheets for 1996 and 1995 in Columns (1) and (2). Take a few minutes to study the balance sheets. Then review Columns (3) and (4), which show the horizontal analysis that would be performed on the comparative balance sheets.

Column (3) shows the change that occurred in each item between December 31, 1995, and December 31, 1996. If the change between the two dates is an increase from 1995 to 1996, the change is a positive figure. If the change is a decrease, the change is a negative figure and is shown in parentheses. Column (4) shows the percentage change in each item. You can calculate the percentage change by dividing the dollar change by the dollar balance of the earlier year (1995). While examining the horizontal analysis in Illustration 17.1 note that:

Analysis of a Balance Sheet

The Colgate-Palmolive Company
The Colgate-Palmolive Company manufactures and markets toothpastes, oral rinses and toothbrushes, bar and liquid soaps, shampoos, conditioners, deodorants, detergents, and cleansers.

1. Total current assets have increased $12.1 million, consisting largely of increases in cash, marketable securities, and other current assets despite a $52.5 million decrease in net receivables, while total current liabilities have increased $151.2 million, largely as a result of increases in the current portion of long-term debt and other accruals.

2. Total liabilities have decreased $95.1 million, while total assets increased by $259.2 million.

Next, study Column (4), which expresses as a percentage the dollar change in Column (3). Frequently, these percentage increases are more informative than absolute amounts, as illustrated by the current asset and current liability changes. Although the absolute amount of current liabilities has increased tremendously over the amount of current assets, the percentages reveal the current assets increased .5%, while current liabilities increased 8.6%. Thus, current liabilities are increasing at a faster rate than current assets. Current assets still exceed current liabilities. This fact indicates that the company will be able to pay its debts as they come due.

ILLUSTRATION 17.1   Comparative Balance Sheets

COLGATE-PALMOLIVE COMPANY
Comparative Balance Sheets
December 31, 1996, and 1995
($ millions)

	December 31		Horizontal Analysis Increase or (Decrease) 1996 over 1995		Vertical Analysis Percent of Total Assets December 31	
	(1) 1996	(2) 1995	(3) Dollars*	(4) Percent*	(5) 1996	(6) 1995
Assets						
Current Assets						
Cash and cash equivalents	$ 248.2	$ 208.8	$ 39.4	18.9%	3.1%	2.7%
Marketable securities	59.6	47.8	11.8	24.7	0.8	0.6
Receivables, net	1,064.4	1,116.9	(52.5)	(4.7)	13.5	14.6
Inventories	770.7	774.8	(4.1)	(0.5)	9.8	10.1
Other current assets	229.4	211.9	17.5	8.3	2.9	2.8
Total current assets	$2,372.3	$2,360.2	$ 12.1	0.5	30.0	30.9
Property, plant and equipment, net	2,428.9	2,155.2	273.7	12.7	30.7	28.2
Goodwill and other intangibles, net	2,720.4	2,741.7	(21.3)	(0.8)	34.4	35.9
Other assets	379.9	385.2	(5.3)	(1.4)	4.8	5.0
	$7,901.5	$7,642.3	$259.2	3.4	100.0	100.0
Liabilities and Shareholders' Equity						
Current Liabilities						
Notes and loans payable	$ 172.3	$ 204.4	($ 32.1)	(15.7)	2.2	2.7
Current portion of long-term debt	110.4	37.0	73.4	198.4	1.4	0.5
Accounts payable	751.7	738.7	13.0	1.8	9.5	9.7
Accrued income taxes	93.1	76.7	16.4	21.4	1.2	1.0
Other accruals	776.8	696.3	80.5	11.6	9.8	9.1
Total current liabilities	$1,904.3	$1,753.1	$151.2	8.6	24.1	22.9
Long-term debt	2,786.8	2,992.0	(205.2)	(6.9)	35.3	39.2
Deferred income taxes	234.3	237.3	(3.0)	(1.3)	3.0	3.1
Other liabilities	942.0	980.1	(38.1)	(3.9)	11.9	12.8
	$5,867.4	$5,962.5	($ 95.1)	(1.6)	74.3	78.0
Shareholders' Equity						
Preferred stock	$ 392.7	$ 403.5	($ 10.8)	(2.7)	5.0	5.3
Common stock, $1 par value (500,000,000 shares authorized, 183,213,295 shares issued)	183.2	183.2	0.0	0.0	2.3	2.4
Additional paid-in capital	1,101.6	1,033.7	67.9	6.6	13.9	13.5
Retained earnings	2,731.0	2,392.2	338.8	14.2	34.6	31.3
Cumulative translation adjustments	(534.7)	(513.0)	(21.7)	4.2	−6.8	−6.7
	$3,873.8	$3,499.6	$374.2	10.7	49.0	45.8
Unearned compensation	(370.9)	(378.0)	7.1	(1.9)	−4.7	−4.9
Treasury stock, at cost	(1,468.8)	(1,441.8)	(27.0)	1.9	−18.6	−18.9
Total shareholders' equity	$2,034.1	$1,679.8	$354.3	21.1	25.7	22.0
	$7,901.5	$7,642.3	$259.2	3.4	100.0	100.0

*Dollars = (1) − (2); Percent = (3)/(2).

Source: Colgate-Palmolive Company, *Annual Report* (New York: Colgate-Palmolive Company, 1996). Used with permission.

Studying the percentages in Column (4) could lead to several other observations. For instance, the 6.9% decrease in long-term debt indicates that interest charges will be lower in the future, having a positive effect on future net income. The 14.2% increase in retained earnings could be a sign of increased dividends in the future; in addition, the increase in cash of 18.9% could support this conclusion.

Now examine Columns (5) and (6) to see the vertical analysis that would be performed. A vertical analysis of Colgate-Palmolive's balance sheet discloses each

ILLUSTRATION 17.2 Comparative Statements of Income and Retained Earnings

COLGATE-PALMOLIVE COMPANY
Comparative Statements of Income and Retained Earnings
For the years ended December 31, 1996 and 1995
($ millions)

	Year Ended December 31		Horizontal Analysis Increase or (Decrease) 1996 over 1995		Vertical Analysis Percent of Net Sales December 31	
	(7) 1996	(8) 1995	(9) Dollars*	(10) Percent*	(11) 1996	(12) 1995
Net sales	$8,749.0	$8,358.2	$ 390.8	4.7%	100.0%	100.0%
Cost of sales	4,451.1	4,353.1	98.0	2.3	50.9	52.1
Gross profit	$4,297.9	$4,005.1	$ 292.8	7.3	49.1	47.9
Selling, general and administrative expenses	3,052.1	2,879.6	172.5	6.0	34.9	34.5
Provision for restructured operations	—	460.5	(460.5)	(100.0)	0.0	5.5
Other expense, net	93.8	96.1	(2.3)	(2.4)	1.1	1.1
Interest expense, net of interest income of $34.3, $30.6 and $34.2, respectively	197.4	205.4	(8.0)	(3.9)	2.3	2.5
Income before income taxes	$ 954.6	$ 363.5	$ 591.1	162.6	10.9	4.3
Provision for income taxes	319.6	191.5	128.1	66.9	3.7	2.3
Net income	$ 635.0	$ 172.0	$ 463.0	269.2	7.3	2.1
Retained earnings, January 1	2,392.2	2,496.7	(104.5)	(4.2)		
	$3,027.2	$2,668.7	$ 358.5	13.4		
Dividends declared:						
Series B Convertible Preference Stock, net of income taxes	20.9	21.1	(0.2)	(0.9)		
Preferred stock	0.5	0.5	0.0	0.0		
Common stock	274.8	254.9	19.9	7.8		
Retained Earnings, December 31	$2,731.0	$2,392.2	$ 338.8	14.2		

*Dollars = (7) − (8); Percent = (9)/(8)

Source: Colgate-Palmolive Company, *1996 Annual Report* (New York: Colgate-Palmolive Company, 1996). Used with permission.

account's significance to total assets or total equities. This comparison aids in assessing the importance of the changes in each account. Columns (5) and (6) in Illustration 17.1 express the dollar amount of each item in Columns (1) and (2) as a percentage of total assets or equities. For example, although other assets declined $5.3 million in 1996, the decrease of 1.4% in the account represents only approximately 4.8% of total assets and, therefore, probably does not have great significance. Vertical analysis also shows that total debt financing decreased from 78.0% of total equities (liabilities and stockholders' equity) in 1995, to 74.3% in 1996. At the same time, the percentage of stockholder financing to total assets of the company increased from 22.0% to 25.7%.

Illustration 17.2 provides the information needed to analyze Colgate-Palmolive's comparative statements of income and retained earnings. Such a statement merely combines the income statement and the statement of retained earnings. Columns (7) and (8) in Illustration 17.2 show the dollar amounts for the years 1996 and 1995, respectively. Study these statements for a few minutes. Then examine Columns (9) and (10) which show the horizontal analysis that would be performed on Colgate-Palmolive's comparative statements of income and retained earnings. Columns (9) and (10) show the absolute and percentage increase and decrease in each item from 1995 to 1996. The absolute change is determined by deducting the 1995 amount from the 1996 amount. If the change between two dates is an increase from 1995 to 1996, the change is a positive figure. If the change is a decrease, the change is a negative figure

Analysis of Statement of Income and Retained Earnings

and is shown in parentheses. You calculate the percentage change by dividing the dollar change by the dollar amount for 1995.

The horizontal analysis shows that sales increased a total of $390.8 million, an increase of 4.7%. Since cost of goods sold increased by a much smaller amount ($98.0 million), gross profit increased by $292.8, or 7.3%. The $460.5 million expense in 1995 was the result of a provision for restructured operations. Although this is not a recurring expense, it does not classify as an extraordinary expense and is treated as part of income from continuing operations.

Now look at Columns (11) and (12) to see the vertical analysis that would be performed. Columns (11) and (12) express the dollar amount of each item in Columns (7) and (8) as a percentage of net sales. Even though cost of goods sold increased in 1996, it remained a fairly constant percentage of net sales. Therefore, gross profit as a percentage of net sales increased only slightly. The percentage of expenses to net sales decreased somewhat, thus yielding an increase in income before income taxes as a percentage of net sales.

Many times, "a picture is worth a thousand words." Bar graphs can show some of the information in the comparative financial statements. Several of the graphs include data from earlier years as well. Illustration 17.3 shows the relationship between net sales and gross profit for the years 1994 through 1996.

Illustration 17.4 shows the percentage of gross profit to sales for the years 1984 through 1996. The percentage has increased almost steadily over that period from 39.2% to 49.1% of net sales.

Illustration 17.5 shows net income for the years 1994 through 1996. The 1995 amount excludes the restructuring charge, since it is considered to be a "one-time" charge.

Reinforcing Problems

E17–1 Perform horizontal and vertical analysis.

P17–1 Perform horizontal and vertical analysis and comment on the results.

P17–1A Perform horizontal and vertical analysis and comment on the results.

Having completed the horizontal analysis and vertical analysis of Colgate-Palmolive's balance sheet and statement of income and retained earnings, you are ready to study trend percentages and ratio analysis. The last section in this chapter discusses some final considerations in financial statement analysis. Professional financial statement analysts use several tools and techniques to determine the solvency and profitability of companies.

TREND PERCENTAGES

Trend percentages, also referred to as *index numbers,* help you to compare financial information over time to a base year or period. You can calculate trend percentages by:

1. Selecting a base year or period.
2. Assigning a weight of 100% to the amounts appearing on the base-year financial statements.
3. Expressing the corresponding amounts on the other years' financial statements as a percentage of base-year or period amounts. Compute the percentages by dividing nonbase-year amounts by the corresponding base-year amounts and then multiplying the result by 100.

The following information for Colgate-Palmolive illustrates the calculation of trend percentages:

($ millions)	1994	1995	1996
Net sales	$7,587.9	$8,358.2	$8,749.0
Cost of goods sold	3,913.3	4,353.1	4,451.1
Gross profit	$3,674.6	$4,005.1	$4,297.9
Operating expenses	2,794.7	3,641.6	3,343.3
Income before income taxes	$ 879.9	$ 363.5	$ 954.6

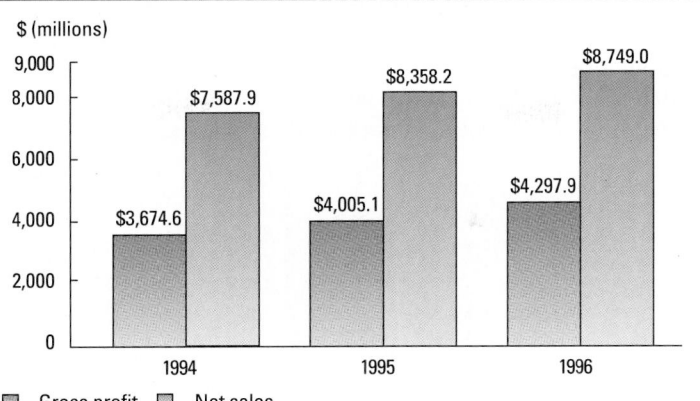

ILLUSTRATION 17.3
Net Sales and Gross
Profit ($ millions)

ILLUSTRATION 17.4   Gross Profit ($ millions; percent to sales)

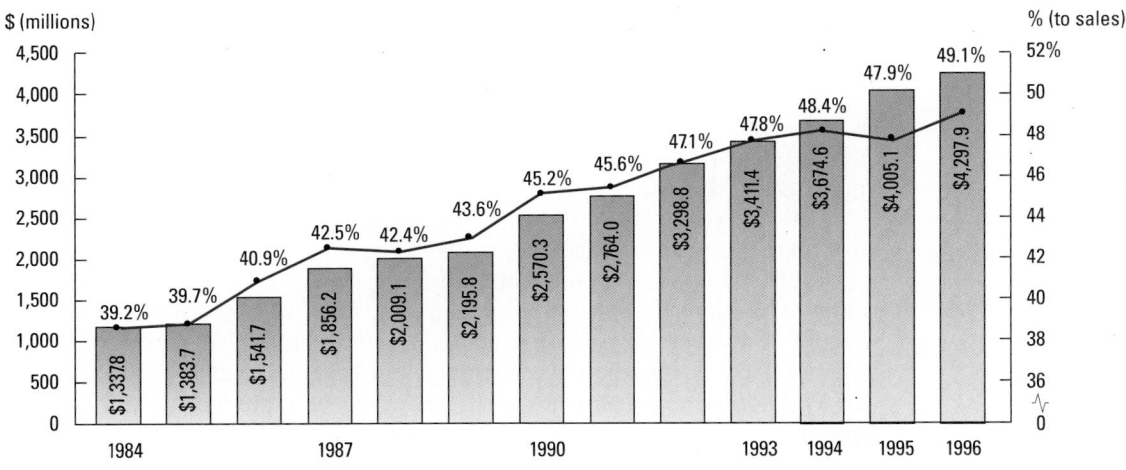

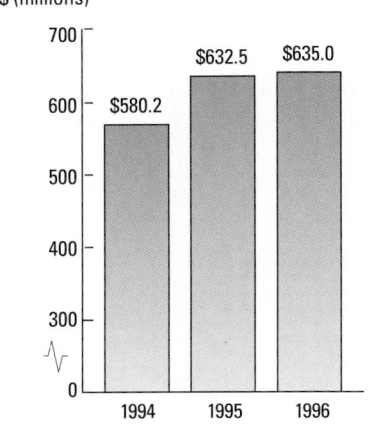

Excluding a restructuring charge in 1995.

ILLUSTRATION 17.5
Net Income ($ millions)

If 1994 is the base year, to calculate trend percentages for each year divide net sales by $7,587.9 million; cost of goods sold by $3,913.3 million; gross profit by $3,674.6 million; operating profit by $2,794.7 million; and income before income taxes by $879.9 million. After all divisions have been made, multiply each result by 100. The resulting percentages reflect trends as follows:

	1994	1995	1996
Net sales	100.0%	110.2%	115.3%
Cost of goods sold	100.0	111.2	113.7
Gross profit	100.0	109.0	117.0
Operating expenses	100.0	130.3	119.6
Income before income taxes	100.0	41.3	108.5

These trend percentages indicate the changes taking place in the organization and highlight the direction of these changes. For instance, the percentage of sales is increasing each year compared to the base year. Cost of goods sold increased at a lower rate than net sales in 1994 and 1996, causing gross profit to increase at a higher rate than net sales. Operating expenses in 1995 increased due to the provision for restructured operations, causing a significant decrease in income before income taxes. Percentages provide clues to an analyst about which items need further investigation or analysis. In reviewing trend percentages, a financial statement user should pay close attention to the trends in related items, such as the cost of goods sold in relation to sales. Trend analysis that shows a constantly declining gross margin (profit) rate may be a signal that future net income will decrease.

As useful as trend percentages are, they have one drawback. Expressing changes as percentages is usually straightforward as long as the amount in the base year or period is positive—that is, not zero or negative. Analysts cannot express a $30,000 increase in notes receivable as a percentage if the increase is from zero last year to $30,000 this year. Nor can they express an increase from a loss last year of $10,000 to income this year of $20,000 in percentage terms.

Proper analysis does not stop with the calculation of increases and decreases in amounts or percentages over several years. Such changes generally indicate areas worthy of further investigation and are merely clues that may lead to significant findings. Accurate predictions depend on many factors, including economic and political conditions; management's plans regarding new products, plant expansion, and promotional outlays; and the expected activities of competitors. Considering these factors along with horizontal analysis, vertical analysis, and trend analysis should provide a reasonable basis for predicting future performance.

RATIO ANALYSIS

Objective 4
Perform ratio analysis on financial statements using liquidity ratios, long-term solvency ratios, profitability tests, and market tests.

Logical relationships exist between certain accounts or items in a company's financial statements. These accounts may appear on the same statement or on two different statements. We set up the dollar amounts of the related accounts or items in fraction form called *ratios*. These ratios include: (1) liquidity ratios; (2) equity, or long-term solvency, ratios; (3) profitability tests; and (4) market tests.

Liquidity Ratios

Liquidity ratios indicate a company's short-term debt-paying ability. Thus, these ratios show interested parties the company's capacity to meet maturing current liabilities.

CURRENT, OR WORKING CAPITAL, RATIO Working capital is the excess of current assets over current liabilities. The ratio that relates current assets to current liabilities is the **current,** or **working capital, ratio.** The current ratio indicates the ability of a company to pay its current liabilities from current assets and, thus, shows the strength of the company's working capital position.

You can compute the current ratio by dividing current assets by current liabilities:

$$\text{Current ratio} = \frac{\text{Current assets}}{\text{Current liabilities}}$$

The ratio is usually stated as a number of dollars of current assets to one dollar of current liabilities (although the dollar signs usually are omitted). Thus, for Colgate-Palmolive in 1996, when current assets totaled $2,372.3 million and current liabilities totaled $1,904.3 million, the ratio is 1.25:1, meaning that the company has $1.25 of current assets for each $1.00 of current liabilities.

The current ratio provides a better index of a company's ability to pay current debts than does the absolute amount of working capital. To illustrate, assume that we are comparing Colgate-Palmolive to Company B. For this example, use the following totals for current assets and current liabilities:

	Colgate-Palmolive	Company B
Current assets (a)	$2,372.3	$120.0
Current liabilities (b)	1,904.3	53.2
Working capital (a − b)	$ 468.0	$ 66.8
Current ratio (a/b)	1.25:1	2.26:1

Colgate-Palmolive has seven times as much working capital as Company B. However, Company B has a superior debt-paying ability since it has $2.26 of current assets for each $1.00 of current liabilities.

Short-term creditors are particularly interested in the current ratio since the conversion of inventories and accounts receivable into cash is the primary source from which the company obtains the cash to pay short-term creditors. Long-term creditors are also interested in the current ratio because a company that is unable to pay short-term debts may be forced into bankruptcy. For this reason, many bond indentures, or contracts, contain a provision requiring that the borrower maintain at least a certain minimum current ratio. A company can increase its current ratio by issuing long-term debt or capital stock or by selling noncurrent assets.

A company must guard against a current ratio that is too high, especially if caused by idle cash, slow-paying customers, and/or slow-moving inventory. Decreased net income can result when too much capital that could be used profitably elsewhere is tied up in current assets.

Refer to Illustration 17.1. The Colgate-Palmolive Company data in Column (4) indicate that current liabilities are increasing more rapidly than current assets. We could also make such an observation directly by looking at the change in the current ratio. Colgate-Palmolive's current ratios for 1996 and 1995 follow:

	December 31		Amount of
($ millions)	**1996**	**1995**	**Increase**
Current assets (a)	$2,372.3	$2,360.2	$ 12.1
Current liabilities (b)	1,904.3	1,753.1	151.2
Working capital (a − b)	$ 468.0	$ 607.1	$(139.1)
Current ratio (a/b)	1.25:1	1.35:1	

Colgate-Palmolive's working capital decreased by $139.1 million, or 22.9% ($139.1/ $607.1), and its current ratio decreased from 1.35:1 to 1.25:1. Together, these figures reflect that its current liabilities increased faster than its current assets.

ACID-TEST (QUICK) RATIO   The current ratio is not the only measure of a company's short-term debt-paying ability. Another measure, called the **acid-test (quick) ratio,** is the ratio of quick assets (cash, marketable securities, and net receivables) to current liabilities. Analysts exclude inventories and prepaid expenses from current assets to compute quick assets because they might not be readily convertible into cash. The formula for the acid-test ratio is:

Reinforcing Problems
E17–2 Determine effects of various transactions on the current ratio.
P17–4 and P17–4A Determine effects of various transactions on working capital and current ratio.

Reinforcing Problems
P17–3 and P17–3A Compute working capital, current ratio, and acid-test ratio.

$$\text{Acid-test ratio} = \frac{\text{Quick assets}}{\text{Current liabilities}}$$

Short-term creditors are particularly interested in this ratio, which relates the pool of cash and immediate cash inflows to immediate cash outflows.

The acid-test ratios for 1996 and 1995 for Colgate-Palmolive are:

($ millions)	December 31		Amount of Increase (or Decrease)
	1996	**1995**	
Quick Assets (a)	$1,372.2	$1,373.5	$ (1.3)
Current Liabilities (b)	1,904.3	1,753.1	151.2
Net quick assets (a − b)	$ (532.1)	$ (379.6)	$(152.5)
Acid-test ratio (a/b)	.72:1	.78:1	

In deciding whether the acid-test ratio is satisfactory, investors consider the quality of the marketable securities and receivables. An accumulation of poor-quality marketable securities or receivables, or both, could cause an acid-test ratio to appear deceptively favorable. When referring to marketable securities, poor quality means securities likely to generate losses when sold. Poor-quality receivables may be uncollectible or not collectible until long past due. The quality of receivables depends primarily on their age, which can be assessed by preparing an aging schedule or by calculating the accounts receivable turnover. (Covered in Chapter 9.)

CASH FLOW LIQUIDITY RATIO   Another approach to measuring short-term liquidity is the **cash flow liquidity ratio.** The numerator, as an approximation of cash resources, consists of (1) cash and marketable securities, or liquid current assets, and (2) net cash provided by operating activities, or the cash generated from the company's operations. This reflects the company's ability to sell inventory and collect accounts receivable. The formula for the cash flow liquidity ratio is:

$$\frac{\begin{array}{c}\text{Cash and marketable} \\ \text{securities}\end{array} + \begin{array}{c}\text{Net cash provided} \\ \text{by operating activities}\end{array}}{\text{Current liabilities}}$$

For 1996, Colgate-Palmolive has $248.2 million in cash and cash equivalents, $59.6 million in marketable securities, $1,904.3 million in current liabilities, and $917.4 million in cash provided by operating activities (taken from the statement of cash flows in its annual report). Its cash flow liquidity ratio is:

$$\frac{\$248.2 + \$59.6 + \$917.4}{\$1,904.3} = .64 \text{ times}$$

This indicates that the company is going to have to rely on some other sources of funding to pay its current liabilities. The company's liquid current assets will only cover about two-thirds of the current liabilities. Possibly net cash provided by operations will be substantially higher in 1997.

ACCOUNTS RECEIVABLE TURNOVER   **Turnover** is the relationship between the amount of an asset and some measure of its use. **Accounts receivable turnover** is the number of times per year that the average amount of receivables is collected. To calculate this ratio, divide net credit sales (or net sales) by average net accounts receivable; that is, accounts receivable after deducting the allowance for uncollectible accounts:

$$\begin{array}{c}\text{Accounts receivable} \\ \text{turnover}\end{array} = \frac{\text{Net credit sales (or net sales)}}{\text{Average net accounts receivable}}$$

When a ratio compares an income statement item (like net credit sales) with a balance sheet item (like net accounts receivable), the balance sheet item should be an average. Ideally, analysts calculate average net accounts receivable by averaging the end-of-month balances or end-of-week balances of net accounts receivable outstanding during the period. The greater the number of observations used, the more accurate the resulting average. Often, analysts average only the beginning-of-year and end-of-year balances because this information is easily obtainable from comparative financial statements. Sometimes a formula calls for the use of an average balance, but only the year-end amount is available. Then the analyst must use the year-end amount.[1]

In theory, the numerator of the accounts receivable turnover ratio consists of only net credit sales because those are the only sales that generate accounts receivable. However, if cash sales are relatively small or their proportion to total sales remains fairly constant, analysts can obtain reliable results by using total net sales. In most cases, the analyst may have to use total net sales because the separate amounts of cash sales and credit sales are not reported on the income statement.

Colgate-Palmolive's accounts receivable turnover ratios for 1996 and 1995 follow. Net accounts receivable on January 1, 1994, totaled $1,049.6 million.

	December 31		Amount of
($ millions)	**1996**	**1995**	**Increase**
Net sales (a)	$8,749.0	$8,358.2	$390.8
Net accounts receivable:			
January 1	$1,116.9	$1,049.6	$ 67.3
December 31	1,064.4	1,116.9	(52.5)
Total (b)	$2,181.3	$2,166.5	$ 14.8
Average net receivables (c) (b/2 = c)	$1,090.7	$1,083.3	
Turnover of accounts receivable (a/c)	8.02	7.72	

The accounts receivable turnover ratio provides an indication of how quickly the company collects receivables. The accounts receivable turnover ratio for 1996 indicates that Colgate-Palmolive collected, or turned over, its accounts receivable slightly more than eight times. The ratio is better understood and more easily compared with a company's credit terms if we convert it into a number of days, as is illustrated in the next ratio.

NUMBER OF DAYS' SALES IN ACCOUNTS RECEIVABLE The **number of days' sales in accounts receivable** ratio is also called the *average collection period for accounts receivable*. Calculate it as follows:

$$\text{Number of days' sales in accounts receivable (average collection period for accounts receivable)} = \frac{\text{Number of days in year (365)}}{\text{Accounts receivable turnover}}$$

The turnover ratios for Colgate-Palmolive show that the number of days' sales in accounts receivable decreased from about 47 days (365/7.72) in 1995 to 46 days (365/8.02) in 1996. The change means that the average collection period for the company's accounts receivable decreased from 47 to 46 days.

Reinforcing Problems
E17–3 Compute average number of days receivables are outstanding; determine effect of increase in turnover.
BDC17–2 Compute turnover ratios for four years and number of days' sales in accounts receivable; evaluate effectiveness of company's credit policy.

BUSINESS INSIGHT The number of days' sales in accounts receivable ratio measures the average liquidity of accounts receivable and indicates their quality. Generally, the shorter the collection period, the higher the quality of receivables. However, the average collection period varies by industry; for example, collection periods are short in utility companies and much longer in some retailing companies. A comparison of the average collection period with the credit terms extended customers by the company provides further insight into the quality of the accounts receivable. For example, receivables with terms of 2/10, n/30 and an average collection period of 75 days need to be investigated further. It is important to determine why customers are paying their accounts much later than expected.

AN ACCOUNTING PERSPECTIVE

---

[1]These general comments about the use of averages in a ratio apply to the other ratios involving averages discussed in this chapter.

INVENTORY TURNOVER A company's inventory turnover ratio shows the number of times its average inventory is sold during a period. You can calculate **inventory turnover** as follows:

Reinforcing Problem
E17–5 Compute inventory turnover.

$$\text{Inventory turnover} = \frac{\text{Cost of goods sold}}{\text{Average inventory}}$$

When comparing an income statement item and a balance sheet item, measure both in comparable dollars. Notice that we measure the numerator and denominator in cost rather than sales dollars. (Earlier, when calculating accounts receivable turnover, we measured both numerator and denominator in sales dollars.) Inventory turnover relates a measure of sales volume to the average amount of goods on hand to produce this sales volume.

Colgate-Palmolive's inventory on January 1, 1995, was $713.9 million. The following schedule shows that the inventory turnover decreased slightly from 5.85 times per year in 1995 to 5.76 times per year in 1996. To convert these turnover ratios to the number of days it takes the company to sell its entire stock of inventory, divide 365 by the inventory turnover. Colgate-Palmolive's average inventory sold in about 63 and 62 days (365/5.76 and 365/5.85) in 1996 and 1995, respectively.

($ millions)	1996	1995	Amount of Increase or (Decrease)
Cost of goods sold (a)	$4,451.1	$4,353.1	$98.0
Merchandise inventory:			
January 1	$ 774.8	$ 713.9	$60.9
December 31	770.7	774.8	(4.1)
Total (b)	$1,545.5	$1,488.7	$56.8
Average inventory (c) (b/2 = c)	$ 772.8	$ 744.35	
Turnover of inventory (a/c)	5.76	5.85	

Other things being equal, a manager who maintains the highest inventory turnover ratio is the most efficient. Yet, other things are not always equal. For example, a company that achieves a high inventory turnover ratio by keeping extremely small inventories on hand may incur larger ordering costs, lose quantity discounts, and lose sales due to lack of adequate inventory. In attempting to earn satisfactory income, management must balance the costs of inventory storage and obsolescence and the cost of tying up funds in inventory against possible losses of sales and other costs associated with keeping too little inventory on hand.

AN ACCOUNTING PERSPECTIVE
——

BUSINESS INSIGHT Cabletron Systems develops, manufactures, installs, and supports a wide range of standards-based LAN and WAN connectivity hardware and software products. For the year ended February 29, 1996, both its number of day's sales in accounts receivable and its inventory turnover rate increased as compared to the prior year. In its 1996 annual report, the company explained these increases as follows:

Accounts receivable, net of allowance for doubtful accounts, were $147.9 million at February 29, 1996 or 42 days of sales outstanding, compared to $91.4 million or 33 days of sales in accounts receivable at February 28, 1995. This increase in receivables reflects higher sales and the timing of collections. The higher days' sales outstanding will be more typical of the Company's business activities in future periods as international sales increase.

The Company has historically maintained higher levels of inventory than its competitors in the LAN industry in order to implement its policy of shipping most orders requiring immediate delivery within 24 to 48 hours. World-wide inventories were $153.6 million at February 29, 1996 or 111 days of inventory, compared to $103.0 million or 104 days of inventory as of the end of the preceding fiscal year. The increase of days in inventory and absolute inventory were the result of increasing inventories in support of global sales growth somewhat offset by improving inventory control procedures.

TOTAL ASSETS TURNOVER **Total assets turnover** shows the relationship between the dollar volume of sales and the average total assets used in the business. We calculate it as follows:

$$\text{Total assets turnover} = \frac{\text{Net sales}}{\text{Average total assets}}$$

This ratio measures the efficiency with which a company uses its assets to generate sales. The larger the total assets turnover, the larger the income on each dollar invested in the assets of the business. For Colgate-Palmolive, the total asset turnover ratios for 1996 and 1995 follow. Total assets as of January 1, 1995, were $6,142.4 million.

($ millions)	1996	1995	Amount of Increase
Net sales (a)	$ 8,749.0	$ 8,358.2	$ 390.8
Total assets:			
January 1	$ 7,642.3	$ 6,142.4	$1,499.9
December 31	7,901.5	7,642.3	259.2
Total (b)	$15,543.8	$13,784.7	$1,759.1
Average total assets (c) (b/2 = c)	$ 7,771.9	$ 6,892.4	
Turnover of total assets (a/c)	1.13:1	1.21:1	

Each dollar of total assets produced $1.21 of sales in 1995 and $1.13 of sales in 1996. In other words, between 1995 and 1996, Colgate-Palmolive had a decrease of $.08 of sales per dollar of investment in assets.

Equity, or long-term solvency, ratios show the relationship between debt and equity financing in a company.

EQUITY (STOCKHOLDERS' EQUITY) RATIO The two basic sources of assets in a business are owners (stockholders) and creditors; the combined interests of the two groups are *total equities*. In ratio analysis, however, the term *equity* generally refers only to stockholders' equity. Thus, the **equity (stockholders' equity) ratio** indicates the proportion of total assets (or total equities) provided by stockholders (owners) on any given date. The formula for the equity ratio is:

$$\text{Equity ratio} = \frac{\text{Stockholders' equity}}{\text{Total assets (or total equities)}}$$

Colgate-Palmolive's liabilities and stockholders' equity from Illustration 17.1 follow. Colgate-Palmolive's equity ratio increased from 22.0% in 1995 to 25.7% in 1996. Illustration 17.1 shows that stockholders increased their proportionate equity in the company's assets due largely to the retention of earnings (which increases retained earnings).

($ millions)	December 31, 1996 Amount	December 31, 1996 Percent	December 31, 1995 Amount	December 31, 1995 Percent
Current liabilities	$1,904.3	24.1%	$1,753.1	22.9%
Long-term liabilities	3,963.1	50.2	4,209.4	55.1
Total liabilities	$5,867.4	74.3	$5,962.5	78.0
Total stockholders' equity	2,034.1	25.7	1,679.8	22.0
Total equity (equal to total assets)	$7,901.5	100.0%	$7,642.3	100.0%

The equity ratio must be interpreted carefully. From a creditor's point of view, a high proportion of stockholders' equity is desirable. A high equity ratio indicates the

Real World Example
At December 31, 1996, General Electric Company reported total assets turnover of 0.32.

Note to the Student
Use any company's annual report to calculate the liquidity ratios for the company.

Equity, or Long-Term Solvency, Ratios

Note to the Student
Use any company's annual report to calculate the equity ratios for the company.

existence of a large protective buffer for creditors in the event a company suffers a loss. However, from an owner's point of view, a high proportion of stockholders' equity may or may not be desirable. If the business can use borrowed funds to generate income in excess of the net after-tax cost of the interest on such funds, a lower percentage of stockholders' equity may be desirable.

To illustrate the effect of higher leveraging (i.e., a larger proportion of debt), assume that Colgate-Palmolive could have financed an increase in its productive capacity with $40 million of 6% bonds instead of issuing 5 million additional shares of common stock. The effect on income for 1996 would be as follows, assuming a federal income tax rate of 40%:

Net income as presently stated (Illustration 17.2)	$635,000,000
Deduct additional interest on debt (0.06 × $40 million)	2,400,000
	$632,600,000
Add reduced taxes due to interest deduction (.4 × 2,400,000)	960,000
Adjusted net income	$633,560,000

As shown, increasing leverage by issuing bonds instead of common stock reduces net income. However, there are also fewer shares of common stock outstanding. Assume the company has 183 million shares of common stock outstanding. Earnings per share (EPS) with the additional debt would be $3.46 (or $633,560,000/183 million shares), and EPS with the additional stock would be $3.38 (or $635,000,000/188 million shares).

Since investors place heavy emphasis on EPS amounts, many companies in recent years have introduced large portions of debt into their capital structures to increase EPS, especially since interest rates were relatively low in the early 1990s.

We should point out, however, that too low a percentage of stockholders' equity (too much debt) has its dangers. Financial leverage magnifies losses per share as well as EPS since there are fewer shares of stock over which to spread the losses. A period of business recession may result in operating losses and shrinkage in the value of assets, such as receivables and inventory, which in turn may lead to an inability to meet fixed payments for interest and principal on the debt. As a result, the company may be forced into liquidation, and the stockholders could lose their entire investments.

STOCKHOLDERS' EQUITY TO DEBT (DEBT TO EQUITY) RATIO   Analysts express the relative equities of owners and creditors in several ways. To say that creditors held a 74.3% interest in the assets of Colgate-Palmolive on December 31, 1996, is equivalent to saying stockholders held a 25.7% interest. Another way of expressing this relationship is the **stockholders' equity to debt ratio:**

$$\text{Stockholders' equity to debt ratio} = \frac{\text{Stockholders' equity}}{\text{Total debt}}$$

Such a ratio for Colgate-Palmolive would be .28:1 (or $1,679.8 million/$5,962.5 million) on December 31, 1995, and .35:1 (or $2,034.1 million/$5,867.4 million) on December 31, 1996. This ratio is often inverted and called the **debt to equity ratio.** Some analysts use only long-term debt rather than total debt in calculating these ratios. These analysts do not consider short-term debt to be part of the capital structure since it is paid within one year.

Profitability Tests

Profitability is an important measure of a company's operating success. Generally, we are concerned with two areas when judging profitability: (1) relationships on the income statement that indicate a company's ability to recover costs and expenses, and (2) relationships of income to various balance sheet measures that indicate the company's relative ability to earn income on assets employed. Each of the following ratios utilizes one of these relationships.

RATE OF RETURN ON OPERATING ASSETS   The best measure of earnings performance without regard to the sources of assets is the relationship of net operating income to operating assets, the **rate of return on operating assets.** This ratio shows the earning power of the company as a bundle of assets. By disregarding both nonoperating assets and nonoperating income elements, the rate of return on operating assets measures the profitability of the company in carrying out its primary business functions. We can break the ratio down into two elements—the operating margin and the turnover of operating assets.

Operating margin reflects the percentage of each dollar of net sales that becomes net operating income. Net operating income excludes **nonoperating income elements** such as extraordinary items, cumulative effect on prior years of changes in accounting principle, losses or gains from discontinued operations, interest revenue, and interest expense. Another name for net operating income is "income before interest and taxes" (IBIT). The formula for operating margin is:

$$\text{Operating margin} = \frac{\text{Net operating income}}{\text{Net sales}}$$

Turnover of operating assets shows the amount of sales dollars generated for each dollar invested in operating assets. **Operating assets** are all assets actively used in producing operating revenues. Typically, we use year-end operating assets, even though in theory an average would be better. **Nonoperating assets** are owned by a company but not used in producing operating revenues, such as land held for future use, a factory building rented to another company, and long-term bond investments.

Analysts do not use these nonoperating assets in evaluating earnings performance. Nor do they use total assets that include nonoperating assets not contributing to the generation of sales. The formula for the turnover of operating assets is:

$$\text{Turnover of operating assets} = \frac{\text{Net sales}}{\text{Operating assets}}$$

The rate of return on operating assets of a company is equal to its operating margin multiplied by turnover of operating assets. The more a company earns per dollar of sales and the more sales it makes per dollar invested in operating assets, the higher is the return per dollar invested. To find the rate of return on operating assets, use the following formulas:

$$\frac{\text{Rate of return}}{\text{on operating assets}} = \frac{\text{Operating}}{\text{margin}} \times \frac{\text{Turnover of}}{\text{operating assets}}$$

or

$$\frac{\text{Rate of return}}{\text{on operating assets}} = \frac{\text{Net operating income}}{\text{Net sales}} \times \frac{\text{Net sales}}{\text{Operating assets}}$$

Because net sales appears in both ratios (once as a numerator and once as a denominator), we can cancel it out, and the formula for rate of return on operating assets becomes:

$$\frac{\text{Rate of return on}}{\text{operating assets}} = \frac{\text{Net operating income}}{\text{Operating assets}}$$

For analytical purposes, the formula should remain in the form that shows margin and turnover separately, since it provides more information.

The rates of return on operating assets for Colgate-Palmolive for 1996 and 1995 are:

Reinforcing Problems
P17–5 and P17–5A Compute rate of return on operating assets and demonstrate effects of various transactions on this rate of return.

Note to the Student
Use any annual report and calculate the profitability ratios.

Reinforcing Problem
E17–6 Compute rate of return on operating assets.

($ millions)	1996	1995	Amount of Increase or (Decrease)
Net operating income (a)*	$1,152.0	$ 568.9	$583.1
Net sales (b)	$8,749.0	$8,358.2	$390.8
Operating assets (c)†	$7,901.5	$7,642.3	$259.2
Operating margin (a/b)	13.17%	6.81%	
Turnover of operating assets (b/c)	1.11 times	1.09 times	
Rate of return on operating assets (a/c)	14.58%	7.44%	

*Calculated as income before income taxes plus net interest expense. This method excludes nonoperating items.

†Colgate-Palmolive Company had no nonoperating assets, so we used total assets in the calculation.

AN ACCOUNTING PERSPECTIVE

BUSINESS INSIGHT   Companies that are to survive in the economy must attain some minimum rate of return on operating assets. However, they can attain this minimum rate of return in many different ways. To illustrate, consider a grocery store and a jewelry store, each with a rate of return of 8% on operating assets. The grocery store normally would attain this rate of return with a low margin and a high turnover, while the jewelry store would have a high margin and a low turnover, as shown here:

	Margin × Turnover =	Rate of Return on Operating Assets
Grocery store	1% × 8.0 times =	8%
Jewelry store	20 × 0.4 =	8

NET INCOME TO NET SALES (RETURN ON SALES) RATIO   Another measure of a company's profitability is the **net income to net sales** ratio, calculated as follows:

$$\text{Net income to net sales} = \frac{\text{Net income}}{\text{Net sales}}$$

This ratio measures the proportion of the sales dollar that remains after deducting all expenses. The computations for Colgate-Palmolive for 1996 and 1995 are:

($ millions)	1996	1995	Amount of Increase or (Decrease)
Net income (a)	$ 635.0	$ 172.0	$463.0
Net sales (b)	$8,749.0	$8,358.2	$390.8
Ratio of net income to net sales (a/b)	7.26%	2.06%	

Although the ratio of net income to net sales indicates that the net amount of profit increased on each sales dollar, exercise care in using and interpreting this ratio. The net income includes all nonoperating items that may occur only in a particular period; therefore, net income includes the effects of such things as extraordinary items, changes in accounting principle, effects of discontinued operations, and interest charges. Thus, a period that contains the effects of an extraordinary item is not comparable to a period that contains no extraordinary items. Also, since interest expense is deductible in the determination of net income while dividends are not, the methods used to finance a company's assets affect net income.

Illustration 17.6 shows graphically what net income to net sales for 1996 would have been without the decrease caused by the one-time restructuring charge. By excluding this item, one can see what the trend of "normal" return on sales was over the three years shown.

RETURN ON AVERAGE COMMON STOCKHOLDERS' EQUITY   From the stockholders' point of view, an important measure of the income-producing ability of a com-

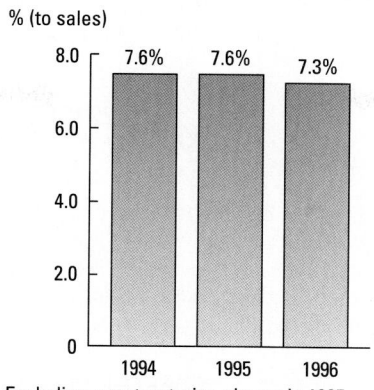

pany is the relationship of **return on average common stockholders' equity,** also called *rate of return on average common stockholders' equity,* or simply the **return on equity (ROE).** Although stockholders are interested in the ratio of operating income to operating assets as a measure of management's efficient use of assets, they are even more interested in the return the company earns on each dollar of stockholders' equity. The formula for return on average common stockholders' equity if no preferred stock is outstanding is:

$$\text{Return on average common stockholders' equity} = \frac{\text{Net income}}{\text{Average common stockholders' equity}}$$

When a company has preferred stock outstanding, the numerator of this ratio becomes net income minus the annual preferred dividends, and the denominator becomes the average book value of common stock. As described in Chapter 12, the book value of common stock is equal to total stockholders' equity minus (1) the liquidation value (usually equal to par value) of preferred stock and (2) any dividends in arrears on cumulative preferred stock. Thus, the formula becomes:

$$\text{Return on average common stockholders' equity} = \frac{\text{Net income} - \text{Preferred stock dividends}}{\text{Average book value of common stock}}$$

The Colgate-Palmolive Company has preferred stock outstanding. The ratios for Colgate-Palmolive follow. Total common stockholders' equity on January 1, 1995, was $1,414.5 million. Preferred dividends were $21.4 million in 1996 and $21.6 million in 1995.

($ millions)	1996	1995	Amount of Increase or (Decrease)
Net income — Preferred stock dividends (a)	$ 613.6	$ 150.4	$ 463.2
Total common stockholders' equity (book value of common stock):*			
January 1	$1,276.3	$1,414.5	$(138.2)
December 31	1,641.4	1,276.3	365.1
Total (b)	$2,917.7	$2,690.8	$ 226.9
Average common stockholder's equity: (c) (b/2 = c)	$1,458.9	$1,345.4	
Return on common stockholders' equity (a/c)	42.06%	11.18%	

*Total stockholders' equity − Par value of preferred stock

The stockholders would regard the increase in the ratio from 11.18% to 42.06% favorably. This ratio indicates that for each dollar of capital invested by a common stockholder, the company earned approximately 42 cents in 1996.

BUSINESS INSIGHT   Sometimes, two companies have the same return on assets but have different returns on stockholders' equity, as shown here:

	Company 1	Company 2
Return on assets	12.0%	12.0%
Return on stockholders' equity	6.4	8.0

The difference of 1.6% in Company 2's favor is the result of Company 2's use of borrowed funds, particularly long-term debt, in its capital structure. Use of these funds (or preferred stock with a fixed return) is called trading on the equity. When a company is trading profitably on the equity, it is generating a higher rate of return on its borrowed funds than it is paying for the use of the funds. The excess, in this case 1.6%, is accruing to the benefit of the common stockholders, because their earnings are being increased.

Companies that magnify the gains from this activity for the stockholders are using *leverage*. Using leverage is a risky process because losses also can be magnified, to the disadvantage of the common stockholders. We discussed trading on the equity and leverage in Chapter 15.

Reinforcing Problem
E17–4 Compute cash flow margin.

CASH FLOW MARGIN   The cash flow margin measures a company's overall efficiency and performance. The **cash flow margin** indicates the ability of a company to translate sales into cash. Measuring the amount of cash a company generates from every dollar of sales is important because a company needs cash to service debt, pay dividends, and invest in new capital assets. The formula for the cash flow margin is:

$$\text{Cash flow margin} = \frac{\text{Net cash provided by operating activities}}{\text{Net sales}}$$

Thus, we calculate Colgate-Palmolive's 1996 cash flow margin as follows:

$$\frac{\$917.4 \text{ million net cash provided by operating activities}}{\$8,749.0 \text{ million net sales}} = 10.49\%$$

Reinforcing Problems
E17–8 Compute EPS.
E17–10 Compute EPS for current and prior year.

EARNINGS PER SHARE OF COMMON STOCK   Probably the measure used most widely to appraise a company's operations is **earnings per share (EPS)** of common stock. EPS is equal to earnings available to common stockholders divided by the weighted-average number of shares of common stock outstanding. The financial press regularly publishes actual and forecasted EPS amounts for publicly traded corporations, together with period-to-period comparisons. The Accounting Principles Board noted the significance attached to EPS by requiring that such amounts be reported on the face of the income statement.[2] (Chapter 13 illustrates how earnings per share should be presented on the income statement.)

The calculation of EPS may be fairly simple or highly complex depending on a corporation's capital structure. A company has a simple capital structure if it has no outstanding securities (e.g., convertible bonds, convertible preferred stocks, warrants, or options) that can be exchanged for common stock. If a company has such securities outstanding, it has a complex capital structure. Discussion of EPS for a corporation with a complex capital structure is beyond the scope of this text.

Real World Example
At October 31, 1996, Hewlett Packard reported net income of $2,586M and EPS of $2.46.

A company with a simple capital structure reports a single basic EPS amount, which is calculated as follows:

$$\text{EPS of common stock} = \frac{\text{Earnings available to common stockholders}}{\text{Weighted-average number of common shares outstanding}}$$

---

[2]Accounting Principles Board, *Opinion No. 15,* "Reporting Earnings per Share" (New York: AICPA, 1969), par. 12. *FASB Statement No. 128,* "Earnings per Share" (Norwalk, Connecticut: FASB, 1997), simplified the standards for computing earnings per share and made them comparable to international EPS standards.

The amount of earnings available to common stockholders is equal to net income minus the current year's preferred dividends, whether such dividends have been declared or not.

Determining the Weighted-Average Number of Common Shares   The denominator in the EPS fraction is the weighted-average number of common shares outstanding for the period. If the number of common shares outstanding did not change during the period, the weighted-average number of common shares outstanding would, of course, be the number of common shares outstanding at the end of the period. The balance in the Common Stock account of Colgate-Palmolive (Illustration 17.1) was $183.2 million on December 31, 1996. The common stock had a $1 par value. Assuming no common shares were issued or redeemed during 1996, the weighted-average number of common shares outstanding would be 183.2 million (or $183.2 million/$1 per share). (Normally, common treasury stock reacquired and reissued are also included in the calculation of the weighted-average number of common shares outstanding. We ignore treasury stock transactions to simplify the illustrations.)

If the number of common shares changed during the period, such a change increases or decreases the capital invested in the company and should affect earnings available to stockholders. To compute the weighted-average number of common shares outstanding, we weight the change in the number of common shares by the portion of the year that those shares were outstanding. Shares are outstanding only during those periods that the related capital investment is available to produce income.

To illustrate, assume that during 1995 Colgate-Palmolive's common stock balance increased by $11.7 million (11.7 million shares). Assume that the company issued 9.5 million of these shares on April 1, 1995, and the other 2.2 million shares on October 1, 1995. The computation of the weighted-average number of common shares outstanding would be:

171.5 million shares × 1 year	171.5 million
9.5 million shares × ¾ year (April–December)	7.125 million
2.2 million shares × ¼ year (October–December)	.55 million
Weighted-average number of common shares outstanding	179.175 million

An alternate method looks at the total number of common shares outstanding, weighted by the portion of the year that the number of shares was outstanding, as follows:

Reinforcing Problem
E17–9 Compute weighted-average number of shares outstanding.

171.5 million shares × ¼ year (January–March)	42.875 million
181.0 million shares × ½ year (April–September)	90.5 million
183.2 million shares × ¼ year (October–December)	45.8 million
Weighted-average number of shares outstanding	179.175 million

Another alternate method is:

171.5 million shares ×	3 months =	514.5 million share-months
181.0 million shares ×	6 months =	1,086.0 million share-months
183.2 million shares ×	3 months =	549.6 million share-months
	12 months	2,150.1 million share-months

2,150.1 million share-months/12 months = 179.175 million shares

Note that all three methods yield the same result. In 1996, the balance in the common stock account did not change as it had during 1995. Therefore, the weighted-average number of common shares outstanding during 1996 is equal to the number of common shares issued, 183.2 million. The EPS of common stock for the Colgate-Palmolive Company are:

($ millions)	1996	1995	Amount of Increase or (Decrease)
Net income—preferred dividends (a)	$613.6	$150.4	$463.2
Average number of shares of common stock outstanding (b)	183.2	179.175	4.025
EPS of common stock (a/b)	$ 3.35	$ .84	

Colgate-Palmolive's stockholders would probably view the increase of approximately 298.8% ([$3.35 − $.84]/$.84) in EPS from $.84 to $3.35 favorably.

EPS and Stock Dividends or Splits   Increases in shares outstanding as a result of a stock dividend or stock split do not require weighting for fractional periods. Such shares do not increase the capital invested in the business and, therefore, do not affect income. All that is required is to restate all prior calculations of EPS using the increased number of shares. For example, assume a company reported EPS for 1999 as $1 (or $100,000/100,000 shares) and earned $150,000 in 2000. The only change in common stock over the two years was a two-for-one stock split on December 1, 2000, which doubled the shares outstanding to 200,000. The firm would restate EPS for 1999 as $0.50 (or $100,000/200,000 shares) and as $0.75 ($150,000/200,000 shares) for 2000.

Basic EPS and Diluted EPS   In the merger wave of the 1960s, corporations often issued securities to finance their acquisitions of other companies. Many of the securities issued were *calls on common* or possessed *equity kickers.* These terms mean that the securities were convertible to, or exchangeable for, shares of their issuers' common stock. As a result, many complex problems arose in computing EPS. Until 1997, *APB Opinion No. 15* provided guidelines for solving these problems. In 1997, *FASB Statement No. 128,* "Earnings per Share" replaced *APB Opinion No. 15.* A company with a complex capital structure must present at least two EPS calculations, basic EPS and diluted EPS. Because of the complexities involved in the calculations, we reserve further discussion of these two EPS calculations for an intermediate accounting text.

Reinforcing Problem
E17–11 Compute times interest earned.

TIMES INTEREST EARNED RATIO   Creditors, especially long-term creditors, want to know whether a borrower can meet its required interest payments when these payments come due. The **times interest earned ratio,** or *interest coverage ratio,* is an indication of such an ability. It is computed as follows:

$$\frac{\text{Times interest}}{\text{earned ratio}} = \frac{\text{Income before interest and taxes (IBIT)}}{\text{Interest expense}}$$

The ratio is a rough comparison of cash inflows from operations with cash outflows for interest expense. Income before interest and taxes (IBIT) is the numerator because there would be no income taxes if interest expense is equal to or greater than IBIT. (To find income before interest and taxes, take net income from continuing operations and add back the net interest expense and taxes.) Analysts disagree on whether the denominator should be (1) only interest expense on long-term debt, (2) total interest expense, or (3) net interest expense. We will use net interest expense in the Colgate-Palmolive Company illustration.

For Colgate-Palmolive, the net interest expense is $197.4 million (interest expense of $231.7 less interest revenue of $34.3). With an IBIT of $1,152 million, the times interest earned ratio is 5.84, calculated as:

$$\frac{\$1,152}{\$197.4} = 5.84 \text{ times}$$

The company earned enough during the period to pay its interest expense almost 6 times over.

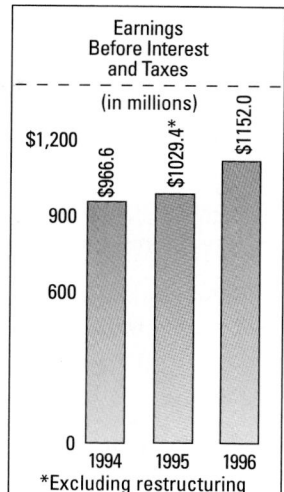

ILLUSTRATION 17.7
Earnings before Interest
and Taxes ($ millions)

Illustration 17.7 shows earnings before interest and taxes for the Colgate-Palmolive Company for the years 1994–1996.

Low or negative interest coverage ratios suggest that the borrower could default on required interest payments. A company is not likely to continue interest payments over many periods if it fails to earn enough income to cover them. On the other hand, interest coverage of 5 to 10 times or more suggests that the company is not likely to default on interest payments.

TIMES PREFERRED DIVIDENDS EARNED RATIO   Preferred stockholders, like bondholders, must usually be satisfied with a fixed-dollar return on their investments. They are interested in the company's ability to make preferred dividend payments each year. We can measure this ability by computing the **times preferred dividends earned ratio** as follows:

$$\text{Times preferred dividends earned ratio} = \frac{\text{Net income}}{\text{Annual preferred dividends}}$$

Colgate-Palmolive has a net income of $635.0 million and preferred dividends of $21.4 million. The number of times the annual preferred dividends are earned for 1996 is:

$$\frac{\$635.0}{\$21.4} = 29.67:1, \text{ or } 29.67 \text{ times}$$

The higher this rate, the higher is the probability that the preferred stockholders will receive their dividends each year.

Analysts compute certain ratios using information from the financial statements and information about the market price of the company's stock. These tests help investors and potential investors assess the relative merits of the various stocks in the marketplace.

Market Tests

The **yield** on a stock investment refers to either an earnings yield or a dividends yield.

EARNINGS YIELD ON COMMON STOCK   You can calculate a company's **earnings yield on common stock** as follows:

$$\text{Earnings yield on common stock} = \frac{\text{EPS}}{\text{Current market price per share of common stock}}$$

Assume Colgate-Palmolive has common stock with an EPS of $4.19 and that the quoted market price of the stock on the New York Stock Exchange is $92.25. The earnings yield on common stock would be:

$$\frac{\$4.19}{\$92.25} = 4.54\%$$

Reinforcing Problem
E17–13 Compute EPS and price-earnings ratio.

PRICE-EARNINGS RATIO   When inverted, the earnings yield on common stock is the **price-earnings ratio.** To compute the price-earnings ratio:

$$\text{Price-earnings ratio} = \frac{\text{Current market price per share of common stock}}{\text{EPS}} = \frac{\$92.25}{\$4.19} = 22.02{:}1$$

Investors would say that this stock is selling at 22 times earnings, or at a multiple of 22. These investors might have a specific multiple in mind that indicates whether the stock is underpriced or overpriced. Different investors have different estimates of the proper price-earnings ratio for a given stock and also different estimates of the future earnings prospects of the company. These different estimates may cause one investor to sell stock at a particular price and another investor to buy at that price.

PAYOUT RATIO ON COMMON STOCK   Using dividend yield, investors can compute the payout ratio on common stock. Colgate-Palmolive's dividends per share were $1.88. To calculate **payout ratio on common stock,** divide the dividend per share of common stock by EPS. The payout ratio for Colgate-Palmolive's stock in 1996 is:

$$\text{Payout ratio on common stock} = \frac{\text{Dividend per share of common stock}}{\text{EPS}} = \frac{\$1.88}{\$4.19} = 44.9\%$$

A payout ratio of 44.9% means that the company paid out 44.9% of its earnings in the form of dividends. Some investors are attracted by the stock of companies that pay out a large percentage of their earnings. Other investors are attracted by the stock of companies that retain and reinvest a large percentage of their earnings. The tax status of the investor has a great deal to do with this preference. Investors in high tax brackets often prefer to have the company reinvest the earnings with the expectation that this reinvestment results in share price appreciation.

DIVIDEND YIELD ON COMMON STOCK   The dividend paid per share of common stock is also of much interest to common stockholders. When the current annual dividend per share of common stock is divided by the current market price per share of common stock, the result is called the **dividend yield on common stock.** Colgate-Palmolive Company's December 31, 1996, common stock price was $92.25 per share. Its dividends per share were $1.88. The company's dividend yield on common stock was:

$$\text{Dividend yield on common stock} = \frac{\text{Dividend per share of common stock}}{\text{Current market price per share of common stock}} = \frac{\$1.88}{\$92.25} = 2.04\%$$

DIVIDEND YIELD ON PREFERRED STOCK   Preferred stockholders, as well as common stockholders, are interested in dividend yields. The computation of the **dividend yield on preferred stock** is similar to the common stock dividend yield computation. Considering Colgate-Palmolive's $4.25 dividend per share of preferred stock

BellSouth Corporation (dollars in millions, except per share data)	1996[a]	1995[b]	1994	1993[c]	1992
Operating Revenues	$19,040	$17,886	$16,845	$15,880	$15,202
Operating Expenses	$14,261	$14,594	$12,787	$13,593	$12,041
Net Income (Loss)	$ 2,863	$ (1,232)	$ 2,160	$ 880	$ 1,618
Earnings (Loss) per Share	$ 2.88	$ (1.24)	$ 2.18	$ .89	$ 1.65
Dividends per Share	$ 1.44	$ 1.41	$ 1.38	$ 1.38	$ 1.38
Book Value per Share	$ 13.37	$ 11.90	$ 14.48	$ 13.60	$ 13.97
Weighted Average Shares Outstanding (millions)	994	993	992	991	981
Total Assets	$32,568	$31,880	$34,397	$32,873	$31,463
Capital Expenditures	$ 4,455	$ 4,203	$ 3,600	$ 3,486	$ 3,189
Return to Average Common Equity	22.4%	(9.2%)	15.4%	6.3%	11.9%
Debt Ratio	43.5%	46.7%	39.3%	40.2%	39.0%
Employees (end of year)	81,241	87,571	92,121	95,084	97,112
Telephone Employees (end of year)	62,425	68,585	73,764	77,958	79,453

A BROADER
PERSPECTIVE
———
BellSouth
Corporation

[a]During 1996, BellSouth recognized a gain of $442 ($344 after tax or $.35 per share) from the sale of its paging operations.

[b]During 1995, BellSouth recognized charges of $4,449 ($2,718 after tax or $2.73 per share) for the discontinuance of Statement of Financial Accounting Standards No. 71, "Accounting for the Effects of Certain Types of Regulations," $1,082 ($663 after tax or $.67 per share) for work force reductions to be completed by the end of 1997 in its telephone operations, and $127 ($78 after tax or $.08 per share) for the refinancing of long-term debt issues.

[c]During 1993, BellSouth recognized a charge of $1,136 ($697 after tax or $.71 per share) for restructuring its telephone operations.

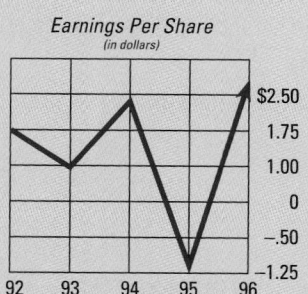

Earnings Per Share
(in dollars)

Record earnings per share of $2.88 in 1996 included 35 cents from the sale of paging operations. Reported EPS in 1995 reflected special charges totaling $3.48, including $2.73 for a required accounting change.

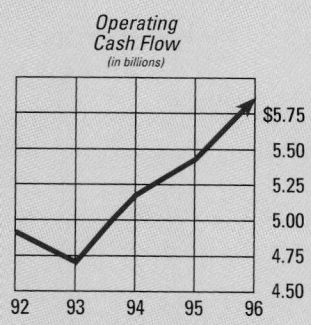

Operating Cash Flow
(in billions)

Cash dividends, an all-time high $1.43 billion, and capital investments were the two primary uses of BellSouth's record 1996 operating cash flow of $5.86 billion.

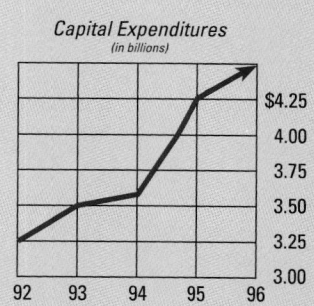

Capital Expenditures
(in billions)

BellSouth invested $4.5 billion in capital expenditures in 1996, reflecting excellent growth opportunities in telecommunications.

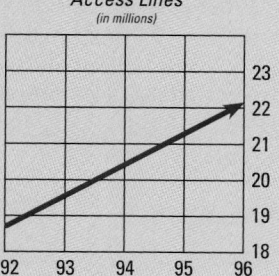

Access Lines
(in millions)

BellSouth became the first company to surpass 22 million U.S. access lines in 1996. Our unprecedented growth included a record 285,000 additional residential lines.

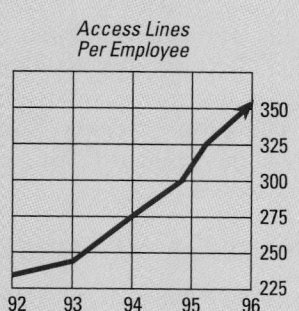

Access Lines Per Employee

This key measure of productivity shows that BellSouth continues to accelerate its initiatives to become even more competitive and efficient.

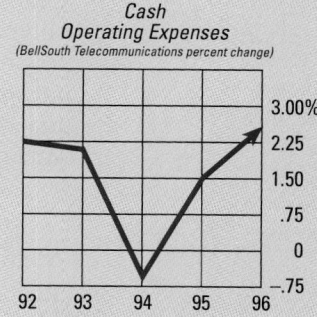

Cash Operating Expenses
(BellSouth Telecommunications percent change)

Cash operating expenses in BellSouth's telephone operations increased in 1996 at less than half the growth rate of network service revenues.

ILLUSTRATION 17.8
Colgate-Palmolive
Company's Cash Flow
per Share of Common
Stock

($ million, except per share data)	Fiscal Year		
	1996	**1995**	**1994**
Operating cash flow data:			
Net income	$635.0	$172.0	$580.2
Restructured operations, net	(105.6)	424.9	(39.1)
Depreciation and amortization	316.3	300.3	235.1
Deferred income taxes and other liabilities	(23.0)	(62.9)	64.7
Cash effect of changes in:			
Receivables	(15.4)	(44.1)	(50.1)
Inventories	(1.2)	(26.1)	(44.5)
Other current assets	0	(42.4)	(7.8)
Payables and accruals	111.3	88.5	90.9
Cash provided by operating activities (a)	$917.4	$810.2	$829.4
Average shares outstanding (b)*	146.6	145.2	146.2
Cash flow per share of common stock (a) ÷ (b)	$6.26	$5.58	$5.67

*As given in the annual report, p. 34.

Reinforcing Problem
E17–12 Compute times dividends
earned and dividend yield.

with a current market price of $70.00 per share, we compute the dividend yield on preferred stock as follows:

$$\text{Dividend yield on preferred stock} = \frac{\text{Dividend per share of preferred stock}}{\text{Current market price per share of preferred stock}} = \frac{\$4.25}{\$70.00} = 6.07\%$$

Through the use of dividend yield rates, we can compare different preferred stocks having different annual dividends and different market prices.

Note to the Student
Calculate the market test ratios for your company. You may want to update the earnings yield on common stock and price-earnings ratio from *The Wall Street Journal*.

CASH FLOW PER SHARE OF COMMON STOCK   Investors calculate the **cash flow per share of common stock** ratio as follows:

$$\text{Cash flow per share of common stock} = \frac{\text{Net cash provided by operating activities}}{\text{Average number of shares of common stock outstanding}}$$

Currently, *FASB Statement No. 95* does not permit the use of this ratio for external reporting purposes. However, some mortgage and investment banking firms do use this ratio to judge the company's ability to pay dividends and pay liabilities. For an example of the cash flow per share of common stock ratio, look at Illustration 17.8 for the Colgate-Palmolive Company. The cash flow per share of common stock decreased in 1995 but increased in 1996.

FINAL CONSIDERATIONS IN FINANCIAL STATEMENT ANALYSIS

Objective 5
Describe the considerations used in financial statement analysis.

Standing alone, a single financial ratio may not be informative. Investors gain greater insight by computing and analyzing several related ratios for a company. Illustration 17.9 summarizes the ratios presented in this chapter, and Illustration 17.10 presents them graphically.

Financial analysis relies heavily on informed judgment. As guides to aid comparison, percentages and ratios are useful in uncovering potential strengths and weaknesses. However, the financial analyst should seek the basic causes behind changes and established trends.

ILLUSTRATION 17.9 Summary of Ratios

Liquidity Ratios	Formula	Significance
Current, or working capital, ratio	Current assets ÷ Current liabilities	Test of debt-paying ability
Acid-test (quick) ratio	Quick assets (Cash + Marketable securities + Net receivables) ÷ Current liabilities	Test of immediate debt-paying ability
Cash flow liquidity ratio	(Cash and marketable securities + Net cash provided by operating activities) ÷ Current liabilities	Test of short-term, debt-paying ability
Accounts receivable turnover	Net credit sales (or net sales) ÷ Average net accounts receivable	Test of quality of accounts receivable
Number of days' sales in accounts receivable (average collection period of accounts receivable)	Number of days in year (365) ÷ Accounts receivable turnover	Test of quality of accounts receivable
Inventory turnover	Cost of goods sold ÷ Average inventory	Test of whether or not a sufficient volume of business is being generated relative to inventory
Total assets turnover	Net sales ÷ Average total assets	Test of whether or not the volume of business generated is adequate relative to amount of capital invested in the business

Equity, or Long-Term Solvency, Ratios		
Equity (stockholders' equity) ratio	Stockholders' equity ÷ Total assets (or total equities)	Index of long-run solvency and safety
Stockholders' equity to debt (debt to equity) ratio	Stockholders' equity ÷ Total debt	Measure of the relative proportion of stockholders' and of creditors' equities

Profitability Tests		
Rate of return on operating assets	Net operating income ÷ Operating assets or Operating margin × Turnover of operating assets	Measure of managerial effectiveness
Net income to net sales (return on sales)	Net income ÷ Net sales	Indicator of the amount of net profit on each dollar of sales
Return on average common stockholders' equity	Net income ÷ Average common stockholders' equity	Measure of what a given company earned for its stockholders from all sources as a percentage of the common stockholders' investment
Cash flow margin	Net cash provided by operating activities ÷ Net sales	Measure of the ability of a firm to translate sales into cash
EPS of common stock	Earnings available to common stockholders ÷ Weighted-average number of common shares outstanding	Measure of the return to investors
Times interest earned ratio	Income before interest and taxes ÷ Interest expense	Test of the likelihood that creditors will continue to receive their interest payments
Times preferred dividends earned ratio	Net income ÷ Annual preferred dividends	Test of the likelihood that preferred stockholders will receive their dividend each year

Market Tests		
Earnings yield on common stock	EPS ÷ Current market price per share of common stock	Comparison with other common stocks
Price-earnings ratio	Current market price per share of common stock ÷ EPS	Index of whether a stock is relatively cheap or expensive based on the ratio
Payout ratio on common stock	Dividend per share of common stock ÷ EPS	Index of whether company pays out a large percentage of earnings as dividends or reinvests most of its earnings
Dividend yield on common stock	Dividend per share of common stock ÷ Current market price per share of common stock	Comparisons with other common stocks
Dividend yield on preferred stock	Dividend per share of preferred stock ÷ Current market price per share of preferred stock	Comparison with other preferred stocks
Cash flow per share of common stock	Net cash provided by operating activities ÷ Average number of shares of common stock outstanding	Test of ability to pay dividends and liabilities

ILLUSTRATION 17.10   Graphic Depiction of Financial Statement Analysis Utilizing Financial Ratios

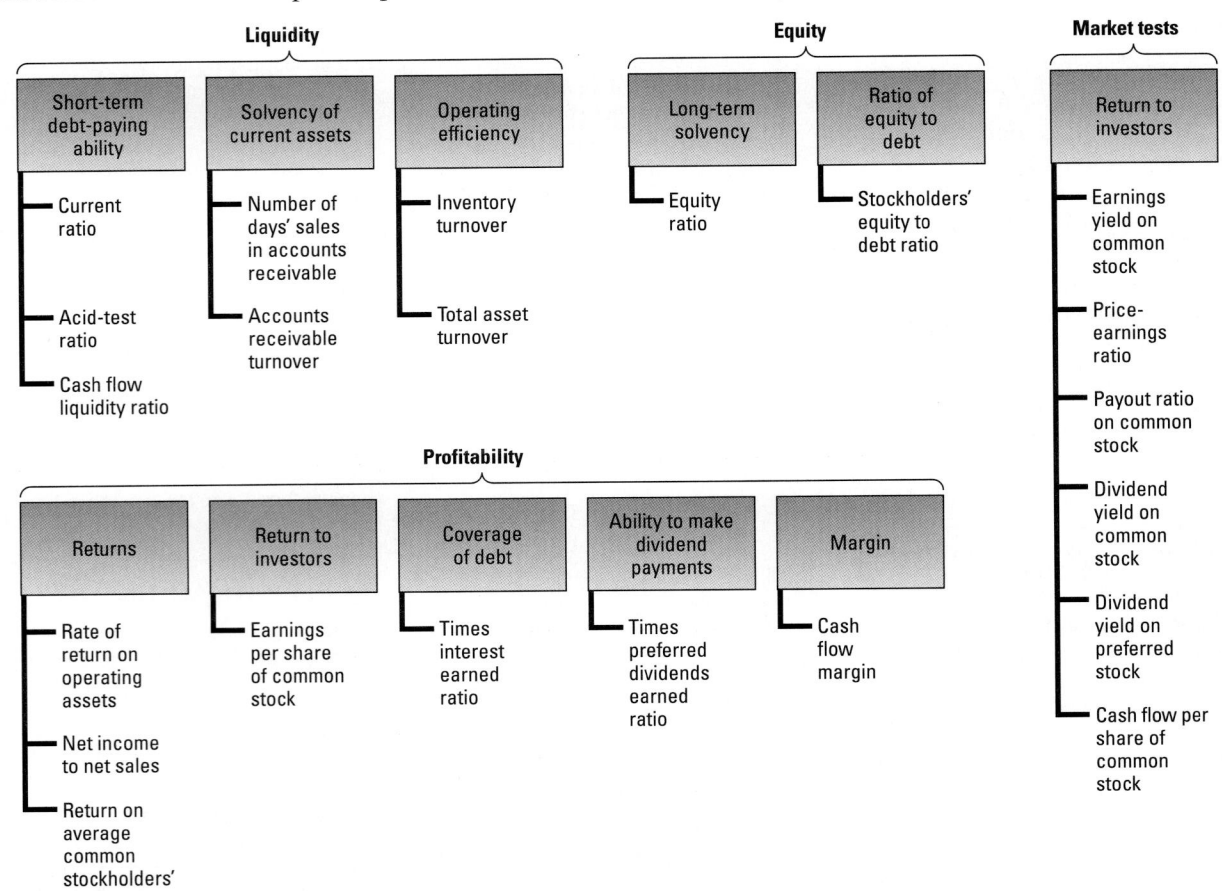

Need for Comparable Data

Analysts must be sure that their comparisons are valid—especially when the comparisons are of items for different periods or different companies. They must follow consistent accounting practices if valid interperiod comparisons are to be made. Comparable intercompany comparisons are more difficult to secure. Accountants cannot do much more than disclose the fact that one company is using FIFO and another is using LIFO for inventory and cost of goods sold computations. Such a disclosure alerts analysts that intercompany comparisons of inventory turnover ratios, for example, may not be comparable.

Also, when comparing a company's ratios to industry averages provided by an external source such as Dun & Bradstreet, the analyst should calculate the company's ratios in the same manner as the reporting service. Thus, if Dun & Bradstreet uses net sales (rather than cost of goods sold) to compute inventory turnover, so should the analyst. Net sales is sometimes preferable because all companies do not compute and report cost of goods sold amounts in the same manner.

Influence of External Factors

Facts and conditions not disclosed by the financial statements may, however, affect their interpretation. A single important event may have been largely responsible for a given relationship. For example, competitors may put a new product on the market, making it necessary for the company under study to reduce the selling price of a product suddenly rendered obsolete. Such an event would severely affect the percentage of gross margin to net sales. Yet there may be little chance that such an event will happen again.

Analysts must consider general business conditions within the industry of the company under study. A corporation's downward trend in earnings, for example, is less alarming if the industry trend or the general economic trend is also downward.

Investors also need to consider the seasonal nature of some businesses. If the balance sheet date represents the seasonal peak in the volume of business, for example, the ratio of current assets to current liabilities may be much lower than if the balance sheet date is in a season of low activity.

Potential investors should consider the market risk associated with the prospective investment. They can determine market risk by comparing the changes in the price of a stock in relation to the changes in the average price of all stocks.

Potential investors should realize that acquiring the ability to make informed judgments is a long process and does not occur overnight. Using ratios and percentages without considering the underlying causes may lead to incorrect conclusions.

Need for Standards of Comparison

Relationships between financial statement items also become more meaningful when standards are available for comparison. Comparisons with standards provide a starting point for the analyst's thinking and lead to further investigation and, ultimately, to conclusions and business decisions. Such standards consist of (1) those in the analyst's own mind as a result of experience and observations, (2) those provided by the records of past performance and financial position of the business under study, and (3) those provided about other enterprises. Examples of the third standard are data available through trade associations, universities, research organizations (such as Dun & Bradstreet and Robert Morris Associates), and governmental units (such as the Federal Trade Commission).

In financial statement analysis, remember that standards for comparison vary by industry, and financial analysis must be carried out with knowledge of specific industry characteristics. For example, a wholesale grocery company would have large inventories available to be shipped to retailers and a relatively small investment in property, plant, and equipment, while an electric utility company would have no merchandise inventory (except for repair parts) and a large investment in property, plant, and equipment.

Even within an industry, variations may exist. Acceptable current ratios, gross margin percentages, debt to equity ratios, and other relationships vary widely depending on unique conditions within an industry. Therefore, it is important to know the industry to make comparisons that have real meaning.

This chapter concludes our coverage of financial accounting. It is likely you will continue on with studies in *managerial* accounting. It is important to realize that it is impossible to completely separate financial and managerial accounting information into neat packages. Managers use both the published financial statements and managerial accounting information in making decisions. Also, some of the concepts covered in managerial accounting (e.g., job costing and process costing) have a direct impact on the formal financial statements. Many accountants are attracted to managerial accounting because it is not constrained by having to conform to generally accepted accounting principles. Instead, management accountants can provide to management whatever information in whatever form management requests.

Reinforcing Problems
P17–8 and P17–8A Determine effects on ratios of change in accounting method (FIFO to LIFO). BDC17–1 Compute net income, identify reason for cash increase, state main sources of financing, and indicate further analyses needed. ARA17–4 Analyze management's objectives and performance from the viewpoints of a creditor and an investor (real world problem).

AN ACCOUNTING PERSPECTIVE	**USES OF TECHNOLOGY** The *Journal of Accountancy* has published articles on Internet resources to encourage greater use of technology by accountants. Five of the articles published in that journal that are very informative for those who want to learn more about the Internet and/or find additional websites regarding accounting are:

Dennis R. Schmidt, Roxanne M. Spindle, and William F. Yancey, "Tapping the World Wide Web," August 1996, pp. 73–77.

John J. Gill, "Where to Find Help Online," March 1997, pp. 45–49.

"Accountant's Online User's Manual: Lesson 3," March 1997, pp. 51–54.

Val D. Steed, "Must Technologies for All CPAs," March 1997, pp. 59–60, 62.

Richard J. Koreto, "When the Bottom Line Is Online," March 1997, pp. 63–65.

You may want to investigate one or more of these articles and then visit some of the websites they list. There is no doubt that the Internet will only grow in importance in the future. The more you know about it, the more marketable you will be upon graduation.

UNDERSTANDING THE LEARNING OBJECTIVES

Objective 1
Describe and explain the objectives of financial statement analysis.

- A company's financial statements are analyzed internally by management and externally by investors, creditors, and regulatory agencies.
- Management's analysis of financial statements primarily relates to parts of the company. Management is able to obtain specific, special-purpose reports to aid in decision making.
- External users focus their analysis of financial statements on the company as a whole. They must rely on the general-purpose financial statements that companies publish.
- Financial statement analysis consists of applying analytical tools and techniques to financial statements and other relevant data to obtain useful information.
- This information is the significant relationships between data and trends in those data assessing the company's past performance and current financial position.
- The information is useful for making predictions that may have a direct effect on decisions made by many users of financial statements.
- Present and potential company investors use this information to assess the profitability of the firm.
- Outside parties and long-term creditors sometimes are interested in a company's solvency, and thus use the information in predicting the company's solvency.

Objective 2
Describe the sources of information for financial statement analysis.

- Published reports are one source of financial information. Published reports include financial statements, explanatory notes, letters to stockholders, reports of independent accountants, and management's discussion and analysis (MDA).
- Government reports are another source of financial information and include Form 10-K, Form 10-Q, and Form 8-K. These reports are available to the public for a small charge.
- Financial service information, business publications, newspapers, and periodicals offer meaningful financial information to external users. Moody's Investors Services; Standard & Poor's; Dun & Bradstreet, Inc.; and Robert Morris Associates all provide useful industry information. Business publications, such as *The Wall Street Journal* and *Forbes*, also report industry financial news.

Objective 3
Calculate and explain changes in financial statements using horizontal analysis, vertical analysis, and trend analysis.

- Horizontal analysis is the calculation of dollar changes or percentage changes in comparative statement items or totals. Use of this analysis helps detect changes in a company's performance and highlights trends.
- Vertical analysis consists of a study of a single financial statement in which each item is expressed as a percentage of a significant total. Use of this analysis is especially helpful in analyzing income statement data such as the percentage of cost of goods sold to sales or the percentage of gross margin to sales.
- Trend analysis compares financial information over time to a base year. The analysis is calculated by:
  1. Selecting a base year or period.
  2. Assigning a weight of 100% to the amounts appearing on the base-year financial statements.

3. Expressing the corresponding amounts shown on the other years' financial statements as a percentage of base-year or period amounts. The percentages are computed by dividing nonbase-year amounts by the corresponding base-year amounts and then multiplying the results by 100.

Trend analysis indicates changes that are taking place in an organization and highlights the direction of these changes.

- **Liquidity ratios** indicate a company's short-term debt-paying ability. These ratios include (1) current, or working capital, ratio; (2) acid-test (quick) ratio; (3) cash flow liquidity ratio; (4) accounts receivable turnover; (5) number of days' sales in accounts receivable; (6) inventory turnover; and (7) total assets turnover.

- **Equity, or long-term solvency, ratios** show the relationship between debt and equity financing in a company. These ratios include (1) equity (stockholders' equity) ratio and (2) stockholders' equity to debt ratio.

- **Profitability tests** are an important measure of a company's operating success. These tests include (1) rate of return on operating assets, (2) net income to net sales, (3) net income to average common stockholders' equity, (4) cash flow margin, (5) earnings per share of common stock, (6) times interest earned ratio, and (7) times preferred dividends earned ratio.

- **Market tests** help investors and potential investors assess the relative merits of the various stocks in the marketplace. These tests include (1) earnings yield on common stock, (2) price-earnings ratio, (3) dividend yield on common stock, (4) payout ratio on common stock, (5) dividend yield on preferred stock, and (6) cash flow per share of common stock.

- For a complete summary and a graphic depiction of all liquidity, long-term solvency, profitability, and market test ratios, see Illustrations 17.9 and 17.10.

- **Need for comparative data:** Analysts must be sure that their comparisons are valid— especially when the comparisons are of items for different periods or different companies.

- **Influence of external factors:** A single important event, such as the unexpected placing of a product on the market by a competitor, may affect the interpretation of the financial statements. Also, the general business conditions and the possible seasonal nature of the business must be taken into consideration, since these factors could have an impact on the financial statements.

- **Impact of inflation:** Since financial statements fail to reveal the impact of inflation on the reporting entity, one must make sure that the items being compared are all comparable; that is, the impact of inflation has been taken into consideration.

- **Need for comparative standards:** In financial statement analysis, remember that standards for comparison vary by industry, and financial analysis must be carried out with knowledge of specific industry characteristics.

Objective 4
Perform ratio analysis on financial statements using liquidity ratios, long-term solvency ratios, profitability tests, and market tests.

Objective 5
Describe the considerations used in financial statement analysis.

Demonstration Problem 17–A

Comparative financial statements of Kellogg Company for 1994 and 1995 follow:

Kellogg Company
Kellogg Company is one of the world's largest breakfast cereal companies.

KELLOGG COMPANY
Comparative Income Statements
For the Years Ended December 31, 1995, and 1994
($ millions)

	1995	1994
Net revenues	$7,003.7	$6,562.0
Cost of goods sold	3,177.7	2,950.7
Gross margin	$3,826.0	$3,611.3
Operating expenses	2,988.5	2,448.7
Nonoperating expense (interest)	41.5	32.6
Income before income taxes	$ 796.0	$1,130.0
Income taxes	305.7	424.6
Net earnings	$ 490.3	$ 705.4

KELLOGG COMPANY
Comparative Balance Sheets
December 31, 1995, and 1994
($ millions)

	1995	1994
Assets		
Cash and temporary investments	$ 221.9	$ 266.3
Accounts receivable, net	590.1	564.5
Inventories	376.7	396.3
Other current assets	240.1	206.4
Property, net	2,784.8	2,892.8
Other assets	201.0	141.0
Total assets	$4,414.6	$4,467.3
Liabilities and Stockholders' Equity		
Current liabilities.	$1,265.4	$1,185.2
Long-term liabilities	1,558.3	1,474.6
Common stock	77.8	77.6
Capital in excess of par value	105.2	68.6
Retained earnings	3,963.0	3,801.2
Treasury stock	(2,361.2)	(1,980.6)
Currency translation adjustment	(193.9)	(159.3)
Total liabilities and stockholders' equity	$4,414.6	$4,467.3

Required   **a.**   Prepare comparative common-size income statements for 1995 and 1994.

b.   Perform a horizontal analysis of the comparative balance sheets.

c.   Comment on the results of **a** and **b**.

SOLUTION TO DEMONSTRATION PROBLEM 17–A

a.

KELLOGG COMPANY
Common-Size Comparative Income Statements
For the Years Ended December 31, 1995, and 1994

	Percent	
	1995	**1994**
Net revenues	100.00%	100.00%
Cost of goods sold.	45.37	44.97
Gross margin	54.63%	55.03%
Operating expenses	42.67	37.32
Nonoperating expense (interest)	.59	.50
Income before income taxes	11.37%*	17.21%
Income taxes	4.36	6.47
Net earnings	7.01%*	10.74%

*Difference due to rounding.

b.

KELLOGG COMPANY
Comparative Balance Sheets
December 31, 1995, and 1994
($ millions)

			Increase or Decrease	
	1995	**1994**	**1995 Amount**	**1994 Percent**
Assets				
Cash and temporary investments	$ 221.9	$ 266.3	$(44.4)	(16.67)%
Accounts receivable, net	590.1	564.5	25.6	4.53
Inventories	376.7	396.3	(19.6)	(4.95)
Other current assets	240.1	206.4	33.7	16.33
Property, net	2,784.8	2,892.8	(108.0)	(3.73)
Other assets	201.0	141.0	60.0	42.55
Total assets	$4,414.6	$4,467.3	$(52.7)	(1.18)%

Liabilities and Stockholders' Equity

Current liabilities	$1,265.4	$1,185.2	$ 80.2	6.77%
Long-term liabilities	1,558.3	1,474.6	83.7	5.68
Common stock	77.8	77.6	.2	.26
Capital in excess of par value	105.2	68.6	36.6	53.35
Retained earnings	3,963.0	3,801.2	161.8	4.26
Treasury stock	(2,361.2)	(1,980.6)	(380.6)	19.22
Currency translation adjustment	(193.9)	(159.3)	(34.6)	21.72
Total liabilities and stockholders' equity	$4,414.6	$4,467.3	$(52.7)	(1.18)

c. The $441.7 million increase in net revenues yielded a $214.7 million increase in gross margin because the gross margin rate slightly declined from 55.03% to 54.63%. Operating expenses increased as a percentage of sales from 37.32% to 42.67%; however, the decrease in gross margin coupled with the large increase in expenses yielded an overall decrease in net income.

　　The balance sheet of Kellogg Company changed significantly. The company probably financed increases in accounts receivable, other current assets, and treasury stock through decreased cash and increased long-term liabilities and retained earnings.

Demonstration Problem 17–B

The balance sheet and supplementary data for Xerox Corporation follow:

XEROX CORPORATION
Balance Sheet with IOFS on an Equity Basis
December 31, 1995
($ millions)

	1995
Assets	
Cash	$ 130
Accounts receivable, net	1,894
Finance receivables, net	4,069
Inventories	2,646
Deferred taxes and other current assets	1,094
Total current assets	$ 9,833
Finance receivables due after one year, net	6,406
Land, buildings, and equipment, net	2,092
Investments in affiliates, at equity	1,328
Goodwill	627
Investment in discontinued operations, net	4,810
Other assets	873
Total assets	$25,969
Liabilities and Shareholders' Equity	
Short-term debt and current portion of long-term debt	$ 3,265
Accounts payable	563
Accrued compensation and benefit costs	731
Unearned income	228
Other current liabilities	2,212
Total current liabilities	$ 6,999
Long-term debt	7,867
Liabilities for postretirement medical benefits	1,018
Deferred taxes and other liabilities	2,436
Discontinued policyholders' deposits and other operations liabilities	2,810
Deferred ESOP benefits	(547)
Minorities' interests in equity of subsidiaries	745
Preferred stock	763
Common shareholders' equity (108.1 million)	3,878
Total liabilities and shareholders' equity	$25,969

Xerox
Xerox Corporation is a global enterprise serving the document processing market.

1. Cost of goods sold, $4,962.
2. Net sales, $16,611.
3. Inventory, January 1, $2,294.
4. Net interest expense, $509.

Supplementary data for 1995 (in millions)

5. Net income before interest and taxes, $2,356.

6. Net accounts receivable on January 1, $1,811.

7. Total assets on January 1, $27,278.

Required   Compute the following ratios:

a. Current ratio.

b. Acid-test ratio.

c. Accounts receivable turnover.

d. Inventory turnover.

e. Total assets turnover.

f. Equity ratio.

g. Times interest earned ratio.

SOLUTION TO DEMONSTRATION PROBLEM 17–B

a. Current ratio:

$$\frac{\text{Current assets}}{\text{Current liabilities}} = \frac{\$9,833,000,000}{\$6,999,000,000} = 1.40{:}1$$

b. Acid-test ratio:

$$\frac{\text{Quick assets}}{\text{Current liabilities}} = \frac{\$6,093,000,000}{\$6,999,000,000} = .87{:}1$$

c. Accounts receivable turnover:

$$\frac{\text{Net sales}}{\text{Average net accounts receivable}} = \frac{\$16,611,000,000}{\$1,852,500,000} = 8.97 \text{ times}$$

d. Inventory turnover:

$$\frac{\text{Cost of goods sold}}{\text{Average inventory}} = \frac{\$4,962,000,000}{\$2,470,000,000} = 2.01 \text{ times}$$

e. Total assets turnover:

$$\frac{\text{Net sales}}{\text{Average total assets}} = \frac{\$16,611,000,000}{\$26,623,500,000} = .62 \text{ times}$$

f. Equity ratio:

$$\frac{\text{Stockholders' equity}}{\text{Total assets}} = \frac{\$4,641,000,000}{\$25,969,000,000} = 17.87\%$$

g. Times interest earned ratio:

$$\frac{\text{Income before interest and taxes}}{\text{Interest expense}} = \frac{\$2,356,000,000}{\$509,000,000} = 4.63 \text{ times}$$

NEW TERMS

Accounts receivable turnover   Net credit sales (or net sales) divided by average net accounts receivable.   *636*

Acid-test (quick) ratio   Ratio of quick assets (cash, marketable securities, and net receivables) to current liabilities.   *635*

Cash flow liquidity ratio   Cash and marketable securities plus net cash provided by operating activities divided by current liabilities.   *636*

Cash flow margin   Net cash provided by operating activities divided by net sales.   *644*

Cash flow per share of common stock   Net cash

provided by operating activities divided by the average number of shares of common stock outstanding.   *650*

Common-size statements   Show only percentages and no absolute dollar amounts.   *627*

Comparative financial statements   Present the same company's financial statements for two or more successive periods in side-by-side columns.   *627*

Current ratio   Also called *working capital ratio*. Current assets divided by current liabilities.   *634*

Debt to equity ratio   Total debt divided by stockholders' equity.   *640*

Dividend yield on common stock Dividend per share of common stock divided by current market price per share of common stock. *648*

Dividend yield on preferred stock Dividend per share of preferred stock divided by current market price per share of preferred stock. *648*

Earnings per share (EPS) The amount of earnings available to common stockholders (which equals net income less preferred dividends) divided by weighted-average number of shares of common stock outstanding. *644*

Earnings yield on common stock Ratio of current EPS to current market price per share of common stock. *647*

Equity (stockholders' equity) ratio The ratio of stockholders' equity to total assets (or total equities). *639*

Horizontal analysis Analysis of a company's financial statements for two or more successive periods showing percentage and/or absolute changes from prior year. This type of analysis helps detect changes in a company's performance and highlights trends. *627*

Inventory turnover Cost of goods sold divided by average inventory. *638*

Liquidity Company's state of possessing liquid assets, such as (1) cash and (2) other assets that will soon be converted to cash. *626*

Net income to net sales Net income divided by net sales. *642*

Nonoperating assets Assets owned by a company but not used in producing operating revenues. *641*

Nonoperating income elements Elements excluded from net operating income because they are not directly related to operations; includes such elements as extraordinary items, cumulative effect on prior year of changes in accounting principle, losses or gains from discontinued operations, interest revenue, and interest expense. *641*

Number of days' sales in accounts receivable The number of days in a year (365) divided by the accounts receivable turnover. Also called the **average collection period for accounts receivable.** *637*

Operating assets All assets actively used in producing operating revenues. *641*

Operating margin Net operating income divided by net sales. *641*

Payout ratio on common stock The ratio of dividends per share of common stock divided by EPS. *648*

Price-earnings ratio The ratio of current market price per share of common stock divided by the EPS of the stock. *648*

Rate of return on operating assets (Net operating income ÷ Net sales) × (Net sales ÷ Operating assets). Result is equal to net operating income divided by operating assets. *641*

Return on average common stockholders' equity Net income divided by average common stockholders' equity; often called **rate of return on average common stockholders' equity,** or simply **return on equity (ROE).** *643*

Return on equity (ROE) Net income divided by average common stockholders' equity. *643*

Stockholders' equity to debt ratio Stockholders' equity divided by total debt; often used in inverted form and called the **debt to equity ratio.** *640*

Times interest earned ratio A ratio computed by dividing income before interest and taxes by interest expense (also called **interest coverage ratio**). *646*

Times preferred dividends earned ratio Net income divided by annual preferred dividends. *647*

Total assets turnover Net sales divided by average total assets. *639*

Trend percentages Similar to horizontal analysis except that a base year or period is selected, and comparisons are made to the base year or period. *627*

Turnover The relationship between the amount of an asset and some measure of its use. See *accounts receivable turnover, inventory turnover,* and *total assets turnover. 636*

Turnover of operating assets Net sales divided by operating assets. *641*

Vertical analysis The study of a single financial statement in which each item is expressed as a percentage of a significant total; for example, percentages of sales calculations. *627*

Yield (on stock) The yield on a stock investment refers to either an earnings yield or a dividend yield. Also see Earnings yield on common stock and Dividend yield on common stock and preferred stock. *647*

Self-Test

True-False

Indicate whether each of the following statements is true or false.

1. An objective of financial statement analysis is to provide information about the company's past performance and current financial position.

2. Vertical analysis helps detect changes in a company's performance over several periods and highlights trends.

3. Common-size statements provide information about changes in dollar amounts relative to the previous periods.

4. Liquidity ratios show a company's capacity to pay maturing current liabilities.

5. A company that is quite profitable may find it difficult to pay its accounts payable.

6. Financial statement analysts must be sure that comparable data are used among companies to make the comparisons valid.

MULTIPLE-CHOICE

Select the best answer for each of the following questions.

The following data were abstracted from the December 31, 2000, balance sheet of Andrews Company (use for questions 1 and 2):

Cash	$136,000
Marketable securities	64,000
Accounts and notes receivable, net	184,000
Merchandise inventory	244,000
Prepaid expenses	12,000
Accounts and notes payable, short term	256,000
Accrued liabilities	64,000
Bonds payable, long term	400,000

1. The current ratio is:
   a. 1:2.
   b. 2:1.
   c. 1.2:1.
   d. 3:1.

2. The acid-test ratio is:
   a. 1:2.
   b. 2:1.
   c. 1.2:1.
   d. 3:1.

Benson Company shows the following data on its 2000 financial statements (use for questions 3–5):

Accounts receivable, January 1	$ 720,000
Accounts receivable, December 31	960,000

Merchandise inventory, January 1	900,000
Merchandise inventory, December 31	1,020,000
Gross sales	4,800,000
Sales returns and allowances	180,000
Net sales	4,620,000
Cost of goods sold	3,360,000
Income before interest and taxes	720,000
Interest on bonds	192,000
Net income	384,000

3. The accounts receivable turnover is:
   a. 5.5 times per year.
   b. 5.714 times per year.
   c. 5 times per year.
   d. 6.667 times per year.

4. The inventory turnover is:
   a. 5 times per year.
   b. 4.8125 times per year.
   c. 3.5 times per year.
   d. 4 times per year.

5. The times interest earned ratio is:
   a. 4.75 times per year.
   b. 3.75 times per year.
   c. 2 times per year.
   d. 3 times per year.

Now turn to page 676 to check your answers.

QUESTIONS

1. What are the major sources of financial information for publicly owned corporations?

2. The higher the accounts receivable turnover rate, the better off the company is. Do you agree? Why?

3. Can you think of a situation where the current ratio is very misleading as an indicator of short-term, debt-paying ability? Does the acid-test ratio offer a remedy to the situation you have described? Describe a situation where the acid-test ratio does not suffice either.

4. Before the Marvin Company issued $20,000 of long-term notes (due more than a year from the date of issue) in exchange for a like amount of accounts payable, its current ratio was 2:1 and its acid-test ratio was 1:1. Will this transaction increase, decrease, or have no effect on the current ratio and acid-test ratio? What would be the effect on the equity ratio?

5. Through the use of turnover rates, explain why a firm might seek to increase the volume of its sales even though such an increase can be secured only at reduced prices.

6. Indicate which of the relationships illustrated in the chapter would be best to judge:
   a. The short-term debt-paying ability of the firm.
   b. The overall efficiency of the firm without regard to the sources of assets.

   c. The return to owners (stockholders) of a corporation.
   d. The safety of long-term creditors' interest.
   e. The safety of preferred stockholders' dividends.

7. Indicate how each of the following ratios or measures is calculated:
   a. Payout ratio.
   b. Earnings per share of common stock.
   c. Price-earnings ratio.
   d. Earnings yield on common stock.
   e. Dividend yield on preferred stock.
   f. Times interest earned.
   g. Times preferred dividends earned.
   h. Return on average common stockholders' equity.
   i. Cash flow margin.

8. How is the rate of return on operating assets determined? Is it possible for two companies with operating margins of 5% and 1%, respectively, to both have a rate of return of 20% on operating assets? How?

9. Cite some of the possible deficiencies in accounting information, especially regarding its use in analyzing a particular company over a 10-year period.

The Coca-Cola Company

10. **Real World Question** From the Consolidated Statements of Income of The Coca-Cola Company in the annual report booklet, determine the percentage change in operating income from 1995 to 1996.

The Coca-Cola Company

11. **Real World Question** From the Consolidated Statements of Income of The Coca-Cola Company in the annual report booklet, determine the 1996 net income per common share.

The Coca-Cola Company

12. **Real World Question** From the "Selected Financial Data" of The Coca-Cola Company in the annual report booklet, determine the 1996 cash dividends per common share.

The Coca-Cola Company

13. **Real World Question** From the financial statements of The Coca-Cola Company in the annual report booklet, determine the 1996 cash flow margin.

EXERCISES*

Income statement data for Boston Company for 2000 and 1999 follow:

	2000	1999
Net sales	$2,610,000	$1,936,000
Cost of goods sold	1,829,600	1,256,400
Selling expenses	396,800	350,000
Administrative expenses	234,800	198,400
Federal income taxes	57,600	54,000

Prepare a horizontal and vertical analysis of the income data in a form similar to Illustration 17.2. Comment on the results of this analysis.

A company engaged in the following three independent transactions:

1. Merchandise purchased on account, $2,400,000.
2. Machinery purchased for cash, $2,400,000.
3. Capital stock issued for cash, $2,400,000.
   a. Compute the current ratio after each of these transactions assuming current assets were $3,200,000 and the current ratio was 1:1 before the transactions occurred.
   b. Repeat part **a** assuming the current ratio was 2:1.
   c. Repeat part **a** assuming the current ratio was 1:2.

A company has sales of $3,680,000 per year. Its average net accounts receivable balance is $920,000.

a. What is the average number of days accounts receivable are outstanding?
b. By how much would the capital invested in accounts receivable be reduced if the turnover could be increased to 6 without a loss of sales?

Columbia Corporation had the following selected financial data for December 31, 1998:

Net sales	$1,800,000
Cost of goods sold	1,080,000
Operating expenses	315,000
Net income	195,000
Total assets	1,000,000
Net cash provided by operating activities	25,000

Compute the cash flow margin.

Exercise 17–1
Perform horizontal and vertical analysis (L.O. 3)

Exercise 17–2
Determine effects of various transactions on the current ratio (L.O. 4)

Exercise 17–3
Compute average number of days receivables are outstanding; determine effect of increase in turnover (L.O. 4)

Exercise 17–4
Compute cash flow margin (L.O. 4)

*By using the ratio module in the General Ledger Applications Software (GLAS) package, you can work any of the exercises or problems that deal with ratios.

Exercise 17–5
Compute inventory turnover (L.O. 4)

From the following partial income statement, calculate the inventory turnover for the period.

Net sales		$2,028,000
Cost of goods sold:		
Beginning inventory	$ 234,000	
Purchases	1,326,000	
Cost of goods available for sale	$1,560,000	
Less: Ending inventory	265,200	
Cost of goods sold		1,294,800
Gross margin		$ 733,200
Operating expenses		327,600
Net operating income		$ 405,600

Exercise 17–6
Compute rate of return on operating assets (L.O. 4)

Eastern, Inc., had net sales of $3,520,000, gross margin of $1,496,000, and operating expenses of $904,000. Total assets (all operating) were $3,080,000. Compute Eastern's rate of return on operating assets.

Exercise 17–7
Compute return on common stockholders' equity (L.O. 4)

Nelson Company began the year 1999 with total stockholders' equity of $2,400,000. Its net income for 1999 was $640,000, and $106,800 of dividends were declared. Compute the rate of return on average stockholders' equity for 1999. No preferred stock was outstanding.

Exercise 17–8
Compute EPS (L.O. 4)

Rogers Company had 60,000 shares of common stock outstanding on January 1, 1999. On April 1, 1999, it issued 20,000 additional shares for cash. The amount of earnings available for common stockholders for 1999 was $600,000. What amount of EPS of common stock should the company report?

Exercise 17–9
Compute weighted-average number of shares outstanding (L.O. 4)

Smith Company started 2000 with 800,000 shares of common stock outstanding. On March 31, it issued 96,000 shares for cash, and on September 30, it purchased 80,000 shares of its own stock for cash. Compute the weighted-average number of common shares outstanding for the year.

Exercise 17–10
Compute EPS for current and prior year (L.O. 4)

A company reported EPS of $2 (or $2,400,000/1,200,000 shares) for 1998, ending the year with 1,200,000 shares outstanding. In 1999, the company earned net income of $7,680,000, issued 320,000 shares of common stock for cash on September 30, and distributed a 100% stock dividend on December 31, 1999. Compute EPS for 1999, and compute the adjusted earnings per share for 1998 that would be shown in the 1999 annual report.

Exercise 17–11
Compute times interest earned (L.O. 4)

A company paid interest of $32,000, incurred federal income taxes of $88,000, and had net income (after taxes) of $112,000. How many times was interest earned?

Exercise 17–12
Compute times dividends earned and dividend yield (L.O. 4)

John Company had 20,000 shares of $600 par value, 8% preferred stock outstanding. Net income after taxes was $5,760,000. The market price per share was $720.

a. How many times were the preferred dividends earned?
b. What was the dividend yield on the preferred stock assuming the regular preferred dividends were declared and paid?

Exercise 17–13
Compute EPS and price-earnings ratio (L.O. 4)

A company had 80,000 weighted-average number of shares of $320 par value common stock outstanding. The amount of earnings available to common stockholders was $800,000. Current market price per share is $720. Compute the EPS and the price-earnings ratio.

PROBLEMS

Problem 17–1
Perform horizontal and vertical analysis and comment on the results (L.O. 3)

Bethlehem Steel Corporation is one of the leading U.S. producers of steel plate and corrosion-resistant coated sheet steel used in the automotive markets. Bethlehem Steel's comparative statements of income and retained earnings and consolidated balance sheet for 1995 and 1994 follow.

BETHLEHEM STEEL CORPORATION
Consolidated Statement of Earnings
For the Years Ended December 31, 1995, and 1994
($ thousands)

	December 31	
	(1) 1995	(2) 1994
Net sales	$4,867.5	$4,819.4
Costs and Expenses:		
Cost of sales	$4,202.8	$4,287.3
Depreciation	284.0	261.1
Estimated restructuring losses	111.8	137.4
Total Costs	$4,598.6	$4,685.8
Income from operations	$ 268.9	$ 133.6
Financing income (expense):		
Interest and other income	7.7	7.1
Interest and other financing costs	(60.0)	(46.2)
Loss before Income Taxes and Cumulative Effect of Changes in Accounting	$ 216.6	$ 94.5
Benefit (Provision) for Income Taxes	(37.0)	(14.0)
Net earnings (loss)	$ 179.6	$ 80.5
Retained Earnings, January 1	(859.4)	(939.9)
	$ (679.8)	$ (859.4)
Dividends	0.0	0.0
Retained Earnings, December 31	$ (679.8)	$ (859.4)

BETHLEHEM STEEL CORPORATION
Consolidated Balance Sheet
As of December 31, 1995, and 1994

	December 31	
	(1) 1995	(2) 1994
Assets		
Current Assets		
Cash and cash equivalents	$ 180.0	$ 159.5
Receivables	374.6	519.5
Total	$ 554.6	$ 679.0
Inventories		
Raw Materials and supplies	$ 335.5	$ 331.9
Finished and semifinished products	604.9	534.9
Contract work in process less billings of $10.9 and $2.3	17.8	16.1
Total inventories	$ 958.2	$ 882.9
Other current assets	$ 13.0	$ 7.2
Total current assets	$1,525.8	$1,569.1
Property, Plant and Equipment less accumulated depreciation of $4329.5 and $4167.8	$2,714.2	$2,759.3
Investments and Miscellaneous Assets	112.3	124.2
Deferred Income Tax Asset — net	885.0	903.2
Intangible Asset — Pensions	463.0	426.6
Total Assets	$5,700.3	$5,782.4

Liabilities and Stockholders' Equity

Current Liabilities

Accounts payable	$ 381.4	$ 387.0
Accrued employment costs	208.0	165.8
Postretirement benefits other than pensions	150.0	138.0
Accrued taxes	72.4	67.6
Debt and capital lease obligations	91.5	88.9
Other current liabilities	146.3	163.9
Total current liabilities	$1,049.6	$1,011.2
Pension Liability	$1,115.0	$1,117.1
Postretirement Benefits Other Than Pensions	1,415.0	1,441.4
Long-term Debt and Capital Lease Obligations	546.8	668.4
Other	335.6	388.5
Total noncurrent liabilities	$3,412.4	$3,615.4
Total Liabilities	$4,462.0	$4,626.6

Common Stockholders' Equity

Preferred Stock—at $1 per share par value (aggregate liquidation preference of $481.2); Authorized 20,000,000 shares	$ 11.6	$ 11.6
Preference Stock—at $1 per share par value (aggregate liquidation preference of $88.2); Authorized 20,000,000 shares	2.6	2.6
Common Stock—at $1 per share par value/Authorized 250,000,000 and 150,000,000 shares; Issued 112,699,869 and 111,882,276 shares	112.7	111.9
Held in Treasury, 1,992,189 and 1,996,715 shares at cost	(59.4)	(59.5)
Additional Paid-in Capital	1,850.6	1,948.6
Accumulated Deficit	(679.8)	(859.4)
Total common stockholders' equity	1,238.3	1,155.8
Total liabilities and stockholders' equity	5,700.3	5,782.4

Required **a.** Perform a horizontal and vertical analysis of Bethlehem Steel's financial statements in a manner similar to Illustrations 17.1 and 17.2.

b. Comment on the results obtained.

Problem 17–2
Perform trend analysis and comment on the results (L.O. 3)

Ford Motor Company is the world's second-largest producer of cars and trucks and ranks among the largest providers of financial services in the United States. The following information pertains to Ford:

(in millions)	1993	1994	1995
Sales	$91,568	$107,137	$110,496
Cost of goods sold	85,280	95,887	101,171
Gross margin	$ 6,288	$ 11,250	$ 9,325
Operating expenses	4,856	5,424	6,044
Net operating income	$ 1,432	$ 5,826	$ 3,281

Required **a.** Prepare a statement showing the trend percentages for each item, using 1993 as the base year.

b. Comment on the trends noted.

Problem 17–3
Compute working capital, current ratio, and acid-test ratio (L.O. 4)

The following data are for Clock Company:

	December 31	
	2000	**1999**
Notes payable (due in 90 days)	$ 75,200	$ 60,000
Merchandise inventory	240,000	208,000
Cash	100,000	128,000
Marketable securities	49,600	30,000
Accrued liabilities	19,200	22,000
Accounts receivable	188,000	184,000
Accounts payable	112,000	72,000
Allowance for uncollectible accounts	24,000	15,200
Bonds payable, due 2001	156,000	160,000
Prepaid expenses	6,400	7,360
Cash flow from operating activities	60,000	40,000

a. Compute the amount of working capital at both year-end dates.

b. Compute the current ratio at both year-end dates.

c. Compute the acid-test ratio at both year-end dates.

d. Compute the cash flow liquidity ratio at both year-end dates.

e. Comment briefly on the company's short-term financial position.

Required

Tulip Products, Inc., has a current ratio on December 31, 1999, of 2:1 before the following transactions were completed:

1. Sold a building for cash.
2. Exchanged old equipment for new equipment. (No cash was involved.)
3. Declared a cash dividend on preferred stock.
4. Sold merchandise on account (at a profit).
5. Retired mortgage notes that would have matured in 2007.
6. Issued a stock dividend to common stockholders.
7. Paid cash for a patent.
8. Temporarily invested cash in government bonds.
9. Purchased inventory for cash.
10. Wrote off an account receivable as uncollectible. Uncollectible amount is less than the balance of the Allowance for Uncollectible Accounts.
11. Paid the cash dividend on preferred stock that was declared earlier.
12. Purchased a computer and gave a two-year promissory note.
13. Collected accounts receivable.
14. Borrowed from the bank on a 120-day promissory note.
15. Discounted a customer's note. Interest expense was involved.

Problem 17–4
Determine effects of various transactions on working capital and current ratio (L.O. 4)

Consider each transaction independently of all the others.

Required

a. Indicate whether the amount of working capital will increase, decrease, or be unaffected by each of the transactions.

b. Indicate whether the current ratio will increase, decrease, or be unaffected by each of the transactions.

The following selected data are for three companies:

Problem 17–5
Compute rate of return on operating assets and demonstrate effects of various transactions on this rate of return (L.O. 4)

	Operating Assets	Net Operating Income	Net Sales
Company 1	$ 1,404,000	$ 187,200	$ 2,059,200
Company 2	8,424,000	608,400	18,720,000
Company 3	37,440,000	4,914,000	35,100,000

a. Determine the operating margin, turnover of operating assets, and rate of return on operating assets for each company.

b. In the subsequent year, the following changes took place (no other changes occurred):

Required

Company 1 bought some new machinery at a cost of $156,000. Net operating income increased by $12,480 as a result of an increase in sales of $249,600.

Company 2 sold some equipment it was using that was relatively unproductive. The book value of the equipment sold was $624,000. As a result of the sale of the equipment, sales declined by $312,000, and operating income declined by $6,240.

Company 3 purchased some new retail outlets at a cost of $6,240,000. As a result, sales increased by $9,360,000, and operating income increased by $499,200.

1. Which company has the largest absolute change in—
    a. Operating margin ratio?
    b. Turnover of operating assets?
    c. Rate of return on operating assets?

2. Which one realized the largest dollar change in operating income? Explain this change in relation to the changes in the rate of return on operating assets.

Problem 17–6
Compute EPS, rate of return on sales and stockholders' equity, and number of times interest earned for two years (L.O. 4)

The largest spice company in the world, McCormick & Company, Inc., produces a diverse array of specialty foods. The following information is for McCormick & Company, Inc.:

($ millions)	**1996**	**1995**
Net sales	$1,732,506	$1,691,086
Income before interest and taxes	95,545	171,904
Net income	41,918	97,521
Interest expense	33,811	39,298
Stockholders' equity	450,043	519,253
Common stock, no par value, November 30	161,030	160,653

Assume average common shares outstanding for 1996 and 1995 are 78,205 and 81,218 (in millions), respectively.

Required   Compute the following for both 1996 and 1995. Then compare and comment. Assume stockholders' equity for 1994 was $435,600.

a. EPS of common stock.

b. Net income to net sales.

c. Return on average common stockholders' equity.

d. Times interest earned ratio.

Problem 17–7
Compute numerous standard ratios (L.O. 4)

Parametric Technology Corporation is in the CAD/CAM/CAE industry and is the top supplier of software tools used to automate a manufacturing company. The following consolidated balance sheet and supplementary data are for Parametric for 1996:

PARAMETRIC TECHNOLOGY CORPORATION
Consolidated Balance Sheet
For September 30, 1996 (in thousands)
Assets

Current Assets	
Cash and cash equivalents	$201,614
Short-term investments	232,602
Accounts Receivable, net of allowances for doubtful accounts of $2,910	117,273
Other current assets	10,561
Total Current Assets	$562,050
Marketable investments	21,896
Property and equipment, net	36,517
Other Assets	38,754
Total Assets	$659,217

Liabilities and Stockholders' Equity

Current Liabilities	
Accounts payable and accrued expenses	$ 39,416
Accrued compensation	32,186
Deferred revenue	56,420
Income taxes	17,970
Total Current Liabilities	$145,992
Other liabilities	793

Stockholders' Equity

Preferred stock, $.01 par value; 5,000 shares authorized; none issued	
Common stock, $.01 par value; 215,000 shares authorized; 127,452 (1996) and 125,129 (1995) shares issued	1,275
Additional paid-in capital	207,039
Foreign currency translation adjustment	(1,316)
Retained earnings	306,638
Treasury stock, at cost, 23 (1996) and 0 (1995) shares	(1,164)
Unrealized loss on investments	(40)
Total Liabilities and Stockholders' Equity	$659,217

1. Net income $137,910.
2. Income before interest and taxes, $204,656.
3. Cost of goods sold, $56,454.
4. Net sales, $600,122.
5. Total interest expense for the year, $11,501.
6. Weighted-average number of shares outstanding, 126,279.

Supplementary data for 1996 (in millions)

Calculate the following ratios and show your computations. For calculations normally involving averages, such as average accounts receivable or average stockholders' equity, use year-end amounts if the information is not available to use averages.

Required

a. Current ratio.
b. Net income to average common stockholders' equity.
c. Number of days' sales in accounts receivable (assume 365 days in 1996).
d. EPS of common stock.
e. Times interest earned ratio.
f. Equity ratio.
g. Net income to net sales.
h. Total assets turnover.
i. Acid-test ratio.

Paper Company is considering switching from the FIFO method to the LIFO method of accounting for its inventory before it closes its books for the year. The January 1 merchandise inventory was $864,000. Following are data compiled from the adjusted trial balance at the end of the year:

Problem 17–8
Determine effects on ratios of change in accounting method (FIFO to LIFO)
(L.O. 4)

Merchandise inventory, December 31 (FIFO)	$1,008,000
Current liabilities	720,000
Net sales	2,520,000
Operating expenses	774,000
Current assets	1,890,000
Total assets (operating)	2,880,000
Cost of goods sold	1,458,000

If the switch to LIFO takes place, the December 31 merchandise inventory would be $900,000.

a. Compute the current ratio, inventory turnover ratio, and rate of return on operating assets assuming the company continues using FIFO.
b. Repeat **a** assuming the company adjusts its accounts to the LIFO inventory method.

Required

ALTERNATE PROBLEMS

Fruit of the Loom is one of the largest manufacturers of knit apparel in the world and has maintained a position of leadership as a vertically integrated low-cost producer in the industry. Fruit of the Loom's comparative statements of income and retained earnings for 1995 and 1994 are given below.

Problem 17–1A
Perform horizontal and vertical analysis and comment on the results
(L.O. 3)

FRUIT OF THE LOOM
Consolidated Statement of Earnings
For the Years Ended December 31, 1995, and 1994
($ Thousands, except per data share)

	December 31	
	(1) 1995	(2) 1994
Net sales	$2,403,100	$2,297,800
Cost of sales	1,885,700	1,651,300
Gross earnings	$ 517,400	$ 646,500
Selling, general and administrative expenses	429,700	376,300
Goodwill amortization	37,300	35,200
Impairment writedown of goodwill	158,500	0
Operating earnings (loss)	$ (108,100)	$ 235,000
Interest expense	(116,900)	(95,400)
Other expense-net	(21,700)	(6,100)
Earnings (loss) before income tax (benefit) expense, extraordinary item and cumulative effect of change in accounting principles	$ (246,700)	$ 133,500
Income tax (benefit) expense	(19,400)	73,200
Earnings (loss) before cumulative effect of change in accounting principles	$ (227,300)	$ 60,300
Cumulative effect of change in accounting principles: Pre-operating costs	(5,200)	0
Net earnings (loss)	$ (232,500)	$ 60,300
Retained Earnings, January 1	680,600	620,300
	$ 448,100	$ 680,600
Dividends	0	0
Retained Earnings, December 31	$ 448,100	$ 680,600

FRUIT OF THE LOOM
Consolidated Balance Sheet
As of December 31, 1995, and 1994
($ Thousands)

	December 31	
	(1) 1995	(2) 1994
Assets		
Current Assets		
Cash and cash equivalents (including restricted cash)	$ 26,500	$ 49,400
Notes and accounts receivable (less allowance for possible losses of $26,600,000 and $20.700,000, respectively)	261,000	295,600
Inventories		
Finished goods	522,300	496,200
Work in process	132,400	141,500
Materials and supplies	44,800	39,100
Other	72,800	54,800
Total current assets	$1,059,800	$1,076,600
Property, Plant and Equipment		
Land	$ 20,100	$ 19,300
Buildings, structures and improvements	486,400	435,600
Machinery and equipment	1,076,600	1,041,300
Construction in progress	24,200	35,200
Total property, plant, and equipment	$1,607,300	$1,531,400
Less accumulated depreciation	578,900	473,200
Net property, plant and equipment	$1,028,400	$1,058,200
Other Assets		
Goodwill (less accumulated amortization of $257,800,000 and $242,400,000, respectively)	$ 771,100	$ 965,800
Other	60,200	62,900
Total other assets	$ 831,300	$1,028,700
Total assets	$2,919,500	$3,163,500

Liabilities and Stockholders' Equity

Current Liabilities

Current maturities of long-term debt	$ 14,600	$ 23,100
Trade accounts payable	60,100	113,300
Accrued insurance obligations	38,800	23,600
Accrued advertising and promotion	23,800	23,400
Interest payable	16,000	18,300
Accrued payroll and vacation pay	15,300	33,100
Accrued pension	11,300	19,800
Other accounts payable and accrued expenses	123,900	77,200
Total current liabilities	$ 303,800	$ 331,800

Noncurrent Liabilities

Long-term debt	1,427,200	1,440,200
Net deferred income taxes	0	43,400
Other	292,900	222,300
Total noncurrent liabilities	$1,720,100	$1,705,900
Total Liabilities	$2,023,900	$2,037,700

Common Stockholders' Equity

Common stock and capital in excess of par value, $.01 par value; authorized, Class A, 200,000,000 shares, Class B, 30,000,000 shares; issued and outstanding:

Class A Common Stock, 69,268,701 and 69,160,349 shares, respectively	$ 465,600	$ 463,700
Class B Common Stock, 6,690,976 shares	4,400	4,400
Retained earnings	448,100	680,600
Currency translation and minimum pension liability adjustments	(22,500)	(22,900)
Total common stockholders' equity	$ 895,600	$1,125,800
Total liabilities and stockholders' equity	$2,919,500	$3,163,500

a. Perform a horizontal and vertical analysis of Fruit of the Loom's financial statements in a manner similar to those illustrated in this chapter.

b. Comment on the results of the analysis in **a**.

Required

Deere & Company manufactures, distributes, and finances a full range of agricultural equipment; a broad range of industrial equipment for construction, forestry, and public works; and a variety of lawn and grounds care equipment. The company also provides credit, health care, and insurance products for businesses and the general public. Consider the following information from the Deere & Company 1995 Annual Report:

Problem 17–2A
Perform trend analysis and comment on the results
(L.O. 3)

(in millions)	1992	1993	1994	1995
Sales	$6,961	$7,696	$8,977	$10,291
Cost of goods sold	4,892	5,369	6,020	6,922
Gross margin	$2,069	$2,327	$2,957	$ 3,369
Operating expenses	2,025	2,055	2,036	2,276
Net operating income	$ 44	$ 272	$ 921	$ 1,093

a. Prepare a statement showing the trend percentages for each item using 1992 as the base year.

b. Comment on the trends noted.

Required

The following data are for Toy Company:

Problem 17–3A
Compute working capital, current ratio, and acid-test ratio (L.O. 4)

| | December 31 | |
	2000	**1999**
Allowance for uncollectible accounts	$ 72,000	$ 57,000
Prepaid expenses	34,500	45,000
Accrued liabilities	210,000	186,000
Cash in Bank A	1,095,000	975,000
Wages payable	–0–	37,500
Accounts payable	714,000	585,000
Merchandise inventory	1,342,500	1,437,000
Bonds payable, due in 2001	615,000	594,000
Marketable securities	217,500	147,000
Notes payable (due in six months)	300,000	195,000
Accounts receivable	907,500	870,000
Cash flow from operating activities	192,000	180,000

Required **a.** Compute the amount of working capital at both year-end dates.

b. Compute the current ratio at both year-end dates.

c. Compute the acid-test ratio at both year-end dates.

d. Compute the cash flow liquidity ratio at both year-end dates.

e. Comment briefly on the company's short-term financial position.

Problem 17–4A
Determine effects of
various transactions on
working capital and current
ratio (L.O. 4)

On December 31, 2000, Energy Company's current ratio was 3:1 before the following transactions were completed:

1. Purchased merchandise on account.

2. Paid a cash dividend declared on November 15, 2000.

3. Sold equipment for cash.

4. Temporarily invested cash in trading securities.

5. Sold obsolete merchandise for cash (at a loss).

6. Issued 10-year bonds for cash.

7. Wrote off goodwill to retained earnings.

8. Paid cash for inventory.

9. Purchased land for cash.

10. Returned merchandise that had not been paid for.

11. Wrote off an account receivable as uncollectible. Uncollectible amount is less than the balance in the Allowance for Uncollectible Accounts.

12. Accepted a 90-day note from a customer in settlement of customer's account receivable.

13. Declared a stock dividend on common stock.

Required Consider each transaction independently of all the others.

a. Indicate whether the amount of working capital will increase, decrease, or be unaffected by each of the transactions.

b. Indicate whether the current ratio will increase, decrease, or be unaffected by each of the transactions.

Problem 17–5A
Compute rate of return on
operating assets and dem-
onstrate effects of various
transactions on this rate
of return (L.O. 4)

Digital Company has net operating income of $500,000 and operating assets of $2,000,000. Its net sales are $4,000,000.

The accountant for the company computes the rate of return on operating assets after computing the operating margin and the turnover of operating assets.

Required **a.** Show the computations the accountant made.

b. Indicate whether the operating margin and turnover increase or decrease after each of the following changes. Then determine what the actual rate of return on operating assets would be. The events are not interrelated; consider each separately, starting from the original earning power position. No other changes occurred.

(1) Sales increased by $160,000. There was no change in the amount of operating income and no change in operating assets.

(2) Management found some cost savings in the manufacturing process. The amount of reduction in operating expenses was $40,000. The savings resulted from the use of less materials to manufacture the same quantity of goods. As a result, average inventory was $16,000 lower than it otherwise would have been. Operating income was not affected by the reduction in inventory.

(3) The company invested $80,000 of cash (received on accounts receivable) in a plot of land it plans to use in the future (a nonoperating asset); income was not affected.

(4) The federal income tax rate increased and caused income tax expense to increase by $20,000. The taxes have not yet been paid.

(5) The company issued bonds and used the proceeds to buy $400,000 of machinery to be used in the business. Interest payments are $20,000 per year. Net operating income increased by $100,000 (net sales did not change).

Polaroid Corporation designs, manufactures, and markets worldwide instant photographic cameras and films, electronic imaging recording devices, conventional films, and light polarizing filters and lenses. The following information is for Polaroid:

Problem 17–6A
Compute EPS, rate of return on sales and stockholders' equity, and number of times interest earned for two years (L.O. 4)

($ millions)	1995	1994
Net sales	$2,236.9	$2,312.5
Income before interest and taxes	149.3	207.3
Net income	(140.2)	117.7
Interest expense	52.1	46.6
Stockholders' equity (on December 31, 1993, $717.6)	717.7	864.4
Common stock, par value $1, December 31	75.4	75.4

Compute the following for both 1995 and 1994. Then compare and comment.

Required

a. EPS of common stock.

b. Net income to net sales.

c. Net income to average common stockholders' equity.

d. Times interest earned ratio.

The Walt Disney Company operates several ranges of products from theme parks and resorts to broadcasting and other creative content. The following balance sheet and supplementary data are for The Walt Disney Company for 1996.

Problem 17–7A
Compute numerous standard ratios (L.O. 4)

THE WALT DISNEY COMPANY
Consolidated Balance Sheet
For September 30, 1996
(in millions)
Assets

Cash and cash equivalents		$ 278
Investments		454
Receivables		3,343
Inventories		951
Total current assets		$ 5,026
Film and television costs		3,912
Theme Parks, Resorts, and other property, at cost		
Attractions, buildings and equipment	$11,019	
Accumulated depreciation	(4,448)	
		6,571
Projects in process		1,342
Land		118
Intangible Assets, net		17,978
Other Assets		2,359
Total Assets		$37,306

Liabilities and Stockholders' Equity

Accounts Payable and other accrued liabilities		$ 6,374
Income Taxes Payable		582
Total current liabilities		$ 6,956
Borrowings		12,342
Unearned royalty and other advances		1,179
Deferred Income Taxes		743
Common shareholders' equity		
Common shares ($.01 par value)	$ 8,576	
Retained Earnings	7,933	
Cumulative translation and other adjustments	39	
Treasury shares	(462)	16,086
Total Liabilities and Stockholders' Equity		$37,306

Supplementary data required for 1996 (in millions)

1. Net income $1,214.
2. Income before interest and taxes, $2,499.
3. Cost of goods sold, $15,406.
4. Net sales, $18,739.
5. Inventory on September 30, 1995, $824.
6. Total interest expense for the year, $438.

Required   Calculate the following ratios and show your computations. For calculations normally involving averages, such as average stockholders' equity, use year-end amounts unless the necessary information is provided.

a.   Current ratio.

b.   Net income to average common stockholders' equity.

c.   Inventory turnover.

d.   Number of days' sales in accounts receivable (assume 365 days in 1996).

e.   EPS of common stock (ignore treasury stock).

f.   Times interest earned ratio.

g.   Equity ratio.

h.   Net income to net sales.

i.   Total assets turnover.

j.   Acid-test ratio.

Problem 17–8A
Determine effects on ratios of change in accounting method (FIFO to LIFO) (L.O. 4)

Cooper Company currently uses the FIFO method to account for its inventory but is considering a switch to LIFO before the books are closed for the year. Selected data for the year are:

Merchandise inventory, January 1	$1,430,000
Current assets	3,603,600
Total assets (operating)	5,720,000
Cost of goods sold (FIFO)	2,230,800
Merchandise inventory, December 31 (LIFO)	1,544,400
Merchandise inventory, December 31 (FIFO)	1,887,600
Current liabilities	1,144,000
Net sales	3,832,400
Operating expenses	915,200

Required   a.   Compute the current ratio, inventory turnover ratio, and rate of return on operating assets assuming the company continues using FIFO.

b.   Repeat **a** assuming the company adjusts its accounts to the LIFO inventory method.

BEYOND THE NUMBERS—CRITICAL THINKING

The comparative balance sheets of the Darling Corporation for December 31, 2000, and 1999 follow:

Business Decision Case 17–1
Compute net income, identify reason for cash increase, state main sources of financing, and indicate further analyses needed (L.O. 3, 4)

DARLING CORPORATION
Comparative Balance Sheets
December 31, 2000, and 1999

	2000	1999
Assets		
Cash	$ 480,000	$ 96,000
Accounts receivable, net	86,400	115,200
Merchandise inventory	384,000	403,200
Plant and equipment, net	268,800	288,000
Total assets	$1,219,200	$902,400
Liabilities and Stockholders' Equity		
Accounts payable	$ 96,000	$ 96,000
Common stock	672,000	672,000
Retained earnings	451,200	134,400
Total liabilities and stockholders' equity	$1,219,200	$902,400

Based on your review of the comparative balance sheets, determine the following:

a. What was the net income for 2000 assuming there were no dividend payments?

b. What was the primary source of the large increase in the cash balance from 1999 to 2000?

c. What are the two main sources of assets for Darling Corporation?

d. What other comparisons and procedures would you use to complete the analysis of the balance sheet?

As Miller Manufacturing Company's internal auditor, you are reviewing the company's credit policy. The following information is from Miller's annual reports for 1997, 1998, 1999, and 2000:

Business Decision Case 17–2
Compute turnover ratios for four years and number of days' sales in accounts receivable; evaluate effectiveness of company's credit policy (L.O. 4)

	1997	1998	1999	2000
Net accounts receivable	$ 1,080,000	$ 2,160,000	$ 2,700,000	$ 3,600,000
Net sales	10,800,000	13,950,000	17,100,000	19,800,000

Management has asked you to calculate and analyze the following in your report:

a. If cash sales account for 30% of all sales and credit terms are always 1/10, n/60, determine all turnover ratios possible and the number of days' sales in accounts receivable at all possible dates. (The number of days' sales in accounts receivable should be based on year-end accounts receivable and net credit sales.)

b. How effective is the company's credit policy?

Wendy Prince has consulted you about the possibility of investing in one of three companies (Apple, Inc., Baker Company, or Cookie Corp.) by buying its common stock. The companies' shares are selling at about the same price. The long-term capital structures of the companies are as follows:

Business Decision Case 17–3
Analyze investment alternatives (L.O. 3, 4)

	Apple, Inc.	Baker Company	Cookie Corp.
Bonds with a 10% interest rate			$2,400,000
Preferred stock with an 8% dividend rate		$2,400,000	
Common stock, $10 par value	$4,800,000	2,400,000	2,400,000
Retained earnings	384,000	384,000	384,000
Total long-term equity	$5,184,000	$5,184,000	$5,184,000
Number of common shares outstanding	480,000	240,000	240,000

Prince has already consulted two investment advisers. One adviser believes that each of the companies will earn $300,000 per year before interest and taxes. The other adviser believes that each company will earn about $960,000 per year before interest and taxes. Prince has asked you to write a report covering these points:

a. Compute each of the following, using the estimates made by the first and second advisers.

   (1) Earnings available for common stockholders assuming a 40% tax rate.

   (2) EPS of common stock.

   (3) Rate of return on total stockholders' equity.

b. Which stock should Prince select if she believes the first adviser?

c. Are the stockholders as a group (common and preferred) better off with or without the use of long-term debt in the companies?

Annual Report Analysis 17–4
Analyze management's objectives and performance from the viewpoints of a creditor and an investor (real world problem)
(L.O. 3, 4)

The following selected financial data excerpted from the 1995 annual report of Maytag Corporation represents the summary information which management presented for interested parties to review:

MAYTAG CORPORATION
Selected Financial Data
($ thousands except per share data)

	1995	1994	1993	1992	1991
Net sales	$3,039,524	$3,372,515	$2,987,054	$3,041,223	$2,970,626
Cost of sales	2,250,616	2,496,065	2,262,942	2,339,406	2,254,221
Income taxes	74,800	90,200	38,600	15,900	44,400
Income (loss) from continuing operations . .	(14,996)	151,137	51,270	(8,354)	79,017
Percent of income (loss) from continuing operations to net sales	(0.5%)	4.5%	1.7%	(0.3%)	2.7%
Income (loss) from continuing operations per share	($0.14)	$ 1.42	$ 0.48	($0.08)	$ 0.75
Dividends paid per share	0.515	0.50	0.50	0.50	0.50
Average shares outstanding (in thousands)	107,062	106,795	106,252	106,077	105,761
Working capital	$ 543,431	$ 595,703	$ 406,181	$ 452,626	$ 509,025
Depreciation of property, plant and equipment	102,572	110,044	102,459	94,032	83,352
Additions to property, plant and equipment . .	152,914	84,136	99,300	129,891	143,372
Total assets	2,125,066	2,504,327	2,469,498	2,501,490	2,535,068
Long-term debt	536,579	663,205	724,695	789,232	809,480
Total debt to capitalization	45.9%	50.7%	60.6%	58.7%	45.9%
Shareowners' equity per share of common stock . .	$ 6.05	$ 6.82	$ 5.50	$ 5.62	$ 9.50

Required a. As a creditor, what do you believe management's objectives should be? Which of the preceding items of information would assist a creditor in judging management's performance?

b. As an investor, what do you believe management's objectives should be? Which of the preceding items of information would assist an investor in judging management's performance?

c. What other information might be considered useful?

Refer to the excerpt from BellSouth Corporation's annual report, in "A Broader Perspective" (page 649). Explain why the dividends per share continued to increase in 1995 and 1996 despite a loss in 1995.

Annual Report Analysis 17–5
Discuss payout ratio
(L.O. 4)

Choose a company the class wants to know more about and obtain its annual report. In groups of two or three students, calculate either the liquidity, equity, profitability, or market test ratios. Each group should select a spokesperson to tell the rest of the class the results of the group's calculations. Finally, the class should decide whether or not to invest in the corporation based on the ratios they calculated.

Group Project 17–6
Analyze an annual report

In a group of two or three students, go to the library and attempt to locate Dun & Bradstreet's Industry Norms and Key Business Ratios. You may have to ask the reference librarian for assistance to see if this item is available at your institution. If it is not available at your institution, ask if it is available through an interlibrary loan. (Obviously, if you cannot obtain this item, you cannot do this project.) Then select and obtain the latest annual report of a company of your choice. Determine the company's SIC Code (a code that indicates the industry in which that company operates). SIC Codes for specific companies are available on COMPACT DISCLOSURE, an electronic source that may be available at your library. As an alternative, you could call the company's home office to inquire about its SIC Code. The annual report often contains the company's phone number. From the annual report, determine various ratios for the company, such as the current ratio, debt to equity ratio, and net income to net sales. Then compare these ratios to the industry norms for the company's SIC Code as given in the Dun & Bradstreet source. Write a report to your instructor summarizing the results of your investigation.

Group Project 17–7
Analyze a company's performance against industry norms

In a group of two or three students, obtain the annual report of a company of your choice (other than one of the companies in the annual reports booklet that came with the text). Identify the major sections of the annual report and the order in which they appear. Would you recommend the order be changed to emphasize the most useful and important information? If so, how? Then describe some specific useful information in each section. Comment on your perceptions of the credibility that a reader of the annual report could reasonably assign to each section of the report. For instance, if such a discussion appears in the annual report you select, would you assign high credibility to everything that appears in the Letter to Stockholders regarding the company's future prospects? Write a report to your instructor summarizing the results of your investigation.

Group Project 17–8
Analyze the major sections of an annual report

USING THE INTERNET—A VIEW OF THE REAL WORLD

Visit the following website for IBM Corporation:
http://www.ibm.com
By following choices on the screen, locate the income statements and balance sheets for the latest two years. Calculate all of the ratios illustrated in the chapter for which the data are available. Compare the ratios to those shown for Colgate-Palmolive as presented in the chapter. Write a report to your instructor showing your calculations and comment on the results of your comparison of the two companies.

Internet Project 17–9
Analyze an annual report retrieved on the Internet

Visit the following website for General Electric Company:
http://www.ge.com
By following choices on the screen, locate the income statements and balance sheets for the latest two years. Calculate all of the ratios illustrated in the chapter for which the data are available. Compare the ratios to those shown for Colgate-Palmolive as presented in the chapter. Write a report to your instructor showing your calculations and comment on the results of your comparison of the two companies.

Internet Project 17–10
Analyze an annual report retrieved on the Internet

ANSWERS TO SELF-TEST

TRUE-FALSE

1. **True.** Financial statement analysis consists of applying analytical tools and techniques to financial statements and other relevant data to obtain useful information.
2. **False.** Horizontal analysis provides useful information about the changes in a company's performance over several periods by analyzing comparative financial statements of the same company for two or more successive periods.
3. **False.** Common-size statements show only percentage figures, such as percentages of total assets and percentages of net sales.

4. **True.** Liquidity ratios such as the current ratio and acid-test ratio indicate a company's short-term debt-paying ability.
5. **True.** The accrual net income shown on the income statement is not cash basis income and does not indicate cash flows.
6. **True.** Analysts must use comparable data when making comparisons of items for different periods or different companies.

MULTIPLE-CHOICE

1. **b.** Current assets:

    $$\$136,000 + \$64,000 + \$184,000$$
    $$+ \$244,000 + \$12,000 = \$640,000$$

    Current liabilities:

    $$\$256,000 + \$64,000 = \$320,000$$

    Current ratio:
    $$\$640,000/\$320,000 = 2{:}1$$

2. **c.** Quick assets:

    $$\$136,000 + \$64,000 + \$184,000 = \$384,000$$

    Current liabilities:

    $$256,000 + \$64,000 = \$320,000$$

    Acid-test ratio:
    $$\$384,000/\$320,000 = 1.2{:}1$$

3. **a.** Net sales:

    $$\$4,620,000$$

Average accounts receivable:

$$(\$720,000 + \$960,000)/2 = \$840,000$$

Accounts receivable turnover:

$$\$4,620,000/\$840,000 = 5.5$$

4. **c.** Cost of goods sold:

    $$\$3,360,000$$

    Average inventory:

    $$(\$900,000 + \$1,020,000)/2 = \$960,000$$

    Inventory turnover:

    $$\$3,360,000/\$960,000 = 3.5$$

5. **b.** Income before interest and taxes $720,000
    Interest on bonds 192,000

    Times interest earned ratio:

    $$\$720,000/\$192,000 = 3.75 \text{ times}$$

CHECK FIGURES

Chapter 1

E1-1	No check figure
E1-2	(b) $12,900
E1-3	(a) $22,500
E1-4	RE at beg. $105,000
E1-5	No check figure
E1-6	No check figure
E1-7	No check figure
E1-8	No check figure
E1-9	No check figure
E1-10	Net income, $105,000
E1-11	RE, Aug. 31, $196,400
E1-12	Total assets, $290,000
E1-13	1995 equity ratio, 35.5%
P1-1	Cash, $78,400
P1-2	(b) Total assets, $208,610
P1-3	(a) Net income, $124,235
P1-4	(d) Total assets, $272,200
P1-5	No check figure
P1-1A	Cash, $148,660
P1-2A	(b) Total assets, $412,000
P1-3A	Net income, $13,500
P1-4A	(b) Net income, $160,000
P1-5A	No check figure
BDC1-1	No check figure
ARA1-2	No check figure
ARA1-3	No check figure
EC1-4	No check figure

Chapter 2

E2-1	No check figure
E2-2	No check figure
E2-3	(a) Dr. Cash, Cr. Capital Stock, $100,000
E2-4	(b) Dr. Cash, Cr. Notes Payable, $30,000
E2-5	(b) Dr. Salaries Expense, Cr. Cash, $24,000
E2-6	(f) Paid rent, $600
E2-7	Trial balance total, $214,600
E2-8	(d) Dr. Cash, Cr. Accts. Rec., $4,800
E2-9	Cash balance, $37,500
E2-10	Trial balance total, $330,720
E2-11	No check figure
E2-12	Cash and cash equivalents increase, 135%
P2-1	Aug. 31, Dr. Dividends, Cr. Cash, $1,000
P2-2	(c) Trial balance total, $758,800
P2-3	(d) Trial balance total, $963,060
P2-4	(d) Trial balance total, $358,100
P2-5	Trial balance total, $624,000
P2-1A	Mar. 2, Dr. Rent Expense, Cr. Cash, $6,000
P2-2A	Trial balance total, $231,400
P2-3A	(d) Trial balance total, $766,400
P2-4A	(d) Trial balance total, $512,340
P2-5A	Trial balance total, $658,800
BDC-2-1	(c) Net income, $9,900
ARA2-2	Short-term investments decrease, 62%
ARA2-3	No check figure
EC2-4	No check figure

Chapter 3

E3-1	No check figure
E3-2	No check figure
E3-3	No check figure
E3-4	Dr. Insurance Expense, $1,000
E3-5	Dr. Rent Expense, $4,000
E3-6	No check figure
E3-7	Supplies expense, $5,500
E3-8	Depreciation expense, $20,000
E3-9	Dec. 31, Dr. Unearned Subscriptions, $40,000
E3-10	June 30, Dr. Unearned Ticket Fees, $30,000
E3-11	Cr. Service Revenue, $30,000
E3-12	Cr. Interest Payable, $300
E3-13	Dr. Salaries Expense, $6,000
E3-14	(a) Net income for 1999 overstated, $8,000
E3-15	No check figure
E3-16	1995, 146
P3-1	Dr. Rent Expense, $20,000
P3-2	(a) Dr. Supplies Expense, $7,000
P3-3	(c) Dr. Insurance Expense, $7,200
P3-4	1999, Corrected net income, $192,100
P3-5	(b) June 5, Dr. Rent Expense, $2,000
P3-1A	Dr. Supplies Expense, $1,800
P3-2A	(a) Cr. Subscriptions Revenue, $5,000
P3-3A	(3) Dr. Depreciation Expense— Buildings, $6,000
P3-4A	1999, Corrected net income, $224,800
P3-5A	(b) Dec. 3, Cr. Subscriptions Revenue, $6,000
BDC3-1	No check figure
BDC3-2	(b) Net income, $66,000
ARA3-3	1996, 374

Chapter 4

E4-1	No check figure
E4-2	No check figure
E4-3	No check figure
E4-4	No check figure
E4-5	No check figure
E4-6	Net income, $182,100
E4-7	RE, Dec. 31, 1999, $116,000
E4-8	(b) Correct net income, $90,000
E4-9	Dec. 31, Cr. to RE, $182,100
E4-10	No check figure
E4-11	RE, ending balance, $860,000
E4-12	Dec. 31, Cr. to RE, $182,563
E4-13	No check figure
E4-14	No check figure
E4-15	Current ratio, 1995, 1.25:1
P4-1	To close the expense accounts Dr. Income Summary, $178,700
P4-2	(a) Net income, $157,600
P4-3	Net income, $35,600
P4-4	Net loss, $49,617
P4-5	Net income, $81,234
P4-1A	June 30, Dr. Income Summary, Cr. RE, $108,700
P4-2A	(a) Net income, $188,950
P4-3A	(a) Net income, $147,184
P4-4A	(a) Net income, $124,410
P4-5A	(a) Net loss, $1,480
BDC4-1	Net income, $56,550
ARA4-2	The Coca-Cola Company, Current ratio, 1996, .80:1
BP4-3	No check figure
CRP4-1	(e) Net income, $61,800

Chapter 5

E5-1	No check figure
E5-2	(b) Net income, $72,000
E5-3	Revenue, $125 million
E5-4	(b) Net income understated by $4,100
E5-5	(b) Gross margin, $2,000,000
E5-6	No check figure
P5-1	No check figure
P5-2	(b) Net income, $322,000
P5-3	(b) Net income, $13,800,000
P5-4	No check figure
P5-5	No check figure
P5-1A	No check figure
P5-2A	(b) Net income, $20,000
P5-3A	(b) Net income, $9,900,000
P5-4A	No check figure
P5-5A	No check figure
BDC5-1	No check figure
ARA5-2	No check figure
EC5-3	No check figure

Chapter 6

E6-1	No check figure
E6-2	(a) Silver Co., Dr. Purchases, $56,000
E6-3	Cash discount, $1,536
E6-4	Gross selling price less cash discount, $17,781.12
E6-5	(a) Cash paid, $32,928
E6-6	(a) Cash paid, $1,881.60
E6-7	(a) June 24, Cr. Cash, $81,480

E6-8	Cost of goods sold, $49,300
E6-9	Case 1, Gross margin, $288,000
E6-10	No check figure
E6-11	No check figure
E6-12	Dr. Income Summary, $822
P6-1	(b) Aug. 14, Cr. Cash, $113,680
P6-2	Cash discount, $2,674.56
P6-3	(d) Net income, $162,144
P6-4	(c) Trial balance total, $997,898
P6-5	(b) Net income, $302,560
P6-1A	(a) Apr. 10, Dr. Cash, $234,259.20
P6-2A	July 31, Cr. Cash, $31,131.18
P6-3A	(c) Trial balance total, $2,770,560
P6-4A	(d) Net income, $124,068
P6-5A	(b) Net income, $122,420
BDC6-1	(a) Net income, 1998, $49,500
BDC6-2	1996, Gross margin percentage, 48.76%
ARA6-3	1996, Operating income, $3,915M
EC6-4	No check figure

Chapter 7

E7-1	Corrected income, 1999, $418,784
E7-2	No check figure
E7-3	Ending inventory, $170,220
E7-4	Ending inventory, $162,480
E7-5	Ending inventory, $5,600
E7-6	(a) Weighted average ending inventory, $18,141.12
E7-7	Sept. 20, Dr. to Cost of Goods Sold, $2,016
E7-8	(6) Dr. to Cost of Goods Sold, $18,816
E7-9	(5) Dr. to Cost of Goods Sold, $4,835
E7-10	Ending inventory, $2,952
E7-11	Paper profits, $3,000
E7-12	No check figure
E7-13	Carrying amount for used auto, $72,000
E7-14	Dr. Loss Due to Decline in Market Value of Inventory, $240
E7-15	Lower of cost or market, $50,640
E7-16	Lower of cost or market, $51,360
E7-17	Estimated inventory, $201,600
E7-18	Estimated inventory, $684,000
E7-19	Estimated inventory at cost, $30,175
P7-1	Corrected income, 1999, $304,800
P7-2	(a) Corrected income, 1996, $270,000
P7-3	(a) Gross margin, $80,500
P7-4	(a) Cost of Goods Sold, $1,776.24
P7-5	(a) (2) LIFO-perpetual, ending inventory, $32,160
	(b) (2) LIFO-periodic, ending inventory, $22,680
P7-6	(a) Oct. 15, Dr. Cost of Goods Sold, $25,800
P7-7	(a) (1) FIFO-perpetual, ending inventory, $46,950 (same as FIFO-periodic)
P7-8	(a) Gross margin, $808,000
P7-9	Lower of cost or market, $189,056

P7-10	(b) Estimated inventory, $802,882
P7-11	Estimated ending inventory at cost, $126,000
P7-1A	Corrected income, 1999, $345,000
P7-2A	(a) Corrected income, 1996, $644,000
P7-3A	(a) Gross margin, $100,920
P7-4A	Mar. 31, Dr. Cost of Goods Sold, $388
P7-5A	(a) (2) LIFO-perpetual, ending inventory, $117,600
	(b) (2) LIFO-periodic, ending inventory, $112,400
P7-6A	(a) Mar. 25, Dr. Cost of Goods Sold, $80,100
P7-7A	(a) (1) FIFO-perpetual, ending inventory, $8,712 (same as FIFO-periodic)
P7-8A	(a) Gross margin, $374,400
P7-9A	Lower of cost or market, $88,848
P7-10A	(b) Net income, first quarter, $36,800
P7-11A	Estimated ending inventory at cost, $47,880
BDC7-1	(a) Green, net income, $6,100
BDC7-2	Estimated inventory, $70,400
ARA7-3	Inventory turnover, 6.51 times
EC7-4	No check figure

Chapter 8

E8-1	No check figure
E8-2	No check figure
E8-3	Adjusted cash balance, $14,915
E8-4	Adjusted cash balance, $14,070
E8-5	Cr. Cash, $126
E8-6	Checks outstanding at March 31, $24,000
E8-7	Deposits in transit, $4,740
E8-8	Adjusted cash balance, $4,401
E8-9	Cr. cash, $340
E8-10	No check figure
E8-11	Dec. 2, Dr. Petty Cash, $900
P8-1	Adjusted cash balance, $28,935
P8-2	Adjusted cash balance, $136,350
P8-3	Mar. 31, Cr. Cash, $258.50
P8-4	June 30, Cr. Cash Short and Over, $2.10
P8-1A	Adjusted cash balance, $30,626.39
P8-2A	Adjusted cash balance, $53,821
P8-3A	Dec. 31, Cr. Petty Cash, $97.95
P8-4A	Apr. 30, Cr. Cash, $156.93
BDC8-1	No check figure
BDC8-2	No check figure
BDC8-3	(b) Corrected cash balance, $23,003.80
ARA8-4	No check figure
ARA8-5	Quick ratio, 1996, .64:1
EC8-6	No check figure
GP8-7	No check figure

Chapter 9

E9-1	(b) Dr. Uncollectible Accounts Expense, $4,750
E9-2	Required allowance balance, $42,075
E9-3	No check figure
E9-4	(a) Dr. Credit Card Expense, $2,400
E9-5	Sales tax payable, $20,000
E9-6	Full amount, $32M
E9-7	No check figure

E9-8	Crawford, Inc., Dr. Interest Expense, $800
E9-9	Dunston, Inc., Dr. Accounts Receivable—Crawford, Inc., $20,800
E9-10	(a) Dr. Discount on Notes Payable, $400
E9-11	(a) Dr. Interest Expense, $400
E9-12	No. of days' sales in accounts receivable, 132.73 days
P9-1	(b) Dr. Uncollectible Accounts Expense, $16,750
P9-2	Dr. Credit Card Expense, $500
P9-3	(a) July 1, Cr. Sales Tax Payable, $1,200
P9-4	(a) Estimated product warranty payable, $12,000
P9-5	July 14, Cr. Interest Revenue, $5,400
P9-6	(a) Nov. 1, Dr. Discount on Notes Payable, $4,500
P9-1A	(b) Dr. Uncollectible Accounts Expense, $2,450
P9-2A	Dr. Cash, $3,880
P9-3A	(a) Jan. 2, Cr. Sales Tax Payable, $4,000
P9-4A	(a) Estimated product warranty payable, $114,000
P9-5A	Sept. 29, Dr. Dishonored Notes Receivable, $104,000
P9-6A	Dec. 31, Dr. Interest Expense, $450
BDC9-1	(a) Total benefit, $96,600
BDC9-2	No check figure
ARA9-3	The Coca-Cola Company, Accounts receivable turnover, 11.12 times

Chapter 10

E10-1	Total cost of land, $702,400
E10-2	Total cost of land, $522,000
E10-3	Total cost of machine, $734,400
E10-4	Cost of machine, $20,000
E10-5	1998, Dec. 31, Dr. Depreciation Expense— Office Furniture, $6,000
E10-6	Double-declining balance, 1998, $180,000
E10-7	Asset cost, $144,000
E10-8	(a) 1999, Depreciation, SOYD method, $20,400
E10-9	Depreciation expense, first year, $2,000
E10-10	Depreciation for 2001, $11,200
E10-11	No check figure
E10-12	Depreciation for 1999, $20,400
E10-13	Depreciation for 2000, $11,200
E10-14	Net income overstated in 1999, $1,000
E10-15	Net income overstated in 1998, $96,000
P10-1	Total cost of machine, $460,400
P10-2	Total cost of land, $1,374,240
P10-3	(a) Total cost of truck, $32,160
P10-4	(a) Total cost of land, $318,000
P10-5	(c) SOYD depreciation expense, $24,444
P10-6	(c) DDB depreciation expense, 1999, $10,200
P10-1A	Total cost of machine, $123,840
P10-2A	Total cost of land, $209,832
P10-3A	(c) Dr. Depreciation Expense— Machinery, $39,583
P10-4A	(a) Total cost of building, $254,080

P10-5A	(c) SOYD depreciation in 1998, $192,000	P12-1	1998 (Assumption A) Preferred dividend, $62,400	P13-2A	Nov. 16, Cr. Paid-In Capital— Stock Dividend, $96,000
P10-6A	(c) DDB depreciation in 1999, $23,438	P12-2	(b) Total assets, $4,000,000	P13-3A	1998, Apr. 2, Cr. Paid-In Capital—Stock Dividend, $25,000
BDC10-1	(a) Cost of land, $771,600	P12-3	(a) Total assets, $1,056,000		
BDC10-2	(a) (4) DDB depreciation, $50,400	P12-4	(b) Total stockholders' equity, $9,216,000	P13-4A	Unappropriated retained earnings, Dec. 31, $1,336,000
BDC10-3	No check figure	P12-5	(b) Total book value of common stock, $615,000	P13-5A	(3) Cr. Paid-In Capital— Common Treasury Stock Transactions, $19,200
BDC10-4	1996 Coca-Cola Company, rate of return, 24.22%	P12-6	(1) Total book value of common stock, $902,400		
ARA10-5	No check figure	P12-7	(c) Total cash payment, $1,017,600	P13-6A	(b) Total stockholders' equity, $17,942,000

Chapter 11

E11-1	(a) Dr. Loss on Disposal of Plant Assets, $2,700	P12-1A	1997 (Assumption A) Preferred dividend, $102,000	P13-7A	(b) Retained earnings, Oct 31, 1998, $36,930
E11-2	Cr. Gain on Disposal of Plant Assets, $2,700	P12-2A	(a) Jan. 29, Dr. Organization Costs, $744,000	P13-8A	(a) Net income, $48,000
E11-3	(b). Dr. Fire Loss, $7,500	P12-3A	(a) Total assets, $191,200	BDC13-1	(a). Cash dividends Jones will receive, $21,120
E11-4	Dr. Loss on Disposal of Plant Assets, $4,050	P12-4A	(b) Total stockholders' equity, $1,769,000	BDC13-2	No check figure
E11-5	(e) Dr. Loss on Disposal of Plant Assets, $30,000	P12-5A	(b) Total book value of common stock, $546,000	ARA13-3	(c) Coca-Cola Company's P-E ratio, 37.59
E11-6	Depletion per ton, $1.08	P12-6A	(b) Total book value of common stock, $2,514,600	EC13-4	No check figure
E11-7	Depletion per ton, $0.72	P12-7A	Book value of preferred stock, $967,500		
E11-8	Depreciation for year, $112,500	BDC12-1	(a) Rudd Co., common stock dividends, $4,320,000	**Chapter 14**	
E11-9	Amortization each year 1995–2000, $5,850	BDC12-2	(a) East Corporation, Book value per share of common, $113	E14-1	Nov. 1, Cr. Realized Gain on Trading Securities, $46,944
E11-10	Dr. Franchise Amortization Expense, $1,350	ARA12-3	1996, Maytag, ratio of net income to ave. s/h equity, 22.53%	E14-2	Dec. 31, 1999, Dr. Unrealized Loss on Trading Securities, $720
E11-11	Dec. 31, Dr. Rent Expense, $54,000	EC12-4	No check figure	E14-3	(c) Dr. Realized Loss on Available-for-Sale Securities, $13,440
E11-12	Goodwill, $180,000			E14-4	Dr. Loss from Sim Company, $93,750
P11-1	(b) Dr. Loss on Disposal of Plant Assets, $2,880	**Chapter 13**		E14-5	(b) Dr. Common Stock (TRD Company), $6,720,000
P11-2	(a) Book value of truck, $24,300	E13-1	Total stockholders' equity, $7,720,000	E14-6	(a) Goodwill = $840,000
P11-3	Dr. Loss on Disposal of Plant Assets, $540	E13-2	Feb. 1, Cr. Dividends Payable, $60,000	E14-7	(b) Dr. Goodwill, $302,400
P11-4	Oct. 1, Dr. Trucks (D), $106,680	E13-3	Dec. 31, Cr. Dividends Payable, $182,000	E14-8	(b) Excess of cost over book value, $506,250
P11-5	Dr. Depletion, $246,000	E13-4	(a) Cr. Stock Dividends Distributed—Common, $900,000	E14-9	(a) Book value of investment, $24,624,000
P11-6	Patent amortization expense, 1999, $14,400	E13-5	(b) Cr. Paid-In Capital—Stock Dividend, $30,000	E14-10	(a) Dec. 31, 1999, balance in investment account, $2,984,400
P11-7	(a) Dr. Patent Amortization Expense, $19,200	E13-6	(a) Dr. Retained Earnings, $900,000	P14-1	(b) Dec. 31, Dr. Unrealized Loss on Market Decline of Available-for-Sale Securities, $18,000
P11-1A	Dr. Loss on Disposal of Plant Assets, $900	E13-7	(a) Book value per share, $40		
P11-2A	(a) Book Value, $42,750	E13-8	Cr. Paid-in Capital— Donations, $62,400	P14-2	(a) Nov. 2, Cr. Realized Gain on Sale of Trading Securities, $6,732
P11-3A	Dr. Moving Vans (new), $30,025	E13-9	(a) Net income, $3,600,000	P14-3	(b) Jan. 1, 1999, Cr. Minority Interest, $840,000
P11-4A	Dec. 31, Dr. Depreciation Expense—Buildings, $124,020	E13-10	Retained earnings, Dec. 31, $99,200	P14-4	(b) Dec. 31, 2001, Investment account balance, $9,025,170
P11-5A	(b) Depreciation for 1998, $10,000	E13-11	Net income per share, $19.03	P14-5	(b) Total assets, $13,590,000
P11-6A	1999, Dec. 31, Dr. Patent Amortization Expense, $22,200	E13-12	(a) Earnings per share, 1999, $10.72	P14-6	Goodwill, $324,000
		P13-1	Total paid-in capital, $7,010,000	P14-7	(a) Net income, $860,892
P11-7A	(c) Dr. Rent Expense, $28,800			P14-1A	(a) Nov. 3, Realized Gain on Trading Securities, $9,504
BDC11-1	(a) Cr. Gain on Disposal of Plant Assets, $33,000	P13-2	Dec. 1, Cr. Paid-In Capital— Stock Dividend, $2,400	P14-2A	(a) Dec. 31, 1999, Dr. Unrealized Loss on Trading Securities, $31,680
BDC11-2	(a) (2) Goodwill, $750,000	P13-3	(4) Cr. Dividends Payable, $140,000		
ARA11-3	1996, 147.33%	P13-4	Aug. 4, Cr. Paid-In Capital— Stock Dividend, $400,000	P14-3A	(b) Jan. 1, 1999, Cr. Minority Interest, $1,008,000
EC11-4	No check figure	P13-5	Unappropriated retained earnings, $6,518,400	P14-4A	(b) Dec. 31, 2001, Investment account balance, $1,488,270
Chapter 12		P13-6	(b) Total stockholders' equity, $1,452,000	P14-5A	(b) Total assets, $7,578,000
E12-1	Preferred dividends, $100,000			P14-6A	Goodwill, $450,000
E12-2	Preferred dividends, $72,000	P13-7	(b) Appropriated retained earnings, $18,000	P14-7A	(a) Net income, $585,000
E12-3	Dr. Cash, $1,120,000	P13-8	Net loss, $36,000	P14-8A	No check figure
E12-4	Dr. Cash, $680,000	P13-1A	Total stockholders' equity, $5,496,000	BDC14-1	No check figure
E12-5	Dr. Land, $72,000			BDC14-2	(b) Total assets, $2,610,000
E12-6	Cr. Common Stock, $18,000			BDC14-3	1995, Dividend yield on common stock, 2.58%
E12-7	Dr. Organization Costs, $480,000			ARA14-4	No check figure
E12-8	Book value, $18 per share				

Chapter 15

E15-1	Sept. 30, 1999, Cr. Bond Interest Payable, $1,200
E15-2	(c) Total price, $1,400,605
E15-3	Bond interest expense, $147,940
E15-4	Dr. Premium on Bonds Payable, $2,471
E15-5	Dr. Loss on Bond Redemption, $24,000
E15-6	Cr. Gain on Bond Redemption, $19,200
E15-7	Dr. Bond Interest Expense, $540
E15-8	Cr. Paid-in Capital in Excess of Par—Common, $20,000
E15-9	1995 times interest earned ratio, 7.04 times
E15-10	Present value, $12,418.40
E15-11	Present value, $77,217.30
E15-12	(c) Present value, $1,434,132
E15-13	Future value, $720,524
P15-1	Dec. 1, 1998, Cr. Bond Interest Payable, $11,250
P15-2	(a) Price to be offered, $958,343
P15-3	Jan. 1, Cr. Discount on Bonds Payable, $377
P15-4	(a) Price received, $564,225
P15-5	(a) Price received, $84,954
P15-6	(a) July 1, 2003, Dr. Bond Interest Expense, $24,000
P15-1A	June 1, 1998, Cr. Bond Interest Payable, $4,800
P15-2A	(a) Price to be offered, $469,169
P15-3A	Jan. 1 Cr. Discount on Bonds Payable, $1,871
P15-4A	(a) Price received, $260,185
P15-5A	(a) Price received, $447,698
P15-6A	July 1, 2003, Dr. Bond Interest Expense, $36,000
BDC15-1	Alternative (1), EPS, $5.83
BDC15-2	No check figure
BDC15-3	No check figure
ARA15-4	The Limited, Inc., times interest earned ratio, 8.44 times
ARA15-5	No check figure
EC15-6	No check figure

Chapter 16

E16-1	No check figure
E16-2	Cost of goods sold, cash basis, $288,000
E16-3	No check figure
E16-4	Net cash provided by operating activities, $193,000
E16-5	Net cash provided by operating activities, $448,000
E16-6	No check figure
E16-7	Purchase of plant assets, $20,000
E16-8	Net cash provided by operating activities, $47,000
E16-9	No check figure
P16-1	(b) Net cash provided by operating activities, $256,000
P16-2	Net cash provided by operating activities, $71,250
P16-3	(i) Cash flow liquidity ratio, 17.37 times
P16-4	(h) Cash flow margin ratio, 10.39%
P16-5	(b) Net cash provided by operating activities, $66,750
P16-1A	(b) Net cash provided by operating activities, $428,000
P16-2A	Net cash provided by operating activities, $39,555
P16-3A	(h) Cash flow margin ratio, 17.67%
P16-4A	(g) Cash flow per share of common stock ratio, $1.40
P16-5A	(b) Net cash provided by operating activities, $217,700
BDC16-1	Net cash provided by operating activities, $(7,500)
BDC16-2	Net cash provided by operating activities, $149,500
ARA16-3	The Coca-Cola Company, 2.78 times
ARA16-4	No check figure
ARA16-5	(a) Maytag Corporation, Cash-flow per share, $2.11

Chapter 17

E17-1	Net income increase, 18.1%
E17-2	(a) (3) Current ratio, 1.75:1
E17-3	(a) 91.25 days
E17-4	Cash flow margin, 1.39%
E17-5	Inventory turnover, 5.2 times
E17-6	Rate of return on operating assets, 19.2%
E17-7	Return on average common stockholders' equity, 24%
E17-8	EPS, $8 per share
E17-9	Weighted-average no. of shares, 852,000
E17-10	EPS for 1998, $1
E17-11	No. of times interest earned, 7.25 times
E17-12	(a) Times preferred dividend earned, 6 times
E17-13	P-E ratio, 72
P17-1	(a) Net sales increase, 1.0%
P17-2	(a) Operating expenses, 1995, 124.46%
P17-3	(c) Acid-test ratio, 2000, 1.52:1
P17-4	No check figure
P17-5	(a) Co. 1, Rate of return on operating assets, 13.38%
P17-6	(a) EPS, 1996, $0.54
P17-7	(g) Equity ratio, 77.7%
P17-8	(a) Inventory turnover, 1.56 times
P17-1A	(a) Net earnings decrease, 485.6%
P17-2A	(a) Cost of goods sold, 1995, 141%
P17-3A	(b) Current ratio, 2000, 2.88:1
P17-4A	No check figure
P17-5A	(a) Rate of return on operating assets, 25%
P17-6A	(a) EPS, 1994, $1.56
P17-7A	(c) Inventory turnover, 17.36 times
P17-8A	(a) Rate of return on operating assets, 12%
BDC17-1	(a) Net income, $316,800
BDC17-2	(a) No. of days' sales in accounts receivable, 1997, 52.14 days
BDC17-3	(a) (2) Apple, Inc., EPS using first advisor's estimate, $0.38
ARA17-4	No check figure
ARA17-5	No check figure

APPENDIX

COMPOUND INTEREST AND ANNUITY TABLES

TABLE A.1 Future Value of \$1 at Compound Interest: 1%–20% $F_{in} = (1 + i)^n$

Period	1%	2%	3%	4%	5%	6%	7%	8%	9%	10%
1	1.01000	1.02000	1.03000	1.04000	1.05000	1.06000	1.07000	1.08000	1.09000	1.10000
2	1.02010	1.04040	1.06090	1.08160	1.10250	1.12360	1.14490	1.16640	1.18810	1.21000
3	1.03030	1.06121	1.09273	1.12486	1.15762	1.19102	1.22504	1.25971	1.29503	1.33100
4	1.04060	1.08243	1.12551	1.16986	1.21551	1.26248	1.31080	1.36049	1.41158	1.46410
5	1.05101	1.10408	1.15927	1.21665	1.27628	1.33823	1.40255	1.46933	1.53862	1.61051
6	1.06152	1.12616	1.19405	1.26532	1.34010	1.41852	1.50073	1.58687	1.67710	1.77156
7	1.07214	1.14869	1.22987	1.31593	1.40710	1.50363	1.60578	1.71382	1.82804	1.94872
8	1.08286	1.17166	1.26677	1.36857	1.47746	1.59385	1.71819	1.85093	1.99256	2.14359
9	1.09369	1.19509	1.30477	1.42331	1.55133	1.68948	1.83846	1.99900	2.17189	2.35795
10	1.10462	1.21899	1.34392	1.48024	1.62889	1.79085	1.96715	2.15892	2.36736	2.59374
11	1.11567	1.24337	1.38423	1.53945	1.71034	1.89830	2.10485	2.33164	2.58043	2.85312
12	1.12683	1.26824	1.42576	1.60103	1.79586	2.01220	2.25219	2.51817	2.81266	3.13843
13	1.13809	1.29361	1.46853	1.66507	1.88565	2.13293	2.40985	2.71962	3.06580	3.45227
14	1.14947	1.31948	1.51259	1.73168	1.97993	2.26090	2.57853	2.93719	3.34173	3.79750
15	1.16097	1.34587	1.55797	1.80094	2.07893	2.39656	2.75903	3.17217	3.64248	4.17725
16	1.17258	1.37279	1.60471	1.87298	2.18287	2.54035	2.95216	3.42594	3.97031	4.59497
17	1.18430	1.40024	1.65285	1.94790	2.29202	2.69277	3.15882	3.70002	4.32763	5.05447
18	1.19615	1.42825	1.70243	2.02582	2.40662	2.85434	3.37993	3.99602	4.71712	5.55992
19	1.20811	1.45681	1.75351	2.10685	2.52695	3.02560	3.61653	4.31570	5.14166	6.11591
20	1.22019	1.48595	1.80611	2.19112	2.65330	3.20714	3.86968	4.66096	5.60441	6.72750
21	1.23239	1.51567	1.86029	2.27877	2.78596	3.39956	4.14056	5.03383	6.10881	7.40025
22	1.24472	1.54598	1.91610	2.36992	2.92526	3.60354	4.43040	5.43654	6.65860	8.14027
23	1.25716	1.57690	1.97359	2.46472	3.07152	3.81975	4.74053	5.87146	7.25787	8.95430
24	1.26973	1.60844	2.03279	2.56330	3.22510	4.04893	5.07237	6.34118	7.91108	9.84973
25	1.28243	1.64061	2.09378	2.66584	3.38635	4.29187	5.42743	6.84848	8.62308	10.83471
26	1.29526	1.67342	2.15659	2.77247	3.55567	4.54938	5.80735	7.39635	9.39916	11.91818
27	1.30821	1.70689	2.22129	2.88337	3.73346	4.82235	6.21387	7.98806	10.24508	13.10999
28	1.32129	1.74102	2.28793	2.99870	3.92013	5.11169	6.64884	8.62711	11.16714	14.42099
29	1.33450	1.77584	2.35657	3.11865	4.11614	5.41839	7.11426	9.31727	12.17218	15.86309
30	1.34785	1.81136	2.42726	3.24340	4.32194	5.74349	7.61226	10.06266	13.26768	17.44940

Period	11%	12%	13%	14%	15%	16%	17%	18%	19%	20%
1	1.11000	1.12000	1.13000	1.14000	1.15000	1.16000	1.17000	1.18000	1.19000	1.20000
2	1.23210	1.25440	1.27690	1.29960	1.32250	1.34560	1.36890	1.39240	1.41610	1.44000
3	1.36763	1.40493	1.44290	1.48154	1.52088	1.56090	1.60161	1.64303	1.68516	1.72800
4	1.51807	1.57352	1.63047	1.68896	1.74901	1.81064	1.87389	1.93878	2.00534	2.07360
5	1.68506	1.76234	1.84244	1.92541	2.01136	2.10034	2.19245	2.28776	2.38635	2.48832
6	1.87041	1.97382	2.08195	2.19497	2.31306	2.43640	2.56516	2.69955	2.83976	2.98598
7	2.07616	2.21068	2.35261	2.50227	2.66002	2.82622	3.00124	3.18547	3.37932	3.58318
8	2.30454	2.47596	2.65844	2.85259	3.05902	3.27841	3.51145	3.75886	4.02139	4.29982
9	2.55804	2.77308	3.00404	3.25195	3.51788	3.80296	4.10840	4.43545	4.78545	5.15978
10	2.83942	3.10585	3.39457	3.70722	4.04556	4.41144	4.80683	5.23384	5.69468	6.19174
11	3.15176	3.47855	3.83586	4.22623	4.65239	5.11726	5.62399	6.17593	6.77667	7.43008
12	3.49845	3.89598	4.33452	4.81790	5.35025	5.93603	6.58007	7.28759	8.06424	8.91610
13	3.88328	4.36349	4.89801	5.49241	6.15279	6.88579	7.69868	8.59936	9.59645	10.69932
14	4.31044	4.88711	5.53475	6.26135	7.07571	7.98752	9.00745	10.14724	11.41977	12.83918
15	4.78459	5.47357	6.25427	7.13794	8.13706	9.26552	10.53872	11.97375	13.58953	15.40702
16	5.31089	6.13039	7.06733	8.13725	9.35762	10.74800	12.33030	14.12902	16.17154	18.48843
17	5.89509	6.86604	7.98608	9.27646	10.76126	12.46768	14.42646	16.67225	19.24413	22.18611
18	6.54355	7.68997	9.02427	10.57517	12.37545	14.46251	16.87895	19.67325	22.90052	26.62333
19	7.26334	8.61276	10.19742	12.05569	14.23177	16.77652	19.74838	23.21444	27.25162	31.94800
20	8.06231	9.64629	11.52309	13.74349	16.36654	19.46076	23.10560	27.39303	32.42942	38.33760
21	8.94917	10.80385	13.02109	15.66758	18.82152	22.57448	27.03355	32.32378	38.59101	46.00512
22	9.93357	12.10031	14.71383	17.86104	21.64475	26.18640	31.62925	38.14206	45.92331	55.20614
23	11.02627	13.55235	16.62663	20.36158	24.89146	30.37622	37.00623	45.00763	54.64873	66.24737
24	12.23916	15.17863	18.78809	23.21221	28.62518	35.23642	43.29729	53.10901	65.03199	79.49685
25	13.58546	17.00006	21.23054	26.46192	32.91895	40.87424	50.65783	62.66863	77.38807	95.39622
26	15.07986	19.04007	23.99051	30.16658	37.85680	47.41412	59.26966	73.94898	92.09181	114.47546
27	16.73865	21.32488	27.10928	34.38991	43.53531	55.00038	69.34550	87.25980	109.58925	137.37055
28	18.57990	23.88387	30.63349	39.20449	50.06561	63.80044	81.13423	102.96656	130.41121	164.84466
29	20.62369	26.74993	34.61584	44.69312	57.57545	74.00851	94.92705	121.50054	155.18934	197.81359
30	22.89230	29.95992	39.11590	50.95016	66.21177	85.84988	111.06465	143.37064	184.67531	237.37631

TABLE A.2   Future Value of an Ordinary Annuity of \$1 per Period: 1%–20% $F_{A_{in}} = \dfrac{(1+i)^n - 1}{i}$

Period	1%	2%	3%	4%	5%	6%	7%	8%	9%	10%
1	1.00000	1.00000	1.00000	1.00000	1.00000	1.00000	1.00000	1.00000	1.00000	1.00000
2	2.01000	2.02000	2.03000	2.04000	2.05000	2.06000	2.07000	2.08000	2.09000	2.10000
3	3.03010	3.06040	3.09090	3.12160	3.15250	3.18360	3.21490	3.24640	3.27810	3.31000
4	4.06040	4.12161	4.18363	4.24646	4.31012	4.37462	4.43994	4.50611	4.57313	4.64100
5	5.10101	5.20404	5.30914	5.41632	5.52563	5.63709	5.75074	5.86660	5.98471	6.10510
6	6.15202	6.30812	6.46841	6.63298	6.80191	6.97532	7.15329	7.33593	7.52333	7.71561
7	7.21354	7.43428	7.66246	7.89829	8.14201	8.39384	8.65402	8.92280	9.20043	9.48717
8	8.28567	8.58297	8.89234	9.21423	9.54911	9.89747	10.25980	10.63663	11.02847	11.43589
9	9.36853	9.75463	10.15911	10.58280	11.02656	11.49132	11.97799	12.48756	13.02104	13.57948
10	10.46221	10.94972	11.46388	12.00611	12.57789	13.18079	13.81645	14.48656	15.19293	15.93742
11	11.56683	12.16872	12.80780	13.48635	14.20679	14.97164	15.78360	16.64549	17.56029	18.53117
12	12.68250	13.41209	14.19203	15.02581	15.91713	16.86994	17.88845	18.97713	20.14072	21.38428
13	13.80933	14.68033	15.61779	16.62684	17.71298	18.88214	20.14064	21.49530	22.95338	24.52271
14	14.94742	15.97394	17.08632	18.29191	19.59863	21.01507	22.55049	24.21492	26.01919	27.97498
15	16.09690	17.29342	18.59891	20.02359	21.57856	23.27597	25.12902	27.15211	29.36092	31.77248
16	17.25786	18.63929	20.15688	21.82453	23.65749	25.67253	27.88805	30.32428	33.00340	35.94973
17	18.43044	20.01207	21.76159	23.69751	25.84037	28.21288	30.84022	33.75023	36.97370	40.54470
18	19.61475	21.41231	23.41444	25.64541	28.13238	30.90565	33.99903	37.45024	41.30134	45.59917
19	20.81090	22.84056	25.11687	27.67123	30.53900	33.75999	37.37896	41.44626	46.01846	51.15909
20	22.01900	24.29737	26.87037	29.77808	33.06595	36.78559	40.99549	45.76196	51.16012	57.27500
21	23.23919	25.78332	28.67649	31.96920	35.71925	39.99273	44.86518	50.42292	56.76453	64.00250
22	24.47159	27.29898	30.53678	34.24797	38.50521	43.39229	49.00574	55.45676	62.87334	71.40275
23	25.71630	28.84496	32.45288	36.61789	41.43048	46.99583	53.43614	60.89330	69.53194	79.54302
24	26.97346	30.42186	34.42647	39.08260	44.50200	50.81558	58.17667	66.76476	76.78981	88.49733
25	28.24320	32.03030	36.45926	41.64591	47.72710	54.86451	63.24904	73.10594	84.70090	98.34706
26	29.52563	33.67091	38.55304	44.31174	51.11345	59.15638	68.67647	79.95442	93.32398	109.18177
27	30.82089	35.34432	40.70963	47.08421	54.66913	63.70577	74.48382	87.35077	102.72313	121.09994
28	32.12910	37.05121	42.93092	49.96758	58.40258	68.52811	80.69769	95.33883	112.96822	134.20994
29	33.45039	38.79223	45.21885	52.96629	62.32271	73.63980	87.34653	103.96594	124.13536	148.63093
30	34.78489	40.56808	47.57542	56.08494	66.43885	79.05819	94.46079	113.28321	136.30754	164.49402

Period	11%	12%	13%	14%	15%	16%	17%	18%	19%	20%
1	1.00000	1.00000	1.00000	1.00000	1.00000	1.00000	1.00000	1.00000	1.00000	1.00000
2	2.11000	2.12000	2.13000	2.14000	2.15000	2.16000	2.17000	2.18000	2.19000	2.20000
3	3.34210	3.37440	3.40690	3.43960	3.47250	3.50560	3.53890	3.57240	3.60610	3.64000
4	4.70973	4.77933	4.84980	4.92114	4.99337	5.06650	5.14051	5.21543	5.29126	5.36800
5	6.22780	6.35285	6.48027	6.61010	6.74238	6.87714	7.01440	7.15421	7.29660	7.44160
6	7.91286	8.11519	8.32271	8.53552	8.75374	8.97748	9.20685	9.44197	9.68295	9.92992
7	9.78327	10.08901	10.40466	10.73049	11.06680	11.41387	11.77201	12.14152	12.52271	12.91590
8	11.85943	12.29969	12.75726	13.23276	13.72682	14.24009	14.77325	15.32700	15.90203	16.49908
9	14.16397	14.77566	15.41571	16.08535	16.78584	17.51851	18.28471	19.08585	19.92341	20.79890
10	16.72201	17.54874	18.41975	19.33730	20.30372	21.32147	22.39311	23.52131	24.70886	25.95868
11	19.56143	20.65458	21.81432	23.04452	24.34928	25.73290	27.19994	28.75514	30.40355	32.15042
12	22.71319	24.13313	25.65018	27.27075	29.00167	30.85017	32.82393	34.93107	37.18022	39.58050
13	26.21164	28.02911	29.98470	32.08865	34.35192	36.78620	39.40399	42.21866	45.24446	48.49660
14	30.09492	32.39260	34.88271	37.58107	40.50471	43.67199	47.10267	50.81802	54.84091	59.19592
15	34.40536	37.27971	40.41746	43.84241	47.58041	51.65951	56.11013	60.96527	66.26068	72.03511
16	39.18995	42.75328	46.67173	50.98035	55.71747	60.92503	66.64885	72.93901	79.85021	87.44213
17	44.50084	48.88367	53.73906	59.11760	65.07509	71.67303	78.97915	87.06804	96.02175	105.93056
18	50.39594	55.74971	61.72514	68.39407	75.83636	84.14072	93.40561	103.74028	115.26588	128.11667
19	56.93949	63.43968	70.74941	78.96923	88.21181	98.60323	110.28456	123.41353	138.16640	154.74000
20	64.20283	72.05244	80.94683	91.02493	102.44358	115.37975	130.03294	146.62797	165.41802	186.68800
21	72.26514	81.69874	92.46992	104.76842	118.81012	134.84051	153.13854	174.02100	197.84744	225.02560
22	81.21431	92.50258	105.49101	120.43600	137.63164	157.41499	180.17209	206.34479	236.43846	271.03072
23	91.14788	104.60289	120.20484	138.29704	159.27638	183.60138	211.80134	244.48685	282.36176	326.23686
24	102.17415	118.15524	136.83147	158.65862	184.16784	213.97761	248.80757	289.49448	337.01050	392.48424
25	114.41331	133.33387	155.61956	181.87083	212.79302	249.21402	292.10486	342.60349	402.04249	471.98108
26	127.99877	150.33393	176.85010	208.33274	245.71197	290.08827	342.76268	405.27211	479.43056	567.37730
27	143.07864	169.37401	200.84061	238.49933	283.56877	337.50239	402.03234	479.22109	571.52237	681.85276
28	159.81729	190.69889	227.94989	272.88923	327.10408	392.50277	471.37783	566.48089	681.11162	819.22331
29	178.39719	214.58275	258.58338	312.09373	377.16969	456.30322	552.51207	669.44745	811.52283	984.06797
30	199.02088	241.33268	293.19922	356.78685	434.74515	530.31173	647.43912	790.94799	966.71217	1181.88157

TABLE A.3   Present Value of $1 at Compound Interest: 1%–20% $P_{i,n} = \dfrac{1}{(1 + i)^n}$

Period	1%	2%	3%	4%	5%	6%	7%	8%	9%	10%
1	0.99010	0.98039	0.97087	0.96154	0.95238	0.94340	0.93458	0.92593	0.91743	0.90909
2	0.98030	0.96117	0.94260	0.92456	0.90703	0.89000	0.87344	0.85734	0.84168	0.82645
3	0.97059	0.94232	0.91514	0.88900	0.86384	0.83962	0.81630	0.79383	0.77218	0.75131
4	0.96098	0.92385	0.88849	0.85480	0.82270	0.79209	0.76290	0.73503	0.70843	0.68301
5	0.95147	0.90573	0.86261	0.82193	0.78353	0.74726	0.71299	0.68058	0.64993	0.62092
6	0.94205	0.88797	0.83748	0.79031	0.74622	0.70496	0.66634	0.63017	0.59627	0.56447
7	0.93272	0.87056	0.81309	0.75992	0.71068	0.66506	0.62275	0.58349	0.54703	0.51316
8	0.92348	0.85349	0.78941	0.73069	0.67684	0.62741	0.58201	0.54027	0.50187	0.46651
9	0.91434	0.83676	0.76642	0.70259	0.64461	0.59190	0.54393	0.50025	0.46043	0.42410
10	0.90529	0.82035	0.74409	0.67556	0.61391	0.55839	0.50835	0.46319	0.42241	0.38554
11	0.89632	0.80426	0.72242	0.64958	0.58468	0.52679	0.47509	0.42888	0.38753	0.35049
12	0.88745	0.78849	0.70138	0.62460	0.55684	0.49697	0.44401	0.39711	0.35553	0.31863
13	0.87866	0.77303	0.68095	0.60057	0.53032	0.46884	0.41496	0.36770	0.32618	0.28966
14	0.86996	0.75788	0.66112	0.57748	0.50507	0.44230	0.38782	0.34046	0.29925	0.26333
15	0.86135	0.74301	0.64186	0.55526	0.48102	0.41727	0.36245	0.31524	0.27454	0.23939
16	0.85282	0.72845	0.62317	0.53391	0.45811	0.39365	0.33873	0.29189	0.25187	0.21763
17	0.84438	0.71416	0.60502	0.51337	0.43630	0.37136	0.31657	0.27027	0.23107	0.19784
18	0.83602	0.70016	0.58739	0.49363	0.41552	0.35034	0.29586	0.25025	0.21199	0.17986
19	0.82774	0.68643	0.57029	0.47464	0.39573	0.33051	0.27651	0.23171	0.19449	0.16351
20	0.81954	0.67297	0.55368	0.45639	0.37689	0.31180	0.25842	0.21455	0.17843	0.14864
21	0.81143	0.65978	0.53755	0.43883	0.35894	0.29416	0.24151	0.19866	0.16370	0.13513
22	0.80340	0.64684	0.52189	0.42196	0.34185	0.27751	0.22571	0.18394	0.15018	0.12285
23	0.79544	0.63416	0.50669	0.40573	0.32557	0.26180	0.21095	0.17032	0.13778	0.11168
24	0.78757	0.62172	0.49193	0.39012	0.31007	0.24698	0.19715	0.15770	0.12640	0.10153
25	0.77977	0.60953	0.47761	0.37512	0.29530	0.23300	0.18425	0.14602	0.11597	0.09230
26	0.77205	0.59758	0.46369	0.36069	0.28124	0.21981	0.17220	0.13520	0.10639	0.08391
27	0.76440	0.58586	0.45019	0.34682	0.26785	0.20737	0.16093	0.12519	0.09761	0.07628
28	0.75684	0.57437	0.43708	0.33348	0.25509	0.19563	0.15040	0.11591	0.08955	0.06934
29	0.74934	0.56311	0.42435	0.32065	0.24295	0.18456	0.14056	0.10733	0.08215	0.06304
30	0.74192	0.55207	0.41199	0.30832	0.23138	0.17411	0.13137	0.09938	0.07537	0.05731
31	0.73458	0.54125	0.39999	0.29646	0.22036	0.16425	0.12277	0.09202	0.06915	0.05210
32	0.72730	0.53063	0.38834	0.28506	0.20987	0.15496	0.11474	0.08520	0.06344	0.04736
33	0.72010	0.52023	0.37703	0.27409	0.19987	0.14619	0.10723	0.07889	0.05820	0.04306
34	0.71297	0.51003	0.36604	0.26355	0.19035	0.13791	0.10022	0.07305	0.05339	0.03914
35	0.70591	0.50003	0.35538	0.25342	0.18129	0.13011	0.09366	0.06763	0.04899	0.03558
36	0.69892	0.49022	0.34503	0.24367	0.17266	0.12274	0.08754	0.06262	0.04494	0.03235
37	0.69200	0.48061	0.33498	0.23430	0.16444	0.11579	0.08181	0.05799	0.04123	0.02941
38	0.68515	0.47119	0.32523	0.22529	0.15661	0.10924	0.07646	0.05369	0.03783	0.02673
39	0.67837	0.46195	0.31575	0.21662	0.14915	0.10306	0.07146	0.04971	0.03470	0.02430
40	0.67165	0.45289	0.30656	0.20829	0.14205	0.09722	0.06678	0.04603	0.03184	0.02209

Period	11%	12%	13%	14%	15%	16%	17%	18%	19%	20%
1	0.90090	0.89286	0.88496	0.87719	0.86957	0.86207	0.85470	0.84746	0.84034	0.83333
2	0.81162	0.79719	0.78315	0.76947	0.75614	0.74316	0.73051	0.71818	0.70616	0.69444
3	0.73119	0.71178	0.69305	0.67497	0.65752	0.64066	0.62437	0.60863	0.59342	0.57870
4	0.65873	0.63553	0.61332	0.59208	0.57175	0.55229	0.53365	0.51579	0.49867	0.48225
5	0.59345	0.56743	0.54276	0.51937	0.49718	0.47611	0.45611	0.43711	0.41905	0.40188
6	0.53464	0.50663	0.48032	0.45559	0.43233	0.41044	0.38984	0.37043	0.35214	0.33490
7	0.48166	0.45235	0.42506	0.39964	0.37594	0.35383	0.33320	0.31393	0.29592	0.27908
8	0.43393	0.40388	0.37616	0.35056	0.32690	0.30503	0.28478	0.26604	0.24867	0.23257
9	0.39092	0.36061	0.33288	0.30751	0.28426	0.26295	0.24340	0.22546	0.20897	0.19381
10	0.35218	0.32197	0.29459	0.26974	0.24718	0.22668	0.20804	0.19106	0.17560	0.16151
11	0.31728	0.28748	0.26070	0.23662	0.21494	0.19542	0.17781	0.16192	0.14757	0.13459
12	0.28584	0.25668	0.23071	0.20756	0.18691	0.16846	0.15197	0.13722	0.12400	0.11216
13	0.25751	0.22917	0.20416	0.18207	0.16253	0.14523	0.12989	0.11629	0.10421	0.09346
14	0.23199	0.20462	0.18068	0.15971	0.14133	0.12520	0.11102	0.09855	0.08757	0.07789
15	0.20900	0.18270	0.15989	0.14010	0.12289	0.10793	0.09489	0.08352	0.07359	0.06491
16	0.18829	0.16312	0.14150	0.12289	0.10686	0.09304	0.08110	0.07078	0.06184	0.05409
17	0.16963	0.14564	0.12522	0.10780	0.09293	0.08021	0.06932	0.05998	0.05196	0.04507
18	0.15282	0.13004	0.11081	0.09456	0.08081	0.06914	0.05925	0.05083	0.04367	0.03756
19	0.13768	0.11611	0.09806	0.08295	0.07027	0.05961	0.05064	0.04308	0.03670	0.03130
20	0.12403	0.10367	0.08678	0.07276	0.06110	0.05139	0.04328	0.03651	0.03084	0.02608
21	0.11174	0.09256	0.07680	0.06383	0.05313	0.04430	0.03699	0.03094	0.02591	0.02174
22	0.10067	0.08264	0.06796	0.05599	0.04620	0.03819	0.03162	0.02622	0.02178	0.01811
23	0.09069	0.07379	0.06014	0.04911	0.04017	0.03292	0.02702	0.02222	0.01830	0.01509
24	0.08170	0.06588	0.05323	0.04308	0.03493	0.02838	0.02310	0.01883	0.01538	0.01258
25	0.07361	0.05882	0.04710	0.03779	0.03038	0.02447	0.01974	0.01596	0.01292	0.01048
26	0.06631	0.05252	0.04168	0.03315	0.02642	0.02109	0.01687	0.01352	0.01086	0.00874
27	0.05974	0.04689	0.03689	0.02908	0.02297	0.01818	0.01442	0.01146	0.00912	0.00728
28	0.05382	0.04187	0.03264	0.02551	0.01997	0.01567	0.01233	0.00971	0.00767	0.00607
29	0.04849	0.03738	0.02889	0.02237	0.01737	0.01351	0.01053	0.00823	0.00644	0.00506
30	0.04368	0.03338	0.02557	0.01963	0.01510	0.01165	0.00900	0.00697	0.00541	0.00421
31	0.03935	0.02980	0.02262	0.01722	0.01313	0.01004	0.00770	0.00591	0.00455	0.00351
32	0.03545	0.02661	0.02002	0.01510	0.01142	0.00866	0.00658	0.00501	0.00382	0.00293
33	0.03194	0.02376	0.01772	0.01325	0.00993	0.00746	0.00562	0.00425	0.00321	0.00244
34	0.02878	0.02121	0.01568	0.01162	0.00864	0.00643	0.00480	0.00360	0.00270	0.00203
35	0.02592	0.01894	0.01388	0.01019	0.00751	0.00555	0.00411	0.00305	0.00227	0.00169
36	0.02335	0.01691	0.01228	0.00894	0.00653	0.00478	0.00351	0.00258	0.00191	0.00141
37	0.02104	0.01510	0.01087	0.00784	0.00568	0.00412	0.00300	0.00219	0.00160	0.00118
38	0.01896	0.01348	0.00962	0.00688	0.00494	0.00355	0.00256	0.00186	0.00135	0.00098
39	0.01708	0.01204	0.00851	0.00604	0.00429	0.00306	0.00219	0.00157	0.00113	0.00082
40	0.01538	0.01075	0.00753	0.00529	0.00373	0.00264	0.00187	0.00133	0.00095	0.00068

TABLE A.4   Present Value of an Ordinary Annuity of $1 per Period: 1%–20% $P_{A_{i,n}} = \dfrac{1 - \dfrac{1}{(1 + i)^n}}{i}$

Period	1%	2%	3%	4%	5%	6%	7%	8%	9%	10%
1	0.99010	0.98039	0.97087	0.96154	0.95238	0.94340	0.93458	0.92593	0.91743	0.90909
2	1.97040	1.94156	1.91347	1.88609	1.85941	1.83339	1.80802	1.78326	1.75911	1.73554
3	2.94099	2.88388	2.82861	2.77509	2.72325	2.67301	2.62432	2.57710	2.53129	2.48685
4	3.90197	3.80773	3.71710	3.62990	3.54595	3.46511	3.38721	3.31213	3.23972	3.16987
5	4.85343	4.71346	4.57971	4.45182	4.32948	4.21236	4.10020	3.99271	3.88965	3.79079
6	5.79548	5.60143	5.41719	5.24214	5.07569	4.91732	4.76654	4.62288	4.48592	4.35526
7	6.72819	6.47199	6.23028	6.00205	5.78637	5.58238	5.38929	5.20637	5.03295	4.86842
8	7.65168	7.32548	7.01969	6.73274	6.46321	6.20979	5.97130	5.74664	5.53482	5.33493
9	8.56602	8.16224	7.78611	7.43533	7.10782	6.80169	6.51523	6.24689	5.99525	5.75902
10	9.47130	8.98259	8.53020	8.11090	7.72173	7.36009	7.02358	6.71008	6.41766	6.14457
11	10.36763	9.78685	9.25262	8.76048	8.30641	7.88687	7.49867	7.13896	6.80519	6.49506
12	11.25508	10.57534	9.95400	9.38507	8.86325	8.38384	7.94269	7.53608	7.16073	6.81369
13	12.13374	11.34837	10.63496	9.98565	9.39357	8.85268	8.35765	7.90378	7.48690	7.10336
14	13.00370	12.10625	11.29607	10.56312	9.89864	9.29498	8.74547	8.24424	7.78615	7.36669
15	13.86505	12.84926	11.93794	11.11839	10.37966	9.71225	9.10791	8.55948	8.06069	7.60608
16	14.71787	13.57771	12.56110	11.65230	10.83777	10.10590	9.44665	8.85137	8.31256	7.82371
17	15.56225	14.29187	13.16612	12.16567	11.27407	10.47726	9.76322	9.12164	8.54363	8.02155
18	16.39827	14.99203	13.75351	12.65930	11.68959	10.82760	10.05909	9.37189	8.75563	8.20141
19	17.22601	15.67846	14.32380	13.13394	12.08532	11.15812	10.33560	9.60360	8.95011	8.36492
20	18.04555	16.35143	14.87747	13.59033	12.46221	11.46992	10.59401	9.81815	9.12855	8.51356
21	18.85698	17.01121	15.41502	14.02916	12.82115	11.76408	10.83553	10.01680	9.29224	8.64869
22	19.66038	17.65805	15.93692	14.45112	13.16300	12.04158	11.06124	10.20074	9.44243	8.77154
23	20.45582	18.29220	16.44361	14.85684	13.48857	12.30338	11.27219	10.37106	9.58021	8.88322
24	21.24339	18.91393	16.93554	15.24696	13.79864	12.55036	11.46933	10.52876	9.70661	8.98474
25	22.02316	19.52346	17.41315	15.62208	14.09394	12.78336	11.65358	10.67478	9.82258	9.07704
26	22.79520	20.12104	17.87684	15.98277	14.37519	13.00317	11.82578	10.80998	9.92897	9.16095
27	23.55961	20.70690	18.32703	16.32959	14.64303	13.21053	11.98671	10.93516	10.02658	9.23722
28	24.31644	21.28127	18.76411	16.66306	14.89813	13.40616	12.13711	11.05108	10.11613	9.30657
29	25.06579	21.84438	19.18845	16.98371	15.14107	13.59072	12.27767	11.15841	10.19828	9.36961
30	25.80771	22.39646	19.60044	17.29203	15.37245	13.76483	12.40904	11.25778	10.27365	9.42691
31	26.54229	22.93770	20.00043	17.58849	15.59281	13.92909	12.53181	11.34980	10.34280	9.47901
32	27.26959	23.46833	20.38877	17.87355	15.80268	14.08404	12.64656	11.43500	10.40624	9.52638
33	27.98969	23.98856	20.76579	18.14765	16.00255	14.23023	12.75379	11.51389	10.46444	9.56943
34	28.70267	24.49589	21.13184	18.41120	16.19290	14.36814	12.85401	11.58693	10.51784	9.60857
35	29.40858	24.99862	21.48722	18.66461	16.37419	14.49825	12.94767	11.65457	10.56682	9.64416
36	30.10751	25.48884	21.83225	18.90828	16.54685	14.62099	13.03521	11.71719	10.61176	9.67651
37	30.79951	25.96945	22.16724	19.14258	16.71129	14.73678	13.11702	11.77518	10.65299	9.70592
38	31.48466	26.44064	22.49246	19.36786	16.86789	14.84602	13.19347	11.82887	10.69082	9.73265
39	32.16303	26.90259	22.80822	19.58448	17.01704	14.94907	13.26493	11.87858	10.72552	9.75696
40	32.83469	27.35548	23.11477	19.79277	17.15909	15.04630	13.33171	11.92461	10.75736	9.77905

Period	11%	12%	13%	14%	15%	16%	17%	18%	19%	20%
1	0.90090	0.89286	0.88496	0.87719	0.86957	0.86207	0.85470	0.84746	0.84034	0.83333
2	1.71252	1.69005	1.66810	1.64666	1.62571	1.60523	1.58521	1.56564	1.54650	1.52778
3	2.44371	2.40183	2.36115	2.32163	2.28323	2.24589	2.20958	2.17427	2.13992	2.10648
4	3.10245	3.03735	2.97447	2.91371	2.85498	2.79818	2.74324	2.69006	2.63859	2.58873
5	3.69590	3.60478	3.51723	3.43308	3.35216	3.27429	3.19935	3.12717	3.05763	2.99061
6	4.23054	4.11141	3.99755	3.88867	3.78448	3.68474	3.58918	3.49760	3.40978	3.32551
7	4.71220	4.56376	4.42261	4.28830	4.16042	4.03857	3.92238	3.81153	3.70570	3.60459
8	5.14612	4.96764	4.79877	4.63886	4.48732	4.34359	4.20716	4.07757	3.95437	3.83716
9	5.53705	5.32825	5.13166	4.94637	4.77158	4.60654	4.45057	3.30302	4.16333	4.03097
10	5.88923	5.65022	5.42624	5.21612	5.01877	4.83323	4.65860	4.49409	4.33893	4.19247
11	6.20652	5.93770	5.68694	5.45273	5.23371	5.02864	4.83641	4.65601	4.48650	4.32706
12	6.49236	6.19437	5.91765	5.66029	5.42062	5.19711	4.98839	4.79322	4.61050	4.43922
13	6.74987	6.42355	6.12181	5.84236	5.58315	5.34233	5.11828	4.90951	4.71471	4.53268
14	6.98187	6.62817	6.30249	6.00207	5.72448	5.46753	5.22930	5.00806	4.80228	4.61057
15	7.19087	6.81086	6.46238	6.14217	5.84737	5.57546	5.32419	5.09158	4.87586	4.67547
16	7.37916	6.97399	6.60388	6.26506	5.95423	5.66850	5.40529	5.16235	4.39770	4.72956
17	7.54879	7.11963	6.72909	6.37286	6.04716	5.74870	5.47461	5.22233	4.98966	4.77463
18	7.70162	7.24967	6.83991	6.46742	6.12797	5.81785	5.53385	5.27316	5.03333	4.81219
19	7.83929	7.36578	6.93797	6.55037	6.19823	5.87746	5.58449	5.31624	5.07003	4.84350
20	7.96333	7.46944	7.02475	6.62313	6.25933	5.92884	5.62777	5.35275	5.10086	4.86958
21	8.07507	7.56200	7.10155	6.68696	6.31246	5.97314	5.66476	5.38368	5.12677	4.89132
22	8.17574	7.64465	7.16951	6.74294	6.35866	6.01133	5.69637	5.40990	5.14855	4.90943
23	8.26643	7.71843	7.22966	6.79206	6.39884	6.04425	5.72340	5.43212	5.16685	4.92453
24	8.34814	7.78432	7.28288	6.83514	6.43377	6.07263	5.74649	5.45095	5.18223	4.93710
25	8.42174	7.84314	7.32998	6.87293	6.46415	6.09709	5.76623	5.46691	5.19515	4.94759
26	8.48806	7.89566	7.37167	6.90608	6.49056	6.11818	5.78311	5.48043	5.20601	4.95632
27	8.54780	7.94255	7.40856	6.93515	6.51353	6.13636	5.79753	5.49189	5.21513	4.96360
28	8.60162	7.98442	7.44120	6.96066	6.53351	6.15204	5.80985	5.50160	5.22280	4.96967
29	8.65011	8.02181	7.47009	6.98304	6.55088	6.16555	5.82039	5.50983	5.22924	4.97472
30	8.69379	8.05518	7.49565	7.00266	6.56598	6.17720	5.82939	5.51681	5.23466	4.97894
31	8.73315	8.08499	7.51828	7.01988	6.57911	6.18724	5.83709	5.52272	5.23921	4.98245
32	8.76860	8.11159	7.53830	7.03498	6.59053	6.19590	5.84366	5.52773	5.24303	4.98537
33	8.80054	8.13535	7.55602	7.04823	6.60046	6.20336	5.84928	5.53197	5.24625	4.98781
34	8.82932	8.15656	7.57170	7.05985	6.60910	6.20979	5.85409	5.53557	5.24895	4.98984
35	8.85524	8.17550	7.58557	7.07005	6.61661	6.21534	5.85820	5.53862	5.25122	4.99154
36	8.87859	8.19241	7.59785	7.07899	6.62314	6.22012	5.86171	5.54120	5.25312	4.99295
37	8.89963	8.20751	7.60872	7.08683	6.62881	6.22424	5.86471	5.54339	5.25472	4.99412
38	8.91859	8.22099	7.61833	7.09371	6.63375	6.22779	5.86727	5.54525	5.25607	4.99510
39	8.93567	8.23303	7.62684	7.09975	6.63805	6.23086	5.86946	5.54682	5.25720	4.99592
40	8.95105	8.24378	7.63438	7.10504	6.64178	6.23350	5.87133	5.54815	5.25815	4.99660

REAL WORLD COMPANIES INDEX

NEW TERMS INDEX

SUBJECT INDEX

CHART OF ACCOUNTS FOR CHAPTERS 1–11

Account Number	Account Title

Asset Accounts

100	Cash
101	Petty Cash
103	Accounts Receivable
104	Allowance for Uncollectible Accounts
105	Merchandise Inventory
106	Repair Parts Inventory
107	Supplies on Hand
108	Prepaid Insurance
109	Store Supplies on Hand
110	Prepaid Advertising
111	Prepaid Printing Expense
112	Prepaid Rent
113	Receivable from Employees
114	Receivable from Insurance Company
115	Rent Receivable
120	Notes Receivable
121	Interest Receivable
125	Salvaged Materials
130	Land
140	Buildings
141	Accumulated Depreciation–Buildings
150	Trucks
151	Accumulated Depreciation–Trucks
152	Automobiles
153	Accumulated Depreciation–Automobiles
160	Office Furniture
161	Accumulated Depreciation–Office Furniture
165	Furniture and Fixtures
166	Accumulated Depreciation–Furniture and Fixtures
170	Equipment
171	Accumulated Depreciation–Equipment
172	Office Equipment
173	Accumulated Depreciation–Office Equipment
174	Store Fixtures
175	Accumulated Depreciation–Store Fixtures
180	Machinery
181	Accumulated Depreciation–Machinery
185	Other Assets
190	Ore Deposits
191	Accumulated Depletion–Ore Deposits
192	Land Improvements
193	Accumulated Depreciation–Land Improvements
194	Leasehold
195	Leasehold Improvements

Number Account	Title

Asset Accounts (concluded)

196	Franchises
197	Patents
198	Copyrights
199	Goodwill

Liability Accounts

200	Accounts Payable
201	Notes Payable
202	Discount on Notes Payable
203	Loan Payable
204	Interest Payable
205	Vouchers Payable
206	Salaries Payable (or Wages Payable)
207	Sales Salaries Payable
208	Office Salaries Payable
209	Officers' Salaries Payable
210	Unearned Delivery Fees
211	Unearned Subscriptions
212	Unearned Ticket Fees
213	Unearned Laundry Fees
214	Unearned Management Fees
215	Unearned Rent
216	Unearned Service Fees
217	Unearned Commissions
218	Mortgage Note Payment
219	Travel Expenses Payable
220	Employees' Federal Income Taxes Payable
221	FICA Taxes Payable
222	Medical Insurance Premiums Payable
223	Employees' State Income Taxes Payable
224	Federal Unemployment Taxes Payable
225	State Unemployment Taxes Payable
226	Sales Tax Payable
227	Federal Excise Tax Payable
230	Estimated Product Warranty Payable
232	Estimated Property Taxes Payable
235	Other Liabilities
240	Commissions Payable

Stockholder's Equity Accounts

300	Capital Stock
310	Retained Earnings
320	Dividends